THE COMPLETE WHO'S WHO OF INTERNATIONAL RUGBY

Terry Godwin
Chief Researcher: John Jenkins

BLANDFORD PRESS
POOLE • NEW YORK • SYDNEY

First Published in the UK 1987 by Blandford Press
Link House, West Street, Poole, Dorset BH15 1LL

Copyright © 1987 Terry Godwin

Distributed in the United States by
Sterling Publishing Co, Inc,
2 Park Avenue, New York, NY 10016

Distributed in Australia by
Capricorn Link (Australia) Pty Ltd
PO Box 665, Lane Cove, NSW 2066

British Library Cataloguing in Publication Data

Godwin, Terry
  The complete who's who of international
  rugby.
  1. Rugby football players— Biography
  I. Title
  796.33'3'0922   GV944.9.A1

ISBN 0 7137 1838 2

Typeset by Wordstream Ltd, Bournemouth

Printed in Great Britain by
Mackays of Chatham Ltd, Kent.

CONTENTS

INTRODUCTION &
ACKNOWLEDGEMENTS

The prime motive in the production of this book was to provide for the first time a source of reference for every player who has played international rugby. It was an inevitable consequence of a lifetime's fascination with and involvement in the most absorbing and thrilling game to spring from man's inventive nature. If the reader derives as much fascination and pleasure from its contents, particularly the biographical side-lines and anecdotes, as was elicited by the research and production, the book will have achieved part of its purpose.

Perhaps the real merit of the book has been to provide identifying substance for the many players, particularly from the distant past, who hitherto had been confined to relatively anonymous one-line entries in rugby annuals. Regrettably resurrection has not been total; some players seem condemned to obscurity, biographical statistics elusively defying the most ardent and thorough investigation. Suffice to say, research is on-going and any biographical titbit that may emanate from long-lost publications, dark attics or even personal memory would be enormously appreciated. Likewise, the pointing out of any error of fact which may have inadvertently crept in would be advantageous for future editions. Please write to me c/o Blandford Press, Link House, West Street, Poole, Dorset BH15 1LL, England.

A book of this nature relies for its production not only on personal knowledge and research but on the labours and expertise of many others similarly fascinated by the character and profile of the game's international players. To these I owe a tremendous debt, the response to queries and confirmation of fact given with generous alacrity. Only one source, the official statistician of the South African Rugby Football Board, surprisingly failed to respond to the desirability of producing a book with obviously beneficial effects to all those concerned with the playing of the game. The South African refusal to help was perplexing, and among other things throws into question the SARB purpose in appointing someone reluctant to fulfil his raison d'être.

Of those who readily responded, and there were many throughout the world, including players themselves, some gave incalculable assistance. These included the New Zealand rugby historians, Rod Chester and Neville McMillan; Ned Van Esbeck of Ireland, Jim Shepherd of Australia; and Chris Thau and Henri Garcia, who supplied details of French players. I am indebted, too, to Tim Auty, the indefatigable English rugby historian, whose father is listed in the book. Tim's painstaking research, particularly regarding births and deaths, was most valuable. John Griffiths, a Welshman with an unsurpassed knowledge of English international rugby, offered much useful guidance. Caroline North, editor of *Rothman's Rugby Yearbook,* offered encouragement and practical help. Many others contributed, incidentally, usually through bibliography, which is acknowledged elsewhere.

But my chief thanks are due to John Jenkins, whose good humour and sense of fun were a major psychological boost when the frustrations and failures loomed. John was a painstaking checker of many accepted facts, and unearthed much that was new. Much of John's probing was done at the National Library of Wales in Aberystwyth, a drop kick from his home in Bow Street, and many a yellowing newspaper file and dusty tome bore his fingerprints. The tidiness and order of the completed text is due largely to the fastidious editing of John Newth. Appointed local researcher, John's failure to discover details of the drowning of Irish international Tom Brand in Poole Harbour in 1938, a short distance from Blandford Press's offices, in no way diminished appreciation of that rare bird in publishing, a real professional.

Terry Godwin
July 1986

HOW TO USE THIS BOOK

The data given in this book is up to date to the end of the northern hemisphere's 1985/86 season: i.e. to the match between Scotland and Romania on 29 March 1986.

The book is confined to the eight countries who are full members of the International Board.

To prevent the book being as thick as it is wide, the entries are given in a concise form, and the list of abbreviations on page 13 should be consulted. Other conventions are given below.

Each entry is divided into six parts:

1. Name and country

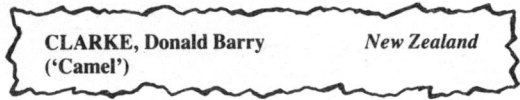

CLARKE, Donald Barry   *New Zealand*
('Camel')

The player's surname and forenames, plus any medals or decorations. The player's common nickname is given as long as it is not one of the usual diminutives of one of his forenames.

2. Clubs

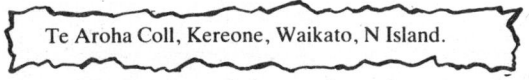

Te Aroha Coll, Kereone, Waikato, N Island.

The school, university, senior clubs and major representative sides for which the player appeared regularly.

3. Birth and death

b 10.11.33 Pihama.

Details of the date and place of the player's birth and death. Throughout the book, nineteenth-century dates are prefixed by '18' as in '1890' but twentieth-century dates are not prefixed by '19', so '71' means 1971.

4. Position, summary of appearances, and scoring record

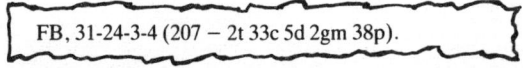

FB, 31-24-3-4 (207 − 2t 33c 5d 2gm 38p).

Since international rugby began in 1871 the description of players' positions understandably has changed often and, in an effort to avoid any confusion, modern equivalents have been used throughout this book, even though the players might have been described differently during their playing days. For example, a player who appeared in, say, the 1950s as a wing-forward is described as he is known today, a flanker, even though that term was quite unknown at the time and is one of the relatively new terms to come into common usage. In the early days, before the introduction of so-called specialised players, every forward was known generically as a forward. That description is used in the book for players of the pre-specialised era and also when it has been impossible to confirm any specific position. By 1932 the scrum had evolved from the old-fashioned 'first up, first down' free-for-all to 3-2-3 in the northern hemisphere and 2-3-2 in New Zealand, with the eighth forward as 'rover'. Eventually, the much more practical 3-4-1 formation, always favoured in South Africa, found popular appeal and even New Zealand, innovators of 2-3-2, adopted it. The hooker, one of the more apt descriptions of a player's duty, entered rugby's phraseology and the front-row forward, as he was hitherto known, either became a prop or a hooker. Loose or side-row forwards ultimately became flankers and no 8s and second-row men became much more precisely lock-forwards.

It should also be noted that when international rugby began, teams were 20-a-side, and usually these early teams comprised of up to three full-backs, a threequarter-back, three half-backs (all of whom often were inter-changeable) and 13 forwards. The reduction to 15-a-side and the subsequent advent of the four-threequarter system (by 1894) would have introduced some universal clarity into positional definition but for the fact that New Zealand and Australia, for reasons best known to themselves, insisted upon a modified version of the four-threequarter system. In simple Antipodean terms, they employed a scrum-half, two five-eighths (equivalent to the northern hemisphere's fly-half and inside centre), a centre and two wings, positions still in currency there today but employed nowhere else in the world. Wherever applicable, southern hemisphere terminology has been adhered to, although it conflicts with the desired consistency regarding players' positions.

The summary of a player's appearances is given in the form: played-won-drawn-lost.

Students of the history of rugby will be aware of discrepancies in scoring and scorers in early international matches. The failure by most formative Rugby Unions to establish statistical records makes reliable information hard to come by in this respect. A certain amount of compromise has been necessary: generally, the accepted reliable publishing sources have been given preference in determining some of the early scorers whose achievements may have been disputed. However, where possible, all 'claimants' have been acknowledged and will continue to be until other evidence comes to light. Interestingly, the question of who scored what and when is not exclusively confined to the dim and distant past when the game was less well publicised than it is today. In recent times there have been several instances of dispute over a score, when even the all-seeing TV eye has been unable to settle the argument. Reflecting modern players' changed attitude to scoring and the importance they attach to it is the number of times, at a push-over for instance, when the scorer will make it his business to collect the ball and display to all and sundry (but particularly to the Press Box) the evidence that it was he and not any of the other seven forwards who physically grounded the ball.

There has been a recent tendency, too, to allocate tries to individuals in cases of penalty tries. Although the Law specifically requires a penalty try to be awarded to the offended team, modern custom often requires that the score be awarded to an individual, usually the player who presumably would have scored but for the offence by the defending side.

By common consent, the most inconsistent area in rugby concerns scoring in the early days, when England, Scotland, Wales and Ireland frequently devised scoring methods and values which suited them but perhaps not their opponents. A classic case was the Wales v England match of 1893. Wales, who played with different scoring values from their opponents, won the match 12-11 because of an agreement to accept newly established IB points values. Had Wales played under their own scoring rules, the match would have been drawn. In examining individual scoring achievements of that period, it should be borne in mind that values for scores not only varied but did not come into being until the 1890/1 season and were the subject of many changes in the course of the next 15 years. As a consequence, some players enjoyed scores under both the 'new' and the 'old' system, some obtaining scores with variable points values and some scores without any points value at all. In all such cases of overlapping, it seemed sensible to avoid unnecessary ambiguity by omitting that player's points total altogether. Creating a false points total by translating all such inconsistent scores into modern values was considered but rejected.

5. **Details of appearances**

56 SA+(1c 2p) SA+(1c 2p); 57 A+(2c 3p)
A+(2c 1gm); 58 A+(2c) A+(1c 4p); 59
BI+(6p) BI+(1t 1c) BI+(2c 1d 1p) BI−(2p); 60
SA− SA+(1c 1d 1p) SA=(1c 2p) SA−(1p); 61
F+(2c 1d) F+(1c) F+(4c 3p); 62 A+(1c 1d 1p)
A+(1c 2p) A=(2p) A+(1p) A+(2c); 63 E+(1t
3c 1d 1p) E+(1gm); 63 I+(1p) W+(1p); 64
E+(1c 2p) S= F+; 64 A+(3c) A−(1c).

A game won is shown by '+', a game lost by '−' and a game drawn by '='. British Lions Test appearances are given at the end of this section.

An appearance as a replacement is indicated by 'r'. Rugby football has taken a long time to adapt in many respects, not the least being with regard to substituting injured players. It is generally accepted that when the IB officially allowed replacements, the first player in an international match to avail himself of the edict was Mike Gibson, when he took over from Barry John for the British Lions in the 1st Test against South Africa in Pretoria on 17 July 1968. What is less well known is that Australia and New Zealand connived at and permitted substitution long before, and there were many such instances from 1907 to the time when the IB formally acknowledged the wisdom of substitution. It is not easy to discover whether Australia and New Zealand obtained special dispensation from the IB in all such cases, although obviously they did in some. Suffice to say that many replacements occurred which were barely publicised and some may have been quietly overlooked; indeed, some instances have only recently been unearthed. No judgements are made in this respect. Where a player is known to have played as a replacement, the fact is conveyed.

It should be stressed that although most of the international appearances recorded in this book concern only matches between the eight IB countries, some countries have accorded official status and have awarded caps for matches against non-IB countries, as well as against representative sides such as a Centenary President's XV. These appearances are credited where applicable, and generally concern Australia and France until the recent recognition of Argentina and Romania as 'official' opposition by some countries. Previous 'non-cap' matches against these countries have not been included.

6. Other biographical details

> Farmer/sales rep. NZ's most capped FB; most pts in Tests. Played in 16 consec matches without losing 61-4. 169 pts (13 apps) NZ > 57 A. 218 pts (23 apps) NZ > 60 A & SA; 173 pts in SA most by any player on tour in SA. 107 pts > 62 A; 149 pts (26 apps) > 63-4 BI,F & C. 781 pts & 89 apps for NZ. Ckt for Auckland. 4 bros Ian, Doug, Brian & Graeme rep Waikato, all five playing once v Thames Valley 61. Ian rep NZ 53-64. Autobiography 'The Boot' pub 66; co-author with Roger Urbahn 'The Fourth Springbok Tour of NZ' pub 63. Moved to Johannesburg, SA.

There are no hard and fast rules about this part of the entry, which aims to give a rounded picture of the subject both as a rugby player and as a man. Among the items which may be found are: profession; major rugby tours undertaken (the symbol '>' is used throughout the book to indicate a tour); achievements at other sports; other members of the same family who played top-class rugby; war record; books written; rugby league career. The list of abbreviations (page 13) is particularly relevant to this section of the entry.

LIST OF ABBREVIATIONS

A: Australia; Albion
AA: anti-aircraft
AAA: Amateur Athletics Association
Acad: Academy
ACT: Australian Capital Territory
ADC: Aide-de-Camp
Adm: Admiral
AFC: Association Football Club; Air Force Cross
Agric: Agricultural; Agriculture
AI: Academical Institute
AIF: Australian Imperial Forces
AM: Albert Medal
app(s): appearance(s)
ARA: Associate of the Royal Academy
Arg: Argentina
ARU: Australian Rugby Union
Assoc: Association
Asst: Assistant; assisted
Ath: Athletic(s)
AW: Anglo-Welsh Team

b: born
BAOR: British Army of the Rhine
Battn: Battalion
Bd: Board
Bde: Brigade
BEC: Bordeaux Etudiants Club
Beds: Bedfordshire
BEF: British Expeditionary Force
BEM: British Empire Medal
Berks: Berkshire
BF: British Forces
BHS: Boys' High School
BI: British Isles (i.e. British Lions)

BOAC: British Overseas Airways Corporation
Brecs: Brecknockshire; Breconshire
Brit: British
bro(s): brother(s)
BS: Board School
BSC: British Steel Corporation
BT: British Team
Bt: Baronet
Bucks: Buckinghamshire
bus: business
BUSF: British Universities Sports Federation

C: Canada
c: conversion(s); circa
Caerns: Caernarvonshire
Cambs: Cambridgeshire
Can: Canada
capt: captain(ed)
Cards: Cardiganshire
Carms: Carmarthenshire
CASG: Club Athlétique des Sports Généraux
CAT: College of Advanced Technology
Cathed: Cathedral
CB: Companion of the Bath; Constituent Body
CBE: Commander of the British Empire
CBC: Christian Brothers' College
CBS: Christian Brothers' School
CCC: County Cricket Club
CCF: Combined Cadet Force
CCS: Casualty Clearing Station; Colonial Civil Service

Cdr: Commander
CEGS: Church of England Grammar School
CES: Church of England School
CGS: County Grammar School
Ch: Chief
Champ(s): Championship(s); Champion(s)
Chmn: Chairman
CIE: Companion of the Order of the Indian Empire; Transport Organisation of Ireland
C in C: Commander in Chief
CIYMS: Church of Ireland Young Men's Society
ckt(er): cricket(er)
CMG: Companion of the Order of St Michael and St George
CO: Commanding Officer
Co(s): County(ies); Company
C of E: Church of England
C of I: Church of Ireland
Col: Colonel
Coll(s): College(s)
Comb: Combined
Comm: Committee
Comp: Comprehensive
consec: consecutive
Corp: Corporation
corr: correspondent
Cpl: Corporal
CS: County School
CUCC: Cambridge University Cricket Club
CURFC: Cambridge University Rugby Football Club
CUS: Catholic University School
CVO: Commander of the Royal Victorian Order
CY: Cricketer of the Year (in *Wisden's Cricketers' Almanack)*
Cz: Czechoslovakia

d: died; drop-goal
DCLI: Duke of Cornwall's Light Infantry
DCM: Distinguished Conduct Medal
DD: Doctor of Divinity
dept: department
Derbys: Derbyshire
DFC: Distinguished Flying Cross
Dir: Director
disqu: disqualified
Dist: District(s)
Div: Division
DL: Deputy Lieutenant
Dr: Doctor
DSC: Distinguished Service Cross
DSM: Distinguished Service Medal
DS: Dental School
DSO: Distinguished Service Order

E: East(ern); England
Educ: Educational
engr(g): engineer(ing)
ENT: ear, nose and throat
equ: equal(led)
ER: East Riding
exec: executive

F: France
FB: full back
FC: Football Club
Fdr: Founder
FFR: Fédération Française de Rugby
Fg Off: Flying Officer
FH: fly-half
FHU: Four Home Unions
Fix: Fixture
Fj: Fiji
FP: Former Pupils

FRCS: Fellow of the Royal
 College of Surgeons
FRCSI: Fellow of the Royal
 College of Surgeons of Ireland
FRGS: Fellow of the Royal
 Geographical Society
FRS: Fellow of the Royal Society
FRU: French Rugby Union
Ft: Flight
ft: feet

G: Germany
GAA: Gaelic Athletic
 Association
GB: Great Britain
GC: Golf Club
GCB: Knight Grand Cross of the
 Bath
Gen: General
Glam: Glamorgan
Glos: Gloucestershire
gm: goal from a mark
GOC: General Officer
 Commanding
govt: government
Gp Capt: Group Captain
GP: general practitioner
GPS: Great Public Schools
 (Australia)
Griq: Griqualand
GS: Grammar School
GSO: General Staff Officer
GWR: Great Western Railway

H: Hornets
HAC: Honourable Artillery
 Company
HE: Higher Education
heavywt: heavyweight
Herts: Hertfordshire
HM: Headmaster
Hon: The Honourable; honorary

Hosp(s): Hospital(s)
HS: High School; highest score
HTV: Harlech Television

I: Ireland
IB: International Board
i/c: in charge of
ICI: Imperial Chemical Industries
IFS: Irish Free State
Imp: Imperial
in: inches
inc: including
inj: injury(ies); injured
Inst: Institute
int(s): international(s)
IOM: Isle of Man
IOW: Isle of Wight
intermed: intermediate
IRU: Irish Rugby Union
ISC: Imperial Service College
ISM: Imperial Service Medal
ISO: Imperial Service Order
It: Italy

J: Japan
Jnr(s): Junior(s)
JP: Justice of the Peace
jt: joint

KBE: Knight of the British
 Empire
KC: King's Counsel
KCB: Knight Commander of the
 Bath
KCIE: Knight Commander of the
 Indian Empire
KCMG: Knight Commander of St
 Michael and St George
KCS: King's College School
KCSI: Knight Commander of the
 Star of India

KCVO: Knight Commander of
   the Royal Victorian Order
KES: King Edward's School
KGS: King's Grammar School
kia: killed in action
KORR: King's Own Royal
   Regiment
KOSB: King's Own Scottish
   Borderers
KPM: King's Police Medal
KR: Kingston Rovers
K St J: Knight of St John
Kt: Knight

Lancs: Lancashire
lb: pound(s)
L/Cpl: Lance-Corporal
ldg: leading
LDV: Local Defence Volunteers
Leics: Leicestershire
Lge: League
LI: Light Infantry
Lib: Liberal
Lincs: Lincolnshire
LlD: Doctor of Letters
Lt: Lieutenant
LTA: Lawn Tennis Association
LTC: Lawn Tennis Club
Ltd: Limited
LTF: Lawn Tennis Federation

M: Maoris
m: minutes; metres
MAC: Motor Ambulance Corps
Maj: Major
Man: Managing
MBE: Member of the Order of
   the British Empire
MC: Military Cross
MCC: Marylebone Cricket Club
Mdx: Middlesex
ME: Middle East

Mem: Member
Met: Metropolitan
Mgr: Manager
MICG: Member of the Institute of
   Civil Engineers
Mil: Military
Min: Ministry
MM: Military Medal
MO: Medical Officer
MOA: Member of the Order of
   Australia
Mod: Modern
Mon: Monmouthshire
MP: Member of Parliament
MRCS: Member of the Royal
   College of Surgeons
Mt: Mount
mth(s): month(s)

N: North(ern)
NAm: North America
Nat: National
NCB: National Coal Board
NE: North-East(ern)
NIFC: Northern Ireland Football
   Club
NLD: Notts, Lincs & Derbys
no: number; not out
Northumb: Northumberland
Notts: Nottinghamshire
nr: near
NSW: New South Wales
NSWRU: New South Wales
   Rugby Union
NU: Northern Union
NW: North-West(ern)
NZ: New Zealand(er)
NZA: New Zealand Army
NZEF: New Zealand
   Expeditionary Force
NZGA: New Zealand Golf
   Association

NZMC: New Zealand Medical
Corps
NZN: New Zealand Native Team
NZRU: New Zealand Rugby
Union
NZS: New Zealand Services

O: Old
OB: Old Boys
OBLI: Oxford & Bucks Light
Infantry
OBE: Order of the British Empire
OFS: Orange Free State
OMT: Old Merchant Taylors
OStJ: Order of St John
OUCC: Oxford University
Cricket Club
OURFC: Oxford University
Rugby Football Club
Oxon: Oxfordshire

P: President's XV
p: penalty goal(s)
PA: personal assistant
PC: Privy Counsellor
PE: physical education
Pembs: Pembrokeshire
Pk: Park
pl: played; plays; playing
Poly: Polytechnic
POW: prisoner of war
Prep: Preparatory
Pres: President
prev: previous
Prmy: Primary
pro: professional
PR(O): Public Relations (Officer)
Prof: Professor
Prov: Province(s)
ptn: partner(ed)
Pte: Private
PTI: Physical Training Instructor

Pt Off: Pilot Officer
pts: points
pub: published
PUC: Paris University Club

QC: Queen's Counsel
QEGS: Queen Elizabeth's
Grammar School
Qld: Queensland
QSM: Queen's Service Medal
(NZ)

R: Romania; Royal; Rovers;
Replacement; Replaced
r: replacement; replaced
RA: Royal Artillery
RAC: Royal Armoured Corps
RADC: Royal Army Dental
Corps
RAE: Royal Aircraft
Establishment
RAEC: Royal Army Education
Corps
RAF: Royal Air Force
RAFVR: Royal Air Force
Volunteer Reserve
RAMC: Royal Army Medical
Corps
RAN: Royal Australian Navy
RAOC: Royal Army Ordnance
Corps
RASC: Royal Army Service
Corps
RBAI: Royal Belfast Academical
Institute
RC: Roman Catholic; Rowing
Club
RCF: Racing Club de France
RCPI: Royal College of
Physicians of Ireland
RCSI: Royal College of Surgeons
of Ireland

RCT: Royal Corps of Transport
RCVS: Royal College of
    Veterinary Surgery
Rd: Road
RDC: Rural District Council
RE: Royal Engineers
rec: record
ref: referee(d)
REME: Royal Electrical &
    Mechanical Engineers
rep: representative; represent(ed)
Rev: Reverend
RFA: Royal Field Artillery
RFC: Rugby Football Club; Royal
    Flying Corps
RFU: Rugby Football Union
RGA: Royal Garrison Artillery
Rgrs: Rangers
RGS: Royal Grammar School
Rgt: Regiment
RHA: Royal Horse Artillery
RHS: Royal High School
RIE: Royal Indian Engineering
RL: Rugby League
rly: railway
RMA: Royal Military Academy;
    Royal Marine Artillery
RMC: Royal Military College
RMS: Royal Military School
RN: Royal Navy
RNAS: Royal Naval Air Service
RNC: Royal Naval College
RNEC: Royal Naval Engineering
    College
RNLI: Royal National Lifeboat
    Institution
RNVR: Royal Naval Volunteer
    Reserve
RNZAF: Royal New Zealand Air
    Force
RNZN: Royal New Zealand Navy
RS: Royal School

Rt Hon: Right Honourable
RU: Rugby Union
RUC: Royal Ulster Constabulary
RUI: Royal University of Ireland

S: Scotland; South(ern)
s: seconds
SA: South Africa(n)
SAAF: South African Air Force
SAAMC: South African Army
    Medical Corps
SAm: South America
SARB: South African Rugby
    Board
SARF: South African Rugby
    Federation
SAus: South Australia
SB: Stade Bordelais
SBUC: Stade Bordelais
    Université Club
SC: Ski Club
sc: score(d)
Sch(s): School(s)
SCUF: Sporting Club
    Universitaire de France
Sec: Secondary; Secretary
sel: selector; selected; selection
Servs: Services
SF: Stade Français
SFU: Scottish Football Union
Sgt: Sergeant
SH: scrum-half
S Ldr: Squadron Leader
SMS: Secondary Modern School
Snr: Senior
Soc: Society
SOE: Stade Olympien des
    Etudiants
Sqn: Squadron
SS: Secondary Schools
St: Street; Saint
st: stone(s)

Staffs: Staffordshire
Surg(s): Surgeon(s)
susp: suspended
SW: South-West(ern)
SWEB: South Wales Electricity
 Board
SWFU: South Wales Football
 Union
Switz: Switzerland

t: try; tries
TA: Territorial Army
TD: Territorial Decoration;
 Teachta Dala (Irish MP)
Tech: Technical (College)
Tg: Training; Tonga
Theol: Theological
Tment: Tournament
TOEC: Toulouse Olympique
 Employés Club
Treas: Treasurer
Trin: Trinity
TTC: Teacher Training College

UAU: Universities Athletics
 Union
UC: University College
UK: United Kingdom
Ump: Umpire(d)
uncap: uncapped
Univ(s): University(ies)

UNO: United Nations
 Organisation
UOFS: University of Orange Free
 State
US: United States of America
USAF: United States Air Force
USARU: United States of
 America Rugby Union
Utd: United
UWIST: University of Wales
 Institute of Science and
 Technology

v: versus
VC: Victoria Cross
V-capt: Vice-captain
VD: Volunteer Decoration
V-pres: Vice-president

W: Wales; West(ern); Wanderers
w: with
WA: Western Australia
Wd: World
WRU: Welsh Rugby Union
WW: World War

y: yard(s)
YMCA: Young Men's Christian
 Association
Yorks: Yorkshire
yr(s): year(s)

A

AARVOLD, Sir Carl Douglas *England*
OBE TD JP
Durham Sch, Cambridge Univ, Headingley, W
Hartlepool, Durham Co, Blackheath,
Barbarians.
b 7.6.07.
Centre/wing, 16-9-1-6 (12 − 4t).
28 NSW+ W+ I+ F+ S+; 29 W+ I− F+(2t);
31 W= S− F−; 32 SA− W− I+ S+(2t); 33 W−;
BI > 30 NZ 4-1-0-3, A 1-1-0-0.
High Court Judge. Blue 25-8. Rugby fives blue.
BT > 27 Arg. Capt BI v NZ 30, 1st BI Test win
(6-3) in NZ. Capt E 6 times. Durham &
Northumb v SA 31. Called to Bar 32. Served
WW2 as Lt Col RA. Pres LTA 62.

ABADIE, André *France*
Pau.
b 27.7.34 Toulouse.
Hooker, 1-1-0-0.
64 I+.
Leather salesman.

ABADIE, Alain *France*
Graulhet.
b 15.8.46 Toulouse.
Prop, 7-4-1-2.
65 R+r; 67 SA− SA+ SA= NZ−; 68 S+ I+.

ABADIE, Lucien *France*
Tarbes.
Prop, 1-0-0-1.
63 R−.

ABBOTT, Harold Louis *New Zealand*
('Bunny')
Taranaki, Wanganui, Wellington, Brit
Columbia.
b 17.6.1882 Camerontown; *d* 16.1.71
Palmerston N.
Wing, 1-1-0-0 (8 − 2t 1c).
06 F+(2t 1c).
Blacksmith/plating inspector Central Racing
Districts. NZ > 05 A, 05-6 BI,F & NAm (played
for & against Brit Columbia). Served Boer War.
Son Lionel played for Wellington 44-54 & NZ
XV 44. Professional sprinter.

ABERCROMBIE, Cecil Halliday *Scotland*
Berkhamsted, US Portsmouth.
b 12.4.1886 India; kia 31.5.16 Jutland.
Forward, 6-2-0-4 (3 − 1t).
10 I+ E−; 11 F−(1t) W−; 13 F+ W−.
RN. Hampshire CCC.

ABERCROMBIE, James Gilbert *Scotland*
Heriot's, Edinburgh Univ.
b 9.5.28.

Hooker, 7-4-0-3 (3 − 1t).
49 F+ W+ I−; 50 F+ W− I− E+(1t).
Medicine.

ABRAHAM, Myles ('Miley') DCM *Ireland*
MM
Bective Rgrs.
b 1887 Dublin.
Centre, 5-2-0-3
12 E− S+ W+ SA−; 14 W−.
Civil service/Irish Dept of Justice. Served WW1,
Sgt RFA.

ABRAHAMS, Anthony Morris *Australia*
Frederick
Cranbrook Sch Sydney, Sydney Univ, NSW.
b 28.3.44.
Lock, 3-0-0-3.
67 NZ−; 68 NZ−; 69 W−.
Solicitor.

ACKERMAN, Robert Angus *Wales*
Christ's Coll Brecon, Welsh SS, St Mary's Coll
Twickenham, Newport, London Welsh, E
Suburbs (A), Cardiff, Barbarians.
b 2.3.61 Ebbw Vale.
Wing/centre, 22-10-0-12 (4 − 1t).
80 NZ−; 81 E+ S− A+; 82 I− F+ E− S−; 83
S+ I+ F− R−; 84 S− I+(1t) F− E+ A−; 85
S+ I− F− E+ Fj+; BI > 83 NZ 2(1r)-0-0-2.
Computer sales. Wales B v F 81. Wales XV v
Maoris 82. RL 86. Son of Doug Ackerman, sec
Newport RFC. Whitehaven RL 86.

ACKERMANN, David Schalk *South Africa*
Pienaar ('Dawie')
Stellenbosch Univ, W Prov.
Flanker, 8-4-0-4 (3 − 1t).
55 BI+(1t) BI− BI+; 56 A+ A+ NZ− NZ−;
58 F−.
PE teacher.

ADAMS, Alan Augustus *England*
Auckland GS, Otago Univ, Otago, S Island,
The London Hosp, London Univ, Barbarians.
b 8.5.1883 Greymouth, NZ; *d* 28.7.63
Greymouth.
Centre, 1-1-0-0.
10 F+.
Medicine. NZ sel 27-8, 34-7. Pres NZRFU 29.

ADAMS, Charles *Ireland*
O Wesley, Barbarians.
b 8.12.1883; *d* 13.11.65 Malahide.
Forward, 16-10-0-6 (3 − 1t).
08 E−; 09 E− F+; 10 F+; 11 E+ S+(1t) W−
F+; 12 S+ W+ SA−; 13 W− F+; 14 F+ E−
S+; BT > 10 SA.
Civil service. Barbarians comm.

ADAMS, Frank Reginald　　　*England*
Wellington Coll, Richmond, Mdx.
b 1853; *d* 32.
Forward, 7-4-3-0 (2t).
1875 I+ S=; 1876 S+; 1877 I+(1t); 1878 S=;
1879 S= I+(1t).
Ship insurer. Son of Maj Gen F. Adams, CB.
E's 1st capt in Calcutta Cup match, v S 1879. In
bus in Australia & US 1894.

ADAMS, Neil Joseph ('Noodles')　　*Australia*
St Joseph's Sch Carrington, Merewether-
Carlton, Newcastle, NSW Country, NSW.
b 26.8.25 Wickham, NSW.
Prop, 1-0-0-1.
55 NZ−.
Brewery worker/seaman. Only player capped
from Merewether-Carlton.

ADAMSON, Robert Wilson　　　*Australia*
Sydney Univ, E Suburbs, NSW.
b 1889; *d* 52.
Wing, 1-1-0-0.
12 US+.
NSW sel.

ADEY, Garry John　　　*England*
Leicester.
b 13.6.47 Loughborough.
2-0-0-2.
76 I− F−.
Engr.

ADKINS, Stanley John ('Akker')　　*England*
Stoke Council Sch, Stoke OB, The Army, Comb
Servs, Coventry, Barbarians, Warwicks.
b 2.6.22 Coventry.
No 8/lock, 7-4-1-2 (3 − 1t).
50 I+ F− S−; 53 W+ I= F+ S+(1t).
Aircraft factory machinist/licensee. Served
WW2, L/Cpl Coldstream Guards, Sgt RASC.
V-pres Coventry. Bowls for Warwicks.

AGAR, Albert Eustace　　　*England*
W Hartlepool GS, Hartlepool R, Durham City,
Lloyds Bank, Durham Co, London Cos,
Harlequins, Mdx.
b 12.11.23 W Hartlepool.
Centre, 7-4-1-2 (6 − 1t 1d).
52 SA− W−(1t) S+(1d) I+ F+; 53 W+ I=.
Banking. Served WW2, navigator in RAF.
England sel 62-71 (chmn 69-71). Mdx CB rep;
IB rep; pres RFU 84-5. Treas of Lloyds Bank.

AGAR, Robert Dunlop　　　*Ireland*
Mountjoy Sch, Kilkenny Coll, Malone,
Barbarians.
b 29.3.20 Fenagh, Co Carlow.
No 8/flanker/lock, 10-5-1-4.
47 F− E+ S+ W−; 48 F+; 49 S+ W+; 50 F=

E− W−.
Police.

AGNEW, Patrick Joseph　　　*Ireland*
St Malachy's Coll Belfast, CIYMS.
b 18.3.42 Belfast.
Prop, 2-0-0-2.
74 Fr−; 76 A−.
Bank mgr.

AGNEW, W.C.C.　　　*Scotland*
Stewart's Coll, Stewart's Coll FP, Barbarians.
Flanker/lock, 2-1-0-1.
30 W+ I−.

AGUERRE, Roger　　　*France*
Biarritz Ol.
b 13.3.57 Mauléon.
FH, 1-1-0-0 (6 − 1d 1p).
79 S+(1d 1p).
Municipal employee.

AGUILAR, David　　　*France*
Pau.
Flanker, 1-1-0-0.
37 G+.

AGUIRRE, Jean-Michel　　　*France*
Bagnères.
b 2.11.51 Tostat.
SH/FB, 39-25-3-11 (123 − 2t 14c 1d 28p).
71 A+; 72 S−; 73 W+ I− J+(1t) R+; 74 I+(1c)
W= Arg+ R− SA−; 76 W−r E+ US+ A+(1t
2c 1p) R−(1c 2p); 77 W+ E+ S+ I+(1c 2p)
Arg+(1p) Arg=(6p) NZ+ NZ− R+; 78 E+(2c
1p) S+(1c 3p) I+(2p) W− R+(2p); 79 I=(1c
1p) W+(2p) E−(1c) S+(1p) NZ−(1c) NZ+(1p)
R+(2c 1d 1p); 80 W− I+(1c 2p).
Schoolmaster.

AHEARN, Thomas　　　*Ireland*
Queen's Coll Cork.
Forward, 1-1-0-0.
1899 E+.
Insurance.

AINCIART, Edouard　　　*France*
Bayonne.
Hooker, 6-5-0-1.
33 G+; 34 G+; 35 G+; 37 G+ It+; 38 G−.

AINSLIE, Robert　　　*Scotland*
Edinburgh Inst, Edinburgh Inst FP.
b 1858; *d* 12.5.06 Sydney, NSW.
Forward, 7-4-2-1 (3t).
1879 I+ E=; 1880 I+ E−; 1881 E=(1t); 1882 I+
E+(2t).
Bro of Thomas.

AINSLIE, Thomas　　　*Scotland*
Edinburgh Inst, Edinburgh Inst FP.

b 1859; *d* 16.3.26.
Forward, 11-7-2-2 (1t).
1881 E=; 1882 I+ E+; 1883 W+ I+ E−; 1884 W+(1t) I+ E−; 1885 W= I+.
Wine trader. Bro of Robert. Touch-judge S v I, S v E 1892. Pres SFU 1891-2.

AITCHISON, G.R.   *Scotland*
Craigmount, Edinburgh W.
Wing, 1-1-0-0.
1883 I+.

AITCHISON, Thomas Graham   *Scotland*
Gala.
b − ; *d* 25.12.77 Clovenfords.
FB, 3-2-0-1.
29 W− I+ E+.

AITKEN, Alexander I.   *Scotland*
Edinburgh Inst, Edinburgh Inst FP.
b − ; *d* 7.7.25 Salisbury, Rhodesia.
Forward, 1-1-0-0.
1889 I+.

AITKEN, George   *New Zealand/Scotland*
Gothard
Westport HS, Westport, Buller, Univ,
Wellington, N Island, NZ Univs, Oxford Univ,
Barbarians (E), London Scottish.
b 2.7.1898 Westport, NZ; *d* 24.8.52
Wellington, NZ.
New Zealand
Centre, 2-1-0-1.
21 SA+ SA−.
Scotland
Wing/centre, 8-7-0-1.
24 W+ I+ E−; 25 F+ W+ I+ E+; 29 F+.
Timber trade/civil service. Capt NZ v SA 21,
youngest NZ capt until Herb Lilburne 29.
Rhodes Scholar. Blue 22-4; capped for S from
Oxford. 440y hurdler.

AITKEN, James   *Scotland*
Penicuik HS, Edinburgh Coll of Commerce,
Gala.
b 22.11.47 Penicuik.
Prop, 23-13-0-10 (4 − 1t).
77 E− I+ F−; 81 A+ F− W+ E− I+ NZ−
NZ− R+; 82 E+ I− F+ W+; 83 F− W− E+;
84 W+(1t) E+ I+ F+ R−.
Co dir. Scotland B. Scottish XV v Japan 76.

AITKEN, Richard   *Scotland*
London Scottish, RN, Barbarians.
b 29.6.14 Dunbar.
Prop, 1-0-0-1.
47 W−.
RN. S's oldest 1st cap until T. Gray 50. Played
in 6 Victory ints.

ALBALADÉJO, Pierre   *France*
('Monsieur Le Drop')
Dax.
b 13.2.33 Dax.
FB/FH, 30-19-3-8 (104 − 16c 12d 12p).
54 E+ It+; 60 W+(1c) I+(3d) It+(2d) R−; 61
S+(1c 1d 1p) SA= E= W+ I+(1d 1p) NZ−(2d)
NZ− A+(2d); 62 S+(1c 2p) E+(2c) W−
I+(1c); 63 S−(1p) I+(3c 1d) E−(1c) W+(1c)
It+; 64 S− NZ−(1p) W=(1c 2p) It+(3p) I+(3c)
SA+(1c 1p) Fj+.
Restaurateur. F's most capped FH. Set world
rec 3d in an int, v I 60.

ALBERTYN, Pieter Kuyper   *South Africa*
('Pierre' or 'PK')
Stellenbosch HS, Stellenbosch Univ, Guy's
Hosp, Barbarians (E), George, SW Dist.
b 27.5.1897 Caledon.
Wing/centre, 4-3-1-0 (3 − 1t).
24 BI+ BI+(1t) BI= BI+.
Dentist. Capt SA v BI (4 Tests) 24. At
Stellenbosch HS when Paul Roos was principal.
6t Stellenbosch Univ v Villagers 19. Knee inj W
Prov Univs v NZ Imp Servs 19 threatened
career; played again in 6 weeks, sc 5t v Som W.
Studied dentistry at Guy's Hosp; declined to
play in England Trial. Returned SA 23.

ALCOCK, Arnold   *England*
Newcastle-under-Lyme HS, Manchester Univ,
Guy's Hosp, Richmond, Blackheath, Surrey.
b 18.8.1882; *d* 7.11.73.
Hooker, 1-0-1-0.
06 SA=.
Medicine. According to rugby historian John
Griffiths, Dr Alcock earned his cap due to
clerical error, confused with Liverpool player,
L.A.N. Slocock, capped in E's next match, v F
07. Rep London Univ at swimming. GP in
Gloucester. Pres Gloucester 24.

ALDERSON, Frederic Hodgson   *England*
Rudd JP
Durham Sch, Cambridge Univ, Tyndale,
Hartlepool R, Blackheath, Northumb, Durham
Co, Barbarians.
b 27.6.1867 Hartford, Northumb; *d* 18.2.25
Hartlepool.
Centre, 6-4-0-2 (1t 4c).
1891 W+(2c) I+ S−(1c); 1892 W+(1t 1c) S+;
1893 W−.
HM. Blue 1887-8. Played for Hartlepool R v
Barbarians, in 1st match played by Barbarians
27.12.1890. Capt E on debut. Blackheath >
1895 Germany. Ref S v I 03. Original mem
Barbarians. Lawn tennis for Co Durham. Asst
master, HM Henry Smith Sch Hartlepool 1892.

ALEXANDER, E.   *South Africa*
Griq W.

23

2-0-0-2.
1891 BT− BT−.

ALEXANDER, Edward Perkins　　　　*Wales*
Llandovery Coll, Cambridge Univ, Brecon,
Wasps, Blackheath.
b 1863 Monknash; *d* 26.10.31 Holt, Wilts.
Forward, 5-1-2-2.
1885 S=; 1886 E− S−; 1887 E= I+.
Farmer. Blue 1884-6. Ckt for S Wales XI.

ALEXANDER, Harry　　　　*England*
Bromborough Sch, Uppingham Sch, Oxford
Univ, Birkenhead Pk, Cheshire, Richmond,
Barbarians, Mdx.
b 6.1.1879 Oxton, Cheshire; kia 17.10.15
Hulluch.
Forward, 7-2-1-4 (7 − 2c 1p).
1900 I+(1c) S=; 01 W− I−(1p) S−; 02 W−(1c)
I+.
Schoolmaster. Contemporary of W. Cobby at
Uppingham. Blue 1897-8. Served WW1, 2nd Lt
in Grenadier Guards; killed on 13th day of
active service. Co hockey; scratch golfer. Also
high-class ice skater & pro singer. Taught at
Stanmore Pk Prep Sch.

ALEXANDER, Robert　　　　*Ireland*
RBAI, Queen's Univ Belfast, NIFC, Police
Union, Barbarians.
b 24.9.10 Belfast; kia 19.7.43 Burma.
Flanker, 11-6-0-5 (3 − 1t).
36 E+ S+ W−; 37 E− S+(1t) W+; 38 E− S−;
39 E+ S+ W−; BI > 38 SA 3-1-0-2.
RUC. Ireland ckter. Served WW2, Capt in R
Inniskillen Fusiliers.

ALEXANDER, William　　　　*England*
Northern, Barbarians, Northumb.
Wing, 1-0-0-1.
27 F−.
Chartered accountant. Employed for time in
Can. Lived in F.

ALEXANDER, William H.　　　　*Wales*
Glynneath, Llwynypia.
b c1878 Glynneath; *d* −.
Forward, 7-3-0-4 (6 − 2t).
1898 I+ E−; 1899 E+ S− I−; 01 S− I+(2t).
Police.

ALLAN, Bryce　　　　*Scotland*
Glasgow Acad, Glasgow Academicals.
b 1859 − ; *d* −.11.22.
Forward, 1-0-0-1.
1881 I−.

ALLAN, James Leslie　　　　*Scotland*
Gala Acad, Edinburgh Univ, Melrose,
Barbarians.
b 4.3.27 Melrose.

Centre, 4-0-0-4.
52 F− W− I−; 53 W−.
Schoolmaster. Nephew of John W.

ALLAN, John Lewis Forsyth　　　　*Scotland*
Rugby Sch, Cambridge Univ.
b 20.8.34.
Wing, 2-0-0-2.
57 I− E−.
Law. Blue 56.

ALLAN, John W.　　　　*Scotland*
Melrose, Barbarians.
b 05; *d* 29.12.58.
Prop, 17-7-1-9 (27 − 9c 3p).
27 F+; 28 I−; 29 F+ W− I+(1c) E+; 30 F−
E=; 31 F+(2p) W−(1c) I−(1c) E+(5c); 32
SA− W− I−(1c); 34 I+(1p) E−.
Nursing. Uncle of James. 5c v E 31, rec for a
Scot (with F.H. Turner).

ALLAN, Richard Campbell　　　　*Scotland*
Hutchesons' GS, Hutchesons' GSFP.
b 16.3.39 Glasgow.
SH, 1-0-0-1.
69 I−.
Wholesale meat salesman.

ALLAN, Trevor　　　　*Australia*
N Sydney Tech HS, Gordon, NSW.
b 26.9.26 Bathurst.
Centre, 14-6-1-7 (22 − 2t 2c 4p).
46 NZ−(1t) M− NZ−; 47 NZ−(1c 3p) S+
I+(1t 1c) W−; 48 E+ F−; 49 M− M= M+
NZ+ NZ+(1p).
Automobile salesman/TV commentator. 66 pts
A > 47-8 BI, F (took over as tour capt after inj
to W.M. McLean in 6th match). Capt A > 49
NZ. Leigh RL (E) 50, £6250 fee; N Sydney.

ALLARDICE, William Dallas　　　　*Scotland*
Aberdeen GS, Aberdeen GSFP.
b 4.11.19 Glasgow.
SH, 8-3-0-5 (5 − 1c 1p).
47 A−; 48 F+ W− I−; 49 F+(1c) W+ I−(1p)
E−.
Schoolmaster.

ALLEN, Charles Elliot　　　　*Ireland*
Merchiston Castle Sch, Foyle Coll, Derry,
Liverpool.
b 14.10.1880 Gibraltar; *d* 15.1.66 Can.
Forward, 21-6-1-14 (3 − 1t).
1900 E− S= W−; 01 E+ S− W−; 03 S− W−;
04 E− S− W+; 05 E+(1t) S+ W− NZ−; 06 E+
S− W+ SA−; 07 S− W−.
Grainbroker. Bro of G.G.

ALLEN, Charles Peter PC MP　　　　*Wales*
Rugby Sch, Oxford Univ, Beaumaris.
b 2.12.1861 Prestwich; *d* 18.9.30 London.

24

Back, 2-0-0-2 (1t).
1884 E−(1t) S−.
Barrister. Blue 1881-3. Sc W's 1st t v E, 1884.
Served WW1, Maj 5th Glos Rgt.

ALLEN, Frederick Richard   *New Zealand*
Phillipstown Sch, Canterbury, Linwood,
Marlborough, Waikato, Auckland, N Island,
Barbarians (E).
b 9.2.20 Oamaru.
1st/2nd five-eighth, 6-4-0-2.
46 A+ A+; 47 A+ A+; 49 SA− SA−.
Dress manufacturer. Capt v A 46, > 47 A. Capt
NZ > 49 SA. Asst mgr NZ > 67 BI,F & Can.
NZRFU sel 64-8, coach 66-8. Served WW2, Lt
Infantry Battn. Co-author 'Fred Allen on
Rugby' pub 70.

ALLEN, G. Glynn   *Ireland*
Merchiston Castle Sch, Derry, Liverpool.
b 14.3.1874; *d* −.
Half-back, 9-6-1-2 (3 − 1t).
1896 E+ S= W+; 1897 E+ S−; 1898 E+ S−;
1899 E+(1t) W+.
Bro of C.E.

ALLEN, H.W.   *Scotland*
Glasgow Acad, Glasgow Academicals.
Forward, 1-0-1-0.
1873 E=.

ALLEN, Nicholas Houghton   *New Zealand*
Remuera Intermed Sch, Auckland GS,
Auckland Univ, Auckland, NZ Univs, NZ Jnrs,
Cos.
b 30.8.58 Auckland; *d* 7.10.84 Woollongong,
NSW.
1st five-eighth, 2-1-0-1 (4 − 1t).
80 A− W+(1t).
Sales rep. NZr > 80 A & Fj; NAm & W. Ckt for
Auckland.

ALLEN, Peter B.   *South Africa*
Jnr Springboks, E Prov.
b 10.4.30.
Lock, 1-1-0-0.
60 S+.
Capt Jnr Springboks > 59 SAm.

ALLEN, T.C.   *Ireland*
NIFC.
Forward, 2-0-0-2.
1885 E− S−.

ALLEN, W.S.   *Ireland*
Wanderers.
Forward, 1-0-0-1.
1875 E−.

ALLEY, Geoffrey Thomas   *New Zealand*
Christchurch Boys' HS, UC Canterbury,

Southland, Canterbury, S Island.
b 4.2.03 Amberley.
No 8, 3-1-0-2.
28 SA− SA+ SA−.
Farmer/librarian. NZ > 26 A, 28 SA. NZ Univs
shot putt champ 28. Dir of National Library
Service & National Librarian 64-7. Wrote 'With
the Brit Rugby Team in New Zealand' pub 30.

ALLISON, Dennis Fenwick   *England*
Dame Allan's Sch Newcastle, Durham Univ,
Northern, Coventry, Barbarians, Northumb,
Warwicks.
b 20.4.31.
FB, 7-3-2-2 (15 − 5p).
56 W−(1p) I+(1p) S+ F−(2p); 57 W+(1p); 58
W= S=.
Research dept ICI/co dir.

ALLISON, James Barnett   *Ireland*
RS Dungannon, Campbell Coll, Queen's Coll
Belfast, Edinburgh Univ.
b 28.6.1880; *d* 31.3.07.
Centre, 12-4-1-7 (4 − 1d).
1899 E+ S+; 1900 E−(1d) S= W−; 01 E+ S−
W−; 02 E− S+ W−; 03 S−.
Capped from sch.

ALLPORT, Alfred   *England*
London Int Coll Isleworth, Guy's Hosp,
Blackheath, Barbarians, Surrey.
b 12.9.1867 Brixton; *d* 2.5.49 London.
Forward, 5-3-0-2.
1892 W+; 1893 I+; 1894 W+ I− S−.
Medicine/RAMC. Consultant surg St Paul's
Hosp.

ALLPORT, Percy   *South Africa*
Villagers, W Prov.
FB, 2-1-0-1 (3 − 1t).
10 BI− BI+(1t).
1st SA FB to sc t in int rugby. Normally centre
for W Prov.

ALVAREZ, André   *France*
Bayonne, Tyrosse.
b 26.5.23 Bayonne.
FH/FB, 21-14-0-7 (25 − 1t 6c 2d 1p).
45 BF+ BF−; 46 BF+ I+ NZS− W+(1d); 47
S+ I+ W− E−; 48 I− A+(2c) S−(1c) W+(1c)
E+(1c); 49 I+ E−(1d) W+(1c) 51 S+ E+
W+(1t 1p).

AMAND, Henri   *France*
SF.
b 17.9.1873; *d* 67.
FH, 1-0-0-1.
06 NZ−.
Heating co draughtsman.

25

AMBERT, Albert *France*
Toulouse.
Flanker, 5-3-0-2 (11 − 1t 4c).
30 S+ I+(1c) E−(1c) G+(1t 2c) W−.

AMESTOY, Jean-Baptiste *France*
Montois.
b 28.8.36 Ustaritz.
Prop, 2-0-0-2.
64 NZ− E−.
Engr.

ANDERSON, Albert *New Zealand*
Canterbury, NZ Colts, NZ Jnrs, NZ Univs, S
Island.
b 5.2.61 Christchurch.
Lock, 5-2-1-2.
83 S= E− ; 84 A− A+ A+.
NZ > 83 S & E, 84 A, 85 Arg.

ANDERSON, Alexander Harvie *Scotland*
Merchiston Castle Sch, Glasgow Academicals.
b 1873; *d* 14.12.39.
Forward, 1-0-0-1.
1894 I−.
Textile manufacturer.

ANDERSON, Darsie G. *Scotland*
London Scottish.
b − ; *d* −.12.37 Guildford.
Half-back, 8-6-0-2 (2 − 1t).
1889 I+ ; 1890 W+(1t) I+ E− ; 1891 W+ E+ ;
1892 W+ E−.
Business. Sc 1st int try w a pts value (2), S v W
1890.

ANDERSON, Ernest *Scotland*
Stewart's Coll, Stewart's Coll FP, Edinburgh
Univ.
b 20.10.18.
SH, 2-0-0-2.
47 I− E−.
Schoolmaster. Played in 1 Servs int 44.

ANDERSON, Frederick Edmund *Ireland*
('Fuzzy')
Coleraine Acad Inst, Queen's Univ Belfast,
Barbarians.
b 29.8.29 Belfast.
Prop, 13-3-2-8.
53 F+ E= S+ W− ; 54 NZ− F− E− S+ W− ; 55
F− E= S− W−.
Medicine. Emigrated to A.

ANDERSON, Henry James *Ireland*
Galway GS, Queen's Coll Galway, O Wesley,
Blackheath, Bedford, Barbarians.
b 17.3.1882; *d* 9.11.49 Dublin.
Wing, 4-2-0-2.
03 E+ S− ; 06 E+ S−.

Dental surg. Played for Blackheath, Bedford v
NZ 05. Pres IRU 45-6.

ANDERSON, J.A. *South Africa*
W Prov.
b Lancs.
1-1-0-0.
03 BT+.

ANDERSON, John Henry *South Africa*
('Biddy')
Diocesan Coll Rondebosch, Villagers, W Prov.
b 26.4.1874; *d* 11.3.26 Bredasdorp.
3-1-0-2.
1896 BT− BT− BT+.
Mining. SA sel. Ckt for SA.

ANDERSON, John W. *Scotland*
Scot's Coll NZ, Merchiston Castle Sch, W of
Scotland, Canterbury NZ.
b 9.5.1850 Edinburgh; *d* 26.5.34 Christchurch,
NZ.
Forward, 1-0-0-1.
1872 E−.
Engr/shipping.

ANDERSON, Stanley *England*
Rockcliff, Northumb.
Centre, 1-0-0-1.
1899 I−.
Licensee. Northumb CCC.

ANDERSON, Thomas *Scotland*
Merchiston Castle Sch.
b 17.5.1863 Ledcamerock; *d* 17.6.38.
FB, 1-1-0-0.
1882 I+.
Stockbroker. Capped from sch. Ckt S v A 1882.

ANDERSON, William Andrew *Ireland*
Omagh Acad, Stranmillis TTC, Dungannon,
Ulster.
b 3.4.55 Sixmilebridge.
Lock, 6-3-1-2.
84 A− ; 85 S+ F= W+ E+ ; 86 F−.
Detained 4 mths in Arg for allegedly insulting
their flag, during Penguins tour

ANDERSON, William Francis *England*
Orrell.
b 45 Ormskirk.
Prop, 1-0-0-1.
73 NZ−.
Engr. 1st Orrell player capped.

ANDERTON, C. *England*
Manchester Free W.
b c1868; *d* c59.
Forward, 1-1-0-0.
1889 NZN+.

Cap in Manchester clubhouse. Capped in 1888 E XV that did not play.

ANDRÉ, Georges ('Le Bison')   *France*
RCF.
 b 13.8.1889 Paris; kia 4.5.43 Tunisia.
Wing, 7-0-0-7 (11 − 3t 1c).
13 SA−(1c) E− W−(1t) I− ; 14 I−(1t) W− E−
(1t).
PE teacher. Served WW2.

ANDREW, Christopher Robert   *England*
Barnard Castle Sch, Cambridge Univ,
Nottingham, Yorks, N Div.
 b 18.2.63 Richmond, Yorks.
FH, 9-4-1-4 (86 − 4c 5d 21p).
85 R+(2d 4p) F= (1d 2p) S+(2p) I−(2p) W−
(1c 1d 2p); 86 W+(1d 6p) S−(2p) I+(3c 1p) F−.
Blue 82-4. E Under 23s v English Students; >
Spain 84. Equ world rec 6p v W 86. Capt
Cambridge Univ at ckt.

ANDREW, J.B.   *South Africa*
Transvaal.
1-0-0-1.
1896 BT−.
Wing, 1-1-0-0 (3 − 1t).

ANDREWS, Frank   *Wales*
Pontypool, Newbridge.
 b 1888; *d* −.
Back−row, 4-2-0-2.
12 SA−; 13 E− S+ I+.
Steelworker. Hunslet RL 13.

ANDREWS, Frederick Graham   *Wales*
Cheltenham Coll, Swansea.
 b 15.9.1864; *d* 2.6.29 Swansea.
Forward, 2-0-0-2.
1884 E− S−.
Engr.

ANDREWS, George E.   *Wales*
Taunton Sch, St Julians HS Newport, Newport.
 b 24.8.04 Newport.
Wing, 5-1-1-3 (9 − 3t).
26 E=(1t) S−; 27 E−(1t) F+(1t) I−.
Dock broker/rep. Leeds RL 27.

ANDREWS, G.   *Ireland*
RBAI, NIFC.
Forward, 2-0-0-2.
1875 E− E−.

ANDREWS, H.W.   *Ireland*
NIFC.
Forward, 3-1-0-2.
1888 NZN−; 1889 S− W+.

ANDURAN, Joé   *France*
SCUF.

b −; kia WW1.
No 8, 1-0-0-1.
10 W−.
Picture gallery employee.

ANGUS, Alexander William   *Scotland*
Watson's, Watsonians.
 b 11.11.1889 Sydney, NSW; *d* 25.3.47
Edinburgh.
Centre, 18-7-0-11 (9 − 3t).
09 W−; 10 F+(1t) W− E−; 11 W− I−(1t); 12
F+ W− I− E+ SA−; 13 F+ W−; 14 E−; 20 F+
W+ I+(1t) E−.
Played either side WW1. Ref W v E 24, I v NSW
27. Ckt for S.

ANLEZARK, Ernest Arthur   *Australia*
('George')
Bathurst Dist Sch, Bathurst, W Union, NSW
Country, Lismore, NSW.
 b 29.12.1882 Bathurst; *d* 56.
Five-eighth, 1-0-0-1.
05 NZ−.
Blacksmith/cotton broker. Qld RL 08, then
Oldham (E).

ANTELME, Michael Joseph   *South Africa*
George
St Charles Coll Maritzburg, Natal Univ,
Transvaal.
 b 23.4.34.
5-2-2-1.
60 NZ+ NZ− NZ= NZ+; 61 F=.
Land surveyor.

ANTHONY, Leslie   *Wales*
Cwmllynfell, Neath.
 b 21.11.21 Rhiwfawr.
Prop, 3-1-1-1.
48 E= S+ F−.
Miner/sheet metal worker. Oldham RL 48. RL
scout.

ANTON, Peter A.   *Scotland*
Perth HS, Dundee HS, St Andrew's Univ.
 b 25.6.1850 Errol; *d* 10.12.11 Kilsyth.
Forward, 1-0-1-0.
1873 E=.
Minister.

APSEY, John T.   *South Africa*
Jnr Springboks, W Prov.
Prop, 3-2-0-1.
33 A+ A−; 38 BI+.
Jnr Springboks > 32 Arg (scored t in each of 2
Tests).

ARAOU, René   *France*
Narbonne.
Prop, 1-1-0-0.
24 R+.

ARCALIS, Roger   *France*
Brive.
b 1.6.27 Tarbes.
FB, 5-2-1-2.
50 S− I=; 51 I− E+ W+.
Switched to RL.

ARCHER, Arthur Montfort JP   *Ireland*
Armagh RS, Trin Coll Dublin, NIFC.
Forward, 1-0-0-1.
1879 S−.
Medicine. Served WW1, Lt Col 1st Cheshire
Rgt.

ARCHER, Herbert   *England*
Blundell's Sch, Guy's Hosp, Bridgwater & A.
b −.8.1884; *d* 26.12.46 Nether Stowey,
Bridgwater.
No 8, 3-2-0-1.
09 W− F+ I+; BT > 08 A, NZ.
Medicine/RAMC. GP at Nether Stowey.

ARCHER, William Roberts   *New Zealand*
('Robin')
Gore HS, Otago, Southland.
b 19.9.30 Gore.
1st five-eighth, 4-4-0-0.
55 A+ A+; 56 SA+ SA+.
Schoolmaster/building co mgr. NZ > 57 A.
Coached Southland 73-80. Father Bill & bro
Watson played for Southland; uncle Jim Archer
All Black 25.

ARGUS, Walter Garland   *New Zealand*
Pleasant Point HS, Linwood, Canterbury, S
Island.
b 29.5.21 Auckland.
Wing, 4-4-0-0 (12 − 4t).
46 A+(2t) A+; 47 A+(1t) A+(1t).
Market gardener/meat co employee. NZ Army
> 45-6 BI. 12t NZ > 47 A.

ARIGHO, John Edward ('Joxer')   *Ireland*
Castleknock Sch, Blackrock Coll, Lansdowne.
b 10.7.07 Dublin.
Wing, 16-8-1-7 (18 − 6t).
28 F+(2t) E−(1t) W+(2t); 29 F+ E+ S−(1t)
W=; 30 F− E+ S+ W−; 31 F− E+ S+ W−
SA−.
Journalism/bus. 5t 28 most by I player in Champ
season.

ARINO, Michel   *France*
Agen.
Wing, 1-0-0-1.
62 R−.

ARISTOUY, Pierre   *France*
Pau.
b 18.19.20 Arette, Béarn; *d* 17.5.74.

Lock, 6-2-1-3.
48 S−; 49 Arg+; 50 S− I= E+ W−.

ARMSTRONG, Reginald OBE   *England*
Newcastle Coll of Medicine, Durham Medicals,
Durham Univ, Northern, Barbarians,
Northumb.
b 6.12.1898; *d* 17.2.68 Morpeth.
Prop, 1-1-0-0 (3 − 1p).
25 W+(1p).
Medicine/RAMC. Served WW2, Lt Col 21st
Army Group & 8th Army. OBE 44. 1st doctor
to describe foot & mouth disease in humans in
UK, 67.

ARMSTRONG, William Kenneth   *Ireland*
Grosvenor HS, Stranmillis TTC, NIFC.
b 22.10.31 Belfast.
FH, 2-1-0-1.
60 SA−; 61 E+.
Schoolmaster.

ARNAL, Jean-Marie   *France*
RCF.
b − ; *d* c60 Toulon.
Lock, 2-0-0-2.
14 I− W−.

ARNAUDET, Michel   *France*
Lourdes.
b 11.3.43 Lourdes.
Wing/centre, 3-3-0-0 (12 − 4t).
64 I+(1t); 67 It+(3t) W+.
Hotelier.

ARNEIL, Rodger James   *Scotland*
Edinburgh Acad, Edinburgh Academicals,
Leicester, Northampton, Barbarians.
b 1.5.44 Edinburgh.
Flanker, 22-8-0-14.
68 I− E− A+; 69 F+ W− I− E− SA+; 70 F−
W− I− E+ A−; 71 F− W− I− E+ E+; 72 F+
W− E+ NZ−; BI > 68 SA 4-0-1-3, 71 A, NZ.
Textiles. Scottish XV v Arg (2) 69.

ARNOLD, Derek Austin ('Bluey')   *New Zealand*
Harewood Airport Sch, Christchurch West HS,
Christchurch, Canterbury, S Island.
b 10.1.41 Balclutha.
2nd five-eighth, 4-4-0-0.
63 I+ W+; 64 E+ F+.
Sports goods retailer. NZ > 63-4 BI,F & Can.
Player-coach Suburbs. Sel Canterbury 75-6.

ARNOLD, Keith Dawson   *New Zealand*
('Killer')
Cambridge Sch, Matamata, Waikato, Hautapu.
b 1.3.20 Feilding.
Flanker, 2-2-0-0 (3 − 1t).
47 A+(1t) A+.
Farmer. NZ Army > 45-6 BI. NZ > 47 A.

Served WW2, Pte in 21st Infantry Battn. Bro
A.J. rep Waikato 47-50.

ARNOLD, William Richard   *Wales*
Morriston, Llanelli, Swansea.
b 7.7.1881 Morriston; *d* 30.7.57 Morriston.
Wing, 1-0-0-1.
03 S−.
Surveyor/architect. In unbeaten Swansea XV
04-5. Glamorgan CCC comm.

ARNOTT, David Taylor   *Ireland*
Cheltenham, Lansdowne, NIFC.
b 1855; *d* 23.7.15 Ryde, IOW.
Forward, 1-0-0-1.
1875 E−.
Journalism. Corr for 'Irish Times'.

AROTCA, René   *France*
Bayonne.
Flanker, 1-1-0-0.
38 R+.
Police.

ARRIETA, Julien   *France*
SF.
b 3.9.24 Irun, Spain.
Hooker, 2-0-0-2.
53 E− W−.
Accountant.

ARTHUR, Sir Allen   *Scotland*
Merchiston Castle Sch, Glasgow Acad, Glasgow
Academicals, Merchistonians.
b 3.4.1857; *d* 9.10.23.
Forward, 2-0-1-1.
1875 E=, 1876 E−.
Business. Bro of John.

ARTHUR, Charles Suckling   *Wales*
Newton Coll Devon, Cardiff.
b 21.4.1866 Kent; *d* 12.12.25 Cardiff.
Back, 3-1-0-2.
1888 I− NZN+; 1891 E−.
Solicitor/schoolmaster. Sec Cardiff RFC 1892-
25. Bros Fred & Willie also played for Cardiff.

ARTHUR, John William   *Scotland*
Glasgow Acad, Glasgow Academicals, Glasgow
Univ.
b 25.4.1848 Glasgow; *d* 15.3.21 St Jean-de-
Luz.
Back, 2-1-0-1.
1871 E+; 1872 E−.
Co dir. Bro of Allen. Played in 1st int, S v E
1871. Renowned philanthropist.

ARTHUR, Terence Gordon   *England*
W Hartlepool GS, W Hartlepool, Manchester
Univ, Cambridge Univ, Wasps, Moseley,
Waterloo, Barbarians, Durham Co, Bucks, N

Midlands.
b 5.9.40.
Centre, 2-0-1-1.
66 W− I=.
Partner in actuarial consultants. Blue 62.

ARTHUR, Tom   *Wales*
Neath.
b 10.1.06 Pontypridd.
Lock/prop/flanker, 18-9-2-7 (12 − 4t).
27 S− F+ I−; 29 E− S+ F+(1t) I=; 30 E− S−
I+(1t) F+; 31 E= S+ F+(1t) I+ SA−; 33 E+
S−(1t).
Police. Heavyweight boxer.

ASH, W.H.   *Ireland*
RBAI, NIFC.
Forward, 3-0-0-3.
1875 E− E−; 1877 S−.

ASHBY, David Lloyd   *New Zealand*
Mataura Primary Sch, Southland Tech Coll,
Southland.
b 15.2.31 Mataura.
FB, 1-0-0-1.
58 A−.
Orchardist. Coach Kaikorai 79.

ASHBY, Roland Clive   *England*
RGS High Wycombe, Harper Adams Agric
Coll, Wasps, Barbarians, Shropshire, Bucks, E
Midlands.
b 24.1.37 Mozambique.
SH, 3-0-1-2 (3 − 1t).
66 I= F−; 67 A−(1t).
Family bus. Of SA parentage. Early education
in SA. Lived in Portuguese E Africa; when
posted by Portuguese authorities as a deserter
for missing National Service, abandoned dual
nationality & declared himself exclusively South
African. After leaving sch, spent 18 mths in
Antarctica.

ASHCROFT, Alan ('Ned')   *England*
Cowley GS, RAF, St Helens, Waterloo,
Barbarians, Lancs.
b 21.8.30 St Helens.
No 8, 16-10-4-2 (3 − 1t).
56 W− I+ S+ F−; 57 W+ I+ S+ F+; 58 W=
A+ I+(1t) F+ S=; 59 I+ F= S=; BI > 59 A 1-
1-0-0, NZ 1-0-0-1.
Schoolmaster. Taught art at Liverpool Coll.

ASHCROFT, Alec Hutchinson   *England*
DSO
Birkenhead Sch, Cambridge Univ, Birkenhead
Pk, Blackheath, Edinburgh W, Cheshire.
b 18.10.1887 Liverpool; *d* 18.4.63 Bath.
FH, 1-0-0-1.
09 A−.
HM. Blue 08-9. Served WW1, Temp Maj S

29

Staffs Rgt. Mentioned in despatches 16, DSO 19. Asst master Fettes Coll 10-14, HM 19-45.

ASHER, Albert Arapeha ('Opai') *New Zealand*
Tauranga Sch, Tauranga, Auckland, City, N Island.
 b 3.12.1879 Tauranga; *d* 8.1.65 Auckland.
Wing, 1-1-0-0 (3 − 1t).
03 A+(1t).
Fireman/groundsman. 5ft 6ins. Scored NZ's 1st int t, v A 03. Rec 17t (played in all 11 matches) NZ > 03 A. RL 08, NZ RL 10, 13. Groundsman at Carlaw Pk 21-43.

ASHER, Sir Augustus Gordon *Scotland*
Grant CBE
Loretto Sch, Oxford Univ, Fettesian-Lorettonians, Edinburgh W.
 b 18.12.1861 India; *d* 15.7.30.
Half-back, 7-4-2-1 (1t 2d).
1882 I+; 1884 W+(1d) I+(1t) E−; 1885 W=; 1886 I+(1d) E=.
Solicitor/Writer to the Signet. Blue 1881-4; ckt & ath blue. Ckt for S. S's pole vault champ. Pres SRU 29-30. Kt 27.

ASHFORD, William OBE JP *England*
St Thomas's Hosp, Richmond, Exeter, Barbarians, Surrey, Devon.
 b 18.12.1871; *d* 1.1.54 Topsham, Devon.
Forward, 4-1-1-2.
1897 W− I−; 1898 S= W+.
Medicine. Served WW1, CO at Topsham Volunteer Auxiliary Hosp. OBE 18. Devon CCC.

ASHLEY, Sydney A. *South Africa*
W Prov.
1-0-1-0.
03 BT=.
Customs official.

ASHTON, Clifford *Wales*
Aberavon.
 b 33.
FH, 7-4-1-2 (3 − 1t).
59 E+ S− I+(1t); 60 E− S+ I+; 62 I=.
Schoolmaster/PT instructor. Coach Chepstow RFC.

ASHWORTH, Abel *England*
Oldham, Rochdale H.
 b 1864 Mossley; *d* 10.1.38 Oldham.
Forward, 1-1-0-0.
1892 I+.
Engr's labourer. Turned RL when his club, Rochdale Hornets, helped form NU 1895.

ASHWORTH, Barry Graeme *New Zealand*
Otahuhu Coll, Auckland, N Island.
 b 23.9.49 Waiuku.

Flanker, 5-3-0-2.
78 A+ A+; 80 A− A+ A−.
Sheet metal co dir. NZ > 78 BI.

ASHWORTH, John Charles *New Zealand*
Linwood, Canterbury, Kaiapoi, S Island.
 b 15.9.49 Makahu.
Prop, 24-18-0-6 (4 − 1t).
78 A+ A+ A−(1t); 80 A− A+ A−; 81 SA+ SA− SA+; 82 A+ A−; 83 BI+ BI+ BI+ BI+ A+; 84 F+ F+ A− A+ A+; 85 E+ E+ A+.
Advertising artist/farmer. NZ > 77 F, 78 BI, 80 A & Fj; NAm & W, 83 & 84 A. NZ (2) v Arg 79. World XV > 86 SA.

ASKEW, John Garbutt *England*
Durham Sch, Durham City, Cambridge Univ, Durham Co, Barbarians.
 b 2.9.08; *d* 31.8.42 Stannington Morpeth, Northumb.
FB, 3-2-0-1.
30 W+ I− F+.
Blue 29-31. Ckt for CUCC & Durham CCC 26-7. CCS in Nyasaland 32; invalided home 33. Farmed in SA from 37.

ASLETT, Alfred Rimbault DSO *England*
Clifton Coll, RMC Sandhurst, Blackheath, Lansdowne, Richmond, The Army, Barbarians, Lancs, Surrey.
 b 14.1.01; *d* −.5.80 Cowfold.
Centre, 6-2-1-3 (6 − 2t).
26 W= I− F+(2t) S−; 29 S− F+.
The Army. Served WW2, reaching rank of Brig in KORR. Twice mentioned in despatches. DSO 45. Dir Army Sports Control Board 46. England sel 48-59. V-pres RFU 58-9.

ASSINDER, Eric Walter *England*
King Edward's Sch Birmingham, O Edwardians, Midland Cos.
 b 29.8.1888; *d* 11.10.74.
Centre, 2-0-0-2.
09 A− W−.
Medicine/RAMC. Served WW1 as Capt.

ASTON, Ferdinand T.D. ('Ferdy') *South Africa*
Transvaal, Blackheath, Barbarians (E).
 b 1871 England; *d* −.
Centre/wing, 4-1-0-3.
1896 BT− BT− BT− BT+.
Capt SA v BT 1st-3rd Tests 1896. Bro of R.L.

ASTON, Herbert Reid *Ireland*
Wesley, Trin Coll Dublin.
 b −; *d* −.1.68.
Half-back, 2-0-0-2 (3 − 1t).
08 E− W−(1t).
Civil engr. Employed by India Public Works Dept.

ASTON, Randolph Littleton　　*England*
Cheltenham Coll, Westminster Sch,
Berkhamsted Sch, Tonbridge Sch, Cambridge
Univ, Blackheath, Barbarians, Kent.
b 6.9.1869 Kensington; *d* 3.11.30 Salisbury.
Centre, 2-2-0-0.
1890 S+ I+; BT > 1891 SA.
Schoolmaster. Blue 1889-90. Bro of 'Ferdy'. 30t
in 19 apps BT > 1891 SA. Taught at Blair Lodge
& Tonbridge Schs.

ASTRE, Richard　　*France*
Béziers.
b 28.8.48 Toulouse.
SH, 11-5-0-6 (10 − 1t 2d).
71 R+; 72 I−; 73 E−r; 75 E+ S+(1d) I− SA−
SA− Arg+(1t); 76 A+(1d) R−.
Commercial traveller. Jt capt (with Jacques
Fouroux) F > 75 SA.

ATKINS, Alfred Patrick ('Slatts')　　*Ireland*
Belvedere, RCSI, Bective Rgrs.
b 9.4.1900; *d* 25.3.79.
Wing, 1-1-0-0 (3 − 1t).
24 F+(1t).
Dental surg. Wing Cdr RAF. Susp sine die by
IRU for playing one match for Huddersfield
RL; not reinstated on appeal.

ATKINSON, Henry　　*New Zealand*
W Coast, Kohinoor, Otago, Southern, S Island.
b 1888 Greymouth; *d* −.
Lock, 1-1-0-0.
13 A+.
NZ > 13 NAm.

ATKINSON, J. Maurice　　*Ireland*
NIFC.
b −; *d* 26.7.80.
Centre, 2-1-0-1.
27 F+ NSW−.
Insurance.

ATKINSON, J.R.　　*Ireland*
Rugby Sch, Dublin Univ.
Back, 2-0-0-2.
1882 W− S−.

ATTEWELL, Stephen Leonard　　*Wales*
Pill Harriers, Newport.
b 31.12.1895 Newport; *d* 26.2.83 Newport.
Prop/lock, 3-1-0-2.
21 E− S− F+.
Farmer.

AUCAMP, J. ('Hans')　　*South Africa*
Potchefstroom Theol Coll, W Transvaal.
Wing, 2-2-0-0 (3 − 1t).
24 BI+(1t) BI+.

AUGE, Joseph　　*France*
Dax.
Flanker/no 8, 2-0-0-2.
29 S− W−.

AUGRAS, Lucien　　*France*
Agen.
b 13.8.12 La Châtre, Indre.
Wing, 3-1-0-2.
31 I+ S− W−.

AULD, William　　*Scotland*
Uppingham Sch, W of S.
b −.4.1868; *d* 19.7.45.
Half-back, 2-2-0-0.
1889 W+, 1890 W+.
Accountant.

AULDJO, L.J.　　*Scotland*
Abertay.
Half-back, 1-0-1-0.
1878 E=.

AUSTIN, Leslie Raymond　　*Australia*
St Aloysius Sch Sydney, N Suburbs, NSW.
b 10.12.35.
Prop, 1-1-0-0.
63 E+.
Printer.

AUTY, Joseph Richard　　*England*
Mill Hill Sch, O Millhillians, Headingley,
Leicester, Barbarians, Yorks.
b 19.8.10 Batley.
FH, 1-0-0-1.
35 S−.
Woollen manufacturer. Father of rugby
historian Tim.

AVEROUS, Jean-Luc　　*France*
La Voulte.
b 22.10.54 La Voulte.
Wing, 25-16-0-9 (28 − 7t).
75 S+ I− SA−(1t) SA−; 76 I+ W−(1t) E+
US+(1t) A+ A+(1t) R−; 77 W+ E+ S+ I+
Arg+ R+; 78 E+(1t) S+ I+; 79 NZ− NZ+(1t);
80 E−(1t) S−; 81 A−.
Economics student.

AVERY, Henry Esau DSO CMG　　*New Zealand*
CBE
Mount Cook Sch, Wellington Coll, Wellington,
N Island.
b 3.10.1885 Wellington; *d* 22.3.61 Wellington.
Flanker, 3-2-0-1.
10 A+ A− A+.
Accountant/Army. Reinforced NZ > 10 A.
Served in 2 WWs; DSO 16 as Lt Col with
NZEF. CMG, CBE & American Legion of
Merit WW2.

AZARÈTE, Jean-Louis　　　　　*France*
Dax, St Jean-de-Luz.
b 8.5.45 Olhete-Urrugue.
Prop, 26-11-5-10.
69 W= R+; 70 S+ I+ W− R+; 71 S+ I= E=
SA− SA= A−; 72 E+ W− I− A= R+; 73
NZ+ W+ I− R+; 74 I+ R− SA− SA−; 75
W−.
Municipal employee.

B

BAARD, Adriaan Pieter　　　　*South Africa*
Stellenbosch Univ, W Prov.
b 17.5.33.
1-1-0-0.
60 I+.
Medicine.

BABROW, Louis　　　　　*South Africa*
Grey Coll Bloemfontein, Cape Town Univ,
Guy's Hosp, W Prov.
b 24.4.15 Smithfield.
Centre, 5-4-0-1 (9 − 3t).
37 A+ A+ NZ− NZ+(1t) NZ+(2t).
Medicine. Completed medical studies at Guy's
Hosp.

BADELEY, Cecil Edward Oliver　　*New Zealand*
Remuera Prmy Sch, Auckland GS, Auckland, N
Auckland, Whangarei HSOB, N & S Island.
b 7.11.1896 Auckland.
1st five-eighth, 2-1-0-1.
21 SA+ SA−.
Licensee. Bro of Victor Badeley, NZ 22-24 (no
Tests). NZ > 20 A. Chosen as capt NZ > 24-5
BI & F, repl by Cliff Porter before team set out.
15 apps for NZ. Served WW1, NZ Rifle Bde.

BADER, Edouard　　　　　　*France*
Primeveres.
SH, 2-0-0-2.
27 I− S−.

BADGER, Owen　　　　　　　*Wales*
Seaside Stars, Llanelli.
b 3.11.1871 Llanelli; *d* 17.3.39 Llanelli.
Centre, 4-1-0-3.
1895 E− S− I+; 1896 E−.
Steel shearer. 5ft 7in, 10st. Swinton RL 1896.

BADIN, Christian　　　　　　*France*
Chalon.
b 11.9.49 Pont-de-Vaux, Ain.
Centre, 3-2-0-1.
73 W+ I−; 75 Arg+.
Draughtsman.

BAGOT, John Christopher　　　*Ireland*
Tuam Sch, Trin Coll Dublin, Lansdowne.

b 1859; *d* −.4.1935.
Back, 5-1-0-4 (1d).
1879 S− E−; 1880 E− S−; 1881 S+(1d).
Medicine. 1d v S 1881 enabled I to record 1st
win.

BAILEY, Aidan Hilary　　　　　*Ireland*
PBC Bray, UC Dublin, Lansdowne.
b 1.1.16 Dublin; *d* 6.6.76 Bray.
Centre/FH, 13-6-0-7 (22 − 4t 2c 2p).
34 W−; 35 E− S+(1t) W+(1p) NZ−(1p); 36
E+(1t) S+ W−; 37 E−(1c) S+(1c) W+(1t); 38
E−(1t) S−.
Solicitor. Capped from school. Uncle of Niall.

BAILEY, Mark D.　　　　　　*England*
Cambridge Univ, Wasps.
Wing, 2-0-0-2.
84 SA− SA−.
Blue 82-5.

BAILEY, Niall　　　　　　　*Ireland*
PBC Bray, Northampton.
b 20.3.1929 Dublin.
Wing, 1-0-0-1.
52 E−.
Builders' merchants mgr. Nephew of Aidan.

BAILLETTE, Marcel　　　　　*France*
Perpignan, Quillan, Toulon.
b 12.10.04 Perpignan.
Centre, 17-7-0-10 (13 − 3t 1d).
25 I− NZ− S−; 26 W− M−; 27 I− W− G−; 29
G+(2t); 30 S+ I+ E− G+; 31 I+ S− E+(1d);
32 G+(1t).

BAIN, David McLaren　　　　　*Scotland*
Edinburgh Acad, Oxford Univ.
b 10.9.1891 Edinburgh; kia 3.6.15 Festubert.
Prop, 11-4-0-7.
11 E−; 12 F+ W− E+ SA−; 13 F+ W− I+
E−; 14 W− I−.
The Army. Blue 10-13. Capt, 3rd Battn Gordon
Highlanders.

BAINBRIDGE, Steve　　　　　*England*
John Marlay Sch, Alsager Coll, Gosforth,
Fylde, Northumb.
b 7.10.56 Newcastle-upon-Tyne.
Lock, 13-4-1-8.
82 F+ W+; 83 F− W= S− I−; NZ+; 84 S− I+
F− W− NZ− NZ−; BI > 83 NZ 2-0-0-2.
Schoolmaster. 6ft 7in. E Under 23s. English
Students. England B v I,F. E > 81 Arg; 82 US,
Can. Refused permission by local education
authority to tour E > 84 SA. Disqu from int
rugby after being sent off in club match 85. Brit
students decathlon champ. Brit Colls high jump
champ, 6ft 7 1/2in.

BAIRD, Gavin Roger Todd   *Scotland*
St Mary's Prep Sch Melrose, Merchiston Castle
Sch, Scottish Schs, Kelso.
 b 12.4.60 Kelso.
Wing, 25-14-1-10.
81 A+; 82 E+ I− F+ W+ A+ A−; 83 I− F−
W− E+ NZ=; 84 W+ E+ I+ F+ A−; 85 I−
W− E−; 86 F+ W− E+ I+ R+; BI > 83 NZ 4-
0-0-4.
Grain merchant. At SH for Scottish Schs v E, I
78. Scotland B v I 79, v F 80, 81. S > 81 NZ.
Scottish XV v Fj 82. At centre for Kelso 85-6.

BAIRD, James Alexander   *New Zealand*
Steenson
Caversham Sch, Otago.
 b 17.12.1893 Dunedin; *d* 7.6.17 France.
Centre, 1-1-0-0.
13 A+.
Served WW1, Pte Otago Infantry Rgt; died as
result of wounds.

BAKER, Albert Melville   *Wales*
Newport.
 b 1885 Newport; *d* −.
Wing, 3-3-0-0 (12 − 4t).
09 S+ F+(3t); 10 S+(1t); BI > 10 SA.
Carpenter.

BAKER, Ambrose   *Wales*
Neath.
 b 7.7.1897; *d* 24.11.76 Oldham.
Flanker/lock, 5-2-0-3 (3 − 1t).
21 I+; 23 E− S− F+(1t) I−.
Miner/licensee. Oldham RL.

BAKER, Douglas George Santley   *England*
Merchant Taylors' Sch, Oxford Univ, OMT,
Barbarians, London Cos, E Midlands, Mdx.
 b 29.11.29 Las Palmas.
FH, 4-1-1-2.
55 W− I= F− S+; BI > 55 SA 2-1-0-1.
Schoolmaster/fuel co. Blue 51-2. Barbarians >
57 Can. Played ckt for Authentics. Asst master
at Oundle; went on teaching exchange to A, 62.

BAKER, Edward Morgan   *England*
Denstone Coll, Oxford Univ, Moseley,
Blackheath, Wolverhampton, Burton,
Barbarians, Midland Cos.
 b 12.8.1874; *d* 25.11.40 Winchester.
Centre, 7-3-0-4.
1895 W+ I+ S−; 1896 W+ I− S−; 1897 W−.
Clergyman/HM. Blue 1893-6. Ordained 1897;
various curacies until Vicar of St Paul's, East
Brisbane, A. Became HM King's Sch
Parramatta 19-32, then returned to UK.

BAKER, Harald William AM   *Australia*
Sydney, E Suburbs, NSW.
 b 29.9.1887 Sydney; *d* 17.10.62.
Lock, 3-0-0-3.
14 NZ− NZ− NZ−.
Co dir. Bro of Reginald. Rep A at boxing,
swimming, water polo & wrestling. Awarded
AM for bravery; with fellow int Jimmy Clarken
he rescued 8 surfers. Served WW1; broke spine
in fall in hold of a troopship. In plaster for 2 yrs
& immobile for 4 yrs. Became ldg boxing ref.

BAKER, Hiatt Cowles JP   *England*
Rugby Sch, Clifton, Glos.
 b 30.6.1863; *d* 19.9.34 Almondsbury, Bristol.
Forward, 1-0-1-0.
1887 W=.
Man dir family clothing & drapery bus. Pro-
chancellor Bristol Univ.

BAKER, Reginald Leslie   *Australia*
('Snowy')
Sydney Univ, NSW.
 b 8.2.1884 Sydney; *d* 1.12.53 Los Angeles.
Half-back, 2-0-0-2.
04 BT− BT−.
Draughtsman/co dir/boxing promoter. Bro of
Harald. Rep A at boxing, polo, diving &
swimming. Reached middleweight boxing finals,
Olympics 08; lost to J.W.H.T. Douglas (later E
Ckt capt) in bout refereed by Douglas's father.
Moved to Hollywood where he taught film stars
to fence, swim & ride.

BAKER-JONES, Paul E.R.   *Wales*
Blundell's Sch, RA, The Army, Newport.
 b 27.12.1894; *d* −.5.34 Quetta.
Centre, 1-0-0-1.
21 S−.
The Army. Capt, RA. Son of Thomas.

BAKER-JONES, Thomas   *Wales*
Monmouth Sch, Newport.
 b 16.9.1862 Newport; *d* 26.5.59 Swansea.
Forward, 6-1-1-4 (1t).
1882 I+(1t) E−; 1883 S−; 1884 S−; 1885 E−
S=.
Solicitor. Sc W's 1st t, v I 1882. Longest lived
Welsh cap. Fdr mem Newport RFC 1874.
Father of Paul.

BALADIÉ, Georges   *France*
Agen.
Wing, 6-3-0-3 (9 − 3t).
45 BF+(1t) BF− W−; 46 BF+(1t) I+ NZS−
(1t).

BALFOUR, Sir Andrew KCMG   *Scotland*
CB FRCP
George Watson's Coll, Edinburgh Univ,
Cambridge Univ, Watsonians.
 b 21.3.1873 Edinburgh; *d* 30.1.31.
Forward, 4-1-1-2.
1896 W− I= E+; 1897 E−.

Scientist/dir London Sch of Tropical Medicine. Blue 1896-7. Served WW1, Lt Col in RAMC; mentioned in despatches. Pres SRU 30-1.

BALFOUR-MELVILLE, Leslie   *Scotland*
Melville
Edinburgh Acad, Edinburgh Academicals, Edinburgh Univ.
b 9.3.1854 Bonnington, Edinburgh; d 16.7.37 N Berwick.
Back, 1-0-0-1.
1872 E−.
Writer to the Signet. Pres SRU 1893-4. Ckt for S.

BALL, Nelson ('Kelly')   *New Zealand*
Foxton Prmy Sch, Feilding Agric HS, Wanganui, Wanganui OB, Wellington, Hutt, N Island.
b 11.10.08 Foxton.
Wing, 5-3-0-2 (12 − 4t).
31 A+(1t); 32 A+(1t) A+; 35 W−(2t); 36 E−.
Meat inspector/coin machine bus. Cousin of Bill Francis. Bros Rex & Ernest rep Wellington. Son Murray rep Manawatu, Wellington & NZ Trials 59-60. NZ > 32 A, 35-6 BI, F. Coach Feilding OB 37. Emigrated to A 48.

BALLARIN, Jacques   *France*
Tarbes, Toulouse.
Wing/centre, 3-0-0-3 (3 − 1t).
24 E−(1t); 25 NZ− S−.

BALLESTY, John Patrick   *Australia*
St Patrick's Coll Strathfield, Sydney Teachers' Coll, Eastwood, NSW.
b 20.5.45.
Five-eighth/centre, 9-1-0-8 (23 − 1t 1c 1d 5p).
68 NZ− NZ− F+(1d) I−(1t) S−; 69 W− SA− (3p) SA−(1p) SA−(1c 1p).
RL club mgr. 89 pts (17 apps) A > 69 SA. E Suburbs RL for 25,000 dollars; later Queanbeyan & Eastwood.

BANCE, John Forsyth   *England*
Radley Coll, Cambridge Univ, Bedford, Barbarians, E Midlands.
b 15.1.25.
Lock, 1-1-0-0.
54 S+.
Farmer. Blue 45. Played in 3 Co Champ finals.

BANCROFT, John ('Jack')   *Wales*
Swansea.
b 1879 Swansea; d 7.1.42 Swansea.
FB, 18-14-0-4 (88 − 38c 4p).
09 E+(1c) S+(1c) F+(6c) I+(3c); 10 F+(8c 1p) E− S+(1c) I+; 11 E+ F+(3c) I+(2c 1p); 12 E− S+(2c) I−(1c); 13 I+(2c 1p); 14 E−(1c) S+(2c 1p) F+(5c).
Copper worker/groundsman/licensee. Rec-equ.

19 pts v F 10 inc world rec 8 cons. Champ rec 11c in season 08-9. Glamorgan CCC. Bro of Billy.

BANCROFT, William John   *Wales*
('Billy')
Swansea.
b 2.3.1871 Swansea; d 3.3.59 Swansea.
FB, 33-16-1-16 (60 − 20c 1d 4p 1gm).
1890 S− E+ I=(1c); 1891 E−(1c) S− I+(1c 1d); 1892 E− S− I−; 1893 E+(1c 1p) S+(1p) I+; 1894 E− S+ I−; 1895 E− S−(1gm) I+(1c); 1896 E− S+ I−; 1897 E+(1c); 1898 I+(1c 1p) E−; 1899 E+(4c) S−(2c) I−; 00 E+(2c 1p) S+ I+; 01 E+(2c) S−(1c) I+(2c).
Cobbler. 5ft 5 1/2in. 33 consec ints. Capt W 11 times. Glamorgan CCC. Bro of Jack.

BANNERMAN, Edward   *Scotland*
Mordaunt
Edinburgh Acad, Edinburgh Academicals.
b 14.1.1850; d −.
Forward, 2-0-1-1.
1872 E−; 1873 E=.
Bus. Ckt for S.

BANNERMAN, Lord John   *Scotland*
Macdonald
Shawlands Acad, Glasgow HS, Glasgow HSFP, Glasgow Univ, Oxford Univ, Barbarians.
b 1.9.01; d 12.4.69.
Lock, 37-22-2-13 (6 − 2t).
21 F− W+ I− E−; 22 F= W= I+ E−; 23 F+ W+ I+ E−; 24 F− W+ I+ E−; 25 F+ W+ I+ E+; 26 F+(1t) W+ I− E+; 27 F+ W+ I− E+ NSW+; 28 F+ W− I− E−; 29 F+ W− I+(1t) E+.
Factor. Blue 27-8. Pres SRU 54-5. Life Peer 67.

BANNON, Desmond Patrick   *Australia*
New England, NSW Country, NSW.
b 23.
Five-eighth, 1-0-0-1.
46 M−.

BAQUET, Jean   *France*
Toulouse.
Wing, 1-1-0-0.
21 I+.

BARBAZANGES, Antonin   *France*
Roanne.
FH/centre, 2-2-0-0.
32 G+; 33 G+.

BARDON, Maurice Edgar   *Ireland*
('Mebs')
Dublin HS, Bohemians.
b 4.8.1907 Greystones, Co Wicklow.
Flanker, 1-0-0-1.
34 E−.
Bank official.

BARKER, Herbert Samuel　　　*Australia*
Bourke St Sch, Randwick, St George, NSW.
b 29 Sydney.
Centre, 7-3-0-4 (24 − 3c 6p).
52 Fj+(1p) Fj− NZ+ NZ−; 53 SA−(2p); 54
Fj+(1c 1p) Fj−(2c 2p).
Clerk/traveller. A > 53 SA. Basketball for NSW
46-56. Rep A in hammer throw in
Commonwealth Games 50; won A hammer title
56.

BARLEY, Bryan　　　*England*
Normanton GS, Yorks SS, England SS, Leeds
Univ, Wakefield, Yorks.
b 4.1.60 Wakefield.
Centre, 4-1-0-3.
84 I+ F− W− A−.
Management trainee. England SS > 79 A.
Yorks > 80 F. E Under 23s 80, 82. English
Students 83. Broke jaw club match 83.

BARLOW, M.　　　*Ireland*
Wanderers, NSW.
Forward, 1-0-0-1.
1875 E−.
Emigrated to A. NSW > NZ 1882.

BARLOW, Thomas Marriott　　　*Wales*
Cardiff.
b 1864 Manchester; *d* 27.1.42 Chester.
FB, 1-1-0-0.
1884 I+.
Solicitor. Sec Welsh Golf Fed. Ckt for Glam
CCC.

BARNARD, A.S.　　　*South Africa*
E Prov.
Prop, 2-2-0-0.
84 SAm+ SAm+.

BARNARD, Johannes Hendrikus　　*South Africa*
('Jannie')
Transvaal.
b 29.1.45 Johannesburg.
FH, 5-1-0-4.
65 S− A− A− NZ+ NZ−.
Clerk. Bro of Robert.

BARNARD, Robert William　　　*South Africa*
Transvaal.
b 26.11.41 Pretoria.
1-0-0-1.
70 NZ−r.
Bro of Jannie. SA > 69-70 BI, 71 A.

BARNARD, Willem Hendrick　　*South Africa*
Minnaar
Upington HS, Stellenbosch Univ, N Transvaal.
b 7.8.23 Upington.
Lock, 2-2-0-0.

49 NZ+; 51 W+.
Cartage contractor.

BARNES, Ian Andrew　　　*Scotland*
Hawick HS, Edinburgh Univ, Hawick.
b 19.4.48 Hawick.
Flanker/lock, 7-2-0-5.
72 W−; 74 F+r; 75 E−r NZ−; 77 I+ F− W−.
Scottish XV v Japan 77.

BARNES, Robert James　　　*Ireland*
Armagh RS, Trin Coll Dublin, Armagh.
b 25.4.11 Armagh.
Centre, 1-1-0-0 (3 − 1t).
33 W+(1t).
Clerk in Holy Orders. Ckt for I 8 times 30-47.

BARNES, Stuart　　　*England*
Welsh SS, Oxford Univ, Newport, Bristol,
Bath, Glos.
b 22.11.62 Grays, Essex.
FH/FB, 6-1-0-5 (18 − 3c 1d 3p).
84 A−; 85 R+r NZ−(1c 1p) NZ−(2c 1d); 86 S−
r F−r(2p).
Blue 81-3. Moved from Essex to W 72. Capt
Welsh SS. Wales Snr Squad 81. Decided to play
for E. E Under 23s > 83 It, R. Missed E > 84
SA because of final exams at Oxford.

BARNETT, John Thomas　　　*Australia*
('Bowser')
Newtown, Hartley, NSW.
b 19.1.1886 Carcour; *d* 51.
Forward, 5-1-1-3.
07 NZ− NZ− NZ=; 08 W−; 09 E+.
Potter. A > 08-9 BI, NAm. Olympic rugby gold
medal 08. RL.

BARR, Ainsworth　　　*Ireland*
Tonbridge Sch, Methodist Coll Belfast.
b 1875; *d* 19.12.34 Belfast.
Half-back, 4-2-0-2.
1898 W−; 1899 S+; 1901 E+ S−.
Stockbroker/solicitor. Pres IRU 08-9.

BARR, Robert John MC TD　　　*England*
Stamford Sch, Leicester, Barbarians, Leics.
b 26.5.07 Blisworth, Northants; *d* 24.9.75.
FB, 3-1-0-2 (2 − 1c).
32 SA− W−(1c) I+.
Insurance broker/textile agent. Served WW2 in
Army.

BARRAU, Max　　　*France*
Beaumont, Toulouse.
b 26.11.50 Beaumont de Lomagne.
SH, 15-8-2-5 (4 − 1t).
71 S+ E= W−; 72 E+ W− A= A+; 73 S+
NZ+ E− I− J+(1t) R+; 74 I+ S−.
Commercial rep. Capt F > 74 Arg.

BARRELL, Robert *Wales*
Penarth, Cardiff.
b 05 Aberaman.
Prop/lock, 4-2-1-1 (3 − 1t).
29 S+ F+(1t) I=; 33 I−.
Police.

BARRERE, Paul *France*
Toulon.
b 05.
Lock, 2-1-0-1.
29 G+; 31 W−

BARRETT, Edward Ivo *England*
Medhurst CIE
Cheltenham Coll, Lennox, RMC Sandhurst,
The Army, Surrey.
b 22.6.1879 Winchester; *d* 10.7.50
Bournemouth.
Centre, 1-0-0-1.
03 S−.
The Army/police/Ministry of Aircraft
Production. Ckt for Hants 1895-25, sc 215 v
Glos 20. Hockey for Hants. Amateur golf
champ J 17. Queen's & King's Medals in SA
War 1899-03. Shanghai Police 07-29. CIE 16.
Served WW2 as 2nd in command of internment
camp, Norfolk.

BARRETT, James ('Buster') *New Zealand*
City, Ponsonby, Marist, Auckland.
b 8.10.1888 Auckland; *d* 31.8.71 Hamilton.
Flanker, 2-1-0-1.
13 A+ A−.
Carpenter/farmer. NZ > 14 A.

BARRIE, Robert William *Scotland*
Hawick HS, Hawick.
b −.7.11 Hawick.
Flanker, 1-0-0-1.
36 E−.
Hosiery.

BARRIÈRE, Raoul *France*
Béziers.
Prop, 1-0-0-1.
60 R−.

BARRINGTON, Thomas James *England*
Mountstevens
Wrekin Coll, Bridgwater & A, Harlequins,
Richmond, Bristol, Som.
b 8.7.08.
FH, 2-0-1-1.
31 W= I−.
Solicitor. Served WW2 with RAF. Som Refs
Soc. Part-time clerk Som River Authority.

BARRINGTON-WARD, Sir *England*
Lancelot Edward KCVO
Westminster Sch, Bromsgrove Sch, Oxford

Univ, Edinburgh Univ.
b 4.7.1884 Worcester; *d* 17.11.53 Bury St
Edmunds.
No 8, 4-3-1-0.
10 W+ I= F+ S+.
Medicine. KCVO 35. Surg to King George VI
36-52. Extra surg to HM The Queen from 52.
Hunterian Professor R Coll of Surgs 52. Grand
Cross Order of St Olaf. Order of St Sava.

BARRON, James Henry *England*
Bingley, Yorks.
b 28.8.1874 Micklethwaite, nr Bingley; *d*
2.12.42 Bingley.
Forward, 3-0-0-3.
1896 S−; 1897 W− I−.
Coal merchant/property owner.

BARRY, Edward Fitzgerald *New Zealand*
Seadown & Monavale Sch, Pleasant Point Dist
HS, Wellington Tech Coll, Marist, Wellington,
Hutt, Wanganui.
b 3.9.05 Temuka.
Flanker, 1-0-1-0.
34 A=.
Accountant/telegraph linesman/police. Son
Kevin rep NZ 62-4; another son P.T. Barry pl
for Cos. NZ > 32 & 34 A. Club sel & coach.

BARRY, J. *South Africa*
W Prov.
3-1-2-0 (3 − 1t).
03 BT= BT= BT+(1t).

BARRY, Michael Joseph *Australia*
Brothers (Brisbane), Qld.
b 21.10.42.
SH, 1-0-0-1.
71 SA−.
Medicine.

BARTHE, E. *France*
SBUC.
Flanker, 2-0-0-2 (3 − 1t).
25 W− E−(1t).

BARTHE, Jean *France*
Lourdes.
b 22.7.32 Lourdes.
Flanker/no 8/lock, 26-17-2-7.
54 Arg+ Arg+; 55 S+; 56 I+ W− It+ E+ Cz+;
57 S− I− E− W− R+ R+; 58 S− E− A+ W+
It+ I+ SA= SA+; 59 S+ E= It+ W+.
Electrical mechanic/bazaar owner. RL.

BARTLETT, Jasper Twining *England*
Birkenhead Inst, Liverpool Univ, N Univs,
Comb Univs, Waterloo, RE, The Army, Comb
Servs, Barbarians, Cheshire.
b 17.10.24; *d* 16.1.69 Liverpool.
Lock, 1-0-0-1.

51 W−.
Civil engr at Mersey Docks. Over 40 apps for Cheshire.

BARTLETT, John Dudley *Wales*
Llandovery Coll, Welsh SS, Cambridge Univ, St David's Coll Lampeter, Llanelli, London Welsh.
 b 07 Carmarthen; *d* 17.1.67 Hayling Island.
Wing, 3-1-0-2 (3 − 1t).
27 S−; 28 E−(1t) S+.
Curate/RN chaplain.

BARTLETT, Richard Michael *England*
('Ricky')
Stowe Sch, KCS Wimbledon, Cambridge Univ, Harlequins, Barbarians, Surrey.
 b 13.2.29; *d* 5.3.84 Liss, Hants.
FH, 7-6-1-0.
57 W+ I+ F+ S+; 58 I+ F+ S=.
Insurance/pig farmer. Blue 51. England sel.

BARTON, John *England*
Caludon Castle Sch, Caludon Castle OB, Coventry, Barbarians, Warwicks.
 b 19.3.43.
Lock, 4-1-0-3 (6 − 2t).
67 I+ F− W−(2t); 72 F−.
Farmer/Brit Motor Corporation. E > 67 Can.

BARTON, Roger Furnivall *Australia*
Daranth
All Saints Coll Bathurst, Sydney Univ, NSW.
 b c1877; *d* −.
Forward, 1-0-0-1.
1899 BT−.
Farmer/mines station mgr.

BASAURI, Robert *France*
Albi.
FH, 1-1-0-0.
54 Arg+.

BASCOU, Paulin *France*
Bayonne.
No 8, 1-0-0-1.
14 E−.
Butcher/bank official.

BASQUET, Guy *France*
Agen.
 b 13.7.21 Layroc.
No 8, 33-17-1-15 (24 − 8t).
45 W−; 46 BF+ I+ NZS− W+; 47 S+ I+ W− E−; 48 I−(1t) A+(2t) S− W+(1t) E+; 49 S− I+(1t) E− W+ Arg+; 50 S− I= E+ W−; 51 S+ I− E+(1t) W+; 52 S+(1t) I− SA− W− E− It+(1t).
F's most capped no 8. Capt F > 49 Arg. Asst mgr F > 61 NZ.

BASSETT, Arthur *Wales*
Aberavon, Cardiff, Derby Police.
 b Kenfig Hill.
Wing, 6-3-1-2.
34 I+; 35 E= S+ I−; 38 E+ S−.
Police/licensee. Bro of Jack. 99t in 101 apps for Cardiff. Halifax RL 39 (64t in 108 apps), York 48. RL Challenge Cup medal 39. 2 GB RL Tests in Australia 46, sc 5t.

BASSETT, John Archibald *Wales*
('Jack')
Penarth, Glamorgan Police, Cardiff, Barbarians.
 b 1905 Pontypridd.
FB, 15-8-2-5 (29 − 10c 3p).
29 E− S+ F+ I=; 30 E− S− I+(1p); 31 E=(1c) S+(2c) F+(5c) I+(1c) SA−; 32 E+(1c 1p) S+(1p) I−; BI > 30 NZ 4-1-0-3, A 1-0-0-1.
Miner/police. Bro of Arthur.

BASTARD, William Eberhardt *South Africa*
('Ebbo')
Hilton Coll, Natal.
 b 12; *d* −.2.49.
Flanker, 6-4-0-2 (6 − 2t).
37 A+(1t) NZ− NZ+(1t) NZ+; 38 BI+ BI−.
Farmer. Died shooting incident.

BASTIAT, Jean-Pierre *France*
Dax.
 b 11.4.49 Dax.
Lock/no 8, 32-21-3-8 (24 − 4t 1c 2p).
69 R+; 70 S+ I+ W−; 71 S+ I= SA=; 72 S− A=; 73 E−; 74 Arg+ Arg+ SA−; 75 W− Arg+ Arg+ R+(1t 1p); 76 S+ I+(1c 1p) W− E+(1t) A+ A+ R−(1t); 77 W+ E+ S+ I+(1t) 78 E+ S+ I+ W−.
Insurance official.

BATCH, Patrick Gerard *Australia*
Qld Univ, Brisbane Univ, Qld.
 b 19.1.53.
Wing, 14-7-0-7 (20 − 5t).
75 S− W−; 76 E− Fj+(2t) Fj+ Fj+(1t) F− F−; 78 W+ W+ NZ−(1t) NZ− NZ+; 79 Arg+(1t).
Veterinarian. A > 75-6 BI, US.

BATCHELOR, Tremlett Brewer *England*
Rugby Sch, Oxford Univ, The London Hosp, Richmond, Utd Hospitals, E Cos.
 b 22.6.1884; *d* 21.12.66 Liverpool.
Wing, 1-1-0-0.
07 F+.
Medicine. Blue 06. MRCS 14. Served WW1, Actg Maj RAMC; mentioned in despatches 18.

BATES, Albert Jacobus *South Africa*
W Transvaal.
 b 18.4.41 Germiston.
Flanker/No 8, 4-1-0-3.

69 E−; 70 NZ+ NZ−; 72 E−.
Platinum mine shift boss. SA > 69-70 BI; 71 A.

BATESON, Alfred Hardy   *England*
Bramley OB, Otley, Yorks.
b 10.8.01 Otley; *d* 21.2.82 Scarborough.
Prop, 4-2-1-1.
30 W+ I− F+ S=.
Millwright/heating & ventilating engr. 1st cap
with fellow Otley player, F.W.S. Malir, 1st
players capped from Otley. Played football until
age 23. Within yr, made 1st of 20 apps for
Yorks.

BATESON, Harold Dingwall JP   *England*
Rugby Sch, Oxford Univ, Blackheath,
Liverpool, Lancs.
b 2.5.1856; *d* 29.10.27 Liverpool.
Forward, 1-1-0-0.
1879 I+.
Solicitor. Blue 1874,5,7. Read Riot Act as
Liverpool JP during police strike 11. Soldiers
opened fire on strikers, killing two.

BATSON, Thomas   *England*
Sydney Coll Bath, Oxford Univ, Blackheath.
b 1852; *d* 5.2.33.
Forward, 3-3-0-0.
1872 S+; 1874 S+; 1875 I+.
Schoolmaster. Ath blue for hammer & shot.
Asst master Blackheath Proprietary Sch, later
Rossall. Cousin of F. & L. Stokes.

BATTEN, John Maxwell   *England*
Haileybury & ISC, Cambridge Univ.
b 28.2.1853 Almora, Kumaon; *d* 15.10.17.
FB, 1-1-0-0.
1874 S+.
Schoolmaster. Blue 1871-4; capt 1873-4.
Rackets for Cambridge. Taught at Kelly Coll,
Newton Abbot Sch & Plymouth Coll.

BATTERHAM, Roderick Paul   *Australia*
('Batters')
N Sydney Tech Coll, Gordon, ACT,
Parramatta, NSW.
b 24.11.47.
Wing, 2-1-0-1 (15 − 4t 1p).
67 NZ−(2t 1p); 70 S+(2t).
PE teacher.

BATTISHALL, Bruce Robert   *Australia*
('Nuts')
St George, Sydney, NSW, Rosslyn Pk (E).
b 3.9.46.
No 8, 1-0-0-1.
73 E−.
Accounts clerk.

BATTY, Grant Bernard   *New Zealand*
St Mary's Convent Sch Masterton, Greytown

Sch, Kurani Coll, Wellington, NZ Jnrs, NZ
Univs, N Island, Tauranga.
b 31.8.51 Greytown.
Wing, 15-9-1-5 (16 − 4t).
72 W+ S+(1t); 73 E+ I= F− E−(1t); 74 A+
A+(1t) I+; 75 S+; 76 SA− SA+ SA− SA−; 77
BI+(1t).
Insurance salesman. 5ft 5in. 21t NZ > 72-3 BI &
F, 74 A & Fj & I,W,E (13t in 7 out of 8
matches), 76 SA. Autobiography 'Grant Batty'
pub 77.

BATTY, Walter DCM   *New Zealand*
Auckland GS, Grammar, Auckland, N Island.
b 1.1.05 Tonga; *d* 10.5.79 Auckland.
Flanker/no 8, 4-3-0-1 (3 − 1t).
30 BI− BI+ BI+(1t); 31 A+.
Insurance salesman. Served WW2, 6th Field
Rgt; DCM in Libya. Five bros played club rugby
in Auckland.

BAUME, John Lea   *England*
Ashville Coll Harrogate, Northern, Headingley,
Harrogate, The Army, Comb Servs, Northumb.
b 18.7.20.
Prop, 1-0-0-1.
50 S−.
The Army/poultry farmer. Served WW2, R
Northumb Fusiliers; later Korean War. Retd 61,
took up poultry farming.

BAXTER, Archibald John   *Australia*
('Tarakan Jack')
Kogarah Marist Bros Sch, Kiwis (Melbourne), E
Suburbs, A Servs, RAN, NSW.
b 30.8.22.
Prop, 9-4-1-4.
49 M− M= M+ NZ+ NZ+; 51 NZ− NZ−; 52
NZ+ NZ−.
RAN/shopkeeper.

BAXTER, James ('Bim')   *England*
Liverpool Inst, Birkenhead Pk, Barbarians,
Cheshire.
b 8.6.1870; *d* 5.7.40 Rock Ferry, Cheshire.
Forward, 3-1-1-1.
1900 W− I+ S=.
Insurance. Served WW2, Lt Cmdr RNVR. Ref
6 ints 20-5. RFU sel; pres 26-7. Mgr RFU > 27
Arg; BI > 30 NZ, A. Mem IB 26-39. Capt
Mersey Rowing Club. Won yachting bronze
medal 08 Olympics as crew mem of 12-metre
'Mouchette'. Capt R Liverpool GC 26; pres
Cheshire Union of Golf Clubs 29.

BAXTER, Thomas J.   *Australia*
Brisbane GS, Qld, Qld Univ, Oxford Univ.
b 28.4.35.
Centre, 1-0-0-1.
58 NZ−.
Exec engr. Rhodes Scholar. Blue 58-9.

BAYLISS, Gwyn   *Wales*
Brynmawr GS, Pontypool.
b −.5.07 Brynmawr; d 10.3.76 Blaina.
FB, 1-0-0-1.
33 S−.
Schoolmaster/journalist.

BAYVEL, Paul Campbell   *South Africa*
Robertson
Parktown Boys HS, Witwatersrand Univ,
Transvaal.
b 28.3.49 Johannesburg.
SH, 10-7-1-2.
74 BI− BI= F+ F+; 75 F+ F+; 76 NZ+ NZ−
NZ+ NZ+.
Rep.

BAZLEY, Reginald Charles   *England*
Barrow GS, Furness, Liverpool Univ,
Waterloo, UAU, The Army, Comb Servs,
Barbarians, Lancs.
b 15.12.29 Barrow.
Wing, 10-6-2-2 (6 − 2t).
52 I+ F+; 53 W+ I= F+ S+(2t); 55 W− I= F−
S+.
Civil engr/contract mgr.

BEAMISH, Charles E. St J.   *Ireland*
Leicester, RAF, Ulster, Barbarians.
b 23.6.08 Cork; d 18.5.84 Templemore, Co
Tipperary.
Prop/hooker, 12-5-0-7 (3 − 1p).
33 W+ S−; 34 S− W−; 35 E− S+ W+ NZ−
(1t); 36 E+ S+ W−; 38 W−.
RAF. Bro of George. Ulster v NZ 35.

BEAMISH, Sir George Robert   *Ireland*
CBE KCB
Coleraine AI, Coleraine, RAF Cranwell,
Leicester, RAF, Midland Cos London Irish,
Barbarians.
b 29.4.1905; d 13.11.67 Castlerock.
No 8, 25-12-2-11.
25 E= S− W+; 28 F+ E− S+ W+; 29 F+ E+
S− W=; 30 F− S+ W−; 31 F− E+ S+ W−
SA−; 32 E− S+ W+; 33 E− W+ S−; BI > 30
NZ 4-1-0-3, A 1-1-0-0.
RAF. Bro of Charles. Capt Midland Cos in 30-
21 win v SA 31, only defeat of their tour & still
most pts ever scored v SA. CBE 42. KCB 55.

BEARNE, Keith Robert Fraser   *Scotland*
Rydal Sch, Cambridge Univ, London Scottish.
b 37 London.
No 8, 2-0-0-2.
60 F− W−.
Rep. Blue 57-9.

BEATTIE, John Armstrong   *Scotland*
Hawick HS, Hawick, Barbarians.
b 5.1.07 Hawick; d 10.2.77 Hawick.
Prop/flanker/lock, 23-9-0-14.
29 F+ W−;30 W+; 31 F+ W− I− E+; 32 SA−
W− I− E−; 33 W+ E+ I+; 34 I+ E−; 35 W−
I− E+ NZ−; 36 W− I− E−.
Joiner.

BEATTIE, John Ross   *Scotland*
Glasgow Acad, Glasgow Academicals, Glasgow
Univ, Heriot's FP, Glasgow.
b 27.11.57 N Borneo.
No 8, 21-9-1-11.
80 I− F+ W− E−; 81 F− W+ E− I+; 83 F−
W− E+ NZ=; 84 E+r R− A−; 85 I−; 86 F+
W− E+ I+ R+; BI > 80 SA; 83 NZ 1r-0-0-1.
Civil engr. Scotland B v I, F. Scottish XV v Fj
82. Knee inj interrupted int career. BI v Rest of
World, Cardiff 86.

BEATTY, George Edward   *New Zealand*
Fitzroy Sch, New Plymouth Boys' HS, HSOB,
Taranaki, N Island.
b 29.3.25 New Plymouth.
1st five-eighth, 1-0-1-0.
50 BI=.
Mgr wine & spirit co. Leigh (E) RL 50-2,
Bellevue R 53-5. Ckt for Taranaki.

BEATTY, W.J.   *Ireland*
NIFC, Richmond, Barbarians.
Prop/lock, 3-3-0-0.
10 F+; 12 F+ W+.

BEAUMONT, William Blackledge   *England*
Ellesmere Coll, Fylde, Lancs, Barbarians.
b 9.3.52 Preston.
Lock, 34-14-3-17.
75 I− A−r A−; 76 A+ W− S− I− F−; 77 S+
I+ F− W−; 78 F− W− S+ I+ NZ−; 79 S= I−
F+ W− NZ−; 80 I+ F+ W+ S+; 81 W− S+
I+ F− Ag= Arg+; 82 A+ S=; BI > 77 NZ 3-1-
0-2; 80 SA 4-1-0-3.
Textile bus/BBC commentator. E's most capped
lock; most ints as capt (21). 33 consec caps. N of
England, E Under 23s v Tg 74. NW Cos > 79
SA. E > 81 Arg. Career ended by inj.
Autobiography 'Thanks to Rugby' pub 82.
Established Sch of Rugby, with sponsorship of
Wimpey Homes, 85.

BEAURIN, Charles   *France*
SF.
Forward, 2-0-0-2.
07 E−; 08 E−.

BEBB, Dewi Iorwerth Ellis   *Wales*
Friars Sch Bangor, Colwyn Bay, Beaumaris,
Trin Coll Carmarthen, Cardiff Tg Coll, RN, R
Marines, US Portsmouth, Swansea, Barbarians.
b 7.8.38 Bangor.
Wing, 34-13-4-17 (33 − 11t).
59 E+(1t) S− I+ F−; 60 E− S+(1t) I+ F−

SA−; 61 E+(2t) S− I+ F−(1t); 62 E= S− F+ I=; 63 E− F− NZ−; 64 E=(2t) S+ F= SA−; 65 E+ S+ I+(1t) F−(1t); 66 F+ A−; 67 S− I− F− (1t) E+(1t); BI > 62 SA 2-0-0-2; 66 A 2-2-0-0, NZ 4-0-0-4.
RN/HTV production. W > 64 SA. Wales XV v Fj 64.

BECK, Jacobus Johannes   *South Africa*
('Colin')
Strand Sch, Stellenbosch Univ, Jnr Springboks, W Prov.
b 27.3.59 Strand.
Centre, 3-2-0-1 (4 − 1t).
81 NZ+r NZ−r US+(1t).

BECKER, Vincent Anthony Mary   *Ireland*
Gonzaga Coll, Mungret Coll, Lansdowne.
b 9.10.47 Dublin.
Wing, 2-0-1-1.
74 F− W=.
Insurance. Ath for I.

BECKETT, Gerald Gordon Paul   *Ireland*
Wesley Coll, Trin Coll Dublin.
b 28.6.1886; *d* 3.9.50.
Centre, 3-1-0-2 (3 − 1t).
1908 E− S+(1t) W−.
Chmn Irish Pensions Appeal Tribunal.

BECKINGHAM, Geoffrey   *Wales*
Barry, Cardiff.
b 29.7.24 Barry.
Hooker, 3-1-0-2.
53 E− S+; 58 F−.
Municipal gardener. Recalled by W 5 yrs after previous cap.

BEDELL-SIVRIGHT, David   *Scotland*
Revell ('Darkie')
Fettes Coll, Cambridge Univ, Edinburgh Univ, Barbarians.
b 8.12.1880 N Queensferry; *d* 5.9.15 Gallipoli.
Forward, 22-12-0-10 (9 − 3t).
1900 W−; 01 W+ I+ E+; 02 W− I− E−; 03 W+ I+; 04 W− I+(2t) E+; 05 NZ−; 06 W− I+(1t) E− SA+; 07 W+ I+ E+; 08 W− I−; BT > 03 SA, 04 & 08 A, NZ.
Medicine. Blue 1899-02. Played with bro John v W 02. Capt BT > 04 A, NZ. Scottish heavywt boxing champ. One-time stock rearer in A. Served WW1, Surg RN; died of blood poisoning in Gallipoli.

BEDELL-SIVRIGHT, John   *Scotland*
Vamdaleur
Fettes Coll, Cambridge Univ.
b −.10.1881 N Queensferry; *d* 21.10.20 Montrose.
Forward, 1-0-0-1.
02 W−.

Estate mgr/farmer. Blue 1900-3. Played with bro Darkie v W 02.

BEDFORD, Harry   *England*
Morley.
b 1866 Gildersome; *d* −.1.29 Leeds.
Forward, 3-3-0-0 (2t).
1889 NZN+(2t); 1890 S+ I+.
Licensee.

BEDFORD, Lawrence Leslie   *England*
Headingley, Barbarians, Yorks.
b 11.2.03 Leeds; *d* 25.11.63 Harewood, Yorks.
FB, 2-0-1-1.
31 W= I−.
Co dir dyeware & chemical co. Capt Headingley & Yorks. Club ckter.

BEDFORD, Thomas Pleydell   *South Africa*
Natal, Oxford Univ, Richmond.
b 8.2.42 Bloemfontein.
No 8/flanker, 25-13-4-8 (3 − 1t).
63 A+(1t) A− A− A+; 64 W+ F−; 65 I− A− A−; 68 BI+ BI= BI+ BI+ F+ F+; 69 A+ A+ A+ A+ S− E−; 70 I= W=; 71 F+ F=.
Architect. Blue 65-7. Scored t on Test debut. SA > 69-70 BI; 71 A (inj early, returned SA). Capt SA v A 2nd, 3rd Tests 69; S 69. 119 apps for Natal.

BEER, Ian David Stafford JP   *England*
Whitgift Sch, O Whitgiftians, Cambridge Univ, Harlequins, Bath, Shropshire, Dorset & Wilts.
b 28.4.31 Croydon.
No 8, 2-1-0-1 (3 − 1t).
55 F− S+(1t).
HM. Blue 52-4. Capt Oxford-Cambridge > 55 US. Camb U CB rep RFU. Taught at Marlborough Coll, Ellesmere Coll, Lancing Coll.

BEESE, Michael Christopher   *England*
Keynsham GS, Liverpool.
b 8.10.48 Bristol.
Centre, 3-0-0-3 (4 − 1t).
72 W− I− F−(1t).
Town planner.

BEGBIE, Thomas Allan   *Scotland*
Merchiston Castle Sch, Edinburgh W.
b 1862; *d* 26.2.1896 London.
FB, 2-0-1-1 (1c).
1881 I− E=(1c).
Veterinary surg.

BEGU, J.   *France*
Dax.
Centre/wing, 3-2-0-1 (8 − 2t).
82 Arg+r(1t); 84 E+(1t) S−.

BEGUERIE, Christian *France*
Agen.
No 8, 1-0-0-1.
79 NZ−.

BEGUET, Louis *France*
RCF.
b 7.12.1894 Neuf-Mesnil; *d* −.3.83.
Prop, 10-3-0-7 (33 − 2t 9c 3p).
22 I−; 23 S−(1p) W−(1c) E−(1p) I+(1t 1c); 24
S+ I− E− R+(1t 7c 1p) US−.
F rec 7c v R 24 (P. Villepreux 5c v E 72, F rec v
IB opposition).

BEHOTEGUY, André *France*
Bayonne, Cognac.
b 19.10.1900 Bayonne; *d* 60 Cognac.
Centre, 20-6-0-14 (28 − 5t 3c 1d 1p).
23 E−; 24 S+ I− E−(1d) W−(1t) R+(2t 1p)
US−; 26 E−; 27 E+ G+ G−(1t); 28 NSW−(1c)
I−(1c) E− G+ W+(1c); 29 S−(1t) W− E−; 30
W−.
Played with bro Henri in 5 ints.

BEHOTEGUY, Henri *France*
RCF, Cognac.
b 18.10.1898 Bayonne.
Centre, 6-2-0-4 (3 − 1t).
23 W−; 28 NSW− I−(1t) E− G+ W+.
Played with bro André in 5 ints.

BEITH, Bruce McNeil ('Jackie') *Australia*
Sydney Univ, A Forces, E Suburbs, NSW.
b 28.9.1893 Mudgee, NSW; *d* −.9.61.
FB, 1-0-0-1.
14 NZ−.
Dentist. Served WW1, Capt Army Medical
Corps. Qld sel.

BEKKER, Hendrik Johannes *South Africa*
('Hennie')
J.G. Meiring Sch, Stellenbosch Univ, Jnr
Springboks, Quaggas, Barbarians, Paarl
Teachers Coll, OFS, Boland, W Prov.
b 12.9.52 Nuwerus.
Lock, 2-0-0-2 (4 − 1t).
81 NZ−(1t) NZ−.
Univ employee. SA tallest player, 6ft 7in.
Scored t on debut. SA > 81 US.

BEKKER, Hendrik P. Jordaan *South Africa*
('Jaap')
N Transvaal.
b 11.2.25 Dordrecht.
Prop, 15-10-0-5 (3 − 1t).
52 E+ F+; 53 A+ A− A+ A+; 55 BI+ BI−
BI+; 56 A+ A+ A+ NZ− NZ+ NZ− NZ−.
Clerk/Native Affairs Dept. Bro of Martiens &
Dolf; played with Dolf 3rd, 4th Tests v A 53.
Sister Corrie rep SA at ath. Bro Daan boxed for
SA.

BEKKER, Martiens J. *South Africa*
N Transvaal.
b Dordrecht.
Flanker, 1-1-0-0.
61 S+.
Bro of Jaap & Dolf.

BEKKER, Rudolph Philippus *South Africa*
('Dolf')
N Transvaal.
b 26.12.26.
Wing, 2-2-0-0 (3 − 1t).
53 A+(1t) A+.
Bro of Jaap & Martiens; played with Jaap 3rd,
4th Tests v A 53.

BELASCAIN, Christian *France*
Bayonne.
b 1.11.53 Biarritz.
Centre, 18-11-1-6 (4 − 1t).
77 R+; 78 E+ S+ I+ W− R+; 79 I= W+ E−
S+(1t); 82 W− E− S− I+; 83 E+ S+ I− W+.
Import agent. Côte Basque > 81 NZ.

BELL, David Lauder *Scotland*
George Watson's, Watsonians, St Andrew's
Univ, Oxford Univ, Barbarians.
b 28.4.49 Edinburgh.
Centre, 4-2-0-2.
75 I+ F− W+ E−.
Blue 70. Ckt for S.

BELL, F.J. *England*
Northern.
Forward, 1-0-0-1.
1900 W−.
Market gardener. Hunslet RL 1900.

BELL, Henry *England*
Liverpool Inst, New Brighton.
b 1860; *d* 20.9.35 Marylebone.
Forward, 1-1-0-0.
1884 I+.
Banker. Fdr Lloyds Bank RFC 13. Extensive
banking career & mem of various important
financial commissions.

BELL, J. Lowthian *England*
Darlington, Durham Co.
Half-back, 1-1-0-0.
1878 I+.

BELL, John Arthur *Scotland*
Dollar Acad, Clydesdale.
b 1882; *d* −.
Forward, 6-3-0-3.
01 W+ I+ E+; 02 W− I− E−.

BELL, Keith Radcliffe *Australia*
CEGS E Brisbane, Qld Univ, Qld.
b 10.6.48 Goondiwindi.

Prop, 1-0-0-1.
68 S−.
Schoolmaster.

BELL, Lewis Hay Irving *Scotland*
Edinburgh Acad, Edinburgh Academicals,
Edinburgh Univ.
b 23.10.1878; *d* 25.6.24.
Forward, 3-1-1-1.
1900 E=; 04 W− I+.
Medicine.

BELL, Peter Joseph *England*
Caterham Sch, Caterham OB, Cirencester Coll,
Cranbrook, Ashford, Blackheath, Barbarians,
Kent, Bay of Plenty (NZ).
b 28.4.37.
Flanker, 4-1-2-1.
68 W= I= F− S+.
Farmer.

BELL, Raymond Henry *New Zealand*
King's HS, Pirates, Otago, S Island.
b 31.12.25 Dunedin.
Wing/FB, 3-2-0-1 (6 − 1t 1p).
51 A+(1t); 52 A−(1p) A+.
Council engr's office. NZ > 51 A. Knee inj 2nd
Test v A 52 ended playing career. Otago sel 68-
71; pres of Pirates club 79.

BELL, Richard J. *Ireland*
RBAI, NIFC.
Back/half-back, 2-0-0-2.
1875 E− E−.
Ump I v S 1877.

BELL, Robert William *England*
Durham Sch, Leeds Clergy Sch, Cambridge
Univ, Northern, Blackheath, Barbarians,
Northumb.
b 19.12.1875 Newcastle-upon-Tyne; *d* 9.6.40
Newcastle-upon-Tyne.
Forward, 3-1-1-1.
1900 W− I+ S=.
Clergyman. Blue 1897-9. Ordained 01. Rowed
in Jesus Coll VIII.

BELL, Sir William Ewart KCB *Ireland*
Methodist Coll Belfast, Collegians, Barbarians.
b 13.11.24 Belfast.
Flanker, 4-2-1-1.
53 F+ E= S+ W−.
Head of NI Civil Service.

BELLETANTE, Guy *France*
Nantes.
b 13.3.27 Périgueux.
Centre, 3-2-0-1.
51 I− E+ W+.

BELLISS, Ernest Arthur ('Moke') *New Zealand*
Moawhanga Huia, Wanganui, Hautapu, N
Island.
b 1.4.1894 Palmerston N; *d* 22.4.74 Taihape.
No 8/flanker, 3-1-1-1 (3 − 1t).
21 SA+(1t) SA− SA=.
Butcher/farmer. NZ > 20 & 22 A. Son E.V. &
grandson P.J. rep Wanganui.

BENDON, Gordon John *England*
KCS Wimbledon, KCS OB, RAF, Wasps,
London Cos, E Cos, Mdx, Surrey.
b 9.4.29.
Prop, 4-1-2-1.
59 W− I+ F= S=.
Sales rep/marketing dir. 20 seasons with Wasps.

BÉNÉSIS, René *France*
Narbonne, Agen.
b 29.8.44 Orthez.
Hooker, 30-15-6-9.
69 W= R+; 70 S+ I+ W− E+ R+; 71 S+ I=
E= W− A+ R+; 72 S− I− E+ W− I− A=
R+; 73 NZ+ E− W+ I− J+ R+; 74 I+ W=
E+ S−.
PE teacher.

BENETIÈRE, Jean *France*
Roanne.
Hooker, 2-2-0-0.
54 It+ Arg+.

BENNET, Robert *New Zealand*
Albany St Sch Dunedin, Alhambra, Otago, S
Island.
b 23.7.1879 Caversham; *d* 9.4.62 Dunedin.
Centre, 1-1-0-0.
05 A+.
Tailor.

BENNETT, Frank *Ireland*
Methodist Coll Belfast, Queen's Univ Belfast,
Collegians.
b 1893 Clonakilty; *d* −.5.81.
Wing, 1-0-0-1.
13 S−.
Methodist minister.

BENNETT, Ivor *Wales*
Aberavon.
b 16.6.13 Aberkenfig.
Prop, 1-0-0-1.
37 I−.
Police/club steward. Warrington RL 37,
Bridgend RL.

BENNETT, Norman Osborn *England*
('Billy')
Epsom Coll, St Mary's Hosp, Waterloo, US
Portsmouth, RN, Barbarians, London Cos,
Hants, Surrey, Lancs.

b 21.9.22.
Centre, 7-3-1-3 (3 − 1t).
47 W+ S+(1t) F+; 48 A− W= I− S−.
Medicine. Served RNVR as Surg Lt. Ckt for Free Foresters, RN, Worcs & MCC.

BENNETT, Percy   *Wales*
Cardiff Harlequins.
Forward, 4-0-0-4.
1891 E− S−; 1892 S− I−.

BENNETT, Philip OBE   *Wales*
Coleshill Sec, Welsh SS, Welsh Youth, Llanelli, Barbarians.
b 24.10.48 Felinfoel.
Wing/centre/FH/FB, 29-19-4-6 (166 − 4t 18c 2d 36p).
69 F=r; 70 SA= S+ F+; 72 S+r NZ−(4p); 73 E+(1c) S−(2p) I+(1c 2p) F−(1d) A+(4p); 74 S+(1c) I=(1c 1p) F=(3p) E−(1c 2p); 75 S−r I+(3c 2p); 76 E+ S+(2c 3p) I+(1t 3c 3p) F+(2p); 77 I+(2c 2p) F− E+ S+(1t 2c 2p); 78 E+(3p) S+(1d 1p) I+ F+(2t 1c); BI > 74 SA 4-3-1-0; 77 NZ 4-1-0-3.
Steelworker/sports shopkeeper/TV reporter. 1st Welshman capped as r, v F 69. W > 68 Arg; 69 NZ A & Fj; 73 Can; 75 Far East. Wales XV v J 73; Arg 76. Welsh XV v NZ 74. W's ldg pts scorer; jt Champ rec 38 pts 76. Career 210 pts (inc BI) one-time world rec. Rec-equ 19 pts v I 76. 103 pts (26 in Tests) BI > 74 SA; 112 pts (18) BI > 77 NZ. Capt BI > 77. Rec 44 pts (8 Tests) for BI. Ptn Gareth Edwards rec 24 times for W. Barbarians v NZ 73, A 76. Barbarians > 76 US, Can. Capt Llanelli 73-9. Autobiog 'Everywhere for Wales' pub 84.

BENNETT, Walter Gordon   *Australia*
CEGS Brisbane, YMCA Brisbane, Qld.
b 26.3.06 Brisbane; 11.9.79 Sydney.
SH, 4-2-0-2 (3 − 1t).
31 M+; 33 SA− SA+(1t) SA−.
Chemist. Bro in law of M.C. Clarke. A > 33 SA. Accomplished wrestler; won many Qld champs 29-31.

BENNETT, William Neil ('Nellie')   *England*
Tiffin Sch, Bedford, Colwyn Bay, London Welsh, Surrey.
b 20.4.51 Ramsey, IOM.
FH, 7-2-1-4 (23 − 2t 5p).
75 S+(1p) A−; 76 S−r; 79 S=(1p) I−(1t 1p) F+(1t 1p) W−(1p).
Schoolmaster. E's most pts (48) on overseas tour (> 75 A) & most pts in any tour match (36 v WA 75). Accomplished ckter.

BENNETTS, Barzillai Beckerleg   *England*
('Barrie') MBE
Bridgend Coll, Penzance, Devonport A, Redruth, Richmond, Barbarians, Cornwall.

b 14.7.1883; *d* 26.7.58 Alverton, Penzance.
Wing, 2-0-0-2.
09 A− W−.
Solicitor. RFU > 10 Arg. Rep Cornwall at ckt, golf & hockey. Distinguished viola player & amateur dramatic actor. County coroner. RNLI Award for servs to Penlee lifeboat comm. MBE 49.

BENT, G.C.   *Ireland*
Portora RS, Trin Coll Dublin.
Half-back, 2-0-1-1.
1882 W− E=.

BENTLEY, John Edmund   *England*
Tonbridge Sch, Gipsies.
b c1847; *d* 12.12.13 Hampstead.
Half-back, 2-1-0-1.
1871 S−; 1872 S+.
Official at R Courts of Justice. Played in 1st int, S v E 1871.

BERBIZIER, Pierre   *France*
Lourdes, Agen.
b 17.6.58 Lannemezan.
SH, 21-12-0-9 (12 − 3t).
81 S+ I+ W+ E+ NZ− NZ−; 82 I+ R−; 83 S+ I−; 84 S−r NZ− NZ−; 85 Arg− Arg+(1t) J+ J+; 86 S−(1t) I+(1t) W+ E+.
Professor of PE. F > 85 Arg.

BEREJNOÏ, Jean-Claude   *France*
Tulle.
b 20.4.39 Decazeville, Aveyron.
Prop/hooker, 27-19-4-4.
63 R=; 64 S− W= It+ I+ SA+ Fj+ R+; 65 S+ I= E− W+ It+ R+; 66 S= I+ E+ W− It+ R+; 67 S− A+ E+ It+ W+ I+ R+.
Insurance agent.

BERESFORD-KNOX, H.J. See
H.J. Knox

BERGÈS, Bernard   *France*
Toulouse.
SH, 1-0-0-1.
26 I−.

BERGÈS-CAU, René   *France*
Lourdes.
b 28.2.49 Tarbes; *d* 83.
FB, 1-1-0-0.
76 E+r.
Rep.

BERGÈSE, Félix   *France*
Bayonne.
Centre, 6-5-0-1 (12 − 4t).
36 G+; 37 G+(2t) It+(1t); 38 G− R+ G+(1t).

BERGH, Willem Ferdinand   *South Africa*
('Ferdie')
Stellenbosch Boys HS, Stellenbosch Univ, SW
Dist.
 b 2.11.06.
Lock, 17-13-0-4 (21 − 7t).
31 W+(1t) I+; 32 E+(1t) S+; 33 A+(2t) A−
A+ A+ A−; 37 A+(1t) A+(1t) NZ− NZ+
NZ+(1t); 38 BI+ BI+ BI−.
Co dir/animal husbandry.

BERGHAN, Trevor   *New Zealand*
Rawene Dist HS, Rotorua HS, Rotorua,
Auckland Univ, Otago Univ, NZ Univs, Otago,
S Island.
 b 13.7.14 Houhora.
1st five-eighth, 3-3-0-0.
38 A+ A+ A+.
Dentist. NZ > 38 A. Served WW2, RNZN.
Coach Univ club in Auckland 47-51.

BERGIERS, Roy Thomas   *Wales*
Edmond
QEGS Carmarthen, Cardiff Coll, Llanelli,
Barbarians.
 b 11.11.50 Carmarthen.
Centre, 11-7-0-4 (8 − 2t).
72 E+ S+(1t) F+ NZ−; 73 E+ S− I+ F− A+;
74 E−; 75 I+(1t); BI > 74 SA.
Schoolmaster/PT instructor. Wales B v F 72. W
> 73 Can; 75 Far East. Welsh XV v NZ 74.
Wales XV v J 73; Arg 76.

BERGOUGNAN, Yves ('Le   *France*
Requin')
Toulouse.
 b 8.5.24 Toulouse.
SH, 17-10-0-7 (12 − 3d).
45 BF+ W−; 46 BF+(1d) I+(1d) NZS− W+;
47 S+ I+ W− E−; 48 S− W+ E+(1d); 49 S−
E− Arg+ Arg+.

BERKELEY, William Vaughan   *Scotland*
Fettes Coll, Oxford Univ.
 b 14.6.04.
Prop, 4-3-0-1.
26 F+; 29 F+ W− I+.
Schoolmaster. Blue 24-6.

BERKERY, Patrick Joseph   *Ireland*
Crescent Sch Limerick, Lansdowne,
Barbarians.
 b 3.2.29 Clonmel.
FB, 11-6-0-5 (5 − 1c 1p).
54 W−; 55 W−; 56 S+ W+; 57 F+ E− S+(1c)
W−; 58 A+ E− S+(1p).
Oil co rep.

BERMINGHAM, John J. ('Big   *Ireland*
Boy')
Blackrock Coll.

 b 19.10.1899; *d* 61.
Prop, 4-1-0-3.
21 E− S+ W− F−.

BERMINGHAM, Vincent John   *Australia*
Tech Coll Warwick, Toowoomba, Qld.
 b 10; *d* −.8.83 Brisbane.
Prop, 3-1-1-1.
34 NZ+ NZ=; 37 SA−.
Farmer.

BERNARD, René   *France*
Bergerac.
 b 11.5.25 Bergerac.
Prop, 4-3-0-1.
51 S+ I− E+ W+.
Switched to RL.

BERNE, John Edward   *Australia*
Pagewood Marist Bros Sch, Randwick, NSW.
 b 14.3.54 Co Antrim.
Centre, 1-0-0-1.
75 S−.
Emigrated to A at 7. A > 75-6 BI; inj on only int
app. S Sydney RL 76; later E Suburbs &
Cronella.

BERNON, Jean   *France*
Lourdes.
Lock/prop, 2-0-0-2.
22 I−; 23 S−.

BÉROT, Jean-Louis   *France*
Toulouse.
 b 28.7.47 Dax.
SH/FH, 21-7-4-10 (23 − 1t 1c 3d 3p).
68 NZ− A−; 69 S− I−; 70 E+(1t 1d) R+; 71
S+ I=(1d) E=(1d) W− SA−(2p) SA=(1c) A−
A+ R+; 72 S− I− E+ W− A=; 74 I+(1p).
Masseur.

BERRIDGE, Michael John   *England*
King's Sch Peterborough, Peterborough,
Northampton, Leicester, Barbarians, E
Midlands.
 b 28.2.23; *d* 2.10.73.
Prop, 2-0-0-2.
49 W− I−.
Farmer. Comb Cos v A 47, SA 51.

BERRY, Charles Walter   *Scotland*
Loretto Sch, Oxford Univ, Fettesian-
Lorettonians.
 b 6.9.1863; *d* 11.10.47.
Forward, 8-4-2-2 (6c 1gm).
1884 I+(2c) E−; 1885 W=; 1887 I+(1c 1gm)
W+(2c) E=; 1888 W− I+(1c).
Merchant. Blue 1883-4. Sc of S's 1st gm, v I
1887.

BERRY, Henry *England*
St Mark's Sch Gloucester, Gloucester, The
Army, Glos.
b 8.1.1883 Gloucester; kia 9.5.15 Festubert, F.
Forward, 4-3-1-0 (6 − 2t).
10 W+ I= F+(1t) S+(1t).
The Army. Served in Glos Rgt in SA War
(Queen's Medal). Served in St Helena, India &
with Army Reserve. Recalled for WW1; served
as Cpl when killed in F.

BERRY, John *England*
Kendal H, Tyldesley, Lancs.
b c1867; *d* −.5.30 Manchester.
Half-back, 3-2-0-1.
1891 W+ I+ S−.
Licensee/builder's labourer. Turned RL when
his club, Tyldesley, helped form NU 1895.

BERRY, Joseph Thomas Wade *England*
Eastbourne Coll, Market Harborough,
Leicester, Barbarians, Leics.
b 17.7.07 Slawston, Leics.
Flanker, 3-2-0-1.
39 W+ I− S+.
Farmer. Leics CB rep RFU 53-68. E sel 51-66.
Pres RFU 68-9 & Leicester. Bro in law of J.
McD. Hodgson. Wife an E int golfer.

BERTRAM, David Minto *Scotland*
George Watson's Coll, Watsonians.
b 24.1.1899 Edinburgh; *d* 10.4.75.
Hooker, 11-6-2-3 (8 − 2t 1c).
22 F= W= I+ E−(1c); 23 F+ W+ I+ E−; 24
W+(1t) I+(1t) E−.
Medicine.

BERTRAND, Pierre *France*
Bourg.
b 27.
Prop, 8-4-0-4 (10 − 2c 2p).
51 I−(1c) E+ W+; 53 S+(1c) I− E− W−(1p)
It+(1p).
Veterinary surg.

BERTRANNE, Roland Gaston *France*
Lycée Bagnères, Bagnères.
b 6.12.49 Ibos, Hautes-Pyrénées.
Centre/wing, 69-38-6-25 (66 − 17t).
71 E=(1t) W− SA=(1t) A−(1t) A+; 72 S− I−;
73 NZ+(1t) E−(1t) J+(1t) R+(1t); 74 I+ W=
E= S− Arg+(1t) Arg+(1t) R− SA−(1t) SA−;
75 W− E+ S+ I− SA− SA− Arg+ Arg+(1t)
R+; 76 S+ I+ W− E+ US+ A+(1t) A+(1t)
R−; 77 W+ E+ S+(1t) I+ Arg+(1t) Arg=
NZ+ NZ− R+; 78 E+ S+ I+ W− R+; 79 I=
W+ E− S+ R+(1t); 80 W− E− S− I+ SA−
R−; 81 S+(1t) I+ W+ E+ R+ NZ− NZ−.
Draughtsman. F's most capped player. F > 71,
80 SA. 7t (6 apps, inc 4t v W Transvaal) F > 71
SA, rec for F.

BESOMO, Keith Scott *Australia*
Enmou HS, E Suburbs, NSW, Associate (WA).
b 54.
No 8, 1-0-0-1.
79 I−.
Accountant. Born deaf. Father Vic was A
swimming champ.

BESSET, Edmond *France*
Grenoble.
FB, 1-1-0-0.
24 S+.

BESSET, Lucien *France*
SCUF.
b 4.1.1892 Paris; *d* 22.4.75 Paris.
Wing, 2-0-0-2 (4 − 2c).
14 W− E−(2c).
Deputy for Paris/public works contractor.
Served WW1. Légion d'Honneur.

BESSON, Marcel *France*
CASG.
b 01 Dijon.
Wing, 6-0-0-6 (3 − 1t).
24 I−; 25 I− E−(1t); 26 S− W−; 27 I−.

BESSON, Pierre *France*
Brive.
b 11.4.40 Saint-Astier, Dordogne.
Wing, 5-2-0-3.
63 S− I+ E−; 65 R+; 68 SA−.
PE teacher.

BESTBIER, Andre *South Africa*
OFS.
b 31.3.46 Potchefstroom.
1-1-0-0.
74 F+r.
Army officer.

BESTER, John L.A. *South Africa*
Jan Van Riebeck Sch, W Prov.
b 18.
Centre/wing, 2-1-0-1 (6 − 2t).
38 BI+(1t) BI−(1t).
Clerk. SA > 37 A, NZ.

BESTER, J.J.N. *South Africa*
W Prov.
2-2-0-0 (3 − 1t).
24 BI+ BI+(1t).

BESWICK, A.M. *South Africa*
Border.
3-1-0-2.
1896 BT− BT− BT+.

BESWICK, Edmund *England*
Swinton, Lancs.
b c1860 Penrith; *d* 22.1.11 Salford.

Back, 2-0-1-1.
1882 I= S−.

BETTS, Terence Neil ('Tiny')   *Australia*
St Laurence CBC Sch Brisbane, W End, Qld.
b 13.4.26.
Prop, 3-0-0-3.
51 NZ− NZ−; 54 Fj−.
Tax inspector. Qld sel, life mem.

BEVAN, Griffith Wilfred   *Wales*
Burry Port, Birmingham Welsh, Llanelli,
Devonport Servs, RN.
b 15.8.14 Burry Port.
Prop, 1-0-0-1.
47 E−.
Steelworker. Fdr mem Birmingham Welsh.

BEVAN, James Alfred   *Wales*
Hereford Cathed Sch, Abergavenny,
Cambridge Univ, Newport, Grosmont.
b 1859 Brisbane (A); *d* 3.2.38 Leytonstone.
Back, 1-0-0-1.
1881 E−.
Minister. Blue 1877, 1880. W's 1st capt, v E
1881.

BEVAN, John Charles   *Wales*
Ferndale GS, Cardiff Coll, Cardiff, Barbarians.
b 28.10.50 Tylorstown.
Wing, 10-8-0-2 (19 − 5t).
71 E+(1t) S+ I+ F+; 72 E+ S+ F+(1t) NZ−
(1t); 73 E+(2t) S−; BI > 71 A, NZ 1-1-0-0.
PT instructor/licensee. 54 pts (18t) BI > 71 A,
NZ, inc rec-equ 17t for NZ tour. Barbarians v
NZ 73. Warrington RL 73. 6 GB RL Tests, 17
Wales RL. Qualified lifeguard.

BEVAN, John David   *Wales*
Neath GS, Bryncoch, Aberavon, Barbarians.
b 12.3.48; *d* 6.6.86.
FH, 4-3-0-1 (3 − 1d).
75 F+ E+ S−(1d) A+; BI > 77 NZ.
Schoolmaster. Wales B v F 74. Wales XV v Tg
74. Welsh XVr v NZ 74. W > 75 Far East.
Barbarians v NZ 74. Asst Mgr Wales B > 83
Spain. Aberavon coach, then WRU coach 82-5.
Retired due to ill health Nov 85. Ckt for Neath
& Wales.

BEVAN, T. Sidney   *Wales*
Swansea.
Back−row, 1-0-0-1.
04 I−; BT > 04 A 1-1-0-0, NZ.
Schoolmaster.

BEVAN, Vincent David   *New Zealand*
Otaki Convent Sch, Wellington Coll OB,
Wellington, Athletic, N Island.
b 24.12.21 Wellington.
SH, 6-3-1-2.

49 A− A−; 50 BI= BI+ BI+ BI+.
Carpenter/milkman/coffee bar proprietor/taxi
driver. NZ > 47 A, 53-4 BI,F & NAm. Barred
from > 49 SA because he was part Maori.

BEYNON, Benjamin   *Wales*
Swansea.
FH, 2-1-0-1.
20 E+ S−.
Docker/painter & decorator. Switched from
rugby to football. Joined Swansea Town. 12
goals in 31 matches 14-22. Changed codes again,
joined Oldham RL 22, won Challenge Cup
medal 25.

BEYNON, George Edward BEM   *Wales*
Swansea.
b 02; *d* 14.10.57 Carshalton.
Flanker, 2-1-0-1.
25 F+ I−.

BEZUIDENHOUDT, Chris E.   *South Africa*
N Transvaal.
Prop, 3-3-0-0.
62 BI+ BI+ BI+.

BEZUIDENHOUDT, Nicholas   *South Africa*
Stephanus Erasmus
N Transvaal.
b 4.3.50 Delmas.
Prop, 9-5-1-3.
72 E−; 74 BI− BI− BI= F+ F+; 75 F+ F+; 77
Wd+.
Accountant.

BIANCHI, Jérôme   *France*
Toulon.
FB, 1-1-0-0.
85 J+.

BIANCO, Antoine   *France*
Auch.
b 7.11.36.
Lock, 1-0-0-1.
61 NZ−r.

BICHENDARITZ, Jean   *France*
Biarritz Ol.
Prop, 3-3-0-0.
54 It+ Arg+ Arg+.

BIDART, Laurent   *France*
La Rochelle.
b 11.1.30 Boucau.
FH, 1-0-0-1.
53 W−.

BIÉMOURET, Paul   *France*
Agen.
b 1.4.43 Mas d'Auvignon, Gens.
Flanker, 19-8-2-9 (4 − 1t).

69 E− W=; 70 I+ W− E+; 71 W− SA− SA=
A−; 72 E+(1t) W− I− A+ R+; 73 S+ NZ+
E− W+ I−.
Farmer.

BIENES, René *France*
Cognac.
b 2.8.23 Toulouse.
Flanker/prop/no 8, 29-16-1-12 (12 − 4t).
50 S− I= E+ W−; 51 S+ I− E+ W+; 52 S+ I−
SA− W− E− It+(1t); 53 S+ I− E−; 54 S+ I+
NZ+ W− E+ Arg+(2t) Arg+(1t); 56 S− I+
W− It+ E+.
Section chief in brandy works. Capt F > 54 Arg
& Chile.

BIERMAN, J. Nicholas *South Africa*
Transvaal.
b 10.
1-1-0-0.
31 I+.
Civil Service. SA > 31-2 BI.

BIGGAR, Alistair Gourlay *Scotland*
Sedbergh Sch, London Scottish, Barbarians.
b 4.8.46 Edinburgh.
Wing, 12-5-0-7 (3 − 1t).
69 SA+; 70 F− I− E+(1t) A−; 71 F− W− I−
E+ E+; 72 F+ W−; BI > 71 NZ.
Foreign Exchange. Cousin of Mike.

BIGGAR, Michael Andrew *Scotland*
Sedbergh Sch, Cambridge Univ, London
Scottish, Barbarians.
b 20.11.49 Aberdeen.
Flanker, 24-6-2-16.
75 I+ F− W+ E−; 76 W− E+ I+; 77 I+ F−
W−; 78 I− F− W− E− NZ−; 79 W− E= I=
F− NZ−; 80 I− F+ W− E−.
Law. Blue 71. Cousin of Alistair. Scottish XV v
J 76, 77.

BIGGS, John Maundy *England*
Univ Coll Hosp, Utd Hosps, Wasps.
b 1855 Reading; *d* 3.6.35 Barnstaple.
Forward, 2-1-1-0.
1878 S=; 1879 I+.
1st int from Wasps, whom he capt 1877-9.

BIGGS, Norman Witchell *Wales*
Cardiff Coll, Cambridge Univ, Richmond,
Cardiff, Barbarians.
b 3.11.1870 Cardiff; *d* 27.2.08 Nigeria.
Back/wing, 8-4-0-4 (4 − 2t).
1888 NZN+; 1889 I−; 1892 I−; 1893 E+(1t)
S+(1t) I+; 1894 E− I−.
Police. W's youngest player, 18 yr 1 mnth v
NZN 22.12.1888. Bro of Selwyn. One of 6 bros
who played for Cardiff 1886-07. Superintendent
in Nigerian Police when killed by poisoned
arrow in native ambush.

BIGGS, Selwyn Hanam *Wales*
Cardiff, Richmond, Barbarians.
b 1875.
FH, 9-4-0-5.
1895 E− S−; 1896 S+; 1897 E+; 1898 I+ E−;
1899 S− I−; 1900 I+.
Co dir. Bro of Norman.

BIGOT, Charles *France*
Quillan, Lézignan.
Hooker/flanker, 4-2-0-2.
30 S+ E−; 31 I+ S−.

BIILMANN, Ronald Regnor *Australia*
All Saints Coll Bathurst, St Joseph's Coll, E
Suburbs, NSW.
b 08; *d* 16.5.63.
Five-eighth, 4-1-0-3 (12 − 3c 2p).
33 SA−(1p) SA+(3c 1p) SA− SA−.
Grazing station mgr. Of Dutch descent. A > 33
SA. Noted ckter; once dismissed Don Bradman,
Bathurst v NSW CA 29. Renowned trout
fisherman.

BILBAO, Louis *France*
St Jean-de-Luz.
b 14.9.56 St Jean-de-Luz.
Wing, 2-1-1-0.
78 I+; 79 I=.
Municipal employee.

BILLAC, Eugène *France*
Bayonne.
b 16.3.1898 Bayonne; *d* 29.11.57.
FH, 9-2-0-7 (6 − 2t).
20 S− E− W− I+ US+(1t); 21 S−(1t) W−; 22
W−; 23 E−.

BILLIÈRE, Michel *France*
Toulouse.
b 16.7.43 Rieumes.
Flanker, 1-0-0-1.
68 NZ−.
Carpenter.

BIOUSSA, Alex *France*
Toulouse.
b 7.3.02 Toulouse.
Flanker, 21-5-0-16 (9 − 3t).
24 W− US−; 25 I− NZ− S− E−; 26 S− I− E−
; 28 E− G+(1t) W+; 29 I− S− W− E−; 30
S+(1t) I+ E− G+(1t) W−.
Bro of Clovis.

BIOUSSA, Clovis ('Le Gosse') *France*
Toulouse.
b 1892 Toulouse; *d* −.
SH, 3-0-0-3.
13 W− I−; 14 I−.
Journalist/PE dir. Bro of Alex. FFR selector.

BIRABEN, Maurice *France*
Dax.
b c1892; *d* 25.3.63.
Prop, 10-4-2-4.
20 W− I+ US+; 21 S+ W− E− I+; 22 S= E=
I−.

BIRCH, James *Wales*
Neath.
b Northampton.
Prop/lock 2-2-0-0.
11 S+ F+.
Police.

BIRKETT, Graham Anthony *Scotland*
Harlequins, London Scottish.
Centre, 1-0-0-1.
75 NZ−.

BIRKETT, John Guy Giberne *England*
Haileybury & ISC, Brighton, Harlequins,
Barbarians, Surrey.
b 27.12.1884 Richmond, Surrey; *d* 16.10.68.
Centre, 21-12-2-7 (34 − 10t 1d).
06 S+ F+ SA=; 07 F+(1t 1d) W− S−; 08
F+(1t) W−(2t) I+ S−(1t); 10 W+ I= S+(2t);
11 W− F+ I− S+(1t); 12 W+ I+(1t) S−
F+(1t).
Land agent. Once E rec cap holder. Son of
Reginald, nephew of Louis. Served WW1, Capt
RFA. Mentioned in despatches 18. Order of
Crown of It, 5th class. Capt Army Claims
Commission for E 43-6.

BIRKETT, Louis *England*
Haileybury & ISC, Clapham R, Mdx.
b 1.1.1853; *d* 11.4.43 Barnstaple.
FB, 3-1-1-1.
1875 S=; 1877 I+ S−.
Played with bro Reginald, v S 1875, I 1877.
Uncle of John. One of E's longest-lived players.

BIRKETT, Reginald Halsey *England*
Lancing Coll, Clapham R.
b 28.3.1849; *d* 30.6.1898.
Forward/back, 4-2-1-1 (1t).
1871 S−(1t); 1875 S=; 1876 S+; 1877 I+.
Hide & skin broker. Sc E's 1st t, v S 1871.
Played with bro Louis, v S 75, I 77. Father of
John. Mem of original RFU comm 1871. A
distinguished footballer, capped as goalkeeper E
v S 1879. FA Cup Winners' medal 1880, for
Clapham R, a club which played football &
rugby.

BIRRELL, R. *Australia*
NSW.
Wing, 1-0-0-1 (3 − 1p).
69 Fj−(1p).

BIRT, Frederick William *Wales*
Newport.
b 10.11.1886 Newport; *d* 5.7.56 Beaufort.
Centre/FB, 7-3-0-4 (7 − 1d 1p).
11 E+(1p) S+; 12 E− S+(1d) I− SA−; 13 E−.
Education officer. Sc all Newport's pts in 9-3
defeat of SA 12. Bowls for Wales. Served WW1,
RE.

BIRT, R. *Australia*
Qld.
Hooker, 1-0-0-1.
14 NZ−.

BIRTWISTLE, William Murray *New Zealand*
Balmoral Intermed Sch, Mt Roskill GS, College
Rifles, Auckland, Canterbury, Christchurch,
Waikato, Hamilton City, S & N Islands.
b 4.7.39 Auckland.
Wing, 7-6-0-1 (12 − 4t).
65 SA+(1t) SA+ SA− SA+(1t); 67 E+(1t)
W+(1t) S+.
Bank official. 9t NZ > 67 BI,F & C.

BISHOP, Colin Charles *England*
Univ Coll Sch, Cambridge Univ, Blackheath,
Barbarians, Mdx.
b 5.10.03; *d* 4.3.80.
FH, 1-0-0-1.
27 F−.
Blue 25.

BISHOP, David John ('Bish') *Wales*
St Cadoc's RC Sch, St Illtyd's Coll, Rhymney
Tech, O Illtydians, Cardiff Youth, Welsh
Youth, Cardiff, Ebbw Vale, Pontypool.
b 31.10.61 Cardiff.
SH, 1-0-0-1 (4 − 1t).
84 A−(1t).
Sales rep. Wales B v F 84. Irish grandmother.
Born in same Newtown dist of Cardiff as Terry
Holmes. Broke neck 81 & told not to play again.
2 bros played for O Illtydians. Recipient of R
Humane Soc Award for rescuing mother & baby
from River Taff, Cardiff 79. Amateur boxer for
Wales.

BISHOP, Edward H. *Wales*
Llandovery Coll, Swansea.
Back, 1-0-0-1.
1889 S−.

BISHOP, J.M. *Scotland*
Glasgow Acad, Glasgow Academicals.
Forward, 1-0-1-0.
1893 I=.

BISSET, Alexander Anderson *Scotland*
Merchiston Castle Sch, RIE Coll.
b 18.10.1883 Duns; *d* 14.2.27 Moffat.
Half-back, 1-0-0-1.

04 W−.
Sudan Forestry.

BISSET, William Montane *South Africa*
Bishops Diocesan Coll Rondebosch, W Prov.
b 1867; d −.2.58.
2-0-0-2.
1891 BT− BT−.

BLACK, Angus William *Scotland*
Dollar Acad, Edinburgh Univ, Barbarians.
b 6.5.25 Dunfermline.
SH, 6-2-0-4.
47 F− W−; 48 E+; 50 W− I− E+; BI > 50 A,
NZ 2-0-0-2.
Medicine. Played in 2 Servs ints.

BLACK, Brian Henry *England*
Oxford Univ, Blackheath, Barbarians.
b 27.5.07; kia 29.7.40 Chilwark, Wilts.
Lock, 10-3-2-5 (30 − 2t 6c 4p).
30 W+(1c 1p) I− F+(1c) S=; 31 W=(2p) I−(1t
1c) S−(2c 1p) F−(1c); 32 S+(1t) 33 W−; BI >
30 NZ 4-1-0-3, A 1-0-0-1.
Articled clerk/solicitor/co dir. Blue 29. Rep GB
in bobsleigh team that won world champ 37.
Won squash rackets champ in S of F. Served
WW2, Pt Off in RAF.

BLACK, James William *Australia*
Manly, Sydney, NSW.
b 10.6.58.
FB/centre, 4-3-0-0 (4 − 1t).
85 C+ C+ NZ−(1t) Fj+.
Bank official. A > 84 Fj; 84 BI.

BLACK, John Edwin *New Zealand*
Timaru Boys' HS, Univ, Canterbury, S Island,
NZ Jnrs, NZ Univs.
b 25.7.51 Timaru.
Hooker, 3-0-0-3.
77 F−; 79 A−; 80 A−.
Freezing co production mgr. NZ > 76 Arg &
Uruguay, 77 F, 78 BI, 79 A, 80 A & Fj

BLACK, Neville Wyatt *New Zealand*
Ngongotaha Primary Sch, Rotorua HS,
Ponsonby, Auckland.
b 25.4.25 Kawakawa.
SH, 1-0-0-1.
49 SA−.
Wool classer/garage proprietor. NZ > 49 SA.
Wigan (E) RL 52, Keighley 57, Ngongotaha 57-
60.

BLACK, Robert Stanley *New Zealand*
Otago Boys' HS, Pirates, Univ, Otago, Buller,
White Star, S Island.
b 23.8.1893 Arrowtown; kia 21.9.16 France.
1st five-eighth, 1-1-0-0.
14 A+.

Banking. NZ > 14 A. Cpl in Otago Mounted
Rifles & Canterbury Infantry Rgt; killed in
Battle of the Somme.

BLACK, William Pollock *Scotland*
Glasgow HS, Glasgow HSFP, Barbarians.
b 27.11.21.
Prop, 5-2-0-3.
48 F+ W− I− E+; 51 E−.
Medicine.

BLACKADDER, William Francis *Scotland*
OBE
Merchiston Castle Sch, Edinburgh Univ, W of
S.
b 23.1.13 Edinburgh.
Prop, 1-1-0-0.
38 E+.
Shipping/RAF. Played in 1 Servs int.

BLACKHAM, J.C. *Ireland*
Queen's Coll Cork.
Hooker, 6-1-1-4.
09 S− W− F+; 10 E= S− W−.

BLACKLOCK, Joseph H. *England*
Aspatria, Cumberland.
b 20.10.1878; d 28.6.45.
Forward, 2-0-0-2.
1898 I−; 1899 I−.
Deputy foreman in coalmine.

BLACKMORE, Jacob Henry *Wales*
('Blood')
Abertillery.
b 1884 Abertillery; d −.
Flanker, 1-1-0-0.
09 E+.
Collier. Hull KR RL.

BLAIKIE, Colin Fraser *Scotland*
Heriot's Coll, Heriot's FP, Barbarians.
b 21.11.41 Edinburgh.
FB, 8-4-0-4 (15 − 5p).
63 I+ E−; 66 E+(1p); 68 A+(2p); 69 F+(1p)
W−(1p) I− E−.
Quantity surveyor. Scottish XV v Arg (2) 69.

BLAIN, Antoine *France*
Carcassonne.
Flanker, 1-1-0-0.
34 G+.

BLAIR, Malcolm Rignold *Australia*
Sydney GS, W Suburbs, NSW, Waratahs.
b 04; d 63.
Prop, 2-1-0-1.
31 M+ NZ−.
Accountant/co dir.

49

BLAIR, Patrick Charles Bentley   *Scotland*
Fettes Coll, Cambridge Univ.
b 18.7.1891 Wanlockhead; kia 6.7.15 Ypres.
Hooker/prop, 5-2-0-3.
12 SA−; 13 F+ W− I+ E−.
Egyptian civil service. Blue 10-13. Served WW1,
2nd Lt in Rifle Bde.

BLAIR, Robert   *South Africa*
Helpmekaar Sch Johannesburg, Grey Coll
Bloemfontein, Stellenbosch Univ, SA Univs,
Wanderers, W Prov, Transvaal.
b 3.6.53 Johannesburg.
FH, 1-1-0-0 (21 − 3c 5p).
77 Wd+(3c 5p).
Rep.

BLAKE, Alan Walter ('Kiwi')   *New Zealand*
Wairarapa HS, Carterton, Wairarapa, N Island,
NZ Maoris, Wairarapa-Bush.
b 3.11.22 Carterton.
Flanker, 1-0-0-1.
49 A−.
Freezing co board walker. Served WW2,
trooper 20th Armoured Rgt. 24 apps for NZEF
XV 45-6. Wairarapa selector 67-8. Bro Rex NZ
trials 57-9. Son Ian played for Wairarapa-Bush
73-8.

BLAKE, Jere ('Jerry')   *Wales*
Cardiff.
b 1875 Cardiff; *d* 15.2.33.
Forward, 9-6-0-3.
1899 E+ S− I−; 1900 E+ S+ I+; 01 E+ S− I+.
Coal trimmer/police. Salford RL. Father of
Jerry Blake, who played for Cardiff 24-6.

BLAKE-KNOX, Stephen Ernest   *Ireland*
Fitzroy
Campbell Coll, Queen's Univ Belfast, Trin Coll
Dublin, NIFC.
b 9.7.48 Dublin.
Wing, 3-1-0-2.
76 E+ S−; 77 Fr−.
Schoolmaster.

BLAKEMORE, Reginald Edward   *Wales*
Newport Saracens, Newport.
b 1.9.24 Newport.
Prop, 1-0-0-1.
47 E−.
Docker/fish & chip shop proprietor. Served
WW2, S Wales Borderers. St Helens RL 47.

BLAKEWAY, Philip John   *England*
King's Sch Sherborne, Cheltenham, Gloucester.
b 31.12.50 Cheltenham.
Prop, 19-11-1-7.
80 I+ F+ W+ S+; 81 W− S+ I+ F−; 82 I− F+
W+; 84 I+ F− W− SA−; 85 R+ F= S+ I−; BI
> 80 SA.

Dir fruit & veg co. E Under 23 v J 73. Broke
neck Gloucester v S Wales Police 78. Broke rib
v F 80; inj curtailed app BI > 80 SA to 1 match.
Announced retirement from game 81 & 82 but
changed his decision each time to regain E
place. E > 82 US, Can. 3rd in Brit Under 21
Mod Pentathlon Champs, 68; res for World Jnr
Champs 68. Sister Gill GB v US Show Pony
team 59. Mother Joyce co lawn tennis player &
qualified for Jnr Wimbledon 39.

BLAKISTON, Sir Arthur   *England*
Frederick Bt MC
Bedford Sch, Trent Coll, Cambridge Univ,
Northampton, Liverpool, Blackheath,
Barbarians, E Midlands, Lancs, Surrey.
b 16.6.1892; *d* −.2.74.
Lock/flanker, 17-13-1-3 (6 − 2t).
20 S+; 21 W+ I+(1t) S+ F+(1t); 22 W−; 23 S+
F+; 24 W+ I+ F+ S+; 25 NZ− W+ I= S− F+;
BI > 24 SA 4-0-1-3.
Farmer. Served WW1, Trooper in King
Edward's Horse, Capt RFA. Wounded.
Inherited father's baronetcy 41.

BLANCO, Serge   *France*
Biarritz Ol.
b 31.1.58 Caracas, Venezuela.
FB/wing, 39-21-2-16 (106 − 14t 4c 14p).
80 SA− R−; 81 S+(1t) W+ E+ A−(1p) A−
R+(1t) NZ− NZ−(1p); 82 W−(1t) E− S−
I+(1t 2p) R− Arg+(1t 1p) Arg+(1t); 83
E+(2c) S+(1c 3p) I−(1t 1c 2p) W+(3p); 84 I+
W+ E+ S− NZ−(1t) NZ− R+; 85 E= S+(2t)
I= W+ Arg−(1t) Arg+(1t) J+; 86 S− I+(1p)
W+(1t) E+(1t).
Office worker. France B v W 78-9; v Spain 78; F
v Tunisia 78, v Yugoslavia, It, Can 79; v Soviet
Union 80. Champ rec 36 pts 83. F > 80 SA; 85
Arg. 1t v E 86 equ Andy Irvine's world rec of 10
for a FB. Rest of World v BI, Cardiff 86, Five
Nations v Overseas XV, Twickenham 86.

BLAND, Alexander Frederick   *Wales*
Cardiff.
b 24.11.1866 Haverfordwest; *d* 18.10.47 Barry.
Forward, 9-4-2-3.
1887 E= S− I+; 1888 S+ I− NZN+; 1890 S−
E+ I=.
Solicitor.

BLAND, Geoffrey Victor   *Australia*
Manly, NSW, Waratahs.
b 05; *d* 61.
Lock, 7-3-0-4.
32 NZ+ NZ− NZ−; 33 SA− SA+ SA− SA+.
Insurance broker.

BLATHERWICK, Thomas   *England*
Epsom Coll, Manchester, Lancs.
b 25.12.1855; *d* 29.1.40.

Forward, 1-1-0-0.
1878 I+.

BLAYNEY, John Joseph　　　　　*Ireland*
Glenstal Abbey Sch, UC Dublin, Wanderers.
b 13.3.25 Dublin.
Centre, 1-1-0-0 (3 − 1t).
50 S+(1t).
Barrister.

BLOMLEY, John　　　　　*Australia*
St Joseph's Coll Sydney, Sydney Univ, NSW.
b 27; *d* 73.
Centre, 7-3-1-3 (3 − 1t).
49 M− M= M+(1t) NZ+ NZ+; 50 BI− BI−.
Medicine. Served with AAMC in Vietnam.

BLOND, Jean　　　　　*France*
SF.
No 8/flanker, 6-5-0-1 (6 − 2t).
35 G+; 36 G+; 37 G+(1t); 38 G− R+(1t) G+.

BLYTH, Leonard　　　　　*Wales*
Dynevor Sch, Gorseinon, Swansea.
b 20.11.20 Swansea.
Flanker, 3-2-0-1.
51 SA−; 52 E+ S+.
Co dir. Father of Roger. Served WW2, RN.

BLYTH, William Roger　　　　　*Wales*
Swansea GS, Swansea, Barbarians.
b 2.4.50 Swansea.
FB/centre, 6-2-0-4 (6 − 1t 1c).
74 E−; 75 S−r; 80 F+ E− S+(1c) I−(1t).
Sales rep. Son of Leonard. Wales B v F 73.
Welsh XVr v NZ 74. W > 75 Far East.

BODY, James Alfred　　　　　*England*
Tonbridge Sch, Gipsies.
b 1846; *d* 9.9.29 Manitoba, Can.
Forward, 2-1-1-0.
1872 S+; 1873 S=.
Brewer/proprietor flax-crushing co. Fdr mem
Gipsies. Emigrated to Can.

BOFFELLI, Victor　　　　　*France*
Aurillac.
b 30.3.47 Arques, Aude.
Flanker, 18-8-2-8 (8 − 2t).
71 A+(1t) R+; 72 S− I−; 73 J+ R+; 74 I+(1t)
W= E= S− Arg+ Arg+ R− SA− SA−; 75
W− S+ I−.
Bank employee.

BOGGS, Eric George　　　　　*New Zealand*
Otahuhu Tech HS, Training College, Auckland,
Army, Ponsonby, Wellington, N Island, Comb
Servs, Barbarians (E).
b 28.3.22 Whangarei.
Wing, 2-1-0-1.
46 A+; 49 SA−.

HM. 15t 22 apps for Comb Servs. NZ > 49 SA.
Auckland sel-coach 53, 73-7.

BOLAND, Simon Bernard DSO　　　　　*Australia*
Past GS Brisbane, Qld.
b 12.7.1875; *d* 54.
Forward, 3-0-0-3.
1899 BT− BT−; 03 NZ−.
Clerk. Served in Boer War. One of fdrs of Qld
RL 07.

BOLTON, Charles Arthur CBE　　　　　*England*
Marlborough Coll, Oxford Univ, US
Portsmouth, Barbarians, Surrey.
b 3.1.1882; *d* 23.11.63 Eastbourne.
Flanker, 1-1-0-0.
09 F+.
The Army. Served WW1, Lt Col in Manchester
Rgt. Mentioned in despatches 3 times. CBE 19.
Joined R Tank Corps 23. Brig 31. Served WW2,
BEF to F 39. ME Forces 40. Mentioned in
despatches twice. Order of the Nile & Order of
the Redeemer (Greece) 3rd class.

BOLTON, Reginald MBE　　　　　*England*
QEGS Wakefield, Wakefield, Univ Coll Hosp,
Harlequins, Barbarians, Yorks.
b 20.11.09.
Flanker, 5-3-0-2 (6 − 2t).
33 W−; 36 S+(1t); 37 S+; 38 W− I+(1t).
Medicine. Rep London Univ at swimming.
Served WW2 RAMC. MBE 44.

BOLTON, Wilfrid Nash ('Baby')　　　　　*England*
OBE
RMC Sandhurst, RNA Gosport, Blackheath,
Kent.
b 14.9.1862 Ireland; *d* 12.8.30 Contrexeville
Vosges, F.
Back, 11-7-1-3 (6t 2c).
1882 I=(1t) S− W+(1t) S+(1t); 1883 I+(1t) S+(1t);
1884 W+(1c) I+(1t) S+(1c); 1885 I+(1t) S+(1t); 1887
I− S−.
The Army. Army ath champ, high-class
gymnast. Served Boer War. Wounded 3 times;
mentioned in despatches twice. Queen's Medal
(3 clasps), King's Medal (2 clasps). Stayed on in
SA after War; became Resident Magistrate,
Transvaal. Later Provost Marshal & Food
Controller of Cyprus.

BOLTON, William Henry　　　　　*Scotland*
Rugby Sch, Oxford Univ, W of S.
b 15.3.1851 Stirling; *d* 5.12.1896.
Forward, 1-0-0-1.
1876 E−.
Barrister. Blue 1873-5.

BONAL, Jean-Marie　　　　　*France*
Toulouse, SF.
b 12.12.45 St-Cirque-de-Jordanne, Cantal.

51

Wing, 14-5-0-9 (15 − 5t).
68 E+ W+ Cz+ NZ− NZ− SA−(1t) SA− R−
(1t); 69 S− I− E−(1t) R+; 70 W−(1t) E+(1t).
PE instructor. RL.

BONAMY, Raoul *France*
SB.
Flanker, 2-0-0-2 (3 − 1t).
28 NSW−(1t) I−.
Switched to RL.

BONAVENTURA, Maurice *England*
Sydney
Cranleigh Sch, HAC, Lensbury, Blackheath,
Barbarians, Surrey.
b 28.4.02.
Prop, 1-0-1-0.
31 W=.
Insurance/petroleum co employee. Also played
rugby for Singapore Ckt & Sports Club; capt R
Bangkok Sports Club 26-7.

BOND, Anthony Matthew *England*
Wellacre Co SS, Sale.
b 3.8.54 Urmston, Manchester.
Centre, 6-1-1-4.
78 NZ−; 79 S= I− NZ−; 80 I+; 82 I−.
Advertising rep. Broke leg E v I 80.

BOND, A.T.W. *Ireland*
Derry Acad Inst, Derry.
b 17.8.1871; d −.
Forward, 2-2-0-0.
1894 S+ W+.

BOND, John Garth Parker *New Zealand*
Hornby Sch, Albion, Canterbury, S Island.
b 24.5.20 Carterton.
Prop, 1-0-0-1.
49 A−.
Freezing co worker. Father Norman rep
Wairarapa 09-11. Served WW2, Pte 26th Battn;
19 apps for Comb Servs 45-6. Racehorse owner
& breeder.

BONHAM-CARTER, Sir Edgar *England*
KCMG CIE
Clifton Coll, Oxford Univ, Blackheath,
Barbarians.
b 2.4.1870; d 24.4.56 Alton, Hants.
Forward, 1-0-0-1.
1891 S−.
The Law/Sudan Civil Service. Blue 1890-1. Won
cap when Ernest Bromet withdrew through inj.
Called to Bar 1895. Various overseas postings.
CIE 19. KCMG 20. Order of the Nile (1st class).

BONIFACE, André *France*
Mont-de-Marsan.
b 14.8.34 Monfort-en-Chalosse, Landes.
Wing/centre, 48-25-5-18 (44 − 11t 1c 2d 1p).

54 I+ NZ+ W− E+(1t) It+(1t) Arg+
Arg+(2t); 55 S+(1t) I+; 56 S− I+(1t) W− It+
Cz+(1t); 57 S− I− W− R+(2t); 58 S− E−; 59
E=; 61 NZ− NZ− A+ R=; 62 E+ W− I+
It+(1p) R−; 63 S−(1d) I+(1d) E− W+ It+
R=; 64 S− NZ− E− W= It+(1t); 65 W+ It+
R+(1c); 66 S= I+ E+(1t) W−.
Sports shopowner. Played with bro Guy in 18
ints. F's longest int career, 13 seasons.

BONIFACE, Guy ('La Souris') *France*
Mont-de-Marsan.
b 6.3.37 Monfort-en-Chalosse, Landes; d
31.12.67.
Centre, 35-19-6-10 (42 − 14t).
60 W+ I+ It+ R− Arg+(1t) Arg+(2t)
Arg+(1t); 61 S+(1t) SA= E= W+(1t) It+ I+
NZ− NZ− NZ− R=; 62 R−; 63 S− I+(1t) E−
(1t) W+(1t) It+ R=; 64 S−; 65 S+ I= E−
W+(2t) It+(1t) R+(2t); 66 S= I+ E+ W−.
Café proprietor. Played with bro André in 18
ints.

BONIS, Edward Tasman *Australia*
S Brisbane HS, YMCA Brisbane, Qld.
b 07; d 22.9.84.
Hooker, 21-10-1-10 (3 − 1t).
29 NZ+ NZ+ NZ+; 30 BI+; 31 M+(1t) NZ−;
32 NZ+ NZ− NZ−; 33 SA− SA+ SA− SA−
SA+; 34 NZ+ NZ= ; 36 NZ− NZ− M+; 37
SA−; 38 NZ−.
Packing co mgr.

BONNES, Etienne *France*
Narbonne.
FB, 3-1-0-2.
24 W− R+ US−.

BONNEVAL, Eric *France*
Toulouse.
b 19.11.63 Toulouse.
Centre, 6-4-0-2 (12 − 3t).
84 NZ−r(1t); 85 W+ Arg−(1t) J+(1t); 86 W+
E+.
F > 85 Arg.

BONNUS, Firmin ('Min') *France*
Toulon.
b 25.8.24 Toulon; d 26.4.70 Toulon.
Lock, 4-1-1-2.
50 S− I= E+ W−.
Café proprietor.

BONNUS, Michel *France*
Toulon.
FB, 5-3-0-2 (4 − 1d).
37 It+(1d); 38 G− R+ G+; 40 BF−.

BONSOR, Frederick DCM *England*
Bradford.
b 1861; d −.2.32.

52

Half-back, 6-3-3-0.
1886 W+ I+ S=; 1887 W= S=; 1889 NZN+.
Farmer. Capped in 1888 E side that did not play.
1st Yorks player to capt E, v NZN 1889. Chose
to play for Bradford in a Yorks Cup-tie rather
than E v S 1890 & never played for E again. His
club, Bradford, helped form NU 1895. DCM in
Boer War.

BONTEMPS, Dominique   *France*
La Rochelle.
b 27.5.46 Rochefort.
Flanker, 1-0-0-1.
68 SA−.
Insurance agent.

BOOBBYER, Brian   *England*
Uppingham Sch, Oxford Univ, Rosslyn Pk,
Barbarians, Mdx, RA.
b 25.2.28 Ealing.
Centre, 9-4-0-5 (6 − 2t).
50 W− I+ F− S−; 51 W− F−(1t) 52 S+ I+(1t)
F+.
MRA. Blue 49-51. Son of doctor. Gave up all
sport 52 to dedicate life to Moral Rearmament,
initially in Asia & US, then at Oxford 62. 4 ckt
blues − 40 apps OUCC 49-52. Grandfather
E.V. Shaw (later Archdeacon of Oxford &
Bishop of Buckingham) sc 78 no Oxford Univ v
A 82. Father also top ckter. 2 of his mother's
sisters rep England at lacrosse. Wife (née Rodd)
related to Tremayne Rodd.

BOON, Ronald Winston   *Wales*
Barry CS, Trin Coll Carmarthen, Dunfermline
Coll of PE, Cardiff, TA, Barbarians, London
Welsh.
b 6.6.09 Barry.
Wing, 12-7-1-4 (20 − 4t 2d).
30 S− F+; 31 E= S+(1t) F+ I+ SA−; 32 E+(1t
1d) S+(1t) I−; 33 E+(1t 1d) I−.
Schoolmaster. Descended from a family of
blacksmiths from Coombe Martin, Devon.
Boon's t & d enabled W to record 1st win at
Twickenham 33. Cardiff v NZ 35. Glamorgan
CCC. Wales AAA sprint champ.

BOOTH, Ernest Edward   *New Zealand*
('General')
Clyde Quay Sch Wellington, Athletic, Otago,
Kaikorai, Southland, NSW, Newtown.
b 24.2.1876 Teschemakers; *d* 18.10.35
Christchurch.
FB, 3-2-1-0.
06 F+; 07 A+ A=.
Journalist. NZ > 05 A, 05-6 BI,F & NAm, 07
A. Moved to A. Served WW1 with Australian
forces. Returned to NZ. Related to D. Jowett
(E).

BOOTH, Joseph   *Wales*
Pontymister, West Hartlepool, Durham Co.
b c1872-4; *d* 28.4.58 Durham.
Forward, 1-1-0-0.
1898 I+.

BOOTH, Lewis Alfred   *England*
Giggleswick Sch, Headingley, Bohemians,
RAF, Barbarians, Yorks.
b 26.9.09 Horsforth, Leeds; kia 25.6.42.
Wing, 7-3-1-3 (9 − 3t).
33 W− I+(1t) S−; 34 S+(1t); 35 W= I+ S−
(1t).
Woollen manufacturer. 56 apps for Yorks.
Served WW2 Pt Off RAF.

BOOTS, John George   *Wales*
Newport.
b 2.7.1874 Aberbeeg; *d* 30.12.28 Newport.
Forward, 16-11-1-4 (3 − 1t).
1898 I+ E−; 1899 I−; 00 E+ S+ I+; 01 E+ S−
(1t) I+; 02 E+ S+ I+; 03 E+ S− I+; 04 E=.
Insurance. 365 apps for Newport, capt 03-4.

BORCHARD, Georges   *France*
RCF.
Forward, 5-0-0-5.
08 E−; 09 E− W− I−; 11 I−.

BORDE, François   *France*
RCF, Toulouse.
b 8.12.1899 Lourdes.
Centre, 12-4-1-7 (3 − 1t).
20 I+ US+(1t); 21 S+ W− E−; 22 S= W−; 23
S− I+; 24 E−; 25 I−; 26 E−.

BORDENAVE, Leon   *France*
Toulon.
b 11.5.20 Udos.
FH, 5-3-0-2.
48 A+ S− W+ E+; 49 S−.

BORNEMANN, Walter William   *Ireland*
Dublin HS,, Wanderers.
b 19.1.36 Dublin.
Wing, 4-0-0-4.
60 E− S− W− SA−.
Administrative supervisor.

BORTHWICK, John Bishop   *Scotland*
Stewart's Coll, Stewart's Coll FP, Edinburgh
Univ.
Prop, 2-2-0-0.
38 W+ I+.
Medicine.

BOS, Frans Herman ten   *Scotland*
Fettes Coll, Oxford Univ, London Scottish,
Barbarians.
b 21.4.37 Richmond, Surrey.
Lock, 17-6-2-9 (3 − 1t).

59 E=; 60 F− W− SA−; 61 F− SA− W+ I+
E−; 62 F− W+(1t) I+ E=; 63 F+ W− I+ E−.
Management consultant. Blue 58-60.

BOSCH, Gerald Raymond *South Africa*
General Smuts HS Vercenagers, Transvaal.
b 12.4.49 Vereeniging.
FH, 9-7-0-2 (89 − 7c 2d 23p).
74 BI−(1d 2p) F+ F+(2c 6p); 75 F+ F+; 76
NZ+(1c 1p) NZ−(3p) NZ+(1c 2p) NZ+(1c 1d
2p).
Medical rep. 132 career pts for SA. 22 pts (inc
equ world rec 6p) v F 75, most by SA in Test.
33pts SA v NZ 76. Currie Cup rec 36 pts,
Transvaal v Far North 7.7.73.

BOSLER, John Morgan *Australia*
Sydney Boys' HS, E Suburbs, NSW.
b 4.2.33 Sydney.
Half-back, 1-0-0-1.
53 SA−.
Gas co mgr. Son in law of Bob Stuart. A > 53
SA. RL.

BOSMAN, N.J.S. *South Africa*
Pretoria Boys HS, Transvaal.
3-2-1-0.
24 BI+ BI= BI+.

BOSWELL, John Douglas *Scotland*
Rugby Sch, Loretto Sch, Oxford Univ, W of S.
b 16.2.1867; *d* 5.1.48.
Forward, 15-11-1-3 (5t 4c 2d).
1889 W+ I+; 1890 W+(1t) I+(1d) E−; 1891
W+(1t) I+(3c) E+; 1892 W+(1t 1c) I+ E−;
1893 I= E+(1d); 1894 I− E+(2t).
Writer to the Signet. Blue 1885-7. Pres SRU
1898-9. Served WW1, Lt Col in R Scots
Fusiliers. Order of the White Eagle (4th class)
(with swords). TD.

BOTHA, Daniel Sarel ('Darius') *South Africa*
Hendrik Verwoerd Sch Pretoria, Pretoria Univ,
Pretoria Police, Jnr Springboks, SA Univs, N
Transvaal.
b 26.6.55 Breyten.
Wing, 1-0-0-1.
81 NZ−.
Police chaplain. Bro of Naas. SA > 81 US.

BOTHA, Hendrik Egnatius *South Africa*
('Naas')
Hendrik Verwoerd Sch Pretoria, Pretoria Univ,
SA Under 19s, Quaggas, Barbarians, N
Transvaal.
b 27.2.58 Breyten.
FH, 17-14-0-3 (173 − 34c 12d 23p).
80 SAm+(3c 1d 1p) SAm+(1c 3d 1p) BI+(3c)
BI+(2c 2p) BI+(1c 1d 1p) BI−(1p) SAm+(2c
1d 1p) SAm+(3c) F+(4c 3p); 81 I+(1c 3p)
I+(3d 1p) NZ−(1c 1d) NZ+(1c 1d 5p) NZ+(2c

2p) US+(3c); 82 SAm+(6c 1d) SAm−(1c 2p).
Police/dir coaching Pretoria Univ. Bro of
Darius. Most pts for SA in all Tests (see P.J.
Visagie). Most pts (35, 3 apps) for SA in series
on tour, v NZ 81, inc 2nd Test 20 pts, most by
any player in Test v NZ. Most pts (31) by SA in
any tour match, v Nelson Bays, NZ 81. Currie
Cup pts rec holder (175) 80. Capt N Transvaal
80-1. SA Player of Year 79. SA Univs, prov
baseball player; prov softball. Reinstated by
SARB after speculative trip to US 83 to consider
becoming kicker in American Football.
Overseas XV v Five Nations, Twickenham 86.

BOTHA, J. *South Africa*
Bishops Diocesan Coll Rondebosch, Transvaal.
1-1-0-0.
03 BT+.
Cousin of D.J. Brink.

BOTHA, Johannes Petrus *South Africa*
Frederick
Wonderboom HS, Stellenbosch Univ, N
Transvaal.
b 11.5.37.
Flanker, 3-3-0-0.
62 BI+ BI+ BI+.
Army. SA > 60-1 BI.

BOTHA, Pieter Hendrik *South Africa*
Transvaal.
b 13.9.35 Florida.
Lock, 2-0-0-2.
65 A− A−.
Constructor.

BOTTING, Ian James *England*
John McGlashan Coll, Christ's Coll NZ,
Ashburton Co, Otago Univ, Otago, NZ Univs,
Oxford Univ, RAF, NLD, Blackheath,
Leicester, Barbarians, New Zealand.
b 18.5.22 Dunedin, NZ; *d* 9.7.80 Christchurch,
NZ.
Wing, 2-1-0-1.
50 W− I+.
Schoolmaster/chaplain. Served WW2 as Lt in
NZ Army & Fg Off RNZAF. On return to NZ,
won blues for ath, ckt & rugby at Otago Univ
48. 9 apps (no ints) NZ > 49 SA. In UK won
blues 49-50; an undergraduate when sel by E.
After graduating, returned to NZ where he took
holy orders (C of E). Chaplain at Christ's Coll,
St Margaret's Coll; precentor Christchurch
Cathed. Died from inj in road accident.

BOUBÉE, Jean *France*
Tarbes.
b 11.10.1900 Biarritz; *d* −.3.73 Paris.
Flanker, 9-3-1-5 (3 − 1t).
21 S+ E− I+(1t); 22 E= W−; 23 E− I+; 25
NZ− S−.

BOUCHER, Arthur William   *Wales*
Clytha Sch, Newport, Barbarians.
b 29.6.1870 Somerset; d 26.4.48 Dinas Powys.
Forward, 13-5-0-8 (3 − 1t).
1892 E− S− I−; 1893 E+ S+ I+; 1894 E−;
1895 E− S− I+; 1896 E− I−; 1897 E+(1t).
Shipping exec.

BOUDREAU, R.   *France*
SCUF.
b − ; kia WW1.
Forward, 2-0-0-2.
10 W− S−.

BOUFFLER, Robert George   *Australia*
Waratahs (Orange), Central W, NSW.
b 1874; d 56.
Forward, 1-0-0-1.
1899 BT−.
Compositor.

BOUGHTON, Harold J.   *England*
Gloucester, Glos.
b 7.9.10 Gloucester.
FB, 3-1-1-1 (14 − 1t 3p).
35 W=(1t) I+(1c 3p) S−.
Omnibus driver.

BOUGUYON, Gérard ('La   *France*
Bouguye')
Grenoble.
b 24.11.35 Quimbech.
Lock/prop, 9-4-2-3 (3 − 1t).
61 SA= E= W+ It+ I+ NZ− NZ− NZ−
A+(1t).
Professor of physics.

BOUJET, Christian   *France*
Grenoble.
b 29.8.42.
FH/FB, 3-0-0-3 (5 − 1t 1c).
68 NZ− A−r(1t 1c) SA−.
Science professor.

BOUQUET, Jacques   *France*
Bourgoin, Vienne.
b 3.7.33 Tullins, Isère.
Centre/FH, 34-21-4-9 (21 − 3t 3c 2d).
54 S+; 55 E+; 56 S+ I+(1d) W−(1t) It+ E+
Cz+; 57 S− E− W−(2c) R+; 58 S− E−; 59 S+
It+(1t) W+ I−; 60 S+ E= W+ I+(1c) R−; 61
S+ SA= E= W+ It+(1t) I+(1d) R=; 62 S+
E+ W− I+.
Merchant.

BOURDEU, Jean-Roger   *France*
Lourdes.
b 6.1.27 Pau.
Flanker/wing, 9-3-0-6 (3 − 1t).
52 S+ I− SA− W− E− It+; 53 S+(1t) I− E−.

BOURGAREL, Roger   *France*
Toulouse.
b 21.4.47 Toulouse.
Wing, 9-6-1-2 (3 − 1t).
69 R+; 70 S+ I+ E+(1t) R+; 71 W− SA−
SA=; 73 S+.
Bank employee. F > 71 SA; 1st black player to
tour SA.

BOURKE, Thomas Kevin   *Australia*
Downlands Coll Toowoomba, Brothers
(Brisbane), Qld.
b 22.
Centre, 1-0-0-1.
47 NZ−.
Radio station technician. A > 47-8 BI, F. Inj on
only int app.

BOUSQUET, Adolphe   *France*
Béziers.
b 14.11.1899 Imarausson, Herault.
FH, 3-2-0-1.
21 E− I+; 24 R+.

BOUSQUET, René   *France*
Albi.
b 02 Albi.
Lock, 9-2-0-7 (3 − 1t).
26 M−; 27 I− S− W− E+ G+(1t); 29 W− E−;
30 W−.

BOWCOTT, Henry Morgan   *Wales*
('Harry')
Cardiff HS, Welsh SS, Cambridge Univ,
Cardiff, London Welsh, Barbarians.
b 30.4.1907 Cardiff.
Centre/FH, 8-4-2-2 (3 − 1t).
29 S+ F+ I=; 30 E−; 31 E= S+; 33 E+ I−(1t);
BI > 30 NZ 4-1-0-3, A 1-1-0-0.
Civil service. Blue 27-8. Cambridge Univ > 34
US. Cardiff v NZ 35. WRU sel 63-74, pres 74-5.
Asst mgr W > 68 Arg. Bros Jackie & Bill also
played for Cardiff.

BOWDEN, Noel James Gordon   *New Zealand*
Auckland GS, Tg Coll, Auckland, Ponsonby,
Waikato, Cambridge Utd, Taranaki, New
Plymouth HSOB, N Island.
b 19.3.26 Whangarei.
FB, 1-1-0-0 (3 − 1p).
52 A+(1p).
Navy/schoolmaster/PE lecturer. Teachers club
coach 68-72. Outstanding long-jumper (rec 22ft
6in at sch) & lawn tennis player (Taranaki &
Wanganui).

BOWDLER, Frederick Arthur   *Wales*
('Lonza')
Abercarn, Cross Keys.
Prop/lock/hooker, 15-5-1-9.
27 NSW−; 28 E− S+ I− F−; 29 E− S+ F+ I=;

30 E−; 31 SA−; 32 E+ S+ I−; 33 I−.
Miner.

BOWEN, Bleddyn *Wales*
Cwmtawe Comp, Welsh SS, Welsh Youth,
Swansea, S Wales Police, Glamorgan,
Barbarians.
b 16.7.61 Swansea.
Centre, 10-5-0-5 (10 − 1t 2p).
83 R−; 84 S− I+(2p) F− E+; 85 Fj+; 86 E−
(1t) S+ I+ F−.
Police. Welsh Youth > 80 SA. Wales B > 80
US, Can; 83 Spain. Wales XV v J 83.

BOWEN, Clifford Alfred *Wales*
Llanelli, Plymouth Albion.
b 1874 Llanelli; *d* 29 Rickmansworth.
Wing, 4-2-0-2 (3 − 1t).
1896 E− S+(1t) I−; 1897 E+.
Dock official, Devonport.

BOWEN, Daniel St James *Ireland*
('Jimmy')
PBC Cork, Cork Constitution.
b 11.2.57 Cork.
Wing, 3-0-0-3.
77 W− E− S−.
Finance co.

BOWEN, David Harry *Wales*
Bangor Normal Coll, Llanelli.
b 1864 Llanelli; *d* 17.8.13 Bynea.
Back, 4-0-1-3.
1882 E−; 1886 E− S−; 1887 E=.
HM. 1st match for Llanelli at 15. Ref E v S 1905.
WRU sel. IB rep 1908. Rugby corr 'Evening
Express' Cardiff.

BOWEN, George E. *Wales*
Swansea.
Half-back/back, 4-2-0-2.
1887 S− I+; 1888 S+ I−.
Mines official.

BOWEN, William Arnold *Wales*
Swansea.
b 1862; *d* 25.8.26 Swansea.
Forward, 13-3-2-8.
1886 E− S−. 1887 E= S− I+; 1888 NZN+;
1889 S− I−; 1890 S− E+ I=; 1891 E− S−.
Docker/builder.

BOWEN, William E. *Wales*
Swansea.
b 1899.
FH, 6-4-1-1 (6 − 2t).
21 S− F+; 22 E+(1t) S=(1t) I+ F+.
Railway checker/groundsman. Leeds RL 22.

BOWERS, Richard Guy *New Zealand*
Nelson Coll, Golden Bay-Motueka, Athletic,

Wellington, S Island.
b 5.11.32 Rawhiti.
1st five-eighth, 2-1-0-1.
54 I+ F−.
Tobacco grower. NZ > 53-4 BI,F & NAm.
Father R. Bowers rep Wellington.

BOWIE, Thomas Chalmers *Scotland*
George Watson's Coll, Watsonians, RAMC.
b 28.4.1889 Edinburgh; *d* 28.11.72.
FH, 4-2-0-2 (7 − 1t 1d).
13 I+(1t) E−; 14 I+ E−(1d).
Medicine.

BOWMAN, Albert William *New Zealand*
New Lynn Sch, Napier Tech Coll, Hawkes Bay,
Nelson, Nelson Coll OB, N Island.
b 5.5.15 Auckland.
Flanker, 3-3-0-0 (6 − 2t).
38 A+ A+(1t) A+(1t).
Plasterer/linesman/oil co branch mgr. NZ > 38
A.

BOYAU, Maurice *France*
SBUC.
b 1889 Dax; kia 16.9.18.
Forward, 6-0-0-6 (4− 2c).
12 I− S− W−(1c) E−(1c); 13 W− I−.
Légion d'Honneur.

BOYCE, Edward Stewart *Australia*
The Scots Coll, Sydney GS, Sydney Univ, NSW,
Oxford Univ.
b 14.12.41.
Wing, 13-5-0-8 (3 − 1t).
62 NZ− NZ−; 64 NZ− NZ− NZ+; 65 SA+
SA+; 66 W+ S−; 67 E+ I−(1t) F− I−.
Medicine. Played with twin bro J.S. in 5 ints. 16t
A > 66-7 BI, F, Can. Post-grad student at
Oxford Univ. Obstetrician & gynaecologist.

BOYCE, James Stewart *Australia*
The Scots Coll, Sydney Univ, E Suburbs, NSW.
b 14.12.41.
Wing, 12-6-1-5 (12 − 4t).
62 NZ= NZ− NZ−; 63 E+ SA− SA+(1t) SA+
SA−; 64 NZ− NZ+(2t); 65 SA+(1t) SA+.
Economist/brewery exec. Played with twin bro
Edward in 5 ints. A > 62 NZ − 6t v Wairarapa,
tour match rec for A; > 63 SA.

BOYD, Alister Forrest *Australia*
McClelland
Southport GS, Qld.
b 35.
Wing, 1-1-0-0.
58 M+.

BOYD, Archibald *Australia*
Pirates, NSW.
b 1872; *d* 6.5.05.

Half-back, 1-0-0-1.
1899 BT−.
Compositor.

BOYD, Cecil Anderson MC   *Ireland*
St Stephens Green Sch, Trin Coll Dublin,
Wanderers, Barbarians.
b 1875; *d* 27.2.42.
FB, 3-0-1-2.
1900 S=; 01 S− W−; BT > 1896 SA.
Medicine. Served WW1.

BOYD, G.M.   *Scotland*
Glasgow HS, Glasgow HSFP.
b 8.3.05.
Wing, 1-1-0-0.
26 E+.

BOYD, J.L.   *Scotland*
US Portsmouth, RN.
FH, 2-1-0-1.
12 E+ SA−.
RN.

BOYER, Paul   *France*
Toulon.
SH, 1-1-0-0.
35 G+.

BOYES, H.C.   *South Africa*
Griq W.
b − ; *d* 1892.
2-0-0-2.
1891 BT− BT−.

BOYLE, Alasdair Hugh Wilson   *Scotland*
Merchiston Castle Sch, London Univ, St
Thomas's Hosp, London Scottish.
b 30.9.45 Glasgow.
No 8, 6-2-0-4 (3 − 1t).
66 A+(1t); 67 F+ NZ−; 68 F− W− I−.
Medicine. Bro of Cameron.

BOYLE, Allan Cameron Wilson   *Scotland*
Merchiston Castle Sch, Kelvinside Acad,
Cambridge Univ, London Scottish.
b 11.11.37 Glasgow.
Prop, 3-2-0-1.
63 F+ W− I+.
Stockbroker. Bro of Alasdair.

BOYLE, Cecil William   *England*
Clifton Coll, Oxford Univ.
b 16.3.1853 London; kia 5.4.1900 Boshof, SA.
Half-back, 1-0-1-0.
1873 S=.
Stockbroker. Served Boer War, Capt Queen's
Own Oxon Hussars, Imperial Yeomanry. Ckt
blue 1873. Mem of Stock Exchange.

BOYLE, Charles Vesey DFC   *Ireland*
Dublin HS, Trin Coll Dublin, Lansdowne,
Barbarians.
b 2.7.15 Dublin.
Wing, 9-4-0-5 (3 − 1t).
35 NZ−; 36 E+(1t) S+ W−; 37 E− S+ W+; 38
W−; 39 W−; BI > 38 SA 2-1-0-1.
Barrister/judge/HM. Served WW2.

BOYLE, Stephen Brent   *England*
Sir Thomas Rich's GS, Sir Thomas Rich's OB,
Gloucester, Moseley.
b 9.8.53 Warrington, Lancs.
Lock, 3-0-1-2.
83 W= S− I−; BI > 83 NZ.
Football for Herefordshire Schs. E Under 23s v
Can, J. England B > 78 R; v F B 79. Played in
Gloucester's John Player Cup final win 78.

BOYLEN, Francis ('Patsy')   *England*
Hartlepool Excelsior, Hartlepool R, Durham
Co.
b 1879; *d* 3.2.38 Hull.
Forward, 4-2-0-2.
08 F+ W− I+ S−.
Driller/plater, later at BOCM Hull. Hartlepool
XV v NZ 09. Hull RL 08; E RL cap & > A, NZ
10. Continued RL until 23.

BRABAZON, H.M.   *Ireland*
Tipperary GS, Trin Coll Dublin.
Forward, 2-0-0-2.
1884 E−; 1886 E−.

BRACE, David Onllwyn   *Wales*
Gowerton GS, UC Cardiff, Aberavon,
Swansea, Oxford Univ, RAF, Newport,
Llanelli, Barbarians.
b 16.11.32 Gowerton.
SH, 9-6-0-3 (3 − 1t).
56 E+ S+ I− F+; 57 E−; 60 S+ I+(1t) F−; 61
I+.
Head of Sport BBC Wales. Blue 55-6.

BRADBY, Matthew Seymour   *England*
MBE
Rugby Sch, RNEC Keyham, Cambridge Univ,
US Portsmouth, RN, Barbarians, Hants.
b 25.3.1899 Rugby.
Centre, 2-1-1-0.
22 I+ F=.
Tea grower/RN. Served WW2 Lt Cmdr. Capt
nautical sch Heswall & Training Ship Mercury,
Hamble River 50.

BRADDOCK, Kenneth James   *Wales*
Greenfield SMS, Newbridge.
b 42 Treowen, Newbridge.
Flanker, 3-0-0-3.
66 A−; 67 S− I−.
Miner/police.

BRADLEY, Michael James   *Ireland*
Dolphin.
 b 1898; *d* 14.7.51.
Prop/lock, 19-9-0-10.
20 W− F−; 22 E− S− W− F+; 23 E− S− W+
F−; 25 F+ S− W+; 26 F+ E+ S+ W−; 27 F+
W+; BI > 24 SA.
Dairy products co owner.

BRADLEY, Michael Timothy   *Ireland*
PBC Cork, Cork Constitution, Munster.
 b 17.11.62 Cork.
SH, 9-3-1-5.
84 A−; 85 S+ F= W+ E+; 86 F− W− E− S−.
Ireland B v S 83.

BRADLEY, Robert   *England*
W Hartlepool, Durham Co.
Forward, 1-0-0-1.
03 W−.

BRADSHAW, George   *Ireland*
Methodist Coll Belfast, Collegians.
Wing, 1-0-0-1.
03 W−.
Lacrosse for I.

BRADSHAW, Harry   *England*
Bramley, Yorks.
 b 17.4.1868 Bramley, Leeds; *d* 31.12.10
Halifax.
Forward, 7-3-0-4 (5 − 2t).
1892 S+; 1893 W− I+(1t) S−; 1894 W+(1t) I−
S−.
Horse teamster/cloth dresser/licensee. Leeds
RL 1895.

BRADSHAW, Keith   *Wales*
Ogmore GS, Tondu, Cefn Cribbwr, Bridgend,
Barbarians.
 b 7.4.39 Cefn Cribbwr.
Centre, 9-5-2-2 (36 − 1t 6c 7p).
64 E= S+(1t 1c 1p) I+(3c) F=(1c 2p) SA−(1p);
66 E+ S+(1c) I−(1p) F+(2p).
NCB draughtsman/schoolmaster. W > 64 SA.
Chmn sel Aberavon 85-6. Son Chris played for
Bridgend 85-6.

BRADSHAW, Robert McNevin   *Ireland*
Wanderers.
 b 1860; *d* −.12.07.
Forward, 2-0-0-2.
1885 E− S−.
Land agent.

BRADY, Aidan Malachy   *Ireland*
Blackrock Coll, UC Dublin, Malone.
 b 16.10.39 Dublin.
Hooker, 4-2-1-1.
66 S−; 68 E= S+ W+.
Medicine.

BRADY, Joseph Anthony   *Ireland*
CBC Monkstown, Wanderers.
 b 9.4.52 Dublin.
Centre, 2-1-0-1.
76 E+ S−.
Insurance.

BRADY, James R.   *Ireland*
Belfast HS, CIYMS, Barbarians.
 b 11.2.31 Belfast.
Lock, 12-6-2-4.
51 S+ W=; 53 F+ E= S+ W−; 54 W−; 56 W+;
57 F+ E− S+ W−.
Bank official.

BRAID, Gary John   *New Zealand*
Bay of Plenty.
 b 25.7.60 Tauranga.
Lock, 2-0-1-1.
83 S= E−.
NZ > 83 S & E, 84 A.

BRAIN, Stephen Edward   *England*
Harold Malley GS Solihull, England SS,
England Colts, Moseley, Coventry.
 b 11.11.54 Moseley.
Hooker, 13-4-1-8.
84 SA− A−r; 85 R+ F= S+ I− W− NZ−
NZ−; 86 W+ S− I+ F−.
Builder. E Under 23s. E > 84 SA. Five Nations
v Overseas XV, Twickenham 86.

BRAITHWAITE, John   *England*
Holbeck, Leicester, Midland Cos.
 b 21.4.1873 Leeds; *d* 15.11.15 Leicester.
Half-back, 1-0-0-1.
05 NZ−.
Engr.

BRAITHWAITE-EXLEY, Bryan   *England*
JP
Sedbergh Sch, RAF, Headingley, N
Ribblesdale.
 b 30.11.27 Wetherby.
No 8, 1-0-0-1.
49 W−.
Co dir family quarrying bus. 18 seasons with
Headingley 46-63. Also played for S Malaya.

BRAMWELL, Thomas   *Ireland*
Bangor GS, NIFC.
Hooker, 1-1-0-0.
28 F+.
Engr.

BRANCA, Gérard   *France*
SF.
 b 29.12.03 Sedan.
No 8, 3-0-0-3.
28 S−; 29 I− S−.

BRAND, Gerhardt Hamilton *South Africa*
Sea Point HS, Hamilton, W Prov.
b 8.10.06 Cape Town.
Wing/FB, 16-13-0-3 (55 − 13c 2d 7p).
28 NZ− NZ+; 31 W+ I+; 32 E+(1d) S+; 33
A+(1c 1p) A−(1p) A+(1c) A+(1p) A−(1d); 37
A+(1p) A+(4c) NZ+(2c 1p) NZ+(1c); 38
BI+(4c 2p).
Clerk/sports outfitter. 293 career pts for SA.
Most pts (190, 20 apps) for SA on tour, A, NZ
37. SA > 31-2 BI; his d v E at Twickenham 31
measured at 85y from point of kick to landing.
His p which clinched SA's 2nd Test win v NZ 37
was greeted with such delight by non-playing
members of tour team that one of them, Howard
Watt, sprained his ankle as he jumped up and
down in stands. Played for Hamilton club, in
honour of whom second Christian name was
suggested by his grandfather.

BRAND, Thomas Norman *Ireland*
Coleraine Acad Inst, NIFC.
b 5.1.1899; *d* −.6.38 Poole, Dorset.
Forward, 1-0-0-1.
24 NZ−; BIuncap > 24 SA 2-0-0-2.
Accidentally drowned.

BRANLAT, Albert *France*
RCF, SBUC.
Forward, 3-0-0-3 (2 − 1c).
06 NZ−(1c) E−; 08 W−.

BRASH, John C. *Scotland*
Fettes Coll, Cambridge Univ, Yorks.
Flanker, 1-0-0-1.
61 E−.
Blue 59-61.

BRASS, John Ellis *Australia*
Sydney Boys' HS, Randwick, NSW.
b 7.10.46 Sydney.
Centre, 12-3-0-9 (9 − 2t 1p).
66 BI− W+ S−(1t); 67 E+(1t) I− F− I− NZ−;
68 NZ− F+ I− S−(1p).
Insurance clerk/shopping centre exec. A > 66-7
BI, F; 68-9 I, S. E Suburbs RL; capt A RL.

BREAKEY, Richard William *Scotland*
Fettes Coll, Gosforth.
b 14.11.56 Consett.
FH, 1-0-0-1.
78 E−.
Accountant.

BRECKENRIDGE, John Wylie *Australia*
Glebe-Balmain, NSW, Waratahs.
b 22.4.03.
Flanker, 4-4-0-0.
29 NZ+ NZ+ NZ+; 30 BI+.
Auditor/co dir. NSW > 27-8 BI, F. Mgr A > 53
SA; 55 NZ. A sel; pres ARU 56.

BREDENKAMP, M. *South Africa*
Griq W.
2-0-0-2.
1896 BT− BT−.

BREJASSOU, René ('La Brejasse') *France*
Tarbes.
b 12.8.29 Aurehan.
Prop/lock, 15-8-0-7 (3 − 1t).
52 S+ I− SA− W− E−; 53 E− W−; 54 S+(1t)
I+ NZ+; 55 S+ I+ E+ W− It+.
Fuel merchant.

BREMNER, Selwyn George ('Mick') *New Zealand*
Tauranga Coll, Mt Albert GS, Auckland,
Grammar, Univ, Canterbury, NZ Univs.
b 2.8.30 Otorohanga.
2nd/1st five-eighth, 2-1-0-1.
52 A+; 56 SA−.
Wool exporter. NZ > 60 A & SA. Coach
Victoria Univ. Ckt for Auckland.

BRENNAN, James Irwin *Ireland*
Belfast HS, Trin Coll Dublin, CIYMS,
Barbarians.
b 22.8.34 Belfast.
Prop, 2-1-0-1.
57 S+ W−.
HM Armagh RS.

BRESNIHAN, Finbarr Patrick K. ('Barrie') *Ireland*
Gonzaga Sch, UC Dublin, Lansdowne, London
Irish, Barbarians.
b 13.3.44 Waterford.
Centre, 25-13-4-8 (15 − 5t).
66 E= W+(1t); 67 A+ E− S+ W+ F−; 68 F−
E= S+(1t) W+ A+(1t); 69 F+ E+(1t) S+(1t)
W−; 70 SA= F− E− S+ W+; 71 F= E− S+
W−; BIr > 66 A, NZ; 68 SA 3-0-1-2.
Medicine. Bro in law of Con Feighery.

BRETHES, Roger *France*
St Sever.
FB, 1-1-0-0 (2 − 1c).
60 Arg+(1c).

BRETT, Jasper Thomas *Ireland*
Monkstown Pk Sch Dublin, Armagh RS,
Monkstown.
b 8.8.1895 Kingstown; *d* 4.2.17.
Wing, 1-0-0-1.
14 W−.
Articled clerk. Died of illness contracted as 2nd
Lt on WW1 active service with R Dublin
Fusiliers.

BRETTARGH, A.T. *England*
Liverpool OB, Barbarians, Lancs.

Centre, 8-1-1-6 (3 − 1t).
1900 W−; 03 I− S−; 04 W=(1t) I+ S−; 05 I−
S−.

BREWER, J.   *England*
Gipsies.
Forward, 1-1-0-0.
1875 I+.

BREWER, Trevor John   *Wales*
Newport HS, Newport, Oxford Univ, London
Welsh.
b 16.8.30 Newport.
Wing, 3-2-0-1 (6 − 2t).
50 E+; 55 E+ S−(2t).
Production services mgr ICI. Blue 51. Welsh
AAA.

BREWIS, Johannes D. ('Hannes')   *South Africa*
N Transvaal.
b 15.6.20 Oudtshoorn.
FH, 10-10-0-0 (18 − 1t 5d).
49 NZ+ NZ+(1t, 1d) NZ+ NZ+(1d); 51
S+(1d) I+(1d) W+(1d); 52 E+ F+; 53 A+.
Pretoria police. SA > 51-2 BI, F.

BREWIS, Nathaniel Thomas   *Scotland*
Edinburgh Inst, Edinburgh Inst FP, Edinburgh
Univ.
b 16.4.1856 Eshott Hall, Northumberland; *d*
21.10.24 Edinburgh.
Forward, 6-2-2-2.
1876 E−; 1878 E=; 1879 I+ E=; 1880 I+ E−.
Medicine. Pres SRU 1885-6.

BREWSTER, Alexander Kinloch   *Scotland*
Melville Coll, Stewart's-Melville FP.
b 3.5.54 Dechmont.
Flanker/prop, 6-4-0-2.
77 E−; 80 I− F+; 86 E+ I+ R+.
Farmer. Converted from flanker to play prop v
E 86.

BRICE, Alfred ('Bobby')   *Wales*
Aberavon, Cardiff.
b 21.9.1872 Som; *d* −.
Forward, 18-12-1-5 (8 − 2t 1c).
1899 E+ S− I−; 1900 E+ S+ I+; 01 E+ S− I+;
02 E+ S+ I+(1c); 03 E+ S− I+(1t); 04 E=
S+(1t) I−.
Police. Susp 8 months for swearing at Crawford
Findlay, ref I v W 04.

BRIDIE, R.H.   *Wales*
St Madras Coll, Newport.
Half-back, 1-1-0-0 (1t).
1882 I+(1t).
Works mgr.

BRIDLE, Owen Lawman   *Australia*
Footscray, Victoria.

b 10 Exmouth, E; *d* −.5.83 Melbourne.
Flanker/no 8, 12-5-1-6 (15 − 5t).
31 M+; 32 NZ+(1t) NZ− NZ−(1t); 33 SA−
SA− SA+(1t); 34 NZ+(1t) NZ=; 36 NZ−
NZ−(1t) M+.
Rep.

BRIERS, Theunis Petrus Daniel   *South Africa*
('Theuns')
Pretoria Univ, W Prov.
b 11.7.29 Otterkuil.
Wing, 7-4-0-3 (15 − 5t).
55 BI−(2t) BI+(1t) BI− BI+(2t); 56 NZ−
NZ+ NZ+.
Wine farmer. 5t v BI 55 series rec for SA in SA.
SAr > 56 A, NZ.

BRIGGS, Arthur ('Spafty')   *England*
Otley, Bradford, Yorks.
b 1871; *d* 18.8.43.
Half-back, 3-3-0-0.
1892 W+ I+ S+.
Iron moulder. His club, Bradford, helped form
NU 1895. Notable swimmer & breeder of
sealyham terriers.

BRINGEON, Adolphe   *France*
Biarritz Ol.
Wing, 1-0-0-1.
25 W−.

BRINK, Danie J. ('Koei')   *South Africa*
W Prov.
b 7.11.1882.
Forward, 3-1-1-1.
06 S− W+ E=.
Town Clerk, Lindley, OFS. Cousin of J. Botha.

BRINN, Alan   *England*
RGS High Wycombe, Gloucester.
b 21.7.42 Ystrad, Rhondda.
Lock, 3-0-0-3.
72 W− I− S−.
Sports outfitter.

BRISCOE, Kevin Charles   *New Zealand*
('Monkey')
New Plymouth Boys' HS, Tukapa, Taranaki,
NZ Colts, N Island.
b 20.8.36 New Plymouth.
SH, 9-5-2-2.
59 BI+; 60 SA− SA+ SA= SA−; 63 I+ W+;
64 E+ S=.
Panel beater/sales rep. NZ > 60 A & SA, 62 A,
63-4 BI,F & Can.

BRISTOW, James Rippingham   *Ireland*
RBAI, NIFC.
b −.10.1858; *d* 4.4.25 Belfast.
Forward, 1-0-0-1.

1879 E−.
Bank man dir.

BRITTON, Gordon R. *Wales*
Newport.
Centre, 1-0-0-1.
61 S−.
Police.

BROAD, Edmund George DFC *Australia*
Southport GS, Qld Univ, Qld.
b 3.1.21 Brisbane.
Five-eighth, 1-0-0-1.
49 M−.
District court judge. Served WW2, S Ldr in
RAAF. Mem of organising comm Olympic
Games, Melbourne 56.

BROADLEY, Tom *England*
Bingley, Bradford, W Riding, Yorks.
b 18.8.1871 Bingley; *d* 26.11.50 Bradford.
Forward, 6-1-0-5.
1893 W− S−; 1894 W+ I− S−; 1896 S−.
Maltster/licensee. Bradford RL 1896.

BROCKHOFF, John David *Australia*
Bellevue Hill Public Sch, The Scots Coll, St
Andrew's Coll, Sydney Univ, E Suburbs, NSW.
b 8.6.28 Ross Bay, Sydney.
Flanker, 8-3-1-4 (6 − 2t).
49 M= M+(2t) NZ+ NZ+; 50 BI− BI−; 51
NZ− NZ−.
Salesman. Asst mgr A > 75-6 BI, US. A coach
74-9.

BROMET, William Ernest *England*
Richmond Sch (Yorks), Oxford Univ,
Richmond, Tadcaster, Yorks, Mdx.
b 17.5.1868 Tadcaster; *d* 23.1.49.
Forward, 12-8-0-4 (2 − 1t).
1891 W+ I+; 1892 W+ I+ S+(1t); 1893 W− I+
S−; 1895 W+ I+ S−; 1896 I−; BT > 1891 SA.
Solicitor/dir R Mint Birmingham. Blue 1889.
App with bro Edward (Cambridge Univ, non-
int) in 2 Tests BT > 1891 SA, 1st bros to play for
BT.

BROOK, Peter Watts Pitt *England*
Whitgift Sch, Westminster Bank, Utd Banks,
Cambridge Univ, Harlequins, Bristol,
Barbarians, Wilts, E Cos, Sussex.
b 21.9.06 Thornton Heath.
Flanker/no 8, 3-1-1-1.
30 S=; 31 F−; 36 S+.
Schoolmaster/clergyman. Blue 28-31. Ordained
35. Served WW2 chaplain XIVth Army in
Burma. Rep Surrey at pole vault & hurdles.
Glos CCC 2nd XI. Councillor for Bath 66.

BROOKE, Terence John *England*
Purley CGS, Battersea CAT, Warlingham,

Richmond, Barbarians, Surrey.
b 8.10.40.
Centre, 2-1-0-1.
68 F− S+.
Chartered structural engr.

BROOKS, D. ('Cocky') *South Africa*
Border.
b 1883.
Forward, 1-0-0-1.
06 S−.

BROOKS, Frederick G. *England*
Bedford GS, Bedford, E Midlands, Rhodesia.
b 1.5.1883; *d* − 9.47.
Wing, 1-0-1-0 (3 − 1t).
06 SA=(1t).
Played for Rhodesia in Currie Cup 06.

BROOKS, Hon Marshall Jones *England*
Rugby Sch, Oxford Univ.
b 30.5.1855; *d* 5.1.44 Tarporley.
FB, 1-1-0-0.
1874 S+.
Son of 1st Baron Crawshaw. Blue 1873. Ath
blue 1874-6. World's best for high jump, 6ft 2
1/2in at Lillie Bridge, London, 4.4.1876.

BROPHY, Niall Henry *Ireland*
O'Connell's CBS, UC Dublin, Blackrock Coll,
Barbarians.
b 19.11.35 Dublin.
Wing, 20-7-2-11 (12 − 4t).
57 F+(1t) E−; 59 E− S+ W− F+(1t); 60 F−
(2t) SA−; 61 S− W−; 62 E− S− W−; 63 E=
W+; 67 E− S+ W+ F− A+; BI > 59 A, NZ; 62
SA 2-0-1-1.
Chartered accountant.

BROPHY, Thomas John *England*
Westpark GS, Liverpool Univ, Liverpool,
Loughborough Colls, Barbarians, Lancs.
b 8.7.42 Liverpool.
FH, 8-2-1-5.
64 I− F+ S−; 65 W− I−; 66 W− I= F+.
Schoolmaster. Barrow RL 66. Taught at Rossall
Sch, Barrow GS.

BROUGH, James Wasdale *England*
Silloth.
b 5.11.03 Silloth.
FB, 2-1-0-1.
25 NZ− W+.
Fisherman/yeast merchants' rep. Leeds RL 25.

BROUGHAM, Henry *England*
Wellington Coll, Oxford Univ, Harlequins.
b 8.7.1888 Wellington Coll; *d* 18.2.23 La Croix.
Wing, 4-3-0-1 (9 − 3t).
12 W+(1t) I+(1t) S− F+(1t).
The Army. Served WW1 Maj RFA; severely

gassed. Died from phthisis contracted while serving in Ireland 18. Rackets & ckt blue 11 (sc 84 v Cambridge). Also Berks CCC 05-14 & Minor Cos v SA 12. All comers singles rackets champ; won doubles Champ with B.S. Foster.

BROUGHTON, Augustus Stephen   *Wales*
Treorchy.
 b 29.4.04 Cardiff; *d* − .9.81 Llwynypia.
Prop/no 8, 2-1-0-1.
27 NSW−; 29 S+.
Police. Son played for Maesteg.

BROWN, Alan Arthur   *England*
Cowley Sch, St Helens, Carnegie Coll, St Luke's Coll Exeter, Exeter, Aldershot Servs, Barbarians, Lancs, Devon.
 b 28.8.11 St Helens.
Flanker, 1-0-0-1.
38 S−.
Snr PE adviser. Served WW2 4th Devonshire Rgt.

BROWN, Alexander Henderson   *Scotland*
Heriot's Coll, Heriot's FP, Edinburgh Dentistry Coll.
 b 12.5.05.
FH, 3-1-0-2 (10 − 1d 2p).
28 E−; 29 F+(1p) W−(1d 1p).
Dentist. Pres SRU 71-2.

BROWN, Archibald   *Wales*
Newport.
 b 1895 Cross Keys.
SH, 1-1-0-0.
21 I+.
Electrician/schoolmaster. Leeds RL 21, then Dewsbury.

BROWN, Arthur Robert   *Scotland*
Gala Acad, Gala.
 b 10.12.49 Galashiels.
FB, 5-4-0-1 (13 − 5c 1p).
71 E+ E+(4c); 72 F+(1c) W− E+(1p).
Lorry driver.

BROWN, Bruce Robert   *Australia*
Brisbane Boys' Coll, Brisbane Univ, Qld.
 b 18.8.44.
Prop, 2-0-0-2.
72 NZ− NZ−.
Accountant/co sec.

BROWN, C.   *South Africa*
W Prov.
3-1-2-0.
03 BT= BT= BT+.

BROWN, Charles   *New Zealand*
Central Sch New Plymouth, Star, Taranaki, Tukapa, N Island, Comb Servs.

 b 19.12.1887 New Plymouth; *d* 2.4.66 New Plymouth.
SH, 2-1-0-1 (3 − 1t).
13 A+(1t) A−.
NZ > 20 A. Leading administrator. Bro Claude NZ Trials 35.

BROWN, Charles H.C.   *Scotland*
Dollar Acad, Dunfermline.
 b −; *d* 25.10.76 Perth.
Wing, 1-1-0-0 (3 − 1t).
29 E+(1t).
Timber.

BROWN, David Ian   *Scotland*
Loretto Sch, Cambridge Univ, Barbarians.
 b 09.
FB, 3-3-0-0.
33 W+ E+ I+.
Schoolmaster. Taught at Stowe Sch.

BROWN, Eric Lawrence ('Bolo')   *Ireland*
RBAI, Queen's Univ Belfast, Instonians.
 b 6.9.30 Belfast.
Flanker, 1-0-0-1.
58 F−.

BROWN, Gordon Lamont   *Scotland*
Marr Coll, W of S, Barbarians.
 b 1.11.47 Troon.
Lock, 30-14-0-16.
69 SA+; 70 F− W−r I− E+ A−; 71 F− W− I− E+ E+; 72 F+ W− E+ NZ−; 73 E−r P+; 74 W− E+ I− F+; 75 I+ F− W+ E− A+; 76 F− W− E+ I+; BI > 71 A & NZ 2-1-0-1; 74 SA 3-3-0-0; 77 NZ 3-1-0-2.
Bank clerk/building soc mgr. Scottish XV v Arg 73, Tg 74. 8 t BI > 74 SA, most by lock on major tour (broke hand 3rd Test). Bro Peter took his place v W 70; Peter inj in match, rep by Gordon. Autobiography 'Broon from Troon' pub 83.

BROWN, G.S.   *Ireland*
Monkstown, US Portsmouth, Barbarians.
Hooker/prop, 3-2-0-1 (3 − 1t).
12 S+ W+(1t) SA−.
The Army.

BROWN, H.   *Ireland*
Windsor.
Back, 1-0-0-1.
1877 E−.
Played with bro T. Brown v E 1877.

BROWN, James   *Wales*
Cardiff.
 b 22.3.01 Cardiff; *d* 30.7.76.
Lock, 1-0-0-1.
25 I−.
Docker.

BROWN, James Victor   *Australia*
Newington Coll, Stanmore, Sydney, Randwick,
NSW.
b 35.
Hooker, 9-0-0-9.
56 SA− SA−; 57 NZ− NZ−; 58 W− I− E− S−
F−.
Personnel.

BROWN, J.A.   *Scotland*
Glasgow Acad, Glasgow Academicals.
Hooker, 2-0-0-2.
08 W− I−.

BROWN, J.B.   *Scotland*
Glasgow Acad, Glasgow Academicals.
Forward, 17-10-3-4 (2t).
1879 I+(1t) E=; 1880 I+ E−; 1881 I− E=(1t);
1882 I+ E+; 1883 W+ E−; 1884 W+ I+ E−;
1885 I+; 1886 W+ I+ E=.

BROWN, John Alfred   *Wales*
Cardiff.
Forward, 7-6-0-1 (3 − 1t).
07 E+(1t) S− I+; 08 E+ S+ F+; 09 E+.
Coal trimmer. 221 apps for Cardiff 1900-10.

BROWN, Leonard Graham   *England*
('Bruno') MC
Brisbane GS (Aus), Oxford Univ, The London
Hosp, Blackheath, Barbarians, Surrey,
Queensland.
b 6.9.1888 Brisbane, Aus; *d* 23.5.50 Charing
Cross Hosp.
Prop, 18-14-0-4 (12 − 4t).
11 W− F+ I− S+; 13 SA− W+ F+ I+ S+(1t);
14 W+(1t) I+ S+ F+; 21 W+ I+(1t) S+(1t)
F+; 22 W−.
Medicine. Rhodes Scholar. Blue 10-12 (capt).
Capt E v W 22. Served WW1, Capt RAMC,
later Lt Col. MC 17. Mentioned in despatches
18. Played either side WW1. Rep NSW on RFU
comm 22-49; pres 48-9. Chmn Dominions
Conference 47. IB rep (responsible for
obtaining IB status for A, NZ & SA). Asst in
founding ARFU 26.11.49. ENT specialist.

BROWN, Mark ('Shaft')   *Wales*
Fairwater Comp, Cwmbran, Pontypool.
b 18.12.58 Newport.
Flanker, 3-1-0-2.
83 R−; 86 E− S+.
Quantity surveyor. Sc t Wales XV v J 83.
Gained 2nd cap after withdrawing from WRU
Squad v Fj 85.

BROWN, Peter Currie   *Scotland*
Marr Coll, W of S, Gala, Barbarians.
b 16.12.41 Troon.
Lock/no 8, 27-13-2-12 (64 − 2t 6c 15p).
64 F+ NZ= W− I+ E+; 65 I− E= SA+; 66

A+; 69 I− E−(1p); 70 W− E+(1c 2p); 71 F−
(1c) W−(4p) I−(1c) E+(1t 2c) E+(1t 1p); 72
F+(1p) W−(1c 1p) E+(1t 3p) NZ−; 73 F−(2p)
W+ I+ E− P+.
Chartered accountant. Took bro Gordon's place
v W 70; inj in match, Gordon came on as r.

BROWN, Robert Charles   *Australia*
Duntroon Military Coll, ACT, NSW Country,
Parramatta, NSW.
b 9.2.53.
FB, 2-2-0-0 (14 − 1c 1d 3p).
75 E+(1d 2p) E+(1c 1p).
Army.

BROWN, Ross Handley   *New Zealand*
Central Sch New Plymouth, HSOB, King's Coll,
NZ Jnrs, Taranaki, N Island.
b 8.9.34 New Plymouth.
Centre/1st/2nd five-eighth, 16-13-0-3 (12 − 3t
1d).
55 A−; 56 SA+ SA−(1t) SA+ SA+; 57 A+
A+(1t 1d); 58 A+ A−(1t) A+; 59 BI+ BI+; 61
F+ F+ F+; 62 A+.
Family timber business mgr. NZ > 57 & 62 A.
Taranaki sel 71-2. Father Handley & uncle
Henry ex-NZ reps. Bro Don rep Taranaki &
King Country.

BROWN, Spencer William   *Australia*
('Spanner')
Manly, NSW.
b 21; *d* 73.
Half-back, 3-1-0-2.
53 SA+ SA− SA−.
Property developer/garage proprietor.

BROWN, T.   *Ireland*
Windsor.
Forward, 2-0-0-2.
1877 E− S−.
Played with bro H. Brown v E 1877.

BROWN, Thomas Gow   *Scotland*
Heriot's Coll, Heriot's FP, Edinburgh Univ.
b 02.
Wing, 1-0-0-1.
29 W−.
Medicine.

BROWN, Thomas W.   *England*
Colston Sch, Bristol Univ, Bristol, Barbarians,
Glos.
b 07; *d* 14.5.61.
FB, 9-5-0-4.
28 S+; 29 W+ I− S− F+; 32 S+; 33 W− I+
S−.
Garage proprietor/licensee. 171 apps for Bristol.
Susp sine die by RFU for contact with RL club
33. Not reinstated on appeal.

63

BROWN, W.H. *Ireland*
Santry Coll, Trin Coll Dublin.
Wing, 1-1-0-0.
1899 E+.

BROWN, William David *Scotland*
Cheltenham Coll, Glasgow Acad, Glasgow
Academicals.
b 29.5.1852; *d* 24.3.1875.
Back/FB, 5-1-2-2.
1871 E+; 1872 E−; 1873 E=; 1874 E−; 1875
E=.
Shipping office. Played in 1st int, S v E 1871.
Killed by train near his home 16 days after capt S
v E at Raeburn Place.

BROWN, William James *Ireland*
Annadale GS, Queen's Univ Belfast, Malone.
b 43.
Wing, 4-2-1-1 (3 − 1t).
70 SA= F− S+(1t) W+.
Schoolmaster/finance co man dir.

BROWN, William Stewart *Ireland*
Wesley Coll, Trin Coll Dublin.
b 1868; *d* −.1.46.
Half-back, 5-3-1-1.
1893 S= W−; 1894 E+ S+ W+.

BROWN, William Storey *Scotland*
(**'Hopper'**)
Edinburgh Inst, Edinburgh Inst FP.
b 1859; *d* 15.9.01 Galashiels.
Half-back, 7-5-0-2 (2t).
1880 I+ E−(1t); 1882 I+(1t) E+; 1883 W+ I+
E−.
Engr/tweed manufacturer. Ump W v S, S v I
1888. Pres SRU 1887-8.

BROWNE, Antony William *Ireland*
RS Dungannon, Trin Coll Dublin.
1-0-0-1.
51 SA−.
Medicine.

BROWNE, Declan ('Decco') *Ireland*
Blackrock Coll.
b 12.1.1900.
Hooker, 1-0-0-1.
20 F−.
Dublin Police.

BROWNE, Hugh Christopher *Ireland*
DSO CBE
US Portsmouth, RN.
b 28.11.05 London; *d* 6.11.83.
Hooker/prop, 3-1-1-1.
29 E+ S− W=.
RN/Queen's Messenger.

BROWNE, William Fraser *Ireland*
(**'Horsey'**)
Campbell Coll, RMC Sandhurst, US
Portsmouth, The Army.
b 29.1.03; *d* 23.5.31 Hartley Grange, Surrey.
Prop/hooker, 12-6-1-5 (3 − 1t).
25 E= S− W+(1t); 26 S+ W−; 27 F+ E− S+
W+ NSW−; 28 E− S+.
The Army. Died of leukaemia at Adrian Stoop's
home, where he had been taken from Aldershot
Mil Hosp to spend his last few days among
friends.

BROWNING, Arthur *Scotland*
Glasgow HS, Glasgow HSFP, Halifax.
b 2.7.1897.
Wing, 7-4-2-1 (22 − 5t 2c 1p).
20 I+(1t); 22 F=(1t) W=(2t 1p) I+; 23 E−
I+(1t 2c) W+.
Medicine. Int career over when played for
Halifax 24.

BROWNING, David R. *Ireland*
Wanderers.
Forward, 2-1-0-1.
1881 E− S+.

BROWNLIE, Cyril James *New Zealand*
Sacred Heart Coll Auckland, Hastings, Hawkes
Bay, Waiau, Wairoa Pirates, N Island.
b 6.8.1895 Wanganui; *d* 7.5.54 Wairoa.
Lock/flanker, 3-3-0-0.
24 W+; 25 E+ F+.
Farmer. Bro of Maurice. Another bro Laurence
1 app for NZ 21. NZ > 24-5 A,BI,F & C, 26 A,
28 SA. 1st player to be sent off in an int, v E 25.
Served WW1, Otago Mounted Rifles.

BROWNLIE, Maurice John *New Zealand*
Sacred Heart Coll Auckland, St Patrick's Coll
Wellington, Hastings, Hawkes Bay, N Island.
b 10.8.1897 Wanganui; *d* 21.1.57 Gisborne.
Lock/flanker, 8-6-0-2 (6 − 2t).
24 I+ W+(1t); 25 E+(1t) F+; 28 SA− SA+
SA− SA+.
Farmer. Bro of Cyril. NZ > 22 & 26 A, 24-5
A,BI,F & C; capt 1st NZ > 28 SA. Served
WW1. NZ amateur heavywt boxing final 21,
beaten by Brian McCleary, with whom he
played > 24-5 A,BI,F & Can.

BRUCE, Charles Russell *Scotland*
Gala Acad, Glasgow Academicals, Barbarians.
b 25.4.18.
Centre/FH, 8-2-0-6.
47 F− W− I− E−; 49 F+ W+ I− E−.
Surveyor. Played in 3 Servs ints.

BRUCE, John Alexander *New Zealand*
Te Aro Sch, St James, Wellington, Athletic,
Auckland, City, N Island, NZ Army.

64

b 11.11.1887 Wellington; *d* 20.10.70
Wellington.
No 8, 2-2-0-0.
14 A+ A+.
Carpenter. NZ > 13 NAm, 14 A. Rep
Wellington at ckt; scored 200 in club match.
Served WW1, sapper Field Engrs. Played for
NZ Army in King's Cup & > SA 18-19.

BRUCE, Norman Scott   *Scotland*
Gala Acad, Gala, Blackheath, The Army,
Comb Servs, London Scottish, Barbarians,
Hants.
b 32 Edinburgh.
Hooker, 31-13-4-14 (9 − 3t).
58 F+ A+ I− E=; 59 F− W+(1t) I− E=; 60
F− W− I+ E− SA−(1t); 61 F− SA− W+ I+
E−; 62 F− W+ I+ E=; 63 F+ W− I+ E−; 64
F+ NZ= W− I+ E+(1t).
The Army. Comb Servs v A 57, SA 61 (capt),
NZ 63.

BRUCE, Oliver Douglas   *New Zealand*
Southbridge Dist HS, Ashburton HS, HSOB,
NZ Jnrs, Mid-Canterbury, Christchurch,
Oxford, Ohoka, Canterbury, S Island.
b 23.5.47 Dunedin.
1st five-eighth, 14-10-0-4 (15 − 5d).
76 SA− SA+(1d) SA−(1d); 77 BI− BI+ BI+;
77 F− F+; 78 A+ A+(1d) I+(2d) W+ E+ S+.
Schoolmaster/TV & radio sports commentator.
NZ > 74 A & Fj & I,W & E, 76 SA, 77 F, 78 BI.
Bro-in-law of H.H. Macdonald.

BRUCE, Robert Mitchell   *Scotland*
Gordon's Coll, Gordonians.
b 19.6.22 Aberdeen.
Prop, 4-1-0-3.
47 A−; 48 F+ W− I−.
Bank mgr/hotelier.

BRUCE, Stewart A.M. DL JP   *Ireland*
King William's Coll IOM, NIFC, The Army.
b 1857; *d* −.4.37.
Forward, 3-0-0-3.
1883 E− S−; 1884 E−.
The Army. Uncle of J.H. Bruce-Lockhart.

BRUCE-LOCKHART, John   *Scotland*
Harold
Sedbergh Sch, Cambridge Univ, London
Scottish, Barbarians.
b 4.3.1889 Beith; *d* 4.6.56 London.
Centre, 2-0-0-2 (4 − 1d).
13 W−; 20 E−(1d).
Schoolmaster. Father of Rab & Logie. Nephew
of S.A.M. Bruce. Blue 10. Ckt for S. Served
WW2, 2nd Lt in Seaforth Highlanders;
mentioned in despatches. (In Cambridge Univ
War List, listed as Lockhart, John Harold
Bruce).

BRUCE-LOCKHART, Logie   *Scotland*
Sedbergh Sch, Cambridge Univ, London
Scottish.
b 12.10.21.
Centre, 5-2-0-3 (2 − 1c).
48 E+; 50 F+(1c) W−; 53 I− E−.
HM. Son of John, bro of Rab. Blue 45-6.

BRUCE-LOCKHART, Rab   *Scotland*
Brougham
Glasgow Acad, Cambridge Univ, London
Scottish.
b 1.12.16 Rugby.
FH, 3-0-0-3.
37 I−; 39 I− E−.
Schoolmaster. Son of John, bro of Logie. Blue
37-8. Ckt for S.

BRUN, Georges   *France*
Vienne.
b 23.12.22 Aix les Bains.
FB/wing/centre, 14-7-0-7.
50 E+ W−; 51 S+ E+ W+; 52 S+ I− SA− W−
E− It+; 53 E− W− It+.
Commercial agent.

BRUNEAU, Maurice ('La Souris')   *France*
SBUC.
b 1.8.1883 Bordeaux; *d* −.
Wing/centre, 4-0-0-4 (3 − 1t).
10 W− E−; 13 SA−(1t) E−.

BRUNET, Yves   *France*
Perpignan.
b 25.8.50 Peyrestortes.
Hooker, 2-1-0-1.
75 SA−; 77 Arg+.
Wine grower.

BRUNKER, Alfred A.   *Ireland*
Lansdowne.
b 1873; *d* −.8.46.
Forward, 2-0-0-2.
1895 E− W−.

BRUNTON, Joseph MC DSO   *England*
N Durham, Rockcliff, The Army, Northumb.
b 21.8.1888; *d* 18.9.71.
Lock, 3-3-0-0.
14 W+ I+ S+.
Chmn, man dir engrg co. Served WW1 Seaforth
Highlanders, Northumb Fusiliers (later Lt Col
commanding). MC 16, & Bar 17. Mentioned in
despatches 3 times. DSO 18. Ref W v NZ 25.
Rep Northumb on RFU 45-54. Pres RFU 53-4.

BRUTTON, Ernest Bartholomew   *England*
Durham Sch, Cambridge Univ, Lichfield Theol
Coll, Northumb, Durham Co.
b 1863 Newcastle-upon-Tyne; *d* 26.2.42
Botleigh, Glastonbury.

Back, 1-0-1-0.
1886 S=.
Clergyman/schoolmaster. Blue 1883,5,6 (capt).
Ath blue 1884. Ckt for Northumb 1891 & Devon
01-4. Ordained 1888. Asst master Lancing Coll
until Vicar of Aylesbeare.

BRYANT, Charles H.   *Ireland*
Cardiff.
Wing, 2-0-0-2.
20 E− S−.
Coach proprietor.

BRYCE, C.C.   *Scotland*
Glasgow Acad, Glasgow Academicals.
b −; d −.2.1895.
Forward, 2-0-1-1.
1873 E=; 1874 E−.

BRYCE, Robert Donaldson   *Scotland*
Hamish
Perth Acad, RE, The Army, W of S,
Barbarians.
b 12.11.41.
Prop, 1-1-0-0.
73 I+r.
The Army/production mgr cigarette co. Capped
at 31.

BRYCE, William Erskine   *Scotland*
St Bees Sch, Selkirk.
b 16.1.01; d 22.2.83 Melrose.
SH, 11-6-1-4 (9 − 3t).
22 W= I+(1t) E−; 23 F+(1t) W+ I+ E−; 24
F− W+(1t) I+ E−.
Tweed manufacturer. Scottish hockey int.

BRYDEN, Charles Cowper   *England*
Cheltenham Coll, Clapham R.
b 16.6.1852; d 20.2.41.
Forward, 2-1-0-1.
1875 I+; 1877 S−.
Business. Bro of Henry.

BRYDEN, Henry Anderson   *England*
Cheltenham Coll, Clapham R.
b 3.5.1854; d 23.9.37 Parkstone, Dorset.
Forward, 1-1-0-0.
1874 S+.
Bro of Charles. Acclaimed long distance runner.
Ran 2nd to Walter Slade (RFU treasurer 1875-
6) when he set world mile best of 4m 24.5s at
Stamford Bridge 19.6.1865. Author of books on
African sport and natural history 1889-36.

BRYDON, William Ritchie   *Scotland*
Crawford ('Wee Willie')
Heriot's Coll, Heriot's FP.
b 6.11.15; d 11.6.80 Edinburgh.
SH, 1-0-0-1.

39 W−.
Scottish Agriculture Industries.

BRYERS, Ronald Frederick   *New Zealand*
Ohakune Dist HS, Raetihi, King Country, NZ
Maoris.
b 14.11.19 Raetihi.
Lock, 1-0-0-1.
49 A−.
Headmaster. NZ Maoris v A 46. Selector for
Bay of Plenty 62-73 & NZ Maoris 57-8.

BRYNARD, Gert Steenkamp   *South Africa*
W Prov.
b 27.10.38.
Wing, 7-3-0-4 (6 − 2t).
65 A− NZ− NZ− NZ+(2t) NZ−; 68 BI+ BI+.
Medicine.

BUCHAN, Arthur John   *Australia*
Sydney Tech HS, Sydney Univ, Randwick, St
George, NSW.
b 24.
No 8/flanker, 10-3-0-7.
46 NZ− NZ−; 47 NZ− NZ− S+ I+ W−; 48
E+ F−; 49 M−.
Schoolmaster/NSW Deputy dir of education.

BUCHANAN, Allan McMillan   *Ireland*
Portora RS, Trin Coll Dublin.
b 21.5.04; d 24.11.56.
Prop, 6-4-0-2.
26 E+ S+ W−; 27 S+ W+ NSW−.
Medicine/schoolmaster. Killed in motor
accident.

BUCHANAN, Angus   *Scotland*
Royal HSFP.
b 15.1.1847 Inverary; d 21.2.27.
Forward, 1-1-0-0 (1t).
1871 E+(1t).
Bank agent. Sc S's 1st t, in 1st int v E 1871.
Uncle of Fletcher. Ump S v E 77, 79. Ref I v S
1877, S v I 1880. Pres SRU 1879-80. Ckt for S.

BUCHANAN, Fletcher Gordon   *Scotland*
Kelvinside Acad, Kelvinside Academicals,
Oxford Univ.
b 23.12.1889; d −.1.67.
FB/centre, 3-1-0-2.
10 F+; 11 F− W−.
Nephew of Angus. Blue 09-10. Scottish long
jump champ. Served WW1, Capt in RE;
mentioned in despatches.

BUCHANAN, John Blacker   *Ireland*
Sherborne Sch, Trin Coll Dublin.
Forward, 3-0-0-3.
1882 S−; 1884 E− S−.
Army Medical Service.

BUCHANAN, Sir John Cecil   *Scotland*
Rankin KCMG
Stewart's Coll, Stewart's Coll FP, Edinburgh
Univ, Barbarians.
b 18.6.1896 SA; *d* 19.2.76.
Hooker, 16-11-0-5 (3 − 1t).
21 W+(1t) I+ E−; 22 W+ I+ E−; 23 F+ W+
I+ E−; 24 F− W+ I+ E−; 25 F+ I+.
Colonial medical service. KCMG 61.

BUCHER, Alfred Moore   *Scotland*
Royal HS, Edinburgh Acad, Edinburgh
Academicals.
b 22.3.1874; *d* 20.8.39 Edinburgh.
Wing, 1-0-0-1 (3 − 1t).
1897 E−(1t); BT > 1899 A.
Wine trade/mgr N British Steam Packet Co.

BUCHET, Eric   *France*
Nice.
Flanker, 5-2-0-3.
80 R−; 82 E− R−r Arg+ Arg+.
Insurance salesman.

BUCHLER, John U.   *South Africa*
Transvaal.
b 7.4.30 Johannesburg.
FB, 10-9-0-1 (8 − 1c 1gm 1p).
51 S+ I+ W+; 52 E+ F+; 53 A+(1c 1p) A−
A+ A+(1gm); 56 A+.
Mine clerk. SA > 51-2 BI, F.

BUCKINGHAM, Ralph Arthur   *England*
BEM
Stoneygate Prep Sch, Rossall Sch, Leicester,
Stoneygate, Barbarians, Leics.
b 07 Blaby, Leicester.
Centre, 1-0-0-1.
27 F−.
Co dir shoe-mercers. Served WW2 Civil
Defence, then Ft Lt with RAF. BEM for
gallantry 42.

BUCKLEY, James Henry   *Ireland*
Terenure Coll, Sunday's Well.
b 44.
Flanker, 2-1-0-1.
73 E+ S−.
Insurance.

BUCKNALL, Anthony Launce   *England*
Ampleforth Coll, Oxford Univ, Richmond,
Middlesex, London Cos, E Cos.
b 7.6.45 Torquay.
Flanker, 10-3-1-6.
69 SA+; 70 I+ W− S− F−; 71 W− I+ F= S−
S−.
Stockbroker. Capt E v W 71. Blue 65-6. Boxing
blue. Bro in law of A.J. Lamb, Northants &
England ckter.

BUDD, Arthur James ('Jimmy')   *England*
Clifton Coll, Cambridge Univ, Bart's Hosp,
Blackheath, Kent.
b 14.10.1853 Bristol; *d* 27.8.1899 SA.
Forward, 5-3-2-0 (1t).
1878 I+; 1879 S= I+; 1881 W+(1t) S=.
Medicine. Touch-judge S v E 1892. Sec London
Soc of Refs 1889-90. Pres RFU 1888-9. Mem IB
1890-5. Emigrated to SA 1893.

BUDD, Thomas Alfred   *New Zealand*
Bluff, Southland, S Island.
b 1.8.22 Bluff.
Lock, 2-1-0-1.
46 A+; 49 A−.
Northland Harbour Board works mgr. Bro
H.G. Budd rep Southland 45.

BUDGE, Grahame Morris   *Scotland*
Edinburgh W, Barbarians.
b 7.11.20 Hamiota, Manitoba; *d* 14.11.79
Vancouver.
Prop, 4-2-0-2 (3 − 1t).
50 F+(1t) W− I− E+; BI > 50 NZ, A 1-0-0-1.
Poultry farmer/real estate co dir.

BUDWORTH, Richard Thomas   *England*
Dutton
Christ's Coll Brecon, Oxford Univ, Blackheath,
London Welsh, Barbarians, Kent, Sussex.
b 17.10.1867; *d* 7.12.37 London.
Forward, 3-1-0-2 (1 − 1t).
1890 W−; 1891 W+(1t) S−.
Clergyman/HM. Blue 1887-9. Ordained 02.
Taught at Lancing Coll, Clifton Coll, Durham
Sch. Original mem Barbarians. Served WW1.
Died at his London Club on morning of 37 Univ
Match with ticket for match in his pocket.

BUISSON, Henri   *France*
Béziers.
b 4.8.04 Béziers.
Prop, 2-2-0-0.
31 E+ G+.

BULGER, Lawrence Quinlivan   *Ireland*
('Fat Cupid')
Blackrock Coll, Trin Coll Dublin, Lansdowne,
Barbarians.
b 5.7.1875; *d* −.3.28.
Wing, 8-4-1-3 (20 − 2t 2c 1gm 2p).
1896 E+(1c) S= W+(1c); 1897 E+(1t 1gm) S−
(1t); 1898 E+(1p) S− W−(1p); BT > 1896 SA.
Medicine. Bro of Michael. 20t BT > SA 1896.
Ath for I. Ref English Public Sch Trial at
Richmond 10 in which his son M.L.Q., from
Univ Coll Sch, played SH.

BULGER, Michael Joseph   *Ireland*
Blackrock Coll, Trin Coll Dublin.
b 15.5.1867; *d* −.

1-0-0-1.
1888 NZN−.
Medicine. Bro of Lawrence.

BULL, Arthur Gilbert　　　　*England*
O Bedford Modernians, Northampton,
Barbarians.
Prop 1-1-0-0.
14 W+.
Medicine.

BULLMORE, Herbert Henry　　　*Scotland*
Edinburgh Univ.
b 1881 Sydney; d −.12.37.
Forward, 1-0-0-1.
02 I−.
Medicine.

BULLOCK-DOUGLAS, George　*New Zealand*
Arthur Hardy
Gonville Sch, Wanganui Collegiate Sch,
Auckland GS, Wanganui, N Island.
b 4.6.11 Wanganui; d 25.8.58 Wanganui.
Wing, 5-2-1-2 (9 − 3t).
32 A−(1t) A+(2t) A+; 34 A− A=.
Bank accountant. 5t N v S Island 32. NZ > 32 &
34 A (7t). Served WW2, Capt 22nd Battn.
Father George fdr/sec Kaierau club in
Wanganui.

BULLOUGH, E.　　　　　　　*England*
Wigan, Lancs.
b Wigan.
Forward, 3-3-0-0.
1892 W+ I+ S+.
His club, Wigan, helped form NU 1895.

BULPITT, Michael Philip　　　*England*
Berkhamsted Sch, Chelmsford, Osterley,
Blackheath, Barbarians, London Cos, E Cos.
b 12.4.44 Richmond, Yorks.
Wing, 1-0-0-1.
70 S−.
Advertising exec.

BULTEEL, A.J.　　　　　　*England*
Manchester.
Forward, 1-1-0-0.
1875 I+.

BUNTING, William Louis　　　*England*
Bromsgrove Sch, Cambridge Univ,
Bromsgrove, Richmond, Moseley, Kent,
Barbarians, Midlands.
b 9.8.1873; d 15.10.47 Odiham, Hants.
Centre, 9-2-2-5.
1897 I− S+; 1898 I− S= W+; 1899 S−; 1900
S=; 01 I− S−.
Schoolmaster. Blue 1894-5. Helped Kent win
County Champ 1897.

BUONOMO, Yvan　　　　　*France*
Béziers.
b 19.9.46 Sete, Herault.
No 8, 3-2-0-1.
71 A+ R+; 72 I−.
Heating & sanitary engr.

BURCHER, David Howard　　　*Wales*
Newport HS, St Luke's Coll Exeter, Newport,
Cardiff, Barbarians.
b 26.10.51 Newport.
Centre, 4-3-0-1.
77 I+ F− E+ S+; BI > 77 NZ 1-0-0-1.
Schoolmaster. Wales B v F 76. Wales B > 80
US, Can.

BURDETT, A.F.　　　　*South Africa*
W Prov.
b 1881.
Forward, 2-1-0-1.
06 S− I+.
SA > 06-7 BI, F.

BURDON, Alexander ('Bluey')　　*Australia*
Glebe, Sydney, NSW.
b 31.3.1880 Sydney; d 13.12.43 Branxton.
Forward, 4-0-0-4 (3 − 1t).
03 NZ−; 04 BT− BT−(1t); 05 NZ−.
Labourer/barber. RL.

BURGE, Albert Bentley ('Son')　　*Australia*
S Sydney, NSW.
b 3.6.1887 Penrith, NSW; d 43.
Forward, 2-0-1-1.
07 NZ=; 08 W−.
Oyster farmer. Played with bro Peter 3rd Test v
NZ 07. Ar > 08 BI.

BURGE, Peter Harold Boyne　　*Australia*
('Emu')
S Sydney, NSW.
b 14.2.1884; d −.7.56.
Forward, 3-0-1-2.
07 NZ− NZ− NZ=.
Groom/boat builder. Played with bro Albert v
NZ 07. RL.

BURGER, Matthys Boshoff　　*South Africa*
('Thys')
Helpmekaar Sch Johannesburg, Pretoria Univ,
Pretoria Police, N Transvaal.
b 10.11.54 Pietersburg.
Flanker/no 8, 3-3-0-0 (8 − 2t).
80 BI+r SAm+(1t); 81 US+r(1t).
Police. SA > 81 NZ. 5t SA v Paraguay Inv XV
80.

BURGER, S.W.P.　　　　*South Africa*
W Prov.
Lock, 2-2-0-0.

84 E+ E+.
Rest of World v BI, Cardiff 86.

BURGER, W.A.G. ('Bingo')　　　*South Africa*
Border.
b 1884.
Forward, 4-2-0-2.
06 S− I+ W+; 10 BI−.
SA > 06-7 BI, F.

BURGES, John Hume　　　*Ireland*
St John's Sch Leatherhead, Rosslyn Pk.
b 26.10.28 Tipperary.
SH, 2-0-1-1 (3 − 1p).
50 F=(1p) E−.
RN/oil co rep.

BURGESS, George Francis　　　*New Zealand*
('Jerry')
Pirates, Southland, S Island.
b 20.9.1883 Invercargill; *d* 2.7.61 Auckland.
Half-back, 1-1-0-0.
05 A+.
Bricklayer. Capt S Island 04.

BURGESS, Gregory Alexander　　　*New Zealand*
John
St Joseph's Convent Sch Onehunga, Marcellin
Coll, Univ, Union, Auckland, Ponsonby,
Wasps, Takapuna.
b 6.7.54 Auckland.
Prop, 1-0-0-1.
81 SA−.
Schoolmaster/insurance sales mgr. NZ v Fj 80.
Coach Onehunga HS 76-9. Runner-up 100 kg
national power lift 78. 11s 100m sprinter.

BURGESS, Robert Balderston　　　*Ireland*
Portora RS, Trin Coll Dublin, Barbarians.
b 25.12.1890; kia 9.12.15 Armentières.
1-0-0-1.
12 SA−.
Irish Bar. Served WW1, Capt in RE.

BURGESS, Robert Clive　　　*Wales*
Glyncoed Sch, Ebbw Vale, Breschia (It).
b 25.11.50 Manmoel.
Flanker, 9-6-0-3 (4 − 1t).
77 I+(1t) F− E+ S+; 81 I+ F+; 82 F+ E− S−.
Merchant seaman/driver. Wales B v F 76.

BURGESS, Robert Edward　　　*New Zealand*
Hastings Boys' HS, Univ, NZ Jnrs, NZ Univs,
Manawatu, Southland, Southland HSOB, N
Island, Lyon (F).
b 26.3.49 New Plymouth.
1st five-eighth, 7-3-1-3 (6 − 2t).
71 BI− BI+(2t) BI−; 72 A+ W+; 73 I= F−.
Lecturer in botany at Massey Univ. NZ > 72-3
BI,F & NAm. Student in F.

BURGUN, Marcel　　　*France*
RCF, Castres Ol.
b 1887; kia 15.
Centre, 11-1-0-10 (3 − 1t).
09 I−; 10 W−(1t) S− I−; 11 S+ E−; 12 I− S−;
13 S− E−; 14 E−.
Engr. Killed in air combat.

BURKE, Cyril Thomas BEM　　　*Australia*
Newcastle Boys' HS, Merewether-Carlton,
Waratahs, Newcastle, NSW Country, NSW.
b 7.11.25 Waratah, Newcastle.
SH, 26-10-0-16 (6 − 2t).
46 NZ−; 47 NZ− NZ− S+ I+(1t) W−; 48 E+
F−; 49 M+ M+ NZ+ NZ+; 50 BI− BI−(1t);
51 NZ− NZ− NZ−; 53 SA+ SA− SA−; 54
Fj+; 55 NZ− NZ− NZ+; 56 SA− SA−.
Civil Service/rep. Served WW2, RAAF in
Borneo.

BURKE, Matthew Peter　　　*Australia*
Australian Schs, Univ of NSW, Randwick,
NSW.
b 15.9.64.
Wing, 7-6-0-1.
84 E+r I+; 85 C+ C+ NZ− Fj+ Fj+.
Student. A > 84 Fj; 84 BI.

BURKE, Peter Standish　　　*New Zealand*
Edgecumbe Sch, Tauranga Coll, Bay of Plenty,
Edgecumbe, Marist, Auckland, Stratford,
Taranaki, Tukapa, Hawera, N Island.
b 22.9.27 Tauranga.
Lock/no 8, 3-3-0-0.
55 A+; 57 A+ A+.
Oil co exec. NZ > 51 & 57 A. NZRFU sel 78-
82. Bay of Plenty lawn tennis 45; with sister Judy
(NZ women's champ) won Taranaki mixed
doubles.

BURKITT, John Colley Smith　　　*Ireland*
Queen's Coll Cork, Cork.
b Kilkee; *d* −.
Forward, 1-0-0-1.
1881 E−.
Medicine.

BURLAND, Donald William　　　*England*
Bristol, Barbarians, Glos.
b 22.1.08; *d* 26.1.76.
Centre, 8-3-1-4 (23 − 3t 4c 2p).
31 W=(1t 1c) I− F−(1t); 32 I+(1t 1c 2p)
S+(2c); 33 W− I+ S−.
Licensee/gift shopkeeper. Served WW2, Maj in
RASC.

BURNET, David Ronald　　　*Australia*
Knox GS, Sydney, Gordon, NSW.
b 8.9.50.
Centre, 6-1-1-4 (4 − 1t).

72 F= F− NZ− NZ− NZ− Fj+(1t).
Manly RL 74.

BURNET, Patrick John   *Scotland*
Edinburgh Acad, Oxford Univ, London
Scottish, Edinburgh Academicals.
b 25.7.39 Edinburgh.
Centre, 1-0-0-1.
60 SA−.
Chartered accountant/stockbroker. Blue 60.

BURNET, William Alexander   *Scotland*
Hawick, Barbarians.
b 6.3.1886; *d* 25.7.58.
Centre, 1-1-0-0.
12 E+.
Nephew of David Patterson. Ref I v E 32, W v I
34.

BURNET, William Alexander   *Scotland*
Loretto Sch, W of S.
b 8.7.12.
Prop/lock, 8-1-0-7.
34 W−; 35 W− I− E+ NZ−; 36 W− I− E−.
Yarn merchant.

BURNETT, James Niven   *Scotland*
Heriot's Coll, Heriot's FP, Edinburgh Univ.
b 12.7.47 Kilmarnock.
Prop, 4-1-0-3.
80 I− F+ W− E−.
Dental surgeon.

BURNETT, Roy   *Wales*
Newport, Barbarians.
b 6.10.26 Abercarn.
FH, 1-0-0-1.
53 E−.
Schoolmaster/steelworker.

BURNS, Benjamin Henry   *England*
Smeston's Private Sch St Andrews, Edinburgh
Acad, Blackheath, Calcutta.
b 28.5.1848 Scotland; *d* 3.6.32.
Forward, 1-0-0-1.
1871 S−.
Played in 1st int S v E 1871. Various overseas
postings in banking profession. Returned UK to
take post as co dir publishers & booksellers.

BURNS, Ian George   *Ireland*
Dublin HS, Wanderers.
b 7.12.55 Dublin.
Centre, 1-0-0-1.
80 E−r.
Accountant.

BURNS, James   *Wales*
Cardiff.
b 02 Newtown, Cardiff; *d* 71.
Lock/prop, 2-1-0-1.

27 F+ I−.
Licensee. 108 apps for Cardiff 24-30. Bro Tom
also played for Cardiff. Cousin of boxer
'Peerless' Jim Driscoll.

BURNS, Patrick James   *New Zealand*
Albion, Canterbury, S Island.
b 10.3.1881 Lyttelton; *d* 24.2.43 Lyttelton.
SH/wing/centre, 5-2-1-2 (6 − 2t).
08 AW=; 10 A+ A− A+(2t); 13 A−.
Boilermaker. NZ > 10 A.

BURRELL, George ('Dod')   *Scotland*
Gala Acad, Gala.
b 21.1.21 Galashiels.
FB, 4-1-0-3.
50 F+ W− I−; 51 SA−.
BP sales rep. Ref E v I 58, W v I 59. Served
WW2, KOSB. Mgr BI > 77 NZ.

BURTON, George William   *England*
Winchester Coll, Blackheath.
b 29.8.1855; *d* 17.9.1890 West Hampstead.
Forward, 6-4-2-0 (6t).
1879 S=(1t) I+; 1880 S+(1t); 1881 I+ W+(4t)
S=.
Solicitor. 1st t in 1st Calcutta Cup match, v S
1879. 4t v W 1881, in 1st E v W int.

BURTON, Hyde Clark   *England*
RNEC Keyham, Bishops Stortford, Richmond,
RN, Barbarians, E Cos.
b 10.6.1898.
Wing, 1-0-1-0.
26 W=.
RN/chartered accountant. Served WW1 with
Grand Fleet. Served WW2 naval control W
Africa; later trade & naval intelligence at
Admiralty.

BURTON, Michael Alan   *England*
Longlevens Sch, Gloucester, Glos.
b 18.12.45 Maidenhead.
Prop, 17-4-1-12.
72 W− I− F− S− SA+; 74 F= W+; 75 S+ A−
A−; 76 A+ W− S− I− F−; 78 F− W−.
Co dir. Autobiography 'Never Stay Down' pub
82. Pub 2 subsequent books. Sent off v A 75, 1st
E int dismissed.

BUSH, James Arthur   *England*
Clifton Coll, Clifton, Glos.
b 28.7.1850 Cawnpore, India; *d* 21.9.24
Clevedon.
Forward, 5-3-2-0.
1872 S+; 1873 S=; 1875 S= I+; 1876 S+.
Glos CCC. Wkt-keeper with W.G. Grace's
touring ckt side in A 1873-4. Gentlemen v
Players 74-5.

BUSH, Percy Frank   *Wales*
Penygraig, UC Cardiff, Cardiff, Nantes (F).
b 23.6.1879 Cardiff; *d* 19.5.55 Cardiff.
FH, 8-7-0-1 (20 − 2t 1c 3d).
05 NZ+; 06 E+ SA−; 07 I+(1t 1d); 08 E+(1t 1c
1d) S+; 10 S+ I+(1d); BTuncap > 04 A, NZ.
Schoolmaster/consular official. 171 apps for
Cardiff 1899-14. Capt Cardiff v NZ 05, & in 17-0
victory v SA 07. Bro Fred also played for
Cardiff. Ckt for Glamorgan II. Vice-consul
Nantes 10, capt local club. In one match v Le
Havre 10 sc 54 pts, inc 10t. On return to Wales
awarded Medaille d'Argent de Gratitude by
French govt.

BUSH, Ronald George   *New Zealand*
Mt Albert GS, Univ, Auckland, NZ Univs,
Otago, S & N Islands.
b 3.5.09 Nelson.
FB, 1-1-0-0 (14 − 1c 4p).
31 A+(1c 4p).
Schoolmaster/indent agent. Father George rep
Canterbury 1898-01. Co-fdr NZ Barbarians 37.
Auckland pres 66-8. NZRFU sel 61-4. Asst mgr
NZ > 62 A. Ckt for Auckland.

BUSH, William Kingita Te Pohe   *New Zealand*
Whakatane HS, City, Horohoro, Suburbs,
Belfast, Canterbury, S Island, NZ Maoris.
b 24.1.49 Napier.
Prop, 12-8-1-3.
74 A+ A=; 75 S+; 76 I+ SA+ SA−; 77 BI−
BI+ BI+r; 78 I+ W+; 79 A−.
Boilermaker/commercial diver. NZ > 74 A & Fj
& I,W & E, 76 SA, 78 BI, 79 A.

BUSTAFFA, Daniel   *France*
Carcassonne.
b 11.1.56 Carcassonne.
Wing, 11-3-1-7 (4 − 1t).
77 Arg+(1t) Arg= NZ+ NZ−; 78 W− R+; 80
W− E− S− SA− R−.
Sports shopowner. 3t (3 apps) F > 80 SA.

BUTCHER, Chris J.S.   *England*
England SS, Harlequins, Mdx, London.
b 19.8.60 Karachi.
No 8, 3-0-0-3.
84 SA− SA− A−.
Labourer/deep sea fisherman. E Schs > 78 A,
NZ. E Under 23s v Netherlands 80. Stayed on in
SA after E > 84 SA. Played with bro John, a
wing, at Harlequins; another bro, David, played
prop for London Scottish.

BUTCHER, Walter Vincent   *England*
Carlisle GS, Bristol, Streatham, Barbarians,
Glos.
b 2.2.1878; *d* 26.8.57 Bexhill.
Half-back, 7-1-1-5.
03 S−; 04 W= I+ S−; 05 W− I− S−.

Rly engr. Served WW1, Capt RE. Surrey CCC
2nd XI. Employed on Indian State Rlys.

BUTLER, Arthur Geoffrey   *England*
R Henley GS, Henley, Harlequins, Barbarians,
Oxon, E Midlands.
b 30.9.14 Oxford.
Wing, 2-2-0-0 (3 − 1t).
37 W+ I+(1t).
Builder/farmer. Oxon rep RFU 50. Pres RFU
63-4. GB ath team Antwerp 37.

BUTLER, Edward Thomas   *Wales*
(**'Bamber'**)
Monmouth Sch, Cambridge Univ, Pontypool,
Barbarians.
b 8.5.57 Newport.
No 8, 16-6-1-9 (8 − 2t).
80 F+ E− S+ I− NZ−r; 82 S−(1t); 83 E= S+
I+ F− R−; 84 S− I+ F−(1t) E+ A−; BIr > 83
NZ.
Schoolmaster/BBC TV production. Blue 76-78.
Wales B v F 77, 79. Wales B > 80 US, Can; 83
Spain. Capt Wales XV v Maoris 82, v J 83. Capt
Pontypool 81-4 (won 130 out of 148).

BUTLER, Lochlann Gerard   *Ireland*
(**'Locky'**)
Blackrock Coll.
b 9.10.35 Bray.
Hooker, 1-0-0-1.
60 W−.
Hotel supplies co dir.

BUTLER, Nick   *Ireland*
Bective Rgrs, Garryowen.
b −; *d* 21.1.52 Limerick.
Prop, 1-0-0-1.
20 E−.

BUTLER, Owen Frederick   *Australia*
Mackville HS, N Suburbs (ACT), NSW
Country, NSW.
b 31.5.44.
Lock, 7-2-0-5.
69 SA− SA−; 70 S+; 71 SA− SA− F+ F−.
Schoolmaster/farmer.

BUTLER, Peter E.   *England*
Crypt GS, Gloucester.
b 23.6.51 Gloucester.
FB, 2-0-0-2 (10 − 2c 2p).
75 A−(1c 1p); 76 F−(1c 1p).

BUTTERFIELD, Jeffrey   *England*
Cleckheaton GS, Cleckheaton, Loughborough
Colls, Northampton, Barbarians, Yorks.
b 9.8.29 Heckmondwike.
Centre, 28-16-5-7 (15 − 5t).
53 F+(1t) S+(1t); 54 W+ NZ− I+(1t) S+ F−;
55 W− I=(1t) F− S+; 56 W− I+(1t) S+ F−; 57

71

W+ I+ F+ S+; 58 W= A+ I+ F+ S=; 59 W−
I+ F= S=; BI > 55 SA 4-2-0-2, 59 A, NZ. .
Schoolmaster/salesman/proprietor 'The Rugby
Club' London. E's most capped centre. 28
consec caps. RFU sel.

BUXTON, John Burns　　　　*New Zealand*
Takapuna GS, Univ, Manawatu, NZ Univs,
Lincoln Coll, Canterbury, Otago, Auckland,
Takapuna, S Island.
b 31.10.33 Auckland.
Flanker, 2-1-0-1.
55 A−; 56 SA+.
Farm appraiser/meat marketing co. Capt NZ
Univs XV that beat SA 56. Coach Hawkes Bay.

BUZY, Eugène　　　　*France*
Lourdes.
b 13.2.17 Benejacq.
Prop, 17-10-0-7.
46 NZS− W+; 47 S+ I+ W− E−; 48 I− A+
S− W+ E+; 49 S− I+ E− W+ Arg+ Arg+.

BYERS, Rowland Morrow　　　　*Ireland*
Campbell Coll, Oxford Univ, NIFC,
Barbarians.
b 18.6.05 Belfast.
Wing, 5-3-1-1.
28 S+ W+; 29 E+ S− W=.
Co dir. Blue 26. Steward Irish Turf Club. Served
WW2, Lt Col in RA.

BYRNE, Edward Michael Joseph　　　*Ireland*
('Ned')
Mt St Joseph Coll Roscrea, Blackrock Coll.
b 14.9.48 Kilkenny.
Prop, 6-0-0-6.
77 S− F−; 78 F− W− E− NZ−.
Licensee/bottling plant co dir. All Ireland
hurling medal 72.

BYRNE, Francis A.　　　　*England*
Moseley, Midland Cos.
b 1873 Penns, Birmingham; *d* −.
Centre, 1-0-0-1.
1897 W−.
Played with bro Fred v W 1897.

BYRNE, James Frederick ('Fred')　　*England*
Moseley, Barbarians, Midland Cos.
b 19.6.1871 Penns, Birmingham; *d* 10.5.54
Birmingham.
FB, 13-4-1-8 (24 − 2c 2d 4p).
1894 W+ I− S−; 1895 I+ S−(1p); 1896 I−(1d);
1897 W− I−(2p) S+(1c 1d); 1898 I−(1p) S=
W+(1c); 1899 I−; BI > 1896 SA.
Co dir/industrialist. Served Boer War 1899-
1900. Played with bro Francis v W 1897. Capt E
3 times. Played in all 21 matches & 127 pts BT >
1896 SA, only player until 60 to reach 100 pts on

tour of SA. Ckt for Warwicks 1897-07 (capt 03-
7); Gentlemen v Players 05.

BYRNE, Noel Francis　　　　*Ireland*
Rockwell Coll Newbridge, UC Dublin.
b 18.12.38 Curragh, Co Kildare.
Wing, 1-0-0-1.
62 F−.
Dental surg. Bro of S.J.

BYRNE, Seamus Joseph　　　　*Ireland*
Newbridge Coll, UC Dublin, Lansdowne.
b 7.6.31 Dublin.
Wing, 3-1-0-2 (9 − 3t).
53 S+(3t) W−; 55 F−.
Medicine. Bro of N.F. 1st I int to score 3t since
Eugene Davy v S 30. Moved to US; lived in
Daytona 84.

BYRON, William G.　　　　*Ireland*
Edinburgh Univ, NIFC.
b −; *d* 61.
Forward, 11-7-1-3.
1896 E+ S= W+; 1897 E+ S−; 1898 E+ S−
W−; 1899 E+ S+ W+.

C

CABANIER, Jean-Michel ('La　　*France*
Cabane')
Montauban.
b 13.5.36 Lavilledieu, Tarn et Garonne.
Hooker/prop, 26-18-3-5 (12 − 4t).
63 R=; 64 S− Fj+; 65 S+ I= W+(1t) It+ R+;
66 S= I+ E+ W− It+ R+; 67 S− A+ E+
It+(1t) W+ I+(1t) SA− SA+(1t) NZ− R+; 68
S+ I+.
Municipal clerk.

CABROL, Henri　　　　*France*
Béziers.
b 11.2.47 Bize, Aude.
FH, 4-2-1-1 (6 − 3c).
72 A=r A+; 73 J+(3c) 74 SA−.
Motor parts salesman.

CADDELL, Ernest Duncan MC　　*Ireland*
Portora RS, Trin Coll Dublin, Wanderers.
b 18.11.1881; *d* 27.5.42.
SH, 13-6-0-7 (6 − 2t).
04 S−; 05 E+ S+ W− NZ−; 06 E+ S− W+
SA−; 07 E+(2t) S−; 08 S+ W−.
Medicine. Served WW1, Lt Col RAMC.

CADENAT, Jules ('Jularo')　　*France*
SCUF.
b −.9.1885 Béziers; *d* 65 Béziers.
Forward, 7-0-0-7.
10 S− E−; 11 W− I−; 12 W− E−; 13 I−.
Printer.

CAGNEY, Stephen J. *Ireland*
London Irish.
b −; d 61.
Lock/prop, 13-9-1-3.
25 W+; 26 F+ E+ S+ W−; 27 F+; 28 E− S+
W+; 29 F+ E+ S− W=.
National Irish Bank official.

CAHUC, François *France*
St Girons.
Flanker, 1-0-1-0.
22 S=.

CAIN, John Joseph MM *England*
St Mary's Coll Crosby, Waterloo, Lancs.
b 12.6.20.
Flanker, 1-0-0-1.
50 W−.
Banking/bus machines. Served WW2 Irish
Guards. MM 44.

CAIN, Michael James *New Zealand*
Clifton, Taranaki, Comb Servs, N Island.
b 7.7.1885 Waitara; d 27.8.51 New Plymouth.
Hooker, 4-4-0-0.
13 US+; 14 A+ A+ A+.
Freezing co employee. Took up rugby at 21. NZ
> 13 NAm, 14 A. Played for Comb Servs in
King's Cup 19.

CAIRNS, Alexander Gordon *Scotland*
George Watson's Coll, Watsonians, Oxford
Univ.
b 26.4.1878 Hamilton; d 8.4.68.
Forward, 12-7-0-5.
03 W+ I+ E+; 04 W− I+ E+; 05 W− I− E+;
06 W− I+ E−.
Writer to the Signet. Blue 1899-01. Served
WW1, Lt in Lothians & Border Horse; Capt &
Adjutant 32 Bde RFA.

CALCRAFT, William Joseph *Australia*
Manly, NSW.
b 23.3.37.
Flanker, 1-1-0-0.
85 C+.
Solicitor at merchant bank. A > 84 Fj; 84 BI.

CALDER, Finlay *Scotland*
Melville Coll, Scottish Schs, Stewart's-Melville
FP, Edinburgh, S of Scotland.
b 20.8.57 Haddington.
Flanker, 5-4-0-1.
86 F+ W− E+ I+ R+.
One of 4 rugby-playing bros. Took twin Jim's
place in S XV v F 86; also S > 84 R when Jim
unavailable. Scotland B.

CALDER, James Hamilton *Scotland*
Melville Coll, Scottish Schs, Stewart's-Melville
FP, Heriot-Watt Univ.

b 20.8.57 Haddington.
Flanker, 27-13-1-13 (12 − 3t).
81 F− W+ E−(1t) I+ NZ− NZ− R+ A+; 82
E+ I− F+ W+(1t) A+ A−; 83 I− F− W− E+
NZ=; 84 W+ E+ I+ F+(1t) A−; 85 I− F−
W−; BI > 83 NZ 1-0-0-1.
Export exec. Twin of Finlay. Scottish XV v Fj
82.

CALE, William Ray *Wales*
Newbridge, Pontypool.
b Usk.
Flanker, 7-5-0-2 (3 − 1t).
49 E+ S− I−; 50 E+(1t) S+ I+ F+.
Greengrocer. St Helens RL 50.

CALLAN, Colm Patrick *Ireland*
St Vincent's Coll Castleknock, Lansdowne,
Barbarians.
b 6.1.23 Port, Co Louth.
Lock, 10-7-0-3.
47 F− E+ S+ W−; 48 F+ E+ S+ W+; 49 F−
E+.
Insurance. Played in 4 Victory ints.

CALLANDER, Gary J. *Scotland*
Kelso High, Kelso Harlequins, Kelso.
Hooker, 1-0-0-1.
84 R−.
Scotland B v F 82.

CALLESEN, John Arthur *New Zealand*
Nelson Coll, Palmerston N HSOB, NZ Jnrs,
Manawatu, N Island.
b 24.5.50 Palmerston N.
Lock, 4-3-1-0.
74 A+ A= A+; 75 S+.
Farmer. 6ft 5in, 15st 8lb. NZ > 74 A & Fj & I,W
& E, 76 Arg & Uruguay.

CALS, Robert *France*
RCF.
Wing, 1-0-0-1.
38 G−.

CALVO, Guy ('Tachine') *France*
Lourdes.
b 13.9.33 Lourdes.
Wing, 2-0-0-2.
61 NZ− NZ−.

CAMBÉRABÉRO, Didier *France*
La Voulte, French Univs, Béziers.
b 9.1.61 La Voulte.
FH, 7-6-0-1 (44 − 2t 12c 1d 3p).
82 R− Arg+(1p) Arg+(1c 1p); 83 E+(1p)
W+(1d); 85 J+(5c) J+(2t 6c).
Professor of PE. Son of Guy, nephew of Lilian.
French Jnrs v G, Soviet Union 80-1. France B v
W 81, 82, E 81. F v G 82. F > 85 Arg.

CAMBÉRABÉRO, Guy *France*
La Voulte.
b 27.5.36 Soubion, Landes.
FH, 14-10-1-3 (113 − 2t 19c 12d 11p).
61 NZ−; 62 R−; 64 R+(1t 1d); 67 A+(1c 1d 4p)
E+(2c 1d 1p) It+(9c 1d 2p) W+(1t 1c 2d 1p)
I+(1c 2d) SA− SA+(2c 2d) SA=(1p); 68
S+(1c) E+(1c 1d 1p) W+(1c 1d 1p).
Tobacconist. Father of Didier, bro of Lilian.
French Champ rec 32 pts, 67. 5d (3 apps) 67,
most in Champ season. F > 67 SA.

CAMBÉRABÉRO, Lilian *France*
La Voulte.
b 15.7.37 St-Vincent-de-Tyrosse.
SH, 13-11-1-1 (6 − 2t).
64 R+; 65 S+ I=; 66 E+ W−; 67 A+(1t) E+
It+ W+ I+; 68 S+ E+ W+(1t).
Tobacconist. Bro of Guy, uncle of Didier.

CAMBRE, Théo *France*
Oloron.
FB, 4-2-0-2.
20 E− W− I+ US+.

CAMEL, André *France*
Toulouse.
b 9.1.05 Toulouse.
Lock/flanker, 15-7-0-8 (9 − 3t).
28 S−(1t) NSW−(1t) I− E− G+ W+; 29 W−
(1t) E− G+; 30 S+ I+ E− G+ W−; 35 G+.
Played with twin bro Marcel v W & E 29.

CAMEL, Marcel *France*
Toulouse.
b 9.1.05 Toulouse.
Lock, 3-0-0-3.
29 S− W− E−.
Played with twin bro André v W & E 29.

CAMERON, Alan Douglas *Scotland*
Hillhead HS, Hillhead HSFP.
b 4.3.24.
Wing/centre, 3-0-0-3.
51 F−; 54 F− W−.
Co dir.

CAMERON, Alan Stewart *Australia*
Newington Coll, NSW.
b 18.11.29 Narranderra, NSW.
Lock, 20-5-0-15 (3 − 1t).
51 NZ− NZ− NZ−; 52 Fj+ Fj− NZ+ NZ−; 53
SA− SA+ SA− SA−; 54 Fj+(1t) Fj−; 55 NZ−
NZ− NZ+; 56 SA− SA−; 57 NZ−; 58 I−.
Stock auctioneer.

CAMERON, Alexander William *Scotland*
Cumming
George Watson's Coll, Watsonians.
b 3.3.1866; *d* 14.3.57 Swansea.
FB, 3-1-0-2.

1887 W+; 1893 W−; 1894 I−.
Medicine. Shared practice in W with E.T.
Morgan.

CAMERON, Angus *Scotland*
Glasgow HS, Glasgow HSFP, Barbarians.
b 24.6.29.
FH/centre/FB, 17-5-0-12 (18 − 2t 1d 3p).
48 W−; 50 I− E+; 51 F− W+ I− E−(1t) SA−;
53 I− E−; 55 F− W+ I+(1d) E−(1t 1p); 56
F+(1p) W−(1p) I−; BI > 55 SA 2-1-0-1.
Wholesale grocer. Capt S in 0-44 defeat by SA,
51. Played with bro Donald v I, E 53. 44 pts (9
apps) BI > 55 SA.

CAMERON, Donald *Scotland*
Glasgow HS, Glasgow HSFP.
b 25.12.27 Glasgow.
Centre, 6-0-0-6.
53 I− E−; 54 F− NZ− I− E−.
Lawyer. Played with bro Angus v I, E 53.

CAMERON, Donald *New Zealand*
Stratford HS, Stratford, Taranaki, N Island.
b 15.7.1887 Waitara; *d* 25.8.47 New Plymouth.
Wing, 3-2-1-0.
08 AW+(1t) AW= AW+.
Farmer. Father R.H. rep Taranaki 1885.

CAMERON, E.D. *Ireland*
Coleraine AI, Bective Rgrs.
Half-back, 2-0-0-2.
1891 S− W−.

CAMERON, Lachlan Murray *New Zealand*
Te Kauwhata Coll, Hamilton Boys' HS, Univ,
NZ Jnrs, NZ Colts, NZ Univs, Manawatu.
b 12.4.59 Hamilton.
2nd five-eighth/centre, 5-3-0-2.
80 A−; 81 SA+r SA− SA+ R+.
Student. NZ v Arg 79. NZ > 80 A & Fj, 81 R &
F.

CAMERON, Neil William *Scotland*
Shrewsbury Sch, Glasgow Univ.
b 2.9.25 Carlisle; *d* 79.
FB, 3-0-0-3 (2 − 1c).
52 E−; 53 F−(1c) W−.
Medicine.

CAMICAS, Fernand *France*
Tarbes.
b −.5.1899 Tarbes; *d* 11.5.73 Toulouse.
Hooker, 10-2-0-8.
27 G−; 28 S− I− E− G+ W+; 29 I− S− W−
E−.

CAMO, Ernest *France*
Villeneuve.
b − ; *d* −.10.78 Villeneuve sur Lot.

No 8/flanker, 6-4-0-2.
31 I+ S− W− E+ G+; 32 G+.

CAMPAÈS, André   *France*
Lourdes.
 b 30.3.44 Lourdes.
Wing, 14-8-1-5 (12 − 4t).
65 W+; 67 NZ−(1t) 68 S+(1t) I+(1t) E+ W+
Cz+ NZ− NZ− A−; 69 S− W=(1t); 72 R+; 73
NZ+.
Accountant.

CAMPBELL, Alister John   *Scotland*
Hawick HS, Hawick.
 b 1.1.59.
Lock, 12-6-0-6.
84 I+ F+ R−; 85 I− F− W− E−; 86 F+ W−
E+ I+ R+.
Scottish XV v Netherlands 78. Scotland B v F
83-4; I 83. S > 84 R.

CAMPBELL, Charles Eric   *Ireland*
Wesley Coll, O Wesley.
 b 12.12.42 Tullow, Co Carlow.
Lock, 1-0-1-0.
70 SA=.
Petroleum distributors exec.

CAMPBELL, David Alfred DFC   *England*
King's Sch Parramatta (A), Cambridge Univ.
 b Adelong, NSW 15; *d* 82.
Flanker, 2-2-0-0.
37 W+ I+.
Poet/grazier. Blue 36. Served WW2. DFC &
bar.

CAMPBELL, Edward   *Ireland*
Fitzhardinge DSO
RS Dungannon, Corrig Coll Kingstown, Trin
Coll Dublin, Monkstown, Leinster.
 b 17.1.1880; *d* 13.12.57.
Wing, 4-2-0-2 (3 − 1t).
1899 S+(1t) W+; 1900 E− W−.
Minister. Scored 1st int t at Inverleith, v S 1899.
Served WW1, Deputy Acting Chaplain General
17; mentioned in despatches 16-17, DSO 17.

CAMPBELL, George Theophilus   *Scotland*
Fettes Coll, London Scottish, Barbarians, Mdx.
 b 17.10.1872; *d* 28.3.24 London.
Wing/centre, 17-9-3-5 (10 − 2t 1d).
1892 W+(1t) I+ E−; 1893 I= E+(1d); 1894
W− I− E+; 1895 W+ I+(1t) E+; 1896 W− I=
E+; 1897 I+; 1899 I−; 1900 E=.
Outstanding athlete, ckter. Played in Mdx XV
with A.J. Gould.

CAMPBELL, H.H.   *Scotland*
Oundle Sch, Cambridge Univ, London Scottish,
Barbarians.
Flanker/lock, 4-1-0-3.

47 I− E−; 48 I− E+.
Blue 46. Played in 2 Servs ints.

CAMPBELL, James Alexander   *Scotland*
Merchiston Castle Sch, Cambridge Univ, W of
S.
 b 1858 Lake Athabasca, C; *d* 20.6.02
Winnipeg.
Back, 5-1-3-1.
1878 E=; 1879 I+ E=; 1881 I− E=.
Fur trader. Capped from sch.

CAMPBELL, John Argentine   *Scotland*
Fettes Coll, Cambridge Univ.
 b 20.10.1877 Arg; *d* 1.12.17 Germany.
Forward, 1-0-1-0.
1900 I=.
Schoolmaster/rancher. Blue 1897-9; ath blue
1898. Served WW1, Lt 17th Lancers, then
Inniskilling Dragoons. Reported missing 1.12.17
in F; died of wounds in German hosp.

CAMPBELL, John Denison   *Australia*
('Dinny')
NSW.
 b 22.7.1889 Penrith, NSW; *d* 31.8.66 Sydney.
Centre, 3-1-0-2.
10 NZ− NZ+ NZ−.
Shopkeeper. RL 10.

CAMPBELL, Norman   *Scotland*
MacDonald
Sherborne Sch, London Univ, London Scottish.
 b 31 Tylorstown.
SH, 2-1-0-1.
56 F+ W−.
Medicine. Served in RAMC.

CAMPBELL, Samuel Burnside   *Ireland*
Boyd MC
Foyle Coll, Edinburgh Univ, Derry.
 b 29.6.1889; *d* 1.3.71.
Forward, 12-7-0-5.
11 E+ S+ W− F+; 12 F+ E− S+ W+ SA−; 13
E− S− F+.
Medicine. Served WW1.

CAMPBELL, Seamus Oliver   *Ireland*
('Ollie')
Belvedere Coll, Dublin Coll of Commerce, O
Belvedere, Leinster.
 b 3.3.54 Dublin.
FH/centre, 22-10-0-12 (217 − 1t 15c 7d 54p).
76 A−; 79 A+(2c 1d 4p) A+(2d 1p); 80 E−(3p)
S+(1c 1d 3p) F−(1c 1d 3p) W+(3c 1p); 81 F−
(3p) W− E−(1d) S−(1c 1p) SA−(2c 1p); 82
W+(1c 2p) E+(1c 2p) S+(1d 6p) F−(3p); 83
S+(1c 3p) F+(1c 4p) W−(2p) E+(1t 1c 5p); 84
F−(4p) W−(3p); BI > 80 SA 3(1r)-1-0-2; 83 NZ
4-0-0-4.
Textiles co dir. I's ldg pts scorer. World's most p

75

(6) in an int, I v S 82. Most p (14) in Champ season (4 apps), 83. Champ rec 52 pts 83, 46pts 81, 82. Champ rec 21 pts v S 82 & E 83. 60 pts I > 79 A, most by I player on tour (inc rec 19 pts v A); I > 81 SA. Top scorer BI > 80 SA (60); 83 NZ (124).

CAMPBELL-LAMERTON, *Scotland*
Jeremy R.F.
London Scottish, Scots Guards, The Army.
Lock, 1-1-0-0.
86 F+.
The Army. Son of M. J.

CAMPBELL-LAMERTON, *Scotland*
Michael John
Ottershaw Sch, Guildford, Halifax, The Army,
Comb Servs, Blackheath, London Scottish,
Barbarians, Surrey, Yorks.
b 1.8.33.
Lock, 23-11-3-9.
61 F− SA− W+ I+; 62 F− W+ I+ E=; 63 F+
W− I+ E−; 64 I+ E+; 65 F− W− I− E=
SA+; 66 F= W− I+ E+; BI > 62 SA 4-1-0-3;
66 A 2-2-0-0, NZ 2-0-0-2.
The Army. Father of Jeremy. Runner-up in shot
& discus All Irish champs 58. Comb Servs v SA
60. Capt BI > 66 NZ. After leaving Army,
Domestic Bursar at Balliol Coll, Oxford.

CAMPESE, David Ian *Australia*
Queanbeyan, ACT.
b 21.10.62.
Wing, 20-12-1-7 (77 − 10t 8c 7p).
82 NZ−(1t) NZ+(1t) NZ−; 83 US+(4t 1c)
Arg−(1p) Arg+(1t 3c 1p) NZ− It+(3c 1p)
F=(1c 1p) F−(1p); 84 Fj+ NZ+ NZ−(1p) NZ−
(1t 1p) E+ I+ W+ S+(2t); 85 Fj+ Fj+.
Trainee mgr. A Under 21s 81-3. A > 82 NZ; 83
It & F; 84 Fj; 84 BI. Australian Player of Year
82. 4t v US 83 equ Greg Cornelsen's A int rec.

CANDLER, Peter Laurence *England*
Sherborne Sch, Cambridge Univ, Bart's Hosp,
Richmond, Barbarians, Mdx.
b 28.1.14.
FH, 10-5-2-3 (6 − 2t).
35 W=; 36 NZ+ W= I− S+(1t); 37 W+ I+ S+;
38 W−(1t) S−.
Medicine. Blue 34. Served WW2, Lt Col in
RAMC.

CANNELL, Lewis Bernard *England*
St Richard's Coll Droitwich, Northampton GS,
Oxford Univ, St Mary's Hosp, Northampton,
RAF, Comb Servs, Barbarians, London Cos, E
Midlands, Mdx.
b 10.6.26 Coventry.
Centre, 19-9-1-9 (6 − 2t).
48 F−; 49 W− I− F+(1t) S+; 50 W− I+ F− S−
; 52 SA− W−; 53 W+(1t) I= F+; 56 I+ S+ F−;

57 W+ I+.
Medicine. Blue 48-50. Radiologist at Addington
Hosp, Durban SA 69.

CANNIFFE, Donal Martin *Ireland*
Cork Constitution, Lansdowne, Munster.
b 14.8.49 Mullingar.
SH, 2-1-0-1.
76 W− E+.
Insurance. Ireland B.

CANNIFFE, William Dennis *Australia*
Qld.
b 1885; *d* 56.
Forward, 1-0-0-1.
07 NZ−.
Marine engr.

CANTONI, Jack ('Canto') *France*
Béziers.
b 11.5.48 Carmaux, Tarn.
Wing/FB, 17-6-3-8 (13 − 3t 1d).
70 W−(1t) R+; 71 S+ I= E=(1t) W− SA−
SA=(1d) A− R+(1t); 72 S− I−; 73 S+ NZ+
W+ I−; 75 W−r.
PE teacher.

CANTRELL, John Leo *Ireland*
Blackrock Coll, UC Dublin, Comb Univs,
Leinster.
b 10.1.54 Limerick.
Hooker, 9-1-0-8.
76 A− F− W− E+ S−; 81 S− SA− SA− A−.
Architect. Ireland B. I > 81 SA.

CAPDOUZE, Jean ('Nono') *France*
Pau.
b 30.8.42 Salies-de-Béarn.
Centre/FH, 6-4-1-1 (6 − 2t).
64 SA+ Fj+(2t) R+; 65 S+ I= E−.
Baker. RL.

CAPENDEGUY, Jean-Michel *France*
Bégles.
b 5.3.44 Ciboure; *d* 1.1.68.
Wing, 2-1-0-1 (3 − 1t).
67 NZ− R+(1t).
PE teacher.

CAPITANI, Philibert *France*
Toulon.
Lock, 2-2-0-0.
54 Arg+ Arg+.

CAPLAN, David William Nigel *England*
Leeds GS, Newcastle Univ, Oxford Univ,
Headingley.
b 5.4.54 Leeds.
FB, 2-2-0-0.
78 S+ I+.
Dentist.

CAPMAU, A. *France*
Toulouse.
Forward, 1-0-0-1 (3 − 1t).
14 E−(1t).

CARABIGNAC, Joseph *France*
Agen.
b 10.10.29 Agen; *d* 22.2.73 Valence d'Agen.
FH, 7-2-0-5 (9 − 3d).
51 S+ I−; 52 SA−(1d) W− E−; 53 S+(1d) I−
(1d).

CARBERRY, Christopher *Australia*
Michael
Sydney Univ, Brisbane, NSW.
b 27.4.51.
Hooker, 13-9-0-4.
73 Tg+ E−; 76 I+ US+ Fj+ Fj+ Fj+; 81 F+
F+ I+ W− S−; 82 E−.
Solicitor. A > 73-4 & 75-6 BI.

CARBONNE, P. *France*
Perpignan.
SH, 1-0-0-1.
27 W−.

CARDUS, Richard Michael *England*
Foxwood Sch, Roundhay, Wasps.
b 23.5.56 Leeds.
Centre, 2-1-0-1.
79 F+ W−.

CARDY, Alan Michael *Australia*
Katoomba HS, NSW.
b 12.9.45.
Wing, 9-2-0-7 (6 − 2t).
66 BI− BI− W+(1t) S−; 67 E+ I− F−; 68
NZ−(1t) NZ−.
PE teacher. RL.

CARELSE, Gabriel ('Gawie') *South Africa*
E Prov.
b 21.7.41 Port Elizabeth.
Lock, 14-9-0-5.
64 W+ F−; 65 I− S−; 67 F+ F+ F−; 68 F+
F+; 69 A+ A+ A+ A+; 69-70 S−.
Garage proprietor.

CAREW, Patrick James ('Paddy') *Australia*
Qld.
b 10.9.1876; *d* 46.
Forward, 4-1-0-3.
1899 BT+ BT− BT− BT−.
Clerk.

CAREY, Godfrey Mohun *England*
Sherborne Sch, Oxford Univ, Blackheath,
Barbarians, Som.
b 17.8.1872 Guernsey; *d* 18.12.27.
Forward, 5-3-0-2 (3 − 1t).
1895 W+(1t) I+ S−; 1896 W+ I−.

Schoolmaster. Blue 1891-2,4. Son of Sir
Godfrey Carey. Barbarians comm. Taught at
Sherborne 1897-27.

CARLETON, John *England*
Upholland GS, Chester Coll, Orrell, Cheshire.
b 24.11.55 Orrell.
Wing, 26-12-3-11 (28 − 7t).
79 NZ−; 80 I+ F+(1t) W+ S+(3t); 81 W− S+
I+ F− Arg= Arg+; 82 A+ S= I− F+(1t)
W+(1t); 83 F− W=(1t) S− I− NZ+; 84 S− I+
F− W− A−; BI > 80 SA 3-1-0-2; 83 NZ 3-0-0-
3.
Schoolmaster/building soc employee. E
Students v J 76. E Under 23s > 77 Can. England
XV v US 78. E > 79 Far East; 81 Arg; 82 US &
Can. Resigned as maths, PE teacher at Park HS,
Hindley, Lancs, to tour BI > 80 SA. Work
prevented his touring with E > 84 SA.

CARLETON, Sydney Russell *New Zealand*
Christchurch Boys' HS, HSOB, Canterbury, S
Island.
b 22.2.04 Christchurch; *d* 23.10.73
Christchurch.
Centre/FB/2nd five-eighth, 6-1-0-5.
28 SA− SA+ SA−; 29 A− A− A−.
Warehouseman. NZ > 28 SA, 29 A.

CARLSON, Raymond Allen *South Africa*
W Prov.
b 2.10.48 E London.
FB, 1-0-0-1.
72 E−.
Rugby administrator.

CARMICHAEL, Alexander *Scotland*
Bennett ('Sandy') MBE
Loretto Sch, W of S, Barbarians.
b 2.2.44 Glasgow.
Prop, 50-19-0-31 (3 − 1t).
67 I− NZ−; 68 F− W− I− E− A+; 69 F+ W−
I− E− SA+; 70 F− W− I− E+ A−; 71 F−
W−(1t) I− E+ E+; 72 F+ W− E+ NZ−; 73
F− W+ I+ E− P+; 74 W− E+ I− F+; 75 I+
F− W− E− NZ− A+; 76 F− W− E+ I+; 77
E− I+r F− W−; 78 I−; BI > 71 NZ; 74 SA.
Plant hire firm. S's most capped prop. Played
twice as flanker S > 69 Arg. Scottish XV v Arg
73; Tg 74. Suffered multiple facial fractures BI v
Canterbury 71; inj ended tour. MBE 77.

CARMICHAEL, James Howden *Scotland*
George Watson's Coll, Watsonians, Edinburgh
Univ.
22.3.1900 Edinburgh.
Wing, 3-1-0-2.
21 F− W+ I−.
Provision merchant.

CARMICHAEL, Philip P.   *Australia*
St Joseph's Coll, Qld.
 b 25.1.1884 Brisbane; *d* −.9.73.
FB, 4-1-0-3 (6 − 1gm 1p).
04 BT−; 07 NZ−(1gm 1p); 08 W−; 09 E+.
Clerk. Ldg scorer, 122 pts, A > BI 08-9.
Olympic rugby gold medal 08.

CAROLIN, Harold William   *South Africa*
('Paddy')
Diocesan Coll Rondebosch, Villagers,
Mooreesburg, W Prov.
 b 1880; *d* −.
Half-back, 3-2-0-1.
03 BT+; 06 S− I+.
Lawyer. Vice-capt SA > 06 BI; capt v S 06.
16pts SA v Yorks 06. Ckt for W Prov 03-8. All−
round sportsman; Victor Ludorum 4 yrs running
at Diocesan Coll. Went in to law partnership in
Mooreesburg with fellow Springbok, Freddie
Luyt.

CARON, Lucien   *France*
Lyon Ol, Castres.
 b 16.12.16 Lyon.
Prop, 10-6-0-4 (3 − 1t).
47 E−; 48 I− A+ W+ E+; 49 S− I+ E− W+
Arg+(1t).

CARPENDALE, Maxwell John   *Ireland*
RMC Sandhurst, Monkstown.
 b 1865; *d* −.1.41.
Wing, 4-1-0-3 (1d).
1886 S−; 1887 W−; 1888 W+(1d) S−.
The Army.

CARPENTER, Alfred Denzel   *England*
Littledean, Cinderford, Gloucester, RAF,
Barbarians, Glos.
 b 23.7.1900 Mitcheldean; *d* 18.4.74.
Prop, 1-0-0-1.
32 SA−.
Collier. Served WW2, RAF Rgt. Early
education in Swansea.

CARPENTER, Macquarie   *Australia*
Gordon ('Max')
Randwick HS, Victoria.
 b 11.
Wing, 2-0-0-2 (20 − 2t 1c 4p).
38 NZ−(3p) NZ−(2t 1c 1p).
Army/wholesale butcher.

CARPENTIER, Manuel   *France*
Lourdes.
 b 14.10.59 Calais.
No 8/lock, 8-2-0-6.
80 E− SA− R−; 81 S+ I+ A−; 82 E− S−.
Locksmith. F > 80 SA.

CARR, Ernest T.A.   *Australia*
NSW.
 b 11.5.1885; *d* 36.
Wing, 6-1-0-5 (3 − 1t).
13 NZ−(1t) NZ− NZ+; 14 NZ− NZ− NZ−.

CARR, Nigel John   *Ireland*
Regent House, Queen's Univ Belfast, Ards,
Ulster.
 b 27.7.59 Belfast.
Flanker, 7-3-1-3.
85 S+ F= W+ E+; 86 W− E− S−.
PhD. I Under 23s; Ireland B v S 79, 84, v E 80,
82. Ulster v A 84. BI v Rest of World, Cardiff
86.

CARR, Robert Stanley Leonard   *England*
MC
Cranleigh Sch, O Cranleighans, Manchester,
Moseley.
 b 11.7.17; *d* c77.
Wing, 3-2-0-1.
39 W+ I− S+.
Co dir. Served WW2 Manchester Rgt & King's
African Rifles. MC 41.

CARRÈRE, Christian Roger   *France*
Tarbes Lycée, Toulon.
 b 27.7.43 Tarbes.
No 8/flanker, 27-15-2-10 (12 − 4t).
66 R+; 67 S−(1t) A+ E+ W+ I+ SA− SA+
SA= NZ− R+; 68 S+ I+ E+ W+(1t) Cz+(1t)
NZ−(1t) A− R−; 69 S− I−; 70 S+ I+ W−
E+; 71 E= W−.
PR exec. Capt F > 68 NZ & A; 71 SA.

CARRÈRE, Jean ('Nonou')   *France*
Vichy, Toulon.
 b 5.4.30 Argeles sur Mer.
Flanker, 8-2-1-5.
56 S−; 57 E− W− R+; 58 S− SA= SA+; 59
I−.
PE instructor.

CARRÈRE, Robert   *France*
Mont-de-Marsan.
 b 21.
Prop, 2-1-0-1.
53 E− It+.
Pork butcher.

CARRICK, James Stewart   *Scotland*
Glasgow Acad, Glasgow Academicals.
 b 4.9.1855; *d* 2.1.23 Seattle, USA.
FB, 2-1-0-1.
1876 E−; 1877 E+.
Ump S v I, S v E 1886, I v S, S v W, E v S 1887.
Pres SRU 1886-7. Ckt for S.

CARRINGTON, Kenneth Roy   *New Zealand*
Opotiki Coll, Rutherford HS, Waitemata, Bay

of Plenty, Edgecumbe, Auckland, N Island, NZ Maoris, Casale (It).
b 3.9.50 Whakatane.
Wing, 3-0-1-2.
71 BI− BI− BI=.
PE & science teacher. Noted sprinter at sch.

CARROLL, Claude   *Ireland*
Belvedere Coll, Bective Rgrs.
b −; *d* 38 Letterkenny.
Lock, 1-0-0-1.
30 F−.
Bank official. Died from perforated ulcer.

CARROLL, Daniel Brendan   *Australia*
St Aloysius Coll, Stanford Univ, NSW.
b 17.11.1889 Melbourne; *d* 55 San Francisco.
Wing/SH, 2-1-0-1 (3 − 1t).
08 W−; 12 US+(1t).
Oil co exec. Won 2 Olympic gold medals for rugby, A v GB, London 08 & US v F, Antwerp 20. A > US 12, stayed behind to study geology. Stanford Univ v NZ 13. Served WW1 initially with US Army. Seconded to Australian Army to play in their King's Cup side at end of WW1. Emigrated to US 19. Became US football coach.

CARROLL, John Charles   *Australia*
Sydney Tech HS, NSW.
b 14.9.25.
Flanker, 1-0-0-1.
53 SA−.
Carpenter.

CARROLL, John Hugh   *Australia*
Newington Coll, NSW.
b 20.3.34.
Lock, 7-1-1-5 (3 − 1t).
58 M= M− NZ− NZ+ NZ−(1t); 59 BI− BI−.
Wool buyer.

CARROLL, Raymond   *Ireland*
Castleknock Sch, Lansdowne.
b 9.2.26 Dublin.
SH, 3-1-0-2.
47 F−; 50 S+ W−.
Co dir.

CARSON, James   *Australia*
Pirates, NSW.
b c1870 Dunedin, NZ; *d* 03 Sydney.
Forward, 1-1-0-0.
1899 BT+.
Fireman. Went to A c1890, died of TB at 33. NSW > NZ 1894. Uncle of Bill Carson, NZ rep at rugby (non Test) & ckt.

CARSON, Peter John   *Australia*
NSW.
b 52.

SH, 2-2-0-0 (3 − 1t).
79 NZ+; 80 NZ+(1t).

CARTWRIGHT, Vincent Henry   *England*
('Lump') DSO
Rugby Sch, Nottingham, Oxford Univ, Harlequins, Barbarians, Midlands.
b 10.9.1882 Nottingham; *d* 25.11.65 Loughborough.
Forward, 14-2-2-10 (8 − 4c).
03 W− I− S−; 04 W= S−; 05 W− I− S− NZ−; 06 W− I− S+ F+(4c) SA=.
Solicitor. Blue 01-4. Capt Nottingham in Midland Cos Cup win 06. Midland Cos v NZ 05. Ref I v S 06, S v I 09, I v S, F v I 10, S v I 11. Ref Centenary Match at Rugby Sch 1.11.23. England sel. Rep SA on RFU 21-9. IB mem 29-31. RFU comm; pres 28-9. Ckt for Notts 01-4. Served WW1, Maj in R Marines; twice mentioned in despatches. DSO 18. Croix de Guerre.

CASEMENT, Brabazon   *Ireland*
Newcomer
RS Dungannon, Trin Coll Dublin.
b 1852 Co Antrim; *d* 10 Macleayshire, A.
Forward/back, 3-0-0-3.
1875 E− E−; 1879 E−.
Medicine/stockbreeder/landowner. Died in coach accident.

CASEMENT, Francis DSO   *Ireland*
Coleraine AI, Trin Coll Dublin.
b 1881; *d* 14.8.67.
Centre, 3-2-0-1.
06 E+ S− W+.
The Army. Served WW1, Army Medical Service; DSO 17.

CASEY, James C. ('Ter')   *Ireland*
Young Munster.
b Limerick.
Hooker, 2-1-0-1.
30 S+; 32 E−.
Timber mill worker.

CASEY, Patrick Joseph   *Ireland*
CBC Monkstown, UC Dublin, Lansdowne.
b 4.8.41 Dublin.
FH/centre/wing, 12-4-2-6 (9 − 3t).
63 F− E= S− W+(1t) NZ−; 64 E+(1t) S− W− F−(1t); 65 F= E+ S+.
Accountant.

CASEY, Stephen Timothy   *New Zealand*
Christian Bros' Sch, Southern, Otago, S Island.
b 24.12.1882 Dunedin; *d* 10.8.60 Dunedin.
Hooker, 8-6-1-1.
05 S+ I+ E+ W−; 07 A+ A+ A=; 08 AW+.
Storeman. NZ > 05 A, 05-6 BI,F & NAm, 07 A. Bro Mick rep Otago 01-8.

CASEY, Terence Vincent   *Australia*
NSW.
b 38.
FB, 6-3-0-3 (34 − 2c 2d 8p).
63 SA+(1p) SA+(1c 1d 1p) SA−(1d 1p); 64
NZ−(2p) NZ− NZ+(1c 3p).
Schoolmaster. 55 pts A > 64 NZ.

CASSAGNE, P.   *France*
Bourgogne.
Centre, 1-1-0-0 (4 − 1t).
85 J+r(1t).

CASSAGNE, Paul   *France*
Pau.
Lock, 1-1-0-0 (10 − 5c).
57 It+(5c).

CASSAYET, Aimé   *France*
Tarbes, Narbonne.
b 1898 Tarbes; *d* 26.5.27 Narbonne.
Lock/no 8, 31-5-2-24 (9 − 3t).
20 S− E− W− US+; 21 W− E− I+(1t); 22 S=
E=(1t) W−; 23 S− W− E− I+ ; 24 S+ E− W−
R+ US−; 25 I− NZ−(1t) S− W−; 26 S− I−
E− W− M−; 27 I− S− W−.

CASSELS, David Young   *Scotland*
Merchiston Castle Sch, W of S.
b 1859; *d* 25.1.23 Bothwell.
Forward, 7-4-1-2.
1880 E=; 1881 I−; 1882 I+ E+; 1883 W+ I+
E−.
Iron master. Pres SRU 08-9.

CASSIÈDE, Marcel ('Titi')   *France*
Dax.
b 24.8.34 Pontoux.
Lock, 3-1-1-1.
61 NZ− A+ R=.

CASTENS, Herbert Hayton   *South Africa*
Rugby Sch, Oxford Univ, Middlesex, S of
England, Villagers, W Prov.
b 23.11.1864 Somerset E; *d* 18.10.29 London.
Forward, 1-0-0-1.
1891 BT−.
Barrister. Blue 1886-7. SA's 1st capt, v BT 1891;
ref BT 1st match, v Cape Town Clubs & SA v
BT 3rd Test. Rugby coach at Diocesan Coll.
Capt Rugby Sch at ckt; also played for W Prov
1890-1 (165 no v E Prov 1891). 1st SA ckt capt;
led 1894 tour to E.

CASTETS, Jean   *France*
Toulon.
Lock, 3-1-0-2.
23 W− E− I+.
Seaman.

CATCHESIDE, Howard Carston   *England*
OBE
Oundle Sch, Percy Pk, Northumb.
b 18.8.1899.
Wing, 8-5-1-2 (18 − 6t).
24 W+(2t) I+(2t) F+(1t) S+(1t); 26 W= I−; 27
I+ S−.
Ship broker/coal exporter. Served WW1 2nd Lt
RFA. Served WW2. Reached rank of Lt Col.
OBE (Mil) 45. E sel 36-62 (chmn 51-62).

CATCHPOLE, Kenneth William   *Australia*
The Scots Coll, Sydney Univ, NSW.
b 21.6.39.
SH, 27-9-1-17 (9 − 3t).
61 Fj+(1t) Fj+ Fj= SA− SA− F−; 62 NZ−
NZ− NZ−; 63 SA+ SA+ SA−; 64 NZ− NZ−
NZ+; 65 SA+ SA+; 66 BI− BI− W+ S−; 67
E+(1t) I− F− I−(1t) NZ−; 68 NZ−.
Chemical engr. Capt A 13 times. Capt A > 67
NZ.

CATHCART, Charles Walker   *Scotland*
CBE
Loretto Sch, Edinburgh Univ.
b 16.3.1853 Edinburgh; *d* 22.2.32.
Forward, 3-0-1-2 (1d).
1872 E−(1d); 1873 E=; 1876 E−.
Surgeon. Bro-in-law of J.G. Tait. Sc S's 1st d, v
E 1872.

CATLEY, Evelyn Haswell   *New Zealand*
Orini Sch, King's Coll, Taupiri, Hamilton OB,
Waikato, Huntley, N Island.
b 23.9.15 Hamilton; *d* 23.3.75 Hamilton.
Hooker, 7-3-0-4.
46 A+; 47 A+ A+; 49 SA− SA− SA− SA−.
Farmer. NZ > 47 A, 49 SA. 22-yr 1st class
career, 35-56. Son Gary rep Waikato 62-7.

CATTELL, Alfred   *Wales*
Cottesmore Sch, St Mark's C of E Coll Chelsea,
Oxford Univ, Llanelli.
b 1857 Cottesmore, Rutland; *d* 10.9.33
Sheffield.
Forward, 2-0-0-2.
1882 E−; 1883 S−.
Headmaster/wholesaler. Lord Mayor of
Sheffield. Chmn Sheff Utd FC.

CATTELL, Richard Henry   *England*
Burdon
Trin Coll Stratford-on-Avon, Oxford Univ,
Blackheath, Moseley, Barbarians, Midland Cos.
b 23.3.1871 Erdington, Birmingham; *d* 19.7.48.
Half-back, 7-3-0-4 (6 − 2t).
1895 W+ I+ S−; 1896 W+(2t) I− S−; 1900
W−.
Clergyman. Blue 1893. Ordained 1897.
Switched to football 1898; played for Welwyn

AFC until 03 & Tring FC until 06. Served WW1 as chaplain to Forces.

CAUGHEY, Sir Thomas   *New Zealand*
Harcourt Clarke ('Pat') OBE OStJ
Mt Albert Prmy Sch, King's Coll, Univ, NZ
Univs, Auckland, N Island.
b 4.7.11 Auckland.
Centre/2nd five-eighth/wing, 9-4-1-4 (9 − 3t).
32 A− A+; 34 A− A=; 35 S+(3t) I+; 36 E−
A+; 37 SA−.
Business. NZ > 32 A (12t); 34 & 36 A; 35-6 BI
& C (18t). All−round sportsman at sch. Cousins
Brian & David rep Auckland. Mem Auckland
Hosp Bd 53-71; kt 72.

CAUJOLLE, Jean   *France*
Tarbes.
b 1888 Tarbes; *d* 46 Tarbes.
FB, 5-0-0-5.
09 E−; 13 SA− E−; 14 W− E−
Café proprietor.

CAULTON, Ralph Walter   *New Zealand*
Wellington Coll, Poneke, Wellington, N Island.
b 10.1.37 Wellington.
Wing, 16-11-1-4 (24 − 8t).
59 BI+(2t) BI+(2t) BI−; 60 SA− SA−; 61 F+;
63 E+(2t) E+; 63 I+ W+; 64 E+(1t) S=
F+(1t) A+ A+ A−.
Clerk/sales rep/mgr wine & spirits co. NZ > 60
A & SA (11t); 63-4 BI,F & C (14t). NZRFU
coaching comm 78-80.

CAUNÈGRE, Robert   *France*
SBUC.
Wing, 2-2-0-0 (6 − 2t).
38 R+(1t) G+(1t).

CAUSSADE, Alain   *France*
Lourdes.
b 27.7.52 Juillan.
FH, 12-6-1-5 (42 − 2t 5c 5d 3p).
78 R+(1d); 79 I=(1t) W+ E− NZ−(1d)
NZ+(1t 1c 1d) R+(1c 2p); 80 W−(1c 1d) E−(1c
1p) S−(1d); 81 S+r(1c) I+.
Municipal employee.

CAUSSARIEU, Georges   *France*
Pau.
b − ; *d* −.9.74 St Pée-sur-Nivelle.
Centre, 1-0-0-1.
29 I−.
Customs inspector. RL.

CAVE, John Watkins   *England*
Wellington Coll, Cambridge Univ, Richmond,
Surrey.
b 5.2.1867 Surbiton; *d* 4.12.49 Wokingham.
Forward, 1-1-0-0.
1889 NZN+.

Schoolmaster. Blue 1887-8. Son of Hon Mr
Justice Cave. Taught at Wellington 1893-23.

CAVE, William Thomas Charles   *England*
Tonbridge Sch, Cambridge Univ, Blackheath,
Barbarians, Kent.
b 24.11.1882; *d* −.
Forward, 1-0-0-1.
05 W−; BT > 03 SA.
Solicitor. Blue 02-4. Served WW1; POW.

CAWKWELL, George Law   *Scotland*
King's Coll NZ, Oxford Univ, Barbarians.
b 25.10.19 Auckland, NZ.
Lock, 1-0-0-1.
47 F−.
University lecturer. Blue 46-7.

CAWSEY, Roy Milton   *Australia*
NSW.
b 22; *d* 6.5.74.
FB, 3-2-0-1 (2 − 1c).
49 M− NZ+(1c) NZ+.
Banking.

CAYREFOURCQ, Edmond   *France*
Tarbes.
Wing, 1-0-0-1.
21 E−.

CAZALS, Pierre   *France*
Mont-de-Marsan.
b 8.12.31 Mont-de-Marsan.
Prop, 3-1-1-1.
61 NZ− A+ R=.

CAZAUX, Louis ('Loulou')   *France*
Tarbes.
b 15.7.38 Tarbes.
Centre/FB, 3-1-1-1 (6 − 2t).
59 I−; 60 It+(2t); 62 S=.
Licensee.

CAZENAVE, Albert   *France*
Pau.
b 7.3.02 Nay; *d* −.9.82.
Flanker, 5-3-0-2 (3 − 1t).
27 E+ G+(1t); 28 S− NSW− G+.

CAZENAVE, Fernand   *France*
RCF.
b 26.11.24 Orthey.
Wing, 6-5-0-1 (3 − 1t).
50 E+(1t); 52 S+; 54 I+ NZ+ W− E+.
Asst mgr F > 71 & 75 SA; 72 A; 79 Fj & NZ.

CELAYA, Michel   *France*
Biarritz Ol, SBUC.
b 27.7.30 Biarritz.
No 8/lock, 50-30-5-15 (18 − 6t).
53 E− W− It+; 54 I+ E+ It+ Arg+ Arg+; 55

S+ I+ E+(1t) W− It+; 56 S− I+ W− It+ E+
Cz+(1t); 57 S− I− E− W− R+; 58 S− E− A+
W+ It+; 59 S+ E=; 60 S+ E= W+(1t) I+(1t)
R− Arg+(2t) Arg+ Arg+; 61 S+ SA= E= W+
It+ I+ NZ− NZ− NZ− A+ R=.
Electricity draughtsman & inspector. Capt F >
58 SA. Asst mgr F > 71 & 75 SA; 72 A. Coach F
> 80 SA.

CELHAY, Maurice   *France*
Bayonne.
Wing, 6-4-0-2 (24 − 8t).
35 G+(2t); 36 G+(1t); 37 G+(1t) It+(4t); 38
G−; 40 BF−.

CERUTTI, William Hector ('Wild   *Australia*
Bill')
NSW.
b 7.5.09; *d* 3.7.65.
Prop, 17-9-0-8 (9 − 3t).
29 NZ+ NZ+ NZ+; 30 BI+; 31 M+ NZ−; 32
NZ+(2t) NZ− NZ−; 33 SA− SA+(1t) SA−
SA− SA+; 36 M+; 37 SA− SA−.
Transport exec/wood carver. A > 36 NZ (inj in
1st match, missed Tests). Asst mgr A > NZ 49,
55. Cousin of Edgar Stapleton.

CESSIEUX, Noel   *France*
FC Lyon.
Forward, 1-0-0-1 (3 − 1t).
06 NZ−(1t).
Sc F's 1st try, v NZ 06.

CESTER, Elie Antoine   *France*
L'Isle Jourdain Lycée, L'Isle Jourdain, TOEC,
Valence.
b 27.7.42 L'Isle Jourdain.
Lock, 35-18-4-13 (3 − 1t).
66 S= I+ E+; 67 W+; 68 S+ I+ E+ W+ Cz+
NZ− NZ− A− SA− SA−(1t) R−; 69 S− I−
E− W=; 70 S+ I+ W− E+; 71 A−; 72 R+; 73
S+ NZ+ W+ I− J+ R+; 74 I+ W= E= S−.
Restaurateur. F's most capped lock.

CHABAN-DELMAS, Jacques   *France*
Pierre Michel
Lycée Lakanal a Sceaux, Faculté de Droit de
Paris, CASG.
b 7.3.15 Paris.
Wing, 1-0-0-1.
45 BF−.
Journalist/politics. Played for French XV v R in
World Fair Tournament, Paris 37; one of the
Romanian players was Ion Papa, who like
Chaban-Delmas became his country's prime
minister. Finalist in French men's doubles lawn
tennis champs 65. Served WW2; Légion
d'Honneur, Croix de Guerre, Rosette de la
Résistance, Commandeur de Virtuti Militari de
Pologne, US Order of Merit, Order of Leopold
of Belgium, Cordon de l'étoile Yugoslavie.

Mem of Military Delegation of provisional govt
of French Republic 43. Various political posts to
end of WW2. Finance & Information minister
45-6. Deputy of Gironde 46-62. Mayor of
Bordeaux 47. French prime minister 69-72.
Unsuccessful candidate for presidency 74. Pres
of National Assembly 78-81. Married 3 times.
Author of two books, "L'Ardeur' pub 75,
"Charles de Gaulle" pub 80.

CHABOWKSI, H.   *France*
Nice.
Prop, 1-1-0-0.
85 Arg+.
F > 85 Arg.

CHADEBECH, P.   *France*
Brive.
Centre, 5-3-0-2.
82 R− Arg+ Arg+; 86 S− I+.
F > 85 Arg.

CHALLIS, Robert   *England*
Cathed Sch Bristol, O Cathedralians, Bristol,
Som.
b 9.3.32.
FB, 3-3-0-0 (10 − 2c 2p).
57 I+(1p) F+ S+(2c 1p).
Builders' merchant sales rep. Credited with
being 1st int player to place kick penalties to
touch, v I 57. Som CCC 2nd XI.

CHALLINOR, Cyril   *Wales*
Neath.
b 13.5.12; *d* 29.11.76 Neath.
Flanker, 1-0-0-1.
39 E−.
Miner.

CHALLONER, Robert L.   *Australia*
NSW.
b 3.10.1872 England; *d* −.
Forward, 1-0-0-1.
1899 BT−.

CHALMERS, Thomas   *Scotland*
Glasgow Acad, Glasgow Academicals.
b 20.3.1850; *d* 25.5.26 Glasgow.
Back, 6-1-2-3.
1871 E+; 1872 E−; 1873 E=; 1874 E−; 1875
E=; 1876 E−.
Ckt for S.

CHAMBERS, Ernest Leonard   *England*
MC
Bedford GS, Cambridge Univ, Blackheath,
Bedford, Kent, E Midlands.
b 24.7.1882 London; *d* 23.11.46 Cheam.
Forward, 3-2-1-0.
08 F+; 10 W+ I=.
Schoolmaster. Blue 04. Ath blue (hammer) 04.

Served WW1 Beds Rgt, Northumb Fusiliers &
Yorks LI. Mentioned in despatches. MC 17.
Taught at Bedford GS.

CHAMBERS, Henry Francis   *Scotland*
Townshend
Cheltenham Coll, Edinburgh Univ.
b 22.5.1865 Victoria, A; d 12.2.34.
FB, 4-3-0-1
1888 W− I+; 1889 W+ I+.
Medicine.

CHAMBERS, Sir Joseph KCB   *Ireland*
CMG
Rathmines Coll, Trin Coll Dublin.
b 1864; d 22.9.35 Roscrea.
Forward, 5-0-1-4.
1886 E− S−; 1887 E= S− W−.
Medicine/RN. Reached rank of Surg Vice Adm.
Pres IRU 1887-8. Ref W v S 1888, I v NZN
1889, S v E 1890, E v S 1891. Ump I v S 1889, S v
I 1890.

CHAMBERS, Richard Rodney   *Ireland*
RBAI, Queen's Univ Belfast, Instonians,
Ulster.
b 15.8.27 Belfast.
Centre, 6-4-1-1.
51 F+ E+ S+ W=; 52 F+ W−.
Barrister.

CHAMP, Eric   *France*
Toulon.
b 8.6.62 Toulon.
Flanker, 7-6-0-1.
85 Arg− Arg+ J+ J+; 86 I+ W+ E+.
Electrician. F > 85 Arg.

CHANTRILL, Bevan Stanislaus   *England*
Bristol GS, Clifton, RAF, Durban R (SA),
Natal, Weston-super-Mare, Bristol, Richmond,
Manchester, Rosslyn Pk, Glos, Som.
b 11.2.1897.
FB, 4-4-0-0
24 W+ I+ F+ S+.
Goldminer. Served WW1 from age of 17,
Queen's Own Hussars, Glos Rgt, RFC.
Goldmining in SA from 29-63. Served WW2
SAAF, RAF.

CHAPMAN, Charles Edward   *England*
Horncastle GS, Trent Coll, St Paul's Sch Stony
Stratford, Oxford Univ, Cambridge Univ, Eden
W, Trojans, Hants.
b 26.8.1860 Swinsted; d −.3.02.
Back, 1-1-0-0.
1884 W+.
Clergyman/schoolmaster. Cambridge blue
1881,4. Ckt for CUCC. Various teaching posts,
inc CEGS Melbourne (A) & Llandovery Coll.
Ordained 1894. Took own life.

CHAPMAN, Frederick Ernest   *England*
S Shields HS, Durham Univ, Westoe,
Hartlepool R, Durham Cos.
b 1888 S Shields; d 8.5.38.
Wing/centre, 7-7-0-0 (20 − 1t 7c 1p).
10 W+(1t 1c 1p) I+ F+(1c) S+(1c); 12 W+(1c);
14 W+(2c) I+(1c); BT > 08 NZ.
Medicine. Scored 1st int t at Twickenham, v W
10. Served WW1, RAMC. Twice wounded.

CHAPMAN, Geoffrey Alexander   *Australia*
Sydney Univ, NSW.
b 2.12.39.
Flanker, 3-0-1-2 (14 − 1c 4p).
62 NZ=(3p) NZ− NZ−(1c 1p).
Medicine/racehorse trainer. 61 pts A > 62 NZ.

CHAPUY, Léon   *France*
SF.
Centre, 1-0-0-1.
26 S−.

CHARPENTIER, Gilbert   *France*
SF.
Wing, 3-0-0-3.
11 E−; 12 W− E−.

CHARTERS, Robert Gray   *Scotland*
('Robin')
Hawick HS, Hawick.
b 29.10.30 Hawick.
Centre, 3-2-0-1.
55 W+ I+ E−.
Knitwear. Chmn SRU sels 84-6.

CHARTON, Pierre   *France*
Montferrand.
No 8, 1-0-0-1.
40 BF−.

CHARVET, Denis   *France*
Toulouse.
b 12.5.62 Cahors.
Centre, 3-3-0-0 (8 − ?t)
85 J+(2t); 86 W+ E+.
Student. F > 85 Arg.

CHASSAGNE, Jean   *France*
Montferrand.
FH, 1-0-0-1.
38 G−.

CHATEAU, Albert   *France*
Bayonne.
SH, 1-0-0-1.
13 SA−.

CHAUD, Eugène   *France*
Toulon.
Wing, 3-3-0-0 (16 − 1t 5c 1p).
32 G+(1t 1c); 34 G+(1c); 35 G+(3c 1p).

CHEESMAN, William Inkersole   *England*
Merchant Taylors' Sch, Oxford Univ, OMT.
b 20.6.1889; *d* 20.11.69.
SH, 4-3-0-1.
13 SA− W+ F+ I+.
Schoolmaster/Sudan Civil Service. Blue 10-11.
Also played ckt, football, hockey & lawn tennis.
Taught at Marlborough Coll & Pembroke
House Sch, Kenya.

CHENEVAY, Claude   *France*
Grenoble.
b 9.2.43 Grenoble.
No 8, 1-0-0-1.
68 SA−.
Chef de service.

CHERRINGTON, Nau Paora   *New Zealand*
('Brownie')
Kawakawa Dist HS, Otiria, N Auckland, NZ
Maoris, N Island.
b 5.3.24 Otiria; *d* 26.6.79 Whangarei.
Wing, 1-0-1-0.
50 BI=.
Carpenter. NZ > 51 A.

CHESTON, Ernest Constantine   *England*
Haileybury & ISC, Oxford Univ, Richmond.
b 24.10.1848; *d* 9.7.13.
Forward, 5-3-2-0 (1t).
1873 S=; 1874 S+; 1875 I+(1t) S=; 1876 S+.

CHEVALLIER, Bernard   *France*
('Cheval')
Montferrand.
b 7.9.25 Bougnat, Creuse.
Lock, 26-15-0-11.
52 S+ I− SA− W− E− It+; 53 E− W− It+; 54
S+ I+ NZ+ W− Arg+; 55 S+ I+ E+ W− It+;
56 S− I+ W− It+ E+ Cz+; 57 S−.
French Railways.

CHIBERRY, Jacques   *France*
Chambery.
Wing, 1-1-0-0.
55 It+.

CHIGNELL, Thomas Wilson   *South Africa*
W Prov.
b 1866; *d* 17.10.52.
1-0-0-1.
1891 BT−.
Electrical engineer.

CHILCOTT, Gareth James   *England*
Aditon Pk Sch Bristol, Bath.
b 20.11.56 Bristol.
Prop, 3-1-0-2.
84 A−; 86 I+ F−.
Lumberjack.

CHILO, André   *France*
RCF.
b 5.7.1898 Toulouse.
FB, 4-0-0-4.
20 S− W−; 25 I− NZ−.
PT instructor. Long jump & triple jump champ
of F.

CHISHOLM, David Hardie   *Scotland*
St Boswells Sch, Melrose, Barbarians.
b 23.1.37 St Boswells.
FH, 14-8-2-4 (15 − 1t 4d).
64 I+ E+; 65 E=(1d) SA+(1d); 66 F= I+ E+
A+(1t); 67 F+ W+(1d) NZ−(1d); 68 F− W−
I−.
Agric salesman. Bro of Robin.

CHISHOLM, Robin William   *Scotland*
Taylor
St Boswells Sch, Melrose, Barbarians.
b 16.10.29 St Boswells.
FB, 11-4-0-7 (5 − 1c 1p).
55 I+ E−; 56 F+ W− I− E−; 58 F+(1c 1p) W−
A+ I−; 60 SA−.
Auctioneer. Bro of David.

CHOLLEY, Gérard   *France*
Castres.
b 6.6.45 Luxeuil-les-Bains.
Prop/lock, 31-22-2-7 (12 − 3t).
75 E+ S+ I− SA− SA− Arg+ Arg+ R+; 76
S+ I+(1t) W− E+ A+(1t) A+(1t) R−; 77 W+
E+ S+ I+ Arg+ Arg= NZ+ NZ− R+; 78 E+
S+ I+ W− R+; 79 I= S+.
Laboratory employee.

CHOY, Joseph   *France*
Narbonne.
Prop, 10-8-0-2 (3 − 1t).
30 S+ I+ E− G+ W−; 31 I+; 33 G+; 34 G+;
35 G+; 36 G+(1t).

CHRISTIAN, Desmond Lawrence   *New Zealand*
Otahuhu, Auckland, N Island.
b 9.9.23 Auckland; *d* 30.8.77 Auckland.
No 8, 1-0-0-1.
49 SA−.
Warehouseman/motel proprietor. Served WW2
1st NZ Div. NZ > 49 SA. Ldg administrator &
sel. NZRFU sel 64-6.

CHRISTOPHERSON, Percy JP   *England*
Marlborough Coll, Bedford Sch, Oxford Univ,
Blackheath, Barbarians, Kent.
b 31.3.1866 Blackheath; *d* 4.5.21 Folkestone.
Back, 2-1-0-1 (2t).
1891 W+(2t) S−.
Schoolmaster. Blue 1886-8. Capt Univ,
Blackheath & Kent. Ckt for Oxford, Berks
CCC, Kent CCC (1887). Taught at Wellington
Coll.

CHURCH, William Campbell *Scotland*
Glasgow Acad, Glasgow Univ, Glasgow
Academicals.
 b 1884 Glasgow; kia 28.6.15 Gallipoli.
Wing, 1-0-0-1.
06 W−.
Selected S v NZ 05, but declined to play. Partly
educated in Switz. Served WW1, Capt Scottish
Rifles.

CILLIERS, Gert D. *South Africa*
UOFS, OFS.
 b 28.7.40.
Wing, 3-2-0-1 (3 − 1t).
63 A+(1t) A− A+.
Schoolmaster. SA > 65 I,S.

CIMAROSTI, Jacques *France*
Castres.
Wing, 1-1-0-0.
76 US+r.

CLAASSEN, Johannes *South Africa*
Theodorus ('Johan')
Christiana HS, Potchefstroom Univ, W
Transvaal.
 b 23.9.30 Prince Albert.
Lock, 28-17-4-7 (10 − 2t 2c).
55 BI− BI+ BI− BI+; 56 A+ A+ NZ− NZ+
NZ− NZ−; 58 F= F−; 60 S+ NZ+ NZ− NZ=;
60 W+ I+; 61 E+ S+(1t) F= I+ A+(2c) A+;
62 BI= BI+ BI+ BI+(1t).
Schoolmaster. 10 lock apps with J.A. Du Rand.
Capt SA 9 times, v F (2) 58; I, A (2) 61; BI (4)
62. 105 apps for W Transvaal. Coach SA > 71
A.

CLAASSEN, Wynand *South Africa*
Middleburg Sch Transvaal, Pretoria Univ,
Durban Collegians, SA Univs, Jnr Springboks,
Marmande (F), N Transvaal, Natal.
 b 16.1.51 Schweize-Reneke.
No 8, 7-5-0-2.
81 I+ I+ NZ+ NZ− US+; 82 SAm+ SAm−.
Architect. Capt SA on all 7 apps. With
Marmande in F 77-8.

CLADY, André *France*
Lezignan.
Lock, 5-4-0-1 (8 − 2t 1c).
29 G+; 31 I+ S− E+(1t) G+(1t 1c).

CLAMP, Michael *New Zealand*
Hutt Valley HS, Petone, Wellington, Wasps,
Centurions, NZ Colts, NZ Jnrs, NZ Maoris.
 b 26.12.61 Wellington.
Wing, 2-2-0-0 (4 − 1t).
84 A+ A+(1t).
NZ > 84 A, 85 Arg. World XV > 86 SA. Maori
Player of Year 84.

CLAPP, Thomas J.S. *Wales*
Monmouth Sch, Nantyglo, Newport.
 b c1855 Somerset.
Forward, 14-4-2-8 (2t).
1882 I+(1t) E−; 1883 S−; 1884 E− S− I+(1t);
1885 E− S=; 1886 S−; 1887 E= S− I+; 1888
S+ I−.
Solicitor. Fdr mem Newport RFC 1874.
Emigrated US 1888.

CLARAC, Henri *France*
St Girons.
Flanker, 1-0-0-1.
38 G−.

CLARE, J. *Wales*
Cardiff.
Back, 1-0-0-1.
1882 E−.
Sailor. His cap is in Cardiff RFC museum.

CLARK, Charles William Henry *England*
Rugby Sch, Liverpool, Lancs.
 b 19.3.1857; *d* 11.5.43 Battersea.
Half-back, 1-1-0-0 (1t).
1875 I+(1t).
Ptn spice millers. Capt Ormskirk GC 14.

CLARK, Donald William *New Zealand*
Timaru Boys' HS, Cromwell, Otago, S Island.
 b 22.2.40 Cromwell.
Flanker, 2-2-0-0.
64 A+ A+.
Farmer. Farm inj ended rugby career 67.

CLARK, James Goode *Australia*
St Joseph's Coll, Qld.
 b 9.9.08; *d* 11.4.79.
Flanker, 5-2-0-3.
31 M+ NZ−; 32 NZ+ NZ−; 33 SA−.

CLARK, Robert Lawson *Scotland*
Melville Coll, Edinburgh Univ, Edinburgh W,
Barbarians, RN.
 b 27.1.44 Edinburgh.
Hooker, 9-5-0-4 (4 − 1t).
72 F+ W−(1t) E+ NZ−; 73 F− W+ I+ E−
P+.
RN.

CLARK, William Henry *New Zealand*
Nelson Coll, Victoria Univ, NZ Univs,
Wellington, N Island.
 b 16.11.29 Motueka.
Flanker, 9-7-0-2 (9 − 3t).
53 W−(1t); 54 I+(1t) E+ S+; 55 A+(1t) A+;
56 SA− SA+ SA+.
Service station mgr. NZ > 53-4 BI,F & NAm.
Bro Tony rep Wellington.

CLARKE, Adrian Hipkins *New Zealand*
Avondale Coll, Waitemata, Auckland.
b 23.2.38 Christchurch.
1st/2nd five-eighth, 3-1-0-2.
58 A+; 59 BI−; 60 SA−.
Clerk/insurance agent/commercial fisherman.
Bro Philip rep NZ 67; father Vernon one of
NZ's leading sports photographers. NZ > 60 A
& SA. Unsuccessfully stood for election to NZ
Parliament.

CLARKE, Allan James *England*
Coventry, Warwicks.
b 21.2.13; *d* 25.9.75 Coventry.
Lock, 6-2-2-2.
35 W= I+ S−; 36 NZ+ W= I−.
Hotelier.

CLARKE, Donald Barry *New Zealand*
('Camel')
Te Aroha Coll, Kereone, Waikato, N Island.
b 10.11.33 Pihama.
FB, 31-24-3-4 (207 − 2t 33c 5d 2gm 38p).
56 SA+(1c 2p) SA+(1c 2p); 57 A+(2c 3p)
A+(2c 1gm); 58 A+(2c) A+(1c 4p); 59
BI+(6p) BI+(1t 1c) BI+(2c 1d 1p) BI−(2p); 60
SA− SA+(1c 1d 1p) SA=(1c 2p) SA−(1p); 61
F+(2c 1d) F+(1c) F+(4c 3p); 62 A+(1c 1d 1p)
A+(1c 2p) A=(2p) A+(1p) A+(2c); 63 E+(1t
3c 1d 1p) E+(1gm); 63 I+(1p) W+(1p); 64
E+(1c 2p) S= F+; 64 A+(3c) A−(1c).
Farmer/sales rep. NZ's most capped FB; most
pts in Tests. Played in 16 consec matches
without losing 61-4. 169 pts (13 apps) NZ > 57
A. 218 pts (23 apps) NZ > 60 A & SA; 173 pts in
SA most by any player on tour in SA. 107 pts >
62 A; 149 pts (26 apps) > 63-4 BI,F & C. 781 pts
& 89 apps for NZ. Ckt for Auckland. 4 bros Ian,
Doug, Brian & Graeme rep Waikato, all five
playing once v Thames Valley 61. Ian rep NZ
53-64. Autobiography 'The Boot' pub 66; co-
author with Roger Urbahn 'The Fourth
Springbok Tour of NZ' pub 63. Moved to
Johannesburg, SA.

CLARKE, Ian James *New Zealand*
Hawera Tech Coll, Kereone, Waikato, N
Island, Barbarians (E).
b 5.3.31 Kaponga.
Prop/no 8, 24-19-1-4.
53 W−; 55 A+ A+ A−; 56 SA+ SA− SA+
SA+; 57 A+ A+; 58 A+ A+; 59 BI+ BI+; 60
SA+ SA−; 61 F+ F+ F+; 62 A+ A+ A=; 63
E+ E+.
Farmer. One of 5 bros who played 1st class
rugby (see Don Clarke). NZ > 53-4 BI,F &
NAm, 57 & 62 A, 60 A & SA, 63-4 BI,F & C.
Capt v A 55. Sc gm for Barbarians (E) v NZ 64.

CLARKE, Joseph A.B. *Ireland*
St Mary's Coll, RCSI, Bective Rgrs.

b −; *d* Dublin.
SH, 7-2-0-5 (3 − 1t).
22 S−(1t) W− F+; 23 F−; 24 E− S− W+.
Dental surgeon.

CLARKE, Ray Lancelot *New Zealand*
Okaiawa Sch, Okaiawa, Taranaki, Stratford,
Waikato, N Island.
b −.7.09 Wairea; *d* 3.6.72 New Plymouth.
Lock, 2-2-0-0.
32 A+ A+.
Cheesemaker. NZ > 32 A. Son, also R.L., rep
Wellington 62 & Taranaki 64-6.

CLARKE, Samuel Simmonds TD *Wales*
Neath.
b 1857 Weymouth; *d* 25.5.47 Mumbles.
Back/FB, 2-2-0-0.
1882 I+; 1887 I+;
The Army. Sec SWFU 1880.

CLARKE, Simon John Scott *England*
Wellington Coll, Cambridge Univ, Hove,
Devonport Servs, RN, Bath, Yokohama (J),
Blackheath, Kent, Devon, Sussex.
b 2.4.38 Westcliff.
SH, 13-4-3-6 (3 − 1t).
63 W+ I= F+ S+ NZ− NZ− A−(1t); 64 NZ−
W= I−; 65 I− F+ S=.
Sales mgr/marketing. Blue 62-3. Ckt for CUCC
61-2, Comb Servs, Kent CCC 2nd XI. Served R
Marines.

CLARKE, W.H. ('Ginger') *South Africa*
Transvaal.
b 11.10.05.
No 8, 1-1-0-0.
33 A+.

CLARKEN, James *Australia*
Glebe, NSW.
b 19.7.1876 Thames, NZ; *d* 31.7.53 Sydney.
Forward, 4-1-0-3.
05 NZ−; 10 NZ− NZ+ NZ−.
Goldminer/car hire owner. A > 12 US, Can.
AIF > 18-19 BI, A. Noted surf-lifesaver.

CLARKSON, Walter A. *South Africa*
Natal.
b 8.7.1896 Durban; *d* 73.
Centre, 3-2-0-1.
21 NZ− NZ+; 24 BI+.
Badly inj 1st Test v BI 24, never played again for
SA.

CLAUDEL, Roger *France*
Lyon.
Flanker, 2-2-0-0.
32 G+; 34 G+.

CLAUSS, Paul Robert Adolph　　　*Scotland*
Loretto Sch, Oxford Univ, Barbarians.
b 22.6.1868 Munich; *d* 21.4.45 Cheltenham.
Wing, 6-5-0-1 (6 − 3t 1d).
1891 W+(2t) I+(1t) E+(1d); 1892 W+ E−;
1895 I+; BT > 1891 SA.
Schoolmaster. Blue 1889-91. Served WW1, Lt
Unattached List TF.

CLAUZEL, François　　　*France*
Béziers, Narbonne.
Flanker, 3-0-0-3.
24 E− W−; 25 W−.

CLAVE, Jean　　　*France*
Agen.
Hooker, 3-3-0-0.
36 G+; 39 R+ G+.

CLAVERIE, Henri　　　*France*
Lourdes.
b 24.
FB, 2-1-0-1.
54 NZ+ W−.
Typographer.

CLAY, Alexander Thomson　　　*Scotland*
Edinburgh Acad, Edinburgh Academicals.
b 27.9.1863 Kelso; *d* 20.11.50.
Forward, 7-4-2-1 (1t).
1886 W+(1t) I+ E=; 1887 I+ W+ E=; 1888
W−.
Writer to the Signet.

CLAYTON, John Henry　　　*England*
Rugby Sch, Liverpool, Lancs.
b 24.8.1849; *d* 21.3.24 London.
Forward, 1-0-0-1.
1871 S−.
Cotton broker. Played in 1st int, S v E 1871.
Capt R Liverpool GC. Died in a taxi-cab.

CLEARY, Michael Arthur　　　*Australia*
Waverley CBC, NSW.
b 30.4.40.
Wing, 6-2-1-3 (12 − 4t).
61 Fj+(1t) Fj+(2t) Fj= SA− SA−(1t) F−.
Co dir. Rep A ath at Commonwealth Games,
Perth 62. A RL v E 62. NSW Parliament;
minister for sport.

CLEAVER, William Benjamin　　　*Wales*
Pentre Sch, Treorchy, Pentre, UC Cardiff,
Cardiff, Barbarians.
b 15.9.21 Treorchy.
Centre/FH/FB, 14-9-1-4 (6 − 1t 1d).
47 E− S+(1t) F+ I+ A+; 48 E= S+ F− I−; 49
I−; 50 E+ S+(1d) I+ F+; BI > 50 NZ 3-0-1-2,
A.
Mining engr. Wales XV v Kiwis 46. Barbarians v
A 48.

CLEGG, Barry G.　　　*Wales*
Swansea, Neath.
b 55.
Lock, 1-0-0-1.
79 F−.
Fireman. W > 75 Far East; 78 A. Wales B v F
75, 77. Wales XV v Arg 76.

CLEGG, Roger James　　　*Ireland*
Bangor GS, Stranmillis, Bangor.
b 4.12.48 Bangor.
Prop, 5-3-0-2.
73 F+; 75 E+ S− F+ W−.
PE teacher.

CLÉMENT, Jean　　　*France*
RCF, Valence.
b 1900 Tarbes; *d* c45.
FB, 10-2-2-6.
21 S+ W− E−; 22 S= E= W− I−; 23 S− W−
I+.
Stood down v E 23 at own request because he
felt he was not in form; Christian Magnanou
took his place.

CLÉMENT, Pierre　　　*France*
RCF.
b c06.
Centre, 1-0-0-1.
31 W−.

CLEMENT, William Harries MC　　　*Wales*
TD OBE
Llanelli CS, Felinfoel, Llanelli.
b 15.
Wing, 6-2-0-4 (3 − 1t).
37 E− S− I−; 38 E+ S− I+(1t); BI > 38 SA.
Local govt/WRU sec 56-81. Served WW2, Maj
in Welch Rgt; MC at Battle of Bulge, 44.

CLEMENTE, Michel　　　*France*
Oloron.
b 30.11.55 Oloron.
No 8, 3-2-0-1.
78 R+; 80 S− I+.
Gamekeeper.

CLEMENTS, Jeffrey Woodward　　　*England*
Cranleigh Sch, O Cranleighans, Cambridge
Univ, RN, Devonport Servs, US Portsmouth,
Barbarians, Hants.
b 18.8.32.
Flanker, 3-1-2-0.
59 I+ F= S=.
Schoolmaster/co dir. Blue 53-55. Taught at
Cranleigh. In bus for many yrs in SE Asia. Ckt
for Singapore & Malaya.

CLEMENTS, Phillip　　　*Australia*
NSW.
b 52.

Lock, 1-0-0-1.
82 NZ−.

CLEVELAND, Sir Charles Raitt   *England*
KCIE KBE
Christ's Coll Finchley, Oxford Univ,
Blackheath, Kent.
b 2.11.1866 Bombay; *d* 18.1.29.
Forward, 2-1-1-0.
1887 W+ S=.
Indian Civil Service/omnibus co sec. Blue 1885-
6. Ath blue (hammer).

CLIBBORN, W.G.   *England*
Richmond.
Forward, 6-3-2-1.
1886 W+ I+ S=; 1887 W+ I− S=.
Capped in 1888 E side that did not play.

CLIFFORD, Jeremiah Thomas   *Ireland*
Limerick CBS, Young Munster, Barbarians.
b 15.11.23 Tipperary.
Prop, 14-8-1-5 (3 − 1t).
49 F− E+ S+ W+; 50 F= E− S+ W−; 51
F+(1t) E+ SA−; 52 F+ S+ W−; BI > 50 NZ 3-
0-1-2, A 2-2-0-0.
Aircraft refueller.

CLIFFORD, Michael   *Australia*
NSW.
b 16; kia 43.
FB, 1-0-0-1.
38 NZ−.
Clerk. Served WW2, RAAF; killed in aeroplane
crash.

CLINCH, Andrew Daniel ('Coo')   *Ireland*
Belvedere Coll, Trin Coll Dublin, Wanderers.
b 28.11.1867 Dublin; *d* −.2.37.
Forward, 10-3-1-6.
1892 S−; 1893 W−; 1895 E− S− W−; 1896 E+
S= W+; 1897 E+ S−; BT > 1896 SA.
Medicine. Father of 'Jammie'. Pres IRU 04-5.

CLINCH, James Daniel   *Ireland*
('Jammie')
Catholic Univ Sch St Andrews, Trin Coll
Dublin, RCSI, Wanderers, Barbarians.
b 28.9.01 Clondalkin, Co Dublin; *d* 1.5.81
Dublin.
Flanker, 30-16-2-12.
23 W+; 24 F+ E− S− W+ NZ−; 25 F+ E= S−
; 26 E+ S+ W−; 27 F+; 28 F+ E− S+ W+; 29
F+ E+ W− S=; 30 F− E+ S+ W−; 31 F− E+
S+ W− SA−; BI > 24 SA.
Medicine/insurance. Son of 'Coo'. Emergency
FB on BI > 24 SA. GP in Gwent, W.

CLOETE, H.A. ('Patats')   *South Africa*
W Prov.

1-1-0-0.
1896 BT+.

CLOUGH, Francis John   *England*
St John Rigby RC VI Coll, England Schs,
Durham Univ, Cambridge Univ, Orrell.
b 1.11.62 Wigan.
Centre, 2-1-0-1.
86 I+ F−.
E Under 23s, England B. Capt Cambridge Univ
86-7.

CLUCHAGUE, Louis ('L'ailier   *France*
myope')
Biarritz Ol.
b − ; *d* −.7.78.
Wing, 2-1-0-1 (3 − 1t).
24 S+; 25 E−(1t).
Primary schoolmaster.

CLUNE, John Joseph   *Ireland*
Blackrock Coll.
b 2.4.1890; *d* 43.
Hooker/lock, 6-3-0-3.
12 SA−; 13 W− F+; 14 F+ E− W+.
Medicine/RAVC.

CLUNIES-ROSS, A.   *Scotland*
St Andrew's Univ.
b Cocos Islands; *d* −.
Back, 1-1-0-0.
1871 E+.
Of Malay-Scottish ancestry. Played in 1st int, S v
E 1871.

COATES, Charles Hutton   *England*
Christ's Coll Finchley, Cambridge Univ, Leeds
& Yorks W, Bishop Auckland, Surrey, Yorks.
b 4.5.1857 Yorks; *d* 14.2.22 Boscombe, Hants.
Forward, 3-1-1-1.
1880 S+; 1881 S=; 1882 S−.
Clergyman. Blue 1877-9. Oarsman, archer.
Ordained 1881. RN chaplain 1885-91.

COATES, Vincent Middleton   *England*
Hope MC
Monkton Combe Sch, Haileybury & ISC,
Cambridge Univ, Bridgwater, Bath, Leicester,
Richmond, Barbarians, Som.
b 18.5.1889; *d* 14.11.34 Maidenhead.
Wing, 5-4-0-1 (18 − 6t).
13 SA− W+(1t) F+(3t) I+(2t) S+.
Medicine. Blue 07. Served WW1, RAMC.
Mentioned in despatches. Awarded MC on field
of battle, The Somme 16. Som CCC. Died in fall
from train.

COBB, Walter George   *Australia*
NSW.
b 1870; *d* 33.
FB, 2-0-0-2.

1899 BT− BT−.
Labourer.

COBBY, William   *England*
Uppingham Sch, Cambridge Univ, Hull,
Castleford, Hull & ER, Barbarians, Yorks.
b 5.7.1877 Swine, Hull; *d* 15.1.57.
Forward, 1-0-0-1.
1900 W−.
Schoolmaster. Blue 1900. Contemporary of H.
Alexander at Uppingham.

COBDEN Donald Gordon   *New Zealand*
Christchurch Boys' HS, HSOB, Canterbury, S
Island, Barbarians (E), Catford Bridge, Kent,
RAF.
b 11.8.14 Christchurch; kia 11.8.40 English
Channel.
Wing, 1-1-0-0.
37 SA+.
Joined RAF 38. Reported missing during Battle
of Britain. Body washed ashore at Ostend where
he was buried by Germans. Bro Alf rep
Canterbury 33-5.

COBNER, Terence John   *Wales*
W Mon GS, Pontypool, Madeley Coll, Staffs,
Barbarians.
b 10.1.46 Blaenavon.
Flanker, 19-13-2-4 (8 − 2t).
74 S+(1t) I= F= E−; 75 F+(1t) E+ S− I+ A+;
76 E+ S+; 77 F− E+ S+; 78 E+ S+ I+ F+ A−
; BI > 77 NZ 3-1-0-2.
Schoolmaster. Wales B v F 73. Wales XV v Tg
74. Welsh XV v NZ 74. W > 75 Far East; 78 A.
Wales XV v Arg 76.

COCKCROFT, Eric Arthur Percy *New Zealand*
Southland Boys' HS, Univ, Otago, S
Canterbury, Pirates, Timaru HSOB, S Island,
Comb Servs.
b 10.9.1890 Clinton; *d* 2.4.73 Ashburton.
Wing/FB, 3-2-0-1.
13 A−; 14 A+ A+.
Headmaster. NZ > 14 A. One of dynasty of
Cockrotts, 4 of whom played 1st class rugby in
NZ. Rep NZ at bowls 53 & S Canterbury at
cricket. Taught at HS of Timaru & Ashburton.
Wrote 'The Modern Method in NZ Football'
pub 24.

COCKERHAM, Arthur   *England*
Bradford Olicana.
Forward, 1-0-0-1.
1900 W−.
Manningham RL 1900.

COCKERILL, Maurice Stanley   *New Zealand*
('Snow')
Hawera Sch, Hawera Tech Coll, Hawera Ath,
Taranaki.

b 8.12.28 Hawera.
FB, 3-3-0-0 (11 − 4c 1p).
51 A+(1c 1p) A+(1c) A+(2c).
Joiner/service station proprietor. NZ > 51 A.
Inj in Taranaki v Waikato 51 ended career. Ckt
for Taranaki.

COCKRELL, Charles Herbert   *South Africa*
W Prov.
b 10.1.39 Cape Town.
Hooker, 3-0-2-1.
69 S−; 70 I= W=.
Telecommunications technician. Bro of Robert.
SA > 69-70 BI.

COCKRELL, Robert James   *South Africa*
J.G. Meiring Sch, Noordelikes, W Prov.
b 4.4.50 Cape Town.
Hooker, 11-8-0-3.
74 F+ F+; 75 F+ F+; 76 NZ+ NZ−; 77 Wd+;
81 NZ− NZ+r NZ− US+.
Rep/Post Office electrician. Bro of Charles. SA
> 80 SAm.

COCKS, Michael Richard   *Australia*
NSW, Qld, W Prov (SA), Natal (SA).
b 1.3.45.
Flanker/no 8, 10-3-1-6.
72 F= F− NZ− NZ− Fj+; 73 Tg+ Tg− W−
E−; 75 J+.
Schoolmaster.

CODERC, Jean   *France*
Chalon.
Centre, 5-5-0-0 (6 − 2t).
32 G+(1t); 33 G+(1t); 34 G+; 35 G+; 36 G+.

CODEY, David   *Australia*
GPS, Brisbane, NSW Country, NSW, Qld.
b 7.7.57.
No 8/flanker, 6-4-0-2.
83 Arg−; 84 E+ W+ S+; 85 C+ NZ−.
Marketing consultant. Inj in debut int. A > 84
BI.

CODLIN, Brett William   *New Zealand*
Tehihi Prmy Sch, King's Coll, Lincoln Coll,
Canterbury, Counties, Ardmore, N Island, NZ
Univs.
b 29.11.56 Pukekohe.
FB, 3-1-0-2 (23 − 1c 7p).
80 A−(3p) A+(1c 2p) A−(2p).
Farmer. NZ > 80 A & Fj (95 pts); NAm & W.
Father M.C. rep Waikato 44; bro Mark NZ trial
79.

CODORNIOU, Didier   *France*
Narbonne.
b 13.2.58 Gruissan.
Centre, 32-19-3-10 (20 − 5t).
79 NZ− NZ+(1t) R+(1t); 80 W− E− S− I+;

81 S+ W+ E+ A−; 83 E+ S+ I− W+ A= A+
R+; 84 I+ W+ E+ S− NZ− NZ− R+; 85 E=
S+ I=(1t) W+ Arg− Arg+(1t) J+(1t).
Bank employee. France B v W 79. F > 85 Arg.
Inj interrupted career.

CODY, Ernest Austin   *Australia*
St Joseph's Coll, NSW.
b 1889; *d* 68.
Prop, 3-1-0-2.
13 NZ− NZ− NZ+.

COETZEE, Johannes Hermanus   *South Africa*
Hugo ('Boland')
W Prov.
b 20.1.45 Porterville.
Flanker, 6-4-0-2.
74 BI−; 75 F+r; 76 NZ+ NZ− NZ+ NZ+.
Wine farmer.

COFFEY, John J.   *Ireland*
Blackrock Coll, Lansdowne, Barbarians.
b 6.5.1877 Dublin; *d* 28.9.45.
Forward, 19-8-0-11.
1900 E−; 01 W−; 02 E− S+ W−; 03 E+ S−
W−; 05 E+ S+ W− NZ−; 06 E+ S− W+
SA−; 07 E+; 08 W−; 10 F+.
Civil service. Retired 07-8 season. Gained 1
more cap v F 10 when visiting Irish dressing−
room to wish team good luck, was persuaded to
take the place of one of the Irish forwards who
was ill. Ref S v F 12. Pres IRU 24-65.

COGAN, William St John   *Ireland*
Queen's Coll Cork, Edinburgh Univ, Glasgow
Univ.
Forward, 2-1-0-1.
07 E+ S−.
Medicine.

COGNET, Lucien   *France*
Montferrand.
No 8, 5-5-0-0.
32 G+; 36 G+ G+; 37 G+ It+.

COLBERT, Raymond   *Australia*
NSW.
b 30.5.31 Brisbane.
FB, 6-2-0-4 (6 − 3c).
52 Fj− NZ+ NZ−; 53 SA+(2c) SA−(1c) SA−.
Chemist.

COLCLOUGH, Maurice John   *England*
Duke of York's RMS, Kent SS, London SS,
Sussex, Liverpool Univ, Lancs, Wasps,
Angoulême, Poitiers (F), Swansea.
b 2.9.53 Oxford.
Lock, 25-14-1-10 (4 − 1t).
78 S+ I+; 79 NZ−; 80 F+ W+ S+; 81 W− S+
I+ F−; 82 A+ S= I− F+ W+; 83 F− NZ+(1t);
84 S− I+ F− W−; 86 W+ S− I+ F−; BI > 80

SA 4-1-0-3; 83 NZ 4-0-0-4.
Cafe proprietor/marina developer. London v
Arg, NZ 78, A 81, NZ 83. E > 79 Far East; 82
US, Can. Moved to Wales 85.

COLDRICK, Albert Percy   *Wales*
Newport.
b 1888 Newport; *d* 26.12.53.
Prop/lock, 6-5-0-1.
11 E+ S+ I+; 12 E− S+ F+.
Rly platelayer. Wigan RL 12.

COLE, John Walter   *Australia*
Maroubra HS, NSW.
b 20.9.46 Sydney.
Wing, 24-4-1-19 (21 − 6t).
68 NZ− NZ− F+ I− S−; 69 W− SA− SA−
SA− SA−; 70 S+(2t); 71 SA− SA− SA−(1t)
F+ F−; 72 NZ− NZ−(1t) NZ−; 73 Tg+(1t)
Tg−(1t); 74 NZ− NZ= NZ−.
Salesman. RL.

COLEMAN, Ernest   *Wales*
Newport.
Prop, 3-1-0-2.
49 E+ S− I−.
Docker.

COLES, Fenton C.   *Wales*
Pontypool.
b 14.9.37 Blaenavon.
Wing, 3-2-0-1.
60 S+ I+ F−.
Miner.

COLEY, Eric OBE TD   *England*
Northampton Town & Country Sch,
Northampton, E Midlands, The Army,
Barbarians.
b 23.7.03 Northampton; *d* 3.5.57
Northampton.
No 8, 2-1-0-1 (3 − 1t).
29 F+; 32 W−(1t).
The Army/hotel proprietor. Served WW2. Brig
in RA. OBE (mil) 52. E sel 37-48. Sec
Northants CCC. Son David played for
Northampton & E Midlands.

COLLIER, Samuel Ruddell   *Ireland*
Queen's Coll Belfast.
b Lisburn; *d* −.
Back, 1-0-0-1.
1883 S−.
Medicine. In practice in Wimbledon for many
years.

COLLINS, Arthur Harold   *New Zealand*
Stratford Prmy Sch, Stratford, Taranaki,
Clifton, N Island.
b 19.7.06 Stratford.
FB, 3-2-0-1 (9 − 3c 1p).

32 A+(1p) A+(2c); 34 A−(1c).
Plasterer. Top scorer 54 pts NZ > 32 A; top scorer 56 pts > 34 A. Coach & administrator after retirement. Son B.A. rep Taranaki 62-3.

COLLINS, John   *Wales*
Aberavon, Barbarians.
b 32.
Wing, 10-4-1-5 (9 − 3t).
58 A+(1t) E= S+(1t) F−(1t); 59 E+ S− I+ F−; 60 E−; 61 F−.
Steelworker. Lives in Majorca.

COLLINS, John Law   *New Zealand*
Tokomaru Bay Dist HS, Marist, Poverty Bay, NZ Maoris, N Island.
b 1.2.39 Tokomaru Nay.
2nd five-eighth, 3-3-0-0.
64 A+; 65 SA+ SA+.
Wool classer.

COLLINS, Paul K.   *Australia*
NSW.
b 16.
Five-eighth, 3-0-0-3 (3 − 1t).
37 SA−; 38 NZ−(1t) NZ−.
Confectioner/co exec.

COLLINS, Philip John   *England*
Camborne, Cornwall.
b 4.11.28.
FB, 3-3-0-0.
52 S+ I+ F+.
Engrg draughtsman.

COLLINS, Tom   *Wales*
Mountain Ash.
Centre, 1-0-0-1.
23 I−.
Miner. Hull RL 23.

COLLINS, William Edward CMG   *England*
VD
Cheltenham Coll, O Cheltonians, St George's Hosp, Oxford Univ.
b 14.10.1853 Monghyr, India; d 11.8.34 Wellington, NZ.
Half-back, 5-4-1-0 (1t).
1874 S+; 1875 I+ S= I+; 1876 S+(1t).
Medicine. Played in 1st Hosp Cup final, St George's v Guy's 1875. Emigrated to NZ 1878. Served WW1 NZ Medical Corps. CMG 17. Mem of Legislative Council of NZ from 07.

COLLIS, William Robert   *Ireland*
Fitzgerald
Rugby Sch, Cambridge Univ, Yale Univ, King's Coll Hosp, Harlequins, Surrey.
b 16.2.1900; d 27.5.75.
Hooker, 7-4-1-2.

24 F+ W+ NZ−; 25 F+ E= S−; 26 F+.
Medicine. Son of W.S. Blue 19-20.

COLLIS, William Stuart   *Ireland*
Wanderers.
b 1860; d 2.1.47.
Forward, 1-0-0-1.
1884 W−.
Father of W.R.F.

COLLOPY, George   *Ireland*
Bective Rgrs.
b −; d −.8.25.
Forward, 2-0-0-2.
1891 S−; 1892 S−.
Father of Richard & William.

COLLOPY, Richard J.   *Ireland*
St Andrews Coll, Bective Rgrs.
b 2.5.1899.
Lock/prop, 13-5-1-7.
23 E− S− W+ F−; 24 F+ E− S− W+ NZ−; 25 F+ E= S− W+.
Accountant. Bro of William, son of George. Huddersfield RL 25.

COLLOPY, William P.   *Ireland*
St Andrews Coll, Bective Rgrs, Barbarians.
b 5.5.1894; d 4.1.72.
Hooker/prop, 19-7-0-12.
14 F+ E− S+ W−; 21 E− S+ W− F−; 22 E− S− W− F+; 23 S− W+ F−; 24 F+ E− S− W+.
Accountant/toiletries rep/guest house proprietor. Son of George & bro of Richard. Served WW1, Cpl in RFA.

COLMAN, John Thomas Henry   *New Zealand*
(**'Ginger'**)
St Joseph's Sch Hawera, Hawera, Taranaki, Waimate, N Island.
b 14.1.1887 Hawera; d 28.9.65 Hawera.
Flanker/FB/wing, 4-4-0-0 (2 − 1c).
07 A | A | ; 08 AW | AW | (1c).
Blacksmith. NZ > 07 A.

COLOMBIER, Jean   *France*
St Junien.
b 23.9.28 St Junien, Haute Vienne.
Wing, 3-0-0-3.
52 SA− W− E−.

COLOMINE, Guy   *France*
Narbonne.
Prop, 1-0-0-1.
79 NZ−.

COLTMAN, Stuart   *Scotland*
Hawick HS, Hawick.
b 27.3.20 Hawick.
Prop, 5-2-0-3.

48 I−; 49 F+ W+ I− E−.
Served in KOSB.

COLTON, A.J. ('Ginger')   *Australia*
Qld.
b 25.3.1875; *d* 46.
Forward, 2-1-0-1 (3 − 1t).
1899 BT+(1t) BT−.
Farmer. Bro of Thomas.

COLTON, Thomas ('Puddin')   *Australia*
Qld.
b 1874; *d* 58.
Forward, 2-0-0-2.
04 BT− BT−.
Farmer. Bro of 'Ginger'.

COLVILLE, Andrew Galbraith   *Scotland*
Merchiston Castle Sch, Blackheath.
b 1847; *d* 17.4.1881 Bournemouth.
Back, 2-1-0-1.
1871 E+; 1872 E−
Invited by E to play in 1st int v S 1871, chose to
play for S.

COMBE, Abram   *Ireland*
RBAI, Rugby Sch, NIFC.
b 16.7.1852; *d* −.
Forward, 1-0-0-1.
1875 E−.
Merchant.

COMBE, Julien   *France*
SF.
FB, 4-1-0-3.
10 S− E− I−; 11 S+.

COMBES, Gaston   *France*
Fumel.
SH, 1-0-0-1.
45 BF−.

COMMUNEAU, Marcel   *France*
SF, Beauvais.
b 11.9.1885 Beauvais; *d* −.
Forward, 20-1-0-19 (9 − 3t).
06 NZ− E−; 07 E−(1t); 08 E− W−; 09 E−
W− I−; 10 S− E−(1t) I−; 11 S+ E− I−; 12 I−
S−(1t) W− E−; 13 SA− E−.
Engr/industrialist. Capt F in 1st int win, v S 11.

CONDOM, Jean   *France*
Boucau, Rouen.
b 15.4.60 St André de Seigneux.
Lock, 26-16-3-7.
82 R−; 83 E+ S+ I− W+ A= A+ R+; 84 I+
W+ E+ S− NZ− NZ− R+; 85 E= S+ I= W+
Arg− Arg+ J+; 86 S− I+ W+ E+.
Farmer/office worker. France B v S 82. France
A v It 82. F > 85 Arg. Five Nations v Overseas
XV, Twickenham 86.

CONDON, Hugh Charles   *Ireland*
London Irish.
b 17.2.55 Leamington.
FH, 1-0-0-1.
84 S−r.
Medicine. Rep English Youth. Ireland B.

CONIL DE BEYSSAC, Jacques   *France*
SBUC.
b 1888 Bordeaux; kia 11.6.18.
Flanker/lock, 5-0-0-5.
12 I− S−; 14 I− W− E−.

CONNELL, Gordon Colin   *Scotland*
Trinity Acad, Trinity Academicals, London
Scottish.
b 3.10.44 Edinburgh.
SH, 5-2-0-3 (3 − 1d).
68 E−(1d) A+; 69 F+ E−; 70 F−; BIr > 68 SA
1-0-0-1.
Investments.

CONNOR, Desmond   *Australia/New Zealand*
Michael
Marist Bros' Coll Brisbane, Marist, Qld,
Auckland, N Island.
b 9.8.35 Ashgrove, Brisbane.
Australia
SH, 12-1-1-10.
57 W− I− E− S− F−; 58 M= M− NZ− NZ+
NZ−; 59 BI− BI−.
New Zealand
SH, 12-10-1-1.
61 F+ F+ F+; 62 A+ A+ A= A+ A+; 63 E+
E+; 64 A+ A−.
PE teacher/footwear co dir. Capt A, v-capt NZ.
A > 57-8 BI & F. Went to NZ 60. NZ > A 62.
Returned to A 66. ARU sel & coach. Asst mgr
A > I & S 68.

CONSIDINE, Stanley George   *England*
Ulick
Blundell's Sch, Bath, Som.
b 11.8.01 India; *d* 31.8.50 Bath.
Wing, 1-1-0-0.
25 F+.
Solicitor. Played in 2 Irish Trials 20. Scored 3000
runs for Som CCC.

CONSTANT, Georges   *France*
Perpignan.
b 1900; *d* −.6.78 Nevers.
Prop, 1-0-0-1.
20 W−.
Business.

CONWAY, Geoffrey Seymour   *England*
MC TD
Fettes Coll, Cambridge Univ, Rugby,
Harlequins, Hartlepool R, Manchester,
Blackheath, Barbarians, Lancs, Durham.

b 15.11.1897.
No 8/lock, 18-15-1-2 (25 − 1t 11c).
20 F+ I+ S+; 21 F+; 22 W− I+ F= S+(1c); 23
W+ I+(2c) S+ F+(1t); 24 W+(1c) I+(1c)
F+(2c) S+(3c); 25 NZ−(1c); 27 W+.
Schoolmaster/schools inspector. Blue 19-21.
Served WW1. MC 17. Served WW2, promoted
Lt Col. England's most c in Champ (7 in 24).
Taught at Rugby Sch. Archaeologist in Greece
61-9. Retd to live in F.

CONWAY, Richard James ('Red')   *New Zealand*
Whakatane HS, Zingari-Richmond, Otago,
Hamilton Tech Coll, Waikato, Whakatane Utd,
Bay of Plenty, N Island.
b 22.4.35 Whakatane.
No 8/flanker, 10-5-1-4 (3 − 1t).
59 BI+ BI+ BI−; 60 SA− SA= SA−; 65 SA+
SA+ SA− SA+(1t).
Carpenter. Suffered septic finger in Trials for
NZ > 60 SA. Advised that normal healing
would take too long for him to be fit to tour.
Decided to take no chances; he had finger
amputated. Coached Whakatane Utd 75-8.
Softball for Rotorua.

CONWAY-REES, John   *Wales*
Llandovery Coll, Oxford Univ, Blackheath,
Richmond, Llanelli, Barbarians, Cardiff,
London Welsh.
b 13.1.1870; *d* 30.8.32 London.
Back, 3-1-0-2.
1892 S−; 1893 E+; 1894 E−.
HM. Blue 1891-3. Originated idea of 4
threequarters at Oxford Univ. Barbarians
comm.

COOK, Bruce P.   *Australia*
NSW.
b 53.
FB, 1-0-0-1.
79 I−.

COOK, H.G.   *Ireland*
Lansdowne.
Forward, 1-0-0-1.
1884 W−.
Ref S v E 1886. Hon Sec IRU 1882-6.

COOK, John Gilbert   *England*
Bedford Sch, Bedford.
b 16.5.11 Houghton Regis, Beds; *d* −.9.79
Overstrand, Norfolk.
Flanker, 1-1-0-0.
37 S+.
Treasury valuer. Bedfordshire CCC &
Gentlemen of Ireland.

COOK, Peter William   *England*
Dulwich Coll, Richmond, Barbarians, Surrey,
London Cos.

b 8.1.43 High Wycombe.
Wing, 2-1-0-1.
65 I− F+.
Sales engr. Surrey comm.

COOK, Terence   *Wales*
New Tredegar Tech, Cardiff.
b 24.6.27 Bedwas.
Wing, 2-0-0-2.
49 S− I−.
Engrg draughtsman/impresario. Halifax RL 49.

COOKE, David Alexander   *England*
Gravesend GS, Harlequins.
b 10.2.49 Malta.
Centre, 4-0-0-4.
76 W− S− I− F−.
Schoolmaster.

COOKE, David Howard   *England*
Haileybury & ISC, NE London Poly,
Harlequins, London, Mdx.
b 19.11.55 Brisbane.
Flanker, 12-5-1-6.
81 W− S+ I+ F−; 84 I+; 85 R+ F= S+ I− W−
NZ− NZ−.
Estate agent. E Under 23s v F 77; > Can, F, It,
Netherlands. England v I 80. E > 82 US & Can.

COOKE, Graham Morven   *Australia*
Qld, Transvaal.
b 3.1.12 Nanango, Qld.
Lock, 13-5-0-8 (3 − 1t).
32 NZ+ NZ− NZ−; 33 SA− SA+ SA−; 46
NZ−; 47 NZ− S+(1t) I+ W−; 48 E+ F−.
Police/taxi driver. Recalled to A team after 14
yrs; world's longest int career, 17 yrs. Lived for
a time in SA.

COOKE, Paul   *England*
St Edward's Oxford, Oxford Univ, Richmond,
Barbarians.
b 18.12.16; kia 1.5.40 Calais.
SH, 2 1 0 1.
39 W+ I−.
Bank official. Blue 36-7. BT > 36 Arg. Served
WW2, 2nd Lt OBLI.

COOKE, Albert Edward   *New Zealand*
Hamilton Boys' HS, Grafton, Auckland, Napier
Tech Coll, Hawkes Bay, Masterton, Wairarapa,
Masterton OB, Wellington, Hutt, Hastings, N
Island.
b 5.10.01 Auckland; 29.9.77 Auckland.
2nd five-eighth/centre, 8-7-0-1 (12 − 4t).
24 I+ W+; 25 E+ F+(2t); 30 BI− BI+ BI+
BI+(2t).
Sales rep/mercer/dockyard worker. After
leaving sch played RL for Post & Telegraph. NZ
> 24-5 BI,F & C (27t in 29 apps); 26 A.
Richmond RL (Auckland) 32; rep NZ v GB 32,

v A 35. Joined RNZAF for WW2; played rugby union again for them 40.

COOKE, Reuben James   *New Zealand*
Merivale, Canterbury, S Island.
b −; *d* 10.5.40 Melbourne.
Flanker, 1-1-0-0.
03 A+.
Hotelier. NZ > 03 A; sent off 1st match, v NSW. Moved to Melbourne 13; coach & administrator of Kiwi club.

COOLICAN, John Edward   *Australia*
NSW.
b 53.
Prop, 4-1-1-2.
82 NZ−; 83 It+ F= F−.

COOP, Thomas   *England*
Tottington, Leigh, Lancs.
b 1865 Tottington, Lancs; *d* −.
FB, 1-1-0-0.
1892 S+.
Turned RL when his club, Leigh, helped form NU 1895.

COOPER, John Graham   *England*
Aston GS, Moseley, Midlands.
b 3.6.1881; *d* 26.10.65.
Forward, 2-0-0-2.
09 A− W−.
Solicitor. Served WW1 R Warwick Rgt. Mentioned in despatches 17. Emigrated to Can.

COOPER, Malcolm McGregor   *Scotland*
CBE
Napier Boys HS NZ, Oxford Univ, Barbarians, Wellington.
b 17.8.10 Napier, NZ.
Flanker, 2-0-0-2.
36 W− I−.
Univ professor. Played for Wellington before going up to Oxford. Blue 34-6. Capt Oxford Univ v NZ 35.

COOPER, Martin John   *England*
Burton-on-Trent GS, Wednesfield GS, Moseley.
b 23.4.48 Burton-on-Trent.
FH, 11-6-0-5 (4 − 1t).
73 F+ S+ NZ+r; 75 F− W−; 76 A+ W−; 77 S+ I+(1t) F− W−.
Building soc employee.

COOPPER, Sidney Frank   *England*
RNEC Keyham, Blackheath, Barbarians, Devon.
b −.10.1878; *d* 16.1.61.
Wing, 7-1-0-6 (6 − 2t).
1900 W−; 02 W− I+(1t); 05 W− I−(1t) S−; 07 W−.

RN. Sec RFU 24-47. Served WW1 as RN engrg officer in destroyers, once sunk. Mentioned in despatches.

COOTE, Patric Bernard   *Ireland*
RAF Cranwell, RAF, Leicester, Surrey.
b 7.1.10; kia 13.4.41.
Centre, 1-0-0-1.
33 S−.
RAF.

COPE, David   *South Africa*
W Prov, Transvaal.
b c1878; *d* 1898 Mostert's Hoek, nr Matjiesfontein.
FB, 1-0-0-1 (2 − 1c).
1896 BT−(1c).
Scored SA's 1st pts from a kick, v BT 2nd Test 1896. Died from inj sustained in rly accident, at Mostert's Hoek, travelling with another Transvaal player, A.M. Tait, for a Currie Cup match in Cape Town. Tait was also killed.

COPE, Sir William Bt KC JP DL   *Wales*
Repton, Cambridge Univ, Cardiff, Blackheath, Barbarians.
b 18.8.1870 Roath; *d* 15.7.46 St Mellons.
Forward, 1-1-0-0.
1896 S+.
Barrister. Blue 1891. Served WW1, Maj Glam Yeomanry. MP 18-29. Bt 28. Ckt for Glam CCC.

CORBETT, Leonard James   *England*
Fairfield Sch, Bristol Saracens, Bristol, Glos.
b 12.5.1897 Bristol; *d* 26.1.83 Taunton.
Centre, 16-11-1-4 (15 − 3t 1gm 1p).
21 F+; 23 W+ I+(1t); 24 W+ I+(1t) F+ S+; 25 NZ−(1p) W+ I= S− F+; 27 W+(1t 1gm) I+ S− F−.
Gen mgr chocolate co/superintendent R Ordnance factory Bridgend. Served WW1 RASC. Capt E 4 times. Glos CCC. Corr on ckt & rugby for 'Sunday Times'.

CORCORAN, James Crothmans   *Ireland*
PBC Cork, UC Cork, London Irish.
b 14.7.22 Cork.
Prop, 2-1-0-1.
47 A−; 48 F+.
Medicine. Played in 2 Victory ints.

CORDIAL, Ian F.   *Scotland*
Edinburgh W.
Centre, 4-0-0-4 (3 − 1t).
52 F−(1t) W− I− E−.
Textiles.

CORFE, Arthur Cecil DSO   *Australia*
Christ's Coll, Toowoomba GS, Past Grammars, Qld.

94

b 12.12.1877 NZ; *d* 30.7.49 England.
Forward, 1-0-0-1.
1899 BT−.
The Army. Went to Brisbane c1898. Served
Boer War & WW1.

CORKEN, Thomas Samuel   *Ireland*
Methodist Coll Belfast, Collegians.
b 15.9.10 Lisburn.
Hooker, 3-2-0-1.
37 E− S+ W+.
Manufacturer's agent.

CORLESS, Barrie James   *England*
Wymondham Coll, Coventry, Moseley.
b 7.11.45 Booton, Norfolk.
Centre, 10-5-0-5 (4 − 1t).
76 A+(1t) I−r; 77 S+ I+ F− W−; 78 F− W−
S+ I+.
Schoolmaster.

CORLEY, Henry Hagarty   *Ireland*
Leeson Sch Brownie, Trin Coll Dublin,
Wanderers, Barbarians.
b 1879; *d* −.2.36.
Half-back/centre, 8-2-0-6 (5 − 1c 1p).
02 E− S+(1c) W−; 03 E+(1p) S− W−; 04 E−
S−.
Ref S v SA 06, S v E 08. Ckt for Gentlemen of
Ireland.

CORMAC, Henry S.T.   *Ireland*
Clontarf, Barbarians.
b 18.5.02.
Wing, 3-1-0-2.
21 E− S+ W−.
Civil engr.

CORNELSEN, Gregory   *Australia*
The Armidale Sch, Australian Schs, NSW
Country, NSW, Brisbane, Qld.
b 29.8.52.
Flanker/lock, 25-9-1-15 (16 − 4t).
74 NZ− NZ−, 75 J+ 3− W−, 76 E− F− F−,
78 W+ W+ NZ− NZ− NZ+(4t); 79 I− I−
NZ+ Arg− Arg+; 80 NZ+ NZ− NZ+; 81 I+
W− S−; 82 E−.
Grazier/pensions consultant/schoolmaster.
Australian Schs > 68 SA. A > 75-6 & B1-2 BI;
78 NZ; 79 Arg. 4t v NZ 78, rec for A in an int.

CORNER, Mervyn Miles Nelson   *New Zealand*
MC OBE
Auckland GS, Grammar, Auckland.
b 5.7.08 Auckland.
SH, 6-4-0-2.
30 BI+ BI+ BI+; 31 A+; 34 A−; 36 E−.
Gen mgr savings bank/chmn NZ Fishing
Industry Bd. NZ > 32 & 34 A, 35-6 BI & C.
Served WW2, 30th Battn; during service played
football for Army v Auckland. NZRFU sel 50-4.

CORNES, John Reginald   *Australia*
Carterton, Teachers, Qld.
b 30.10.47 Cambridge, NZ.
SH, 1-1-0-0.
72 Fj+.
Shearing overseer. A > NZ 72. Inj on only int
app.

CORNFORTH, Roger George   *Australia*
Warcup
NSW.
b 19.1.19 Sydney; *d* 30.3.76 Sydney.
Flanker/lock, 2-0-0-2 (3 − 1t).
47 NZ−(1t); 50 BI−.
Schoolmaster. At 18st 12lb reputed to be
heaviest Australian first-grade player. Rep A
water polo at Olympics, London 48. Noted
swimmer, cktr.

CORNISH, Frederick Henry   *Wales*
Cardiff.
b 1876 Bridgwater; *d* 27.4.40 Cardiff.
Forward, 4-2-0-2.
1897 E+; 1898 I+ E−; 1899 I−.
Boilermaker. Hull RL. Uncle of Arthur. One of
6 mem of Grangetown family who played for
Cardiff.

CORNISH, Robert Arthur   *Wales*
Canton HS, Welsh SS, Cardiff Univ, RN,
Cardiff.
b 30.6.1897; *d* 29.7.48 Cardiff.
Centre, 10-3-1-6 (7 − 1t 1d).
23 E− S−; 24 E−; 25 E− S−(1t) F+; 26 E= S−
I+ F+(1d).
Schoolmaster. 149t for Cardiff 19-28. Played in
Centenary Match at Rugby Sch 23. Nephew of
Fred.

COSCOLL, Gilbert   *France*
Béziers.
b −; *d* −.8.21.
Lock/prop, 2-1-0-1
21 S+ W−.

COSLETT, Kelvin   *Wales*
Welsh Youth, Aberavon, Llanelli.
b 14.1.42 Bynea.
FB, 3-1-1-1 (3 − 1p).
62 E= S− F+(1p).
Steelworker/haulage contractor. St Helens RL
62, then Rochdale H. Lance Todd Trophy 72.
Coached W RL.

COSSEY, Raymond Reginald   *New Zealand*
('Mick')
Helensville Dist HS, Otahuhu Coll, Ardmore
Coll, Poverty Bay, Gisborne HSOB, Counties,
Pukekohe, N Island.
b 21.1.35 Papakura.

Wing, 1-1-0-0.
58 A+.
Schoolmaster/commercial cleaner.

COSTANTINO, Jean   *France*
Montferrand.
Prop, 1-1-0-0.
73 R+.

COSTELLO, Patrick Joseph   *Ireland*
CBS Synge St, Bective Rgrs.
b 18.8.31 Dublin.
Lock, 1-0-0-1.
60 F−.
Carpets co dir.

COSTELLO, Paul Patrick Scott   *Australia*
Downlands Coll Toowoomba, Qld.
b 27.
FB, 1-0-0-1.
50 BI−.
Golf Club sec-mgr.

COSTES, Frederic   *France*
Montferrand.
b 27.6.57 La Rochelle.
Wing, 7-4-0-3 (4 − 1t).
79 E−(1t) S+ NZ− NZ+ R+; 80 W− I+.
PE instructor.

COTTER, James Logan   *Scotland*
Hillhead HS, Hillhead HSFP, Glasgow Univ.
b 6.1.07 Motherwell.
FH, 2-1-0-1.
34 I+ E−.
Minister.

COTTINGTON, Gordon S.   *Scotland*
Kelso HS, Kelso, Barbarians, Yorks.
b 2.4.11.
Hooker, 5-1-0-4.
34 I+ E−; 35 W− I−; 36 E−.
Automobile salesman/motor engr. Castleford
RL 36.

COTTON, Francis Edward   *England*
Newton-le-Willows GS, Liverpool,
Loughborough Colls, Coventry, Sale, Lancs,
Barbarians.
b 3.1.48 Wigan.
Prop, 31-13-0-18 (4 − 1t).
71 S− S− P−; 73 W− I− F+ S+ NZ+ A+; 74
S−(1t) I−; 75 I− F− W−; 76 A+ W− S− I−
F−; 77 S+ I+ F− W−; 78 S+ I+; 79 NZ−; 80
I+ F+ W+ S+; 81 W−; BI > 74 SA 4-3-0-1, 77
NZ 3-1-0-2.
Mining engr/lecturer/sports goods. E's most
capped prop. E Under 25s v Fj 70.
Autobiography 'Fran, an autobiography' pub
81.

COTTON, J.   *Ireland*
Wanderers.
Forward, 1-1-0-0 (1t).
1889 W+(1t)

COTTRELL, Anthony Ian   *New Zealand*
('Beau') CBE
Christ's Coll, Christchurch, Canterbury, S
Island.
b 10.2.07 Westport.
Hooker/prop, 11-6-0-5.
29 A− A− A−; 30 BI− BI+ BI+ BI+; 31 A+;
32 A− A+ A+.
Barrister. NZ > 29 & 32 A. Canterbury
administrator 30-9.

COTTRELL, Neville Vincent   *Australia*
St Laurence CBC Sch Brisbane, Qld.
b 16.3.27.
Hooker, 14-5-1-8 (13 − 2c 3p).
49 M− M= M+ NZ+ NZ+; 50 BI− BI−; 51
NZ− NZ− NZ−(1p); 52 Fj+ Fj− NZ+(1c 1p)
NZ−(1c 1p).
Salesman/engrg.

COTTRELL, Wayne David   *New Zealand*
W Christchurch HS, Suburbs, NZ Jnrs,
Canterbury, S Island.
b 30.9.43 Christchurch.
2nd/1st five-eighth, 9-5-1-3 (6 − 1t 1d).
68 A+ A+ F+ F+(1d); 70 SA−; 71 BI− BI+
BI− BI=(1t).
Baker. NZ > 67 BI,F & C, 68 A & Fj, 70 A &
SA.

COTTY, W.   *South Africa*
Diocesan Coll Rondebosch, Griq W.
1-0-0-1.
1896 BT−.

COUCH, Manuera Benjamin   *New Zealand*
Riwai
Pirinoa Sch, Christchurch Tech Sch, Greytown,
Wairarapa, Gladstone, NZ Maoris, N Island.
b 27.6.25 Christchurch.
1st five-eighth, 3-1-0-2.
47 A+; 49 A− A−.
Farmer/shearing contractor/MP. Served WW2,
RNZAF. NZ > 47 A. Wairarapa sel, chmn &
pres. Mem of NZRFU council 72-9. National
Party MP for Wairarapa 75; became Postmaster
Gen & Minister of Maori Affairs & Police.

COUGHLAN, Thomas Desmond   *New Zealand*
St Kevin's Coll, Temuka, S Canterbury, Aria-
Mokauiti, King Country, S Island.
b 9.4.34 Temuka.
Flanker, 1-1-0-0.
58 A+.
Farmer. Mid-Canterbury sel 73-4.

COUGHTRIE, Stanley *Scotland*
Edinburgh Acad, Edinburgh Academicals.
b 19.7.35 Hamilton.
SH, 11-4-1-6 (8 − 1c 1d 1p).
59 F− W+ I− E=; 62 W− I+(1d) E−; 63 F+
W− I+(1p) E−(1c); BI > 59 NZ.

COULMAN, Michael John *England*
Risingbrook SMS Stafford, Stafford, Staffs
Police, Moseley, Brit Police, Staffs, N
Midlands.
b 6.5.44 Stafford.
Prop, 9-3-2-4 (3 − 1t).
67 A− I+ F− S+ W−; 68 W= I= F− S+(1t).
Police/restaurant mgr. Midlands Police heavywt
boxing champ, 64-5. Staffs Police 100y, 220y
champ 67. Salford RL 68. 3 GB RL Tests.
England RL in World Champs 75. Salford coach
83-4.

COULON, J. *France*
Grenoble.
Centre, 1-0-0-1.
28 S−.

COULSON, Thomas John *England*
Gloucester, Coventry, Warwicks, Midland Cos.
b 31.12.1896; *d* 26.3.48.
Prop/no 8, 3-3-0-0.
27 W+; 28 NSW+ W+.
Aircraft fitter. Served WW1 4th Hussars.

COULTER, Henry Herbert *Ireland*
Methodist Coll Belfast, Queen's Univ Belfast.
b 1898 Glastry, Co Down; *d* 13.7.65 Bristol.
Hooker, 3-0-0-3.
20 E− S− W−.
Medicine.

COUPER, J.H. *Scotland*
Blairlodge Sch, W of S.
b −; *d* c17.
Forward, 3-0-1-2.
1896 W− I=; 1899 I−.

COURT, Edward Darlington *England*
Rugby Sch, Oxford Univ, Blackheath, Kent.
b 22.6.1862; *d* 2.4.35.
Forward, 1-1-0-0.
1885 W+.
Home Civil Service. Blue 1882-3.

COURTNEY, Anthony William *Ireland*
('Andy')
CBS Nenagh Clongowes, UC Dublin.
b 19.5.1899 Nenagh; *d* 3.1.70 Limerick.
Prop, 7-1-0-6.
20 S− W− F−; 21 E− S+ W− F−.
Medicine.

COUTTS, Frank Henderson CBE *Scotland*
DL
Glasgow Acad, Melrose, Barbarians, The
Army.
b 8.7.18 Glasgow.
Lock, 3-0-0-3.
47 W− I− E−.
The Army. Brig in KOSB. 2 Servs ints. Pres
SRU 77-8.

COUTTS, Ian Douglas Freeman *Scotland*
Dulwich Coll, O Alleynians, Oxford Univ.
b 27.4.28 Herne Hill.
Centre, 2-0-0-2.
51 F−; 52 E−.
Schoolmaster. Blue 51. Ckt blue.

COVERDALE, Harry *England*
Rossall Sch, Hartlepool R, Blackheath,
Barbarians, Durham Cos, Surrey.
b 22.3.1889 Hartlepool; *d* 64 SA.
FH, 4-3-0-1 (4 − 1d).
10 F+; 12 I+ F+(1d); 20 W−.
Shipowner. Football for Rossall. Served WW1,
The Army & RFC. E sel 31-48. Served WW2
RAF. Emigrated to SA 49.

COVE-SMITH, Ronald *England*
Merchant Taylors' Sch, OMT, Cambridge Univ,
King's Coll Hosp, London Univ, Utd Hospitals,
Mdx.
b 26.11.1899.
Lock, 29-22-2-5 (3 − 1t).
21 S+ F+; 22 I+ F= S+; 23 W+ I+ S+ F+; 24
W+ I+ S+ F+; 25 NZ−(1t) W+ I= S− F+; 27
W+ I+ S− F−; 28 NSW+ W+ I+ F+ S+; 29
W+ I−; BI > 24 SA 4-0-1-3.
Medicine. Blue 19-21. Swimming & water polo
half blue. Capt E 7 times. Played on 6 winning
sides v W. Capt BI > 24 SA. Various eminent
medical appointments 19-56.

COWAN, Ronald C. *Scotland*
Selkirk HS, Selkirk, Barbarians.
b 26.11.41 Selkirk
Wing, 5-2-1-2 (3 − 1t).
61 F−; 62 F− W+ I+(1t) E=; BI > 62 SA 1-0-
0-1.
Tweed. Leeds RL 62.

COWEY, Bernard Turing *Wales*
Vionnee ('Bun') DSO
Wellington Coll, RMC Sandhurst, Welch Rgt,
The Army, Newport, Barbarians, London
Welsh.
b 20.11.11 Tidworth, Hants.
Wing, 4-2-1-1 (9 − 3t).
34 E− S+(2t) I+(1t); 35 E=.
The Army.

COWIE, William Lorn Kerr *Scotland*
Fettes Coll, Glasgow Univ, Edinburgh W,
Cambridge Univ.
 b 1.6.26 Glasgow.
No 8, 1-0-0-1.
53 E−.
Advocate/judge.

COWLING, Robin James *England*
Sidcot Sch, Leicester.
 b 24.3.44 Ipswich.
Prop, 8-2-1-5.
77 S+ I+ F− W−; 78 F− NZ−; 79 S= I−.
Farm mgr.

COWMAN, Alan Richard *England*
Workington GS, Newcastle Univ, UAU,
Loughborough Colls, Coventry, Cumberland &
Westmorland.
 b 18.3.49 Workington.
FH, 5-0-0-5 (6 -- 2d).
71 S− S−(1d) P−; 73 W−(1d) I−.
Schoolmaster.

COWNIE, William Brodie *Scotland*
George Watson's Coll, Watsonians.
 b 1871; d −.12.32.
Forward, 9-5-1-3.
1893 W− I= E+; 1894 W− I− E+; 1895 W+
I+ E+.
Chartered accountant.

COWPER, Denis Lawson *Australia*
Newington Coll, Victoria.
 b 28.12.08; d 5.12.81.
Centre/wing, 9-3-0-6 (18 − 4t 1c 1d).
31 NZ−(1t); 32 NZ+(1t) NZ− NZ−(1t 1c); 33
SA− SA+ SA−(1t) SA− SA+(1d).
Business exec. Only Victorian to capt A. Asst
mgr A > 57-8 BI, F, US & Can.

COX, Brian Phillip *Australia*
Sydney CEGS, NSW, Rosslyn Pk (E).
 b 24.9.28 Sydney.
SH, 9-2-0-7 (3 − 1t).
52 Fj+ Fj−(1t) NZ+ NZ−; 54 Fj−; 55 NZ−; 56
SA−; 57 NZ− NZ−.
Surveyor. Father of Michael & Phillip. Spent
time in UK c49.

COX, H.L. *Ireland*
Brentwood Sch, Trin Coll Dublin.
FB/forward, 4-0-0-4.
1875 E− E−; 1877 E− S−.

COX, Michael Hunter *Australia*
NSW.
 b 26.10.58.
Wing, 2-0-0-2 (4 − 1t).
81 W−(1t) S−.
Distribution mgr/car sales mgr. Bro of Phillip,

son of Brian. A > 80 Fj; B1-2 BI. Played most
State matches at centre & for club at FH. RL.

COX, Norman Simpson *England*
Repton Sch, Sunderland, Barbarians, Durham
Cos.
 b 3.9.1877; d 29.3.30 Sunderland.
Centre, 1-0-0-1.
01 S−.
Co dir.

COX, Phillip Anthony *Australia*
Balgowllah HS, Manly, Sydney, NSW.
 b 2.8.57 Sydney.
SH, 16-7-0-9.
79 Arg− Arg+; 80 Fj+ NZ+ NZ−; 81 W−r
S−; 82 S− S+ NZ− NZ+ NZ−; 84 Fj+ NZ+
NZ− NZ−.
Bro of Michael, son of Brian. Added as extra
player A > 80 Fj; > 81-2 & 84 BI; 84 Fj.

CRABBIE, George Ernest *Scotland*
Edinburgh Acad, Edinburgh Academicals.
 b 23.7.1882; d 23.10.21.
Centre, 1-0-0-1.
04 W−.
Merchant. Bro of John.

CRABBIE, John Edward OBE *Scotland*
Edinburgh Acad, Edinburgh Academicals,
Oxford Univ.
 b 11.4.1879; d 21.8.37 Port of Monteith.
Wing, 6-3-0-3 (6 − 2t).
1900 W−; 02 I−; 03 W+ I+(1t); 04 E+(1t); 05
W−.
Advocate. Bro of George. Blue 1898-01. Served
WW1, Capt in Black Watch.

CRABOS, René ('Le Crabe') *France*
RCF, St-Sever.
 b 7.2.1899 St-Sever, Côte Basque; d 64.
Centre, 17-6-2-9 (19 − 1t 5c 2p).
20 S− E−(1t) W− I+ US+; 21 S+ W− E−(2p)
I+(4c); 22 S= E=(1c) W− I−; 23 S− I+; 24 S+
I−.
Son of St-Sever businessman. 1st rugby match at
13. Played for miltary side, 'Ascas' of Lyon &
Joinville Mil Sch, nr Paris. Capt French Army &
F. Mgr F > 49 Arg, 54 & 60 Arg & Chile.

CRAIG, John Binnie *Scotland*
Gala Acad, Heriot's Coll, Heriot's FP.
 b 7.12.18 Calcutta.
Wing, 1-0-0-1.
39 W−.
Sales mgr. Played in 1 Servs int.

CRAIG, Robert Robertson *Australia*
NSW, London Welsh (E).

b 1.9.1881 Sydney; *d* 5.3.35 Broughton, Hull.
Forward, 1-0-0-1.
08 W−.
Boilermaker/licensee. Olympic rugby gold
medal 08. RL in E.

CRAIG, Ronald G. *Ireland*
RBAI, Queen's Univ Belfast.
FB, 2-0-0-2.
38 S− W−.
Minister. Moderator of Presbyterian Church.

CRAMPAGNE, Jacques *France*
Bégles.
Wing, 1-0-1-0.
67 SA=.

CRAMPTON, G. *South Africa*
Griq W.
1-0-1-0.
03 BT=.

CRANCÉE, Roland *France*
Lourdes.
b 24.9.32 Treveray, Meuse.
No 8, 2-2-0-0 (3 − 1t).
60 Arg+(1t); 61 S+.
Petrol station mgr.

CRANMER, Peter *England*
St Edward's Oxford, Oxford Univ, Richmond,
Moseley, Barbarians.
b 10.9.14 Acocks Green, Birmingham.
Centre, 16-10-2-4 (14 − 1t 2d 1p).
34 W+ I+ S+; 35 W= I+ S−(1d); 36 NZ+(1d)
W= I− S+(1t); 37 W+ I+(1p) S+; 38 W− I+
S−.
Stockbroker/journalist. Blue 33-4. Capt E twice.
Brit Army v French Army 40. Served WW2. Ckt
Warwicks; 166 apps 34-54; Bombay Europeans;
Servs 44-5. Served WW2 in Egypt & Burma.
Corr for BBC & 'Sunday Times'.

CRANSTON, Alastair Gerald *Scotland*
Hawick HS, Hawick.
b 11.12.49 Hawick.
Centre, 11-2-0-9.
76 W− E+ I+; 77 E− W−; 78 F−r W− E−
NZ−; 81 NZ− NZ−.
Farmer. Scottish XV v Japan 77.

CRAUSTE, Michel ('Attila') *France*
RCF, Lourdes.
b 6.7.34 St-Laurent de Gasse, Landes.
No 8/flanker, 63-38-9-16 (33 − 11t).
57 R+ R+(1t); 58 S− E− A+(1t) W+ It+ I+;
59 E= It+ W+ I−; 60 S+ E= W+ I+ It+ R−
Arg+ Arg+; 61 S+ SA= E=(1t) W+ It+ I+
NZ− NZ− NZ−(1t) A+ R=(1t); 62 S+ E+(3t)
W− I+(1t) It+ R−; 63 S− I+ E− W+ It+ R=;
64 S− NZ− E− W=(1t) It+ I+(1t) SA+ Fj+

R+; 65 S+ I= E− W+ It+ R+; 66 S= I+ E+
W− It+.
Electricity technician. Capt F > 64 SA.

CRAVEN, Daniel Hartman *South Africa*
('Danie')
Lindley Sch, Stellenbosch Univ, W Prov, E
Prov, N Transvaal.
b 11.10.10 Lindley, OFS.
FH/SH/centre/no 8, 16-12-0-4 (6 − 2t).
31 W+ I+; 32 S+(1t); 33 A+(1t) A− A+ A+
A−; 37 A+ A+ NZ− NZ+ NZ+; 38 BI+ BI+
BI−.
Schoolmaster/dir of PE SA Defence Force.
Yorkshire grandfather went to SA as diamond
prospector. One-time theological student. SA's
'Mr Rugby'. Capped from Stellenbosch; played
for SA before prov. Capt SA v NZ 1st Test 37;
BI (3) 38. SA > 31-2 BI. Played in 4 different
positions in 4 consec Tests v A 33. Coach SA >
51-2 BI, F. Mgr SA > 56 A, NZ. SA selector.
Pres SARB 56−. Biography 'Ek Speel Vir Suid-
Afrika' pub 49.

CRAWFORD, E.C. *Ireland*
Cheltenham Coll, Trin Coll Dublin.
b 26.1.1861; *d* 20.4.23 London.
Half-back, 1-0-0-1.
1885 E−.

CRAWFORD, John Archibald *Scotland*
Cheltenham Coll, RMA Sandhurst, RE, The
Army, London Scottish.
b 20.11.10; *d* 10.1.73.
Flanker, 1-1-0-0 (3 − 1t).
34 I+(1t).
The Army.

CRAWFORD, W.H. *Scotland*
US Portsmouth, RN.
Flanker, 5-3-0-2 (21 − 1t 3c 4p).
38 W+(1t 1c 1p) I+(2c) E+(2p); 39 W−(1p)
E−.
RN.

CRAWFORD, William Ernest *Ireland*
Methodist Coll Belfast, Malone, Ulster,
Lansdowne, Cardiff, Barbarians.
b 17.11.1891 Belfast; *d* 12.1.59 Belfast.
FB, 30-12-1-17 (18 − 6c 2p).
20 E− S− W− F−; 21 E− S+ W− F−; 22 E−
S−; 23 E−(1c) S− W+(1c) F−(1c); 24 F+ E−
W+(2c) NZ−; 25 F+(1p) E= S−(1c 1p) W+;
26 F+ E+ S+ W−; 27 F+ E− S+ W+.
Accountant/Belfast City treasurer. Ulster v SA
12. Played football for Bohemians &
Cliftonville. Pres IRU 57-8. Father in law of J.S.
Ritchie.

CREAN, Thomas Joseph VC *Ireland*
DSO

Clongowes Coll, Wanderers, Johannesburg Wanderers.
b 19.4.1873 Dublin; *d* 25.3.23.
Forward, 9-5-1-3 (6 − 2t).
1894 E+ S+ W+; 1895 E− S− W−(1t); 1896 E+ S= W+(1t); BT > 1896 SA.
Medicine. Won VC in SA War 01, in which he served with 1st Imperial Light Horse Bde & although severely wounded led bayonet charge against Boers at Elandslaagte (see Robert Johnston & F.M. Harvey). Served WW1; DSO 15.

CREED, Roger Norman   *England*
Solihull GS, O Sillhillians, Moseley, Coventry, Warwicks.
b 19.11.45 Solihull.
Flanker, 1-0-0-1.
71 P−.
Buyer in family power tools co. E Under 25s v Fj 70.

CREIGHTON, John Neville   *New Zealand*
Christchurch Boys' HS, Univ, NZ Univs, NZ Jnrs, Canterbury, S Island.
b 10.3.37 Rotherham.
Hooker, 1-1-0-0.
62 A+.
Solicitor. NZ > 62 A. Coach Univ club (Christchurch) 69-78 & Merivale-Papanui 79.

CREMASCHI, Michel   *France*
St Jean-de-Luz, Lourdes.
b 26.4.56 Urrugne.
Prop, 11-5-1-5.
80 R−; 81 R+ NZ− NZ−; 82 W− S−; 83 A= A+ R+; 84 I+ W+.
Restaurateur/chef. Jaw broken during F > 81 A, missed Tests.

CREMIN, John Francis ('Mick')   *Australia*
NSW.
b 23.
Five-eighth, 3-0-0-3.
46 NZ− NZ−; 47 NZ−.
Clerk.

CRESSWELL, Brian   *Wales*
Newport St Julians HS, Newport.
b 34.
Flanker, 4-2-0-2 (3 − 1t).
60 E− S+ I+(1t) F−.
Steelworker. Some sources state Cresswell scored t v F 60 but Newport team-mate Brian Jones was official scorer.

CRICHTON, Robert Young   *Ireland*
('John Willy')
Campbell Coll Belfast, Trin Coll Dublin, Barbarians.
b 18.8.1897; *d* 29.7.40.

Lock/prop, 15-3-1-11.
20 E− S− W− F−; 21 F−; 22 E−; 23 W+ F−; 24 F+ E− S− W+ NZ−; 25 E= S−.
Medicine/stockbroker. One of I's heaviest forwards, 18st.

CRICHTON, Scott   *New Zealand*
Wellington, NZ Maoris, Southern Maoris.
b 31.8.61 Wanganui.
Prop, 2-0-1-1.
83 S= E−.
NZ > 83 S & E (inj v E); 85 Arg. World XV > 86 SA.

CRICHTON, W.H.   *France*
Le Havre.
b England.
FB, 2-0-0-2.
06 NZ− E−.

CRICHTON-MILLER, Donald   *Scotland*
Fettes Coll, Cambridge Univ, TA, Barbarians, Gloucester.
b 7.12.06.
Flanker, 3-1-0-2 (6 − 2t).
31 W−(2t) I− E+.
Schoolmaster. Blue 28.

CRIDLAN, Arthur Gordon   *England*
Uppingham Sch, Oxford Univ, Blackheath, Barbarians, Mdx.
b 9.7.09 Ealing.
Flanker, 3-1-1-1.
35 W= I+ S−.
Man dir food manufacturers. Blue 28-30. Alpine Ski Club mem. Served WW2 with RE. Order of Crown of Belgium 46.

CRISTINA, Jacques   *France*
Montferrand.
No 8, 1-1-0-0.
79 R+.

CRITTLE, Charles Peter   *Australia*
Sydney HS, Sydney Univ, NSW.
b 21.7.39.
No 8/flanker, 15-6-0-9.
62 NZ− NZ−; 63 SA+ SA+ SA−; 64 NZ− NZ− NZ+; 65 SA+ SA+; 66 BI− BI− S−; 67 E+ I−.
Barrister. Climbed Mount Kilimanjaro on 40th birthday.

CROKER, E.W.D.   *Ireland*
Limerick.
Forward, 1-0-0-1.
1878 E−.
The Army. Served in 93rd Highlanders.

CROLE, Gerard Bruce MC   *Scotland*
Edinburgh Acad, Oxford Univ.

b 7.6.1894 Edinburgh; *d* 31.3.65 Aberdeen.
Wing, 4-3-0-1 (9 − 3t).
20 F+(1t) W+ I+(2t) E−.
Sudan political service/schoolmaster. Half-bro
of Phipps Turnbull. Blue 13 & 19. Served WW1,
2nd Lt Dragoon Guards & RFA; MC 17. POW.
Ckt for S.

CROMEY, George Ernest　　*Ireland*
Methodist Coll Belfast, Queen's Univ Belfast,
Collegians, Barbarians.
b 8.5.13 Ahogil, Ballymena.
FH, 9-4-0-5 (6 − 2t).
37 E− S+ W+; 38 E−(1t) S−(1t) W−; 39 E+
S+ W−; BI > 38 SA 1-1-0-0.
Minister.

CROMPTON, Charles Arthur　　*England*
Cheltenham Coll, RMA Woolwich, RE,
Blackheath.
b 21.10.1848; *d* 6.7.1875 Bengal.
Forward, 1-0-0-1.
1871 S−.
The Army. Played in 1st int, S v E 1871. Played
football for E 1871. Died while serving as RE Lt
in India.

CRONJE, Peter Arnold　　*South Africa*
Transvaal.
b 21.9.49.
Centre, 7-4-2-1 (10 − 3t).
71 F+ F=(1t) A+ A+ A+(1t); 74 BI−
BI=(1t).

CRONYN, A.P.　　*Ireland*
Monaghan Coll, UC Dublin, Lansdowne.
b 3.9.1855; *d* −.4.37.
Back/half-back, 3-0-0-3.
1875 E− E−; 1880 S−.
The Army/minister. Served with 97th Rgt. Last
survivor of 1st Irish XX.

CROSBY, J.H.　　*South Africa*
Transvaal.
1-0-0-1.
1896 BT−.
SA selector.

CROSBY, Nicholas J.　　*South Africa*
Transvaal.
2-2-0-0.
10 BI+ BI+.

CROSS, James Robert　　*Australia*
NSW.
b 27.10.30.
Hooker, 3-1-0-2.
55 NZ− NZ− NZ+.
Clerk.

CROSS, Keith Austin　　*Australia*
Sydney HS, NSW.
b 8.6.28.
Flanker/no 8, 19-5-0-14 (18 − 6t).
49 M− NZ+ NZ+; 50 BI−(1t) BI−; 51 NZ−
NZ−; 52 NZ+; 53 SA− SA+(1t) SA−(1t)
SA−; 54 Fj+(1t) Fj−(1t); 55 NZ−; 56 SA−
SA−; 57 NZ−(1t) NZ−.
Accountant.

CROSS, Malcolm　　*Scotland*
Merchiston Castle Sch, Merchistonians,
Manchester.
b 16.6.1855 Glasgow; *d* 20.12.19 Gatehouse of
Fleet.
Back, 9-4-3-2 (8c 2d).
1875 E=; 1876 E−; 1877 I+(4c) E+(1d); 1878
E=; 1879 I+(2c 1d) E=; 1880 I+(1c) E−(1c).
Merchant trader. Bro of William. Ump S v I, S v
W 1885. Pres SRU 1884-5.

CROSS, Thomas ('Angry')　　*New Zealand*
Kaikorai, Otago, Linwood, Canterbury,
Poneke, Wellington, Petone, S & N Islands.
b 21.1.1876 Dunedin; *d* −.
Flanker, 2-2-0-0 (3 − 1t).
04 BT+; 05 A+(1t).
Meat worker. Susp for season after being sent
off in club match 07. Turned RL.

CROSS, William　　*Scotland*
Glasgow Acad, Merchiston Castle Sch,
Merchistonians.
b −; *d* 16.10.1890 Bournemouth.
Back, 2-1-0-1 (1t 1c).
1871 E+(1t 1c); 1872 E−.
Bro of Malcolm. Sc S's 1st c, in 1st int v E 1871.
Ref S v E 1877. Ump S v I 1882, S v W 1883.
Pres SRU 1882-3.

CROSSAN, Keith Derek　　*Ireland*
RBAI, Instonians, Ulster.
b 29.12.59 Belfast.
Wing, 11-4-1-6 (4 − 1t).
82 S+; 84 F− W− E− S−; 85 S+ F= W+(1t)
E+; 86 E− S−.
Bank official. I > 81 SA.

CROSSE, Charles William　　*England*
Rugby Sch, Oxford Univ, RMC Sandhurst.
b 13.6.1854; *d* 28.5.05 Paris.
Forward, 2-2-0-0.
1874 S+; 1875 I+.
The Army. Blue 1874. With E.H. Nash, refused
permission by Oxford Univ to play E v S 1875.
Ckt for OUCC. Maj in 6th Dragoon Guards.
Served in Transvaal campaign 1881.

CROSSMAN, Owen Clive　　*Australia*
Sydney CEGS, NSW.
b 03; *d* 63.

Wing, 2-2-0-0 (3 − 1t).
29 NZ+(1t); 30 BI+.
Accountant.

CROWE, James Fintan ('Golly')   *Ireland*
Blackrock Coll, UC Dublin.
b 21.11.52 Dublin.
Centre, 1-0-0-1.
74 NZ−.
Accountant. Son of Morgan.

CROWE, Louis   *Ireland*
Belvedere Coll, O Belvedere.
b −; *d* −.9.68.
Wing, 3-1-0-2 (3 − 1t).
50 E− S+(1t) W−.
Medicine. Ath for I.

CROWE, Morgan Patrick   *Ireland*
Blackrock Coll, RCSI, Lansdowne, Barbarians.
b 5.3.07 Dublin.
Centre, 13-6-1-6 (6 − 2t).
29 W=; 30 E+ S+(1t) W−; 31 F− S+ W−
SA−; 32 S+ W+; 33 W+ S−(1t); 34 E−.
Medicine/Army. Father of J.F. & bro of Philip.

CROWE, Philip Martin   *Ireland*
Blackrock Coll.
b 24.8.10 Dublin.
Centre/FB, 2-0-0-2 (2 − 1c).
35 E−; 38 E−(1c).
Licensed vintner. Bro of Morgan.

CROWE, Phillip John   *Australia*
The Scots Coll, NSW.
b 27.10.55 London, England.
Wing, 6-3-0-3 (8 − 2t).
76 F−; 78 W+(1t) W+; 79 I− NZ+ Arg−(1t).
Medicine.

CROWLEY, Kieran James   *New Zealand*
Kaponga, Taranaki, NZ Colts, NZ Barbarians,
N Island.
b 31.8.61.
FB, 5-4-1-0 (58 − 5c 16p).
85 E+(6p) E+(3c 3p) A+(2p) Arg+(1c 4p)
Arg=(1c 1p).
NZ > 83 S & E, 85 Arg (48 pts).

CROWLEY, Patrick Joseph   *New Zealand*
Bourke
Marist Bros' Sch Wanganui, Wanganui Tech
Coll, St Patrick's Coll Silverstream, Marist,
Auckland, N Island.
b 20.10.23 Wanganui.
Flanker, 6-3-1-2 (3 − 1t).
49 SA− SA−; 50 BI= BI+(1t) BI+ BI+.
Meat inspector/farmer.

CULLEN, Thomas Joseph   *Ireland*
Blackrock Coll, Clongowes Coll, UC Dublin.

b 5.9.26 Dublin.
SH, 1-0-0-1.
49 F−.
Architect.

CULLEN, William John MBE   *Ireland*
Christ's Hosp Sch, Oxford Univ, Monkstown,
Manchester, Barbarians.
b 7.12.1894; *d* 60.
Centre, 1-0-0-1.
20 E−.

CULLITON, Michael Gerard   *Ireland*
Mount St Joseph's Sch Roscrea, Wanderers,
Barbarians.
b 15.6.36 Clonaslee, Laois.
Lock/no 8, 19-4-0-15 (3 − 1t).
59 E− S+ W− F+; 60 E−(1t) S− W− F−
SA−; 61 E+ S− W− F−; 62 S− F−; 64 E+ S−
W− F−.
Farmer.

CUMBERLEGE, Barry   *England*
Stephenson OBE
Durham Sch, Cambridge Univ, Blackheath,
Barbarians, Northumb.
b 5.6.1891 Newcastle upon Tyne; *d* 22.9.70
Folkestone.
FB, 8-6-0-2 (2 − 1c).
20 W− I+ S+; 21 W+ I+(1c) S+ F+; 22 W−.
Lloyd's underwriter. Declined invitation BT >
10 SA because he was still at school. Blue 10-13.
Ref 16 ints 26-34. Ckt for Cambridge Univ,
Durham, Northumb, Kent CCC. Served WW1
RASC, later NZ Div. Twice mentioned in
despatches. OBE (Mil) 18. Served WW2 R
Observer Corps.

CUMMING, Sir Duncan   *England*
Cameron KBE CB
Giggleswick Sch, Cambridge Univ, Blackheath,
Barbarians.
b 10.8.03; *d* 10.12.79.
No 8, 2-1-0-1.
25 S− F+.
Sudan Political Service/man dir. Blue 22-4. CB
48. KBE 53.

CUMMING, Sir Ronald S. TD   *Scotland*
Uppingham Sch, Aberdeen Univ.
b 1900 Speyside; *d* 17.11.82.
Hooker/prop, 2-1-0-1.
21 F− W+.
Co chmn. Kt 65.

CUMMINGS, William   *New Zealand*
Marist Bros' Sch, Waltham Sch, Linwood,
Canterbury.
b 13.3.1889 Timaru; *d* 28.5.55 Christchurch.
Lock, 2-1-0-1 (3 − 1t).
13 A+(1t) A−.

Newspaper & publishing employee. Bro Ernie rep Canterbury 13 & 21.

CUMMINS, William   *Wales*
Treorchy.
No 8, 4-3-1-0 (3 − 1t).
22 E+ S= I+ F+(1t).
Police.

CUMMINS, William Edward   *Ireland*
Ashley
Queen's Coll Cork.
b 1858; *d* 18.10.23.
Forward, 3-0-1-2.
1879 S−; 1881 E−; 1882 E=.
Medicine.

CUNDY, Rawi Tama   *New Zealand*
Nelson Coll, Featherston Utd, Wairarapa, Featherston, Southern Utd, Greytown.
b 15.8.01 Featherston; *d* 9.2.55 Hinakura.
2nd five-eighth, 1-0-0-1 (3 − 1p).
29 Ar−(1p).
Sheep farmer. NZ > 29 A. 1st NZ player to reach 100 pts in domestic 1st-class rugby, 110 pts 27 (inc 4p which helped Wairarapa defeat Hawkes Bay in Ranfurly Shield challenge).

CUNLIFFE, Foster Lionel   *England*
Rugby Sch, RMA Woolwich, RA.
b 20.4.1854; *d* 15.4.27.
Forward, 1-1-0-0.
1874 S+.
The Army. Served Afghan War 1878-9 & NW Frontier 1897-8. Lt Col RHA 1899.

CUNNINGHAM, Dunlop   *Ireland*
McCosh
RBAI, Fettes Coll, NIFC.
b 20.2.01 Belfast; *d* −.1.85.
Flanker/lock, 6-3-1-2.
23 E− S− W+; 25 F+ E= W+.
Tobacco co dir.

CUNNINGHAM, Gary Richard   *New Zealand*
Takapuna GS, N Shore, NZ Jnrs, Auckland, N Island.
b 12.5.55 Auckland.
Wing/centre/2nd five-eighth, 5-3-0-2.
79 A−; 79 S+ E+; 80 A− A+.
Sales rep. NZ > 79 A, 79 E,S & It, 80 A & Fj.
NZ (2) v Arg 79.

CUNNINGHAM, Sir George   *Scotland*
GCIE KCSI OBE
Fettes Coll, Oxford Univ.
b 23.3.1888 Broughty Ferry; *d* 8.12.63.
Half-back, 8-3-0-5 (9 − 3c 1p).
08 W− I−; 09 W−(1p) E+(3c); 10 F+ I+ E−; 11 E−.

Indian civil service. Blue 07-9. Served WW1, Punjab Light Horse.

CUNNINGHAM, Leonard John   *Wales*
Aberavon Quins, Aberavon, Barbarians.
b 3.1.32 Port Talbot.
Prop, 14-5-4-5.
60 E− S+ I+ F−; 62 E= S− F+ I=; 63 NZ−; 64 E= S+ I+ F= SA−.
Steelworker/licensee. Served RAF. W > 64 SA. Barbarians v NZ 64. Aberavon comm.

CUNNINGHAM, Martin John   *Ireland*
('Marney')
PBC Cork, UC Cork, Cork Constitution, Barbarians.
b 23.6.33 Cork.
Flanker, 7-2-1-4 (3 − 1t).
55 F− E= S− W−; 56 F− S+ W+(1t).
Civil engr/priest.

CUNNINGHAM, Robert Fraser   *Scotland*
Preston Lodge Sch, Gala.
b 4.1.53 Musselburgh.
Prop, 3-0-1-2.
78 NZ−; 79 W− E=.
Industrial relations officer. Scottish XV v J 77.

CUNNINGHAM, William   *New Zealand*
Waihi West, Auckland, City, Waitete, Ponsonby, NZ Maoris, N Island.
b 8.7.1874 Rangiaohia; *d* 3.9.27 Auckland.
No 8/flanker, 9-7-2-0 (3 − 1t).
05 S+(1t) I+; 06 F+; 07 A+ A+ A=; 08 AW+ AW= AW+.
Blacksmith. NZ > 05 A, 05-6 BI,F & NAm, 07 A. Auckland selector 20.

CUNNINGHAM, William A.   *Ireland*
Belvedere Coll, Lansdowne.
b 27.3.1900; *d* 59.
FH/SH, 8-2-0-6 (3 − 1t).
20 W−; 21 E− S+(1t) W− F−; 22 E−; 23 S− W+; Blr > 24 SA 1-0-1-0.
Dentist. Emigrated SA 23. Living in Johannesburg when invited to join BI > 24 SA, after 2 FB, W.F. Gaisford and T.E. Holliday, ruled out by inj early in tour.

CUPPAIDGE, John Loftus   *Ireland*
Rossall Sch, Trin Coll Dublin, Wanderers.
b 1858; *d* −.11.34 A.
Forward, 3-0-0-3 (1t).
1879 E−; 1880 E−(1t) S−.
Medicine. Scored I's 1st int pts, 1t v E 1880. Emigrated to Qld.

CUPPLES, Leslie Frank MM   *New Zealand*
Otautau Sch, Tokaanu, Bay of Plenty, N Island.
b 8.2.1898 Otautau; *d* 10.8.72 Hamilton.
No 8, 2-2-0-0.

24 I+ W+.
Post & Telegraph employee/farmer. Served
WW1, Field Ambulance. NZ > 22 A, 24-5
A,BI,F & C.

CURLEY, Terrence George　　　*Australia*
NSW.
b 6.6.38.
FB, 11-2-0-9 (11 − 1c 1d 2p).
57 NZ− NZ−; 58 W− I− E−(1d) S− F− M+
NZ− NZ+(1p) NZ−(1c 1p).
Solicitor/priest. 47 pts A > 58 NZ.

CURRAN, Declan James　　　*Australia*
Sydney Univ, Sydney, Newcastle, NSW.
b 15.4.52.
Prop, 5-3-0-2.
80 NZ+; 81 F+ F+ W−; 83 Arg−.
Lawyer.

CURRELL, J.　　　*Ireland*
RBAI, NIFC.
Forward, 1-0-0-1.
1877 S−.

CURREY, Frederick Innes　　　*England*
Marlborough Coll, Marlborough Nomads.
b 3.5.1849; *d* 18.12.1896 London.
Forward, 1-1-0-0.
1872 S+.
Solicitor. Fdr mem Marlborough Nomads 1868.
Ref S v W 1887. Pres RFU 1884-6. IB mem
1891-2. Shared with A.G. Guillemard
distinction of serving RFU in all five chief
offices.

CURRIE, C.　　　*South Africa*
Diocesan Coll Rondebosch, Griq W.
1-0-1-0.
03 BT=.

CURRIE, Clive James　　　*New Zealand*
Rongotai Coll, Oriental-Rongotai, Canterbury,
Christchurch HSOB, NZ Jnrs, N & S Islands.
b 25.12.55 Wellington.
FB, 2-2-0-0.
78 I+ W+.
Schoolmaster. Broken jaw v W allowed him to
make only 4 apps NZ > 78 BI. NZ Schs ckt.

CURRIE, L.R.　　　*Scotland*
Dunfermline.
Lock, 8-3-0-5.
47 A−; 48 F+ W− I−; 49 F+ W+ I− E−.
Chemist.

CURRIE, Ernest William　　　*Australia*
Qld.
b 9.4.1875; *d* −.

Half-back, 1-0-0-1.
1899 BT−.
Clerk.

CURRIE, John David　　　*England*
Bristol GS, Oxford Univ, Harlequins, Bristol,
Barbarians.
b 3.5.32 Clifton, Bristol.
Lock, 25-14-6-5 (16 − 2c 4p).
56 W− I+(1c 2p) S+(1c 2p) F−; 57 W+ I+ F+
S+; 58 W= A+ I+ F+ S=; 59 W− I+ F= S=;
60 W+ I+ F= S+; 61 SA−; 62 W= I+ F−.
Asst factory mgr. Blue 54-7. Ptn David Marques
in 22 consec ints 56-61. 9 apps OUCC 56-7; 1
app Som CCC 53.

CURTIS, Arthur Bryan DFC　　　*Ireland*
Eastbourne Coll, Oxford Univ.
b 27.3.24 Shanghai.
Flanker, 3-1-1-1 (3 − 1t).
50 F= E− S+(1t).
HM. Served WW2, RAF. DFC 45. Blue 49.
Emigrated to Rhodesia 54.

CUSCADEN, William Andrew　　　*Ireland*
ISO DSO
Diocesan Sch Wexford, Trin Coll Dublin, Bray.
b 1.11.1853; *d* 5.8.36.
Forward, 1-0-0-1.
1875 E−.
Inspector Gen of Police, Straits Settlements.

CUSSAC, Pierre　　　*France*
Biarritz Ol.
Wing, 1-1-0-0.
34 G+.

CUSSEN, Denis John　　　*Ireland*
Blackrock Coll, Trin Coll Dublin, Barbarians.
b 19.7.01 Newcastle W, Co Limerick; *d*
15.12.80 Richmond.
Wing, 15-6-0-9 (15 − 5t).
21 E− S+(1t) W− F−; 22 E−; 23 E− S−(1t)
W+(1t) F−; 26 F+ E+(2t) S+ W−; 27 F+ E−.
Medicine. Ath for I.

CUSWORTH, Leslie　　　*England*
Normanton GS, W Midlands TTC, English
Colls, Brit Colls, Wakefield, Moseley,
Leicester, Yorks, NE Cos, N Midlands,
Barbarians.
b 3.7.54 Wakefield.
FH, 10-4-1-5 (9 − 3d).
79 NZ−; 82 F+ W+; 83 F−(1d) W=(1d) NZ+;
84 S− I+(1d) F− W−.
Schoolmaster/insurance. England B > 78 R. E
> 82 US & Can. In 3 John Player Cup Final wins
with Leicester 79-81. 23d for Wakefield 75-6.

CUTHBERTSON, William　　　*Scotland*
('Gulliver')

Marr Coll Troon, Kilmarnock, Harlequins.
b 6.12.49 Kilwinning.
Lock, 21-10-1-10.
80 I−; 81 W+ E− I+ NZ− NZ− R+ A+; 82
E+ I− F+ W+ A+ A−; 83 I− F− W− NZ=;
84 W+ E+ A−.
Engr/co rep. Scotland B. Scottish XV v Fj 82.
Basketball int.

CUTHILL, John Elliot ('Jock')   *New Zealand*
Otago Boys' HS, Taieri, Univ, NZ Univs,
Otago, S Island.
b 21.8.1892 Inverleithen, Scotland; *d* 22.4.70
Invercargill.
FB, 2-2-0-0.
13 A+ US+.
Partner in firm of public secretaries. NZ > 13
NAm. Studies prevented his accepting captaincy
NZ > 14 A. Served WW1 Otago Rgt; invalided
home 16. Sec of Southland Racing Club &
Southland Trotting Club.

CUTLER, Stephen Arthur   *Australia*
Geoffrey
Sydney Univ, Gordon, Sydney, NSW.
b 28.7.60.
Lock, 13-10-0-3.
82 NZ+r; 84 NZ+ NZ− NZ− E+ I+ W+ S+;
85 C+ C+ NZ− Fj+ Fj+.
Research student. 6ft 7in, 17st 5lb. A > 82 NZ;
83 It & F; 84 BI. Rest of World v BI, Cardiff 86.
Overseas XV v Five Nations, Twickenham 86.

CUTZACH, Amédée   *France*
Quillan.
FH, 1-1-0-0.
29 G+.

D

DACEY, Malcolm   *Wales*
Cefn Hengoed 3ch, Swansea 3chs, Welsh
Youth, Bonymaen, Swansea.
b 12.7.60 Swansea.
FH, 10-4-1-5 (9 − 3d).
83 E=(1d) S+ I+ F− R−; 84 S− I+ F−
E+(2d) A−.
Marketing sales rep. Wales B v A 81, v F 81, 82.
Wales B > 83 Spain. Wales XV v Maoris 82, v J
83. BIr v Rest of World, Cardiff 86. Five
Nations v Overseas XV, Twickenham 86.

DAGUERRE, Francis   *France*
Biarritz Ol.
Prop, 1-1-0-0 (3 − 1t).
36 G+(1t).

DAGUERRE, Jean   *France*
CASG.

FH, 1-1-0-0.
33 G+.

D'AGUILAR, Francis Burton   *England*
Grant
Cheltenham Coll, RMA Woolwich, RE, The
Army.
b 11.12.1849; *d* 24.7.1896 Bath.
Forward, 1-1-0-0 (1t).
72 S+(1t).
The Army. Maj RE. Served Afghan War 1878-
80.

DALGLEISH, Adam   *Scotland*
Gala.
b −; *d* −.10.38.
Forward, 8-4-0-4.
1890 W+ E−; 1891 W+ I+; 1892 W+; 1893
W−; 1894 W− I−.
Millworker. 1st player capped from a Border
club.

DALGLEISH, Kenneth James   *Scotland*
Fettes Coll, Edinburgh W, Cambridge Univ,
RAF.
b 7.6.31; *d* 74.
Wing/centre, 4-0-0-4.
51 I− E−; 53 F− W−.
RAF. Blue 51-3.

DALLAS, John Dewar   *Scotland*
George Watson's Coll, Watsonians.
b 1878; *d* 31.7.42.
Forward, 1-1-0-0 (3 − 1t).
03 E+(1t).
Law. Ref W v NZ 05; I v W 08; W v E, I v E 09;
E v W, I v W 10; I v E 11; I v W 12. SRU comm.
Pres SRU 12-13. Sheriff.

DALLEY, William Charles   *New Zealand*
Christchurch Boys' HS, Leeston, Canterbury,
Ellesmere, Christchurch HSOB, S Island.
b 18.11.01 Lyttelton.
SH, 5-3-0-2.
24 I+; 28 SA− SA+ SA− SA+.
Stock co employee. NZ > 24-5 A,BI,F & C, 26
& 29 A, 28 SA. Inj limited apps > 29 A.
Leading administrator. Rep Canterbury bowls
& ckt. Bro H.G. rep Canterbury 21-4.

D'ALTON, George   *South Africa*
Diocesan Coll Rondebosch, W Prov.
Flanker, 1-1-0-0.
33 A+.

DALTON, Andrew Grant   *New Zealand*
('Froggy')
Selwyn Coll, Lincoln Coll, Eastern, Bombay,
Counties, N Island.
b 16.11.51 Dunedin.
Hooker, 35-30-0-5 (12 − 3t).

77 F+; 78 A+ A+ A− I+(1t) W+ E+ S+; 79
F+ F− S+; 81 S+ S+ SA+ SA− SA+ R+(1t)
F+ F+; 82 A+ A− A+; 83 BI+ BI+ BI+ BI+
A+; 84 F+ F+(1t) A− A+ A+; 85 E+ E+
A+.
Farm advisory officer. Son of R.A. NZ's most
capped hooker. NZ > 77 F, 78 BI, 79 A, 79 E,S
& It, 80 NAm & W, 81 R & F, 83 A. NZ v Fj 80.
Capt v SA 81, BI & A 83; A 84. Capt Overseas
XV v Five Nations, Twickenham 86.

DALTON, Douglas   *New Zealand*
Napier Tech Coll, Napier Tech Coll OB,
Hawkes Bay, Trentham Army, Wellington, N
Island.
b 18.1.13 Napier.
Prop, 9-6-0-3.
35 I+ W−; 36 A+ A+; 37 SA+ SA− SA−; 38
A+ A+.
Plasterer/Charolais stud owner. NZ > 35-6 BI &
C (inj limited apps), 36 & 38 A. Selector for
Hawkes Bay & N Island; fdr mem & pres of
Saracens club. Pres Napier GC. OStJ for
services to St John's Ambulance Assoc.

DALTON, Raymond Alfred   *New Zealand*
Te Awamutu Coll, Wellington, Pirates, Otago,
Comb Servs, S Island.
b 14.7.19 Te Awamutu.
Prop, 2-2-0-0.
47 A+ A+.
Advertising exec. Father of Andy. Served
WW2, Ft Lt RNZAF. Rep Comb Servs in BI 44-
6. NZ > 47 A, 49 SA.

DALTON, Timothy J.   *England*
Warwick Sch, Kenilworth, Coventry, Rugby,
Warwicks.
Wing, 1-1-0-0.
69 S+r.
E's 1st r.

DALY, John Christopher   *Ireland*
Presentation Coll Cobh, London Irish,
Barbarians.
b 12.12.16 Cobh.
Prop, 7-5-0-2 (3 − 1t).
47 F− E+ S+ W−; 48 E+ S+ W+(1t).
Engr. Served WW2. Huddersfield RL 48.

DALY, Maurice J.   *Ireland*
Haberdashers' Aske's Sch, Harlequins.
Wing, 1-0-0-1 (3 − 1t).
38 E−(1t).
Farmer. Reserve for England trial. Farmed in
Kenya.

DALZELL, George Nelson   *New Zealand*
Culverden Sch, Culverden, Canterbury, S
Island.
b 26.4.21 Rotherham.

Lock, 5-3-0-2 (3 − 1t).
53 W−; 54 I+ E+(1t) S+ F−.
Sheep farmer. Served WW2, 3rd NZ Div in
Pacific; severely wounded. NZ > 53-4 BI,F &
NAm. Breeder & trainer of trotting ponies.
Father-in-law of Graeme Higginson.

DANBY, Thomson   *England*
Barnard Castle Sch, St John's Coll York,
Durham City, Gosport, Harlequins, The Army,
Comb Servs, Barbarians, Durham Cos, Hants.
b 10.8.26.
Wing, 1-0-0-1.
49 W−.
Schoolmaster. Master i/c rugby at Shebbear
Coll, Devon. Salford RL.

DANEEL, George M.   *South Africa*
Robertson Boys HS, Cape Town Univ,
Stellenbosch Univ, W Prov.
b 29.8.04 Calvinia.
No 8/flanker, 8-6-0-2 (6 − 2t).
28 NZ+ NZ− NZ+(1t) NZ−; 31 W+(1t) I+;
32 E+ S+.
Dutch Reform Church minister. SA > 31-2 BI.
Nephew of Henry J. Father Marthinus played
for Stellenbosch v BT 1891.

DANEEL, Henry J.   *South Africa*
W Prov.
b −; *d* 46.
Forward, 4-2-1-1.
06 S− I+ W+ E=.
Uncle of George.

DANIEL, David John ('Dai Sam')   *Wales*
Llanelli.
b 1871; *d* 30.4.48 Llanelli.
Forward, 8-3-0-5.
1891 S−; 1894 E− S+ I−; 1898 I+ E−; 1899
E+ I−.
Mason/brewery worker. Father of Gipsy Daniel,
British light-heavyweight boxing champ 27.

DANIEL, Laurence Thomas   *Wales*
David
Abersychan GS, Blaenavon, Pontypool Utd,
Ebbw Vale, Pontypool, Newport.
b 5.3.42 Pontypool.
Wing, 1-1-0-0 (3 − 1t).
70 S+(1t).
Schoolmaster. W > 68 Arg.

DANIELL, John ('The Prophet')   *England*
Clifton Coll, Cambridge Univ, Richmond,
Barbarians, Mdx, Som.
b 12.12.1878 Bath; *d* 24.1.63 Holway, Som.
Forward, 7-4-1-2.
1899 W−; 1900 I+ S=; 02 I+ S+; 04 I+ S−.
Schoolmaster/tea planter. Blue 1898-1900. Capt
E 6 times. Inj interrupted int career. E sel 13-39

(chmn 32-9). RFU pres 45-7. IB mem 45-7. Ckt blue; Som CCC 04-12. England ckt sel 21, 24. Served WW1 as Pte in Sportsmans Battalion; Capt RASC.

DANIELS, Patrick Charles Thomas *Wales*
Millfield Sch, Welsh Youth, Glamorgan W, Cardiff.
 b 15.5.57 Cardiff.
Centre, 2-1-0-1.
81 A+; 82 I−.
Wales B v F 78. Wales B > 80 US, Can. W > 78 A. Wales v Overseas XV 80.

DANION, Jean *France*
Toulon.
Prop, 1-0-0-1.
24 I−.

DANOS, Pierre *France*
Toulon, Béziers.
 b 4.6.29 Toulouse.
SH, 17-11-3-3 (15 − 3t 2d).
54 Arg+(1d) Arg+; 57 R+; 58 S− E− W+(1t) It+(1t) I+(1t) SA=(1d) SA+; 59 S+ E= It+ W+ I−; 60 S+ E=.
Café proprietor.

DARBISHIRE, Godfrey *Wales*
Rugby Sch, Oxford Univ, Bangor.
 b 26.9.1854 Manchester; *d* 29.10.1889 Florida.
Forward, 1-0-0-1.
1881 E−.
Civil engr. Played in W's 1st int, v E 1881. Emigrated US 1881.

DARBOS, Pierre *France*
Dax.
Flanker, 1-1-0-0.
69 R+.

DARBY, Arthur John Lovett *England*
Cheltenham Coll, Cambridge Univ, Sorbonne, Birkenhead Pk, Richmond, Barbarians, Surrey.
 b 9.1.1876; *d* 16.1.60 Dartmouth.
Forward, 1-0-0-1.
1899 I−.
Schoolmaster. Blue 1896-8. Served WW1 as RNVR Lt with battle cruisers at Dogger Bank & Battle of Jutland. Languages master at RNC Dartmouth.

D'ARCY, Anthony Michael William *Australia*
Nudgee Coll, Australian Schs, Brisbane, Qld.
 b 10.10.59.
Prop, 10-6-0-4.
80 Fj+ NZ+; 81 F+ F+ I+ W− S−; 82 E− S− S+.

Student. Australian Schs > 77-8 BI. A > 79 Arg. Penrith RL, Brisbane.

DARGAN, Michael James *Ireland*
Belvedere Coll, Glongowes Coll, O Belvedere, UC Dublin.
 b 9.10.28 Dublin.
Flanker, 2-1-0-1.
52 S+ W−.
Pharmaceutical chemist. Ckt for I; played v MCC 54.

DARRACQ, Roland *France*
Dax.
Flanker, 1-1-0-0.
57 It+.

DARRIEUSSECQ, André *France*
Biarritz Ol.
 b 4.6.47 St-Jean-de-Luz.
Prop, 1-0-0-1.
73 E−.
Municipal employee.

DARRIEUSSECQ, Jean *France*
Mont-de-Marsan.
SH, 1-1-0-0.
53 It+.

DARROUY, Christian ('Eliacin') *France*
Mont-de-Marsan.
 b 13.1.37 Pouydesseaux, Landes.
Wing, 40-22-6-12 (69 − 23t).
57 I− E−(1t) W− It+(2t) R+; 59 E=; 61 R=; 63 S− I+(3t) E− W+ It+(1t); 64 NZ− E−(1t) W= It+ I+(2t) SA+(1t) Fj+(2t) R+; 65 S+(2t) I=(1t) E−(1t) It+(2t) R+; 66 S= I+(2t) E+ W− It+(1t) R+; 67 S− A+ E+ It+(1t) W+ I+ SA− SA− SA=.
Schoolmaster. With Jean Dupuy, F's most capped wing. F's leading t-scorer. Capt F > 67 SA.

DARVENIZA, Paul *Australia*
NSW.
 b 19.9.45 Brisbane.
Hooker, 4-0-0-4.
69 W− SA− SA− SA−.
Medicine/politics. Qld Labor MP.

DAUDIGNON, Georges *France*
SF.
SH, 1-0-0-1.
28 S−.

DAUGA, Benoit ('Le Grand Ferre') *France*
Mont-de-Marsan.
 b 8.5.42 Montgaillard, Landes.
Lock/no 8/flanker, 63-30-7-26 (34 − 11t).
64 S− NZ− E− W= It+ I+ SA+ Fj+ R+; 65

S+ I= E− W+ It+ R+; 66 S= I+ E+ W−
It+(1t) R+; 67 S− A+ E+ It+(1t) W+(1t) I+
SA− SA− SA+ SA= NZ− R+; 68 S+ I+(1t)
NZ− NZ− NZ− A− SA−(2t) SA− R−; 69 S−
I− E− R+(1t); 70 S+(1t) I+ W− E+(1t) R+;
71 S+ I= E= W−(1t) SA− SA= A− A+ R+;
72 S−(1t) I− W−.
Restaurateur. F > 67, 71 SA.

DAUGER, Jean   *France*
Bayonne.
b 12.11.19 Cambo.
Centre, 3-2-0-1 (6 − 2t).
45 BF+(2t) BF−; 53 S+.
9 yrs between caps. Switched to RL, later
reinstated.

DAULOUEDE, Pierre   *France*
Tyrosse.
Prop, 4-2-0-2.
37 G+ It+; 38 G−; 40 BF−.

DAUNCEY, Frederick Herbert   *Wales*
Abergavenny GS, Newport.
b 1.12.1871 Pontypool; *d* 30.10.55 Newport.
Wing, 3-1-0-2.
1896 E− S+ I−.
Solicitor. Hockey & lawn tennis for Wales.

DAVENPORT, Alfred   *England*
Rugby Sch, Oxford Univ, Ravenscourt Pk.
b 5.5.1849; *d* 2.4.32.
Forward, 1-0-0-1.
1871 S−.
Solicitor. 1st capt Oxford Univ 1869. Played in
1st int, S v E 1871.

DAVEY, E. Claude   *Wales*
Ystalyfera CS, Swansea Univ, Swansea, Sale,
Lancs, London Welsh, Berks, Barbarians,
Rosslyn Pk.
b 14.12.08 Garnant.
Centre, 23-14-2-7 (15 − 5t).
30 F+; 31 E= S+ F+(1t) I+(1t) SA−; 32 E+
S+ I−(1t); 33 E+ S−; 34 E− S+ I+; 35 E= S+
I− NZ+(1t); 36 S+(1t); 37 E− I−; 38 E+ I+.
Schoolmaster/electrical engr. Father English. 2t
Swansea v NZ 35.

DAVEY, James ('Maffer')   *England*
Trewirgie Sch, Redruth, Cornwall, Coventry,
Mines RFC (Transvaal), Transvaal.
b 25.12.1880 Redruth; *d* 21.10.51.
FH, 2-0-0-2.
08 S−; 09 W−; BT > 08 A, NZ.
Gold miner/bootmaker. Capt Transvaal 04.
Olympic silver medal for rugby, GB (Cornwall)
v A 08. Bowls for Cornwall. In SA 01-7.

DAVEY, Richard Frank   *England*
Wellington Sch, Wellington, Teignmouth,

Wanstead, Leytonstone, Exeter, London Cos,
Devon, E Cos.
b 22.9.05.
Flanker, 1-0-1-0.
31 W=.
Chartered surveyor/Inland Revenue valuer.

DAVID, Richard J.   *Wales*
Cardiff.
b 1876.
SH, 1-1-0-0.
07 I+.
Window cleaner. 112 apps for Cardiff 03-7.
Cardiff v NZ 05. Wigan RL 07.

DAVID, Thomas Patrick   *Wales*
Hawthorn SMS, Pontypridd, Llanelli,
Barbarians.
b 2.4.49 Pontypridd.
Flanker, 4-3-0-1.
73 F− A+; 76 I+ F+; BI > 74 SA.
Fitter/co dir. Wales B v Can 71, v F 71, 72 (2).
W > 73 Can. Wales XV v J 73. Barbarians v NZ
73. Cardiff RL 82. RL rec 26t for a prop, 83. 2
Wales RL caps. Business ptn with Steve
Fenwick.

DAVIDGE, Glyn David   *Wales*
Welsh Youth, Newport.
b 34.
No 8/flanker, 9-5-0-4.
59 F−; 60 S+ I+ F− SA−; 61 E+ S− I+; 62
F+; BIr > 62 SA.

DAVIDSON, Cecil T.   *Ireland*
NIFC.
b US; *d* 60.
Wing, 1-0-0-1.
21 F−.
Irish sprint champ.

DAVIDSON, Ian G.R.   *Ireland*
RBAI, NIFC.
b 10.8.1879; *d* −.6.39.
Wing, 9-3-1-5 (6 − 2t).
1899 E+; 1900 S= W−; 01 E+(1t) S− W−(1t);
02 E− S+ W−; BT > 03 SA.
Emigrated to Can.

DAVIDSON, James   *England*
Aspatria, Cumberland.
b 28.12.1868; *d* 23.12.45.
Forward, 5-2-1-2.
1897 S+; 1898 S= W+; 1899 I− S−.
Stonemason/builder. Played with bro Joseph v S
1899. RFU comm.

DAVIDSON, James Charles   *Ireland*
St Brendan's Bristol, Queen's Univ Belfast,
Bristol, Dungannon, BUSF, Irish Comb. Univs,
Ulster.

b 23.10.42 Armagh.
Flanker, 6-3-1-2.
69 F+ E+ S+ W−; 73 NZ=; 76 NZ−.
Schoolmaster/PE lecturer. Debut for Bristol as 17-yr-old schoolboy. Coach of Queen's Univ, Comb Univs & Ulster.

DAVIDSON, James Norman   *Scotland*
Grieve
Hawick HS, Edinburgh Univ, Barbarians.
b 28.1.31 Hawick.
FH, 7-0-0-7 (3 − 1t).
52 F− W− I−(1t) E−; 53 F− W−; 54 F−.
Medicine. Ckt for S 51. Moved to NZ.

DAVIDSON, John Alexander   *Scotland*
Waid Acad, London Scottish, Edinburgh W.
b 6.8.32 Avoch, Ross.
No 8, 3-1-1-1.
59 E=; 60 I+ E−.
Oil.

DAVIDSON, Joseph   *England*
Aspatria, Cumberland.
b 5.10.1878; *d* 8.10.10.
Forward, 2-0-0-2.
1899 W− S−.
Stonemason/builder. Played with bro James v S 1899. Adept at boxing & ath. Killed in accident in sand quarry.

DAVIDSON, J.P.   *Scotland*
RIE Coll.
b 3.9.1851; *d* −.
Forward, 2-0-1-1.
1873 E=; 1874 E−.

DAVIDSON, Max   *South Africa*
Stellenbosch Univ, E Prov.
1-1-0-0.
10 BI+.

DAVIDSON, Robert Alfred   *Australia*
Lewars
NSW.
b 18.10.26.
Prop, 13-3-0-10.
52 Fj+ Fj− NZ+ NZ−; 53 SA−; 57 NZ−
NZ−; 58 W− I− E− S− F− M+.
Oil co man dir. Capt A > BI, F, US & C 57-8.

DAVIDSON, Roger Stewart TD   *Scotland*
Royal HS, Royal HSFP, Aberdeen Univ.
b 17.2.1869 Kinfauns; *d* 18.2.55 Perth.
Forward, 1-1-0-0.
1893 E+.
Minister. Pres SRU 02-3.

DAVIE, Murray Geoffrey   *New Zealand*
Canterbury, S Island.
b 19.9.55 Christchurch.

Prop, 1-1-0-0 (4 − 1t).
83 E−r(1t).
NZ > 83 S & E.

DAVIES, Abel Christmas   *Wales*
London Welsh, Utd Hosps.
b 1861 Narberth; *d* 18.6.14 Gowerton.
Wing, 1-0-0-1.
1889 I−.
Medicine.

DAVIES, Alun E.   *Wales*
Welsh SS, Llanelli.
Flanker, 1-0-0-1.
84 A−.
Won 8 consec Welsh SS caps. Wales B v F 79.

DAVIES, Benjamin   *Wales*
Llanelli.
b 1873 Llanelli; *d* −.6.30 Llanelli.
Half-back, 2-0-0-2.
1895 E−; 1896 E−.
Licensee. Sec Llanelli RFC. Coach Llandovery Coll. Sons Wilfred & Harry became journalists in Llanelli.

DAVIES, Cecil Rhys   *Wales*
Cardiff HS, Cardiff HSOB, Bedford, RAF, London Welsh.
b −; kia 25.12.1941.
Prop, 1-0-0-1.
34 E−.
RAF. Bro Selby also played for Cardiff.

DAVIES, Charles Lynn   *Wales*
('Cowboy')
QEGS Carmarthen, Trin Coll Carmarthen, Blaengarw, Cardiff, Llanelli, Glam W.
b 29 Banc-y-Felin.
Wing, 3-2-0-1 (6 − 2t).
56 E+(1t) S+(1t) I−
Schoolmaster/electrical engr. Won Welsh SS 100y 47, beating Trevor Brewer into 2nd place.

DAVIES, Christmas Howard   *Wales*
Swansea, Llanelli.
b 25.12.16 Burry Port.
FB, 6-5-0-1.
39 S+ I+; 47 E− S+ F+ I+.
Steelworker. Played either side of WW2. 2 Servs ints.

DAVIES, Clifton ('Bard of   *Wales*
Kenfig')
Cardiff, Barbarians.
b 12.12.19 Kenfig Hill; *d* 28.1.67.
Prop, 16-10-2-4 (3 − 1t).
47 S+ F+ I+ A+; 48 E= S+ F− I−; 49 F−; 50
E+(1t) S+ I+ F+; 51 E+ S− I=.
BI > 50 A, NZ 1-0-0-1.

Miner. 190 apps for Cardiff 45-52. Bro Willie played FH 31 times for Cardiff.

DAVIES, Cyril Allan Harvard　　　*Wales*
Amman Valley GS, Cardiff Univ, Swansea, Llanelli, Cardiff, Barbarians.
b 21.11.36 Ammanford.
Centre, 7-5-1-1.
57 I+; 58 A+ E= S+ I+; 60 SA−; 61 E+.
Electrical engr/computer officer. Played for Swansea while still at sch. Knee inj v E 61 ended int career.

DAVIES, Daph　　　*Wales*
Bridgend, Cardiff.
b Bridgend; *d* c65.
Centre, 2-1-0-1.
21 I+; 25 I−.
GPO telephone engr.

DAVIES, David Bailey MC　　　*Wales*
St David's Coll Sch Lampeter, St David's Coll, Oxford Univ, Llanelli, London Welsh.
b 3.12.1884 Llanwenog; *d* 24.8.68 Hendon.
FB, 1-1-0-0.
1907 E+.
Schoolmaster/minister. Son of farmer. Blue 05-7. Served WW1, 2nd Lt in Welsh Guards, MC 18. Ordained 26.

DAVIES, David Brian　　　*Wales*
Llanelli GS, UC Swansea, Llanelli, Cardiff, Neath, Pentyrch.
b 7.7.41 Weston-super-Mare.
Centre, 3-1-1-1.
62 I=; 63 E− S+.
Lecturer. Played for Llanelli while at school. Son of D.I. Davies.

DAVIES, David G.　　　*Wales*
Treorchy, Cardiff, Rugby.
b 1897 Treorchy.
Lock/prop, 2-0-0-2.
23 E− S−.
Carpenter. Joined Cardiff after failing to make Treorchy 1st XV.

DAVIES, David Hunt　　　*Wales*
Aberavon.
b 11.11.1896 Port Talbot; *d* 8.5.79 Port Talbot.
Centre, 1-0-0-1.
24 E−.
Wounded WW1.

DAVIES, David Idwal　　　*Wales*
Pontarddulais, Swansea.
b 10.11.15.
Centre, 1-0-0-1.
39 E−.
Schoolmaster. Father of D.B. Davies. Leeds RL 39. RL organiser in S Wales 49.

DAVIES, David John　　　*Wales*
Neath.
b 20.2.41; *d* 16.4.69 Dewsbury.
Flanker, 1-0-1-0.
62 I=.
Schoolmaster. Leeds RL 62. Collapsed & died during match.

DAVIES, David Maldwyn　　　*Wales*
Somerset Police, Barbarians.
b 2.5.25 Penygraig.
Hooker, 17-12-1-4.
50 E+ S+ I+ F+; 51 E+ S− I= F− SA−; 52 E+ S+ I+ F+; 53 I+ F+ NZ+; 54 E−; BI > 50 NZ 2-0-1-1, A 1-1-0-0.
Miner/police. Barbarians v SA 52.

DAVIES, D.H.　　　*Wales*
Neath.
Back−row, 1-1-0-0.
04 S+.
Police.

DAVIES, Douglas S.　　　*Scotland*
Ashkirk Sch, Hawick.
b 23.7.1899 Ashkirk; *d* −.
No 8, 20-12-2-6 (3 − 1p).
22 F= W= I+ E−; 23 F+ W+ I+ E−; 24 F− (1p) E−; 25 W+ I+ E+; 26 F+ W+ I− E+; 27 F+ W+ I−; BI > 24 SA 4-0-1-3.
Farmer.

DAVIES, Eirwynne Gwynne　　　*Wales*
Kenfig Hill, Cardiff, Cheltenham.
b 23.6.08 Aberkenfig.
Wing, 3-0-0-3.
28 F−; 29 E−; 30 S−.
Furniture manufacturer. 67 apps for Cardiff 27-30. Wigan RL 30.

DAVIES, Emlyn　　　*Wales*
Aberavon.
Prop, 2-1-0-1.
47 A+; 48 I−.
Locomotive driver.

DAVIES, Evan　　　*Wales*
Maesteg.
b 1892 Maesteg; *d* 46.
FB, 1-0-0-1.
19 NZA−.
Miner.

DAVIES, Ewan Gibson　　　*Wales*
Cardiff HS, Llandovery Coll, UC London, Cardiff.
b 23.6.1887 Cardiff; *d* 2.9.79 Cardiff.
Wing, 2-1-0-1 (6 − 2t).
12 E− F+(2t).
Solicitor.

DAVIES, Frederick E. *Ireland*
Trin Coll Dublin, Lansdowne.
b 1866; *d* 11.5.51.
Half-back, 5-1-1-3 (2 − 1t).
1892 S− W+(1t); 1893 E− S= W−.

DAVIES, Geoffrey Huw *England*
King Edward VI GS Stourbridge, England SS,
UWIST, Cambridge Univ, Coventry, Cardiff,
Wasps.
b 18.2.59 Eastbourne.
FH/centre/FB, 21-7-3-11 (16 − 4t).
81 S+(1t) I+ F− Arg=(1t) Arg+(1t); 82 A+
S= I−; 83 F− W= S−; 84 S− SA− SA−; 85
R+r NZ− NZ−; 86 W+ S− I+(1t) F−.
Chartered surveyor. Blue 80-1. Of Welsh
parents. Son of a lecturer. Played with Tony
Swift (E) & Gareth Roberts (W) UWIST v
Exeter UAU Final 80. E Under 23s, English
Students. E > 80 J, Fj; 81 Arg; 84 SA; 85 NZ.
England B v F. Capt, scored t in 100th Univ
Match 81.

DAVIES, George *Wales*
Swansea.
b 25.12.1875.
Centre/FB, 9-8-0-1 (11 − 1t 4c).
1900 E+ S+ I+(1t); 01 E+ S− I+; 05 E+(2c)
S+ I+(2c).
Mason. KO'd as he scored t v I 1900, and carried
off.

DAVIES, Glyn R. *Wales*
Pontypridd GS, Cilfynydd, Cambridge Univ, R
Corps of Signals, The Army, Yorks,
Pontypridd, Barbarians.
b 24.8.27 Cilfynydd; *d* −.11.76 Bristol.
FH, 11-5-1-5.
47 S+ A+; 48 E= S+ F− I−; 49 E+ S− F−; 51
E+ S−.
Wine merchant. Blue 48-50. Bro in law opera
singer Sir Geraint Evans. Played in 2 Victory
ints.

DAVIES, Harold Joseph *Wales*
Newport St Julians HS, Newport.
b 5.12.1899; *d* 29.3.76.
Wing, 1-0-0-1.
24 S−; BIr > 24 SA 1-0-0-1.
Butcher. Normally wing or centre, played twice
at FB BI > 24 SA.

DAVIES, Harry Graham *Wales*
Llandovery Coll, Guy's Hosp, New Dock Stars,
Llanelli, London Welsh.
b 19.4.1899 Llanelli.
Centre, 3-3-0-0.
21 F+ I+; 25 F+.
Medicine.

DAVIES, Haydn John *Wales*
Cowbridge GS, Cambridge Univ, Aberavon.
b 34.
Centre, 2-1-0-1.
59 E+ S−.
Law.

DAVIES, Henry Stanley *Wales*
Treherbert.
b 23.4.1895 Ystrad; *d* 14.2.66 Ystrad.
Prop, 1-0-0-1.
23 I−.
HM. Served WW1.

DAVIES, Hopkin *Wales*
Swansea.
Forward, 4-2-0-2.
1898 I+ E−; 1901 S− I+.

DAVIES, Howell *Wales*
Kenfig Comp, Pyle, Bridgend, Glamorgan.
b 6.6.59 Pyle.
FB, 4-2-0-2 (39 − 1t 4c 9p).
84 S−(1c 1p) I+(1c 2p) F−(1t 1c 2p) E+(1c 4p).
Welder. Wales B v F 83. Wales B > 83 Spain.
Wales Champ rec 39 pts 84.

DAVIES, Howell John *Wales*
Neath.
Hooker, 2-1-0-1.
12 E− S+.
Huddersfield RL 12.

DAVIES, Ivor Thomas *Wales*
QEGS Carmarthen, Carmarthen Harlequins, St
David's Coll Sch Lampeter, St David's Coll,
Llanelli, London Welsh.
b 6.4.1892 Carmarthen; *d* 54 Hampstead.
Wing, 3-3-0-0 (6 − 2t).
14 S+(1t) F+ I+(1t*).
Civil Service. Entered St David's Coll 13.10.11,
same day as fellow future int J.G. Stephens.
Served WW1 7th Lancers, 2nd Dragoon
Guards, Machine Gun Corps. * some sources
credit this t to W.H. Evans.

DAVIES, Jenkin Alban *Wales*
St John's Leatherhead, Llandovery Coll, Oxford
Univ, Swansea, Cardiff, London Welsh,
Llanelli.
b 5.9.1885; *d* −.8.76 Los Angeles.
Prop, 7-6-0-1 (6 − 2t).
13 S+ F+(1t) I+; 14 E− S+ F+(1t) I+.
Minister/schoolmaster. Served WW1, chaplain
to Forces, attached to RFA. Capt of 'Terrible
Eight' v I 14.

DAVIES, J.L. *Ireland*
Monkstown.
Forward, 2-1-0-1.
1898 E+ S−.

DAVIES, John Henry *Wales*
Aberavon.
Flanker, 1-0-0-1.
23 I−.
Steelworker/engr's clerk.

DAVIES, Jonathan *Wales*
Gwendraeth GS, Trimsaran Youth, Trimsaran, Welsh Dists, Neath.
b 24.10.62 Trimsaran.
FH, 6-4-0-2 (13 − 1t 3d).
85 E+(1t 1d) Fj+; 86 E−(1d) S+(1d) I+ F−.
Painter/contracts mgr. Wales B v F 84.

DAVIES, Leonard Morris *Wales*
Stradey Sch, Bynea, RE, Kent, Llanelli.
b 30 Bynea; d 23.9.57 Morriston.
Flanker, 3-3-0-0.
54 F+ S+; 55 I+.
Clerk. Bro of Terry. One of 1st specialist blind-side flankers. Died at 27 after long illness.

DAVIES, Leslie ('Bychan') *Wales*
Bonymaen, Swansea.
b 13.7.13 Swansea; d −.9.84.
Prop/lock, 2-2-0-0.
39 S+ I+.
Wagon repairer.

DAVIES, Lyn ('Tanky') *Wales*
Bridgend Sports, BAOR, The Army, Bridgend.
b 2.2.40 Blaengarw.
Wing, 3-2-0-1.
66 E+ S+ I−.
Colliery worker.

DAVIES, Mark *Wales*
Maesteg Comp, Nantyffyllon, Swansea.
b 9.7.58 Maesteg.
Flanker, 3-2-0-1.
81 A+; 82 I−; 85 Fj+.
Physiotherapist. Swansea v NZ 80, v A 81.
Wales B v A 81, v F 81, v Spain 85. Wales B > 83 Spain. Wales XV v Maoris 82, J 83.

DAVIES, Michael John *Wales*
Diocesan Coll Cape Town, Cape Town Univ, Oxford Univ, Blackheath, Barbarians.
b 7.10.18 ?SA; d 8.7.84 SA.
Centre, 2-2-0-0.
39 S+ I+.
Colonial Service. Rhodes Scholar. Played in WW2-time University Match, no blue. Govt minister Tanganyika. Sec Imperial Coll London.

DAVIES, N. Glyn ('Shorty') *Wales*
Blackheath, London Welsh, Barbarians.
b 28 Blackwood.
Flanker, 1-1-0-0.
55 E+.
Schoolmaster/professor. Basketball int.

DAVIES, Patrick Harry *England*
Denstone Coll, Manchester, Sale, Cheshire.
b 17.3.03; d 21.2.79 Ware, Herts.
Flanker, 1-1-0-0.
27 I+.
Building manufacturer. Served WW2 with RAF. Pres of Sale (centenary 61) & Cheshire (58-60).

DAVIES, Philip Thomas *Wales*
Llangatwg Comp, Neath Schools, Welsh SS, Seven Sisters, Llanelli, S Wales Police.
b 19.10.63 Seven Sisters.
No 8, 6-4-0-2 (12 − 3t).
85 E+ Fj+ (2t); 86 E− S+ I+(1t) F−.
Police/sales rep.

DAVIES, Robin Harvard *Wales*
KCS Wimbledon, Oxford Univ, London Welsh, Surrey, Barbarians.
b 12.1.34.
Flanker, 6-3-1-2 (3 − 1t).
57 S−(1t) I+ F+; 58 A+; 62 E= S−.
Industrial research. Blue 55-7. Barbarians > 58 SA. Fix sec London Welsh.

DAVIES, Terence John *Wales*
Stradey Sch, Devonport Servs, R Marines, RN, Swansea, Bynea, Llanelli, Barbarians.
b 24.9.33 Llwynhendy, Llanelli.
FB, 21-10-1-10 (50 − 7c 12p).
53 E−(1p) S+(1p) I+(1c) F+; 57 E− S−(1p) I+(2p) F+(2c 1p); 58 A+(1p) E=(1p) S+(1c) F−(1p); 59 E+(1c) S−(1c) I+(1c) F−(1p); 60 E−(2p) SA−; 61 E+ S− F−; BI > 59 A, NZ 2-1-0-1.
Timber merchant/co dir. Bro of Leonard. Barbarians > 57 Can.

DAVIES, Thomas Gerald Reames *Wales*
QEGS Carmarthen, Loughborough Coll, Cambridge Univ, Cardiff, London Welsh, Barbarians.
b 7.2.45 Llansaint.
Centre/wing, 46-29-3-14 (72− 20t).
66 A−; 67 S− I− F− E+(2t); 68 E= S+; 69 S+ I+ F= NZ− NZ− A+(1t); 71 E+(2t) S+(1t) I+(2t) F+; 72 E+ S+(1t) F+(1t) NZ−; 73 E+(1t) S− I+ F− A+(1t); 74 S+ F= E−; 75 F+(1t) E+(1t) S− I+(1t); 76 E+ S+ I+(2t) F+; 77 I+(1t) F− E+ S+; 78 E+ S+ I+ A−(1t) A−(1t); BI > 68 SA 1-0-0-1; 71 A, NZ 4-2-1-1.
Schoolmaster/HTV/'The Times' corr. Blue 68-70. Wales most capped threequarter, 11 at centre, 35 on wing. With Gareth Edwards sc most t for W. W > 69 A, NZ & Fj; 73 Can; 75 Far East. Wales XV v Fj 69; J 73; Tg 74; Arg 76. Welsh XV v NZ 74. Barbarians v A 67, NZ 67,74, A 76. Declined 2 BI tours > SA 74, NZ 77.

DAVIES, Thomas Mervyn *Wales*
Penlan CS, Swansea Coll of Ed, O.
Guildfordians, London Welsh, Surrey,
Swansea, Barbarians.
 b 9.12.46 Swansea.
No 8, 38-26-4-8 (7 − 2t).
69 S+ I+ F= E+ NZ− NZ− A+; 70 SA= S+
E+(1t) I− F+; 71 E+ S+ I+ F+; 72 E+ S+ F+
NZ−; 73 E+ S− I+ F− A+; 74 S+ I= F= E−
(1t); 75 F+ E+ S− I+ A+; 76 E+ S+ I+ F+;
BI > 71 A, NZ 4-2-1-1; 74 SA 4-3-1-0.
Rep/business. World's most capped no 8 (46 inc
8 BI). W > 69 NZ, A & Fj; 73 Can; 75 Far East.
Wales XV v J 73. Welsh XV v NZ 74.
Barbarians v SA 70, NZ 74, A 76 (capt). Son of
D. Davies, 'Victory' int 46. Career ended by
brain haemorrhage.

DAVIES, Vivian Gordon *England*
Marlborough Coll, Harlequins, Barbarians,
Surrey.
 b 22.1.1899 Durham; kia 23.12.41 England.
FH/centre, 2-0-0-2.
22 W−; 25 NZ−.
Served WW1 DCLI. Served WW2 Capt RA.

DAVIES, W. *Wales*
Cardiff.
Forward, 1-1-0-0.
1896 S+.

DAVIES, William ('Sgili') *Wales*
Swansea, Amman Utd.
 b 14.2.06 Cwmgors; *d* 5.10.75 Cwmgors.
Flanker, 4-3-0-1 (3 − 1t).
31 SA−(1t); 32 E+ S+ I+.
Miner/colliery deputy.

DAVIES, William Anthony *New Zealand*
King's Coll, Otago Univ, Auckland, NZ Jnrs,
NZ Univs, Otago, Blackheath (E), London
Irish.
 b 16.9.39 Auckland.
1st/2nd five-eighth, 3-2-0-1.
60 SA−; 62 A+ A+.
Medicine. 94 pts NZ > 60 A & SA. Continued
medical studies in England 71-4. Moved to A;
coached various sides. Uncles Morris Davies rep
Auckland, Waikato & Poverty Bay & Leslie
Davies rep N Auckland.

DAVIES, William Avon *Wales*
Port Talbot CS, Exeter Univ, Aberavon,
Plymouth, Devon.
 b 27.12.1890 Aberavon; *d* 18.9.67 Exeter.
Centre, 2-1-0-1 (3 − 1t).
12 S+ I−(1t).
Schoolmaster. Leeds RL 13, then Keighley.

DAVIES, William Gareth *Wales*
Gwendraeth GS, Tumble, Welsh SS,

Carmarthenshire, Llanelli, UWIST, Cardiff,
Oxford Univ, Barbarians.
 b 29.9.56 Tumble.
FH, 21-9-0-12 (40 − 2c 7d 5p).
78 A− A−(1d 2p) NZ−(3p); 79 S+ I+ F−
E+(1d); 80 F+(1c) E− S+ NZ−; 81 E+(1d)
S− A+(1d); 82 I− F+ E−(1d) S−; 85 S+(1d)
I−(1c 1d) F−; BI > 80 SA 1-0-0-1.
Building soc mgr. Barbarians > 76 US, Can (inc
rec 31 pts v Quebec). Blue 77. Wales XV v R 79.
W > 78 A. Cardiff pts in season (383 83-4) & dg
in career (53 74-85) rec. Welsh SS, Glamorgan
CCC 2nd ckt. Barbarians' comm 85.
Autobiography 'Standing Off' pub 86.

DAVIES, William John Abbott *England*
('Dave') OBE
RNEC Keyham, RNC Greenwich, US
Portsmouth, RN, Hants.
 b 21.6.1890 Pembroke; *d* 26.4.67.
FH, 22-20-1-1 (24 − 4t 3d).
13 SA− W+ F+ I+ S+; 14 I+(1t) S+ F+(1t);
20 F+(1t) I+ S+; 21 W+(1d) I+ S+ F+; 22 I+
F= S+(1t); 23 W+ I+(1d) S+ F+(1d).
RN. E's most capped FH. Capt E 11 times. At
Greenwich won Champions Cup as best athlete
of year. Served WW1 with 'Iron Duke' in Grand
Fleet, transferred to 'Queen Elizabeth', staff of
C in C Grand Fleet. Made 1st of many apps with
Cyril Kershaw Grand Fleet v Rest of Navy 19;
made half-back rec 14 apps with Kershaw for E.
Played in Centenary Match at Rugby Sch 23.
Teetotaller. Wrote 2 books 'Rugby Football'
pub 23 & 'Rugby Football & How To Play It'
pub 33.

DAVIES, William John Nixon *Ireland*
Edinburgh Univ, Bessbrook.
 b 1870; *d* −.1.62 Chicago, US.
Forward, 9-0-1-8.
1890 S− W= E−; 1891 E− S− W−; 1892 E−
S−; 1895 S−.
Medicine. Emigrated to US. Great uncle of
J.W.S. Irwin.

DAVIES, William Philip Cathcart *England*
Denstone Coll, RAF, Cambridge Univ,
Cheltenham, Harlequins, Barbarians, Sussex, N
Midlands.
 b 6.8.28 Abberley, Worcs.
Centre, 11-5-2-4 (3 − 1t).
53 S+; 54 NZ− I+; 55 W− I= F− S+; 56 W−;
57 F+ S+(1t); 58 W=; BI > 55 SA 3-2-0-1.
HM. Ath for Cambridge. Taught at Christ's
Hosp, Denstone Coll & Cheltenham Coll.

DAVIES, William Thomas *Wales*
Harcourt
Gowerton CS, Swansea, London Welsh.
 b 28.3.16 Penclawdd.
Centre/FH 6-3-0-3 (7 − 1t 1d).

36 I+; 37 E− I−; 39 E− S+ I+(1t 1d).
Schoolmaster. Bradford N RL 39. GB RL v NZ
3 apps 46-7. Wales RL 10 apps. Lance Todd
Trophy 47.

DAVIS, Alec Michael   *England*
Torquay GS, St Luke's Exeter, RN, Devonport
Servs, Harlequins, Barbarians, Staffs, Devon.
b 23.1.42 Lichfield.
Lock, 16-5-2-9.
63 W+ I= S+ NZ− NZ−; 64 NZ− W= I− F+
S−; 66 W−; 67 A−; 69 SA+; 70 I+ W− S−.
Schoolmaster. E coach. Co-author with Donald
Ireland 'Science of Rugby Football' pub 85.

DAVIS, Clarence Clive   *Australia*
NSW.
b 28.3.28 Auburn, NSW.
Wing, 4-1-0-3.
49 NZ+; 51 NZ− NZ− NZ−.
Travel agent. Bro of Gordon.

DAVIS, Clive Enoch   *Wales*
Blackwood SMS, Newbridge.
b 17.9.49 Tredegar.
No 8/lock, 3-1-0-2 (4 − 1t).
78 A−; 81 E+(1t) S−.
Brewery engr. W > 78 A. Wales Br v F 77.
Wales B > 80 US, Can.

DAVIS, Eric Hamilton   *Australia*
Victoria.
b 17 England.
Prop, 4-1-1-2.
47 S+ W−; 49 M− M=.
Clerk.

DAVIS, Gordon Walter Gray   *Australia*
NSW.
b 19.6.27.
Five-eighth/centre, 2-1-0-1.
55 NZ− NZ+.
Grazier/wool broker. Bro of Clarence.

DAVIS, Gregory Victor   *Australia*
Sacred Heart Coll Auckland, Thames Valley,
Auckland, Bay of Plenty, Drummoyne, NSW.
b 27.7.39 Matamata, NZ; *d* 24.7.79 Rotorua,
NZ.
No 8, 39-10-1-28 (6 − 2t).
63 E+(1t) SA− SA+ SA+ SA−; 64 NZ− NZ−
NZ+; 65 SA+; 66 BI− BI− W+ S−; 67 E+ I−
F−(1t) I− NZ−; 68 NZ− NZ− F+ I− S−; 69
W− SA− SA− SA− SA−; 70 S+; 71 SA−
SA− SA− F+ F−; 72 F= F− NZ− NZ− NZ−.
Wholesale meat/wool classer. Moved to A 63.
Capt A 16 consec Tests. Capt A > 71 F, 72 NZ.
Died of brain tumour.

DAVIS, Keith   *New Zealand*
Sacred Heart Coll Auckland, Marist, NZ

Maoris, Auckland, N Island.
b 21.5.30 Whakatane.
SH, 10-7-0-3.
52 A+; 53 W−; 54 I+ E+ S+ F−; 55 A+; 58
A+ A− A+.
Hotelier/commission agent. NZ > 53-4 BI,F &
NAm. NZ Maoris selector 67. Bro Morris rep
Waikato & half-bro Mita Johnson rep
Manawhenua.

DAVIS, Lyndon John   *New Zealand*
Cashmere HS, Suburbs, NZ Jnrs, Canterbury, S
Island.
b 22.12.43 Christchurch.
SH, 3-3-0-0.
76 I+; 77 BI+ BI+.
Tomato grower. 1st cap at 33 & inj v I 76. NZ >
76 SA. Rep Canterbury v BI 66, 71 & 77. Coach
Suburbs club.

DAVIS, Roger Andrew   *Australia*
King's Sch Sydney, Oxford Univ, NSW.
b 23.10.51 Sydney.
Lock, 3-0-1-2.
74 NZ− NZ= NZ−.
Academic research. Blue 74-5.

DAVIS, Walter   *Australia*
NSW.
b −; *d* −.
Forward, 3-1-0-2.
1899 BT+ BT− BT−.
Engr.

DAVIS, William Edward Norman   *Wales*
('Wendy')
Cardiff HS, HSOB, Penarth, Cardiff,
Barbarians.
b 7.9.13 Birmingham.
Prop, 3-2-0-1.
39 E− S+ I+.
Business. 119 apps for Cardiff 34-40. Played in 3
Servs ints.

DAVIS, William Leslie   *New Zealand*
Hastings Boys' HS, HSOB, Hawkes Bay,
Taradale, NZ Colts, N Island.
b 15.12.42 Hastings.
Centre, 11-11-0-0 (12 − 4t).
67 A+(1t); 67 E+ W+(1t) F+ S+(1t); 68 A+
A+(1t) F+; 69 W+ W+; 70 SA+.
Salesman. NZ > 63-4 & 67 BI,F & C, 68 A &
Fj, 70 A & SA. Sprint rep for Hawkes Bay 60-3;
rep NZ softball 73,76. Rec includes penalty t v
A 68.

DAVISON, W.   *Ireland*
Belfast Acad.
Forward, 1-0-0-1.
1887 W−.

DAVY, Eugene O'Donnell   *Ireland*
Belvedere Coll, UC Dublin, Lansdowne.
b 26.7.04 Dublin.
FH/centre, 34-19-1-14 (36 − 8t 3d).
25 W+; 26 F+ E+ S+ W−; 27 F+(1t) E− S+
W+ NSW−; 28 F+ E− S+(1t) W+; 29 F+(1t)
E+(1t) S−(1d) W=(1t); 30 F− E+ S+(3t) W−
(1d); 31 F− E+ S+ W− SA−; 32 E− S+ W+;
33 E− W+(1d) S−; 34 E−.
Stockbroker. Pres IRU 67.

DAWES, Sydney John OBE   *Wales*
Lewis Sch Pengam, Newbridge UC
Aberystwyth, Welsh Univs, UAU,
Loughborough Colls, London Welsh, Surrey,
Barbarians, Leics.
b 29.4.40 Newbridge.
Centre, 22-13-2-7 (12 − 4t).
64 I+(1t) F= SA−; 65 E+ S+ I+ F−(1t); 66
A−(1t); 68 I− F−; 69 E+ NZ− A+; 70 SA=
S+(1t) E+ I− F+; 71 E+ S+ I+ F+; BI > 71
A, NZ 4-2-1-1.
Schoolmaster/business/WRU nat coaching
organiser. W > 64 SA; 68 Arg; 69 NZ, A & Fj.
Wales XV v Fj 69. Asst mgr W > 75 Far East, A
78. Capt Barbarians v NZ 73. Capt BI > 71 A,
NZ. Coach BI > 77 NZ. Wrote book 'Rugby
Union' pub 75.

DAWSON, Alfred Ronald   *Ireland*
St Andrews Coll, Wanderers, Barbarians.
b 5.6.32 Dublin.
Hooker, 27-7-1-19 (3 − 1t).
58 A+(1t) E− S+ W− F−; 59 E− S+ W− F+;
60 F− SA−; 61 E+ S− W− F− SA−; 62 S−
F− W−; 63 F− E= S− W+ NZ−; 64 E+ S−
F−; BI > 59 A 2-2-0-0 & NZ 4-1-0-3.
Architect. BI most ints as capt, 6. Capt BI > 59
A, NZ. Asst mgr BI > 68 SA. Barbarians comm
mem.

DAWSON, Ernest Frederick   *England*
RIE Coll, Richmond, Surrey.
b 10.5.1858; *d* 7.4.04 Hampstead.
Forward, 1-1-0-0.
1878 I+.

DAWSON, James Cooper   *Scotland*
Strathallan Sch, Glasgow Acad, Glasgow
Academicals, Oxford Univ, Barbarians.
b 29.10.25.
Prop, 20-6-0-14 (3 − 1t).
47 A−; 48 F+ W−; 49 F+ W+ I−; 50 F+ W−
I− E+ SA−; 51 F− W+(1t) I− E− SA−; 52
F− W− I−; 53 E−.
Chartered accountant/man dir. Blue 43.

DAWSON, Walter Laird   *Australia*
NSW.
b 24.
Lock, 2-0-0-2.

46 NZ− NZ−.
Engr.

DAY, Harold Lindsay Vernon   *England*
Bedford Mod Sch, Leicester, The Army, RA,
Midlands, Hants, Leics.
b 12.8.1898 Darjeeling; *d* 15.6.72 Hadley
Wood.
Wing, 4-0-1-3 (16 − 2t 2c 2p).
20 W−(1t 1c); 22 W−(1t) F=(1c 2p); 26 S−.
Schoolmaster/The Army. Won 1st cap in
unusual circumstances, replaced W.M. Lowry
after Lowry had been photographed with team
shortly before kick-off v W 20. The sels
explained that Day would be better suited to wet
conditions. Ref S v W 34. Ckt for The Army,
Hants & Beds. Served WW1 RA. Taught at
Felsted Sch. Wrote on rugby for several
newspapers.

DAY, Harry T.   *Wales*
Newport.
Forward, 5-3-0-2.
1892 I−; 1893 E+ S+; 1894 S+ I−.
Carpenter.

DAY, Hubert Charles   *Wales*
Newport.
b 8.5.08 Griffithstown, Newport; *d* 27.6.77
Salford.
Hooker, 5-3-1-1.
30 S− I+ F+; 31 E= S+.
Carpenter/licensee. Salford RL 31-48.

DAY, Thomas Brynmor   *Wales*
Swansea.
b 29.12.07 Glanamman; *d* −.9.80 Swansea.
Lock/prop, 13-8-2-3.
31 E= S+ F+ I+ SA−; 32 E+ S+ I−; 34 S+
I+; 35 E= S+ I−.
Oil refinery worker/police. Son in law of Billy
Trew.

DEACON, J. Thomas   *Wales*
Swansea.
b 1868 Monmouth; *d* −.
Forward, 4-1-0-3.
1891 I+; 1892 E− S− I−.
Carpenter/stonemason.

DEAN, Geoffrey John MC   *England*
Rugby Sch, Cambridge Univ, The Army,
Harlequins, Barbarians, Sussex.
b 12.11.09.
SH, 1-0-0-1.
31 I−.
The Army. Served WW2. MC 40. Lost leg N
Africa. POW. Noted tennis & hockey player.

DEAN, Paul Michael   *Ireland*
St Mary's Coll, Irish Schs.

b 28.6.60 Dublin.
FH/centre, 14-6-1-7.
81 SA− SA− A−; 82 W+ E+ S+ F−; 84 A−;
85 S+ F= W+ E+; 86 F− W−.
Sales rep. Ireland B 80. I > 81 SA.

DEANE, Ernest Cotton MC   *Ireland*
Corrig Coll Kingstown, Coll of Surgs,
Monkstown.
b 4.5.1887 Limerick; kia 25.9.15 Neuve
Chapelle.
Wing, 1-0-0-1.
09 E−.
RAMC. Capt 1st Indian Expeditionary Force;
mentioned in despatches & MC.

DEANS, Colin Thomas   *Scotland*
Hawick HS, Hawick, S of Scotland.
b 3.5.55 Hawick.
Hooker, 44-18-3-23 (8 − 2t).
78 F− W− E− NZ−; 79 W− E= I= F− NZ−;
80 I− F+; 81 F− W+ E− I+ NZ−(1t) NZ−
R+ A+; 82 E+ I− F+ W+ A+ A−; 83 I− F−
W− E+ NZ=; 84 W+ E+ I+ F+ A−; 85 I−
F− W− E−; 86 F+ W− E+ I+ R+(1t); BI >
83 NZ.
Fuel injection specialist. S's most capped
hooker. Capt S 86. Scottish Select v Netherlands
75. S Under 21 75, 76; Scotland B. S > 77 Far
East; 81 NZ. Scottish XV v Japan 77, Fj 82.
Capt S of Scotland v A 84. Capt Hawick, S club
champs 84-5. Capt BI v Rest of World, Cardiff
86.

DEANS, Derek Thomas   *Scotland*
R Gordons Sch, Edinburgh Univ, Hawick,
Barbarians.
b 30.4.45 Hawick.
Hooker, 1-0-0-1.
68 E−.
Chartered accountant.

DEANS, Robert George   *New Zealand*
Christchurch Boys' HS, HSOB, Canterbury, S
Island.
b 19.2.1884 Christchurch; *d* 30.9.08
Christchurch.
Centre, 5-4-0-1 (9 − 3t).
05 S+ I+(2t) E+ W−; 08 AW+(1t).
Farmer. NZ > 05 A (Youngest mem, 20 apps),
05-6 BI,F & NAm. Centre of controversy over
non-try v W 05. Died 2 months after 3rd Test v
AW 08 following appendix operation, aged 24.
Plaque perpetuates his memory at Christchurch
Boys' HS; also Robert Deans Scholarship.

DEANS, Robert Maxwell   *New Zealand*
Canterbury, NZ Colts, NZ Jnrs, S Island.
b 4.9.59 Cheviot.
FB, 5-2-1-2 (50 − 4c 14p).
83 S=(2c 3p) E−(1c 1p); 84 A−r A+(5p)

A+(1c 5p).
NZ > 83 E & S, 84 A, top scorer 52 pts 85 Arg.
World 1st-class best 43 pts (3t 14c 1p) v S
Australia 84. World XV > 86 SA.

DEAS, David Wallace   *Scotland*
Heriot's Coll, RDVC, Heriot's FP.
b 30.3.19.
No 8/lock, 2-0-0-2.
47 F− W−.
Veterinary surgeon.

DE BRUYN, Johan   *South Africa*
OFS.
b 12.10.48 Revilo.
Lock, 1-0-0-1.
74 BI−.
Technician/diesel mechanic. SA > 74 F.

DEDET, Jacques   *France*
SF.
b 4.3.1887 Hougilon, New Caledonia; *d* 4.3.71.
Centre/SH, 8-0-0-8.
10 S− E− I−; 11 W− I−; 12 S−; 13 E− I−.
Medicine.

DEDEYN, Paul   *France*
RCF.
Forward, 1-0-0-1.
06 NZ−.

DEDIEU, Paul   *France*
Béziers.
b 8.5.33 Toulouse.
FB, 12-8-2-2 (25 − 8c 1d 2p).
63 E− It+(1c); 64 W= It+ I+(1d) SA+
Fj+(3c) R+; 65 S+(2c) I= E−(1p) W+(2c 1p).
Panel beater.

DEE, John Mackenzie   *England*
Henry Smith Sch Hartlepool, English SS,
Hartlepool R, Barbarians, Durham Cos.
b 22.10.38 Hartlepool.
Centre/wing, 2-0-1-1.
62 S=; 63 NZ−; BI > 62 SA.
Schoolmaster.

DEERING, Mark Joseph   *Ireland*
Mount St Joseph's Coll Roscrea, Bective Rgrs.
b 6.3.1900 Dunlavin, Co Wicklow; *d* 26.4.73.
Lock, 1-0-1-0.
29 W=.
Farmer. Bro of S.J. & uncle of S.M. TD for
Wicklow.

DEERING, Seamus Joseph   *Ireland*
Mount St Joseph Coll Roscrea, Bective Rgrs,
Barbarians.
b 18.11.06 Dunlavin.
Lock/prop, 9-5-0-4.

35 E− S+ W+ NZ−; 36 E+ S+ W;− 37 E−
S+.
Civil service. Bro of M.J. & father of S.M.

DEERING, Seamus Mary ('Shay')　　*Ireland*
St Mary's Coll, UC Dublin, Garryowen, St
Mary's Coll.
　b 5.8.48 Dublin.
Flanker, 8-1-1-6.
74 W=; 76 F− W− E+ S−; 77 W− E−; 78
NZ−.
Veterinary surgeon. Son of S.J. & nephew of
M.J.

DE GRÉGORIO, Jean　　*France*
Grenoble.
　b 9.12.35 Romans.
Hooker, 22-14-3-5 (3 − 1t).
60 S+ E= W+ I+ It+ R− Arg+(1t) Arg+; 61
S+ SA= E= W+ It+ I+; 62 S+ E+ W−; 63
S− W+ It+; 64 NZ− E−.
Electrician/café proprietor.

DEHEZ, Jean-Louis　　*France*
Agen.
　b 6.5.44.
FH, 2-1-0-1 (11 − 1c 1d 2p).
67 SA−; 69 R+(1c 1d 2p).
19 pts v SW Dist, F > 67 SA, most pts by F in
any tour match (see Patrick Estève).

DE JONGH, Hermanus Paul　　*South Africa*
Kruger ('Manus')
W Prov.
Wing, 1-1-0-0 (3 − 1t).
28 NZ+(1t).
Broke nose 3rd Test v NZ 28, returned after
treatment to score t.

DE JOUVENCAL, Etienne　　*France*
SF.
FB, 2-0-0-2.
09 W　I　.

DE KLERK, Izak Johannes　　*South Africa*
Stellenbosch Univ, Transvaal.
　b 28.10.38 Calvinia.
Lock, 3-0-2-1.
69 E−; 70 I= W=.
PRO. SA > 69-70 BI.

DE KLERK, Kevin Brian Henry　　*South Africa*
Hill HS Johannesburg, Alberton, Jnr
Springboks, Gazelles, Natal, Transvaal.
　b 6.5.50 Johannesburg.
Lock, 13-9-0-4.
74 BI− BI− BI−r; 75 F+ F+; 76 NZ−r NZ+
NZ+; 80 SAm+ SAm+ BI+; 81 I+ I+.
Office worker/rep. Gazelles > 72 Arg. SA > 74
F.

DE KOCK, Arthur　　*South Africa*
Hopetown, Stellenbosch Univ, Griq W.
　b 11.1.1866; *d* 6.7.57.
1-0-0-1.
1891 BT−.

DE KOCK, J.S. ('Sas')　　*South Africa*
Stellenbosch Univ, W Prov.
FH, 2-0-2-0.
21 NZ=; 24 BI=.
Broke ankle 1st match SA > 21 NZ, v
Wanganui.

DE LABORDERIE, Marcel　　*France*
RCF.
　b 11.1.1899 Buenos Aires, Arg; *d* 53.
Wing/centre, 4-1-0-3 (3 − 1t).
21 I+; 22 I−; 25 W−(1t) E−.

DE LACY, Hugh　　*Ireland*
Ranelagh Coll Athlone, Trin Coll Dublin,
Harlequins, Barbarians.
　b −; *d* 8.11.79.
SH, 2-2-0-0.
48 E+ S+.

DELAGE, C.　　*France*
Agen.
FH, 3-2-0-1.
83 S+ I−; 85 J+r.

DELAHAY, William James　　*Wales*
('Bobby')
Bridgend, Cardiff, Torquay Ath, Devon.
　b 2.9.1900; *d* 12.9.78 Bridgend.
SH/FH/centre, 18-7-2-9 (3 − 1t).
22 E+ S= I+ F+; 23 E− S− F+ I−; 24 NZ−;
25 E− S− F+(1t) I−; 26 E= S− I+ F+; 27 S−.
Building worker. Capt Cardiff 26-7.

DELAIGUE, Gilles　　*France*
Toulon.
Centre, 2-2-0-0 (4 − 1t).
73 J+(1t) R+.

DELAMORE, Graham Wallace　　*New Zealand*
('Red')
Thames HS, Napier Tech Coll, Hawkes Bay,
Manawatu, Hutt, Wellington, RNZAF, Comb
Servs, N Island.
　b 3.4.20 Thames.
1st five-eighth, 1-0-0-1.
49 SA−.
GS principal. Served WW2, Fg Off (PE)
RNZAF. NZ > 49 SA.

DELANEY, Michael Gilbert　　*Ireland*
Blackrock Coll, Bective Rgrs.
　b 1872; *d* −.6.38.

Half-back, 1-0-0-1.
1895 W−.
Master tailor. Ref S v W 1899, S v E 1900.

DELPORT, Willem Hendrik   *South Africa*
Stellenbosch Univ, E Prov.
b 5.11.20 Kirkwood, Cape Prov.
Hooker, 9-8-0-1 (6 − 2t).
51 S+(1t) I+(1t) W+; 52 E+ F+; 53 A+ A−
A+ A+.
Solicitor/lawyer. Father of Jakobus, E Prov
hooker 77-81. SA > 51-2 BI, F.

DELQUE, Antonin   *France*
Toulouse.
Lock, 4-3-0-1 (6 − 2t).
37 It+(2t); 38 G− R+ G+.

DE MALHERBE, Henri   *France*
CASG.
Flanker, 2-2-0-0 (6 − 2t).
32 G+; 33 G+(2t).

DE MALMANN, René   *France*
RCF.
Forward, 7-0-0-7.
08 E− W−; 09 E− W− I−; 10 E− I−.

DE MELKER, Sydney Clarence   *South Africa*
Griq W.
b 1884; *d* 3.11.53 Springs.
Centre, 2-0-2-0.
03 BT=; 06 E=.
Mining.

DE MUIZON, Jacques   *France*
SF.
FB, 1-0-0-1.
10 I−.

DENNISON, Seamus Patrick   *Ireland*
Mungret Coll, UC Galway, UC Cork,
Garryowen.
b 26.1.50 Abbeyfeale, Co Limerick.
Wing, 3-2-0-1 (4 − 1t).
73 F+; 75 E+ S−(1t).
Schoolmaster.

DESCAMPS, Paul   *France*
RCF.
b − ; kia WW1.
Forward, 1-1-0-0 (4 − 2c).
11 S+ (2c).
Played in F's 1st int win, v S 11.

DESCAMPS   *France*
SBUC.
No 8, 1-0-0-1.
27 G−.

DESCLAUX, Francis   *France*
RCF.
Centre, 3-3-0-0 (7 − 2c 1d).
49 Arg+ Arg+; 53 It+(2c 1d).

DESCLAUX, Joseph   *France*
Perpignan.
Centre, 10-9-0-1 (23 − 3t 7c).
34 G+(1t 1c); 35 G+; 36 G+(2t) G+; 37 G+
It+(3c); 38 G− R+(1c) G+(1c); 45 BF+(1c).

DESNOYER, Laurent   *France*
Brive.
Wing, 1-0-0-1.
74 R−.

DESTARAC, Louis   *France*
Tarbes, Quillan.
b 1.9.02 Tarbes.
FB, 9-2-0-7 (10 − 5c).
26 S− I− E− W− M−; 27 W− E+ G+(3c) G−
(2c).

DESVOUGES, Robert   *France*
SF.
Lock, 1-0-0-1.
14 W−.

DETREZ, P.-E.   *France*
Nîmes.
Prop, 2-2-0-0 (4 − 1t).
83 A+r; 85 J+(1t).
F > 85 Arg.

DEVENISH, Charles   *South Africa*
Griq W.
1-0-0-1.
1896 BT−.

DEVENISH, George St Leger   *South Africa*
('Long George')
Transvaal.
1-0-0-1.
1896 BT−.
SA selector.

DEVENISH, M. ('Tiger')   *South Africa*
Transvaal.
1-0-0-1.
1891 BT−.

DEVEREUX, Donald   *Wales*
Welsh Youth, Neath, London Welsh.
b 31.
Prop, 3-2-1-0.
58 A+ E= S+.
Schoolmaster. Huddersfield RL, then Leeds.

DEVEREUX, John Anthony   *Wales*
('Dalek')
Ffaldau Jnr Sch, Ynysawdre Comp, Blaengarw,

S Glamorgan Inst, Bridgend.
b 20.3.66 Pontycymmer.
Centre, 4-2-0-2.
86 E− S+ I+ F−.
Student. FH, FB at Ynysawdre Sch under ex-Wales coach John Lloyd. Won 2 Boys Clubs of Wales football caps as centre-forward. Capped at 19 after less than a season with S Glamorgan Inst & Bridgend, whom he joined 84. Played only 2 matches (1 aband) for Bridgend when selected by W. BI v Rest of World, Cardiff 86.

DE VILLIERS, D.I. ('Dirkie')   *South Africa*
Wellington HS Cape Town, Cambridge Univ, Transvaal.
Centre, 3-2-0-1 (3 − 1t).
10 BI+(1t) BI− BI+.
Blue 13.

DE VILLIERS, David Jacobus   *South Africa*
('Dawie')
Stellenbosch Univ, W Prov, Jnr Springboks.
b 10.7.40 Burgersdorp.
SH, 25-15-4-6 (9 − 3t).
62 BI+ BI+; 65 I− NZ− NZ+ NZ−; 67 F+ F+ F− F=; 68 BI+(1t) BI= BI+ BI+ F+ F+; 69 A+ A+; 69 E−; 70 I= W= NZ+(1t) NZ− NZ+ NZ+.
Minister/diplomat. Serious knee inj threatened career. SA's most capped SH. 17 half-back apps with P.J. Visagie. Most ints as SA capt (22). Tour capt 65 A, NZ; 68 F; 69-70 BI; v F (4) 67; BI (4) 68; A (1st & 4th Tests) 69; NZ (4) 70. Capt 1st Gazelles > 65 SAm. SA Ambassador in London.

DE VILLIERS, H.A. ('Boy' later   *South Africa*
'Bekkies')
W Prov.
b − ; *d* 40.
Centre, 3-1-1-1.
06 S− W+ E=.
Auctioneer. Cousin of J.D. Krige. SA > 06-7 BI, F. Coach Cape Town Univ.

DE VILLIERS, Henry Oswald   *South Africa*
W Prov.
b 10.3.45 Johannesburg.
FB, 14-8-3-3 (26 − 7c 4p).
67 F+(4c 1p) F+(2c) F− F=(1p); 68 F+ F+; 69 A+ A+ A+ A+ S− E−; 70 I=(1c 1p) W=(1p).
Insurance agent. 16 apps SA > 69-70 BI. Inj ended career.

DE VILLIERS, Pierre du P.   *South Africa*
Gymnasium Boys HS Paarl, W Prov.
b −.6.05.
SH, 8-6-0-2.
28 NZ+ NZ+ NZ−; 32 E+; 33 A+; 37 A+ A+ NZ−.
Clerk/schoolmaster. SA > 31-2 BI.

DEVINE, Dauncey   *South Africa*
Stellenbosch Univ, Transvaal.
SH, 2-0-1-1.
24 BI=; 28 NZ−.
Trialist for SA > 37 A, NZ 14 seasons after 1st played for SA.

DEVITT, Sir Thomas Gordon Bt   *England*
Sherborne Sch, Cambridge Univ, Blackheath, The Army, Barbarians, Mdx.
b 27.12.02 Bishopsgate, Surrey.
Wing, 4-3-0-1.
26 I− F+; 28 NSW+ W+.
The Army/co dir. Blue 23-5. Ath blue (long jump) 23-4. Served WW2.

DE VOS, Dirk Johannes Jacobus   *South Africa*
W Prov.
b 8.4.41 Kroonstad.
SH, 3-1-0-2.
65 S−; 69 A+; 69 S−.
Personnel officer/schoolmaster. SA > 69-70 BI, 71 A.

DE WAAL, Albertus Nicholas   *South Africa*
W Prov.
b 14.2.42.
No 8, 4-2-1-1.
67 F+ F+ F− F=.

DE WAAL, P.   *South Africa*
Stellenbosch Univ, W Prov.
1-1-0-0.
1896 BT+.

DEWAR, Henry ('Norkey')   *New Zealand*
Newtown Sch, Berhampore Sch, Melrose, Wellington, Hawera, Star, Stratford, Taranaki, N Island.
b 13.10.1883 Wellington; kia 19.8.15 Chunuk Bair, Gallipoli.
No 8, 2-2-0-0.
13 A+ US+.
Moulder. NZ > 13 NAm. Capt in Wellington Mounted Rifles.

DE WET, Andre Eloff   *South Africa*
W Prov.
b 1.8.46 Kokstad.
Lock, 3-2-0-1.
69 A+ A+ E−.
Pharmacist. SA > 69-70 BI.

DE WET, Pieter   *South Africa*
Stellenbosch Univ, W Prov.
Centre, 3-2-0-1.
38 BI+ BI+ BI−.

DEWHURST, John Henry MBE   *England*
Mill Hill Sch, Cambridge Univ, Richmond, St Thomas's Hosp, Surrey.

b 27.12.1863 Skipton; *d* 22.4.47.
Forward, 4-1-1-2.
1887 W+ I− S=; 1890 W−.
Medicine. Blue 1885-6. Capped in 1888 E side that did not play.

DE WINTON, Robert Francis *England*
Chippini
Summer Fields Sch, Marlborough Coll, Marlborough Nomads, Oxford Univ, Blackheath.
b 9.9.1868 Newport, Gwent; *d* 14.3.23 Porterville, California.
Half-back, 1-0-0-1.
1893 W−.
HM. Blue 1888-90. Served WW1 with Lancs Fusiliers. Died from fall from window of hotel bedroom.

DEYGAS, Marcel *France*
Vienne.
Centre, 1-1-0-0.
37 It+.

DIACK, Ernest Sinclair ('Tuppy') *New Zealand*
Napier Boys' HS, Gore HS, Univ, Otago, Zingari-Richmond, Pukerau-Maitland, Southland, NZ Univs, S Island.
b 22.7.32 Invercargill.
Wing, 1-1-0-0.
59 BI+.
Schoolmaster. Father Charlie rep Otago & Marlborough. Ckt for Otago.

DIBBLE, Robert *England*
Bridgwater & A, Newport, Som.
b Bridgwater.
Forward, 19-11-1-7.
06 S+ F+ SA=; 08 F+ W− I+ S−; 09 A− W− F+ I+ S−; 10 S+; 11 W− F+ S+; 12 W+ I+ S−.
Licensee. Served in Boer War. 73 apps Som 01-21.

DICK, Charles John ('Ian') *Ireland*
Ballymena Acad, Queen's Univ Belfast, Ballymena, Barbarians.
b 26.1.37 Ballymena.
Lock/no 8, 8-1-2-5.
61 W− F− SA−; 62 W=; 63 F− E= S− W+.
Medicine. Bro of James.

DICK, James *Ireland*
Ballymena Acad, Queen's Univ Belfast.
b 24.10.39 Ballymena.
Hooker, 1-0-0-1.
62 E−.
Medicine. Bro of 'Ian'.

DICK, John *New Zealand*
Auckland GS, Grafton, Auckland, Air Force,

RNZAF, Canterbury, N Island.
b 3.10.12 Auckland.
Wing, 3-2-0-1 (3 − 1t).
37 SA+(1t) SA−; 38 A+.
Warehouseman. NZ > 38 A (original selection, withdrew when contracted measles, ultimately joined team when supporters paid his fare). Father of Malcolm.

DICK, John Stanley *Ireland*
Queen's Coll Cork, Barbarians.
b −.4.1865; *d* −.
Forward, 3-0-1-2.
1887 E= S− W−.
Medicine.

DICK, Lewis Gibson *Scotland*
Morrison's Sch, Loughborough Colls, Jordanhill, Swansea, Barbarians.
b 20.12.50 Perth.
Wing, 14-6-0-8 (8 − 2t).
72 W−r E+; 74 W− E+ I− F+(1t); 75 I+ F− W+ E− NZ− A+(1t); 76 F−; 77 E−.
PE teacher. Scottish XV v Tg 74, J 77.

DICK, Malcolm John *New Zealand*
Bayfield Sch, Auckland GS, Ponsonby, Auckland, N Island.
b 3.1.41 Auckland.
Wing, 15-11-1-3 (12 − 4t).
63 I+ W+; 64 E+ S= F+; 65 SA−; 66 BI+(1t); 67 A+ E+(1t) W+ F+(1t); 69 W+(1t) W+; 70 SA− SA−.
Accountant. Son of John. NZ > 63-4 (19t) & 67 BI,F & C, 70 A & SA (14t). 40t in 54 NZ apps. Chmn Auckland RFU.

DICK, R.C.S. *Scotland*
Cambridge Univ, Guy's Hosp, Barbarians.
Centre, 14-6-0-8 (18 − 6t).
34 W− I+(2t) E−; 35 W− I− E+ NZ−(1t); 36 W− I− E−; 37 W+(2t); 38 W+ I+ E+(1t).
Medicine. Blue 33.

DICKS, John *England*
Northampton GS, O Northamptonians, Wellingborough, Northampton, Barbarians, E Midlands.
b 12.9.12 Ecton, Northants.
Lock/prop, 8-5-2-1.
34 W+ I+ S+; 35 W= I+ S−; 36 S+; 37 I=.
Farmer.

DICKSON, Gordon *Scotland*
Gala Acad, Gala.
b 10.12.54 Galashiels.
No 8, 9-1-2-6 (4 − 1t).
78 NZ−; 79 W− E= I= F−(1t) NZ−; 80 W−; 81 F−; 82 W+r.
Civil engr. Scottish XV v J 77.

DICKSON, James Alfred *Ireland*
Nicholson
Portora RS, Trin Coll Dublin.
b 12.3.1897 Enniskillen; *d* 24.11.63
Enniskillen.
Wing, 3-0-0-3 (3 − 1t).
20 E−(1t) W− F−.
Dental surg.

DICKSON, Maurice Rhynd DSO *Scotland*
Marlborough Coll, Edinburgh Univ, Oxford
Univ, Barbarians.
b 2.1.1882 Panbride; *d* 10.1.40 Arbroath.
Forward, 1-0-0-1.
05 I−.
Writer to the Signet. Blue 03. Served WW1. Ckt
for S.

DICKSON, Walter Michael *Scotland*
SA Coll Rondebosch, Oxford Univ,
Blackheath, Barbarians.
b 23.11.1884 SA; kia 26.9.15 Gallipoli.
FB, 7-4-0-3.
12 F+ W− E+ SA−; 13 F+ W− I+.
Surveyor. Rhodes Scholar. Blue 12, along with
another SA-born Scottish int, SSL Steyn; both
killed WW1. In same Oxford XV were Lionel
Brown, Australian-born E player & 4 other
South Africans, K.C.M. Hands, N. Reid, L.R.
Broster & W.E. Thomas. Served WW1, Lt
Argyle & Sutherland Highlanders. Noted
bulldog breeder; also raced cars at Brooklands.

DIETT, Leonard John *Australia*
NSW.
b 27.8.39.
Centre, 2-0-0-2.
59 BI− BI−.
PE teacher. RL.

DILLON, Edward Wentworth *England*
Rugby Sch, Oxford Univ, Blackheath,
Harlequins, Barbarians, Kent.
b 15.2.1881 Surrey; *d* 20.4.41.
Centre, 4-1-1-2.
04 W= I+ S−; 05 W−.
Ship & insurance broker. Ckt blue 01-2. 110 no
on 1st 1st-class app, London v Worcs 1900; Kent
1900-14 (capt 09-14). Served WW1, Capt R
West Kent Rgt, mentioned in despatches,
wounded.

DINGLE, Arthur James ('Mud') *England*
Bow Sch Durham, Durham Sch, Oxford Univ,
Hartlepool R, Richmond, Barbarians, Durham
Cos, Surrey.
b 1892 Hetton le Hole, Co Durham; kia 22.8.15
Gallipoli.
Centre/wing, 3-3-0-0.
13 I+; 14 S+ F+.
Schoolmaster. Blue 11. 55t in 13-14. Noted

oarsman. Missing, presumed killed at Suvla
Bay, Gallipoli.

DINKELMANN, Ernst E. *South Africa*
Pretoria Univ, N Transvaal.
b 14.5.27 Ermelo.
Flanker/lock, 6-5-0-1 (6 − 2t).
51 S+(1t) I+; 52 E+ F+; 53 A+ A−
Medicine. SA > 51-2 BI, F.

DINTRANS, Phillippe *France*
Tarbes.
b 29.1.57 Tarbes.
Hooker, 44-24-3-17 (12 − 3t).
79 NZ− NZ+ R+; 80 E− S− I+ SA−(1t) R−;
81 S+ I+ W+ E+ A− A− R+ NZ− NZ−; 82
W− E− S− I+ R− Arg+ Arg+; 83 E+ W+
A= A+ R+; 84 I+ W+ E+ S− NZ− NZ−
R+; 85 E= S+ I= W+ Arg− Arg+ J+ J+(2t).
PE instructor. F's most capped hooker. F > 79
NZ; 80 SA; 85 Arg (capt).

DIRKSEN, Corra W. *South Africa*
N Transvaal.
b 22.1.38.
Wing, 10-4-3-3 (9 − 3t).
63 A+; 64 W=; 65 I− S−; 67 F+(2t) F+(1t) F−
F=; 68 BI+ BI=.
Chemist.

DIX, William *Australia*
NSW.
b 19.11.1887; *d* 44.
Centre/FB/wing, 4-1-1-2.
07 NZ− NZ− NZ=; 09 E+.
Engr.

DIXON, Ernest Joseph *Australia*
Qld.
b 1885; *d* 41.
Forward, 1-0-0-1.
04 BT−.
Schoolmaster.

DIXON, Maurice James *New Zealand*
Sydenham Sch, Christchurch Tech Coll,
Sydenham, Canterbury, S Island.
b 6.2.29 Christchurch.
Wing, 10-8-0-2 (6 − 2t).
54 I+ E+ S+ F−; 56 SA+ SA− SA+(1t) SA+;
57 A+ A+(1t).
Railway fitter/licensee. NZ > 53-4 BI,F & NAm
(7t), 57 A. Canterbury & S Island sel.

DIXON, Peter John *England*
St Bees Coll, Durham Univ, Workington,
UAU, Oxford Univ, Harlequins, Gosforth,
Barbarians, Cumberland & Westmorland.
b 30.4.44 Keighley.
Flanker, 22-7-1-14 (16 − 4t).
71 P−; 72 W− I− F− S−; 73 I− F+ S+(2t); 74

121

S− I− F= W+; 75 I−; 76 F−(1t); 77 S+ I+ F−
W−; 78 F− S+ I+(1t) NZ−; BI > 71 A, NZ 3-
2-1-0.
Social anthropologist. Blue 67-70. Oxford Univ
CB rep on RFU.

DIZABO, Pierre ('Pepe')   *France*
Tyrosse.
 b 4.10.29 St Vincent de Tyrosse.
Centre/FH, 13-8-1-4 (6 − 1t 1d).
48 A+ S− E+; 49 S− I+ E− W+ Arg+; 50 S−
I=; 60 Arg+ Arg+(1d) Arg+(1t).
Recalled for F > 60 Arg after 10 yr absence.

DOBBIN, Frederick James   *South Africa*
('Uncle')
Griq W.
 b 1879 Bethulie; *d* −.2.50.
FH/SH, 9-5-3-1 (3 − 1t).
03 BT=(1t) BT=; 06 S− W+ E=; 10 BI+; 12
S+ I+ W+.
SA > 06 BI, 12-13 BI, F. Capt SA v S 12. Scored
t on Test debut.

DOBBS, George Eric Burroughs   *England*
St Stephen's Green Sch Dublin, Shrewsbury
Sch, RMA Woolwich, Plymouth A, Devonport
A, Llanelli, RE, The Army, Barbarians,
Devon.
 b 21.7.1884; *d* 17.6.17 Poperinghe.
Flanker, 2-0-0-2.
06 W− I−.
The Army. Capt Shrewsbury Sch football XI.
Served WW1, Lt Col in RE. Awarded Legion
d'Honneur, Mons 14. Mentioned in despatches
3 times. Died of wounds.

DOBIE, John A.R.   *South Africa*
Transvaal.
 b 4.8.05.
Wing, 1-0-0-1.
28 NZ−.

DOBLE, Samuel Arthur   *England*
Regis Sch, Moseley.
 b 9.3.44 Wolverhampton; *d* −.9.77
Birmingham.
FB, 3-1-0-2 (20 − 1c 6p).
72 SA+(1c 4p); 73 NZ− W−(2p).
Schoolmaster. 47 pts (5 apps) E > 72 SA. Died
of cancer.

DOBSON, Denys Douglas   *England*
Newton Coll, Cheltenham Coll, Oxford Univ,
Newton Abbot, Devonport A, Barbarians,
London Welsh, Devon.
 b 28.10.1880; *d* 10.7.16 Ngama, Nyasaland.
Forward, 6-2-0-4 (9 − 3t).
02 W−(1t) I+ S+; 03 W−(1t) I− S−(1t); BT >
04 A, NZ.
Colonial civil service. Blue 1899-01. Sent off for

'obscene language' during one match on BT >
04 A, NZ. Killed by a charging rhinoceros when
District Resident at Ngama.

DOBSON, George   *Wales*
Cardiff.
 b 1873 Pontypridd.
Forward, 1-1-0-0.
1900 S+.
Bro of Tom.

DOBSON, James Donald   *Scotland*
Glasgow Acad, Glasgow HS, Glasgow
Academicals.
 b 1889; *d* −.
Wing, 1-1-0-0 (3 − 1t).
10 I+(1t).

DOBSON, John MC   *Scotland*
Glasgow Acad, Glasgow Academicals.
 b 1887; *d* 14.7.36.
Hooker, 6-2-0-4.
11 E−; 12 F+ W− I− E+ SA−.
Co dir. Served WW1.

DOBSON, Ronald Leslie   *New Zealand*
Wellesley Sch, Ponsonby, Auckland, Northcote,
Comb Servs, Barbarians (E).
 b 26.3.23 Auckland.
2nd five-eighth, 1-0-0-1.
49 A−.
House painter/textile production planner.
Served WW2; 8t (18 apps) Comb Servs.
Coached various clubs.

DOBSON, Thomas   *Wales*
Cardiff.
 b c1872; *d* 4.7.36 Cardiff.
Forward, 4-2-0-2 (3 − 1t).
1898 I+(1t) E−; 1899 E+ S−.
Coal trimmer. Bro of George.

DOBSON, Thomas Hyde   *England*
Bowling FC, Bradford, Yorks.
 b −.2.1872; *d* 12.11.02 Bradford.
Centre, 1-0-0-1.
1895 S−.
Tailor. Won many events at Yorks ath meetings.
Turned RL when his club, Bradford, helped
form NU 1895. His father, Harry, trained the
Bradford XV which won Yorks Challenge Cup
1884.

DOBSON, William Goldie   *Scotland*
Heriot's Coll, Heriot's FP, Edinburgh Univ.
 b 9.2.1894; *d* 11.3.73.
Prop, 3-1-1-1.
22 W= I+ E−.
Medicine.

122

DOCHERTY, James Thomas　　　　*Scotland*
Glasgow HS, Glasgow HSFP.
b 5.6.31 Glasgow.
FH/centre, 8-3-1-4 (3 − 1d).
55 F− W+(1d); 56 E−; 58 F+ W− A+ I− E=.
Sportswear co dir.

DODD, Ernest Henry　　　　*New Zealand*
Wellington Coll, OB, Wellington, N Island.
b 21.3.1880 Wellington; kia 11.9.18 France.
Forward, 1-1-0-0.
05 A+.
Clerk. NZ Rifle Bde.

DODGE, Paul William　　　　*England*
Wreake Sch, Leics SS, England Colts, Leicester,
Midland Cos.
b 26.5.58 Leicester.
Centre, 32-14-5-13 (15 − 1t 1c 3p).
78 W− S+(1p) I+ NZ−; 79 S= I− F+ W−; 80
W+ S+; 81 W− S+ I+(1t) F− Arg= Arg+; 82
A+(1c) S=(2p) F+ W+; 83 F− W= S− I−
NZ+; 85 R+ F= S+ I− W− NZ− NZ−; BIr >
80 SA 2-1-0-1.
Bookbinder. Midland Cos v A 75. Midlands &
North v Arg 76. E Under 23s v J; > 77 Can. E >
79 Far East; v Fj 82. Broke leg 83. Played for
Leicester in 3 consec John Player Cup final wins.

DODS, Francis Palliser　　　　*Scotland*
Edinburgh Acad, Edinburgh Academicals.
b 23.2.1879; *d* 29.6.10.
Forward, 1-1-0-0.
01 I+.
Stockbroker. Bro of J.H.

DODS, John Henry　　　　*Scotland*
Edinburgh Acad.
b 30.9.1875; kia 30.12.15.
Forward, 8-5-1-2.
1895 W+ I+ E+; 1896 W− I= E+; 1897 I+
F−
Factor. Bro of F.P. Served WW1; killed on
board HMS 'Natal' which blew up at Cromarty.

DODS, Peter William　　　　*Scotland*
Galashiels Acad, Gala.
b 6.1.58 Galashiels.
FB, 15-5-1-9 (150 − 2t 14c 38p).
83 I−(2p) F−(1c 1p) W−(1c 3p) E+(1c 3p)
NZ=(5p); 84 W+(2c 1p) E+(2c 2p) I+(1t 3c
2p) F+(1c 5p) R−(1t 1c 3p) A−(4p); 85 I−(4p)
F−(1p) W−(2c 1p) E−(1p).
Joiner. Scottish XV v Netherlands 78, Fj 82.
Scotland B v I 79, F 80-2. S > 81 NZ, 82 A. 50
pts 84 Champ.

DOHERTY, Alan Edward　　　　*Ireland*
Kilkenny Coll, O Wesley.

b 31.7.45 Enniscorthy.
1-0-1-0.
74 P=r.
Pensions consultant.

DOHERTY, William David　　　　*Ireland*
Dulwich Coll, O Alleynians, Cambridge Univ,
Guy's Hosp, Surrey, Barbarians.
b 17.7.1893; *d* 31.3.66.
Flanker/no 8/lock, 7-1-0-6.
20 E− S− W−; 21 E− S+ W− F−.
Medicine. Blue 13.

DOMEC, Albert　　　　*France*
Carcassonne.
Wing, 1-0-0-1.
29 W−.

DOMEC, Henri　　　　*France*
Lourdes.
b 9.8.32 Lourdes.
Flanker, 20-15-0-5 (3 − 1t).
53 W− It+(1t); 54 S+ I+ NZ+ W− E+ It+; 55
S+ I+ E+ W−; 56 I+ W− It+; 58 E− A+ W+
It+ I+.
Engrg fitter.

DOMENECH, Amédée ('Le Duc')　　　*France*
Vichy, Brive.
b 3.5.33 Narbonne.
Prop/no 8, 52-32-4-16 (24 − 8t).
54 W− E+ It+; 55 S+(1t) I+(1t) E+ W−; 56
S− I+ W− It+ E+ Cz+(1t); 57 S− I− E− W−
It+(1t) R+ R+; 58 S− E− It+; 59 It+; 60 S+
E= W+ I+(1t) It+ R− Arg+(2t) Arg+ Arg+;
61 S+ SA= E= W+ It+(1t) I+ NZ− NZ−
NZ− A+ R=; 62 S+ E+ W− I+ It+ R−; 63
W+ It+.
Hotelier.

DOMERCQ, Jean　　　　*France*
Bayonne.
Hooker, 2 0 0 2.
12 I− S−.
Army.

DONALD, Andrew John　　　*New Zealand*
Wanganui, NZ Colts, NZ Jnrs, N Island, NZ
Barbarians.
b 11.5.57 Wanganui.
SH, 7-4-1-2.
83 S= E−; 84 F+ F+ A− A+ A+.
NZ > 81 R & F, 83 S & E, 84 A. World XV >
86 SA.

DONALD, Sir David Grahame　　　*Scotland*
KCB DFC AFC
Dulwich Coll, O Alleynians, Oxford Univ,
Barbarians.
b 27.7.1891; *d* 23.12.76.

Prop, 2-0-0-2.
14 W− I−.
RAF. Blue 11-13. Served WW1. Contemporary
at Dulwich of E's Cyril Lowe (MC DFC), who
also had a distinguished WW1 record in RFC;
E's John Greenwood (mentioned in
despatches); & fellow Scot E.G. Loudoun-
Shand (MC). A 5th int at Dulwich was I's W.D.
Doherty, a doctor.

DONALD, James George　　　*New Zealand*
Wellington Coll, Gladstone, Wairarapa,
Featherston Liberal, Southern Utd, Masterton,
Greytown, N Island.
b 4.6.1898 Featherston.
Flanker, 2-1-0-1.
21 SA+ SA−.
Farmer. Bro of Quentin. NZ > 20, 22 & 25
(capt) A.

DONALD, Kenneth John　　　*Australia*
Ipswich GS Qld, Qld.
b 9.8.36.
Wing, 9-0-1-8 (21 − 1t 6p).
57 NZ−; 58 W− I− E− S−(1t) M=(1p) M−
(2p); 59 BI−(2p) BI−(1p).
Medicine.

DONALD, Quentin　　　*New Zealand*
Wellington Coll, Gladstone, Wairarapa,
Featherston Utd, Featherston, Southern Utd, N
Island.
b 13.3.1900 Featherston; *d* 27.12.65 Greytown.
Hooker, 4-4-0-0.
24 I+ W+; 25 E+ F+.
Farmer. Bro of James. NZ > 24-5 A,BI,F & C.
Wairarapa sel 35.

DONALD, Russell L.H.　　　*Scotland*
Glasgow HS, Glasgow HSFP.
b 9.9.1898; *d* 31.12.32.
FH, 3-1-0-2.
21 W+ I− E−.

DONALDSON, James Albert　　　*Ireland*
Methodist Coll Belfast, Collegians.
b 16.9.36 Belfast.
Flanker, 4-2-0-2.
58 A+ E− S+ W−.
Farmer/insurance/property.

DONALDSON, Mark William　　　*New Zealand*
New Plymouth Boys' HS, HSOB, NZ Colts,
Manawatu, Celtic, Hawkes Bay, N Island.
b 6.11.55 Palmerston N.
SH, 13-9-0-4 (4 − 1t).
77 F− F+; 78 A+ A+ A− I+ E+ S+; 79
F+(1t) F− A− S+r; 81 SA+r.
Bank clerk/sports shop mgr. NZ > 77 F, 78 BI,
79 A, 79 E,S & It, 80 A & Fj (broken jaw
limited him to 2 apps); NAm & W. NZ v Fj 80.

DONALDSON, William Patrick　　　*Scotland*
Loretto Sch, Oxford Univ, W of S, Fettesian-
Lorettonians, Barbarians.
b 4.3.1871; *d* 27.3.23 Dollar.
Half-back, 6-2-2-2 (3 − 1p).
1893 I=; 1894 I−; 1895 E+; 1896 I= E+; 1899
I−(1p).
Iron merchant. Blue 1892-4.

DONNELLY, Martin Paterson　　　*England*
('Squib')
New Plymouth Boys' HS (NZ), Canterbury
Univ, Canterbury, NZ Univs, Oxford Univ,
Blackheath, Barbarians.
b 17.10.17 Ngaruawahia, NZ.
Centre, 1-0-0-1.
47 I−.
Sales marketing mgr. Served WW2 NZEF, Maj
4th Armoured Bde. Bursary to Oxford. Blue 46.
Rep rugby at SH, FH, centre, FB. Ckt blue − 23
apps OUCC 46-7; 1 app Mdx CCC 46; 20 apps
Warwicks CCC 48-50. Has distinction of scoring
centuries at Lord's in Varsity Match (142 in 46),
Gentlemen v Players (162 n.o. 47) & in a Test
match (206 for NZ v E, 49). One of NZ's finest
batsmen − NZ > 37, 49 England; v Australia
37-8, 38-9. 59 matches, 7 Tests, for NZ (3745
runs at 46.81, HS 206).

DONOVAN, Alun John　　　*Wales*
Maesydderwen CS, St Paul's Coll Cheltenham,
Swansea, Breconshire, Cardiff.
b 5.10.55 Abercrave.
FB/centre, 5-2-0-3.
78 A−; 81 I+r A+; 82 E− S−.
Schoolmaster. W > 78 A. Wales B v F 77. Wales
B > 80 US, Can.

DONOVAN, Richard　　　*Wales*
Welsh Youth, S Wales Police.
Wing, 1-0-0-1.
83 F−r.
Police. Wales B > 83 Spain.

DONOVAN, Thomas M.　　　*Ireland*
Queen's Coll Cork.
Forward, 1-0-0-1.
1889 S−.

DON WAUCHOPE, Andrew　　　*Scotland*
Ramsay ('Bunny')
Fettes Coll, Fettesian-Lorettonians, Cambridge
Univ.
b 29.4.1861; *d* 16.1.48.
Half-back, 12-8-3-1 (6t).
1881 E=; 1882 E+; 1883 W+(1t); 1884 W+
I+(1t) E−; 1885 W= I+(1t); 1886 W+(1t)
I+(2t) E=; 1888 I+.
Stockbroker/lawyer. Blue 1880-1. Played with
bro P.H. v I 1885, v W 1886. Ref W v I 1889, E v

I 1890, I v E 1893. Ump S v W, 1889, S v I, W v S, S v E 1890. Pres SRU 1889-90. Ckt for S.

DON WAUCHOPE, Patrick   *Scotland*
Hamilton
Fettes Coll, Fettesian-Lorettonians.
b 1.5.1863; *d* 11.1.39.
Half-back, 5-4-1-0 (1t).
1885 I+; 1886 W+; 1887 I+ W+(1t) E=.
Writer to the Signet. Played with bro A.R. v I 1885, v W 1886.

DOOLEY, John Francis   *Ireland*
St Joseph's Coll Galway, Galwegians.
b 10.8.34 Galway.
Centre, 3-1-0-2 (3 − 1t).
59 E− S+(1t) W−.
Played football for Irish Univs.

DOOLEY, Wade Anthony   *England*
Beaumont St Sch Warrington, Preston
Grasshoppers, Brit Police, Lancs.
b 2.10.57 Warrington.
Lock, 10-4-1-5 (4 − 1t).
85 R+ F= S+ I− W− NZ−r; 86 W+ S− I+ F− (1t).
Police. 6ft 8in − one of tallest players to rep E. Played RL at sch, switched to RU when a police cadet 75. 1st Lancs Policeman to be capped; Lancs Constabulary Sportsman of Yr 85. N of England v R 84. Brit Police v NZ Comb Servs 86.

DORAN, Bertie R.W.   *Ireland*
Lansdowne.
b 1876; *d* 22.3.48.
Centre, 8-2-1-5 (3 − 1t).
1900 S= W−; 01 E+ S−(1t) W−; 02 E− S+ W−.
Solicitor.

DORAN, Edward F.   *Ireland*
Lansdowne.
Forward, 2-0-1-1.
1890 S− W=.
Bro of 'Blucher'.

DORAN, Gerald Percy ('Blucher')   *Ireland*
Lansdowne.
b 1877; *d* 31.3.43.
Wing, 8-3-1-4 (6 − 2t).
1899 S+ W+(1t); 1900 E− S=; 02 S+(1t) W−; 03 W−; 04 E−; BT > 1899 A.
Solicitor. Bro of Edward.

DORE, Edmund ('Eric')   *Australia*
Qld.
b 1880; *d* 64.
Forward, 1-0-0-1.
04 BT−.
Clerk. Bro of Michael.

DORE, Michael Joseph   *Australia*
St Joseph's Coll Brisbane, Qld.
b c1883; *d* 13.8.10.
Half-back, 1-0-0-1.
05 NZ−.
Saddler. Bro of Eric. RL.

DORMEHL, Pieter J.   *South Africa*
Stellenbosch Univ, W Prov.
2-1-0-1.
1896 BT− BT+.

DOROT, Jacques   *France*
RCF.
Lock, 1-1-0-0.
35 G+.

DORR, Rudolph William   *Australia*
Victoria.
b 10; *d* 61.
Wing, 2-1-0-1.
36 M+; 37 SA−.
Master butcher.

DORWARD, Arthur Fairgrieve   *Scotland*
Gala Acad, Sedbergh Sch, Cambridge Univ, Gala, Barbarians.
b 3.3.25.
SH, 15-3-0-12 (3 − 1d).
50 F+; 51 SA−; 52 W− I− E−; 53 F− W− E−; 55 F−; 56 I− E−; 57 F+ W+(1d) I− E−.
Tweed. Bro of Tommy. Blue 47-9.

DORWARD, Thomas Fairgrieve   *Scotland*
Gala Acad, Sedbergh Sch, Gala, RAF.
b 27.3.16; kia 5.3.41.
SH, 5-3-0-2 (4 − 1d).
38 W+ I+(1d) E+; 39 I− E−.
RAF/tweed. Bro of Arthur.

DOSPITAL, Pierre   *France*
Bayonne.
b 15.5.50 Ainhoa.
Prop, 24-16-2-6.
77 R I; 80 I+; 81 S+ I+ W+ E+; 82 I+ R− Arg+ Arg+; 83 E+ S+ I− W+; 84 E+ S− NZ− NZ− R+; 85 E= S+ I= W+ Arg−.
Municipal employee. F > 80 SA; 85 Arg.

DOUGLAS, George   *Scotland*
Jedburgh GS, Jedforest.
b 1897; *d* 26.10.57 Jedburgh.
Lock, 1-1-0-0.
21 W+.
Baker. Served WW1 KOSB. Batley RL 21.

DOUGLAS, James Alexander   *Australia*
Victoria.
b 39.
Wing, 3-0-1-2.

62 NZ= NZ− NZ−.
Electrician.

DOUGAN, John Patrick   *New Zealand*
St Michael's Sch Taita, St Bernard's Coll,
Petone, Wellington, Taradale, NZ Jnrs, Hawkes
Bay, Havelock, N Island.
b 22.12.46 Lower Hutt.
1st five-eighth, 2-1-0-1 (4 − 1t).
72 A+(1t); 73 E−.
Co dir. Sc NZ's 1st 4-pt try v A, 19.8.72. Ckt for
Hutt Valley & Hawkes Bay. Uncles Jackie &
Bill rep Wellington.

DOUGLAS, Arthur Coates   *Ireland*
RBAI, Instonians.
b 16.8.02; *d* −.6.37.
Wing, 5-0-0-5 (6 − 2t).
23 F−(1t); 24 E−(1t) S−; 27 NSW−; 28 S−.
Sports master. Ckt for I.

DOUGLAS, John   *Scotland*
Stewart's Coll, Stewart's Coll FP, Kent.
b 18.12.34 Woolwich.
No 8, 12-6-1-5 (3 − 1t).
61 F− SA− W+ I+(1t) E−; 62 F− W+ I+ E=;
63 F+ W− I+; BI > 62 SA.
Glasgow-Edinburgh v SA 61. Owner of
'Rubstic', winner of Grand National 79.

DOUGLAS, Mark Henry James   *Wales*
Lampeter Comp, Welsh SS, Lampeter,
Carmarthen Ath, Llanelli, W Wales, Carms,
Barbarians, London Welsh.
b 10.12.60 Aberystwyth.
SH, 3-1-0-2.
84 S− I+ F−.
Butcher. Wales B v F 82-4, v Spain 85. Wales B
> 83 Spain. With Gary Pearce at Carmarthen
Ath. Bro Carl played for Swansea.

DOUGLAS, William M.   *Wales*
Cardiff.
b 2.7.1863; *d* 45.
Back, 4-0-1-3.
1886 E− S−; 1887 E= S−.
Colliery official. Ref I v E 1891, 1894, S v E
1896, 1903. IB rep 14.

DOUGLASS, Frank W.   *South Africa*
E Prov.
1-0-0-1.
1896 BT−.

DOURTHE, Claude ('Le   *France*
Chameau')
Dax.
b 20.11.48 Magescq, Landes.
Centre, 33-17-3-13 (39 − 10t 1d).
66 R+; 67 S− A+ E+(1t) W+(1t) I+ SA−(1t)
SA− SA+ NZ−; 68 W+ NZ−(1d) SA− SA−;
69 W=; 71 SA=r R+(1t); 72 I− I− A= A+
R+; 73 S+(1t) NZ+(1t) E−; 74 I+ Arg+(1t)
Arg+(1t) SA− SA−(1t); 75 W− E+ S+(1t).
Dentist. F > 67 SA.

DOUSSEAU, Emile   *France*
Angoulême.
Prop, 1-1-0-0.
38 R+.

DOUTY, Peter Sime   *Scotland*
Sedbergh Sch, Cambridge Univ, London
Scottish.
b 26.10.03 Leeds; *d* 18.7.48.
SH, 3-2-0-1 (3 − 1t).
27 NSW+; 28 F+(1t) W−.
Insurance. Blue 24.

DOVEY, Beverley Alfred   *England*
Lydney GS, Lydney, Cambridge Univ, Rosslyn
Pk, Barbarians, Glos, Herts, Yorks.
b 24.10.38.
Prop, 2-1-1-0.
63 W+ I=.
Schoolmaster. Blue 60.

DOWELL, William Henry   *Wales*
Newport, Pontypool.
b 21.5.1885 Pontypool.
Flanker/lock, 7-6-0-1.
07 E+ S− I+; 08 E+ S+ F+ I+.
Licensee. Warrington RL 12.

DOWN, Percy John   *England*
Dr Kempe's Sch Long Ashton, Redland,
Bristol, Som.
b 14.10.1883 Clifton; *d* 22.7.54.
Prop, 1-0-0-1.
09 A−; BT(uncap) > 08 A, NZ.
Farmer. Capt & chmn (45-54) of Bristol.

DOWNING, Albert Joseph   *New Zealand*
('Doolan')
Marist, Hawkes Bay, Auckland, N Island.
b 12.7.1886 Napier; kia 8.8.15 Gallipoli.
Lock/no 8, 5-5-0-0.
13 A+ US+; 14 A+ A+ A+.
Clerk. NZ > 13 NAm, 14 A. 1st NZ int casualty
WW1; killed during landing at Suvla Bay.

DOWNING, Arthur Joseph   *Ireland*
Rugby Sch, Trin Coll Dublin.
b 16.11.1891.
Forward, 1-0-0-1.
1882 W−.
Civil engr.

DOWSE, John Cecil Alexander   *Ireland*
Monkstown, Trin Coll Dublin.
Forward, 3-2-0-1.

126

14 F+ S+ W−.
RAMC.

DOWSE, John Henry *Australia*
NSW.
b 35.
Five-eighth, 4-2-0-2 (25 − 5c 5p).
61 Fj+(3c) Fj+(1c 2p) SA−(1p) SA−(1c 2p).

DOWSON, Aubrey Osler MC *England*
Rugby Sch, Oxford Univ, Moseley, Manchester,
Midlands.
b 10.11.1875; d 5.10.40.
Forward, 1-0-0-1.
1899 S−.
Manufacturer/farmer. Blue 1896. Mem of New
Coll VIII which won Grand Challenge Cup
Henley 1897. Ath blue (shot & hammer) 1895-7.
Served WW1, 12th Rifle Bde. Mentioned in
despatches 17. MC 18.

DOYLE, James Anthony Paul *Ireland*
PBC Bray, Greystones.
b 26.4.58 Dublin.
SH, 2-0-0-2.
84 E− S−.
Licensee.

DOYLE, J.T. *Ireland*
PBC Bray, Bective Rgrs.
Wing, 1-1-0-0 (3 − 1t).
35 W+(1t).
Licensed vintner/racehorse buyer.

DOYLE, Michael Gerard Martin *Ireland*
Newbridge Coll, UC Dublin, Cambridge Univ,
Blackrock Coll, Edinburgh W, Barbarians.
b 13.10.41 Castleisland.
Flanker, 20-10-3-7 (6 − 2t).
65 F=(1t) E+ S+ W− SA−; 66 F− E= S−
W+; 67 A+ E− S+ W+ F− A+; 68 F− E= S+
W+(1t) A+; BI > 68 SA 1-0-0-1.
Veterinary surg. Bro of T.J. Blue 65. IRU coach
84-6.

DOYLE, Thomas Joseph *Ireland*
Newbridge Coll, UC Cork, Wanderers.
b 9.6.44 Castleisland.
Flanker, 3-2-1-0.
68 E= S+ W+.
Co dir/pension broker. Bro of Michael.

DRAKE-LEE, Nicholas James *England*
Stonyhurst Coll, Kettering, Cambridge Univ,
Rosslyn Pk, Leicester, Manchester, Waterloo, E
Midlands, Lancs.
b 7.4.42.
Prop, 8-3-2-3 (3 − 1t).
63 W+ I= F+ S+(1t); 64 NZ− W= I−; 65 W−.
Schoolmaster/landscaper/construction. Blue 61-
3.

DREW, D. *Scotland*
Glasgow Acad, Glasgow Academicals.
b −; d −.12.11.
Forward, 2-1-0-1.
1871 E+; 1876 E−.
Played in 1st int, S v E 1871.

DROITECOURT, Michel *France*
Montferrand.
b 30.10.49 Maux, Paris.
FB/wing, 17-9-2-6 (10 − 1t 3c).
72 R+; 73 NZ+r E−; 74 E= S− Arg+ SA−; 75
SA− SA− Arg+ Arg+(1t) R+; 76 S+ I+ W−
A+(3c); 77 Arg=.
Tyre co employee.

DRUMMOND, Archibald Hugh *Scotland*
OBE
Kelvinside Acad, Kelvinside Academicals.
b 2.4.15 Glasgow.
Wing, 2-2-0-0 (6 − 1t 1p).
38 W+ I+(1t 1p).
Ironmonger.

DRUMMOND, Charles William *Scotland*
Gala Acad, Melrose, Barbarians.
b 26.5.23 St Boswells.
Wing, 11-4-0-7 (3 − 1t).
47 F− W− I− E−; 48 F+ I− E+(1t); 50 F+
W− I− E+.
Banker. Pres SRU 74-5.

DRYBROUGH, Andrew Stanley *Scotland*
Merchiston Castle Sch, Edinburgh W,
Merchistonians.
b 1879; d 12.9.46.
Centre, 2-1-0-1.
02 I−; 03 I+.
Brewer.

DRYBURGH, Royden Gladstone *South Africa*
Stellenbosch Univ, W Prov, Natal.
b 1.11.29 Cape Town.
FB/wing, 8-4-0-4 (28 − 3t 3c 3p).
55 BI+(1t 2c) BI−(2p) BI+(2c); 56 A+(1t)
NZ−(1p) NZ−(1t); 60 NZ+(1c) NZ−.
Sales rep. Capt SA v NZ (2) 60. 6t v Qld, 56,
most for SA in any tour match.

DRYDEN, Robert Hunter *Scotland*
George Watson's Coll, Watsonians, Barbarians.
b 10.1.18 Edinburgh.
Wing, 1-0-0-1.
37 E−.
Solicitor.

DRYSDALE, Daniel *Scotland*
Heriot's Coll, Oxford Univ, Edinburgh Univ,
Heriot's FP, Barbarians.
b 18.5.01 Kippen, Stirlingshire.
FB, 26-18-0-8 (45 − 19c 1d 1p).

23 F+(2c) W+(1c) I+ E−; 24 F− W+(4c 1p)
I+(2c) E−; 25 F+(1c) W+(1c 1d) I+(1c)
E+(1c); 26 F+(1c) W+(1c) I− E+; 27 F+(1c)
W+ I− E+ NSW+(2c); 28 F+ W− I−(1c) E−;
29 F+; BI > 24 SA 4-0-1-3.
Timber merchant. Blue 25. Pres SRU 51-2.

DUBERTRAND, André   *France*
Montferrand.
 b 25.4.50 Saubion, Landes.
Wing, 12-8-2-2 (20 − 5t).
71 A+ R+(1t); 72 I−; 74 I+ W= E= SA−; 75
Arg+ Arg+ R+(3t); 76 S+(1t) US+.
PE instructor.

DUBOIS, Daniel   *France*
Bégles.
 b 17.6.44 Le Havre.
No 8, 1-1-0-0.
76 S+.
Industrial designer.

DUBROCA, Daniel   *France*
Agen.
 b 25.4.54 Aigullon.
Prop/hooker, 14-9-0-5 (4 − 1t).
79 NZ+; 81 NZ−r; 82 E− S−; 84 W+ E+ S−;
85 Arg+ J+(1t) J+; 86 S− I+ W+ E+.
Fruit farmer. F > 79 NZ; 80 SA; 85 Arg. Capt 4
Champ matches 86. Son in law of Jean Ranno,
French RL int.

DUCHE, André   *France*
Limoges.
Wing, 1-1-0-0 (9 − 1t 3c).
29 G+(1t 3c).

DUCKETT, Horace   *England*
Bradford, Yorks.
 b 11.10.1867 Thornton, Bradford; *d* 3.3.39
Todmorden.
Half-back, 2-1-0-1.
1893 I+ S−.
Shuttle maker. Turned RL when his club,
Bradford, helped form NU 1895.

DUCKHAM, David John   *England*
King Henry VIII GS Coventry, Coventry,
Warwicks, Barbarians.
 b 28.6.46 Coventry.
Centre/wing, 36-10-2-24 (36 − 10t).
69 I−(1t) F+ S+(2t) W− SA−; 70 I+ W−(1t)
S− F−; 71 W− I+ F= S− S− P−; 72 W− I−
F− S−; 73 NZ− W− I− F+(2t) S+ NZ+ A+;
74 S− I− F=(1t) W+(1t); 75 I− F−(1t) W−; 76
A+(1t) W− S−; BI > 69 SA, 71 NZ 3-1-1-1
Bank official. 6t BI v West Coast-Buller NZ 71.
Autobiography 'Dai for England' pub 80.

DUCLOS, Antoine   *France*
Lourdes.

Prop, 1-0-0-1.
31 S−.

DUCOUSSO, Jean   *France*
Tarbes.
 b 12.5.1900 Tarbes.
FB, 3-0-0-3 (4 − 2c).
25 S− W−(1c) E−(1c).

DUDGEON, Herbert William   *England*
Guy's Hosp, Durham Univ, Richmond,
Northern, Barbarians, Surrey.
Forward, 7-2-1-4.
1897 S+; 1898 I− S= W+; 1899 W− I− S−.
Medicine. Early education in Switz; capt
Association Geneva for 2 seasons.

DUFAU, Gérard ('Zeze')   *France*
RCF.
 b 27.8.24 Dax.
SH, 38-21-0-17 (6 − 2t).
48 I− A+; 49 I+ W+; 50 S− E+ W−; 51 S+ I−
E+ W+; 52 SA− W−; 53 S+ I− E− W−; 54
S+ I+ NZ+ W− E+ It+; 55 S+(1t) I+ E+
W− It+(1t); 56 S− I+ W− It+; 57 S− I− E−
W− It+ R+.
Physical culture instructor. F's most capped SH.

DUFAU, Julien   *France*
Biarritz Ol.
 b −; kia WW1.
Wing, 4-0-0-4 (6 − 2t).
12 I−(1t) S− W− E−(1t).

DUFF, Benjamin   *South Africa*
W Prov.
FB, 3-0-0-3.
1891 BT− BT− BT−.

DUFF, Peter Laurence   *Scotland*
Glasgow Acad, Glasgow Academicals,
Barbarians.
 b 12.11.12.
Lock, 6-3-0-3.
36 W− I−; 38 W+ I+ E+; 39 W−; BI > 38 SA
2-1-0-1.
Farmer. Flanker in 3rd Test BI > 38 SA. Played
in 3 Servs ints.

DUFF, Robert Hamilton   *New Zealand*
Lyttelton Dist HS, Christchuch Boys' HS,
Christchurch, Canterbury, S Island.
 b 5.8.25 Lyttelton.
Lock, 11-8-0-3.
51 A+ A+ A+; 52 A− A+; 55 A+ A−; 56
SA+ SA− SA+ SA+.
Public accountant. NZ > 51 A. NZRFU
selector 71-3. Asst mgr, coach NZ > 72-3 BI,F
& NAm.

DUFFAULT, Yves — *France*
Agen.
Flanker, 2-2-0-0.
54 Arg+ Arg+.

DUFFOURCQ, Jacques — *France*
SBUC.
b 19.8.1881 Salies-de-Béarn; *d* 75 Salies-de-Béarn.
Forward, 4-0-0-4.
06 NZ– E–; 07 E–; 08 W–.
Medicine.

DUFFY, Bernard A.A. — *South Africa*
Border.
Centre, 1-1-0-0.
28 NZ+.

DUFFY, Hugh — *Scotland*
Jedburgh GS, Jedforest.
b 1.4.34 Shotts.
No 8, 6-3-0-3.
36 W– I–; 38 W+ I+ E+; 39 W–.
Licensee. Salford RL 55.

DUFOUR, René — *France*
Tarbes.
b 13.9.1881 Tarbes; *d* –.
No 8, 1-0-0-1.
11 W–.
Business.

DUGDALE, John Marshall JP — *England*
Rugby Sch, Oxford Univ, Ravenscourt Pk.
b 15.10.1852; *d* 30.10.18.
Forward, 1-0-0-1.
1871 S–.
Barrister. Played in 1st int, S v E 1871. JP for Montgomeryshire.

DUGGAN, Alan Thomas Anthony — *Ireland*
Castleknock Coll, Lansdowne, Barbarians.
b 11.6.42 Dublin.
Wing, 25-14-3-8 (30 – 10t).
63 NZ–; 64 F–; 66 W+; 67 A+(1t) S+ W+(1t) A+; 68 F– E= S+(2t) W+; 69 F+ E+ S+(1t) W–; 70 SA=(1t) F– E– S+ W+(1t); 71 F= E–(1t) S+(2t) W–; 72 F+.
Sales rep. I's most capped wing (with Tom Grace).

DUGGAN, William — *Ireland*
CBC Cork, UC Cork.
b 14.6.1890 Skahabeg, Cork; *d* –.
FH/centre, 2-0-0-2.
20 S– W–.
Medicine.

DUGGAN, William Patrick — *Ireland*
Rockwell Coll, Blackrock Coll.
b 12.3.50 Kilkenny.
No 8/flanker, 41-12-1-28 (4 – 1t).
75 E+ S– F+ W–(1t); 76 A– F– W– S– NZ–; 77 W– E– S– F–; 78 S+ F– W– E– NZ–; 79 E+ S= A+ A+; 80 E–; 81 F– W– E– S– SA– SA– A–; 82 W+ E+ S+; 83 S+ F+ W– E+; 84 F– W– E– S–; BI > 77 NZ 4-1-0-3.
Electrical contractor. I's most capped no 8. I > 81 SA. Sent off with Geoff Wheel v W 15.1.77.

DUHARD, Yves — *France*
Bagnères.
b 11.7.55 Aste.
Lock, 1-0-0-1.
80 E–.
Hospital employee.

DUHAU, Jean — *France*
SF, SBUC.
b 1.5.06 Ondres, Landes; *d* 24.9.73..
No 8, 7-4-0-3 (14 – 1t 4c 1p).
28 I–; 30 I+ G+; 31 I+ S– W–; 33 G+(1t 4c 1p).
Switched to RL.

DUKE, Alfred — *Scotland*
Royal HS, Royal HSFP.
b 1866; *d* 11.12.45 Felton, Northumb.
Forward, 6-5-0-1.
1888 W– I+; 1889 W+ I+; 1890 W+ I+.
Medicine.

DULAURANS, Clément — *France*
Toulouse.
Wing, 3-0-0-3.
26 I–; 28 S–; 29 W–.

DULUC, André — *France*
Béziers.
Wing, 1-1-0-0 (3 – 1t).
34 G+(1t).

DU MANOIR, Yves — *France*
RCF.
b 11.8.04 Vaucresson; *d* 2.1.28.
FH, 8-0-0-8 (4 – 1d).
25 I– NZ– S–(1d) W– E–; 26 S–; 27 I– S–.
Served in French Flying Corps. Killed when plane crashed shortly before kick-off F v S 28. Colombes Stadium, owned by his club, RCF, was re-named Stade Yves du Manoir in his memory.

DUN, Andrew Frederick — *England*
Bristol GS, England SS, Bart's Hosp, English Students, Bristol, Glos, London Scottish, Wasps, Mdx.
b 26.11.60 Bristol.

Flanker, 1-0-0-1.
84 W−.
Medicine. England SS > 79 A, NZ. London Div
v A 81. Capt E Under 23s > 81 It & F; R 83.
Capt English Students > 83 J.

DUNBAR, A. Robert *Australia*
NSW.
b 1888; d 54.
Wing/FB, 4-2-0-2.
10 NZ− NZ+ NZ−; 12 US+.
Education officer.

DUNCAN, Alexander William *Scotland*
Merchiston Castle Sch, Edinburgh Univ.
b 19.6.1881 Crichton; d 18.11.34 Angmering.
FB, 6-3-0-3.
01 W+ I+ E+; 02 W− I− E−.
Medicine. Ckt for S.

DUNCAN, Denoon D. *Scotland*
SA Coll Rondebosch, Oxford Univ.
b −; d 55.
Prop, 4-3-0-1.
20 F+ W+ I+ E−.
Solicitor. Blue 19-20.

DUNCAN, James *New Zealand*
Kaikorai, Otago, S Island.
b 12.11.1869 Dunedin; d 19.10.53 Dunedin.
1st five-eighth, 1-1-0-0.
03 A+.
Saddler. Believed to have originated NZ's five-
eighths alignment. NZ's 1st tour capt, NZ > 03
A. Coach NZ > 05-6 BI,F & NAm. Ref NZ v
AW 08.

DUNCAN, Macbeth Moir *Scotland*
Fettes Coll, Fettesian-Lorettonians, Cambridge
Univ.
b −.9.1866; d 2.10.42.
Wing, 1-0-0-1.
1888 W−.
Advocate/The Army. Blue 1885-7. Pres SRU
27-8.

DUNCAN, Matthew Dominic *Scotland*
Fletcher
Douglas Acad, Alsager Coll, Midland Colls, W
of S.
b 29.8.59 Glasgow.
Wing, 5-4-0-1 (8 − 2t).
86 F+ W−(1t) E+(1t) I+ R+.
Scotland B v F, I 85. Glasgow v Netherlands 85.
Held Scottish Schs hurdles rec; rep Glasgow at
swimming. 3t on debut for W of S 78.

DUNCAN, Michael Gordon *New Zealand*
Elsthorpe Sch, Lindisfarne Coll, Hastings
HSOB, NZ Jnrs, Hawkes Bay, N Island.
b 8.8.47 Waipawa.

1st five-eighth/centre, 2-0-1-1.
71 BI−r BI=.
Farmer.

DUNCAN, Robert Francis Hugh *England*
Cardiff Univ, Guy's Hosp, Barbarians, Mdx.
b 10.6.1896 Wenvoe, Glamorgan.
Lock/prop, 3-2-1-0.
22 I+ F= S+.
Sales rep. Son of R.T. Duncan (Cardiff,
Barbarians). Served WW1, Capt Welch Rgt;
mentioned in despatches. Served WW2 Lt Col R
Welch Fusiliers in Far East.

DUNCAN, William Dow *New Zealand*
Kaikorai, Otago, S Island.
b 11.6.1892 Port Chalmers; d 14.12.61
Dunedin.
Hooker, 3-1-1-1.
21 SA+ SA− SA=.
Telephone linesman & cable joiner. NZ > 20 A.
Otago selector 46-50. Son Bert rep Otago 41.

DUNCAN, William Robert *Ireland*
Orangefield BS, Cregagh Tech Coll, Malone.
b 14.7.57 Belfast.
Flanker, 2-0-0-2.
84 W− E−.
Engr.

DUNKLEY, Philip Edward *England*
('Pop')
O Laurentians, Leicester, Harlequins,
Barbarians, Warwicks.
b 9.8.04.
Flanker/no 8, 6-2-1-3.
31 I− S−; 36 NZ+ W= I− S+.
Bank official.

DUNLOP, Sir Ernest Edward *Australia*
CMG OBE
Benalla HS, Melbourne Univ, St Bartholomew's
Hosp, Victoria.
b 12.7.07 Wangaratta.
No 8/lock, 2-1-0-1.
32 NZ−; 34 NZ+.
Medicine.

DUNLOP, James W. CB CMG *Scotland*
Cheltenham Coll, RA, The Army, W of S.
b 16.10.1854; d 30.11.28.
Forward, 1-0-1-0.
1875 E=.
The Army.

DUNLOP, Quintin *Scotland*
Merchiston Castle Sch, W of S.
b 9.3.43 Ayr.
Hooker, 2-2-0-0.
71 E+ E+.
Farmer.

DUNLOP, Robert CBE   *Ireland*
Coleraine AI, Trin Coll Dublin.
b −; *d* 30.11.35.
Centre/wing, 11-2-1-8 (1t).
1889 W+; 1890 S− W=(1t) E−; 1891 E− S−
W−; 1892 E− S−; 1893 W−; 1894 W+.

DUNN, Edward   *New Zealand*
Dargaville HS, Teachers' Coll, NZ Colts, NZ
Maoris, N Auckland, Whangarei, N Island.
b 19.1.55 Te Kopuru.
1st five-eighth, 2-2-0-0 (4 − 1t).
79 S+(1t); 81 S+.
Schoolmaster. Bro of Ian. NZ > 78 BI, 79 E,S
& It. NZ (2) v Arg 79. Won Tom French Cup
for outstanding Maori player, 78.

DUNN, Ian Thomas Wayne   *New Zealand*
NZ Colts, N Auckland, NZ Maoris.
b 11.6.60 Te Kopuru.
1st five-eighth, 3-3-0-0.
83 BI+ BI+ A+.
Bro of Eddie. NZ > 83 & 84 A; 83 S & E.

DUNN, John Markham   *New Zealand*
Ararimu Sch, Drury Papakura, Pukekohe,
Manukau, Auckland, Grafton, N Island.
b 17.11.18 Otahuhu.
Wing, 1-1-0-0.
46 A+.

DUNN, Peter E.F.   *Ireland*
Belvedere Coll, Bective Rgrs.
b 21.2.1894; *d* −.4.65.
Lock, 1-0-0-1.
23 S−.
Dentist.

DUNN, Peter Keith   *Australia*
NSW.
b 36.
Prop, 5-1-0-4.
58 NZ− NZ+ NZ−; 59 BI− BI−.
Commercial traveller.

DUNN, Thomas Brown   *Ireland*
Campbell Coll, NIFC.
b −; *d* 22.12.75.
1-0-0-1.
35 NZ−.
Printing co man dir.

DUNNE, Michael J.   *Ireland*
Castleknock Coll, Trin Coll Dublin,
Lansdowne, Barbarians.
b −; *d* 7.2.67 Dublin.
Lock, 16-7-0-9.
29 F+ E+ S−; 30 F− E+ S+ W−; 32 E− S+
W+; 33 E− W+ S−; 34 E− S− W−; BI > 30
NZ, A.
Bank solicitor.

DUNWORTH, David Anthony   *Australia*
St Joseph's Coll, Qld.
b 29.8.46.
Prop, 5-2-1-2.
71 F+ F−; 72 F= F−; 76 Fj+.
Real estate.

DU PLESSIS, Carel Johan   *South Africa*
Gill Coll, Boys HS Paarl, Stellenbosch Univ,
Gazelles, Merignac (F), W Prov.
b 24.6.60 Somerset E.
Wing, 6-5-0-1 (12 − 3t).
82 SAm+(1t) SAm−; 84 E+(1t) E+ SAm+
SAm+(1t).
Student. Bro of Willie. SA > 81 NZ, US.
Overseas XV v Five Nations, Twickenham 86.

DU PLESSIS, Daniel Coenraad   *South Africa*
N Transvaal.
b 9.8.48 Potchefstroom.
Prop, 2-2-0-0.
77 Wd+; 80 SAm+.
Medicine.

DU PLESSIS, Felix   *South Africa*
N Transvaal, Transvaal.
b 19 Steynsburg, OFS; *d* 1.5.78.
Lock, 3-3-0-0.
49 NZ+ NZ+ NZ+.
Wine & spirit merchant. Capt SA v NZ (3) 49.
Father of Morne, nephew of Nic. Served WW2,
navigator SAAF. Played SA Forces v NZ
Forces, Rome 44.

DU PLESSIS, Morne   *South Africa*
Klerksdorp Prmy Sch, Grey Coll Bloemfontein,
Stellenbosch Univ, Villagers, W Prov.
b 21.10.49 Krugersdorp, Vereeniging.
No 8/flanker, 22-18-0-4 (12 − 3t).
71 A+ A+ A+; 74 BI− BI− F+ F+; 75 F+
F+; 76 NZ+ NZ− NZ+ NZ+; 77 Wd+; 80
SAm+ SAm+(1t) BI+ BI+ BI+ BI−
SAm+(1t) F+.
SA Navy/dir sports goods co. Capt SA 15 times.
Tour capt SAm 80; v F (2) 75; NZ (4) 76; Wd 77;
SAm (in SA), BI (4), F 80. Born few months
after father Felix capt SA to 3 consec wins v NZ
49. 1st father & son to capt SA. Mother Pat SA
hockey capt; uncle Horace Smethurst capt SA
football XI; another uncle Eric Smethurst also
played football for SA. At sch, Victor Ludorum
in ath; also tennis & swimming champ. Capt SA
Schs at ckt; ckt for W Prov.

DU PLESSIS, M.J.   *South Africa*
W Prov.
Centre, 2-2-0-0.
84 SAm+ SAm+.

DU PLESSIS, N.J. ('Nic')   *South Africa*
W Transvaal.

131

b −; d 49.
5-3-2-0.
21 NZ+ NZ=; 24 BI+ BI+ BI=.
Schoolmaster. Uncle of Felix. SA > 21 NZ.

DU PLESSIS, Pieter George　　　*South Africa*
N Transvaal.
b 23.7.47 Nylstroom.
Lock, 1-0-0-1.
72 E−.
Lecturer.

DU PLESSIS, Thomas　　　*South Africa*
Dannhauser
Middleburg Sch, Pretoria Univ, Transvaal Club,
N Transvaal.
b 29.6.53 Elsburg.
SH, 2-2-0-0 (4 − 1t).
80 SAm+(1t) SAm+.
Sports shop owner.

DU PLESSIS, Willem ('Willie')　　*South Africa*
Gill Coll, Stellenbosch Univ, Defence Club
(Cape Town), Barbarians, W Prov.
b 4.9.55 Somerset E.
Centre, 14-10-0-4 (12 − 3t).
80 SAm+ SAm+ BI+(1t) BI+ BI+ BI−(1t)
SAm+ SAm+ F+; 81 NZ− NZ+ NZ−; 82
SAm+(1t) SAm−.
Sailor. Bro of Carel. SA > 81 US.

DU PLOOY, Abraham Johannes J.　*South Africa*
Stellenbosch Univ, E Prov.
Prop, 1-0-0-1.
55 BI−.

DU PREEZ, Frederik Christoffel　*South Africa*
Hendrik ('Frik')
Standerton HS, N Transvaal.
b 28.11.35 Rustenberg.
Lock/flanker, 38-24-6-8 (11 − 1t 1c 2p).
61 E+(1c) S+(2p) A+ A+; 62 BI= BI+ BI+
BI+; 63 A+; 64 W+ F−; 65 A− A− NZ−
NZ− NZ+ NZ−; 67 F=; 68 BI+(1t) BI= BI+
BI+ F+ F+; 69 A+ A+ S−; 70 I= W=; 70
NZ+ NZ− NZ+ NZ+; 71 F+ F= A+ A+ A+.
Army/SAAF. SA's most capped player (with JH
Ellis). 87 apps for SA. SA > 60-1 BI, F; 69-70
BI.

DU PREEZ, Jan Gysbert　　　*South Africa*
Hermanus
Stellenbosch Univ, W Prov.
b 6.10.30.
1-0-0-1.
56 NZ−.
Lecturer at Stellenbosch Univ.

DUPONT, Clément　　　　　*France*
Lourdes, Rouen, SBUC.

b 11.4.1899 Argeles.
SH, 16-7-0-9.
23 S− W− I+; 24 S+ I− W− R+ US−; 25 S−;
27 E+ G+ G−; 28 NSW− G+ W+; 29 I−.

DUPONT, J.-L.　　　　　*France*
Agen.
Hooker, 1-1-0-0.
83 S+.

DUPONT, Louis　　　　　*France*
RCF.
No 8, 6-6-0-0.
34 G+; 35 G+; 36 G+ G+; 38 R+ G+.

DUPOUY, A.　　　　　　*France*
SB.
Centre, 2-1-0-1 (3 − 1t).
24 W− R+(1t).

DUPRAT, Bernard ('Begnat')　　*France*
Bayonne.
b 17.7.43 Bayonne.
Wing, 15-9-1-5 (31 − 9t).
66 E+ W−(1t) It+ R+(1t); 67 S−(1t) A+
E+(1t) SA− SA+; 68 S+(1t) I+; 72 E+(2t)
W− I−(2t) A=.
Meat inspector.

DUPRÉ, Paul　　　　　*France*
RCF.
b −; kia WW1.
Hooker, 1-0-0-1.
09 W−.

DUPUY, Jean ('Pipiou')　　　*France*
Tarbes.
b 25.5.34 Vic-Bigorre.
Wing, 40-22-6-12 (57 − 19t).
56 S− I+ W− It+ E+(1t) Cz+(1t); 57 S− I−
E− W−(1t) It+(2t) R+(3t); 58 S−(1t) E−
SA= SA+; 59 S+ E= It+(2t) W+ I−(1t); 60
W+(1t) I+ It+ Arg+ Arg+(2t); 61 S+ SA=
E= NZ−(1t) R=; 62 S+ E+ W− I+ It+; 63
W+ It+(2t) R=(1t); 64 S−.
Insurance agent. With Christian Darrouy, F's
most capped wing.

DU RAND, Jacobus Abraham　*South Africa*
('Salty')
Stellenbosch Univ, Rhodesia, N Transvaal.
b 16.1.26 Hofmeyr; d 79.
Lock, 21-15-0-6 (12 − 4t).
49 NZ+ NZ+; 51 S+(1t) I+ W+; 52 E+ F+; 53
A+(1t) A−(1t) A+ A+; 55 BI− BI+ BI−
BI+; 56 A+ A+ NZ− NZ+(1t) NZ− NZ−.
SA > 51-2 BI, F. 10 lock apps with J.T.
Claassen. Capt SA v NZ 1st Test 56. Much
publicised fracas with fellow Springbok, Jan
Pickard, during Trials cost him captaincy of SA
> 56 A, NZ.

132

DU SOUICH, Charles *France*
SCUF.
Centre, 2-0-0-2.
11 W− I−.

DUTHIE, James *England*
W Hartlepool, Winlaton Vulcans, Durham.
b 1878; *d* 29.5.46 W Hartlepool.
Forward, 1-0-0-1.
03 W−.
Shipyard worker.

DUTIN, Bernard *France*
Mont-de-Marsan.
b 9.12.44.
Flanker, 4-0-0-4.
68 NZ− Λ− SA− R−.
Clerk.

DU TOIT, A.F. *South Africa*
Stellenbosch Univ, W Prov.
b 12.5.1899.
Prop, 2-1-0-1.
28 NZ+ NZ−.

DU TOIT, Benjamin Abraham *South Africa*
Paarl Boys HS, Stellenbosch Univ, Transvaal.
b 10.11.12.
3-2-0-1 (3 − 1t).
38 BI+ BI+(1t) BI−.
Govt chemist. Suffered inj vertebra early in SA
> 37 A, NZ. Declined to tour initially; attended
Trials, watched from stands. Changed his mind,
joined in and selected to tour.

DU TOIT, Pieter Alfonso *South Africa*
('Fonnie')
N Transvaal.
b 13.3.20.
SH, 8-8-0-0 (6 − 2t).
49 NZ+ NZ+ NZ+(1t); 51 S+ I+ W+; 52
E+(1t) F+.
Insurance clerk, SA > 51-2 BI, F.

DU TOIT, Pieter Gerhard *South Africa*
('Hempies')
Paul Roos Gymnasium Sch Stellenbosch,
Stellenbosch Univ, Jnr Springboks, W Prov.
b 23.8.52 Villiersdorp.
Prop, 5-3-0-2.
81 NZ−; 82 SAm+ SAm−; 84 E+ E+.
Wine producer. SA > 80 SAm, 81 US.

DU TOIT, Pieter Stephanus *South Africa*
('Spiere')
Paarl Boys HS, Stellenbosch Univ, W Prov.
b 9.10.35 Petrusville.
Prop, 14-9-3-2.
58 F= F−; 60 NZ+ NZ− NZ= NZ+ W+ I+;
61 E+ S+ F= I+ A+ A+.
Farmer/wine & spirit rep. SA > 60-1 BI, F.

DUTOUR, François Xavier *France*
Toulouse.
b 6.11.1886 Moissat, Puy de Dôme; d− .
FB, 6-0-0-6 (2 − 1c).
11 E− I−(1c); 12 S− W− E−; 13 S−.
Veterinary surg.

DUTRAIN, Henri *France*
Toulouse.
b 23 Toulouse.
Centre, 8-5-0-3.
45 W−; 46 BF+ I+; 47 E−; 49 I+ E− W+
Arg+.

DUTREY, Joseph *France*
Lourdes.
Lock, 1-0-0-1.
40 BF−.

DUVAL, René *France*
SF.
Forward, 6-0-0-6.
08 E− W−; 09 E−; 11 E− W− I.

DUVENHAGE, Floris P. *South Africa*
Griq W.
b 6.11.17 Vryburg.
2-2-0-0.
49 NZ+ NZ+.

DWYER, Laurence Joseph *Australia*
NSW.
b 1884; *d* 64.
Centre, 8-3-0-5 (4 − 1d).
10 NZ− NZ+ NZ−; 12 US+; 13 NZ+; 14 NZ−
NZ− NZ−(1d).
Law clerk. Capt A > 13 NZ.

DWYER, Patrick Joseph *Ireland*
Garbally Coll Ballinasloe, UC Dublin, UC
Galway.
b 24.5.40 Clonee, Co Galway.
Prop, 5 0 1 4.
62 W=; 63 F− NZ−; 64 S− W−.
Veterinary surg.

DYKE, John Charles Meredith *Wales*
Christ's Coll Brecon, Penarth, Barbarians.
b 20.6.1885 Llangasty.
FB, 1-0-0-1.
06 SA−; BI > 08 A, NZ.
Solicitor's clerk.

DYKE, Louis Meredith *Wales*
Penarth, Cardiff, Barbarians.
b 1888 Cardiff; *d* 12.7.61 Llandough.
Centre, 4-4-0-0 (7 − 1t 2c).
10 I+(1t); 11 S+(2c) F+ I+.
Docks official. 33t in 107 apps for Cardiff 1908-
12. One of 4 Cardiff threequarters v S, F & I 10.

DYKES, Andrew Spencer OBE   *Scotland*
Loretto Sch, Glasgow Acad, Glasgow
Academicals, Barbarians.
b 04.
FB, 1-0-0-1.
32 E−.
Co dir. Bro of J.C., nephew of J.M.

DYKES, James Carroll   *Scotland*
Glasgow Acad, Loretto Sch, Glasgow
Academicals, Barbarians.
b 4.7.01.
FH/centre, 20-14-1-5 (17 − 3t 2c 1d)
22 F= E−(1t); 24 I+; 25 F+ W+ I+(1c); 26 F+
W+ I− E+(1d); 27 F+ W+ I− E+(1t) NSW+;
28 F+(1t) I−; 29 F+ W− I+(1c).
Insurance. Bro of A.S., nephew of J.M.

DYKES, John Morton   *Scotland*
Glasgow HS, Clydesdale, Glasgow HSFP.
b −; *d* 12.10.55 Bearsden.
Forward, 10-6-2-2 (3 − 1t).
1898 I+ E=; 1899 W+ E+; 1900 W−(1t) I=; 01
W+ I+ E+; 02 E−.
Man dir clothiers. Uncle of J.C. & A.S. SRU
comm; pres 20-2.

DYSON, John William   *England*
Skelmanthorpe, Huddersfield, Yorks.
b 6.9.1866 Skelmanthorpe; *d* 3.1.09
Huddersfield.
Wing, 4-3-0-1 (1t).
1890 S+(1t); 1892 S+; 1893 I+ S−.
Licensee. All−round athlete & noted sprinter.
30t 6d for Yorks 1899-1900. Turned RL when
club, Huddersfield, helped form NU 1895.

E

EAGLES, Harry   *England*
Salford.
Forward, 0-0-0-0.
BT > 1888 A, NZ.
With Percy Robertshaw, awarded an E cap in
the 1888 side that never played, because of
dispute over setting up IB. Neither player made
an int app.

EASTES, Charles Colbram   *Australia*
Manly HS, NSW.
b 12.6.25 Epping, NSW.
Wing, 6-0-1-5 (6 − 2t).
46 NZ−(1t) NZ−(1t); 47 NZ− NZ−; 49 M−
M=.
Insurance. Mgr A > 69 SA.

EASTGATE, Barry Peter   *New Zealand*
Richmond Sch, Hokitika HS, Hokitika Kiwi, W
Coast, Linwood, Canterbury, S Island.

b 10.7.27 Nelson.
Prop, 3-2-0-1.
52 A− A+; 54 S+.
Carpenter/co dir. NZ > 53-4 BI,F & NAm.
Retired on medical advice 54. Bro R.R.
Eastgate rep W Coast & Auckland.

EBDON, Percy John   *England*
Wellington, Som.
b 16.3.1874 Milverton, Som; *d* 16.2.43
Wellington, Som.
Forward, 2-0-0-2.
1897 W− I−.
Som CCC 1894.

ECHAVÉ, Louis   *France*
Agen.
b 11.6.34 Ciboure.
Lock, 1-1-0-0.
61 S+.

EDDISON, John Horncastle MC   *England*
Ilkley GS, Bromsgrove Sch, Headingley,
Barbarians, Yorks.
b 25.8.1888 Edinburgh; *d* 18.11.82 Edinburgh.
Forward, 4-3-0-1 (3 − 1t).
12 W+ I+ S− F+(1t).
Insurance official. Served WW1 Lt RFA.
Mentioned in despatches, MC 16. Top ref. One
of the longest lived int players.

EDGAR, Charles Stuart   *England*
Birkenhead Pk, Barbarians, Cheshire.
b 1876; *d* 26.5.49 Chester.
Forward, 1-0-0-1.
01 S−.
Cotton broker.

EDWARDS, Arthur Bernard   *Wales*
Ebbw Vale GS, UC Aberystwyth, London
Univ, London Welsh, The Army.
b 7.10.27 Bynea; *d* 19.9.84.
FB, 2-1-0-1 (3 − 1p).
55 E+(1p) S−.
The Army/college principal.

EDWARDS, Benjamin Oswald   *Wales*
Newport, Ebbw Vale.
b 29.5.23; *d* 2.9.78 Cheltenham.
Lock, 1-0-1-0 (3 − 1p).
51 I=(1p).
Factory foreman. 115 apps Newport.

EDWARDS, David   *Wales*
Glynneath.
b 21.3.1896 Glynneath; *d* 24.8.60 Glynneath.
Lock, 1-0-0-1.
21 E−.
Builder's labourer/collier. Served WW1, Welsh
Guards. Rhigos coach. Rochdale Hornets RL
21.

EDWARDS, Douglas Baxter *Scotland*
Heriot's Coll, Heriot's FP.
b 19.3.30.
Flanker, 3-1-0-2.
60 I+ E− SA−.

EDWARDS, Gareth Owen *Wales*
Pontardawe Tech Sch, Millfield, Cardiff Coll,
Cardiff, Barbarians.
b 12.7.47 Gwaun-cae-Gurwen.
SH, 53-34-5-14 (85 − 20t 2c 3d).
67 F− E+ NZ−; 68 E=(1t) S+ I−(1d) F−; 69
S+(1t) I+ F=(1t) E+ NZ− NZ− A+; 70
SA=(1t) S+(2c) E+ I− F+; 71 E+ S+(1t)
I+(2t) F+(1t); 72 E+ S+(2t) F+ NZ−; 73
E+(1t) S− I+(1t) F− A+; 74 S+ I= F=(1d)
E−; 75 F+(1t) E+ S− I+(1t) A+(1t); 76
E+(1t) S+(1t) I+(1t) F−; 77 I+ F− E+(1t)
S+; 78 E+ S+(1t) I+ F+(1d); BI > 68 SA 2-0-
1-1; 71 A, NZ 4-2-1-1; 74 SA 4-3-1-0.
Business/BBC TV commentator. W > 69 NZ, A
& Fj; 73 Can; 75 Far East. Welsh XV v NZ 74.
Wales XV v Arg 76. World's most capped SH
(63 inc 10 BI). With Gerald Davies sc most t for
W. Barbarians v NZ 67, SA 70 (capt), NZ 73-4,
A 76. Bro Gethin played for Cardiff & Neath.

EDWARDS, H.G. *Ireland*
Rossall Sch, Trin Coll Dublin.
Forward, 2-0-0-2.
1877 E−; 1878 E−.

EDWARDS, Peter ('Pink *South Africa*
Panther')
Afrikaans Hoer Seuns Sch Pretoria, Pretoria
Univ, SA Univs, Quaggas, Barbarians,
Harlequins Club, N Transvaal.
b 23.5.53 George.
FB, 2-2-0-0.
80 SAm+ SAm+.
Schoolmaster. Northern Univs 76. Married to
Aryna Edwards, SA hockey player.

EDWARDS, Reginald *England*
Preswell Sch Newport, Newport, Som.
b 11.12.1887 in Pontypool; d .8.51.
Prop, 11-8-1-2 (3 − 1t).
21 W+ I+ S+(1t) F+; 22 W− F=; 23 W+; 24
W+ F+ S+; 25 NZ−.
Master butcher. His t v S 21 is credited to E.R.
Gardner by some sources. Emigrated to Can.

EDWARDS, R.W. *Ireland*
Malone.
Forward, 1-1-0-0.
04 W+; BT > 04 A & NZ.
Only Irish int player on BT > 04 A & NZ.

EDWARDS, T. *Ireland*
Lansdowne.
Wing, 6-1-1-4.

1888 NZN−; 1890 S− W= E−; 1892 W+; 1893
E−.

EDWARDS, William Victor *Ireland*
Thanet Col Margate, Coleraine AI, Campbell
Coll, Belmont Sch, Malone, Knock, Ulster.
b 16.10.1887 Strandtown; kia 29.12.17
Jerusalem.
Forward, 2-1-0-1.
12 F+ E−.
Accountant. Irish 220y swimming champ; water
polo int. 1st man to swim Belfast Lough,
16.8.12. Served WW1, R Irish Fusiliers.

EGAN, James T. *Ireland*
Clongowes Coll, Cork Constitution, The Army.
FB, 3-1-0-2.
31 F− E+ SA−.
The Army.

EGAN, John D. *Ireland*
Bective Rgrs.
b −; d −.3.50 Arg.
Flanker, 1-0-0-1.
22 S−.

EGAN, Michael Stanislaus *Ireland*
Sacred Heart Coll Limerick, Garryowen.
b 12.4.1872; d 2.1.54.
Forward, 2-0-0-2.
1893 E−; 1895 S−.

EIDMAN, Ian Harold *Wales*
Penarth GS, Welsh SS, Glamorgan SS, UWIST,
UAU, Dinas Powys, Cardiff.
b 31.10.57 Cardiff.
Prop, 13-7-0-6.
83 S+ R−; 84 I+ F− E+ A−; 85 S+ I− Fj+; 86
E− S+ I+ F−.
Office equipment sales rep. Wales B v F 82.
Wales B > 83 Spain. Wales XV v J 83.

EKIN, W. *Ireland*
RBAI, Queen's Coll Belfast.
Forward, 2-1-0-1.
1888 W+ S−.

ELGIE, Michael Kelsey *Scotland*
Michaelhouse Sch, St Andrew's Univ, London
Scottish.
b 6.3.33 Durban.
Centre, 8-2-0-6 (14 − 1t 1c 3p).
54 NZ− I− E−(1t) W−; 55 F− W+(1c 1p)
I+(2p) E−.

ELISSALDE, Edmond *France*
Bayonne.
FH/centre, 2-1-0-1.
36 G+; 40 BF−.

135

ELISSALDE, Jean-Pierre　　　　*France*
La Rochelle.
b 54.
SH, 5-1-0-4 (11 − 2t 1d).
80 SA− R−; 81 A− A−(1t 1d) R+(1t).
F > 80 SA.

ELLA, Gary Albert　　　　*Australia*
Matraville HS, Univ of NSW, Randwick,
Sydney, NSW.
b 23.7.60 La Perouse, Sydney.
Centre, 4-1-1-2 (4 − 1t).
82 NZ− NZ+(1t); 83 F= F−.
Field officer Dept of Aboriginal Affairs. Bro of
Glen & Mark; cousin of Steve Ella, Australian
RL int. A > 83 F. Played RL at primary sch.
Australian Schs > 77-8 BI. A Under 21s. A >
81-2 BI.

ELLA, Glen Joseph　　　　*Australia*
Matraville HS, Australian Schs, Randwick,
Sydney, NSW.
b 5.6.59 La Perouse, Sydney.
FB, 4-3-0-1.
82 S−; 83 It+; 85 C+r Fj+.
Sales rep. Twin of Mark, bro of Gary. Played
RL at primary sch. A Schools > 77-8 BI. Capt A
Under 21s v NZ 80.

ELLA, Mark Gordon MOA　　　　*Australia*
Matraville HS, Australian Schs, Sydney,
Randwick, NSW.
b 5.6.59 La Perouse, Sydney.
Five-eighth, 25-13-1-11 (75 − 6t 3c 7d 8p).
80 NZ+(1d) NZ− NZ+(1d); 81 F+ S−; 82 E−
S− NZ− NZ+ NZ−; 83 US+(1d) Arg− Arg+
NZ− It+(1t) F=(1d) F−(1d); 84 Fj+ NZ+(1c
1p) NZ−(1t 1c 2p) NZ−(1c 5p) E+(1t) I+(1t
2d) W+(1t) S+(1t).
Management. Twin of Glen, bro of Gary.
Played RL at primary sch. A Schs > 77-8 BI.
Australian Player of Year 81-2. A > 79 Arg, 80
Fj, 84 BI. Capt A > 82 NZ; 83 It & F; 84 BI. 1st
touring player to score t in each of 4 ints in UK,
84. MOA 84. Biography 'Ella, Ella, Ella' pub
84.

ELLEM, Michael Anthony　　　　*Australia*
NSW.
b 52.
No 8, 1-1-0-0.
76 Fj+r.

ELLIOT, Charles Henry　　　　*England*
Repton Sch, Sunderland, Blackheath, Durham
Cos.
b 31.5.1861; *d* 1.4.34 Bristol.
Forward, 1-1-0-0.
1886 W+.
Uncle of Edgar William. Made mark which
A.E. Stoddart goaled to give E victory v W 1886

(any player then could take kick after mark had
been called).

ELLIOT, Christopher　　　　*Scotland*
Langholm, Barbarians.
b 24.2.33.
Wing, 12-3-2-7 (8 − 1c 2p).
58 E=(1p); 59 F−; 60 F−(1c 1p); 63 E−; 64 F+
NZ= W− I+ E+; 65 F− W− I−.
Tweed mill employee. Bro of T.G.

ELLIOT, Edgar William　　　　*England*
Wellington Coll, Sunderland, Barbarians,
Durham Cos.
b 9.7.1879; *d* 31.
Wing, 4-0-1-3 (6 − 2t).
01 W− I− S−; 04 W=(2t).
Soda mines mgr. Nephew of Charles Henry.
Worked in California.

ELLIOT, Matthew　　　　*Scotland*
Hawick.
b 1871 Hawick; *d* 3.12.45.
Half-back, 6-4-1-1.
1895 W+; 1896 E+; 1897 I+ E−; 1898 I+ E=.
Mason.

ELLIOT, Thomas　　　　*Scotland*
Gala.
b 1880; *d* −.11.48 Forest Row, Sussex.
Wing, 1-1-0-0.
05 E+.
Textile worker.

ELLIOT, Thomas　　　　*Scotland*
Loretto Sch, Gala, Barbarians.
b 6.4.26 nr Gala.
Prop, 14-6-0-8.
55 W+ I+ E−; 56 F+ W− I− E−; 57 F+ W+
I− E−; 58 W− A+ I−; BI > 55 SA.
Farmer.

ELLIOT, Thomas Grieve　　　　*Scotland*
Langholm Acad, Langholm, Barbarians.
b 1.3.41 Langholm.
Flanker, 5-3-0-2.
68 W− A+; 69 F+ W−; 70 E+.
Textile worker. Bro of Christopher. Scottish
Dist v NZ 67.

ELLIOT, Walter DSC MP　　　　*England*
HMS Conway, RNEC Keyham, US
Portsmouth, RN.
b 17.2.10.
FH, 7-5-0-2 (3 − 1t).
32 I+ S+; 33 W−(1t) I+ S−; 34 W+ I+.
RN/bus/MP. Served WW2. Mentioned in
despatches, DSC 44. Retd from RN 58. Tory
MP Carshalton & Banstead 60, re-elected 64, 66
& 70.

136

ELLIOT, W.I. Douglas　　　　　　　*Scotland*
Edinburgh Acad, Edinburgh Academicals,
Barbarians.
b 18.4.23 Stow, Midlothian.
Flanker, 29-7-0-22 (6 − 2t).
47 F− W−(1t) E− A−; 48 F+ W− I− E+; 49
F+(1t) W+ I− E−; 50 F+ W− I− E+; 51 F−
W+ I− E− SA−; 52 F− W− I− E−; 54 NZ−
I− E− W−.
Farmer. S's most capped flanker.

ELLIOTT, Albert Ernest　　　　　　*England*
Cheltenham Coll, Cambridge Univ, St Thomas's
Hosp, Barbarians, Mdx.
b 5.3.1869 Basset Mount, Southampton;　d
1.12.1900 Middelburg, SA.
Forward, 1-0-0-1.
1894 S−.
Medicine. Blue 1891. Served in Boer War as
civil surgeon with RA. Died of fever on active
service.

ELLIOTT, Francis Michael　　　　　*Australia*
('Max')
The Scots Coll, NSW.
b 20.12.30.
Prop, 1-0-0-1.
57 NZ−.
Medicine.

ELLIOTT, John E. JP　　　　　　　　*Wales*
Cardiff.
b −; d 30.3.38.
Centre/SH 3-1-0-2.
1894 I−; 1898 I+ E−.
Docks man dir.

ELLIOTT, Kenneth George　　　*New Zealand*
Clyde Quay Sch, Wellington Coll, OB,
Wellington, Univ, Manawatu, Hamilton OB,
Waikato, Comb Servs, N Island.
b 3.3.22 Wellington.
Lock/no 8, 2 2 0 0 (3 − 1t).
46 A+(1t) A+.
Farm appraiser/insurance mgr.

ELLIOTT, William Ronald　　　　　*Ireland*
Joseph
Regent House Newtownards, Queen's Univ
Belfast, Bangor.
FB, 1-0-1-0.
79 S=.
Schoolmaster.

ELLIS, Charles Seymour　　　　　*Australia*
King's Sch, NSW.
b 1.9.1879; d −.
Forward, 4-1-0-3.
1899 BT+ BT− BT− BT−.
Clerk.

ELLIS, Jack　　　　　　　　　　　*England*
Wakefield.
b 28.10.12 Rothwell Haigh, Leeds.
SH, 1-1-0-0.
39 S+.
Schoolmaster.

ELLIS, Jacobus Hendrik ('Jan')　*South Africa*
SW Africa.
b 5.1.43 Brakpan.
Flanker, 38-22-6-10 (21 − 7t).
65 NZ− NZ− NZ+ NZ−; 67 F+(1t) F+ F−(1t)
F=; 68 BI+ BI= BI+ BI+(1t) F+ F+; 69
A+(1t) A+ A+(1t) A+ S−; 70 I= W= NZ+
NZ− NZ+ NZ+; 71 F+ F= A+(1t) A+
A+(1t); 72 E−; 74 BI− BI− BI− BI= F+ F+;
76 NZ+.
Agent. SA's most capped player (with Frik du
Preez). 74 apps for SA. 32 career t for SA. SA >
69-70 BI.

ELLIS, Keith James　　　　　　　*Australia*
NSW.
b 30.3.27.
Prop, 5-1-0-4.
58 NZ− NZ+ NZ−; 59 BI− BI−.
Police.

ELLIS, Mervyn　　　　　　　*South Africa*
Transvaal.
b c1892.
6-4-2-0.
21 NZ+ NZ=; 24 BI+ BI+ BI= BI+.

ELLIS, Sidney S. JP　　　　　　　*England*
Dulwich Coll, Faversham, Queen's House,
Blackheath, Kent.
b 13.3.1859; d 1.12.37.
Forward, 1-1-0-0 (1t).
1880 I+(1t).
Stockbroker. Mem London Stock Exchange
1882-37; 'father' of the Stock Exchange. JP for
Croydon.

ELLWOOD, Beresford Jon　　　　*Australia*
The Scots Coll, NSW.
b 24.7.37.
Centre/five-eighth, 20-7-2-11 (29 − 2t 1c 7p).
58 NZ−(1t) NZ+ NZ−; 61 Fj+(1t) Fj= SA−
F−(1c 1p); 62 NZ− NZ− NZ= NZ− NZ−; 63
SA− SA+ SA+ SA−; 64 NZ+; 65 SA+(4p)
SA+(2p); 66 BI−.
Cattle farmer.

ELSEY, W.J.　　　　　　　　　　　*Wales*
Cardiff.
b 1871 Roath; d −.
Forward, 1-0-0-1 (3 − 1t).
1895 E−(1t).

ELSOM, Allan Edwin George   *New Zealand*
N Linwood Sch, Albion, Canterbury, S Island.
b 18.7.25 Christchurch.
Centre/wing, 6-3-0-3 (3 − 1d).
52 A− A+; 53 W−; 55 A+ A+(1d) A−.
Real estate agent. NZ > 53-4 BI,F & NAm.

ELVIDGE, Ronald Rutherford   *New Zealand*
John McGlashan Coll, Univ, NZ Univs, Otago,
Union, S Island.
b 2.3.23 Timaru.
2nd five-eighth/centre, 9-4-1-4 (12 − 4t).
46 A+ A+(1t); 49 SA− SA− SA− SA−(1t); 50
BI=(1t) BI+ BI+(1t).
Obstetrician & gynaecologist. NZ > 49 SA.
Capt 1st 3 Tests v BI 50; inj in 3rd Test.
Continued medical studies in E, returning NZ
56.

EMANUEL, David Maurice   *Australia*
Sydney GS, NSW.
b 23.6.34.
No 8/lock, 9-1-1-7.
57 NZ−; 58 W− I− E− S− F− M+ M= M−.
Salesman/co dir.

EMERY, Neville Allen   *Australia*
Sydney Coll of EGS, NSW.
b 24 Lismore.
Five-eighth, 10-6-1-3 (3 − 1t).
47 NZ− S+ I+ W−; 48 E+ F−; 49 M= M+
NZ+ NZ+(1t).
Schoolmaster. RL in E.

EMMOTT, Charles   *England*
Bradford, Yorks.
b 1868; *d* 10.3.27 Saltaire.
Half-back, 1-1-0-0.
1892 W+.
Furniture broker. His club, Bradford, helped
form NU 1895.

EMSLIE, William Douglas   *Scotland*
Royal HS, Royal HSFP.
FH, 2-0-0-2.
30 F−; 32 I−.

ENGELBRECHT, Jan Pieter   *South Africa*
Paul Roos Gymnasium Sch, Stellenbosch Univ,
W Prov.
b 10.11.38.
Wing, 33-19-3-11 (24 − 8t).
60 S+ W+ I+; 61 E+ S+ F= A+(1t) A+; 62
BI+ BI+ BI+; 63 A− A−; 64 W+ F−; 65 I−
S−(1t) A−(2t) A− NZ− NZ− NZ+ NZ−; 67
F+ F+(1t) F− F=; 68 BI+ BI= F+ F+; 69 A+
A+(1t).
Farmer/economist. SA's most capped wing.
With J.L. Gainsford, most t (8) in ints v IB
countries. SA > 60-1 BI, F; 15t in 15 apps SA >

65 NZ (most by SA in NZ). 5t (inc 4 v Littoral-
Provence) SA > 68 F. Career 44t for SA.

ENGLISH, Michael Anthony   *Ireland*
Francis
Rockwell Coll, Lansdowne, Bohemians,
Barbarians.
b 2.6.33 Limerick.
FH, 16-3-2-11 (9 − 3d).
58 W− F−; 59 E− S+ F+(1d); 60 E− S−; 61
S− W− F−; 62 F− W=(1d); 63 E= S−
W+(1d) NZ−; BI > 59 A, NZ.
Insurance.

ENNIS, Francis Noel Gerard   *Ireland*
('Frank')
St Paul's Coll Raheny, Trin Coll Dublin,
Wanderers.
b 24.12.55 Dublin.
FB, 1-1-0-0.
79 A+r.
Accountant.

ENSOR, Anthony Howard   *Ireland*
Gonzaga Coll, UC Dublin, Wanderers,
Barbarians.
b 17.8.49 Dublin.
FB, 22-7-2-13 (28 − 1t 8p).
73 W− F+; 74 F−(2p) W=(3p) E+(1p) S+ P=
NZ−(2p); 75 E+ S− F+(1t) W−; 76 A− F−
W− E+ NZ−; 77 E−; 78 S+ F− W− E−.
Solicitor.

ENTHOVEN, H.J.   *England*
Richmond.
Back, 1-1-0-0.
1878 I+.

ENTRICAN, John C.   *Ireland*
RS Dungannon, Queen's Univ Belfast.
FB, 1-1-0-0.
31 S+.

ERBANI, Dominique   *France*
Agen.
b 16.8.56 Bergerac.
Flanker/no 8, 22-14-2-6 (4 − 1t).
81 A− A− NZ− NZ−; 82 Arg+ Arg+; 83 S+r
I− W+ A= A+ R+; 84 W+ E+ R+; 85 E=
W+r Arg+(1t); 86 S− I+ W+ E+.
Police. F > 85 Arg.

ERCEG, Charles Percy   *New Zealand*
Sacred Heart Coll Auckland, Aupouri, N
Auckland, Awanui, Kaitaia Pirates, Grafton,
NZ Maoris, Auckland, N Island.
b 28.11.28 Waipapakauri.
Wing, 4-3-0-1.
51 A+ A+ A+; 52 A−.
Insurance agent. NZ > 51 A. NZ Maoris
selector 72-80. Mgr Maoris > A, Fj & Tg 79.

ESCAFFRE, Pierre *France*
Narbonne.
Prop, 2-2-0-0 (3 − 1t).
33 G+; 34 G+(1t).

ESCOMMIER, Michel *France*
Montelimar.
Hooker, 1-1-0-0.
55 It+.

ESPONDA, Jean-Michel *France*
RCF.
b 24.4.43 Hendaye.
Prop, 10-1-0-9.
67 SA− SA− R+; 68 NZ− NZ− SA− R−; 69
S− I−r E−.
Technician.

ESTCOURT, Noel Sidney Dudley *England*
Plumtree Sch Rhodesia, Rhodes Univ, E Prov
(SA), Cambridge Univ, Blackheath,
Barbarians.
b 7.1.29 Selukwe, S Rhodesia.
FB, 1-1-0-0.
55 S+.
Schoolmaster. Ckt blue − 21 apps CUCC 53-4.
Returned to Rhodesia 55.

ESTÈVE, Alain ('Le Grand') *France*
Béziers.
b 15.9.46 Castelnaudary, Aude.
Lock, 21-8-2-11.
71 SA− R+; 72 I− E+ W− I− A+ R+; 73 S+
NZ+ E− I−; 74 I+ W= E= S− R− SA−
SA−; 75 W− E+.
Restaurateur.

ESTÈVE, Patrick *France*
Narbonne.
b 14.2.59 Lavelanet.
Wing, 23-14-3-6 (44 − 11t).
82 R− Arg+(1t) Arg+; 83 E+(1t) S+(2t) I−
(1t) W+(1t) A= A+(1t) R+(1t); 84 I+ W+
E+(1t) S− NZ− NZ− R+; 85 E= S+ I=(1t)
W+(1t); 86 S− I+.
Agricultural technician. 5t 83, most by F in
Champ (inc a t in each match, feat achieved only
by P. Sella, H.C. Catcheside & A.C. Wallace).
France B v W,E,S 80. France A v It, Soviet
Union 81. F > 84 J (8t v E Japan; see J-L
Dehez). Broke leg in unofficial match in Rio de
Janeiro, during F's journey to Arg for 85 tour.
Rest of World v BI, Cardiff 86.

ETCHEBERRY, Jean *France*
Rochefort, Cognac, Vienne.
b 27.8.01 Boucau.
Flanker/no 8, 16-3-0-13 (3 − 1t).
23 W− I+; 24 S+ I− E− W− R+(1t) US−; 26
S− I− E− M−; 27 I− S− W− G−.

ETCHENIQUE, Jean *France*
Biarritz Ol.
b 17.1.54 Ustaritz.
Centre, 4-2-0-2 (4 − 1t).
74 R− SA−; 75 E+(1t) Arg+.
Municipal employee.

ETCHEPARE, Jean *France*
Bayonne.
b 8.11.1898 Biandos, Landes; *d* c70 Boucau.
Flanker, 1-0-0-1.
22 I−.

ETCHEVERRY, Marc *France*
Pau.
b 23.8.42 Pau.
Prop, 2-1-1-0.
71 S+ I=.
Municipal employee.

ETLINGER, T.E. *South Africa*
W Prov.
1-1-0-0.
1896 BT+.

EUTROPE, A. *France*
SCUF.
b −; kia WW1.
Prop, 1-0-0-1.
13 I−.

EVANS, Arthur Candy *Wales*
Pontypool.
b 19.2.04 Pontypool; *d* 7.1.52 Pontypool.
Flanker/lock, 3-1-0-2.
24 E− I− F+.
Collier. Halifax RL.

EVANS, Brinley *Wales*
Welsh SS, Llanelli.
b 27.9.05 Felinfoel; *d* 6.10.78 Felinfoel.
Hooker, 6-3-1-2.
33 E+ S−; 36 E= S+ I+; 37 E−.
Miner/steelworker.

EVANS, Brinley Samuel MC *Wales*
London Univ, Llanelli.
b 21.1.1894; *d* 28.6.64 Llanelli.
Wing/centre, 5-4-1-0.
20 E+; 22 E+ S= I+ F+.
Schoolmaster.

EVANS, Bryn *Wales*
Penclawdd, Swansea.
b 1900; *d* 29.4.70.
SH, 1-0-0-1.
33 S−.
Schoolmaster.

EVANS, Colin *Wales*
Pontypool.
b 36.
SH, 1-0-0-1.
60 E−.
Engr's fitter. Leeds RL 60.

EVANS, David *Wales*
Penygraig.
b 1872 Maenclochog.
Forward, 4-2-0-2.
1896 S+ I−; 1897 E+; 1898 E−.
Collier/police.

EVANS, David Alexander *New Zealand*
City, Hawkes Bay, Scinde Dist, Napier, Napier
HSOB.
b 4.10.1886 Napier; *d* 12.10.40 Napier.
No 8, 1-0-0-1.
10 A−.
Freezing works employee. NZ > 10 A. Turned
RL 11; rep NZ 11-12. Son Eric rep Hawkes Bay
34.

EVANS, David Daniel *Wales*
Barry CGS, Cardiff Univ, New Brighton,
Cheshire.
b 7.4.09 Barry.
SH, 1-0-0-1.
34 E−.
Headmaster. Ckt for Cheshire.

EVANS, Sir David William *Wales*
Llandovery Coll, Oxford Univ, Cardiff,
Barbarians, London Welsh.
b 4.11.66 Dowlais; *d* 17.3.26 Cardiff.
Forward, 5-1-1-3.
1889 S− I−; 1890 E+ I=; 1891 E−.
Solicitor. Blue 1887-8. Kt 25.

EVANS, D.B. *Wales*
Amman Utd, Swansea.
FB, 1-0-1-0.
26 E=.
Colliery fireman.

EVANS, Denis Pritchard *Wales*
Tredegar GS, UC Aberystwyth, Oxford Univ,
Ebbw Vale, Llanelli.
b 19.3.36 Scunthorpe.
Wing, 1-0-0-1.
60 SA−.
Education & tg off SWEB/management
consultant. Blue 59. Chmn Ebbw Vale.
Administrative sec Hong Kong Sevens.

EVANS, Emrys *Wales*
Cwmgors, Amman Utd, The Army, Llanelli.
b 24.4.11 Gwaun-cae-Gurwen; *d* −.6.83
Bristol.
Prop/flanker, 3-2-0-1.

37 E−; 39 S+ I+.
Haulage contractor. Played in 2 Servs ints.
Salford RL 39.

EVANS, Eric *England*
O Aldwinians, Loughborough Coll, Sale,
Barbarians, Lancs.
b 1.2.25 Droylesden, Manchester.
Hooker, 30-17-3-10 (15 − 5t).
48 A−; 50 W−; 51 I− F− S+; 52 SA− W−
S+(1t) I+ F+; 53 I=(1t) F+(1t) S+; 54 W+
NZ− I+ F−; 56 W− I+(1t) S+ F−; 57 W+ I+
F+(1t) S+; 58 W= A+ I+ F+ S=.
Schoolmaster/industrial relations officer. Capt E
13 times. 105 apps for Lancs. RFU sel. Served
WW2, Sgt in Border Rgt.

EVANS, Frank *Wales*
Llanelli.
b 3.4.1897 Dafen; *d* 30.11.72 Llanelli.
Wing, 1-0-0-1.
21 S−.
Power station worker/storeman. Swinton RL 21.
GB RL > 24 Australia. Coached Acton,
Willesden RL clubs.

EVANS, Gareth L. *Wales*
Newport HS, Cross Keys, Newport.
b 54.
Wing, 3-1-0-2.
77 F−r; 78 F+; A−r; BI > 77 NZ 3-0-0-3.

EVANS, Geoffrey William *England*
Bablake Sch, Manchester Univ, Coventry.
b 10.12.50 Coventry.
Centre, 9-4-1-4 (7 − 1t 1d).
72 S−; 73 W−r F+ S+(1t) NZ+; 74 S− I−
F=(1d) W+.

EVANS, G. Rosser *Wales*
Llandovery Coll, Cardiff.
Half-back, 1-0-0-1.
1889 S−.

EVANS, Gwyn *Wales*
Clydach, Cardiff, Barbarians.
Flanker, 12-6-1-5 (3 − 1t).
47 E−(1t) S+ F+ I+ A+; 48 E= S+ F− I−; 49
E+ S− I−.
Police. Became Ch Superintendent S Wales
Police. 1st Cardiff City policeman to gain cap.

EVANS, Gwyn *Wales*
Maesteg Comp, Welsh SS, Swansea Univ,
UAU, Brit Univs, Maesteg.
b 6.9.57 Maesteg.
Wing/FB/centre, 10-3-0-7 (74 − 4c 22p).
81 S−r I+(2p) F−(1c 3p) A+(1c 3p); 82 I−(1c
1p) F+(6p) E− S−(1c 4p); 83 F−(1p) R−(2p);
BI > 83 NZ 2-0-0-2.
Sports centre mgr. Wales B v Fr 77, 79, 81.

Wales B > 80 US, Canada. Equ world rec, 6p v F 82. Wales pts rec for season (48 in 82). W's most pg in Champ season (11 in 82).

EVANS, Harry Loft MBE   *Scotland*
Clifton Coll, Edinburgh Univ.
b −; *d* −.
Wing, 1-1-0-0.
1885 I+.
Medicine.

EVANS, Iorwerth   *Wales*
Caerleon, Bedford Ath, London Welsh, Bedford.
Hooker, 2-2-0-0.
34 S+ I+.
Schoolmaster.

EVANS, Islwyn   *Wales*
Swansea.
Centre, 4-3-1-0 (13 − 3t 1d).
22 E+(1t) S=(1d) I+(1t) F+(1t).
Tinplater.

EVANS, Jack   *Wales*
Blaina.
Forward, 1-0-1-0.
04 E=.
Colliery farrier/farmer.

EVANS, Jack Elwyn   *Wales*
Brynamman, Amman Utd, Swansea, Llanelli.
b 1897 Brynamman; *d* 41 Swansea.
Centre, 1-0-0-1.
24 S−.
Miner/club steward. Broughton Rgrs RL 24.

EVANS, Jack H.   *Wales*
Pontypool.
Centre, 3-2-0-1.
07 E+ S− I+.
Miner/shop assistant.

EVANS, John ('Jack')   *Wales*
Llanelli, Llwynypia.
b 1871 Ammanford; *d* 24 Swinton.
Forward, 3-2-0-1.
1896 S+ I−; 1897 E+.
Collier/tram track layer. Swinton RL 1897. Won RL Cup medal 1900. Sons Jack & Bryn played RL.

EVANS, John David   *Wales*
Pengeulan Sch Mountain Ash, Mountain Ash, Cardiff, Barbarians.
b 28 Mountain Ash.
Prop, 2-1-0-1.
58 I+ F−.
NCB official/sales mgr/bus. 338 apps for Cardiff 51-61. Cardiff v NZ 53.

EVANS, John R.   *Wales*
Newport HS, Newport, London Welsh, Barbarians.
b 12.9.13 Newport; kia −.2.43 Middle East.
Hooker, 1-0-0-1.
34 E−.
Business in Gold Coast. Served WW2, S Wales Borderers, Maj in Welsh Guards. Capt Wales XV with 13 new caps, on only int appearance. Capt Newport v NZ 35 (1c).

EVANS, Llewellyn John   *Australia*
Brisbane GS, Qld.
b 19.2.1881; *d* −.
Five-eighth, 3-0-0-3.
03 NZ−; 04 BT− BT−.
Clerk. Bro of 'Poley'.

EVANS, Nevill Lloyd ('Barney')   *England*
Eltham Coll, RNEC Keyham, Devonport Servs, US Portsmouth, Comb Servs, RN, Barbarians, Hants, Devon.
b 16.12.08.
Prop, 5-3-0-2.
32 W− I+ S+; 33 W− I+.
RN. Served WW2 engr officer, later Lt Cmdr. Sec St Enodoc GC 66.

EVANS, O.J.   *Wales*
Cardiff.
Half-back, 4-1-1-2.
1887 E= S−; 1888 S+ I−.
Mem of the outstanding Cardiff side which won 26, lost 1 the last, against Moseley, 1885-6, scoring 533 pts against 18. In contrast played W v S 1887, in which George Lindsay scored 5 of Scotland's 12t, both still records.

EVANS, Peter Denzil   *Wales*
St Michael's Sch Bryn, Llanelli.
b 29 Llanelli.
Flanker, 2-1-0-1.
51 E+ F−.
Concrete blocks business. Emigrated NZ.

EVANS, Robert Thomas   *Wales*
Newport.
b 16.2.21 Rhymney.
Flanker, 10-7-1-2 (3 − 1t).
47 F+ I+(1t); 50 E+ S+ I+ F+; 51 E+ S− I= F−; BI > 50 NZ 4-0-1-3, A 2-2-0-0.
CID. Played in 5 Victory ints. Capt Mon team which beat 46 Kiwis 15-0.

EVANS, Ronald BEM   *Wales*
Bridgend, Welsh Police, Glam, Brit Police, Bridgend Sports, Cowbridge.
b 6.11.41 Bridgend.
Centre, 3-1-0-2.
63 S+ I− F−.
Police. BEM 78.

EVANS, Stuart *Wales*
Dumbarton House Sch Swansea, BSC Port
Talbot, Welsh Youth, Resolven, Swansea,
Western Suburbs (Aus), Neath.
b 14.6.63 Neath.
Prop, 2-1-0-1.
85 F− E+.
BSC apprentice.

EVANS, Thomas *Wales*
Swansea, Breconshire.
b Neyland.
Centre, 1-0-0-1.
24 I−.
Civil Service.

EVANS, Thomas Geoffrey *Wales*
Pembrey Comp, Llandovery Coll, UC Bangor
Llanelli, Bridgend, Neath, London Welsh,
Surrey, Barbarians.
b 1.5.43 Pembrey.
Lock, 7-5-1-1.
70 SA=; S+ E+ I−; 72 E+ S+ F+; BIr > 71 A,
NZ.
Polytechnic lecturer. London Welsh coach 78-
82, chmn sel 85-6.

EVANS, Thomas Henry *Wales*
Ammanford CS, Llanelli.
b 31.12.1882 Ammanford; *d* 19.3.55 Llanelli.
Flanker/lock, 18-15-0-3 (3 − 1t).
06 I−; 07 E+ S− I+; 08 I+ A+; 09 E+ S+ F+
I+; 10 F+ E− S+ I+; 11 E+ S+ F+ I+(1t).
Police. 3 W Triple Crown sides. Capt Llanelli in
8-3 win v A 08. Capt Llanelli 09-11.

EVANS, Thomas Wynne *Wales*
Llandybie, Llanelli.
b 13.8.26 Llandybie.
SH, 1-1-0-0.
58 A+.
Miner/licensee. Capt Llanelli 56-7.

EVANS, Trevor Pryce *Wales*
Welsh Youth, Swansea, Barbarians.
b 26.11.47.
Flanker, 10-9-0-1 (8 − 2t).
75 F+ E+ S−(1t) I+ A+; 76 E+ S+(1t) I+ F+;
77 I+; BI > 77 NZ 1-0-0-1.
Estate agent. Wales B v F 74. Wales XV v Tg
74, Arg 76. Welsh XV v NZ 74. Barbarians v A
76.

EVANS, Vivian *Wales*
Neath, Barbarians.
b 14.7.19 Cross Inn, Skewen.
FB, 3-3-0-0 (25 − 2c 7p).
54 I+(3p) F+(2c 3p) S+(1p).
Steelworker/aged persons home superintendent.
Capped at 34. POW WW2.

EVANS, W.H. *Wales*
Llwynypia.
b 9.2.1892 Tonypandy; *d* 79 Bryncethin.
Centre, 4-3-0-1 (6 − 2t).
14 E− S+ F+(1t) I+(1t*).
Miner. Welch Rgt WW2. *Some sources cr this t
to I.T. Davies.

EVANS, Wilfred J. *Wales*
Pontypool.
b 12.5.14 Griffithstown.
Prop, 1-1-0-0.
47 S+.
Police. Played in 5 Victory ints.

EVANS, William Frederick *Wales*
Christ's Coll Brecon, Sherborne, Rhymney,
Oxford Univ, Newport.
b c1856; *d* −.
Back/half-back, 2-1-0-1 (1t).
1882 I+(1t); 1883 S−.
Headmaster. Emigrated Australia.

EVANS, William George *Wales*
Brynmawr.
b c1886; *d* 49 Port Talbot.
Forward, 1-1-0-0.
11 I+.
Miner. Leeds RL 1911.

EVANS, William Roderick *Wales*
Cowbridge Sch, Cambridge Univ, Cardiff,
Bridgend, Barbarians, London Welsh.
b 19.12.34 Porthcawl.
Lock, 13-6-2-5.
58 A+ E= S+ I+ F−; 60 SA−; 61 E+ S− I+
F−; 62 E= S− I+; BI > 59 A 1-1-0-0, NZ 3-0-0-
3.
Solicitor. Blue 55. Barbarians v A 58, SA 61.
Barbarians > 58 SA.

EVANS, William Thomas *Australia*
('Poley')
Qld.
b 9.4.1876; *d* 19.7.64 Brisbane.
Five-eighth, 2-1-0-1 (3 − 1t).
1899 BT+(1t) BT−.
Engr. Bro of Llewellyn. Rep Qld ckt & bowls.

EVERSON, William Aaron *Wales*
Caerphilly GS, Newport.
b −.3.06 Machen; *d* 26.3.66 Newport.
FB, 1-0-0-1 (2 − 1c).
26 S−(1c).
Police/tobacconist. 314 apps Newport. Sec
Newport RFC. Snelling's Sevens fdr 54; Bill
Everson Award to outstanding player named in
his honour.

EVANSON, Arthur Macdonnell *England*
JP
Oundle Sch, Oxford Univ, Richmond, Mdx.
b 1859; *d* 31.12.34.
Back, 4-4-0-0 (3c).
1882 W+(2c); 1883 I+(1c) S+; 1884 S+.
HM. Bro of Wyndham. Blue 1880-1 (capt 82 but did not play). Ath blue (shot) 1880-2.

EVANSON, Wyndham Alleyn *England*
Daubney
St John's Sch Leatherhead, Owls, Civil Service, Richmond.
b 1851; *d* 30.10.34.
Back, 5-1-3-1 (1t).
1875 S=; 1877 S−; 1878 S=; 1879 S= I+(1t).
Civil Service. Bro of Arthur. Distinguished oarsman & sculler. Became scratch golfer at 60 at Crowborough GC.

EVELEIGH, Kevin Alfred *New Zealand*
Otorohanga Coll, Palmerston N Tech Coll OB, Feilding, Manawatu, N Island, Rhodesia, Zimbabwe.
b 8.11.47 Palmerston N.
Flanker, 4-2-0-2.
76 SA+ SA−; 77 BI+ BI−.
Timber worker/farm contractor. NZ > 74 A & Fj & I,W & E, 76 SA, 77 F. Settled in Rhodesia 79.

EVERSHED, Frank *England*
Burton-on-Trent GS, Amersham Hall Sch Reading, Oxford Univ, Burton, E Sheen, Blackheath, Barbarians, Midland Cos.
b 6.9.1866 Winshill, Staffs; *d* 29.6.54 Winshill.
Forward, 10-7-0-3 (4t).
1889 NZN+(1t); 1890 W− S+(1t) I+; 1892 W+(1t) I+(1t) S+; 1893 W− I+ S−.
Solicitor. Son of S. Evershed, MP, & father of Rt Hon Lord Evershed. 1st Midland Cos player to be capped. Derbys CCC 1889-94. Hockey for Derbys 06, when he was 40.

EWART, E.N. *Scotland*
Glasgow Acad, Glasgow Academicals.
b −; *d* 02.
Forward, 3-1-1-1 (2t).
1879 E=; 1880 I+(2t) E−.

EYRES, Wallace C.T. *England*
US Portsmouth, Richmond, RN, Barbarians, Hants.
No 8, 1-1-0-0.
27 I+.
RN/mgr White City Stadium. Played at centre for Richmond. Served WW2 as aide to Adm Bonham Carter.

F

FABRE, Emile *France*
Toulouse.
Lock, 3-2-0-1.
37 It+; 38 G− G+.

FABRE, Jean *France*
Toulouse.
b 7.11.35 Rodez, Aveyron.
Flanker/no 8, 8-3-0-5.
63 S− I+ E− W+ It+; 64 S− NZ− E−.
Mathematics professor.

FABRE, Lolo *France*
Lezignan.
Hooker, 1-1-0-0.
30 G+.

FABRE, Michel *France*
Béziers.
Wing, 8-4-0-4 (8 − 2t).
81 A− R+ NZ− NZ−; 82 I+ R−; 85 J+(1t) J+(1t).

FAGAN, Arthur Robert St Leger *England*
Guy's Hosp, Utd Hosps, Richmond, Tiverton, Devon, Mdx.
b 24.11.1862; *d* −.
FB, 1-1-0-0.
1887 I+.
Medicine. Capped in 1888 E side that did not play.

FAGAN, George Lantie *Ireland*
Kingstown Sch, Rugby Sch, Trin Coll Dublin.
b 27.11.1859; *d* 1885.
Half-back, 1-0-0-1.
1878 E−.

FAGAN, William Barnard Cecil *Ireland*
('Buzzer')
Blackrock Coll, Trin Coll Dublin, Wanderers, Morley.
b 23.4.27 Dublin.
Prop, 3-1-0-2.
56 F− E− S+.
Medicine.

FAHEY, Edward Joseph *Australia*
St Joseph's Coll, NSW.
b 1882; *d* 23.8.50.
Lock, 4-1-0-3.
12 US+; 13 NZ− NZ−; 14 NZ−.

FAHMY, Ernest Chalmers *Scotland*
Eltham Coll, Edinburgh Univ, Abertillery.
b 28.11.1892 Amoy, China; *d* 25.8.82 Edinburgh.
Centre/FH, 4-3-0-1.

20 F+ W+ I+ E−.
Medicine. Father Egyptian, mother Scottish.
GP in Western Valley, Gwent; played for
Abertillery 19-22.

FAILLIOT, Pierre ('La *France*
Locomotive')
RCF.
b 21.2.1889 Paris; *d* 21.12.35.
Wing, 8-1-0-7 (12 − 4t).
11 S+(1t) W− I−(1t); 12 I− S− E−(1t); 13 E−
W−(1t).
Paper manufacturer.

FAIRBROTHER, Keith Eli *England*
('Batman')
Caludon Castle Sch Coventry, Stoke OB,
Nuneaton, Coventry, Warwicks.
b 8.5.44 Coventry.
Prop, 12-5-1-6.
69 I− F+ S+ W− SA+; 70 I+ W− S− F−; 71
W− I+ F=; BI > 69 SA.
Fruiterer. Leigh RL 75.

FAIRFAX, Russell Lance *Australia*
Matraville HS, NSW.
b 29.3.52.
FB, 8-2-1-5 (27 − 1d 8p).
71 F+ F−; 72 F=(2p) F−(5p) NZ− Fj+(1d); 73
W− E−(1p).
Club exec/RL coach. RL.

FAITHFULL, Charles Kirke *England*
Tindal ('Chubby')
Wellington Coll, Devonport Servs, US
Portsmouth, Halifax, Harlequins, Comb Servs,
The Army, Barbarians, Surrey, Hants, Yorks.
b 6.1.03; *d* 8.8.79.
Prop, 3-2-0-1.
24 I+; 26 F+ S−.
The Army. Ref 29-36. Amateur boxer. Served
WW2, reaching rank of Lt Col.

FALLAS, Herbert *England*
Wakefield Trin.
Back, 1-1-0-0.
1884 I+.
Clerk.

FANNING, Alfred Henry *New Zealand*
Netherwood
Marist Bros' Sch Christchurch, Linwood,
Canterbury.
b 31.3.1890 Linwood; *d* 11.3.63 Christchurch.
No 8, 1-0-0-1 (3 − 1t).
13 A−(1t)
Carpenter. Bro of Bernard; another bro Leo
wrote rugby book 'Players & Slayers'. Nephew
Louis Peterson rep NZ 21-3 (no Tests). Fdr
mem Marist club, Christchurch.

FANNING, Bernard John *New Zealand*
Kaiapoi, Linwood, Canterbury, Poneke,
Wellington, S Island.
b 11.11.1874 Christchurch; *d* 9.7.46
Christchurch.
No 8, 2-2-0-0.
03 A+; 04 BI+.
Blacksmith. Bro of Alfred.

FARGUES, Hector *France*
Dax.
Flanker, 1-1-0-0.
23 I+.

FARMER, E.H. *Australia*
Qld.
Flanker, 1-0-0-1.
10 NZ−.
Farmer/miner.

FARR-JONES, Nicholas *Australia*
Campbell
Sydney Univ, Australian Univs, Sydney, NSW.
b 18.4.62.
SH, 9-8-0-1 (4 − 1t)
84 E+ I+ W+ S+(1t); 85 C+ C+ NZ− Fj+
Fj+.
Law student. A > 84 Fj; 84 BI. Rest of World v
BI, Cardiff 86.

FARRELL, Colin Paul *New Zealand*
St Paul's Coll Auckland, Suburbs, NZ Colts,
Auckland.
b 19.3.56 Auckland.
FB, 2-1-0-1.
77 BI+ BI−.
Fencing contractor.

FARRELL, James Leo *Ireland*
Castleknock Coll, Bective Rgrs, Barbarians.
b 7.8.03; *d* 24.10.79 Cirencester.
Lock/flanker, 29-17-1-11.
26 F+ E+ S+ W−; 27 F+ E− S+ W+ NSW−;
28 F+ E− S+ W+; 29 F+ E+ S− W=; 30 F−
E+ S+ W−; 31 F− E+ S+ W− SA−; 32 E−
S+ W+; BI > 30 NZ 4-1-0-3 & A 1-0-0-1.
Farmer.

FASSON, Francis Hamilton MBE *Scotland*
JP
Merchiston Castle Sch, London Scottish,
Edinburgh W, Barbarians.
b 21.9.1877; *d* 23.10.55.
Half-back, 5-2-0-3.
1900 W−; 01 W+ I+; 02 W− E−.
Writer to the Signet.

FAULKNER, Anthony George *Wales*
('Charlie')
St Mary's Sch Newport, Newport Saracens,
Cross Keys, Pontypool, Monmouthshire,

Barbarians.
b 27.2.41 Newport.
Prop, 19-14-0-5 (4 − 1t).
75 F+ E+ S− I+(1t) A+; 76 E+ S+ I+ F+; 78
E+ S+ I+ F+ A− A− NZ−; 79 S+ I+ F−; BIr
> 77 NZ.
Steelworker/brewery rep. Wales B v F 74. W >
75 Far East; 78 A. Welsh XV v NZ 74. Wales
XV v Arg 76. Judo black belt. Mem of
legendary Pontypool Front Row. Called up as r
BI > 77 NZ whilst on WRU coaching course
Aberystwyth. Newport coach 82-86.

FAULL, John   *Wales*
Bromsgrove Sch, Swansea, Barbarians.
b 30.6.33 Morriston.
No 8/lock, 12-7-1-4 (3 − 1t).
57 I+ F+(1t); 58 A+ E= S+ I+ F−; 59 E+ S−
I+; 60 E− F−; BI > 59 A 1-1-0-0, NZ 3-0-0-3.
Co dir. Barbarians v A 58. Son of Wilfred Faull,
int ref & pres WRU 62-3.

FAURE, Felix   *France*
Tarbes.
b−; kia WW1.
No 8/flanker, 3-0-0-3.
14 I− W− E−.

FAUVEL, Jean-Pierre   *France*
Tulle.
b 56.
Flanker, 1-0-0-1.
80 R−.
F > 80 SA.

FAVRE, G.   *France*
Lyon.
Flanker, 2-0-0-2.
13 E− W−.

FAWCETT, Christopher Louis   *New Zealand*
('Kit')
Matamata Coll, Univ, Otago, Waikato, NZ
Jnrs, NZ Univs, Auckland, S Island, Natal
Univ, Wasps (E).
b 28.10.54 Matamata.
FB, 2-1-0-1.
76 SA+ SA−.
Schoolmaster. NZ > 76 SA. Lived and taught
for a time in SA & BI.

FAY, Garrick   *Australia*
Sydney (Shore) CES, NSW, Wasps (E).
b 11.4.48.
Lock, 24-9-1-14 (4 − 1t).
71 SA−; 72 NZ− NZ− NZ−; 73 Tg+ Tg− W−
E−; 74 NZ− NZ= NZ−; 75 E+ E+(1t) J+ S−
W−; 76 I+ US+; 78 W+ W+ NZ− NZ− NZ+;
79 I−.
Co exec.

FEA, William Rognvald   *New Zealand*
Otago Boys' HS, Univ, Comb Servs, NZ Univs,
Otago, S Island.
b 5.10.1898 Dunedin.
1st five-eighth, 1-0-1-0.
21 SA=.
Medicine. Played for Comb Servs team which
won King's Cup. Coached Timaru HSOB 26-30.
Served WW2, Lt Col 8th Field Ambulance. NZ
squash champ 36-7.

FEAR, Albert   *Wales*
Abertillery, Newport.
Flanker, 4-3-0-1 (3 − 1t).
34 S+ I+(1t); 35 S+ I−.
Miner.

FEDDIS, Noel   *Ireland*
PBC Glasthule, CBS Dun Laoghaire,
Lansdowne.
b 29.12.32 Dublin.
Flanker, 1-0-0-1.
56 E−.
Chartered accountant.

FEGAN, John Herbert Craugle   *England*
Blackheath Proprietary Sch, Cambridge Univ,
Blackheath, Barbarians, Kent.
b 20.1.1872 Old Charlton, Kent; *d* 26.7.49.
Wing, 3-2-0-1 (3 − 1t).
1895 W+ I+(1t) S−.
Medicine.

FEIGHERY, Conleth Francis   *Ireland*
Castleknock Coll, UC Dublin, Lansdowne,
Leinster.
b 13.8.46 Dublin.
Lock, 3-3-0-0.
72 F+ E+ F+.
Medicine. Bro of T.A.O.; bro in law of Barrie
Bresnihan.

FEIGHERY, Thomas Anthony   *Ireland*
Oliver
Clongowes Wood Coll, UC Dublin, St Mary's
Coll, Leinster.
b 16.1.45 Dublin.
Prop, 2-0-0-2.
77 W− E−.
Medicine. Bro of Con. Ireland B.

FELL, Alfred Nolan   *Scotland*
Nelson Coll, Edinburgh Univ.
b 17.1.1878 Nelson, NZ; *d* 20.4.53 Colchester.
Wing, 7-5-0-2 (6 − 2t).
01 W+ I+ E+(1t); 02 W− E−(1t); 03 W+ E+.
Medicine. Selected for S v NZ 05, but withdrew
out of 'loyalty' to his birthplace.

FENDER, Norman   *Wales*
Cardiff.

b 2.9.10 Cardiff; *d* −.10.83 York.
Flanker, 6-5-1-0 (3 − 1t).
30 I+ F+; 31 E= S+ F+(1t) I+.
Labourer/licensee. York RL 31. RL for E & W.

FENWICK, Steven Paul   *Wales*
Caerphilly GTS, Borough Road Coll, Bridgend,
Barbarians.
  b 23.7.51 Nantgarw.
Centre, 30-20-0-10 (152 − 4t 11c 3d 35p).
75 F+(1t 1c 1p) E+(1t) S−(2p) A+(2c 1p); 76
E+(3c) S+(1d) I+ F+(2p); 77 I+(1d) F−(3p)
E+(2p) S+; 78 E+ S+(1t) I+(1t 4p) F+(1d)
A− A− NZ−(1p); 79 S+(1c 3p) I+ (2c 4p) F−
(3p) E+(1c); 80 F+ E− S+(1p) I−(1p) NZ−
(1p) 81 E+(1c 4p) S−(2p); BI > 77 NZ 4-1-0-3.
Schoolmaster/business. W's most capped centre.
Champ rec-equ 38 pts 79. W's pts rec on
overseas tour − 55 A 78. W > 75 Far East; 78
A. Wales B v F 74. Wales B > 80 US, Can 80.
Wales XV v Tg 74, R 79. Barbarians > 76 US,
Can. Cardiff RL 81 £20,000 fee. 2 Wales RL
caps. Business ptn with Tommy David.

FENWICKE, Peter Thomas   *Australia*
King's Sch Paramatta, NSW.
  b 14.11.32.
No 8/flanker, 6-0-0-6.
57 NZ−; 58 W− I− E−; 59 BI− BI−.
Grazier.

FERGUSON, James Huck   *Scotland*
Portobello Sch, Heriot's Coll, Gala.
  b 19.10.03.
Prop, 1-0-0-1.
28 W−.
Dir tweed co.

FERGUSON, William Gordon   *Scotland*
Royal HS, Royal HSFP.
Prop, 5-2-0-3.
27 NSW+; 28 F+ W− I− E−.

FERGUSSON, Ewen Alastair   *Scotland*
John
Rugby Sch, Oxford Univ, Barbarians.
  b 28.10.32.
Lock, 5-0-0-5.
54 F− NZ− I− E− W−.
Foreign Office. Blue 52-3. Ambassador to S.A.
82-4. Deputy Under-sec at F.O. 85-6.

FERNANDES, Charles Walker   *England*
Luis
Rossall Sch, Wakefield, Leeds, Yorks W,
Yorks.
  b 3.4.1857 Wakefield; *d* 12.8.44 Thirsk.
Forward, 3-2-1-0 (1t).
1881 I+ W+(1t) S=.
Landowner. His club, Leeds, helped form NU
1895.

FERRAND, Lucien   *France*
Chalon.
Flanker, 1-0-0-1.
40 BF−.

FERREIRA, P.S.   *South Africa*
W Prov.
Flanker, 2-2-0-0 (4 − 1t).
84 SAm+ SAm+(1t).

FERRIEN, Roger   *France*
Tarbes.
  b 9.11.24 Rucles.
Prop, 4-1-1-2.
50 S− I= E+ W−.

FERRIS, J. Hugh   *Ireland/South Africa*
RBAI, Queen's Coll Belfast, Transvaal.
  b 30.7.1876; *d* −.
Ireland
SH, 4-0-1-3.
1900 E− S= W−; 01 W−.
South Africa
SH, 1-1-0-0.
03 BT+.

FIDLER, John E.   *England*
Cheltenham, Gloucester, Glos.
  b 16.9.48 Cheltenham.
Lock, 4-1-1-2.
81 Arg= Arg+; 84 SA− SA−.
Police. England B > 78 R. E > 81 Arg, 84 SA.
Appeared in 9 County Champ finals with Glos.

FIELD, Edwin   *England*
Clifton Coll, Cambridge Univ, Mdx W,
Richmond, Barbarians, Mdx.
  b 16.12.1871 Hampstead; *d* 9.1.47 Bromley.
FB, 2-1-0-1.
1893 W− I+.
Solicitor. Blue 1892-4. Ckt blue 1894; played
also for Berks 1895 & Mdx 04, 06.

FIELDING, Keith John   *England*
KES Five Ways, Loughborough Colls, Moseley,
N Midlands.
  b 8.7.49 Birmingham.
Wing, 10-4-0-6 (3 − 1t).
69 I− F+(1t) S+ SA+; 70 I+ F−; 72 W− I−
F− S−.
Schoolmaster. Salford RL 73.

FIHELLY, John Arthur   *Australia*
St Joseph's Coll, Qld.
  b 7.11.1882 Timoleague, Ireland; *d* 2.3.45.
Forward, 2-0-1-1.
07 NZ− NZ=r.
Civil service/journalist. RL.

FINAT, René   *France*
CASG.

Wing, 2-2-0-0 (15 − 5t).
32 G+(2t); 33 G+(3t).

FINCH, Ernest JP   *Wales*
Pembroke Dock CS, Monmouthshire Tg Coll,
Pembroke Dock Harlequins, Llanelli.
b 16.7.1899 Pembroke Dock; *d* 1.10.83
Haverfordwest.
Wing, 7-3-0-4 (12 − 4t).
24 F+(1t) NZ−; 25 F+(2t) I−; 26 F+; 27
NSW−(1t); 28 I−.
Schoolmaster. Played football before taking up
rugby.

FINCH, Richard Tanner   *England*
Sherborne Sch, Cambridge Univ, St George's
Hosp, Richmond, Surrey, Kent.
b 1857 Kensington; *d* 12.1.21 Seaton.
Half-back, 1-1-0-0.
1880 S+.
Medicine. Blue 1876-9, capt 79-80.
Contemporary of A.S. Taylor at Pembroke
Coll. GP at Salisbury. E cap at RFU
Twickenham.

FINLAN, John Frank   *England*
Saltley GS, O Saltleians, Coventry, Moseley,
Barbarians, N Midlands.
b 9.9.41.
FH, 13-4-2-7 (9 − 3d).
67 I+ F−(1d) S+(1d) W− NZ−; 68 W=
I=(1d); 69 I− F+ S+ W−; 70 F−; 73 NZ−.
Electricity Bd buying dept/systems analyst. E >
67 Can. England sel.

FINLAY, Arthur Bannatyne   *Scotland*
Edinburgh Acad, Edinburgh Academicals.
b 21.4.1854; *d* 10.9.21.
Forward, 1-0-1-0.
1875 E=.
Sheep farmer. Bro of J.F. & Ninian. Farmed in
US.

FINLAY, Arthur Noel ('Huck')   *Australia*
Sydney GS, NSW.
b 25.12.03 Sydney; *d* 20.9.81.
Lock, 4-4-0-0.
29 NZ+ NZ+ NZ+; 30 BI+.
Radio station exec. NSW > BI & F 27-8.

FINLAY, Brian Edward Louis   *New Zealand*
Marist Bros' Sch Miramar, St Patrick's Coll,
Univ, Manawatu, Marist, N Island.
b 7.11.27 Cromwell.
Flanker, 1-1-0-0.
59 BI+.
Joiner. Cousin of Jack. Coached Marist &
Ashhurst clubs.

FINLAY, Jack MC   *New Zealand*
Christchurch Boys' HS, Feilding Agric Coll,

Feilding OB, Manawatu, Hutt Army,
Wellington, N Island.
b 31.1.16 Normanby.
No 8, 1-1-0-0 (3 − 1t).
46 A+(1t).
Merchandise supervisor. Served WW2, Maj in
25th Infantry Battn. V-capt Comb Servs 44-5.
NZRFU selector 61-4. Cousin of Brian.

FINLAY, James Ernest MC   *Ireland*
Queen's Coll Belfast, Cardiff.
Forward, 6-0-0-6.
13 E− S− W−; 20 E− S− W−.
Medicine. Served WW1. In practice in Wales for
a time.

FINLAY, James Fairbairn   *Scotland*
Edinburgh Acad, Edinburgh Academicals,
Edinburgh Univ.
b 8.4.1852; *d* 25.1.30.
Forward, 4-1-1-2 (1t).
1871 E+; 1872 E−; 1874 E−(1t); 1875 E=.
Indian Civil Service. Played in 1st int, S v E
1871. Bro of A.B. & Ninian.

FINLAY, Ninian Jamieson   *Scotland*
Edinburgh Acad, Edinburgh Academicals,
Edinburgh Univ.
b 31.1.1858 Edinburgh; *d* 7.3.36.
Back, 9-2-4-3 (3d).
1875 E=; 1876 E−; 1878 E=; 1879 I+ E=(1d);
1880 I+(2d) E−; 1881 I− E=.
Writer to the Signet. Bro of J.F. & A.B.
World's youngest int player, 17yrs 36 days when
capped from sch. Fellow-Scot Charles Reid was
same age when 1st capped, but Finlay was
reckoned to be a day younger because of 4 leap
yrs in his lifetime compared with Reid's 5.

FINLAY, Robert   *Scotland*
George Watson's Coll, Watsonians.
b 9.4.23 Edinburgh.
Lock, 1-1-0-0.
48 E+.
Mining engr.

FINLAY, W.   *Ireland*
RBAI, Windsor, NIFC.
Forward, 8-0-0-8.
1875 E−; 1877 E− S−; 1878 E−; 1879 S− E−;
1880 S−; 1882 S−.

FINLAYSON, Alexander A.J.   *Wales*
Cardiff, Barbarians.
b 18.3.48.
Centre, 3-0-2-1.
74 I= F= E−.
Police. Wales B v F 72. Wales XV v Tg 74. 135t
for Cardiff 67-76.

147

FINLAYSON, Ian ('Bunny')   *New Zealand*
Maungaturoto Sch, Kamo, Maungakaramea, N
Auckland, Auckland, N Island.
b 4.7.1899 Maungaturoto; *d* 29.1.80
Whangarei.
Flanker/lock, 6-3-0-3.
28 SA− SA+ SA− SA+; 30 BI− BI+.
Farmer. 1st class debut in N Auckland's 1st
match, v S Island Country, 20. NZ > 25 & 26 A,
28 SA (sent off v Transvaal). N Auckland
selector 33-40. Three bros Bain, Tote & Angus
rep N Auckland; bro Jack was pres 50 & another
bro Callum rep Otago 27-30.

FINLEY, Francis George ('Pony')   *Australia*
NSW.
b 27.2.1884; *d* 43.
Half-back, 1-0-0-1.
04 BT−.
Grazier.

FINLINSON, Horace William   *England*
Bedford Mod Sch, Blair Lodge, Blackheath,
Barbarians, Kent, E Cos.
b 9.6.1871 Bedford.
Forward, 3-2-0-1.
1895 W+ I+ S−.

FINN, Maurice Cornelius   *Ireland*
('Moss')
PBC Cork, Irish Schs, UC Cork, Cork
Constitution.
b 29.3.57 Cork.
Wing, 14-7-0-7 (16 − 4t).
79 E+; 82 W+(2t) E+ S+ F−; 83 S+ F+(2t)
W− E+; 84 E− S− A−; 86 F− W−.
Business. Ireland B 77, 79; Under 23s.

FINN, Raymond Gerard Andrew   *Ireland*
Belvedere Coll, Newbridge Coll, UC Dublin.
b 25.11.53 Dublin.
Centre, 1-0-0-1.
77 F−.
Vet.

FINNANE, Stephen Charles   *Australia*
Vaucluse HS, NSW.
b 3.7.52.
Prop, 6-5-0-1.
75 E+ J+ J+ E−; 78 W+ W+.
Law clerk. Author 'The Game They Play in
Heaven' pub 79.

FINNEY, Sir Stephen CIE   *England*
Clifton Coll, RIE Coll.
b 8.9.1852; *d* 1.3.24.
Half-back, 2-1-1-0 (1t).
1872 S+(1t); 1873 S=.
Rly mgr. CIE 04. KB 13. Indian public works
dept 1874. E Bengal State Rly 1891-9; Indian
NW Rly 1899-07.

FIRTH, Frederick   *England*
Halifax.
b c1870 Cleckheaton; *d* −.2.36 Olneyville, US.
Wing, 3-1-0-2.
1894 W+ I− S−.
Machine shop foreman. Mem of E's 1st 4-
threequarters line, v W 1894. Turned RL when
his club, Halifax, helped form NU 1895.
Emigrated US c08.

FISHER, Alastair Thomson   *Scotland*
George Watson's Coll, Waterloo, Watsonians.
b 3.9.16 Edinburgh; *d* 26.1.83.
Hooker, 2-0-0-2.
47 I− E−.
Quantity surveyor. Father of Colin.

FISHER, Colin Douglas   *Scotland*
Merchant Taylors' Sch Crosby, Liverpool Poly,
Waterloo.
b 27.12.49 Liverpool.
Hooker, 5-3-0-2.
75 NZ− A+; 76 W− E+ I+.
Surveyor. Son of Alastair. Scottish XV v J 76.

FISHER, D.   *Scotland*
Glasgow HS, W of S.
Forward, 1-0-1-0.
1893 I=.

FISHER, James Pringle   *Scotland*
Royal HS, Royal HSFP, Edinburgh DS,
London Scottish, The Army, Comb Servs,
Barbarians.
b 17.3.39 Edinburgh.
No 8/flanker, 25-9-3-13.
63 E−; 64 F+ NZ= W− I+ E+; 65 F− W− I−
E= SA+; 66 F= W− I+ E+ A+; 67 F+ W+
I− E− NZ−; 68 F− W− I− E−.
Dentist/The Army. Comb Servs v NZ 63. Rep
GB in Olympics basketball.

FITE, Roger   *France*
Brive.
b 13.10.38 Cabrerolles, Herault.
Lock, 2-2-0-0.
63 W+ It+.
Rly employee.

FITZGERALD, Charles Conway   *Ireland*
MC
RS Dungannon, Glasgow Univ, Dungannon.
Wing, 3-1-0-2.
02 E−; 03 E+ S−.
Served WW1.

FITZGERALD, Ciaran Fintan   *Ireland*
St Joseph's Coll Ballinasloe, Garbally Coll, UC
Galway, Irish Univs, Connacht, St Mary's Coll,
Barbarians.
b 4.6.52 Galway.

Hooker, 25-13-1-11 (4 − 1t).
79 A+ A+; 80 E− S+ F− W+(1t); 82 W+ E+
S+ F−; 83 S+ F+ W− E+; 84 F− W− A−; 85
S+ F= W+ E+; 86 F− W− E− S−; BI > 83
NZ 4-0-0-4.
Army. Ireland B. I > 79 A. Capt BI > 83 NZ.

FITZGERALD, Desmond　　　　*Ireland*
Christopher
De La Salle Coll Churchtown, Trin Coll Dublin,
Lansdowne.
b 20.12.57 Dublin.
Prop, 5-0-0-5.
84 E− S−; 86 W− E− S−.
Computer science/oil co sales rep. I > 81 SA.

FITZGERALD, Gerald David　　　　*Wales*
Cardiff.
b 1873 Cardiff; *d* 30.11.51 Cardiff.
Centre, 2-1-0-1 (7 − 1t 1d).
1894 S+(1t 1d) I−.
Coal agent/marine store. Leigh RL 1895, Batley
1896. 1st RU int to win RL Cup Final medal.

FITZGERALD, James Train　　　*New Zealand*
Hutt Valley HS, Univ, Otago, NZ Univs,
Wellington, N Island.
b 6.8.28 Petone.
2nd five-eighth, 1-0-0-1 (3 − 1t).
52 A−(1t).
PE teacher/co mgr/assurance agent. NZ > 53-4
BI,F & NAm.

FITZGERALD, J.　　　　　　　*Ireland*
Wanderers.
Forward, 1-0-0-1.
1884 W−.

FITZPATRICK, Brian Bernard　*New Zealand*
James
Gisborne Boys' HS, HSOB, Poverty Bay, Univ,
Wellington, Auckland, NZ Univs, N Island.
b 5.3.31 Opotiki.
2nd five-eighth, 3-1-0-2.
53 W−; 54 I+ F−.
Clerk/customs agent. NZ > 51 A, 53-4 BI,F &
NAm.

FITZPATRICK, Michael Patrick　　*Ireland*
St Paul's Coll, Trin Coll Dublin, Wanderers.
b 25.11.50 Dublin.
Prop, 10-3-1-6.
78 S+; 80 S+ F− W+; 81 F− W− E− S− A−;
85 F=r.
Market research exec.

FLANAGAN, Peter　　　　　*Australia*
St Joseph's Coll, Qld.
b 1886 Dublin; *d* 52 California, US.
Forward, 2-0-0-2.
07 NZ− NZ−.

FLEMING, Charles James Nicol　　*Scotland*
Fettes Coll, Oxford Univ, Edinburgh W.
b 5.4.1868; *d* 13.11.48.
Back, 3-2-1-0 (3 − 1t).
1896 I= E+(1t); 1897 I+.
Inspector of schools. Blue 1888-90. Pres SRU
11.

FLEMING, G.R.　　　　　　*Scotland*
Glasgow Acad, Glasgow Academicals.
Forward, 2-0-1-1.
1875 E=; 1876 E−.
Pres SRU 1878-9. Ref S v E 1879.

FLEMING, John Kingsley　　*New Zealand*
Auckland GS, Grammar, NZ Colts, Marist-St
Pat's, NZ Jnrs, Wellington, Marist, Waikato, N
Island.
b 2.5.53 Auckland.
Lock, 5-3-0-2 (4 − 1t).
79 S+ E+(1t); 80 A− A+ A−.
Contractor/farmer. NZ > 78 BI, 79 A, 79 E,S &
It, 80 A & Fj. NZ (2) v Arg 79. Broke ankle in
1st match for Waikato 80.

FLETCHER, Charles John　　*New Zealand*
Compton
Waimauku Sch, King's Coll, Coll Rifles,
Auckland, Waimauku, N Auckland, N Island.
b 9.5.1894 Rewiti; *d* 9.9.73 Auckland.
No 8, 1-0-1-0.
21 SA=.
Farmer. Inj in NZ before tour, did not play NZ
> 20 A. Bro Bert rep N Auckland 21-30.

FLETCHER, Hugh Nethersole　　*Scotland*
Charterhouse Sch, Edinburgh Univ.
b 27.4.1877; *d* −.
Forward, 2-1-0-1.
04 E+; 05 W−.
Medicine.

FLETCHER, Nigel Corbet OBE　　*England*
Merchant Taylors' Sch, Cambridge Univ, OMT,
Univ Coll Hosp, Barbarians, Mdx.
b 3.8.1877 London; *d* 21.12.51 Hampstead.
Forward, 4-0-0-4.
01 W− I− S−; 03 S−.
Medicine. Blue 1897-9. Asst Surg-in-Ch St John
Ambulance Bde.

FLETCHER, Thomas　　　　　*England*
Northside Council Sch, Seaton.
b 1874 Seaton, Cumberland; *d* 28.8.50 High
Harrington.
Wing, 1-0-0-1.
1897 W−.
Tobacconist/quarrymaster. Seaton RL 97.

FLETCHER, William Robert   *England*
Badger
Marlborough Coll, Oxford Univ, Blackheath,
Marlborough Nomads.
b 10.12.1851; *d* 20.4.1895 London.
Forward, 2-0-2-0.
1873 S=; 1875 S=.
Merchant. Blue 1871,3,4.

FLETCHER, W.W.   *Ireland*
Kingstown.
Half-back, 3-0-0-3.
1882 W− S−; 1883 E−.

FLETT, Andrew Binny   *Scotland*
The Leys Sch, Edinburgh Univ.
b 1875; *d* −.
Forward, 5-3-0-2 (5 − 1t 1c).
01 W+(1t 1c) I+ E+; 02 W− I−.
Medicine. Pres SRU 07-8; sec & treasurer 14.

FLOOD, Robert Stanislaus   *Ireland*
('Tamsy')
Belvedere Coll, Trin Coll Dublin.
b 03; *d* 22.4.55.
No 8, 1-1-0-0.
25 W+.
Licensed vintner.

FLYNN, James P.   *Australia*
St Joseph's Coll, Qld.
b 18.6.1894; *d* −.
Centre, 2-0-0-2.
14 NZ− NZ−.
Brewery dir. Capt Qld v NZ 14.

FLYNN, Michael Kevin   *Ireland*
Terenure Coll, Wanderers, Barbarians.
b 20.3.39 Dublin.
Centre, 22-7-4-11 (13 − 4t).
59 F+; 60 F−; 62 E− S− F− W=; 64 E+(2t)
S− W− F−; 65 F= E+ S+ W−(1t) SA−; 66
F− E= S−; 72 F+ E+(1t) F+; 73 NZ=.
Insurance. Int career spanned 15 yrs.

FOGARTY, John Raymond   *Australia*
Patrick
Qld.
b 29.
Wing, 2-1-1-0 (3 − 1t).
49 M=(1t) M+.

FOGARTY, Richard MM   *New Zealand*
Union, Otago, Hawera, Auckland, Coll Rifles,
Taranaki, Comb Servs.
b 12.12.1891 Matakanui; *d* 9.9.80 Dunedin.
No 8/hooker, 2-1-1-0.
21 SA+ SA=.
Carpenter. Served WW1, NZ Rifle Bde. NZ
Army team in King's Cup & > SA 19. Oldest
All Black at time of his death.

FOGARTY, Thomas   *Ireland*
Garryowen.
Forward, 1-0-0-1.
1891 W−.

FOLEY, Brendan Oliver   *Ireland*
St Mary's CBS Limerick, Shannon.
b 6.8.50 Limerick.
Lock, 11-2-0-9.
76 F− E+; 77 W−r; 80 F− W+; 81 F− E− S−
SA− SA− A−.
Rep/licensee. I > 81 SA.

FOOKES, Ernest Faber   *England*
New Plymouth Boys HS (NZ), Heath GS,
Owen's Coll Manchester, Manchester Univ,
Halifax, Sowerby Bridge, Yorks, Taranaki,
Tukapa, Taranaki-Wanganui-Manawatu.
b 31.5.1874 Wairoa, NZ; *d* 3.3.48 New
Plymouth, NZ.
Wing, 10-3-0-7 (15 − 5t).
1896 W+(2t) I− S−; 1897 W− I− S+(1t); 1898
I− W+(2t); 1899 I− S−.
Medicine. NZ-born, went to E to study. When
Halifax helped form NU 1895, switched to
Sowerby Bridge. Returned NZ 1900. Sel NZ >
05 BI, could not travel. Pres Taranaki RFU 33.
3 sons played 1st class rugby, Ken in NZ Trials
34.

FORBES, Colin Francis   *Australia*
St Joseph's Coll, Qld.
b 32.
Flanker/prop, 6-2-0-4.
53 SA+ SA− SA−; 54 Fj+; 56 SA− SA−.
Banking.

FORBES, H.H.   *South Africa*
Transvaal.
1-0-0-1.
1896 BT−.
Mining.

FORBES, John Lockhart   *Scotland*
George Watson's Coll, Watsonians.
b 11.4.1883 Edinburgh; *d* 10.2.67.
Centre, 3-1-0-2.
05 W−; 06 I+ E−.
Horticulturalist.

FORBES, R.E.   *Ireland*
RBAI, Malone.
b 11.12.1880; *d* −.
Forward, 1-1-0-0.
07 E+.

FORD, Brian Robert   *New Zealand*
Rangiora HS, Kaikoura, Shirley, Canterbury,
Marlborough, S Island.
b 10.7.51 Kaikoura.
Wing, 4-4-0-0.

77 BI+ BI+; 78 I+; 79 E+.
Crushing & cartage contractor. NZ > 77 F, 78
BI (4 apps only), 79 E,S & It. NZ (2) v Arg 79.
High-class sprinter, inc 10.7s 100m, 21.9s 200m.

FORD, Brian William　　　　　*Australia*
St Columba's, Qld.
b 39.
Wing, 1-0-0-1.
57 NZ−.
Co dir.

FORD, Drummond St Clair　　　　*Scotland*
RNC Pangbourne, US Portsmouth, Barbarians,
RN.
b 16.12.07; kia 12.12.42.
Wing, 5-1-1-3 (6 − 2t).
30 I−(1t) E=; 31 E+(1t); 32 W− I−.
RN.

FORD, Eric Exell　　　　　　*Australia*
St Joseph's Coll, NSW.
b 2.6.04; *d* 83.
Wing, 2-2-0-0.
29 NZ+ NZ+.
Civil service. Bro of John. NSW > BI & F 27-8.

FORD, Frederick John Vivian　　　*Wales*
Welch Rgt, Newport, The Army, Harlequins.
b 13.10.17 Redcar.
Wing, 1-0-0-1.
39 E−.
The Army/school administrator, Imperial
Service College. Maj in Welch Rgt.

FORD, Ian G.　　　　　　　*Wales*
Newport, Barbarians.
b 29.
Lock, 2-1-0-1.
59 E+ S−.
Market gardener/plant scientist. Son Roger
played for London Welsh 83-86.

FORD, James Robert　　　　　*Scotland*
Gala.
Forward, 1-0-1-0.
1893 I=.
Builder.

FORD, John Alfred ('Jack')　　　*Australia*
St Joseph's Coll, NSW.
b 17.2.06; *d* 20.2.85.
Flanker/no 8, 4-4-0-0 (6 − 2t).
29 NZ+ NZ+(1t) NZ+(1t); 30 BI+.
Brewery rep. Bro of Eric. NSW > 27 BI, F; sent
off v Cardiff 3.12.27.

FORD, Peter John　　　　　*England*
Central Mod Sch Gloucester, Gloucester, RAF,
Barbarians, Glos.
b 2.5.32.

Flanker, 4-1-1-2.
64 W= I− F+ S−.
Wholesale fruit merchant. RFU sel.

FORESTIER, Jacques　　　　　*France*
SCUF.
b 1890; *d* 27.3.78 Paris.
Flanker, 1-0-0-1.
12 W−.
Medicine.

FORGUES, Fernand　　　　　*France*
Bayonne.
b 30.11.1884 Pau; *d* 12.4.77 Bayonne.
Lock/prop, 11-1-0-10.
11 S+ E− W−; 12 I− W− E−; 13 S− SA−
W−; 14 I− E−.
Garage proprietor. FFR selector. One of F's
longest lived players.

FORMAN, Terrence Robert　　　*Australia*
NSW.
b 12.1.48.
Wing, 7-0-0-7 (3 − 1t).
68 I− S−; 69 W− SA−(1t) SA− SA− SA−.
Min of agric.

FORREST, A.J.　　　　　　*Ireland*
Cheltenham Coll, Wanderers, Leeds St Johns,
Yorks.
b 13.10.1859 Dublin; *d* 13.7.36 Thorp Arch,
Glos.
Forward, 7-1-1-5 (1t).
1880 E− S−; 1881 E− S+; 1882 W− E=; 1883
E−(1t).
Land agent.

FORREST, Edward G.　　　　*Ireland*
Reading Sch, King William's Coll IOM,
Wanderers.
b.5.10.1870 Dublin; *d* −.
Forward, 13-5-1-7 (4 − 1d).
1888 NZN−; 1889 S− W+; 1890 S− E−; 1891
E−; 1893 S=; 1894 E+(1d) S+ W+; 1895 W−;
1897 F+ S−
Medicine. Played with bro H. Forrest v S 1893.

FORREST, H.　　　　　　*Ireland*
Coleraine AI, King William's Coll IOM,
Cheltenham Coll, Wanderers.
b 4.2.1864; *d* −.
Forward, 2-0-1-1.
1893 S= W−.
Bus. Played with bro Edward v S 1893.

FORREST, James Edmiston　　　*Scotland*
Sedbergh Sch, Glasgow Acad, Glasgow
Academicals, TA, Barbarians.
b 3.2.07; *d* 2.4.81.
Wing, 3-1-0-2.

32 SA−; 35 E+ NZ−.
Timber.

FORREST, John Gordon Scott *Scotland*
Strathallan Sch, Cambridge Univ, RN,
Barbarians.
b 28.4.17; kia −.9.42.
Wing, 3-3-0-0 (6 − 2t).
38 W+ I+(2t) E+.
RN. Blue 36-8.

FORREST, J.W. *England*
US Portsmouth, RN, Comb Servs, Hants.
Lock, 10-4-2-4 (2 − 1c).
30 W+ I− F+ S=; 31 W= I− S− F−(1c); 34 I+
S+.
RN. Capt of RN 32-5.

FORREST, Reginald *England*
Christ's Coll Blackheath, Blackheath,
Wellington, Taunton, Barbarians, Som.
b 12.5.1878 Bristol; *d* 11.4.03 Minehead.
Wing, 6-2-1-3 (3 − 1t).
1899 W−; 1900 S=; 02 I+ S+; 03 I− S−(1t).
Electrical engr. Died of typhoid fever
contracted during E's visit to Dublin 14.2.03.

FORREST, Walter Torrie MC *Scotland*
Kelso HS, Hawick, Kelso.
b 14.11.1880 Kelso; kia 19.4.17 Gaza,
Palestine.
FB, 8-5-0-3 (2 − 1c).
03 W+ I+ E+; 04 W− I+ E+; 05 W− I−(1c).
Maj in KOSB. Mentioned in despatches & MC.

FORSAYTH, Hector Henry *Scotland*
King's Sch Parramatta, Oxford Univ,
Barbarians.
b 18.12.1899 Sydney; *d* 7.3.52 Gladstone, Qld.
FB, 7-2-1-4.
21 F− W+ I− E−; 22 W= I+ E−.
Stockbroker. Blue 21.

FORSYTH, Ian William *Scotland*
Stewart's Coll, Stewart's Coll FP, Barbarians.
b 4.7.46 Edinburgh.
Centre, 6-3-0-3 (4 − 1t).
72 NZ−; 73 F− W+ I+(1t) E− P+.
Chartered accountant/investment analyst.

FORSYTH, J. *Scotland*
Edinburgh Univ.
Forward, 1-1-0-0.
1871 E+.
Played in 1st int, S v E 1871.

FORT, Jacques *France*
Agen.
b 16.1.38 Bordeaux.
Lock/prop, 7-4-1-2.

67 It+ W+ I+ SA− SA− SA+ SA=.
Sheet-iron works mgr.

FORTUNE, John Joseph *Ireland*
St Joseph's CBS Fairview, Clontarf.
b 1.12.33 Dublin.
Wing, 2-0-0-2.
63 NZ−; 64 E−.
Purchasing official Electricity Supply Bd.

FORWARD, Allen *Wales*
Pontypool, Mon Police, Barbarians.
Flanker, 6-4-0-2.
51 S− SA−; 52 E+ S+ I+ F+.
Police.

FOSTER, Alexander Roulston *Ireland*
Foyle Coll, Queen's Coll Belfast, Derry.
b 22.6.1890 Londonderry; *d* 24.8.72.
Wing/centre, 17-9-1-7 (12 − 4t).
10 E= S− F+; 11 E+ S+(1t) W− F+; 12
F+(1t) E− S+(1t) W+; 14 E− S+ W−(1t); 21
E− S+ W−; BI > 10 SA 3-1-0-2.
HM. Played either side WW1.

FOSTER, R.A. *Scotland*
Wilton Sch, Hawick.
b 7.12.07.
Prop, 4-1-0-3.
30 W+; 32 SA− I− E−.

FOULDS, Robert Thompson *England*
King William's Coll IOM, Birmingham,
Furness, Moseley, Waterloo, Barbarians, N
Midlands, Lancs.
b 27.4.06.
Prop/no 8, 2-1-0-1.
29 W+ I−.
Wholesale meat co dir.

FOURCADE, Georges *France*
BEC.
Prop, 2-0-0-2.
09 E− W−.
Medicine.

FOURES, Henri *France*
Toulouse.
b 29.8.25 Issus.
Lock, 4-3-0-1.
51 S+ I− E+ W+.
Asst mgr F > 68 NZ, A; 74 Arg.

FOURIE, Carel *South Africa*
E Prov.
b 1.8.50 Uitenhage.
Wing, 4-4-0-0 (10 − 1t 2p).
74 F+ F+; 75 F+ F+(1t 1p).
Schoolmaster. Bro of Polla.

FOURIE, Theodorus Thenuis *South Africa*
('Polla')
SE Transvaal.
b 19.7.45 Uitenhage.
Flanker, 1-0-0-1.
74 BI−.
Bro of Carel. SA > 74 F.

FOURIE, Willem L. ('Lofty') *South Africa*
Oudtshoorn HS, SW Africa.
b 23.7.36 Oudtshoorn.
Wing, 2-0-1-1 (3 − 1t).
58 F= F−(1t).
Schoolmaster/brewery rep.

FOURNET, Franck *France*
Montferrand.
b 26.11.22 Clermont Ferrand; *d* −.7.82.
FH, 1-0-0-1.
50 W−.

FOUROUX, Jacques *France*
La Voulte, Auch.
b 24.7.47 Auch.
SH, 27-17-3-7 (20 − 5t).
72 I− R+; 74 W= E= Arg+(1t) Arg+ R−
SA− SA−; 75 W− Arg+(1t) R+(1t); 76 S+
I+(1t) W− E+(1t) US+ A+; 77 W+ E+ S+
I+ Arg+ Arg= NZ+ NZ− R+.
Technician. Jt capt F > 75 SA. Asst mgr F > 85
Arg. Coach F > 81 A. FFR coach 85-6.

FOWLER, Isaac John ('Ike') *Wales*
Tycroes, Llanelli.
b 27.8.1894 Pantyffynnon; *d* 17.6.81 Batley.
SH, 1-0-0-1.
19 NZA−.
Miner/textile pattern cutter. WW1 ints. Batley
RL 19 £250 fee. Wales RL 26. Touch-judge RL
Cup Final 35. Received WRU cap 75.

FOWLER, Frank Dashwood *England*
Cheltenham Coll, RIE Coll, Manchester,
Lancs.
b 16.8.1855; *d* −.
Forward, 2-0-2-0.
1878 S=; 1879 S=.
Engr. Oarsman at RIE Coll. Public Works dept
of India 1878. Sec for Rlys to Govt of India,
Madras 08.

FOWLER, Howard *England*
Clifton Coll, Oxford Univ, Walthamstow,
Blackheath, Mdx.
b 20.10.1857 Tottenham; *d* 6.5.34 Burnham on
Sea.
Forward, 3-1-2-0.
1878 S=; 1881 W+ S=.
Barrister. Blue 1877-8. Ckt blue 1877,9,80; also
played for Essex CCC. Skilled golfer and
billiards player. Called to Bar 1883.

FOWLER, R. Henry *England*
Leeds.
Forward, 1-1-0-0.
1877 I+.
His club, Leeds, helped form NU 1895.

FOX, Francis Hugh JP *England*
Marlborough Coll, Marlborough Nomads,
Wellington, Som, Barbarians.
b 12.6.1863 Wellington; *d* 28.5.52.
Half-back, 2-1-0-1.
1890 W− S+.
Manufacturer. Capped in 1888 E side that did
not play. Sec & treasurer of Som 1883-91. IB
mem 01. Pres RFU 1900-2.

FOX, Grant James *New Zealand*
Auckland GS, NZ Schs, NZ Colts, NZ Univs,
NZ Jnrs, N Island, Auckland.
b 6.6.62 New Plymouth.
1st five-eighth, 1-1-0-0 (3 − 1d).
85 Arg+(1d).
NZ > 85 Arg. World XV > SA 86.

FOX, John *Scotland*
Gala.
b 30.8.21.
Prop/hooker, 4-0-0-4.
52 F− W− I− E−.
Wine & whisky blender.

FOX, Otto George ('Tony') *Australia*
Sydney GS, NSW.
b 34.
Centre, 1-0-0-1.
58 F−.
Bank clerk.

FRAME, John Neil Munro *Scotland*
Glenalmond Acad, Scottish Schs, Edinburgh
Univ, Scottish Univs, Gala, N Midlands.
b 8.10.46 Edinburgh.
Centre, 23-7-0-16 (13 − 4t).
67 NZ−, 68 F− W I E ; 69 W I− E−
SA+; 70 F− W− I− E+ A−; 71 F− W− I−(1t)
E+ E+(2t); 72 F+(1t) W E I ; 73 P+r.
Stockbroker.

FRANCE, C. *Scotland*
Kelvinside Acad, Kelvinside Academicals.
Wing, 1-1-0-0.
03 I+.

FRANCIS, Arthur Reginald Howe *New Zealand*
('Bolla')
Auckland GS, Ponsonby, Auckland, N Island.
b 8.6.1882 Wanganui; *d* 15.6.57 Takapuna.
Lock/flanker, 10-7-2-1 (16 − 3t 2c 1p).
05 A+(1c); 07 A+(1t) A+(1t) A=; 08
AW+(1c) AW=(1p) AW+(1t); 10 A+ A−
A+.

Engr. NZ > 05, 07 & 10 A. RL in BI: Newton Rangers 11; later Wigan & Hull (E). Won RL Cup Final medal. Returned to NZ & reinstated by NZRFU. Coach Grammar club 30-5. Bro-in-law of Dave Gallaher.

FRANCIS, David Gwyn   *Wales*
Gowerton GS, UC Cardiff, Llanelli, Oxford Univ, London Welsh, Leicester, Surrey, London Cos.
b 2.2.1896 Gorseinon.
Lock/flanker, 2-0-0-2.
19 NZA−; 24 S−.
Schoolmaster. Blue 19. Ref. Served WW1, Staff Sgt, R Welsh Fusiliers.

FRANCIS, Eric   *Australia*
Ipswich GS Qld, Qld.
b 17.6.1894.
Wing, 2-0-0-2.
14 NZ− NZ−.
Schoolmaster. Believed to be A's oldest living int.

FRANCIS, Joseph A.J.   *South Africa*
Transvaal.
b 1888; *d* −.1.25 Johannesburg.
Prop, 5-5-0-0 (6 − 2t).
12 S+ I+(1t) W+; 13 E+ F+(1t).
Mining. SA > 12-13 BI, F.

FRANCIS, Thomas Egerton   *England*
Seymour ('Tim') OBE
Tonbridge Sch, Cambridge Univ, Blackheath, Som, Transvaal.
b 21.11.02 SA; *d* 24.2.69 Bulawayo.
Centre, 4-1-1-2 (8 − 4c).
26 W= I−(3c) F+(1c) S−.
Co dir. Blue 22-5. Played for Transvaal 26. Ckt blue 25; also played for Som CCC. Served WW2, reached rank of Lt Col. OBE 65.

FRANCIS, William Charles   *New Zealand*
New Plymouth Convent Sch, Tukapa, Wellington Club, Oriental, Wellington, N Island.
b 4.2.1894 New Plymouth.
Hooker, 5-4-0-1 (6 − 2t).
13 A+ A−; 14 A+ A+ A+(2t).
Plumber/Army. Cousin of Nelson Ball. NZ > 14 A; youngest ever forward to rep NZ, 18yrs 7mths.

FRANKCOM, Geoffrey Peter   *England*
KES Bath, Cambridge Univ, Bedford, Headingley, Bath, RAF, Barbarians, Som.
b 5.4.42 Bath.
Centre, 4-1-1-2.
65 W− I− F+ S=.
Schoolmaster/RAF. Blue 61,3,4. Over 100 apps

for Bath. Taught at Bedford Sch 65-7. Served in RAF, Ft Lt Strike Command 67.

FRANKS, James Gordon   *Ireland*
Clifton Coll, Trin Coll Dublin, Monkstown, Barbarians.
b 1878; *d* −.11.41.
Forward, 3-1-0-2.
1898 E+ S− W−.
Solicitor.

FRANQUENELLE, André ('Le   *France*
Sioux')
SCV.
b 15.8.1889 Rochefort-sur-Mer; *d* −.
Centre, 3-1-0-2.
11 S+; 13 W− I−.
Army/sports organiser.

FRASER, Bernard Garfield   *New Zealand*
St Paul's Coll Auckland, Marist Hutt Valley, Wellington, N Island.
b 21.7.53 Lautoka, Fiji.
Wing, 23-17-1-5 (24 − 6t).
79 S+ E+; 80 A−(1t) W+(1t); 81 S+ S+ SA+ SA− SA+ R+ F+ F+; 82 A+(1t) A−(1t) A+; 83 BI+ BI+ BI+ BI+ A+ S=(2t) E−; 84 A−.
Truck driver. NZ (2) v Arg 79. NZ > 79 E,S & It, 80 A & Fj (16t), NAm & W, 81 R & F, 83 & 84 A; 83 S & E. World XV > 86 SA. Wrote (with Stu Wilson) 'Ebony & Ivory. The Stu Wilson, Bernie Fraser Story' pub 84.

FRASER, C.F.P.   *Scotland*
Glasgow Univ.
Half-back, 2-1-0-1.
1888 W−; 1889 W+.

FRASER, Sir Edward Cleather   *England*
CMG
Blackheath Proprietary Sch, Oxford Univ, Blackheath.
b 1853; *d* 15.10.27.
Forward, 1-1-0-0.
1875 I+.
Business/Council of Govt Mauritius. Blue 1872-5. CMG 12.

FRASER, George   *England*
Godolphin Sch Hammersmith, Richmond, Barbarians, Surrey, Mdx.
b −.8.1878; *d* 20.8.50.
Forward, 5-2-0-3.
02 W− I+ S+; 03 W− I−.
Mem of Stock Exchange 04-49.

FRASER, James William   *Scotland*
Edinburgh Inst, Edinburgh Inst FP, Edinburgh Univ.
Forward, 1-0-1-0.

1881 E=.
Medicine. In practice in Yorks.

FRASER, Rowland   *Scotland*
Merchiston Castle Sch, Edinburgh Univ,
Cambridge Univ.
b 10.1.1890 Perth; kia 1.7.16 The Somme.
Hooker/prop, 4-0-0-4.
11 F− W− I− E−.
Blue 08-10. Served WW1, Capt Rifle Brigade.
Perthshire CCC.

FRAZER, Edward Fitzgerald   *Ireland*
Bective Rgrs.
b 1869; *d* −.9.43.
Forward, 2-0-0-2.
1891 S−; 1892 S−.
Medicine. I jersey in Bective clubhouse.

FRAZER, Harry Frederick   *New Zealand*
Napier Boys' HS, Pirates, Hawkes Bay, Army,
Auckland, RNZAF, Comb Servs, N Island.
b 21.4.16 Wanganui.
Prop/lock, 5-4-0-1 (3 − 1t).
46 A+ A+; 47 A+(1t) A+; 49 SA−.
Carpenter. NZ > 47 A, 49 SA. Coach, pres
Pirates club. Rec includes penalty t v A 47.

FREAKES, Hubert Dainton   *England*
Maritzburg Coll SA, Rhodes Univ, Oxford
Univ, Harlequins, Barbarians.
b 2.2.14; kia −.3.42 England.
FB, 3-1-0-2 (2 − 1c).
38 W−(1c); 39 W+ I−.
Business/RAF. Rhodes Scholar. Blue 36-8 (capt
38). Ath blue 38. In business in Johannesburg
39-40. Served WW2, Fg Off in RAF.

FREDERICKSON, Cornelius   *South Africa*
Abraham ('Ringo')
Transvaal.
b 17.8.50 Lichtenburg.
Hooker, 3 2 0 1.
74 BI−; 80 SAm+ SAm+.

FREEAR, Arthur Edward   *Ireland*
Lansdowne, Aberavon, Swansea.
Wing, 3-1-0-2 (3 − 1t).
01 E+ S− W−(1t).
Licensee. Played in W 02-4. Hull RL 04.

FREEDMAN, John Edward   *Australia*
Canterbury HS, NSW.
b 25.6.35.
Prop, 4-0-1-3.
62 NZ= NZ− NZ−; 63 SA−.
Bank official. Mgr A > W & E 73. Sailed in 3
America's Cup Challenge crews for Australia.

FREEMAN, Eric   *Australia*
NSW.
b 22.
Flanker, 2-0-0-2.
46 NZ−r M−.
Real estate.

FREEMAN, Harold   *England*
Marlborough Coll, Oxford Univ, Marlborough
Nomads.
b 15.1.1850; *d* 15.7.16 London.
Back, 3-2-1-0 (2d).
1872 S+(1d); 1873 S=; 1874 S+(1d).
E's lst d, v S 1872. Mem of 1st OURFC comm
1869.

FREMAUX, André   *France*
PUC.
b 6.11.28 Paris.
Centre, 1-0-1-0.
58 SA=r.

FRENCH, J.   *Scotland*
Glasgow Acad, Glasgow Academicals.
Forward, 4-3-1-0.
1886 W+; 1887 I+ W+ E=.

FRENCH, Raymond James   *England*
Cowley Sch, Leeds Univ, St Helens, Barbarians,
Lancs.
b 23.12.39 St Helens.
Lock, 4-1-1-2.
61 W− I− F= S+.
Schoolmaster/TV commentator. St Helens RL
61-8; also v-capt GB in World Cup 68.

FRENEY, Michael Ernest   *Australia*
Nudgee Coll Brisbane, Qld.
b 10.5.48.
Hooker, 6-1-0-5.
72 NZ− NZ− NZ−; 73 Tg+ W− E−r.
Law/insurance.

FREW, Alexander   *Scotland/South Africa*
Edinburgh Univ, Transvaal.
b Kilmarnock, Scotland; *d* −.4.47.
Scotland
Forward 3-3-0-0.
01 W+ I+ E+.
South Africa
Front row, 1-0-1-0 (3 − 1t).
03 BT=(1t).
Medicine. At Edinburgh Univ 01; mem of
Scotland's Triple Crown side 01, under capt
Mark Morrison. Played v Morrison when capt
SA v BT 1st Test 03.

FREW, George M.   *Scotland*
Glasgow HS, Glasgow HSFP.
b 9.9.1883 Larkhall; *d* −.
Forward, 15-9-0-6 (3 − 1t).

06 SA+; 07 W+ I+(1t) E+; 08 W− I− E+; 09 W− I+ E+; 10 F+ W− I+; 11 I− E−.

FRIEBE, John Percy *Scotland*
Glasgow HS, Glasgow HSFP.
b 9.5.31.
No 8, 1-0-0-1.
52 E−.
Chartered accountant.

FRONEMAN, Dirk Cornelius *South Africa*
OFS.
b 14.4.54 Wynburg.
1-1-0-0.
77 Wd+.
Army.

FRONEMAN, Innes Lyndon *South Africa*
('Fronie')
Border.
b 18.12.07.
Flanker, 1-1-0-0.
33 A+.

FRY, Henry Arthur TD *England*
Liverpool Coll, Liverpool, Fylde, Waterloo, Rosslyn Pk, The Army, Barbarians, Lancs.
b 22.12.10; d 3.1.77 Formby.
Flanker, 3-3-0-0 (6 − 2t).
34 W+ I+(2t) S+.
Solicitor. Served WW2, reached rank of Lt Col. TD 46.

FRY, Stephen Perry *South Africa*
Cape Town Univ, W Prov.
b 14.7.24.
Flanker, 13-10-0-3.
51 S+ I+ W+; 52 E+ F+; 53 A+ A− A+ A+; 55 BI− BI+ BI− BI+.
Engr. SA > 51-2 BI, F. Capt SA v BI (4) 55. Bro of Dennis SA 51-2 (no Tests).

FRY, Thomas William *England*
Queen's House.
FB, 3-3-0-0 (1t).
1880 I+ S+(1t); 1881 W+.
E's 1st sole FB, v S 1880. Queen's House Club (dissolved 1883) was part of Royal palace at Greenwich. Emigrated to Can.

FRYER, Frank Cunningham *New Zealand*
Christ's Coll, Christchurch, Canterbury, S Island.
b 2.11.1886 Riccarton; d 22.9.58 Hastings.
Wing, 4-2-2-0.
07 A+ A+ A=; 08 AW=.
Dentist. NZ > 07 A. Ckt for Hawkes Bay. NZGA amateur foursomes winner 27; NZGA pres 54.

FULLER, Herbert George *England*
Christ's Coll Finchley, Cambridge Univ, Bath, Som.
b 4.10.1856 Finchley; d 2.1.1896 Streatham.
Forward, 6-4-1-1.
1882 I= S− W+; 1883 I+ S+; 1884 W+.
Univ employee. Won rec 6 blues 1878-83; CURFC rules thereafter (1886-72) altered, to stop 5th yr students from playing in Univ Match. Abroad 1884-6; returned to be elected Pres CURFC 1885.

FULLER, William Bennett *New Zealand*
Merivale, Canterbury, S Island.
b 9.4.1883 Christchurch; d 25.7.57 Christchurch.
2nd, 1st five-eighth, 2-1-0-1 (3 − 1t).
10 A+(1t) A−.
Rly workshops employee. NZ > 10 A. Ref Wellington v BI 30.

FULTON, Adam Kelso *Scotland*
Dollar Acad, Edinburgh Univ, Dollar Academicals, RAMC.
b 29.
SH, 2-0-0-2.
52 F−; 54 F−.
Medicine.

FULTON, John *Ireland*
Methodist Coll Belfast, NIFC.
b 1871; d 17.4.48 Portrush.
FB, 16-6-0-10.
1895 S− W−; 1896 E+; 1897 E+; 1898 W−; 1899 E+; 1900 W−; 01 E+; 02 E− S+ W−; 03 E+ S− W−; 04 E− S−.
Woollen mills co mgr.

FURCADE, Roger *France*
Perpignan.
b 22.1.28 St Nazaire.
FH, 1-1-0-0.
52 S+.

FURLONG, Blair Donald Marie *New Zealand*
Dannevirke HS, Marist, Hawkes Bay, Wellington, Kawerau Utd, Bay of Plenty.
b 10.3.45 Dannevirke.
1st five-eighth, 1-0-0-1.
70 SA−.
Co mgr. NZ > 70 A (7c 1p v WA) & SA. Leading administrator. Central Districts ckt 65-70.

FURNESS, Donald Charles *Australia*
NSW.
No 8, 1-0-0-1.
46 M−.
Banking/bookmaking. Ar > NZ 46. Ref A v Fj (2) 52 & A v Fj 54.

FUTTER, Francis Cuthbert　　　　　*Australia*
King's Sch Paramatta, NSW.
b −; *d* 13.11.41.
Centre, 1-0-0-1.
04 BT−.
Mining engr/grazier.

FYFE, Kenneth Carmichael　　　　　*Scotland*
Oundle Sch, Cambridge Univ, Sale, London
Scottish, Barbarians.
b −; *d* −.2.74 Johannesburg.
Wing, 10-3-0-7 (25 − 3t 5c 2p).
33 W+(1c 1p) E+(1t); 34 E−; 35 W− I−(1c)
E+(1t 2c) NZ−(1t); 36 W− E−(1c 1p); 39 I−.
Blue 32-5. Capt Cambridge Univ v NZ 35.

G

GABE, Rhys Thomas　　　　　*Wales*
Llanelli Intermed Sch, Llanelli, Borough Road
Coll, London Welsh, Cardiff.
b 22.6.1880 Llangennech; *d* 15.9.67 Cardiff.
Wing/centre/extra back, 24-18-1-5 (33 − 11t).
01 I+; 02 E+(1t) S+(2t) I+; 03 E+ S− I+(1t);
04 E= S+(1t) I−(1t); 05 E+(1t) S+ I+ NZ+;
06 E+ I−(1t) SA−; 07 E+ S− I+(1t); 08
E+(2t) S+ F+ I+; BT > 04 A, NZ.
Schoolmaster. Played in 3 Triple Crown XVs.
'Marked' David Lloyd George when PM kicked
off at Cardiff v Blackheath 25.1.08.

GABERNET, Serge　　　　　*France*
Toulouse.
b 6.2.55 Montréjeau.
FB, 14-8-0-6 (48 − 2t 2c 1d 11p).
80 E− S−(1t 1p); 81 S+(1p) I+(1p) W+(1t 2p)
E+ A−(1c 1p) A− R+(2p) NZ−(1d) NZ−; 82
I+(1c 2p); 83 A+(1p) R+.
PE teacher. F > 80 SA.

GACHASSIN, Jean ('Peter Pan')　　　　　*France*
Lourdes.
b 23.12.41 Bagnères.
Wing/FH/centre/FB, 32-19-4-9 (32 − 8t 1c 2d).
61 S+ I+(1t); 63 R=(1t); 64 S− NZ− E− W=
It+ I+ SA+ Fj+ R+(1t); 65 S+(1t) I= E− W+
It+ R+; 66 S= I+ E+(1t) W−; 67 S−(1c) A+
It+(2t) W+ I+ NZ−(1d) 68 I+(1d) E+(1t); 69
S− I−.
Schoolmaster.

GADNEY, Bernard C.　　　　　*England*
Dragon Sch Oxford, Stowe Sch, Richmond,
Leicester, Headingley, Barbarians, Leics, E
Midlands, Oxon, Yorks.
b 16.7.09 Oxford.
SH, 14-9-1-4 (3 − 1t).
32 I+ S+; 33 I+(1t) S−; 34 W+ I+ S+; 35 S−;
36 NZ+ W= I− S+; 37 S+; 38 W−.

HM. Bro of Cyril Gadney (Pres RFU 62-3). BT
> 36 Arg. Served WW2 RNVR.

GAFFIKIN, W.　　　　　*Ireland*
RBAI, Windsor.
Forward, 1-0-0-1.
1875 E−.

GAGE, John H.　　　　　*Ireland/South Africa*
('Jack') MC
Queen's Univ Belfast, OFS.
b 2.4.07 Worcester, Cape Prov.
Ireland
Wing, 4-3-0-1 (3 − 1t).
26 S+(1t) W−; 27 S+ W+.
South Africa
Wing, 1-1-0-0.
33 A+.
Government official/journalist/life insurance
agent. Served WW2. MC 44.

GAINSFORD, John L.　　　　　*South Africa*
Lansdown HS Cape Town, W Prov.
b 4.8.38.
Centre, 33-18-3-12 (24 − 8t).
60 S+ NZ+ NZ− NZ=(2t) NZ+ W+ I+(1t);
61 E+ S+ F= A+(1t) A+; 62 BI=(1t) BI+
BI+ BI+(1t); 63 A+ A− A− A+(1t); 64 W+
F−; 65 I− S− A− A−(1t) NZ− NZ− NZ+
NZ−; 67 F+ F+ F−.
Insurance inspector/wine trade. SA's most
capped centre. 10 centre apps with A.I.
Kirkpatrick. 71 apps for SA. Most t for SA (with
J.P. Engelbrecht) v IB countries. SA > 60-1 BI,
F.

GALAU, Henri　　　　　*France*
Toulouse.
b 17.7.1897 Villefranche de Conflans; *d* 1.2.50.
FH, 5-1-0-4 (6 − 2t).
24 S+(1t) I− E− W− US−(1t).

GALBRAITH, Edward　　　　　*Ireland*
Portora RS, Trin Coll Dublin.
Forward, 1-0-0-1.
1875 E−.
Bro of Richard.

GALBRAITH, Hugh Tener　　　　　*Ireland*
Derry AI, Belfast Acad.
Forward, 1-0-1-0.
1890 W=.
Medicine.

GALBRAITH, Richard　　　　　*Ireland*
Portora RS, Trin Coll Dublin.
Half-back/forward/FB, 3-0-0-3.
1875 E− E−; 1877 E−.
Bro of Edward.

GALE, Norman Reginald *Wales*
Gowerton GS, Gorseinon, Llanelli, Swansea.
b 24.7.39 Gorseinon.
Hooker, 25-12-3-10 (6 − 1t 1p).
60 I+; 63 E− S+ I− NZ−; 64 E= S+ I+ F=
SA−; 65 E+ S+(1t) I+ F−; 66 E+ S+ I− F+
A−; 67 E+ NZ−(1p); 68 E=; 69 NZ− NZ−
A+.
Fitter/licensee. Wales XV v Fj 64. W > 64 SA;
68 Arg; 69 NZ, A & Fj. Coach Llanelli 73-4.

GALIA, Jean *France*
Quillan, Villeneuve.
b 20.3.05 Ille-sur-Têt; d 18.1.49 Toulouse.
Lock, 20-9-0-11 (9 − 3t).
27 E+ G+(1t) G−; 28 S− NSW− I− E−(1t)
W+; 29 I− E− G+; 30 S+ I+ E− G+ W−; 31
S− W− E+(1t) G+.
Switched to RL.

GALLACHER, Ian Stuart *Wales*
Llanelli GS, Welsh Youth, Felinfoel, Llanelli,
Barbarians.
b 22.5.46 Llanelli.
Lock, 1-1-0-0.
70 F+.
Sales rep/police/co dir. Wales B v F 70.
Barbarians > 69 SA. Barbarians v SA 70.
Bradford N RL 70.

GALLAHER, David *New Zealand*
Katikati Sch, Parnell, Ponsonby, Auckland, N
Island.
b 30.10.1873 Ramelton, Ireland; d 4.10.17
Belgium.
Flanker, 6-5-0-1.
03 A+; 04 BT+; 05 S+ E+ W−; 06 F+.
Freezing works foreman. Went to NZ 1878. Jt
capt NZ > 05 A, capt 05-6 BI,F & NAm.
NZRFU sel 07-14. Bro-in-law of Bolla Francis.
Served Boer War & WW1; died of wounds
received at Passchendaele. Co-author with Billy
Stead of 'The Complete Rugby Footballer' pub
06. Auckland RU presented the Gallaher Shield
for clubs in his memory, 22.

GALLIE, George Holmes MC *Scotland*
Fettes Coll, Edinburgh Univ, Edinburgh
Academicals.
b 17.9.17; kia 16.1.44.
Prop, 1-0-0-1.
39 W−.
Son of R.A. Served WW2.

GALLIE, Robert Arthur MC *Scotland*
Glasgow Acad, Fettes Coll, Glasgow
Academicals.
b −.1.1893; d 25.5.48.
Hooker, 8-4-0-4.
20 F+ W+ I+ E−; 21 F− W+ I− E−.
Flour miller. Father of G.H.

GALLION, Jérôme *France*
Toulon.
b 4.4.55 Toulon.
SH, 26-15-4-7 (40 − 10t).
78 E+(1t) S+(1t) I+(1t) W−; 79 I= W+ E−
S+ NZ−(1t) R+; 80 W− E− S−(1t) I+; 83 A=
A+ R+(1t); 84 I+(1t) W+ E+(1t) S−(1t) R+;
85 E= S+ I= W+(1t).
Dentist. F Under 23s v E 78. F > 77 Arg; 80 SA.

GALY, Joseph *France*
Perpignan.
b 22.12.29 Bages.
Centre, 1-0-0-1.
53 W−.

GAMMELL, William Benjamin *Scotland*
Bowring
Fettes Coll, Edinburgh W, Stirling Univ.
b 29.12.52 Edinburgh.
Wing, 5-1-0-4 (8 − 2t).
77 I+(2t) F− W−; 78 W− E−.
Chartered accountant. Scottish XV v J 76, 77.

GAMLIN, Herbert Tremlett *England*
('Octopus')
Wellington Sch, Wellington, Devonport A,
Blackheath, Som.
b 12.2.1878 Wellington, Som; d 12.7.37
London.
FB, 15-4-2-9 (3 − 1p).
1899 W− S−; 1900 W− I+ S=; 01 S−; 02 W−
I+ S+; 03 W− I− S−; 04 W=(1p) I+ S−.
Civil service clerk. 6ft, 14st. Played for Som at
rugby & ckt from age of 16; his catch ended one
of the most remarkable innings in 1st class ckt,
dismissing A.C. MacLaren (son of RFU pres
James MacLaren) after the Lancs player had
scored 424 at Taunton 1895.

GANLY, James Blandford *Ireland*
St Columba's Coll, Trin Coll Dublin,
Monkstown, Barbarians.
b 7.3.04 Dublin; d −.7.76 Galway.
Wing, 12-7-0-5 (21 − 7t).
27 F+ E− S+(1t) W+(2t) NSW−; 28 F+(2t)
E− S+(1t) W+(1t); 29 F+ S−; 30 F−.
Cattle salesman. Ckt & lawn tennis for I. Killed
in shooting accident.

GARD, Philip Charles *New Zealand*
Kurow Dist HS, Kurow, N Otago, S Island.
b 20.11.47 Kurow.
2nd five-eighth, 1-0-1-0.
71 BI=.
Co rep. Bro Neville rep N Otago 62. Cousin
Ross rep Otago & NZ Univs; another cousin Ian
rep N Otago 77-80.

GARDINER, Ashley John *New Zealand*
New Plymouth Boys' HS, Tukapa, NZ Jnrs,

Taranaki, N Island.
b 10.12.46 New Plymouth.
Prop, 1-1-0-0.
74 A+.
Warehouse mgr. NZ > 74 A & Fj & I,W & E.

GARDINER, Ernest Robert *England*
Devonport Servs, RN, Devon.
b 6.10.1886 ?Wales; d 26.1.54.
Hooker, 10-8-1-1 (6 − 2t).
21 W+ I+ S+(1t); 22 W− I+(1t) F=; 23 W+
I+ S+ F+.
RN. His t v S 21 is credited to R. Edwards by
some sources.

GARDINER, Frederick *Ireland*
Lurgan Coll, NIFC, Barbarians.
b 31.5.1874 Armagh; d −.6.21.
Forward, 22-8-1-13 (10 − 2t 2c).
1900 E− S=; 01 E+(1t) W−; 02 E−(1t) S+
W−; 03 E+ W−; 04 E− S− W+; 06 E+(1c) S−
W+(1c); 07 S− W−; 08 S+ W−; 09 E− S− F+.
Linen manufacturer. Ref S v E 12.

GARDINER, James Burnett *Ireland*
Campbell Coll, NIFC, Rhodesia.
b 27.10.02; d 11.4.61 George, Cape Prov, SA.
SH/centre, 13-5-1-7.
23 E− S− W+ F−; 24 F+ E− S− W+ NZ−; 25
F+ E= S− W+.
Cattle rancher. Moved to Rhodesia.

GARDINER, S. *Ireland*
Belfast A.
FB, 2-0-1-1.
1893 E− S=.

GARDINER, William *Ireland*
Lurgan Coll, NIFC.
b −; d 21.3.24 Dungannon.
Wing/centre, 17-6-2-9 (6 − 2t).
1892 E− S−; 1893 E− S− W , 1894 E I S
W+; 1895 E− S− W−; 1896 E+ S= W+; 1897
E+(2t) S−; 1898 W−.
Flax factory proprietor.

GARDNER, Herbert Prescott JP *England*
Wellington Coll, Richmond, Mdx.
b 1855; d 38.
Forward, 1-1-0-0 (1t).
1878 I+(1t).
Dairy farmer/grazier. Emigrated to A; became
JP in Qld.

GARDNER, William Charles *Australia*
NSW.
b 2.3.29.
FB, 1-0-0-1 (3 − 1p).
50 BI−(1p).

GARNER, Ralph Lindsay *Australia*
de la Salle Coll, NSW.
b 20.1.27 Yass, NSW.
Wing, 2-2-0-0 (6 − 2t).
49 NZ+(2t) NZ+.
Surg.

GARNETT, Harry Wharfedale *England*
Tennant
Blackheath Proprietary Sch, Bradford, Yorks.
b 16.9.1851 Otley; d 27.4.28.
Forward, 1-0-0-1.
1877 S−.
Paper manufacturer. Often played without
stockings. 1st pres of Yorks. Pres RFU 1889-90.
His club, Bradford, helped form NU 1895.

GARRETT, Richard Marks *Wales*
Penarth.
b c1865; d 08 Penarth.
Back, 8-3-1-4.
1888 NZN+; 1889 S−; 1890 S− E+ I=; 1891
S− I+; 1892 E−.
Docks coal tipper. Killed in accident at Penarth
Docks.

GARRY, Michael G. *Ireland*
Crescent Coll Limerick, RCSI, Bective Rgrs.
b −; d 17.9.67.
Forward, 7-3-0-4.
09 E− S− W− F+; 11 E+ S+ W−.
Medicine.

GARUET, Jean-Pierre *France*
Lourdes.
b 15.6.53 Lourdes.
Prop, 16-9-3-4.
83 A= A+ R+; 84 I+ NZ− NZ− R+; 85 E=
S+ I= W+ Arg−; 86 S− I+ W+ E+.
F > 85 Arg. Sent off v I 84.

GASC, Jacques *France*
Graulhet.
b 24.12.49 Graulhet, Tarn.
Flanker, 1-0-0-1.
77 NZ−.
Draughtsman.

GASPAROTTO, Guy *France*
Montferrand.
b 48.
Lock, 2-1-0-1.
76 A+ R−.
Agricultural technician.

GASTON, Joseph Tate *Ireland*
Ballymena Acad, Trin Coll Dublin,
Monkstown.
b 28.11.30 Cloughmills, Ballymena.
Wing, 8-1-0-7 (3 − 1t).

54 NZ− F− E− S+ W−(1t); 55 W−; 56 F−
E−.
Medicine.

GAUBY, Georges *France*
Perpignan.
SH, 1-1-0-0.
56 Cz+.

GAUDERMEN, Pierre *France*
RCF.
b −; *d* 48.
Forward, 1-0-0-1.
06 E−.

GAVIN, Kenneth *Australia*
NSW.
b 20.1.1883 Cudal, NSW; *d* 56.
Forward, 1-1-0-0.
09 E+.
Farmer. Ar > BI 08. RL.

GAVIN, Thomas J. *Ireland*
Cotton Coll Staffs, Cambridge Univ, Moseley,
London Irish.
Centre, 2-1-0-1.
49 F− E+.
Priest/HM.

GAVINS, Michael Neil *England*
Roundhay Sch, Loughborough Colls, Leeds
Univ, Leeds, Middlesbrough, Moseley,
Leicester, Leics, Midland Cos, N Midlands.
b 14.10.34 Leeds.
FB 1-0-0-1.
61 W−.
Schoolmaster. Various teaching appointments,
including Uppingham.

GAY, David John *England*
Oldfield Boys Sch, City of Bath Tech Sch, Bath,
Harlequins, Barbarians, Som.
b 10.3.48.
No 8, 4-1-2-1.
68 W= I= F− S+.
Solicitor's articled clerk.

GAYRAUD, William *France*
Toulouse.
Forward, 1-1-0-0 (3 − 1t).
20 I+(1t).

GEDDES, Irvine Campbell *Scotland*
George Watson's Coll, London Scottish.
b 9.7.1882; *d* 18.5.62.
Forward, 6-5-0-1 (10 − 5c).
06 SA+; 07 W+ I+(2c) E+(1c); 08 W−(1c)
E+(1c).
Shipping. Father of Keith.

GEDDES, John Herbert *New Zealand*
Southland Boys' HS, Pirates, Southland, S
Island.
b 9.1.07 Invercargill.
Wing, 1-0-0-1.
29 A−.
Clerical employee. 7t NZ > 29 A. Otago sprint
champ. Father Arthur leading NZ
administrator.

GEDDES, Keith Irvine DFC *Scotland*
Loretto Sch, Cambridge Univ, London Scottish.
b 18.
FB, 4-0-0-4 (10 − 2c 2p).
47 F−(1p) W−(1c 1p) I− E−(1c).
Farmer. Son of Campbell. Blue 38.

GEDDES, William McKail MC *New Zealand*
Auckland GS, Univ, Auckland, N Island.
b 13.5.1893 Auckland; *d* 1.7.50 Auckland.
1st five-eighth, 1-1-0-0.
13 A+.
Man dir food processing co. Served WW1, NZ
Field Artillery.

GEDGE, Henry Theodore Sidney *Scotland*
Loretto Sch, Dulwich Coll, Oxford Univ,
London Scottish, Edinburgh W, Barbarians.
b 19.8.1870 London; *d* 5.12.43.
Wing, 6-4-0-2 (10 − 2t 1d).
1894 W− I− E+; 1896 E+(1t); 1899 W+(1t 1d)
E+.
Church. Father of P.M.S. Blue 1893.

GEDGE, Peter Maurice Sydney *Scotland*
Loretto Sch, Cambridge Univ, Edinburgh W.
b 18.5.10 York.
Wing, 1-1-0-0.
33 I+.
Schoolmaster/minister. Son of H.T.S. Fencing
champion.

GEEL, P.J. ('Flip') *South Africa*
OFS.
b 10 Boshof; *d* −.6.71.
Lock, 1-1-0-0.
49 NZ+.

GEEN, William Purdon *Wales*
Haileybury & ISC, Oxford Univ, Newport,
Barbarians.
b 14.3.1891 Newport; kia 31.7.15 Hooge,
Belgium.
Wing/centre, 3-1-0-2.
12 SA−; 13 E− I+.
Nephew of F.J. Purdon. Blue 1910-12. Mon
CCC. 2nd Lt in KRRC.

GEERE, V. *South Africa*
Transvaal.
b 9.9.06.

Lock, 5-3-0-2.
33 A+ A− A+ A+ A−.
Bank clerk. SA > 31-2 BI.

GEFFIN, Aaron Okey ('Ox')   *South Africa*
Johannesburg Pirates, Transvaal.
b 28.5.21 Johannesburg.
Prop, 7-7-0-0 (48 − 9c 10p).
49 NZ+(5p) NZ+(1p) NZ+(3p) NZ+(1c 1p);
51 S+(7c) I+(1c) W+.
Building contractor. Of Jewish stock. Born close
to Ellis Pk Stadium. Kicking skills taught by ex-
Springbok Freddie Turner at Pirates club; often
practised in bare feet. SA > 51-2 BI, F. 121
career pts for SA. Most cons (7) for SA in an int,
v S 51. Served WW2. With fellow Springbok Bill
Payn helped organise 'internationals' v NZ in
German POW camp, Thorn, Poland.
Registered without a given name as a child;
registered himself later as 'Aaron Okey', the
latter adopted from nickname. Known also as
'Ox' when POW.

GELDENHUYS, Schalk Burger   *South Africa*
Agric High Sch Kroonstad, Pretoria Univ,
Marmande (F), Jnr Springboks, SA Univs,
Quaggas, Barbarians, N Transvaal.
b 18.5.56 Kroonstad.
Flanker, 5-3-0-2 (4 − 1t).
81 NZ+ NZ− US+(1t); 82 SAm+ SAm−.
Student. With Marmande 77-8. Played in 5
Currie Cup finals. Jnr Springboks v BI 80.

GELLING, Anthony Massey   *Australia*
NSW.
b 1.12.46.
Flanker, 2-1-0-1.
72 NZ− Fj+.
Farmer.

GEMMELL, Bruce McLeod   *New Zealand*
Auckland GS, NZ Jnrs, Auckland.
b 12.5.50 Auckland.
SH, 2-1-1-0.
74 A+ A=.
Sales rep. NZ > 74 A & Fj. Retired on medical
advice 79. Ckt for Auckland.

GEMMILL, Robert   *Scotland*
Glasgow HS, Glasgow HSFP, Barbarians.
Lock, 7-3-0-4.
50 F+ W− I− E+; 51 F− W+ I−.

GENESTE, Robert   *France*
BEC, Bègles.
Wing, 2-2-0-0.
45 BF+; 49 Arg+.

GENSANNE, Roger   *France*
Béziers.
b 4.2.34 Severac, Tarn.

GENT, David Robert   *England*
St Paul's Coll Cheltenham, Gloucester, Glos.
b 9.1.1883 Llandovery; *d* 16.1.64 Hellingly,
Sussex.
Half-back/FH, 5-1-1-3.
05 NZ−; 06 W− I−; 10 W+ I=.
Schoolmaster/journalist. Welsh Trial 05; Welsh
reserve. Cornwall CCC. Rugby corr 'Sunday
Times'.

GENTH, J.S.M.   *England*
Manchester.
Forward, 2-1-1-0.
1874 S+; 1875 S=.

GENTLES, Thomas Alexander   *South Africa*
Diocesan Coll Rondebosch, Stellenbosch Univ,
W Prov.
b 31.5.34.
SH, 6-3-0-3.
55 BI− BI+ BI+; 56 NZ+ NZ−; 58 F−.
SA shortest player, 5ft 3in. Wigan (E) RL.

GEORGE, Ernest Edward   *Wales*
Cardiff, Pontypridd.
b 1871 Llantwit Major; *d* 28.11.52 Cardiff.
Forward, 3-1-0-2.
1895 S− I+; 1896 E−.
Mason/hotelier.

GEORGE, Harold W.   *Australia*
NSW.
b 1887; kia 16.
Prop, 8-3-0-5.
10 NZ− NZ+ NZ−; 12 US+; 13 NZ− NZ+; 14
NZ− NZ−.
Clerk.

GEORGE, James Thomas   *England*
Falmouth, Barbarians, Cornwall.
b 24.8.18.
Lock, 3-2-0-1.
47 S+ F+; 49 I−.
RN/shipyard fitter.

GEORGE, Victor Leslie   *New Zealand*
Otago Boys' HS, Invercargill, Southland, S
Island.
b 5.6.08 Invercargill.
Prop, 3-3-0-0.
38 A+ A+ A+.
Farmer/storeman. NZ > 38 A. NZRFU sel 64-
70 & administrator. Bro Cyril NZ trial 34.

GERAGHTY, E.M. ('Carrots')   *South Africa*
Stellenbosch Univ, Border.
b 20.4.27.

Wing, 1-1-0-0.
49 NZ+.

GÉRALD, Georges　　　　　　*France*
RCF.
b 17.3.04 Aix-Vienne; *d* 9.11.77.
Centre, 13-5-0-8 (4 − 1d).
27 E+; 28 S−; 29 I− S− W− E−; 30 S+ I+ E−
W−; 31 I+ S− E+(1d).

GERBER, Daniel Mattheus　　　*South Africa*
('Danie')
Despatch Sch, SA Schs, Despatch, Jnr
Springboks, OFS, E Prov.
b 14.4.58 Port Elizabeth.
Centre, 15-12-0-3 (58 − 14t 1c).
80 SAm+(1t) SAm+(1t) F+; 81 I+(2t) I+
NZ− NZ+ NZ− US+; 82 SAm+(3t) SAm−
(1t); 84 E+(1t) E+(3t) SAm+(1t 1c)
SAm+(1t).
Clerk/sports organiser. Most t for SA in all ints
(see J.P. Engelbrecht, J.L. Gainsford).
Overseas XV v Five Nations, Twickenham 86.

GERBER, Michael C.　　　　　*South Africa*
E Prov.
b 12.10.35 Port Elizabeth.
FB, 3-1-1-1 (8 − 4c).
58 F= F−(1c); 60 S+(3c).
Accountant.

GERICKE, F.W. ('Mannetjies')　*South Africa*
Transvaal.
b 8.6.33.
SH, 1-1-0-0 (3 − 1t).
60 S+(1t).
Fitter.

GERINTES, Gilbert　　　　　　*France*
CASG.
Flanker, 3-1-0-2 (6 − 2t).
24 R+(1t); 25 I−; 26 W−(1t).

GERMISHUYS, Johannes　　　*South Africa*
Servaas ('Gerrie')
Brandwag Sch Benoni, Goudstad Teachers Coll,
SA Univs, SA Colls, OFS, Jnr Springboks,
Gazelles, Transvaal.
b 29.10.49 Port Shepstone.
Wing, 20-16-0-4 (48 − 12t).
74 BI−; 76 NZ+(1t) NZ− NZ+ NZ+; 77
Wd+; 80 SAm+(1t) SAm+ BI+(1t) BI+(1t)
BI+(1t) BI− SAm+ SAm+(2t) F+(1t); 81 I+
I+ NZ+(1t) NZ− US+(2t).
Schoolmaster/sports official. Gazelles > 72 Arg.

GERRARD, Ronald Anderson　　*England*
DSO
Taunton Sch, Bath, Barbarians, Som.
b 26.1.12 Hong Kong; kia 22.1.43 Libya.
Centre, 14-8-1-5.

32 SA− W− I+ S+; 33 W− I+ S−; 34 W+ I+
S+; 36 NZ+ W= I− S+.
Civil engr. Public Schs & TA champ at putting
the shot. Capt Glos/Som v NZ 35. Som CCC 35.
Served WW2, DSO 42. The Gerrard Memorial
Fund at Taunton Sch set up in his memory.
After WW2 wife Molly became pres of Bath;
believed to be only woman to have given radio
commentary on a rugby match.

GESCHWIND, Pierre　　　　　　*France*
RCF.
Wing, 2-2-0-0 (6 − 2t).
36 G+(1t) G+(1t).

GETHING, Glyn Ivor　　　　　　*Wales*
Neath.
b 16.6.1892 Neath; *d* 20.3.77 Neath.
FB, 1-1-0-0.
13 F+.
Banking.

GIACCARDY, Marc　　　　　　*France*
SBUC.
b −; kia WW1.
Forward, 1-0-0-1.
07 E−.
Journalist.

GIBBONS, Eric de Courcy　　　*Australia*
NSW.
b 13; *d* 62.
SH, 3-1-0-2 (2 − 1c).
36 NZ− NZ− M+(1c).
Bank clerk.

GIBBS, B.　　　　　　　　　*South Africa*
Griq W.
1-0-1-0.
03 BT=.

GIBBS, George Anthony TD　　　*England*
Clifton Coll, Bristol, Northern, Barbarians,
Glos, Northumb.
b 31.3.20.
Prop, 2-1-0-1.
47 F+; 48 I−.
Tobacco co factory mgr. Bro of Nigel. Served
WW2.

GIBBS, John Clifford JP　　　　*England*
Queen's Coll Taunton, Harlequins, Kent.
b 10.3.02.
Wing, 7-4-0-3 (6 − 2t).
25 NZ− W+; 26 F+; 27 W+ I+(1t) S−(1t) F−.
Printer/publisher. Bro of W.D. Gibbs (Pres
RFU 55-6). Son, John D. Cambridge blue 65.
Played football for Bromley in Athenian Lge 32-
34.

GIBBS, Nigel *England*
Clifton Coll, Oxford Univ, Guildford &
Godalming, Bristol, Harlequins, London Cos,
Glos, Surrey.
b 24.9.22.
FB, 2-1-0-1 (4 − 2c).
54 S+(2c) F−.
HM. Bro of George. Ckt blue 41. Served WW2,
RNVR Lt in submarines. Mentioned in
despatches. Various teaching posts, inc
Charterhouse (50-62) & Colston's (HM from
65).

GIBBS, Paul Roderick *Australia*
King Edward's Sch Birmingham, Victoria.
b 6.12.41 Birmingham, England.
Five-eighth, 1-0-0-1.
66 S−.
Sales rep.

GIBBS, Reginald Arthur *Wales*
Queens Coll Taunton, Cardiff, Barbarians.
b 1882 Cardiff; *d* 28.11.38 Cardiff.
FH/extra back/wing, 16-13-0-3 (53 − 17t 1c).
06 S+ I−; 07 E+(1t) S−; 08 E+(1t) S+ F+(4t
1c) I+(1t); 10 F+(3t) E−(1t) S+ I+(1t); 11
E+(1t) S+(3t) F+ I+(1t); BT > 08 A, NZ.
Shipowner. W's t rec (4 v F 08) equ with Willie
Llewellyn & Maurice Richards. Equ W's rec
most t (6) in season, 07-8. 90t for Cardiff 01-11
& 30 pts (4t 9c) Cardiff v Moseley 7.1.11. Ckt
Glam CCC.

GIBLIN, Lyndhurst Falkiner *England*
DSO MC
Hutchins Sch Hobart, London Univ, Cambridge
Univ, Blackheath, Barbarians, Mdx.
b 29.11.1872 Hobart, Tasmania; *d* 2.3.51.
Forward, 3-2-0-1.
1896 W+ I−; 1897 S+.
Gold miner/fruit grower/professor. Blue 1894-6.
Served WW1. MC & DSO 18. Worked in the
Klondyke & Can's NW Territories. Fruit grower
in Tasmania. Professor of economics Melbourne
Univ 29-40.

GIBSON, Arthur Sumner *England*
Marlborough Coll, Oxford Univ, Manchester,
Lancs.
b 14.7.1844 Hants; *d* 23.1.27 Binfield, Berks.
Forward, 1-0-0-1.
1871 S−.
Civil engr. Played in 1st int, S v E 1871.

GIBSON, Cameron Michael *Ireland*
Henderson
Campbell Coll, Trin Coll Dublin, Cambridge
Univ, NIFC, Barbarians.
b 3.12.42.
FH/centre/wing, 69-28-9-32 (115 − 9t 7c 6d
17p).

64 E+ S− W− F−(1d); 65 F= E+ S+(1d) W−
SA−; 66 F−(1p) E= S− W+(1d 1p); 67 A+(1t
2d) E− S+ W+ F− A+; 68 E= S+ W+(1d)
A+; 69 E+ S+(1t) W−(1t); 70 SA= F− E−
S+(1t) W+; 71 F= E− S+(1c 2p) W−(3p); 72
F+ E+ F+; 73 NZ= E+ S− W−(1t) F+(2p);
74 F− W= E+(2t 2c) S+(1c) P=(2c 2p); 75
E+(1t) S− F+ W−; 76 A− F− W− E+ S−
NZ−; 77 W−(3p) E− S−(1t 1c 2p) F−(1p); 78
F− W− E− NZ−; 79 S= A+ A+; BI > 66 A,
NZ 4-0-0-4; 68 SA 4(1r)-0-1-3; 71 A, NZ 4-2-1-1;
74r SA; 77 NZ.
Solicitor. Blue 63-5. World's most capped
player, 81 (12 BI). 69 apps for BI. World's 1st
int r (r Barry John 1st Test BI > 68 SA).

GIBSON, Charles Osborne Provis *England*
MC DL
Uppingham Sch, Oxford Univ, Northern,
Barbarians, Northumb.
b −.10.1876; *d* 9.11.31 Stocksfield, Northumb.
Forward, 1-0-0-1.
01 W−.
Solicitor. Bro of G.R. & T.A. Gibson. Served
WW1. Col Northumb Fusiliers (TA). MC 16.
Mentioned in despatches 15 & 18.

GIBSON, George Ralph *England*
Uppingham Sch, Northern, Barbarians,
Northumb.
b −.3.1878; *d* −.10.39.
Forward, 2-0-0-2.
1899 W−; 01 S−; BT > A 1899.
Timber merchant. Bro of Charles & T.A.
Gibson.

GIBSON, Michael Edward *Ireland*
St Andrews Coll, Trin Coll Dublin, Lansdowne.
b 3.3.54 Dublin.
No 8/lock, 5-1-2-2.
79 F= W− E+ S=; 81 W−r.
Laboratory technician.

GIBSON, Thomas Alexander *England*
Uppingham Sch, Cambridge Univ, Northern,
Barbarians, Northumb.
b 30.1.1880 Gateshead; *d* 27.4.37.
Forward, 2-0-0-2.
05 W− S−; BT > 03 SA.
Timber merchant. Blue 01-2. Bro of Charles &
G.R. Gibson.

GIBSON, William Ross *Scotland*
Royal HS, Royal HSFP.
b 1865; *d* 1.1.24 Edinburgh.
Forward, 14-9-1-4 .
1891 I+ E+; 1892 W+ I+ E−; 1893 W− I=
E+; 1894 W− I− E+; 1895 W+ I+ E+.
Banker.

GIFFORD, H.P. *Ireland*
Wanderers.
FB, 1-0-0-1.
1890 S−.

GILBERT, F.G. *England*
Devonport Servs, RN.
b c1885; d −.
FB, 2-2-0-0.
23 W+ I+.
RN.

GILBERT, Graham Duncan *New Zealand*
McMillan ('Mike')
Westport Tech Coll, Westport OB, Buller,
Greymouth Utd, W Coast, S Island.
b 1.3.11 Rothesay, Scotland.
FB, 4-2-0-2 (20 − 5c 1d 2p).
35 S+(3c) I+(1c 2p) W−(1c 1d); 36 E−.
Post Office linesman & overseer. Top scorer 125
pts, 27 apps NZ > 35-6 BI & Can. Bradford
Northern RL (E) 37. Returned NZ 40.

GILBERT, Herbert *Australia*
NSW.
b 1888 Gulgong, NSW; d 5.1.72.
Wing, 3-1-0-2 (9 − 3t).
10 NZ− NZ+(2t) NZ−(1t).
Rly examiner. RL.

GILBERT, R. *England*
Devonport Albion, RN.
Forward, 3-1-0-2.
08 W− I+ S−.
RN. Reached rank of Petty Officer; 1st non-
commissioned regular to be capped by E.

GILBERT-SMITH, David Stuart *Scotland*
St Edward's Sch Oxford, Glasgow Univ,
London Scottish, The Army.
b 3.12.31.
Flanker, 1-0-0-1.
52 E−.
The Army/medicine. Served with Duke of
Wellington's Rgt.

GILCHRIST, James *Scotland*
Glasgow Acad, Glasgow Academicals,
Barbarians.
b 03; d 72.
Hooker, 1-1-0-0.
25 F+.
Engr.

GILES, James Leonard *England*
Coventry, Warwicks.
b 10 Coventry; d 28.3.67 Coventry.
SH, 6-4-1-1 (6 − 2t).
35 W= I+(1t); 37 W+ I+; 38 I+(1t) S−; BI >
38 SA 2-1-0-1.
Centre in 3rd Test BI > 38 SA.

GILES, Raymond *Wales*
Welsh Youth, Aberavon.
b 15.1.61 Pyle.
SH, 2-1-0-1.
83 R−; 85 Fj+r.
Capt Welsh Youth > 80 SA. Wales B v A 81.
Wales B > 83 Spain.

GILL, Andrew Davidson *Scotland*
Gala Acad, Gala, Barbarians.
b 30.8.49 Edinburgh.
Wing, 5-3-0-2 (8 − 2t).
73 P+(2t); 74 W− E+ I− F+.
Mgr wholesale newsagents. Scottish XV v Arg
69, 73.

GILLESPIE, Charles Theodore *New Zealand*
MC
Oriental, Wellington, N Island.
b 24.6.1883 Masterton; d 22.1.64 Masterton.
No 8, 1-1-0-0.
13 A+.
Army/farmer. Served WW1, farrier-sgt NZ
Artillery; commissioned in the field. Gassed &
wounded at Passchendaele. Retired as officer
commanding Northern Command 38.

GILLESPIE, John Imrie *Scotland*
Edinburgh Acad, Edinburgh Academicals.
b 16.1.1879; d 5.12.43.
Half-back, 10-6-1-3 (27 − 5t 6c).
1899 E+(1t); 1900 W− E=; 01 W+(2t 2c)
I+(1t) E+(1t 3c); 02 W−(1c) I−; 04 I+ E+; BT
> 03 SA.
Chartered accountant. Ref W v E 07; W v E 11.

GILLESPIE, Joseph Cecil *Ireland*
Wesley Coll, Trin Coll Dublin, Wanderers,
Barbarians.
b 1897; d −.3.45.
Prop, 2-1-0-1.
22 W− F+.
Medicine. Emigrated to SA.

GILLESPIE, William David *New Zealand*
Waimate Dist HS, Pirates, Otago, Onslow,
Wellington, S Island.
b 6.8.34 Cromwell.
Flanker, 1-1-0-0.
58 A+.
Truck driver/salesman. NZ > 57 A, 60 A & SA.
Capt Otago to beat BI 59. Son-in-law of Charlie
Oliver.

GILLETT, George Arthur *New Zealand*
Hamilton E Sch, Karangahake, Thames,
Auckland, Merivale, Ponsonby, S & N Islands.
b 23.4.1877 Leeston; d 12.9.56 Onehunga.
FB/flanker, 8-6-1-1 (7 − 1t 2c).
05 S+ I+ E+ W−; 07 A+ A=; 08 AW+(2c)
AW+(1t).

Tramways & rlys employee/licensee. NZ > 05 A, 05-6 BI,F & NAm, 07 A. Went to Kalgoolie & rep WA at Australian Rules. Returned NZ 05. Turned RL 11, toured E with Australasian team. Became full-time RL organiser in N Island, establishing RL in Wellington & Thames. Reinstated to rugby union; Poverty Bay sel 17-18. Bro Jack rep Auckland 1897-9.

GILLIES, Alexander Campbell　　*Scotland*
George Watson's Coll, Watsonians.
b 25.3.1900; *d* 22.1.80.
No 8, 12-10-0-2 (26 − 1t 7c 3p).
24 W+ I+ E−; 25 F+(1t 1c) W+ E+(1c); 26 F+(1p) W+(1p); 27 F+(3c 1p) W+(1c) I− E+(1c).
Medicine.

GILLIES, Colin Cuthbert　　*New Zealand*
Waitaki Boys' HS, Otago, Univ, Matakanui, NZ Univs, S Island.
b 8.10.12 Oamaru.
1st five-eighth, 1-1-0-0.
36 A+.
Schoolmaster/accountant. NZ > 36 A. N Otago sel 56. Ckt for N Otago. Bros A.J. & D.H. rep N Otago.

GILPIN, Francis Gerald　　*Ireland*
RBAI, Queen's Univ Belfast.
b 20.10.40 Belfast.
FH/FB, 3-0-0-3.
62 E− S− F−.
Economist. Cousin of David Hewitt.

GILRAY, Colin　　*New Zealand/Scotland*
MacDonald MC OBE
Otago Boys' HS, Univ, Otago, S Island, Oxford Univ, London Scottish.
b 17.3.1885 Broughty Ferry, S; *d* 15.7.74 Melbourne.
New Zealand
Wing, 1-1-0-0.
05 A+.
Scotland
Centre, 4-2-0-2 (3 − 1t).
08 E+; 09 W− E+(1t); 12 I−.
Lawyer/college principal. Rhodes Scholar; blue 08-9. Served WW1, Capt Rifle Bde. Principal John McGlashan Coll 22-34; HM Scotch Coll, Melbourne, 34-53 & deputy chancellor Univ of Melbourne.

GIRLING, B.E.　　*Wales*
Cardiff.
Forward, 1-0-0-1.
1881 E−.
Played in W's 1st int, v E 1881. Played for Cardiff in their 1st season 1876-7; club capt 1881-2.

GITTINGS, William John　　*England*
Barker Butts Sch, Coventry, Warwicks, Midland Cos.
b 5.10.39 Coventry.
SH, 1-0-0-1.
67 NZ−.
Aircraft sheet metal fabricator.

GLASGOW, Francis Turnbull　　*New Zealand*
Wellington Coll, Athletic, Taranaki, Hawera, Southland, Eltham, Hawkes Bay, Waipawa, Star, N Island.
b 17.8.1880 S Dunedin; *d* 20.2.39 Wellington.
Flanker/lock, 6-5-0-1 (9 − 3t).
05 S+(1t) I+ E+ W−; 06 F+(1t); 08 AW+(1t).
Bank mgr. NZ > 05 A, 05-6 BI,F & NAm.
NZRFU management comm 31-6, exec 37-9.
Liaison off for SA 37.

GLASGOW, Ronald James　　*Scotland*
Cunningham
Knox Acad, Dunfermline, Barbarians.
b 5.11.30.
Flanker, 10-5-1-4 (9 − 3t).
62 F− W+(1t) I+ E=; 63 I+ E−(1t); 64 I+ E+(1t); 65 W− I−.
Schoolmaster.

GLASS, Dion Caldwell　　*Ireland*
Methodist Coll Belfast, Queen's Univ Belfast, Collegians, Barbarians.
b 15.5.34 Belfast.
FB/wing/centre, 4-0-0-4.
58 F−; 60 W−; 61 W− SA−.
Accountant.

GLEN, William Sutherland　　*Scotland*
Merchiston Castle Sch, Edinburgh W.
b 13.3.32.
Flanker, 1-1-0-0.
55 W+.
Farmer.

GLENN, William Spiers MC　　*New Zealand*
Manaia Sch, Waimate, Taranaki, N Island.
b 21.2.1877 Greymouth; *d* 5.10.53 Wanganui
No 8, 2-2-0-0.
04 BT+; 06 F+.
NZ > 05 A, 05-6 BI,F (did not tour in NAm).
Served WW1, Maj in RFA. NZRFU comm 22-3. 1st All Black to enter NZ parliament, for Rangitikei 19-28. Racehorse breeder & owner; steward & trustee Wanganui Jockey Club.

GLENNON, James Joseph　　*Ireland*
De La Salle Coll Skerries, Cistercian Sch Roscrea, Skerries.
b 7.7.53 Dublin.
Lock, 2-1-0-1.
80 E− S+.
Solicitor.

GLOAG, Laurie G.   *Scotland*
Oundle Sch, Cambridge Univ, Barbarians.
Centre, 4-2-0-2 (3 − 1t).
49 F+ W+(1t) I− E−.
Blue 48.

GLOVER, Peter Bernard   *England*
De Aston Sch, RAF Cranwell, RAF, Bedford,
Bath, Comb Servs, Barbarians, Yorks.
b 25.9.45.
Wing, 3-0-1-2.
67 A−; 71 F= P−.
RAF pilot. Rep RAF at ath 66.

GODDARD, Maurice Patrick   *New Zealand*
Marist Bros' Sch Timaru, Timaru Boys' HS,
Ashburton Co, Zingari, S Canterbury, Comb
Servs.
b 28.9.21 Timaru; *d* 19.6.74 Christchurch.
Centre/wing, 5-3-0-2 (3 − 1t).
46 A+; 47 A+ A+; 49 SA−(1t) SA−.
Furrier/menswear store owner. Rep E v S in 2
WW2 ints. NZ > 47 A, 49 SA. Bro Jack > 49
SA. Son Tony rep S Canterbury 66-78.

GODFRAY, Reginald Edmund   *England*
Victoria Coll Jersey, Pk House, Richmond,
Mdx.
b 10.5.1880; *d* 4.2.67.
Centre, 1-0-0-1.
05 NZ−.
Stockbroker. Mem of Stock Exchange 14-68.
Pres Chiswick Pk LTC.

GODFREY, Robin Patrick   *Ireland*
Stonyhurst Coll, UC Dublin.
b 16.9.31 Tilbury, Essex.
Centre, 2-1-0-1.
54 S+ W−.
Medicine.

GODWIN, Herbert O.   *England*
Broadway SMS, Standard, Coventry, The
Army, Comb Servs, Barbarians, Warwicks.
b 21.12.35 ?Blaenavon, Gwent.
Hooker, 11-2-2-7 (3 − 1t).
59 F= S=; 63 S+ NZ− NZ− A−(1t); 64 NZ−
I− F+ S−; 67 NZ−; BIr > 62 SA.
Machine fitter.

GOING, Sidney Milton MBE   *New Zealand*
Northland Coll, Church Coll, Mid-Northern, N
Auckland, NZ Maoris, N Island.
b 19.8.43 Kawakawa.
SH, 29-17-2-10 (44 − 10t 1c 2p).
67 A+; 67 F+(1t); 68 F+(2t); 69 W+ W+; 70
SA− SA−r; 71 BI− BI+(1t) BI− BI=; 72
A+(1t) A+ A+(1t) W+ S+(1t); 73 E+ I=(1t)
F− E−; 74 I+; 75 S+; 76 I+r SA− SA+(1c 2p)
SA− SA−(1t); 77 BI+(1t) BI−.
Farmer. NZ's most capped SH. NZ > 67 BI,F &

C, 68 A & Fj, 70 A & SA, 72-3 BI,F & NAm, 74
I,W & E, 76 SA. Bros Ken (NZ 74 − no Tests)
& Brian rep N Auckland. Maori Player of Year
67-72. Bob Howitt's biography 'Super Sid' pub
78.

GOLDSWORTHY, Samuel James   *Wales*
Swansea.
b − c1855; *d* 28.9.1889 Swansea.
Forward, 3-1-1-1.
1884 I+; 1885 E− S=.

GOMMES, Jacques   *France*
RCF.
Prop, 1-0-0-1.
09 I−.

GONNET, Charles-Albert   *France*
Albi, RCF.
b 3.11.1897 Laon, Aisne; *d* −.
Hooker, 16-4-1-11 (5 − 1c 1p).
21 E− I+; 22 E= W−; 24 S+ E−; 26 S−(1p) I−
E− W−(1c) M−; 27 I− S− W− E+ G+.

GOODALL, Kenneth George   *Ireland*
Foyle Coll, Newcastle Univ, City of Derry.
b 23.2.47 Leeds.
No 8, 19-12-2-5 (9 − 3t).
67 A+ E− S+ W+ F− A+; 68 F− E= S+ W+
A+(1t); 69 F+ E+ S+; 70 SA= F− E− S+(1t)
W+(1t); BI > 68 SA.
Schoolmaster/chemical engr. Workington RL.

GOODFELLOW, John   *Scotland*
Langholm.
b 06; *d* 2.4.51.
Wing, 3-0-0-3.
28 W− I− E−.

**GOODHUE, Frederick William Scotland
Jervis**
Merchiston Castle Sch, Cambridge Univ,
London Scottish, Barbarians.
b 26.4.1867 London, Ontario; *d* 30.12.40.
Forward, 9-7-0-2 (1 − 1t).
1890 W+ I+ E−; 1891 W+(1t) I+ E+; 1892
W+ I+ E−.
Medicine. Blue 1885-6.

GOOSEN, Cornelius Petrus   *South Africa*
('Piet')
Diocesan Coll Rondebosch, OFS.
b 3.2.37.
Lock, 1-0-0-1.
65 NZ−.
Schoolmaster/executive.

GORDON, Alexander   *Ireland*
Trin Coll Dublin.

Forward, 1-0-0-1.
1884 S−.
Medicine.

GORDON, George Campbell　　　*Australia*
Trinity GS, NSW.
b 11.9.03 Bowral.
Wing, 1-1-0-0 (3 − 1t).
29 NZ+(1t).
Insurance.

GORDON, Keith Milton　　　*Australia*
Sydney HS, NSW.
b 23.4.27.
Prop, 2-0-0-2.
50 BI− BI−.
Chartered accountant.

GORDON, Rick J.　　　*Scotland*
London Scottish.
b 16.3.58 Lahore.
Centre, 2-1-0-1.
82 A+ A−.
Surveyor.

GORDON, Robert　　　*Scotland*
Loretto Sch, Edinburgh W.
b 25.7.30.
Wing, 6-1-0-5 (6 − 2t).
51 W+(2t); 52 F− W− I− E−; 53 W−.
Chartered accountant.

GORDON, Roland Elphinstone　　　*Scotland*
King's Sch Canterbury, RMA Woolwich, RA,
The Army.
b 22.1.1893 Selangor; *d* 30.8.18.
Centre, 3-2-0-1 (6 − 2t).
13 F+(2t) W− I+.
The Army. Served WW1, Maj RA; died of
wounds.

GORDON, Thomas Gisborne　　　*Ireland*
Rugby Sch, NIFC.
b 15.12.1852; *d* 8.7.35
Half-back, 3-0-0-3.
1877 E− S−; 1878 E−.
Wine merchant. Played without right hand, lost
in gun accident.

GORDON-SMITH, Gerald W.　　　*England*
Camborne Sch of Mines, Redruth, Cornwall,
Blackheath, Barbarians, Kent.
b −; *d* 23.1.11 Carbis Bay.
Centre, 3-1-1-1 (7 − 1t 1d).
1900 W− I+(1t 1d) S=.
1st Cornishman to be capped.

GORE, A. Fraser C.　　　*Scotland*
London Scottish.
Forward, 1-1-0-0.
1882 I+.

GORE, John Henry ('Jack')　　　*Wales*
Blaina.
b 16.6.1899 Blaina; *d* 18.3.71 Bedwellty.
Back−row/lock/prop, 4-1-0-3.
24 I− F+ NZ−; 25 E−.
Licensee. Father of Billy. Salford RL 25. Played
RL for E.

GORE, William ('Billy')　　　*Wales*
Newbridge.
b 19.11.19 Blaina.
Hooker, 3-3-0-0.
47 S+ F+ I+.
Foundryman/licensee. Son of Jack. Warrington
RL 47.

GORTON, H.C.　　　*South Africa*
Transvaal.
1-0-0-1.
1896 BT−.

GOSSMAN, Bryan M.　　　*Scotland*
Ardrossan Acad, Strathclyde Univ, W of
Scotland.
b 5.5.51.
FH, 3-0-0-3 (6 − 2d).
80 W−; 83 F−(2d) W−.
Building soc mgr. Bro of J.S.

GOSSMAN, J.S.　　　*Scotland*
Cambridge Univ, London Scottish.
Wing, 1-0-0-1.
80 E−r.
Bro of B.M.

GOT, Raoul ('Le Boulet de　　　*France*
Canon')
Perpignan.
b 11.10.1900 Perpignan.
Wing, 13-4-2-7 (18 − 6t).
20 I+(2t) US+(1t); 21 S+ W−; 22 S= E=(1t)
W− I−; 24 I− E− W− R+(2t) US−.

GOTLEY, A.L.H. See Henniker-
Gotley

GOTTO, Robert Porter Corry　　　*Ireland*
('Bertie') OBE
Campbell Coll, Uppingham Sch, Methodist Coll
Belfast.
b 20.1.1881; *d* 5.8.60 Belfast.
1-0-0-1.
06 SA−.
Timber importer.

GOULD, Arthur Joseph　　　*Wales*
('Monkey')
Newport Juniors, Newport, London Welsh,
Richmond, Middlesex, Southampton Trojans,
Hampshire.
b 10.10.1864 Newport; *d* 2.1.19 Newport.

Back/centre, 27-10-3-14 (4t 1c 2d).
1885 E−(1c) S=; 1886 E− S−; 1887 E= S−
I+(1d); 1888 S+; 1889 I−; 1890 S−(1t) E+ I=;
1892 E− S− I−; 1893 E+(2t) S+ I+; 1894 E−
S+; 1895 E− S− I+; 1896 E− S+(1t) I−(1d);
1897 E+.
Public works contractor/brewery rep. Capt W
rec 18 times, inc 1st Triple Crown XV 1893.
Once W rec cap holder. WRU comm 1897, sel
1898. Renowned athlete. 1st match for Newport
at 16. Father Joseph came from Oxford to work
in brass foundry in Newport. One of 6 bros who
played for Newport, 3 for W. Was at centre of
major controversy when WRU granted him
deeds to house to mark retirement, which other
Unions considered an act of proessionalism. As
a result I & S refused to play W in 1897. Gould
did not play again, and took up refereeing. W
were accepted back into the fold but did not
played S again until 1899.

GOULD, George Herbert   *Wales*
Newport.
b 1870 Newport; *d* 18.12.13 Germiston, SA.
Centre, 3-2-0-1 (4 − 2t).
1892 I−; 1893 S+(1t) I+(1t).
Civil engr. Bro of Arthur & Bob.

GOULD, Robert   *Wales*
Newport, London Welsh.
b 1863; *d* −.4.32
Forward, 11-2-2-7.
1882 I+ E−; 1883 S−; 1884 E− S− I+; 1885
E− S=; 1886 E−; 1887 E= S−.
Civil engr/brewery exec. Bro of Arthur & Bert.
IB rep 1892.

GOULD, Rodney Lloyd   *South Africa*
Natal.
b 10.8.42.
FB, 4-3-1-0 (3 − 1d).
68 BI+ BI= BI+ BI+(1d).
Rep. SA > 68 F.

GOULD, Roger George   *Australia*
Brisbane, Qld, Petrarca (It).
b 4.4.57.
FB, 22-11-1-10 (80 − 3t 13c 2d 12p).
80 NZ+(1c) NZ−(1p) NZ+(2c 1p); 81 I+(1d)
W− S−; 82 S+(2t) NZ−(1c 2p) NZ+(1c 3p)
NZ−(1t 1c 3p); 83 US+(4c) Arg− F= F−; 84
NZ+(1d) NZ− NZ− E+ I+ W+(3c 2p) S+; 85
NZ−.
Co dir. A > 78 NZ; inj prevented his playing. A
> 79 Arg; 80 Fj; 81-2 & 84 BI. Rec 35 pts in 3
Tests v NZ 82. Australian Player of Year 82.
Played some club rugby in Arg. Overseas XV v
Five Nations, Twickenham 86.

GOULDING, Sir William Joshua   *Ireland*
Bt JP DL
Cork, Munster.
b 7.3.1856; *d* 12.7.25.
Half-back, 1-0-0-1.
1879 S−.
Banking. Bt 04. Pres IRU 1880-1. Steward of
Irish Turf Club.

GOURDON, Jean-François   *France*
RCF, Bagnères.
b 8.9.54 Paris.
Wing, 22-13-0-9 (48 − 12t).
74 S− Arg+ Arg+(2t) R−(1t) SA− SA−(1t);
75 W−(1t) E+(1t) S+ I− R+; 76 S+ I+ W−
(1t) E−(1t); 78 E+ S+; 79 W+(2t) E− S+ R+;
80 I+(2t).
Accountant. F > 74 Arg.

GOWANS, James Jollie DSO   *Scotland*
Harrow Sch, Cambridge Univ, London Scottish,
Barbarians.
b 23.4.1872; *d* 27.4.36 SA.
Wing, 8-5-1-2 (6 − 2t).
1893 W−; 1894 W− E+; 1895 W+(1t) I+ E+;
1896 I= E+(1t).
The Army. Blue 1892-3. Served WW1.

GOWLLAND, Geoffrey Cathcart   *Scotland*
Fettes Coll, RMA Sandhurst, RE, The Army,
London Scottish.
b 27.5.1885; *d* 9.10.80.
Forward, 7-3-0-4 (3 − 1t).
08 W−; 09 W− E+; 10 F+(1t) W− I+ E−.
The Army.

GOYARD, André   *France*
Lyon U.
Prop, 7-6-0-1 (3 − 1t).
36 G+ G+; 37 G+ It+(1t); 38 G− R+ G+.

GRACE, Thomas Oliver   *Ireland*
Newbridge Coll, UC Dublin, St Mary's Coll,
Barbarians.
b 24.10.48 Dublin.
Wing, 25-9-3-13 (20 − 5t).
72 F+ E+(1t); 73 NZ= E+(1t) S= W−; 74 E+
S+ P= NZ−; 75 E+ S−(1t) F+(1t) W−; 76 A−
F− W− E+(1t) S− NZ−; 77 W− E− S− F−;
78 S+; BI > 74 SA.
Accountant. I's most capped wing (with Alan
Duggan). 4t v Griq W on BI > 74 SA.

GRACIE, Archibald Leslie MC   *Scotland*
OBE
Eltham Coll, Oxford Univ, Harlequins,
Manchester.
b 15.10.1896 Colombo; *d* 2.8.82 Northants.
Centre, 13-5-2-6 (6 − 2t).
21 F− W+ I− E−; 22 F= W= I+ E−; 23 F+
W+(1t) I+ E−(1t); 24 F−.

Carried shoulder high by Welsh spectators after scoring a remarkable late t, which won the match v Wales 3.2.23. The ingredients of what was described as one of rugby's greatest tries were an overhead pass, a diagonal scything run, a final dummy pass and a perilous run back inside along the dead-ball line with Welsh defenders in hot pursuit. So close to the dead-ball line was Gracie that when he eventually grounded, one of his boots struck a small boy who lost some teeth. Asked to play last match before retirement, for Harlequins v Cardiff at Arms Park, Easter Monday, 29. Served WW1 60th Rifles.

GRACIET, René   *France*
SBUC.
FH/centre, 6-1-0-5 (3 − 1t).
26 I− W−; 27 S− G+(1t); 29 E−; 30 W−.

GRAHAM, Charles Stewart   *Australia*
Melbourne Univ, Qld.
b 1876; d 44.
Forward, 1-0-0-1.
1899 BT−.
Clerk.

GRAHAM, David   *England*
Aspatria H, Aspatria, Keswick, Rochdale, New Brighton, Cumberland.
b −.6.1875 Aspatria; d −.1.62 Carlisle.
Forward, 1-0-0-1.
01 W−.
HM.

GRAHAM, David John   *New Zealand*
New Plymouth Boys' HS, Univ, Auckland, NZ Univs, Christchurch HSOB, Canterbury, S Island.
b 1.1.35 Stratford.
No 8/flanker, 22-17-3-2 (6 − 2t).
58 A+(1t) A−; 60 SA+ SA=; 61 F+ F+ F+(1t); 62 A+ A+ A= A+ A+; 63 E+ E+; 63 I+ W+; 64 E+ S− F+ A+ A+ A .
HM. NZ > 60 A & SA, 62 A, 63-4 BI,F & C. Capt v A 64. Appointed HM Auckland GS 73. Bros Jim & Bob NZ trials.

GRAHAM, Ian N.   *Scotland*
Edinburgh Acad, Edinburgh Academicals, Barbarians.
b 8.5.18.
Hooker, 2-0-0-2.
39 I− E−.
Farmer. Played in 3 Servs ints.

GRAHAM, James   *Scotland*
Kelso HS, Edinburgh Agricultural Coll, Kelso, Barbarians.
b 19.6.02 Selkirk.
Flanker, 15-6-1-8 (3 − 1t).

26 I− E+; 27 F+ W+ I− E+ NSW+(1t); 28 F+ W− I− E−; 30 I− E=; 32 SA− W−.
Farmer.

GRAHAM, James Buchan   *New Zealand*
Lawrence HS, Zingari-Richmond, Otago, Southern, S Island.
b 23.4.1884 Dunedin; d 15.5.41 Auckland.
Flanker, 3-3-0-0 (10 − 5c).
13 US+(4c); 14 A+(1c) A+.
Boilermaker/rly workshops mgr. Top scorer, 66 pts NZ > 13 NAm; > 14 A. Son J.B. rep Otago 45-50. Ckt for Otago.

GRAHAM, James Hope Stewart   *Scotland*
Edinburgh Acad, Edinburgh Academicals.
b 16.4.1856; d 17.10.22 Dumfries.
Forward, 10-4-3-3 (1t).
1876 E−; 1877 I+ E+; 1878 E=; 1879 I+ E=; 1880 I+ E−; 1881 I−(1t) E=.
Writer to the Signet. Ump E v S 1882, S v E 1883, S v I, E v S 1884, I v S 1885. Pres SRU 1883-4.

GRAHAM, H.J.   *England*
Wimbledon H, Surrey.
Forward, 4-3-1-0.
1875 I+ S= I+; 1876 S+.
Played with bro J.D.G. v I 1875. Treasurer RFU 1876-8.

GRAHAM, John Duncan George   *England*
Wellington Coll, Wimbledon H, Surrey.
b 1856.
Forward, 1-1-0-0.
1875 I+.
Played with bro H.J. v I 1875.

GRAHAM, Richard Irvine   *Ireland*
Campbell Coll Belfast, Trin Coll Dublin.
b 22.7.1889; d 15.4.12.
Forward, 1-1-0-0.
11 F+.

GRAHAM, Ronald   *Australia*
NSW.
b 21.12.46.
Prop, 18-9-1-8.
73 Tg+ Tg− W− E−; 74 NZ= NZ−; 75 E+ J+ J+ S− W−; 76 I+ US+ Fj+ Fj+ Fj+ F− F−.

GRAHAM, Thomas Cooper   *Wales*
Newport.
b 1866 Newcastle-upon-Tyne; d 1.12.45 Cardiff.
Forward, 12-5-1-6 (3 − 1t).
1890 I=; 1891 S− I+; 1892 E− S−; 1893 E+ S+ I+; 1894 E− S+; 1895 E−(1t) S−.
Minister. Originator of organised forward play; can claim to have been W's 1st coach as he directed practice before W v E 1899.

GRAHAM, Wayne Geoffrey *New Zealand*
Tauranga Boys' Coll, Univ, NZ Colts, NZ Jnrs,
NZ Univs, Otago, Clinton, Ranfurly, S Island.
b 13.4.57 Tauranga.
Lock, 1-1-0-0.
79 F+r.
Stock & station agent. NZ > 78 BI. NZ v Arg
79. Ckt for NZ Schs.

GRALTON, Austin Sarsfield *Australia*
Qld.
b 9.2.1878; *d* 19.
Half-back, 3-1-0-2.
1899 BT+ BT−; 03 NZ−.
Farmer/joiner.

GRANT, Derrick *Scotland*
Hawick HS, Hawick, Barbarians.
b 19.4.38 Hawick.
Flanker, 14-6-2-6 (3 − 1t).
65 F− E= SA+; 66 F= W− I+(1t) E+ A+; 67
F+ W+ I− E− NZ−; 68 F−; BI > 66 A & NZ.
Hosiery. Bro of T.O. SRU asst coach 82-3, 84-5.

GRANT, D.M. *Scotland*
Elstow Sch, E Midlands.
b −.1.1893; *d* −.
Wing, 2-0-0-2.
11 W− I−.
Bank official. Capped from school. Served
WW1. Emigrated to Can.

GRANT, Edwin Leslie *Ireland*
Belfast HS, CIYMS.
b 13.4.46 Belfast.
Wing, 4-1-1-2 (9 − 3t).
71 F=(1t) E−(1t) S+(1t) W−.
Insurance surveyor.

GRANT, Lachlan Ashwell *New Zealand*
('Goldie')
Clandeboye Sch, Timaru Boys' HS, Temuka, S
Canterbury, Comb Servs, S Island.
b 4.10.23 Temuka.
Lock/flanker, 4-2-0-2.
47 A+ A+; 49 SA− SA−.
Farmer. Served WW2; 13 apps for Comb Servs
44-5. NZ > 47 & 51 A, 49 SA. Pres S
Canterbury 76. Father & two bros rep S
Canterbury.

GRANT, Malcolm Leith *Scotland*
Norwich Sch, Cambridge Univ, Harlequins,
Barbarians.
b 8.11.27.
Centre/FH, 4-2-0-2.
55 F−; 56 F+ W−; 57 F+.
Brewer.

GRANT, Patrick J. *Ireland*
Tullabeg Coll, Clongowes Coll, Bective Rgrs.

b −.12.1871 Dublin; *d* −.
FB, 2-2-0-0.
1894 S+ W+.
Solicitor.

GRANT, Thomas Oliver *Scotland*
Hawick HS, Hawick, Barbarians.
b 5.9.32 Hawick.
Lock/No 8, 6-2-1-3.
60 I+ E− SA−; 64 F+ NZ= W−.
Production study mgr/hosiery. Bro of Derrick.

GRANT, William St Clair *Scotland*
RHS Craigmount.
b 1853 Bengal; *d* −.
Back, 2-0-1-1.
1873 E=; 1874 E−.
Ckt for S.

GRATTON, J. *France*
Agen.
Flanker/No 8, 12-6-2-4.
84 NZ− NZ− R+; 85 E= S+ I= W+ Arg−
Arg+ J+ J+; 86 S−.
F > 85 Arg.

GRAULE, Vincent *France*
Perpignan.
b 22.1.04 Perpignan.
Centre, 6-1-0-5.
26 I− E− W−; 27 S− W−; 31 G+.

GRAVELL, Raymond William *Wales*
Robert
Burry Port SMS, QEGS Carmarthen, Welsh
Youth, Llanelli, Barbarians.
b 12.9.51 Mynyddygarreg.
Centre, 23-16-0-7 (4 − 1t).
75 F+ E+ S− I+ A+; 76 E+ S+ I+ F+; 78 E+
S+(1t) I+ F+ A− A− NZ−; 79 S+ I+; 81 I+
F−; 82 F+ E− S−; BI > 80 SA 4(1r)-1-0-3.
Sales rep/community service/TV. Wales B v F
72, 74. W > 75 Far East; 78 A. Wales XV v Tg
74, Arg 76, R 79. Barbarians v A 76. Barbarians
> 76 Can.

GRAVES, Charles Robert Arthur *Ireland*
Bishop Foy Sch Waterford, Wanderers,
Barbarians.
Hooker, 15-5-0-10.
34 E− S− W−; 35 E− S+ W+ NZ−; 36 E+ S+
W−; 37 E− S+; 38 E− S− W−; BI > 38 SA 2-
1-0-1.
Bank of I official. Played prop in 3rd Test BI >
38 SA.

GRAVES, Robert Henderson *Australia*
NSW.
b 1.9.1880 Sydney; *d* 15.2.57.

Forward, 1-0-0-1.
07 NZ−r.
Switched to RL.

GRAY, Anthony John   *Wales*
Friars Sch Bangor, Cardiff Coll, London Welsh,
Barbarians, Newbridge, Maesteg, Bridgend, E
Cos, London Cos.
b 14.6.42 Stoke on Trent.
Flanker, 2-1-1-0.
68 E= S+.
Schoolmaster/lecturer. W > 68 Arg. WRU N
Wales dist rep. Coach, capt London Welsh 71-2.
WRU sel 79-82, 85-6. Succeeded John Bevan as
WRU coach Dec 85.

GRAY, Arthur   *England*
Otley, Yorks.
b 4.9.17 Leeds.
FB, 3-2-0-1 (2 − 1c).
47 W+(1c) I− S+.
Fruit merchants mgr. Served WW2. Wakefield
Trin RL 47.

GRAY, B. Geoffrey   *South Africa*
Diocesan Coll Rondebosch, Cape Town Univ,
W Prov.
b 28.7.09.
Centre, 4-3-0-1.
31 W+; 32 E+ S+; 33 A−.
Lawyer. SA > 31-2 BI.

GRAY, David   *Scotland*
Kilmarnock Acad, W of Scotland.
b 28.3.53 Kilmarnock.
Lock, 9-1-1-7.
78 E−; 79 I= F− NZ−; 80 I− F+ W− E−; 81
F−.
Finance co rep.

GRAY, George Donaldson   *New Zealand*
('Doddy')
Albion, Canterbury, Poneke, Wellington, S
Island.
b c1880; *d* 16.4.61 Christchurch.
1st five-eighth, 3-2-1-0 (9 − 3t).
08 AW=; 13 A+(1t) US+(2t).
Timber yard employee. NZ > 13 NAm. 56 apps
for Canterbury, 14 for Wellington.

GRAY, George Leitch   *Scotland*
Gala.
Hooker, 4-1-0-3.
35 NZ−; 37 W+ I− E−.
Plumber. Huddersfield RL 37.

GRAY, Kenneth Francis   *New Zealand*
Wellington Coll, Paremata, Petone, Wellington,
N Island.
b 24.6.38 Porirua.
Prop, 24-21-1-2 (12 − 4t).

63 I+ W+; 64 E+ S= F+(1t); 64 A+ A+(1t)
A−; 65 SA+ SA+ SA− SA+(1t); 66 BI+ BI+
BI+ BI+; 67 W+ F+ S+; 68 A+ F+ F+; 69
W+(1t) W+.
Farmer. NZ > 63-4 BI,F & C (4 apps at lock),
67 > BI,F & C, 68 A & F.

GRAY, Robert Disney   *Ireland*
Wesley Coll, O Wesley, Barbarians.
b 2.1.1896 Ballybay, Co Monoghan; *d* 80.
Flanker/no 8, 4-2-0-2.
23 E− S−; 25 F+; 26 F+.
Ulster Bank official.

GRAY, Thomas   *Scotland*
Heriot's Coll, Northampton, Heriot's FP,
Barbarians.
b 20.1.17.
FB, 3-1-0-2 (10 − 2c 2p).
50 E+(2c); 51 F−(2p) E−.
Protective clothing salesman. Played in 5 Servs
ints.

GRAY, William Ngataiawhio   *New Zealand*
Te Puke HS, HSOB, Bay of Plenty, Rotorua
HSOB, Whakarewarewa, Ngongotaha, NZ
Maoris, N Island, N Suburbs (Sydney).
b 23.12.32 Te Puke.
2nd five-eighth, 6-4-0-2.
55 A+ A−; 56 SA+ SA− SA− SA+ SA+.
Surveyor. NZ > 57 A. Broke leg during NZ
Maoris > 58 A. NZ Maori jnr lawn tennis
champ 50. Played in A 60-2.

GREEN, Craig Ivan   *New Zealand*
Glenmark, Mid-Canterbury, NZ Colts,
Canterbury, S Island, NZ Univs.
b 23.3.61 Christchurch.
2nd five-eighth/centre, 10-6-2-2 (16 − 4t).
83 S=r E−; 84 A− A+ A+; 85 E+ E+(2t)
A+(1t) Arg+ Arg=(1t).
NZ > 83 S & E, 84 A, 85 Arg. World XV > 86
SA.

GREEN, John   *England*
Giggleswick Sch, Skipton, Yorks.
b 17.9.1881 Silsden; *d* 27.12.68.
Forward, 8-3-1-4.
05 I−; 06 S+ F+ SA=; 07 F+ W− I− S−.
Timber merchant.

GREEN, Joseph Fletcher   *England*
Rugby Sch, W Kent.
b 28.4.1847 W Ham; *d* 28.8.23 Leeds.
Half-back, 1-0-0-1.
1871 S−.
Shipowner. Inj in 1st int, S v E 1871, never
played again. Bro in law of Fred Stokes.

GREENE, Ernest H. ('Swallow') *Ireland*
Kingstown Sch, Trin Coll Dublin, Kingstown, Wanderers.
b 1862; *d* −.11.37.
Wing, 5-0-0-5 (1t).
1882 W−; 1884 W−; 1885 E−(1t) S−; 1886 E−.
Irish 100y champ 1885.

GREENLEES, H.D. *Scotland*
Rossall Sch, Leicester.
b −; *d* c77.
FH, 6-4-1-1.
27 NSW+; 28 F+ W−; 29 I+ E+; 30 E=.
Shoe shops.

GREENLEES, James Robertson *Scotland*
Campbell
Loretto Sch, Kelvinside Acad, Cambridge Univ, Kelvinside Academicals.
b 14.12.1878; *d* 16.5.51.
Forward, 7-3-1-3.
1900 I=; 02 W− I− E−; 03 W+ I+ E+.
Medicine/schoolmaster. Blue 1898-01. Ref I v E 13; E v W 14. Pres SRU 13-14.

GREENSLADE, Desmond *Wales*
Cwmcarn, Abercrave, Newbridge Youth, Newport, Barbarians.
b 11.1.33 Cwmcarn.
Prop, 1-0-0-1.
62 S−.
Coalminer.

GREENWELL, John Henry *England*
Rockcliff, Tynemouth, Barbarians, Northumb.
b 1864; *d* 42.
Forward, 2-1-0-1.
1893 W− I+.
Builder/public works contractor. More than 100 apps for Northumb; 1st to receive county cap. Received long service medal as a special constable.

GREENWOOD, Colin M. *South Africa*
Villagers, W Prov.
b 25.1.36.
Centre, 1-1-0-0 (6 − 2t).
61 I+(2t).
Wakefield Trin (E) RL.

GREENWOOD, James Thomson *Scotland*
Dunfermline HS, Dunfermline, Edinburgh Univ, RAF, Perthshire Academicals, Harlequins, E Cos, Barbarians.
b 28 Dunfermline.
Flanker/no 8, 20-8-1-11.
52 F−; 55 F− W+ I+ E−; 56 F+ W− I− E−; 57 F+ W+ E−; 58 F+ W− A+ I− E=; 59 F− W+ I−; BI > 55 SA 4-2-0-2.
Schoolmaster/lecturer. Capt S 9 times.

Barbarians > 57 Can, 58 SA. Coach at Loughborough Colls.

GREENWOOD, John Eric *England*
('Jenny') JP
Dulwich Coll, O Alleynians, Cambridge Univ, Leicester, Harlequins, Barbarians, Surrey.
b 23.7.1891; *d* −.7.75.
Forward, 13-11-0-2 (30 − 12c 2p).
12 F+; 13 SA− W+(1c) F+(1c) I+(1p) S+; 14 W+ S+ F+(6c); 20 W− F+(1c 1p) I+(1c) S+(2c).
Chartered accountant/co dir Boots Chemists. Blue 10-13, 19, capt Cambridge 12 & 19. Intended to retire from serious rugby after 19 Univ Match, dissuaded by Maj Stanley, to capt England 20. Pres of Hawks Club. With G.W. Parker, most c in an int (6 v F 14). Rep Univ on RFU 19-37. IB mem 37. Pres RFU 35-7, Trustee 48. Served WW1 Artists' Rifles, then E Surrey Rgt & Capt Grenadier Guards. Mentioned in despatches, wounded battle of Nieppe 18. JP for Nottingham 47-53.

GREENWOOD, John Richard *England*
Heaton
Merchant Taylors' Crosby, Cambridge Univ, Waterloo, Coventry, Barbarians, Lancs.
b 11.9.41.
Flanker, 5-0-1-4 (3 − 1t).
66 I=(1t) F− S−; 67 A−; 69 I−.
Schoolmaster. Blue 62-3. E coach. Taught at Stonyhurst Coll.

GREER, R. *Ireland*
Kingstown.
Forward, 1-0-0-1.
1875 E−.

GREEVES, Thomas Jackson *Ireland*
Campbell Coll, NIFC.
b 1.7.1886; *d* 28.8.74.
Centre, 5-2-0-3.
07 E+ S− W−; 09 W− F+.
Linen merchant. Pres IRU 29-30.

GREFFE, Michel *France*
Grenoble.
b 27.10.40 Lyon.
No 8/flanker, 5-2-0-3.
68 W+ Cz+ NZ− NZ− SA−.
Salesman.

GREG, Walter *England*
Marlborough Coll, Marlborough Nomads, Manchester, Lancs.
b 14.2.1851 Bollington, Cheshire; *d* 6.2.06 Assouan.
Forward, 2-2-0-0.
1875 I+; 1876 S+.

172

Solicitor. England cap & jersey in Manchester clubhouse.

GREGG, Robin Johnston *Ireland*
Ballymena Acad, Queen's Univ Belfast.
b 28.11.30 Carnlough, Ballymena.
FB, 7-3-1-3 (12 − 6c).
53 F+(2c) E= S+(4c) W−; 54 F− E− S+.
Civil engr. 4c v S 53 most by I player (with Paul Murray).

GREGORY, Gordon George *England*
Huish's Sch Taunton, Taunton, Reading Univ, Bath, Bristol, Som.
b 8.12.08 Taunton; d 4.12.63 Newton Abbot.
Hooker, 13-6-0-7 (4 − 2c).
31 I− S− F−; 32 SA− W− I+ S+; 33 W− I+ S−; 34 W+ I+(2c) S+.
Farmer.

GREGORY, John Arthur *England*
St Andrew's Coll Dublin, Rydal Sch, Dublin W, Clifton, Blackheath, Bristol, The Army, Barbarians, Glos.
b 22.6.23.
Wing, 1-0-0-1.
49 W−.
Cigarette co employee/snr sales rep. All Ireland 100y & 220y champ 47-9. Rep GB 48 Olympics (silver medal 4 x 100 relay); 50 European Champs; 52 Olympics. Joined Huddersfield RL 47; applied for reinstatement. RFU originally refused. Ultimately suspended 1 yr, until April 48. Gained his only cap following season. Pres Bristol Ath Club.

GREGORY, Stuart Carlton *Australia*
Qld.
b 18.9.46.
Lock/no 8, 16-3-1-12.
68 NZ− F+ I− S−; 69 SA− SA−; 71 SA− SA− F+ F−; 72 F= F−; 73 Tg+ Tg− W− E−.
Accountant.

GREIG, A. *Scotland*
Glasgow HS, Glasgow HSFP.
b 27.10.1889; d −.
FB, 1-0-0-1.
11 I−.

GREIG, Sir Louis Leisler KBE *Scotland*
CVO
Merchiston Castle Sch, Glasgow Acad, Glasgow Univ, RN.
b 17.11.1880; d 1.3.53.
Half-back, 5-2-0-3.
05 NZ−; 06 SA+; 07 W+; 08 W− I−; BT > 03 SA.
RN. 3rd choice S v NZ 05, after A.N. Fell & W.C. Church declined to play.

GREIG, R.C. *Scotland*
Glasgow Acad, Glasgow Academicals, Glasgow Univ.
Half-back, 2-1-0-1.
1893 W−; 1897 I+.
Pres SRU 03-4.

GRENSIDE, Bertram Arthur *New Zealand*
Taradale Sch, Pukehou Sch, Mohaka Sch, Hastings, Hawkes Bay, N Island.
b 9.4.1899 Hastings.
Wing, 6-2-0-4 (9 − 3t).
28 SA− SA+ SA−(1t) SA+; 29 A−(1t) A− (1t).
Farmer. 8t NZ > 28 SA. 30t, 141 pts Hawkes Bay 22-7.

GREVILLE, Handel *Wales*
Gwendraeth GS, Cefneithin, Tumble, Llanelli, Swansea.
b 13.9.21 Drefach.
SH, 1-1-0-0.
47 A+.
County council clerk. Swansea v SA 51. Fix sec, chmn Llanelli.

GREY, Gareth Owen *Australia*
NSW.
b 29.9.47.
SH, 5-1-0-4.
72 F−r NZ− NZ− NZ− Fj+r.
Farmer. Ar > BI & US 75-6.

GREYLING, Pieter Johannes Frederik ('Piet') *South Africa*
OFS.
b 16.5.42 Zastron.
Flanker, 25-16-4-5 (15 − 5t).
67 F+(2t) F+ F− F=; 68 BI+ F+ F+; 69 A+(1t) A+ A+ A+ S− E−(1t); 70 I=(1t) W= NZ+ NZ− NZ+ NZ+; 71 F+ F= A+ A+ A+; 72 E−.
Rep. SA > 69-70 BI. Capt SA v E 72.

GRIEVE, Charles Frederick *Scotland*
Ampleforth Coll, Oxford Univ, Barbarians, Duke of Wellington's Rgt, The Army.
b 1.10.13 Philippines.
FH, 2-0-0-2.
35 W−; 36 E−; BI > 38 SA 2-1-0-1.
The Army. Blue 34-6; Oxford Univ v NZ 35. FB 2nd & 3rd Tests BI > 38 SA.

GRIEVE, Robert George Moir *Scotland*
Kelso HS, Kelso, Barbarians.
b 1.2.11 Maxton, St Boswells.
Prop, 7-1-0-6.
35 W− I− E+ NZ−; 36 W− I− E−.
Builder.

GRIFFARD, Joseph *France*
Lyon U.
Prop/lock, 3-3-0-0.
32 G+; 33 G+; 34 G+.

GRIFFIN, A. *Wales*
Edinburgh Univ.
Forward, 1-0-0-1.
1883 S−.
Medicine. Drafted in after W had arrived in
Edinburgh a player short.

GRIFFIN, Cornelius S. *Ireland*
St Joseph's Sch Highgate, London Irish.
Wing, 2-2-0-0.
51 F+ E+.

GRIFFIN, Leslie John *Ireland*
St Andrews Coll, Wanderers, Barbarians.
b 14.9.22 Arklow.
Lock, 2-2-0-0.
49 S+ W+.
Brewery exec.

GRIFFIN, Thomas Sydney *Australia*
NSW.
b 1884; *d* 50.
Forward, 6-2-1-3.
07 NZ− NZ=; 08 W−; 10 NZ− NZ+; 12 US+.
Warehouseman. Olympic rugby gold medal 08.

GRIFFITHS, Clive Ronald *Wales*
Gowerton GS, Welsh SS, Cardiff Coll, British
Colls, Penclawdd, Llanelli.
b 2.4.54 Loughor.
FB, 1-1-0-0.
79 E+r.
Schoolmaster. Wales B v F 78. St Helens RL 79
£25,000 fee. 2 Wales RL caps, both as r.

GRIFFITHS, Daniel *Wales*
Llanelli.
b 1858 Llanelli; *d* 29.10.36 Llanelli.
Forward, 2-1-0-1.
1888 NZN+; 1889 I−.
Dock worker.

GRIFFITHS, Gareth M. *Wales*
Porth CS, St Luke's Coll, Cardiff, London
Welsh, Barbarians.
b 27.11.31 Penygraig.
Wing/centre, 12-9-0-3 (15 − 5t).
53 E− S+ I+(1t) F+(2t) NZ+; 54 I+ F+(1t)
S+; 55 I+(1t) F+; 57 E− S−; BIr > 55 SA 3-2-
0-1.
Schoolmaster/PRO. Barbarians v NZ 54.
Barbarians > 57 Can.

GRIFFITHS, Griffith ('Gitto') *Wales*
Llanelli.

b 1864 Llanelli; *d* 38 Llanelli.
Half-back, 1-0-0-1.
1889 I−.
Tinplate mill worker/foreman.

GRIFFITHS, Jack Lester MC *New Zealand*
Wellington Coll, Poneke, Wellington, N Island.
b 9.4.12 Wellington.
2nd/1st five-eighth, 7-5-1-1.
34 A=; 35 S+ I+ W−; 36 A+ A+; 38 A+.
Bank mgr. NZ > 34, 36 & 38 (capt) A, 35-6 BI
& Can. Served WW2; mentioned in despatches
& MC. Reached Maj, ADC to General
Freyberg. Capt 2nd NZEF v Comb Servs 40.
Ckt for Wanganui 20-3. NZRFU council 61-5,
exec comm 65-72. Father A.J. rep Wellington
04-5 & NZRFU sel 20-3. Uncles Jim & Fred
Tilyard NZ reps (Fred played no Tests).

GRIFFITHS, Vincent M. *Wales*
Bristol Univ, Newport.
b 29.5.01; *d* 7.1.67 Newport.
FH, 3-1-0-2 (7 − 1t 1d).
24 S−(1t) I− F+(1d); BI > 24 SA 2-0-0-2.
Schoolmaster.

GRIFFITHS, W. *Ireland*
Limerick.
Forward, 1-0-0-1.
1878 E−.

GRIGG, Peter Clive *Australia*
Townsville, Qld Country, Qld.
b 20.7.58.
Wing, 15-11-0-4 (8 − 2t).
80 NZ+(2t); 82 S+ NZ− NZ+ NZ−; 83 Arg+
NZ−; 84 Fj+ W+ S+; 85 C+ C+ NZ− Fj+
Fj+.
Insurance salesman. A > 80 Fj; 81-2 & 84 BI.

GRIMMOND, David Noel *Australia*
NSW.
b 44.
Wing, 1-0-0-1.
64 NZ−.
Co exec. RL.

GRIMSHAW, Colin *Ireland*
Methodist Coll, Queen's Univ Belfast.
b 20.3.47.
SH, 1-1-0-0.
69 E+r.
Pharmacist.

GROBLER, Cornelius Johannes *South Africa*
('Kleintjie')
OFS.
b 24.8.44 Pretoria.
3-2-1-0 (4 − 1t).
74 BI=; 75 F+ F+.
SAAF technician. SA > 74 F.

GRONOW, Benjamin *Wales*
Bridgend.
b 10.5.1889? Bridgend; *d* 24.11.67
Huddersfield.
Forward, 4-3-0-1 (3 − 1t).
10 F+(1t) E− S+ I+.
Stonemason/road haulier. Kicked off for W, in
1st int at Twickenham 15.1.10, E scoring from it
through F.E. Chapman inside a minute.
Huddersfield RL 10, later Featherstone R,
Batley. 7 GB RL Tests, 8 Wales RL.

GRUARIN, Arnaldo ('La *France*
Gruche')
Toulon.
b 5.2.38 Baguera, Italy.
Prop, 26-19-3-4 (6 − 2t).
64 W= It+ I+ SA+ Fj+ R+; 65 S+ I= E− W+
It+(1t); 66 S= I+ E+(1t) W− It+ R+; 67 S−
A+ E+ It+ W+ I+ NZ−; 68 S+ I+.
Sports shop proprietor.

GRYLLS, William Michell *England*
Haileybury & ISC, RMC Sandhurst, Redruth,
The Army, Cornwall.
b 9.1.1885; *d* −.
Lock, 1-0-0-1.
05 I−.
The Army. Served as regular with Indian Army.
Reached rank of Lt Col. Father fdr mem
Redruth 1875.

GUDSELL, Keith Eric *Australia*
Wanganui Tech Coll, Manawatu, University,
Wanganui TCOB, NZ Univs, Wanganui,
Sydney Univ, NSW.
b 19.10.24 Wanganui, NZ.
Centre, 3-0-0-3.
51 NZ− NZ− NZ−.
Veterinary surg. 6 apps NZ > SA 49 & A 50.
Went to Sydney to study.

GUELORGET, Pierre *France*
RCF.
Wing, 2-2-0-0 (6 − ?t)
31 E+ G+(2t).

GUERASSIMOFF, Jules *Australia*
Rockhampton GS, Brisbane Univ.
b 28.6.40 Thangool.
Lock/no 8, 12-5-0-7.
63 SA+ SA+ SA−; 64 NZ− NZ− NZ+; 65
SA+; 66 BI− BI−; 67 E+ I− F−.
Agricultural scientist.

GUERIN, Brendan Noel *Ireland*
Castleknock Coll, Galwegians.
b 2.1.30 Cappoquin, Co Waterford.
Lock, 1-1-0-0.
56 S+.
Bank official.

GUEST, Richard Heaton *England*
Cowley Sch, St Helens, Liverpool Univ,
Waterloo, Barbarians, Lancs.
b 12.3.18.
Wing, 13-7-1-5 (15 − 5t).
39 W+ I− S+; 47 W+ I− S+(1t) F+(1t); 48
A− W= I−(2t) S−; 49 F+ S+(1t).
Business. E sel 63-66. Served WW2, Capt RA.
Played in same E team as cousin J. Heaton in 6
ints either side WW2 (39-47).

GUICHEMERRE, Abel *France*
Dax.
b 23.8.1889 Dax; *d* 26.4.46.
No 8/flanker, 4-1-0-3.
20 E−; 21 E− I+; 23 S−.

GUILBERT, Alain *France*
Toulon.
b 28.9.50 St Maur, Val-de-Marne.
Lock/No 8, 14-7-2-5 (4 − 1t).
75 E+(1t) S+ I− SA− SA−; 76 A+; 77 Arg+
Arg= NZ+ NZ− R+; 79 I= W+ E−.
Electrical engr.

GUILLEMAN, Pierre *France*
RCF.
b −; kia WW1.
Forward, 11-1-0-10 (3 − 1t).
08 E− W−; 09 E− I−; 10 W− S− E− I−(1t);
11 S+ E− W−.

GUILLEMARD, Arthur George *England*
Rugby Sch, W Kent.
b 18.12.1846; *d* 7.8.09.
FB, 2-1-0-1.
1871 S−; 1872 S+.
Solicitor. Of French Protestant refugee stock.
Played in 1st int, S v E 1871. Ref E v I 1877, E v
S 1878, E v I 1879, E v S 1880, E v I, E v W
1881. Ump S v E 1873. Original mem RFU
1871. Pres RFU 1878-82 (held all 5 chief RFU
offices). England cap in RFU Museum.

GUILLEUX, Pierre *France*
Agen.
b 24 Usecau.
FB, 2-1-0-1.
52 SA− It+.
Handball int.

GUIRAL, Marius *France*
Agen.
FB, 3-3-0-0 (8 − 4c).
31 G+(4c); 32 G+; 33 G+.

GUMMER, Charles Henry *England*
Alexander
Plymouth A, Moseley, Brit Police, Devon.
b 20.11.05; *d* 4.2.74 Bishop's Waltham.
No 8, 1-1-0-0 (3 − 1t).

29 F+(1t).
Police/Civil Service/RAF. Served with police 27-44, WW2 as Maj in Army. RAF 52-57, then Ministry of Defence.

GUNN, Alexander William MVO   *Scotland*
Royal HS, Royal HSFP, Edinburgh Univ.
b 16.11.1890; *d* −.4.80 Stowlangtoft Hall, Suffolk.
FH, 5-2-0-3 (3 − 1t).
12 F+(1t) W− I− SA−; 13 F+.
RN surg.

GUNNER, Charles Richards   *England*
Marlborough Coll, Marlborough Nomads.
b 7.1.1853; *d* 4.2.24.
Back, 1-1-0-0.
1875 I+.
Solicitor/banker.

GUNTHER, William John   *Australia*
St Joseph's Coll, NSW.
b 34.
Flanker, 1-0-0-1.
57 NZ−.
Grazier.

GURDON, Charles   *England*
Haileybury & ISC, Cambridge Univ, Richmond, Mdx.
b 3.12.1855 Barnham Broom, Norfolk; *d* 26.6.31 Mdx.
Forward, 14-10-3-1.
1880 I+ S+; 1881 I+ W+ S=; 1882 I= S−; 1883 S+; 1884 W+ S+; 1885 I+; 1886 W+ I+ S=.
County Court Judge. Blue 1877. Rowing blue 1876-8. Played with bro Temple 10 times for E. Called to Bar 1881. Co-author of Centenary Book on Oxford & Cambridge Boat Race 27.

GURDON, Edward Temple   *England*
Haileybury & ISC, Cambridge Univ, Richmond.
b 25.1.1854 Barnham Broom, Norfolk; *d* 12.6.29 London.
Forward, 16-12-3-1 (1t).
1878 S=; 1879 I+; 1880 S+(1t); 1881 I+ W+ S=; 1882 S− W+; 1883 I+ S+; 1884 W+ I+ S+; 1885 W+ I+; 1886 S=.
Public Record office/solicitor. Of old East Anglian stock, eldest son of Rev Edward Gurdon; bro of Charles. Entered Trin Coll 1873; played in last XX to rep Cambridge. Blue 1874-6; capt 1875-6. RFU comm (1877) before being capped. Once rec apps for an English player. In 9 matches as capt, E won 8 and drew 1. Capt of 1st Champ winning side and 1st Triple Crown winners, 1883. Capt Richmond 10 yrs. Ref I v S 1898, S v I 1899; touch-judge E v S 1891. RFU sel. IB rep 1890-1928. Pres Richmond & RFU 1890-2.

GUTHRIE, F.H.   *South Africa*
Diocesan Coll Rondebosch, W Prov.
Half-back, 3-0-0-3.
1891 BT− BT−; 1896 BT−.

GUY, Richard Alan   *New Zealand*
Henderson HS, Waipu Dist HS, Waipu, N Auckland, N Island.
b 6.4.41 Lower Hutt.
Prop, 4-1-1-2.
71 BI− BI+ BI− BI=.
Dairy farmer. N Auckland comm, chmn Whangarei Dist comm. Father R.E. rep Wellington 39.

GWILLIAM, John Arthur   *Wales*
Monmouth Sch, Cambridge Univ, Newport, Barbarians, London Welsh, Gloucester, Edinburgh W.
b 28.2.23 Pontypridd.
Lock/no 8, 23-15-1-7.
47 A+; 48 I−; 49 E+ S− I− F−; 50 E+ S+ I+ F+; 51 E+ S− I= SA−; 52 E+ S+ I+ F+; 53 E+ I+ F+ NZ+; 54 E−.
HM. Blue 47-8. Taught at Glenalmond & Birkenhead Schs.

GWYNN, Arthur Percival   *Ireland*
St Columba's Coll, Trin Coll Dublin.
b 11.6.1874 Ramelton, Co Donegal; *d* 14.2.1898 Rangoon.
Wing, 1-0-0-1.
1895 W−.
Indian Civil Service. Bro of Lucius. Ckt for Gentlemen of I.

GWYNN, David   *Wales*
Swansea, Oldham, Lancs.
b c1861; *d* −.3.10 Swansea.
Back, 6-1-1-4.
1882 E−; 1887 S−; 1890 E+ I=; 1891 E− S−.
Moved to Oldham pre-1895. Later RL.

GWYNN, Lucius Henry   *Ireland*
St Columba's Coll, Trin Coll Dublin, Monkstown, Barbarians.
b 25.5.1873 Ramelton, Co Donegal; *d* 23.12.02 Davos Platz, Switz.
Wing, 7-4-1-2.
1893 S=; 1894 E+ S+ W+; 1897 S−; 1898 E+ S−.
Univ lecturer. Bro of Arthur. Ckt for Gentlemen of I.

GWYNN, William Henry   *Wales*
Battersea Coll, Swansea.
b 1856; *d* 1.4.1897 Bridgend.
Half-back, 5-1-1-3.
1884 E− S− I+; 1885 E− S=.
Schoolmaster. WRU sec 1892-6. IB rep 1892-5. Ex-footballer.

H

HADEN, Andrew Maxwell   *New Zealand*
Wanganui Intermed Sch, Wanganui Boys' Coll,
Univ, NZ Jnrs, Ponsonby, Auckland, Algida
(It), Harlequins (E).
  b 26.9.50 Wanganui.
Lock, 41-31-1-9 (8 − 2t).
77 BI+ BI− BI+(1t) BI+; 77 F− F+; 78 A+
A+ A− I+ W+ E+ S+; 79 F+ F− A− S+ E+;
80 A− A+ A− W+; 81 S+ SA+ SA− SA+; 81
R+ F+ F+; 82 A+ A− A+; 83 BI+ BI+ BI+
BI+(1t) A+; 84 F+ F+; 85 Arg+ Arg=.
Salesman/property officer/journalist. 6ft 61/2in,
believed to be tallest All Black. Rec 117 apps for
NZ. NZ > 72-3 BI,F & NAm, 76 Arg &
Uruguay, 77 F, 78 BI, 79 A, 79 E,S & It, 80 A &
Fj (14 out of 16 apps), NAm & W, 81 R & F, 83
A, 85 Arg. Played for Overseas XV v Five
Nations, Twickenham 86. World XV > 86 SA.
Autobiog 'Boots'n All' pub 84.

HADLEY, Adrian Michael   *Wales*
Lady Mary HS Cardiff, Cardiff Schools, S
Glamorgan Schools, Welsh Youth, Cardiff.
  b 1.3.63 Cardiff.
Wing, 12-6-0-6 (12 − 3t).
83 R−; 84 S− I+ F− E+(1t); 85 F− E+
Fj+(1t); 86 E− S+(1t) I+ F−.
Civil Service. Wales XV v J 83. Wales B > 83
Spain.

HADLEY, Swinbourne   *New Zealand*
Marist Bros' Sch Auckland, Marist, Auckland,
N Island, Manukau.
  b 19.9.04 Whangaroa; *d* 30.4.70 Auckland.
Hooker, 4-2-0-2.
28 SA− SA+ SA− SA+.
Harbour Board employee. NZ > 28 SA. Served
WW2; POW & invalided home. Bro of W.E.

HADLEY, William Edward   *New Zealand*
Marist Bros' Sch Auckland, Marist, Te Puke,
Bay of Plenty, Auckland, N Island, Takapuna.
  b 11.3.10 Auckland.
Hooker, 8-4-1-3 (6 − 2t).
34 A− A=; 35 S+(1t) I+ W−; 36 E− A+(1t)
A+.
Carpenter/plasterer. NZ > 34 & 36 A, 35-6 BI
& C (broke jaw in opening match). Bro of
Swinbourne.

HAGET, André   *France*
PUC.
  b 26.4.31 Biarritz.
FH, 14-10-0-4 (3 − 1t).
53 E−; 54 I+ NZ+ E+ Arg+; 55 E+ W− It+;
57 I− E− It+(1t) R+; 58 It+ SA+.
Dentist. Son of Henri.

HAGET, Francis   *France*
Agen, Biarritz.
  b 1.10.49 Sauveterre-de-Béarn.
Lock, 32-19-3-10 (4 − 1t).
74 Arg+ Arg+; 75 SA− Arg+ Arg+ R+; 76
S+; 78 S+(1t) I+ W− R+; 79 I= W+ E− S+
NZ− NZ+ R+; 80 W− S− I+; 84 S− NZ−
NZ− R+; 85 E= S+ I=; 86 S− I+ W+ E+.
Casino croupier. F > 74, 85 Arg; 79 NZ. Career
interrupted by back inj.

HAGET, Henri   *France*
CASG, Biarritz Ol.
  b −; *d* 68.
FH, 2-1-0-1 (7 − 1t 1p).
28 S−(1t); 30 G+(1p).
Father of André.

**HAHN, C.H.L. ('Hudie' or   *South Africa*
'Cocky')**
Transvaal.
Wing, 3-2-0-1 (3 − 1t).
10 BI+(1t) BI− BI+.

HAIG, James Scott   *New Zealand*
Kaitangata Sch, Kaitangata Crescent, S Otago,
Otago, Kaikorai, S Island.
  b 7.12.24 Prestonpans, Scotland.
SH, 2-2-0-0 (3 − 1t).
46 A+(1t) A+.
Storeman/co rep. Went to NZ at early age.
Turned RL, rep NZ 47-54 (only player to have
been All Black cap at both codes since WW2).
Bro of Laurie. Another bro Bert rep Otago. Son
Barry NZ Colts 79.

HAIG, Laurence Stokes   *New Zealand*
Kaitangata Sch, S Otago, Kaitangata Crescent,
Otago, S Island.
  b 18.10.22 Prestonpans, Scotland.
1st five-eighth, 9-8-0-1 (5 − 1t 1c).
50 BI+(1c) BI+ BI+; 51 A+ A+ A+(1t); 53
W−; 54 E+ S+.
Coalminer/food corpn branch mgr. NZ > 51 A,
v-capt 53-4 BI,F & NAm (19 apps). Bro of J.S.

HAIGH, Leonard   *England*
Sandringham House Southport, Manchester,
Barbarians, Lancs.
  b 19.10.1880 Prestwich; *d* 6.8.16 Woolwich.
Prop, 7-4-1-2.
10 W+ I= S+; 11 W− F+ I− S+.
Cadet Officer. Died in training for active service
WW1.

HAKIN, Ronald Frederick   *Ireland*
Regent House Newtownards, Stranmillis Tech
Coll, CIYMS.
  b 3.9.50 Belfast.
Lock, 6-0-0-6.

76 W− S− NZ−; 77 W− E− F−.
Schoolmaster.

HALE, Peter Martin   *England*
Solihull Sch, Solihull, Moseley, Midland Cos, N Midlands.
b 12.8.43 Hall Green, Birmingham.
Wing, 3-2-0-1.
69 SA+; 70 I+ W−.
Accountancy clerk/sales rep. Rep Warwicks at lawn tennis.

HALES, Duncan Alister   *New Zealand*
Dannevirke HS, Dannevirke OB, Hawkes Bay, Lincoln Coll, NZ Univs, Canterbury, Palmerston N HSOB, Manawatu, S Island.
b 22.11.47 Dannevirke.
Wing/centre, 4-4-0-0.
72 A+ A+ A+ W+.
Govt land valuer/chiropractor. NZ > 72-3 BI,F & NAm. Studied chiropractic at Palmer Coll, US.

HALET, René   *France*
Strasbourg.
b 17.3.1899 Mans.
Wing, 3-0-0-3.
25 NZ− S− W−.

HALL, C.   *England*
Gloucester.
Forward, 2-0-0-2.
01 I− S−.
Hotelier.

HALL, Duncan A.   *Australia*
Brisbane, Qld.
b 16.3.56 Qld.
Flanker/lock, 15-10-0-5 (4 − 1t).
80 Fj+ NZ+ NZ+ NZ−; 81 F+ F+(1t); 82 S− S+; NZ− NZ+; 83 US+ Arg− Arg+ NZ− It+.
PE instructor. A > 79 Arg; 81-2 BI. Father Duncan played RL for A.

HALL, Ian   *Wales*
Aberavon, S Wales Police, Barbarians.
b 4.11.46 Gilfach Goch.
Centre/wing, 8-4-3-1.
67 NZ−; 70 SA= S+ E+; 71 S+; 74 S+ I= F=.
Police. Wales XV v Tg 74. Welsh XV v NZ 74.

HALL, John   *England*
Gateshead Inst, N Durham, Hartlepool R, Blackheath, Durham Co.
Forward, 3-1-0-2.
1894 W+ I− S−.

HALL, John Peter   *England*
Beechen Cliff Sch, E Colts, Oldfield OB, Bath.
b 15.3.62 Bath.

Flanker, 15-4-1-10 (4 − 1t).
84 S−r I+ F− SA− SA− A−; 85 R+ F= S+ I− W− NZ− NZ−(1t); 86 W+ S−.
Sportswear salesman. E > 84 SA. Broke thumb v S 86, missed remainder of int season.

HALL, Norman Macleod ('Nim')   *England*
Worksop Coll, St Mary's Hosp, The Army, Huddersfield, Comb Servs, Barbarians, Richmond, Yorks, Mdx.
b 2.8.25 Huddersfield; d 26.6.72 London.
FH/centre/FB, 17-9-2-6 (39 − 8c 3d 4p).
47 W+(1d) I− S+(1d) F+; 49 W−(1d) I−; 52 SA− W− S+(2c) I+ F+(2p); 53 W+(1c) I=(2p) F+(1c) S+(4c); 55 W− I=.
Medical student/insurance broker/licensee. Capt E 13 times.

HALL, R.O.N.   *Ireland*
Trin Coll Dublin.
Forward, 1-0-0-1.
1884 W−.

HALL, William Herdman   *Ireland*
RBAI, Instonians.
b 16.8.01 Belfast; d 20.10.83.
FH/SH, 6-2-0-4.
23 E− S− W+ F−; 24 F+ S−.
Chartered accountant/building soc mgr.

HALLARAN, Charles Francis   *Ireland*
George Thomas AM
Eastman's Coll, RNC Dartmouth, US Portsmouth, RN, Barbarians, Surrey.
b 10.6.1897; kia 21.3.41.
Flanker/lock/prop, 15-6-0-9.
21 E− S+ W−; 22 E− S− W−; 23 E− F−; 24 F+ E− S− W+; 25 F+; 26 F+ E+.
RN.

HALLIDAY, Simon John   *England*
Downside Sch, Oxford Univ, Bath.
b 13.7.60 Haverfordwest, Pembs.
Centre, 2-1-0-1.
86 W+ S−.
Blue 79-81. Also ckt blue, 9 apps OUCC 80-2; also Minor Cos, Free Foresters. England Under 23s > Far East 82; R 83. England XV v Can 83. Out of rugby for yr with broken leg. England B v I 85.

HALPIN, Thomas   *Ireland*
Garryowen.
b 1888; d −.1.54.
Forward, 13-6-1-6.
09 S− W− F+; 10 E= S− W−; 11 E+ S+ W− F+; 12 F+ E− S+.

HAMALAINEN, Harold Arwit   *Australia*
('Hamma')
Qld.

178

b 03; d 75.
Flanker, 3-3-0-0.
29 NZ+ NZ+ NZ+.
Truck driver.

HAMERSLEY, Alfred St George   *England*
KC (Can) MP
Marlborough Coll, Marlborough Nomads,
Canterbury (NZ).
b 8.10.1848 Great Haseley, Oxon; d 25.2.29
Bournemouth.
Forward, 4-2-1-1 (1t).
1871 S−; 1872 S+(1t); 1873 S=; 1874 S+.
Lawyer/MP. Played in 1st int, S v E 1871. Called
to Bar 1873. Tory MP for Woodstock 10-18. In
WW1 recruited & trained artillery batteries; in
17, at age 68, went to France as CO of Heavy
Artillery. Reached rank of Lt Col. Credited
with furthering game of rugby in NZ and Can on
visits there. Capt Canterbury in NZ. Legal
adviser to City of Vancouver & Canadian Pacific
Rly.

HAMILTON, A.J.   *Ireland*
Lansdowne.
Forward, 1-0-0-1.
1884 W−.

HAMILTON, Andrew Steven   *Scotland*
Ripon GS, Headingley, Barbarians.
b 8.3.1893 Hamilton; d 3.11.75 Leeds.
Centre/FH, 2-1-0-1.
14 W−; 20 F+.
Civil engr.

HAMILTON, Bruce G.   *Australia*
NSW.
Lock, 1-0-0-1.
46 M−.
Ar > NZ 46.

HAMILTON, Donald Cameron   *New Zealand*
Southland Boys' HS, Pirates, Southland, S
Island.
b 19.1.1883 Invercargill; d 14.4.25 Invercargill.
Flanker, 1-0-1-0.
08 AW=.
Chemist. Banned sine die by Southland RFU
after participating in RL exhibition match with
his RU club Pirates v Britannia 09. Capt
Southland at ckt 10-11; nominated for NZ 14.
Served WW1, NZ Medical Corps.

HAMILTON, F.   *South Africa*
E Prov.
1-0-0-1.
1891 BT−.

HAMILTON, Hugh Montgomerie   *Scotland*
Marlborough Coll, W of Scotland.
b 26.6.1854; d 11.8.30 Australia.

Back, 2-0-1-1.
1874 E−; 1875 E=.
Judge. Ump E v S 1876.

HAMILTON, Rex Lamont   *Ireland*
Campbell Coll Belfast, NIFC.
b 30.4.1898 Belfast; d 2.6.84 Belfast.
Wing, 1-1-0-0.
26 F+.
Flax merchant.

HAMILTON, Robert Wallace   *Ireland*
Trin Coll Dublin, Wanderers.
b 1870; d 23.8.46.
Forward, 1-0-0-1.
1893 W−.

HAMILTON, Willoughby J.   *Ireland*
Harrow Sch, Trin Coll Dublin.
Forward, 1-0-0-1.
1877 E−.

HAMILTON-HILL, Edward A.   *England*
OBE
HMS Conway, Harlequins, RN, Surrey.
b 22.11.08; d 23.10.79.
Flanker, 3-1-1-1.
36 NZ+ W= I−.
RN/Merchant Navy. Served WW2 in RN. Lived
in Malta from 46; man dir Radio & TV Services.
OBE 61.

HAMILTON-WICKES, Richard   *England*
Henry
Bilton Grange Sch, Wellington Coll, Cambridge
Univ, Harlequins.
b 31.12.01 Northwood, Mdx; d 2.6.63.
Wing, 10-4-2-4 (12 − 4t).
24 I+(1t); 25 NZ− W+(1t) I= S−(1t) F+(1t);
26 W= I− S−; 27 W+.
Blue 20-3 (capt 22-3).

HAMLET, George Thomas   *Ireland*
Wesley Coll, O Wesley
b 9.4.1881 Balbriggan; d 10.10.59.
Forward, 30-12-1-17.
02 E− S+ W− NZ−; 04 S− W+; 05
E+ S+ W− NZ−; 06 SA−; 07 E+ S− W−; 08
E− S+ W−; 09 E− S− W− F+; 10 E= S− F+;
11 E+ S+ W− F+.
Pres IRU 26-7.

HAMMAND, Charles Ackroyd   *Australia*
NSW.
b 9.5.1888 Waverley; d −.
Forward, 2-1-0-1.
08 W−; 09 E+.
Medicine.

HAMMETT, Ernest Dyer   *England*
Galbraith

179

Newport Intermed Sch, Newport HS, Newport, Cardiff, Blackheath, Barbarians, Surrey, Som. *b* 15.10.1891 Radstock; *d* 23.6.47. Centre, 8-6-0-2 (12 − 6c). 20 W− F+ S+; 21 W+(1c) I+ S+(3c) F+(2c); 22 W−. Schoolmaster. Offered WRU Trial 19. Elected to play for E. W v E lawn tennis.

HAMMON, John Douglas *Australia* **Campbell ('Bill')** Palmerston N BHS, Auckland GS, Auckland, St Kilda, Victoria. *b* 3.3.14 Invercargill, NZ. Centre, 1-0-0-1. 37 SA−. A > NZ 36.

HAMMOND, Charles Edward *England* **Lucas ('Curly')** Bedford GS, Oxford Univ, Harlequins, Barbarians, Mdx. *b* 3.10.1879; *d* 15.4.63. Forward, 8-3-0-5. 05 S− NZ−; 06 W− I− S+ F+; 08 W− I+. Schoolmaster. Blue 1899-1900. Mdx v NZ 05. Various teaching posts inc Wellington Coll 06-7 & Felsted 40-3. Uncle of Robin Prescott (RFU sec 63-71).

HAMMOND, Ian Arthur *New Zealand* Marlborough. *b* 25.10.25 Blenheim. Hooker, 1-1-0-0. 52 A+. Farmer. NZ > 51 A. Marlborough RU comm & pres.

HANCOCK, Andrew William *England* Framlingham Coll, London Univ, Sidcup, Cambridge, Northampton, Stafford, Barbarians, Wasps, London Cos, Staffs, E Cos. *b* 19.6.39. Wing, 3-1-1-1 (3 − 1t). 65 F+ S=(1t); 66 F−. Town & country planning. Scored memorable t v S 65. In the final moments he received the ball inside his own 25 and ran 95y for a score which drew the match.

HANCOCK, Francis Escott *Wales* Cardiff, Somerset. *b* 7.12.1859 Wiveliscombe; *d* 29.10.43 Wiveliscombe. Back, 4-1-1-2. 1884 I+; 1885 E− S=; 1886 S−. Brewery dir. Credited as fdr of 4 threequarter system at Cardiff 1884; introduced it W v S 1886. Bro of Froude Hancock; 2 other bros played for Cardiff.

HANCOCK, George Edward *England* Rock Ferry HS, O Rockferrians, Birkenhead Pk, RAF, Mount Hope (Can), Cheshire. *b* 21.3.12. Centre, 3-2-0-1. 39 W+ I− S+; BT > 36 Arg. Solicitor. Served WW2, Ft Lt in RAF.

HANCOCK, Patrick Sortain *England* Dulwich Coll, Leytonstone, Streatham, Richmond, E Cos, Surrey. *b* 1883; *d* −. FH, 3-1-1-1. 04 W= I+ S−; BT > 03 SA. Farmer. Emigrated Can. Served WW1 with Canadian Forces; lost leg.

HANCOCK, Philip Froude *England* **('Baby')** Cavendish Coll, Cambridge Univ, Wiveliscombe, Blackheath, Barbarians, Som. *b* 29.8.1865 Wellington, Som; *d* 16.10.33 Clifton, Som. Forward, 3-2-0-1. 1886 W+ I+; 1890 W−; BT > 1891 SA; 1896 SA. Brewery dir. At 6ft 5in & 17st one of biggest of early forwards. One of 5 bros to play for Wiveliscombe & Som. Bro Frank was Cardiff & W capt, with whom he originated 4-threequarters system, 1886. Capped in 1888 E side that did not play. Only int player to tour with both BT teams to SA 1891 & 1896. Travelled from Som to London (170 miles each way) to play for Blackheath. Often had to walk final 10 miles of journey home. Introduced S.M.J. Woods to Som CCC (Woods studied brewing at Hancock's brewery).

HANCOCK, William Jack Henry *England* The Army, R Signals, Cross Keys, Newport. *b* 26.9.32 Newport, Gwent. Lock, 2-0-1-1. 55 W− I=. The Army/ICI. Salford RL 55.

HANDFORD, Frank G. *England* The Leys Sch, Kersal, Manchester, Barbarians, Lancs. *b* 1884. Flanker, 4-2-0-2. 09 W− F+ I+ S−; BI > 10 SA. Emigrated SA.

HANDS, Reginald Harold *England* **Myburgh** Diocesan Coll Rondebosch SA, Oxford Univ, Manchester, Blackheath, Barbarians, Mdx. *b* 26.7.1888 Cape Town; *d* 20.4.18 France. Forward, 2-2-0-0. 10 F+ S+.

180

Lawyer. Rhodes Scholar. Blue 08-9. Bros K.C.M. & P.A.M. also Oxford blues. All 3 bros played Test ckt for SA v E 13-14. Called to Bar 11. Served WW1 with SA Heavy Artillery in German SW Africa & F; died of wounds.

HANDY, Christopher Bernard   *Australia*
('Buddha')
Qld.
 b 28.3.50.
Prop, 6-4-0-2.
78 NZ+; 79 NZ+ Arg− Arg+; 80 NZ+ NZ−.
Hotel mgr/tv broadcaster.

HANLEY, Joseph ('Jerry')   *England*
Plymouth A, Civil Service, Devon.
 b 14.9.01.
Flanker, 7-5-0-2 (3 − 1t).
27 W+ S− F−; 28 W+ I+ F+ S+(1t).
Fitter HM Dockyard Devonport.

HANLEY, Ross Gregory   *Australia*
Brothers, Brisbane, Qld.
 b 6.12.61.
Wing/centre, 2-2-0-0 (4 − 1t).
83 US+r(1t) It+r.
Civil servant. A Under 21s. A > 82 NZ; 83 It & F; 84 Fj; 84 BI.

HANNAFORD, Ronald Charles   *England*
Crypt Sch, Gloucester, Durham Univ, Cambridge Univ, Rosslyn Pk, Bristol, Durham Co, Glos.
 b 19.10.44 Gloucester.
No 8, 3-1-1-1 (3 − 1t).
71 W−(1t) I+ F=.
Schoolmaster. Blue 67. Taught at Clifton Coll.

HANNAH, Ronald S.M.   *Scotland*
W of Scotland.
Wing, 1-0-0-1.
71 I−.

HANNAN, James   *Wales*
Newport, London Welsh.
 b 1864 Newport; d 22.6.05 Newport.
Forward, 19-7-1-11 (2t).
1888 NZN+(1t); 1889 S− I−; 1890 S− E+ I=; 1891 E−; 1892 E− S−(1t) I−; 1893 E+ S+ I+; 1894 E− S+ I−; 1895 E− S− I+.
Boilermaker/foreman.

HANRAHAN, Charles J.   *Ireland*
Castleknock Coll, Dolphin, Barbarians.
 b −; d 28.2.69.
Prop/no 8, 20-11-1-8 (3 − 1t).
26 S+ W−(1t); 27 E− S+ W+ NSW−; 28 F+ E− S+; 29 F+ E+ S− W=; 30 F− E+ S+ W−; 31 F−; 32 S+ W+.
Bank mgr. Pres IRU 54-5.

HANVEY, Robert Jackson   *England*
Aspatria, Blennerhasset, Cumberland & Westmorland.
 b 16.8.1899.
Prop, 4-1-1-2.
26 W= I− F+ S−.
Shoe repairer. Ref. Served WW1.

HARBISON, Harry Thomas   *Ireland*
Blackrock Coll, UC Dublin, Bective Rgrs.
 b 19.8.57 Dublin.
Hooker, 3-0-0-3.
84 W−r E− S−.
I > 81 SA.

HARDCASTLE, Philip Angus   *Australia*
St George's Coll Buenos Aires, NSW.
 b 23.12.19 Buenos Aires; d 62.
Lock, 3-1-0-2.
46 NZ− NZ−; 49 M+.
Medicine.

HARDCASTLE, William Robert   *Australia*
Petone HS, Wellington, Melrose, Glebe, NSW.
 b 30.8.1874 Wellington, NZ; d 11.7.44 Randwick.
Forward, 2-0-0-2.
1899 BT−; 03 NZ−.
Miner/grocer. NZ > A 1897. Australia RL > E 08-9.

HARDING, Arthur Flowers   *Wales*
('Boxer')
Christ's Coll Brecon, London Welsh, Barbarians.
 b 8.8.1878 Market Rasen; d 15.5.47 Martinborough, NZ.
Forward, 20-15-1-4 (3 − 1t).
02 E+ S+ I+; 03 E+ S− I+; 04 E= S+ I−; 05 E+(1t) S+ I+ NZ+; 06 E+ S+ I− SA−; 07 I+; 08 E+ S+; BT > 04 A, NZ; 08 A, NZ.
Articled clerk/station mgr. Middlesex v NZ 05. Capt BT > 08 A, NZ. Emigrated to NZ 10.

HARDING, Charles Theodore   *Wales*
Monmouth Sch, Newport.
 b 1860 Chorlton; d 13.7.19 Newport.
Forward, 3-1-0-2.
1888 NZN+; 1889 S− I−.
Docksman. Fdr mem Newport. Bro of George.

HARDING, Ernest Harold   *England*
Devonport Servs, RN.
 b 22.5.1899; d 25.12.80 Liskeard.
No 8, 1-0-0-1.
31 I−.
RN.

HARDING, George Frederick JP   *Wales*
Monmouth Sch, Newport.
 b 1858 Chorlton; d 8.7.27 Newport.

Forward/back/half-back, 4-1-0-3.
1881 E−; 1882 I+ E−; 1883 S−.
Co dir. Fdr mem Newport. Mon CCC. Bro of
Theo.

HARDING, M.A.　　　　　　　　*Australia*
NSW.
b 28.12.55 Wellington, NZ.
1-1-0-0.
83 It+.

HARDING, Richard M.　　　　　　*England*
Bristol.
SH, 3-2-1-0.
85 R+ F= S+.

HARDING, Victor Sydney James　　*England*
St Marylebone GS, The Army, Cambridge
Univ, Sale, Saracens, Barbarians, London Cos,
Harlequins, Edinburgh W, Mdx.
b 18.6.32.
Lock, 6-2-3-1 (3 − 1t).
61 F=(1t) S+; 62 W= I+ F− S=.
Sales mgr/NCB. Blue 58-60.

HARDING, W. Rowe　　　　　　　*Wales*
Gowerton CS, Cambridge Univ, Swansea,
London Welsh, Llanelli, Barbarians.
b 10.9.01 Birchgrove, Swansea.
Wing, 17-6-1-10 (15 − 5t).
23 E− S− F+(1t) I−; 24 I− F+ NZ−; 25 F+
I−; 26 E= I+(1t) F+; 27 E−(1t) S− F+(2t) I−;
28 E−; BI > 24 SA 3-0-1-2.
Circuit judge. Blue 24-7. Capt W 4 times.
WRU, Barbarian comm. Chmn Swansea RFC,
Glamorgan CCC. Chancellor Diocese of St
David's 49.

HARDWICK, Peter F.　　　　　　*England*
Percy Pk, Northumb.
b 1877; d −.2.24 N Shields.
Forward, 8-3-1-4.
02 I+ S+; 03 W− I− S−; 04 W= I+ S−.
Marine engr. Served WW1, superintendent of
repair of damaged warships.

HARDY, Evan Michael Pearce　　*England*
OBE
Ampleforth Coll, Blackheath, The Army, Comb
Servs, Headingley, Barbarians, Yorks.
b 3.11.27 Bareilly, India.
FH, 3-1-0-2.
51 I− F− S+.
The Army. Served in Korea. Reached rank of
Col. Army rep on RFU. Comb Servs, Army
ckter.

HARDY, Gerald Gabriel　　　　　*Ireland*
Castleknock Coll, Bective Rgrs.
b 29.3.37 Omeath, Co Louth; d −.10.63
Gormanston, Co Meath.

FH, 1-0-0-1.
62 S−.
Licensee/fish merchant. Killed in road accident.

HARE, William Henry ('Dusty')　　*England*
Magnus GS Newark, Nottingham, Leicester,
Newark, E Midlands.
b 29.11.52 Newark.
FB, 25-11-2-12 (240 − 2t 14c 1d 67p).
74 W+; 78 F− NZ−(1d 1p); 79 NZ−(3p); 80
I+(3c 2p) F+(1p) W+(3p) S+(2c 2p); 81 W−
(1t 5p) S+(1c 3p) Arg=(2c 1p) Arg+(1c 2p); 82
F+(2c 5p) W+(3p); 83 F−(4p) W=(2p) S−(3p)
I−(5p) NZ+(1c 3p); 84 S−(2p) I+(3p) F−(1t 2c
2p) W−(5p) SA−(4p) SA−(3p); BI > 83 NZ.
Farmer. E's most capped FB, most pts in ints,
most pts in Champ (44 in 84), most p in Champ
(14 in 83). Failed to score in only 1st 2 ints.
Passed Sam Doble's world rec pts (3651) 81. 10
apps Notts CCC 71-77. Autobiography (with
David Norrie) 'Dusty' pub 85.

HARIZE, Dominique　　　　　　　*France*
Cahors, Toulouse.
b 26.2.56 St Cere.
Wing, 9-6-0-3 (16 − 4t).
75 SA−(1t) SA−; 76 A+(1t) A+ R−; 77
W+(1t) E+ S+(1t) I+.

HARMAN, George Richard　　　　*Ireland*
Aniacke
Monmouth GS, Trin Coll Dublin, Barbarians.
b 6.6.1874 Crosshaven, Co Cork; d 14.12.75
Totnes Point, Devon.
Centre, 2-2-0-0.
1899 E+ W+.
Medicine. Longest lived int player.

HARPER, Sir Charles Henry KBE　　*England*
CMG
Blundell's Sch, Oxford Univ, Blackheath,
Exeter, Devon.
b 24.2.1876; d 14.5.50 Heswall.
Forward, 1-0-0-1.
1899 W−.
Colonial Service. Blue 1897-8. Called to Bar 09.
OBE 19. CMG 21. KBE 30. Died on golf
course.

HARPER, Eric Tristram　　　　*New Zealand*
St Patrick's Coll Wellington, Christchurch Boys'
HS, Christchurch, Canterbury, S Island.
b 1.12.1877 Papanui; kia 30.4.18 Palestine.
Centre/wing, 2-2-0-0 (6 − 2t).
04 BT+; 06 F+(2t).
Solicitor. Won NZ champs at 400y hurdles 01 &
880y 02. NZ > 05-6 BI,F & NAm. Ckt for
Canterbury 07; noted mountaineer who
discovered a pass to the West Coast at head of
Rangitata River 08. Canterbury RU comm 10-
11. Bro Cuthbert rep Canterbury 06. Served

WW1, Canterbury Mounted Rifles; killed whilst quietening horses during artillery bombardment.

HARPER, John   *Ireland*
RBAI, Instonians, RAF.
b 15.8.21 Belfast.
Centre, 3-2-0-1.
47 F− E+ S+.
RAF/merchant.

HARPUR, Thomas Gerald OBE   *Ireland*
Trin Coll Dublin.
ab 30.10.1887; *d* −.
Forward, 3-1-0-2.
08 E− S+ W−.
Medicine. Emigrated to NZ. Served WW1, NZMC & 2nd Auckland Rgt.

HARRIS, Daniel J.E.   *Wales*
Ferndale GS, Pontypridd, London Welsh, Cardiff.
b 36.
Lock, 8-4-0-4.
59 I+ F−; 60 S+ I+ F− SA−; 61 E+ S−.
Schoolmaster/hotelier. Leigh RL.

HARRIS, Perry Colin   *New Zealand*
Feilding Agric HS, Te Kawau, Manawatu.
b 11.1.46 Feilding.
Prop, 1-0-0-1.
76 SA−.
Farmer/insurance agent. NZr > 76 SA for inj B.R. Johnstone. Father Rex & bro Graham rep Manawatu.

HARRIS, Stanley Wakefield CBE   *England*
Bedford GS, Blackheath, E Midlands, Pirates (SA), Kenya, Transvaal.
b 13.12.1893; *d* Cape Town 73.
Wing, 2-2-0-0 (3 − 1t).
20 I+ S+(1t); BI > 24 SA 2-0-0-2.
The Army. Played for Pirates in Johannesburg when chosen as wing BI > 24 SA; took over as FB because of spate of inj. Spent most of life in SA. Played for Transvaal 14. Served WW1, badly wounded as gunnery officer in Battle of Somme. Took up dancing whilst recuperating; progressed to finals of world ballroom champs. Declined to rep GB in 20 Olympic mod pentathlon in order to concentrate on rugby. Won SA amateur light-heavywt boxing title 21. Rep SA in Davis Cup; won All-England Mixed Doubles title. Rep E at polo. Served WW2, POW of Japanese 3 1/2 yrs, working on notorious 'Rly of Death' in Siam. CBE 46.

HARRIS, Tal   *Wales*
Aberavon.

SH, 1-0-0-1.
27 NSW−
Docker.

HARRIS, Terence Anthony   *South Africa*
CBC Kimberley, Transvaal.
b 27.8.16 Kimberley.
FH, 5-4-0-1 (3 − 1t).
37 NZ+ NZ+; 38 BI+(1t) BI+ BI−.
Clerk. Ckt for SA (3 Tests 47-9); scored 114 no Griq W v OFS when 17yrs 4mths, world's youngest debut century in 1st class ckt. 5 times Griq W lawn tennis champ.

HARRIS, Thomas William   *England*
Barry Road Sch Northampton, Northampton.
b 06 Northampton; *d* −.11.58 Northampton.
Lock/no 8, 2-1-0-1.
29 S−; 32 I+.
Fish & fruit salesman.

HARRISON, Arthur Clifford TD   *England*
Hartlepool R, Barbarians, Durham Co.
b 10.5.11.
Wing, 2-0-0-2.
31 I− S−.
Accountant/brewery co sec. Also played for Mombasa Sports Club & Selangor Sports Club. Served WW2.

HARRISON, Arthur Leyland VC   *England*
Dover Coll, RNC Dartmouth, US Portsmouth, RN, Hants.
b 3.2.1886 Torquay; kia 23.4.18 Zeebrugge.
Forward, 2-2-0-0.
14 I+ F+.
RN. Served WW1; fought at Battle of Jutland. Mentioned in despatches 16. Posthumous VC for part in blocking of Zeebrugge 18.

HARRISON, Gilbert ('Gillie')   *England*
Cheltenham Coll, Hull, Yorks.
b 13.6.1858 Cottingham; *d* 9.11.1894.
Forward, 7-5-1-1.
1877 I+ S−; 1879 S= I+; 1880 S+; 1885 W+ I+.
Corn merchant. His club, Hull, helped form NU 1895.

HARRISON, Harold Cecil   *England*
('Dreadnought') CB DSO
KES Birmingham, RMA Woolwich, US Portsmouth, R Marines, The Army, RN, Barbarians, Kent.
b 26.2.1889; *d* 26.3.40 Marylebone.
Forward, 4-3-0-1 (4 − 2c).
09 S−; 14 I+ S+(2c) F+.
The Army. Served WW1, commanded SA Siege Battery; DSO 16. CB 39. Known in Army as 'Tiny' and 'Dreadnought' by seamen. Ref F v S 22.

HARRISON, Michael E.   *England*
QEGS Wakefield, Loughborough Univ,
Wakefield, Yorks.
b 19.4.56 Barnsley.
Wing, 5-1-0-4 (8 − 2t).
85 NZ−(1t) NZ−(1t); 86 S− I+ F−.
Banking. Right wing for Yorks, left for E. High-
class sprinter − 10.7s 100 metres. Car accident
inj kept him out of rugby for 2 yrs.

HARRISON, T.   *Ireland*
Cork.
FB/back, 3-0-0-3.
1879 S−; 1880 S−; 1881 E−.

HARROWER, P.R.   *Scotland*
London Scottish.
b 19.1.1860; *d* −.
FB, 1-0-1-0.
1885 W=.

HART, Augustine Henry   *New Zealand*
Marist Bros' Sch Auckland, Sacred Heart Coll,
New Plymouth Tech Coll, Tukapa, Taranaki, N
Island.
b 28.3.1897 Auckland; *d* 1.2.65 Auckland.
Wing, 1-1-0-0.
24 I+.
Fancy goods shop proprietor. Top t scorer 23t
(17 apps) NZ > 24-5 A,BI,F & Can.

HART, George Fletcher   *New Zealand*
Waitaki Boys' HS, Canterbury B, Christchurch,
Canterbury, S Island.
b 10.2.09 Christchurch; *d* 3.6.44 Sora, It.
Wing, 11-8-0-3 (21 − 7t).
30 BI−(1t) BI+(1t) BI+ BI+; 31 A+(1t); 34
A−; 35 S+ I+(1t) W−; 36 A+(1t) A+(2t).
Commercial traveller/real estate agent. Broken
collar bone restricted him to only 1 app NZ > 32
A. NZ > 34 & 36 A, 35-6 BI & Can. NZ 100y
champ 31 with 10.4s. Capt in 20th Armoured
Rgt; died of wounds received during advance
from Cassino to Avezzano.

HART, John Garrow Maclachlan   *Scotland*
George Watson's Coll, Watsonians, Edinburgh
Univ, RAF, Comb Servs, E Midlands, London
Scottish. ·
b 7.4.28 Balfron, Stirling.
Wing, 1-0-0-1.
51 SA−.
Trading in steel-making raw materials. Five
Nations comm. FHU tours comm sec, sec IB 71-
86. World-class hurdler; S 120y hurdles rec
stood for 20yrs; rep S in Empire Games,
Auckland 50; rep GB 49 & 52.

HART, Thomas Mure   *Scotland*
Strathallan Sch, Glasgow Univ, Oxford Univ.
b 1.3.09 Glasgow.

Centre/FH, 2-1-0-1.
30 W+ I−.
Colonial service. Blue 31. Ckt for S.

HART, Walter   *Scotland*
Newtown Sch, Melrose.
b 30.3.35 Newton St Boswells.
Flanker, 1-0-0-1.
60 SA−.
Upholstery.

HARTLEY, A.J.   *South Africa*
W Prov.
1-0-0-1.
1891 BT−.

HARTLEY, Bernard Charles   *England*
(**'Jock'**) CB OBE
Dulwich Coll, Cambridge Univ, Blackheath,
Barbarians, Sussex, Kent.
b 16.3.1879 Woodford; *d* 24.4.60.
Forward, 2-1-0-1.
01 S−; 02 S+.
Stockbroker. Blue 1900. Ath blue (hammer)
1899-01. Twice rowed for Jesus Coll at Henley.
Rep Cambridge on RFU 07-8; The Army 21-22
& 28-48. E sel 23-4. Mgr BI > 37 SA. IB rep 45-
54. Pres RFU 47-8. Served WW1, Herts Rgt;
gassed & wounded. Sec Army Sports Control
Bd 18-41. OBE 25. National Playing Fields
Assoc 26-46. CB 46.

HARVEY, Frederick Maurice   *Ireland*
Watson VC MC Croix de Guerre
Portora RS, Ellesmere Coll, Wanderers.
b 1.9.1888; *d* 21.8.80 Calgary, Can.
FH/FB, 2-1-0-1.
07 W−; 11 F+.
The Army. Served WW1; VC 17. One of 3
Wanderers players (see Tommy Crean & Robert
Johnston) to win VC. Emigrated to Can.

HARVEY, George Alfred Duncan   *Ireland*
CB CMG
Portora RS, Wanderers.
b 27.10.1882; *d* 22.9.57.
Centre, 5-4-0-1.
03 E+ S−; 04 W+; 05 E+ S+.
The Army. Served WW1, Maj Gen in RAMC.

HARVEY, Ian Hamilton   *New Zealand*
Tinui, Wairarapa, Masterton, N Island.
b 1.1.03 Masterton; *d* 22.10.66 Wellington.
No 8, 1-1-0-0.
28 SA+.
Licensee. NZ > 24-5 A,BI,F & C, 26 A, 28 SA
(struck down by various illnesses on all 3 tours;
apps restricted).

HARVEY, Laurence   *Scotland*
Greenock Coll, Greenock W.

Forward, 1-0-0-1.
1899 I−.
Shipwright.

HARVEY, Lester Robert   *New Zealand*
Waitaki Boys' HS, Vincent, Matakanui, Otago,
S Island.
b 14.4.19 Dunedin.
Lock, 8-3-1-4.
49 SA− SA− SA− SA−; 50 BI= BI+ BI+
BI+.
Farmer. 18 apps NZ > 49 SA.

HARVEY, Patrick ('Peter')   *New Zealand*
Rakaia, Christchurch, Canterbury, S Island.
b 3.4.1880 S Rakaia; *d* 29.10.49 Christchurch.
SH, 1-1-0-0.
04 BT+.
Unable to tour NZ > 05-6 BI because he was
unable to obtain leave from his job as a lip−
reading teacher at Sumner Sch for the Deaf.
Matter taken up in House of Representatives,
Premier Seddon declaring that Harvey could not
be spared because he was the only lip−reading
teacher in the country. Canterbury & S Island
sel. Sec of S Island Motor Union from 35.

HARVEY, Patrick B.   *Australia*
Qld.
No 8, 2-0-1-1.
49 M− M=.

HARVEY, Ronald Mason   *Australia*
NSW.
b 26.10.33 Newcastle.
Five-eighth, 2-0-0-2.
58 F− M−.
Traveller. Ckt for NSW; bro of Neil Harvey, A
Test ckter.

HARVEY, Thomas Arnold   *Ireland*
Portora RS, St Oswald's Coll, Trin Coll Dublin,
Barbarians.
b 17.4.1878 Dublin; *d* 25.12.66 Dublin.
Forward, 8-2-0-6.
1900 W−; 01 S− W−; 02 E− S+ W−; 03 E+
W−.
Bishop of Cashel. Ckt for Gentlemen of I.

HASELL, Edward William ('Nut')   *New Zealand*
Normal Sch Christchurch, Merivale,
Canterbury, S Island, Comb Servs.
b 26.4.1889 Christchurch; *d* 7.4.66
Christchurch.
Hooker, 2-1-0-1 (3 − 1t).
13 A+(1t) A−.
Law/brewery sec & accountant. Served WW1,
Bombardier in NZ Field Artillery. Played in
King's Cup with Comb Servs 19.

HASLETT, Leslie Woods   *England*
Cheltenham Coll, RMA Woolwich, Blackheath,
Birkenhead Pk, E Cos.
b 5.6.1900.
Lock, 2-1-0-1 (3 − 1t).
26 I−(1t) F+.
Chartered accountant. Moved to Can.

HASTIE, Alexander James   *Scotland*
Melrose GS, Melrose, Barbarians.
b 29.7.35.
SH, 18-10-2-6.
61 W+ I+ E−; 64 I+ E+; 65 E= SA+; 66 F=
W− I+ E+ A+; 67 F+ W+ I− NZ−; 68 F−
W−.
Painter.

HASTIE, Ian Robert   *Scotland*
Kelso HS, Kelso.
b 7.9.29.
Prop, 6-2-1-3 (3 − 1t).
55 F−; 58 F+(1t) E=; 59 F− W+ I−.
Emigrated to NZ.

HASTIE, John Dickson Hart   *Scotland*
Gala Acad, Melrose.
Hooker, 3-3-0-0.
38 W+ I+ E+.
Bank mgr. Played in 3 Servs ints.

HASTINGS, Andrew Gavin   *Scotland*
George Watson's Coll, Scottish Schs,
Cambridge Univ.
b 3.1.62 Edinburgh.
FB, 5-4-0-1 (83 − 1t 6c 19p).
86 F+(6p) W−(1t 1p) E+(3c 5p) I+(2p) R+(3c
5p).
Student. Blue 84-5. Capt Cambridge Univ 85. S
Under 21, Scotland B. S > NAm 85. 22 pts Final
Scottish Trial 86. One of 4 bros at George
Watson's Coll. Capped with bro Scott v F 86, 1st
bros to make debut in same match for S since
G.T. & W. Neilson v W 1891. Equ world rec 6p
on debut v F 86. Champ best 52 pts inc rec 14p
86; 21pts v E & R 86 most by S player.

HASTINGS, George William D.   *England*
O Patesians, Gloucester, Barbarians, Glos.
b 7.11.24 Dursley.
Prop, 13-8-3-2 (11 − 1t 1c 2p).
55 W− I=(1t) F− S+; 57 W+ I+ F+ S+; 58
W= A+ I+ F+(1c 1p) S=(1p).
Purchasing mgr/farmer. Barbarians > 57 Can,
58 SA.

HASTINGS, Scott   *Scotland*
George Watson's Coll, Watsonians, Newcastle
Poly, Anglo-Scots, Northumberland,
Edinburgh.
b 4.12.64 Edinburgh.
Centre, 5-4-0-1 (8 − 2t).

86 F+ W− E+(1t) I+ R+(1t).
Capped with bro Gavin v F 86, 1st bros to make debut in same match for S since G.T. & W. Neilson v W 1891. Capt school, Edinburgh Schs, Scottish Schs. Deputised for Gavin at FB Scotland B v Italy 85.

HATHERELL, William Ian   *Australia*
Qld.
b 30.
Prop, 2-1-0-1.
52 Fj+ Fj−.
Dentist.

HATHWAY, George Frederick   *Wales*
Newport, London Welsh.
b 23.1.1897; *d* 30.1.71 Newport.
Hooker, 2-1-0-1.
24 I− F+.

HATTINGH, L.B. ('Lappies')   *South Africa*
Lindley Sch, OFS.
Lock, 1-0-0-1.
33 A−.
Clerk.

HAUC, Jules   *France*
Toulon.
b 20.5.05 Maureilhan.
Prop, 5-2-0-3 (6 − 2t).
28 E− G+(1t); 29 I− S− G+(1t).

HAUSER, Michel   *France*
Lourdes.
b 45.
Flanker, 1-0-0-1.
69 E−.

HAUSER, Rodney Graham   *Australia*
Qld.
b 31.3.52.
SH, 15-9-0-6 (4 − 1t).
75 J+r J+(1t) W−r; 76 E− I+ US+; 76 Fj+ Fj+ Fj+ F− F−; 78 W+ W+; 79 I− I−.
Sports dir.

HAVARD, William Thomas DSO   *Wales*
MC DD
Brecon SS, UC Aberystwyth, Oxford Univ, St Michael's Theol Coll Llandaff, Llanelli, London Welsh.
b 23.10.1889; *d* 17.8.56 Gwbert-on-Sea.
Prop, 1-0-0-1.
19 NZA−.
Bishop. Played football & rugby for Aberystwyth Univ and town. Played football for Swansea Town and scored their 1st goal. Served WW1, Chaplain to Forces. DSO 16. Blue 19. Bishop of St Asaph 34-50 & St David's 50-6.

HAVELOCK, Harold   *England*
Hartlepool R, W Hartlepool, Durham Co.
Flanker, 3-2-0-1.
08 F+ W− I+.
Hull RL 08.

HAWCRIDGE, John Joseph   *England*
('Artful Dodger')
Manningham A, Manningham, Bradford.
b 1863 Macclesfield; *d* 1.1.05 San Francisco.
Back, 2-2-0-0 (2t).
1885 W+(1t) I+(1t).
Hatter. 38t for Bradford 1884-5. Emigrated US 1892.

HAWKER, Michael John   *Australia*
Sydney GS, Sydney, Australian Univs, NSW.
b 11.11.59 NSW.
Centre, 24-12-1-11 (29 − 5t 2d 1p).
80 Fj+ NZ+(1t) NZ− NZ+; 81 F+ F+ I+ W−; 82 E− S−(1t 1p) S+ NZ−(1t) NZ+ NZ−(1d); 83 US+ Arg− Arg+ NZ− It+(2t) F=(1d) F−; 84 NZ+ NZ− NZ−.
Schoolmaster. Top scorer, 52 pts, A Schs > 77-8 BI. A > 80 Fj; 81-2 & 84 BI; 83 It & F. Vice-capt A v NZ 80 at age of 20. Australian Player of Year 81.

HAWKINS, Frank   *Wales*
Pontypridd.
Back−row/lock, 2-1-0-1.
12 I− F+.
Police.

HAWTHORNE, Phillip Francis   *Australia*
Newcastle BHS, NSW.
b 24.10.43.
SH/five-eighth, 21-8-1-12 (34 − 2c 7d 3p).
62 NZ= NZ− NZ−; 63 E+ SA− SA−(1p) SA+ SA−;.64 NZ− NZ− NZ+(1d); 65 SA+ SA+; 66 BI− BI− W+(1c 1d); 67 E+(3d 1p) I−(1d) F−(1c 1d 1p) I− NZ−.
Accountant. 28 pts in Tests A > BI, F & Canada 66-7, rec for A on tour. One of 4 players to score 3d in an int (P. Albaladejo, F v I 60; H.E. Botha, SA v I 81; J.-P. Lescarboura, F v E 85). RL.

HAY, Bruce Hamilton   *Scotland*
Liberton SS, Boroughmuir.
b 23.5.50.
FB/wing, 23-4-2-17 (12 − 3t).
75 NZ− A+; 76 F−; 78 I− F− W− E− NZ−(1t); 79 W− E= I= F− NZ− NZ−; 80 I− F+ W− E−; 81 F− W+ E− I+(1t) NZ− NZ−(1t); BI > 77 NZ; 80 SA 3-0-0-3.
Commercial rep.

HAYES, Edward Sautelle   *Australia*
('Dooney')
Toowoomba GS, Qld Univ, Qld.

b 11; kia 43 N Africa.
Centre, 5-1-0-4 (3 − 1p).
34 NZ+ NZ=; 38 NZ− NZ− NZ−(1p).
Capt A > 36 NZ (he & Bill Cerutti inj 1st
match; neither played in Tests). Served WW2,
RAAF.

HAY-GORDON, John Robert *Scotland*
Edinburgh Acad, Harrow Sch, Edinburgh
Academicals, Edinburgh Univ.
b 9.11.1849; *d* −.1.34.
Back, 3-2-1-0.
1875 E=; 1877 I+ E+.
Hon sec Nice GC (F) for over 30 yrs.

HAYWARD, David John *Wales*
Crumlin High Level Sch, Newbridge GS, Welsh
SS, Loughborough Colls, Crumlin, Newbridge,
Cardiff, Wolfhounds, Co-optimists.
b 1.3.34 Crumlin.
Flanker, 6-2-1-3 (3 − 1t).
63 E−(1t) NZ−; 64 S+ I+ F= SA−.
Schoolmaster/sales rep/mgr cider, whisky
trade/interior design. W > 64 SA. Wales XV v
Fj 64. Original mem WRU coaching advisory
comm 66. Coach E Wales v NZ 67. Chmn
Cardiff 85-6. Son Cennydd played for
Newbridge Utd.

HAYWARD, Donald James *Wales*
Newbridge.
b 30.6.25 Pontypool.
Lock/prop, 15-10-1-4.
49 E+ F−; 50 E+ S+ I+ F+; 51 E+ S− I= F−
SA−; 52 E+ S+ I+ F+; BI > 50 A, NZ 3-0-1-2.
Rly engr/butcher. Wigan RL 54. To RL in NZ.

HAYWARD, George *Wales*
Swansea.
b 1887.
Prop/back−row, 5-5-0-0.
08 S+ F+ I+ A+; 09 E+.
Wigan RL 13.

HAYWARD, Harold Owen *New Zealand*
('Circus')
Thames City, Auckland, N Island.
b 23.5.1883 Blenheim; *d* 25.7.70 Thames.
No 8, 1-1-0-0 (3 − 1t).
08 AW+(1t).
Commercial fisherman. RL 11, rep NZ 12-13.
Reinstated after WW1, playing at club level
until 24. Bro Morgan rep NZ at RL 12-13 &
resumed RU for Auckland 20-3.

HAYWARD, Leslie William *England*
Cheltenham GS, Cheltenham, Glos.
b 17.5.1886 Cheltenham.
Centre, 1-0-1-0.
10 I=.

HAZELL, David St George *England*
Taunton Sch, Loughborough Coll, Leicester,
Bristol, Barbarians, Leics, Som.
b 23.4.31 Taunton.
Prop, 4-1-1-2 (9 − 3p).
55 W− I= F−(2p) S+(1p).
Schoolmaster. Master i/c rugby & ckt Taunton
Sch from 55.

HAZLETT, Edward John *New Zealand*
Winchester Sch Waihi, Christ's Coll, Mossburn,
Drummond, Southland, S Island.
b 21.7.38 Invercargill.
Prop, 6-6-0-0.
66 BI+ BI+ BI+ BI+; 67 A+; 67 E+.
Farmer/hide co mgr. NZ > 67 BI,F & Can. Bro
D.L. rep Southland 66. Nephew of W.E.;
another uncle J.S. NZ trial 24.

HAZLETT, William Edgar *New Zealand*
Waihope Sch, Waitaki Boys' HS, Pirates,
Lumsden, Southland, S Island.
b 8.11.05 Invercargill; *d* 13.4.78 Gore.
Flanker/no 8, 8-5-0-3.
28 SA− SA+ SA− SA+; 30 BI− BI+ BI+
BI+.
Sheep farmer. NZ > 26 A, 28 SA. Noted sheep
dog trialist & thoroughbred horse owner.
Headed owners' list with $900,000 racehorse
winnings 65-9. Bro J.S. NZ trial 24; uncle of
E.J.

HEADON, Thomas Anthony *Ireland*
Aloysius
O'Connell CBS, UC Dublin.
b 18; *d* 21.8.66.
Prop, 2-1-0-1.
39 S+ W−.
Physicist/dir of chocolate co.

HEALEY, Patrick *Ireland*
Limerick.
b 1070, *d* .6.18.
Forward, 10-3-0-7.
01 E+ S W ; 02 E− S+ W−; 03 E+ S− W−;
04 S−.

HEARN, Robert Daniel *England*
Cheltenham Coll, Trin Coll Dublin, Oxford
Univ, Bedford, Barbarians.
b 12.8.40.
Centre, 6-2-0-4.
66 F− S−; 67 I+ F− S+ W−.
Schoolmaster. Blue 64. Irish Univs
middleweight boxing champ 63. Rugby career
ended when broke neck in tackle, Midlands,
London & Home Cos v NZ 67. Confined to
wheelchair. Conquered total paralysis to
continue teaching economics at Haileybury.
Autobiog 'Crash Tackle' pub 72.

HEATH, Arthur Howard JP MP   *England*
Clifton Coll, Oxford Univ.
b 29.5.1856 Newcastle under Lyme, Staffs; *d* 24.4.30 London.
FB, 1-1-0-0.
1876 S+.
Colliery proprietor/iron master/MP. Son of Robert Heath, MP for Stoke. Blue 1875,7-9. Ckt for Oxford (3 yrs), Glos CCC, Mdx CCC, Staffs CCC. Contested Henley as Tory candidate 1892, 1895; won in 1900, but was defeated in 06. Won Leek 10. Served WW1 as Lt Col on Staff of RFA; mentioned in despatches for valuable services by Sec of State for War 17.

HEATLIE, Barry Heatlie ('Fairy') *South Africa*
Diocesan Coll Rondebosch, Diocesan OB, Gardens, Villagers, W Prov.
b 25.4.1872 Glen Heatlie, Worcester, Cape Prov; *d* 19.8.51 Cape Town.
Forward, 6-2-1-3 (6 − 3c).
1891 BT− BT−; 1896 BT− BT+; 03 BT=(2c) BT+(1c).
Gen mgr sugar co in Arg. Capt SA in 1st win, v BT 4th Test 1896; capt v BT 3rd Test 03. When SA capt 1896, supplied his team with green-coloured Diocesan OB club jerseys, and thereafter they became Springbok national colours. Longest SA int career (13 seasons, with J.M. Powell). SA sel. 41 apps for W Prov, never on losing side in 21 Currie Cup matches. Moved to Buenos Aires 05, helped establish rugby in Arg. Was still playing there at 49, when inj ended career. Returned SA 25. Died from inj received when hit by a car en route to Diocesan OB Annual Dinner 51.

HEATON, John JP   *England*
Cowley Sch, Liverpool Univ, Notts, Waterloo, Barbarians, Lancs.
b 30.8.12.
Centre, 9-5-1-3 (17 − 4c 3p).
35 W= I+ S−; 39 W+ I− S+(3p); 47 I− S+(4c) F+.
Architect. E's longest int career − 13 seasons. Played with cousin Dicky Guest for E in 6 ints either side of WW2 (39-47).

HEDEMBAIGT, Maurice   *France*
Bayonne.
b −; kia WW1.
FH, 3-0-0-3.
13 S− SA−; 14 W−.
House painter.

HEEPS, Thomas Roderick   *New Zealand*
Mt Albert GS, Athletic, Wellington, Petone, N Island.
b 7.3.38 Hamilton.
Wing, 5-4-1-0 (3 − 1t).

62 A+ A+ A= A+ A+(1t).
Chemist. NZ > 62 A (14t); 8t v Northern NSW 62, most for NZ in any tour match. NZ sprint champ 61-3, best time of 9.8s for 100y.

HEFFERNAN, Michael R.   *Ireland*
Cork Constitution.
b −; *d* 20.11.70.
Forward, 4-3-0-1 (3 − 1t).
11 E+ S+ W− F+(1t).
Bank official.

HEGARTY, Charles Brian   *Scotland*
Hawick HS, Hawick.
b 29.11.50.
Flanker, 4-0-0-4.
78 I− F− W− E−.
Hosiery worker. Son of J.J.

HEGARTY, John Jackson   *Scotland*
Hawick HS, Hawick, Barbarians.
b 13.4.25 Hawick.
Flanker/lock, 6-0-0-6.
51 F−; 53 F− W− I− E−; 55 F−.
Painter. Father of C.B.

HEINRICH, Edward Laurence   *Australia*
St Joseph's Coll, NSW.
b 25.6.40.
Flanker, 10-3-2-5 (6 − 2t).
61 Fj+ Fj+ Fj= SA− F−(1t); 62 NZ− NZ− NZ=; 63 E+(1t) SA−.
Co dir. RL.

HEKE, Wiremu Rika ('Bill')   *New Zealand*
Maniopoto, Tangowahine, N Auckland, Mangakahia, NZ Maoris.
b 3.9.1894.
Flanker, 3-0-0-3.
29 A− A− A−.
Farmer. NZ Maoris > 26 Europe. NZ > 29 A. Bro Mundy & son Kea rep N Auckland. Played under name of Wiremu Rika.

HELLINGS, Dick   *Wales*
Llwynypia.
b 1.12.1874 Tiverton; *d* 9.2.38.
Forward, 9-5-0-4 (3 − 1t).
1897 E+; 1898 I+ E−; 1899 S− I−; 1900 E+(1t) I+; 1901 E+ S−.
Coal cutter/police.

HEMI, Ronald Courtney   *New Zealand*
Hamilton Boys' HS, Frankton, Waikato, N Island.
b 15.5.33 Whangarei.
Hooker, 16-12-0-4 (3 − 1t).
53 W−; 54 I+ E+ S+ F−; 55 A+ A+ A−; 56 SA+ SA+ SA+; 57 A+(1t) A+; 59 BI+ BI+ BI−.
Chartered accountant. NZ > 53-4 BI,F & NAm

(22 apps), 57 A, 60 A & SA (rib inj restricted apps). Tendon inj ended career 61. Ckt for Auckland 50-1.

HEMPHILL, Robert DSO   *Ireland*
Armagh RS, Trin Coll Dublin.
b 26.8.1888; *d* 21.4.35 Cornwall.
Forward, 4-3-0-1.
12 F+ E− S+ W+.
The Army. Served WW1, Maj RAMC.

HENDERSON, A.P.   *England*
Taunton Sch, Cambridge Univ, Edinburgh W.
b Kirkintilloch, Scotland.
Hooker, 9-3-0-6 (3 − 1t).
47 W+ I− S+(1t) F+; 48 I− S− F−; 49 W− I−.
Blue 45-7.

HENDERSON, Brian Carlyle   *Scotland*
Dalkeith HS, Edinburgh W, Barbarians.
b 39.
Centre, 12-5-2-5 (6 − 2t).
63 E−; 64 F+ I+ E+; 65 F−(2t) W− I− E=; 66 F= W− I+ E+.
Insurance.

HENDERSON, Frederick William   *Scotland*
Loretto Sch, St Andrew's Univ, London Scottish.
b 3.1.1879; *d* 50.
Forward, 2-0-1-1.
1900 W− I=.
Minister.

HENDERSON, Ian C.   *Scotland*
Edinburgh Acad, Edinburgh Academicals, Edinburgh W, Barbarians.
b 31.10.18.
Prop/hooker, 8-1-0-7.
39 I− E−; 47 F− W− E− A−; 48 I− E+.
Farmer. Bro of J.M. Played either side WW2.

HENDERSON, James Young   *Scotland*
Milne ('JY')
George Watson's Coll, Watsonians.
b 9.3.1891 Edinburgh; kia 31.7.17 Flanders.
SH, 1-0-0-1.
11 E−.
Business in India. Played rugby for Madras. Lt in Highland Light Infantry.

HENDERSON, J.M.   *Scotland*
Edinburgh Acad, Edinburgh Academicals, Barbarians.
b 1.5.07.
Flanker/lock, 3-3-0-0.
33 W+ E+ I+.
Farmer. Bro of I.C. Moved to NZ.

HENDERSON, John Hamilton   *Scotland*
Michaelhouse Sch SA, Oxford Univ,

Barbarians, Richmond.
b 9.2.30.
Lock/flanker, 9-0-0-9 (9 − 3t).
53 F− W− I−(1t) E−(1t); 54 F− NZ− I− E− W−(1t).
Industrial engr/co dir. Blue 52.

HENDERSON, M.M.   *Scotland*
Dunfermline, Barbarians.
Prop, 3-1-0-2.
37 W+ I− E−.
PT teacher.

HENDERSON, Nelson Faviell   *Scotland*
Dulwich Coll, Oxford Univ, London Scottish.
b 24.9.1865; *d* 16.6.43.
Forward, 1-1-0-0.
1892 I+.
Publishing. Blue 1886.

HENDERSON, Noel Joseph   *Ireland*
Foyle Coll, Queen's Univ Belfast, Barbarians.
b 10.8.28 Drumahoe, Co Derry.
Centre/FB, 40-18-4-18 (54 − 4t 1d 13p).
49 S+ W+; 50 F=; 51 F+(1p) E+ S+(1d) W= SA−; 52 F+(1p) S+(1t 1p) W− E−; 53 F+ E=(2p) S+(1t) W−; 54 NZ− F− E− S+ W−(1p); 55 F−(1p) E=(1p) S− W−(1p); 56 S+(1t) W+; 57 F+ E− S+ W−; 58 A+(1t) E− S+(1p) W−(1p) F−(2p); 59 E− S+ W− F+; BI > 50 NZ 1-0-0-1, A.
Sales supt petroleum co. Bro in law of Jackie Kyle.

HENDERSON, Peter ('Sammy')   *New Zealand*
Gisborne Boys' HS, Wairoa Celtic, Hawkes Bay, Kaierau, Wanganui, N Island.
b 18.4.26 Gisborne.
Wing, 7-3-0-4 (6 − 2t).
49 SA−(1t) SA− SA− SA−; 50 BI+ BI+ BI+(1t).
Dental mechanic/farmer. NZ sprint champ 49, 10.0s 100y; 9.9s in winning heat at Empire Games 50. Top try scorer 7t NZ > 49 SA. Huddersfield RL (E) (214t in 258 RL apps 50-7). Bro Ron rep Poverty Bay 35-6 & Southland 37.

HENDERSON, Robert Gordon   *Scotland*
Durham Sch, Durham Univ, Newcastle, Northern.
b 8.1.1900 Coldstream; *d* 24.2.77.
Prop/lock, 2-1-0-1.
24 I+ E−; BI > 24 SA 2-0-0-2.
Nigerian police.

HENDERSON, Sir Robert Samuel   *England*
Findlay KCMG CB
Bedford GS, Fettes Coll, Edinburgh Univ, Blackheath, St Mary's Hosp.

b 11.12.1858 Calcutta; *d* 5.10.24 Millbank, London.
Forward, 5-5-0-0 (1t).
1882 W+(1t); 1883 S+; 1884 W+ S+; 1885 W+.
Medicine/The Army Medical Service. Served chiefly overseas 1885-98, inc SA War 01-2. Served WW1; mentioned in despatches 17. CB 17. KCMG 19.

HENDRIE, K.G.P.   *Scotland*
Heriot's Coll, Heriot's FP.
b 2.7.1898; *d* −.12.53.
Flanker/no 8, 3-2-0-1.
24 F− W+ I+; BI > 24 SA 1-0-0-1.
Shopkeeper.

HENDRY, T.L.   *Scotland*
Clydesdale, Barbarians.
Forward, 4-2-1-1.
1893 W− I= E+; 1895 I+.

HENEBREY, Geoffrey Joseph   *Ireland*
Garryowen.
b 1880; *d* 22.2.45.
FB, 6-3-0-3.
06 E+ S− W+ SA−; 09 W− F+.

HENNIKER-GOTLEY, Anthony   *England*
Lefroy Henniker
Tonbridge Sch, Oxford Univ, Blackheath, Barbarians, Surrey, Kent.
b 2.3.1887 Tysoe; *d* −.5.72.
SH, 6-4-0-2.
10 F+ S+; 11 W− F+ I− S+; BT > 10 Arg.
Political officer in Tanganyika/schoolmaster. Blue 09. To Rhodesia 11. Served WW1 in E Africa. Called to Bar 23. Served WW2 in RAFVR.

HENRICH, Vincent William   *Australia*
NSW.
b 34.
Flanker, 2-1-0-1.
54 Fj+ Fj−.

HEMING, Robin John   *Australia*
N Sydney HS, NSW.
b 11.12.32 Solomon Islands.
Lock, 21-7-2-12.
61 Fj+ Fj= SA− SA− F−; 62 NZ− NZ= NZ− NZ−; 63 SA+ SA+ SA−; 64 NZ− NZ− NZ+; 65 SA+ SA+; 66 BI− BI− W+; 67 F−.
Optometrist.

HEMINGWAY, Wilfred Hubert   *Australia*
Sydney GS, Sydney Univ, NSW.
b 22.9.08 Auckland.
Wing, 3-1-0-2 (3 − 1t).
31 M+ NZ−; 32 NZ−(1t).
7t NSW > NZ 28. A > 31 NZ.

HENRIKSEN, E.H.   *Scotland*
Royal HS, Royal HSFP.
No 8, 1-0-0-1.
53 I−.

HENRY, Arthur   *Australia*
Brisbane GS, Qld.
Centre, 1-0-0-1.
1899 BT−.

HEPBURN, D.P.   *Scotland*
Eastbourne Coll, Woodford, Barbarians.
FH/centre, 9-4-0-5 (4 − 1d).
47 A−(1d); 48 F+ W− I− E+; 49 F+ W+ I− E−.

HEPBURN, T.   *South Africa*
Stellenbosch Univ, W Prov.
1-1-0-0 (2 − 1c).
1896 BT+(1c).

HEPPELL, W.G.   *England*
Devonport A, Devon.
Prop, 1-0-0-1.
03 I−.

HERBERT, A. John   *England*
Marling Sch, Cambridge Univ, Wasps.
b 1.1.33.
Flanker, 6-2-3-1.
58 F+ S=; 59 W− I+ F= S=.
ICI. Blue 54-6 (capt). Oxford-Cambridge > 55 SAm.

HERD, Harold Vincent   *Australia*
NSW.
b 10; *d* 61.
Centre, 1-1-0-0.
31 M+.

HEREWINI, Macfarlane   *New Zealand*
Alexander
Wesley Prep Sch, Otahuhu Coll, Otahuhu, Auckland, Manukau, NZ Maoris, N Island.
b 17.10.40 Mokai.
1st/2nd five-eighth, 10-9-1-0 (21 − 1t 5d 1p).
62 A+(1t 1d); 63 I+; 64 S= F+(1p); 65 SA+(1d); 66 BI+(1d) BI+ BI+ BI+(1d); 67 A+(1d).
Drainage contractor/shop proprietor/waterside worker. 74 pts (19 apps, 6 at FB) NZ > 63-4 BI,F & C; 6 apps > 67 BI,F & Can. Coach Manukau & NZ Maoris sel since 59. Son Mackie NZ Schs rep.

HÉRICÉ, Daniel   *France*
Bègles.
b 7.9.21.
Flanker, 1-0-1-0.
50 I=.
Decathlete & discus champ.

HERON, Archibald George　　　*Ireland*
RBAI, Queen's Coll Belfast.
b 21.10.1875;　*d* –.
Forward, 1-1-0-0.
01 E+.
Medicine. Served WW1, civil surgeon SA Field
Force, RAMC.

HERON, G.　　　*Scotland*
Glasgow Acad, Glasgow Academicals.
Forward, 2-0-1-1.
1874 E–; 1875 E=.

HERON, James　　　*Ireland*
RBAI, NIFC.
Half-back, 2-0-0-2.
1877 S–; 1879 E–.
Bro of W.T.

HERON, W.T.　　　*Ireland*
NIFC.
Half-back, 2-0-0-2.
1880 E– S–.
Bro of James.

HERRERA, Ronald C.　　　*Wales*
Wattsville, Cross Keys, Newport.
b 16.1.05;　*d* 16.3.73 Newport.
Prop/hooker/lock, 8-3-1-4 (6 – 2t).
25 S– F+ I–; 26 E= S–(1t) I+(1t) F+; 27 E–.
Motor mechanic/police. Sc W's 1st t at
Murrayfield, 6.2.26. R Humane Soc citation for
saving woman from drowning in River Usk.

HERRERO, André　　　*France*
Toulon.
b 28.1.38 Puisserguier, Herault.
No 8/flanker/lock, 22-14-3-5 (6 – 2t).
63 R=; 64 NZ– E– W= It+ I+(1t) SA+ Fj+
R+; 65 S+ I= E– W+(1t); 66 W– It+ R+; 67
S– A+ E+ It+ I+ R+.
Restaurateur.

HERRERO, Bernard　　　*France*
Nice.
b 57.
Hooker, 1-0-0-1.
83 I–.
F > 80 SA.

HERRICK, Robert Warren　　　*Ireland*
Galway GS, Trin Coll Dublin.
Half-back, 1-0-0-1.
1886 S–.
Medicine.

HESFORD, Robert　　　*England*
Arnold Sch Blackpool, Bristol.
b 26.3.52.
Flanker/no 8, 10-5-2-3.

81 S+r; 82 A+ S= F+r; 83 F–r; 85 R+ F= S+
I– W–.
Schoolmaster. E Under 23s. Father Bob
Huddersfield Town goalkeeper FA Cup Final
38. Bro Steve, ex-Fylde RU, Warrington RL.
Bro Iain Football Lge goalkeeper.

HETHERINGTON, James Gilbert　　　*England*
George
Churcher's Sch Petersfield, Trojans, Cambridge
Univ, Northampton, Hants, E Midlands.
b 3.3.32.
FB, 6-3-2-1 (9 – 3p).
58 A+(1p) I+(1p); 59 W– I+ F=(1p) S=.
Management consultant/co dir. Blue 55.
Oxford-Cambridge > 55 SAm.

HEUNIS, Johan Wilhelm　　　*South Africa*
Outenique Sch George, Pretoria Univ, E Prov,
N Transvaal.
b 26.1.58 George.
FB, 8-6-0-2 (37 – 1t 6c 7p).
81 NZ–r US+; 82 SAm+(1p) SAm–; 84 E+(3c
5p) E+(3c 1p) SAm+(1t) SAm+.
Military trainee/law student. Chosen SA > 81
NZ within month of 1st app for N Transvaal.
Bro Chris was N Transvaal centre.

HEUSTON, Frederick Samuel　　　*Ireland*
CMG
Kingstown.
3-0-0-3.
1882 W–; 1883 E– S–.
Army Medical Service.

HEWITT, David　　　*Ireland*
RBAI, Queen's Univ Belfast, Instonians,
Barbarians, Ulster.
b 9.9.39 Belfast.
Centre/wing, 18-5-0-13 (16 – 1t 2c 3p).
58 A+ E– S+ F–; 59 S+(1c 1p) W–(1p)
F+(1p); 60 E– S–(1c) W– F–; 61 E+ S–(1t)
W– F–; 62 S– F–; 65 W–; BI > 59 A 2-2-0-0,
NZ 3-0-0-3; 62 SA 1-0-0-1.
Solicitor. Son of Tom; cousin of F.G. Gilpin &
W.J. Hewitt.

HEWITT, Edwin Newbury　　　*England*
Barker Butts Sch, Coventry Tech Coll,
Coventry, Sphinx, Vikings, Warwicks.
b 22.4.24.
FB, 3-0-0-3 (2 – 1c).
51 W–(1c) I– F–.
Co mgr locksmiths.

HEWITT, Francis Seymour　　　*Ireland*
RBAI, Instonians, Ulster.
b 3.10.06.
FH/centre, 9-5-1-3 (6 – 2t).
24 W+(1t) NZ–; 25 F+ E= S–; 26 E+(1t); 27
E– S+ W+.

Bank mgr. Bro of Tom & V.A. I's youngest int player, 17yrs 5mths 5days v W 24. Retired from game at 21 on religious grounds.

HEWITT, John Arthur   *Ireland*
Carrickfergus GS, NIFC.
b 21.11.60 Carrickfergus.
FH/centre, 2-0-0-2.
81 SA−r SA−r.
PE teacher. I > 81 SA.

HEWITT, Thomas R.   *Ireland*
RBAI, Queen's Univ Belfast, Ulster.
b 12.3.05.
Wing/centre, 9-5-1-3 (8 − 2t 1c).
24 W+(1t) NZ−; 25 F+ E=(1t) S−; 26 F+(1c) E+ S+ W−.
Solicitor. Father of David. Bro of Frank & V.A.

HEWITT, Victor Alexander   *Ireland*
RBAI, Instonians, Ulster.
b 23.3.13 Belfast.
FH, 6-4-0-2 (4 − 1d).
35 S+ W+ NZ−; 36 E+ S+(1d) W−.
Dental surgeon. Bro of F.S. & V.A. Ulster v NZ 35.

HEWITT, Walter W.   *England*
Queen's House.
Forward, 4-2-2-0.
1881 I+ W+ S=; 1882 I=.
Renowned oarsman.

HEWITT, William John   *Ireland*
RBAI, Instonians, Barbarians, Ulster.
b 6.6.28 Belfast.
FH/wing, 4-1-0-3.
54 E−; 56 S+; 59 W−; 61 SA−.
Chartered accountant/dir shipping co. Cousin of David.

HEWSON, Allan Roy   *New Zealand*
Hutt Valley HS, Wellington Colts, Petone, Wellington.
b 6.6.54 Lower Hutt.
FB, 19-16-0-3 (201 − 4t 22c 4d 43p).
81 S+(1p) S+(2t 6c) SA+ SA−(4p) SA+(3p) R+(1p) F+(1d 2p) F+(2c 2p); 82 A+(2c 1p) A−(1c 2p) A+(1t 2c 1d 5p); 83 BI+(1d 3p) BI+(1c 1p) BI+(1c 3p) BI+(1t 4c 2p) A+(1c 4p); 84 F+(2p) F+(2c 5p) A−(1d 2p).
Marketing asst/insurance broker. World's most pts (26) in a Test, v A 82. NZ's most cons (6) in a Test, v S 81. 21 pts NZ v SA 81, rec for NZ in series. NZ > 79 E,S,It, 81 R & F, 83 & 84 A. NZ series best 46 pts v BI 83. Bro Kevin rep Wellington. Ckt for Wellington & NZ.

HEWSON, Francis Thomas   *Ireland*
Marlborough Coll, Wanderers.
b 9.10.1852; *d* 10.8.1886 Bombay.

Forward, 1-0-0-1.
1875 E−.
Indian Civil Service.

HIAMS, Harry   *Wales*
Swansea, London Welsh.
Prop, 2-1-0-1.
12 I− F+.
Served WW1, RFA.

HICKEY, John Joseph   *Australia*
NSW.
b 4.1.1887; *d* 15.5.50.
Centre, 2-1-0-1.
08 W−; 09 E+.
Butcher. Olympic rugby gold medal 08. RL.

HICKMAN, Arthur   *Wales*
Neath CS, Neath.
b 6.8.10 Skewen.
Wing, 2-0-0-2.
30 E−; 33 S−.
Transport mgr building co. Swinton RL.

HICKIE, Denis Joseph   *Ireland*
St Mary's Coll, Barbarians.
b 12.4.43 Dublin.
No 8, 6-3-1-2.
71 F= E− S+ W−; 72 F+ E+.
Insurance.

HICKSON, John Lawrence   *England*
Bingley, Bradford, Barbarians, Yorks.
b 1860; *d* 4.8.20.
Forward, 6-3-1-2.
1887 W+ I− S=; 1890 W− S+ I+.
Co chmn. Capped in 1888 E side that did not play. His club, Bradford, helped form NU 1895.

HIDDLESTONE, David   *Wales*
Neath.
b 14.6.1890 Hendy; *d* 16.11.73 Hendy.
Flanker, 5-3-1-1 (3 − 1t).
22 E+(1t) S= I+ F+; 24 NZ−.
Tinplate bar cutter. Grandfather of Terry Price. At 31 one of the oldest players capped by W. Led Welsh XV in novel form of 'Haka' before kick-off v NZ 24.

HIGGINS, J.A. Dudley   *Ireland*
Mountjoy Coll Dublin, Ulster Civil Service, Lansdowne.
b Rathdrum, Co Wicklow.
FB, 6-4-0-2.
47 S+ W− A−; 48 F+ S+ W+.
Civil service.

HIGGINS, Reginald   *England*
Wade Deacon HS Widnes, Leeds Univ, UAU, The Army, Comb Servs, Liverpool, Barbarians, Lancs.

b 11.7.30 Widnes; *d* 29.12.79 Frodsham.
Flanker, 13-8-1-4 (6 − 2t).
54 W+ NZ− I+ S+; 55 W− I= F−(1t) S+; 57
W+ I+ F+ S+(1t); 59 W−; BI > 55 SA 1-1-0-0.
Commercial rep. Knee inj 1st Test BI > 55 SA
prevented his playing until 56. Father & uncle
RL ints.

HIGGINS, W.W.   *Ireland*
RBAI, NIFC.
Half-back, 2-0-0-2.
1884 E− S−.

HIGGINSON, Graeme   *New Zealand*
Rangiora HS, Glenmark, Canterbury,
Culverden, Hawkes Bay, NZ Barbarians, S
Island.
b 14.12.54 Rangiora.
Lock, 6-5-0-1.
80 W+; 81 S+ SA+; 82 A+ A−; 83 A+.
Farmer. NZ > 80 A & Fj; NAm & W, 83 A. NZ
v Fj 80. Bro Bryan rep Canterbury 75-6. Son-in-
law of Nelson Dalzell.

HIGNELL, Alastair James   *England*
Denstone Coll, Cambridge Univ, Bristol.
b 4.9.55 Cambridge.
FB, 15-4-1-10 (48 − 3c 14p).
75 A− A−; 76 A+(1c 3p) W−(3p) S− I−; 77
S+(2c 2p) I+ F−(1p) W−(3p); 78 W−(2p); 79
S= I− F+ W−.
BBC. Blue 74-77. Ckt blue. 137 apps for Glos
CCC 74-83.

HILL, Algernon Frank   *Wales*
Clifton Coll, Cardiff.
b 13.1.1866; *d* 20.4.27 Lisvane, Cardiff.
Forward, 15-6-2-7.
1885 S=; 1886 E− S−; 1888 S+ I− NZN+;
1889 S−; 1890 S− I=; 1893 E+ S+ I+; 1894 E−
S+ I−.
Solicitor. Capt W 4 times. Served Cardiff as
player & administrator 1883 95.

HILL, Sir Basil Alexander KBE   *England*
CB DSO JP
Newenheim Coll Heidelburg, RNEC Keyham,
The Army, US Portsmouth, Blackheath,
Barbarians, Kent.
b 23.4.1880; *d* 31.7.60.
Forward, 9-2-2-5 (2 − 1c).
03 I− S−; 04 W= I+; 05 W− NZ−; 06 SA=; 07
F+(1c) W−.
The Army. Maj Gen. Helped Kent win Co
Champ 04. 2-handicap golfer. Army rep on
RFU 26-39. IB mem 38. Pres RFU 37-9. Served
with R Marines Artillery from 1897 & at Siege of
Tsingtau 14. Served WW1 Gallipoli. Mentioned
in despatches 3 times. DSO 17. CB 37. KBE 41.
Col Commandant REME 42-47. JP for Surrey.

HILL, Colin Cecil Pitcairn   *Scotland*
Fettes Coll, St Andrew's Univ.
Forward, 2-1-0-1.
12 F+ I−.

HILL, Richard John ('Duracell')   *England*
Bishop Wordsworth Sch Salisbury, Exeter Univ,
English Students, English Univs, Bath.
b 4.5.61 Birmingham.
SH, 5-0-0-5.
84 SA− SA−; 85 I−r NZ−r; 86 F−r.
Schoolmaster. E > 84 SA. Five Nations v
Overseas XV, Twickenham 86.

HILL, Ronald Andrew   *South Africa*
Milton HS Bulawayo, Rhodesia.
b 20.12.34.
Hooker, 7-6-0-1.
60 W+ I+; 61 I+ A+ A+; 62 BI+; 63 A−.
Hardware salesman. SA > 60-1 BI, F.

HILL, Stanley Frank ('Tiny')   *New Zealand*
Okato Prmy Sch, Christchurch, Canterbury,
Counties, NZ Army, NZ Maoris, S Island.
b 9.4.27 New Plymouth.
Flanker/no 8/lock, 11-9-0-2.
55 A−; 56 SA+ SA+ SA+; 57 A+ A+; 58 A+;
59 BI+ BI+ BI+ BI−.
Army. NZ > 57 A. Canterbury sel 75-9.
NZRFU sel 81-3. Bro Brian rep Taranaki 54-5;
sons Stan & John rep NZ at basketball.

HILLARD, Ronald Johnstone   *England*
CMG
St Paul's Sch, Oxford Univ, O Paulines,
Barbarians.
b 6.5.03 Durham.
Prop, 1-0-0-1.
25 NZ−.
Colonial service/co dir. Blue 23-4. CMG 50.

HILLARY, Michael Francis   *Ireland*
Clongowes Coll, UC Dublin.
b 6.6.25 Malaya.
Wing, 1-0-0-1.
52 E−.
Architect.

HILLER, Robert   *England*
Bec Sch, Birmingham Univ, Oxford Univ,
Harlequins, Surrey.
b 14.10.42 Woking.
FB, 19-6-3-10 (138 − 3t 12c 2d 33p).
68 W=(1c 1p) I=(2p) F−(2p) S+(1c 1p); 69 I−
(4p) F+(2c 3p) S+(1c) W−(3p) SA+(1c 1p); 70
I+(2d) W−(2c 1p) S−(1c); 71 I+(3p) F=(1t 1c
3p) S−(1t 3p) S−(1p) P−(1t 1c 2p); 72 W−(1p)
I−(1c 2p); BI > 68 SA, 71 A, NZ.
Schoolmaster/business. Blue 65. Ckt blue 66
(HS 64 v Essex, BB 4-53 v Leics). Once E's most

193

capped FB & ldg scorer. Sc on every E app. E >
67 Can. Capt E 7 times. 68 apps for Surrey.

HILLHOUSE, David William   *Australia*
Qld.
b 13.7.55.
No 8/lock, 16-8-1-7.
75 S−; 76 E− Fj+ Fj+ Fj+ F− F−; 78 W+
W+; 83 US+ Arg− Arg+ NZ− It+ F= F−.
Airline pilot. Recalled 83 after 5 yr absence.

HILLS, Ernest Fryers ('Nigger')   *Australia*
Otahuhu Coll, Otahuhu, Melbourne, Victoria.
b 3.3.30 Auckland.
Wing, 2-0-0-2.
50 BI− BI−.
Engrg. Jnr & snr sprint champ; later pro sprinter
in A.

HILTON-JONES, P.F. See
JONES, P.F.

HINAM, Sidney   *Wales*
Cardiff.
b 29.8.1898 Blaina; d 18.8.82 Cardiff.
Flanker/lock, 5-2-1-2.
25 I−; 26 E= S− I+ F+.
Rly employee/police. Rochdale Hornets RL 26.

HIND, Alfred Ernest   *England*
Uppingham Sch, Cambridge Univ, Leicester,
Nottingham, Midland Cos.
b 7.4.1878 Preston; d 21.3.47 Leicester.
Wing, 2-0-0-2.
05 NZ−; 06 W−; BT(uncap) > 03 SA.
Solicitor. Blue 1900. Ath blue 1898-01. Twice
ran 100y in 9.8s. Midland Co v NZ 05. Notts
CCC 1900-1.

HIND, Guy Reginald   *England*
Haileybury & ISC, Guy's Hosp, Blackheath,
Barbarians, Kent.
b 4.4.1887 Stoke on Trent; d 8.11.70.
Prop, 2-1-0-1.
10 S+; 11 I−; BTuncap > 08 NZ.
Medicine. Son of doctor. London v SA 12.

HINDMARSH, James Charles   *Australia*
The Scots Coll, NSW.
b 11.4.52.
Wing, 9-5-0-4 (12 − 3c 2p).
75 J+ S− W−; 76 US+(3c 2p) Fj+ Fj+ Fj+ F−
F−.
Dairy farmer. 23 pts v Glamorgan 75, A tour
match rec. Penrith RL 77.

HINDMARSH, John A.   *Australia*
The Scots Coll, Qld.
Centre, 1-0-0-1.
04 BT−.
Clerk/insurance. RL.

HINES, Geoffrey Robert   *New Zealand*
St Paul's Collegiate Hamilton, Tokoroa, NZ
Colts, Waikato.
b 10.10.60 Tokoroa.
Flanker, 1-0-0-1.
80 A−.
Bushman. NZ Schs 110m hurdles champ 77. NZ
> 80 A & Fj; NAm & W.

HINGERTY, Daniel Joseph   *Ireland*
O'Connell CBS, UC Dublin.
b 11.1.20 Dublin.
Flanker, 4-2-0-2.
47 F− E+ S+ W−.
Prof of clinical biochemistry UC Dublin. Played
in 3 Victory ints.

HINSHELWOOD, Alexander   *Scotland*
James Watt ('Sandy')
Stewart's Coll, Kirkcaldy HS, Stewart's Coll FP,
London Scottish, Barbarians.
b 23.3.42.
Wing, 21-8-1-12 (15 − 5t).
66 F= W− I+(2t) E+ A+; 67 F+ W+(1t) I−
E−(1t) NZ−; 68 F− W− I− E− A+(1t); 69 F+
W− I− SA+; 70 F− W−; BI > 66 A, NZ 2-0-0-
2; 68 SA 1-0-0-1.
Pharmaceuticals. Glasgow-Edinburgh v NZ 63.

HINTON, T.J.   *Wales*
Cardiff.
Forward, 1-1-0-0.
1884 I+.
66 apps for Cardiff 1879-85.

HINTON, William Peart   *Ireland*
Wesley Coll, O Wesley, Barbarians.
b 27.10.1882; d 29.8.53.
FB, 16-6-1-9 (4 − 2c).
07 W−; 08 E− S+(1c) W−; 09 E− S−; 10 E=
S− W− F+; 11 E+ S+(1c) W−; 12 F+ E−
W+.
Ref S v F 21. Pres IRU 20-1.

HIPWELL, John Noel Brian   *Australia*
Wallsend HS, NSW.
b 24.1.48 Mayfield, NSW.
SH, 36-11-2-23 (14 − 4t).
68 NZ−r NZ−(1t) F+ I− S−; 69 W− SA−
SA− SA− SA−; 70 S+(1t); 71 SA− SA− F+
F−; 72 F= F−; 73 Tg+(1t) W− E−; 74 NZ−
NZ=(1t) NZ−; 75 E+ E+ J+ S− W−; 78 NZ−
NZ− NZ+; 81 F+ F+ I+ W−; 82 E−.
Fitter/schoolmaster. A > 66-7 BI; 68-9 & 72 F;
69 SA; 69 I & S; 73-4 E & W. Capt A > BI &
US 75-6. Ar > NZ 78. Retired 81, but returned
to play v F.

HIPWELL, Michael Louis   *Ireland*
Terenure Coll, Barbarians.
b 15.7.40 Bagenalstown, Co Carlow.

Flanker, 12-5-1-6.
62 E− S−; 68 F− A+; 69 F+r S+r W−; 71 F=
E− S+ W−; 72 F+; BI > 71 A, NZ.
Pilot. I's 1st r, took over from N.A.A. Murphy v
F 25.1.69.

HIQUET, Jean-Claude   *France*
Agen.
b 4.11.39 Soustons, Landes.
FH, 1-0-0-1.
64 E−.
Storekeeper.

HIRSCH, John Gauntlett   *South Africa*
('Baron')
Shrewsbury Sch, Cambridge Univ, E Prov.
b 20.2.1883 Port Elizabeth; *d* −.2.58 Cape
Town.
2-2-0-0.
06 I+; 10 BI+.

HIRSCHBERG, William   *Australia*
Adolphous
NSW.
Forward, 1-0-0-1.
05 NZ−.
Jeweller.

HIRST, George Littlewood   *Wales*
Emmanuel Sch Wandsworth, Newport.
b 5.5.1890 Merthyr; *d* 30.7.67 Abergavenny.
Wing, 6-5-0-1 (17 − 3t 2d).
12 S+(1t); 13 S+; 14 E−(1d) S+(1t 1d) F+(1t)
I+.
Wholesale fruiterer.

HOBBS, Michael James Bowie   *New Zealand*
('Jock')
Canterbury, Vale of Lune (E).
b 15.2.60 Christchurch.
Flanker, 17-13-2-2 (16 − 4t).
83 BI+ BI+ BI+ BI+ DI I (1t) A I S−(1t) F−; 84
F+ F+ A− A+ A+; 85 E+ E+(1t) A+
Arg+(1t) Arg=.
Solicitor. NZ > 83 & 84 A; 83 S & E, capt 85
Arg. World XV > 86 SA. Played in E 82-3.

HOBBS, Reginald Francis Arthur   *England*
CB CMG DSO
Wellington Coll, RMA Woolwich, RE, The
Army, Blackheath, Barbarians, Kent.
b 30.1.1878; *d* 10.7.53.
Forward, 2-0-0-2.
1899 S−; 03 W−.
The Army. Brig Gen. Father of R.G.S.; 2 other
sons kia WW2. Top athlete at RMA Woolwich.
1897. Served SA War 1899-02; DSO 02. Served
WW1. Mentioned in despatches 5 times. CMG
15. CB 31.

HOBBS, Reginald Geoffrey   *England*
Stirling ('Pooh') CB DSO OBE
Wellington Coll, RMA Woolwich, The Army,
Richmond, Barbarians, Kent.
b 8.8.08.
Lock, 4-2-0-2.
32 SA− W− I+ S+.
The Army. Maj Gen. Son of R.F.A. Served
WW2. DSO 42. OBE 44. CB 46. Croix de
Guerre 58. Pres RFU 61-2.

HOBBS, T.H.M.   *Ireland*
Wellington Coll, Trin Coll Dublin.
Forward, 2-0-0-2.
1884 S−; 1885 E−.

HOBSON, Edward Wallis   *Ireland*
Atherstone R Sch Dungannon, Trin Coll
Dublin.
b 5.12.1851, *d* 17.4.24.
Back, 1-0-0-1.
1875 E−.
C of I Archdeacon of Armagh.

HOBSON, Thomas E.C.   *South Africa*
Stellenbosch Univ, Hamiltons, W Prov.
Half-back, 1-1-0-0.
03 BT+.

HOCHE, Michel   *France*
PUC.
b 20.9.32 Levallois-Perret, Seine.
Lock, 5-2-0-3.
57 I− E− W− It+ R+.
Electrical engr.

HODDER, Wilfred   *Wales*
Pontypool.
b 6.5.1898 Abersychan; *d* 12.11.57
Morecambe.
Flanker/lock, 3-1-0-2 (3 − 1t).
21 E− S− F+(1t).
Miner/hotelier. Served WW1 in R Field
Artillery. Wigan RL 21, later dir.

HODGENS, Charles H.   *Australia*
NSW.
Five-eighth, 3-1-0-2 (3 − 1t).
10 NZ− NZ+(1t) NZ−.

HODGES, Harold Augustus   *England*
Roclareston House Nottingham, Sedbergh Sch,
Oxford Univ, Sorbonne Univ, Nottingham,
Blackheath, Midland Cos.
b 22.1.1886 Mansfield Woodhouse; kia 24.3.18
nr Mons.
Prop, 2-0-0-2.
06 W− I−.
Schoolmaster. Blue 05-8. Notts CCC 11. Taught
at Tonbridge 09-14. Served WW1, 3rd Mon Rgt.
Twice mentioned in despatches.

195

HODGES, Jehoida Joseph   *Wales*
Newport.
b 1877 Newport; *d* 13.9.30 Ebbw Vale.
Back−row/lock, 23-17-1-5 (18 − 6t).
1899 E+ S− I−; 1900 E+ S+ I+; 01 E+(1t)
S−; 02 E+ S+ I+; 03 E+(3t) S− I+; 04 E=
S+; 05 E+ S+ I+ NZ+; 06 E+(1t) S+(1t) I−.
Collier/insurance agent/hotelier. 3t W v E 03
after switch from pack to wing during match.

HODGSON, Aubrey John   *Australia*
Newington Coll NSW, NSW.
b 9.3.12 Lockhart, NSW; *d* 28.8.82 Sydney.
No 8, 11-3-0-8 (3 − 1t).
33 SA+ SA− SA−; 34 NZ+; 36 NZ− NZ−
M+; 37 SA−(1t); 38 NZ− NZ− NZ−.
Co dir.

HODGSON, Charles Gordon   *Scotland*
Glasgow HS, London Scottish.
b 11.5.38.
Wing, 2-0-0-2.
68 I− E−.
Civil engr.

HODGSON, Grahame Thomas   *Wales*
Robert
Ogmore GS, Neath, Barbarians.
b 38.
FB, 15-5-3-7 (12 − 4p).
62 I=(1p); 63 E−(1p) S+(1p) I− F−(1p) NZ−;
64 E= S+ I+ F= SA−; 66 S+ I− F+; 67 I−.
Schoolmaster. W > 64 SA.

HODGSON, John McDonald   *England*
Northern, Leicester, Northumb.
b 13.2.09; *d* −.4.70.
Flanker/no 8, 7-4-0-3.
32 SA− W− I+ S+; 34 W+ I+; 36 I−;
BI(uncap) > 30 NZ 2-0-0-2.
Bus/Ministry of Supply. Bro in law of J.T.W.
Berry. Northumb/Durham v NZ 35. 2-handicap
golfer. Served WW2 in Turkey.

HODGSON, Stanley Arthur   *England*
Murray
Durham City, Barbarians, Durham Co.
b 14.5.28.
Hooker, 11-4-4-3.
60 W+ I+ F= S+; 61 SA− W−; 62 W= I+ F−
S=; 64 W=; BI > 62 SA.
Maintenance fitter.

HOFFMAN, Richard Stephanus   *South Africa*
Boland.
b 2.12.31.
Wing, 1-1-0-0.
53 A+.
Tailor/cannery co.

HOFMEYR, Murray Bernard   *England*
Pretoria HS, Rhodes Univ, Grahamstown,
Oxford Univ, Barbarians.
b 9.12.25 Pretoria, SA.
FB, 3-0-0-3 (7 − 2c 1p).
50 W−(1c) F− S−(1c 1p).
Schoolmaster/business mgr. Rhodes Scholar.
Blue 48-50. Ckt blue, 35 apps OUCC 49-51 −
carried bat through innings in Varsity Match 49,
only 2nd such instance; 9 apps NE Transvaal.
Moved to Zambia 65.

HOGARTH, Thomas Bradley   *England*
Hartlepool Creelers, Hartlepool R, W
Hartlepool, Leicester, Gray's Ath, Durham
City, Durham Co.
b 1877; *d* 61.
Forward, 1-1-0-0 (3 − 1t).
06 F+(1t).
Shipyard blacksmith. Late call-up for only cap.
Played football for Southampton &
Huddersfield.

HOGG, Charles Graham   *Scotland*
Hawick HS, Boroughmuir.
b 2.3.48 Hawick.
Wing, 2-0-0-2.
78 F−r W−r.
Civil Service. Both caps won as r for David
Shedden.

HOGG, W.   *Ireland*
Trin Coll Dublin.
Forward, 1-0-0-1.
1885 S−.

HOLDER, Edward Catchpole   *New Zealand*
Nelson Coll, Westport OB, Buller, S Island.
b 26.7.08 Seddonville; *d* 2.7.74 Christchurch.
Wing, 1-0-1-0.
34 A=.
Servs car driver/bookshop proprietor. NZ > 32
& 34 A. RL in E for Streatham & Mitcham 35,
later Wigan. Returned NZ, reinstated & rep
Buller 42. Rep Buller at ath & ckt.

HOLFORD, G.   *England*
Linden Sch, Gloucester, Glos.
b 1886.
Lock, 2-1-0-1.
20 W− F+.
The Army/omnibus driver. Capped at 34.

HOLLAND, David   *England*
Devonport A, Gloucester.
b 1886 Gloucester; *d* 7.3.45 Gloucester.
Forward, 3-2-0-1 (3 − 1t).
12 W+ I+ S−(1t).
RN/licensee. Served WW1 HMS Colossus.
Oldham RL 12.

HOLLAND, Jeremiah Joseph　　　*Ireland*
CBC Cork, UC Cork, Wanderers.
b 24.11.55 Cork.
Lock, 3-0-0-3.
81 SA− SA−; 86 W−.
Sales exec. I > 81 SA.

HOLLIDAY, Thomas E. ('Toff')　　*England*
Aspatria, Cumberland & Westmorland.
b 13.7.1898; d 19.7.69.
FB, 7-4-1-2.
23 S+ F+; 25 I= S− F+; 26 F+ S−; BI > 24
SA.
Draper & ironmonger. Hurt in 1st match BI >
24 SA, missed rest of tour. Capt Cumberland &
Westmorland in Co Champ win v Kent 24.
Oldham RL.

HOLLINGDALE, Albert　　　*Wales*
Swansea.
Back−row/lock 2-0-0-2.
12 SA−; 13 E−.
Bro of T.H.

HOLLINGDALE, Thomas Henry　　*Wales*
Gowerton, Neath.
b 12.11.1900 Swansea; d 14.4.78 Hounslow.
Flanker/no 8, 6-1-0-5.
27 NSW−; 28 E− S+ I− F−; 30 E−.
Police/minister. Bro of Albert.

HOLMES, Cyril Butler　　　*England*
Wrekin Coll, Manchester Univ, Manchester,
RMC Sandhurst, The Army, Barbarians, NW
Cos, Lancs.
b 11.1.15.
Wing, 3-1-0-2 (3 − 1t).
47 S+(1t); 48 I− F−.
Dir family oil co. One of outstanding sprinters
of his generation. AAA sprint champ. GB 100m
Olympic Games 36. Won 100y, 220y Empire
Games, Sydney, 38. Served WW2 Army PT
Corps & Co Sgt Maj Instructor at Sandhurst.

HOLMES, Edgar　　　　*England*
Manningham, Yorks.
b 1863; d −.
Forward, 2-2-0-0.
1890 S+ I+.
Cabinetmaker/upholsterer. His club,
Manningham, helped form NU 1895.

HOLMES, G.W.　　　　*Ireland*
Trin Coll Dublin.
Centre, 3-0-0-3.
12 SA−; 13 E− S−.

HOLMES, Luke Jackson　　*Ireland*
Methodist Coll Belfast, Lisburn.
b 1867; d 39 Antrim.
FB, 2-1-0-1.

1889 S− W+.
Solicitor.

HOLMES, Terence David　　　*Wales*
Bishop Hannon Sch, Welsh SS, Welsh Youth,
Cardiff Youth, Cardiff, Barbarians.
b 10.3.57 Cardiff.
SH, 25-13-1-11 (36 − 9t).
78 A−(1t) NZ−; 79 S+(1t) I+ F−(1t) E+; 80
F+(1t) E− S+(1t) I− NZ−; 81 A+; 82 I−(1t)
F+(1t) E−; 83 E= S+ I+(1t) F−; 84 E+; 85 S+
I− F− E+ Fj+(1t); BI > 80 SA; 83 NZ 1-0-0-1.
Scrap metal dealer/dir engrg co. W > 78 A.
Wales XV v R 79, Maoris 82. Career hampered
by inj. Bradford N RL 85, believed for rec
£80,000 fee. One of Northern's major Welsh
signings, Terry Price (67), was a spectator at
Holmes's last RU match, Cardiff v Llanelli,
Stradey Pk, 23.11.85. 195 apps (123t) for
Cardiff. Autobiography due to be pub 87.

HOLMES, Walter Alan　　　*England*
Vicarage Street Sch, Nuneaton, Barbarians,
Warwicks.
b 10.9.25 Nuneaton.
Prop, 16-8-1-7.
50 W− I+ F− S−; 51 W− I− F− S+; 52 SA−
S+ I+ F+; 53 W+ I= F+ S+.
Tool machinist/miner/tractor factory employee.
Capt Nuneaton 52-5.

HOLMES, William Barry　　　*England*
St George's Sch Buenos Aires, Cambridge
Univ, Richmond, Barbarians, Argentina.
b 6.1.28 Buenos Aires; d 10.11.49 Salta, Arg.
FB, 4-2-0-2 (4 − 2c).
49 W− I−(1c) F+(1c) S+.
Blue 47-8. Returned to Arg 49 to play twice for
Arg v F. Two mths later & within week of
getting married, d of typhoid fever.

HOLMS, William Frederick CIE　　*Scotland*
Blairlodge Sch, RIE Coll, Edinburgh W.
b 27.8.1866; d 30.9.50.
Wing/FB, 6-4-2-0.
1886 W+ E=; 1887 I+ E=; 1889 W+ I+.
Indian civil service.

HOLT, Nigel Colin　　　*Australia*
E Dist, Brisbane, Qld.
b 28.11.61.
Lock, 1-1-0-0.
84 Fj+.
Family businessman. A Schs > 78 BI. A Under
21s 82. A > 83 It & F; 84 Fj; 84 BI.

HOLTON, Douglas Norman　　*South Africa*
Wynberg Boys HS, E Prov.
b 23.9.32.

197

Prop, 1-1-0-0.
60 S+.
SA > 60-1 BI (inj, returned SA).

HONAN, Barry David *Australia*
Ashgrove Marist Coll, Qld Univ, Qld.
b 47.
Centre, 9-1-0-8.
68 NZ−r NZ− F+ I− S−; 69 SA− SA− SA−
SA−.
Science master. Bro of Bob.

HONAN, Robert Emmett *Australia*
Ashgrove Marist Coll, Qld.
b 44.
Centre, 2-0-0-2.
64 NZ− NZ−.
Insurance. Bro of Barry. RL.

HOOK, Llewellyn Simpkin *New Zealand*
Thames HS, Ponsonby, Auckland, Hamilton
Technical OB, Waikato, N Island.
b 4.5.05 Puni; d 4.8.79 Auckland.
Flanker/centre/wing, 3-0-0-3.
29 A− A− A−.
Bank clerk/tobacconist. 9 apps NZ > 29 A. Bro
L.R. rep Auckland 28-35; another bro Glen rep
Auckland & N Auckland.

HOOK, William Gordon *England*
Sir Thomas Rich's Sch, Gloucester, Glos.
b 21.12.20 Gloucester.
FB, 3-1-0-2 (2 − 1c).
51 S+(1c); 52 SA− W−.
Shop proprietor. Played for Gloucester at 15
1/2. Rep Glos at ath & ckt (2nd XI). Served
WW2 in N Africa. Son played for Rosslyn Pk.

HOOKS, Kenneth John *Ireland*
Bangor GS, Queen's Univ Belfast.
b 1.1.60 Markethill, Co Armagh.
Wing, 1-0-0-1.
81 S−.
Schoolmaster. Taught at Armagh RS.

HOOPER, Charles Alexander *England*
Clifton Coll, Cambridge Univ, Richmond, Mdx
W, Gloucester, Glos, Barbarians, Mdx.
b 6.6.1869 Stonehouse, Glos; d 16.9.50
Taplow, Bucks.
Centre, 3-1-0-2.
1894 W+ I− S−.
Solicitor. Blue 1890. Mem of E's 1st 4-
threequarters line, v W 1894. Emigrated to
Hong Kong 14. Served WW1 Hong Kong
Special Police.

HOOPER, John Alan *New Zealand*
Merivale, Canterbury, Greymouth Utd, W
Coast, Sunnyside, S Island.
b 20.11.13 Christchurch.

2nd five-eighth, 3-1-0-2.
37 SA+ SA− SA−.
NZ > 38 A. Served WW2, NZ Infantry Battn.

HOPKIN, William H. *Wales*
Newport.
b 1.7.14 Newport.
Wing, 1-0-0-1.
37 S−.
Accident compensation officer omnibus co/BR
Newport buffet. Played football for Newport Co
AFC. Swinton RL 38.

HOPKINS, Kevin *Wales*
Maesydderwen Comp, Welsh SS, S Glam Inst,
Neath, Cardiff, Swansea.
b 29.9.61 Cwmllynfell.
Centre, 1-1-0-0.
85 E+.
Wales B v A 81, v F 81-4. Wales XV v J 83.

HOPKINS, Philip Lewis *Wales*
Collegiate Sch Tanyrallt Alltwen, Pontardawe,
UC Bangor, Swansea.
b 21.1.1882 Pontardawe; d 26.9.66 Swansea.
Wing, 4-3-0-1 (9 − 3t).
08 A+(1t); 09 E+(1t) I+(1t); 10 E−.
Works foreman. Reserve for Wales amateur
football XI & hockey XI. Rowed for UC Bangor
at Henley. Accomplished at ckt, lawn tennis,
ath & golf (4 handicap Pontardawe GC).

HOPKINS, Raymond ('Chico') *Wales*
Welsh Youth, Maesteg.
b 8.7.48.
SH, 1-1-0-0 (3 − 1t).
70 E+r(1t); BI > 71 A, NZ 1r−0-0-1.
Fitter. Swinton RL 72. W > 69 NZ, A & Fj.
Wales B v F 70.

HOPKINS, Thomas *Wales*
Swansea.
b 20.1.03; d 26.1.80 Ystradgynlais.
Prop/flanker, 4-2-1-1 (3 − 1t).
26 E= S− I+(1t) F+.
Colliery fireman. Sec Ystradgynlais RFC 46-70.

HOPKINS, William John *Wales*
Aberavon.
b 1898.
FH, 2-0-0-2 (3 − 1t).
25 E− S−(1t).
Docker/rly mechanic.

HOPKINSON, Alister Ernest *New Zealand*
S Otago HS, Timaru HSOB, S Canterbury,
Darfield, Canterbury, Cheviot, Amberley, S
Island.
b 30.5.41 Mosgiel.
Prop, 9-7-0-2.
67 S+; 68 A+ F+ F+ F+; 69 W+; 70 SA−

SA+ SA−.
Stock agent/auctioneer. NZ > 67 BI,F & C, 68
A & Fj, 70 A & SA. Canterbury sel & coach 75-
9. Father rep S Canterbury 37.

HOPLEY, Frederick John van der   *England*
Byl DSO
Harrow Sch, Cambridge Univ, Blackheath,
Villagers (SA), Barbarians, Kent.
b 28.8.1883 Grahamstown, SA; *d* 16.8.51
Salisbury, Rhodesia.
Flanker, 3-2-0-1.
07 F+ W−; 08 I+.
Son of Mr Justice Hopley. Public Schools
heavywt boxing champ 01-2. Ath (03-5) & ckt
(04) blue. Reserve for SA > 12-13 BI, F. Served
WW1, Lt Grenadier Guards. Twice mentioned
in despatches. DSO 16 for 'conspicuous
gallantry despite wounds' at Beaumont Hamel.
Schools PT & ath adviser to Rhodesian Govt.

HOPWOOD, Douglas J.   *South Africa*
Wynberg Boys HS, W Prov.
b 3.6.34.
No 8, 22-15-3-4 (15 − 5t).
60 S+ NZ= NZ+ W+; 61 E+(1t) S+(1t) F=
I+ A+(1t) A+; 62 BI= BI+ BI+ BI+; 63 A+
A− A+; 64 W+(1t) F−; 65 S− NZ+ NZ−.
Diesel mechanic/rep. SA > 60-1 BI, F.

HORAN, Arthur Kevin   *Ireland*
Blackheath Proprietary Sch, Cambridge Univ,
Blackheath, Barbarians.
b 13.10.1886; *d* 15.1.70.
SH, 2-0-0-2.
20 E− W−.

HORDERN, Peter Cotton AFC   *England*
Brighton Coll, Oxford Univ, Newport,
Gloucester, Blackheath, Barbarians, Devon, N
Midlands, Hants.
b 13.5.07.
Prop/flanker/no 8, 4-1-0-3.
31 I− S− F−; 34 W+; BT > 36 Arg.
Schoolmaster. Blue 28. Coached by Ernie
Hammett at Brighton Coll. Taught at
Monmouth & Bromsgrove. Served WW2 as
RAF flying instructor. AFC 44. Sec of
Appointments Bd Birmingham Univ 45;
Warden of Chancellor's Hall 45-63.

HORE, John   *New Zealand*
King Edward Tech Coll, Southern, Otago, S
Island.
b 9.8.07 Dunedin; *d* 7.7.79 Dunedin.
Hooker/prop, 10-6-1-3 (9 − 3t).
30 BI+ BI+ BI+; 32 A−(1t) A+ A+; 34 A−
(1t) A=(1t); 35 S+; 36 E−.
Butcher. NZ > 28 SA, 32 & 34 A, 35-6 BI & F
(broke hand v S).

HORLEY, Charles Henry   *England*
Pendlebury R, Swinton, Lancs.
b 1861 Pendlebury; *d* 10.5.24 Birkdale.
Forward, 1-1-0-0.
1885 I+.
Engr's Dept, Lancs & Yorks Rly, Manchester.

HORNBY, Albert Neilson   *England*
('Monkey') JP
Harrow Sch, Preston Grasshoppers,
Manchester, Lancs.
b 10.2.1847 Blackburn; *d* 17.12.25 Nantwich.
Back, 9-4-3-2 (1t).
1877 I+(1t) S−; 1878 S= I+; 1880 I+; 1881 I+
S=; 1882 I= S−.
Landowner. 1st cap 5 days before 30th birthday.
Refused to play v S 1883 because it would have
interfered with plans for a shooting week-end.
Lancashire CCC. 1st to capt E at rugby (v S) and
ckt (v A) concurrently, 1882. Also capt E v A,
1st Test 1884. 3 Test apps.

HORODAM, A. David   *Australia*
Qld.
Flanker, 1-0-0-1.
13 NZ−.

HORROCKS-TAYLOR, John   *England*
Philip
Heath GS, Cambridge Univ, Halifax, Wasps,
Leicester, Middlesbrough, Barbarians, Yorks.
b 27.10.34 Halifax.
FH, 9-2-3-4 (3 − 1p).
58 W= A+; 61 S+(1p); 62 S=; 63 NZ− NZ−
A−; 64 NZ− W=.
Building products co dir. Blue 56-7.

HORSBURGH, George B.   *Scotland*
London Scottish, Barbarians.
b 10 Stirling.
Lock, 9-4-0-5.
37 W+ I− E−; 38 W+ I+ E+; 39 W− I− E−.
Co dir. Played for British Army v French Army
40.

HORSFALL, Edward Luke   *England*
Giggleswick Sch, Huddersfield, Bedford,
Gloucester, Headingley, Harlequins, Percy Pk,
Cardiff, RAF, Comb Servs, Yorks, Hants.
b 11.8.17 Huddersfield; *d* 81 Bracknell.
Flanker, 1-0-0-1.
49 W−.
RAF/schoolmaster. Won Norwegian gold medal
for cross country skiing. Served WW2, S Ldr
RAF. Remained in service until 67 with rank of
Wg Cmdr. Took up teaching.

HORSLEY, Gavan Rex   *Australia*
Qld.
b 33.
Wing, 1-0-0-1.

54 Fj−.
14t (12 apps) inc 4t v W Tansvaal, tour rec for A > 53 SA. Rep A at surfing.

HORSLEY, Ronald Hugh *New Zealand*
Rongotai Coll, Wellington, Kia Toa, Manawatu, N Island.
b 4.7.32 Wellington.
Lock, 3-1-1-1.
60 SA+ SA= SA−.
Hotel proprietor. NZ > 60 A & SA, 63-4 BI,F & Can. Leading administrator; chmn Wellington club 75.

HORTOLAND, Jean-Pierre *France*
Béziers.
Prop, 1-1-0-0.
71 A+.

HORTON, Anthony Lawrence *England*
('Pinky')
Stonyhurst Coll, R Marines, Blackheath, Van der Stel (SA), Barbarians, London Cos, Surrey.
b 13.7.38 Chiswick.
Prop, 7-1-1-5.
65 W− I− F+ S=; 66 F− S−; 67 NZ−.
Co mgr/insurance broker's consultant. National Service with 45 Commando R Marines 57-9. Lived in SA for some years, employed in wine trade.

HORTON, John Philip *England*
Cowley Sch, Didsbury Coll, St Helens, Sale, Bath, Bristol, Lancs, Som.
b 11.4.51 St Helens.
FH, 13-6-0-7 (12 − 4d).
78 W− S+ I+ NZ−; 80 I+ F+(2d) W+ S+; 81 W−; 83 S−(1d) I−; 84 SA−(1d) SA−.
Schoolmaster. England v US 77.

HORTON, Nigel Edgar *England*
Wheelers Lane SMS Birmingham, King's Norton, Birmingham City Police, Moseley, Toulouse (F), N Midlands.
b 13.4.48.
Lock, 20-7-2-11 (4 − 1t).
69 I− F+ S+ W−; 71 I+ F= S−; 74 S−; 75 W−(1t); 77 S+ I+ F− W−; 78 F− W−; 79 S= I− F+ W−; 80 I+.
Police/bar keeper. Water polo player.

HORTON, Peter Alan *Australia*
NSW.
b 20.7.45 London, England.
Hooker, 19-8-1-10.
74 NZ− NZ= NZ−; 75 E+ E+ J+ J+ S− W−; 76 E− F− F−; 78 W+ W+ NZ− NZ− NZ+; 79 NZ+ Arg−.
Schoolmaster.

HOSEN, Roger Wills *England*
Falmouth Sch, Penryn, Loughborough Coll, UAU, Plymouth A, Wasps, Cheltenham, Bristol, Northampton, Barbarians, Hants, Midland Cos, Cornwall.
b 12.6.33 Falmouth.
FB/wing, 10-3-0-7 (63 − 6c 17p).
63 NZ−(1c 2p) NZ−(1p) A−; 64 F+(1p) S−(1p); 67 A−(1c 2p) I+(1c 1p) F−(3p) S+(3c 2p) W−(4p).
Schoolmaster. Champ rec 38 pts 67. Ckt − 1 app Minor Cos v SA 65; Cornwall CCC 55-69. Taught at Northampton GS, Warwick & Cheltenham Coll, from 66.

HOSKING, Geoffrey Robert *England*
d'Aubrey
Cheltenham Coll, Devonport Servs, RN.
b 11.3.22.
Lock, 5-2-0-3 (3 − 1t).
49 W− I− F+ S+(1t); 50 W−.
Farmer. Served WW2 Capt in R Marines. Farming in S Aus.

HOTOP, John *New Zealand*
King's Sch, Waitaki Boys' HS, Coast, Bush, Univ, Manawatu, Lincoln Coll, NZ Univs, Canterbury, Christchurch, Darfield, Otago, Clutha, Cromwell, S Island.
b 7.12.29 Alexandra.
1st five-eighth, 3-1-0-2 (6 − 1t 1d).
52 A− A+(1t 1d); 55 A−.
Fat lamb buyer/sales rep/finance co area mgr.

HOUBLAIN, H. *France*
SCUF.
Centre, 2-0-0-2.
09 E−; 10 W−.

HOUDET, Robert *France*
SF.
Wing, 10-4-0-6 (21 − 7t).
27 S− W− G+(2t); 28 G+(2t) W+(2t); 29 I− S− E−(1t); 30 S+ E−.

HOUGHTON, Samuel *England*
Birkenhead W, Runcorn, Cheshire.
b 16.8.1870 Runcorn; *d* 17.8.20 Runcorn.
FB, 2-2-0-0.
1892 I+; 1896 W+.
Carpenter/licensee. Runcorn RL 1896.

HOURDEBAIGHT, M. *France*
SBUC.
Forward, 5-0-0-5 (3 − 1t).
09 I−(1t); 10 W− S− E− I−.

HOUSTON, Kenneth James *Ireland*
RBAI, Queen's Univ Belfast, Oxford Univ, London Irish, Barbarians.
b 20.7.41.

200

Wing/centre, 6-1-1-4.
61 SA−; 64 S− W−; 65 F= E+ SA−.
Schoolmaster. Blue 64.

HOW, Richard Alfred   *Australia*
New England Univ, NSW.
b 44.
Wing, 1-0-0-1.
67 I−.

HOWARD, John   *Australia*
CBS Brisbane, Qld.
b 14; *d* 44.
Wing, 2-0-0-2.
38 NZ− NZ−.
Died as POW.

HOWARD, John Leslie Patrick   *Australia*
St Joseph's Coll, Sydney Univ, NSW.
b 30.8.45.
Prop, 7-2-0-5.
70 S+; 71 SA−; 72 NZ− F−r; 73 Tg+ Tg−
W−.
Showman.

HOWARD, Peter Dunsmore   *England*
Mill Hill Sch, O Millhillians, Oxford Univ.
b 20.12.08 Maidenhead; *d* 25.2.65 Lima, Peru.
No 8/flanker, 8-2-2-4.
30 W+ I− F+ S=; 31 W= I− S− F−.
Solicitor/author/farmer. Blue 29-30. Capt E v I
31. Mem GB bobsleigh team that broke world
rec, World Champs, Cortina d'Ampezzo 39.
Left Oxford 31 without degree; accepted post of
National Sec of New Party Youth Movement
from Sir Oswald Mosley. Stood as New Party
candidate at Bristol, Gen Election Oct 31.
Married 32, Doris Metaxa, French jnr lawn
tennis champ & Wimbledon Ladies Doubles
winner 32. Rugby corr 'Sunday Express' 34,
later became political corr. Also wrote regularly
for 'Daily Express' & 'Evening Standard'. Left
Fleet Street to devote life to Oxford Group
(Moral Rearmament). Author of 16 books, 14
plays.

HOWE, Bennett Frederick   *South Africa*
('Peewee')
Dale Coll, Border.
b 30.8.32 Port Nolloth.
Centre, 2-0-0-2 (3 − 1t).
56 NZ−(1t) NZ−.
Wool broker. Ckt for Border.

HOWE-BROWNE, Noel Richard   *South Africa*
Frank George
Oxford Univ, W Prov.
b 24.12.1884; *d* 3.4.43 Tanganyika.
3-2-0-1.
10 BI+ BI− BI+.
Barrister/cotton planter. Blue 05-6.

HOWELL, Maxwell Leo   *Australia*
NSW.
b 23.7.27.
Centre, 5-2-0-3 (3 − 1t).
46 NZ−r; 47 NZ− S+(1t) I+ W−.
Univ professor. Under IB dispensation, 1st A
player to play as r, taking over from T. Allan v
NZ 46. Emigrated to California; returned to
Brisbane.

HOWELLS, Brynmor   *Wales*
Hendy, Llanelli.
b 9.2.11 Hendy; *d* −.6.83 Llangyfelach.
FB, 1-0-0-1.
34 E−.
Steelworker/licensee. Broughton Rgrs 34. Ckt
Lancs Lge (Enfield).

HOWELLS, W.H.   *Wales*
Swansea, Tunbridge Wells.
Forward, 2-1-0-1.
1888 S+ I−.

HOWELLS, William Geoffrey   *Wales*
Loughor, Swansea, Llanelli.
b 29.10.29 Loughor.
Wing, 4-2-0-2 (3 − 1t).
57 E− S− I+ F+(1t).
Steelworker.

HOWIE, David Duchie   *Scotland*
Kirkcaldy HS, Kirkcaldy.
b 1888 Rosebery Temple, Midlothian; kia
19.1.16 Cairo.
Lock/prop, 7-3-0-4.
12 F+ W− I− E+ SA−; 13 F+ W−.
Bro of Robert.

HOWIE, Robert A.   *Scotland*
Kirkcaldy HS, Kirkcaldy, Edinburgh Univ.
b 11.6.1898.
Prop, 7-5-0-2.
24 F− W+ I+ E−; 25 W+ I+ E+; BI > 24 SA
4-0-1-3.
Farmer. Bro of David. Served WW1, 2nd Lt
RFA (1st Highland Bde).

HOYER-MILLAR, Gurth   *Scotland*
Christian
Harrow Sch, Oxford Univ.
b 13.12.29.
Hooker, 1-0-0-1.
53 I−.
Co dir. Blue 52.

HUBBARD, George Cairns   *England*
('Scatter')
Tonbridge Sch, Blackheath, Barbarians, Kent.
b 23.11.1867; *d* 18.12.31 Eltham.
Back, 2-2-0-0 (2 − 1t).
1892 W+(1t) I+.

Stockbroker. Father of John. 74t in 121 apps for Blackheath. Capped in 1888 E side that did not play. Kent CCC.

HUBBARD, John Cairns　　　　*England*
Tonbridge Sch, Blackheath, Harlequins, Barbarians, Kent.
 b 27.6.02.
FB, 1-0-1-0.
30 S=.
Stockbroker. Son of George. Mem of Stock Exchange 21-71. Served WW2, Capt in RAOC.

HUBERT, Albert　　　　*France*
ASF.
SH, 7-0-0-7.
06 E−; 07 E−; 08 E− W− ; 09 E− W− I−.

HUDSON, Arthur　　　　*England*
Gloucester, Devonport, Harwich, RN, Comb Servs, Glos.
 b 27.10.1882 Gloucester; d 27.7.73.
Wing, 8-4-0-4 (27 − 9t).
06 W−(1t) I− F+(4t); 08 F+ W− I+(2t) S−; 10 F+(2t).
Rly official/sports outfitter. Not originally sel v F 06, match in which he scored 4t. 41t for Gloucester 05-6 season. Sec of Gloucester for 40 yrs.

HUGGAN, James Laidlaw　　　　*Scotland*
George Watson's Coll, QEGS Darlington, Wakefield, Darlington, Edinburgh Univ, RAMC, The Army, London Scottish.
 b 11.10.1888 Jedburgh; kia 16.9.14 Aisne.
Wing, 1-0-0-1 (3 − 1t).
14 E−(1t).
Medicine. Served WW1, Lt RAMC (attached to Coldstream Guards).

HUGHES, Arthur Maitland　　　　*New Zealand*
Nelson Coll, Grammar, Auckland, N Auckland.
 b 11.10.24 Auckland.
Hooker, 6-3-1-2.
49 A− A−; 50 BI= BI+ BI+ BI+.
Man dir wine & spirits co. NZr > 47 A.
Auckland Racing Club comm; pres NZ Racing Conference from 74.

HUGHES, Bryan Desmond　　　　*Australia*
NSW.
 b 1887; kia 14.
Prop, 2-1-0-1 (4 − 2c).
13 NZ− NZ+(2c).
Clerk.

HUGHES, Dennis　　　　*Wales*
Pengam GS, UC Aberystwyth, Newbridge, Barbarians.
 b 3.7.41 Markham, Gwent.
Flanker, 6-2-1-3.

67 NZ−; 69 NZ−; 70 SA= S+ E+ I−.
Bank cashier/business exec. W > 68 Arg; 69 NZ, A & Fj. Wales XV v Fj 69.

HUGHES, Edward ('Ned')　　　　*New Zealand*
Southland, Wellington.
 b 26.4.1881 Invercargill; d 1.5.28 NSW.
Hooker, 6-4-1-1 (3 − 1t).
07 A+(1t) A+ A=; 08 AW+; 21 SA+ SA−.
Cooper. With Colin Meads, NZ's longest int career; 15 yrs between caps. Oldest player to play in int, 40yrs 123 days NZ v SA 2nd Test 21. NZ > 07 A. Turned RL, rep NZ 10. Regained amateur status after WW1 service with NZ Rifle Bde.

HUGHES, George Edgar　　　　*England*
Barrow, Otley, Yorks.
 b 24.2.1870 Otley; d 6.10.47 Walney, Barrow.
Forward, 1-0-0-1.
1896 S−.
Shipbuilding rate fixer.

HUGHES, Gomer　　　　*Wales*
Penarth.
 b 13.5.10 Neath; d 14.11.74 Salford.
Lock, 3-2-0-1.
34 E− S+ I+.
Builder's labourer. Swinton RL 34.

HUGHES, Hugh ('Sawdust')　　　　*Wales*
Cardiff.
FB, 2-0-0-2.
1887 S−; 1889 S−.

HUGHES, James C.　　　　*Australia*
NSW.
 b 1885; d 43.
Forward, 2-0-1-1.
07 NZ− NZ=.
Medicine.

HUGHES, Keith　　　　*Wales*
Llanelli GS, Welsh SS, New Dock Stars, Cambridge Univ, Westminster Hosp, Llanelli, London Welsh, Barbarians, London Cos, Surrey.
 b 15.12.49 Glanamman.
Wing/centre, 3-2-0-1.
70 I−; 73 A+; 74 S+.
Medicine. Blue 68-9. Played with John O'Driscoll in Westminster Hosp XV which won Hospitals Cup 1st time 74. Capped from New Dock Stars. Wales B v F 70. W > 73 Can. Wales XV v J 73. GP practice at Ystradgynlais.

HUGHES, Norman McLauran　　　　*Australia*
Sydney CEGS, NSW.
 b 18.11.32 Albury.
Flanker, 14-2-0-12 (3 − 1t).
53 SA− SA+ SA− SA−; 55 NZ− NZ−

NZ+(1t); 56 SA− SA−; 58 W− I− E− S− F−.
Architect.

HUGHES, Robert Wood   *Ireland*
('Barney')
Methodist Coll Belfast, Windsor, NIFC.
b −; *d* 15.1.27.
Forward, 12-1-1-10.
1878 E−; 1880 E− S−; 1881 S+; 1882 E= S−;
1883 E− S−; 1884 E− S−; 1885 E−; 1886 E−.
Snr schs inspector.

HULLIN, William G.   *Wales*
Dynevor GS, Welsh SS, Aberavon, Cardiff,
London Welsh, Surrey, Barbarians.
b 2.1.42 Loughor.
SH, 1-0-0-1.
67 S−.
Bank official. Barbarians > 69 SA.

HULME, Frank Croft   *England*
Birkenhead Sch, Birkenhead Pk, Blackheath,
Liverpool, Barbarians, Cheshire.
b 31.8.1881 Oxton; *d* −.
Half-back, 4-0-0-4.
03 W− I−; 05 W− I−; BT > 04 A, NZ.
Reputation as otter hunter.

HUME, John ('Jenny')   *Scotland*
Royal HS, Royal HSFP.
b 17.3.1890 Edinburgh; *d* 20.12.69 Leeds.
SH, 7-3-1-3 (3 − 1t).
12 F+; 20 F+; 21 F− W+ I−(1t) E−; 22 F=.
University lecturer. Played either side WW1; 9
yrs between caps.

HUME, John William Gardner   *Scotland*
Mill Hill Sch, Oxford Univ, Edinburgh W,
Barbarians.
b 13.6.06; *d* 23.3.76.
Centre, 2-0-0-2.
28 I−; 30 F−
Wine merchant. Blue 27-8.

HUNT, Edward William Francis   *Ireland*
de Vere ('Ted')
Rugby Sch, The Army, Rosslyn Pk, Wanderers,
Barbarians.
b 12.12.08; kia −.12.41.
FB/centre, 5-2-0-3 (6 − 2t).
30 F−; 32 E− S+(1t) W+; 33 E−(1t).
The Army. Served WW2, Maj in RA.

HUNT, James Thomas   *England*
Preston Grasshoppers, Manchester, Lancs.
Forward, 3-1-1-1.
1882 I= S−; 1884 W+.
Bro of Robert & W.H.; played with Robert E v
I 1882.

HUNT, Robert   *England*
Preston GS, Owen's Coll, Preston
Grasshoppers, Manchester, Blackheath, Lancs.
b 21.1.1856; *d* 19.3.13.
Back, 4-2-2-0 (2t 1c 1d).
1880 I+; 1881 W+(1t 1c 1d) S=; 1882 I=(1t).
GP in Blackburn. Bro of J.T. & W.H.; played
with J.T. E v I 1882.

HUNT, William Henry   *England*
Preston Grasshoppers, Manchester, Lancs.
b 11.5.1854 Preston.
Forward, 4-3-0-1.
1876 S+; 1877 I+ S−; 1878 I+.
The Army. Bro of J.T., Robert. Commanded
5th Lancs Artillery Volunteers. Won R Mil
Tournament lance v sword (mounted) 1889.

HUNTER, Bruce Anthony   *New Zealand*
Waitaki Boys' HS, Pirates, Otago, S Island.
b 16.9.50 Oamaru.
Wing, 3-1-0-2.
71 BI− BI+ BI−.
Schoolmaster. 5t Otago v Marlborough 69. NZ
> 70 A & SA (inj limited him to 5 apps).
NZAAA 800m winner 70-1, 75; best time 1m
51s.

HUNTER, D.V.   *Ireland*
Trin Coll Dublin.
Half-back, 1-0-0-1.
1885 S−.

HUNTER, Frank   *Scotland*
Fettes Coll, Edinburgh Univ.
b −.7.1858; *d* −.10.30.
Back, 1-1-0-0.
1882 I+.
Ckt for S.

HUNTER, I.G.   *Scotland*
Selkirk.
FH/wing, 4-1-0-3.
84 I+1, 85 F−1 W C .

HUNTER, James   *New Zealand*
Hawera Sch, Wanganui Collegiate, Taranaki.
b 6.3.1879 Hawera; *d* 14.12.62 Wanganui.
2nd five-eighth, 11-8-2-1 (15 − 5t).
05 S+ I+ E+ W−; 06 F+(2t); 07 A+ A+(1t)
A=; 08 AW+(1t) AW= AW+(1t).
Farmer. NZ > 05 (Jt capt) A; > 05-6 BI,F &
NAm (44t in 24 apps, best tour total ever for
NZ); 07 (capt) A.

HUNTER, John Murray   *Scotland*
Fettes Coll, Cambridge Univ.
b −.11.20.
Lock, 1-0-0-1.
47 F−.
Foreign Office. Blue 46.

203

HUNTER, Laurence Mervyn　　　　*Ireland*
Wallace HS Lisburn, Ulster Civil Service.
b 10.10.43 Dunmurry, Co Antrim.
Centre, 2-2-0-0.
68 W+ A+.
Civil service. Bro of W.R.

HUNTER, Michael Douglas　　　　*Scotland*
Glasgow HS, Glasgow HSFP.
b 45.
Centre, 1-1-0-0.
74 F+.
Scottish XV v Arg 73.

HUNTER, William John　　　　*Scotland*
Hawick HS, Hawick, Barbarians.
b 5.6.34.
Lock, 7-3-1-3.
64 F+ NZ= W−; 67 F+ W+ I− E−.
Hosiery.

HUNTER, William Raymond　　　　*Ireland*
Wallace HS Lisburn, CIYMS, Barbarians.
b 3.4.38 Belfast.
Centre/wing, 10-0-3-7 (6 − 1t 1p).
62 E− S−(1t 1p) F− W=; 63 F− E= S−; 66 F−
E= S−; BI > 62 SA.
Insurance. Bro of L.M.

HUNTSMAN, Robert Paul　　　　*England*
Hymers Coll Hull, Bulmershe Coll Reading,
Maidenhead, Headingley, Yorks, Wasps, N
Div.
b 5.5.57 Beverley.
Prop, 2-0-0-2.
85 NZ− NZ−.
PE teacher. E > 85 NZ.

HURRELL, John　　　　*Wales*
Welsh Youth, Newport, Cross Keys.
b 17.8.33 Cwmcarn.
Centre, 1-0-0-1.
59 F−.
Electrician.

HURST, Andrew Charles Brunel　　　　*England*
Dragon Sch Oxford, Abbotsholme Sch, Malta,
Oxford Univ, Wasps, Barbarians, Mdx.
b 1.10.35 Cairo.
Wing, 1-0-1-0.
62 S=.
Management trainee/solicitor. National Service
in RN. Oxford-Cambridge > 59 Far East.

HURST, Ian Archibald　　　　*New Zealand*
Waitaki Boys' HS, Oamaru OB, N Otago,
Lincoln Coll, NZ Univs, Canterbury, S Island.
b 27.8.51 Oamaru.
2nd five-eighth/centre, 5-1-2-2 (8 − 2t).
73 I= F− E−(1t); 74 A+ A=(1t).
NZ > 72-3 BI,F & NAm, 74 A & Fj & I,W & E.

HUSKISSON, Thomas Frederick　　　　*England*
MC MBE
Merchant Taylors' Sch, OMT, The Army,
Barbarians, London Cos, E Cos, Lancs.
b 1.7.14.
Lock, 8-6-0-2.
37 W+ I+ S+; 38 W− I+; 39 W+ I− S+; BT >
36 Arg.
Co dir. Served WW2 Duke of Wellington's Rgt.
MC & bar 40. MBE 45.

HUTCHINSON, Eric E.　　　　*Australia*
NSW.
b 16; kia 42.
Lock/flanker, 2-0-0-2.
37 SA− SA−.
Served WW2, RAAF.

HUTCHINSON, Francis　　　　*Australia*
Ebsworth
NSW.
b 27.12.17; kia 4.1.43 over Netherlands.
Lock, 4-0-0-4.
36 NZ− NZ−; 38 NZ− NZ−.
RAAF.

HUTCHINSON, Frank MC　　　　*England*
Leeds GS, O Leodiensians, Headingley.
b 1885 Wakefield; *d* 5.3.60 Leeds.
FH, 3-2-0-1 (3 − 1t).
09 F+(1t) I+ S−.
Hotel proprietor. Yorks CCC 2nd XI. Served
WW1. MC 19.

HUTCHINSON, Fred　　　　*Wales*
Maesteg, Neath.
b c1867 Maesteg.
Forward, 3-1-0-2.
1894 I−; 1896 S+ I−.

HUTCHINSON, James E.　　　　*England*
Barnard Castle Sch, Durham City, Northumb.
b 1884; *d* −.
Wing, 1-0-0-1.
06 I−.
Farmer. Handicapped by deformity of hand
following childhood accident with a harvesting
machine.

HUTCHINSON, W.C.　　　　*England*
Christ's Coll Finchley, RIE Coll.
b 1856; *d* c1892 India.
Half-back, 2-2-0-0 (2t).
1876 S+; 1877 I+(2t).
The Army.

HUTCHINSON, William Henry　　　　*England*
Heap ('The Baron')
Rugby Sch, Hull, Yorks.
b 31.10.1850; *d* 4.7.29 Brough.
Forward, 2-2-0-0.

1875 I+ I+.
Shipowner. Capt Yorks. England cap at Hull &
ER club. His club, Hull, helped form NU 1895.

HUTCHISON, William Ramsay   *Scotland*
Glasgow HS.
 b 16.1.1889 Glasgow; kia 22.3.18 France.
Lock, 1-0-0-1.
11 E−.
Capt in R Scots Fusiliers.

HUTH, Henry   *England*
London Int Coll, Huddersfield, Yorks.
 b 1859; d −.12.29 London.
FB, 1-0-1-0.
1879 S=.
Woollen merchant. One of 3 bros who played
for Yorks. His club, Huddersfield, helped form
NU 1895.

HUTIN, Robert   *France*
CASG.
 b 03.
Prop, 3-0-0-3 (3 − 1t).
27 I− S−(1t) W−.

HUTTON, Alexander Harry M.   *Scotland*
Dunfermline.
 b 30.12.07; d 23.12.81.
FB, 1-0-0-1.
32 I−.
Tobacconist.

HUTTON, John Edward   *Scotland*
Harlequins.
Centre, 2-1-1-0.
30 E=; 31 F+.
Bank official.

HUTTON, Samuel Allen   *Ireland*
Belfast Acad, Malone.
 b 40.
Prop, 4-3-0-1.
67 S+ W+ F− A I−.
Textile worker. Emigrated to SA.

HUXTABLE, Richard   *Wales*
Swansea.
 b 13.10.1890 Swansea; d 29.8.70 Swansea.
No 8/flanker, 2-2-0-0.
20 F+ I+.
Tinplater/miner.

HUZZEY, Henry Vivian Pugh   *Wales*
Cardiff.
 b 1876; d 16.8.29 Cardiff.
Wing, 5-2-0-3 (16 − 4t 1d).
1898 I+(1t) E−(1t 1d); 1899 E+(2t) S− I−.
Licensee. W baseball cap. Oldham RL 1900.

HYBART, Albert John JP   *Wales*
Cardiff.
 b 1865 Cardiff; d 28.1.45 Cardiff.
Forward, 1-0-1-0.
1887 E=.
Timber importer.

HYDE, John Phillip   *England*
Wellingborough GS, Northampton, The Army,
Comb Servs, Barbarians, E Midlands.
 b 8.6.30.
Wing, 2-0-0-2.
50 F− S−.
Schoolmaster.

HYNES, William Baynard DSO   *England*
CBE
US Portsmouth, RN.
 b 1889; d 2.3.68.
Lock, 1-1-0-0.
12 F+.
RN/barrister. Served WW1. DSO 21. CBE 43.
Dir of Naval Intelligence, R Canadian Navy 31-
33. Called to Bar 38. Served WW2. Officer of
US Legion of Merit 45. R Humane Soc bronze
medal.

I

IBBITSON, Ernest Denison   *England*
Wesley Coll Sheffield, Headingley, Yorks.
 b 1.2.1882 Leeds; d c56 Can.
Lock, 4-2-0-2.
09 W− F+ I+ S−.
Woollen merchant.

ICARD, J.   *France*
SF.
Forward, 2-0-0-2.
09 E− W−.

IDE, Winston Philip James   *Australia*
Qld.
 b 17.9.14 Brisbane; kia 12.9.44 Thailand.
Centre, 2-0-0-2.
38 NZ− NZ−.
Salesman.

IFWERSEN, Karl Donald   *New Zealand*
St John's Coll Auckland, Auckland GS, College
Rifles, Grammar, Auckland.
 b 6.1.1893 Auckland; d 19.5.67 Auckland.
2nd five-eighth, 1-0-1-0.
21 SA=.
Commercial traveller. After 1 season with
Auckland, turned RL & rep NZ 13-20.
Reinstated 21 to capt Auckland/N Auckland v
SA 21. Unable to tour 24-5 > BI because of
RFU bye-laws regarding professionalism. Sel

for Auckland & N Auckland. Bro Neil rep Auckland 24-6.

IGUINITZ, Emmanuel *France*
Bayonne.
b –; kia WW1.
No 8, 1-0-0-1.
14 E–.
Jeweller.

IHINGOUE, Daniel *France*
BEC.
b –; kia WW1.
Centre, 2-0-0-2.
12 I– S–.
Medical student.

IMBERNON, Jean-François *France*
Perpignan.
b 17.10.51 Perpignan.
Lock, 23-18-2-3.
76 I+ W– E+ US+ A+; 77 W+ E+ S+ I+
Arg+ Arg= NZ+ NZ–; 78 E+ R+; 79 I=; 81
S+ I+ W+ E+; 82 I+; 83 I– W+.
Municipal employee/café owner. F > 76 US.

IMMELMAN, J.H. *South Africa*
W Prov.
b 2.8.1888.
1-1-0-0.
13 F+.
SA > 12-13 BI, F.

IMRIE, Henry Marshall *England*
Durham YMCA, Durham City, Durham Co.
b 1877; *d* 16.10.38 Middleton St George, Co
Durham.
Wing, 2-0-0-2 (3 – 1t).
05 NZ–; 07 I– (1t).
Iron co mgr/colliery mgr.

INGLEDEW, Hugh Murray *Wales*
St Edward's Oxford, Oxford Univ, Cardiff,
Barbarians.
b 26.10.1865 Cardiff; *d* 1.2.37 Cardiff.
Half-back, 3-0-1-2.
1890 I=; 1891 E– S–.
Solicitor. Original Mem of Barbarians. Ckt for
Glam CCC. Played leading part in acquisition of
Arms Park from Bute Estate.

INGLIS, Hamish MacFarlan *Scotland*
Edinburgh Acad, Edinburgh Academicals,
Barbarians.
b 3.8.31 Calcutta.
Lock, 7-1-0-6 (2 – 1c).
51 F– W+(1c) I– E– SA–; 52 W– I–.
Chartered accountant.

INGLIS, James Mercer *Scotland*
Selkirk HS, Selkirk.

b 20.3.28.
Prop, 1-0-0-1.
52 E–.
Tweed.

INGLIS, Rupert Edward *England*
Rugby Sch, Oxford Univ, Blackheath, Mdx.
b 17.5.1864; kia 18.9.16 Ginschy.
Forward, 3-2-1-0.
1886 W+ I+ S=.
Clergyman. Son of Sir John Inglis, the Defender
of Lucknow. Blue 1883-4. Ordained 1899.
Served WW1 as chaplain to Forces. Killed (aged
52) while bringing in wounded under heavy fire.

INGLIS, William Murray *Scotland*
Rugby Sch, Cambridge Univ, RE, The Army.
b 20.1.15.
Prop, 6-4-0-2.
37 W+ I– E–; 38 W+ I+ E+.
The Army. Blue 35-6.

INNES, Gordon Donald *New Zealand*
Waltham Sch, Christchurch Boys' HS, HSOB,
Canterbury, Sydenham.
b 8.9.10 Caversham.
2nd five-eighth, 1-1-0-0.
32 A+.
Schoolmaster/vocational guidance off. NZ > 32
A. Wigan (E) RL 33, later Castleford; rep E v F
35, the only All Black to play RL for E.
Returned NZ to coach a RU schoolboy team at
Karori club; later assisted in coaching at
Sydenham club & Wellington sel.

INNES, John Robert Stephen *Scotland*
Aberdeen GS, Aberdeen GSFP, Aberdeen
Univ, Barbarians.
b 16.9.17 Aberdeen.
Wing/centre, 8-2-0-6 (3 – 1t).
39 W– I–(1t) E–; 47 A–; 48 F+ W– I– E+.
Medicine. Pres SRU 73-4. Played either side
WW2.

IRAÇABAL, Jean *France*
Bayonne.
b 6.7.41 Larressore.
Prop, 34-15-4-15.
68 NZ– NZ– SA–; 69 S– I– W= R+; 70 S+
I+ W– E+ R+; 71 W– SA– SA= A–; 72 E+
W– I– A+ R+; 73 S+ NZ+ E– W+ I– J+;
74 I+ W= E= S– Arg+ Arg+ SA–r.
Municipal employee/chauffeur.

IRELAND, James Cecil Hardin *Scotland*
Glasgow HS, Glasgow HSFP, Barbarians.
b 10.12.03.
Hooker, 11-9-0-2.
25 W+ I+ E+; 26 F+ W+ I– E+; 27 F+ W+
I– E+.

Brewer. Ref I v E, W v I 38; E v W, E v I, I v W 39. Pres SRU 50-1.

IRELAND, John   *Ireland*
RBAI, Windsor.
Forward, 2-0-0-2.
1875 E−; 1877 E−.

IRVIN, Samuel Howell   *England*
Hartlepool OB, Devonport A, Devon.
b 1880 Hartlepool; d 39 Oldham.
FB, 1-0-0-1.
05 W−.
Licensed victualler. Oldham RL.

IRVINE, Andrew Robertson   *Scotland*
Heriot's Coll, Scottish Schs, Heriot's FP,
Edinburgh Univ, Barbarians.
b 16.9.51 Edinburgh.
FB/wing, 51-19-3-29 (273 − 10t 25c 61p).
72 NZ−(2p); 73 F− W+ I+ E−(1c) P+(2c 1p);
74 W− E+(1t 1c 2p) I−(2p) F+(1c 2p); 75
I+(2p) F−(3p) W+ E− NZ− A+; 76 F− W−
(1t) E+(2c 2p) I+(4p); 77 E−(2p) I+(2p) F−
(1p) W−(1t 1c); 78 I− F−(1t) E− NZ−(1c); 79
W−(1t 3p) E=(1p) I=(1t 1p) F−(1t 1c 1p) NZ−
(2p); 80 I−(2c 1p) F+(2t 1c 2p) W−(1c) E−(2c
2p); 81 F−(1p) W+(1t) E−(1c 1p) I+(1p) NZ−
NZ−(1c 2p) R+(4p) A+(1c 5p); 82 E=(2p) I−
(1c) F+(3p) W+(4c) A+(1c 1p) A−(3p); BI >
74 SA 2-2-0-0; 77 NZ 4-1-0-3; 80 SA 3-0-0-3.
Actuary/chartered surveyor. World's int rec pts
scorer (301, inc 28 for BI). S's most capped FB.
Scottish XV v Arg 73, Tg 74, J 76. Champ rec 35
pts 80, 32 (79), 26 (74). 156 pts (15 apps) BI >
74 SA. 5t BI v King Country-Wanganui 77, rec
for FB. Barbarians > 76 Can. Rec includes
penalty t v W 81. Autobiography 'Andy Irvine,
an autobiography' pub 85.

IRVINE, Duncan Robertson   *Scotland*
Edinburgh Acad, Edinburgh Academicals.
b 2.4.1851; d 17.3.14.
Forward, 3-1-2-0.
1878 E=; 1879 I+ E=.
Engr. Bro of R.W., cousin of T.W. Worked for
Govt of Brit Columbia.

IRVINE, Harry Augustus Stewart   *Ireland*
Methodist Coll Belfast, Collegians.
Forward, 1-0-0-1 (2 − 1c).
01 S−(1c).
Took up refereeing.

IRVINE, Ian Bruce   *New Zealand*
Whangarei Boys' HS, HSOB, N Auckland, N
Island.
b 6.3.29 Carterton.
Hooker, 1-0-0-1.
52 A−.

Farmer. Son of W.R. Bro Bob is a rugby
commentator with NZ Radio.

IRVINE, John Gilbert ('Sal')   *New Zealand*
Southern, Otago, S Island.
b 1.7.1888 Dunedin; d 10.6.39 Queenstown.
No 8, 3-3-0-0.
14 A+ A+ A+.
Fireman. NZ > 14 A.

IRVINE, Robert William   *Scotland*
('Bulldog')
Edinburgh Acad, Edinburgh Academicals,
Edinburgh Univ.
b 19.4.1853 Blair Atholl; d 18.4.1897.
Forward, 13-5-4-4 (1t).
1871 E+; 1872 E−; 1873 E=; 1874 E−; 1875
E=; 1876 E−; 1877 I+(1t) E+; 1878 E=; 1879
I+ E=; 1880 I+ E−.
Medicine. 17yr 11mths when capped. Bro of
D.R., cousin of T.W. Played in S's 1st 13 ints.
Capt in S's 1st Calcutta Cup match, v E 1879.
Capt S 8 times.

IRVINE, Thomas Walter   *Scotland*
Edinburgh Acad, Edinburgh Academicals,
Edinburgh Univ.
b 21.10.1865; d 26.1.19.
Forward, 10-7-2-1.
1885 I+; 1886 W+ I+ E=; 1887 I+ W+ E=;
1888 W− I+; 1889 I+.
Medicine. Lt Col in Indian Medical Service.
Cousin of D.R. & R.W.

IRVINE, William Richard ('Bull')   *New Zealand*
Terrace Sch Wellington, Featherston Liberal,
Hawkes Bay, Carterton, Wairarapa, N Island.
b 2.12.1898; d 26.4.52 Whangarei.
Hooker, 5-4-0-1 (9 − 3t).
24 I+ W+(2t); 25 E+ F+(1t); 30 BI−.
Farmer. Father of I.B. NZ > 24-5 A,BI,F &
Can, 26 A.

IRWIN, David George   *Ireland*
RBAI, Queen's Univ Belfast, Ulster.
b 1.2.59 Belfast.
Centre, 16-5-0-11 (8 − 2t).
80 F− W+(1t); 81 F− W− E− S−(1t) SA−
SA− A−; 82 W+; 83 S+ F+ W− E+; 84 F−
W−; BI > 83 NZ 3-0-0-3.
Medicine. I > 81 SA.

IRWIN, John Walker Sinclair   *Ireland*
Campbell Coll, NIFC, Barbarians, Ulster.
b 13.
No 8/flanker, 5-2-0-3 (3 − 1t).
38 E− S−; 39 E+(1t) S+ W−.
Medicine. Son of Samuel. Pres IRFU 69-70.

IRWIN, Mark William   *New Zealand*
Wanganui Collegiate, Univ, Otago, NZ Univs,

207

Gisborne HSOB, Poverty Bay, Rotorua HSOB, Bay of Plenty, S Island.
b 10.2.35 Gisborne.
Prop, 7-4-0-3.
55 A+ A+; 56 SA+; 58 A−; 59 BI+ BI−; 60 SA−.
Medicine. NZ > 60 A & SA. NZ Univs rowing blue; mem of NZ eight 56.

IRWIN, Sir Samuel Thompson *Ireland*
CBE DL
Foyle Coll, Queen's Coll Belfast, London Univ.
b 3.7.1877; *d* 21.6.61.
Forward, 9-2-1-6 (4 − 2c).
1900 E− S= W−; 01 E+(2c) W−; 02 E− S+ W−; 03 S−.
Medicine. Father of J.W.S. Pres IRFU 35-6. Kt 57. Ulster MP.

ISAAC, Henri *France*
RCF.
b −; kia WW1.
FB, 2-0-0-2.
07 E−; 08 E−.

ISAACS, Iorwerth *Wales*
Cilfynydd, Cardiff.
b 12.10.11 Cilfynydd; *d* 25.4.66 Oswestry.
Flanker, 2-1-0-1.
33 E+ S−.
Police/headmaster. Leeds RL 33.

ISHERWOOD, Francis William *England*
Rugby Sch, Oxford Univ, Ravenscourt Pk.
b 16.10.1852; *d* 30.4.1888 Southsea.
Forward, 1-1-0-0 (1c).
1872 S+(1c).
Oil prospector. Blue 1871. Ckt blue 1872; also played for Essex. E's 1st c, v S 1872. Worked in the Carpathian Mountains.

ITHURRA, Etienne *France*
Biarritz Ol.
Lock, 3-3-0-0.
36 G+ G+; 37 G+.

IVES, Walter Norman *Australia*
Sydney GS, NSW.
b 10.11.06.
Flanker, 1-1-0-0.
29 NZ+.
Co exec.

J

JACK, Henry Walter MBE *Ireland*
CBC Cork, UC Cork.
b 14.6.1891 Cork; *d* 19.12.77.
FH/SH, 3-1-0-2.
14 S+ W−; 21 W−.

Dir of agric & forests in Fiji. Played v Wales 14 as r for Dicky Lloyd, who withdrew because of inj sustained during warm-up before kick-off. Fdr Malaya RFU. Pres Fiji RFU.

JACKETT, Edward John *England*
Falmouth, Leicester, Cornwall, Devonport A, Transvaal (SA), De Beers, Kimberley.
b 4.7.1882 Falmouth; *d* 35 Middlesbrough.
FB, 13-4-1-8 (4 − 2c).
05 NZ−; 06 W− I− S+ F+ SA=; 07 W− I− S−; 09 W− F+(2c) I+ S−; BT > 08 A, NZ.
Theatre mgr. Transvaal v BT 03. Olympic silver medal for rugby, GB (Cornwall) v A 08. Dewsbury RL 11. Cycling champ of Cornwall. Artist's model to H.S. Tuke, ARA.

JACKSON, A.H. *England*
Guy's Hosp, Blackheath.
Half-back, 2-2-0-0.
1878 I+; 1880 I+.
Medicine. 22t in 37 apps Blackheath 1877-81.

JACKSON, A.R.V. *Ireland*
Portora RS, Wanderers, Barbarians.
b 25.8.1890 Dublin; *d* 31.1.69.
Wing/centre, 10-6-0-4 (9 − 3t).
11 E+ S+ W− F+(2t); 13 W− F+; 14 F+ E− (1t) S+ W−.

JACKSON, Barry S. *England*
Broughton Pk, Lancs.
Flanker/prop, 2-0-0-2.
70 S−r F−.
Engrg draughtsman. 1st E player capped direct from Broughton Pk.

JACKSON, Dirk Cloete ('Mary') *South Africa*
Diocesan Coll, W Prov.
b 21.4.1885; *d* 17.9.76 nr Pretoria.
SH, 3-2-1-0 (3 − 1p).
06 I+(1p) W+ E=.
Solicitor. Ckt for W Prov 08-13.

JACKSON, Everard Stanley *New Zealand*
Te Araroa Native Sch, Rerekohu Dist HS, Tolaga Bay Country, E Coast, Hikurangi, Hawkes Bay, Whakaki, Wellington, NZ Maoris, N Island.
b 12.1.14 Hastings; *d* 20.9.75 Hastings.
Prop, 6-4-0-2.
36 A+ A+; 37 SA+ SA− SA−; 38 A+.
Labourer. NZ > 36 & 38 A. Served WW2, Capt in Maori Battn; lost leg in Western Desert campaign. Father Frederick rep Leicester v NZ 05, toured NZ with AW 08 & stayed, rep NZ at RL 10. Bro Selwyn rep Hawkes Bay & NZ Maoris 38.

JACKSON, Finlay William *Ireland*
RBAI, NIFC.

b 22.11.01 Belfast; *d* 13.3.41 Belfast.
Centre, 1-0-0-1.
23 E−.
Ckt for I.

JACKSON, Howard W. *Ireland*
Monoghan Sch, Trin Coll Dublin.
Forward, 1-0-0-1.
1877 E−.
Ckt for I 1895.

JACKSON, J.S. *South Africa*
W Prov.
1-0-1-0.
03 BT=.

JACKSON, Kenneth Leslie *Scotland*
Tattersall
Rugby Sch, Oxford Univ, Barbarians.
b 17.11.13; *d* 21.3.82.
FH, 4-3-0-1 (7 − 1t 1d).
33 W+(1t) E+ I+(1d); 34 W−.
HM. Blue 32-3. Ckt blue 34.

JACKSON, Peter Barrie *England*
King Edward VI Sch, O Edwardians, Coventry,
Aldershot Servs, The Army, N Midlands,
Warwicks.
b 22.9.30 Birmingham.
Wing, 20-12-5-3 (18 − 6t).
56 W− I+(1t) F−; 57 W+ I+(1t) F+(2t) S+; 58
W= A+(1t) F+(1t) S=; 59 W− I+ F= S=; 61
S+; 63 W+ I= F+ S+; BI > 59 A 2-2-0-0, NZ
3-1-0-2.
Chocolate co trainee/packing co man dir. Sc t in
4th Test BI v NZ 59.

JACKSON, T.G.H. *Scotland*
R Corps of Signals, The Army, Barbarians.
Wing, 12-4-0-8 (6 − 2t).
47 F− W− E−(1t) A−; 48 F+(1t) W− I− E+;
49 F+ W+ I− E−.
Played in 1 Servs int.

JACKSON, T.H. *Wales*
Swansea.
Forward, 1-0-0-1.
1895 E−.

JACKSON, Walter Jesse *England*
Gloucester, Halifax, Yorks.
b 16.3.1870 Gloucester; *d* 1.12.58 Halifax.
Centre, 1-0-0-1.
1894 S−.
Boilermaker. 1st int player from Gloucester,
although a Halifax player when capped. Turned
RL when his club, Halifax, helped form NU
1895.

JACKSON, William Douglas *Scotland*
Hawick.

b 5.12.41.
Wing, 8-4-1-3.
64 I+; 65 E= SA+; 68 A+; 69 F+ W− I− E−.
Sales rep.

JACOB, Frederick *England*
Sandwich Sch, Thanet W, Cambridge Univ,
Gottingen Univ, London Univ, Blackheath,
Richmond, Cheltenham, Barbarians, Glos,
Kent.
b 4.1.1873 Northbourne, Kent; *d* 1.9.45
Srinagar, Kashmir.
Forward, 8-2-1-5.
1897 W− I− S+; 1898 I− S= W+; 1899 W−
I−.
Schoolmaster. Blue 1895-6. Water polo blue.
Taught at Bradfield Coll, Cheltenham Coll &
Felsted.

JACOB, Herbert Percy *England*
Cranleigh Sch, Oxford Univ, Blackheath.
b 12.10.02.
Wing, 5-5-0-0 (12 − 4t).
24 W+ I+(1t) F+(3t) S+; 30 F+.
Schoolmaster. Blue 23-5. Contemporary with
Scottish int threequarters G. Aitken, G.P.S.
Macpherson, I.S. Smith and A.C. Wallace at
Oxford. Taught at Worksop Coll & Cranleigh.
Sec R Blackheath GC.

JACOB, Philip Gordon *England*
Bedford GS, Cambridge Univ, Blackheath,
Kent.
b 14.5.1875 Seoni, India; *d* −.
Half-back, 1-0-0-1.
1898 I−.
Blue 1894-6. Examiner of local fund accounts,
Accountant Gen's Office, Punjab.

JACOBS, Charles Ronald *England*
Oakham Sch, Nottingham Univ, Northampton,
Barbarians, E Midlands.
b 28.10.28 Whittlesey, Cambs.
Prop, 29-14-5-10.
56 W− I+ S+ F−; 57 W+ I+ F+ S+; 58 W=
A+ I+ F+ S=; 60 W+ I+ F= S+; 61 SA− W−
I− F= S+; 63 NZ− NZ− A−; 64 W= I− F+
S−.
Farmer. RFU sel; E Midlands CB rep.

JAFFRAY, John Lyndon *New Zealand*
Kaikorai Valley HS, Green Island, Otago,
Eastern, S Canterbury, Timaru HSOB, S
Island.
b 17.4.50 Dunedin.
1st/2nd five-eighth, 7-4-0-3 (4 − 1t).
72 A+; 75 S+; 76 I+ SA−(1t); 77 BI−; 79 F+
F−.
Lamb drafter. NZ > 76 SA, 78 BI, 79 A (did not
play in any match). Bro Murray NZ > 76 Arg.

JAGO, Raphael Anthony *England*
Devonport A, Devon.
b 20.1.1882 Chaddock, Dorset; *d* −.
SH, 5-0-1-4 (3 − 1t).
06 W− I−(1t) SA=; 07 W− I−.
Blacksmith. 320 apps for Devonport A (1899-19), 59 for Devon.

JAMES, Boyo John *Wales*
Pontycymmer, Bridgend, Glam.
b 4.9.38 Blaengarw.
Prop, 1-0-1-0.
68 E=.
Blacksmith's striker. Coach Nantymoel.

JAMES, Carwyn Rees *Wales*
Gwendraeth GS, Welsh SS, Cefneithin, UC
Aberystwyth, Llanelli, London Welsh,
Devonport Servs, Barbarians.
b 2.11.29 Cefneithin; *d* 10.1.83 Amsterdam.
FH/centre, 2-1-0-1 (3 − 1d).
58 A+(1d) F−.
Schoolmaster/lecturer/journalist. Coach BI > 71
A, NZ. Coach, pres Llanelli. Wrote (with John
Reason) 'The World of Rugby', pub 79. Corr for
'The Guardian'.

JAMES, David *Wales*
St Thomas Harlequins, Swansea.
b 1867 Swansea; *d* 2.1.29 Swansea.
Half-back, 4-2-0-2.
1891 I+; 1892 S− I−; 1899 E+.
Copper worker/fuel works employee. Bro of
Evan. 5ft 6in, 10st. Declared pro by RFU 1892,
reinstated 1896. Broughton Rgrs RL 1899.

JAMES, D.R. *Wales*
Treorchy.
b 7.10.06 Treorchy; *d* −.11.84.
Prop/hooker, 2-2-0-0.
31 F+ I+.
Colliery fireman. Leeds RL 31.

JAMES, Evan *Wales*
St Thomas Harlequins, Swansea.
b 1869; *d* 02.
Half-back, 5-2-0-3.
1890 S−; 1891 I+; 1892 S− I−; 1899 E+.
Copper worker/fuel works employee. Bro of
David. 5ft 7in, 10st 7lb. Declared pro by RFU
1892, reinstated 1896. Broughton Rgrs RL 1899.
Died of TB.

JAMES, Maldwyn *Wales*
Cilfynydd, Cardiff.
b 28.6.13 Cilfynydd.
Hooker, 5-2-1-2.
47 A+; 48 E= S+ F− I−.
NCB official.

JAMES, Peter Michael *Australia*
Qld.
b 35.
Centre, 2-0-1-1.
58 M= M−.

JAMES, Thomas Owen *Wales*
Aberavon.
b 6.10.04 Aberavon; *d* −.4.84 Neath.
FB, 2-0-0-2 (3 − 1p).
35 I−(1p); 37 S−.
Steelworker. Bro of W.P.

JAMES, William John *Wales*
Dyffryn Comp, Welsh SS, Welsh Youth,
Aberavon, Barbarians.
b 18.7.56 Port Talbot.
Hooker, 15-7-1-7 (4 − 1t).
83 E= S+ I+ F− R−; 84 S−; 85 S+ I− F− E+
Fj+(1t); 86 E− S+ I+ F−.
Architectural assistant. Wales B v F 82. Wales B
> 80 US, Can; 83 Spain. Wales XV v Maoris 82,
J 83. Capt Aberavon 79-81.

JAMES, William P. *Wales*
Aberavon.
b 02.
Wing, 2-0-0-2 (3 − 1t).
25 E−(1t) S−.
Dock worker. Bro of T.O. Leeds RL 25.

JAMESON, Joseph Singer *Ireland*
Trin Coll Dublin, Lansdowne.
Forward, 7-2-1-4.
1888 NZN−; 1889 S− W+; 1891 W−; 1892 E−
W+; 1893 S=.
Medicine.

JAMIESON, J. *Scotland*
Craigmount Educ Inst, W of Scotland.
Forward, 8-5-1-2 (1t).
1883 W+ I+ E−; 1884 W+ I+ E−(1t); 1885
W= I+.
Sc t in abandoned match, I v S 1885. Settled in
NZ.

JANECZEK, T. *France*
Tarbes.
Flanker, 2-2-0-0.
82 Arg+ Arg+.

JANION, Jeremy Paul A.G. *England*
St Edmund's Coll Ware, Saffron Walden,
Bedford, Richmond, London Cos, E Cos.
b 25.9.46 Bishop's Stortford.
Wing/centre, 12-3-1-8.
71 W− I+ F= S− S− P−; 72 W− S− SA+; 73
A+; 75 A− A−.
Brewery accountant. England Under 25s v Fj
70.

JANSEN, Ebenhaeser *South Africa*
Griekwastad Sch, UOFS, Jnr Springboks,
Gazelles, SA Univs, OFS.
b 5.6.54 Griekwastad.
Flanker, 1-0-0-1.
81 NZ−.
Student. Bro of Joggie. SA > 80 SAm, 81 US.

JANSEN, Joachim Scholtz *South Africa*
('Joggie')
UOFS, OFS.
b 5.2.48 Griekwastad.
Centre, 10-7-1-2 (3 − 1t).
70 NZ+ NZ−(1t) NZ+ NZ+; 71 F+ F= A+
A+ A+; 72 E−.
Bro of Ebenhaeser.

JARASSE, Auguste *France*
Brive.
Hooker, 1-1-0-0.
45 BF+.

JARDEL, Jean *France*
Bordelais.
Wing, 2-0-0-2.
28 I− E−.

JARDEN, Ronald Alexander *New Zealand*
Hutt Valley HS, Univ, Wellington, NZ Univs, N
Island.
b 14.12.29 Lower Hutt; *d* 18.2.77 Wellington.
Wing, 16-11-0-5 (42 − 7t 6c 3p).
51 A+ A+(2t); 52 A− A+(1p); 53 W−(1c 1p);
54 I+ E+ S+ F−; 55 A+(1t 2c 1p) A+(1t 1c)
A−(1t); 56 SA+(1t 2c) SA− SA+(1t) SA+.
Oil co employee/sharebroker. Top scorer 88 pts
(inc 15t, & inc 38 pts v Central West) NZ > 51 A
& 94 pts > 53-4 BI,F & NAm. NZ career rec 945
pts (145t, 141c, 76p). NZ jnr 440y champ 49.
Rep NZ in Admiral's Cup in his yacht 'Barnacle
Bill', Cowes 75. Wrote 'Rugby on Attack', pub
61.

JARMAN, Henry *Wales*
Newport.
b 1883; *d* 13.12.28 Talywain.
Forward, 4-3-0-1.
10 E− S+ I+; 11 E+; BI > 10 SA 3-1-0-2.
Miner. Reputed the outstanding forward BI >
10 SA. Died a hero's death, throwing himself in
front of a runaway coal truck as it careered
towards a group of playing children.

JARMAN, J. Wallace *England*
Merchant Venturers, Bristol, Glos.
b 15.7.1872; *d* −.9.50 Vancouver.
Forward, 1-0-0-1.
1900 W−; BT(uncap) > 1899 A.
Rep. 1st player capped from Bristol. In Can 20-
50.

JARRETT, Keith Stanley *Wales*
Monmouth Sch, Newport, London Welsh.
b 18.5.48 Newport.
FB/centre, 10-6-2-2 (73 − 2t 17c 11p).
67 E+(1t 5c 2p); 68 E=(1c) S+(1c); 69 S+(1c
2p) I+(3c 1p) F=(1c) E+(3c 2p) NZ− NZ−(1t
2p) A+(2c 2p); BI > 68 SA.
Scrap merchant. Father H.H. ckter
Warwickshire CCC, Glamorgan CCC. With J.
Bancroft & P. Bennett most pts (19) in int, W v
E 67. W's most pts (15) in tour match, v Otago
NZ 69. W > 69 NZ, A & Fj. 2 apps Glamorgan
CCC 67, HS 18 no v Pakistan. Barrow RL.

JAUREGUY, Adolphe *France*
RCF, Toulouse.
b 18.2.1898 Ostabat; *d* 4.9.77.
Wing, 31-8-1-22 (42 − 14t).
20 S− E− W−(1t) I+(2t) US+(1t); 22 S=(1t)
W−(1t); 23 S− W− E− I+(2t); 24 S+(1t) W−
R+(4t) US−; 25 I− NZ−; 26 S− E− W− M−;
27 I− E+; 28 S− NSW− E−(1t) G+ W+; 29
I− S− E−.
Bro of Pierre. Asst mgr F > 49 Arg.

JAUREGUY, Pierre *France*
Toulouse.
Wing, 4-0-0-4.
13 S− SA− W− I−.
Veterinary surgeon. Bro of Adolphe.

JEANGRAND, Henri *France*
Tarbes.
Centre, 1-1-0-0.
21 I+.

JEANJEAN, Pierre *France*
Toulon.
b 3.2.24 Port Vendres.
Wing, 1-0-0-1.
48 I−.
Medicine/Army.

JEAVONS, Nicholas Clive *England*
Berkhamsted Prep, Wolverhampton GS, Staffs
Schools, English SS, Tettenhall Coll,
Wolverhampton Poly, Moseley, Midlands.
b 12.11.57 Calcutta.
Flanker, 14-6-3-5 (4 − 1t).
81 S+ I+ F− Arg= Arg+; 82 A+(1t) S= I−
F+ W+; 83 F− W= S− I−; BI > 83 NZ.
Engr. E Under 23 v F 77; > 78 F. English
Students v Arg. E > 81 Arg; 83 Can, US.

JEEPS, Richard Eric Gautrey *England*
CBE JP
Bedford Mod Sch, Cambridge, Northampton,
Barbarians, London Cos, E Cos.
b 25.11.31 Willingham, Cambs.
SH, 24-13-6-5.
56 W−; 57 W+ I+ F+ S+; 58 W= A+ I+ F+

211

S=; 59 I+; 60 W+ I+ F= S+; 61 SA− W− I−
F= S+; 62 W= I+ F− S=; BI(uncap) > 55 SA
4-2-0-2; 59 A 2-2-0-0, NZ 3-0-0-3; 62 SA 4-0-1-3.
Fruit farmer/chmn Sports Council. Capt E 13
times. 13 BI Tests, inc 4 before 1st app for E.
RFU sel 65-71, pres 76-7. Cambridgeshire CCC.
County councillor & JP.

JEFFARES, Ernest William   *Ireland*
Wanderers.
Forward, 2-0-0-2.
13 E− S−.

JEFFERD, Andrew Charles   *New Zealand*
Reeves
Wanganui Collegiate Sch, Lincoln Coll, NZ
Univs, Canterbury, Glenmark, Tokomaru Bay,
E Coast.
b 13.6.53 Gisborne.
2nd five-eighth, 3-3-0-0.
81 S+ S+ SA+.
Farmer. NZr > 80 A & Fj.

JEFFERY, John J.   *Wales*
Pontllanfraith GS, Cardiff Coll, Newport,
Blackwood, Barbarians.
b 45.
No 8, 1-0-0-1.
67 NZ−.
Schoolmaster. W > 68 Arg. Barbarians v SA 70.
Barbarians > 69 SA. Blamed for loose pass
'blunder' which cost a t v NZ 67.

JEFFREY, George Luxton   *England*
St John's Wood Sch, Cambridge Univ,
Harlequins, Blackheath, Barbarians, Mdx.
b 1863; *d* 4.11.37.
Forward, 6-2-3-1 (1t).
1886 W+ I+ S=; 1887 W= I− S=(1t).
Stockbroker. Blue 1884-5. Capped in 1888 E
side that did not play.

JEFFREY, John   *Scotland*
Merchiston Castle Sch, Newcastle Univ, British
Univs, S of Scotland, Kelso.
b 25.3.59 Kelso.
Flanker, 8-4-0-4 (8 − 2t).
84 A−; 85 I− E−; 86 F+ W−(1t) E+ I+
R+(1t).
Scotland B v F 83-4, I 84. Five Nations v
Overseas XV, Twickenham 86.

JENKINS, Albert   *Wales*
Llanelli.
b 1895 Llanelli; *d* 7.10.53 Llanelli.
Centre, 14-7-0-7 (47 − 4t 7c 3d 3p).
20 E+ S−(1t 1c) F+ I+(1t 2c 1d); 21 S−(2d)
F+(2p); 22 F+(1c); 23 E− S−(1c 1p) F+(2c)
I−; 24 NZ−; 28 S+(1t) I−(1t).
Docker/tinplater. Served WW1, 38th Welsh Div
in F.

JENKINS, Albert Mortimer   *Wales*
Swansea.
b 1872 Ringwood, Lancs; *d* 3.7.61 Bromley.
Forward, 2-1-0-1.
1895 I+; 1896 E−.
Archdeacon of Pretoria, SA.

JENKINS, David Morgan   *Wales*
Treorchy.
b c01 Tonypandy; *d* −.4.68 Bridgend.
Lock/prop, 4-2-1-1.
26 E= S− I+ F+.
Police/licensee. Hunslet RL 26, Leeds 31.

JENKINS, David Rees   *Wales*
Resolven, Neath, Swansea.
b 12.4.04 Resolven; *d* 13.8.51 Whitley Bay.
Hooker/prop, 2-0-0-2.
27 NSW−; 29 E−.
Miner/licensee. Leeds RL 29.

JENKINS, Edward Macdonald   *Wales*
Aberavon.
b 28.7.04 Tonyrefail.
Flanker/lock/prop, 21-10-1-10.
27 S− F+ I− NSW−; 28 E− S+ I− F−; 29 F+;
30 E− S− I+ F+; 31 E= S+ F+ I+ SA−; 32
E+ S+ I−.
Police. Welsh shot & discus champion.

JENKINS, Ernest   *Wales*
Newport.
Flanker, 2-2-0-0.
10 S+ I+.
Docker. Rochdale Hornets RL 10.

JENKINS, J.C.   *Wales*
London Welsh, Newport, Newbridge, Mdx,
Mon, Barbarians.
b 19.4.1880.
Lock, 1-0-0-1.
06 SA−.

JENKINS, John Llewellyn   *Wales*
Senghenydd, Aberavon.
b 12.3.03 Maesteg.
No 8, 2-1-0-1.
23 S− F+.
Steelworker/police.

JENKINS, Leighton H.   *Wales*
Mon Tg Coll, Newport, RAF, London Welsh.
b 31.
No 8/lock, 5-4-0-1.
54 I+; 56 E+ S+ I− F+.
RAF. S Ldr (retired 86).

JENKINS, Vivian Gordon James   *Wales*
Llandovery Coll, Oxford Univ, Bridgend,
London Welsh, Kent, Barbarians, London Cos.
b 2.11.11 Port Talbot.

FB, 14-8-2-4 (36 − 1t 10c 1d 3p).
33 E+ I−(1c); 34 S+(2c) I+(1t 2c); 35 E=
S+(1d) NZ+(2c); 36 E= S+(2c) I+(1p);
37 E−; 38 E+(1c 2p) S−; 39 E−; BI > 38 SA 1-
0-0-1.
Schoolmaster/journalist. Blue 30-2. Barbarians
comm. London Counties v NZ 35. Ckt blue 33
& Glamorgan CCC. Ex-editor 'Rothman's
Rugby Yearbook' & ex rugby corr 'Sunday
Times'.

JENKINS, William J.　　　　　　*Wales*
Cardiff.
b 1882; *d* 56.
Flanker/lock/prop, 4-3-0-1.
12 I− F+; 13 S+ I+.
House repairer.

JENNINGS, Cecil B.　　　　　*South Africa*
Dale Coll, Border.
b 16.8.14.
1-0-0-1.
37 NZ−.
Clerk. Father of Mike SA 69-70 (no Tests).

JENNINS, Christopher Robert　　*England*
Rydal Sch, Liverpool Univ, Waterloo, Lancs.
b 5.2.42.
Centre, 3-1-0-2.
67 A− I+ F−.
Chartered accountant.

JÉRÔME, Georges　　　　　　*France*
SF.
Forward, 2-0-0-2 (3 − 1t).
06 NZ−(1t) E−.
Rly Chef de Service.

JESSEP, Evan　　*New Zealand/Australia*
Morgan ('Ted')
Newtown Sch, S Wellington Sch, Poneke,
Wellington, Victoria.
b 11.10.04 Leichhard, NSW; *d* 10.1.83 Sydney.
New Zealand
Hooker, 2-1-0-1.
31 A+; 32 A−.
Australia
Prop, 2-1-1-0.
34 NZ+ NZ=.
Mechanic/E Suburbs clubroom employee. NZ's
1st int hooker in 3-2-3 scrum. Played for &
against both NZ & A. Moved to NZ 08.
Returned to A 33. Wellington v BI 30. NZ > 32
A. Broken ankle ended playing career 37.
Coach E Suburbs (Sydney) 40-55.

JEWITT, J.　　　　　　　　*England*
Hartlepool R, Durham Co.
Lock, 1-0-0-1.
02 W−.
According to Hartlepool R historian was sel by

E owing to case of mistaken identity. Broughton
Rgrs RL.

JOHN, Barry ('BJ')　　　　　　*Wales*
Cefneithin Sch, Gwendraeth GS, Cefneithin,
Trin Coll Carmarthen, Llanelli, Cardiff,
Barbarians.
b 6.1.45 Cefneithin.
FH, 25-14-3-8 (90 − 5t 6c 8d 13p).
66 A−; 67 S− NZ−(1d); 68 E=(1d) S+ I− F−;
69 S+(1t) I+(1d) F= E+(1t 1d) NZ− NZ−
A+; 70 SA= S+ E+(1t 1d) I−; 71 E+(2d)
S+(1t 1c 1p) I+(1c 1d 2p) F+(1t 1p); 72 E+(1c
2p) S+(3c 3p) F+(4p); BI > 68 SA 1-0-0-1; 71
A, NZ 4-2-1-1.
Schoolmaster/co dir/journalist. W > 69 NZ, A
& Fj. Broke collarbone 1st Test BI > 68 SA.
Rec 188 pts BI 71. Champ rec 35 pts 72.
Barbarians v NZ 67, SA 70. Wrote 'World of
Rugby' pub 78.

JOHN, David Arthur　　　　　　*Wales*
Gowerton, Bedford, Llanelli.
b 05 Gowerton; *d* 16.8.29 London.
SH, 4-1-0-3.
25 I−; 28 E− S+ I−.
Steelworker. Suffered physical breakdown 29,
died aged 24.

JOHN, David Evan　　　　　　*Wales*
Llanelli.
b 1.3.02 Loughor; *d* 20.11.73 Loughor.
FH, 5-2-0-3 (9 − 3t).
23 F+ I−; 28 E−(1t) S+(1t) I−(1t).
Steelworker. Capt Llanelli 28-9. Llanelli comm.

JOHN, Ernest Raymond ('Roy')　　　*Wales*
Neath GS, Neath, Glam, Barbarians.
b 3.12.25 Neath; *d* 28.9.81 Neath.
Lock/flanker, 19-13-1-5 (3 − 1t).
50 E+ S+ I+ F+(1t); 51 E+ S− I= F− SA−;
52 E+ S+ I+ F+; 53 E− S+ I+ F+ NZ+; 54
E−; BI > 50 NZ 4-0-1-3, A 2-2-0-0.
Quantity surveyor. Served in RN. Barbarians >
52 SA.

JOHN, Glyndwr　　　　　　　*Wales*
Garw SS, Welsh SS, St Luke's Coll, London
Welsh.
b 22.3.32 Neath; *d* 7.6.83.
Centre/FH, 2-1-0-1.
54 E− F+.
Schoolmaster. Football for Welsh Youth. Leigh
RL as schoolboy, repaid £400 signing fee &
reinstated by WRU. Taught at Monmouth Sch.

JOHN, John Hywel　　　　　　*Wales*
Swansea.
Hooker, 8-3-1-4.
26 E= S− I+ F+; 27 E− S− F+ I−.
Police.

JOHNS, William Alexander   *England*
Sir Thomas Rich's Sch Gloucester, Gloucester,
Glos.
 b 1.2.1882 Gloucester; *d* −.
Forward, 7-4-1-2 (3 − 1t).
09 W− F+(1t) I+ S−; 10 W+ I= F+.
Stevedore/hotelier.

JOHNSON, Adrian Paul   *Australia*
NSW.
 b 6.12.24.
Centre, 2-0-0-2.
46 NZ− M−.
Medicine.

JOHNSON, Brian Bernard   *Australia*
NSW.
 b 29.4.30; *d* 29.8.66 New Guinea.
Flanker/no 8/prop, 9-3-0-6 (6 − 2t).
52 Fj+(1t) Fj− NZ+ NZ−; 53 SA+(1t) SA−
SA−; 55 NZ− NZ−.
Dental mechanic. Bro of Peter.

JOHNSON, Lancelot Matthew   *New Zealand*
Lusmden Sch, Southland Boys' HS, Wellington,
Celtic, Hawkes Bay, N Island.
 b 9.8.1897 Lumsden.
1st/2nd five-eighth, 4-2-0-2.
28 SA− SA+ SA− SA+.
Accountant. NZ > 25 A, 28 SA.

JOHNSON, Peter George   *Australia*
Sydney HS, NSW.
 b 13.9.37 Sydney.
Hooker, 42-13-2-27 (3 − 1t).
59 BI− BI−; 61 Fj+ Fj+ Fj= SA− SA− F−; 62
NZ− NZ− NZ= NZ− NZ−; 63 E+ SA− SA+
SA+ SA−; 64 NZ− NZ− NZ+; 65 SA+ SA+;
66 BI− BI− W+ S−; 67 E+ I− F−(1t) I−
NZ−; 68 NZ− NZ− F+ I− S−; 70 S+ 71 SA−
SA− F+ F−.
Economist. Bro of Brian. A's most capped
player. Capt A > I & S 68.

JOHNSON, Thomas Albert   *Wales*
(**'Codger'**)
S Church St Docks Sch, Welsh SS, Cardiff,
Penarth.
 b 1893; *d* −.5.48.
Wing/FB, 12-4-0-8 (6 − 1t 1p).
21 E− F+ I+(1p); 23 E− S− F+; 24 E−(1t) S−
NZ−; 25 E− S− F+.
Marine stores dealer. 187 apps for Cardiff 20-7.
1st r in Welsh rugby: replaced Llanelli's Dai
John v Cardiff when John was inj early in match
at Arms Park 9.2.29. Both clubs mildly rebuked
by WRU for allowing breach of Laws.

JOHNSON, William Dilwyn   *Wales*
Gowerton GS, Swansea, Pontardulais.
 b 5.12.23 Swansea.

Flanker, 1-0-0-1.
53 E−.
Police.

JOHNSTON, David Ian   *Scotland*
George Watson's Coll, Scottish Schs, Edinburgh
Univ, Watsonians.
 b 20.10.58 Edinburgh.
Centre, 27-15-1-11 (16 − 4t).
79 NZ−; 80 I−(2t) F+ W− E−; 81'R+ A+; 82
E+ I− F+ W+(1t) A+ A−; 83 I− F− W−
NZ=; 84 W+ E+(1t) I+ F+ R−; 86 F+ W−
E+ I+ R+.
Law. Scottish XV v Fj 82. Capt Scottish Schs v F
77. Joined Hibernian FC at 16; then
Meadowbank Thistle & Rangers before
transferring to Hearts. 18 months a pro
footballer, switched back to rugby. Inj
interrupted int career. S > 82 A; R 84. Bro
Stuart played FH in Scottish Trial 86.

JOHNSTON, Henry Halcro CB   *Scotland*
CBE CM
Dollar Acad, Edinburgh Collegian FP,
Edinburgh Univ, Army Medical Staff.
 b 13.9.1856 Kirkwall; *d* 13.10.39.
FB/wing, 2-2-0-0.
1877 I+ E+.
Medicine/The Army.

JOHNSTON, Jack   *Ireland*
Armagh RS, Belfast Acad, NIFC.
 b −; *d* 11.
Forward, 8-1-1-6.
1881 S+; 1882 S−; 1884 S−; 1885 S−; 1886 E−;
1887 E= S− W−.
Pres IRFU 02-3.

JOHNSTON, James   *Scotland*
Gala Acad, Melrose.
 b 17.9.25 St Boswells.
Lock, 5-0-0-5 (3 − 1t).
51 SA−; 52 F− W− I− E−(1t).
Oil distributor.

JOHNSTON, Meredith   *Ireland*
Armagh RS, Trin Coll Dublin.
 b 1860; *d* −.4.44.
Half-back, 8-1-1-6 (1t).
1880 E− S−; 1881 E− S+; 1882 E=(1t); 1884
E− S−; 1886 E−.

JOHNSTON, Ralph William   *Ireland*
Foyle Coll, Trin Coll Dublin.
Centre, 3-0-1-2.
1890 S− W= E−.
Medicine. Ckt for I.

JOHNSTON, Robert VC   *Ireland*
King William's Coll IOM, Wanderers,
Johannesburg Wanderers.

b 13.8.1872; *d* 24.3.50 Kilkenny.
Forward, 2-0-0-2.
1893 E− W−; BT > 1896 SA.
The Army. One of 2 forwards on BT > 1896 SA
(see Tommy Crean) to be awarded VC in later
SA War 1899-01.

JOHNSTON, T.J.   *Ireland*
Queen's Coll Belfast.
Forward, 6-1-1-4.
1892 E− S− W+; 1893 E− S=; 1895 E−.

JOHNSTON, W.G.S.   *Scotland*
Cambridge Univ, Richmond, Barbarians.
Wing, 5-1-0-4.
35 W− I−; 37 W+ I− E−.
Blue 32-4.

JOHNSTON, William ('Massa')   *New Zealand*
Alhambra, Otago, S Island.
b 13.9.1881 Dunedin; *d* 9.1.51 Sydney, NSW.
Flanker, 3-2-1-0.
07 A+ A+ A=.
NZ > 05 A, 05-6 BI,F (missed NAm because of
illness), 07 A. RL 07; joined Wigan (E) 08,
Warrington 10. Moved to A, where he became
commissionaire at R Sydney Agric Showground.

JOHNSTON, William C.   *Scotland*
Glasgow HS, Glasgow HSFP.
b 16.12.1896; *d* 6.10.83.
FB, 1-0-1-0.
22 F=.

JOHNSTON, William R.   *England*
Colston's Sch Bristol, Bristol, Gloucester.
b 1887; *d* −.
FB, 16-13-1-2.
10 W+ I= S+; 12 W+ I+ S− F+; 13 SA− W+
F+ I+ S+; 14 W+ I+ S+ F+.
Leather co rep. Once E's most capped FB. Was
still playing after WW1.

JOHNSTONE, Bradley Ronald   *New Zealand*
Takapuna GS, N Shore, NZ Jnrs, Auckland, N
Island.
b 30.7.50 Auckland.
Prop, 13-10-0-3 (8 − 2t).
76 SA+; 77 BI+(1t) BI−; 77 F− F+; 78 I+ W+
E+(1t) S+; 79 F+ F− S+ E+.
Builder. NZ > 76 SA, 77 F, 78 BI, 79 A (did not
play in any match), 79 E,S & It, 80 A & Fj.
Father Ron rep Auckland 48-52 & NZ trials.

JOHNSTONE, Paul Geoffrey   *South Africa*
Stellenbosch Univ, Cape Town Univ, Oxford
Univ, W Prov.
b 30.6.30.
Wing, 9-7-0-2 (11 − 2t 1c 1p).

51 S+ I+ W+; 52 E+ F+; 56 A+ NZ− NZ+
NZ−.
Brewery rep. Blue 52-4. SA > 51-2 BI, F.

JOHNSTONE, Peter   *New Zealand*
Mosgiel Dist HS, Canterbury Cavalry,
Ashburton Co, Taieri, Otago, S Island.
9.8.22 Mosgiel.
No 8/flanker, 9-6-1-2 (3 − 1t).
49 SA− SA−(1t); 50 BI= BI+ BI+ BI+; 51
A+ A+ A+.
Bridge building contractor. NZ > 49 SA, 51 A
(capt). Otago sel 59-61 & pres. Held most
offices at Taieri club; their ground named in his
honour. Bro Jim rep Wellington 55-7.

JOHNSTONE, W.E.   *Ireland*
St Columba's Coll, Trin Coll Dublin.
Forward, 1-0-0-1.
1884 W−.

JOHNSTONE-SMYTH, T.R.   *Ireland*
Lansdowne.
Forward, 1-0-1-0.
1882 E=.

JOINEL, Jean-Luc   *France*
Brive.
b 21.9.53 St Vincent-de-Cosse, Dordogne.
Flanker/No 8, 46-26-3-17 (4 − 1t).
77 NZ+; 78 R+; 79 I= W+ E− S+ NZ− NZ+
R+(1t); 80 W− E− S− I+ SA−; 81 S+ I+ W+
E+ R+ NZ− NZ−; 82 E− S− I+ R−; 83 E+
S+ I− W+ A= A+ R+; 84 I+ W+ E+ S−
NZ− NZ−; 85 S+ I= W+ Arg−; 86 S− I+ W+
E+.
Rep. F > 80 SA; 85 Arg.

JOL, Marcel   *France*
Biarritz.
b 16.5.23 Biarritz; *d* 81.
Hooker, 10-6-0-4.
47 S+ I+ W− E−; 49 S− I+ E− W+ Arg+
Arg−.
Switched to RL.

JONES, Arthur Hugh   *Wales*
Llandovery Coll, Cardiff, London Welsh.
b c08 Bridgend; *d* 26.6.64 Porthcawl.
Wing, 2-1-0-1.
33 E+ S−.
Manufacturer. Father in law of Howard
Nicholls.

JONES, Benjamin Lewis   *Wales*
Gowerton GS, Welsh SS, Neath, Devonport
Servs, RN, Llanelli.
b 11.4.31 Gorseinon.
FB/centre/wing, 10-8-0-2 (36 − 9c 6p).
50 E+(1c 1p) S+(1p) I+ F+(3c 1p); 51 E+(4c)
S− SA−; 52 E+ I+(1c 1p) F+(2p); BIr > 50

215

NZ 1-0-0-1, A 2-2-0-0.
Lorry driver/schoolmaster. Ckt Cornwall. Leeds RL 52 £6000 fee, later Wentworthville (A). 15 GB RL Tests. Wrote book 'King of Rugger' pub 58.

JONES, Brian James   *Wales*
Cwmcarn Sch, Pontywaun GS, Cwmcarn Utd, Newport, Devonport Servs, Devon, Comb Servs, RN, Barbarians.
b 10.10.35 Cwmcarn.
Centre, 2-1-0-1 (3 − 1t).
60 I+ F−(1t*).
Production clerk/marketing dir building co. Served R Marines. Only living player to have played on winning side v all three major touring teams, A, NZ & SA. Newport v NZ 53 & 63, v A 57. Barbarians v SA 61. Barbarians > 58 SA (only uncap back on tour). Coach Newport 67-9 (won Welsh champ, beat SA). Coach Oxford Univ 68-9. Newport Centenary chmn 74-5, 83-86; sec 75. *This t erroneously credited to Brian Cresswell.

JONES, Charles W.   *Wales*
Bridgend, Newport, Birkenhead Pk, The Army, Harlequins.
b 18.6.1893; *d* c59 Preston.
Flanker, 3-2-0-1.
20 E+ S− F+.
The Army/schoolmaster. Served WW1, Sgt-maj Welch Rgt. Played in Mother Country XV 19. PE teacher at Birkenhead Sch.

JONES, C.H.   *South Africa*
Transvaal.
2-0-2-0.
03 BT= BT=.

JONES, Clifford W. OBE   *Wales*
Porth CS, Llandovery Coll, Welsh SS, Cambridge Univ, Cardiff, Barbarians, London Welsh.
FH, 13-8-2-3 (6 − 2t).
34 E− S+ I+; 35 E= S+(1t) I− NZ+; 36 E= S+(1t) I+; 38 E+ S− I+.
Barrister/antique dealer. Uncle of Kingsley Jones. Blue 33-5. WRU comm 56, sel 57-78, pres 80-1. Team-mate with Vivian Jenkins & Arthur Rees in Llandovery XV. Wrote book 'Rugby Football' pub 37.

JONES, Dan   *Wales*
Neath.
b 2.3.07 Neath Abbey.
Wing, 1-0-0-1.
27 NSW−.
Rly blacksmith.

JONES, Daniel   *Wales*
Aberavon.

b 1875; *d* 1.1.59 Taibach.
Half-back, 1-1-0-0 (3 − 1t).
1897 E+(1t).
Millman at tinplate works.

JONES, David   *Wales*
Morriston, Swansea.
b 30.4.16 Swansea.
Prop, 7-3-0-4.
47 E− F+ I+; 49 E+ S− I− F−.
Post Office employee.

JONES, David ('Tarw')   *Wales*
Treherbert, Aberdare.
b 1881; *d* −.1.33.
Forward, 13-11-0-2.
02 E+ S+ I+; 03 E+ S− I+; 05 E+ S+ I+ NZ+; 06 E+ S+ SA−.
Collier/police. Treherbert RL. Suspended by WRU 07. Wounded WW1.

JONES, David Kenneth   *Wales*
Gwendraeth GS, Llanelli, UC Cardiff, Oxford Univ, Cardiff, Barbarians, London Welsh.
b 7.8.41 Cross Hands.
Centre/wing, 14-6-2-6 (6 − 2t).
62 E= S− F+ I=; 63 E− F− NZ−; 64 E+ S+ SA−; 66 E+ S+(2t) I− F+; BI > 62 SA 3-0-1-2; 66 A 2-2-0-0, NZ 1-0-0-1.
Industrialist. Blue 63. W > 64 SA. CBI Welsh Council mem.

JONES, David L.   *Wales*
Newport.
b 01.
No 8/flanker/lock/prop, 5-2-1-2.
26 E= S− I+ F+; 27 E−.
Steelworker/fitter's labourer. Wigan RL 27.

JONES, David Phillips ('Ponty')   *Wales*
Pontypool, London Welsh, Barbarians.
b −.1.1882 Pontypool; *d* 11.1.36 Llantarnam.
Wing, 1-1-0-0 (3 − 1t).
07 I+(1t); BT > 08 A, NZ; 10 SA.
Coal merchant. Bro of J.P. ('Jack') & J.P. ('Tuan').

JONES, Edgar Lewis   *Wales*
Gowerton, Llanelli.
b 4.5.10 Sketty; *d* 9.2.86.
Prop, 5-2-1-2.
30 F+; 33 E+ S− I−; 35 E=.
Miner/steelworker/docker. Leeds RL 35. Served WW2 Welch Rgt. V-pres Glam CCC.

JONES, Elvet Lewis   *Wales*
Llanelli CS, Llanelli.
b 29.4.13 Llanelli.
Wing, 1-1-0-0.
39 S+; BI > 38uncap SA 2-1-0-1.

216

Magistrate's clerk. BI Test player before Welsh cap. Chmn, pres Llanelli.

JONES, Frederick Phelp *England*
Wallasey GS, New Brighton, Birkenhead Pk.
b 1873; *d* 14.8.44.
Wing, 1-0-0-1.
1893 S−.
Brick manufacturer.

JONES, Garth Glennie *Australia*
Nundah Sch Brisbane, Qld.
b 18.11.31 Childers.
Wing, 12-4-0-8 (12 − 4t).
52 Fj+(1t) Fj−; 53 SA− SA+(1t) SA− SA−;
54 Fj+(1t) Fj−; 55 NZ−(1t) NZ− NZ+; 56
SA−.
Insurance clerk.

JONES, Graham ('Bunner') *Wales*
Abersychan GS, Abersychan Tech,
Garndiffaith, Pontypool, Ebbw Vale.
Flanker, 3-1-0-2 (3 − 1t).
63 S+ I−(1t) F−.
Garage supervisor. 145 consec apps for Ebbw
Vale.

JONES, Graham Glyn *Wales*
Llandovery Coll, Cardiff.
b 24.11.06 Morriston.
Centre, 2-0-0-2 (7 − 1t 1d).
30 S−(1t 1d); 33 I−.
Clerk.

JONES, Harold James *Wales*
Maesteg, Neath.
b 18.12.08 Maesteg; *d* 16.10.55 Keighley.
Lock, 2-1-0-1.
29 E− S+.
Police/licensee. Wigan RL 30.

JONES, Harry *Wales*
Penygraig.
b 1870 Porthcawl, *d* −.
Forward, 2-2-0-0.
02 S+ I+.

JONES, Herbert Arthur *England*
Barnstaple.
b 22.8.18 Landkey, Barnstaple.
Lock, 3-1-0-2.
50 W− I+ F−.
Farmer.

JONES, Howie *Wales*
Neath GS, Swansea, Neath.
b 8.9.07 Glynneath.
Wing, 2-2-0-0 (3 − 1t).
30 I+(1t) F+.
Lloyds Bank official. Son of Howell. Try v I 30

scored jointly with Harry Peacock, the players grounding ball simultaneously.

JONES, Hubert A. *Australia*
Newcastle, NSW.
b 1888; kia 18.
Centre, 3-1-0-2 (9 − 3t).
13 NZ− NZ−(2t) NZ+(1t).
Medical student.

JONES, Hywel *Wales*
Glynneath, Neath.
b 1882; *d* 1.12.08.
Forward, 1-0-0-1.
04 I−.
Surveyor to Neath RDC. Father of Howie.

JONES, Ian Conin *Wales*
Malmesbury Sch Stellenbosch, Oxford Univ,
London Welsh, Surrey.
b 2.3.40 Vryburg, SA.
Lock, 1-0-0-1.
68 I−.
Merchant banker. Blue 62-4.

JONES, Iorwerth *Wales*
Llanelli.
b 3.4.03 Loughor; *d* 31.8.83 Penclawdd.
No 8, 5-1-0-4.
27 NSW−; 28 E− S+ I− F−.
Steelworker/greengrocer. Played amateur
football for Swansea AFC. Leeds RL 32.

JONES, Ivor Egwad CBE *Wales*
Gowerton, Loughor, Swansea, Llanelli,
Birmingham, N Midlands.
b 10.12.01 Loughor; *d* 16.11.82 Swansea.
Flanker, 16-4-1-11 (13 − 1t 5c).
24 E− S−(1t); 27 S− F+ I− NSW−; 28 E−(1c)
S+ I−(2c) F−; 29 E− S+(1c) F+ I=; 30 E− S−
(1c); BI > 30 NZ 4-1-0-3, A 1-0-0-1.
Furnaceman. Capt Wales 3 times. Scored over
1200 pts for Llanelli. IB rep 62-5. WRU pres
68-9.

JONES, Jack Bedwellty *Wales*
Abertillery.
Prop, 4-3-0-1 (3 − 1t).
14 E− S+ F+ I+(1t).
Miner. Oldham RL. Mem of 'Terrible Eight'.

JONES, James *Wales*
Aberavon.
b 1893; *d* −.
No 8/flanker, 6-3-0-3.
19 NZA−; 20 E+ S−; 21 S− F+ I+.
Licensee.

JONES, James Phillips ('Tuan') *Wales*
Christ's Coll Brecon, Guy's Hosp, London
Welsh, Barbarians.

b 1884 Pontypool; *d* −.
Centre, 1-1-0-0 (3 − 1t).
13 S+(1t); BT > 08uncap A, NZ.
Medicine. Bro of D.P. & J.P. ('Jack').
Emigrated A.

JONES, J. Arthur   *Wales*
Monmouth Sch, Cardiff.
b 1857 Risca; *d* 20.1.19 Llandaff.
Forward, 1-0-0-1.
1883 S−.
Cardiff Exchange. High Sheriff of Glam.

JONES, John ('Bala')   *Wales*
Aberavon.
SH, 1-1-0-0.
01 E+.
General dealer. 5ft 5in.

JONES, John ('Strand')   *Wales*
Lampeter Sch, St David's Coll Lampeter,
Oxford Univ, Llanelli, Liverpool, London
Welsh.
b 2.12.1877 Caio, Carms; *d* 3.4.58
Pyllaucrynion.
FB, 5-4-0-1 (11 − 4c 1p).
02 E+(1p) S+(1c) I+; 03 E+(3c) S−.
Chaplain/farmer. Son of farmer. Blue 1899-01.
Ordained Deacon 03, priest 04. Army chaplain
in India 09-26. Chmn Lampeter RFC 47-8.

JONES, John Phillips ('Jack')   *Wales*
Christ's Coll Brecon, Pontypool, London
Welsh, Newport, Barbarians.
b 2.3.1887 (or 1886) Pontypool; *d* 19.3.51
Newport.
Centre/wing, 14-11-0-3 (18 − 6t).
08 A+; 09 E+ S+ F+(2t) I+(1t); 10 F+(1t)
E−; 12 E− F+(1t); 13 F+ I+(1t); 20 F+ I+; 21
E−.
Coal merchant. Bro of D.P. & J.P. ('Tuan')
Jones.

JONES, Joseph   *Wales*
Swansea.
15.3.1899 Pontardawe; *d* 27.1.60.
Centre, 1-1-0-0.
24 F+.
Licensee. Won only cap because WRU
suspended B.O. Male two days before match v F
in Paris. Melville Rosser moved to FB with
Jones at centre. Leeds RL 24.

JONES, Kenneth Jeffrey   *Wales*
W Mon GS, Newport, Barbarians.
b 30.12.21 Blaenavon.
Wing, 44-28-2-14 (51 − 17t).
47 E− S+(2t) F+ I+ A+; 48 E=(1t) S+(1t) F−
I−; 49 E+ S− I− F−(1t); 50 E+ S+(1t) I+(1t)
F+(2t); 51 E+(1t) S− I= F−(1t) SA−; 52
E+(2t) S+(1t) I+(1t) F+; 53 E− S+(1t) I+ F+

NZ+(1t); 54 E− I+ F+ S+; 55 E+ S− I+ F+;
56 E+ S+ I− F+; 57 S−; BI > 50 NZ 3-0-1-2,
A.
Schoolmaster/newspaper columnist. Victor
Ludorum W Mon GS 39. World's most capped
wing (47 inc 3 BI). Barbarians v SA 52, NZ 54.
Welsh 100y, 220y sprint champ 7 yrs in succ.
Sprinted for GB in Olympics 48 & for Wales in
Empire Games 54. Capt Brit team European
Games, Berne 54. Rugby corr 'Sunday Express'.

JONES, Kenyon William James   *Wales*
MBE US Bronze Star
Monmouth Sch, Oxford Univ, London Welsh.
b 5.9.11.
No 8, 1-0-0-1.
34 E−.
Chmn, man dir Ronson Products. Blue 31-2.

JONES, Kingsley D.   *Wales*
Llandovery Coll, Cardiff, Barbarians.
b 35.
Prop, 10-4-1-5.
60 SA−; 61 E+ S− I+; 62 E= F+; 63 E− S+
I− NZ−; BI > 62 SA 4-0-1-3.
Fruiterer. Nephew of Cliff Jones.

JONES, Murray Gordon   *New Zealand*
N Shore, Auckland, Omaha, NZ Jnrs, N
Auckland, N Island.
26.10.42 Warkworth; *d* 12.2.75 Auckland.
Prop, 1-0-0-1.
73 E−.
Carpenter/concrete co proprietor. Drowned in
Auckland Harbour trying to rescue his 2-yr-old
son who had fallen overboard from a yacht. Bro
Rod rep N Auckland 68-75.

JONES, Percy   *Wales*
Newport, Pontypool, London Welsh.
Lock/no 8, 8-5-0-3.
12 SA−; 13 E− S+ F+; 14 E− S+ F+ I+.
Hotelier. Mem of 'Terrible Eight'.

JONES, Percy Sydney Twentyman   *South Africa*
Diocesan Coll Rondebosch, Grahamstown,
Albany, Diocesans OB, Villagers, W Prov.
b 13.9.1876 Beaufort W; *d* 8.3.54 Cape Town.
3-1-0-2 (3 − 1t).
1896 BT− BT− BT+(1t).
Judge. SA sel. Ckt for SA 02. Judge Pres of the
Cape.

JONES, Peter Anthony   *Australia*
Waverley Coll Sydney, NSW.
b 15.8.42.
Centre, 2-1-0-1 (3 − 1t).
63 E+(1t) SA−.
Estate agency clerk. RL.

218

JONES, Peter Frederick ('Tiger')   *New Zealand*
Kaitaia Coll, Awanui, N Auckland, N Island.
24.3.32 Kaitaia.
Flanker/no 8, 11-9-0-2 (6 − 2t).
54 E+ S+; 55 A+ A+; 56 SA+ SA+(1t); 58
A+(1t) A− A+; 59 BI+; 60 SA−.
Family name was Hilton-Jones.
Farmer/fisherman. NZ > 53-4 BI,F & NAm
(10t), 60 A & SA. Mangonui club sel & N
Auckland RU mem. Mem N Auckland Harbour
Bd from 78. Norman Harris wrote his biography
'It's Me, Tiger' pub 65.

JONES, Raymond Bark   *Wales*
Uppingham Sch, Anglesey, Cambridge Univ,
Lancs.
b 29.8.11 Blundellsands.
Lock, 2-1-0-1.
33 E+ S−.
Solicitor. Blue 31-3.

JONES, Richard   *Wales*
Swansea.
b 27.11.1879; *d* −.
Half-back, 15-12-1-2 (9 − 3t).
01 I+; 02 E+; 04 E= S+(1t) I−; 05 E+(1t); 08
F+(1t) I+ A+; 09 E+ S+ F+ I+; 10 F+ E−.
Police/licensee.

JONES, Richard ('Chink')   *Wales*
London Welsh.
Flanker, 1-0-0-1.
29 E−.
Bank clerk. Bro of Robert.

JONES, Robert   *Wales*
Northampton.
b 26.10.1893 Shanghai; *d* −.
FH, 3-1-1-1.
26 E= S− F+.
Schoolmaster. Chinese mother, Welsh father.
Bro of Richard ('Chink').

JONES, Robert   *Wales*
Llwynypia.
Forward, 1-1-0-0.
01 I+.
Police.

JONES, Robert Nicholas   *Wales*
Cwmtawe Comp, Welsh SS, Swansea.
b 10.11.66 Trebanos.
SH, 4-2-0-2.
86 E− S+ I+ F−.
Solicitor's clerk/liaison officer. Born, bred in
village of Trebanos, which produced Bleddyn
Bowen and Glam & E fast bowler Greg
Thomas. 12 schools caps. Ckt for Welsh SS &
Glamorgan Colts. Wales B v F 85. 2 bros also
SHs, Anthony at Penarth & Rhodri a schoolboy

at Cwmtawe Comp. Works with Malcolm Dacey
& Clive Thomas, ex-int football ref.

JONES, Ronald E.   *Wales*
Coventry.
b 44.
Flanker/no 8, 5-2-0-3.
67 F− E+; 68 S+ I− F−.
Schoolmaster.

JONES, Stephen Thomas ('Staff')   *Wales*
Mill Street Comp Pontypridd, Welsh Youth, E
Glam, Pontypool.
b 4.1.59 Ynysybwl.
Prop, 5-2-0-3 (4 − 1t).
83 S+(1t) I+ F− R−; 84 S−; BI > 83 NZ 3-0-0-
3.
NCB. Wales B v A 81, v F 80, 81, 82. Wales B >
80 US, Can. Played 13 out of 18 matches BI >
83 NZ.

JONES, Tom   *Wales*
Newport.
b 13.12.1895 Pontnewydd.
Prop/lock, 6-3-1-2 (3 − 1t).
22 E+ S= I+ F+; 24 E−(1t) S−.
Police.

JONES, W. ('Pussy')   *Wales*
Cardiff.
Centre, 2-1-0-1.
1898 I+ E−.
Labourer.

JONES, Walter Idris   *Wales*
Llanelli CS, UC Aberystwyth, Cambridge Univ,
Llanelli, Barbarians, London Welsh.
b 18.1.1900 Llanelli; *d* 5.7.71 Llandaff.
Flanker/lock, 4-1-0-3 (3 − 1t).
25 E− S−(1t) F+ I−.
NCB research chemist. Blue 1923-5. Bro of
Lord Chancellor, Lord Elwyn Jones.

JONES, William Desmond   *Wales*
Gwendraeth GS, Tumble, Aberavon, Llanelli.
b 25 Tumble.
Lock, 1-0-1-0.
48 E=.
Miner/police.

JONES, William Herbert   *Wales*
Llanelli.
b 1.5.06 Llanelli; *d* 31.7.82.
SH, 2-2-0-0.
34 S+ I+.
Miner. St Helens RL 34.

JONES, William John   *Wales*
QEGS Carmarthen, Carmarthen Tg Coll,
Carmarthen Harlequins, Llanelli.
b 4.2.1894 Cefneithin; *d* − .7.78 Llanarthney.

Flanker, 1-0-0-1.
24 I−.
HM. Served WW1. Taught at Cefneithin village sch when Carwyn James & Barry John were pupils.

JONES, William Keri   *Wales*
Ystalyfera GS, Cardiff, Barbarians.
b 13.1.45.
Wing, 5-1-1-3 (6 − 2t).
67 NZ−; 68 E= S+(1t) I− F−(1t); BI > 68 SA.
Schoolmaster. Barbarians v NZ 67. Wigan RL 68.

JONES, William Roy   *Wales*
Swansea.
b 22.2.03 Swansea.
Centre, 2-0-0-2.
27 NSW−; 28 F−.
Oil executive.

JONES, Wyndham   *Wales*
Mountain Ash.
b 1883; d 4.9.53
Half-back, 1-1-0-0 (3 − 1t).
05 I+(1t).
Sec to collier mgr. WRU sel 25-6.

JONES-DAVIES, Thomas Ellis   *Wales*
QEGS Carmarthen, St George's Sch Harpenden, Cambridge Univ, London Welsh, Barbarians.
b 06 Llandilofawr; d 25.8.60 Swansea.
Centre, 4-2-1-1 (6 − 2t).
30 E−(1t) I+; 31 E=(1t) S+; BI > 30 NZ, A.
Medicine.

JORDAAN, R.P. ('Jorrie')   *South Africa*
Cradock HS, N Transvaal.
b 13.7.20.
Hooker, 4-4-0-0.
49 NZ+ NZ+ NZ+ NZ+.
Police.

JORDAN, Henry Martyn   *Ireland/Wales*
Newport, London Welsh.
b 7.3.1865 Clifton; d −.
Ireland
Back, 1-0-0-1.
1884 W−.
Wales
Back, 3-0-1-2 (2t).
1885 E−(2t) S=; 1889 S−.
One of smallest ever int players. Played for I with another Welshman F. Purdon when I arrived in Cardiff two players short (See J. McDaniel).

JORDEN, Anthony Mervyn   *England*
Monmouth Sch, Cambridge Univ, Blackheath,

Harlequins, Bedford, Barbarians, E Cos.
b 28.1.47 Radlett, Herts.
FB, 7-3-1-3 (22 − 5c 4p).
70 F−(2c 1p); 73 I−(1c 1p) F+(2p) S+(2c); 74 F=; 75 W− S+.
Schoolmaster. Blue 68-9. Pres of Hawks Club 70. E Cos CB rep. Ckt blue − 28 apps CUCC 68-70. 60 apps Essex CCC 66-70.

JOSEPH, Howard Thornton   *New Zealand*
Christchurch Boys's HS, Univ, NZ Univs, Canterbury.
b 25.8.49 Christchurch.
Centre, 2-1-0-1.
71 BI+ BI−.
Knee inj ended playing career 71.

JOSEPH, William   *Wales*
Morriston, Swansea.
b 10.5.1878 Morriston.
Forward, 16-12-1-3.
02 E+ S+ I+; 03 E+ S− I+; 04 E= S+; 05 E+ S+ I+ NZ+; 06 E+ S+ I− SA−.
Steelworker. Quoits W v E 01-2.

JOUBERT, Stephen J.   *South Africa*
W Prov.
b 1887; d −.4.39.
Wing/FB, 3-2-1-0 (8 − 1t 1c 1p).
06 I+(1p) W+(1t 1c) E=.
Medicine. Studying in Netherlands at time of selection for SA > 06-7 BI, F. Joined team in E.

JOWETT, Donald   *England*
Heckmondwike.
b 4.12.1866 Bradford; d 27.8.08
Heckmondwike.
Forward, 6-5-0-1 (1c).
1889 NZN+; 1890 S+(1c) I+; 1891 W+ I+ S−.
Licensee. Heckmondwike RL 1896. Relative of E.E. Booth, NZ 05-7.

JOWETT, William Frederick   *Wales*
Swansea.
b 1879 Swansea; d 5.10.39 Clydach.
Wing, 1-1-0-0.
03 E+; BT > 04 A, NZ.
Schoolmaster. Hull KR RL.

JOYCE, James Emerton   *Australia*
NSW.
Forward, 1-0-0-1.
03 NZ−.
Tailor.

JUDD, Harold Augustus   *Australia*
NSW.
b 11.4.1880; d 65.
Forward, 5-0-0-5.
03 NZ−; 04 BT− BT− BT−; 05 NZ−.
Brick co employee.

JUDD, Peter Bruce   *Australia*
NSW.
b 07; *d* 70.
Lock, 2-1-0-1 (3 − 1t).
31 M+(1t) NZ−.
Oyster farmer/grazier. NSW > BI & F 27-8.

JUDD, Philip Edward   *England*
Broad St Sch Coventry, Broad St OB, Coventry,
RAF, Barbarians, Warwicks.
b 8.4.34.
Prop, 22-4-4-14.
62 W= I+ F− S=; 63 S+ NZ− NZ− A−; 64
NZ−; 65 I= F− S−; 66 W− I= F− S−; 67 A−
I+ F− S+ W− NZ−.
Fdr engrg co. E > 63 A, NZ; 67 Can. County
water polo & squash rackets player.

JUDD, Sydney   *Wales*
Cardiff HS, Cardiff, Barbarians.
b 29 Cardiff; *d* 24.2.59 Llanrumney.
Flanker/no 8, 10-7-0-3 (3 − 1t).
53 E− S+ I+ F+ NZ+(1t); 54 E− F+ S+; 55
E+ S−.
Schoolmaster. Cardiff v NZ 53. Barbarians v
NZ 54. Died after long illness, aged 30.

JUDSON, J.H.   *Wales*
Llandovery Coll, Llanelli, London Welsh.
Forward, 2-0-0-2 (1t).
1882 E−; 1883 S−(1t).
Schoolmaster. 1st treas of London Welsh.

JUNOR, J.E.   *Scotland*
Glasgow Acad, Glasgow Academicals.
Forward, 6-2-2-2.
1876 E−; 1877 I+ E+; 1878 E=; 1879 E=; 1881
I−.

JUNQUAS, Louis   *France*
Tyrosse.
b 11.11.20 St Vincent-de-Tyrosse, Landes.
Centre, 13-7-0-6.
45 BF+ BF− W−; 46 BF+ I+ NZS− W+; 47
S+ I+ W− E−; 48 S− W+.

K

KACZOROWKSI, Daniel   *France*
Le Creusot.
b 31.10.52 Le Creusot, Bourgogne.
Flanker, 1-1-0-0.
74 I+r.

KAEMPF, Albert   *France*
St Jean-de-Luz.
Centre, 1-1-0-0.
46 BF+.

KAHTS, Wilhelm Julius Heinrich   *South Africa*
N Transvaal.
b 20.2.47 Valksrust.
Hooker, 11-10-0-1 (4 − 1t).
80 BI+ BI+ BI+ SAm+ SAm+ F+(1t); 81 I+
I+ NZ+; 82 SAm+ SAm−.
SA > 81 US.

KAMINER, J.   *South Africa*
Transvaal.
b 25.1.34.
1-0-0-1.
58 F−.
Medicine.

KARAM, Joseph Francis   *New Zealand*
St Patrick's Coll Silverstream, Marist, Marist-St
Pat's, Wellington, Horowhenua, Paraparaumu,
NZ Jnrs, N Island.
b 21.11.51 Taumarunui.
FB, 10-7-2-1 (65 − 1t 11c 13p).
72 W+(5p) S+(1c); 73 E+(1c) I=(1c) F−(2p);
74 A+(1p) A=(1c 2p) A+(2c); 74 I+(1t 1c 3p);
75 S+(4c).
Salesman/proprietor carpet dyeing co. Moved to
Horowhenua 71 to give Union its 1st All
Black. Top scorer 145 pts (20 apps) NZ > 72-3
BI,F & NAm. 139 pts > 74 A & Fj. 48 pts > 74
I,W & E. Glenora RL 76; Auckland & N Island
RL 76-7.

KASSULKE, N.   *Australia*
Qld.
2-2-0-0.
85 C+ C+.

KATENE, Thomas   *New Zealand*
Matapu Sch, Karioi, Hikurangi, King Country,
Petone, Wellington, NZ Maoris, N Island.
b 14.8.29 Okaiawa.
Wing, 1-1-0-0.
55 A+.

KAVANAGH, James Ronald   *Ireland*
Blackrock Coll, UC Dublin, Wanderers,
Barbarians.
b 21.1.31 Dublin.
No 8/flanker, 35-12-2-21 (12 − 4t).
53 F+ E= S+(1t) W−; 54 NZ− S+ W−; 55 F−
E=; 56 E− S+ W+; 57 F+ E− S+ W−(1t); 58
A+ E− S+ W−; 59 E− S+ W− F+; 60 E− S−
W− F− SA−; 61 E+(1t) S−(1t) W− F− SA−;
62 F−.
Chartered accountant. Bro of Patrick. Water
polo for I.

KAVANAGH, Patrick Joseph   *Ireland*
Blackrock Coll, UC Dublin, Wanderers,
Barbarians.
b 2.9.29 Dublin.
Flanker, 2-0-0-2.

52 E−; 55 W−.
Manufacturer. Bro of Ronald. Water polo for I.

KAY, A. Robert   *Australia*
Victoria.
b 35.
Centre, 2-1-0-1.
58 NZ+; 59 BI−.
The Army.

KAYLL, Henry Edward   *England*
Richmond Sch Yorks, Sunderland, Durham Co.
b 16.7.1855 Sunderland; *d* 14.2.10 Vancouver.
FB, 1-0-1-0.
1878 S=.
Glassworks/farmer. One of 6 bros who play for
Sunderland. English pole vault champ; set
world's best 11ft 1in 1877. Emigrated Can 1880.

KEANE, Maurice Ignatius   *Ireland*
('Moss')
St Brendan's Coll Killarney, UC Dublin,
Lansdowne, Barbarians.
b 27.7.48 Currow, Co Kerry.
Lock, 51-17-4-30 (4 − 1t).
74 F− W= E+ S+ P= NZ−; 75 E+ S− F+
W−; 76 A− F− W− E+ S− NZ−; 77 W− E−
S− F−; 78 S+ F− W− E− NZ−; 79 F= W−
E+ S= A+ A+; 80 E− S+(1t) F− W+; 81 F−
W− E− S−; 82 W+ E+ S+ F−; 83 S+ F+ W−
E+; 84 F− W− E− S−; BI > 77 NZ 1-0-0-1.
Dept of Agric. MSc in Dairy Science. Replaced
Geoff Wheel on BI > 77 NZ when Wheel failed
fitness test.

KEARNEY, James Charles   *New Zealand*
Ranfurly Public Sch, St Kevin's Coll, Ranfurly,
Otago, Brigade, Canterbury, S Island.
b 4.4.20 Naseby.
1st five-eighth, 4-1-0-3 (9 − 1t 2d).
47 A+(1t); 49 SA−(1d) SA−(1d) SA−.
Farmer. NZ > 47 A, 49 SA. Cousin of K.C. &
R.C. Stuart.

KEARNEY, Kenneth Howard   *Australia*
NSW.
b 3.5.24.
Hooker, 7-3-0-4 (3 − 1t).
47 NZ− NZ− S+(1t) I+ W−; 48 E+ F−.
Life assurance exec. Leeds (E) RL 48; RL for
A.

KEARNEY, Ronan Kieran   *Ireland*
Newbridge Sch, UC Dublin, Wanderers.
b 5.3.57 Kilkenny.
Flanker, 4-0-0-4.
82 F−; 84 A−; 86 F− W−.
Accountant/farmer. I > 81 SA.

KEDDIE, Robert Ramsay   *Scotland*
George Watson's Coll, Watsonians, Edinburgh
Univ.
b 19.7.45 Edinburgh.
Wing, 1-0-0-1.
67 NZ−.
Vet.

KEDZLIE, Quentin D.   *Wales*
Cardiff.
Forward, 2-1-0-1.
1888 S+ I−.
119 apps for Cardiff 1881-93.

KEEFFE, Ernest   *Ireland*
St Nicholas Coll Cork, Sunday's Well,
Barbarians.
b 16.3.19 Cork.
Lock, 6-3-0-3.
47 F− E+ S+ W− A−; 48 F+.
Farmer/fabricating engr. Played in 3 Victory
ints. I boxing rep.

KEELING, J.H.   *England*
Guy's Hosp.
Hooker, 2-0-1-1.
48 A− W=.
Medicine.

KEEN, Brian Warwick   *England*
Hardye's Sch Dorchester, Dorchester,
Newcastle Univ, Northern, Moseley,
Barbarians, Northumb.
b 1.6.44.
Prop, 4-1-2-1.
68 W= I= F− S+.
Technical rep. Moved to SAm; 4 apps for Brazil
71.

KEEN, Leslie   *Wales*
Sandfields Comp Cardiff, Cardiff Coll,
Aberavon, Penarth.
b 13.11.54 Port Talbot.
Wing, 4-2-0-2 (4 − 1t).
80 F+ E− S+(1t) I−.
Schoolmaster. Bro in law of Allan Martin.
Wales B v F 79.

KEETON, George Haydn   *England*
Oakham Sch, Cambridge Univ, Richmond,
Leicester, Midland Cos.
b 13.10.1878; *d* 7.1.49 Menton, France.
Hooker, 3-1-1-1.
04 W= I+ S−.
HM. Blue 1899-1900. Various teaching posts inc
Fettes Coll & Reading Sch. Buried in same
cemetery in Menton as William Webb Ellis &
Percy Carpmael, fdr of the Barbarians.

KEITH, George James ('Hamish')   *Scotland*
Dollar Acad, Wasps, Mdx.
b 41.
Wing, 2-0-0-2(3 − 1t).
68 F−(1t) W−.
Accountant. London v Paris & A 67.

KELAHER, John Desmond   *Australia*
('Jockey')
St Joseph's Coll, Drummoyne, Manly, NSW.
b 5.2.12 Barraba, NSW..
Wing/centre, 13-4-0-9 (9 − 3t).
33 SA− SA+ SA− SA− SA+(1t); 34 NZ+
NZ−; 36 NZ− NZ− M+(1t); 37 SA− SA−(1t);
38 NZ−.
Oil co rep. A > 33 SA, 36 NZ.

KELLEHER, Rodney James   *Australia*
Mana Coll, Qld.
b 8.11.47 Wellington, NZ.
Flanker, 2-0-0-2.
69 SA− SA−.
Carpenter. A > 69 SA (sent off v Rhodesia).

KELLER, Douglas   *Australia/Scotland*
Holcombe
Sydney GS, Sydney Univ, Drummoyne, NSW,
Guy's Hosp, London Scottish (E), Barbarians
(E), Sheffield (E).
b 18.6.22 Wee Waa, NSW.
Australia
Flanker/lock, 6-3-0-3.
47 NZ− S+ I+ W−; 48 E+ F−.
Scotland
Flanker, 7-3-0-4.
49 F+ W+ I− E−; 50 F+ W− I−.
Medicine. Played for & against S. World
authority on urology.

KELLY, Alexander J. ('Tiger')   *Australia*
Wallaroos, E Suburbs (Sydney), NSW.
b −; *d* 13.
Forward, 1-1-0-0.
1899 BT I .
Labourer.

KELLY, E.W.   *South Africa*
Griq W.
1-0-0-1.
1896 BT−.

KELLY, Geoffrey Arnold   *England*
Perse Sch, Letchworth, Bedford, Barbarians, E
Midlands, E Cos.
b 9.2.14.
Prop, 4-2-1-1.
47 W+ I− S+; 48 W=.
Fertiliser sales rep.

KELLY, Hugh C.   *Ireland*
RBAI, NIFC.

b 1849; *d* −.11.44.
Forward, 6-0-0-6.
1877 E− S−; 1878 E−; 1879 S−; 1880 E− S−.
Sheriff of Co Down. Ref I v S, S v E 1883, S v I
1885; ump S v I 84.

KELLY, James Charles   *Ireland*
St Mary's Coll, UC Dublin, Barbarians.
b 8.4.40 Dublin.
SH, 11-2-2-7.
62 F− W=; 63 F− E= S− W+ NZ−; 64 E+ S−
W− F−.
Veterinary surgeon.

KELLY, John Wallace   *New Zealand*
Ashburton HS, Univ, Canterbury, Tg Coll, NZ
Univs, Auckland, N Island.
b 7.12.26 Ashburton.
Wing/FB, 2-0-0-2 (3 − 1p).
49 A−(1p) A−.
Headmaster. NZ > 53-4 BI,F & NAm. Coached
various sides. Canterbury & Auckland Univ ath
blue (shot & discus). Bro G.A.K. rep
Ashburton Co 38-46. HM of Takapuna GS.

KELLY, Robert Forrest   *Scotland*
George Watson's Coll, Watsonians, Barbarians.
b 12.3.07 Edinburgh; 23.2.75 Edinburgh.
Centre/wing, 4-2-0-2.
27 NSW+; 28 F+ W− E−.
Co dir.

KELLY, Russell Lindsay   *Australia*
Frederick
Sydney HS, Canterbury HS, NSW.
b 25.1.09; *d* 25.12.43 Sydney.
Flanker, 7-1-0-6 (2 − 1c).
36 NZ− NZ− M+(1c); 37 SA− SA−; 38 NZ−
NZ−.
Bank official. Served WW2; died of wounds.

KELLY, Seamus   *Ireland*
Clongowes Coll, Lansdowne.
b 15.3.31 Wexford.
FH, 5-1-0-4 (12 − 4p).
54 S+ W−(1p), 55 S−(1p), 60 W−(2p) F−.
General draper. Played Gaelic Football for
Wexford 49-50.

KELLY, Thomas Stanley   *England*
Blundell's Sch, Exeter, London Devonians,
Devon.
b 1882 Tiverton; *d* −.
Lock/prop, 12-5-1-6.
06 W− I− S+ F+ SA=; 97 F+ W− I− S−; 08
F+ I+ S−.
Civil service.

KELLY, W.   *Ireland*
Wanderers.
Forward, 1-0-0-1.

223

1884 S−.
Bank of I.

KEMBER, Gerald Francis   *New Zealand*
Nelson Coll, Victoria Univ, NZ Univs, N Island, Wellington.
 b 15.11.45 Wellington.
FB, 1-0-0-1 (14 − 1c 4p).
70 SA−(1c 4p). ·
Solicitor. Normally five-eighth, played FB in only Test. NZ > 67 BI,F & C; 70 A & SA (34 pts v NE Cape, rec for NZ player in SA). 158 career pts for NZ (19 apps). Ckt for NZ Univs & Wellington.

KEMBLE, Arthur Twiss   *England*
Appleby GS, Liverpool, Leics, Lancs.
 b 3.2.1862 Cumberland; *d* 13.3.25 Crawley, Sussex.
Forward, 3-2-0-1.
1885 W+ I+; 1887 I−.
Wkt keeper for Lancs CCC for 20 seasons.

KEMP, Dudley Thomas   *England*
King Edward VI Sch Southampton, Blackheath.
 b 18.1.10.
No 8, 1-0-1-0.
35 W=.
Rep. Pres RFU 69-70. Hants CCC 2nd XI.

KEMP, James William Young   *Scotland*
('Hamish')
Glasgow HS, Glasgow HSFP, RA, Barbarians.
 b 13.2.33 Glasgow.
Lock, 27-9-2-16 (6 − 2t).
54 W−; 55 F− W+ I+ E−; 56 F+(2t) W− I− E−; 57 F+ W+ I− E−; 58 F+ W− A+ I− E=; 59 F− W+ I− E=; 60 F− W− I+ E− SA−.
Grain merchant.

KEMP, Thomas Arthur   *England*
Denstone Coll, Cambridge Univ, St Mary's Hosp, Richmond, Manchester, The Army, Barbarians, London Cos, Lancs, Mdx.
 b 12.8.15.
FH, 5-3-1-1.
37 W+ I+; 39 S+; 48 A− W=.
Medicine. Blue 36. Rep Cambridge on RFU 53. Sel 55-62. Pres RFU 71-2. Served WW2, Lt Col with RAMC. Chmn RFU Centenary Congress at Cambridge Univ 70.

KENDALL, Percy Dale ('Toggie')   *England*
Elleray Sch New Brighton, Tonbridge Sch, Cambridge Univ, Blackheath, Birkenhead Pk, Cheshire.
 b 21.8.1878 Prescot, Lancs; kia 25.1.15 Ypres.
FH/SH, 3-0-0-3.
01 S−; 02 W−; 03 S−.
Solicitor. Capt Cheshire v NZ 05. Served WW1 King's Liverpool Rgt.

KENDALL-CARPENTER, John   *England*
MacGregor Kendall
Truro Sch, Oxford Univ, Bath, Penzance & Newlyn, Barbarians, Cornwall.
 b 25.9.25 Cardiff.
Prop/no 8, 23-12-1-10 (3 − 1t).
49 I− F+ S+; 50 W− I+ F− S−; 51 I− F− S+; 52 SA− W− S+(1t) I+ F+; 53 W+ I= F+ S+; 54 W+ NZ− I+ F−.
HM. Blue 48-50. Capt every side for which he played. RFU Schools comm mem. FHU rep. Served WW2, RNVR. Taught at Cranbrook & Eastbourne Coll. HM at Wellington, Som.

KENDREW, Douglas Andrew   *England*
DSO CBE CB KCMG
Uppingham Sch, Woodford, Leicester, The Army, Ulster, Comb Servs, Barbarians, E Cos.
 b 22.7.10.
Prop, 10-5-2-3 (2 − 1c).
30 W+ I−; 33 I+(1c) S−; 34 S+; 35 W= I+; 36 NZ+ W= I−; BI > 30 A, NZ.
The Army/Governor of W Aus. Ulster v NZ 35. Served WW2. DSO 43, & 3 bars. CBE 44. CB 58. KCMG 63.

KENNEDY, Adrian George   *Ireland*
Foyle Coll, Queen's Univ Belfast, Collegians.
 b 4.11.32 Londonderry.
No 8, 1-0-0-1.
56 F−.
Univ administrator. Worked for a time at Methodist Coll Belfast.

KENNEDY, Alexander Euan   *Scotland*
George Watson's Coll, Watsonians, Edinburgh Univ.
 b 30.7.54 Edinburgh.
Centre, 4-2-1-1 (4 − 1t).
83 NZ=; 84 W+ E+(1t) A−.
6ft 5ins. Originally FB. S Under 21s 74. Scottish XV v Netherlands 75. S > 77 Far East. Capt Scotland B v F 81. Edinburgh v R 81; Fj 82; NZ 83.

KENNEDY, A. Paul   *Ireland*
St Luke's Coll Exeter, London Irish.
Prop, 2-0-0-2.
86 W− E−.
Married to Welsh girl.

KENNEDY, F.   *Ireland*
Wanderers.
Forward, 3-0-0-3.
1880 E−; 1881 E−; 1882 W−.
Bro of J.M.P.

KENNEDY, F.A.   *Ireland*
Wanderers.

b 2.1.1879.
Half-back, 2-1-0-1.
04 E− W+.

KENNEDY, Finlay DCM   *Scotland*
Stewart's Coll, Stewart's Coll FP.
b 23.1.1892; *d* 8.3.25 Edinburgh.
Prop/lock, 5-3-0-2 (15 − 3c 3p).
20 F+(1c) W+(2p) I+(2c 1p) E−; 21 E−.
Hotelier. Served WW1.

KENNEDY, Hector   *Ireland*
RBAI, Queen's Univ Belfast, Bradford, Yorks.
b −; *d* 15.1.75.
Prop, 2-0-0-2.
38 S− W−.
Medicine.

KENNEDY, John Murray Prior   *Ireland*
Wanderers.
Forward, 2-0-0-2.
1882 W−; 1884 W−.
Medicine. Bro of F.

KENNEDY, Kenneth William   *Ireland*
Campbell Coll, Queen's Univ Belfast, CIYMS,
London Irish, Barbarians, Surrey.
b 10.5.41 Rochester, Kent.
Hooker, 45-22-7-16.
65 F= E+ S+ W− SA−; 66 F− E= W+; 67
A+ E− S+ W+ F− A+; 68 F− A+; 69 F+ E+
S+ W−; 70 SA= F− E− S+ W+; 71 F= E−
S+ W−; 72 F+ E+ F+; 73 NZ= E+ S− W−
F+; 74 F− W= E+ S+ P= NZ−; 75 F+ W−;
BI > 66 A 2-2-0-0, NZ 2-0-0-2; 74 SA.
Medicine. World's most capped hooker, 49 (4
BI), with J.V. Pullin.

KENNEDY, Norman CBE   *Scotland*
Rugby Sch, Oxford Univ, W of Scotland.
b 17.3.1881 Ayr; *d* 15.1.60.
Forward, 3-3-0-0.
03 W+ I+ E+.
Timber merchant. Blue 01.

KENNEDY, Robert Day   *England*
Camborne Sch of Mines, Cornwall.
b 14.8.25; *d* −.5.79 Rhodesia.
Wing, 3-2-0-1 (3 − 1t).
49 I− F+ S+(1t).
Mining engr. Killed in ambush.

KENNEDY, Terence Joseph   *Ireland*
St Mary's Coll, UC Dublin.
b 19.10.54 Dublin.
Wing, 13-5-1-7 (4 − 1t).
78 NZ−; 79 F= W− E+r A+ A+; 80 E−
S+(1t) F− W+; 81 SA− SA− A−.
Sales dir. I > 81 SA. Ckt for Leinster.

KENT, Allan W.   *Australia*
Toowoomba, Darling Downs, Qld.
b 1891; *d* 66.
Forward, 1-1-0-0.
12 US+.

KENT, Charles Philip   *England*
Blundell's Sch, Oxford Univ, Rosslyn Pk.
b 4.8.53 Bridgwater.
Centre, 5-2-0-3 (4 − 1t).
77 S+(1t) I+ F− W−; 78 F−r.
Medicine. Blue 72-5.

KENT, Thomas   *England*
Salford, Lancs.
b 19.6.1864 Nottingham; *d* 29.1.28.
Forward, 6-5-0-1.
1891 W+ I+ S−; 1892 W+ I+ S+; BT > 1888
A, NZ.
Builder/contractor.

KENYON, Basil John   *South Africa*
Border.
b 17.6.18 Umtata.
Flanker, 1-1-0-0.
49 NZ+.
Wool broker/farmer. Capt v NZ 4th Test 49.
Tour capt SA > 51-2 BI; suffered eye inj at
Pontypool early in tour. Operation saved his
sight, but he never played again. Hennie Muller
took over as tour capt. SA sel.

KEOGH, Fergus Stephen   *Ireland*
Newbridge Coll, Bective Rgrs.
b 28.6.39 Dublin.
FB, 2-0-0-2 (6 − 2p).
64 W−(2p) F−.
Rep. Emigrated to A.

KEON, Jack J.   *Ireland*
Limerick.
Forward, 1-0-0-1.
1879 E−.

KER, Hugh Torrance MICE   *Scotland*
OBE
Merchiston Castle Sch, Glasgow Acad, Glasgow
Academicals, Glasgow Univ.
b 1865; *d* 19.3.38 Rye.
Forward, 7-5-1-1 (1t).
1887 I+ W+ E=; 1888 I+; 1889 W+(1t); 1890
I+ E−.
Engr.

KERR, David S.   *Scotland*
Heriot's Coll, Heriot's FP.
b 3.2.1899; *d* −.3.69.
Prop, 10-5-0-5 (6 − 2t).
23 F+ W+; 24 F−; 26 I− E+; 27 W+(1t) I−
E+; 28 I−(1t) E−.
Grain merchant. Pres SRU 60-1.

KERR, Fredrick R. *Australia*
Melbourne HS, Power House, Victoria.
b 18; kia 43 Middle East.
No 8, 1-0-0-1.
38 NZ−.
Played Victoria Rules football. Served WW2.

KERR, Graham Carmichael *Scotland*
Durham Sch, O Dunelmians, Edinburgh W,
Cambridge Univ, Barbarians.
b 29.4.1872 Aberdeen; *d* 18.8.13.
Forward, 8-3-3-2.
1898 I+ E=; 1899 I− W+ E+; 1900 W− I=
E=.
Schoolmaster/Sudan civil service.

KERR, James Mitchell *Scotland*
Heriot's Coll, Heriot's FP, Edinburgh Univ.
b 12.5.10.
FB, 5-1-0-4.
35 NZ−; 36 I− E−; 37 W+ I−.
Medicine. Ckt for S.

KERR, Walter *Scotland*
Loretto Sch, London Scottish.
b 14.9.30 Purley.
Flanker, 1-0-0-1.
53 E−.
Shipping.

KERSHAW, Cecil Ashworth ('K') *England*
Wharfedale Sch Ilkley, RNC Osborne, RNC
Dartmouth, US Portsmouth, Blackheath, RN,
Barbarians.
b 3.2.1895; *d* −.11.72.
SH, 16-14-1-1 (6 − 2t).
20 W− F+ I+ S+(1t); 21 W+(1t) I+ S+ F+; 22
W+ I+ F= S+; 23 W+ I+ S+ F+.
RN/commercial mgr. Son of Sir Lewis Kershaw,
KCSI. Capt in RN. E rec 14 half-back apps with
W.J.A. Davies. Played in Centenary Match at
Rugby Sch 23. Fenced GB Antwerp Olympics
20; GB v US 21. Distinguished hockey player,
ckter. Served WW1 in submarines in Baltic.
Served WW2, Naval planning staff for D-day
landings.

KETELS, Rodney Clive *New Zealand*
Pukekohe HS, Pukekohe, NZ Jnrs, NZ Colts,
Counties, N Island.
b 11.11.54 Papakura.
Prop, 5-5-0-0.
80 W+; 81 S+ S+; 81 R+ F+.
Co rep. NZ > 79 E,S & It, 80 NAm & W, 81 R
& F. NZ v Fj 80.

KEWLEY, Edward *−England*
Marlborough Coll, Liverpool, Lancs.
b 20.6.1852 Farnham Royal, Bucks; *d* 17.4.40.
Forward, 7-4-2-1 (1t).

1874 S+; 1875 S= I+(1t); 1876 S+; 1877 I+ S−;
1878 S=.
Cotton broker. 1st northern club player to capt
E, v I 1877, when E fielded XV 1st time. V-pres
RFU 1878-9.

KEWNEY, Alfred Lionel *England*
('Kicking Ginger') OBE
Rockcliff, Leicester, Barbarians, Northumb.
b 1883; *d* 16.12.59.
Forward, 16-7-0-9 (6 − 2t).
06 W− I− S+ F+(1t); 09 A− W− F+ I+ S−;
11 W−(1t) F+ I− S+; 12 I+ S−; 13 SA−.
Marine engr.

KEY, Alan OBE TD *England*
Cranleigh Sch, O Cranleighans, HAC,
Barbarians, London Cos, Mdx.
b 4.6.08.
SH, 2-0-0-2.
30 I−; 33 W−.
Banking/stockbroker/the Army. Hockey for
English Schs. Served WW2, mentioned in
despatches 40. OBE 45.

KEYES, R.P. *Ireland*
Cork Constitution.
FH, 1-0-0-1.
86 E−.

KEYWORTH, Mark *England*
Ellesmere Coll, Cirencester Agric Coll, N
Midlands, Shropshire, Swansea, Cards,
Aberystwyth.
b 19.2.48 Bridgnorth.
Flanker, 4-1-0-3.
76 A+ W− S− I−.
Farmer in Dyfed.

KIDD, Frederick W. *Ireland*
Dundalk Coll, Trin Coll Dublin, Lansdowne.
Back, 3-0-0-3.
1877 E− S−; 1878 E−.
Master of Coombe Hospital.

KIDSTON, D.W. *Scotland*
Glasgow Acad, Glasgow Academicals.
FB, 2-1-0-1.
1883 W+ E−.

KIDSTON, William Hamilton *Scotland*
Dreghorn Sch, Glasgow Univ, W of Scotland.
b 29.4.1852 Glasgow; *d* 4.6.29 Falmouth.
Back, 1-0-0-1.
1874 E−.
Iron merchant. Pres SRU 1876-7.

KIELY, Matthew David *Ireland*
CBC Cork, UC Cork, Lansdowne.
b 34.
Flanker, 5-1-2-2.

62 W=; 63 F− E= S− W+.
Medicine.

KIERNAN, Henry Arthur *New Zealand*
Douglas ('Mickey')
Kaierau, Wanganui, Grafton, Auckland, N
Island.
b 24.7.1876 Wanganui; *d* 15.1.47 Otahuhu.
SH, 1-1-0-0.
03 A+.
Rly fitter. NZ > 03 A.

KIERNAN, Michael Joseph *Ireland*
PBC Cork, Dolphin, Lansdowne.
b 17.1.61 Cork.
Centre, 19-9-1-9 (94 − 2t 7c 2d 22p).
82 W+r E+ S+ F−; 83 S+(1t) F+ W− E+; 84
E− S−(1t) A−(3p); 85 S+(2c 1d 1p) F=(5p)
W+(2c 3p) E+(1d 2p); 86 F−(3p) W−(1c 2p)
E−(1c 2p) S−(1c 1p); BI > 83 NZ 3-0-0-3.
Finance mgr. Nephew of Michael Lane. 5t I >
81 SA. Five Nations v Overseas XV,
Twickenham 86.

KIERNAN, Thomas Joseph *Ireland*
PBC Cork, UC Cork, Cork Constitution,
Barbarians.
b 7.1.39 Cork.
FB, 54-22-7-25 (135 − 2t 22c 2d 26p).
60 E−(1c) S− W− F− SA−; 61 E+ S− W− F−
(1p) SA−(1t 1c 1p); 62 E− W=; 63 F−(1c) S−
W+(1c 2p) NZ−; 64 E+(3c) S−(1p); 65 F=
E+(1c) S+(2c) W−(1c 1p) SA−; 66 F−(1d)
E=(1p) S−(1p) W+; 67 A+(1p) S−(1p)
S+(1c) W+ F−(1p) A+(1c 1d); 68 F− E=(3p)
S+(1c 1p) W+(1p) A+(1c); 69 F+ E+(1c 2p)
S+ W−(1c 2p); 70 SA=(1c 1p) F− E−(1p)
S+(2c) W+(1c 1p); 71 F=; 72 F+(2p) E+(1c
1p) F+; 73 NZ= E+ S−(1t); BI > 62 SA 1-0-0-
1; 68 SA 4-0-1-3.
Chartered accountant. I's most capped FB; most
times as I capt, 24. Capt BI > 68 SA (17 pts 1st
Test; BI most pts in series, 35). 5t (3 apps) rec
for I > SA 61. Asst mgr I > 81 SA.

KILBY, Francis David *New Zealand*
Southland Boys' HS, Star, Wellington, Pirates,
Wanganui, Taranaki, N Island.
b 24.4.06 Invercargill; *d* 3.9.85 Wellington.
SH, 4-2-1-1 (3 − 1t).
32 A− A+ A+(1t); 34 A=.
Bank mgr. NZ > 28 SA, 32 & 34 A (capt). Mgr
NZ Maoris 58 A & NZ > 63-4 BI,F & C.
Various administrative posts, inc NZRFU exec
55-74; life mem 76.

KILGOUR, Ian James *Scotland*
Cheltenham Coll, RMA Sandhurst, Northumb
Fusiliers, The Army.

b 23.10.1900; *d* 77.
Wing, 1-0-0-1.
21 F−.
The Army.

KILLEEN, Brian Alexander *New Zealand*
('Shorty')
Wellington Coll, Hutt, Wellington, Grafton,
Auckland, New Plymouth HSOB, Taranaki, N
Island.
b 13.4.11 Wellington.
2nd five-eighth, 1-1-0-0.
36 A+.
Bank mgr. NZ > 36 A. Coached Motueka Utd,
Gisborne Marist & Grafton. Sec Motueka &
Golden Bay-Motueka. Medals for boxing at sch,
25-6.

KILLEEN, George Valentine *Ireland*
Mount St Joseph's Coll Roscrea, Garryowen.
b 1884 Kilrush, Co Clare; *d* −.9.33 Tipperary.
Forward, 10-4-0-6.
12 E− S+ W+; 13 E− S− W− F+; 14 E− S+
W−.
Agent for Bank of I.

KILNER, Barron JP *England*
Wakefield Trin, Yorks.
b 11.10.1852 Dewsbury; *d* 28.12.22 Wakefield.
Forward, 1-1-0-0.
1880 I+.
Glass bottle manufacturer. Ldg ref,
administrator. Pres Yorks 1891-2. Touch-judge
Yorks v NZ 05. His club, Wakefield Trin,
helped form NU 1895.

KINDERSLEY, Richard Stephen *England*
Clifton Coll, Oxford Univ, Exeter, Devon.
b 27.9.1858; *d* 26.9.32.
Forward, 3-3-0-0 (2t).
1882 W+; 1884 S+(1t); 1885 W+(1t).
Schoolmaster. Blue 1882-3. Rowing blue 1880-
1. Sc controversial t v S 1884, which led to
break off in fixtures between countries and
ultimately formation of IB. Taught at Radley
Coll & Eton.

KING, Henry *Ireland*
Armagh RS, Trin Coll Dublin.
Forward, 2-0-0-2.
1883 E− S−.

KING, Ian *England*
Loretto Coll, Harrogate, Yorks.
b 23.
FB, 3-2-0-1 (5 − 1c 1p).
54 W+ NZ− I+(1c 1p).
Commercial traveller/licensee.

KING, John Abbott *England*
Giggleswick Sch, Durbanville, Som W (SA),

Headingley, Barbarians, Yorks.
b 21.8.1883 Leeds; kia 9.8.16 Guillemont.
No 8/lock/hooker, 12-8-0-4.
11 W− F+ I− S+; 12 W+ I+ S−; 13 SA− W+
F+ I+ S+.
Farmer. At 5ft 5in, one of E's smallest players.
Broke ribs v S 12. Served WW2.

KING, John Hope Fairbairn   *Scotland*
Selkirk HS, Selkirk.
b 10.4.25; *d* 8.9.82.
Hooker, 4-0-0-4.
53 F− W− E−; 54 E−.
Tweed.

KING, Quentin Eric Moffitt Ayres   *England*
('Quemma')
St Edward's Sch Oxford, Blackheath, The
Army, Barbarians.
b 8.7.1895 Bedford; *d* 30.10.54.
Wing, 1-1-0-0 (3 − 1t).
21 S+(1t).
The Army. Served WW1, Maj in RFA.

KING, Ronald Russell   *New Zealand*
Hokitika Dist HS, Hokitika Excelsior, West
Coast, Cobden, S Island.
b 19.8.09 Waiuta.
Lock, 13-8-1-4.
34 A=; 35 S+ I+ W−; 36 E− A+ A+; 37 SA+
SA− SA−; 38 A+ A+ A+.
Hotel proprietor. NZ > 34, 36 & 38 A, 35-6 BI
& C. Capt v SA 37. NZRFU sel 57-60. Bro A.
King rep W Coast.

KING, Sydney Charles   *Australia*
NSW.
b 21.3.05; *d* 30.3.70.
Centre, 6-5-0-1 (3 − 1t).
29 NZ+ NZ+ NZ+(1t); 30 BI+; 32 NZ+
NZ−.
Journalist. NSW > BI & F 27-8.

KINGSTON, Peter   *England*
Lydney GS, Moseley, Gloucester.
b 24.7.51 Lydney.
SH, 5-1-0-4.
75 A− A−; 79 I− F+ W−.
Schoolmaster.

KINGSTONE, Charles Napoleon   *New Zealand*
('Nipper')
Grafton Sch, Grafton, Taranaki, Clifton, N
Island.
b 2.7.1895 Auckland; *d* 6.5.60 New Plymouth.
FB, 3-1-1-1.
21 SA+ SA− SA=.
Storeman. Rep Taranaki at ckt. Nephew Colin
rep Auckland, Wellington & Canterbury.

KININMONTH, Peter Wyatt   *Scotland*
Sedbergh Sch, Oxford Univ, Richmond,
Barbarians.
b 23.6.24 Bebington, Cheshire.
No 8/flanker, 21-5-0-16 (6 − 1t 1d).
49 F+(1t) W+ I− E−; 50 F+ W− I− E+; 51
F− W+(1d) I− E− SA−; 52 F− W− I−; 54 F−
NZ− I− E− W−; BI > 50 NZ 3-0-1-2 & A.
Lloyds broker. Blue 47-8. Capt S 8 times.

KINNEAR, Roy Muir   *Scotland*
Heriot's Coll, Heriot's FP, Barbarians.
b 3.2.04; *d* 22.9.42.
Centre, 3-2-0-1.
26 F+ W+ I−; BI(uncap) > 24 SA 4-0-1-3.
Motor salesman/garage proprietor. Wigan RL
27. Died during match while on active service
with RAF.

KIPLING, Herbert George   *South Africa*
Griq W.
b 05; *d* 81 E London.
Hooker, 9-7-0-2.
31 W+ I+; 32 E+ S+; 33 A+ A− A+ A+ A−.
Electrician. SA > 31-2 BI. Deputy Mayor E
London.

KIRK, David Edward   *New Zealand*
Wanganui Collegiate Sch, Wanganui, Otago
Univ, Otago, NZ Univs, S Island, Auckland,
Oxford Univ.
b 5.10.60 Wellington.
SH, 4-4-0-0.
85 E+ E+ A+ Arg+.
Medical student. NZ > 83 S & E, 84 A, 85 Arg.
NZ Univs > 85 Europe. Houseman Auckland
Gen Hosp.

KIRKPATRICK, Alexander Ian   *South Africa*
Kimberley Boys HS, Griq W.
b 25.7.30.
FH/centre, 13-8-3-2.
53 A−; 56 NZ+; 58 F=; 60 S+ NZ+ NZ−
NZ= NZ+ W+ I+; 61 E+ S+ F=.
Administrative adviser/coach. Bro in law of R.J.
Lockyear. SA > 60-1 BI, F. 10 centre apps with
J.L. Gainsford for SA. SA sel. Full-time coach
of Transvaal.

KIRKPATRICK, Ian Andrew   *New Zealand*
MBE
King's Coll, Ngatapa, Poverty Bay, Rangiora,
Canterbury, S & N Islands.
b 24.5.46 Gisborne.
Flanker/no 8, 39-25-3-11 (57 − 16t).
67 F+(1t); 68 A+r(3t) A+ F+ F+ F+; 69 W+
W+(1t); 70 SA− SA+(1t) SA− SA−; 71 BI−
BI+(1t) BI− BI=; 72 A+ A+(2t) A+(1t) W+
S+; 73 E+(1t) I= F− E−; 74 A+(1t) A=
A+(1t); 74 I+; 75 S+; 76 I+(1t) SA− SA+
SA− SA−(1t); 77 BI+ BI− BI+(1t) BI+.

Farmer. NZ's most capped flanker (36, with Kel Tremain). 16t in Tests rec for NZ (115t in 289 1st-class apps). 3t v A 68 most by a r. NZ > 67 BI,F & C, 68 A & Fj, 71 A & SA, 72-3 BI,F & NAm (capt), 74 A & Fj & I,W & E, 76 SA. Mgr World XV > 86 SA. Bros David, Colin & John rep Poverty Bay, David also having NZ trial & rep NZ at polo. Biography 'Kirky' written by Lindsay Knight pub 79.

KIRTON, Earle Weston   *New Zealand*
St Joseph's Convent Sch, St Patrick's Coll Silverstream, Upper Hutt, Univ, Otago, NZ Univs, S Island, Harlequins (E), Barbarians (E), Mdx.
b 29.12.40 Taumarunui.
1st five-eighth, 13-12-0-1 (12 − 4t).
67 E+(2t) W+ F+ S+; 68 A+(1t) A+ F+(1t) F+ F+; 69 W+ W+; 70 SA+ SA−.
Dental surgeon. Experienced only Test defeat in 13th & final match. NZ > 63-4 & 67 BI,F & C, 68 A & Fj. Coached Harlequins & Mdx in UK where he is in practice.

KIRWAN, John James Patrick   *New Zealand*
Auckland, NZ Colts, N Island, NZ Barbarians.
b 16.12.64 Auckland.
Wing, 7-6-1-0 (20 − 5t).
84 F+ F+; 85 E+ E+(1t) A+ Arg+(2t) Arg=(2t).
Sports goods sales exec. 6ft 4in, tallest back to rep NZ. NZ > 84 A (inj shoulder), 85 Arg (6t). Played for Rest of World v BI, Cardiff 86 & Overseas XV v Five Nations, Twickenham 86.

KIRWAN-TAYLOR, William   *England*
John OBE
Epsom Coll, Cambridge Univ, Blackheath, Barbarians, Surrey.
b 29.6.05.
Wing, 5-5-0-0 (6 − 2t).
28 NSW+(1t) W+(1t) I+ F+ S+.
Co dir, Blue 26. Served WW2, Rifle Bde, GSO 1 (Lt Col) Airborne Forces. OBE 46. Ckt for MCC, Crusaders CC. Skiing for Kandahar SC, Marden's SC.

KITCHING, Alfred Everley   *England*
Oundle Sch, Cambridge Univ, Blackheath, Barbarians.
b 6.5.1889; *d* 17.3.45.
Lock, 1-1-0-0.
13 I+.
Blue 10-11. Served WW1, E African Field Force.

KITTERMASTER, Harold James   *England*
Rugby Sch, Oxford Univ, Harlequins.
b 7.1.02; *d* 28.3.67 Broughton By Biggar, Lanarkshire.
FH, 7-2-2-3 (9 − 3t).

25 NZ−(1t) W+(1t) I=; 26 W= I− F+(1t) S−. HM. Blue 22,24. Various teaching posts inc Sherborne & Rugby.

KIVELL, Alfred Louis   *New Zealand*
Stratford HS, Stratford, Taranaki, N Island.
b 12.4.1897 Thames.
Lock/flanker, 2-0-0-2.
29 A− A−.
Farmer. Served WW1. NZ > 29 A.

KNIGHT, Arthur ('Bubs')   *New Zealand*
Ellerslie Sch, Grammar, Auckland, N Island.
b 26.1.06 Auckland.
Lock, 1-0-0-1 (3 − 1t).
34 A−(1t).
Butcher. NZ > 26 & 34 A. Bro of L.A.G. Knight (NZ 25 − no Tests), uncle of Laurie Knight. Cousin Wally Knight rep Auckland 37-9.

KNIGHT, Arnold S.   *South Africa*
SA Teachers Coll, Stellenbosch Univ, Transvaal.
b 1887; *d* 2.7.46 White River.
No 8, 5-5-0-0.
12 S+ I+ W+; 13 E+ F+.
Mines mgr. Early education in UK. SA > 12-13 BI, F.

KNIGHT, Frederick   *England*
Devonport, Plymouth, Devon.
Flanker, 1-0-0-1.
09 A−.
Draughtsman HM Dockyard. Plymouth RL 12.

KNIGHT, Gary Albert   *New Zealand*
Mana Coll, Paraparaumu, Horowhenua, Wellington, Freyberg HSOB, Manawatu, Palmerston N HSOB, N Island.
b 26.8.51 Wellington.
Prop, 34-26-0-8 (4 − 1t)
77 F− F+; 78 A+ A+ A− E+ S+; 79 F+ F− A−; 80 A− A+ A− W+; 81 3+ 3+ 3A I SA+(1t); 82 A+ A− A+; 83 BI+ BI+ BI+ BI+ A+; 84 F+ F+ A− A+ A+; 85 E+ E+ A+.
Farmer. NZ's most capped prop. NZ > 77 F, 78 BI, 79 A, 80 A & Fj; NAm & W, 83 A, 85 Arg. Played for Rest of World v BI, Cardiff 86. Inj during crowd trouble at Lautoka during Fj v NZ 80. Commonwealth Games wrestling bronze medal 74.

KNIGHT, Laurence Gibb   *New Zealand*
Auckland GS, Grammar, Auckland, Ngatapa, Poverty Bay, N Island, Paris Univ (F).
b 24.9.49 Auckland.
No 8/flanker, 6-4-0-2 (4 − 1t).
77 BI+ BI− BI+ BI+(1t); 77 F− F+.
Medicine. NZ > 74 A & Fj & I,W & E, 76 SA,

229

77 F. Played for a time in France & SA. Rep Auckland GS at ckt & ath. Nephew of Arthur.

KNIGHT, Martin   *Australia*
Parramatta, NSW.
b 55; *d* 84.
Centre, 3-2-0-1.
78 W+ W+ NZ−.

KNIGHT, Peter Michael   *England*
Bristol Cathed Sch, Durham Univ, St Luke's Coll, Bristol.
b 7.10.47 Bristol.
FB/wing, 3-1-0-2.
72 F− S− SA+.
Schoolmaster.

KNIGHT, Stephen Oliver   *Australia*
Manly HS, NSW.
b 24.7.48 Sydney.
Centre, 6-1-0-5 (3 − 1t).
69 SA− SA−(1t); 70 S+; 71 SA− SA− SA−.
PE teacher. RL for A. 16st.

KNILL, Franklyn Michael David   *Wales*
Cardiff, Barbarians.
Prop, 1-1-0-0.
76 F+r.
Wales B v F 75. Barbarians v A 76. Barbarians > 76 Can.

KNOWLES, Edward   *England*
Millom, Cumberland.
b 1868; *d* 17.3.45.
Forward, 2-1-0-1.
1896 S−; 1897 S+.
Millom RL 1897.

KNOWLES, Thomas Caldwell   *England*
Ampleforth Coll, Birkenhead Pk, Barbarians, Cheshire.
b 6.5.08.
FH, 1-0-0-1.
31 S−; BI > 30 A, NZ.
Co chmn. Served WW2 with RAF. Left-handed golfer; holed in one at Dunedin. BT > 36 Arg.

KNOX, D.   *Australia*
NSW.
2-2-0-0.
85 Fj+ Fj+.

KNOX, Hercules John   *Ireland*
Dublin HS, Trin Coll Dublin, Lansdowne.
b 2.8.1880 Gortnor Abbey, Crossmolina; *d* 11.3.75 Liverpool.
Forward, 10-6-0-4.
04 W+; 05 E+ S+ W− NZ−; 06 E+ S− W+; 07 W−; 08 S+.
Medicine. Changed name by deed poll to Beresford-Knox 12.

KNOX, John   *Scotland*
Kelvinside Acad, Merchiston Castle Sch, Kelvinside Academicals.
b 5.8.1880; *d* 20.4.64.
SH, 3-3-0-0.
03 W+ I+ E+.
Textiles co dir.

KOCH, Augustus Cristoffel   *South Africa*
Boland.
b 21.9.27.
Prop, 22-15-1-6 (15 − 5t).
49 NZ+ NZ+ NZ+; 51 S+(2t) I+ W+; 52 E+ F+; 53 A+ A− A+(1t); 55 BI−(1t) BI+ BI− BI+; 56 A+ NZ+ NZ−; 58 F= F−; 60 NZ+ NZ−.
Farmer/insurance. 112 apps for Boland. SA > 51-2 BI, F.

KOCH, H.V. ('Bubbles')   *South Africa*
Stellenbosch Univ, W Prov.
b 13.6.21.
Flanker/lock, 4-4-0-0.
49 NZ+ NZ+ NZ+ NZ+.
Farmer.

KOTEKA, Tohoa Tauroa ('Paul')   *New Zealand*
Waikato, NZ Jnrs, NZ Maoris.
b 30.9.56 Tokoroa.
Prop, 2-2-0-0.
81 F+; 82 A+.
NZ > 81 R & F.

KOTZE, G.J.M. ('Gert')   *South Africa*
W Prov.
b 12.8.40.
4-2-1-1.
67 F+ F+ F− F=.
Insurance.

KRAEFFT, Donald F. ('Joe')   *Australia*
Sydney Univ, NSW.
b 22.
Lock, 6-3-0-3.
47 NZ− S+ I+ W−; 48 E+ F−.
Engr.

KRANTZ, Eduard Friedrich   *South Africa*
Wilhelm ('Edrich')
Sentraal Sch Bloemfontein, UOFS, SA Univs, Gazelles, Jnr Springboks, N Transvaal, Oribis, OFS.
b 10.8.54 Senekal.
Wing, 2-2-0-0 (4 − 1t).
76 NZ+(1t); 81 I+.
Medicine. Capt SA Under 21s > 75 SAm. SA > 80 SAm, 81 NZ, US. 6 yrs between caps.

KREFT, Anthony John   *New Zealand*
Ranfurly Dist HS, Ranfurly, Otago, S Island.
b 27.3.45 Milton.

Prop, 1-1-0-0.
68 A+.
Transport stock mgr. NZr > 68 A & Fj. Coach,
sel Maniototo RU.

KREUTZER, Simon David   *Australia*
St Joseph's Coll, Qld.
 b 1894; d 71.
Flanker, 1-0-0-1.
14 NZ−.
Police. RL.

KRIGE, J.A.   *England*
Victoria Coll Stellenbosch (SA), Guy's Hosp,
Barbarians.
 b 6.6.1897; d 27.9.46.
Centre, 1-0-0-1.
20 W−.
Medicine.

KRIGE, Jacob Daniel ('Japie')   *South Africa*
Stellenbosch Univ, W Prov.
 b 5.7.1879 Caledon.
Centre, 5-3-1-1 (3 − 1t).
03 BI= BI+; 06 S− I+(1t) W+.
One of 8 sons of Dutch Reform Church
minister. Cousin of H.A. De Villiers. SA > 06-7
BI, F. Underwent appendectomy shortly after
Wales match 06; never played for SA again.
Prov debut at 17; never on losing W Prov side.
Younger bro Willie toured with SA > 12-13 BI,
F.

KRITZINGER, Johannes   *South Africa*
Lordewyk ('Klippies')
Transvaal.
 b 1.3.48 Harrismith.
Flanker, 7-5-1-1 (4 − 1t).
74 BI− BI= F+ F+; 75 F+ F+; 76 NZ+(1t).
Commercial rep. 18st.

KROON, Colin Maxwell   *South Africa*
Kingswood Coll Grahamstown, Stellenbosch
Univ, E Prov.
 b 22.2.31 Graaff Reiner.
Hooker, 1-0-0-1.
55 BI−.
Medicine.

KRUGER, Theuns Lodewicus   *South Africa*
Stellenbosch Univ, Transvaal.
 b 17.6.1896; d 6.7.57 Pretoria.
8-5-1-2.
21 NZ− NZ+; 24 BI+ BI+ BI= BI+; 28 NZ+
NZ−.
Under Sec for Agriculture.

KUHN, Stephanus Petrus ('Fanie') *South Africa*
Jan De Klerk HS Krugersdorp, Transvaal.
 b 12.6.35.
Prop, 19-12-3-4.

60 NZ= NZ+ W+ I+; 61 E+ S+ F= I+ A+
A+; 62 BI= BI+ BI+ BI+; 63 A+ A− A−; 65
I− S−.
Boilermaker/rep. 17 consec Tests 60-3. SA >
60-1 BI, F.

KYLE, John Wilson ('Jackie')   *Ireland*
RBAI, Queen's Univ Belfast, NIFC,
Barbarians.
 b 10.1.26 Belfast.
FH, 46-23-4-19 (24 − 7t 1d).
47 F− E+ S+ W− A−; 48 F+ E+(1t) S+(1t)
W+; 49 F− E+ S+ W+; 50 F= E− S+ W−; 51
F+ E+ S+ W=(1t) SA−; 52 F+ S+(1t) W−
E−; 53 F+(1t) E= S+ W−; 54 NZ− F−; 55 F−
E= W−; 56 F− E− S+(1t) W+(1d); 57 F+(1t)
E− S+ W−; 58 A+ E− S+; BI > 50 NZ 4-0-1-3
& A 2-2-0-0.
Medicine. Bro in law of Noel Henderson.
World's most capped FH, 52 (6 BI). Played in 2
Victory ints. Lives in Zambia.

KYLE, William Elliot   *Scotland*
Buccleuch Sch Hawick, Hawick.
 b 13.7.1881 Hawick; d 11.12.59.
Forward, 21-10-0-11 (6 − 2t).
02 W− I− E−; 03 W+(1t) I+ E+; 04 W− I+
E+; 05 W− I− E+ NZ−; 06 W− I+ E−; 08
E+; 09 W− I+(1t) E+; 10 W−.
Coal merchant.

L

LABADIE, Paul ('Popaul')   *France*
Bayonne.
 b 27.4.28 Bayonne.
Hooker, 21-13-0-8.
52 S+ I− SA− W− E− It+; 53 S+ I− It+; 54
S+ I+ NZ+ W− E+ Arg+; 55 S+ I+ E+ W−;
56 I+; 57 I−.
Accountant.

LABARTHÈTE, Robert   *France*
Pau.
 b 5.20.24 Pau.
FB, 1-1-0-0.
52 S+.

LABAZUY, Antoine   *France*
Lourdes.
 b 9.2.29 Carcassonne, Aude.
FH, 11-8-1-2 (37 − 8c 1d 6p).
52 I−; 54 S+ W−; 56 E+(2p); 58 A+(2c 1d)
W+(2c) I+(1c 1p); 59 S+ E=(1p) It+(2c 1p)
W+(1c 1p).
Hotelier.

LABORDE, Claude ('Coco')   *France*
RCF.
 b 25.8.40.

SH/wing, 5-2-1-2.
62 It+ R−; 63 R=; 64 SA+; 65 E−.
Physical culture monitor.

LABUSCHAGNE, Nicholas *England*
Arthur
Hilton Coll Cape Town, Cape Town Univ,
Guy's Hosp, Harlequins, Barbarians, Mdx, W
Prov (SA), Natal (SA).
b 26.5.31 Durban.
Hooker, 5-2-1-2.
53 W+; 55 W− I= F− S+.
Dental surg/co dir. Mem of Natal RFU exec.
Fdr mem SA Barbarians.

LACANS, Pierre *France*
Béziers.
b 23.4.57 Lezignan.
Flanker, 6-3-0-3 (8 − 2t).
80 SA−; 81 W+ E+(1t) A−(1t) R+; 82 W−.
France B v S 80. F > 80 SA. Played FH for
Béziers in French Cup final v Montferrand 78.

LACASSAGNE, André *France*
SBUC.
b −; kia WW1.
SH, 2-0-0-2.
06 NZ−; 07 E−.

LACAUSSADE, Roger ('Coco') *France*
Bègles, SBUC.
b 30.1.27 Captieux, Gironde.
Wing, 2-1-0-1 (3 − 1t).
48 A+ S−(1t).

LACAZE, Claude ('Papillon') *France*
Lourdes, Angoulême.
b 5.3.40 Pontacq.
FB/FH, 33-18-4-11 (62 − 1t 13c 6d 5p).
61 NZ− NZ− A+ R=(1c); 62 E+ W− I+(1t)
It+; 63 W+ R=; 64 S− NZ− E−; 65 It+(3c)
R+; 66 S=(1p) I+(1c 1p) E+(2c) W−(1c)
It+(3c 1d) R+(1p); 67 S− E+ SA− SA+(1p)
SA=(1d) R+(1c 1d 1p); 68 S+ E+(1d) W+
Cz+ NZ−(1d); 69 E−(1c 1d).
Rep. Bro of Pierre. F > 67 SA; d from halfway
line 3rd Test.

LACAZE, Henri *France*
Périgueux.
Lock, 5-2-0-3
28 I− G+ W+; 29 I− W−

LACAZE, Pierre ('Papillon') *France*
Lourdes.
b 4.5.34 Pontacq.
FB, 7-4-2-1 (14 − 1c 3d 1p)
58 SA= SA+(1d 1p); 59 S+(2d) E= It+ W+
I−(1c).
Commercial traveller. Bro of Claude. RL.

LACAZEDIEU, Charles *France*
Dax.
FH, 5-1-0-4.
23 W− I+; 28 NSW− I−; 29 S−.

LACOME, Michel *France*
Pau.
Centre, 1-1-0-0.
60 Arg+.

LACOSTE, Robert *France*
Tarbes.
Wing, 3-0-0-3 (3 − 1t).
14 I−(1t) W− E−.
Professor.

LACRAMPE, Félix *France*
Béziers.
No 8, 1-1-0-0.
49 Arg+.

LACROIX, Pierre ('Pottiolo') *France*
Mont-de-Marsan, Agen.
b 23.1.35 Houeilles, Landes.
SH, 27-16-3-8 (12 − 4t).
58 A+; 60 W+(1t) I+ It+ R− Arg+(1t) Arg+
Arg+(1t); 61 S+ SA= E= W+ I+ NZ− NZ−
NZ− A+(1t) R=; 62 S+ E+ W− I+ R−; 63
S− I+ E− W+.
PE teacher.

LAFARGE, Yves *France*
Montferrand.
SH/centre, 3-2-0-1.
78 R+; 79 NZ−; 81 I+r.

LAFFOND, André ('Joconde') *France*
Bayonne.
Wing, 1-0-1-0.
22 E=.

LAFFONT, Honoré *France*
Narbonne.
b −; d −.2.75.
SH, 1-0-0-1.
26 W−.

LAFITTE *France*
SCUF.
Forward, 2-0-0-2 (3 − 1t).
10 W−(1t) S−.

LAFOND, Jean-Baptiste *France*
RCF.
b 29.12.61 Paris.
FB/wing, 9-6-1-2 (38 − 8t 2d).
83 A=(1d); 85 Arg− Arg+ J+(4t) J+(2t); 86
S− I+(1d) W+(2t) E+.
8t 4c F > 85 Arg.

LAGDEN, Ronald Owen *England*
Mr Pellat's Sch Swanage, Marlborough Coll,
Oxford Univ, Richmond.
b 21.11.1889 Maseru, Basutoland; kia 1.3.15 St
Eloi.
Lock, 1-1-0-0 (4 − 2c).
11 S+(2c).
Schoolmaster. Rhodes Scholar. Blue 09-11.
Also blues at ckt (09-12), hockey (10-11) &
rackets (09). Taught at Harrow. Served WW1,
Capt then Maj KRRC. Mentioned in despatches
15.

LAGISQUET, Patrice *France*
Bayonne.
b 4.9.62 Arcachon.
Wing, 7-4-1-2 (4 − 1t).
83 A= A+ R+(1t); 84 I+ W+ NZ− NZ−.
Noted sprinter; once recorded 10.8s for 100m.

LA GRANGE, J.B. *South Africa*
Stellenbosch Univ, W Prov.
2-1-1-0.
24 BI= B+.

LAGRANGE, Jean-Claude *France*
RCF.
Centre, 1-1-0-0 (3 − 1t).
66 It+(1t).

LAIDLAW, Alexander Smith *Scotland*
Hawick.
b 13.8.1877 Edinburgh; *d* 12.9.33 Bradford.
Forward, 1-1-0-0.
1897 I+.
Stonemason/licensee. Bradford RL 1899; 1st S
player to turn pro.

LAIDLAW, Christopher Robert *New Zealand*
King's HS Dunedin, Univ, Otago, Shirley, NZ
Univs, NZ Colts, Canterbury, S Island, Oxford
Univ, Lyon Univ (F).
b 16.11.43 Dunedin.
SH, 20-15-0-5 (12 − 3t 1d).
63 F+(1d); 64 A+; 65 SA− SA+(1t) SA−
SA−; 66 BI+ BI+ BI+ BI+; 67 E+(1t) W+
S+; 68 A+(1t) A+ F+ F+; 70 SA− SA+ SA−.
Diplomat. NZ > 63-4 & 67 BI,F & C, 68 A &
Fj, 70 A & SA. Rhodes Scholar; blue 68-9 (capt
to beat SA 69). Autobiography'Mud in Your
Eye' pub 73. NZ High Commission in Fj 73;
then Commonwealth Secretariat in London.

LAIDLAW, Francis Andrew *Scotland*
Linden
Melrose GS, Melrose, Barbarians.
b 20.9.40 Hawick.
Hooker, 32-10-2-20.
65 F− W− I− E= SA+; 66 F= W− I+ E+
A+; 67 F+ W+ I− E− NZ−; 68 F− W− I−
A+; 69 F+ W− I− E− SA+; 70 F− W− I−

E+ A−; 71 F− W− I−; BI > 66 A, NZ 2-0-0-2;
71 A, NZ.
Joiner. Scottish XV v Arg (2) 69. Barbarians >
69 SA.

LAIDLAW, Kevin Francis *New Zealand*
Nightcaps Convent, St Kevin's Coll, Collegiate,
Marist, Southland, Nightcaps.
b 9.8.34 Nightcaps.
Centre/2nd five-eighth, 3-1-1-1.
60 SA+ SA= SA−.
Electrician. NZ > 60 A & SA. Southland sel 69-
72. Won 2 NZ gundog champs.

LAIDLAW, Roy James *Scotland*
Jedburgh GS, Jedforest.
b 5.10.53 Jedburgh.
SH, 36-18-1-17 (20 − 5t).
80 I− F+ W− E−; 81 F− W+ E− I+ NZ−
NZ− R+ A+; 82 E+ I− F+ W+ A+ A−; 83
I−(1t) F− W− E+(1t) NZ=; 84 W+ E+ I+(2t)
F+ R− A−; 85 I− F−; 86 F+ W− E+ I+(1t)
R+; BI > 83 NZ 4(1r)-0-0-4.
Electrician. S's most capped SH. 7 apps
Scotland B. S > 77 Far East; 81 NZ. Scottish
XV v J 77, Fj (capt) 82. 13 times r before 1st
cap. World rec half-back partnership with John
Rutherford (30 apps to R 86).

LAING, Arthur Douglas *Scotland*
('Podger')
Royal HS, Royal HSFP.
b 1892; *d* 24.11.27.
Prop/lock, 7-3-0-4 (2 − 1c).
14 W−(1c) I− E−; 20 F+ W+ I+; 21 F−.
Brewer.

LAIRD, Henri Colin Campbell *England*
Nautical Coll Pangbourne, Harlequins,
Barbarians, Mdx.
b 3.8.08.
FH, 10-8-0-2 (15 − 5t).
27 W+ I+(1t) S−(1t); 28 NSW+(1t) W+(1t) I+
F+ S+(1t); 29 W+ I−.
Stockbroker/marketing co dir. E's youngest
player − 18 yrs 134 days v W 27.

LALANDE, Max ('L'Autobus de *France*
Chateaurenard')
RCF.
Wing, 3-1-0-2 (3 − 1t).
23 S− W−(1t) I+.

LAMBERT, Douglas ('Daniel') *England*
St Edward's Oxford, Eastbourne Coll,
Harlequins, Barbarians, Mdx.
b 4.10.1883 Cranbrook; kia 13.10.15 Loos.
Wing, 7-3-0-4 (46 − 8t 8c 2p).
07 F+(5t); 08 F+(1t) W− S−(2c); 11 W−(1c)
F+(2t 5c 2p) I−.
With George Lindsay, world rec 5t in an int, E v

233

F 07. E's most pts in an int (22 v F 11). Played
football for Corinthians. Served WW1, Lt in
Buffs. Son born 2 months after he was killed.

LAMBERT, Kent King   *New Zealand*
Te Aute Coll, Univ, NZ Colts, Manawatu, QE
Coll OB, NZ Maoris, N Island.
b 23.3.52 Wairoa.
Prop, 11-5-1-5.
72 S+r; 73 E+ I= F− E−; 74 I+; 76 SA− SA−
SA−; 77 BI+ BI+.
Shearer. NZ > 72-3 BI,F & NAm, 74 I,W & E,
76 SA. Appendicitis prevented his playing final
2 Tests v BI 77. Penrith RL (Sydney) 78; knee
inj forced his retirement.

LAMBERT, Noel Hamilton   *Ireland*
('Ham')
Sandford Pk Sch, Rossall Sch, RCVS Dublin,
Lansdowne.
b 5.6.10 Dublin.
Wing/centre, 2-0-0-2.
34 S− W−.
Veterinary surg. Ref 11 ints 47-52. Ckt for I.

LAMBIE, Ian Kerr   *Scotland*
George Watson's Coll, Watsonians.
b 13.4.54 Edinburgh.
No 8, 4-0-1-3.
78 NZ−r; 79 W− E= NZ−.
Surveyor.

LAMBIE, John Kenneth   *Australia*
Port Hacking HS, Wollongong Teachers' Coll,
Casino, NSW.
b 27.3.51 Sydney.
Flanker, 4-0-1-3.
74 NZ− NZ= NZ−; 75 W−.
Schoolmaster.

LAMBIE, Lindsay B.   *Scotland*
Glasgow HS, Glasgow HSFP.
b 30.5.10.
Hooker/flanker, 7-2-0-5 (3 − 1t).
34 W− I+ E−; 35 W− I− E+(1t) NZ−.
Brewery rep.

LAMBOURN, Arthur   *New Zealand*
Petone Central Sch, Petone HS, Petone,
Wellington, N Island.
b −.1.10.
Prop/hooker, 10-4-1-5.
34 A− A=; 35 S+ I+ W−; 36 E−; 37 SA+
SA− SA−; 38 A+.
Photo-engraver. NZ > 34 & 38 A, 35-6 BI & C.
Served WW2. Petone club coach.

LAMOND, George A.W.   *Scotland*
Kelvinside Acad, Kelvinside Academicals, RE.
b 1878; *d* 25.2.18 Colombo.
Centre, 3-3-0-0 (4 − 1d).

1899 W+(1d) E+; 05 E+.
Civil engr. 6 yrs between caps. Served WW1, Lt
Col RE; died on active service. Decorated with
Orders of Medjidieh & Osmaieh by Govts of
Egypt & Turkey. Employed on construction of
King Edward Dock, Avonmouth. Played in
Amateur Golf Champ, St Andrews 13.

LAMONT, Ronald Arthur   *Ireland*
RBAI, Instonians, Barbarians.
b 18.11.41.
No 8, 12-4-3-5 (3 − 1t).
65 F= E+(1t) SA−; 66 F− E= S− W+; 70
SA= F− E− S+ W+.
BI > 66 A & NZ 4-0-0-4.
Schoolmaster.

LAMPKOWSKI, Michael Stanley   *England*
('Lamb Chop')
St Bedes Sch Scunthorpe, Headingley.
b 4.1.53 Scunthorpe.
SH, 4-1-0-3 (4 − 1t).
76 A+(1t) W− S− I−.
Electrician. Wakefield RL 77.

LANDERS, Maurice F.   *Ireland*
Cork Constitution.
b 1871; *d* 7.3.48.
FB, 5-3-0-2.
04 W+; 05 E+ S+ W− NZ−.
Journalist. Corr for 'Cork Examiner'.

LANE, David J.   *Ireland*
CBC Cork, UC Cork.
b 30.9.13 Cork.
Wing, 4-1-0-3.
34 S− W−; 35 E− S+.
Engr.

LANE, Gaston   *France*
RCF.
b 1883; kia 24.9.14 Stenay/Lerouville.
Wing/centre, 16-1-0-15 (3 − 1t).
06 NZ− E− ; 07 E−; 08 E− W−; 09 E− W−
I−(1t); 10 W− E−; 11 S+ W−; 12 I− W− E− ;
13 S−.
Engr.

LANE, Michael Francis   *Ireland*
CBC Cork, UC Cork, Barbarians.
b 3.4.26.
Wing, 17-9-3-5 (3 − 1t).
47 W−; 49 F− E+ S+ W+; 50 F= E− S+ W−;
51 F+ S+ W= SA−; 52 F+ S+(1t); 53 F+ E=;
BI > 50 NZ 1-0-0-1 & A 1-1-0-0.
Engr. Uncle of Michael Kiernan.

LANE, Patrick   *Ireland*
Crescent Coll, O Crescent.

b 7.9.34 Parteen, Co Clare.
Hooker, 1-0-0-1.
64 W−.
Farmer. Pres Irish Farmers Assoc.

LANE, Stuart Morris   *Wales*
Tredegar GS, Cardiff Coll, Cardiff, Newbridge.
b 12.11.52 Tredegar.
Flanker, 5-2-0-3.
78 A−r A−; 79 I+r; 80 S+ I−; BI > 80 SA.
Wales B v F 77. W > 78 A. Inj in 1st match BI >
80 SA, ruled out of rest of tour.

LANE, Timothy Alan   *Australia*
W Dist, Brisbane, Qld.
b 24.11.59.
Centre, 3-2-0-1.
85 C+ C+ NZ−.
PE teacher. A > 82 NZ; 83 It & F; 84 Fj.

LANG, Clifford W.P. ('Haggis')   *Australia*
Dollar Acad (S), Bedford (E), Victoria.
b − Karachi; *d* 44 Far East.
Prop, 2-0-0-2.
38 NZ− NZ−.
Served WW2, Lt in infantry rgt.

LANG, D.   *Scotland*
Paisley.
Forward, 2-1-0-1.
1876 E−; 1877 I+.

LANG, James   *Wales*
Hendy, Llanelli, Swansea.
b 1.10.09 Garnant.
No 8, 12-8-2-2 (3 − 1t).
31 F+(1t) I+; 34 S+ I+; 35 E= S+ I− NZ+; 36
E= S+ I+; 37 E−.
Steelworker.

LANGAN, Daniel Joseph   *Ireland*
CB Fairview, Clontarf.
b 19.3.10 Dublin.
FB, 1-0-0-1.
34 W−.
Pres of Texaco Oil co.

LANGRISH, Reginald W.   *Scotland*
London Scottish, Barbarians.
b −; *d* 15.3.86 Fowey.
FB, 4-1-0-3.
30 F−; 31 F+ W− I−.

LAPAGE, Walter Nevill OBE   *England*
RNC Greenwich, US Portsmouth, RN, Surrey.
b 5.2.1883; *d* 17.5.39.
Centre/wing, 4-2-0-2 (6 − 2t).
08 F+(1t) W−(1t) I+ S−.
RN. Served WW1.

LAPORTE, Guy   *France*
Graulhet.
b 15.12.52 Beaufort.
FH, 10-7-0-3 (88 − 1t 6c 7d 17p).
81 I+(2d 3p) W+(3p) E+(1c 2d) R+(1d) NZ−
(2p) NZ−(1p); 86 S−(1d 2p) I+(1c 3p) W+(1d
2c) E+(1t 2c 3p).

LARARD, Alfred   *South Africa*
Transvaal.
b c1877 Kingston upon Hull, E; *d* 15.8.36
Helston, E.
Half-back, 2-1-0-1 (3 − 1t).
1896 BT− BT+(1t).
Commercial traveller. Scored winning t in SA's
1st win, v BT 4th Test 1896. Went to SA at 17.
Served in Boer War, Imperial Light Horse.
Huddersfield RL 01.

LARKIN, Edward Rennix   *Australia*
Newtown, NSW.
b 1880; kia 25.4.15 Gallipoli.
Forward, 1-0-0-1.
03 NZ−.
Police/journalist. Labor MP. Sec NSW RL.

LARKIN, Kerry Kelsall   *Australia*
Qld.
b 36.
Prop, 2-0-1-1.
58 M= M−.
Medicine.

LARRÉGUY, Pierre   *France*
Bayonne.
Flanker, 1-1-0-0 (3 − 1t).
54 It+(1t).

LARRIBEAU, Léon   *France*
Périgueux, Biarritz.
b 1889 Anglet; kia 13.12.16 Poivre.
FH/wing, 7-0-0-7.
12 I− S− W− E−; 13 S−; 14 I− E−.

LARRIEU, Jean   *France*
Tarbes.
Flanker/no 8, 7-3-0-4.
20 I+ US+; 21 W−; 23 S− W− E− I+.

LARRIEU, Maurice   *France*
SBUC.
Lock, 1-0-0-1.
27 G−.

LARRUE, Hervé   *France*
Carmaux.
b 5.7.35 Boisserou.
Lock, 7-6-0-1.
60 W+ I+ It+ R− Arg+ Arg+ Arg+.
Pork butcher. RL.

LARTER, Peter John *England*
Churston Ferrers GS, Northampton, RAF,
Weston-super-Mare, Comb Servs, Barbarians,
Leics.
b 7.9.44.
Lock, 24-7-3-14 (6 − 1t 1p).
67 A− NZ−(1p); 68 W= I= F− S+; 69 I− F+
S+ W− SA+(1t); 70 I+ W− S− F−; 71 W− I+
F= S− S− P−; 72 SA+; 73 NZ− W−.
RAF technician. Rep RAF at basketball.

LASAOSA, Paul ('Popaul') *France*
Dax.
b 13.7.27 Dax.
SH/centre, 6-3-1-2.
50 I=; 52 S+ I− E− It+; 55 It+.

LASSÈGUE, Jean ('The French *France*
Buffalo')
Toulouse.
b 15.2.24 Rieumes.
Wing, 9-7-0-2 (15 − 5t).
46 W+; 47 S+(1t) I+(2t) W−; 48 W+; 49
I+(1t) E− W+(1t) Arg+.

LASSERRE, Jean-Claude *France*
('Titou')
Dax.
b 12.4.38 Hussein-Dey, Algeria.
SH, 13-8-1-4 (3 − 1d).
63 It+; 64 S− NZ− E− W= It+ I+ Fj+; 65
W+(1d) It+ R+; 66 R+; 67 S−.
Schoolmaster.

LASSERRE, Michel ('L'Obus') *France*
Agen.
b 21.1:40 Beaumont, Tarn et Garonne.
Prop/no 8/lock, 15-5-1-9.
67 SA− SA+; 68 E+ W+ Cz+ NZ− A− SA−
SA−; 69 S− I− E−; 70 E+; 71 E= W−.
Transport agent.

LASSERRE, René ('Poulet') *France*
Bayonne, Cognac, Grenoble.
b 9.10.1895 Bayonne; d c50.
FB/flanker/centre, 16-4-2-10 (10 − 2t 1d).
14 I− W−; 20 S−; 21 S+ W−(1d) I+; 22 S=
E=(1t) W− I−; 23 W−(1t) E−; 24 S+ I− R+
US−.
Cognac works. Served WW1, pilot French
Flying Corps.

LATEGAN, Marthinus Theunis *South Africa*
('Tjol')
Stellenbosch Boys HS, Stellenbosch Univ, W
Prov.
b −.9.25 Stellenbosch.
Centre, 11-10-0-1 (9 − 3t).
49 NZ+ NZ+(1t) NZ+ NZ+; 51 S+(1t) I+
W+; 52 E+ F+; 53 A+(1t) A−.

Accountant. 10 centre apps with Ryk Van
Schoor. SA > 51-2 BI, F.

LATERRADE, G. *France*
Tarbes.
b −; d −.7.29.
FH, 5-1-0-4 (3 − 1t).
10 E− I−; 11 S+(1t) E− I−.
Schoolmaster.

LATIMER, Neil Buchanan *Australia*
Gordon, NSW.
b 32.
Lock, 1-0-0-1.
57 NZ−.
Builder/plantation owner. Worked in Papua
New Guinea.

LAUDER, Wilson *Scotland*
Bridgend GS, Llantwit Major, Neath, Maesteg,
Barbarians.
b 4.11.48 Thornton, Fife.
Flanker, 18-5-0-13 (19 − 2t 4p).
69 I− E− SA+; 70 F−(2p) W−(1p) I−(1t) A−
(1p); 73 F−; 74 W− E+(1t) I− F+; 75 I+ F−
NZ− A+; 76 F−; 77 E−.
Plant engr. Scottish XV v Arg (2) 69, Tg 74. 56
pts S > 70 A. Coach of Maesteg, Llantwit
Major.

LAUDOUAR, Jean *France*
Soustons, SBUC.
b 3.1.34 Soustons, Landes.
Hooker, 5-1-1-3.
61 NZ− NZ− R=; 62 I+ R−.

LAUGA, Pierre *France*
Vichy.
b 17.1.22 Lucq-de-Béarn.
FH, 4-1-1-2 (3 − 1d).
50 S−(1d) I= E+ W−.
PE teacher.

LAUGHLAND, Ian Hugh Page *Scotland*
Merchiston Castle Sch, London Scottish,
Barbarians, E Midlands.
b 29.10.35.
Centre/FH, 31-13-4-14.
59 F−; 60 F− W− I+ E−; 61 SA− W+ I+ E−;
62 F− W+ I+ E=; 63 F+ W− I+; 64 F+ NZ−
W− I+ E+; 65 F− W− I− E= SA+; 66 F=
W− I+ E+; 67 E−.
Business. National Service in Army in Egypt.
Played football for Nairn County in Highland
League. Ckt for The Army.

LAURENT, Auguste *France*
Biarritz Ol.
b 18.4.01 Anglet.
Flanker/lock, 5-0-0-5.
25 NZ− S− W− E−; 26 W−.

LAURENT, Joseph   *France*
Bayonne.
Flanker, 3-0-0-3.
20 S− E− W−.

LAURENT, Marcel   *France*
Auch.
Hooker/prop, 5-5-0-0.
32 G+; 33 G+; 34 G+; 35 G+; 36 G+.
Asst mgr F > 54 Arg & Chile; 58 SA. Mgr F >
60 Arg & Chile; 61 NZ. FFR v-pres 82-3.

LAVAIL, Gilbert   *France*
Perpignan.
FH, 2-1-0-1.
37 G+; 40 BF−.

LAVAUD, Pierre   *France*
Carcassonne.
Forward, 2-0-0-2.
14 I− W−.

LAVERGNE, Pierre   *France*
Limoges.
b 23.
Prop, 1-0-0-1.
50 S−.

LAVERY, Patrick   *Ireland*
London Irish.
b 49.
Wing/centre, 2-0-1-1.
74 W=; 76 W−.
Accountant.

LAVIGNE, Bernard   *France*
Dax.
Centre, 2-0-0-2.
20 E− W−.

LAVIGNE, B.   *France*
Agen.
Wing, 2-1-1-0.
84 R+; 85 E=.

LAW, Sir Archibald Fitzgerald   *England*
KB
Wellington Coll, Oxford Univ, Richmond,
Mdx.
b 1853; *d* 26.6.21.
Forward, 1-0-0-1.
1877 S−.
Barrister/Judicial Comm. Blue 1875. Called to
Bar 1879. KB 08.

LAW, Douglas Edward   *England*
Birkenhead Sch, Birkenhead Pk, Cheshire.
b 12.10.02.
Prop, 1-1-0-0.
27 I+.
Cattle food merchant. RFU > 27 Arg.

LAW, Vivian J.   *Wales*
Newport, The Army.
b 11.6.10 Cardiff.
Prop, 1-1-0-0.
39 I+.
Rep. Played in I trial.

LAWLER, Patrick Joseph   *Ireland*
O'Brien's Inst Artane, Clontarf.
Lock, 12-5-1-6 (3 − 1t).
51 S+ SA=; 52 F+ S+ W− E−; 53 F+(1t); 54
NZ− E− S+; 56 F− E−.
Police. Oil co official. Moved to Arg.

LAWLESS, Michael John   *South Africa*
W Prov.
b 17.9.42 Cape Town.
FH, 4-0-2-2 (3 − 1t).
64 F−(1t); 69 E−r; 70 I= W=.
Rep. SA > 69-70 BI.

LAWLOR, Patrick Joseph   *Ireland*
Mt St Joseph's Coll Roscrea, Bective Rgrs.
b Dunlavin, Co Wicklow; *d* 30.10.65.
Flanker, 6-4-0-2 (3 − 1t).
35 E− S+(1t) W+; 37 E− S+ W+.
Farmer.

LAWRENCE, Hon Henry Arnold   *England*
Wellington Coll, Richmond.
b 17.3.1848; *d* 16.4.02 Minchinhampton.
Forward, 4-2-2-0.
1873 S=; 1874 S+; 1875 I+ S=.
Son of 1st Baron Lawrence, GCB. Capt E v S
1874. V-pres RFU 1875-6.

LAWRENCE, Stephen David   *Wales*
('Sid')
Bridgend, Pontycymmer.
b 5.8.1899 Pontycymmer; *d* 13.2.78 Merthyr.
Flanker/prop/no 8, 6-2-0-4.
25 S− I−; 26 S− I+ F+; 27 E−.
Ironmonger/police.

LAWRIE, James Ruthven   *Scotland*
Gala Acad, Melrose.
b 11.8.1900 Melrose; *d* 9.7.81 Folkestone.
Flanker, 11-6-2-3.
22 F= W= I+ E−; 23 F+ W+ I+ E−; 24 W+
I+ E−.
Commercial traveller.

LAWRIE, Kenneth Graham   *Scotland*
Gala Acad, Gala.
b 31.7.51 Gala.
Hooker, 3-1-0-2.
80 F+r W− E−.
PO engr.

LAWRIE, Percy William   *England*
Wyggeston Sch, Leicester, Midlands,

Barbarians, Leics.
b 26.9.1888 Lutterworth; *d* 27.12.56 Leicester.
Wing, 2-2-0-0 (3 − 1t).
10 S+; 11 S+(1t).
Served WW1, Lt RA. Served WW2, Home
Guard.

LAWSON, Alan James   *Scotland*
Macgregor
Falkirk HS, Strathclyde Univ, Edinburgh W,
London Scottish, Barbarians.
b 19.5.48 Kirkcaldy.
SH, 15-5-2-8 (12 − 3t).
72 F+r E+; 73 F−(1t); 74 W− E+; 76 E+(2t)
I+; 77 E−; 78 NZ−; 79 W− E= I= F− NZ−;
80 W−r.
Chartered accountant. Scottish XV v J 76.
Barbarians > 76 Can. London Cos v NZ 78.

LAWSON, Richard Gordon   *England*
St Bees Sch, Workington, Cumberland.
b 1.9.01; *d* 3.1.61 Cockermouth.
No 8, 1-0-1-0.
25 I=.
Sales dir. Bro of Thomas. 60 apps for
Cumberland. Served WW1, RFC; shot down
over F. POW. Served WW2, Capt in Coastal
Defence Battery.

LAWSON, Thomas Mattocks   *England*
St Bees Sch, Workington, Cumberland.
b 1900 Cockermouth; *d* 21.10.51 Workington.
Flanker, 2-2-0-0.
28 NSW+ W+.
Sales dir/brass founders co chmn. Bro of
Richard. 50 apps for Cumberland. Welterweight
boxing champ W Command during WW1.

LAWTHER, Thomas Hope   *Scotland*
Brendan
Mill Hill Sch, O Millhillians, R Sch of Mines.
b 6.10.09 Rothesay, Bute.
FB, 2-0-0-2.
32 SA− W−.
Mining engr.

LAWTON, Thomas   *Australia*
Oxford Univ, Blackheath, NSW, W Suburbs,
Qld.
b 16.1.1899 Qld; *d* 1.7.78 Brisbane.
Five-eighth, 6-5-0-1 (30 − 3c 8p).
29 NZ+(2p) NZ+(1c 2p) NZ+(2p); 30 BI+; 32
NZ+(2c 2p) NZ−.
Business/farming. Grandfather of T.A. Rhodes
Scholar. Blue 21-3. 127 pts NSW > 27-8 BI, F.

LAWTON, Thomas Anthony   *Australia*
Australian Schs, Souths, Brisbane, Qld.
b 27.11.62.
Hooker, 14-9-1-4 (4 − 1t).
83 F=r F−; 84 Fj+ NZ+ NZ− NZ− E+ I+

W+(1t) S+; 85 C+ C+ NZ− Fj+.
Grandson of Tommy. A Under 21s 81-3. A > 83
It & F; 84 Fj; 84 BI.

LAZIÈS, Henri   *France*
Auch.
b 1.11.29 Belloc.
Lock/prop/flanker, 4-3-0-1.
54 Arg+; 55 It+; 56 E+; 57 S−.

LEADBETTER, Michael Morris   *England*
Broughton Pk, Barbarians, NW Cos, Lancs.
b 25.7.47.
Lock, 1-0-0-1.
70 F−.
Printer. Rochdale Hornets RL.

LEADBETTER, Victor H.   *England*
Kettering GS, Cambridge Univ, Edinburgh W.
b −.9.29 Stanion, Northants.
Lock, 2-1-0-1.
54 S+ F−.
Iron & steel co proprietor. Blue 51-2.

LEAHY, Michael William   *Ireland*
Woodford Normal Sch, UC Cork.
b 6.6.35 Woodford, Co Galway.
Lock, 1-0-0-1.
64 W−.
Garda Siochana superintendent.

LEAKE, William Robert Martin   · *England*
Clifton Coll, Dulwich Coll, Cambridge Univ, O
Alleynians, Harlequins, Barbarians, Surrey.
b 31.12.1865 Ceylon; *d* 14.11.42.
Half-back, 3-2-0-1.
1891 W+ I+ S−.
Clergyman/schoolmaster. Blue 1885-7. 1st
player to play for E direct from Harlequins.
Original mem Barbarians. Taught at Dulwich
where rugby coach of Cyril Lowe & John
Greenwood.

LEATHER, George ('Jumbo')   *England*
Liverpool Coll, Liverpool, Lancs.
b 22.2.1881; *d* 2.1.57 Liverpool.
Forward, 1-0-0-1.
07 I−.
Chartered accountant. Cousin of Wilfred
Stoddart. Sons W.H. & W.J. won blues at
Cambridge.

LE BOURHIS, René   *France*
La Rochelle.
Lock, 1-0-1-0.
61 R=.

LECOINTRE, Michel   *France*
Nantes.
FH, 1-1-0-0.
52 It+.

LEDGER, Septimus Heyns   *South Africa*
Kimberley HS, Griq W.
b 29.4.1889 Kimberley; kia 13.4.17 Arras.
Lock, 4-4-0-0 (3 − 1t).
12 S+ I+; 13 E+ F+.
SA > 12-13 BI, F. Served WW1, Sgt in 2nd
Battn SA Infantry.

LEDINGHAM, George Alexander   *Scotland*
MC
Aberdeen GS, Aberdeen GSFP.
Lock, 1-1-0-0.
13 F+.
Served WW1.

LE DROFF, Jean   *France*
Auch.
b 22.6.39 Ordan-Larroque, Gers.
Lock, 9-4-2-3.
63 It+ R=; 64 S− NZ− E−; 70 E+ R+; 71 S+
I=.
Farmer.

LEE, Frederick Hugh   *England*
Marlborough Coll, Oxford Univ, Marlborough
Nomads.
b 14.9.1855; *d* 6.2.24 Aberdeen.
Forward, 2-2-0-0 (1t).
1876 S+(1t); 1877 I+.
Solicitor/Registrar. Blue 1874-77. Worcs CCC,
Suffolk CCC.

LEE, Harry   *England*
Tettenhall Coll, Cambridge Univ, Guy's Hosp,
Blackheath, Barbarians, Kent.
b 8.12.1882 Batley; *d* 11.1.33 Leeds.
FB, 1-1-0-0.
07 F+.
Medicine. Blue 04. Served WW1, Capt RAMC.
Found dead in his car.

LEE, Samuel   *Ireland*
RBAI, NIFC.
b 26.9.1871; *d* 5.1.44.
Centre, 19-8-2-9 (1 − 1t).
1891 E− S− W−(1t); 1892 E− S− W+; 1893
E− S= W−; 1894 E+ S+ W+; 1895 E− W−;
1896 E+ S= W+; 1897 E+; 1898 E+.
Ref S v E 04. Pres IRU 1899-1900.

LEES, James Blanch   *Scotland*
Selkirk HS, Gala.
b 11.8.19 Selkirk.
No 8/flanker, 5-2-0-3.
47 I− A−; 48 F+ W− E+.
Newsagent. Played in 1 Servs int.

LE FANU, Victor Charles JP   *Ireland*
Haileybury & ISC, Cambridge Univ,
Lansdowne.
b 14.10.1865; *d* 9.8.39.

Forward, 11-3-0-8.
1886 E− S−; 1887 E+ W−; 1888 S−; 1889 W+;
1890 E−; 1891 E−; 1892 E− S− W+.
Schoolmaster/agent to Lord Meath/co dir. Son
of novelist Sheridan le Fanu. Blue 1884-6; 1st
Irish int to play in Univ Match. Played in several
E trials.

LEFÈVRE, Roland   *France*
Brive.
b 19.9.36 La Flamegne.
No 8, 1-0-0-1.
61 NZ−.

LE FLEMING, John   *England*
Tonbridge Sch, Cambridge Univ, Blackheath,
Barbarians, Kent.
b 23.10.1865; *d* 9.10.42 Montreux.
Back, 1-1-0-0.
1887 W+.
Schoolmaster. Blue 1884-6. AAA 120y hurdles
champ 1887; ath blue (hurdles 1886-8, hammer
1887). Won Davos Bowl for ice skating 1893.
Kent CCC 1890-9. Taught at Tonbridge. Served
WW1 Queen's Own Rgt.

LEFORT, Jean-Baptiste   *France*
Biarritz Ol.
No 8, 1-0-0-1.
38 G−.

LEGGATT, Herbert Thomas   *Scotland*
Owen
George Watson's Coll, Watsonians.
b 1869; *d* 23.5.45.
Forward, 9-7-0-2 (1 − 1t).
1891 W+(1t) I+ E+; 1892 W+ I+; 1893 W−
E+; 1894 I− E+.
Insurance.

LEGGE, Walter George   *Wales*
Cross Keys, Newport, Risca, Weston-super-
Mare.
b 11.11.11 Newport; *d* 85.
FB, 2-1-0-1 (5 − 1c 1p).
37 I−(1p); 38 I+(1c).
Steelworker.

LE GOFF, Raymand   *France*
Métro.
Wing, 2-2-0-0 (3 − 1t).
38 R+(1t) G+.

LEGRAIN, Marcel   *France*
SF.
b −; kia WW1.
Forward, 13-1-0-12.
09 I−; 10 I−; 11 S+ E− W− I−; 13 S− SA−
E− W− I−; 14 I− W−.

239

LELEU, John *Wales*
Bishop Gore Sch, Mumbles, London Welsh,
Swansea.
b 13.3.35.
Flanker, 4-1-0-3.
59 E+ S−; 60 F− SA−.
Sales rep.

LE LIEVRE, Jules Mathew *New Zealand*
Akaroa Convent Sch, St Bede's Coll
Christchurch, Akaroa, Marist, Canterbury,
Culverden, S Island.
b 17.8.33 Akaroa.
Prop, 1-1-0-0.
62 A+.
Farmer/broiler chicken grower. NZ > 62 A, 63-
4 BI,F & C. Various selection & coaching posts.

LELY, William Gerald *Scotland*
Fettes Coll, Cambridge Univ, London Scottish.
b −.7.1886; *d* −.
Prop, 1-1-0-0.
09 I+.
Bombay-Burmah Trading Co. Blue 06-8.

LEMON, Arthur *Wales*
Neath.
b 15.4.05 Tonna; *d* −.6.82 Neath.
No 8/flanker, 13-7-2-4.
29 I=; 30 S− I+ F+; 31 E= S+ F+ I+ SA−; 32
E+ S+ I−; 33 I−.
Tinplater/police. St Helens RL 33.

LENDRUM, Robert Noel *New Zealand*
Papakura HS, Papakura, NZ Jnrs, Counties, N
Island.
22.3.48 Waiuku.
FB, 1-0-0-1 (2 − 1c).
73 E−(1c).
Schoolmaster.

LENEHAN, James Kenneth *Australia*
Michael
Riverview Coll, St Ignatius Coll Sydney, NSW.
b 29.4.38.
FB, 24-5-2-17 (44 − 4t 4c 8p).
58 W− E−(1p) S−(1c) F− M+(4p) M= M−;
59 BI− BI−; 61 SA− SA− F−; 62 NZ− NZ=
NZ− NZ−(1t); 65 SA+(1t) SA+(2p); 66
W+(1t 1p) S−(1c); 67 E+(1t 1c) I−(1c) F− I−.
Grazier. 117 pts A > BI, F, US & C 57-8.

LENIENT, Jean-Jacques *France*
Vichy.
Wing, 1-1-0-0.
67 R+.

LENIHAN, Donal Gerard *Ireland*
CBC Cork, UC Cork, Cork Constitution.
b 12.9.59 Cork.
Lock, 22-9-1-12.

81 A−; 82 W+ E+ S+ F−; 83 S+ F+ W− E+;
84 F− W− E− S− A−; 85 S+ F= W+ E+; 86
F− W− E− S−; BIr > 83 NZ.
Bank official. Capt Five Nations v Overseas
XV, Twickenham 86.

LEPATEY, Jacques *France*
Mazamet.
b 25.9.29 Sallières l'Aude.
Wing, 5-4-0-1 (6 − 2t).
54 It+(2t); 55 S+ I+ E+ W−.
Vineyard proprietor. Nephew of Louis.

LEPATEY, Louis *France*
Mazamet.
Prop, 3-1-0-2.
24 S+ I− E−.
Uncle of Jacques.

LE ROUX, Marthinus ('Martiens') *South Africa*
Wessel Maree Sch Odendalsrus, UOFS, Jnr
Springboks, Barbarians, SA Univs, OFS.
b 30.3.51 Wesselsbron.
Prop, 8-7-0-1.
80 BI+ BI+ BI+ BI− SAm+ SAm+ F+; 81
I+.
Schoolmaster. 117 apps for OFS. Barbarians >
79 BI.

LE ROUX, Pieter A. *South Africa*
Stellenbosch Univ, W Prov.
b 1885.
Forward, 3-2-1-0.
06 I+ W+ E=.
Bro of Japie SA 06 (no Tests). SA > 06-7 BI, F.

LESCARBOURA, Jean-Patrick *France*
Dax.
b 12.3.61 Monein.
FH, 20-10-3-7 (150 − 3t 15c 10d 26p).
82 W− E−(1d) S− I+; 83 A=(1d 3p) A+(1c
2p) R+(1t 2c 2p); 84 I+(1c 1d 4p) W+(1c 1d 4p)
E+(3c 1d 1p) S−(1c 1d 1p) NZ−(1c 1d) NZ−
(2t 2p) R+; 85 E=(3d) S+(1p) I=(2c 1p)
W+(2p) Arg−(1c 2p) Arg+(2c 1p).
Town planning employee. Côte Basque > 81
NZ. Champ rec 54 pts (4 apps) 84. Reached 100
int pts v NZ, 2nd Test 84. Equ int match rec 3d v
E 85. 49 pts F > 85 Arg.

LESIEUR, Emile *France*
SF.
b 16.9.1885 Paris; *d* −.
Centre/wing, 12-0-0-12 (3 − 1t).
06 E−(1t); 08 E− W−; 09 E− W− I−; 10 S−
E− I−; 11 E− I−; 12 W−.
Companies administrator. Served WW1; Légion
d'Honneur & Medaille Militaire. French 100,
400m champ.

LESLIE, Andrew Roy　　　　*New Zealand*
Hutt Valley Memorial Tech Coll, Petone,
Wellington, N Island.
b 10.11.44 Lower Hutt.
No 8, 10-6-1-3 (4 − 1t).
74 A+ A=(1t) A+; 74 I+; 75 S+; 76 I+ SA−
SA+ SA− SA−.
Mercer. Capt NZ > 74 A & Fj. Capt & played
in 7 out of 8 matches NZ > 74 I,W,E. Capt > 76
SA. Rep NZ at softball 66 & water polo.
Formerly in partnership as a mercer with
another NZ player, Bob Scott. Father played
football for NZ.

LESLIE, David George　　　　*Scotland*
Dundee HS, Glenalmond Acad, Scottish
Schools, Dundee Univ, Dundee HSFP, W of
Scotland, Gala, Barbarians.
b 14.4.52 Dundee.
No 8/flanker, 32-15-0-17 (8 − 2t).
75 I+ F− W+ E− NZ− A+; 76 F− W−
E+(1t) I+; 78 NZ−; 80 E−; 81 W+ E− I+
NZ− NZ− R+ A+; 82 E+; 83 I− F− W− E+;
84 W+ E+ I+ F+ R−(1t); 85 F− W− E−.
Architect. Scotland B v F 73-4. Scottish XV v J
76. S > 75, 81 NZ. Injs interrupted int career,
inc broken leg 82.

LESLIE-JONES, Frederick　　　　*England*
Archibald CBE
Hereford Cathed Sch, Bromsgrove Sch, Oxford
Univ, Blackheath, Richmond, Barbarians.
b 9.7.1874; *d* 24.1.46.
Centre, 2-2-0-0 (3 − 1t).
1895 W+(1t) I+.
Clergyman/schoolmaster. Blue 1894-6. Various
teaching posts, inc Marlborough. Served WW1,
India Defence Force. Author of 'A View of
English History'.

L'ESTRANGE, Laurence Perot　　　　*Ireland*
Farrar
Blackrock Coll, Chicago Univ, Sorbonne Univ,
Trin Coll Dublin.
b 1.11.34 Lytham, Lancs.
Wing, 1-0-0-1.
62 E−.
Army/stockbroker.

L'ESTRANGE, Rex David　　　　*Australia*
Ashgrove Marist Coll, Qld.
b 25.5.48.
Centre, 16-4-1-11.
71 F+ F−; 72 NZ− NZ− NZ−; 73 Tg+ Tg−
W− E−; 74 NZ− NZ= NZ−; 75 S− W−; 76
I+ US+.
Solicitor.

LEUVIELLE, Maurice　　　　*France*
SBUC.
b −; *d* c58 Bordeaux.
Centre, 7-0-0-7.
08 W−; 13 S− SA− E− W−; 14 W− E−.
Engr/chemist.

LEVASSEUR, Robert　　　　*France*
SF.
b −; *d* 74 Biarritz.
Lock, 2-0-0-2.
25 W− E−.

LEVÉE, Henri　　　　*France*
RCF.
Centre, 1-0-0-1.
06 NZ−.

LEVIS, F.H.　　　　*Ireland*
Wanderers.
Forward, 1-0-0-1.
1884 E−.

LEWIS, Alec Ormonde　　　　*England*
R Masonic Sch, O Masonians, Wells, Bath,
Barbarians, Som.
b 20.8.20 Brighton.
Flanker, 9-5-1-3.
52 SA− W− S+ I+ F+; 53 W+ I= S+; 54 F−.
Sales mgr Shell-Mex & BP. Served WW2
London Rifle Bde & 8th Army. Owing to
wounds unable to play rugby & so played
football with Swindon Town. Resumed rugby
48; capped at 31. E sel.

LEWIS, Allan Robert　　　　*Wales*
Welsh Youth, Abertillery.
b 7.10.42.
SH, 6-3-0-3
66 E+ S+ I− F+ A−; 67 I−; BI > 66 A, NZ 3-
0-0-3.
Carpenter/police/school welfare offcr. W > 64
SA Wales XV v Fj 64

LEWIS, Arthur John　　　　*Wales*
Ebbw Vale.
b 26.9.41.
Centre, 11-9-0-2 (4 − 1t).
70 F+; 71 E+ I+ F+; 72 E+ S+ F+; 73 E+(1t)
S− I+ F−; BI > 71 A, NZ.
Electrician. Wales B v F 70. W > 73 Can.

LEWIS, Brinley Richard　　　　*Wales*
Swansea GS, Cambridge Univ, Pontardawe,
Swansea, London Welsh.
b 4.1.1891 Pontardawe; kia 2.4.17 Ypres.
Wing, 2-1-0-1 (6 − 2t).
12 I−; 13 I+(2t).
Glamorgan Yeomanry. Blue 09-11. Wales XV v
Barbarians 15. Served WW1, Maj in R Field

Artillery, mentioned in despatches. Cousin of G. Michael.

LEWIS, Charles Prytherch JP　　　*Wales*
Llandovery Coll, Oxford Univ.
b 20.8.1853 Llangadoc; *d* 28.5.23 Llandovery.
FB, 5-1-0-4 (4c).
1882 I+(2c) E−; 1883 S−(1c); 1884 E−(1c) S−.
Schoolmaster/solicitor. 3 ath blues. Ckt for
Oxford Univ. 1st vice-pres WRU 1881. Ref W v
E 1885. Mayor of Llandovery 1894-5, 04-05.

LEWIS, D.H.　　　*Wales*
Cardiff.
Forward, 2-0-0-2.
1886 E− S−.

LEWIS, Edward John　　　*Wales*
Llandovery Coll, Cambridge Univ.
b 5.12.1859 Llandovery; *d* 8.6.25 London.
Half-back, 1-0-0-1.
1881 E−.
Surg.

LEWIS, E.W.　　　*France*
Le Havre.
Centre, 1-0-0-1.
06 E−.
British Army.

LEWIS, Howell　　　*Wales*
Swansea.
Wing, 4-3-0-1.
13 S+ F+ I+; 14 E−.

LEWIS, John Gouldstone　　　*Wales*
('Johnny Bach')
Llanelli.
b 1860 Llanelli; *d* 35 Llanelli.
Half-back, 1-1-0-0.
1887 I+.
Tinplater. With bro G.P. played rugby & ckt for
Llanelli; 1st man to score century at Stradey
Park.

LEWIS, John Morris Clement　　　*Wales*
Cambridge Univ, Cardiff, Barbarians.
b 22.6.1890; *d* 27.10.44 Porthcawl.
FH, 11-7-0-4 (19 − 3t 3c 1d).
12 E−; 13 S+(1t 1c) F+(1t 1c) I+; 14 E−
S+(1d) F+ I+(1c); 21 I+; 23 E− S−(1t).
Colliery salesman Cardiff Docks/schoolmaster.
Blue 13, 19. Mother Country XV 19. Distinction
of playing for Cambridge, Cardiff & W before &
after WW1. Sc 2t in same match as bro Ivor sc
4t, Cardiff v Pontypridd 15.1.21. Served WW1,
Lt in Welch Rgt; wounded.

LEWIS, John Rhodri　　　*Wales*
Maesteg Comp, S Glam Inst, Maesteg, Cardiff.
b 25.2.59 Maesteg.

Flanker, 7-3-0-4 (4 − 1t).
81 E+ S− I+ F−; 82 F+ E−(1t) S−.
Wales B v F 81. Wales B > 80 US, Can.

LEWIS, Llewellyn Stanley　　　*Australia*
('Wally')
Brisbane State HS, Qld.
b 12.
Five-eighth/centre, 4-1-1-2.
34 NZ+ NZ=; 36 NZ−; 38 NZ−.
Dentist.

LEWIS, Mark　　　*Wales*
Treorchy, Llwynypia.
b ?Treorchy; *d* Llwynypia.
Wing, 1-1-0-0.
13 F+.
Miner.

LEWIS, Phillip Ivor　　　*Wales*
QEGS Carmarthen, Welsh SS, Crewe &
Alsager Coll, English Colls, British Colls,
Carms, Llanelli.
b 6.1.61 Swansea.
Wing, 8-4-0-4 (8 − 2t).
84 A−; 85 S+ I−(1t) F− E+; 86 E− S+ I+(1t).
Police. Wales B v F 83-4. Played for Llanelli
while still at sch.

LEWIS, Thomas William　　　*Wales*
Cardiff.
b 7.6.02 Taff's Well.
Prop/lock, 3-0-1-2.
26 E=; 27 E− S−.
Police.

LEWIS, William　　　*Wales*
UC Aberystwyth, Swansea, Llanelli.
b 1899 Morriston; *d* −.2.27 Swansea.
Flanker, 1-1-0-0.
25 F+.
Schoolmaster.

LEWIS, Windsor Hopkin　　　*Wales*
Christ's Coll Brecon, Cambridge Univ, London
Welsh, Maesteg.
b 11.11.06 Maesteg; *d* −.11.82.
FH, 6-2-0-4 (7 − 1t 1d).
26 I+; 27 E− F+ I−(1d) NSW−(1t); 28 F−.
Medicine/univ lecturer. Blue 26-7. Father of
Geoff Windsor-Lewis.

LEYLAND, Roy ('Bus') OBE　　　*England*
Wigan GS, Wigan OB, Liverpool Univ,
Waterloo, Leicester, Richmond, The Army,
Comb Servs, Barbarians, Lancs, Hants.
b 6.3.12 Wigan; *d* 4.1.84 Pewsey.
Wing/centre, 3-1-1-1.
35 W= I+ S−; BI > 38 SA.
Schoolmaster/the Army. Served WW2, BEF

242

Dunkirk; then Parachute Rgt. Rep Army on
RFU from 64. OBE 57.

LEYS, Eric Tiki ('Tiny')   *New Zealand*
Wellington Coll, Univ, Wellington, NZ Univs.
b 25.5.07 Wellington.
SH, 1-0-0-1.
29 A−.
Govt Audit Office accountant. NZr > 29 A.
Accomplished ckter, lawn tennis & bowls
player. Father R.R. rep Wanganui &
Manawatu.

LIBAROS, Georges   *France*
Tarbes.
Centre, 2-1-0-1.
36 G+; 40 BF−.

LIDDELL, Eric Henry   *Scotland*
Eltham Coll, Edinburgh Univ.
b 16.1.02 Tientsin, China; *d* 21.1.45 China.
Wing, 7-4-2-1 (12 − 4t).
22 F= W= I+(1t); 23 F+(1t) W+(1t) I+(1t)
E−.
Medical missionary. Liddell made his int debut
at Stade Colombes, Paris, coincidentally the
same stadium in which he set world rec figures of
47.6 secs in winning Olympic Games 440yds title
2 yrs later, after he had given up rugby. The
deeply religious Liddell, who had refused to run
in the Olympic 100y because the heats were
staged on a Sunday, later became a missionary
in China, where he was born. His career was the
subject of a highly acclaimed film of the early
80s, 'Chariots of Fire'. He died, aged 43, in a
Japanese internment camp in China.

LIGHTFOOT, Edward John   *Ireland*
Castleknock Coll, Lansdowne.
b 29.11.07 Dublin; *d* 25.3.81.
Wing, 11-5-0-6 (9 − 3t).
31 F− E+ S+ W− SA−; 32 E− S+(2t)
W+(1t); 33 E− W+ S−.
Wholesale merchant.

LILBURNE, Herbert Theodore   *New Zealand*
Woolston Sch, Albion, Canterbury, Hutt,
Wellington, S & N Islands.
b 16.3.08 Burnham; *d* 12.7.76 Dunedin.
1st/2nd five-eighth/FB, 10-3-1-6 (4 − 2c).
28 SA− SA+; 29 A− A− A−(2c); 30 BI−
BI+; 31 A+; 32 A−; 34 A=.
Rly worker/fruiterer. Youngest NZ Test capt,
21yrs 112days v A 29. NZ > 28 SA, 29 A (top
scorer with 40 pts); 32 & 34 A. Switched to RL
35, rep NZ v A. Reinstated after WW2; coached
Zingari-Richmond.

LILLICRAP, Cameron Paul   *Australia*
Australian Schs, Qld Univ, Brisbane, Qld.
b 19.4.63.

Prop, 1-1-0-0.
85 Fj+.
Student. A Under 21s 83. A > 84 Fj; 84 BI.

LIND, Harry   *Scotland*
Dunfermline HS, Dunfermline, Barbarians.
b 27.3.06.
FH/centre, 16-6-0-10 (7 − 1t 1d).
28 I−; 31 F+ W− I− E+; 32 SA−(1t) W− E−;
33 W+ E+ I+(1d); 34 W− I+ E−; 35 I−; 36
E−.
Architect. N of Scotland v NZ 35.

LINDSAY, Andrew Alexander   *Scotland*
Bonar OBE MC
Southland HS NZ, University (Dunedin), The
London Hosp, London Univ, Barbarians.
b 19.7.1885 Otepopo, NZ; *d* 15.5.70 Auckland,
NZ.
SH, 2-1-0-1.
10 I+; 11 I−.
Surg. Returned NZ 12. Served WW1, Maj
RAMC. Spent time in India & Can. OBE for
work WW2.

LINDSAY, David Frederick   *New Zealand*
Waimate Dist HS, Timaru Boys' HS, Univ,
Otago, NZ Univs.
b 9.12.06 Studholm; *d* 7.3.78 Timaru.
FB, 3-1-0-2 (3 − 1p).
28 SA− SA+(1p) SA−.
Hospital dentist. Top scorer 63 pts NZ > 28 SA.
S Canterbury sel 45-6.

LINDSAY, George Campbell   *Scotland*
Loretto Sch, Oxford Univ, London Scottish.
b 3.1.1863; *d* 5.4.05 Hampstead.
Back, 3-2-1-0 (5t).
1884 W+; 1887 W+(5t) E=.
Accountant/journalist/Lloyds underwriter. Blue
1882-4. Rec 5t S v W 1887 − not originally
selected but regained place after match
postponed.

LINDSAY, Harry   *Ireland*
Santry Coll, Trin Coll Dublin, Armagh.
b Armagh.
Forward, 13-6-2-5 (3 − 1t).
1893 E− S= W−; 1894 E+ S+ W+; 1895 E−;
1896 E+ S= W+; 1898 E+(1t) S− W−.

LINDSAY, Roy Thomas George   *Australia*
Qld.
b 05; *d* 72.
Wing, 1-0-0-1.
32 NZ−.
RL for Toowoomba before cap. Reinstated.

LINDSAY-WATSON, Robert   *Scotland*
Hamilton
Glenalmond Acad, Cambridge Univ, Hawick.

b 4.10.1886; *d* 26.1.56 Hawick.
Wing, 1-1-0-0 (3 − 1t).
09 I+(1t).
Tweed manufacturer. Rep GB in Olympic
hammer throw.

LINEEN, Terence Raymond　　　*New Zealand*
Vermont St Marist Bros' Sch, Sacred Heart Coll
Auckland, Marist, Auckland, N Island.
b 5.1.36 Auckland.
2nd five-eighth/centre, 12-8-1-3.
57 A+ A+; 58 A+ A− A+; 59 BI+ BI+ BI+
BI−; 60 SA− SA+ SA=.
Carpenter/sales rep. NZ > 57 A; 10t NZ > 60 A
& SA.

LIRA, Maurice　　　*France*
La Voulte.
b 30.4.41 La Mure, Isère; *d* 25.1.86 La Voulte.
Lock/flanker/no 8, 13-8-3-2 (6 − 2t).
62 R−; 63 I+ E− W+ It+(1t) R=; 64 W= It+
I+(1t) SA+; 65 S+ I= R+.
Transport business/bar owner.

LISLE, Ronald James　　　*Australia*
NSW.
b 19.9.39 Grafton.
Centre, 4-2-1-1 (6 − 2t).
61 Fj+(1t) Fj+ Fj=(1t) SA−.
Schoolmaster. RL for A.

LISTER, Thomas Norman　　　*New Zealand*
Waitaki Boys' Sch, HSOB, S Canterbury, NZ
Colts, NZ Jnrs, Athletic, Wellington, S Island.
b 27.10.43 Ashburton.
Flanker, 8-5-1-2 (6 − 2t).
68 A+ A+(1t) F+; 69 W+ W+; 70 SA− SA−;
71 BI=(1t).
Freezing co worker/fisherman. NZ > 68 A & Fj,
70 A & SA. Bro John a pro golfer.

LITTLE, Anthony W.　　　*Scotland*
Hawick.
b 1882; *d* −.
Forward, 1-0-0-1 (1t).
05 W−(1t).
Wigan RL 05.

LITTLE, E.M.M.　　　*South Africa*
Griq W.
b −; *d* 45.
2-0-0-2.
1891 BT− BT−.

LITTLE, Paul Francis　　　*New Zealand*
Vermont St Marist Bros' Sch, Marist, Auckland
Colts, Auckland, N Island.
b 14.9.34 Auckland
Centre, 10-8-2-0 (3 − 1t).

61 F+ F+(1t); 62 A+ A= A+; 63 I+ W+; 64
E+ S= F+.
Hairdresser. NZ > 62 A, 63-4 BI,F & C.

LITTLE, Thomas Joseph　　　*Ireland*
Belvedere Coll, Bective Rgrs.
Forward, 7-3-1-3.
1898 W−; 1899 S+ W+; 1900 S= W−; 01 E+
S−.
Medicine. Bro in law of Louis Magee.

LIVERMORE, Alan Edward　　　*Australia*
Qld.
b 19; *d* 56.
Prop, 2-0-0-2 (2 − 1c).
46 NZ−(1c) M−.
Costing clerk.

LIVESAY, Robert O'Hara CMG　　　*England*
DSO
Wellington Coll, RMC Sandhurst, Blackheath,
The Army, Barbarians, Kent.
b 27.6.1876; *d* 23.3.46.
Half-back, 2-1-0-1.
1898 W+; 1899 W−.
The Army. Served SA War 1899-02 (Queen's
Medal, King's Medal), DSO 02. Served WW1.
Mentioned in despatches 6 times. CMG 19;
Legion d'Honneur & American DSM. Reached
rank of Brig Gen. Kent CCC.

LLARY, Roger　　　*France*
Carcassonne.
b −; *d* 20.12.73.
SH, 1-0-0-1.
26 S−.

LLEWELLYN, Philip David　　　*Wales*
Welsh Youth, Swansea.
b 12.5.48.
Prop, 5-3-0-2.
73 I+ F− A+; 74 S+ E−.
Electrician. W > 73 Can. Wales XV v J 73.
Barbarians > 76 Can.

LLEWELLYN, William Morris　　　*Wales*
Christ's Coll Brecon, Llwynypia, Glamorgan,
London Welsh, Surrey, Newport, Penygraig.
b 1.1.1879 Tonypandy; *d* 12.3.73 Pontyclun.
Wing, 20-15-1-4 (48 − 16t).
1899 E+(4t) S−(1t) I−; 1900 E+ S+(2t) I+; 01
E+ S− I+; 02 E+ S+(2t) I+(1t); 03 I+(2t); 04
E=(1t) S+ I−; 05 E+(1t) S+(2t) I+ NZ+; BT
> 04 A, NZ.
Pharmacist. Rec 4t W v E 1899; 50t·1897-8
season. Nephew of Thomas Williams.

LLEWELYN, Donald Barry　　　*Wales*
Llanelli GS, Loughborough Colls, Caerleon
Coll, Newport, Llanelli, Pembrokeshire,
Barbarians.

244

b 1.6.48 Manchester.
Prop, 13-10-1-2 (3 − 1t).
70 SA= S+(1t) E+ I− F+; 71 E+ S+ I+ F+;
72 E+ S+ F+ NZ−.
Schoolmaster/sports shopkeeper. W > 69 NZ,
A & Fj; 75 Far East. Wales XV v Tg 74. Welsh
XV v NZ 74. Barbarians v SA 70.

LLOYD, David John   *Wales*
Garw GS, Welsh SS, Pontycymmer, Cardiff Tg
Coll, Bridgend, Glam.
b 29.3.43 Pontycymmer.
Prop, 24-14-1-9.
66 E+ S+ I− F+ A−; 67 S− I− F− E+; 68 S+
I− F−; 69 S+ I+ F= E+ NZ− A+; 70 F+; 72
E+ S+ F+; 73 E+ S−.
Schoolmaster. Wales XV v Fj 64. W > 68 Arg;
69 NZ, A & Fj. Wales B v F 70. Asst mgr Wales
B > 80 US, Can.

LLOYD, David Percy M.   *Wales*
Carmarthen GS, Pontardawe, Llanelli.
b 1871 Llandilofawr; *d* −.3.59 Llanwrtyd
Wells.
Wing, 4-2-0-2.
1890 S− E+; 1891 E− I+.
Hotelier. Noted athlete, horseman, angler.

LLOYD, Evan   *Wales*
Llanelli.
1871 Llanelli; *d* 28.2.51 Llanelli.
Wing, 1-0-0-1.
1895 S−.
Tinplater. Notable sprinter.

LLOYD, George Llewellyn   *Wales*
The Leys Sch, Newport.
b 1877 Newport; *d* 1.8.57 Newport.
Half-back, 12-7-0-5 (9 − 3t).
1896 I−; 1899 S−(1t) I−; 1900 E+ S+; 01 E+
S−(1t); 02 S+ I+(1t); 03 E+ S− I+.
Solicitor. Officer in RA. Mon CCC.

LLOYD, Richard Averil   *Ireland*
Armagh RS, Trin Coll Dublin, Liverpool.
b 4.8.1891 Tamnamore, Dungannon; *d*
23.12.50 Belfast.
FH, 19-8-1-10 (73 − 2t 15c 7d 3p).
10 E= S−; 11 E+ S+(1c) W− F+(3c 1d); 12
F+(1t) E− S+(1d 1p) W+(1c 1d) SA−; 13 E−
(1d) S−(2c 1d) W−(2c 1p) F+(3c); 14 F+(1c)
E−(1c 1d); 20 E−(1t 1c 1p) F−(1d).
The Army. Most c (7) by I player in Champ
season, 13. Ref E v S, S v W 22. Photographed
with Irish team v Wales 14, but did not play after
injuring himself during warm-up. Place taken by
Harry Jack. Ckt for I.

LLOYD, Robert   *Wales*
Pontypool.
b 1888; *d* 18.1.30 Halifax.

SH, 7-6-0-1.
13 S+ F+ I+; 14 E− S+ F+ I+.
Miner/licensee. Halifax RL 14.

LLOYD, Robert Hoskins   *England*
Cheltenham Coll, Clifton, Harlequins,
Barbarians, Surrey.
b 3.3.43.
Centre, 5-1-2-2 (6 − 2t).
67 NZ−(2t); 68 W= I= F− S+.
Civil engr. Unable to tour BI > 68 SA because
of exams.

LLOYD, Thomas C.   *Wales*
Neath.
Forward, 7-6-0-1.
09 F+; 13 F+ I+; 14 E− S+ F+ I+.
Mem of 'Terrible Eight'.

LLOYD, Trevor   *Wales*
E Sch Taibach, Aberavon, Cwmavon, Maesteg,
Bristol, Crawshay's, Glam.
b 5.9.24 Taibach.
SH, 2-2-0-0.
53 I+ F+; BI > 55 SA.
Blast furnaceman. Schoolmate of actor Richard
Burton & Welsh int Gerwyn Williams. RN
submariner WW2. Capt unbeaten Maesteg 50.
Capt Wales v BI 75th anniversary match 55.
Maesteg coach 56-9.

LOADER, Colin James   *New Zealand*
Queen's Pk Sch Wanganui, Eastern Sch Hutt,
Univ, Wellington, Hutt.
b 10.3.31 Dannevirke.
Centre, 4-3-0-1.
54 I+ E+ S+ F−.
Mercer/builder. NZ > 53-4 BI,F & NAm.
Coached Hutt. Father P.J. rep Hawkes Bay.

LOANE, Mark Edward   *Australia*
Nudgee Coll, Brisbane, Qld, Natal.
b 11.7.54.
No 8/flanker, 28-16-0-12 (8 − 2t).
73 Tg+ Tg−; 74 NZ−; 75 E+(1t) E+ J+; 76
E− I+ Fj+ Fj+ Fj+ F− F−; 78 W+ W+(1t);
79 I− I− NZ+ Arg− Arg+; 81 F+ F+ I+ W−
S−; 82 E− S− S+.
Medicine. State & int debut at 18. A > 75-6 &
81-2 BI; 76 F; 79 Arg. Toured NZ 78 but
returned early because of inj. Out of int rugby
during 80 because of medical studies in SA.
Australian Player of Year 81.

LOBIES, Jean   *France*
RCF.
Wing, 3-1-0-2.
21 S+ W− E−.

LOCHNER, George Philip   *South Africa*
('Butch')
W Prov.
b 1.2.31 Stellenbosch.
No 8, 9-3-1-5 (6 − 2t).
55 BI−; 56 A+ A+ NZ− NZ+ NZ−(1t) NZ−;
58 F=(1t) F−.
Farmer.

LOCHNER, George Philippus   *South Africa*
('Flappie')
Stellenbosch Univ, E Prov.
b 11.1.14 Van Rhynsdorp.
Centre, 3-3-0-0 (3 − 1t).
37 NZ+; 38 BI+ BI+(1t).
Schoolmaster. Mgr SA > 71 A. Chmn SA sels.

LOCHORE, Brian James OBE   *New Zealand*
Wairarapa Coll, Masterton, Wairarapa, N
Island.
b 3.9.40 Masterton.
No 8/lock, 25-19-1-5 (6 − 2t).
64 E+ S=; 65 SA+ SA+ SA− SA+; 66
BI+(1t) BI+ BI+ BI+; 67 A+ E+ W+ F+ S+;
68 A+ F+ F+; 69 W+(1t) W+; 70 SA− SA+
SA− SA−; 71 BI−.
Farmer. Capt NZ 18 times. NZ > 63-4 BI,F &
C. Capt v BI 66, A 67, 67 BI,F & C (14 apps, 1
at lock), 68 A & Fj, A & SA. Capt v W 69.
Masterton & Wairarapa-Bush coach. NZRFU
sel 83-5. Coach NZ > 85 Arg. Coached Rest of
World v BI, Cardiff 86. Rep Wairarapa lawn
tennis 57-61, 79-80.

LOCKE, Harold Meadows   *England*
Birkenhead Pk, Cheshire.
b 1898; *d* 23.3.60 Birmingham.
Centre, 12-9-1-2 (3 − 1t).
23 S+ F+; 24 W+(1t) F+ S+; 25 W+ I= S−
F+; 27 W+ I+ S−.
Civil service.

LOCKWOOD, Richard Evison   *England*
Dewsbury, Heckmondwike, Yorks.
b 11.11.1867 Crigglestone, Wakefield; *d*
10.11.15 Leeds.
Back, 14-8-2-4 (31 − 5t 8c).
1887 W= I− S=; 1889 NZN+; 1891 W+ I+(2t
2c) S−(1t); 1892 W+(2c) I+ S+(1c); 1893 W−
I+; 1894 W+(1t 3c) I−(1t).
Woollen printer/wire rope engr. Also known as
the 'Little Marvel'. Wakefield Trin RL 1895.

LOCKWOOD, T.W.   *Wales*
Newport.
Forward, 3-1-1-1.
1887 E= S− I+.

LOCKYEAR, Richard John   *South Africa*
Kimberley Boys HS, Cape Town Univ, Griq W.
b 26.6.32.

SH, 6-3-2-1 (20 − 4c 4p).
60 NZ+(1c 1p) NZ− NZ=(1c 2p) NZ+(1c 1p)
I+(1c); 61 F=.
Sales mgr. Bro in law of A.I. Kirkpatrick. SA >
60-1 BI, F.

LOGAN, Donald Leslie   *Australia*
NSW.
b 53.
SH, 1-1-0-0.
58 M+.

LOGAN, William Ross   *Scotland*
Merchiston Castle Sch, Edinburgh Univ,
Edinburgh W, Barbarians.
b 24.11.09 Edinburgh.
SH, 20-7-0-13 (6 − 2t).
31 E+(1t); 32 SA− W− I−; 33 W+ E+ I+; 34
W−(1t) I+ E−; 35 W− I− E+ NZ−; 36 W−
I− E−; 37 W+ I− E−.
Farmer. Pres SRU 64-5. Ckt for S.

LOGIN, Spencer Henry Metcalfe   *England*
CVO
Wellington Coll, RN Coll Dartmouth.
b 24.9.1851; *d* 22.1.09.
FB, 1-1-0-0.
1875 I+.
RN. Rear Adm. Commanded various warships.
Fdr mem RN RFU 06. CVO 05.

LOHDEN, Frederick Charles   *England*
OBE JP
Durham Sch, Hartlepool R, Blackheath,
Barbarians, Durham Cos Surrey.
b 13.6.1871; *d* 13.4.54 Cheam.
Forward, 1-0-0-1 (2 − 1t).
1893 W−(1t).
The Army/ship broker. OBE 19. Lawn tennis
for Surrey. Chmn LTA 33, V-pres 34; rep GB
on Int LTF 34. Won London badminton doubles
champ 21; E Badminton comm 20-8. Councillor,
mayor Sutton & Cheam. JP 43-5.

LOMBARD, A.C.   *South Africa*
E Prov.
1-0-0-1.
10 BI−.

LOMBARD, François   *France*
Narbonne.
SH, 2-2-0-0.
34 G+; 37 It+.

LOMBARTEIX, René   *France*
Montferrand.
Prop/lock, 2-2-0-0.
38 R+ G+.

LONDIOS, Jacques   *France*
Montauban.

b 14.1.44 Montauban.
Wing, 1-1-0-0.
67 SA+.
Office worker.

LONG, A.J. ('Paddy')   *New Zealand*
Auckland.
Flanker, 1-1-0-0.
03 A+.
Suspended by Auckland 04 for involvement in a
bribe to a player from City club; suspension
lifted 11.

LONG, Edgar Cecil   *Wales*
Swansea.
b 08; *d* 31.1.58 Swansea.
Flanker, 7-4-1-2.
36 E= S+ I+; 37 E− S−; 39 S+ I+.
Grocer.

LONGLAND, Raymond John   *England*
('Rastus')
Olney, Buckingham, Bedford, RAF,
Northampton, Comb Servs, Barbarians, E
Midlands.
b 29.12.08; *d* 21.9.75.
Prop, 19-11-2-6.
32 S+; 33 W− S−; 34 W+ I+ S+; 35 W= I+
S−; 36 NZ+ W= I− S+; 37 W+ I+ S+; 38 W−
I+ S−.
Carpenter/licensee/schoolmaster. Served WW2
as PTI in RAF.

LORIEUX, Alain   *France*
Grenoble.
b 26.3.56 Paris.
Lock, 12-7-0-5.
81 A− R+ NZ− NZ−; 82 W−; 83 A+ R+; 84
I+ W+ E+; 85 Arg− Arg+r.
Neck inj prevented touring with F > 80 SA.
France B v S 81. F > 85 Arg.

LORRAINE, Herbert Derrick Bell   *Scotland*
Glenalmond Acad, Oxford Univ.
b 4.1.13; *d* 19.3.82.
Centre, 3-3-0-0.
33 W+ E+ I+.
Oil merchant. Blue 32-4.

LOTZ, Jan W.   *South Africa*
Krugersdorp HS, Transvaal.
b 26.8.10.
Hooker, 8-6-0-2 (3 − 1t).
37 A+ A+ NZ− NZ+ NZ+; 38 BI+ BI+ BI−
(1t).
Miner. SA > 37 NZ. Nephew of Phil Mostert.

LOUBSER, John Albertus ('Bob')   *South Africa*
Stellenbosch Univ, W Prov.
b 6.8.1884 Klipheuvel; *d* −.
Wing, 7-5-1-1 (9 − 3t).

03 BT+; 06 S− I+(2t) W+(1t) E=; 10 BI+
BI+.
SA's youngest Test player, 19yr 1mth v BT 03.
24t (21 apps) SA > 06 BI, rec for SA on tour.

LOUDON, Robert Briton   *Australia*
Christ's Coll, Great Public Schs OB, Manly,
NSW.
b 24.3.02 Leeston, NZ.
No 8/lock, 6-3-1-2 (6 − 2t).
29 NZ+; 33 SA+(1t) SA− SA− SA+; 34
NZ=(1t).
Bank clerk/real estate. Served WW2, capt AIF
Tank Corps.

LOUDOUN-SHAND, Eric   *Scotland*
Gordon MC
Dulwich Coll, O Alleynians, Oxford Univ,
Barbarians.
b 31.3.1893.
Centre, 1-0-0-1.
13 E−.
Broker. Blue 13 & 19. Missed S v SA & Univ
Match 12 because of appendicitis. Served WW1.

LOURENS, Matthys Johannes   *South Africa*
('Thys')
N Transvaal.
b 5.5.43 Vryheid.
Flanker, 3-2-1-0 (3 − 1t).
68 BI= BI+(1t) BI+.
SA > 68 F, 71 A.
Army/insurance. 168 apps for N Transvaal.

LOURY, André   *France*
RCF.
b 11.5.1900 Paris; *d* 3.12.68.
Prop, 6-2-0-4.
27 E+ G+ G−; 28 S− NSW− I−.

LOUSTEAU, Marcel   *France*
Dax.
Wing, 1-0-0-1.
23 E−.

LOUW, J.S.   *South Africa*
Transvaal.
3-0-0-3.
1891 BT− BT− BT−.
Uncle of Boy.

LOUW, Marthinus Johannes   *South Africa*
Stellenbosch Univ, N Transvaal.
b 20.4.38 Germiston.
Prop, 2-2-0-0.
71 A+ A+.
Quantity surveyor.

LOUW, Matthys Michael ('Boy') *South Africa*
Paarl Boys HS, W Prov.
b 21.2.06 Wellington Dist, Boland.

247

Prop, 18-14-0-4 (3 − 1t).
28 NZ+ NZ−; 31 W+ I+; 32 E+ S+; 33 A+
A− A+(1t) A+ A−; 37 A+ A+ NZ+ NZ+; 38
BI+ BI+ BI−.
Bank clerk. 5th of 10 bros & 4 sisters. 9 bros
played snr rugby. Bro of Fanie. Nephew of J.S.
SA > 31-2 BI.

LOUW, Robert James   *South Africa*
Wynberg Boys HS, Stellenbosch Univ, Defence
(Cape Town), Gazelles, Barbarians, Oribis, W
Prov.
b 26.3.55 Cape Town.
Flanker, 19-15-0-4 (20 − 5t).
80 SAm+ SAm+ BI+(1t) BI+(1t) BI+ BI−
SAm+ SAm+ F+; 81 I+(1t) I+ NZ− NZ−; 82
SAm+ SAm−; 84 E+(1t) E+ SAm+(1t)
SAm+.
Defence Force. SA > 81 US. Signed Wigan RL
(E) with fellow Springbok Ray Mordt, 85.

LOUW, Stephanus Cornelius   *South Africa*
('Fanie')
Paarl Boys HS, W Prov.
b 09; *d* 39.
12-8-0-4 (6 − 2t).
33 A+ A− A+ A+(1t) A−; 37 A+ NZ− NZ+
NZ+; 38 BI+(1t) BI+ BI−.
Bro of Boy. Nephew of J.S. SA > 31-2 BI.
Collapsed, died after capt W Prov v Transvaal
39.

LOVE, Eden William   *Australia*
Newington Coll, Sydney Univ, NSW.
Prop, 3-1-0-2.
32 NZ+ NZ− NZ−.

LOVERIDGE, David Steven   *New Zealand*
Inglewood HS, Inglewood, Univ, Auckland, NZ
Jnrs, Taranaki, N Island.
b 22.4.52 Stratford.
SH, 24-19-1-4 (12 − 3t).
78 W+; 79 S+(1t) E+; 80 A− A+ A− W+; 81
S+(1t) S+ SA+ SA− SA+ R+ F+ F+; 82 A+
A− A+; 83 BI+(1t) BI+ BI+ BI+ A+; 85
Arg=.
Pig farmer. NZ > 78 BI, 79 A, 79 E,S & It, 80 A
& Fj (capt), NAm & W, 81 R & F, 85 Arg. Capt
NZ (2) v Arg 79. Played for Overseas XV v Five
Nations, Twickenham 86. Rep Taranaki &
Auckland at ckt. Biography 'Dave Loveridge −
Master Halfback' pub 86.

LOWE, Cyril Nelson ('Kit') MC   *England*
DFC
Dulwich Coll, Cambridge Univ, O Alleynians,
Richmond, Blackheath, Surrey, W of Scotland,
RAF.
b 7.10.1891 Holbeach; *d* −.2.83 Surrey.
Wing, 25-21-1-3 (58 − 18t 1d).
13 SA− W+ F+ I+ S+; 14 W+(2t) I+ S+(3t)

F+(3t); 20 W−(1t) F+ I+ S+(1t); 21 W+(1t)
I+(1t 1d) S+ F+(1t); 22 W−(1t) I+(1t) F=
S+(2t); 23 W+ I+(1t) S+ F+.
RAF. Blue 11-13. Son of Lincs clergyman.
Served WW1 in 1st Reserve Horse Transport,
RASC, then volunteered for RFC, claiming 31
enemy aircraft shot down, but officially credited
with 9. In a Letter to the Editor of 'The
Sportsman', 29.1.13, a 'Lover of Rugby'
asserted: 'I think it the utmost folly to persist in
playing Lowe as he is much too small for int
games'. The response from the 5ft 6in, 8st 7lb
Lowe was to become E's ldg t scorer, inc most in
Champ season (8 in 14). All caps consec; once
E's most capped player. Inspired poem 'The
Great Day' by P.G. Wodehouse. Played
football at Dulwich until 16. Excelled at ath,
ckt, swimming & boxing. Rep RAF on RFU; sel
34-8.

LOWE, J. Douglas   *Scotland*
Heriot's Coll, Heriot's FP.
b 28.5.06; *d* 7.11.36.
Lock, 1-0-0-1.
34 W−.
Farrier.

LOWRIE, Frederick William   *England*
Wakefield Collegiate Sch, Batley, Wakefield
Trin.
b 1.3.1868 Wakefield; *d* 9.8.02 Leeds.
Forward, 2-1-0-1.
1889 NZN+; 1890 W−.
Licensee. Batley RL 1895.

LOWRY, Wilfrid Malbon   *England*
The Leys Sch, O Leysians, Birkenhead Pk,
Waterloo, Cheshire.
b 14.7.1900; *d* 4.7.74 Heswall.
Wing, 1-1-0-0.
20 F+.
Cotton broker. Served WW2, RA Lt. See
H.L.V. Day.

LOWTH, Donald R.   *Australia*
NSW.
b 32.
Flanker, 1-0-0-1.
58 NZ−.
Clerk. RL.

LOZOWSKI, Robert Andrew   *England*
Peter
Gunnersbury Sch, Wasps.
b 18.11.60.
Centre, 1-0-0-1.
84 A−.
Father Polish, mother Italian. E Under 23s 84.

LUBIN-LEBRÈRE, Marcel-   *France*
Frederic ('Monsieur Le Maire')
Toulouse.
b 21.7.1891 Agen; *d* 11.7.72.
Prop/lock, 14-3-2-9 (6 − 2t).
14 I− E−(1t); 20 S− E− W− I+ US+; 21 S+;
22 S= E= W−; 24 W−(1t) US−; 25 I−.
Rep. Served WW1; wounded, lost an eye. 17
bullets extracted from body.

LUBRANO, André   *France*
Béziers.
b 19.9.46 Sete, Herault.
Hooker, 2-2-0-0.
72 A+; 73 S+.
Restaurateur.

LUCAS, Basil C.   *Australia*
Qld.
Forward, 1-0-0-1.
05 NZ−.

LUCAS, Frederick William   *New Zealand*
Seddon Memorial Tech Coll, Ponsonby,
Auckland, N Island.
b 30.1.02 Auckland; *d* 17.9.57 Auckland.
Centre/wing, 7-6-0-1 (3 − 1t).
24 I+; 25+; 28 SA+; 30 BI− BI+ BI+(1t)
BI+.
Menswear store owner. NZ > 24-5 BI,F & C, 28
SA. Fdr mem NZ Barbarians. Ponsonby coach;
Auckland & N Island sel. NZRFU sel 45-6. Rep
Piha Surf Club in NZ lifesaving champs. Won
Auckland B grade lawn tennis singles title. Bro
'Snow' rep Auckland. Son 'Buddy' NZ
swimming champ & Empire Games rep, winning
gold medal in 4 x 220 relay 50.

LUCAS, Peter William   *Australia*
Sydney, Detroit (US), Hong Kong, NSW
Country, NSW.
b 24.9.56.
Flanker, 3-1-0-2.
82 N7− N7+ N7−
Schoolmaster. Played for Detroit at age of 14;
played for Hong Kong in Asian Games. A > 81-
2 BI.

LUDDINGTON, William George   *England*
Ernest
Devonport Servs, RN, Devon.
b 8.2.1894; kia 10.1.41 Mediterranean.
Prop/lock, 13-10-2-1 (16 − 5c 1gm 1p).
23 W+ I+ S+(1c) F+(1c); 24 W+ I+ F+ S+;
25 W+ I= S−(1c 1p) F+(2c 1gm); 26 W=.
RN. Served WW2, Master-at-Arms.

LUMSDEN, Ian James Michael   *Scotland*
George Watson's Coll, Bath, Watsonians,
Barbarians.
b 6.4.23 Edinburgh.

FH/FB, 7-2-0-5.
47 F− W− A−; 49 F+ W+ I− E−.
Ckt for S.

LUNN, William Albert   *New Zealand*
Alexandra Dist HS, Lincoln Coll, Alexandra,
Otago, Pirates, Ellesmere.
b 17.9.26 Alexandra.
Flanker, 2-0-0-2.
49 A− A−.
Farm advisory officer with NZ Min of Agric.
Coach Alexandra & Ranfurly clubs.

LUSCOMBE, Francis   *England*
Tonbridge Sch, Gipsies.
b 1846; *d* 17.7.26.
Forward, 6-4-2-0.
1872 S+; 1873 S=; 1875 I+ S= I+; 1876 S+.
Bro of Sir John. One of the prime movers in
acceptance of S's challenge to play 1st int, 1871.
Original mem RFU 1871. V-pres RFU 1877-8.
Celebrated racehorse owner, winning
Cambridgeshire twice with Marco (1895) &
Marcovil (08). Marcovil was grandsire of two
Derby winners, Captain Cuttle (22) & Coronach
(26).

LUSCOMBE, Sir John Henry   *England*
Tonbridge Sch, Gipsies.
b 1848 Cuckfield; *d* 3.4.37 Worth, Sussex.
Forward, 1-0-0-1.
1871 S−.
Chmn Lloyds. Bro of Francis. Longest lived
survivor of E's 1st int, v S 1871. Kt 02. HM Lt
for City of London. High Sheriff 13. Chmn
'Lloyds Register of Shipping' 21. JP for Sussex.

LUTGE, Denis ('Dinny')   *Australia*
NSW.
b 1879 Sydney; *d* 18.2.53.
Forward, 4-0-0-4.
03 NZ−; 04 BT− BT− BT−.
Stevedore/beach inspector. RL.

LUX, Jean-Pierre   *France*
Tyrosse, Dax.
b 9.1.44 St Vincent-de-Tyrosse.
Centre/wing, 47-22-6-13 (39 − 11t).
67 E+ It+(1t) W+ I+ SA− SA− SA= R+; 68
I+ E+ Cz+(2t) NZ−(1t) A− SA− SA−; 69 S−
I− E−; 70 S+(1t) I+ W− E+ R+; 71 S+ I=
E= W− A− A+; 72 S− I−(1t) E+(1t) W− I−
(1t) A=(2t) A+ R+; 73 S+ NZ+ E−; 74 I+
W=(1t) E= S− Arg+ Arg+; 75 W−.
Dentist.

LUXMOORE, Rt Hon Sir Arthur   *England*
Fairfax Charles Coryndon KC PC Kt JP
King's Sch Canterbury, Cambridge Univ,
Richmond, Barbarians, Kent.
b 27.2.1876; *d* 25.9.44 Hammersmith.

Forward, 2-0-1-1.
1900 S=; 01 W1−.
Law. Lord Justice. Blue 1896-7. Called to Bar
1899. KC 19. PC 38. Kt 29. Lib candidate for
Isle of Thanet, Gen Election 24.

LUYA, Humphrey Fleetwood   *England*
Merchant Taylors' Sch Crosby, Waterloo,
Carlisle, Headingley, Barbarians, Lancs.
b 3.2.18.
Lock, 5-0-1-4.
48 W= I− S− F−; 49 W−.
Co dir. Served WW2. POW in Crete.

LUYT, Frederick Pieter   *South Africa*
Stellenbosch Univ, SA Teachers Coll,
Mooreesburg, W Prov.
b 26.2.1888 Ceres; *d* −.
FH, 7-6-0-1 (8 − 2t 1c).
10 BI+(1t) BI− BI+(1t); 12 S+ I+(1c) W+; 13
E+.
Lawyer. Son of farmer. Played with bros John &
Richard, v S W E, 12-13. Rep Stellenbosch & W
Prov at rugby & ckt. Knee inj ended career;
went in to law partnership in Mooreesburg with
fellow Springbok Paddy Carolin.

LUYT, John Douglas   *South Africa*
SA Teachers Coll, Stellenbosch Univ, E Prov.
b 1885; *d* −.
Lock, 4-4-0-0.
12 S+ W+; 13 E+ F+.
Played with bros Pieter & Richard, v S W E, 12-
13. After retirement, became rugby corr for
several SA newspapers.

LUYT, Richard Robin   *South Africa*
SA Teachers Coll, Stellenbosch Univ, W Prov.
b 16.4.1886 Ceres; *d* −.
Centre, 7-6-0-1 (3 − 1t).
10 BI− BI+; 12 S+ I+ W+; 13 E+ F+.
Played with bros John & Pieter, v S W E, 12-13.
Excelled at swimming, golf, ckt & billiards. SA
ckt sel.

LYALL, George G.   *Scotland*
Gala.
b 23.5.21.
Hooker, 5-2-0-3.
47 A−; 48 F+ W− I− E+.
Plumber.

LYALL, William John Campbell   *Scotland*
Edinburgh Acad, Edinburgh Academicals.
b 27.1.1848; *d* −.
Forward, 1-1-0-0.
1871 E+.
Played in 1st int, S v E 1871. Settled in US 1871.

LYDON, Charles Thomas John   *Ireland*
Mt St Joseph's Coll Roscrea, Galwegians.

b 31.8.33 Lecanvey, Westport.
Flanker, 1-1-0-0.
56 S+.
Veterinary surg.

LYLE, Robert Knox   *Ireland*
St Andrews Coll, Trin Coll Dublin.
b 22.6.1884; *d* −.
Centre, 2-1-0-1
10 W− F+.

LYLE, Sir Thomas Ranken   *Ireland*
Coleraine AI, Trin Coll Dublin.
b 26.8.1860 Coleraine; *d* 31.3.44.
Forward, 5-0-1-4.
1885 E− S−; 1886 E−; 1887 E= S−.
University prof. Ref E v S 1887. FRS 12. Kt 22.

LYNAGH, Michael Patrick   *Australia*
Australian Schs, Qld Univ, Brisbane, Qld.
b 25.10.63 Brisbane.
Centre, 8-7-0-1 (42 − 2t 5c 1d 7p)
84 Fj+ E+(1t 2c 1p) I+(1d 1p) W+(1t) S+(3c
5p); 85 C+ C+ NZ−.
A > 83 It & F; 84 Fj; 42 pts in Tests A > 84 BI,
rec for A on tour. Equ Paul McLean's rec int
match total of 21 pts, v S 84. 98 pts in total on 84
tour. Spent childhood in US; played gridiron
football.

LYNCH, John Francis ('Sean')   *Ireland*
St Mary's Coll, Barbarians.
b 22.9.42 Dublin.
Prop, 17-7-4-6.
71 F= E− S+ W−; 72 F+ E+ F+; 73 NZ= E+
S− W−; 74 F− W= E+ S+ P= NZ−; BI > 71
NZ 4-2-1-1.
Licensee.

LYNCH, Leo Michael   *Ireland*
Castleknock Coll, Trin Coll Dublin,
Lansdowne.
b 7.5.30 Dublin.
Lock, 1-1-0-0.
56 S+.
Electrical engr.

LYNCH, Thomas William   *New Zealand*
('Tiger')
St Patrick's Coll Wellington, Celtic, S
Canterbury, Northern, Southland, S Island.
b 6.3.1892 Milton; *d* 6.5.50 Clyde.
Wing, 4-4-0-0 (12 − 4t).
13 A+(3t); 14 A+ A+(1t) A+.
Clerk/farmer. 17t NZ > 13 NAm; 16t > 14 A.
Served WW1. Father T.W. rep Otago 1888-90.
Father of T.W. (next entry).

LYNCH, Thomas William   *New Zealand*
Alexandra Dist HS, Southern, Otago, Marist,
Canterbury, S Island.

b 20.7.27 Naseby.
2nd five-eighth, 3-3-0-0 (9 − 2t 1d).
51 A+ A+(1t 1d) A+(1t).
Stock agent. Son of 'Tiger'. NZ > 51 A. Halifax
RL (E) 52-6. Grandfather Tom rep Otago.
Cousin Tom Coughlan rep NZ 58 & bro-in-law
J.F. Anderson rep Otago 58.

LYNE, Horace Sampson MBE   *Wales*
Plymouth Sch, RN Coll, Newport.
b 31.12.1860 Newport; *d* 1.5.49 Newport.
Forward, 5-1-0-4.
1883 S−; 1884 E− S− I+; 1885 E−.
Solicitor. Ref E v I 1885. With I's R.G. Warren,
longest serving IB rep, 1887-1938. WFU pres 06-
47. Freedom of Newport 32.

LYON, Arthur   *England*
Rugby Sch, Liverpool, Lancs.
b 4.8.1852; *d* 4.12.05 NZ.
Back, 1-0-0-1.
1871 S−.
Merchant. Played in 1st int, S v E 1871.

LYON, George Hamilton d'Oyly   *England*
KCB
King's Sch Bruton, HMS Britannia, US
Portsmouth, RN, Barbarians, Surrey, Hants.
b 3.10.1883 Cupra, India; *d* 20.8.47 Midhurst,
Sussex.
FB, 2-0-0-2.
08 S−; 09 A−.
RN Adm. KCB 40. Fdr mem RN RFU 06. Ckt
for RN & Hants. Served WW1, HMS Monarch
at Battle of Jutland. CB 36. KCB 40.

LYONS, D.   *South Africa*
E Prov.
1-0-0-1.
1896 BT−.

LYSTER, Patrick James   *South Africa*
CBS Kimberley, Natal.
b 31.5.13
Wing, 3-0-0-3.
33 A− A−; 37 NZ−.
Solicitor.

LYTLE, James Hill   *Ireland*
Merchiston Castle Sch, Methodist Coll Belfast,
NIFC.
b 18.5.1875 Belfast; *d* −.
Forward, 12-8-1-3 (3 − 1t).
1894 E+ S+ W+; 1895 W−; 1896 E+ S=
W+(1t); 1897 E+ S−; 1898 E+ S−; 1899 S+.
Merchant. Bro of John.

LYTLE, John N.   *Ireland*
Methodist Coll Belfast, NIFC.
Forward, 8-4-0-4 (8 − 1t 1c 1p)
1888 NZN−; 1889 W+; 1890 E−; 1891 E− S−;

1894 E+(1t) S+(1c) W+(1p).
Bro of James.

LYTTLE, Victor Johnston   *Ireland*
Methodist Coll Belfast, Collegians, Bedford,
RAF, Barbarians.
b 17.7.11 Belfast.
Wing, 3-2-0-1.
38 E−; 39 E+ S+.
Area sales mgr Kodak. Served WW2, RAF.

M

MABON, John Thomas   *Scotland*
Jedburgh GS, Jedforest.
b 13.2.1874; *d* 2.6.45 Jedburgh.
Half-back, 4-1-2-1.
1898 I+ E=; 1899 I−; 1900 I=.
Auctioneer.

MACARTHUR, J.P.   *Scotland*
Ruthin Sch, Waterloo.
SH, 1-0-0-1.
32 E−.
Timber.

MACAULAY, John   *Ireland*
Limerick.
b 1866; *d* 17.8.57.
Forward, 2-1-0-1.
1887 E+ S−.
Miller's agent. Pres IRU 1894-5. Believed to be
1st int to be married when capped.

MACBRIDE, John William   *Australia*
Terrence
The Scots Coll, NSW.
b 27.
Wing, 10-3-0-7 (3 − 1t).
46 NZ− M− NZ−(1t); 47 NZ− NZ− S+ I+
W−; 48 E+ F−.
Investments. 13t A ⊱ BI & F 47-8.

MACCALLUM, John Cameron   *Scotland*
George Watson's Coll, Watsonians.
b 1883; *d* 29.11.57.
Forward, 26-13-0-13 (22 − 2t 8c).
05 E+ NZ−(1t); 06 W− I+(2c) E− SA+; 07
W+ I+ E+; 08 W− I− E+; 09 W− I+ E+; 10
F+(3c) W− I+ E−(1c); 11 F−(1t) I− E−(1c);
12 F+ W− I− E+(1c).
Medicine.

MACDONALD, Andrew William   *South Africa*
Rhodesia.
b 27.8.34.
Flanker, 5-1-0-4.
65 A− NZ− NZ− NZ+ NZ−.
Farmer.

MACDONALD, Donald C. *Scotland*
RDVC Edinburgh, Edinburgh Univ.
b 31.
No 8/flanker, 4-0-1-3.
53 F− W−; 58 I− E=.
College lecturer.

MACDONALD, Donald Shaw *Scotland*
Mackinnon
Diocesan Coll Cape Town, Stellenbosch Univ,
Oxford Univ, London Scottish, W of Scotland.
b 25.9.51 Durban.
No 8, 7-1-0-6.
77 E− I+ F− W−; 78 I− W− E−.
Blue 74-6. Bro of D.A. Scottish XV v J 77.

MACDONALD, Dugald *South Africa*
Alexander
Oxford Univ, W Prov.
b 20.1.50 Durban.
Flanker, 1-0-0-1.
74 BI−.
Blue 75-6. Bro of Donald & Neil, Oxford Univ
capt 85.

MACDONALD, Hamish Hugh *New Zealand*
King's Coll, Ngatapa, Poverty Bay, Rangiora,
Canterbury, Lincoln Coll, Oxford, Kaikohe, N
Auckland, S & N Islands.
b 11.1.47 Rawene.
Lock, 12-7-1-4 (4 − 1t).
72 W+ S+; 73 E+ I= F− E−; 74 I+; 75 S+(1t);
76 I+ SA− SA+ SA−.
Farmer. Played in 7 out of 8 matches NZ > 74
I,W,E. NZ > 72-3 BI,F & NAm, 74 I,W & E,
76 SA. Father H.J. & bro Rod rep N Auckland.
Bro-in-law of Doug Bruce.

MACDONALD, James Alexander *Ireland*
Methodist Coll Belfast, RUI.
b 1849; *d* 23.4.28 Taunton.
Forward, 13-1-1-11.
1875 E− E−; 1877 S−; 1878 E−; 1879 S−; 1880
E−; 1881 S+; 1882 E= S−; 1883 E− S−; 1884
E− S−.
Medicine. Chmn BMA Council.

MACDONALD, John Donald *Scotland*
George Watson's Coll, RMA Sandhurst,
London Scottish, Barbarians, The Army, Comb
Servs, Hants.
b 38.
Prop, 8-4-1-3.
66 F= W− I+ E+; 67 F+ W+ I− E−.
The Army. Served with RCT. London Cos &
Comb Servs v NZ 63; SE Cos v NZ 64.

MACDONALD, James Stirling *Scotland*
Edinburgh Univ.
Wing, 5-3-0-2 (10 − 2t 2c).

03 E+; 04 W− I+(1t 2c) E+(1t); 05 W−.
Medicine. S Rhodesia medical service 13.

MACDONALD, John Mackinnon *Scotland*
OBE TD
Fettes Coll, Edinburgh W.
b −.12.1890; *d* 1.6.80 Portree.
Wing, 1-0-0-1.
11 W−.
The Army/tea planter.

MACDONALD, Keith Roy *Scotland*
Stewart's Coll, Stewart's Coll FP, Barbarians.
b 13.5.33 Dundee.
Centre, 6-2-0-4.
56 F+ W− I−; 57 W+ I− E−.

MACDONALD, Ranald *Scotland*
Coatham Sch, Edinburgh Univ, Barbarians.
b 18.1.28 Consett.
Centre, 4-2-0-2 (3 − 1t).
50 F+(1t) W− I− E+; BI > 50 NZ 1-0-0-1, A 1-
1-0-0.

MACDONALD, W.A. *Scotland*
Royal HS, Glasgow Univ.
b 1862; *d* −.
Forward, 3-2-0-1.
1889 W+; 1892 I+ E−.

MACDONALD, William Gordon *Scotland*
Oundle Sch, London Scottish, Barbarians.
b 30.12.38 Glasgow.
FB, 1-0-0-1.
69 I−r.
Co proprietor.

MACDOUGALL, Graeme Donald *Australia*
NSW.
b 40.
Prop, 2-1-0-1.
61 Fj+ SA−
Co dir. Bro of Stuart. RL.

MACDOUGALL, John Bowes *Scotland*
Greenock Acad, Glasgow Univ, Greenock W,
Wakefield.
Flanker/lock, 5-1-0-4.
13 F+; 14 I−; 21 F− I− E−.
Medicine. Played either side WW1.

MACDOUGALL, Stuart Grant *Australia*
Newington Coll, NSW, ACT.
b 1.6.47.
Prop, 8-2-1-5.
71 SA−; 73 E−; 74 NZ− NZ= NZ−; 75 E+
E+; 76 E−.
Co dir. Bro of Graeme.

MACEWAN, Ian Neven　　　　*New Zealand*
Nelson Coll, Athletic, Wellington, N Island,
Blackheath (E).
b 1.5.34 Auckland.
No 8/lock/prop, 20-14-2-4 (6 − 2t).
56 SA−; 57 A+(1t) A+; 58 A+ A− A+; 59
BI+ BI+ BI+; 60 SA− SA+ SA= SA−; 61 F+
F+ F+; 62 A+(1t) A+ A= A+.
Schoolmaster/clerk/travel
agent/PRO/bookseller. 133 apps for Wellington.
NZ > 57 A, 60 A & SA, 62 A. Played in E 63-4.
Pres NZRFU Rugby Museum.

MACEWAN, Nairn Alexander　　　*Scotland*
Morrison's Sch Crieff, Gala, Highland,
Barbarians.
b 12.12.41 Dar-es-Salaam.
Flanker, 20-9-0-11 (4 − 1t).
71 F− W− I− E+ E+; 72 F+ W− E+(1t)
NZ−; 73 F− W+ I+ E− P+; 74 W− E+ I−
F+; 75 W− E−.
Insurance. Scottish XV v Arg 73, Tg 74.

MACEWAN, Robert Kenneth　　　*Scotland*
Gillespie
Bristol GS, Clifton Coll, Cambridge Univ,
London Scottish, Lansdowne, Barbarians.
b c33 Oxford.
Hooker, 13-3-0-10.
54 F− NZ− I− W−; 56 F+ W− I− E−; 57 F+
W+ I− E−; 58 W−.
Clothiers co dir. Blue 53-4.

MACFARLAN, David James　　　*Scotland*
Loretto Sch, London Scottish.
b 1.3.1862; *d* 2.1.40 Pyford Heath, Surrey.
Back, 8-7-0-1 (4t 3c).
1883 W+(2t); 1884 W+ I+ E−; 1886 W+ I+(1t
3c); 1887 I+; 1888 I+(1t).
Merchant.

MACFARLANE, John L.H.　　　*Scotland*
Craigmount Educ Inst, Edinburgh Univ.
b c1851 Jamaica; *d* .2.1074.
Forward, 3-1-1-1.
1871 E+; 1872 E−; 1873 E=.
Medicine. Played in 1st int, v E 1871.

MACGREGOR, Duncan Grant　　　*Scotland*
George Watson's Coll, Pontypridd, Watsonians,
Barbarians.
b 20.5.1887 Pontypridd; *d* 5.10.71.
Centre, 3-3-0-0.
07 W+ I+ E+.
Draper. Scottish father. Bro of J.R. Selected as
reserve for W v S 07, decided to played for S
instead.

MACGREGOR, Gregor　　　*Scotland*
Uppingham Sch, Cambridge Univ, Barbarians.
b 31.8.1869; *d* 20.8.19.

Back, 13-8-1-4 (1t 2c).
1890 W+ I+(1t) E−(2c); 1891 W+ I+ E+; 1893
W− I= E+; 1894 W− I− E+; 1896 E+.
Blue 1889-90. Ckt for S, Mdx & E.

MACGREGOR, Ian Allan　　　*Scotland*
Alexander
Hillhead HS, Hillhead HSFP, RAF Pembrey,
Llanelli, Barbarians.
b 9.8.31 Glasgow.
Flanker, 9-4-0-5.
55 I+ E−; 56 F+ W− I− E−; 57 F+ W+ I−.
Schoolmaster. Chmn SRU sels 83-4.

MACGREGOR, John Roy　　　*Scotland*
Edinburgh Univ, Newport, Barbarians.
b 27.8.1885 Pontypridd; *d* 24.7.40.
FH, 1-1-0-0 (3 − 1t).
09 I+(1t).
Medicine. Bro of Duncan. Employed at R
Gwent Hosp, Newport, 11-12.

MACILWAINE, Alfred Herbert　　　*England*
MC DSO
Clifton Coll, Hull & ER, The Army, US
Portsmouth, Harlequins, Yorks.
b 27.3.1889; *d* − SA.
Prop/lock, 5-4-0-1.
12 W+ I+ S− F+; 20 I+.
The Army/farmer. 8 yrs between caps. Served
WW1. DSO 18; Croix de Guerre. Served WW2,
Maj commanding S Rhodesia Light Battn.
Farmed in Inyanga Mountains of Rhodesia after
leaving Army.

MACINTYRE, Ian　　　*Scotland*
Royal HS, Fettes Coll, Edinburgh Univ,
Edinburgh W.
b −.11.1869; *d* 29.6.46.
Forward, 6-5-0-1.
1890 W+ I+ E−; 1891 W+ I+ E+.
Writer to the Signet/MP. Pres SRU 1899-1900.

MACKAY, E.B.　　　*Scotland*
Glasgow Acad, Glasgow Academicals.
Wing, 2-1-0-1.
20 W+; 22 E−.

MACKENZIE, A.D.G.　　　*Scotland*
Selkirk.
Prop, 1-0-0-1.
84 A−.

MACKENZIE, Cecil James　　　*Scotland*
Granville
Inverness R Acad, RNEC Keyham, US
Portsmouth, RN.
b 26.2.1889; *d* 7.12.59.
Centre, 1-0-0-1.
21 E−.
RN.

253

MACKENZIE, David Douglas *Scotland*
Merchiston Castle Sch, Edinburgh Univ, RN,
Barbarians.
b 28.12.21.
Wing, 6-1-0-5.
47 W− I− E−; 48 F+ W− I−.
RN/HM. Outstanding athlete.

MACKENZIE, Donald Kenneth *Scotland*
Andrew
Inverness R Acad, Edinburgh W, RAF.
b 30.11.16; kia 12.6.40.
No 8, 2-0-0-2.
39 I− E−.
RAF.

MACKENZIE, James Moir *Scotland*
Fettes Coll, Edinburgh Univ, Barbarians.
b 17.10.1886 Sunderland; *d* 22.1.63 Sussex.
Forward, 9-3-0-6.
05 NZ−; 09 W− I+ E+; 10 W− I+ E−; 11 W−
I−.
Writer to the Signet. Pres SRU 48-9.

MACKENZIE, Sir Robert *Scotland*
Campbell KBE CB VD DL
Glasgow Acad, Uppingham Sch, Glasgow
Academicals, Glasgow Univ.
b 12.1.1856 Glasgow; *d* 26.5.45.
Back, 4-2-1-1 (3t 2d).
1877 I+(3t 2d) E+; 1881 I− E=.
Chartered accountant. Pres SRU 24-5.

MACHALE, Sean *Ireland*
Clongowes Coll, Lansdowne.
b 6.4.36 Ballina.
Prop, 12-5-2-5.
65 F= E+ S+ W− SA−; 66 F− E= S− W+; 67
S+ W+ F−.
Sales rep.

MACIVOR, C.V. *Ireland*
Portora RS, Trin Coll Dublin.
b 12.2.1891 W Indies; *d* −.10.13.
Wing, 7-4-0-3 (3 − 1t).
12 F+ E− S+ W+(1t); 13 E− S− F+.
Student. Died aged 22 after a kick in a practice
match at Trin Coll Dublin.

MACKIE, George Yuill *Scotland*
Highland.
b 19.4.49 Aberdeen.
No 8, 4-1-0-3.
75 A+; 76 F− W−; 78 F−.
Building constructor.

MACKIE, Osbert Gadesden *England*
Haileybury & ISC, Cambridge Univ, Wakefield
Trin, Barbarians, Yorks.
b 23.8.1869 Wakefield; *d* 25.1.27 Redcar.
Centre, 2-1-0-1.

1897 S+; 1898 I−; BT > 1896 SA.
Clergyman. Blue 1895-7. Ordained 1899.

MACKINLAY, James Egan *England*
Harrison
Rugby Sch, St George's Hosp.
b 17.12.1850 Guildford; *d* 1.7.17.
Forward, 3-2-1-0.
1872 S+; 1873 S=; 1875 I+.
Surg.

MACKINNON, Andrew *Scotland*
Rugby Sch, London Scottish.
b 30.4.1873; *d* −.
Forward, 6-3-2-1.
1898 I+ E=; 1899 I− W+ E+; 1900 E=.
Stockbroker.

MACKINTOSH, Charles Ernest *Scotland*
Whistler Christopher
Eastbourne Coll, Oxford Univ, London
Scottish.
b 31.10.03; *d* 74.
Wing, 1-0-0-1.
24 F−.
Co chmn. Blue 25. GB sprint team at Paris
Olympics 24.

MACKINTOSH, Hugh Stewart *Scotland*
CBE LlD
Helmsdale Sch, Glasgow Univ, W of Scotland,
Barbarians.
Prop/hooker, 16-6-1-9 (9 − 3t).
29 F+ W− I+ E+; 30 F− W+ I− E=; 31 F+
W− I−(1t) E+(2t); 32 SA− W− I− E−.
Dir of education for Glasgow.

MACKNEY, Walter Arthur *Australia*
Reginald
NSW.
b 20.7.03; *d* 5.10.75 Sydney.
No 8/flanker, 4-2-1-1.
33 SA− SA+; 34 NZ+ NZ=.
Police/shopkeeper. Rep A rowing Berlin
Olympics 36. Noted surf-boarder, heavywt
boxer.

MACKRELL, William Henry *New Zealand*
Clifton
Newton, Auckland, N Island.
b 20.7.1881 Milton, A; *d* 15.7.17 Auckland.
Hooker, 1-1-0-0.
06 F+.
Printer. NZ > 05 A, 05-6 BI,F & NAm. RL 07,
rep NZ 07-11. Died of paralytic seizure, aged
35.

MACKY, John Victor *New Zealand*
Bayfield Sch, Auckland GS, Univ, Auckland.

b 3.9.1887 Auckland; d 15.9.51 Auckland.
Wing, 1-1-0-0.
13 A+.
Public accountant. Served WW1. Winner of
Shaw Prize 08 for accountancy with highest
marks in NZ; entered practice with RL
administrator Grey Campbell.

MACLACHLAN, Lachlan Patrick   *Scotland*
Plumtree Sch, Oxford Univ, London Scottish,
Barbarians.
b 16.3.28.
SH, 4-0-0-4.
54 NZ− I− E− W−.
HM/architect. Blue 53.

MACLAGAN, William Edward   *Scotland*
Edinburgh Acad, Edinburgh Academicals.
b 5.4.1858; d 10.10.26.
Wing, 25-14-5-6 (3t 4c).
1878 E=; 1879 I+ E=; 1880 I+ E−; 1881 I−
E=; 1882 I+ E+; 1883 W+(3c) I+(1c) E−;
1884 W+ I+ E−; 1885 W= I+; 1887 I+(1t)
W+(1t) E=; 1888 W− I+; 1890 W+(1t) I+
E−; BT > 1891 SA.
Stockbroker. Touch-judge S v E 1894. Capt S 8
times. Capt BT > 1891 SA. Fdr mem London
Scottish. Once rec cap holder. Ckt for S.

MACLAREN, William   *England*
Manchester.
Back, 1-0-0-1.
1871 S−.
Played in 1st int, S v E 1871. Bro of James
MacLaren, RFU pres 1882-4. Uncle of A.C.
MacLaren, Lancs & England ckter. See H.T.
Gamlin.

MACLEAR, Basil   *Ireland*
Bedford Sch, RMC Sandhurst, Cork County,
Monkstown, Blackheath, Bedford, Cork
Constitution.
b 7.4.1881 Portsmouth; kia 26.5.15 Ypres.
Centre/wing, 11-5-0-6 (18 − 4t 3c).
05 E+(1t 1c) S+(1c) W− NZ−; 06 E+(1t 1c)
S− W+(1t) SA−(1t); 07 E+ S− W−.
The Army. Capt R in Dublin Fusiliers;
mentioned in despatches & Queen's Medal.
Beds co sprint champ. 4 apps v 05 NZ −
Blackheath, Bedford, Munster, Ireland. Wore
white kid gloves when playing. Played in E trial,
but rejected as 'not good enough'.

MACLENNAN, Roderick Ross   *England*
Forrest
Merchant Taylors' Sch, OMT, Headingley,
London Scottish, Mdx.
b 23.12.03 Glasgow.
Prop, 3-1-1-1.
25 I= S− F+.
Insurance broker/co dir. Ldg ref. Public Schools

middleweight boxing champ 21. Served WW2,
Intelligence Corps.

MACLENNAN, William Donald   *Scotland*
George Watson's Coll, Watsonians, Edinburgh
Univ, US Portsmouth.
b 4.4.21 Edinburgh.
Wing, 2-0-0-2.
47 F− I−.
Surgeon.

MACLEOD, Duncan Archibald   *Scotland*
Loretto Sch, Glasgow Univ.
b 12.6.1866; d 9.12.07 India.
Forward, 2-1-1-0.
1886 I+ E=.
Planter.

MACLEOD, George W.L.   *Scotland*
Edinburgh Acad, Edinburgh Academicals.
b 1860; d −.
Forward, 2-1-1-0.
1878 E=; 1882 I+.

MACLEOD, Kenneth Grant   *Scotland*
('Grunt')
Fettes Coll, Cambridge Univ.
b 2.2.1888; d 7.3.69.
Centre/wing, 10-6-0-4 (25 − 4t 2c 2p 1gm).
05 NZ−; 06 W−(1p) I+(1gm) E− SA+(1t); 07
W+ I+(1c) E+; 08 I−(1t 1c 1p) E+(2t).
17yr 9mths when capped. Blue 05-8. Played with
bro Lewis Cambridge Univ v NZ & S v NZ 05.
Univ freshmen's sprint champ. Ckt for Lancs
CCC.

MACLEOD, Lewis Macdonald   *Scotland*
Fettes Coll, Cambridge Univ, Barbarians.
b −.6.1885; d 12.11.07 Cambridge.
Centre, 6-2-0-4.
04 W− I+ E+; 05 W− I− NZ−.
Blue 03-5. Capt Camb Univ v NZ 05 with bro
Kenneth; also S v NZ 05.

MACLEOD, William Mackintosh   *Scotland*
Fettes Coll, Fettesian-Lorettonians, Edinburgh
W, Edinburgh Univ, Cambridge Univ.
b −.6.1861 Glasgow; d 30.6.31.
Forward, 2-2-0-0 (2c).
1886 W+(2c) I+.
Stockbroker. Blue 1880-2.

MACLOS, Paul   *France*
SF.
Centre, 2-0-0-2 (7 − 2c 1p).
06 E−; 07 E−(2c 1p).

MACMILLAN, Donald Ian   *Australia*
Toowoomba GS, Qld.
b 30; d 81 New Caledonia.
Flanker, 2-0-0-2.

255

50 BI− BI−.
Stock mgr.

MACMILLAN, Robert Gordon *Scotland*
Merchiston Castle Sch, London Scottish.
b 3.4.1865; *d* 3.4.36.
Forward, 21-14-1-6 (1t).
1887 I+ W+(1t) E=; 1890 W+ I+ E−; 1891
W+ E+; 1892 W+ I+ E−; 1893 W− E+; 1894
W− I− E+; 1895 W+ I+ E+; 1897 I+ E−; BT
> 1891 SA.
Lloyds underwriter. Capt S 6 times. Pres SRU
1900-1.

MACMYN, David James *Scotland*
Fettes Coll, Cambridge Univ, London Scottish,
Barbarians.
b 18.2.03; *d* 16.3.78.
Lock, 11-10-0-1 (6 − 2t).
25 F+ W+ I+(1t) E+; 26 F+(1t) W+ I− E+;
27 E+ NSW+; 28 F+.
Medicine. Blue 21-4. Pres SRU 58-9.

MACNEILL, Hugh Patrick *Ireland*
('Hugo')
Blackrock Coll, Trin Coll Dublin, Oxford Univ,
London Irish.
b 16.9.58 Dublin.
FB, 25-9-1-15 (19 − 4t 1p).
81 F−(1t) W−(1t) E−(1t) S− A−; 82 W+
E+(1t) S+ F−; 83 S+ F+ W−(1p) E+; 84 F−
W− E− A−; 85 S+ F= W+ E+; 86 F− W−
E− S−; BI > 83 NZ 3(1r)-0-0-3.
Economics student. Blue 82-3.

MACPHAIL, J.A.R. *Scotland*
Edinburgh Acad, Edinburgh Academicals,
Barbarians.
b 14.10.23.
Hooker, 2-0-0-2.
49 E−; 51 SA−.
Chartered accountant.

MACPHERSON, Donald *New Zealand/Scotland*
Gregory
Otago Univ, Otago, The London Hosp.
b 23.7.1882 Waimate, NZ; *d* 26.11.56
Waimate.
New Zealand
Wing, 1-1-0-0.
05 A+.
Scotland
Wing, 2-1-0-1 (3 − 1t).
10 I+ E−(1t).
Medicine. Capped by S when continuing
medical studies in London.

MACPHERSON, George Philip *Scotland*
Stewart CBE TD
Edinburgh Acad, Fettes Coll, Oxford Univ,
Edinburgh Academicals, Barbarians.

b 14.12.03 Newtonmore; *d* 2.3.81 Thame,
Oxon.
Centre, 26-13-3-10 (12 − 4t).
22 F= W= I+ E−; 24 W+(1t) E−; 25 F+ W+
E+; 27 F+ W+ I− E+(1t); 28 F+ W− E−; 29
I+(1t) E+; 30 F− W+ I−(1t) E=; 31 W− E+;
32 SA− E−.
Chartered accountant/merchant banker. Blue
22-4. Capt S 12 times. A clock in his memory,
given by his widow, is installed at rear of East
Stand, Murrayfield. International long jumper.

MACPHERSON, Neil Clark OBE *Scotland*
Durham Road Sch Newport, Newport.
b 26.9.1892 Cardiff; *d* 11.11.57 Newport.
Lock/flanker/prop, 7-3-0-4.
20 W+ I+ E−; 21 F− E−; 23 I+ E−; BI > 24
SA 4-0-1-3.
Haulage contractor/civil service. Played for
Newport before and after WW1. Served WW1
NAC Platoon, S Wales Borderers. Susp sine die
24 by SRU for accepting gift of gold watch from
Newport. Reinstated.

MACRAE, Duncan James MC *Scotland*
St Andrew's Univ, Barbarians.
b 4.11.14.
Centre, 9-4-0-5 (3 − 1t).
37 W+ I− E−; 38 W+ I+(1t) E+; 39 W− I−
E−; BI > 38 SA 1-0-0-1.
Medicine. Served WW2.

MACRAE, Ian Robert *New Zealand*
Rangiora HS, Marist, NZ Colts, W Coast, St
Michael's OB, Bay of Plenty, Hawkes Bay, N
Island.
b 6.4.43 Christchurch.
2nd five-eighth/centre, 17-14-0-3 (9 − 3t).
66 BI+ BI+ BI+ BI+(1t); 67 A+; 67 E+ W+
F+ S+(1t); 68 F+ F+; 69 W+ W+(1t); 70 SA−
SA+ SA− SA−.
Timber co exec. NZ > 63-4 & 67 BI,F & C. Bro
Malcolm rep W Coast 63-72.

MACSWEENEY, David Anthony *Ireland*
Rockwell Coll, Cambridge Univ, Blackrock
Coll.
b 26.1.36 Cappoquin, Co Waterford.
Flanker, 1-0-0-1.
55 S−.
Medicine/poet. Blue 57-9.

MADDEN, Michael N. *Ireland*
North Monastery Cork, Sunday's Well.
b 24.11.29 Cork.
Lock, 3-0-1-2.
55 E= S− W−.
Accountant.

MADDOCK, Hopkin Thomas   *Wales*
MC
Christ's Coll Brecon, London Welsh.
b 1881 Pontycymmer; *d* 15.12.21 Cardiff.
Wing, 6-4-0-2 (18 − 6t).
06 E+(1t) S+(1t) I−; 07 E+(2t) S−; 10 F+(2t).
London Co Council. Served WW1, died owing to effects of wounds.

MADDOCKS, Keith   *Wales*
Neath.
b 16.6.27 Resolven.
Wing, 1-0-0-1.
57 E−.
Schoolmaster.

MADGE, Richard John Palmer   *England*
Exeter Sch, Exeter, Devon.
b 19.12.14.
SH, 4-0-1-3.
48 A− W= I− S−.
Capt Devon either side of WW2. Served with RA, Middle East & It.

MADSEN, Duncan Frederick   *Scotland*
Fettes Coll, Gosforth, Barbarians.
b 16.4.47 Gosforth.
Hooker, 14-5-0-9 (4 − 1t).
74 W− E+ I− F+; 75 I+ F− W+ E−; 76 F−;
77 E− I+(1t) F− W−; 78 I−.
Solicitor. Scottish XV v Arg 73, Tg 74.

MAGEE, Joseph Thomas   *Ireland*
St Finians Coll, Navan CUS, Bective Rgrs.
b 25.3.1870 Dublin; *d* 18.5.24.
Wing/centre, 2-0-0-2.
1895 E− S−; BT > 1896 SA.
Journalist/grocer/schoolmaster. Bro of Louis.
Ref E v S 1897, 1899, E v W 1898.

MAGEE, Louis   *Ireland*
CUS Clongowes, R Dick Edinburgh, Bective Rgrs, London Irish.
b −.5.1874 Dublin; *d* 4.4.45 Dunboyne.
Half-back, 27-11-2-14 (9 − 2t 1p).
1895 E−(1t) S− W−; 1896 E+ S= W+; 1897 E+ S−; 1898 E+(1t) S− W−; 1899 E+(1p) S+ W+; 1900 E− S= W−; 01 E+ S− W−; 02 E− S+ W−; 03 E+ S− W−; 04 W+; BT > 1896 SA.
Veterinary surgeon. Bro of Joseph; bro in law of T.J. Little.

MAGINISS, R.M.   *Ireland*
Monaghan Coll, Trin Coll Dublin.
Forward, 2-0-0-2.
1875 E− E−.

MAGNANOU, Christian   *France*
RCF, Bayonne.
b 15.1.03 Bousquet l'Alles des Mines.

FB/centre/FH, 10-2-0-8 (4 − 1d).
23 E−; 25 W− E−; 26 S−; 29 S− W−; 30 S+(1d) I+ E− W−.
Took place of J. Clement v E 23 when Clement at his own request stood down because he felt he was not in form.

MAGNOL, Louis   *France*
Toulouse.
b −; *d* −.5.79 Foix.
FB, 4-0-0-4.
28 S−; 29 S− W− E−.
Pharmacist.

MAGOIS, Henri   *France*
La Rochelle.
b 1.1.47 La Rochelle.
FB, 3-0-0-3.
68 SA− SA− R−.
Accountant.

MAGRATH, Edward   *Australia*
NSW.
b 39.
Wing, 3-1-0-2 (3 − 1t).
61 Fj+(1t) SA− F−.

MAGRATH, Richard Michael   *Ireland*
Cork Constitution.
b 1877; *d* 9.10.72.
Wing, 1-0-0-1.
09 S−.
Cinema mgr/co rep. Ref F v S 28. Pres IRU 21-2.

MAGUIRE, James Richard   *New Zealand*
City, Auckland, Grafton.
b 6.2.1886 Auckland; *d* 1.12.66 Lower Hutt.
Hooker, 3-2-0-1.
10 A+ A− A+.
NZ > 10 A. Mem of Waitemata rowing crew which won NZ fours title 09.

MAGUIRE, J.F.   *Ireland*
Cork.
Forward, 1-0-0-1.
1884 S−.
Pres IRU 1897-8.

MAHONEY, Atholstan ('Tonk')   *New Zealand*
St Anne's Convent, Marist Bros' Sch Newtown, St Patrick's Coll Wellington, Konini, Bush, N Island.
b 15.7.08 Woodville; *d* 13.7.79 Pahiatua.
No 8, 4-2-0-2.
35 S+ I+ W−; 36 E−.
Farmer. NZ > 29 & 34 A, 35-6 BI & C. Played with 2nd NZEF in Egypt during WW2. Son Peter rep Wairarapa-Bush 76-7. Cousin of Charlie Quaid. Killed in motor accident.

MAHONY, Jack *Ireland*
CBC Cork, Dolphin.
b −; *d* 14.7.74.
No 8, 1-0-0-1.
23 E−.
Civil service.

MAIN, Derek R. *Wales*
St Luke's Coll, London Welsh.
b 33 Abergavenny.
Prop, 4-2-0-2.
59 E+ S− I+ F−.
Schoolmaster.

MAINS, Laurence William *New Zealand*
King's HS, Southern, NZ Jnrs, Otago.
b 16.2.46 Dunedin.
FB, 4-2-1-1 (21 − 1t 3c 4p).
71 BI+(2c 1p) BI−(1t) BI=(1c 2p); 76 I+(1p).
Real estate agent. Top scorer 132 pts NZ > 76
SA. Coached Southern in Dunedin.

MAINWARING, Haydn James *Wales*
Swansea, Barbarians, RN, London Welsh.
b 10.6.33 Swansea.
Centre, 1-0-0-1.
61 F−.
RN/bank official. Barbarians v SA 61.

MAINWARING, William T. *Wales*
E Sch Taibach, Taibach, Aberavon,
Crawshay's, Barbarians.
b 24.1.41 Port Talbot.
Lock, 6-1-1-4.
67 S− I− F− E+ NZ−; 68 E=.
Undertaker's asst/steelworker. W > 68 Arg.
Aberavon comm, sel.

MAIR, Norman George *Scotland*
Robertson
Merchiston Castle Sch, Edinburgh Univ.
b 7.10.28 Edinburgh.
Hooker, 4-1-0-3.
51 F− W+ I− E−.
Journalist. Ckt for S. Corr for 'The Scotsman'.
Wrote, narrated 'The Butcher's Legacy', BBC
documentary on story of 7s rugby. Author of
'The Year of the Thistle. S's Grand Slam 1983-
4', pub 84.

MAITLAND, Gardyne *Scotland*
Edinburgh Inst, Edinburgh Inst FP.
Wing/centre, 2-1-1-0.
1885 W= I+.
Bro of Robert.

MAITLAND, Robert *Scotland*
Edinburgh Inst, Edinburgh Inst FP.
Forward, 5-3-2-0.
1881 E=; 1882 I+ E+; 1884 W+; 1885 W=.
Bro of Gardyne.

MAITLAND, Reginald Paynter *Scotland*
Wellington Coll, RA, The Army.
b 6.3.1851; *d* 10.4.26 Bentley, Southampton.
Back, 1-0-0-1.
1872 E−.
The Army.

MAJERUS, Richard *France*
SF.
b 10.6.05 Paris.
Lock, 8-4-0-4 (6 − 2t).
28 W+; 29 I− S−; 30 S+ I+ E− G+(2t) W−.

MAJOR, John *New Zealand*
Waitara HS, Inglewood, Taranaki, N Island.
b 8.8.40 Whakatane.
Hooker, 1-1-0-0.
67 A+.
Farmer. NZ > 63-4 & 67 BI,F & C.

MAJOR, Windsor Cynwyd ('The *Wales*
Flying Carpenter')
Cwmfelin Sch, Maesteg Comp, Bridgend Tech,
Maesteg Celtic, Maesteg, Welch Rgt, London
Welsh, The Army, Comb Servs, Bridgend,
Neath, Aberavon, Glam.
b 15.6.30 Llangynwyd.
Wing, 2-1-0-1.
49 F−; 50 S+.
Carpenter/farmer. 1st match Maesteg at 16,
alongside father Gwilym, v Briton Ferry 46.
Pres Maesteg 79-86.

MALAN, Avril Stefan *South Africa*
Wonderboom HS, Stellenbosch Univ,
Transvaal.
b 9.4.37 Pretoria.
Lock, 16-8-3-5.
60 NZ+ NZ− NZ= NZ+ W+ I+; 61 E+ S+
F=; 62 BI=; 63 A+ A− A−; 64 W+; 65 I− S−.
Production mgr. SA's youngest capt, aged 23 v
NZ 3rd Test 60. Capt SA 10 times. Tour capt 60-
1 > BI, F, 65 I,S; v NZ 3rd, 4th Tests 60; A, 3rd
Test 63. Coach SA > 69-70 BI, F.

MALAN, Ewoud *South Africa*
Ben Viljoen Sch Groblersdal, Pretoria Univ, W
Transvaal, SA Univs, Barbarians, N Transvaal.
b 4.7.53 Groblersdal.
Prop/hooker, 2-1-0-1.
80 BI+r BI−.
Student. Barbarians > 79 BI.

MALAN, Gabriel Frederick *South Africa*
('Abie')
Kenhardt HS, Stellenbosch Univ, W Prov,
Transvaal.
b 18.11.35.
Hooker, 18-9-3-6 (3 − 1t).
58 F−; 60 NZ+ NZ= NZ+; 61 E+ S+ F=; 62
BI= BI+ BI+; 63 A+ A− A+(1t); 64 W+; 65

A– A– NZ– NZ–.
Agricultural adviser. SA's most capped hooker.
SA > 60-1 BI, F. Capt SA v A (3) 63; W 64.

MALAN, Piet   *South Africa*
Gymnasium GS Potchesfroom, Transvaal.
b 13.2.19 Parys.
Flanker, 1-1-0-0.
49 NZ+.
Schoolmaster.

MALBET, Jean-Claude   *France*
Agen.
b 28.8.37.
Hooker, 2-0-1-1.
67 SA– SA=.
Rep.

MALCOLM, A.G.   *Scotland*
Glasgow Univ.
Forward, 1-1-0-0.
1888 I+.

MALCOLM, Sydney James   *Australia*
NSW.
b 03.
SH, 12-7-1-4 (3 – 1t).
29 NZ+ NZ+ NZ+; 30 BI+(1t); 31 NZ–; 32
NZ+ NZ– NZ–; 33 SA– SA+; 34 NZ+ NZ=.
Oil co rep. NSW > 27-8 BI, F. Capt A > 31 NZ.

MALCOLMSON, George Leslie   *Ireland*
RAF, NIFC.
b 2.5.10 Lurgan.
FB, 7-4-0-3.
35 NZ–; 36 E+ S+ W–; 37 E– S+ W+.
RAF.

MALE, Benjamin Oswald   *Wales*
Cross Keys, Cardiff.
b 31.12.1893; *d* 23.2.75 Risca.
FB, 11-3-0-8 (15 – 6c 1p).
21 F+; 23 S–; 24 S–(2c) I–; 27 E–(1p) S–
F+(2c) I–; 28 S+(2c) I– F–.
HM. Selected v F 24 in Paris, sent home from
Paddington after WRU meeting on board train
decided to suspend him for playing for Cardiff
the previous Saturday, within week of int,
contrary to bye-laws. 3 yrs before selected
again. Capt v S & F 28.

MALEIG, Alain   *France*
Oloron, Tarbes.
b 10.7.52 Oloron.
Lock/no 8, 7-2-0-5.
79 W+ E– NZ+; 80 W– E– SA– R–.
Aircraft engr. F > 80 SA.

MALIR, Frank William Stewart   *England*
Heriot's Sch, Stanley House Bridge of Allan,
Woodhouse Grove Sch Abberley Bridge, Otley,

Barbarians, Yorks.
b 4.8.05 India; *d* 22.1.74 Boroughbridge.
Centre, 3-1-1-1.
30 W+ I– S=.
Woollen mills dyer. 1st cap with fellow Otley
player A.H. Bateston, 1st int players from
Otley.

MALLETT, N.V.H.   *South Africa*
W Prov.
No 8, 2-2-0-0 (4 – 1t).
84 SAm+(1t) SAm+.
Bro in law of Peter Whipps.

MALONE, John Hawkes   *Australia*
St Joseph's Coll, NSW.
b 12; *d* 49.
Prop, 4-1-0-3.
36 NZ– NZ– M+; 37 SA–.
Police. Killed in motorcycle accident.

MALOUF, Bruce Paul   *Australia*
St Joseph's Coll, NSW.
b 56.
Hooker, 1-0-0-1.
82 NZ–.
Suffered broken jaw NSW v NZ 80. Broke ankle
A > BI 81-2, did not play a match.

MALQUIER, Yves   *France*
Narbonne.
b 7.5.56 Sigean.
No 8, 1-1-0-0 (8 – 2t).
79 S+(2t).
Draughtsman.

MANCHESTER, John Eaton   *New Zealand*
('Jack')
Timaru Boys' HS, Christchurch, Canterbury, S
Island, Harlequins (E).
b 29.1.08 Waimate; *d* 6.9.83 Dunedin.
Flanker, 9-4-1-4 (3 – 1t).
32 A– A+ A+(1t); 34 A– A=; 35 S+ I+ W–;
36 E–.
Stock firm mgr. Canterbury v BI 30.
Contemporary at Timaru HS with Jack
Lovelock, 36 Olympics 1500m gold medallist.
NZ > 32 & 34 A, 35-6 BI & Can (capt). Coach
Otago Univ 47-52.

MANDIBLE, Edward Francis   *Australia*
St Aloysius Coll, NSW.
b 11.5.1885 Sydney; *d* 36.
Five-eighth, 3-0-1-2.
07 NZ– NZ=; 08 W–.
Plumber.

MANFIELD, Leslie DFC   *Wales*
Welsh SS, Cardiff Univ, Mountain Ash, Cardiff.
b 10.11.15 Mountain Ash.
No 8, 7-4-1-2.

39 S+ I+; 47 A+; 48 E= S+ F− I−.
Deputy HM. Played in England trial Dec 38,
then Welsh trial. Played either side of WW2.
Wales XV v Kiwis 46. Son John played for
London Welsh.

MANGLES, Roland Henry DSO   *England*
CMG CB
Marlborough Coll, Richmond, The Army,
Barbarians, Surrey.
b 9.2.1874; *d* 29.9.48.
Forward, 2-0-0-2.
1897 W− I−.
The Army. Brig Gen. Son of Ross L. Mangles,
one of only 4 civilians to win VC. Served in SA
War. DSO 02. Served WW1; mentioned in
despatches 8 times. CMG 19. CB 24.

MANLEY, Donald Charles   *England*
('Dick')
Hele's Sch Exeter, Exeter, Barbarians, Devon.
b 17.2.32.
Flanker, 4-3-1-0.
63 W+ I= F+ S+.
Cabinet maker.

MANN, B.B.   *Wales*
Cardiff.
Forward, 1-0-0-1.
1881 E−.

MANN, William Edgar DSO   *England*
Marlborough Coll, RMA Woolwich, US
Portsmouth, The Army, Surrey.
b 19.1.1885; *d* 14.2.69.
Forward, 3-1-0-2 (3 − 1t).
11 W− F+(1t) I−.
The Army/dairy farmer. Son of Sir Edward
Mann. Served WW1. DSO 17. Worcs CCC.

MANNING, John   *Australia*
Sydney HS, NSW.
Five-eighth, 1-0-0-1.
04 BT−.

MANNING, Russell Charles   *Australia*
Sylvester
Brisbane Boys Coll, Qld.
FB, 1-0-0-1.
67 NZ−.
Solicitor.

MANS, Wynand Jacobus   *South Africa*
W Prov.
b 21.2.42.
Centre, 2-0-0-2 (5 − 1t 1c).
65 I−(1t) S−(1c).
Rep. SA > 65 A, NZ. 123 career pts for SA.

MANSFIELD, Brian William   *Australia*
NSW.
b 48.
Lock, 1-1-0-0.
75 J+.
Agricultural inspector.

MANTELL, Neil Dennington   *England*
Reigate GS, Rosslyn Pk.
b 13.10.53.
Lock, 1-0-0-1.
75 A−.
Accountant.

MANTEROLA, Thomas   *France*
Lourdes.
No 8/prop, 2-2-0-0.
55 It+; 57 R+.

MANTLE, John T.   *Wales*
Welsh Loughborough Coll, Newport.
Flanker/no 8, 2-0-1-1.
64 E= SA−.
W > 64 SA. St Helens RL 64, Salford, Leigh,
Barrow, Keighley, Cardiff. 13 GB RL Tests 66-
73. 16 Wales RL Tests 68-78. 3 RL Cup Finals
for St Helens, all won.

MANTOULAN, Claude   *France*
Pau.
b 5.3.36 Pau; *d* 9.11.83 Perpignan.
FH, 1-0-0-1.
59 I−.
Switched to RL.

MARAIS, Franswa Pierre ('Buks')   *South Africa*
Boland.
b 13.12.27 Worcester, Cape Prov.
Wing, 5-4-0-1 (10 − 1t 2c 1p).
49 NZ+ NZ+; 51 S+; 53 A+(1t 1c 1p) A−(1c).
Salesman. SA > 51-2 BI, F.

MARAIS, Johannes Frederick   *South Africa*
Klopper ('Hannes')
W Prov, E Prov.
b 21.9.41 Somerset E.
Prop, 35-19-5-11 (3 − 1t).
63 A−; 64 W+(1t) F−; 65 I− S− A−; 68 BI+
BI= BI+ BI+ F+ F+; 69 A+ A+ A+ A+; 69-
70 S− E− I= W=; 70 NZ+ NZ− NZ+ NZ+;
71 F+ F= A+ A+ A+; 74 BI− BI− BI− BI=
F+ F+.
Agricultural counsellor. SA's most capped prop.
Capt SA 11 times. Tour capt SA > 71 A, 74 F; v
F (2) 71; BI (4) 74. Played prop with J.L.
Myburgh for SA in 16 Tests. 75 career apps for
SA.

MARCET, Jean   *France*
Albi.

Hooker, 7-0-0-7.
25 I− NZ− S− W− E−; 26 I− E−.

MARCHAL, Jean-François *France*
Lourdes.
b 16.12.49 Paris.
Lock, 5-3-0-2 (4 − 1t).
79 S+ R+; 80 W−(1t) S− I+.
Hotelier.

MARCHAND, Robert *France*
Poitiers.
Hooker, 2-0-0-2.
20 S− W−.

MARE, Dietlof Siegfredt *South Africa*
Transvaal.
b −; *d* 14.10.13.
Forward, 1-0-0-1.
06 S−.
Lawyer. Named as half-back for SA > 06-7 BI,
F, played 9 times as forward in 12 tour apps. 22
pts SA v F, unofficial int, Paris 07. Wrote 1st
book on rugby in Afrikaans, 'Hints on Rugby
Football', 07. Killed in motor accident.

MARGRAVE, Frederick *Wales*
Lofthouse
Llanelli.
b 25.12.1858 Llanelli; *d* 1.1.46 Llanelli.
Forward, 2-0-0-2.
1884 E− S−.
Wine merchant. Sec Llanelli 1876.

MARKENDALE, Ellis T. *England*
Uppingham Sch, Manchester Rgrs, Lancs.
b −.11.1856; *d* −.
Forward, 1-1-0-0 (1t).
1880 I+(1t).
Hide & skin dealer.

MARKS, Hyram A. *Australia*
NSW.
b 8.6.1872; *d* 57
Forward, 2-1-0-1.
1899 BT+ BT−.
Schoolmaster.

MARKS, Richard James Pickett *Australia*
Brisbane GS, Brisbane Univ, Qld.
b 6.9.42 Bundaberg.
Centre, 17-8-0-9 (3 − 1t).
62 NZ− NZ−; 63 E+ SA+ SA+ SA−; 64 NZ−
(1t) NZ− NZ+; 65 SA+ SA+; 66 W+ S−; 67
E+ I− F− I−.
Clerk. ARU nat dir of coaching.

MAROCCO, Philippe *France*
Montferrand.
b 14.6.60 Saverdun.
Prop, 5-4-0-1 (4 − 1t).

85 J+; 86 S− I+ (1t) W+ E+.
France B v W 85.

MAROT, Alain ('Caly') *France*
Brive.
b 11.3.48 Bergerac.
Centre/FB/FH, 7-4-0-3.
69 R+; 70 S+ I+ W−; 71 SA−; 72 I−; 76 A+.
Business.

MARQUES, Reginald William *England*
David
Yandle Court Sch, Tonbridge Sch, Cambridge
Univ, RE, The Army, Comb Servs, Harlequins,
Herts, Barbarians, Surrey.
b 9.12.32 Hertford.
Lock, 23-13-5-5 (3 − 1t).
56 W− I+ S+ F−; 57 W+ I+ F+ S+; 58 W=
A+ I+ F+ S=; 59 W− I+ F= S=; 60 W+
I+(1t) F= S+; 61 SA− W−.
Refinery engr/manufacturer. Blue 54-7. Mother
from Llanelli. Ptn John Currie in 22 consec ints.
Rugby at Tonbridge directed by L. Bruce-
Lockhart. Herts CCC. Crewman on yacht
'Sovereign' in America's Cup challenge 66.

MARQUESUZAA, Arnaud ('Le *France*
Bison')
RCF.
b 14.6.34 St Palais.
Centre, 10-7-3-0 (3 − 1t).
58 It+ SA= SA+; 59 S+ E= It+ W+; 60 S+
E= Arg+(1t).
Electrical engr.

MARQUIS, John Campbell *England*
Birkenhead Pk, Barbarians.
b 1876; *d* − 28.1.28 Birkenhead.
SH, 2-1-1-0.
1900 I+ S=.
Shipping.

MARRACQ, Henri *France*
Pau
Flanker, 1-0-1-0.
61 R=.

MARRIOTT, Charles John Bruce *England*
Blackheath Proprietary Sch, Tonbridge Sch,
Cambridge Univ, Gipsies, Blackheath, Mdx.
b 15.7.1861 Rensham, Suffolk; *d* 25.12.36
Ipswich.
Forward, 7-5-1-1.
1884 W+ I+ S+; 1886 W+ I+ S=; 1887 I−.
Schoolmaster/landowner. Blue 1881-3. Rep
Cambridge on RFU 1897-07. IB mem 1899. Sec
RFU 07-24. Sec of Queen's Club. Originated a
rugby annual 13. Served WW1, Capt in RASC.

MARRIOTT, Ernest Edward *England*
Rugby Sch, Manchester, Lancs.

b 15.1.1857; *d* 17.
Forward, 1-1-0-0.
1875 I+.
Bus. Son of Henry Marriott, fdr & 1st pres
Manchester club 1860.

MARRIOTT, Victor Robert   *England*
Balham GS, Harlequins, The Army, Comb
Servs, London Cos, Surrey.
b 29.1.38.
Flanker, 4-0-0-4.
63 NZ– NZ– A–; 64 NZ–.
Auditor/computer salesman.

MARSBERG, Arthur Frederick   *South Africa*
W.
Griq W.
b 1883 Sterkstroom; *d* –.3.42.
FB/wing, 3-1-1-1.
06 S– W+ E=.
Theatre employee. Named as understudy to
Arthur Burmeister SA > 06-7 BI, F; became no
1 choice when Burmeister broke rib early in
tour. Known as 'The Lion of the Plains'. Bro of
Peter.

MARSBERG, Peter A.   *South Africa*
Griq W.
1-1-0-0.
10 BI+.
Bro of Arthur.

MARSDEN, George Herbert   *England*
Fylde, Morley, Yorks.
b 16.10.1880 Morley; *d* 7.7.48 Lytham St
Annes.
FH, 3-1-1-1.
1900 W– I+ S=.
Co sec. Fdr mem Fylde. Bradford RL 1900.

MARSDEN-JONES, Douglas   *Wales*
CBE
Bishop Gore GS Swansea, UC Swansea,
Cardiff, London Welsh.
b 1894; *d* 5.1.55 London.
No 8/lock, 2-0-0-2.
21 E–; 24 NZ–; BI > 24 SA 2-0-0-2.
Business mgr/civil engr. Served WW1 Glos
Yeomanry, Tank Corps. Dir of Factories Min of
Supply WW2. Later mgr labour relations div
Ford Motor Co. CBE 52.

MARSH, Henry CIE   *England*
Rev Dr Stacpoole's Sch Kingstown (I), RIE
Coll.
b 8.9.1850; *d* 25.4.39.
Forward, 1-0-1-0.
1873 S=.
Civil engr. Posts in India, Mexico & Arg. CIE
1900.

MARSH, James H.   *Scotland/England*
Edinburgh Inst, Edinburgh Inst FP, Edinburgh
Univ, Swinton.
Scotland
Wing, 2-2-0-0.
1889 W+ I+.
England
Centre, 1-1-0-0.
1892 I+.
Medicine. Only player capped by S & E.

MARSHALL, Arthur   *Scotland*
Edinburgh Acad, Loretto Sch, Edinburgh
Academicals.
b 27.4.1855; *d* 9.12.09.
Forward, 1-0-1-0.
1875 E=.
Tea & coffee planter.

MARSHALL, Brian David   *Ireland*
Edward
Campbell Coll, Queen's Univ Belfast.
b 25.7.40 Egypt.
FB, 1-0-1-0.
63 E=.
Dental surgeon.

MARSHALL, Howard OBE   *England*
Elham Sch, Cambridge Univ, Barnard Castle,
Sunderland, Bart's Hosp, Blackheath,
Barbarians, London, Kent.
b 20.12.1870 Sunderland; *d* 9.10.29
Westminster.
Half-back, 1-0-0-1 (6 – 3t).
1893 W–(3t); BTuncap > 1891 SA.
Medicine. 8t 1gm BT > 1891 SA. Surg to
Circencester Hosp. OBE 20.

MARSHALL, John Campbell   *Scotland*
Rugby Sch, Oxford Univ, London Scottish,
Barbarians.
b 30.1.29.
FB, 5-0-0-5.
54 F– NZ– I– E– W–.
Schoolmaster. Blue 53.

MARSHALL, John Samuel   *Australia*
NSW.
b 21.3.26.
Wing, 1-0-0-1.
49 M–.

MARSHALL, Kenneth Walker   *Scotland*
Edinburgh Acad, Edinburgh Academicals, TA,
Barbarians.
b 23.7.11 Kimberley, SA.
FB, 8-2-0-6.
34 W– I+ E–; 35 W– I– E+; 36 W–; 37 E–.
Ckt for S.

MARSHALL, Murray Wyatt *England*
Wellington Coll, Blackheath, Surrey.
b 1853; *d* 28.7.30.
Forward, 10-6-3-1.
1873 S=; 1874 S+; 1875 I+ S= I+; 1876 S+;
1877 I+ S−; 1878 S= I+.
Timber merchant. Once E's rec cap holder.
Mem of Surrey CCC comm.

MARSHALL, Robert Mackenzie *England*
DSC
Giggleswick Sch, Oxford Univ, Scarborough,
Harlequins, Barbarians.
b 18.5.17; kia 12.5.45.
Lock, 5-3-0-2 (3 − 1t).
38 I+(1t) S−; 39 W+ I− S+.
RNVR. Blue 36-8. Served WW2, Lt in RNVR.
Bar to DSC.

MARSHALL, Thomas Roger *Scotland*
Edinburgh Acad, Edinburgh Academicals,
Edinburgh Univ.
b 26.6.1849; *d* 27.6.13 Penton, Carlisle.
Back, 4-1-1-2.
1871 E+; 1872 E−; 1873 E=; 1874 E−.
Coffee planter. Played in 1st int, S v E 1871.
With bro William v E 1872. Ckt for S.

MARSHALL, William *Scotland*
Edinburgh Academicals.
b 22.6.1852; *d* −.10.07.
Forward, 1-0-0-1.
1872 E−.
Coffee planter. With bro T.R. v E 1872.

MARTHEZE, W.C. ('Rajah') *South Africa*
Griq W.
b 1878.
Forward, 3-2-1-0.
03 BT=; 06 I+ W+.

MARTIN, Allan Jeffrey *Wales*
Sandfields Comp, Cardiff Coll, Aberavon,
Penarth, Barbarians.
b 11.12.48 Port Talbot.
Lock, 34-23-1-10 (25 − 1t 3c 5p).
73 A+; 74 S+ I=; 75 F+ E+(1c 2p) S− I+
A+(1c); 76 E+(1p) S+ I+(1p) F+(1p); 77 I+
F− E+ S+; 78 E+ S+ I+ F+ A− A− NZ−; 79
S+ I+(1t) F− E+(1c); 80 F+ E− S+ I− NZ−;
81 I+ F−; BI > 77 NZ 1-0-0-1; 80 SA.
Finance co rep/business. Bro in law of Les
Keen. W's most capped lock. Wales B v F 72,
73. W > 73 Can; 75 Far East; 78 A. Wales XV v
J 73; Tg 74; R 79. Barbarians v A 76. Partnered
Geoff Wheel 28 times. Over 600 apps for
Aberavon 65-85.

MARTIN, Charles *France*
Lyon.

SH, 3-0-0-3.
09 I−; 10 W− S−.

MARTIN, Chris R. *England*
Bath.
FB, 4-1-1-2.
85 F= S+ I− W−.

MARTIN, Harry J. ('Kalfie') *South Africa*
Grey Coll Bloemfontein, Transvaal.
b 10.6.10.
Prop, 1-1-0-0.
37 A+.
General SA Army/Ch of Staff SAAF.

MARTIN, Henri *France*
SBUC.
b 29.8.1888 Bordeaux; *d* −.
Centre/FB, 2-0-0-2.
07 E; 08 W−.

MARTIN, Hugh DSO *Scotland*
Edinburgh Acad, George Watson's Coll,
Edinburgh Academicals, Oxford Univ,
Barbarians.
b 9.4.1888; *d* 6.1.70.
Wing, 5-2-0-3.
08 W− I− E+; 09 W− E+.
In bus in Shanghai. Blue 07-9. Served WW1;
DSO 17.

MARTIN, Jean-Louis *France*
Béziers.
b 17.4.48 Béziers.
Prop, 4-2-0-2.
71 A+ R+; 72 S− I−.
Chemist/physicist.

MARTIN, Lucien *France*
Pau.
b 28.9.20 Pau.
Hooker, 6-3-0-3.
48 I− A+ S− W+ E+; 50 S−.

MARTIN, Michael Clayton *Australia*
Parramatta, Sydney, NSW.
b 5.5.56.
Wing, 6-4-0-2 (8 − 2t).
80 Fj+(1t) NZ+(1t) NZ−; 81 F+ F+ W−r.
Building contractor. A > 80 Fj; 81-2 BI.

MARTIN, Nicholas O. *England*
Cambridge Univ, Harlequins, Bedford.
b 46.
Lock, 1-0-0-1.
72 F−r.
Blue 65-7.

MARTIN, Walter John DCM *Wales*
Newport HS, Newport.

263

b 14.5.1883 Woodford, Essex; *d* 30.4.33
Newport.
FH, 3-1-0-2 (8).
12 I− F+; 19 NZA−.
Rly official. Served WW1 S Wales Borderers. 7
yrs between caps.

MARTINDALE, Samuel Airey　　*England*
Kendal, Cumberland & Westmorland.
b 5.5.05.
Lock, 1-1-0-0.
29 F+; BI > 30 A, NZ.
Joiner/co dir. County water polo player.

MARTINE, Roger ('Bichon')　　*France*
Lourdes.
b 3.1.30 Bellocq.
Centre/FH, 25-20-2-3 (6 − 1t 1d).
52 S+ I− It+; 53 It+; 54 S+ I+ NZ+ W−(1t)
E+ It+ Arg+; 55 S+ I+ W−; 58 A+ W+ It+
I+ SA= SA+(1d); 60 S+ E= Arg+; 61 S+ It+.
Electricity Board. F > 58 SA.

MARTINEZ, Gérald　　*France*
Toulouse.
b 30.3.55 Montréjeau.
SH, 7-4-0-3 (3 − 1p).
82 W−(1p) E− S− Arg+ Arg+; 83 E+ W+.
Dir of swimming pool. France B v W,S 75; Cz
77. France A v G 75; Poland 77.

MAS, Francis　　*France*
Béziers.
b 8.11.38 Cazouls les Béziers.
Prop, 5-2-0-3.
62 R−; 63 S− I+ E− W+.
Transport business. RL.

MASO, Joseph Jean　　*France*
Lycée Arago Perpignan, Marseilles Univ,
Perpignan, Narbonne.
b 27.12.44 Toulouse.
Centre/FH, 25-12-2-11 (15 − 4t).
66 It+(1t) R+; 67 S− R+; 68 S+ W+ Cz+
NZ− NZ− NZ− A− R−; 69 S− I− W=; 71
SA− SA= R+(1t); 72 E+ W− A+(2t); 73 W+
I− J+ R+.
Rep/men's fashion shop proprietor.

MASON, David Frank ('Tim')　　*New Zealand*
Wellington Coll, Wellington Coll OB,
Wellington.
b 21.11.23 Wellington.
Wing, 1-1-0-0 (3 − 1t).
47 A+r(1t).
Insurance co exec. NZ > 47 A. Moved to SA 47.

MASSARE, Jean　　*France*
PUC.
Prop, 6-4-0-2 (3 − 1t).
45 BF+ BF−(1t) W−; 46 BF+ I+ W+.

MASSÉ, Alphonse　　*France*
SBUC.
Forward, 7-0-0-7.
08 W−; 09 E− W−; 10 W− S− E− I−.

MASSÉ, Henri　　*France*
Grenoble.
FB, 1-1-0-0.
37 G+.

MASSEY, Edward John　　*England*
Ampleforth Coll, Liverpool, Leicester,
Barbarians, Lancs, Leics.
b 2.7.1900; *d* 30.4.40 Woking.
SH, 3-1-1-1.
25 W+ I= S−.
Merchant/farmer. Broke collarbone v S 25.
Overseas pre-WW2; served in RASC.

MASSEY-WESTROPP, Montagu　　*Australia*
King's Sch Parramatta, Glebe, NSW.
b 1891; *d* 74.
Wing, 1-0-0-1.
14 NZ−.
Post Office clerk.

MASSEY-WESTTROPP, R.H.　　*Ireland*
Limerick, Monkstown.
Forward, 1-0-0-1.
1886 E−.

MASTERS, Robin Read　　*New Zealand*
Awatere, Oriental, Albion, Canterbury, S
Island.
b 19.10.1900 Picton; *d* 24.8.67 Christchurch.
No 8, 4-4-0-0.
24 I+ W+; 25 E+ F+.
Clerk. NZ > 24-5 BI,F & C. Illness enforced
retirement 25. Various administrative posts, inc
NZ sel 49 & NZRFU pres 55. Editor of 'Rugby
Almanack of NZ' 35-67.

MASTERS, William Hay　　*Scotland*
Royal HS, Dollar Acad, Edinburgh Inst,
Edinburgh Inst FP.
Half-back, 3-2-0-1 (1t).
1879 I+; 1880 I+(1t) E−.

MATAIRA, Hawea Karepa　　*New Zealand*
Nuhaka Native Sch, Maori Agric Coll, Nuhaka,
Hawkes Bay, NZ Maoris.
b 3.12.10 Nuhaka; *d* 15.11.79 Wairoa.
No 8, 1-0-1-0.
34 A=.
Farmer. NZ > 34 A. City R RL 37 & NZ > 39
BI. Served WW2; played RU in Egypt.

MATHERS, Michael John　　*Australia*
Sydney GS, Sydney, NSW.
b 1.3.55.
Lock, 2-1-0-1.

80 Fj+ NZ−r.
Agric teacher. Mem of 1st A Schs touring side, > 73-4 BI. Capt Sydney & NSW. A > 79 Arg; 80 Fj; 81-2 BI. Australian Player of Year 81.

MATHESON, Jeffrey David　　　*New Zealand*
Waitaki Boys' HS, Lincoln Coll, Pirates, Otago, Maheno, N Otago, S Island.
b 30.3.48 Palmerston.
Prop, 5-5-0-0.
72 A+ A+ A+ W+ S+.
Farmer. NZ > 72-3 BI,F & NAm (inj v S ruled him out of rest of tour). Coach N Otago 77-80.

MATHEU, Jean　　　*France*
Agen, Castres.
b 23.6.20 Gelos.
Flanker, 24-14-0-10 (3 − 1t).
45 W−; 46 BF+ I+ NZS− W+; 47 S+ I+ W− E−; 48 I− A+ S− W+ E+; 49 S− I+ E− W+ Arg+ Arg+; 50 E+ W−; 51 S+ I−(1t).

MATHEWS, Alfred Augustus　　　*Wales*
Christ's Hosp, Llandovery Coll, St David's Coll Lampeter, Lampeter.
b 7.2.1864 Rhymney; *d* 12.8.46 Malpas.
Half-back, 1-0-0-1.
1886 S−.
Minister. Ordained deacon 1887, priest 1888. Rural Dean Newport 30-33; Canon Newport Cathedral 30-39.

MATHIAS, John Lloyd　　　*England*
Bristol, Glos.
b 1878; *d* 21.11.40.
Prop/lock, 4-0-0-4.
05 W− I− S− NZ−.
Rep. Bristol v NZ 05. 187 apps for Bristol.

MATHIAS, Roy　　　*Wales*
Stebonheath Sch, Welsh Youth, Welsh SS, Felinfoel, Llanelli.
b 2.9.49 Llanelli.
Wing, 1-1-0-0.
70 F+.
Electrician. St Helens RL 72. 1 GB RL Test. 20 Wales RL.

MATIER, R.N.　　　*Ireland*
NIFC.
Back, 2-0-0-2.
1878 E−; 1879 S−.

MATTERS, John Charles　　　*England*
RNEC Keyham, Barbarians, Devon.
b 1879; *d* 24.4.49 Oxted, Surrey.
Wing, 1-0-0-1.
1899 S−.
RN. Engr Rear Adm. Served WW1. Rugby career interrupted by overseas posting.

MATTHEWS, Christopher　　　*Wales*
Bridgend, Cardiff.
b −; *d* 60.
Wing, 1-1-0-0.
39 I+.
Commission agent. Won Powderhall Sprint 32.

MATTHEWS, Jack OBE　　　*Wales*
Bridgend CS, Welsh SS, Cardiff Univ, Cardiff, The Army, Barbarians.
b 21.6.20 Bridgend.
Centre/wing, 17-9-2-6 (12 − 4t).
47 E− A+; 48 E= S+(1t) F+; 49 E+ S− I− F−; 50 E+ S+ I+ F+(1t); 51 E+(2t) S− I= F− ; BI > 50 NZ 4-0-1-3, A 2-2-0-0.
Medicine. Welsh SS sprint champ. 5 'Victory' ints. Hon physician to WRU. Medical officer BI > 80 SA.

MATTHEWS, John Robert Clive　　　*England*
Sutton Valence Sch, Guy's Hosp, RN, Comb Servs, Harlequins, Barbarians, London Cos, Mdx.
b 14.6.22 Hastings.
Lock, 10-6-0-4.
49 F+ S+; 50 I+ F− S−; 52 SA− W− S+ I+ F+.
Dental surg. Capt London Cos v SA 52, the tourists' only defeat. Served WW2, Surg Lt RNVR, Arctic convoys, stationed at Murmansk & Naval Mission to Moscow 44-5.

MATTHEWS, Philip Michael　　　*Ireland*
Regent House, Irish Schs, Queen's Univ Belfast, Ards, Ulster.
b 24.1.60 Gloucester.
Flanker, 5-0-0-5.
84 A−; 85 S− F− W− E−.
1st player capped from Ards.

MATTSSON, John Alfred　　　*Ireland*
Middleton Coll, Mountjoy Sch, Wanderers.
FB, 1-1-0-0.
48 E+.

MAUD, Philip CMG CBE　　　*England*
Leamington Coll, RMC Woolwich, RE, Blackheath, Barbarians, Kent.
b 8.8.1870; *d* 28.2.47.
Forward, 2-1-0-1.
1893 W− I+.
The Army. Reached rank of Brig Gen. Served NW Frontier 1889. CMG 03. Served WW1. CBE 19. With Frank Stout & M.P. Atkinson, holds rec of 24 apps for Barbarians. Chief officer London Co Council Parks Dept.

MAUDUY, Gérard　　　*France*
Périgueux.
b 10.12.37 Périgueux.
Wing, 7-5-0-2 (6 − 2t).

57 It+(2t) R+ R+; 58 S− E−; 61 W+ It+.
Draughtsman.

MAUND, John Williams   *Australia*
All Saints Coll Bathurst, NSW.
b 1876; *d* 62.
FB, 1-0-0-1.
03 NZ−.
Solicitor.

MAURAN, Jacques   *France*
Castres.
b 29.
Centre, 6-1-0-5.
52 SA− W− E− It+; 53 I− E−.
Notary.

MAURIAT, Paul   *France*
Lyon.
b 27.5.1887 Neuville sur Saone.
Forward, 19-1-0-18 (2 − 1c).
07 E−; 08 E− W−; 09 W− I−(1c); 10 W− S−
E− I−; 11 S+ E− W− I−; 12 I− S−; 13 S−
SA− W− I−.
Commercial agent.

MAURIN   *France*
SF.
Forward, 1-0-0-1.
06 E−.

MAURONVAL, Francis   *France*
SF.
Wing, 1-0-0-1.
09 I−

MAURY, André   *France*
Toulouse.
Prop,8-0-0-8.
25 I− NZ− S− W− E−; 26 S− I− E−.

MAX, Donald Stanfield   *New Zealand*
Hope Sch, Nelson Coll, Nelson Coll OB,
Nelson, Brightwater Pirates, S Island.
b 7.3.07 Nelson; *d* 4.3.72 Brightwater.
Flanker, 3-1-1-1 (3 − 1t).
31 A+; 34 A−(1t) A=.
Farmer. NZ > 32 (inj limited him to 2 apps) &
34 A. NZRFU pres 49. Bro L. Max rep Nelson.
Rep Nelson at ckt & golf. Governor Nelson Coll
& Lincoln Coll; mem of Nelson Harbour Bd.

MAXWELL, Andrew William   *England*
Caldy Grange GS, New Brighton, Headingley.
b 3.3.51 West Kirby.
Centre, 7-1-0-6.
75 A−; 76 A+ W− S− I− F−; 78 F−.
Rep.

MAXWELL, F.T.   *Scotland*
RMA Sandhurst, RE.

b 10.1.1849; *d* 15.1.1881.
Forward, 1-0-0-1.
1872 E−.
The Army.

MAXWELL, Georgius Henry   *Scotland*
Hope Patrick
Sedbergh Sch, Edinburgh Acad, Edinburgh
Academicals, Edinburgh Univ, RAF, London
Scottish.
b 18.10.1892; *d* 21.2.61.
Prop/hooker/flanker, 13-3-1-9 (7 − 2c 1p).
13 I+ E−; 14 W− I− E−; 20 W+ E−; 21 F−
W+(1c 1p) I−(1c) E−; 22 F= E−.
Gp Capt, RAF Medical Service.

MAXWELL, James Macmillan   *Scotland*
Langholm, Barbarians.
b 30.4.32.
FH, 1-0-0-1.
57 I−.
Builder & plasterer.

MAXWELL-HYSLOP, John   *England*
Edgar
Wellington Coll, Oxford Univ, Richmond,
Sussex.
b 31.3.1899.
Prop/flanker, 3-2-1-0.
22 I+ F= S+.
HM. Blue 20-2. Served WW1, 2nd Lt RFA.
Head Rottingdean Sch 23-61. Served WW2 with
RAF, fitter & Intelligence.

MAYNARD, Alfred Frederick   *England*
Seaford Sch, Durham Sch, Cambridge Univ,
Harlequins, Durham City, Durham Cos.
b 23.3.1894 Anerley, Kent; kia 13.11.16
Beaumont Hamel.
Hooker, 3-3-0-0.
14 W+ I+ S+.
RNVR. Blue 12-13. Durham CCC.

MAYNE, R.H.   *Ireland*
Belfast Acad.
Forward, 2-1-0-1.
1888 W+ S−.

MAYNE, Robert Blair DSO   *Ireland*
Regent House Newtownards, Queen's Univ
Belfast, The Army, Barbarians.
b 11.1.15 Newtownards; *d* 14.12.55 nr
Newtownards.
Lock, 6-3-0-3 (3 − 1t).
37 W+; 38 E−(1t) W−; 39 E+ S+ W−; BI > 38
SA 3-1-0-2.
Lawyer/The Army. Served WW2; DSO & 3 bars
& Legion d'Honneur. Died in car accident.

MAYNE, Thomas   *Ireland*
RBAI, NIFC.

SH, 3-1-0-2.
21 E− S+ F−.
Co dir.

MAYS, Kevin Michael Andrew　　*Ireland*
St Paul's Coll Raheny, UC Dublin.
b 9.8.49 London.
Lock, 4-1-1-2.
73 NZ= E+ S− W−.
Accountant.

MAYSONNIE, Alfred ('Gastofer')　　*France*
Toulouse.
b 10.4.1884 Lavernosse; kia 16 Verdun.
SH, 3-0-0-3.
08 E− W−; 10 W−.
Artisan.

MCALLAN, George Herbert　　*Ireland*
RS Dungannon, Dungannon.
b 1878; *d* 1.2.18 Johannesburg.
FB, 2-1-1-0.
1896 S= W+.
Schoolmaster/bank official. 1st schoolboy to
play for I.

MCARTHUR, Malcolm　　*Australia*
NSW.
b 30.7.1884; *d* −.
No 8, 1-1-0-0.
09 E+.
Insurance. Olympic rugby gold medal 08.

MCATAMNEY, Francis Stevens　　*New Zealand*
Strath Taieri HS, St Kevin's Coll, Strath Taieri,
Otago, S Island.
b 15.5.34 Middlemarch.
Prop, 1-0-0-1.
56 SA−.
Farmer. NZ > 57 A. Coach Ranfurly 60-2 &
Geraldine 71-9.

MCBAIN, Mark Ian　　*Australia*
Brothers, Brisbane, Qld.
b 3.10.59 Qld.
Hooker, 3-2-1-0.
83 It+ F=; 85 Fj+.
Student. A Under 21s 81. A > 83 It & F
(fractured skull v F); 84 Fj; 84 BI. Sent off (with
ex-E hooker Peter Wheeler) A v Midlands, 84.

MCBRIDE, William James　　*Ireland*
('Willie John')
Ballymena Acad, Ballymena, Abertillery,
Barbarians.
b 6.6.40 Toombridge, Co Antrim.
Lock, 63-27-10-26 (4 − 1t).
62 E− S− F− W=; 63 F− E= S− W+ NZ−; 64
E+ S− F−; 65 F= E+ S+ W− SA−; 66 F− E=
S− W+; 67 A+ E− S+ W+ F− A+; 68 F− E=
S+ W+ A+; 69 F+ E+ S+ W−; 70 SA= F−

E− S+ W+; 71 F= E− S+ W−; 72 F+ E+ F+;
73 NZ= E+ S− W− F+; 74 F− W= E+ S+ P=
NZ−; 75 E+ S− F+(1t) W−; BI > 62 SA 2-0-0-
2; 66 A, NZ 3-0-0-3; 68 SA 4-0-1-3; 71 A, NZ 4-
2-1-1; 74 SA 4-3-1-0.
Bank official. World's most capped lock, 80 (inc
rec 17 BI Test apps). Capt BI > 74 SA. Mgr BI
> 83 NZ.

MCCABE, Arthur John Michael　　*Australia*
NSW.
b 1887 Tamworth; *d* −.5.25.
Five-eighth, 1-1-0-0.
09 E+.
Clerk. Olympic rugby gold medal 08. RL.

MCCALL, Barney Ernest Wilford　　*Wales*
MC
Weymouth Sch, RMC, Welch Rgt, Newport.
b 13.5.13 Clifton.
Wing, 3-2-1-0.
36 E= S+ I+.
The Army. Served WW2. Ckt The Army 36,
Minor Counties 48.

MCCALL, B.W.　　*Ireland*
London Irish.
No 8/lock, 3-0-1-2 (4 − 1t).
85 Fr=; 86 E−(1t) S−.
The Army.

MCCALLAN, Barton　　*Ireland*
RBAI, Queen's Univ Belfast, Ballymena.
b 18.7.36 Belfast.
Hooker, 2-0-0-2.
60 E− S−.
Industrial exec.

MCCALLUM, Ian Duncan　　*South Africa*
Cape Town Univ, W Prov.
b 30.7.44 K'Kana, Zambia.
FB, 11-7-1-3 (62 − 10c 14p).
70 NZ+(1c 2p) NZ−(1c 1p) NZ+(1c 2p)
NZ+(1c 4p); 71 F+(?c 3p) F=(1c) A+(?c 1p)
A+(1c 1p) A+; 74 BI− BI−.
Medicine. Played with bro Roy v BI, 1st Test 74.
35 pts (inc 65y p) SA v NZ 70, rec for SA v
NNZ. 84pts SA > 71 A. 134 career pts for SA.

MCCALLUM, Roy James　　*South Africa*
W Prov.
b 12.4.46 Kitwe, Zambia.
SH, 1-0-0-1.
74 BI−.
Medicine. SA > 74 F. Played with bro Ian v BI,
1st Test 74.

MCCANLIS, Maurice Alfred　　*England*
Cranleigh Sch, Oxford Univ, O Cranleighans,
Gloucester, Northampton, Barbarians, Glos.
b 17.6.06 Quetta, India.

Centre, 2-0-1-1.
31 W= I−.
Schoolmaster/farmer. Blue 26-7. Ckt blue 26-8;
Surrey CCC, Glos CCC. Taught at Cheltenham
Coll. Sec N Cotswold Hunt 69.

MCCARLEY, Allan   *Wales*
Neath.
b −; *d* 55.
Flanker, 3-2-0-1 (9 − 3t).
38 E+(1t) S−(2t) I+.
Steelworker.

MCCARTEN, Ronald James   *Ireland*
Workington GS, St Mary's Coll Twickenham,
London Irish.
b 6.8.35 Seaton, Cumberland.
Wing, 3-1-0-2.
61 E+ W− F−.
PE teacher. Taught at Castleknock.

MCCARTHY, Edward A.   *Ireland*
Kingstown.
b −; *d* 28.3.48.
Forward, 1-0-0-1.
1882 W−.

MCCARTHY, Fabian Joseph   *Australia*
Charles
Qld.
b 19.
Prop, 1-0-0-1.
50 BI−.
Wheat farmer.

MCCARTHY, James Stephen   *Ireland*
CBC Cork, Dolphin, Barbarians.
b 30.1.26 Cork.
Flanker, 28-15-3-10 (24 − 8t).
48 F+(1t) E+ S+ W+; 49 F− E+ S+(2t)
W+(1t); 50 W−; 51 F+ E+ S+ W= SA−; 52
F+(2t) S+ W− E−; 53 F+(1t) E= S+(1t); 54
NZ− F− E− S+ W−; 55 F− E=; BI > 50 NZ,
A.
Decorator/business. Business colleague of Tony
O'Reilly.

MCCARTHY, T.   *Ireland*
Cork.
Forward, 1-0-0-1.
1898 W−.

MCCARTHY, Thomas St George   *Ireland*
Trin Coll Dublin.
Centre, 1-0-0-1.
1882 W−.
Dist inspector RIC Tipperary. Co fdr GAA
1884.

MCCAW, William Alexander   *New Zealand*
Marist Bros' HS Invercargill, St Kevin's Coll,

Marist, Southland.
b 26.8.27 Gore.
Flanker/no 8, 5-3-0-2.
51 A+ A+ A+; 53 W−; 54 F−.
HM. NZ > 51 A, 53-4 BI,F & NAm. Capt,
coach & pres Marist. Softball for Southland & S
Island.

MCCLELLAND, Thomas   *Ireland*
Alexander
Ballymena Acad, Queen's Univ Belfast.
Flanker/lock/prop, 16-5-0-11 (6 − 2t).
21 E− S+ W− F−; 22 E− W− F+; 23 E−(1t)
S− W+ F−(1t); 24 F+ E− S− W+ NZ−.
Medicine.

MCCLENAHAN, Robert Orr   *Ireland*
RBAI, Instonians.
b 10.5.02; *d* 57.
Wing, 3-1-0-2.
23 E− S− W+.
Chartered accountant.

MCCLINTON, Arthur Norman   *Ireland*
RBAI, NIFC.
b 16.8.1886; *d* −.
FH, 2-1-0-1 (2 − 1c).
10 W− F+(1c); BI > 10 SA.
Seed merchant.

MCCLUNG, Thomas   *Scotland*
Edinburgh Acad, Sedbergh Sch, Edinburgh
Academicals, Cambridge Univ, Edinburgh
Univ, Barbarians.
b 14.2.33.
Centre/FH, 9-2-0-7 (4 − 2c).
56 I−(2c) E−; 57 W+ I− E−; 59 F− W+ I−;
60 W−.
Farmer/potato merchant. Blue 54.

MCCLURE, G.B.   *Scotland*
Glasgow Acad, W of Scotland.
Half-back, 1-0-1-0.
1873 E=.
Bro of J.H.

MCCLURE, J.H.   *Scotland*
Glasgow Acad, W of Scotland.
Forward, 1-0-0-1.
1872 E−.
Bro of G.B.

MCCOMBE, William McMachan   *Ireland*
Campbell Coll Belfast, Trin Coll Dublin,
Bangor.
b 6.2.49 Uganda.
FH, 5-2-0-3 (32 − 1t 5c 2d 4p).
68 F−(2p); 75 E+(1t 2c) S−(1c 1p) F+(2c 2d
1p) W−.
Civil service/estate agent.

MCCONNELL, Albert Arthur   *Ireland*
McGown
Methodist Coll Belfast, Queen's Univ Belfast,
Collegians, Barbarians.
b 29.10.19 Belfast.
Prop, 7-5-0-2.
47 A−; 48 F+ E+ S+ W+; 49 F− E+.
Medicine. Served with RNVR 42-6.

MCCONNELL, George   *Ireland*
Foyle Coll, RS Dungannon, Edinburgh Univ,
Derry.
b 1.8.1889; *d* 24.3.48.
Forward, 4-2-0-2.
12 F+ E−; 13 W− F+.
Medicine. Served WW1, Capt RAMC attached
Serbian Army & Brit Salonika Force.

MCCONNELL, J.W.   *Ireland*
Lansdowne.
FB, 1-0-0-1.
13 S−.

MCCOOL, Michael John   *New Zealand*
Kereru Sch, St Patrick's Coll Silverstream, NZ
Jnrs, Celtic, Hawkes Bay, Ponoroa Utd,
Wairarapa-Bush.
b 15.9.51 Hastings.
Lock, 1-0-0-1.
79 A−.
Farmer. NZ > 79 A.

MCCORMAC, Frederick Maxwell   *Ireland*
Masonic Sch Dublin, Wanderers.
b 21.5.1884 Dalkey; *d* −.
SH, 3-1-0-2.
09 W−; 10 W− F+.

MCCORMICK, William Fergus   *New Zealand*
Christchurch Boys' HS, Linwood, Canterbury, S
Island.
b 24.4.9 Ashburton.
FB, 16-13-0-3 (121 − 23c 1d 24p).
65 SA+(1c); 67 E+(4c) W+(2o 1p) F | (3o 1p)
S+(1c 2p); 68 A+(3c 1p) A+(2c 2p) F+(3p)
F+(3p) F+(2c 2p); 69 W+(2c 1p) W+(3c 1d
5p); 70 SA−(1p) SA+(1p) SA−; 71 BI−(1p).
Plasterer/slaughterman/sports goods store
employee. Top scorer 118 pts NZ > 67 BI,F &
C; 120 pts > 68 A & Fj. 28 pts v F 68. Top scorer
151 pts > 70 SA. Rep S Island softball. Father
Archie rep NZ 25 (no Tests). Sister Helen NZ
hockey rep. Alex Veysey wrote biography
'Fergie' pub 76.

MCCORMICK, William John   *Ireland*
Newbridge Coll Kildare, Wanderers.
b 18.12.05 Kilrea, Co Derry.
No 8, 1-1-0-0.
30 E+.
Bank official.

MCCOULL, H.C.   *Ireland*
RBAI, Belfast A.
b 20.11.1873; *d* 17.
Forward, 4-1-0-3.
1895 E− S− W−; 1899 E+.

MCCOURT, Desmond   *Ireland*
RBAI, Queen's Univ Belfast.
b 23.
No 8, 1-0-0-1.
47 A−.
Univ administrator.

MCCOWAN, David CBE   *Scotland*
Glasgow Acad, W of Scotland.
b 1860; *d* 15.5.37.
Forward, 10-5-1-4 (1t).
1880 I+ E−; 1881 I− E=; 1882 I+(1t) E+; 1883
I+ E−; 1884 I+ E−.
Broker. Pres SRU 28-9.

MCCOWAN, Robert H.   *Australia*
Brisbane GS, Qld.
b 28.2.1875 Renfrewshire; *d* 41 Murwillumbah.
FB/wing, 3-1-0-2.
1899 BT+ BT− BT−.
Solicitor. Sentenced to 14 yrs gaol for
fraudulently misappropriating £15,000 from a
Trust Fund. After release worked as a bar-room
cleaner.

MCCOWAT, R.H.   *Scotland*
Glasgow Acad, Glasgow Academicals.
Wing, 1-0-0-1.
05 I−.

MCCOY, James Joseph   *Ireland*
Portora RS, Bangor, Brit Police.
b 28.6.58 Enniskillen.
Prop, 7-3-1-3.
84 W− A−; 85 S+ F= W+ E+; 86 F−.
Civil service/police.

MCCRACKEN, Herbert Lowry   *Ireland*
Banbridge Acad, Queen's Univ Belfast, NIFC,
Barbarians.
b 8.7.27 Belfast.
SH, 1-0-0-1.
54 W−.
Solicitor. Won only cap in bizarre
circumstances, replacing John O'Meara who had
to withdraw after ricking a back muscle in bed
on the morning of the match.

MCCRAE, Ian George   *Scotland*
Robert Gordon's Sch, Gordonians, Barbarians.
b 19.5.41.
SH, 6-2-0-4.
67 E−; 68 I−; 69 F+r W−; 72 F+ NZ−.
Insurance. S's 1st int r, v F 69.

MCCROW, John William Stuart *Scotland*
Edinburgh Acad, Edinburgh Academicals.
b 11.5.1899 Chirnside; *d* 25.2.50 Edinburgh.
Wing, 1-0-0-1.
21 I−.
Esparto importer.

MCCUE, Patrick Aloysius *Australia*
('Paddy')
NSW.
b −.6.1883; *d* 10.9.62 Cronulla.
Forward, 4-1-1-2.
07 NZ− NZ=; 08 W−; 09 E+.
Agent/skin dealer. Olympic rugby gold medal
08. RL.

MCCULLOCH, J. Duncan *South Africa*
Griq W.
b 11.4.1884; *d* 19.4.53.
SH, 2-2-0-0.
13 E+ F+.
Mining. SA > 12-13 BI, F.

MCCULLOUGH, John Francis *New Zealand*
Stratford Tech HS, Stratford, Taranaki, Clifton,
Tukapa, N Island.
b 8.1.36 Stratford.
1st five-eighth, 3-2-0-1.
59 BI+ BI+ BI−.
Farmer. Coach Stratford 74-5. Father W.
McCullough rep Taranaki 31-2.

MCCUTCHEON, William *Wales*
Morgan
Swansea, Oldham.
b 1870 Swansea; *d* 3.7.49 Oldham.
Back, 7-3-0-4 (2 − 1t).
1891 S−; 1892 E− S−; 1893 E+ S+(1t) I+;
1894 E−.
Clerk. Moved to Oldham Nov 1888. Later
prominent in NU administration. Ref.

MCDANIEL, J. *Ireland*
Newport.
Forward, 1-0-0-1.
1884 W−.
McDaniel not F.J. Purdon is believed to have
played v W 1884. McDaniel became a club
official with Bath.

MCDERMOTT, Lloyd Clive *Australia*
CEGS Brisbane, Qld.
b 11.11.39.
Wing, 2-0-0-2.
62 NZ− NZ−.
Solicitor. Aborigine. RL.

MCDERMOTT, Sean J. *Ireland*
Blundell's Sch, St Luke's Coll Exeter, London
Irish.
b 28.3.32 Kinsale.

SH, 2-0-0-2.
55 S− W−.
PE officer/sports master/business.

MCDONALD, Alexander *New Zealand*
George St Sch, Kaikorai, Otago, S Island.
b 23.4.1883 Dunedin; *d* 4.5.67 Wellington.
No 8/lock, 8-7-0-1 (11 − 3t 1c).
05 S+ I+(1t) E+ W−; 07 A+; 08 AW+; 13 A+
US+(2t 1c).
Brewery worker. NZ > 05 A, 05-6 BI,F &
NAm, 07 A, 13 NAm (capt). NZRFU sel 30-49.
Co-mgr NZ > 38 A; asst mgr > 49 SA. Life
mem NZRFU 51.

MCDONALD, Barry Stuart *Australia*
Sydney Univ, Randwick, NSW.
b 9.6.40 Matamata, NZ.
Flanker/no 8, 2-1-0-1.
69 SA−; 70 S+.
Real estate. NZ triallist.

MCDONALD, Charles *Scotland*
Jedburgh GS, Jedforest.
b 19.4.19 Jedburgh.
Wing, 1-0-0-1 (3 − 1p).
47 A−(1p).
Rep. Uncle of D.M. Rose. Served WW2,
KOSB.

MCDONALD, J. Andre J. *South Africa*
Stellenbosch Univ, W Prov.
b 17.2.09.
No 8, 4-4-0-0.
31 W+ I+; 32 E+ S+.
Minister. SA > 31-2 BI.

MCDONALD, John Charles *Australia*
('Cracker')
Toowoomba GS, Qld.
b 14; *d* 83.
Flanker, 2-0-0-2.
38 NZ − NZ−.
Printing co owner. Son John shared with Herb
McKinley world rec 46.7s for 400 metres.

MCDONNELL, Alaster Colla *Ireland*
Armagh RS, Trin Coll Dublin.
b 20.1.1867; *d* 15.10.50.
Half-back, 4-1-0-3 (1t).
1889 W+(1t); 1890 S− W−; 1891 E−.

MCDOWELL, John Craig *Ireland*
RBAI, Instonians.
b 8.5.1896; *d* 23.11.78.
FH, 2-1-0-1.
24 F+ NZ−.
Belfast Harbour engr/groundsman RBAI.

MCDOWELL, Steven Clark *New Zealand*
Kahukura, Bay of Plenty, Auckland, NZ Jnrs.

270

b 27.8.61 Rotorua.
Prop, 2-2-0-0.
85 Arg+ Arg=.
NZ > 85 Arg. World XV > 86 SA.

MCELDOWNEY, John　　　*New Zealand*
Thompson
New Plymouth Boys' HS, HSOB, Taranaki, N
Island.
b 26.10.47 New Plymouth.
Prop, 2-2-0-0.
77 BI+ BI+.
Bitumen worker. NZ > 76 Arg & Uruguay, 77
F. Bro Bryce rep Taranaki 72-80.

MCEWAN, Matthew Clark　　　*Scotland*
Edinburgh Acad, Edinburgh Academicals.
b 5.10.1865; *d* 13.4.1899 Chicago.
Forward, 15-10-2-3 (2t 2c 1d).
1886 E=; 1887 I+(1t) W+(1t) E=; 1888 W−
I+; 1889 W+ I+; 1890 W+(1c) I+ E−; 1891
W+(1c) I+(1d) E+; 1892 E−.
Chartered accountant. Bro of W.M.C. Touch-
judge S v I 1895.

MCEWAN, William　　*Scotland/South Africa*
Maclean Clark
Edinburgh Acad, Edinburgh Academicals,
Transvaal.
b 24.10.1875; *d* −.5.34 Cape Town.
Scotland
Forward, 16-8-3-5 (3 − 1t).
1894 W− E+; 1895 W+ E+; 1896 W− I= E+;
1897 I+ E−; 1898 I+ E=(1t); 1899 I− W+ E+;
1900 W− E=.
South Africa
Forward, 2-1-1-0.
03 BT= BT+.
Stockbroker. Bro of Matthew. Emigrated SA.

MCFADYEAN, Colin William　　　*England*
Bristol, Loughborough Colls, UAU, Moseley,
Som.
b 11.3.43.
Centre, 11-2-3-6 (15 − 4t 1d).
66 I= F− S−(1d); 67 A− I+(1t) F− S+(2t) W−
NZ−; 68 W=(1t) I=; BI > 66 A, NZ 4-0-0-4.
PE lecturer at Alsager Tg Coll 67. Rep
Loughborough at ath.

MCFARLAND, Sir Basil　　　*Ireland*
Alexander Talbot CBE
Bedford GS, Derry.
b 18.2.1898.
Wing, 4-0-0-4 (4 − 1d).
20 S− W−(1d) F−; 22 W−.
Co dir. CBE 54.

MCGANN, Barry John　　　*Ireland*
PBC Cork, Lansdowne, Cork Constitution,
Barbarians.

b 28.5.48.
FH, 25-11-3-11 (60 − 1t 3c 6d 11p).
69 F+(1d) E+(1d) S+(1t) W−; 70 SA= F− E−
S+ W+(1d); 71 F= E− S+ W−; 72 F+ E+(1d)
F+; 73 NZ= E+(2c 1d 1p) S−(2p) W−(1c 1p);
76 F− W−(3p) E+(1d 2p) S−(2p) NZ−.
Finance co. Played football for Shelbourne
AFC.

MCGAUGHEY, Sean Kieran　　　*Scotland*
Hawick HS, Hawick W, Hawick.
b Dumfries.
Flanker, 1-0-0-1.
84 R−.
Wool trade. Scotland B v F 84. Born of Irish
parents.

MCGEECHAN, Ian Robert　　　*Scotland*
Allerton Grange Sch Leeds, Carnegie Coll,
Headingley, Barbarians, Yorks.
b 30.10.46 Leeds.
FH/centre, 32-11-2-19 (21 − 7d).
72 NZ−(1d); 73 F−(1d) W+ I+(1d) E− P+; 74
W− E+ I− F+; 75 I+(1d) F− W+(1d) E−
NZ− A+; 76 F− W− E+ I+; 77 E− I+ F−
W−(1d); 78 I− F− W− NZ−(1d); 79 W− E=
I= F−; BI > 74 SA 4-3-1-0; 77 NZ 4-0-1-3.
Schoolmaster. Capt S 9 times. Scottish XV v Tg
74, J 76. S asst coach 85-6.

MCGHIE, Gordon H.　　　*Australia*
Drummoyne HS, Qld.
b 14.10.07.
Wing, 3-3-0-0 (6 − 2t).
29 NZ+(1t) NZ+; 30 BI+(1t).
Insurance. 5ft 2in.

MCGILL, Arthur Neil　　　*Australia*
Sydney Boys HS, NSW.
b 5.12.44.
FB, 21-4-1-16 (72 − 1t 9c 17p).
68 NZ−(2c 2p) NZ−(5p) F+(1c 1p); 69 W−(1t
2c 2p) SA− SA− SA− SA−; 70 S+(1c 1p); 71
3A=(1c 2p) 3A=(2p) 3A= F+(1c) F=(1p); 72
F= F− NZ− NZ− NZ−; 73 Tg+(2c) Tg−(1p).
Rep/NSW dir of coaching.

MCGLASHAN, Thomas Perry　　　*Scotland*
Lang
Royal HS, Royal HSFP, Edinburgh Univ,
Barbarians.
b 29.12.25 Edinburgh.
Prop, 8-0-0-8.
47 F− I− E−; 54 F− NZ− I− E− W−.
Dentist. 8 yrs between caps.

MCGOWN, Thomas Melville　　　*Ireland*
Whitson
Coleraine AI, Merchiston Castle Sch,
Cambridge Univ, NIFC.
b 22.2.1876 Belfast; *d* 15.7.56.

Forward, 3-2-0-1.
1899 E+ S+; 01 S−; BT > 1899 A.
Solicitor. Blue 1896.

MCGRATH, Derek George   *Ireland*
St Michael's Coll, UC Dublin.
b 3.5.60 Dublin.
Flanker, 1-0-0-1.
84 S−.
Vet.

MCGRATH, Noel Fitzgerald   *Ireland*
Stonyhurst Coll, Oxford Univ, London Irish,
Headingley, Yorks.
b 6.2.09 Wakefield, Yorks; *d* −.
Prop, 1-0-0-1.
34 W−.
Solicitor/local govt officer. Blue 34-6.

MCGRATH, Patrick John   *Ireland*
Rockwell Coll, UC Cork, Barbarians.
b 20.8.41 Burma.
Wing/centre, 10-5-1-4 (9 − 3t).
65 E+ S+(1t) W− SA−; 66 F− E=(1t) S−
W+; 67 A+ A+(1t).
Medicine. Moved to Can.

MCGRATH, Robert John   *Ireland*
Murray ('Robbie')
Newbridge Coll, Wanderers.
b 18.7.51 Dublin.
SH, 16-6-0-10.
77 W− E− F−r; 81 SA−(1t) SA− A−; 82 W+
E+ S+ F−; 83 S+ F+ W− E+; 84 F− W−.
Optician. I > 81 SA.

MCGRATH, Timothy   *Ireland*
Rockwell Coll, UC Cork, Garryowen.
b 3.10.33 Cork; *d* 23.9.78 Dungarvan.
No 8, 7-1-0-6.
56 W+; 58 F−; 60 E− S− W− F−; 61 SA−.
Creamery mgr.

MCGRATTAN, Brian   *New Zealand*
Wellington, N Island.
b 31.12.59 Wellington.
Prop, 4-1-2-1.
83 S= E−; 85 Arg+ Arg=.
NZ > 83 S & E, 84 A, 85 Arg.

MCGREGOR, Alwin John   *New Zealand*
('Dougie')
Ponsonby, Auckland, N Island.
b 16.12.1889 Thames; *d* 15.4.63 Auckland.
Wing, 2-2-0-0 (3 − 1t).
13 A+ US+(1t).
Joiner. NZ > 13 NAm. RL 15 & after serving
WW1; rep NZ 19-20. Coach RL in Otago &
Auckland. Nephew of 'Dick' McGregor.

MCGREGOR, Duncan   *New Zealand*
Kaiapoi, Canterbury, Linwood, Petone,
Southland, S & N Islands.
b 16.7.1881 Kaiapoi; *d* 11.3.47 Timaru.
Centre/wing, 4-3-0-1 (21 − 7t).
03 A+(1t); 04 BT+(2t); 05 E+(4t) W−.
NZ's most t (4) in a Test, v E 05. NZ > 05 A, 05-
6 BI,F & NAm (16t, 14 apps). NZ RL > 07 BI;
stayed behind to play for Merthyr. Ankle inj
ended career but returned to NZ 13 to become
RL ref & sel.

MCGREGOR, Neil Perriam   *New Zealand*
Gore HS, Pirates, Wellington, Christchurch,
Canterbury, S Island.
b 29.12.01 Lowburn; *d* 12.7.73 Hokitika.
2nd/1st five-eighth, 2-2-0-0.
24 W+; 25 E+.
Customs dept clerk. NZ > 24-5 BI,F & C (20
apps), 28 SA (inj restricted him to 4 apps).
Nelson & S Island sel 61-8.

MCGREGOR, Robert Wylie   *New Zealand*
('Dick')
Thames, Auckland, Grafton, N Island.
b 31.12.1874 Thames; *d* 22.11.25 Sydney,
NSW.
Centre/FB, 2-2-0-0.
03 A+; 04 BT+.
Steelworker/insurance agent. Plagued by ill
health in later life. Benefit match arranged for
him before he moved to A. Uncle of 'Dougie'.

MCGUIRE, Eamonn Paul   *Ireland*
St Joseph's Coll Galway, UC Galway.
b 28.6.39 Galway.
Flanker, 8-2-1-5.
63 E= S− W+ NZ−; 64 E+ S− W− F−.
Chief Fire Officer Dundalk.

MCGUINNESS, Gerald M.   *Scotland*
St Aloysius Sch Glasgow, W of Scotland.
b 14.9.53.
Prop, 7-1-0-6.
82 A+ A−; 83 I−; 85 I− F− W− E−.
Newsagent. Scottish XVr v J 77, Fj 82.

MCHARDY, Evelyn Edgar   *South Africa*
('Boetie')
Grey Coll, OFS.
b 11.6.1890 Bloemfontein; *d* 60.
Wing, 5-5-0-0 (18 − 6t).
12 S+(1t) I+(3t) W+; 13 E+ F+(2t).
1st SA to score hat-trick of t in Test, v I 12. 6t (5
apps) SA > 12-13 BI, F, most by SA in int series
on tour. Prov debut 10; played for OFS for 14
seasons. Later coach, sel. OFS sprint champ.
Also played football, hockey.

MCHARG, Alastair Ferguson   *Scotland*
Irvine R Acad, W of Scotland, London Scottish,
Barbarians.
 b 17.6.44 Irvine.
Lock/no 8, 44-17-1-26 (8 − 2t).
68 I− E− A+; 69 F+ W− I− E−; 71 F− W−
I− E+ E+; 72 F+ E+ NZ−; 73 F− W+ I+ E−
P+(1t); 74 W− E+ I− F+(1t); 75 I+ F− W+
E− NZ− A+; 76 F− W− E+ I+; 77 E− I+ F−
W−; 78 I− F− W− NZ−; 79 W− E=.
Buyer. S's most capped lock (42 apps). Scottish
XV v Arg (2) 69, 73; Tg 74.

MCHUGH, Maurice James   *New Zealand*
Sacred Heart Coll Auckland, Marist, Auckland,
N Island, City.
 b 19.2.17 Auckland.
Flanker/no 8, 3-2-0-1.
46 A+ A+; 49 SA−.
Cartage contractor/insurance agent. NZ > 49
SA. NZ amateur heavywt boxing champ 38,
runner-up 46. Father Andy rep Auckland 15-21.

MCILDOWIE, George   *Ireland*
Sedbergh Sch, Malone.
 b 3.11.1886 Strandtown, Belfast; *d* 28.12.53.
Forward, 4-0-1-3 (3 − 1t).
06 SA−; 10 E= S− W−(1t).
Civil engr Midland Rly.

MCILRATH, John Alexander   *Ireland*
('Ian')
Ballymena Acad, Stranmillis Coll, Ballymena.
 b 10.3.46 Ballymena.
Centre, 5-0-0-5.
76 A− F− NZ−; 77 W− E−.
Schoolmaster. Ulster v A 74.

MCILWAINE, E.H.   *Ireland*
RBAI, NIFC.
Forward, 2-0-0-2.
1895 S− W−.
Bro of J.E.

MCILWAINE, E.N.   *Ireland*
NIFC.
Half-back/forward, 2-0-0-2.
1875 E− E−.

MCILWAINE, John Elder   *Ireland*
RBAI, NIFC.
 b 3.8.1874 Belfast; *d* −.
Forward, 7-4-0-3.
1897 E+ S−; 1898 E+ S− W−; 1899 E+ W+.
Medicine. Bro of E.H.

MCINDOE, F.   *Scotland*
Glasgow Acad, Glasgow Academicals.
FB, 2-2-0-0.
1886 W+ I=.

MCINTOSH, Donald Neil   *New Zealand*
Featherston Dist HS, Petone, Wellington, N
Island.
 b 1.4.31 Lower Hutt.
Flanker, 4-3-0-1.
56 SA+ SA−; 57 A+ A+.
Wine & spirits salesman/shepherd. NZ > 57 A.
Coach Petone & Featherston clubs.

MCINTOSH, Louis Maxwell   *Ireland*
Cavan RS, Trin Coll Dublin.
Wing, 1-0-0-1 (1t).
1884 S−(1t).
Medicine.

MCINTYRE, Andrew John   *Australia*
Qld Univ, Brisbane, Qld.
 b 23.12.55.
Prop, 18-11-1-6.
82 NZ− NZ+ NZ−; 83 F= F−; 84 Fj+ NZ+
NZ− NZ− E+ I+ W+ S+; 85 C+ C+ NZ−
Fj+ Fj+.
Surveyor. A > 82 NZ; 83 It & F; 84 Fj; 84 BI.

MCKAY, Donald William   *New Zealand*
Takapuna GS, N Shore, Auckland, N Island.
 b 7.8.37 Auckland.
Wing, 5-5-0-0 (6 − 2t).
61 F+(1t) F+ F+; 63 E+ E+(1t).
Chemist. 16t NZ > 62 A. 1st All Black from N
Shore club, Auckland. Auckland sel 73-6.

MCKAY, James William   *Ireland*
Coleraine AI, Queen's Univ Belfast,
Barbarians.
 b 12.7.21 Waterford.
No 8/flanker, 23-14-2-7 (9 − 3t).
47 F−(1t) E+(1t) S+ W− A−; 48 F+ E+(1t)
S+ W+; 49 F− E+ S+ W+; 50 F= E− S+
W−; 51 F+ E+ S+ W= SA−; 52 F+; BI > 50
NZ 4-0-1-3, A 2-2-0-0.
Medicine.

MCKEATING, Edward   *Scotland*
Heriot's Coll, Heriot's FP.
 b 1.9.36 Edinburgh.
Centre, 6-4-0-2.
57 F+ W+; 61 SA− W+ I+ E−.
Packing sales mgr.

MCKECHNIE, Brian John   *New Zealand*
Southland Boys' HS, Star, Southland, S Island.
 b 6.11.53 Gore.
FB/1st five-eighth, 10-7-0-3 (46 − 5c 1d 11p).
77 F−(1p) F+(1c 1d 1p); 78 A+ A−r(1c 2p)
W+r(3p) E+(1c 2p) S+(2c 2p); 79 A−; 81
SA+r F+.
Accountant. Selected as five-eighth NZ > 77 F,
played both Tests at FB; top scorer 89 pts 78 BI.
Also > 79 A, 81 R & F. Otago ckter, rep NZ 75-
81.

MCKEE, William Desmond   *Ireland*
St Columba's Coll Dublin, NIFC.
b 27.8.23; *d* 28.1.82.
Centre, 12-7-1-4 (6 − 2t).
47 A−; 48 F+ E+(1t) S+ W+; 49 F− E+(1t)
S+ W+; 50 F= E−; 51 SA−.
Co dir. Ckt for I 46.

MCKELLAR, Gerald Forbes   *New Zealand*
Otago Boys's HS, Scinde, Hawkes Bay,
Wellington, Pirates, Otago.
b 9.1.1884 Cromwell; *d* 16.1.60 Dunedin.
Flanker, 3-2-0-1.
10 A+ A− A+.
Customs collector. NZ > 10 A. Volunteered to
serve Boer War from sch.

MCKELVEY, James Moorshead   *Ireland*
Campbell Coll Belfast, Queen's Univ Belfast.
b 2.4.33 Belfast.
FB, 2-0-0-2.
56 F− E−.
Medicine. Ckt for I 54.

MCKENDRICK, J.A.   *South Africa*
W Prov.
1-0-0-1.
1891 BT−.

MCKENDRICK, J.G.   *Scotland*
Glasgow Acad, W of Scotland.
Forward, 1-1-0-0.
1889 I+.

MCKENZIE, Richard John   *New Zealand*
('Jock')
St Patrick's Coll Wellington, Petone,
Wellington, Marist, Auckland, N Island.
b 15.3.1892 Lyttelton; *d* 25.9.68 Mt
Maunganui.
2nd/1st five-eighth, 4-4-0-0 (15 − 5t).
13 A+(2t) US+(2t); 14 A+ A+(1t).
Licensee/farmer. NZ > 13 NAm, 14 A. Badly
wounded WW1, but believed to have rep
Waikato subsequently at hockey. Waikato sel
37-8.

MCKENZIE, Roderick   *New Zealand*
McCulloch
Kakariki Sch, Feilding Convent Sch, Kia Toa,
Manawhenua, Palmerston N, Manawatu, N
Island.
b 16.9.09 Rakaia.
Lock/flanker, 9-6-0-3.
34 A−; 35 S+; 36 A+; 37 SA+ SA− SA−; 38
A+ A+ A+.
Post Office supervisor. NZ > 34, 36 & 38 A, 35-
6 BI & Can. Served WW2; played in BI for NZ
Comb Servs, Comb Dominions & twice for S in
servs ints. Bro Jack rep Manawatu.

MCKIBBIN, Alistair Richard   *Ireland*
RBAI, Instonians, St Mary's Hosp, London
Irish.
b 13.1.58 Belfast.
Centre, 14-3-2-9.
77 W− E− S−; 78 S+ F− W− E− NZ−; 79 F=
W− E+ S=; 80 E− S+.
Medicine. Son of H.R., bro of C.H.

MCKIBBIN, Christopher Henry   *Ireland*
RBAI, Instonians, Trin Coll Dublin.
b 24.6.48 Belfast.
Centre, 1-0-0-1.
76 S−r.
Solicitor. Son of H.R., bro of A.R.

MCKIBBIN, Desmond   *Ireland*
RBAI, Instonians, Barbarians.
Prop/lock, 8-4-2-2 (3 − 1p).
50 F= E− S+ W−; 51 F+ E+(1p) S+ W=.
Civil engr/dir of technical services for Belfast.
Bro of H.R. Pres IRFU 85-6.

MCKIBBIN, Henry Roger   *Ireland*
RBAI, Queen's Univ Belfast, Barbarians.
b 13.7.15 Belfast.
Centre, 4-2-0-2 (7 − 2c 1p).
38 W−(1c); 39 E+(1c) S+(1p) W−; BI > 38 SA
3-1-0-2.
Solicitor. Bro of Desmond, father of A.R. &
C.H. Asst mgr BI > 62 SA. IB rep. Centenary
Pres IRU 74-5.

MCKID, William Alexander   *Australia*
('Snakebite')
NSW.
b 27.1.53.
Centre, 6-3-0-3.
75 E+; 76 Fj+; 78 NZ− NZ+; 79 I− I−.
Grazier.

MCKINNEY, Stewart Alexander   *Ireland*
RS Dungannon, Dungannon, Stranmillis Coll,
Barbarians.
b 20.11.46 Strabane.
Flanker, 25-9-1-15 (11 − 2t 1p).
72 F+ E+ F+; 73 W− F+; 74 F− E+ S+(1p)
P=(1t) NZ−; 75 E+ S−; 76 A− F− W− E+
S− NZ−; 77 W− E− S−; 78 S+r(1t) F− W−
E−; BI > 74 SA.
Schoolmaster.

MCKINNON, Alexander   *Australia*
Qld.
b 1878; *d* 44.
Forward, 1-0-0-1.
04 BT−.
Draughtsman.

MCKIVAT, Christopher Hobart   *Australia*
Glebe, NSW.

b 27.11.1879 Orange; *d* 4.5.47 Sydney.
Five-eighth, 4-1-1-2.
07 NZ− NZ=; 08 W−; 09 E+.
Freight co employee. Olympic rugby gold medal
08. RL.

MCLACHLAN, Jon Stanley　　*New Zealand*
Orakei Sch, Selwyn Coll, College Rifles,
Auckland, Eastern.
b 23.6.49 Auckland.
Wing, 1-0-1-0.
74 A=.
Signwriting co mgr. NZ > 74 A & Fj (4t v S
Australia).

MCLAREN, David Alexander　　*Scotland*
Durham Sch, Durham City, Durham Co.
b 29.8.10; *d* 78.
Lock, 1-1-0-0.
31 F+.
Farmer.

MCLAREN, Edward　　*Scotland*
Royal HS, London Scottish, Royal HSFP,
Barbarians.
b 28.5.02; *d* 30.3.50.
Centre, 5-3-0-2 (9 − 3t).
23 F+(2t) W+ I+ E−(1t); 24 F−.

MCLAREN, Hugh Campbell　　*New Zealand*
Auckland GS, Grammar, Auckland, Matamata,
Waikato, N Island.
b 8.6.26 Auckland.
No 8, 1-0-0-1.
52 A−.
Farmer. Appeared in every position in scrum
during career. Withdrew from 2nd Test v A 52
with nose inj.

MCLAUCHLAN, John ('Ian')　　*Scotland*
Ayr Acad, Jordanhill Coll, Jordanhill,
Barbarians.
b 14.4.42 Tarbolton.
Prop, 43-15-2-26.
69 E− SA+; 70 F− W−; 71 F− W− I− E+
E+; 72 F+ W− E+ NZ−; 73 F− W+ I+ E−
P+; 74 W− E+ I− F+; 75 I+ F− W+ E− NZ−
A+; 76 F− W− E+ I+; 77 W−; 78 I− F− W−
E− NZ−; 79 W− E= I= F− NZ−; BI > 71 A,
NZ 4-2-1-1; 74 SA 4-3-1-0.
Schoolmaster. Capt S rec 19 times. Scottish XV
v Arg (2) 69, 73; Tg 74, J 77. Began career as
flanker.

MCLAUGHLIN, James Henry　　*Ireland*
Derry AI, Derry.
b 23.4.1864; *d* −.12.42.
Half-back, 4-1-1-2.
1887 E= S−; 1888 W+ S−.

MCLAUGHLIN, Reginald　　*Australia*
Edward Miller ('Bill')
Newington Coll, NSW.
b 14.
Centre, 2-0-0-2 (6 − 2t).
36 NZ−(1t) NZ−(1t).
Squash court proprietor. Asst mgr A > 58 NZ.
Mgr A > 63 SA & 66-7 BI, F & Can. Pres ARU.

MCLEAN, Alexander Douglas　　*Australia*
Qld.
b −.12.12; *d* 61.
Wing, 10-4-1-5 (12 − 4t).
33 SA− SA+ SA− SA− SA+; 34 NZ+(1t)
NZ=; 36 NZ− NZ− M+(3t).
Cabinet maker/licensee. Bro of Bill. RL.

MCLEAN, Andrew Leslie　　*New Zealand*
Auckland GS, Grammar, Auckland, College
Rifles, Whakatane, Bay of Plenty, Te Puke
Rvrs, N Island.
b 31.10.1898 Auckland; *d* 18.1.64 Auckland.
Lock, 2-0-1-1 (3 − 1t).
21 SA−(1t) SA=.
Farmer/oil co & brewery sales rep. Bro Neil rep
Auckland 18-24.

MCLEAN, Duncan Ian　　*Scotland*
Royal HS, Royal HSFP.
b 1.5.23; *d* 21.3.62.
Flanker/no 8, 2-0-0-2.
47 I− E−.
Civil engr.

MCLEAN, Hugh Foster　　*New Zealand*
Hastings Boys' HS, Napier Boys' HS, Hastings,
Wellington, Star, Taranaki, Grafton, Auckland,
Papakura Army, N Island.
b 18.7.07 Wanganui.
Flanker/no 8, 9-5-0-4 (9 − 3t).
30 BI+(2t) BI+; 32 A− A+ A+(1t); 34 A−; 35
I+ W−; 36 E−.
Carpet trade. NZ > 32 & 34 A, 35-6 BI & F. Co-
fdr NZ Barbarians 37; capt in 1st match v
Auckland 38. Father Jack & four uncles rep
Wanganui. Bros Gordon & Bob rep Taranaki.
Another bro Terry is rugby writer & author of
many rugby books. Mem NZ rowing eight 28. N
Shore GC capt 48-9.

MCLEAN, James Douglas　　*Australia*
Qld.
b 15.4.1880; *d* −.12.47.
Wing, 3-0-0-3 (3 − 1t).
04 BI− BI−; 05 NZ−(1t).
Rly employee. Father of Doug & Bill. RL.

MCLEAN, Jeffrey James　　*Australia*
St Mary's CBC Ipswich, Qld.
b 26.1.47 Ipswich, Qnsld.
Wing, 13-2-1-10 (31 − 2t 1c 7p).

71 SA− SA−(1p) F+(1p) F−(2p); 72 F= F−
NZ−(2p) NZ−(2t 1c) NZ−(1p) Fj+; 73 W−
E−; 74 NZ−.
Hotel mgr. Bro of Paul. 85 pts A > NZ 72.

MCLEAN, John Kenneth   *New Zealand*
Thames HS, Training Coll, Auckland, Thames
Utd, RNZAF, Canterbury, Waikato,
Taumarunui, Comb Servs, King Country, N
Island.
 b 3.10.23 Thames.
Wing, 2-1-0-1.
47 A+; 49 A−.
Schoolmaster. NZ > 47 A. Auckland long jump
champ 43 (22ft 9in); Waikato sprint & long jump
champ 47. Coach Thames HS, Thames Valley
Schs 73-6. Bro Gilbert & son John rep Thames
Valley.

MCLEAN, Paul Edward   *Australia*
Qld.
 b 12.10.53.
Five-eighth/FB, 30-15-1-14 (257 − 2t 27c 3d
62p).
74 NZ−(1c) NZ=(1c 2p) NZ−(2p); 75 J+(2t 5c
1p) J+(6c 2p) S−(1p) W−(1p); 76 E−(2p)
I+(1c 2p) Fj+(2p) Fj+(2c 2p) Fj+(5p) F−(1d
4p) F−(2p); 78 W+(1c 4p) W+(1d 3p) NZ−; 79
I−(1c 2p) I−(1p) NZ+(3p) Arg−(2p) Arg+(1c
1p); 80 Fj+(1c 1d 3p); 81 F+(1c) F+(2c 4p)
I+(3p) W−(1c 1p) S−(1p); 82 E−(1p) S+(3c
5p).
Club mgr/travel mgr. Mem of A's most
celebrated rugby family; grandfather J.D., three
uncles A.D., R.A. & W.M., bro Jeffrey &
cousin Peter all played for A. 154 pts A > BI &
US 75-6, rec for A on tour. Rec 21 pts v S 82. A
pts rec holder. 12 pts World XV v SA 77.
Australian Player of Year 82. Autobiography
'Paul McLean' pub 86.

MCLEAN, Peter William   *Australia*
Brisbane, Qld.
 b 8.2.54.
Lock, 16-7-0-9.
78 NZ− NZ− NZ+; 79 I− I− NZ+ Arg−
Arg+; 80 Fj+r NZ+; 81 I+ W− S−; 82 E− S−
S+.
Hotel mgr. Cousin of Paul, son of Bill. A > 78
NZ; 79 Arg; 80 Fj; 81-2 BI.

MCLEAN, Robert Alexander   *Australia*
NSW.
 b 21.1.49.
Flanker, 5-1-0-4 (3 − 1t).
71 SA−(1t) SA− SA− F+ F−.
Schoolmaster.

MCLEAN, Robert Edward   *Ireland*
RBAI, Trin Coll Dublin.
 b −; *d* −.10.36.

Wing/back, 9-1-1-7.
1881 S+; 1882 W− E= S−; 1883 E− S−; 1884
E− S−; 1885 E−.
Solicitor. Served WW2, Ulster Div.

MCLEAN, William Malcolm   *Australia*
Qld.
 b 28.2.18 Ipswich, Qld.
Lock/no 8, 5-0-0-5 (3 − 1t).
46 NZ− M− NZ−; 47 NZ− NZ−(1t).
Draughtsman/hotelier. Bro of Doug. Capt A >
46 NZ (inj, no Tests), 47-8 BI & F (inj in 6th
match, T. Allan took over as tour capt).

MCLENNAN, Alfred Charles   *Ireland*
('Freddie')
Newbridge Coll, Wanderers.
 b 8.2.51 Dublin.
Wing, 18-2-2-14 (16 − 4t).
77 F−; 78 S+ F− W− E− NZ−; 79 F= W−(1t)
E+(1t) S=; 80 E− F−(1t); 81 F− W− E− S−
SA−(1t) SA−.
Architect. I > 81 SA.

MCLEOD, Bruce Edward   *New Zealand*
Otahuhu Coll, Manrewa, Counties, Colenso-
Pirates, Hawkes Bay, N Island.
 b 30.1.40 Auckland.
Hooker, 24-21-0-3 (12 − 4t).
64 A+(1t) A+ A−; 65 SA+ SA+(1t) SA−
SA+; 66 BI+(1t) BI+ BI+ BI+; 67 E+ W+
F+ S+; 68 A+ A+ F+ F+ F+; 69 W+(1t) W+;
70 SA− SA+.
Co mgr. NZ > 67 BI,F & Can, 68 A & Fj, 70 A
& SA.

MCLEOD, Hugh Ferns ('The   *Scotland*
Abbot')
Hawick HS, Hawick, The Army, Barbarians,
Yorks.
 b 8.6.32 Hawick.
Prop, 40-13-3-24.
54 F− NZ− I− E− W−; 55 F− W+ I+ E−; 56
F+ W− I− E−; 57 F+ W+ I− E−; 58 F+ W−
A+ I− E=; 59 F− W+ I− E=; 60 F− W− I+
E− SA−; 61 F− SA− W+ I+ E−; 62 F− W+
I+ E=; BI > 55 SA; 59 A 2-2-0-0, NZ 4-1-0-3.
Sports shop owner. Uncle of C.M. Telfer.
Barbarians > 58 SA. Served with R Scots
Greys.

MCLEOD, Norman Frederick   *England*
Clifton Coll, RIE Coll.
 b 30.6.1856 Madras; *d* 20.4.21 S Kensington.
Forward, 2-1-1-0.
1879 S= I+.
Civil engr. Son of Gen W.C. McLeod.

MCLOUGHLIN, Gerald Anthony   *Ireland*
Joseph ('Ginger')
CBC Limerick, UC Galway.

b 11.6.52 Limerick.
Prop, 18-9-2-7 (4 − 1t).
79 F= W− E+ S= A+ A+; 80 E−; 81 SA−
SA−; 82 W+ E+(1t) S+ *r*−; 83 S+ F+ W−
E+; 84 F−; BIr > 83 NZ.
Schoolmaster/licensee. I > 79 A, 81 SA.

MCLOUGHLIN, Phelim   *Ireland*
Garbally Coll, Northern, Barbarians.
b 8.8.41 Ballinasloe.
Flanker, 1-0-0-1.
76 A−.
Co dir. Ireland B. Bro of Ray.

MCLOUGHLIN, Raymond John   *Ireland*
Garbally Coll, Newcastle Univ, UC Dublin,
Blackrock Coll, Gosforth, Barbarians.
b 24.8.39 Ballinasloe.
Prop, 40-15-7-18 (4 − 1t).
62 E− S− F−; 63 E= S− W+ NZ−; 64 E+ S−;
65 F= E+ S+ W− SA−; 66 F− E= S− W+; 71
F= E− S+ W−; 72 F+(1t) E+ F+; 73 NZ=
E+ S− W− F+; 74 F− W= E+ S+ P= NZ−;
75 E+ S− F+ W−; BI > 66 A 2-2-0-0, NZ 1-0-
0-1; 71 A, NZ.
Chemical engr. Bro of Phelim.

MCMAHON, Laurance B.   *Ireland*
Blackrock Coll, UC Dublin.
b 4.12.11 London.
Centre/wing, 12-5-0-7 (9 − 3t).
31 E+(1t) SA−; 33 E−; 34 E−; 36 E+ S+(1t)
W−; 37 E− S+(1t) W+; 38 E− S−.
Solicitor. Pres IRU 61-2.

MCMAHON, Michael James   *Australia*
Qld.
b 29.7.1889; *d* 61.
FB, 1-0-0-1 (2 − 1c).
13 NZ−(1c).
Clerk of court.

MCMASTER, Arthur Wallace   *Ireland*
Ballymena Acad, Ballymena, Barbarians.
b 2.12.45 Ballymena.
Wing/centre, 18-8-2-8 (8 − 2t).
72 F+ E+ F+; 73 NZ= E+ S−(1t) W− F+; 74
F− E+ S+ P=; 75 F+ W−; 76 A−(1t) F− W−
NZ−.
Co dir.

MCMASTER, Robert Edward   *Australia*
('Wallaby Bob')
Qld.
b 5.1.21.
Prop, 7-1-0-6 (2 − 1c).
46 NZ− M− NZ−; 47 NZ− NZ− I+(1c) W−.
Licensee. Leeds (E) RL; also pro wrestler.
Served WW2 ME, New Guinea and Borneo.

MCMILLAN, Keith Henry   *Scotland*
Douglas
H & H Coll Natal, Cape Town Univ, Sale.
b 26.
Flanker, 4-0-0-4.
53 F− W− I− E−.
Engr.

MCMINN, Archibald Forbes   *New Zealand*
Carterton, Wairarapa, Palmerston N Inst,
Manawatu, Kia Toa, N Island.
b 14.8.1880 Marton; *d* 23.4.19 Porirua.
Forward, 2-2-0-0 (6 -2t).
03 A+; 05 A+(2t).
Fishmonger. Provincial ref & Manawatu sel.
Bro of 'Paddy'.

MCMINN, Francis Alexander   *New Zealand*
('Paddy')
Albion, Pirates, Manawatu, Alhambra, College
St OB, Napier, Hawkes Bay, Wellington.
b 10.11.1874 Turkina; *d* 8.8.47 Auckland.
Hooker, 1-1-0-0.
04 BI+.
Plasterer. Bro of Archie.

MCMORDIE, J.   *Ireland*
Queen's Coll Belfast.
Forward, 1-0-0-1.
1886 S−.

MCMORROW, Angus   *Ireland*
Terenure Coll, Garryowen.
b 6.11.27 Sligo.
FB, 1-0-1-0.
51 W=.
Aer Lingus sales mgr.

MCMULLEN, Alfred Robinson   *Ireland*
Clifton Coll, Cork.
b 1860; *d* − .2.38.
Forward, 2-1-0-1.
1881 E− S+.
Business. Pres IRU 1003-4.

MCMULLEN, Kenneth Victor   *Australia*
Wagga HS, NSW.
b 16.4.41; *d* 6.2.86.
SH, 4-1-1-2 (3 − 1t).
62 NZ= NZ−; 63 E+ SA−(1t).
Salesman. RL.

MCMULLEN, Raymond Frank   *New Zealand*
Pasadena Intermed Sch, Seddon Memorial Tech
Coll, Eden, Otahuhu, Auckland, N Island.
b 18.1.33 Auckland.
Centre/wing, 11-8-1-2 (12 − 4t).
57 A+(1t) A+(1t); 58 A+(1t) A− A+; 59 BI+
BI+ BI+; 60 SA+ SA=(1t) SA−.
Carpenter/roofing co mgr. NZ > 57 A, 60 A &
SA. Ref NZ v E 73.

MCNAB, John Ronald *New Zealand*
Owaka Dist HS, Owaka, Otago, S Island.
b 26.3.24 Owaka.
Flanker, 6-2-1-3.
49 SA− SA− SA−; 50 BI= BI+ BI+.
Farmer. NZ > 49 SA. Sel & coach in Otago.
Otago pres 80.

MCNAMARA, Vincent *Ireland*
PBC Cork, CBC Cork, UC Cork, Munster.
b 11.4.1891 Blackrock, Co Cork; kia 29.11.15
Gallipoli.
SH, 3-1-0-2 (3 − 1t).
14 E− S+(1t) W−.
Engrg student. Served WW1, 2nd Lt in RE.

MCNAUGHTON, Alan Murray *New Zealand*
Rotorua Boys' HS, Kahukura, NZ Jnrs, Bay of
Plenty, N Island.
b 20.9.50 Christchurch.
Flanker, 3-1-0-2.
71 BI− BI+ BI−.
Builder.

MCNAUGHTON, Paul Peter *Ireland*
Rockwell Coll, Trin Coll Dublin, Greystones.
b 18.11.52 Bray.
Centre, 15-6-2-7.
78 S+ F− W− E−; 79 F= W− E+ S= A+ A+;
80 E− S+ F− W+; 81 F−.
Planning exec. Played football for Shelbourne
AFC.

MCNEECE, James *New Zealand*
Middle Sch Invercargill, Waikiwi, Southland, S
Island.
b 24.12.1885; *d* 21.6.17 Messines, Belgium.
Flanker, 5-4-0-1 (3 − 1t).
13 A+ A−; 14 A+(1t) A+ A+.
Farmer. NZ > 14 A. Rep Southland at ckt.
Served WW1; died of wounds. Bro A.M. rep
Southland.

MCNEIL, Alastair Simpson Bell *Scotland*
George Watson's Coll, Watsonians.
b 28.1.15 Edinburgh; kia 26.1.44 Anzio.
Prop, 1-0-0-1.
35 I−.
Medicine. Surg Lt RNVR. Ckt for S.

MCPARTLIN, Joseph James *Scotland*
('Joker')
KCS Wimbledon, Surrey Schools, Oxford Univ,
Harlequins, Barbarians, Dorset & Wilts,
Surrey.
b 12.6.38.
Centre, 6-2-1-3.
60 F− W−; 62 F− W+ I+ E=.
Schoolmaster. Blue 60-2. Taught at St Edward's
Sch Oxford.

MCPHAIL, Bruce Eric *New Zealand*
Ashburton Borough Sch, Ashburton HS,
HSOB, Mid-Canterbury, Christchurch,
Canterbury, Nelson Coll, Nelson, S Island.
b 26.1.37 Ashburton.
Wing, 2-1-0-1.
59 BI+ BI−.
Flour mills mgr. Coached various sides; ref in
Mid-Canterbury 72-6.

MCQUEEN, Samuel Brown *Scotland*
Merchant Taylors' Sch Crosby, Waterloo,
Barbarians.
b 1896; *d* 16.10.83.
FH, 4-3-0-1 (3 − 1t).
23 F+ W+ I+(1t) E−.

MCRAE, John Alexander *New Zealand*
Marist, Southland, S Island.
b 29.4.14 Springhills; *d* 24.2.77 Invercargill.
Prop, 1-1-0-0.
46 A+r.
Normally a hooker, r H.F. Frazer at prop v A
46. Southland sel 59.

MCSHANE, Jan Melville *Australia*
Oxford Univ, NSW.
b 11.12.10; *d* 75.
SH, 2-0-0-2.
37 SA− SA−.
Man dir. Rhodes Scholar. Blue 33-5.

MCVICKER, Hugh *Ireland*
Colerine AI, Edinburgh Univ, The Army,
Richmond, Barbarians.
b 9.2.01 Ballymoney; *d* 19.1.31 India.
Lock, 5-3-0-2 (3 − 1t).
27 E−(1t) S+ W+ NSW−; 28 F+.
Medicine. Bro of Jim & Samuel. Played for I 4
times with bro Jim.

MCVICKER, James M. OBE *Ireland*
Coleraine AI, Queen's Univ Belfast, Edinburgh
Univ, Collegians, Barbarians.
b 1.10.1896 Ballymoney; *d* −.
No 8/lock, 20-11-1-8.
24 F+ E− S− W+ NZ−; 25 F+ E= S− W+; 26
F+ E+ S+ W−; 27 F+ E− S+ W+ NSW−; 28
W+; 30 F−; BI > 24 SA 3-0-1-2.
Medicine. Played for I 4 times with bro Hugh.

MCVICKER, Samuel *Ireland*
Coleraine AI, Queen's Univ Belfast.
b 12.12.1890 Ballymoney; *d* 23.7.71 Strood,
Kent.
Lock, 4-1-0-3.
22 E− S− W− F+.
Methodist minister. Bro of Hugh & James.
Hockey for I 13-14.

MCWILLIAMS, Ruben George　　*New Zealand*
Eureka Sch Waikato, Ponsonby, Auckland, N Island.
b 12.6.01 Paeroa; *d* 27.1.84 Auckland.
Flanker/no 8, 10-5-0-5 (3 − 1t).
28 SA+ SA− SA+; 29 A− A− A−(1t); 30 BI− BI+ BI+.
Linesman. NZ > 28 SA, 29 A. Asst coach Ponsonby.

MEADOWS, John Ernest Charles　　*Australia*
Melbourne, Victoria.
b 2.2.49 London.
Prop, 22-9-0-13.
74 NZ−; 75 S− W−; 76 I+ US+; 76 Fj+ Fj+ F− F−; 78 NZ− NZ− NZ+; 79 I− I−; 81 I+ W−; 82 E− NZ+ NZ−; 83 US+ Arg+ NZ−.
Building supervisor. Lived in Sheppey, Kent, before family emigrated to A. A > 75-6 BI; 78 NZ. Only Victorian A > 81-2 BI.

MEADOWS, Ronald W.　　*Australia*
N Sydney BHS, Sydney Univ, NSW.
b 12.2.31.
Hooker, 6-2-1-3.
58 M+ M= M− NZ− NZ+ NZ−.
Civil engr.

MEADS, Colin Earl ('Pine Tree')　　*New Zealand*
MBE
Te Kuiti HS, NZ Colts, Waitete, King Country, N Island.
b 3.6.36 Cambridge.
Flanker/lock/no 8, 55-41-4-10 (21 − 7t).
57 A+ A+(1t); 58 A+ A− A+(1t); 59 BI+ BI+(1t) BI−; 60 SA− SA+(1t) SA= SA−; 61 F+ F+ F+(1t); 62 A+ A+ A= A+; 63 E+ E+; 63 I+ W+; 64 E+(1t) S= F+ A+ A+ A−; 65 SA+ SA+ SA− SA+; 66 BI+ BI+(1t) BI+ BI+; 67 A+ E+ W+ F+ S+; 68 A+ A+ F+ F+ F+; 69 W+ W+; 70 SA− SA−; 71 BI− BI+ BI− BI=.
Farmer. NZ's most capped player; with Ned Hughes, NZ's longest int career (15 seasons). NZ > 57 & 62 A, 60 A & SA, 63-4 & 67 BI,F & C, 68 A & Fj, 70 A & SA (inj restricted him to 15 apps). Sent off v S 67. Coach World XV > 86 SA. Bro of Stan. Alex Veysey wrote biography 'Colin Meads All Black' pub 74. MBE 71.

MEADS, Stanley Thomas　　*New Zealand*
Te Kuiti HS, Waitete, King Country, N Island.
b 12.7.38 Arapuni.
Flanker/lock/no 8, 15-13-0-2.
61 F+; 62 A+ A+; 63 I+; 64 A+ A+ A−; 65 SA+ SA+ SA− SA+; 66 BI+ BI+ BI+ BI+.
Farmer. NZ > 62 A, 63-4 BI,F & C (9 apps; needed appendix operation during tour). 15 apps for NZ with bro Colin.

MEARES, Arthur William　　*Ireland*
Devenish ('Newry')
Methodist Coll Belfast, Drogheda GS, Trin Coll Dublin.
b 1874 Mullingar; *d* 23.5.35 Newry.
Forward, 4-2-0-2.
1899 S+ W+; 1900 E− W−; BT > 1896 SA.
Solicitor/estate agent.

MEATES, Kevin Francis　　*New Zealand*
Marist Bros' Sch Greymouth, St Bede's Coll, Marist, Canterbury, S Island.
b 20.2.30 Greymouth.
Flanker, 2-1-0-1.
52 A− A+.
Co dir. Broken leg ended career 57. Fdr mem Cantabrian club. Bro of Bill.

MEATES, William Anthony　　*New Zealand*
Marist Bros' Sch, St Bede's Coll, Ath-Univ, Canterbury, Teachers Coll, Otago, Ranfurly, S Island, NZEF, Barbarians (E).
b 26.5.23 Greymouth.
Wing, 7-3-1-3.
49 SA− SA− SA−; 50 BI= BI+ BI+ BI+.
Schoolmaster. NZ > 49 SA. Bro of Kevin.

MEGAW, John CBE QC TD　　*Ireland*
RBAI, Cambridge Univ, Richmond, Instonians.
b 16.11.09.
Flanker/No 8, 2-0-0-2.
34 W−; 38 E−.
Judge. TD 51. QC 53 (NI 54). CBE 56.

MEIBUSCH, John Henry　　*Australia*
Qld.
b 11.12.1878 Qld; *d* 55.
Forward, 1-0-0-1.
04 BT−.
Labourer. Bro of Ludwig.

MEIBUSCH, Ludwig Samuel　　*Australia*
Qld.
b 1893; *d* 65.
Wing, 1-1-0-0 (6 − 2t).
12 US+(2t).
Bro of John Henry.

MEIKLE, Graham William　　*England*
Churchill
St Bees Sch, Cambridge Univ, Waterloo, Leicester, Barbarians, Lancs.
b 14.10.11 Waterloo.
Wing, 3-3-0-0 (12 − 4t).
34 W+(2t) I+(1t) S+(1t).
Schoolmaster. Bro of Stephen. Taught at KES Birmingham & Wellington Coll.

MEIKLE, Stephen Spencer　　*England*
Churchill

St Bees Sch, Waterloo, Barbarians, Lancs.
b 6.7.04; *d* 4.6.60 Liverpool.
FH, 1-0-0-1 (3 − 1t).
29 S−(1t).
Chandler. Bro of Graham. Ldg ref. Rep Lancs
on RFU 55-60.

MEIN, James Andrew Whitelock   *Scotland*
Edinburgh Acad, Edinburgh Academicals.
b 1.7.1852; *d* 2.3.18.
Forward, 5-1-2-1.
1871 E+; 1872 E−; 1873 E=; 1874 E−; 1875
E=.
Farmer. Played in 1st int, S v E 1871.

MELLETT, T.   *South Africa*
Griq W.
1-0-0-1.
1896 BT−.

MELLISH, Frank   *England/South Africa*
Whitmore MC JP
Wynberg Boys HS, Rondebosch Boys HS, SA
Coll Sch, Cape Town Highlanders, Villagers,
Blackheath, Barbarians, W Prov.
b 26.4.1897 Rondebosch, W Prov; *d* 21.8.65.
England
Flanker/lock, 6-5-0-1 (3 − 1t).
20 W− F+ I+(1t) S+; 21 W+ I+.
South Africa
Flanker, 6-3-2-1.
21 NZ− NZ=; 24 BI+ BI+ BI= BI+.
Bus exec/flower farmer. Served WW1 German
SW Africa, then with SA Heavy Artillery,
reaching rank of Col. MC 16. Served WW2 SA
Armoured Div. Absence abroad on bus
prevented his playing E v S, F 21. Returned to
SA to play on their 1st tour to A, NZ 21. Rep
SA on RFU 45-6. SA sel. Mgr SA > 51 BI, F.

MELROSE, Tony Christopher   *Australia*
NSW.
b 7.9.59.
Five-eighth, 6-3-0-3 (11 − 1c 3d).
78 NZ+(1c 1d); 79 I− I− NZ+(1d) Arg−(1d)
Arg+.
Salesman. Ar > NZ 78. RL.

MELVILLE, Christian Landale   *Scotland*
DSO
Black Watch Rgt, The Army, London Scottish,
Barbarians.
b −; *d* 23.4.84 Dorset.
Lock, 3-1-0-2.
37 W+ I− E−.
The Army. Served WW2. Played in 6 Servs ints.

MELVILLE, Nigel David   *England*
Aireborough GS, England SS, England Colts,
NE London Poly, Otley, Wakefield, Wasps,
Yorks.

b 6.1.61 Leeds.
SH, 9-2-0-7.
84 A−; 85 I− W− NZ− NZ−; 86 W+ S− I+
F−; BIr > 83 NZ.
Advertising mgr/Nike sports goods rep. England
Under 23s > 83 R. England B v F 81. E > 81
Arg, 82 US, Can. Capt E on debut, v A 84.
Spinal inj BI > NZ 83, played only 1 match. 5
operations because of knee problems.

MENRATH, J.   *France*
SCUF.
FB, 1-0-0-1 (8 − 1c 2p).
10 W−(1c 2p).

MENTHILLER, Yves ('Zizi')   *France*
Romans.
b 7.1.41 Bourg, Ain.
Hooker, 5-3-1-1.
64 W= It+ SA+ R+; 65 E−.
Accountant.

MENZIES, Henry Fisher   *Scotland*
Fettes Coll, Royal HS, W of Scotland.
b −.6.1867 London, Ontario; *d* 31.7.38.
Forward, 4-1-1-2.
1893 W− I=; 1894 W− E+.
HM.

MEREDITH, Alun   *Wales*
Devonport Servs.
b 19 Ystrad.
Lock, 3-1-0-2 (3 − 1t).
49 E+(1t) S− I−.
RN. Dir RN PT & Sports.

MEREDITH, Brinley Victor   *Wales*
('Beetle')
W Mon GS, Welsh SS, St Luke's Coll, London
Welsh, Newport, Barbarians.
b 21.11.30 Cwmbran.
Hooker, 34-20-3-11 (9 − 3t).
54 I+ F+ S+(1t); 55 E+ S− I+ F+; 56 E+ S+
I− F+; 57 E− S− I+ F+(1t); 58 A+ E= S+
I+(1t); 59 E+ S− I+ F−; 60 E− S+ F− SA−;
61 E+ S− I+; 62 E= S− F+ I=; BI > 55 SA 4-
2-0-2; 62 SA 4-0-1-3.
Schoolmaster/sales rep. W's most capped
hooker. 41 apps for BI. Taught in St Albans 56-
7.

MEREDITH, Courtenay Charles   *Wales*
Neath, Barbarians.
b 29 Crynant.
Prop, 14-9-0-5 (3 − 1t).
53 S+ NZ+; 54 E− I+ F+ S+; 55 E+ S−
I+(1t) F+; 56 E+ I−; 57 E− S−; BI > 55 SA 4-
2-0-2.
Steelworks official.

MEREDITH, John　　　　　　　*Wales*
Swansea.
b 1864; *d* 30.9.20.
Forward, 4-2-0-2.
1888 S+ I−; 1890 S− E+.

MERET, François　　　　　　*France*
Tarbes.
Prop, 1-0-0-1.
40 BF−.

MÉRICQ, Serge　　　　　　　*France*
Agen.
b 16.5.37 La Réole, Gironde.
Wing, 5-3-1-1 (6 − 2t).
59 I−; 60 S+(1t) E= W+(1t); 61 I+.

MERQUEY, Jacques　　　　　*France*
Toulon.
b 26.9.29 Souillac, Lot.
Centre, 4-1-1-2 (3 − 1t).
50 S−(1t) I= E+ W−.
Switched to RL.

MERRIAM, Sir Laurence Pierce　*England*
Brooke MC JP
St Paul's Sch, Oxford Univ, Blackheath,
Barbarians.
b 28.1.1894; *d* 27.7.66 London.
Lock, 2-1-0-1.
20 W− F+.
Solicitor/co chmn. Blue 13. Blues for swimming
& water polo (13-14). Served WW1, Rifle Brig.
Twice wounded; mentioned in despatches. MC
16. Kt 49. JP for Essex.

MERRY, J.　　　　　　　*South Africa*
E Prov.
1-0-0-1.
1891 BT−.

MERRY, J. Augustus　　　　　*Wales*
Pill Harriers.
Hooker, 2-1-0-1.
12 I− F+.
Hull RL 12.

MESNY, Patrick　　　　　　*France*
Grenoble.
b 54.
Centre, 14-7-0-7 (12 − 3t).
79 NZ−(1t) NZ+; 80 SA− R−; 81 I+ W+r A−
(1t) A− R+ NZ− NZ−; 82 I+(1t) Arg+ Arg+.
Professor of PE. F > 80 SA.

MESSENGER, Henry Herbert　*Australia*
('Dally')
NSW.
b 12.4.1883 Sydney; *d* 24.11.59.
Wing, 2-0-1-1 (7 − 1t 2c).
07 NZ−(1t 1c) NZ=(1c).

Boat builder/club mgr. Grandfather a
bargemaster to Queen Victoria. NZ RL 07.

METCALF, H.D.　　　　　*South Africa*
Border.
1-0-1-0.
03 BT=.

METCALFE, Thomas Charles　*New Zealand*
Pirates, Southland, S Island.
b 13.5.09 Invercargill; *d* 26.5.69 Dunedin.
No 8/flanker, 2-1-0-1.
31 A+; 32 A−.
Butcher. NZ > 32 A.

METHUEN, Alfred　　　　　*Scotland*
Fettes Coll, Cambridge Univ, London Scottish,
Barbarians.
b 15.2.1868; *d* 5.3.49 Isle of Wight.
Forward, 2-2-0-0.
1889 W+ I+.
Blue 1886-8.

MEXTED, Graham George　*New Zealand*
Wellington Coll, Tawa, Wellington, Athletic, N
Island.
b 3.2.27 Greytown.
No 8, 1-1-0-0.
50 BI+.
Service station mgr/car dealer. NZ > 51 A.
Father of Murray.

MEXTED, Murray Graham　*New Zealand*
Tawa Coll, Tawa, Wellington, N Island.
b 5.9.53 Wellington.
No 8/flanker, 34-26-2-6 (16 − 4t).
79 S+(1t) E+; 80 A− A+ A− W+; 81 S+ S+
SA+ SA− SA+ R+ F+ F+; 82 A+(1t) A−
A+; 83 BI+ BI+ BI+ BI+ A+ S= E−; 84 F+
F+ A− A+ A+; 85 E+ E+(1t) A+ Arg+
Arg=(1t).
Garage mgr. NZ's most capped No 8 (31 apps).
NZ (2) v Arg 79. NZ > 79 S,E & It, 80 A & Fj;
NAm & W, 83 & 84 A, 83 S & E, 85 Arg. Played
for Rest of World v BI, Cardiff 86. Over 100
apps for Wellington. Son of Graham.

MEYER, Charles du P.　　*South Africa*
Stellenbosch Univ, W Prov.
b −; *d* 80.
FH, 3-1-1-1.
21 NZ− NZ+ NZ=.

MEYER, P.J.　　　　　*South Africa*
Griq W.
1-0-0-1.
1896 BT−.

MEYER, Sylvain　　　　　　*France*
Périgueux.
b 1.6.34 Strasbourg.

Flanker/no 8/wing, 5-3-1-1 (6 − 2t).
60 S+(1t) E= It+(1t) R− Arg+.
Publicist.

MEYNARD, Jacques *France*
Cognac.
Centre/FB, 2-2-0-0 (10 − 2c 2p).
54 Arg+; 56 Cz+(2c 2p).

MIAS, Lucien *France*
Mazamet.
b 28.9.30 St Germaine de Calherbe Lozere.
Lock, 29-17-1-11 (3 − 1t).
51 S+(1t) I− E+ W+; 52 I− SA− W− E− It+;
53 S+ I− W− It+; 54 S+ I+ NZ+ W−; 57 R+;
58 S− E− A+ W+ I+ SA= SA+; 59 S+ It+
W+ I−.
Schoolmaster/medicine. Took over as capt F >
58 SA when Michel Celaya inj.

MICHAEL, Gwilym Morgan *Wales*
Pontardawe, Swansea.
Flanker/lock, 3-1-0-2 (3 − 1t).
23 E−(1t) S− F+.
Clerk/tinplate co mgr. Cousin of Brinley Lewis.
Played in Centenary Match Rugby School 23.

MICHAELSON, Roger Carl *Wales*
Brandon
Clifton Sch, Cambridge Univ, Aberavon,
London Welsh, Surrey, Barbarians.
b 39.
No 8, 1-0-0-1.
63 E−.
Wholesale fruiterer. Blue 60-2.

MICHAU, J.M. ('Baby') *South Africa*
Transvaal.
b − ; *d* 45.
1-0-0-1.
21 NZ−.

MICHAU, J.P. ('Mannetjies') *South Africa*
Stellenbosch Univ, W Prov.
3-1-1-1.
21 NZ− NZ+ NZ=.

MICHELL, Arthur Tompson *England*
Rugby Sch, Oxford Univ, Ravenscourt Pk.
b 16.9.1853; *d* 13.8.23.
Half-back, 3-2-1-0 (1t).
1875 I+(1t) S=; 1876 I+.
Clergyman. Son of Rev Richard Michell,
Principal of Hertford Coll, Oxford. Blue 1871-4.
Won univ sculls 1884. Ordained 1879. Edited
Rugby Sch Register (3 vols). England cap in
RFU Museum.

MICHIE, Ernest James Stewart *Scotland*
('Fourteen')
Aberdeen GS, Aberdeen Univ, Aberdeen

GSFP, London Scottish, RE, The Army,
Barbarians.
b 7.11.33.
Lock, 15-5-0-10 (3 − 1t).
54 F− NZ− I− E−; 55 W+ I+ E−; 56 F+ W−
I−(1t) E−; 57 F+ W+ I− E−; BI > 55 SA.
The Army/forestry. Barbarians > 57 Can.

MIDDLETON, Bernard Boswell *England*
Marlborough Coll, Marlborough Nomads,
Birkenhead Pk, Cheshire.
b 25.12.1858; *d* 22.10.47.
Forward, 2-1-1-0.
1882 I=; 1883 I+.
Bus.

MIDDLETON, John Alan OBE *England*
St Andrew's Coll Dublin, Wanderers,
Richmond, The Army, Hants.
b 11.1.1894.
FB, 1-1-0-0.
22 S+.
The Army. Served WW1, RASC. Served WW2.
POW in Italy 41-3; escaped 43. Retd after 35 yrs
service with rank of Col.

MIDDLETON, Sydney Albert *Australia*
NSW.
b 24.2.1884; *d* 45.
Lock/no 8, 4-2-0-2.
09 E+; 10 NZ− NZ+ NZ−.
Clerk. Olympic rugby gold medal 08.

MILES, John Henry *England*
Medway Street Sch Leicester, Medway Ath,
Stoneygate, Leicester, Northampton, Midlands.
b 1880 Grimsby; *d* 23.1.53.
Wing, 1-0-0-1.
03 W−.
Farmer/chemist's valuer. 1st player capped from
Leicester. Ref I v F, F v W 13; W v F 14.

MILL, James Joseph *New Zealand*
Napier Boys' HS, Nelson Coll, Poverty Bay,
Marist, Hawkes Bay, E Coast, Masterton, NZ
Maoris, Wairarapa, N Island.
b 19.11.1899 Tokomaru Bay; *d* 29.3.50
Gisborne.
SH, 4-3-0-1.
24 W+; 25 E+ F+; 30 BI−.
Sheep farmer. NZ > 24-5 BI,F & C, 26 A. Rep
Poverty Bay at ckt.

MILLAR, A. *Ireland*
Kingstown.
Forward, 3-0-0-3.
1880 E− S−; 1883 E−.
Medicine.

MILLAR, Henry J. *Ireland*
Monkstown.

b −; *d* 4.4.59.
4-3-0-1.
04 W+; 05 E+ S+ W−.
Co dir. Pres IRU 28-9.

MILLAR, John Neill   *Scotland*
Merchiston Castle Sch, W of Scotland.
b 9.3.1873; *d* 9.11.21 Paisley.
Forward, 6-4-0-2 (2 − 1t).
1892 W+ I+(1t) E−; 1893 W−; 1895 I+ E+.
Yarn merchant.

MILLAR, Robert Kirkpatrick CB   *Scotland*
DSO DL
Edinburgh Acad, RMA Woolwich, RE, The
Army, London Scottish.
b 29.6.01; *d* 17.4.81.
Wing, 1-1-0-0.
24 I+.
The Army.

MILLAR, Sidney   *Ireland*
Ballymena Acad, Belfast Nautical Coll,
Ballymena, Barbarians.
b 23.5.34 Ballymena.
Prop, 37-12-3-22.
58 F−; 59 E− S+ W− F+; 60 E− S− W− F−
SA−; 61 E+ S− W− F− SA−; 62 E− S− F−;
63 F− E= S− W+; 64 F−; 68 F− E= S+ W+
A+; 69 F+ E+ S+ W−; 70 SA= F− E− S+
W+; BI > 59 A 2-2-0-0, NZ; 62 SA 4-0-1-3; 68
SA 2-0-1-1.
Industrial sales rep. 44 apps for BI. Asst mgr BI
> 74 SA. Mgr BI > 80 SA.

MILLAR, William Alexander   *South Africa*
SA Coll Sch, W Prov.
b 6.11.1883 Bedford, E Cape; *d* −.
Flanker/no 8, 6-4-1-1 (6 − 2t).
06 E=(1t); 10 BI− BI+; 12 I+(1t) W+; 13 F+.
Clerk, Rly Dept/prospector. Served in SA War
1899; discharged after being badly wounded.
Took up mountaineering, distance walking &
boxing in effort to regain full fitness. Never lost
a bout as amateur heavywt boxer. Won many
walking races before resuming rugby career, for
W Prov 06. Not originally selected for SA > 06-
7 BI, but won place when Bertie Mosenthal
withdrew. Tour capt SA > 12-13 BI, F; capt v
BI 2nd, 3rd Tests 10. Served WW1, wounded
again. Ref 2 Tests SA v BI 24.

MILLAR, William Henry Jordan   *Ireland*
Regent House Newtownards, Queen's Univ
Belfast.
b 9.1.24 Bangor, Co Down.
Wing, 5-3-1-1.
51 E+ S+ W=; 52 S+ W−.
Medicine.

MILLER, Anthony Robert MBE   *Australia*
CEGS Sydney, NSW, Warringah.
b 28.4.29 Manly.
Lock/prop, 41-9-2-30 (6 − 2t).
52 Fj+ Fj− NZ+ NZ−; 53 SA− SA+ SA−
SA−; 54 Fj+ Fj−; 55 NZ− NZ− NZ+; 56 SA−
SA−; 57 NZ− NZ−; 58 W−(1t) E− S− F−
M+ M= M−; 59 BI− BI−; 61 Fj+ Fj+ Fj=
SA− F−; 62 NZ− NZ−; 66 BI−(1t) BI− W+
S−; 67 I− F− I− NZ−.
Electrical engr. 16 yrs Test career. 345 first-
grade matches. Finished playing 85, aged 56;
took up coaching.

MILLER, D.G. See Schultze,
D.G.

MILLER, Sir Francis Henry   *Ireland*
Foyle Coll, Wanderers.
b 5.10.1865; *d* 16.6.36.
Forward, 1-0-0-1.
1886 S−.
Solicitor/town clerk. Mayor of Londonderry 01-
2. Kt 02.

MILLER, Frederick   *Wales*
Mountain Ash.
b 1873 Talybont.
Forward, 7-5-0-2.
1896 I−; 1900 E+ S+ I+; 1901 E+ S− I+.
Miner/police. Hull RL.

MILLER, James Muir   *Australia*
NSW.
b 6.4.39.
Lock, 6-3-0-3.
62 NZ−; 63 E+ SA−; 66 W+ S−; 67 E+.
Stock station agent.

MILLER, Sydney W.J.   *Australia*
NSW.
b −; *d* −.12.09.
Wing, 1-0-0-1.
1899 BT−.

MILLETT, Harry   *England*
Univ Coll Sch Hampstead, Guy's Hosp,
Richmond, Harlequins, Barbarians, London
Cos, Mdx.
b 2.4.1892 London; *d* 26.5.74.
FB, 1-1-0-0.
20 F+.
Medicine. London Cos v SA (2) 12. Served
WW1, R Marines; mentioned in despatches.
Surg at Guy's Hosp.

MILLIAND, Pierre   *France*
Grenoble.
Wing, 3-3-0-0 (9 − 3t).
36 G+; 37 G+(2t) It+(1t).

MILLICAN, John Gilbert   *Scotland*
Berwickshire HS, Edinburgh Univ.
b 21.8.51 Edinburgh.
Flanker, 3-2-0-1.
73 W+ I+ E−.
Chemical engr.

MILLIKEN, Harold Maurice   *New Zealand*
St Andrew's Coll, Springfield, Canterbury,
Sunnyside, S Island.
b 27.2.14 Christchurch.
Lock, 3-3-0-0 (3 − 1t).
38 A+ A+(1t) A+.
Dairy farmer. NZ > 38 A. Papakura & NZ RL
39. Served WW2; reinstated RU 50 & played for
Clevedon & Grafton clubs, before coach of
Leamington. Son Roger rep Waikato Under 21
72-3.

MILLIKEN, Richard Alexander   *Ireland*
Bangor GS, Queen's Univ Belfast, Bangor,
Barbarians.
b 2.9.50.
Centre, 14-6-2-6 (8 − 2t).
73 E+(1t) S− W− F+; 74 F− W= E+ S+(1t)
P= NZ−; 75 E+ S− F+ W−; BI > 74 SA 4-3-1-
0.
Accountant.

MILLIN, Terence John   *Ireland*
St Andrews Coll, Trin Coll Dublin.
b 9.1.03; *d* 3.7.80.
Centre, 1-1-0-0 (3 − 1t).
25 W+(1t).
Medicine.

MILLS, Frank   *Wales*
Swansea, Cardiff.
b 1873 Mountain Ash; *d* 17.2.25 Porthcawl.
Forward, 13-5-0-8.
1892 E− S− I−; 1893 E+ S+ I+; 1894 E− S+
I−; 1895 E− S− I+; 1896 E−.
Licensee.

MILLS, Frederick William   *England*
Marlborough Coll, Marlborough Nomads,
Bradford, Yorks.
b 5.5.1849 Chertsey; *d* 2.2.04 London.
FB, 2-1-1-0.
1872 S+; 1873 S=.
Solicitor.

MILLS, Stephen G.F.   *England*
Gloucester.
b 25.2.53 Cirencester.
Hooker, 5-1-2-2.
81 Arg= Arg+; 83 W=; 84 SA− SA−.
R inj Peter Wheeler v W 83.

MILLS, Walter J.   *South Africa*
Stellenbosch Univ, W Prov.

b 16.6.1891.
Wing, 1-0-0-1 (3 − 1t).
10 BI−(1t).
Toured with cousin, Louis Louw SA > 12-13 BI.

MILLS, William Alonzo   *England*
Devonport A, Devon.
b 2.2.1879 Devonport; *d* −.
Lock/no 8, 11-4-1-6 (12 − 4t).
06 W− I−(1t) S+(1t) F+(1t) SA=; 07 F+ W−
I− S−; 08 F+(1t) W−.
Inspector of shipwrights HM Dockyard. Some
sources credit his t v I 06 to C.H. Milton.

MILMAN, Sir Dermot Lionel   *England*
Kennedy Bt
Uppingham Sch, Cambridge Univ, Bedford,
Edinburgh W, Barbarians, E Midlands.
b 24.10.12.
No 8, 4-2-0-2.
37 W+; 38 W− I+ S−.
Schoolmaster. Ckt for Beds. Taught at Epsom
Coll & Fettes Coll pre-WW2; served RASC.
Mentioned in despatches. Brit Council officer in
SAm, It & Pakistan from 46. Succeeded father
as 8th Bt 62.

MILNE, Charles James Barclay   *Scotland*
Fettes Coll, Fettesian-Lorettonians, W of
Scotland.
b −.5.1864 Kingston, Jamaica; *d* 6.5.1892
Chertsey, Surrey.
Forward, 3-2-1-0.
1886 W+ I+ E=.
College lecturer/inspector of schools. Killed on
the rly, aged 28.

MILNE, Iain Gordon ('Bear')   *Scotland*
George Heriot's Sch, Heriot Watt Univ,
Heriot's FP, Harlequins, Barbarians, Mdx.
b 17.6.58 Edinburgh.
Prop, 33-16-2-15.
79 I= F− NZ−; 80 I− F+; 81 NZ− NZ− R+
A+; 82 E+ I− F+ W+ A+ A−; 83 I− F− W−
E+ NZ=; 84 W+ E+ I+ F+ A−; 85 F− W−
E−; 86 F+ W− E+ I+ R+; BI > 83 NZ.
Laboratory technician/printing works mgr. Capt
Edinburgh Under 23s. Missed 81 int season
through inj. Scottish XV v Fj 82. One of 3 bros
to play for Heriot's FP. Five Nations v Overseas
XV, Twickenham 86.

MILNE, William Murray   *Scotland*
Glasgow Acad, Glasgow Academicals.
b 27.7.1883; *d* 16.12.82.
Forward, 4-2-0-2.
04 I+ E+; 05 W− I−.
Minister. One of int rugby's longest lived
players.

MILNER, Henare Pawhara　　　*New Zealand*
('Buff')
Tokomaru Bay HS, United, NZ Jnrs, NZ Colts,
E Coast, NZ Maoris, Waiouru Army, Comb
Servs, Wanganui, Counties.
b 12.2.46 Tokomaru Bay.
Wing, 1-0-0-1.
70 SA−.
Army. Played centre, wing, FB & 2nd five-
eighth NZ > 70 A & SA.

MILROY, Eric ('Puss')　　　*Scotland*
George Watson's Coll, Watsonians, Edinburgh
Univ.
b 4.12.1887 Edinburgh; kia 18.7.16 Delville
Wood.
SH, 12-3-0-9 (3 − 1t).
10 W−; 11 E−; 12 W−(1t) I− E+ SA−; 13 F+
W− I+ E−; 14 I− E−; BI > 10 SA.
Chartered accountant. Illness allowed him to
play only 3 matches BI > 10 SA. Lt, Black
Watch Rgt.

MILTON, Cecil Henry　　　*England*
Bedford GS, Camborne Sch of Mines,
Barbarians, Cornwall.
b 7.1.1884; *d* 61
Centre, 1-0-0-1 (3 -1t).
06 I−(1t).
Son of Sir William, bro of J.G. Another bro,
N.W. Milton won blues at Oxford (05-7). Some
sources credit his t v I 06 to W.A. Mills.

MILTON, J.G. ('Jumbo')　　　*England*
Bedford GS, Camborne Sch of Mines,
Barbarians, E Midlands, Cornwall.
b 1.5.1885; *d* 15.6.15.
Forward, 5-1-1-3.
04 W= I+ S−; 05 S−; 07 I−.
Son of Sir William, bro of C.H. 1st 3 caps at 18
while at school. 1st player to follow father into E
team. Emigrated SA 07.

MILTON, Sir William Henry　　　*England*
KCMG KCVO
Marlborough Coll, Marlborough Nomads.
b 3.12.1854 Little Marlow; *d* 6.3.30 Cannes.
Back, 2-2-0-0.
1874 S+ I+.
Colonial Service. Father of C.H. & J.G. Ckt for
SA, 1888. Pte sec to Cecil Rhodes 1890-6; other
posts in Rhodesia 1898-14. KCMG 03; KCVO
10.

MINCH, John Berchmans　　　*Ireland*
Clongowes Wood Coll, UC Dublin, Bective
Rgrs, The Army, Barbarians.
b 29.7.1890 Athy, Co Kildare; kia −.2.43.
Centre, 5-1-0-4.
12 SA−; 13 E− S−; 14 E− S+.
Medicine. Served WW2, Lt Col in RAMC.

MINJAT, Roger　　　*France*
Lyon.
FB, 1-1-0-0.
45 BF+.

MIR, Jean-Henri　　　*France*
Lourdes.
b 21.2.45 Tarbes.
SH, 2-2-0-0.
67 R+; 68 I+.
PE teacher.

MIR, Jean-Pierre　　　*France*
Lourdes.
b 6.7.47 St-Lary, Haute-Gironne.
Centre, 1-1-0-0.
67 A+.
PE teacher.

MITCHELL, Frank　　　*England*
St Peter's Sch York, Cambridge Univ,
Blackheath, Yorks, Kent, Barbarians, Sussex.
b 13.8.1872 Market Weighton; *d* 11.10.35
Lewisham.
Forward, 6-3-0-3 (5 − 1t 1c).
1895 W+(1c) I+ S−; 1896 W+(1t) I− S−.
Stockbroker. Blue 1893-5. Ath blue (shot) 1896.
Ckt blue (1894-6); capt CUCC > 1895 US. On
their return presented team's colours (dark blue,
light blue & white) to Barbarians who adopted
them. 2 Tests E v SA 04; capt SA (3) v E 04 &
12; 5 seasons with Yorks CCC (1894-04, average
34.35 runs). Also Bucks CCC, Kent CCC. CY
02. Barbarians comm. Pte in SA War; later Lt
Yorks Dragoons. Fought at Boshof and
Schwartz Koffeefontein (Queen's Medal).
Remained in SA on bus. Served WW1, W
Riding RFA, promoted Lt Col. Author of
'Rugby Football' in Badminton Library series.

MITCHELL, George Willis Earle　　*Scotland*
George Watson's Coll, Edinburgh W,
Edinburgh Univ, Barbarians.
b 23.11.43 Edinburgh.
Lock, 3-0-0-3.
67 NZ−; 68 F− W−.
Medicine.

MITCHELL, J. Gordon　　　*Scotland*
Craigmount Inst, W of Scotland.
b Hamilton.
Forward, 2-1-1-0.
1885 W= I+.
Touch-judge S v W, I v S 1891.

MITCHELL, Neville Alfred　　*New Zealand*
('Brushy')
Southland Boys' HS, Old Boys, Southland,
Alhambra, Otago, S Island.
b 22.11.13 Invercargill.
Wing/centre, 8-5-0-3 (12 − 4t).

285

35 S+ I+(1t) W−; 36 E− A+(2t); 37 SA−; 38
A+ A+(1t).
Hotel mgr/bookseller/wholesale liquor
merchant. NZ > 35-6 BI & C (22 apps), 36 & 38
A (capt). Father Alf rep Otago & Southland.
Uncle Jack rep Otago.

MITCHELL, Terry William　　　*New Zealand*
Takaka Dist HS, Takaka, NZ Jnrs, Golden Bay-
Motueka, Celtic, Linwood, Canterbury, S
Island, NZ Maoris.
b 11.9.50 Takaka.
Wing, 1-0-0-1.
76 SA−r.
Carpenter/tobacco co rep. NZ > 74 I,W & E, ⁷6
SA. Father M.D.I. rep Golden Bay-Motueka.

MITCHELL, William Grant　　　*England*
Bromsgrove Sch, Cambridge Univ, Guy's Hosp,
Richmond, Barbarians, Mdx.
b 23.5.1865; *d* 14.1.05 Vancouver.
FB, 7-4-0-3.
1890 W− S+ I+; 1891 W+ I+ S−; 1893 S−;
BT > 1891 SA.
Medicine/gold mining. Blue 1886. Ath blue
(shot) 1887. His gm won 2nd Test BT v SA,
Kimberley 1891. Played in all 19 tour matches.
Original mem Barbarians. Joined gold rush in
Alaska.

MITCHELL, William James　　　*New Zealand*
Merivale, Canterbury.
b − Melbourne; *d* 2.6.59 Christchurch.
Wing, 2-1-0-1 (3 − 1t).
10 A− A+(1t).
Rly workshops employee/taxi driver/fruiterer.
NZr > 10 A. RL 11; NZ 13-19. Son Murray rep
Canterbury RU 44-5.

MITCHINSON, Frank Edwin　　　*New Zealand*
Berhampore Sch, Newtown Sch, Southern,
Wellington, Poneke, Wanganui, Raetihi, N
Island.
b 3.9.1884 Lawrence; *d* 27.3.78 Wanganui.
Centre/wing/2nd five-eighth, 11-8-2-1 (32 − 10t
1c).
07 A+(3t) A+ A=(1t); 08 AW+(2t) AW=
AW+(3t);; 10 A+ A− A+(1t); 13 A+r
US+(1c).
Farmer. NZ > 07 & 10 A, 13 NAm. Bro Charles
rep Hawkes Bay 05. Son Neil rep King Country
40-8. Grandsons Grant (Wanganui) & Bruce
(Wairarapa-Bush) also played rep rugby.

MOBBS, Edgar Robert DSO　　　*England*
Bedford Mod Sch, Olney, Northampton, E
Midlands, Barbarians.
b 29.6.1882 Northampton; kia 29.7.17
Zillebeke.
Wing/centre, 7-3-1-3 (12 − 4t).

09 A−(1t) W− F+(1t) I+(1t) S−(1t); 10 I=
F+.
Capt Northampton 07-13 (177t). Rep E
Midlands on RFU. Capt Barbarians v W in war-
time fund−raiser, Cardiff 15. Served WW1 as
Lt. At outset, was refused commission because
of his age, 32. Enlisted as a pte. Raised his own
corps of 264 men, known as 'D' Company 7th
Northants Rgt, and included many rugby
players, including E.R. Butcher, the Devon
capt, & H. Willett, capt of Bedford. Of total of
over 400 volunteers who served with 'Mobbs's
Army' 85 survived. DSO 17. In July 21 20ft high
statue unveiled in his memory in Northampton's
Market Square. 1st Mobbs Memorial Match, E
Midlands v Barbarians, played 10.2.21. RFU &
Barbarians comm. Bucks CCC.

MOBERLEY, William Octavius　　　*England*
Rugby Sch, Oxford Univ, Clifton, Ravenscourt
Pk, Glos.
b 14.11.1851 Shoreham; *d* 2.2.14 Mullion,
Cornwall.
Back, 1-1-0-0.
1872 S+.
Schoolmaster. Blue 1871-3 (capt). Ckt for
OUCC; also Glos CCC (1876-83 & 1886).
Taught at Clifton Coll 1874-13.

MOFFAT, James　　　*Ireland*
Methodist Coll Belfast, Belfast Acad.
Forward, 7-1-1-5.
1888 W+ S− NZN−; 1889 S−; 1890 S− W=;
1891 S−.
Manufacturer's agent.

**MOFFAT-PENDER, I.M. (See
PENDER, I.M.)**

MOFFATT, John Edward　　　*Ireland*
O Wesley.
b 3.3.1882; *d* −.
Wing, 4-2-0-2 (12 − 4t).
04 S−(1t); 05 E+(2t) S+(1t) W−.
Medicine. Served in W African Medical Service.

MOFFETT, Jonathan William　　　*Ireland*
Campbell Coll Belfast, Aberdeen Univ,
Ballymena.
b 30.4.37 Belfast.
SH, 2-1-0-1 (10 − 2c 2p).
61 E+(1c 2p) S−(1c).
Forestry officer.

MOFFITT, James Edward　　　*New Zealand*
St James, Wellington, Oriental, Comb Servs, N
Island.
b 3.6.1889 Waikaia; *d* 16.3.64 Auckland.
No 8, 3-1-1-1.
21 SA+ SA− SA=.
Tailor's cutter/hotel mgr. Served WW1,

286

Auckland Infantry Rgt; Comb Servs in King's Cup & toured SA 19. NZ > 20 A. Bro Joe leading ref.

MOGA, Alban ('Bamby') *France*
Bègles.
b 1.5.23 Bordeaux.
Lock, 22-13-0-9.
45 BF+ BF− W−; 46 BF+ I+ NZS− W+; 47 S+ I+ W− E−; 48 I− A+ S− W+ E+; 49 S− I+ E− W+ Arg+ Arg+.

MOLL, T.M. ('Toby') *South Africa*
SA Coll, Cape Colony, Transvaal, W Prov.
b 20.7.1890 Cape Town; *d* 14.7.16.
1-0-0-1.
10 BI−.
Bank employee. Served WW1, 2nd Lt in Leics Rgt; died of wounds.

MOLLOY, Michael Gabriel *Ireland*
Garbally Park Coll Ballinasloe, UC Galway, London Irish, The Army, Barbarians, Surrey.
b 27.9.44 Cornamona, Co Galway.
Lock, 27-14-3-10 (6 − 2t).
66 F− E=; 67 A+ E− S+ W+ F−(1t) A+; 68 F− E= S+ W+ A+; 69 F+ E+ S+ W−; 70 F− E− S+(1t) W+; 71 F= E− S+ W−; 73 F+; 76 A−.
Medicine. Served in RAMC. Medical officer IRU.

MOLONEY, John Joseph *Ireland*
St Mary's Coll, Barbarians.
b 27.8.49.
SH, 27-14-3-10 (12 − 3t).
72 F+(1t) E+ F+; 73 NZ= E+ S− W− F+; 74 F− W= E+(1t) S+ P= NZ−; 75 E+ S− F+ W−; 76 S−; 78 S+ F− W−(1t) E−; 79 A+ A+; 80 S+ W+; BI > 74 SA.
Sales rep/dir office equipment co.

MOLONEY, Lawrence Anthony *Ireland*
St Munchins Coll, Munster Schs, Garryowen, Munster.
b 14.6.51.
FB, 4-1-0-3.
76 W−r S−; 78 S+r NZ−.
Bank official.

MOLONY, Jack Ursula ('Jacko') *Ireland*
Mount St Joseph Coll Roscrea, UC Dublin.
b 21.10.24 Thurles.
Lock, 1-1-0-0.
50 S+.
Medicine.

MOMMÉJAT, Bernard *France*
Cahors.
b 18.5.34 Paris.
Lock, 22-14-3-5 (6 − 2t).

58 It+(1t) I+ SA= SA+; 59 S+ E= It+ W+ I−; 60 S+ E= I+ R−; 62 S+ E+ W− I+(1t) It+ R−; 63 S− I+ W+.
Draughtsman/restaurateur.

MONCLA, François *France*
RCF, Pau.
b 1.4.32 Louvie-Juzon.
Lock/flanker, 31-18-5-8 (21 − 7t).
56 Cz+; 57 I− E− W− It+ R+; 58 SA= SA+; 59 S+(1t) E= It+(1t) W+(2t) I−; 60 S+(1t) E= W+ I+(1t) It+ R−(1t) Arg+ Arg+ Arg+; 61 S+ SA= E= W+ It+ I+ NZ− NZ− NZ−.
Electricity technician. Capt F > 60 Arg & Chile; 61 NZ.

MONCRIEFF, Hon Francis Jeffrey *Scotland*
Edinburgh Acad, Edinburgh Academicals.
b 27.8.1849; *d* 30.5.1900 Edinburgh.
Forward, 3-1-1-1.
1871 E+; 1872 E−; 1873 E=.
Chartered accountant. S's 1st capt, v E 1871. Pres SRU 1875-6.

MONIÉ, René *France*
Perpignan.
b 2.1.34 Theza.
Centre, 2-1-0-1 (3 − 1t).
56 Cz+(1t); 57 E−.

MONNIER, Robert ('L'Agneau') *France*
SBUC.
Flanker/no 8, 2-0-0-2.
11 I−; 12 S−.

MONNIOT, Marcel *France*
RCF.
Lock/flanker, 2-0-0-2.
12 W− E−.

MONOGHAN, Laurence Edward *Australia*
St Joseph's Coll, NSW.
b 19.5.52.
FB, 17-6-1-10 (11 − 2t 1d).
73 E−; 74 NZ− NZ=(1t) NZ−; 75 E+ E+(1t) S− W−; 76 E− I+ US+; 76 F−; 78 W+ W+(1d) NZ−; 79 I− I−.
Insurance assessor.

MONTADE, Camille *France*
Perpignan.
Prop, 5-0-0-5.
25 I− NZ− S− W−; 26 W−.

MONTEITH, Hugh Glencairn *Scotland*
Fettes Coll, Cambridge Univ, London Scottish, RAMC.
b −.5.1883; *d* −.

Forward, 8-6-0-2 (3 − 1t).
05 E+; 06 W− I+ E− SA+; 07 W+(1t) I+; 08 E+.
Medicine. Blue 03-5. Selected S v NZ 05, but could not play.

MONTEITH, Jack Deryk Erle   *Ireland*
Coleraine AI, Queen's Univ Belfast.
b 24.8.22 Ballymoney.
Centre, 3-2-0-1.
47 E+ S+ W−.
Dental surgeon.

MONTGOMERY, A.   *Ireland*
RBAI, NIFC.
b 26.9.1871; *d* −.1.28.
Centre, 1-0-0-1.
1895 S−.
Bro of Robert.

**MONTGOMERY, Sir Frank   *Ireland*
Percival** MC
RBAI, Campbell Coll, Queen's Univ Belfast.
b 10.6.1892; *d* 11.8.72.
FB, 3-1-0-2.
14 E− S+ W−.
Medicine. Served WW1, Capt RAMC.

MONTGOMERY, Robert   *Ireland*
Queen's Coll Belfast, Cambridge Univ, NIFC.
b 1.2.1866; *d* −.
Wing, 5-2-0-3 (4t).
1887 E+(1t) S− W−(3t); 1891 E−; 1892 W+.
Schoolmaster. Blue 1891. Bro of A.
Montgomery. 1st I int to score 3t, v W 1887.

MONTI, Carrabo Italo Ansell   *Australia*
Qld.
b 14; *d* 77.
Lock, 1-0-0-1.
38 NZ−.
Chemist.

MONTINI, Patrick Evan   *South Africa*
Stellenbosch Univ, W Prov.
b 15.6.29.
Centre, 2-2-0-0.
56 A+ A+.

**MONYPENNY, Douglas   *Scotland*
Blackwell**
Fettes Coll, London Scottish.
b −.6.1878; *d* 22.2.1900 Paardeburg, SA.
Centre, 3-2-0-1 (3 − 1t).
1899 I− W+(1t) E+.
The Army. Served Boer War; died of wounds.

MOODIE, Alexander Reid   *Scotland*
Dundee HS, St Andrew's Univ.
b 30.9.1886 Balmuirfield, Dundee; *d* −.
Forward, 3-2-0-1.

09 E+; 10 F+; 11 F−.
Medicine.

MOOLMAN, Louis Christiaan   *South Africa*
A.H.S. Lyttleton Sch, Pretoria Univ, Pretoria, SA Univs, SA Forces, Jnr Springboks, N Transvaal.
b 21.1.51 Pretoria.
Lock, 20-16-0-4.
77 Wd+; 80 SAm+ SAm+ BI+ BI+ BI+ BI− SAm+ SAm+ F+; 81 I+ I+ NZ− NZ+ NZ− US+; 82 SAm+ SAm−; 84 SAm+ SAm+.
Farmer.

MOON, Brendan Joseph   *Australia*
Australian Schs, Brothers, Brisbane, Qld.
b 10.10.58.
Wing, 31-16-1-14 (52 − 13t).
78 NZ− NZ+; 79 I−(1t) I− NZ+ Arg− Arg+(2t); 80 Fj+(1t) NZ+ NZ−(1t) NZ+; 81 F+(1t) F+ I+ W− S−; 82 E−(2t) S−(1t) S+; 83 US+ Arg− Arg+(2t) NZ− It+(1t) F= F−; 84 Fj+ NZ+(1t) NZ− NZ− E+.
A's most capped wing. A Schs 76. A > 78 NZ; 79 Arg; 80 Fj; 81-2 & 84 BI; broke arm v E 84, returned early. A rec 12t A > 81-2 BI.

MOONEY, Thomas Paul   *Australia*
Qld.
b 29.
Hooker, 2-1-0-1.
54 Fj+ Fj−.

MOORE, C. Malcolm   *Ireland*
Armagh RS, Trin Coll Dublin.
Forward, 3-1-0-2.
1887 S−; 1888 W+ S−.
The Army.

MOORE, D. Frank   *Ireland*
Wanderers.
Forward, 4-0-0-4.
1883 E− S−; 1884 E− W−.
Solicitor. Ref E v W, W v S 1886.

MOORE, Edward James CB VD   *England*
Epsom Coll, Oxford Univ, Bart's Hosp, Blackheath, Kent.
b 25.5.1862; *d* 7.3.25 Lewisham.
Forward, 2-2-0-0.
1883 I+ S+.
Medicine. Blue 1882-3. CB 11. Served WW1, Lt Col RAMC; mentioned in despatches. VD 17. GP at Blackheath.

MOORE, Sir Frederick William   *Ireland*
Trin Coll Dublin, Wanderers.
b 3.9.1857;; *d* 23.8.49.
Forward, 4-0-0-4.
1884 W−; 1885 E− S−; 1886 S−.

Keeper R Botanical Gardens Glasnevin. Pres
IRU 1889-90. Kt 11.

MOORE, Graham John Tarr *New Zealand*
Dannevirke HS, Hawkes Bay, Univ, NZ Univs,
Otago, S Island.
b 18.3.23 Wellington.
Wing, 1-0-0-1 (3 − 1t).
49 A−(1t).
Medicine. Hon physician to Wairarapa RU
since 55. Bro Colin rep Otago & Southland.

MOORE, Herbert *Ireland*
RS Dungannon, Queen's Univ Belfast.
b −.6.1890 Downpatrick; d −.
Forward, 8-4-0-4.
10 S−; 11 W− F+; 12 F+ E− S+ W+ SA−.

MOORE, Herbert *Ireland*
RS Dungannon, RBAI, Windsor.
FB, 2-0-0-2.
1875 E−; 1877 S−.
Medicine.

MOORE, Norman J.N. Hope *England*
Bristol, Glos, Som.
b 1877 Lewisham; d 8.3.38 Scargill, Skipton.
Forward, 3-1-1-1 (6 − 2t).
04 W= I+(2t) S−.
231 apps for Bristol 01-10.

MOORE, Lord Philip Brian Cecil *England*
GCVO KCB CMG PC
Dragon Sch Oxford, Cheltenham Coll, Oxford
Univ, Blackheath, Barbarians, Oxon.
b 6.4.21.
No 8, 1-0-0-1.
51 W−.
Civil service. Blue 45-6. Hockey blue 46.
Keeper of the Queen's Archives. Oxon CCC.
Served WW2, 106 Sqn Bomber Command.
POW in Germany 42-5. Entered Admiralty 47;
Asst Pte Sec to First Lord 50-1; Principal Pte Sec
57-8. Brit High Commissioner Singapore 63-5.
CMG 65. Pte Sec to HM The Queen. Peer 86.

MOORE, Terence Anthony *Ireland*
Patrick
North Monastery Cork, Highfield, Barbarians.
b 29.4.45 Cork.
No 8, 12-5-3-4 (4 − 1t).
67 A+; 73 NZ= E+ S− W− F+; 74 F− W=
E+(1t) S+ P= NZ−.
Clerk.

MOORE, W.D. *Ireland*
RBAI, Queen's Coll Belfast, Windsor.
Forward, 1-0-0-1.
1878 E−.

MOORE, William John *Wales*
Bridgend.
b 17.2.08 Garw Valley; d 31.3.76 Oldham.
Lock, 1-0-0-1 ().
33 I−.
Quarryman. Oldham RL. Sparring partner to
boxer Jackie Paterson.

MOORE, William Kenneth *England*
Thomas
Wyggeston Sch, O Wyggestonians, Devonport
Servs, Leicester, Barbarians, RN, Cornwall,
Leics.
b 24.2.21.
SH, 7-4-0-3.
47 W+ I−; 49 F+ S+; 50 I+ F− S−.
Shoe co sales mgr. E Midlands & Staffs Soc ref.
Served WW2 RN.

MORAITIS, Basil *France*
Toulon.
b 2.1.46 Marseilles.
Wing, 2-0-1-1.
69 E− W=.
Electrician.

MORAN, Frederick George *Ireland*
CUS, Clontarf, Barbarians.
b 13; d 17.10.79.
Wing, 9-5-0-4 (18 − 6t).
36 E+; 37 E−(2t) S+(1t) W+; 38 S−(1t) W−
(1t); 39 E+ S+(1t) W−.
Hotelier/wholesale grocer. Irish ath & clay
pigeon shooting teams.

MORAN, Herbert Michael *Australia*
NSW.
b 1885 Sydney; d 20.11.45 Cambridge, E.
Forward, 1-0-0-1.
08 W−.
Medicine. Capt A > 08 BI.

MORDELL, Robert John *England*
Thames Valley GS, Wasps, Rosslyn Pk,
b 2.7.51 Twickenham.
Flanker, 1-0-0-1.
78 W−.
Schoolmaster. Conceded p which enabled W to
beat E 78 & never played for E again. Oldham
RL 79, later Kent Invicta RL as player/coach
£13,500 fee.

MORDT, Raymond Herman *South Africa*
Churchill Sch, Zimbabwe-Rhodesia,
Wanderers, N Transvaal, Transvaal.
b 15.2.57 Cape Town.
Wing, 18-14-0-4 (48 − 12t).
80 SAm+(1t) SAm+ BI+ BI+ BI+ BI−
SAm+ SAm+(2t) F+; 81 I+ NZ− NZ+ NZ−
(3t) US+(3t); 82 SAm+(2t) SAm−; 84 SAm+
SAm+(1t).

SA Army. Signed Wigan RL (E) with fellow Springbok Rob Louw, 85.

MOREL, André   *France*
Grenoble.
Wing, 1-1-0-0 (3 − 1t).
54 Arg+(1t).

MORELL, Henry Brown   *Ireland*
RS Dungannon, Trin Coll Dublin.
b 1858; *d* −.3.34.
Forward, 4-1-1-2.
1881 E− S+; 1882 W− E=.
Chief insp RIC. Won RIC middleweight boxing title.

MORÈRE, Jean   *France*
Toulouse.
Prop, 4-2-0-2.
27 E+ G+; 28 S− NSW−.

MORETON, Raymond Claude   *New Zealand*
Southland Boys' HS, HSOB, Southland, Univ, NZ Colts, NZ Univs, Canterbury, S Island.
b 30.1.42 Invercargill.
2nd five-eighth/centre, 7-4-1-2 (9 − 2t 1d).
62 A= A+; 64 A+(1d) A+(1t) A−; 65 SA+ SA−(1t).
Chartered accountant. NZ > 62 A.

MORFITT, Samuel   *England*
W Hartlepool, Hull KR, Durham Cos, Yorks.
b −.12.1868 Hull; *d* 1.1.54 Hull.
Back/wing, 6-2-0-4 (9 − 3t).
1894 W+(1t) I− S−; 1896 W+(2t) I− S−.
Shipyard rivetter/licensee. Turned RL when Hull KR changed codes 1897.

MORGAN, Charles Henry   *Wales*
Clifton Coll, Royal Navy, Carmarthen Ath, Llanelli.
b 32 Carmarthen.
Prop, 2-2-0-0.
57 I+ F+.
Textile merchant. Wales XV v Rest of Britain 58.

MORGAN, Clifford Isaac OBE   *Wales*
CVO
Tonyrefail GS, Welsh SS, Cardiff, Bective Rgrs, Barbarians.
b 7.4.30 Porth.
FH, 29-19-2-8 (9 − 3t).
51 I= F− SA−; 52 E+ S+ I+; 53 S+ I+ F+ NZ+; 54 E− I+ S+(1t); 55 E+ S− I+(1t) F+; 56 E+ S+(1t) I− F+; 57 E− S− I+ F+; 58 E= S+ I+ F−; BI > 55 SA 4-2-0-2.
BBC Head of Outside Broadcasts. W's most capped FH. Barbarians v SA 52, NZ 54, A 58. Barbarians > 57 Can; SA 58. Offered £6500 to join Wigan RL 55. Refused nomination to

captain Cardiff. Retired 58. Ed 'Rugby, The Great Ones' pub 70. OBE 77. CVO 86.

MORGAN, D.   *Wales*
Swansea.
Forward, 7-1-2-4 (1t).
1885 S=; 1886 E− S−; 1887 E= S− I+(1t); 1889 I−.

MORGAN, David   *Wales*
Llanelli.
b 1872 Llanelli; *d* 33 Pemberton.
Half-back, 2-1-0-1.
1895 I+; 1896 E−.
Tinplater.

MORGAN, David Edgar   *Wales*
New Dock Stars, Llanelli.
b 17.5.1896 Llanelli; *d* 9.9.83 Llanelli.
Flanker, 4-2-0-2.
20 I+; 21 E− S− F+.
Police. Served WW1. W v E Schs 07 at 11 yrs old. Goalkeeper with Llanelli AFC 14. Hull RL 21. 2 GB RL Tests; 36 days after turning pro, played for GB v A.

MORGAN, David Robert Ruskin   *Wales*
Gwendraeth GS, Cardiff Coll, Pontyberem, Llanelli, Barbarians, Cardiff.
b 41 Pontyberem.
Wing, 9-2-2-5.
62 E= S− F+ I=; 63 E− S+ I− F− NZ−.
Schoolmaster/supervisor BP.

MORGAN, Douglas Waugh   *Scotland*
Melville Coll, Stewart's-Melville FP, Barbarians.
b 9.3.47 Edinburgh.
SH, 21-8-0-13 (71 − 4c 6d 15p).
73 W+(1c) I+(2d 2p) E−(1p) P+; 74 I− F+(1p); 75 I+(1d) F− W+(3p) E−(2p) NZ− A+(1c); 76 F−(1d) W−(1c); 77 I+(1d) F− W−; 78 I−(3p) F−(1c 1d 1p) W−(2p) E−; BI > 77 NZ 2(1r)-0-0-2.⁄
Chiropodist. Scottish XV v Arg 73, Tg 74. 24 pts S v Wellington, NZ, 75.

MORGAN, Edgar MC   *Wales*
Collegiate Sch Tanyrallt, Alltwen, UC Bangor, Pontardawe, Swansea.
b −.4.1882 Pontardawe; *d* −.4.62 Pontardawe.
No 8, 4-3-0-1.
14 E− S+ F+ I+; BTuncap > 08 A, NZ.
Mem of 'Terrible Eight'. Served WW1, infantry officer, Brecknock Rgt, transferred to RE.

MORGAN, Edward T.   *Wales*
Christ's Coll Brecon, Guy's Hosp, London Welsh, Surrey, Sketty.
b 22.5.1880 Abernant; *d* 1.9.49 N Walsham.
Wing, 16-12-1-3 (42 − 14t).

02 E+ S+ I+; 03 I+(2t); 04 E=(1t) S+(1t) I−(2t); 05 E+(2t) S+ I+(1t) NZ+(1t); 06 E+(1t) S+ I−(1t) SA−; 08 F+(2t); BT > 04 A, NZ. Medicine. Bro of W.L., uncle of W. Guy. One of outstanding t scorers of all time; 14t in 13 matches 03-06. GP at Sketty, Swansea.

MORGAN, Frederick Luther   *Wales*
Gwendraeth GS, Llanelli.
b 11.2.15 Pontyberem.
Lock, 4-2-0-2.
38 E+ S− I+; 39 E−.
Police. 1st Gwendraeth GS cap.

MORGAN, George Joseph   *Ireland*
Belvedere Coll, Clontarf, Barbarians.
b 24.3.12; *d* 16.4.79.
SH, 19-8-0-11 (6 − 2t).
34 E−(1t) S− W−; 35 E− S+ W+ NZ−; 36 E+ S+ W−; 37 E− S+ W+; 38 E− S−(1t) W−; 39 E+ S+ W−; BI > 38 SA 1-1-0-0.
Bank official. 19 consec apps for I. Ckt for I.

MORGAN, Harry P.   *Wales*
Wycliffe Coll, Cambridge Univ, Newport.
b 16.6.30 Goytre, Pontypool.
Centre, 4-3-0-1 (3 − 1t).
56 E+ S+(1t) I− F+.
Business house rep. Blue 52-3.

**MORGAN, Haydn John ('Red   *Wales*
Devil')**
Abertillery, Wolfhounds, REME, The Army, Barbarians.
b 30.7.36 Oakdale, Gwent.
Flanker, 27-13-3-11 (9 − 3t).
58 E= S+ I+(1t) F−; 59 I+ F−; 60 E−; 61 E+ S− I+ F−; 62 E= S− F+ I=; 63 S+ I− F−; 65 E+(1t) S+ I+ F−; 66 E+ S+ I− F+ A−(1t); BI > 59 A, NZ 2-0-0-2; 62 SA 2-0-1-1.
Car salesman. W > 64 SA. Barbarians v SA 61. Barbarians > 58 SA. Nickname 'Red Devil' from days as REME cpl when attached to Airborne Div. Emigrated SA.

MORGAN, Ivor   *Wales*
Danygraig Board Sch, Swansea.
b −.8.1884 Pembs; *d* −.12.43.
Flanker, 13-12-0-1 (18 − 6t).
08 A+; 09 E+ S+ F+ I+; 10 F+(2t) E− S+(1t) I+; 11 E+(1t) F+(1t) I+; 12 S+(1t).
Coal trimmer.

MORGAN, James Rydiard   *England*
Hawick.
b c1890 Cockermouth; *d* 29.4.61 Hawick.
Hooker, 1-0-0-1.
20 W−.
Wool merchant. E cap in Hawick clubhouse.

MORGAN, John L. ('Jack')   *Wales*
Oriental Stars, Llanelli.
b 1892 Patagonia.
Flanker, 2-0-0-2.
12 SA−; 13 E−.
Of Welsh parentage, came to W as youth. Played for Oriental Stars v Bordeaux in Bordeaux 26.12.10. Joined Llanelli 11. Returned SAm 13.

MORGAN, Joseph Edmund   *New Zealand*
Whangarei Boys' HS, Mid-Northern, N Auckland, N Island.
b 7.8.45 Whangarei.
2nd five-eighth, 5-3-0-2 (4 − 1t).
74 A+; 74 I+; 76 SA+(1t) SA− SA−.
Fitter/welder. NZ > 74 A & Fj & I, W & E, 76 SA. N Auckland's 'Sports Personality of Year' 76.

MORGAN, Morgan Edgar   *Wales*
Swansea.
b −; *d* c82.
Prop, 4-2-0-2.
38 E+ S− I+; 39 E−; BI > 38 SA 2-0-0-2.
Police/farmer. Suffered broken rib, damaged lung v S 38.

MORGAN, Norman H.   *Wales*
Newport, Barbarians.
b 34.
FB, 3-2-0-1 (14 − 4c 2p).
60 S+(1c 1p) I+(2c) F−(1c 1p).
Steelworker/police.

MORGAN, Peter John   *Wales*
Haverfordwest SMS, Welsh Youth, Llanelli, Pembs, Sydney Welsh (A).
b 1.1.59 Broadhaven.
Centre/FH/wing, 4-2-0-2.
80 S+r I− NZ−r; 81 I+; BI > 80 SA.
Builder. Wales B v Arg 78, v F 78. Wales XV v R 79.

MORGAN, Philip E.J.   *Wales*
Welsh Youth, Steel Co of Wales, Aberavon.
b 21.12.37 Hereford.
Prop, 3-1-0-2.
61 E+ S− F−.
Steelworker.

MORGAN, Rhys   *Wales*
Newport.
Prop, 1-0-0-1.
84 S−.
Wales B v F 83.

MORGAN, Thomas   *Wales*
Morfa Rangers, Llanelli.

b c1866 Llanelli; *d* 1899 Bridgend.
Back, 1-0-0-1.
1889 I−.
Colliery check weigher. Died in Bridgend Asylum.

MORGAN, William George   *England*
Derek
Lewis Sch Pengam, Durham Univ, Medicals, UAU, Newbridge, Percy Pk, Barbarians, Mon, Northumb.
b 30.11.36 Maesycwmmer, Gwent.
No 8, 9-4-2-3.
60 W+ I+ F= S+; 61 SA− W− I− F= S+.
Dentist. Sec Newbridge RFC. Co-opted Higher Education rep RFU; chmn sel. Mgr E > 85 NZ.

MORGAN, William Guy   *Wales*
Christ's Coll Brecon, Welsh SS, Cambridge Univ, Guy's Hosp, Swansea.
b 26.12.07 Garnant; *d* 27.7.73 Carmarthen.
Centre, 8-4-2-2 (13 − 3t 1d).
27 F+(1t) I−(1t); 29 E− S+(1t) F+ I=; 30 I+ F=(1d).
Schoolmaster. Blue 26-9. Nephew of E.T. & W.L. Glamorgan CCC. Later known as W.G. Stewart-Morgan.

MORGAN, William Llewellyn   *Wales*
Christ's Coll Brecon, Cardiff, London Welsh.
b 1885 Abernant; *d* −.
SH, 1-1-0-0.
10 S+; BT > 08uncap A, NZ.
RN. Bro of E.T., uncle of W. Guy.

MORIARTY, Cecil Charles   *Ireland*
Hudson OBE
Trin Coll Dublin, Monkstown.
b 28.1.1877; *d* 7.4.58.
Forward, 1-1-0-0.
1899 W+.
Police. OBE 25.

MORIARTY, Paul William
Morriston, Swansea, W Suburbs (A).
b 16.7.64 Morriston.
Flanker, 2-1-0-1.
86 I+ F−.
Machine operator. Of Irish, English & Welsh ancestry. Wales B. Bro of Richard.

MORIARTY, Richard Daniel   *Wales*
Bishop Vaughan Sch Morriston, Morriston, Swansea, W Suburbs (A).
b 1.5.57 Gorseinon.
Lock/flanker/no 8, 13-5-1-7 (4 − 1t).
81 A+(1t); 82 I− F+ E− S−; 83 E=; 84 S− I+ F− E+; 85 S+ I− F−.
Electrician. Wales B v Arg 78, v A, F 81. Wales B > 80 US, Can; 83 Spain. Wales XV v Maoris 82. Sent off 3 times, Swansea v Llanelli (by Clive

Norling 78, Les Peard 84, Owen Jones 86). Disq from sel for W 85-86 season. Bro of Paul.

MORKEL, Andrew O.   *South Africa*
Transvaal.
b − ; *d* 23.2.46.
1-0-1-0.
03 BT=.
SA > 06-7 BI, F. 1st of 10 mems of Morkel family to rep SA. At one time, 22 Morkels were playing regularly throughout SA. Famous Morkel dynasty began in 1691 when bros Philip & Willem settled in Cape Province after leaving Hamburg because their father did not want them to be conscripted in to German army.

MORKEL, Douglas Francis   *South Africa*
Theodore ('Dougie')
Kimberley, Witwatersrand, Transvaal.
b 1886; *d* 20.2.50 Johannesburg.
Prop/hooker, 9-8-1-0 (38 − 3t 7c 5p).
06 I+ E=; 10 BI+(1t 1c) BI+(3c 1p); 12 S+(1c) I+ W+(1p); 13 E+(2p) F+(2t 2c 1p).
Mining co, Germiston. Played with bro W.S. v I, E 06. Capt SA v BI 1st Test 10; E 13. 140 career pts for SA. Died in motor accident.

MORKEL, Harry J.   *South Africa*
W Prov.
b 14.10.1883; *d* 56.
1-0-0-1.
21 NZ−.
Bro of Royal.

MORKEL, Henry William   *South Africa*
W Prov.
b 14.7.1894.
Wing, 2-1-0-1.
21 NZ− NZ+.

MORKEL, J.A. ('Royal')   *South Africa*
W Prov.
b 22.3.1896; *d* −.10.26.
Lock, 2-1-1-0.
21 NZ+ NZ=.
Bro of Harry.

MORKEL, Jan Willem Hunter   *South Africa*
('Jackie')
W Prov.
b 13.11.1891 Somerset W; *d* 15.5.16 E Africa.
Centre, 5-5-0-0 (16 − 4t 2c).
12 S+ I+(2t) W+; 13 E+(1t) F+(1t 1c).
Bro of Pieter Gerhard. SA > 12-13 BI, F. Served WW1, Trooper in 1st Mounted Bde Scout Corps; died of dysentery.

MORKEL, Pieter Gerhard   *South Africa*
Somerset West, W Prov.
b 15.10.1888 Somerset W; *d* −.
FB, 8-6-1-1 (16 − 6c 1d).

12 S+(1c) I+(3c) W+; 13 E+ F+; 21 NZ−(1c)
NZ+(1c 1d) NZ=.
Bro of Jackie. SA > 12-13 BI, F; 21 NZ. His d
from half-way won 2nd Test v NZ 21; presented
with gold medal by Auckland RU to mark feat.

MORKEL, P.K.   *South Africa*
W Prov.
Wing, 1-0-0-1.
28 NZ−.

MORKEL, William Henry ('Boy')   *South Africa*
Diggers, W Prov.
b 2.1.1886 Somerset W; d 54 Worcester, Cape
Prov.
Flanker/no 8, 9-7-1-1 (6 − 2t).
10 BI+; 12 S+(1t) I+ W+; 13 E+ F+; 21 NZ−
NZ+ NZ=.
Farmer. SA > 12-13 BI, F; 21 NZ. Recalled at
35 after 8yr absence to capt SA 1st Test side v
NZ (3) 21; tour capt Theo Pienaar failed to
make Test team. Four other Morkels in team,
Gerhard, Henry, Harry & Royal.

MORKEL, W.S. ('Sommie')   *South Africa*
Transvaal.
b 1880.
Forward, 4-2-1-1.
06 S− I+ W+ E=.
Played with bro Dougie v I, E 06.

MORLEY, Alan John MBE   *England*
Colston's Sch Bristol, Bristol, Glos.
b 25.6.50 Bristol.
Wing, 7-2-0-5 (8 − 2t).
72 SA+(1t); 73 NZ− W− I−; 75 S+(1t) A−
A−.
Auctioneer/valuer. Scored 475t, world's rec in
1st-class rugby. With P.S. Preece, E's most t in
any tour match (4 v W Aus 75). Over 516 apps
for Bristol 59-86. MBE 85.

MORLEY, John Cuthbert ('Jack')   *Wales*
Newport Sec Sch, Welsh SS, Newport.
b 28.7.09 Newport; d 7.3.72 Newport.
Wing, 14-8-2-4 (15 − 5t).
29 E−(1t) S+ F+ I=; 30 E− I+; 31 E=(1t)
S+(1t) F+ I+(2t) SA−; 32 E+ S+ I−; BI > 30
NZ 3-1-0-2, A.
Dentist. Wigan RL 32. RL for E & W.

MORONEY, John Christopher   *Ireland*
M.
Rockwell Coll, UC Dublin, London Irish,
Garryowen.
b 28.10.45 Clogheen, Co Tipperary.
Wing, 6-5-0-1 (20 − 1t 4c 3p).
68 W+ A+(1c); 69 F+(1t 1c 3p) E+ S+(2c)
W−.
PE instructor.

MORONEY, Rory Joseph   *Ireland*
Matthew
Clongowes Wood Coll, Dublin Coll of
Marketing, Lansdowne.
b 3.10.57 Clonmel.
Centre, 3-0-1-2.
84 F− W−; 85 F=.
Manager.

MORONEY, Thomas Aloysius   *Ireland*
CUS, UC Dublin, London Irish, Surrey, The
Army.
b 27.7.41 Kilmihil, Co Clare.
Prop, 3-1-0-2.
64 W−; 67 A+ E−.
Medicine. Served in RAMC.

MORPHY, E. McG.   *Ireland*
Portora RS, Trin Coll Dublin.
b 28.1.1886; d −.
Forward, 1-0-0-1.
08 E−.

MORRIS, Alfred Drummond   *England*
Warrington CB CMG OBE
Alverstoke Sch, US Portsmouth, RN,
Barbarians.
b 1883; d 24.3.62 Chelsea.
Forward, 3-1-0-2.
09 A− W− F+.
RN. Joined RN 1899; served WW1 RN Air
Service, till joining RAF. OBE 18. CMG 19.
Served WW2, Air Commodore. CB 43. Rep
RAF on RFU 23-5 & 27-45.

MORRIS, Dermot Patrick   *Ireland*
Belvedere Coll, UC Dublin, Bective Rgrs.
b 31.1.08 Dublin.
FB, 6-2-0-4.
31 W−; 32 E−; 35 E− S+ W+ NZ−.
Solicitor.

MORRIS, Sir George Lockwood   *Wales*
Bt
Clifton Coll, Swansea.
b 29.1.1859; d 23.11.47 Henley.
Forward, 5-1-0-4.
1882 I+ E−; 1883 S−; 1884 E− S−.
Engrg works mgr. Bt 47.

MORRIS, Haydn Thomas   *Wales*
Cardiff, Barbarians.
b 28 Mountain Ash.
Wing, 3-2-0-1 (6 − 2t).
51 F−; 55 I+(1t) F+(1t); BI > 55 SA.
Sportsmaster/lecturer.

MORRIS, Joseph Ifor ('Glyn')   *Wales*
Swansea.
b 4.8.01 Burry Port.

No 8/prop, 2-0-0-2.
24 E− S−.
Police.

MORRIS, Martyn Stuart　　　　*Wales*
St Joseph's Comp Port Talbot, Welsh Youth, S
Wales Police, Neath.
b 23.8.62 Neath.
Flanker, 3-1-0-2.
85 S+ I− F−.
Wales B v F 83, 84.

MORRIS, Ronald Rhys　　　　*Wales*
QEGS Carmarthen, Swansea, Bristol.
b 13.6.13 Carmarthen; *d* −.2.83 Westbury on
Trym.
FH, 2-0-0-2.
33 S−; 37 S−.
Rep. Chmn, life mem Bristol.

MORRIS, Stephen　　　　*Wales*
Cross Keys.
b 1896; *d* −.6.65.
Lock/flanker, 19-9-1-9.
20 E+ S− F+ I+; 22 E+ S= I+ F+; 23 E− S−
F+ I−; 24 E− S− F+ NZ−; 25 E− S− F+.
Collier.

MORRIS, Trevor James　　　　*New Zealand*
Nelson Coll, Univ, Canterbury, Motueka Huia,
Nelson-Bays, S Island.
b 3.1.42 Nelson.
FB, 3-3-0-0 (33 − 9c 1d 4p).
72 A+(3c 1d) A+(2c 2p) A+(4c 2p).
Schoolmaster. NZ > 72-3 BI,F & NAm.

MORRIS, Will　　　　*Wales*
Abertillery, London Welsh.
No 8/prop, 3-2-0-1.
19 NZA−; 20 F+; 21 I+.

MORRIS, William ('Bill Cute')　　　　*Wales*
Llanelli.
b 1869 Seaside, Llanelli; *d* 46 Gellideg,
Llanelli.
Forward, 3-2-0-1.
1896 S+ I−; 1897 E+.
Plasterer. Manningham (or Broughton Rgrs)
RL 1897. Uncle of British light-heavyweight
boxing champ, Gipsy Daniel.

MORRIS, William David ('The　　　*Wales*
Shadow')
Neath, Barbarians.
b 11.11.42.
No 8/flanker, 34-20-5-9 (19 − 6t).
67 F− E+(1t); 68 E= S+ I− F−; 69 S+ I+(1t)
F= E+ NZ− NZ− A+(1t); 70 SA= S+(1t) E+
I− F+(1t); 71 E+ S+ I+ F+; 72 E+ S+ F+
NZ−; 73 E+ S− I+ A+(1t); 74 S+ I= F= E−.

Colliery welder. W's most capped flanker. W >
68 Arg; 69 NZ, A & Fj; 73 Can.

MORRIS, William J.　　　　*Wales*
Ardwyn GS, Aberystwyth, Pontypool.
b 40.
Wing, 2-1-0-1.
63 S+ I−.
PE teacher. Cousin of John Morris, MP.

MORRIS, William John　　　　*Wales*
New Brighton, Wrexham, Newport, ˙
Barbarians.
b 16.6.41 Melbourne.
Lock, 2-2-0-0.
65 S+; 66 F+.
Solicitor. Barbarians > 69 SA.

MORRISON, Mark Coxon　　　*Scotland*
Royal HS, Royal HSFP.
b 2.4.1877; *d* 10.5.45.
Forward, 23-12-3-8.
1896 W− I= E+; 1897 I+ E−; 1898 I+ E=;
1899 I− W+ E+; 1900 W− E=; 01 W+ I+ E+;
02 W− I− E−; 03 W+ I+; 04 W− I+ E+; BT
> 03 SA.
Farmer. Capt S 15 times. Capt BT > 03 SA.
Pres SRU 34-5.

MORRISON, Piercy Henderson　　*England*
('Dolly')
Loretto Sch, Cambridge Univ, Northern,
Barbarians, Northumb.
b 30.7.1868; *d* 12.7.36.
Back, 4-3-0-1 (1t).
1890 W− S+ I+(1t); 1891 I+.
Co dir. Blue 1887-90. Read medicine, but did
not take finals. Served WW1 as special
constable & motor driver.

MORRISON, Reginald Herbert　　*Scotland*
Edinburgh Univ.
Wing, 3-2-1-0 (2t).
1886 W+ I+(2t) E=.
Medicine. Lecturer at Melbourne Univ. Noted
sprinter.

MORRISON, Terry Geoffrey　　*New Zealand*
Matamata Coll, Univ, Otago, Ponsonby,
Auckland, S Island, NZ Univs, Harlequins (E),
Mdx.
b 16.6.51 Hamilton.
2nd five-eighth, 1-0-0-1.
73 E−r.
Marketing consultant. Went to UK 78. NZ
sprint champ 76 (21.95s 200m).

MORRISON, Thomas Clarence　　*New Zealand*
CBE
Central Sch Gisborne, Main Sch Timaru, Star, S
Canterbury, Trentham Army, Wellington,

Onslow, Comb Servs, S & N Islands.
b 28.7.13 Gisborne; *d* 31.8.85 Wellington.
Wing, 3-3-0-0 (4 − 1d).
38 A+ A+(1d) A+.
Menswear shop mgr. NZ > 38 A. Served WW2;
rep Comb Servs & ME Army XV. Rep S
Canterbury at swimming & athletics. NZ
selector 50-6. Chmn NZRFU 62-8 (served on
NZRFU 46-68). In business partnership with
Ivan Vodanovich.

MORRISON, William Henry   *Scotland*
Edinburgh Acad, Blair Lodge Sch, Edinburgh
Academicals.
b 26.12.1875 Edinburgh; *d* 9.2.44.
Centre, 1-0-0-1.
1900 W−.
Stockbroker.

MORRISSEY, Peter John   *New Zealand*
Christchurch Boys' HS, HSOB, Canterbury,
Pirates, Kaikorai, Otago, S Island.
b 18.7.39 Christchurch.
Wing, 3-2-1-0 (6 − 2t).
62 A=(1t) A+ A+(1t).
Co mgr. Prov 440y champ 61.

MORRISSEY, William   *Australia*
Qld.
Flanker, 1-0-0-1.
14 NZ−.
Salesman.

MORROW, Robert David   *Ireland*
Bangor GS, Bangor.
Flanker, 3-0-0-3.
86 F− E− S−.
Bank official.

MORROW, Robert Whiteside   *Ireland*
Queen's Coll Belfast, Edinburgh Univ.
FB, 9-0-0-9.
1882 S−; 1883 F− S−; 1884 E− W−; 1885 S−;
1886 E− S−; 1888 S−.
Medicine.

MORSE, Sydney   *England*
Marlborough Coll, Marlborough Nomads, Law
Club.
b 1.6.1854; *d* 27.1.29.
Back, 3-1-2-0.
1873 S=; 1874 S+; 1875 S=.
Solicitor.

MORTELL, Maurice P.   *Ireland*
PBC Bray, Bective Rgrs, Dolphin.
b 13.3.30 Bandon, Co Cork.
Wing, 9-3-1-5 (15 − 5t).
53 F+(1t) E=(1t) S+(1t) W−; 54 NZ− F− E−
S+(2t) W−.
Oil co rep/co dir.

MORTIMER, William   *England*
Marlborough Coll, Cambridge Univ,
Marlborough Nomads, Blackheath, Barbarians,
Kent, Lancs.
b 2.5.1874; *d* 31.10.16 Crowborough.
Forward, 1-0-0-1.
1899 W−; BTuncap > 1896 SA.
Stockbroker. Blue 1895-6. Hockey blue 1895-6.
CUCC > US 1895.

MORTON, Alan Ridley   *Australia*
Canberra HS, Queanbeyan HS, NSW.
b 10.9.34 Queanbeyan.
Wing, 11-2-1-8 (9 − 3t).
57 NZ− NZ−(1t); 58 F− M+(1t) M= M−
NZ− NZ+(1t) NZ−; 59 BI− BI−.
Physiology lecturer.

MORTON, David Simson   *Scotland*
Albany Acad, W of Scotland.
b −; *d* 21.5.37.
Forward, 9-6-1-2 (3t).
1887 I+(1t) W+(1t) E=(1t); 1888 W− I+; 1889
W+ I+; 1890 I+ E−.
Paint manufacturer. Touch-jidge E v S 1893.
Pres SRU 1892-3. Ref W v E 1893.

MORTON, Harold James Storrs   *England*
Uppingham Sch, Cambridge Univ, The London
Hosp, Utd Hosps, Blackheath, Barbarians,
Kent.
b 31.1.1886 Sheffield; *d* 3.1.55 Whitechapel.
Prop, 4-2-1-1.
09 I+ S−; 10 W+ I=.
Medicine. Blue 08. Served WW1, Capt RAMC.

MORTON, William Andrews   *Ireland*
St Columba's Coll, Trin Coll Dublin.
b 1865; *d* 19.3.48.
Forward, 1-0-0-1.
1888 S−.
Medicine.

MOSS, Cecil   *South Africa*
Stellenbosch Univ, Natal.
b 12.2.25.
4-4-0-0.
49 NZ+ NZ+ NZ+ NZ+.
Medicine.

MOSS, F.   *England*
Broughton.
Forward, 3-3-0-0.
1885 W+ I+; 1886 W+.

MOSSOP, Rex Peers   *Australia*
NSW.
b 18.2.28 Sydney.
Flanker/lock, 5-2-0-3.
49 NZ+ NZ+; 50 BI− BI−; 51 NZ−.
TV commentator. Leigh (E) RL 51; later A RL.

295

MOSTERT, Phillipus Jacobus   *South Africa*
Somerset W, W Prov.
b 30.10.1898 Krugersdorp.
Prop/hooker, 14-9-1-4 (6 − 1t 1gm).
21 NZ− NZ+ NZ=; 24 BI+ BI+(1t) BI−; 28
NZ+ NZ−(1gm) NZ+ NZ−; 31 W+ I+; 32 E+
S+.
Clerk. Capt SA v NZ (4) 28. SA > 31-2 BI.
Only SA forward to have scored gm, 2nd Test v
NZ 28. Uncle of Jan Lotz.

MOUNICQ, Paul   *France*
Toulouse.
b 9.2.1887 Luz Saint; *d* c67.
Flanker, 9-1-0-8.
11 S+ E− W− I−; 12 I− E−; 13 S− SA− E−.
Medicine.

MOURE, Henri   *France*
SCUF.
Lock, 1-0-0-1.
08 E−.

MOUREU, Pierre   *France*
Béziers.
b 24.8.1895 Larran; *d* −.
Prop/lock, 17-5-1-11 (6 − 2t).
20 I+ US+; 21 W− E− I+; 22 S= W− I−; 23
S− W− E− I+(1t); 24 S+(1t) I− E− W−; 25
E−.
Légion d'Honneur 56.

MOURIE, Graham Neil Kenneth   *New Zealand*
Opunake HS, New Plymouth Boys' HS,
Victoria Univ, Wellington, Opunake, NZ Jnrs,
NZ Colts, NZ Univs, PUC (F), Taranaki, N
Island.
b 8.9.52 Opunake.
Flanker, 21-17-0-4 (16 − 4t).
77 BI+ BI+; 77 F− F+; 78 I+ W+ E+ S+; 79
F+ F−(1t) A−; 79 S+ E+; 80 W+(1t); 81 S+
S+(1t) F+ F+; 82 A+(1t) A− A+.
Farmer. Capt NZ 19 times. Capt NZ > 76 Arg
& Uruguay, 77 F, 78 BI (14 apps), 79 A, 79 E,S
& It, 80 NAm & W, 81 R & F. Capt v F 79, Fj
80, S 81, A 82.

MOURNET, Adrien   *France*
Bagnères.
SH, 1-0-0-1.
81 A−r.

MOURONVAL, Francis   *France*
SF.
Wing, 1-0-0-1.
09 I−.

MOUTRAY, Ian Edmund Joseph   *Australia*
Fort Street HS, Waverley Coll, NSW.
b 2.7.36.
Wing, 1-1-0-0.

63 SA+.
PE teacher.

MOWAT, Sir John Gunn Bt   *Scotland*
Glasgow Acad, Glasgow Academicals, Glasgow
Univ.
b 1859 Glasgow; *d* 1.1.35 Cleckheaton, Yorks.
Forward, 2-1-0-1.
1883 W+ E−.
Chmn clothing co.

MOYERS, L.W.   *Ireland*
Portarlington Coll, Trin Coll Dublin.
Forward, 1-0-0-1.
1884 W−.

MUHR, Allan H. ('Le Sioux')   *France*
RCF.
b 1880 Chicago, US; *d* WW2 Hamburg.
Forward, 3-0-0-3 (6 − 2t).
06 NZ− E−(1t); 07 E−(1t).
Interpreter. FFR pres & selector. Worked for
US Red Cross. Died while WW2 internee.

MUIR, Douglas E.   *Scotland*
Heriot's Coll, Heriot's FP, Barbarians.
b 17.3.25.
Lock, 7-2-0-5.
50 F+ W− I− E+; 52 W− I− E−.

MULCAHY, William Albert   *Ireland*
('Wigs')
St Munchins Coll Limerick, UC Dublin, Bective
Rgrs, Bohemians, Barbarians.
b 7.1.35 Rathkeale, Co Limerick.
Lock, 35-9-3-23.
58 A+ E− S+ W− F−; 59 E− S+ W− F+; 60
E− S− W− SA−; 61 E+ S− W− SA−; 62 E−
S− F− W=; 63 F− E= S− W+ NZ−; 64 E+
S− W− F−; 65 F= E+ S+ W− SA−; BI > 59
A 1-1-0-0, NZ 1-1-0-0; 62 SA 4-0-1-3.
Medicine.

MULLAN, Bernard ('Barney')   *Ireland*
Clontarf, Barbarians.
Wing, 8-6-0-2 (36 − 6t 6c 2p).
47 F−(1c 1p) E+(2t 2c 1p) S+(1t) W−; 48
F+(1t 2c) E+(1c) S+(1t) W+(1t).
Cattle salesman. Barbarians comm. Irish clay
pigeon shooting team.

MULLANE, Jerome P.   *Ireland*
Blackrock Coll, UC Cork, Limerick
Bohemians.
Flanker, 2-2-0-0.
28 W+; 29 F+.
Creamery mgr.

MULLEN, Karl Daniel   *Ireland*
Belvedere Coll, RCSI, O Belvedere,
Barbarians.

b 26.11.26 Courtown Harbour, Co Wexford.
Hooker, 25-15-2-8.
47 F− E+ S+ W− A−; 48 F+ E+ S+ W+; 49
F− E+ S+ W+; 50 F= E− S+ W−; 51 F+ E+
S+ W= SA−; 52 F+ S+ W−; BI > 50 NZ 2-0-
1-1, A 1-1-0-0.
Medicine. Played in 4 Victory ints. Capt BI > 50
NZ & A.

MULLER, Brian Leo ('Jas')   *New Zealand*
Eltham Convent Sch, Eltham, Taranaki, N
Island.
b 11.6.42 Eltham.
Prop, 14-9-1-4.
67 A+ E+ W+ F+; 68 A+ F+; 69 W+; 70
SA− SA+ SA−; 71 BI− BI+ BI− BI=.
Freezing worker. NZ's heaviest player, 18st in
70. NZ > 67 BI,F & C, 68 A & Fj, 70 A & SA.

MULLER, Gert Hendrik   *South Africa*
W Prov.
b 10.5.48 Vryheid, Natal.
Wing, 14-6-3-5 (12 − 4t).
69 A+ A+ S−; 70 W= NZ+ NZ− NZ+(2t)
NZ+(1t); 71 F+(1t) F=; 72 E−; 74 BI− BI−
BI=.
SA > 69-70 BI, F (flew home for funeral of
father, rejoined tour); 71 A (inj early, returned
SA). 3t SA v NZ 70, series rec for SA v NZ. 4t
SA v North/Mid Scotland 69, & v Victoria (A)
71.

MULLER, Hendrik Scholtz   *South Africa*
Vosloo ('Hennie')
Transvaal, W Prov.
b 26.3.22 Witbank, Transvaal; *d* −.5.77 Cape
Town.
No 8/flanker, 13-12-0-1 (16 − 3t 2c 1p).
49 NZ+ NZ+ NZ+ NZ+; 51 S+(1t) I+ W+;
52 E+(1c 1p) F+; 53 A+(1t) A− A+ A+.
Compound asst in mines/sports shop owner.
Capt SA 9 times, 51-2 (5) & 53 A (4). Coach SA
> 65 A, NZ. Died of heart attack.

MULLIGAN, Andrew Armstrong   *Ireland*
Gresham's Sch, Cambridge Univ, London Irish,
Barbarians.
b 4.2.36 Kasauli, India.
SH, 22-6-0-16.
56 F− E−; 57 F+ E− S+ W−; 58 A+ E− S+
F−; 59 E− S+ W− F+; 60 E− S− W− F−
SA−; 61 W− F− SA−; BIr > 59 A, NZ 1-1-0-0.
Business exec/journalist/EEC rep in
Washington. Blue 55-7.

MULLIN, Brendan John   *Ireland*
Irish Schs, Leinster Schs, Blackrock Coll, Trin
Coll Dublin.
b 30.10.63 Israel.
Centre, 8-3-0-5 (8 − 2t).

84 A−; 85 S+ W+ E+(1t); 86 F− W− E−(1t)
S−.
Law student. Ireland B. Irish int hurdler;
competed v S & Spain 84; v Spain 86.

MUMM, William John   *New Zealand*
Ngakawau, Buller, S Island.
b 26.3.22 Mokihunui.
Prop, 1-0-0-1.
49 A−.
Sawmiller. Buller selector 60-74. Father W.J.
rep Buller 19-21, as did bro Peter 52-7 & nephew
Rex 78-80.

MUNNOCH, Norman McQueen   *Scotland*
George Watson's Coll, Watsonians.
b 4.1.29 Polmont.
Hooker, 3-0-0-3.
52 F− W− I−.

MUNRO, Patrick   *Scotland*
Leeds GS, Oxford Univ, London Scottish,
Barbarians.
b 9.10.1883; *d* 3.5.42 London.
Half-back/FH 13-5-0-8 (14 − 2t 2d).
05 W− I− E+ NZ−; 06 W− I+(1t) E− SA+;
07 I+ E+; 11 F−(1t) W−(1d) I−(1d).
Sudan Civil Service/MP. Blue 03-5. Capt Oxford
Univ v NZ 05. Pres SRU 39-40. Killed on Home
Guard duty.

MUNRO, R.   *Scotland*
St Andrew's Univ.
Forward, 1-1-0-0.
1871 E+.
Minister. Played in 1st int, S v E 1871.

MUNRO, Stephen   *Scotland*
Ayr Acad, Scottish Schools, Ayr, W of
Scotland.
b 11.6.58 Ayr.
Wing, 10-5-0-5 (8 − 2t).
80 I− F+; 81 F− W+ E−(2t) I+ NZ− NZ−
R I I 84 W+.
Production controller/life insurance co
inspector. Glasgow v NZ 79. Scotland B v I, F
79. S > 81 NZ.

MUNRO, William Hutton   *Scotland*
Glenalmond Acad, Glasgow HS, Glasgow
HSFP.
FH/centre, 2-0-0-2.
47 I− E−.
Played in 4 Servs ints.

MURDOCH, Keith   *New Zealand*
King Edward Tech Coll, Zingari-Richmond,
Otago, Marist, Hawkes Bay, Ponsonby,
Auckland, S Island.
b 9.9.43 Dunedin.
Prop, 3-2-0-1 (4 − 1t).

297

70 SA−; 72 A+ W+(1t).
Truck driver/barman. NZ > 70 A & SA, 72-3
BI,F & NAm (played in 9 out of 1st 13 matches;
sent home for disciplinary reasons).

MURDOCH, Peter Henry　　　*New Zealand*
Otahuhu Coll, Otahuhu, NZ Colts, Auckland,
N Island.
b 17.6.41 Auckland.
1st five-eighth, 5-3-0-2 (6 − 2t).
64 A+(1t) A−(1t); 65 SA+ SA+ SA−.
Panelbeater. Father 'Doc' Murdoch rep
Auckland 34-6 & masseur to various sides
touring NZ.

MURDOCH, William Copeland　　　*Scotland*
Wood
Hillhead HS, Hillhead HSFP, Barbarians.
b 3.10.14 Old Kilpatrick.
Centre/wing/FB, 9-3-0-6 (15 − 1t 1c 1d 2p).
35 E+ NZ−(1c); 36 W− I−(1d); 39 E−(1t); 48
F+(2p) W− I− E+.
Banker. 1p 1c Glasgow/Edinburgh v NZ 35.
Played either side WW2; returned to S team
after 10 yr absence. S's longest int career.
Played in 5 Servs ints. Ref W v I, I v SA 51; E v
SA, F v E 52.

MURILLO, Gérard　　　*France*
Dijon.
Wing/centre, 2-2-0-0 (9 − 3t).
54 It+(2t) Arg+(1t).

MURPHY, Cornelius Dennis　　　*Wales*
('Con')
Cross Keys.
b 3.9.08 Aberfan; *d* 13.7.64 Leeds.
Hooker, 3-1-1-1.
35 E= S+ I−.
Miner/licensee. Acton & Willesden RL 35,
Streatham & Mitcham, Leeds 36.

MURPHY, Cornelius Joseph　　　*Ireland*
CUS Leeson Street, Lansdowne, Barbarians.
b 19.9.14 Dublin.
FB, 5-3-0-2.
39 E+ S+ W−; 47 F− E+.
Accountant. Played in 4 Victory ints. Capt I in
opening matches after WW2. Played football for
Bohemians AFC & Irish jnr team.

MURPHY, John Gervase Maurice　　　*Ireland*
Walker
Methodist Coll Belfast, Trin Coll Dublin,
London Irish, The Army, Barbarians.
b 20.8.26 Bangor, Co Down.
FB, 6-1-0-5 (3 − 1p).
51 SA−; 52 S+ W−(1p) E−; 54 NZ−; 58 W−.
Minister/R Army Chaplain's Dept. Chaplain to
HM the Queen, Sandringham.

MURPHY, John Joseph　　　*Ireland*
PBC Bray, Greystones.
b 27.8.57 Bray.
Centre/FB, 3-1-0-2 (5 − 1c 1p).
81 SA−; 82 W+r; 84 S−(1c 1p).
Co dir. Top scorer 36 pts I > 81 SA. Had
football trials with Arsenal.

MURPHY, Noel Arthur　　　*Ireland*
Augustine
CBC Cork, Cork Constitution, Barbarians.
b 22.2.37 Cork.
Flanker, 41-14-2-25 (15 − 5t).
58 A+ E− S+ W− F−; 59 E− S− W− F+; 60
E− S− W−(1t) F− SA−; 61 E+ S− W−; 62
E−; 63 NZ−; 64 E+(1t) S− W− F−; 65 F= E+
S+(1t) W− SA−; 66 F− E= S− W+; 67 A+
E− S+(1t) W+ F−; 69 F+ E+(1t) S+ W−; BI
> 59 A 1-1-0-0, NZ 3-1-0-2; 66 A 2-2-0-0, NZ 2-
0-0-2.
Insurance. Son of N.F. Asst mgr BI > 80 SA.

MURPHY, Noel Francis　　　*Ireland*
North Monastery Coll, Cork Constitution.
b 27.12.04 Cork.
Flanker/lock, 11-5-0-6.
30 E+ W−; 31 F− E+ S+ W− SA−; 32 E− S+
W+; 33 E−.
Father of N.A.A. Pres IRU 60-1.

MURPHY, Patrick Joseph　　　*Australia*
Qld.
Lock, 9-2-0-7.
10 NZ− NZ+ NZ−; 13 NZ− NZ− NZ+; 14
NZ− NZ− NZ−.
Labourer. Bro of William.

MURPHY, William　　　*Australia*
Qld.
b 1880; *d* 57.
Forward, 1-1-0-0.
12 US+.
Bro of Patrick.

MURPHY-O'CONNOR, James　　　*Ireland*
Colman
Prior Coll Bath, RCSI, Bective Rgrs.
No 8, 1-0-0-1 (3 − 1p).
54 E−(1p).
Medicine. Bro in law of W.A. O'Neill.

MURRAY, George M.　　　*Scotland*
Glasgow Acad, Glasgow Academicals.
b 21.6.1900 Glasgow; *d* 26.12.81.
Flanker/prop, 2-1-0-1.
21 I−; 26 W+.
Bro of Ronald.

MURRAY, Harold Vivian　　　*New Zealand*
('Toby')
Christ's Coll, Irwell, Canterbury, Springfield,

Comb Servs, S Island.
b 9.2.1888 Christchurch; d 4.7.71 Amberley.
Flanker, 4-4-0-0 (9 − 3t).
13 A+(1t) US+(2t); 14 A+ A+.
Farmer. NZ > 13 NAm, 14 A. Served WW1;
rep Comb Servs in King's Cup 19.

MURRAY, Henry Walker   *Ireland*
Trin Coll Dublin.
b 12.5.1854; d 25.10.42.
Forward, 3-0-0-3.
1877 S−; 1878 E−; 1879 E−.
Medicine. Served in Indian Medical Service.

MURRAY, H.M.   *Scotland*
Edinburgh Acad, Glasgow Univ.
b 3.5.12.
Centre, 2-0-0-2 (3 − 1t).
36 W−(1t) I−.
Medicine.

MURRAY, John Brendan   *Ireland*
Castleknock Coll, UC Dublin, Barbarians.
b 3.4.42 Dublin.
Centre, 1-0-0-1.
63 F−.
Medicine. Son of Paul. Tennis for I. Emigrated
to Can.

MURRAY, Keith T.   *Scotland*
Hawick, British Police.
Centre, 3-0-0-3.
85 I− F− W−.
Police.

MURRAY, Paul Finbarr   *Ireland*
Blackrock Coll, RCSI, Wanderers, Barbarians.
b 29.6.05 Dublin; d 1.6.81 Dublin.
Centre/SH, 19-10-0-9 (33 − 1t 7c 1d 4p).
27 F+; 29 F+ E+ S−; 30 F− E+(1d) S+(1c)
W−(1p); 31 F− E+(1p) S+(1c) W− SA−; 32
E−(1c 1p) S+(4c) W+; 33 E−(1p) W+ S−(1t),
BI > 30 NZ 3-1-0-2, A 1-0-0-1.
Medicine. Father of John. 4c v S 32, most by I
player (with R.J. Gregg). Pres IRU 65-6.

MURRAY, Peter Chapman   *New Zealand*
Wanganui Collegiate Sch, College OB,
Wanganui, N Island.
b 23.1.1884 Southern Grove; d 6.2.68
Auckland.
Hooker, 1-0-1-0.
08 AW=.
Farmer/stock agent. Mem of Waimarino Co
Council.

MURRAY, Ronald Ormiston   *Scotland*
Loretto Sch, Cambridge Univ.

b 14.11.12 Glasgow.
Prop, 2-1-0-1.
35 W− E+.
Medicine. Bro of George. Blue 33-4.

MURRAY, William Alexander   *Scotland*
Kininmonth OBE
Merchiston Castle Sch, London Scottish, The
Army, Kelvinside Academicals.
b 17.4.1894.
Lock/flanker, 3-2-0-1.
20 F+ I+; 21 F−.
The Army.

MURTAGH, Charles William,   *Ireland*
Portadown.
Lock, 1-0-0-1.
77 S−.

MYBURGH, F.R.   *South Africa*
E Prov.
Half-back, 1-0-0-1.
1896 BT−.

MYBURGH, Johannes   *South Africa*
Lodewikus ('Mof')
Senekal HS, N Transvaal.
b 24.8.36 Senekal.
Prop, 18-12-4-2.
62 BI=; 63 A+; 64 W+ F−; 68 BI+ BI= BI+
F+ F+; 69 A+ A+ A+ A+ E−; 70 I= W=
NZ+ NZ+.
Police. SA > 60-1 BI, F; 69-70 BI. Played prop
with J.F.K. Marais for SA 16 Tests. 109 apps for
N Transvaal.

MYBURGH, W.H. ('Champion')   *South Africa*
W Transvaal.
SH, 1-1-0-0.
24 BI+.

MYCOCK, Joseph   *England*
Giggleswick Sch, Sale, Vale of Lune,
Harlequins, RAF, Comb Servs, Barbarians,
Lancs.
b 17.1.16.
Lock, 5-3-0-2.
47 W+ I− S+ F+; 48 A−.
Man dir. Served WW2, RAF. In bus in Chile,
Peru, Phillipines & Nigeria.

MYERS, Edward MC   *England*
Dollar Acad, Leeds Univ, Headingley,
Leicester, Bradford, Yorks.
b 23.9.1895 New York; d 29.3.56 Bradford.
Centre/FH, 18-15-1-2 (13 − 3t 1d).
20 I+(1t) S+; 21 W+ I+; 22 W− I+ F= S+; 23
W+ I+ S+ F+; 24 W+(1t) I+ F+ S+(1t 1d); 25
S− F+.
Textiles co dir. Born of Yorks parents in US.
Not chosen v F, S 21 because of family

bereavement. Served WW1, W Yorks Rgt;
wounded 3 times.

MYERS, Harry   *England*
Keighley.
b 3.2.1875 Horsforth, Leeds; *d* 19.12.06
Keighley.
SH, 1-0-0-1.
1898 I−.
Licensee. Turned RL when Keighley changed
codes 1900. Died as result of spinal inj sustained
in RL match at Dewsbury 3.11.06.

MYERS, Richard George   *New Zealand*
Cambridge HS, NZ Jnrs, Univ, NZ Univs,
Manawatu, Leamington, Waikato.
b 6.7.50 Hamilton.
Flanker, 1-0-0-1.
78 A−.
Farmer. NZ > 77 F.

MYLES, John   *Ireland*
Dr Hall's Coll Limerick, Trin Coll Dublin.
b c1854; *d* −.4.34.
Half-back, 1-0-0-1.
1875 E−.
Medicine. FRCSI.

MYNOTT, Harry Jonas ('Simon') *New Zealand*
Central Sch New Plymouth, Tukapa, Newton,
Taranaki, N Island.
b 4.6.1876 Auckland; *d* 2.1.24 New Plymouth.
Wing/1st five-eighth, 8-6-1-1.
05 I+ W−; 06 F+; 07 A+ A+ A=; 10 A+ A+.
Tinsmith. NZ > 05 A, 05-6 BI,F & NAm, 07 &
10 A. NZRFU sel 13.

N

NAMUR, René   *France*
Toulon.
b 12.12.09 Montauban.
Hooker, 2-2-0-0.
31 E+ G+.

NANSON, William Moore Bell   *England*
Lowther St Sch Carlisle, Carlisle, Cumberland.
b 12.12.1880 Carlisle; kia 4.6.15 El Krithia.
Forward, 2-1-0-1 (3 − 1t).
07 F+(1t) W−.
Oldham RL 08. Served SA War, Border Rgt
(Queen's & King's Medal). Served WW1,
Manchester Rgt in Egypt & Gallipoli. Went
missing El Krithia, declared dead 13 mths later.

NAPIER, H.M.   *Scotland*
Glasgow HS, W of Scotland.
Forward, 5-3-2-0.
1877 I+ E+; 1878 E=; 1879 I+ E=.

NASH, David   *Wales*
Nantyglo GS, Ebbw Vale, Barbarians.
No 8/lock, 6-3-0-3.
60 SA−; 61 E+ S− I+ F−; 62 F+; BI > 62 SA.
Schoolmaster/dir leisure activities. W's lst
national coach 67, resigned 68.

NASH, Edward Henry   *England*
Rugby Sch, Oxford Univ, Richmond.
b 20.12.1854; *d* 18.9.32 Beaconsfield.
Half-back, 1-1-0-0 (1d).
1875 I+(1d).
Solicitor. Blue 1874-5. Ckt blue. With C.W.
Crosse, refused permission by Dean of Trin Coll
to play E v S 1875. Fdr mem of the Hockey
Association 1885, later v-pres & pres.

NASH, L.C.   *Ireland*
Queen's Coll Cork.
Forward, 6-0-1-5.
1889 S−; 1890 W= E−; 1891 E− S− W−.

NATHAN, Waka Joseph   *New Zealand*
Otahuhu Coll, Otahuhu, NZ Maoris, Auckland,
N Island.
b 8.7.40 Auckland.
Flanker, 14-13-1-0 (12 − 4t).
62 A+ A+(1t) A= A+ A+; 63 E+ E+; 63
W+; 64 F+; 66 BI+ BI+ BI+(2t) BI+(1t); 67
A+.
Freezer worker/brewery promotions officer.
Never on losing NZ Test side. NZ > 62 A; 63-4
(11t − broke jaw v Llanelli) & 67 BI,F & Can
(broke jaw again). NZ Maoris sel 71-77.

NAUDE, Jacobus Pieter ('Tiny')   *South Africa*
W Prov.
b 2.11.36.
Lock, 14-7-2-5 (47 − 2t 4c 11p).
63 A+(1t); 65 A−(1c 1p) A−(1c) NZ− NZ+(2c
1p) NZ−(1p); 67 F+ F+(1p) F−(2p) F=; 68
BI+(1t 2p) BI=(1p) BI+(1p) BI+.
SAr > 68 F. 69y p W Prov v A 63

NEALE, Bruce Alan   *England*
Emanuel Sch Battersea, Rosslyn Pk, The Army,
Comb Servs, London Cos, Surrey, Durham Co.
b 15.9.23.
Lock, 3-1-0-2.
51 I− F− S+.
The Army/ICI. Served WW2, RA.

NEALE, Maurice Edward   *England*
Blackheath, Barbarians.
b 1886 Bristol; *d* 9.7.67 Bristol.
Centre, 1-1-0-0.
12 F+.

NEAME, Stuart   *England*
Cheltenham Coll, O Cheltonians, Blackheath, Kent.
b 15.6.1856; *d* 16.11.36 Bromley, Kent.
Forward, 4-3-1-0.
1879 S= I+ ; 1880 I+ S+.
Hop factor. Pres Cheltonian Soc 21-2.

NEARY, Anthony ('Nero')   *England*
De La Salle Coll Salford, England SS, Liverpool Univ, UAU, Brit Univs, Broughton Pk, Lancs.
b 25.11.49 Manchester.
Flanker, 43-15-3-25 (19 − 5t).
71 W− I+ F= S−(1t) S− P−; 72 W− I− F− S− SA+; 73 NZ− W− I−(1t) F+ S+ NZ+(1t) A+(1t); 74 S−(1t) I− F= W+; 75 I− F− W− S+ A−; 76 A+ W− S− I− F−; 77 I+; 78 Fr−; 79 S= I− F+ W− NZ−; 80 I+ F+ W+ S+.
Articled clerk. E's most capped player. E Under 25s v Fj 70. English Schs basketball.

NEELY, Matthew Robert   *Ireland*
Foyle Coll, Methodist Coll Belfast, Queen's Univ Belfast, Collegians.
b 24.12.19 Craigs, Ballymena.
Prop, 4-2-0-2.
47 F− E+ S+ W−.
Medicine. Served WW2, RN. Played in 4 Victory ints.

NEETHLING, Jacobus Burger   *South Africa*
('Tiny')
W Prov.
b 6.7.38 Rawsonville.
Prop, 8-4-1-3.
67 F+ F+ F− F=; 68 BI+; 69 S−; 70 NZ+ NZ−.
Rep. SA > 65 I, S; 68 F; 69-70 BI.

NEILL, Harry James   *Ireland*
NIFC.
b 1861; *d* 27.6.49.
Forward, 8-1-1-6.
1885 E− S−; 1886 S−; 1887 E= S− W−; 1888 W+ S−.
Co dir.

NEILL, John Brian   *Scotland*
Edinburgh Acad, Edinburgh Academicals, Barbarians.
b 28.7.37.
Prop, 7-3-1-3.
63 E−; 64 F+ NZ= W− I+ E+; 65 F−.
Capt S 6 times.

NEILL, Joseph McFerran   *Ireland*
RBAI, Queen's Univ Belfast, Instonians.
Flanker, 1-1-0-0.
26 F+.
Civil engr. Bro in law of Beamish bros.

NEILL, Robert Miln   *Scotland*
Edinburgh Acad, Edinburgh Academicals.
b 5.9.1882; *d* 14.9.14 Kuala Lumpur.
SH, 2-1-0-1.
01 E+; 02 I−; BT > 03 SA.
Chartered accountant. Died of appendicitis.

NEILL, William   *Wales*
Cardiff.
b 5.6.1878 Cardiff; *d* 2.4.55 Cardiff.
Forward, 11-10-0-1.
04 S+ I−; 05 E+ S+ I+; 07 E+ I+; 08 E+ S+ F+ I+.
Dock crane driver. Warrington RL 08.

NEILSON, George Thomson   *Scotland*
Merchiston Castle Sch, W of Scotland, Barbarians.
b 22.1.1872; *d* −.
Forward, 14-8-1-5 (6 − 1t 1p).
1891 W+ I+ E+; 1892 W− E−; 1893 W−; 1894 W− I−; 1895 W+ I+ E+(1t 1p); 1896 W− I= E+.
Ironmaster. Bro of William, Walter & Robert; played with William for S 8 times. Pres SRU 01-2.

NEILSON, J.A.   *Scotland*
Glasgow Acad, Glasgow Academicals.
Wing, 2-0-2-0.
1878 E=; 1879 E=.

NEILSON, Robert Thomson   *Scotland*
Merchiston Castle Sch, Glasgow Univ, W of Scotland.
b 17.11.1878; *d* 16.7.45.
Centre/half-back, 6-2-3-1.
1898 I+ E=; 1899 I− W+; 1900 I= E=.
Engr. Bro of George, William & Walter. Pres SRU 23-4.

NEILSON, T.   *Scotland*
W of Scotland.
Forward, 1-0-0-1.
1874 E−.

NEILSON, Walter Gordon DSO   *Scotland*
CMG
Merchiston Castle Sch, Merchistonians.
b 1.10.1876; *d* 29.4.27.
Forward, 1-1-0-0.
1894 E+.
The Army. Capped from sch at 17yrs 5mths. Bro of George, William & Robert; played with William v E 1894. Served with Argyle & Sutherland Highlanders.

NEILSON, William   *Scotland*
Merchiston Castle Sch, Cambridge Univ, London Scottish, Barbarians.
b 18.8.1873; *d* 16.3.60.

Centre, 14-10-2-2 (4 − 1t 1d).
1891 W+(1d) E+(1t); 1892 W+ I+ E−; 1893
I= E+; 1894 E+; 1895 W+ I+ E+; 1896 I=;
1897 I+ E−.
Barrister. Blue 1891-3. Capped at school (17yrs
5mths). Bro of George, Walter & Robert;
played with George for S 8 times & with Walter
once, v E 1894. Pres SRU 05-6. WW1 Tank
Corps; wounded. POW.

NEL, Jeremy John *South Africa*
Potchefstroom Boys HS, Stellenbosch Univ,
Rhodes Univ, W Prov.
Centre/FH, 8-3-1-4 (3 − 1t).
56 A+(1t) A+ NZ− NZ+ NZ− NZ−; 58 F=
F−.

NEL, Johannes Arnoldus *South Africa*
('Lofty')
Transvaal.
b 11.8.34.
No 8/flanker, 11-5-0-6.
60 NZ+ NZ−; 63 A+ A−; 65 A− NZ− NZ−
NZ+ NZ−; 70 NZ+ NZ+.
Oldest player to rep SA (36yrs 1mth, v NZ 70)

NEL, P.A.R.O. *South Africa*
Transvaal.
3-1-2-0.
03 BT= BT= BT+.

NEL, Philip Jacobus ('Flip') *South Africa*
Pietermaritzburg Coll, Natal.
b 17.6.02 Kranskop, Greytown, Natal; *d*
12.2.84 Pietermaritzburg.
Lock, 16-13-0-3 (3 − 1t).
28 NZ+ NZ− NZ+(1t) NZ−; 31 W+ I+; 32
E+ S+; 33 A+ A+ A+ A−; 37 A+ A+ NZ+
NZ+.
Farmer. Capt SA v A 33 (4), > A, NZ 37.
Proclaimed retirement by throwing his boots
into sea from ship bringing team back from NZ
37. In SA Trials 28, younger bro Maritz collided
with ref, ex SA capt & selector Theo Pienaar,
who was taken to hospital. Maritz never played
for SA.

NELMES, Barry George *England*
Portway SMS, Bristol, Cardiff.
b 17.4.48 Bristol.
Prop, 6-2-0-4 (4 − 1t).
75 A− A−; 78 W− S+(1t) I+ NZ−.
Licensee. Er > 75 A − r for inj Fran Cotton.
Capt Cardiff 78-9.

NELSON, James Benzie *Scotland*
Glasgow Acad, Glasgow Academicals,
Barbarians.
b 9.2.03 Glasgow; *d* −.10.81 Inverness.
SH, 25-15-1-9 (6 − 2t).
25 F+ W+ I+ E+(1t); 26 F+ W+ I− E+; 27

F+ W+ I− E+; 28 I− E−; 29 F+ W− I+
E+(1t); 30 F− W+ I− E=; 31 F+ W− I−.
Hotelier/accountant.

NELSON, James Edward *Ireland*
Armagh RS, Malone, Barbarians.
b 16.9.21 Belfast.
Lock, 16-9-2-5 (3 − 1t).
47 A−; 48 E+ S+ W+; 49 F− E+ S+ W+; 50
F= E− S+ W−; 51 F+(1t) E+ W=; 54 F−;
BI > 50 NZ 2-0-0-2, A 2-2-0-0.
Accountant.

NELSON, Keith Alister *New Zealand*
Auckland GS, NZ Jnrs, Univ, Otago, NZ
Univs, Clutha, Ponsonby, N & S Islands.
b 26.11.38 Auckland.
No 8, 2-2-0-0.
62 A+ A+.
Dentist. NZ > 63-4 BI,F & C. Inj on NZ
Univs > NAm 60 kept him out of rugby until 62.
Served on Auckland comm since 75. Father Jack
rep Auckland 31-2.

NELSON, Robert *Ireland*
Queen's Coll Belfast.
Forward, 4-0-1-3.
1882 E= S−; 1883 S−; 1886 S−.
Medicine.

NELSON, Thomas Arthur *Scotland*
Edinburgh Acad, Oxford Univ, Barbarians.
b 1876; kia 9.4.17 Arras.
Centre, 1-0-1-0.
1898 E=.
Publisher. Blue 1897-8. Capt in 1st Lothians &
Border Horse; mentioned in despatches 3 times.

NEPIA, George *New Zealand*
Nuhaka Native Sch, Maori Agricultural Coll,
Hawkes Bay, Nuhaka, NZ Maoris, E Coast, N
Island.
b 25.4.05 Wairoa.
FB, 9-7-0-2 (5 − 1c 1p).
24 I+ W+; 25 E+ F+; 29 A−(1c 1p); 30 BI−
BI+ BI+ BI+.
Farmer/electrical appliance factory employee.
NZ > 24-5 BI,F & C (pl in all 38 matches), 29
A. 39 consec apps for NZ. Streatham &
Mitcham RL (E) 35, Halifax 36. Returned NZ
37 & rep NZ v A. Reinstated RU & pl twice for
E Coast, 47, at age of 42. Became oldest New
Zealander to play in 1st class match when he
capt Olympian club v Poverty Bay (capt by his
son George) 50. Became ref.

NESBIT, Steven Roberto *New Zealand*
St Peter's Coll Auckland, Marist, Auckland.
b 13.2.36 Auckland.
1st five-eighth, 2-1-1-0.
60 SA+ SA=.

302

Barman. NZ > 60 A & SA. Went to US; toured NZ with Californian Univs.

NESDALE, Thomas Jude　　　　　*Ireland*
PBC Cork, Garryowen.
b 18.8.33 Cork.
Flanker, 1-0-0-1.
61 F−.
Bank official.

NEVILLE, William C.　　　　　*Ireland*
Dundalk Coll, Trin Coll Dublin.
Forward, 2-0-0-2.
1879 S− E−.
Medicine. Ump S v I 1880, ref I v E 1882. Pres IRU 1879-80.

NEWBOLD, Charles Joseph DSO　　*England*
Uppingham Sch, Cambridge Univ, Wanderers, Blackheath, Barbarians, Kent.
b 12.1.1881 Tunbridge Wells; *d* 26.10.46.
Prop/hooker, 6-1-1-4.
04 W= I+ S−; 05 W− I− S−.
The Army/man dir. Blue 02-3. Served WW1, Lt Col RE; mentioned in despatches 3 times. DSO 17. Man dir Arthur Guinness & Sons. Chmn Brewers Soc.

NEWMAN, Charles Henry　　　　*Wales*
Monmouth Sch, Cambridge Univ, Newport, Durham.
b 28.2.1857 Newport; *d* 28.9.22 Lucerne, Switz.
Back/half-back, 10-1-2-7.
1881 E−; 1882 I+ E−; 1883 S−; 1884 E− S−; 1885 E− S=; 1886 E−; 1887 E=.
Minister. Blue 1882. Capt W 6 times. Fdr mem Newport.

NEWMAN, Sydney Charles　　　*England*
Christian Bros Coll Pretoria, Witwatersrand Univ, Oxford Univ, Barbarians.
b 27.7.19.
FB, 3-1-1-1 (3 − 1p).
47 F+; 48 A− W=(1p).
Chmn, man dir mining co. Rhodes Scholar. Blue 46-7. Served WW2 SA Engrs Corps; POW at Tobruk 42.

NEWTON, Arthur Winstanley　　*England*
Blackheath, The Army, Barbarians.
b 12.9.1879; *d* −.
Wing, 1-0-0-1.
07 S−.
The Army. Believed to have been killed WW1.

NEWTON, Frederick ('Fatty')　*New Zealand*
Linwood, Canterbury, White Star, Buller, S Island.
b 7.5.1881 Christchurch; *d* 10.12.55 Christchurch.

No 8/lock, 3-2-0-1 (3 − 1t).
05 E+(1t) W−; 06 F+.
Rly fitter. NZ > 05 A, 05-6 BI,F & NAm.

NEWTON, Philip Arthur　　　　*England*
Blackheath Proprietary Sch, Oxford Univ, Blackheath, Kent.
b 11.4.1860; *d* 25.12.46.
Forward, 1-0-0-1.
1882 S−.
Sen ptn patent agents. Blue 1879-80.

NEWTON-THOMPSON, John　　　*England*
Oswald DFC
Diocesan Coll Rondebosch SA, Cape Town Univ, Oxford Univ.
b 2.12.20 Paddington, London; *d* 3.3.74 SW Africa.
SH, 2-2-0-0.
47 S+ F+.
Law/MP. Bro of C.L. Newton-Thompson, Cambridge blue 37-8 & SA rep on RFU 47-8. Rhodes Scholar. Blue 45-6. Ckt blue − 7 apps OUCC 46; W Prov 48-9 v MCC. Served WW2, Wg Cmdr SAAF. DFC. Ref from 56. Rep Rhodesia on SARB. SA United Party MP 61-74. Died in air crash.

NICHOL, James Alastair　　　　*Scotland*
Royal HS, Royal HSFP.
b 12.2.32 Edinburgh.
SH, 3-2-0-1 (3 − 1t).
55 W+(1t) I+ E−.
Quantity surveyor.

NICHOL, William　　　　　　　*England*
Brighouse Rgrs.
b 30.10.1868 Raistrick; *d* 10.4.22 Brighouse.
Forward, 2-2-0-0 (2 − 1t).
1892 W+(1t) S+.
Licensee. Turned RL when his club, Brighouse Rgrs, helped form NU 1895.

NICHOLAS, David Llewellyn　　　*Wales*
('Dai Nick')
Stradey Sch, Welsh SS, Welsh Youth, Llanelli, Felinfoel.
b 3.3.55 Llanelli.
Wing, 4-2-0-2.
81 E+ S− I+ F−.
BSC engr/sports therapist. Wales B v F 75, 78. Player−coach Felinfoel 85-6.

NICHOLAS, Philip Leach　　　　*England*
Monmouth Sch, Oxford Univ, Exeter, Barbarians, Devon.
b 30.5.1876; *d* 31.1.52 Barnstaple.
Wing, 1-0-0-1.
02 W−.
Clergyman/schoolmaster. Blue 1897-9. Ordained 08.

NICHOLAS, Trevor J. *Wales*
Cardiff.
Wing, 1-0-0-1.
19 NZA−.
Solicitor. WW1 38th Welsh Div.

NICHOLL, Charles Bowen *Wales*
('Boomer') .
Llandovery Coll, Cambridge Univ, Blackheath,
Llanelli, Barbarians.
b 19.6.1870 Llanegwad; *d* 9.7.39 Clayhidon,
Somerset.
Forward, 15-7-0-8.
1891 I+; 1892 E− S− I−; 1893 E+ S+ I+; 1894
E− S+; 1895 E− S− I+; 1896 E− S+ I−.
Rector/schoolmaster. Blue 1890-3. Bro of D.W.
Barbarians comm.

NICHOLL, David Wilmot *Wales*
Llandovery Coll, Llanelli.
b 1871 Llandilofawr; *d* 11.3.18 Llanelli.
Forward, 1-0-0-1.
1894 I−.
Bank cashier. Bro of C.B.

NICHOLLS, Erith Gwyn *Wales*
Newport, Cardiff Stars, Cardiff, Barbarians.
b −.6.1874 Westbury on Severn; *d* 24.3.39
Dinas Powys.
Centre, 24-16-1-7 (13 − 3t 1d).
1896 S+ I−; 1897 E+; 1898 I+ E−; 1899 E+
S− I−; 1900 S+(1t) I+; 1901 E+(1t) S− I+;
1902 E+ S+ I+(1t 1d); 1903 I+; 1904 E=; 1905
I+ NZ+; 1906 E+ S+ I− SA−; BT > 1899 A.
Laundry owner. Capt W 10 times. Only
Welshman BT > 1899 A. 18 seasons for Cardiff
1892-1910 (capt 1898-01, 03-4). Scored t Cardiff
v NZ 05. WRU selector 25-31. Ref E v S 09. Bro
of S.H., bro in law of Bert Winfield. Wrote 'The
Modern Rugby Game and how to play it' pub
c16.

NICHOLLS, F.E. *Wales*
Cardiff Harlequins.
Centre, 1-0-0-1.
1892 I−.
Cap and jersey in Bridgend RFC.

NICHOLLS, Harry Edgar *New Zealand*
('Ginger')
Petone W Sch, Wellington Coll, Petone,
Wellington, N Island.
b 21.1.1900 Wellington; *d* 1.4.78 Wellington.
SH, 1-1-0-0.
21 SA+.
Council employee. NZ > 22 A. Father Syd rep
Wellington 1889; bro of Marcus; another bro
Harold rep NZ 23 (no Tests); another bro Guy
rep N Auckland.

NICHOLLS, Howard *Wales*
Hereford Cathedral Sch, Maesteg, Bridgend,
Cardiff.
b Maesteg.
Wing, 1-1-0-0.
58 I+.
Butcher. Son in law of Arthur Hugh Jones. An
x−ray many yrs later showed he had fractured a
knee when inj v I 58.

NICHOLLS, Marcus Frederick *New Zealand*
Petone W Sch, Petone HS, Wellington Coll,
Petone, Wellington, Grafton, Auckland, N
Island.
b 13.7.01 Greytown; *d* 10.6.72 Tauranga.
2nd/1st five-eighth/centre, 10-8-1-1 (48 − 11c 2d
1gm 5p).
21 SA+(2c) SA−(1c) SA=; 24 I+(1p) W+(2c
1p); 25 E+(1c 1p) F+(3c); 28 SA+(1d 2p); 30
BI+(2c 1gm) BI+(1d).
Rly clerk/licensee. NZ > 22 & 26 A (top scorer
with 41 pts), 24-5 BI (top scorer with 121 pts); v-
capt 1st NZ > 28 SA. NZRFU sel 36-7. Wrote
'With the All Blacks in Springbokland' pub 28.
Father Syd & son rep Wellington.

NICHOLLS, Sidney H. *Wales*
Cardiff.
Forward, 4-1-0-3.
1888 NZN+; 1889 S− I−; 1891 S−.
Licensee. Bro of E.G. Chmn Cardiff City AFC
1920s.

NICHOLSON, Basil Ellard *England*
Whitgift Sch, O Whitgiftians, Harlequins,
Barbarians, Surrey.
b 1.1.13.
Centre, 2-1-0-1 (3 − 1t).
38 W− I+(1t); BI > 38 SA 1-0-0-1.
Man dir. Served WW2, Lt Col RE, involved
with planning Normandy invasion.

NICHOLSON, Edward Sealy *England*
MBE
Marlborough Coll, Oxford Univ, Guy's Hosp,
Leicester, Blackheath, Barbarians, Surrey.
b 10.6.12.
Hooker, 5-2-2-1.
35 W= I+ S−; 36 NZ+ W=.
Medicine. Blue 31-4. Served WW2, S Ldr RAF.
GP at Beccles.

NICHOLSON, Elliot Tennant *England*
Liverpool Coll, Liverpool, Birkenhead Pk,
Cheshire.
b 13.12.1871; *d* 1.12.53.
Wing, 2-1-0-1 (3 − 1t).
1900 W−(1t) I+.

NICHOLSON, Frank Villeneuve *Australia*
Brisbane GS, Qld.

304

b 15.10.1878; *d* 70.
Forward, 2-0-0-2.
03 NZ−; 04 BT−.
Solicitor. Bro of Fred. One of A's longest lived players.

NICHOLSON, Frederick Charles　　*Australia*
Brisbane GS, Qld.
b 19.4.1885; *d* 75.
Wing, 1-0-0-1.
04 BT−.
Grazier. Bro of Frank.

NICHOLSON, George William　　*New Zealand*
Newton E Sch, City, Ponsonby, Auckland, N Island.
b 3.8.1878 Auckland; *d* 13.9.68 Auckland.
No 8/lock/flanker, 4-3-1-0.
03 A+; 04 BT+; 07 A+ A=.
Bootmaker. NZ > 05 A, 05-6 BI,F & NAm, 07r A. Ref NZ v A 13. NZRFU selector 20-37.

NICHOLSON, Percy Claude　　*Ireland*
Trin Coll Dublin.
b 1879; *d* −.8.48.
Forward, 3-0-1-2.
1900 E− S= W−.
Early education in E.

NICHOLSON, Thomas　　*England*
Rockcliff, Northumb.
Back, 1-1-0-0.
1893 I+.
Retailer. Won pro sprint champ at Powderhall.

NIMB, Charles Frederick　　*South Africa*
Voortrekker HS Wynberg, W Prov.
b 6.9.38.
FH, 1-1-0-0 (9 − 3c 1p).
61 I+(3c 1p).
Bank clerk. SA > 60-1 BI. RL in UK. Lives in Zambia.

NIMMO, Charles Stuart　　*Scotland*
George Watson's Coll, Watsonians.
b 10.6.1895 Edinburgh; *d* 20.2.43 Jedburgh.
SH, 1-0-0-1.
20 E−.
Medicine.

NINNES, Barry Francis　　*England*
Hayle GS, Camborne Tech Coll, St Ives, Coventry, Cornwall, Warwicks.
b 23.3.48 St Ives.
Lock, 1-0-0-1.
71 W−.
Toolmaker.

NOBLE, Jean-Claude　　*France*
La Voulte.
b 29.12.44 Marseilles.

Prop, 6-3-0-3.
68 E+ W+ Cz+ NZ− A− R−.
Draughtsman.

NOMIS, Sydney Harold　　*South Africa*
Transvaal.
b 14.11.41 Johannesburg.
Wing/centre, 25-16-5-4 (18 − 6t).
67 F=; 68 BI+ BI= BI+ BI+(1t) F+ F+; 69 A+(2t) A+ A+ A+ S− E−; 70 I= W=(1t) NZ+(1t) NZ− NZ+ NZ+; 71 F+ F= A+ A+ A+; 72 E−.
Rep. Of Jewish stock. SA > 65 A, NZ; 69-70 BI. 25 consec Tests (3 as centre), a rec for SA.

NORMAN, Douglas James　　*England*
Medway Sch, Medway Ath, Oadby, Leicester, Barbarians, Leics.
b 12.6.1897; *d* 27.12.71.
Hooker, 2-0-0-2.
32 SA− W−.
Pres Leics Schs RU. Served WW1, RA. Served WW2, Home Guard.

NORMAND, Adrien　　*France*
Toulouse.
Lock, 1-1-0-0.
57 R+.

NORRIS, Charles Howard　　*Wales*
Cardiff.
b 11.6.34 Porth.
Prop, 2-1-0-1.
63 F−; 66 F+; BI > 66 A, NZ 3-0-0-3.
Schoolmaster. Barbarians v NZ 67. Chmn Cardiff.

NORSTER, Robert Leonard　　*Wales*
Nantyglo GS, Gwent Coll of HE, S Glamorgan Inst, UC Wales, Abertillery, Welsh Academicals, Barbarians, Cardiff.
b 23.6.57 Ebbw Vale.
Lock, 15-7-1-7.
82 S−; 83 E= S+ I+ F−; 84 S− I+ F− E+ A−; 85 S+ I− F− E+ Fj+; BI > 83 NZ 2-0-0-2.
Account mgr Rank Xerox. Wales XV v R 79. Wales B v F 79, 80. Wales B > 80 Can, US. Sent off Cardiff v S Wales Police 30.11.85, so disqu from W sel 85-86 season.

NORTH, Eustace Herbert Guest　　*England*
St Paul's Sch, Blackheath Proprietary Sch, Oxford Univ, Blackheath, Barbarians, Sussex, Kent.
b 4.11.1868; *d* 17.3.42.
Forward, 3-2-0-1.
1891 W+ I+ S−.
Schoolmaster. Blue 1888-90. Ckt for Oxford Authentics. Chmn Prep Schs Assoc 20-8, treasurer 31-42.

NORTHMORE, S. *England*
Millom, Cumberland.
FH, 1-0-0-1.
1897 I−.
Broughton Rgrs RL.

NORTON, George William *Ireland*
St Mary's Coll, Bective Rgrs, Barbarians.
b 1.4.20 Dublin.
FB, 11-7-1-3 (41 − 7c 9p).
49 F−(3p) E+(1c 2p) S+(2c 1p) W+(1c); 50 F=
E− S+(3c 2p) W−(1p); 51 F+ E+ S+; BI > 50
NZ, A.
Insurance.

NORTON, Rangitane Will *New Zealand*
Methven Convent Sch, Methven Dist HS,
Methven, Mid-Canterbury, Linwood, NZ
Maoris, Canterbury, S Island.
b 30.3.42 Waikari.
Hooker, 27-16-3-8.
71 BI− BI+ BI− BI=; 72 A+ A+ A+ W+ S+;
73 E+ I= F− E−; 74 A+ A= A+; 74 I+; 75
S+; 76 I+ SA− SA+ SA− SA−; 77 BI+ BI−
BI+ BI+.
Bank off/insurance rep. NZ > 72-3 BI,F &
NAm, 74 A & Fj & I,W & E, 76 SA. Capt v BI
77. Capt NZ Maoris > 73 Pacific. Outstanding
Maori Player of Year 73-4.

NORTON, William Barron *Wales*
Carmarthen, Cardiff.
b 1862 Carmarthen; *d* 17.12.1898 Niger.
Back, 6-2-0-4 (1t)
1882 I+ E−; 1883 S−; 1884 E− S− I+(1t).

NOTLEY, John Robert *Ireland*
Masonic Sch Dublin, Wanderers.
b 25.6.26 Drumsna, Co Roscommon.
FB/centre, 2-2-0-0 (2 − 1c).
52 F+(1c) S+.
Insurance. Ckt for I 56.

NOVAK, Michael John *England*
Eastbourne GS, Eastbourne, Harlequins,
Sussex, Surrey.
b 27.9.47 Stratford on Avon.
Wing, 3-0-0-3 (3 − 1t).
70 W−(1t) S− F−.

NOVÈS, Guy *France*
Toulouse.
b 5.2.54 Toulouse.
Wing, 7-4-1-2.
77 NZ+ NZ− R+; 78 W− R+; 79 I= W+.
PE instructor.

NOVIS, Anthony Leslie MC *England*
Epsom Coll, Oxford Univ, Blackheath, The
Army, Comb Servs, Headingley, Barbarians,
Surrey.
b 22.9.06.
Wing, 7-4-0-3 (12 − 4t).
29 S−(1t) F+; 30 W+ I−(1t) F+; 33 I+(2t) S−;
BI > 30 NZ 2-0-0-2, A 1-1-0-0.
The Army. Blue 27. Capt Comb Servs v NZ 35.
Served WW2, twice wounded. Retd 45, Lt Col.

NYKAMP, Joseph L. *South Africa*
Transvaal.
b − ; *d* 68.
1-0-0-1.
33 A−.
Car sales mgr. Capt 1st Jnr Springboks > 32
Arg.

O

OAKELEY, Francis Eckley *England*
Hereford Sch, Eastman's Sch, RNC Osborne,
RNC Dartmouth, US Portsmouth, RN.
b 5.2.1891 Hereford; kia between 25.11.14 &
1.12.14 at sea.
SH, 4-4-0-0.
13 S+; 14 I+ S+ F+.
RN. Joined RN 08. Served WW1, Lt RN. Lost
life in submarine.

OAKES, Robert Frederick *England*
Hartlepool Trin, Hartlepool R, Headingley,
Durham Co.
b 1873 Hartlepool; *d* 23.10.52 Adel, Leeds.
Forward, 8-2-1-5.
1897 W− I− S+; 1898 I− S= W+; 1899
W− S−.
Timber merchant. Son of army sgt, born at
Hartlepool Militia Barracks. Became ldg
administrator, dedicated to amateur principles
of game. Sec Yorks 07-47, pres 22-4. Rep Yorks
on RFU 20-45. E sel 29-39. IB mem 36. Pres
RFU 33-4. E cap in Hartlepool R club.

**OAKLEY, Lionel Frederick
Lightborn** *England*
Bedford Sch, Bedford, The Army, Barbarians,
E Midlands.
b 24.1.25; *d* 81.
Centre, 1-0-0-1.
51 W−.
Fertiliser co sales mgr. Served WW2, RA; 2nd
Indian Airborne Div; & 6th Airborne Div.

OBOLENSKY, Prince Alexander *England*
('Obo')
Trent College, Oxford Univ, Rosslyn Pk,
Barbarians, NLD.
b 17.2.16 St Petersburg, Russia; *d* 29.3.40
Norfolk.
Wing, 4-2-1-1 (6 − 2t).

36 NZ+ (2t) W= I− S+; RFU > 36 SAm. RAF. Blue 35, 37. Only Russian to play rugby for England, was the 1st int to lose life during WW2. Killed in flying training accident. Pioneer of lightweight rugby boots. Has claims to have scored most t in rep match, 17 for RFU v Brazilian XV, Niteroi 31.8.36.

O'BRIEN, Brian   *Ireland*
Foyle Coll, Trin Coll Dublin, Derry.
b 12.7.1872; *d* 16.
Forward, 2-0-1-1.
1893 S= W−.
Medicine.

O'BRIEN, Brian Anthony Philip   *Ireland*
CBS Limerick, Shannon.
b 5.7.39 Limerick City.
Centre, 3-1-1-1.
68 F− E= S+.
Co mgr.

O'BRIEN, Desmond Joseph   *Ireland*
Belvedere Coll, Edinburgh Univ, London Irish, Cardiff, O Belvedere, Barbarians.
b 22.5.19 Dublin.
Flanker/no 8, 20-12-2-6 (3 − 1t).
48 E+ S+ W+; 49 F− E+ S+ W+; 50 F= E− S+ W−; 51 F+ E+ S+(1t) W= SA−; 52 F+ S+ W− E−.
Brewery rep. Squash for I.

O'BRIEN, Frank William Hall   *Australia*
NSW.
b 10.
Wing, 2-0-0-2 (3 − 1t).
37 SA−(1t); 38 NZ−.
Salesman. 440 Y Champ of A, 32.

O'BRIEN, John Gerald   *New Zealand*
Marist, Auckland, Comb Servs, N Island.
b 9.12.1889 Wellington; *d* 9.1.58 Kiwitahi.
FB, 1-1-0-0.
14 A+.
Post & Telegraph employee/farmer. NZ > 14 & 20 A. Comb Servs 19.

O'BRIEN, Kevin Anthony   *Ireland*
De La Salle Sch Salford, Ashton Coll, Broughton Pk.
b 5.6.55 Manchester.
FB, 3-0-0-3 (4 − 1t).
80 E−; 81 SA−r SA−(1t).
Sales rep/life insurance. I > 81 SA.

O'BRIEN-BUTLER, P.E.   *Ireland*
Monkstown.
b −; kia 02 Wynberg, SA.
FB, 6-3-0-3.
1897 S−; 1898 E+ S−; 1899 S+ W+; 1900 E−.
The Army.

O'CALLAGHAN, Cyril Tate MC   *Ireland*
Merchant Taylor's Sch, Carlow.
b 9.9.1889 Carlow; *d* −.
Wing, 7-5-0-2 (3 − 1t).
10 W− F+; 11 E+ S+ W− F+(1t); 12 F+.
The Army. Served WW1, Lt Col 10th R Hussars.

O'CALLAGHAN, Michael Paul   *Ireland*
PBC Cork, Sunday's Well.
b 36.
Prop, 3-1-1-1.
62 W=; 64 E+ F−.
Electrician.

O'CALLAGHAN, Philip ('Philo')   *Ireland*
Greymouth PBS, Dolphin, Barbarians.
b 25.3.46 Cork.
Prop, 21-10-2-9.
67 A+ E− A+; 68 F− E= S+ W+; 69 F+ E+ S+ W−; 70 SA= F− E− S+ W+; 76 F− W− E+ S− NZ−.
Commercial rep.

O'CALLAGHAN, Michael   *New Zealand*
William
Culverden Dist HS, Christchurch Boys' HS, Lincoln Coll, NZ Jnrs, Massey Univ, NZ Univs, Manawatu, Matamata, Waikato, S Poitevin (F), S Toulousain (F), Cambridge Univ, Barbarians (E).
b 27.4.46 Culverden.
Wing, 3-3-0-0.
68 F+ F+ F+.
Veterinary surgery lecturer. Went to France to study 71, then Cambridge where he won blues 74-7.

O'CALLAGHAN, Thomas   *New Zealand*
Raymond
St Joseph's Convent Sch, Marist Bros' HS Greymouth, Canterbury, Celtic, W Coast, Marist, Auckland, Comb Servs, Wellington, S & N Islands.
b 19.1.25 Wellington.
2nd five-eighth, 1-0-0-1 (3 − 1p).
49 A−(1p).
Bank officer. Coach Marist 64-66. Rep W Coast at ckt & hockey.

OCHSE, Johannes Karl ('Chum')   *South Africa*
W Prov.
b 9.2.25 Graaf-Reinet.
Wing, 7-6-0-1 (9 − 3t).
51 I+(1t) W+(1t); 52 E+ F+; 53 A+ A−(1t) A+.
Schoolmaster. SA > 51-2 BI, F.

O'CONNELL, Patrick   *Ireland*
Mount St Joseph's Coll Roscrea, UC Dublin, Derry, Bective Rgrs.

b 27.3.1892 Lixnaw, Co Kerry.
Forward, 6-3-0-3.
13 W− F+; 14 F+ E− S+ W−.
Medicine.

O'CONNELL, William Joseph   *Ireland*
St Munchins Coll Limerick, Lansdowne.
b 22.4.30 Limerick.
Lock, 1-0-0-1.
55 F−.
Bank mgr.

O'CONNOR, Anthony   *Wales*
Duffryn GS, Aberavon, Oxford Univ,
Barbarians.
b 24.4.34.
SH, 5-2-1-2.
60 SA−; 61 E+ S−; 62 F+ I=; BI > 62 SA.
Research mgr. Blue 58.

O'CONNOR, Hubert Stephen   *Ireland*
Terenure Coll, Trin Coll Dublin.
b 2.9.33 Dublin.
Flanker, 4-2-0-2.
57 F+ E− S+ W−.
Medicine.

O'CONNOR, Jack   *Ireland*
Garryowen.
Wing, 1-0-0-1.
1895 S−.

O'CONNOR, Joseph   *Ireland*
Rockwell Coll, UC Cork.
b 27.10.11 Castleisland.
Wing, 11-3-0-8 (9 − 3t).
33 S−; 34 E− S−(1t) W−; 35 E−(1t) S+(1t)
W+ NZ−; 36 S+ W−; 38 S−.
Engr.

O'CONNOR, Joseph J.   *Ireland*
Garryowen.
Wing, 1-1-0-0.
09 F+.

O'CONNOR, Michael David   *Australia*
Phillip Coll, Australian Schs, ACT, Brisbane,
Qld.
b 30.11.60.
Centre/wing, 12-8-0-4 (20 − 5t).
79 Arg− Arg+; 80 Fj+ NZ+ NZ− NZ+(1t); 81
F+(1t) F+(1t) I+(1t); 82 E− S− S+(1t).
A Schs > 77-8 BI & capt 78 NZ. A > 79 Arg; 80
Fj; 81-2 BI. St George RL 82 & A RL.

O'CONNOR, P.J.   *Ireland*
Blackrock Coll, Lansdowne.
b 18.4.1863; d 26.12.19 Dublin.
Half-back, 1-0-0-1.
1887 W−.
Auctioneer.

O'CONNOR, Rory   *Wales*
Welsh Youth, Aberavon.
b −; d −.3.86.
Flanker, 1-0-0-1.
57 E−.
Steelworker. 1st Welsh Youth player to be
capped.

O'CONOR, John Hamilton   *Ireland*
Bective Rgrs.
b 1866 Letterkenny; d 23.5.53 Rathgar.
Forward, 17-6-3-8.
1888 NZN−; 1890 S− W= E−; 1891 E− S−;
1892 E− W+; 1893 E− S=; 1894 E+ S+ W+;
1895 E−; 1896 E+ S= W+.
Pres IRU 11-12.

ODBERT, Reginald Vere Massey   *Ireland*
Blackrock Coll, RAF.
b 9.2.04; d 18.7.43.
Centre, 1-1-0-0.
28 F+.
Served in RAF as Gp Capt.

O'DONNELL, Claude Augustus   *Australia*
NSW.
b 30.1.1886 Paddington; d 4.8.53 Sydney.
No 8, 2-0-0-2.
13 NZ− NZ−.
Tailor's presser.

O'DONNELL, Desmond Hillary   *New Zealand*
St Patrick's Coll Silverstream, OB, Army,
Wellington, Comb Servs, N Island, Raetihi.
b 7.10.21 Palmerston N.
Prop, 1-0-0-1.
49 A−.
Schoolmaster. Last match for Raetihi 64 at age
of 43, having coached club 52-8 & served as
treasurer 52-6. Coach Marist-St Pat's 71. Ckt for
Ruapehu 52-6.

O'DONNELL, Ignatius Charles   *Australia*
St Ignatius Coll Riverview, NSW.
b 27.5.1876; d 46.
SH, 2-0-0-2.
1899 BT− BT−.
Clerk.

O'DONNELL, James M.   *Australia*
Canterbury, Otago, Invercargill, NSW.
Forward, 1-0-0-1.
1899 BT−.
Farmer/police/schoolmaster. NZ > A 1884.
(Arrested shortly before tour departure when
several Invercargill townspeople claimed he
owed them money.) Remained in A; Rep NSW
v BT 1888.

O'DONNELL, Rodney   *Ireland*
Christopher

St Mary's Coll.
b 16.8.56 Dublin.
FB, 5-4-0-1.
79 A+ A+; 80 S+ F− W+; BI > 80 SA 1-0-0-1.
Sales rep.

O'DONOGHUE, Patrick Joseph   *Ireland*
CBC Dun Laoghaire, Bective Rgrs.
b 22.11.31 Dun Laoghaire.
Prop, 11-4-1-6.
55 F− E= S− W−; 56 W+; 57 F+ E−; 58 A+
E− S+ W−.
Civil service.

O'DRISCOLL, Barry Joseph   *Ireland*
Stonyhurst Sch, Manchester Univ, Manchester,
Barbarians.
b 18.9.43 Dublin.
FB, 4-1-1-2 (6 − 2p).
71 F=r(2p) E− S+ W−.
Medicine.

O'DRISCOLL, John Brian   *Ireland*
Stonyhurst Sch, Westminster Hosp, London
Irish, Manchester, Barbarians.
b 26.11.53 Dublin.
Flanker, 26-11-0-15 (4 − 1t).
78 S+; 79 A+ A+; 80 E− S+ F− W+(1t); 81
F− W− E− S− SA− SA− A−; 82 W+ E+ S+
F−; 83 S+ F+ W− E+; 84 F− W− E− S−; BI
> 80 SA 4-1-0-3; 83 NZ 2-0-0-2.
Medicine. I > 81 SA. Played with Keith Hughes
of W in Westminster Hosp XV which won
Hosps' Cup 1st time 74.

OELOFSE, Johannes S.A.   *South Africa*
('Hansie')
Transvaal.
b 16.12.26 Johannesburg; *d* 78.
SH, 4-3-0-1 (6 − 2t).
53 A+(1t) A− A+ A+(1t).
Mining surveyor. SA > 51-2 BI

O'FLANAGAN, Kevin Patrick   *Ireland*
CBS Synge St, UC Dublin, London Irish.
b −.6.19 Dublin.
Wing, 1-0-0-1.
47 A−.
Medicine. Bro of Michael. Football for
Bohemians, Arsenal & I.

O'FLANAGAN, Michael   *Ireland*
CBS Synge St, Lansdowne.
b 29.9.22 Dublin.
Centre, 1-1-0-0.
48 S+.
Vintner. Bro of Kevin. Football for I.

OGILVY, Charles   *Scotland*
Hawick.
b 1889; *d* −.9.58 London.

Centre/FB, 3-0-0-3.
11 I− E−; 12 I−.
Tweed co dir.

O'GORMAN, John Francis   *Australia*
St Joseph's Coll, Sydney Univ, NSW.
b 1.6.36.
Lock, 18-8-0-10.
61 Fj+ SA− SA− F−; 62 NZ−; 63 E+ SA−
SA+ SA+ SA−; 65 SA+ SA+; 66 W+ S−; 67
E+ I− F− I−.
Medicine.

O'HANLON, Bartholomew   *Ireland*
Reginald ('Bertie')
Rockwell Coll, Dolphin, Barbarians.
b 23.10.24 Cork.
Wing, 12-9-1-2 (9 − 3t).
47 E+(2t) S+ W−; 48 F+ E+ S+ W+; 49 F−
E+(1t) S+ W+; 50 F=.
Insurance area mgr.

OLD, Alan Gerald Bernard   *England*
Acklam Hall GS Middlesbrough, London Univ,
Middlesbrough, Leicester, Sheffield, Yorks.
b 23.9.45 Middlesbrough.
FH, 16-3-1-12 (98 − 1t 8c 3d 23p).
72 W− I− F−(1c 2p) S−(3p) SA+; 73 NZ−
A+(1t); 74 S−(1p) I−(1c 5p) F=(1c 1p) W+(1c
2p); 75 I−(1c 1d) A−(2c 3p); 76 S−(1c 2p) I−
(4p); 78 F−(2d); BI > 74 SA.
Schoolmaster. 37 pts BI v SW Dist 74, most by
BI player on any tour & rec by any player on
tour of SA. 1 app Warwicks CCC 69; Durham
CCC. Bro of Chris, Yorks, Warwicks & E ckter.

OLD, Geoffrey Haldane   *New Zealand*
New Plymouth Boys' HS, Eltham, NZ Jnrs,
Taranaki, Palmerston N HSOB, Manawatu.
b 22.1.56 Eltham.
Flanker/No 8/lock, 3-3-0-0.
81 SA+ R+r; 82 A+r.
Police. NZ v Fj 80. NZ > 80 NAm & W, 81 R &
F, 83 S & E.

OLDHAM, W.L.   *England*
Coventry, Midland Cos.
b Coventry; *d* −.
Forward, 2-0-0-2.
08 S−; 09 A−.
Workhouse master.

O'LEARY, Arthur Finbarr   *Ireland*
('Archie')
PBC Cork, Cork Constitution.
b 30.11.29 Cork.
Lock, 3-1-0-2.
52 S+ W− E−.
Insurance.

O'LEARY, Michael Joseph   *New Zealand*
Masterton, Wairarapa, Ponsonby, Auckland, N
Island.
 b 29.9.1883 Masterton; *d* 12.12.63 Masterton.
FB, 4-3-0-1 (12 − 6c).
10 A+ A+(2c); 13 A+(3c) A−(1c).
Blacksmith. NZ > 10 A. Wairarapa sel 22-5.
Bro Humphrey capt NZ Univs 08-9 & later
became Chief Justice.

OLIVE, Dacien   *France*
Montferrand.
 b 12.7.24 Claira.
Wing, 2-0-0-2 (3 − 1t).
51 I−(1t); 52 I−.

OLIVER, Charles Joshua   *New Zealand*
Waltham Sch, Merivale, Canterbury, S Island.
 b 1.11.05 Wanganui; *d* 25.8.77 Brisbane.
2nd five-eighth/centre, 7-2-0-5 (6 − 2t).
29 A−(1t) A−; 34 A−; 35 S+ I+(1t) W−; 36
E−.
Carpenter. NZ > 29 & 34 A; 35-6 BI & C (v-
capt). Ckt for Canterbury 23-7 & NZ > 25-6 A
& 27 E. Father-in-law of David Gillespie. Co-
author with fellow All Black Eric Tindill of 'The
Tour of the Third All Blacks' pub 36.

OLIVER, Desmond Oswald   *New Zealand*
Marist Bros' Sch, Palmerston N Boys' HS,
Victoria Univ, Otago Univ, Otago, NZ Univs, S
Island.
 b 26.10.30 Palmerston N.
Flanker, 2-1-0-1.
54 I+ F−.
Medicine. NZ > 53-4 BI,F & NAm. Went to E
60; dir of renal unit, Churchill Hosp, Oxford.

OLIVER, Donald Joseph   *New Zealand*
Heriot Sch, Kaikorai, Otago, Wellington,
Carterton, Wairarapa, Waikeria, Waikato,
Pirates, Southland, S Island.
 b c07.
Wing, 2-1-0-1 (3 − 1t).
30 BI− BI+(1t).
Prison officer/hydatids inspector. Horowhenua
sel 48-50.

OLIVER, Francis James   *New Zealand*
Lawrence Dist HS, Marist, NZ Jnrs, Southland,
Waiau, Tokomairo, Comb Servs, Otago,
Manawatu, S & N Islands.
 b 24.12.48 Dunedin.
Lock, 17-11-0-6 (4 − 1t).
76 SA−; 77 BI+ BI− BI+ BI+; 77 F− F+; 78
A+ A+ A− I+ W+ E+(1t) S+; 79 F+ F−; 81
SA−.
Police/forestry contractor/fisherman/foreman.
NZ > 76 SA, 77 F, 78 F, 80 NAm & W. Capt v
A 78. NZ v Fj 80. Bro Paul rep Otago 74-80.

OLIVER, George   *Wales*
Pontypool.
Lock/flanker, 4-3-0-1.
20 E+ S− F+ I+.
Hull RL 20; later Pontypridd RL.

OLIVER, George Kenneth   *Scotland*
Gala Acad, Gala.
 b 4.3.46 Galashiels.
No 8, 1-0-0-1.
70 A−.
Chartered architect.

OLIVER, John F.   *South Africa*
Transvaal.
 b − ; *d* 80.
Prop, 2-1-0-1.
28 NZ+ NZ−.

OLIVIER, Ebenhaeser   *South Africa*
W Prov.
 b 10.4.44 Kirkswood.
Wing/centre, 16-11-2-3 (15 − 5t).
67 F+ F+(1t) F−(1t) F=; 68 BI+ BI= BI+
BI+(1t) F+ F+; 69 A+ A+ A+ A+(1t) S−
E−.
Professor. SA > 65 A, NZ; 69-70 BI.

O'LOUGHLIN, David   *Ireland*
Bonaventure
Blackrock Coll, UC Cork, Garryowen.
 b 13.7.16 Kilmallock; *d* 17.7.71 Glenbeigh, Co
Kerry.
Prop/lock, 6-2-0-4 (3 − 1t).
38 E− S−(1t) W−; 39 E+ S+ W−.
Dairy creamery dir. Played in 2 Victory ints.

OLVER, E.   *South Africa*
E Prov.
1-0-0-1.
1896 BT−.

O'MEARA, John Anthony   *Ireland*
CBC Cork, Clongowes Coll, UC Cork,
Dolphin.
 b 26.6.29 Cork.
SH, 22-10-3-9 (6 − 2t).
51 F+ E+ S+ W= SA−; 52 F+ S+ W− E−; 53
F+ E= S+ W−; 54 NZ− F− E− S+; 55 F−
E=; 56 S+(1t) W+; 58 W−(1t).
Solicitor.

O'NEILL, A.   *England*
Torquay Ath, Bart's Hosp, Devon.
 b Teignmouth; *d* −.
Forward, 3-0-0-3.
01 W− I− S−.

O'NEILL, Dallas John   *Australia*
Nudgee Coll, Qld.
 b 43.

310

Flanker, 2-0-0-2.
64 NZ− NZ−.
Switched to RL.

O'NEILL, Henry O'Hara   *Ireland*
Coleraine AI, UC Cork, Queen's Univ Belfast.
b 1.7.07 Portstewart.
Prop, 6-3-0-3.
30 E+ S+ W−; 33 E− W+ S−; BI > 30 NZ 4-1-
0-3 & A.
Civil Service.

O'NEILL, James Bowman   *Ireland*
Methodist Coll Belfast, Queen's Univ Belfast.
b 21.8.1895 Belfast; *d* 19.4.68 Bangor.
SH, 1-0-0-1.
20 S−.
Civil Service/asst to NI Minister of Home
Affairs. Wrote 'Criticus' column in 'Belfast
Telegraph'.

O'NEILL, John Michael   *Australia*
St Mary's CBS Toowoomba, Qld.
b 26.4.32 Warwick, Qld.
Wing/FB, 4-1-0-3.
52 NZ+ NZ−; 56 SA− SA−.
Medicine.

O'NEILL, William Arthur   *Ireland*
('Boldy')
Willow Pk Coll, UC Dublin, Barbarians.
b 15.11.28 Dublin.
Prop, 6-2-1-3.
52 E−; 53 F+ E= S+ W−; 54 NZ−.
Bus/accountant. Bro in law of J.C. Murphy-
O'Connor.

OOSTHUIZEN, Jacobus   *South Africa*
Johannes
W Prov.
b 4.7.51 Worcester, Cape Prov.
Centre, 9-7-0-2 (8 − 2t).
74 BI− F+ F+; 75 F+ F+; 76 NZ+ NZ
NZ+(1t) NZ+.
Police.

OOSTHUIZEN, Ockert Wessel   *South Africa*
('Osie')
Volkskool Sch Heidelberg, Potchefstroom
Univ, W Transvaal, RAU Club, N Transvaal,
SA Forces, Gazelles, Transvaal.
b 1.4.55 Johannesburg.
Prop, 9-7-0-2 (4 − 1t).
81 I+r I+ NZ+ NZ− US+; 82 SAm+(1t)
SAm−; 84 E+ E+.
Sports officer.

OPENSHAW, William Edward   *England*
Harrow Sch, Manchester, Lancs.
b c1851; *d* 15.2.15 Warrington.

Half-back, 1-1-0-0.
1879 I+.
Merchant. Ckt for Harrow v Eton 1869-70. Won
half-mile, 1 mile at Harrow 1870.

O'REILLY, Anthony Joseph   *Ireland*
Francis Kevin
Belvedere Coll, UC Dublin, O Belvedere,
Leicester, Barbarians.
b 7.5.36 Dublin.
Centre/wing, 29-10-1-18 (15 − 5t).
55 F− E=(1t) S− W−; 56 F−(1t) E− S+(1t)
W+; 57 F+ E− S+ W−; 58 A+ E− S+ W−
F−; 59 E− S+ W−(1t) F+; 60 E−; 61 E+ F−
SA−; 63 F−(1t) S− W+; 70 E−; BI > 55 SA 4-
2-0-2; 59 A 2-2-0-0, NZ 4-1-0-3.
Solicitor/pres of Heinz Corp/newspaper
proprietor. I's equ longest int career (16
seasons, with Mike Gibson). Recalled v E 70
after 8 yr gap and arrived at Twickenham by
chauffeur-driven Rolls Royce. BI most t in ints,
6 (10 ints); most t on a tour, 22 (23 apps), A, NZ
59. Son Cameron treasurer of Oxford Union.
Celebrated 50th birthday with a dinner for 450 at
home in Castlemartin, Co Kildare, 7.5.86.

ORR, Charles Edward   *Scotland*
Loretto Sch, W of Scotland, Barbarians.
b 21.11.1866; *d* 6.4.35 Los Angeles.
Half-back, 16-12-1-3 (3t).
1887 I+ W+(1t) E=; 1888 W− I+; 1889
W+(1t) I+; 1890 W+(1t) I+ E−; 1891 W+ I+
E+; 1892 W+ I+ E−.
Farmer.

ORR, Hugh James   *Scotland*
London Scottish, RN, Barbarians.
b 21.1.1878 Australia; *d* 16.5.46.
Centre/wing, 5-4-0-1 (3 − 1t).
03 W+ I+ E+; 04 W−(1t) I+.
RN.

ORR, John E.   *Scotland*
Uppingham Sch, W of Scotland.
Forward, 12-9-1-2 (2t).
1889 I+; 1890 W+ I+(1t) E−; 1891 W+ I+
E+(1t); 1892 W+ I+ E−; 1893 I= E+.

ORR, John Henry OBE   *Scotland*
Heriot's Coll, Edinburgh City Police.
b 13.6.18.
Flanker, 2-0-0-2.
47 F− W−.
Police. Pres SRU 75-6.

ORR, Philip Andrew   *Ireland*
Dublin HS, Trin Coll Dublin, O Wesley,
Barbarians.
b 14.12.50 Dublin.
Prop, 50-16-3-31.
76 F− W− E+ S− NZ−; 77 W− E− S− F−; 78

S+ F− W− E− NZ−; 79 F= W− E+ S= A+
A+; 80 E− S+ F− W+; 81 F− W− E− S−
SA− SA− A−; 82 W+ E+ S+ F−; 83 S+ F+
W− E+; 84 F− W− E− S− A−; 85 S+ F=
W+ E+; 86 F− S−; BI > 77 NZ 1-0-0-1; 80 SA.
Clothing manufacturer. I's most capped prop. I
> 79 A, 81 SA. Dropped after making 49 consec
apps for I.

ORR, Rex William   *New Zealand*
Gore HS, Tg Coll, Otago, Zingari-Richmond,
Ponsonby, Auckland, Comb Servs, S Island.
b 19.6.24 Gore.
FB, 1-0-0-1.
49 A−.
RNZAF/schoolmaster. Capt Comb Servs 53-5.

ORSO, Jean-Charles   *France*
Nice.
b 6.1.58 Cannes-les-Bocca.
Lock, 12-8-2-2.
82 Arg+ Arg+; 83 E+ S+ A=; 84 E+r S−
NZ−; 85 I=r W+ J+ J+.
Horticultural agent. France B v W 81, 2; S 82.
France A v It, Soviet Union 82. High-class
basketball player.

ORWIN, John   *England*
Gloucester, RAF.
Lock, 7-2-1-4.
85 R+ F= S+ I− W− NZ− NZ−.
RAF/Licensee.

OSBORNE, Douglas Hugh   *Australia*
Victoria.
b 19.7.52 Thames, NZ.
Wing, 3-3-0-0 (4 − 1t).
75 E+ E+ J+(1t).
Real estate.

OSBORNE, Richard R.   *England*
Hurstpierpoint Coll, Rochdale, Manchester,
Lancs.
b 20.5.1848 Ashgill, Yorks; *d* 4.11.26
Rochdale.
Back, 1-0-0-1.
1871 S−.
Solicitor. Played in 1st int, S v E 1871; cap &
jersey, oldest in existence, in Manchester club.
Bro of jockey & racehorse trainer, John ('The
Pusher') Osborne.

OSBORNE, Sidney Herbert   *England*
Fettes Coll, Oxford Univ, Harlequins, St Bees,
Mdx, Cumberland.
b 26.2.1880 London; *d* 15.7.39.
Forward, 1-0-0-1.
05 S−.
HM. Blue 1900-2.

OSBORNE, William Michael   *New Zealand*
Wanganui HS, Kaierau, NZ Colts, Wanganui,
NZ Maoris, N Island.
b 24.4.55 Wanganui.
Centre/2nd five-eighth/wing, 16-13-0-3.
75 S+; 76 SA+r SA−r; 77 BI+ BI− BI+ BI+;
77 F− F+r; 78 I+ W+ E+ S+; 80 W+; 82 A+
A+.
Contractor. NZ > 76 SA, 77 F, 78 BI, NAm &
W. NZ v Fj 80. World XV > 86 SA. Rep sch at
ckt, basketball, rowing & ath. Maori Player of
Year 77.

OSBORNE, W.T.   *Wales*
Mountain Ash.
b 1880 Mountain Ash.
Forward, 6-5-0-1 (3 − 1t).
02 E+(1t) S+ I+; 03 E+ S− I+.
Miner/police. Huddersfield RL 03.

O'SHEA, John Patrick ('Tess')   *Wales*
Cardiff, Barbarians.
b 2.6.40.
Prop, 5-1-0-4.
67 S− I−; 68 S+ I− F−; BI > 68 SA 1-0-0-1.
Rep. Sent off BI v E Transvaal 68. Barbarians >
69 SA.

OSLER, Benjamin Louwrens   *South Africa*
('Benny')
W Prov Prep Sch, Rondebosch Boys HS,
Kingswood Coll Grahamstown, Hamiltons,
Villagers, Stellenbosch Univ, Cape Town Univ,
W Prov.
b 23.11.01 Aliwal North; *d* 23.4.60 Belville.
FH, 17-12-1-4 (46 − 2t 6c 4d 4p).
24 BI+(1d) BI+(1c 1p) BI= BI+; 28 NZ+(2d
2p) NZ−(1p) NZ+(1c) NZ−(1c); 31 W+(1c)
I+(1c); 32 E+ S+(1t); 33 A+(1t) A− A+(1d)
A+(1c) A−.
Lawyer. Tour capt SA > 31-2 BI; 2nd Test A
33. 17 consec Tests. Played v bro Stanley, SA v
Oxford Univ 31.

OSLER, F.L.   *Scotland*
Edinburgh Acad, Edinburgh Univ.
SH, 2-0-0-2.
11 F− W−.

OSLER, Stanley Gordon   *South Africa*
('Sharkie')
Stellenbosch Univ, Oxford Univ, W Prov.
b 31.1.07; *d* −.4.80.
1-1-0-0.
28 NZ+.
HM/barrister. Rhodes Scholar. Blue 31. Played
v bro Benny, Oxford Univ v SA 31. Inj cut short
career.

O'SULLIVAN, Alexander Charles   *Ireland*
RS Dungannon, Trin Coll Dublin.

b 1858; *d* 24.
Forward, 1-0-0-1.
1882 S−.
Medicine/professor at Trin Coll Dublin.

O'SULLIVAN, James Michael *New Zealand*
Matapa Sch, Okaiawa, Taranaki, Kaponga, N Island.
b 5.2.1883 Okaiawa; *d* 21.12.60 Hawera.
No 8/flanker, 5-3-1-1.
05 S+ I+ E+ W−; 07 A=.
Farmer. NZ > 05 A, 05-6 BI,F & NAm (broke collarbone v Cardiff), 07 A.

O'SULLIVAN, John Michael *Ireland*
Limerick, Cork.
FB, 2-0-0-2.
1884 S−; 1887 S−.
Pres IRU 1900-1.

O'SULLIVAN, Patrick Joseph *Ireland*
Antony
St Joseph's Coll Galway, Galwegians.
b 2.6.33 Galway.
No 8, 15-5-1-9 (3 − 1t).
57 F+ E− S+(1t) W−; 59 E− S+ W− F+; 60 SA−; 61 E+ S−; 62 F− W=; 63 F− NZ−.
Victualler.

O'SULLIVAN, Terence Patrick *New Zealand*
Anthony
St Patrick's Coll Silverstream, Okato, NZ Jnrs, NZ Colts, Taranaki, N Island.
b 27.11.36 New Plymouth.
Centre/2nd five-eighth, 4-3-0-1 (3 − 1t).
60 SA−; 61 F+(1t); 62 A+ A+.
Farmer. NZ > 60 A & SA (broke wrist v Rhodesia), 62 A. Coached Okata 72-8.

O'SULLIVAN, William *Ireland*
St Brendan's Coll Killarney, Queen's Coll Cork, Edinburgh Univ.
b 1874; *d* 3.3.53.
Forward, 1-0-0-1.
1895 S−.
Medicine. Pres Irish Medical Assoc. Senator IFS.

OTHATS, Jean *France*
Dax.
Wing, 2-2-0-0.
60 Arg+ Arg+.

OUGHTRED, Bernard *England*
W Hartlepool GS, King Edward VI Sch Birmingham, O Edwardians, Hartlepool R, Hull & ER, Furness, Barrow, Barbarians, Westmorland, Durham Co, Yorks.
b 22.8.1888 W Hartlepool; *d* 12.11.49.
SH, 6-2-0-4.
01 S−; 02 W− I+ S+; 03 W− I−.

Naval architect. Contracted typhoid fever during E's visit to Dublin 14.2.03, and made a full recovery, unlike fellow-player R. Forrest and R.S. Whalley, ex-Pres RFU, both of whom died. Attached to RN during WW1; present at Battle of Jutland.

OULD, W.J. *Wales*
Aberavon, Cardiff.
b 6.5.1899 Glyncorrwg.
Lock, 2-0-0-2.
24 E− S−.
Collier/police.

OUTTERSIDE, Robert *Australia*
NSW.
b 6.3.32 Sydney.
Flanker/no 8, 2-0-0-2.
59 BI− BI−.
Schoolmaster.

OWEN, Albert *Wales*
UC Cardiff, Swansea.
b 01.
FH, 1-0-0-1 (3 − 1t).
24 E−(1t).
Schoolmaster.

OWEN, Garfield David *Wales*
Cowbridge GS, Newport, Barbarians.
b 20.3.32 Llanharan.
FB, 6-5-0-1 (26 − 7c 4p).
55 I+(3c 1p) F+(2c 2p); 56 E+(1c) S+ I−(1p) F+(1c).
Schoolmaster/motor sales dir. Halifax RL 56. Welsh javelin champ.

OWEN, John Ernest *England*
Oundle Sch, Cambridge Univ, Blackheath, Moseley, Coventry, Barbarians, Warwicks.
b 21.9.39.
Lock, 14-4-3-7 (3 − 1t).
63 W+(1t) I= F+ S+ A−; 64 NZ−; 65 W− I− F+ S=; 66 I= F− S−; 67 NZ−.
Market research/man dir family engrg co. Blue 61. Ath blue (shot).

OWEN, Richard Morgan *Wales*
Hafod Rgrs, Swansea.
b 1876 Laugharne; *d* 27.2.32 Swansea.
SH, 35-27-1-7 (6 − 2t).
01 I+; 02 E+ S+ I+; 03 E+(1t) S− I+; 04 E= S+ I−; 05 E+ S+ I+ NZ+; 06 E+ S+ I− SA−; 07 E+ S−; 08 F+ I+ A+; 09 E+ S+ F+ I+; 10 F+ E−; 11 E+ S+ F+(1t) I+; 12 E− S+.
Steelworker/licensee. 5ft 4in, 9st 10lb. Once rec cap holder. Penalised so often for incorrect feed of scrum, E v W 04, ultimately asked England's SH, W.V. Butcher, to put ball in at every scrum. Took own life.

OWEN-SMITH, Harold Geoffrey   *England*
Owen ('Tuppy')
Diocesan Coll Rondebosch, Cape Town Univ,
Oxford Univ, St Mary's Hosp, Barbarians.
b 18.2.09 Cape Town.
FB, 10-8-1-1.
34 W+ I+ S+; 36 NZ+ W= I− S+; 37 W+ I+
S+.
Medicine. Capt E 3 times. Rhodes Scholar. Blue
32-3. Blues for ath 31-3 & boxing 31-2. Ckt for
SA 29. Served WW2, SAAMC in Middle East.
GP in Rondebosch.

OWENS, Reuben H. ('Pussy')   *Ireland*
St Andrews Coll, Trin Coll Dublin.
Hooker/flanker, 2-0-0-2.
22 E− S−.

OXENHAM, Anselm McEvoy   *Australia*
Qld.
b 20.7.1882; *d* 19.
Forward, 2-0-0-2.
04 BT−; 07 NZ−.
Clerk.

OXLADE, Allen Martindale   *Australia*
Qld.
b 18.6.1882; *d* 32.
Forward, 4-0-0-4.
04 BT− BT−; 05 NZ−; 07 NZ−.
Printer/paint salesman.

OXLADE, Boyd Davies   *Australia*
Geelong GS Brisbane, Qld.
b 14.
Flanker, 3-0-0-3.
38 NZ− NZ− NZ−.
Printer.

OXLEE, Keith   *South Africa*
Maritzburg Coll, Natal.
b 17.12.34.
FH, 19-13-2-4 (88 − 5t 14c 1d 14p).
60 NZ+ NZ−(1t) NZ=(1t) NZ+ W+(1p) I+;
61 S+ A+(1t) A+(1t 1c 3p); 62 BI= BI+(1p)
BI+(1t 1c 1p) BI+(5c 2p); 63 A+(1c 2p) A−
(1c) A+(2c 2p); 64 W+(3c 2p); 65 NZ−(1d)
NZ−.
Wallpaper co rep. SA > 60-1 BI, F; 65 I, S. 27
pts v BI 62, most by SA in series v BI. 201 career
pts for SA.

P

PACKER, Henry   *Wales*
W Buckland Sch, Newport.
b 3.9.1868 Chipping Norton; *d* 25.5.46
Newport.
Forward, 7-3-0-4.

1891 E−; 1895 S− I+; 1896 E− S+ I−; 1897
E+.
Wholesale grocer. WRU comm, sel. Mgr BI >
24 SA.

PACO, Alain   *France*
Béziers.
b 1.5.52 Béziers.
Hooker, 35-24-1-10 (4 − 1t).
74 Arg+ Arg+ R− SA− SA−; 75 W− E+
Arg+ Arg+ R+; 76 S+ I+ W− E+ US+ A+
A+ R−; 77 W+ E+ S+(1t) I+ NZ+ NZ− R+;
78 E+ S+ I+ W− R+; 79 I= W+ E− S+; 80
W−.
Rep.

PAGE, James Russell ('Rusty')   *New Zealand*
DSO CBE
Southland Boys' HS, RMC Sandhurst (E),
London Scottish, Wellington, N Island.
b 10.5.08 Dunedin; *d* 22.5.85 Auckland.
Centre/1st five-eighth, 6-3-1-2 (3 − 1t).
31 A+; 32 A− A+(1t) A+; 34 A− A=.
Army. RMC Sandhurst 27-30; reserve for S
while playing for London Scottish. Returned
NZ 30. NZ > 32 & 34 A, 35-6 BI & F (made
only 3 apps). Wellington pres 63-7. Lt Col at age
33, CO 2nd NZEF 26th Battn WW2; DSO 42.
Retired from Army with rank of Brig, 63. CBE
54.

PAGE, John Jackson ('Jacko')   *England*
Cambridgeshire HS, O Cantabrians,
Cambridge Univ, Bedford, Northampton, E
Cos.
b 16.4.47 Brighton.
SH, 5-2-1-2.
71 W− I+ F= S−; 75 S+.
Engr. Blue 68-70. E Under 25s v Fj 70.

PALAT, Jacques   *France*
Perpignan.
Flanker, 1-1-0-0.
38 G+.

PALLANT, John Noel   *England*
High Pavement GS, Loughborough Coll, UAU,
Notts, NLD, Midland Co.
b 24.12.44.
No 8/lock, 3-2-0-1.
67 I+ F− S+.
Dir of PE at Merchant Taylors' Sch 68. All E
Schs hammer champ 58. Co basketball.

PALFREYMAN, James Richard   *Australia*
Leonard
NSW.
b 9.5.05; *d* 9.9.73.
No 8/flanker, 4-2-0-2.
29 NZ+; 30 BI+; 31 NZ−; 32 NZ−.
Brewer's maltster.

314

PALMER, Alexander Croydon *England*
OBE
Waitaki Boys HS (NZ), Otago Univ, The London Hosp, RAMC, Harlequins, Barbarians, E Cos.
 b St Clair, Dunedin 2.7.1887; d 16.10.63 Walton.
Wing, 2-1-0-1 (10 − 2t 2c).
09 I+(2t 1c) S−(1c).
Medicine. Served WW1 as Maj in RAMC. Gynaecological & obstetric surg King's Coll Hosp, London for 35 yrs.

PALMER, Bertram Pitt *New Zealand*
Ponsonby, Auckland, Otahuhu, N Island.
 b 14.11.01 Mosstown; d 4.9.32 Auckland.
Hooker, 3-2-0-1 (3 − 1t).
29 A−; 32 A+ A+(1t).
NZ > 29 & 32 A. Suffered head inj Otahuhu v Univ 32 & died following day. Bert Palmer Memorial Trophy presented to Auckland RU for sportsmanship among junior teams.

PALMER, F.H. *England*
Bedford GS, Richmond, Barbarians, Mdx..
 b 6.8.1877.
Wing, 1-0-0-1.
05 W−.

PALMER, Frank MC *Wales*
Swansea.
 b 1896; d 16.10.25 Swansea.
Wing, 3-2-1-0 (3 − 1t).
22 E+(1t) S= I+.
Estate agent. Served WW1.

PALMER, Godfrey Vaughan *England*
CBE TD
Monmouth Sch, RMC Sandhurst, The Army, NIFC, Cross Keys, Harlequins, Richmond, Comb Servs, Barbarians, Mon, Hants.
 b 21.2.1900; d 28.4.72.
Wing, 3-3-0-0 (6 − 2t).
28 I+ F+(2t) S+.
The Army/sales dir. Served WW2, Lt Col; mentioned in despatches 3 times. OBE & US Legion of Merit 44; CBE & TD 45. Reached rank of Brig. 1st Brit Governor of Vienna 45. Went in to bus after war.

PALMER, John Anthony *England*
Prior Pk Coll Bath, St Mary's Coll Twickenham, Bath.
 b 13.2.57 Malta.
Centre, 3-1-0-2.
84 SA− SA−; 86 I+r.
Schoolmaster. E Under 23 > 77 Can, US. England B > 78 R.

PALMIE, Michel *France*
Béziers.
 b 1.12.51 Béziers.
Lock, 23-17-1-5.
75 SA− SA− Arg+ Arg+ R+; 76 S+ I+ W− E+ US+; 77 W+ E+ S+ I+ Arg+ Arg= NZ+ NZ− R+; 78 E+ S+ I+ W−.
Pharmacist. Fined 64,000 Francs after being found guilty by French court of attacking another player in club match. Banned sine die by FFR.

PAOLI, Raymond *France*
SF.
 b 24.12.1889 Courtalain; d −.
Forward, 3-0-0-3 (3 − 1t).
11 I−; 12 I−(1t) S−.
Actor.

PAPAREMBORDE, Robert *France*
Pau.
 b 5.7.48 Luruns.
Prop, 55-34-1-20 (32 − 8t).
75 SA−(1t) SA−(1t) Arg+ Arg+ R+; 76 S+ I+ W− E+(2t) US+ A+(1t) A+ R−; 77 W+ E+ S+(1t) I+ Arg+ NZ+(1t) NZ−; 78 E+ S+ I+ W− R+; 79 I= W+ E− S+ NZ− NZ+ R+; 80 W− E− S− SA− R−; 81 S+ I+ W+ E+ A− A− R+ NZ− NZ−; 82 W− I+ R− Arg+ Arg+; 83 E+(1t) S+ I− W+.
Farmer/shopkeeper. F's most capped prop. World's leading try-scoring prop. F > 80 SA (v-capt). FFR comm mem.

PAPWORTH, Brett *Australia*
NSW.
 b 3.11.63.
2-2-0-0.
85 Fj+ Fj+.
Trainee mgr.

PARDO, Laurent *France*
Hendaye.
 b 19.11.1897 Hendaye; d 14.8.79 Hendaye.
FB, 2-0-0-2.
24 I− E−.

PARDO, Laurent *France*
Bayonne.
 b 19.1.58 Hendaye.
Wing, 14-6-2-6 (8 − 2t).
80 SA− R−; 81 S+ I+(1t) W+ E+ A−; 82 W− E−(1t) S−; 83 A=r; 85 S+ I= Arg+.
Customs officer. F Under 23s v E 79. F > 79 NZ (inj en route, in Fj); 80 SA; 85 Arg (r Patrick Estève).

PARFITT, Frederick Charles *Wales*
Newport.
 b 12.8.1869 Pontnewydd; d 20.3.53 Newport.
Half-back, 9-5-0-4 (3 − 1t).
1893 E+ S+ I+; 1894 E−(1t) S+ I−; 1895 S−;

1896 S+ I−.
Builder.

PARFREY, Padraic Seosamh   *Ireland*
CBC Cork, UC Cork.
b 12.8.50 Cork.
1-0-0-1.
74 NZ−.
Medicine.

PARGADE, Jean-Henri   *France*
Lyon U.
Centre, 1-1-0-0.
53 It+.

PARGETTER, Thomas Alfred   *England*
King Edward VI Sch Stratford on Avon,
Stratford on Avon, Cambridge Univ, Moseley,
Coventry, Warwicks, Midland Cos.
b 21.7.32.
Lock 3-1-1-1.
62 S=; 63 F+ NZ−.
Baker in family bus. Warwicks CCC 2nd XI.

PARIÈS, Lucien   *France*
Biarritz Ol.
b 4.8.47 Biarritz.
FH, 8-4-0-4 (46 − 8c 4d 6p).
68 SA−(1c 1d) R−(1c 3p); 70 S+(1c 1d) I+(1c
1d) W−; 75 E+(4c 1p) S+(1p) I−(1d 1p).
Water authority.

PARK, Jack   *Scotland*
Royal HS, Royal HSFP, Edinburgh Univ.
b 2.4.13 Edinburgh.
Wing, 1-0-0-1.
34 W−.
Medicine.

PARKE, James Cecil   *Ireland*
Lurgan Coll, Trin Coll Dublin, Monkstown,
Barbarians.
b 26.7.1881 Clones, Co Monagahan; *d* 27.2.46.
Centre, 20-6-0-14 (31 − 2t 5c 1gm 4p).
03 W−; 04 E− S− W+(1c); 05 W− NZ−; 06
E+ S−(1t) W+ SA−(1p); 07 E+(1c 1gm) S−
(1p) W−; 08 E−(1p) S+(1c) W−(1c); 09 E−
(1t) S−(1p) W−(1c) F+.
Top-class lawn tennis player:won Irish singles
champ 10-13, Australian singles champ 12 &
All-England mixed doubles 10,12-13. Competed
in Davis Cup & won Olympic silver medal in
doubles 08.

PARKER, Anthony Joseph   *Australia*
Brisbane, Australian Univs, Qld.
b 12.4.61.
SH, 3-1-0-2.
83 Arg−r Arg+ NZ−.
Medical student. A Under 21s 81. A Univs > 81
J. Youngest mem A > 81-2 BI.

PARKER, David   *Wales*
Swansea.
b Pontnewydd; *d* 65.
Prop/hooker/flanker/lock, 10-3-1-6 (11 − 4c 1p).
24 I− F+ NZ−; 25 E− S−(1c 1p) F+(1c) I−; 29
F+(1c) I=(1c); 30 E−; BI > 30 NZ 4-1-0-3, A 1-
0-0-1.
Bro of Thomas.

PARKER, Graham Wilshaw OBE   *England*
TD
Crypt Sch Gloucester, Cambridge Univ,
Gloucester, Blackheath, Barbarians, Glos.
b 11.2.12 Bristol.
FB, 2-1-0-1 (24 − 6c 4p).
38 I+(6c 1p) S−(3p).
Schoolmaster. Blue 32-5; capt v NZ 35. With
J.E. Greenwood, E's most c in an int (6 v I 38).
Ckt blue − 18 apps CUCC 34-5; 70 apps Glos
CCC 32-51; sec from 68. Taught at Dulwich Coll
& Blundell's Sch.

PARKER, James Hislop MM   *New Zealand*
CBE
Christchurch Boys' HS, HSOB, Canterbury, S
Island.
b 1.2.1897 Lyttelton; *d* 11.9.80 Auckland.
Flanker, 3-3-0-0 (3 − 1t).
24 I+ W+; 25 E+(1t).
Orchardist. NZ > 24-5 BI,F & NZ. Mgr NZ >
49 SA. Served WW1, NZ Army. NZRFU exec
39-56; life mem 59. Chmn NZ Apple & Pear
Marketing Board 54-64.

PARKER, Hon Sydney   *England*
Rugby Sch, Liverpool, Lancs.
b 3.10.1853; *d* 21.5.1897 London.
Forward, 2-1-1-0.
1874 S+; 1875 S=.
Tea planter. 5th son of 6th Earl of Macclesfield.

PARKER, Thomas   *Wales*
Swansea.
b 1893 Llansamlet.
Flanker/no 8/lock, 15-8-1-6 (6 − 2t).
19 NZA−; 20 E+ S− I+(1t); 21 E− S− F+ I+;
22 E+(1t) S= I+ F+; 23 E− S− F+.
Tinplate factory dept head. Bro of David.

PARKER, Walter Hambly   *South Africa*
E Prov.
b 13.4.34.
Prop, 2-0-0-2.
65 A− A−.
Engr.

PARKER, William   *Wales*
Swansea.
Forward, 2-1-0-1.
1899 E+ S−.
Fuel works.

PARKHILL, Allan Archibald　　*New Zealand*
Palmerston Dist HS, Palmerston, Otago,
Pirates, Canterbury, Army, S Island.
b 22.4.12 Palmerston.
No 8, 6-4-0-2 (3 − 1t).
37 SA+ SA− SA−; 38 A+(1t) A+ A+.
Butcher. NZ > 38 A.

PARKINSON, Charles Esmond　　*Australia*
Brisbane GS, Qld.
b 3.10.1886 Colinton, NSW; *d* −.
Wing, 1-0-0-1.
07 NZ−.
Civil engr.

PARKINSON, Ross Michael　　*New Zealand*
Wairoa Coll, Gisborne Boys' HS, HSOB,
Poverty Bay, NZ Maoris, N Island.
b 30.5.48 Wairoa.
2nd five-eighth, 7-6-0-1.
72 A+ A+ A+ W+ S+; 73 E+ E−.
Freezing worker. Son-in-law of J.B. Smith. NZ
> 72-3 BI,F & NAm.

PARR, John S.　　*Ireland*
Wanderers.
b 21.8.1889; *d* 59.
No 8/flanker, 4-2-0-2.
14 F+ E− S+ W−.
Bro in law of G.V. & H.W.V. Stephenson.

PARSONS, Ernest Ian DFC　　*England*
Christchurch Boys HS NZ, Canterbury Univ,
RAF, Hull & ER, Yorks.
b 24.10.12 Christchurch, NZ; kia 14.10.40
Turin.
FB, 1-1-0-0.
39 S+.
RAF. Played in last int before outbreak of
WW2, E v S 18.3.39. Served as Pt Off Bomber
Command. DFC 40.

PARSONS, George W.　　*Wales*
Abertillery, Newport.
b 21.4.26 Newbridge.
Lock, 1-0-0-1.
47 E−.
Glassworker. Played in 2 Victory ints. St Helens
47.

PARSONS, Michael James　　*England*
King's Sch Canterbury, Oxford, Northampton,
Oxon.
b 13.3.43.
Lock, 4-1-2-1.
68 W= I= F− S+.
Farmer.

PARTRIDGE, J.E.C. ('The Bird')　　*South Africa*
Dulwich Coll, Newport, Blackheath, London
Welsh, Welch Rgt, The Army, Pretoria

Harlequins, Transvaal.
b 13.6.1879; *d* 61.
1-0-1-0.
03 BT=.
The Army. E trial. Ex-capt Blackheath. Served
as Lt in Welch Rgt in Boer War. Qualified for
SA after playing for Pretoria Harlequins at end
of war. Cap in Regimental Museum, Cardiff.

PASCALIN, Pierre　　*France*
Mont-de-Marsan.
b 21.9.26 St Cein, Landes.
Hooker, 7-4-1-2.
50 I= E+ W−; 51 S+ I− E+ W+.

PASCAREL, A.　　*France*
TOEC.
No 8, 6-0-0-6.
12 W− E−; 13 S− SA− E− I−.
Dentist.

PASCOE, Daniel　　*Wales*
Llanharan, Bridgend, Neath.
b 7.7.1900 Llanharan; *d* 19.5.71 Leeds.
Flanker/lock, 2-1-0-1.
23 F+ I−.
Miner/licensee. Leeds RL 27.

PASCOT, Jep　　*France*
Perpignan.
FH, 6-0-2-4 (3 − 1t).
22 S= E= I−(1t); 23 S−; 26 I−; 27 G−.

PASHLEY, John James　　*Australia*
NSW.
b 31.8.33.
Flanker, 5-2-1-2.
54 Fj+ Fj−; 58 M+ M= M−.
Bank mgr.

PASK, Alun Edward Islwyn　　*Wales*
('Itty')
Pontllanffraith GS, Abertillery, Barbarians.
b 10.9.37.
Flanker/no 8, 26-10-4-12 (6 − 2t).
61 F−(1t); 62 E= S− F+ I=; 63 E− S+ I− F−
NZ−; 64 E= S+ I+ F= SA−; 65 E+ S+ I+ F−
; 66 E+(1t) S+ I− F+ A− 67 S− I−; BI > 62
SA 3-0-1-2; 66 A 2-2-0-0, NZ 3-0-0-3.
Schoolmaster/BBC production. W reserve 13
times. W > 64 SA. Wales XV v Fj 64.
Barbarians v NZ 64.

PATERSON, Alexander Marshall　　*New Zealand*
('Sandy')
Zingari-Richmond, Otago, S Island.
b 31.10.1885 Dunedin; *d* 29.7.33 Dunedin.
Lock/no 8, 5-3-1-1 (3 − 1t).
08 AW= AW+; 10 A+ A− A+(1t).

317

Taxi driver. Collapsed & died while watching a rugby match at Carisbrook.

PATERSON, Duncan Sinclair　　　*Scotland*
Gala Acad, Gala.
b 27.3.43 Galashiels.
SH, 10-4-0-6 (6 − 1t 1d).
69 SA+; 70 I− E+ A−; 71 F− W− I− E+(1t 1d) E+; 72 W−.
Tweed. Scottish XV v Arg (2) 69.

PATERSON, George Quentin　　　*Scotland*
Edinburgh Acad, Edinburgh Academicals, Edinburgh Univ.
Half-back, 1-0-0-1.
1876 E−.

PATERSON, John Rimmer　　　*Scotland*
Loretto Sch, Birkenhead Pk.
b 1900; *d* 25.9.70.
Flanker, 21-13-0-8 (6 − 2t).
24 F− W+ I+ E−; 26 F+ W+ I− E+; 27 F+ W+ I− E+ NSW+; 28 F+(1t) W− I− E−; 29 F+(1t) W− I+ E+.
Estate agent/chartered surveyor.

PATON, Henry　　　*New Zealand*
Waitaki Boys' HS, Dunedin, Otago, Oriental, Wellington, S Island.
b 12.2.1881 Dunedin; *d* 21.1.64 Dunedin.
No 8, 2-2-0-0 (3 − 1t).
10 A+ A+(1t).
Clerk. NZ > 07 A & 10. NZRFU management comm 20-1. Provincial ref.

PATTERSON, Colin Stewart　　　*Ireland*
RBAI, Bristol Univ, Instonians.
b 3.3.55 Belfast.
SH, 11-5-2-4 (20 − 5t).
78 NZ−; 79 F= W−(1t) E+ S=(2t) A+(2t) A+; 80 E− S+ F− W+; BI > 80 SA 3-0-0-3.
Solicitor.

PATTERSON, David　　　*Scotland*
Hawick.
b 11.12.1873; *d* 21.1.45.
Half-back, 1-0-0-1.
1896 W−.
Auctioneer/cattle dealer. Uncle of W. Burnet.

PATTERSON, R. D'Arcy　　　*Ireland*
Manchester Univ, Wanderers, Manchester, Liverpool, Ulster, Leinster.
b Belfast; *d* −.11.30.
Forward, 8-4-0-4 (3 − 1t).
12 F+ S+ W+ SA−; 13 E− S− W− F+(1t).
Uncle of W.E. Pratten.

PATTERSON, William Michael　　　*England*
Sale GS, Sale, Wasps, Barbarians, Cheshire.
b 11.4.36 Newcastle on Tyne.

Centre, 2-1-0-1.
61 SA− S+; BI(uncap/r) > NZ 59 1-0-0-1.
Technical sales engr. E > 67 Can.

PATTISSON, Richard Murrills　　　*England*
Tonbridge Sch, Cambridge Univ, Gipsies, Blackheath.
b 5.8.1860 Tonbridge; *d* 28.11.48 Cambridge.
Forward, 2-2-0-0.
1883 I+ S+.
Barrister. Blue 81-2. Examiner in law & modern history at Cambridge 1888. Called to Bar 1888.

PATTULLO, Gordon L.　　　*Scotland*
Stanley House Sch, Panmure.
b −.9.1892 Colombo; *d* 66.
FB, 4-3-0-1.
20 F+ W+ I+ E−.
Electrical engr.

PAUL, J.E.　　　*England*
RIE Coll.
Forward, 1-0-1-0.
1875 S=.

PAUL, Roger　　　*France*
Montferrand.
Hooker, 1-0-0-1.
40 BF−.

PAULING, Thomas Percival　　　*Australia*
Sydney HS, NSW.
b 26.4.12; *d* 79.
Centre, 2-0-0-2.
36 NZ−; 37 SA−.
Civil service/co sec. Son of NZ player (Non-Test) Tom Pauling.

PAUTHE, Guy　　　*France*
Graulhet.
b 24.10.32 Graulhet.
SH, 1-1-0-0 (3 − 1t).
56 E+(1t).

PAXTON, Iain Angus McLeod　　　*Scotland*
Beath HS Cowdenbeath, Glenrothes, Selkirk, S of Scotland.
b 29.12.57 Dunfermline.
No 8/lock, 25-14-1-10 (12 − 3t).
81 NZ− NZ− R+ A+; 82 E+ I− F+ W+ A+ A−; 83 I− E+ NZ=; 84 W+(1t) E+ I+ F+; 85 I−r F− W−(2t) E−; 86 W− E+ I+ R+; BI > 83 NZ 4-0-0-4.
Electronics technician. Scotland B 79. Sr > 79 NZ; 82 A. Five Nations v Overseas XV, Twickenham 86. Basketball for Scottish Schs.

PAXTON, R. Eric　　　*Scotland*
Kelso HS, Kelso.
b 4.4.57.
Lock/flanker, 2-0-0-2.

318

82 I− A−r.
Agricultural eng. Replaced unrelated Iain
Paxton 2nd Test v A 82.

PAYN, Cecil ('Bill')   *South Africa*
Natal.
b −; *d* 31.10.59 Durban.
Forward, 2-2-0-0.
24 BI+ BI+.
Schoolmaster. Served WW2. Organised rugby
'internationals' v NZ in German POW camp,
Thorn, Poland, with Okey Geffin, also Billy
Millar & Peter Pienaar, both sons of ex-SA capts.

PAYNE, Arthur Thomas   *England*
Dings Crusaders, Bristol, Glos.
b 11.11.08; *d* 7.6.68.
No 8, 2-1-0-1.
35 I+ S−.
Aircraft engr. 163 apps for Bristol 31-8. Much
work for Nat Assoc of Boys Clubs.

PAYNE, Charles Trevor ('Fats')   *Ireland*
Malvern Coll, NIFC.
b −; *d* 12.7.80.
Hooker, 16-10-1-5.
26 E+; 27 F+ E− S+ NSW−; 28 F+ E− S+
W+; 29 F+ E+ W=; 30 F− E+ S+ W−.
Bus.

PAYNE, Colin Martin   *England*
Sherborne Sch, Oxford Univ, Harlequins, W of
Scotland, Barbarians, Warwicks, Surrey.
b 19.5.37.
Lock, 10-2-2-6 (3 − 1t).
64 I− F+ S−; 65 I− F+(1t) S=; 66 W− I= F−
S−.
Engrg administrator. Blue 60.

PAYNE, Gareth W.   *Wales*
The Army, Pontypridd, Newport, Barbarians.
b 8.9.35.
Lock, 3-2-0-1.
60 E− S+ I+.
Civil engr/RE.

PAYNE, Harry   *Wales*
Swansea, RN.
b 10.12.07 Treboeth, Swansea.
Prop, 1-1-0-0.
35 NZ+.
Municipal employee. Played in 2 Servs ints. Son
Jeffrey was mgr of Swansea City FC during
club's fight for Lge survival 86.

PAYNE, John Henry   *England*
Manchester GS, Cambridge Univ, Broughton
Rgrs, Lancs.
b 19.3.1858 Broughton; *d* 24.1.42 Manchester.
Half-back, 7-6-0-1 (1c).
1882 S− W+; 1883 I+ S+; 1884 I+; 1885

W+(1c) I+.
Solicitor. Blue 1879. His club, Broughton Rgrs,
helped form NU 1895. Ckt for CUCC & Lancs.

PEACOCK, Harry   *Wales*
Newport.
Flanker/no 8, 6-4-1-1 (6 − 2t).
29 S+(1t) F+ I=; 30 S− I+(1t) F+.
Police.

PEAKE, Edward   *Wales*
Marlborough Coll, Oxford Univ, Chepstow,
Newport.
b 29.3.1860 Tidenham; *d* 3.1.45 Bluntisham,
Hunts.
Back, 1-0-0-1.
1881 E−.
Minister/schoolmaster. Played in W's 1st int, v E
1881. Noted athlete, broke leg in hurdle race
Oxford, inj which curtailed rugby career. Ath
blue 1883. Cricket blue 81-3. Glos CCC with
W.G. & E.M. Grace. Welsh cap in Welsh Folk
Museum, St Fagan's.

PEARCE, Gareth Peter   *Wales*
Laugharne Sch, Ysgol St Clare's, Welsh SS,
Welsh Youth, Laugharne, Pembs, Carmarthen
Ath, Bridgend, Llanelli, Sydney Welsh (A),
Barbarians.
b 11.11.61 Laugharne.
FH, 3-1-0-2 (6 − 2d).
81 I+(1d) F−; 82 I−r(1d).
Man dir chemical co./distributor of sports
goods. Wales B v F 81, 82. W > 80 US, Can.
With Mark Douglas at Carmarthen Ath. Rec
420 pts for Llanelli 85-6.

PEARCE, Gary Stephen   *England*
Mandeville CS Aylesbury, Aylesbury, Bucks,
Northampton, Midlands.
b 2.3.56 Dinton, Bucks.
Prop, 28-8-5-15.
79 S= I− F+ W−; 81 Arg= Arg+; 82 A+ S=;
83 F− W= S− I− NZ+; 84 S− SA− SA− A−;
85 R+ F= S+ I− W− NZ− NZ−; 86 W+ S−
I+ F−.
Surveyor. E > Far East 79; 81 Arg; 84 SA; 85
NZ. England XV v Can 83.

PEARSE, Gary Keith   *Australia*
N Sydney Tech, NSW, Natal (SA)..
b 8.2.53.
Lock, 9-6-0-3 (12 − 3t).
75 W−r; 76 I+ US+(1t) Fj+(1t) Fj+ Fj+; 78
NZ− NZ− NZ+(1t).
Engineer/liquor industry sales promotion mgr.

PEARSON, A.W.   *England*
Blackheath Proprietary Sch, Guy's Hosp,
Blackheath.
b 1854; *d* −.

FB, 7-4-2-1 (4c).
1875 I+(1c) S= I+(1c); 1876 S+; 1877 S−; 1878
S= I+(2c).
Medicine.

PEARSON, James　　　　　　　*Scotland*
George Watson's Coll, Watsonians.
b 24.2.1889 Edinburgh; kia 22.5.15 Hooge,
Belgium.
Centre/wing, 12-6-0-6 (10 − 1t 1d 1p).
09 I+ E+; 10 F+ W− I+ E−; 11 F−(1d); 12
F+(1t 1p) W− SA−; 13 I+ E−.
Pte, 9th R Scots; shot by sniper.

PEARSON, Thomas William CB　　　*Wales*
DSO TD DL
Mill Hill Sch, Cardiff, Newport, Blackheath.
b 10.5.1872 Bombay; *d* 12.9.57 Newport.
Wing, 13-6-0-7 (12 − 4t).
1891 E−(1t) I+; 1892 E− S−; 1894 S+ I−; 1895
E− S− I+(1t); 1897 E+(1t); 1898 I+ E−; 1903
E+(1t).
Docks engr. Served WW1, Lt Col 4th Welsh
Bde RFA. 40t 1892-3 season, Cardiff rec until
Bleddyn Williams (41) 48. 20 Wales hockey
caps. Welsh lawn tennis doubles champ.

PEART, Thomas George　　　　　*England*
Anthony Hunter
Sedbergh Sch, Blackheath, The Army,
Hartlepool R, Barbarians, Durham Co.
b 10.9.36.
No 8, 2-1-0-1.
64 F+ S−.
Fuel & timber merchant.

PEASE, Frank Ernest　　　　　　*England*
Harrow Sch, Darlington, Hartlepool R,
Barbarians, Durham Co.
b 17.1.1864 Darlington; *d* 27.6.57.
Forward, 1-0-0-1.
1887 I−.
Wine & spirits merchant. Original mem of
Barbarians. Died at 93, one of the longest lived
int players.

PEBEYRE, Elie　　　　　　　　　*France*
Fumel, Brive.
b 27.1.23 Seilhac.
Wing, 8-4-0-4 (3 − 1t).
45 W−; 46 I+ NZS−(1t) W+; 47 S+ I+ W−
E−.
Mgr F > 71 SA. Asst mgr F > 77 Arg.

PEBEYRE, Michel　　　　　　　　*France*
Vichy, Montferrand.
b 21.6.48 Brive.
SH, 7-3-2-2 (3 − 1t).
70 E+ R+(1t); 71 I= SA− SA= A−; 73 W+.
Medical masseur.

PÉCUNE, Joel　　　　　　　　　　*France*
Tarbes.
b 3.3.51 Ibos.
Centre/wing, 10-6-2-2 (16 − 4t).
74 W= E= S−; 75 Arg+(2t) Arg+ R+(1t); 76
I+(1t) W− E+ US+.
PE teacher.

PÉDEUTOUR, Pierre　　　　　　　*France*
Bègles.
b 30.3.55 Tunisia.
FH, 1-1-0-0 (3 − 1d).
80 I+(1d).
Dentist.

PEDLOW, Alexander Cecil　　　　*Ireland*
Campbell Coll Belfast, Queen's Univ Belfast,
CIYMS, Barbarians.
b 20.1.34 Lurgan.
Wing/centre, 30-6-2-22 (31 − 3t 5c 4p).
53 W−(1t); 54 NZ− F− E−; 55 F− E= S− W−
; 56 F−(1c 1p) E− S+(1c) W+(1c 1p); 57 F+(1c
1p) E− S+ W−(1c); 58 A+(1p) E− S+(2t) W−
F−; 59 E−; 60 E− S− W− F− SA−; 61 S−; 62
W=; 63 F−; BI > 55 SA 2-1-0-1.
Dentist. Career handicapped by poor eyesight.
Squash for I.

PEDLOW, Joseph　　　　　　　　*Ireland*
Bessbrook.
Wing, 2-0-0-2.
1882 S−; 1884 W−.
Bro of Robert & Thomas.

PEDLOW, Robert　　　　　　　　*Ireland*
Lurgan Coll, Bessbrook.
b 16.8.1868; *d* 10.2.43.
Wing, 1-0-0-1.
1891 W−.
Bro of Joseph & Thomas.

PEDLOW, Thomas Bowen　　　　　*Ireland*
Lurgan Coll, Queen's Coll Belfast.
b 9.7.1866; *d* 16.7.52.
Centre/wing, 2-1-0-1.
1889 S− W+.
Medicine. Bro of Joseph & Robert.

PEEL, T.　　　　　　　　　　　　*Ireland*
Limerick, Bective Rgrs.
FB, 3-1-0-2.
1892 E− S− W+.

PEGGE, Edward Vernon　　　　　*Wales*
Neath.
b 1864 Briton Ferry; *d* 21.3.15 Neath.
Forward, 1-0-0-1.
1891 E−.
Medicine. WFU comm 1892.

PEIRCE, William   *Ireland*
Cork.
b 1861; d −.3.36.
Back, 1-0-0-1.
1881 E−.

PELLISSIER, Louis   *France*
RCF.
b 12.2.06 San Fernando, Spain; d 16.3.73 Paris.
FB, 5-2-0-3.
28 NSW− I− E− G+ W+.

PELSER, Hendrik Jacobus   *South Africa*
Martin
Rossmore Jnr HS Johannesburg, Transvaal.
b 23.3.34.
Flanker, 11-7-3-1 (6 − 2t).
58 F=; 60 NZ+ NZ− NZ= NZ+(1t) W+ I+;
61 F= I+ A+(1t) A+.
Fitter/turner. Lost an eye in boyhood accident.
SA > 60-1 BI, F.

PENDER (later MOFFAT-   *Scotland*
PENDER), Ian MacAlister
Dollar Acad, Edinburgh Univ, London Scottish,
Barbarians.
b 18.8.1894; d −.10.61.
Prop, 1-0-0-1.
14 E−.

PENDER, Norman Ewart Ker   *Scotland*
Hawick HS, Hawick.
b 1.2.48 Bridlington.
Prop, 4-1-0-3.
77 I+; 78 F− W− E−.
Sales rep. Scottish XV v J 76.

PENMAN, Arthur Percival   *Australia*
Sydney Univ, NSW.
b 1885; d 44.
FB, 1-0-0-1.
05 NZ−.
The Army.

PENMAN, William Mitchell   *Scotland*
Royal HS, US Portsmouth, RAF, Barbarians.
b 12.5.17; kia 3.10.43.
FB, 1-0-0-1.
39 I−.
RAF.

PENNY, Sidney Herbert   *England*
Leicester, Midland Cos.
b 1875 Barnet; d 65 Leicester.
Hooker, 1-0-0-1.
09 A−.
500 apps for Leicester (inc 246 consec). 68 apps
for Midland Cos.

PENNY, W.J.   *England*
King's Coll Hosp, Utd Hosps.

FB, 3-2-1-0 (1t).
1878 I+(1t); 1879 S= I+.
Medicine. 1st int t from FB, v I 1878.

PERCIVAL, The Rev. Launcelot   *England*
Jefferson KCVO
Clifton Coll, Oxford Univ, Rugby, Barbarians,
Midlands.
b 22.5.1869; d 22.6.41 Woking.
Forward, 3-2-0-1 (2 − 1t).
1891 I+; 1892 I+(1t); 1893 S−.
Minister. Blue 1889-91. Ordained 1895. Various
appointments, inc Priest in Ordinary to HM The
King 10. CVO 26. Deputy Clerk to the Closet to
the King from 31. KCVO 36. Knighted in Holy
Orders, title 'Sir' therefore not used.
Herefordshire CCC 1895, 01.

PERITON, Harold Greaves   *England*
('Joe')
Merchant Taylors' Sch Crosby, Waterloo,
Barbarians, Lancs.
b 8.3.01; d −.4.80.
Flanker, 21-12-2-7 (18 − 6t).
25 W+; 26 W= I−(1t) F+ S−; 27 W+ I+ S−
F−; 28 NSW+(1t) I+ F+(2t) S+; 29 W+ I− S−
F+(1t); 30 W+ I− F+(1t) S=.
Stockbroker. Of Irish descent. Capt E 4 times.
Served WW2, RAF liaison officer.

PERKINS, Sydney John ('Perky') *Wales*
Blaenavon SS, Blaenavon, Pontypool, Gwent.
b 27.2.54 Blaenavon.
Lock, 18-9-0-9.
83 S+ I+ F− R−; 84 S− I+ F− E+ A−; 85 S+
I− F− E+ Fj+; 86 E− S+ I+ F−.
Carpenter. Wales B v F 77, 78, 82. Wales B > 83
Spain. Wales XV v Maoris 82. Wales XV v J 83.
Gwent v A 76, NZ 78, Maoris 82. Wales B v F
77-8, 82. W > Spain 83. Capt Pontypool 85-6.

PÉRON, Patrice   *France*
RCF.
b 20.6.49 Colombes, Paris.
Flanker, 2-0-0-2 (4 − 1t).
75 SA−(1t) SA−.
PE teacher.

PERRETT, Frederick Leonard   *Wales*
Neath.
b 1893; d 1.12.18 France.
Hooker/prop, 5-3-0-2.
12 SA−; 13 E− S+ F+ I+.
Leeds RL 13. Served WW1, R Welch Fusiliers,
later London Rgt. Died of wounds after
Armistice.

PERRIER, Patrick   *France*
Bayonne.
b 10.1.57 Bayonne.

Centre, 4-1-0-3.
82 W− E− S− I+r.
France A v NZ 81. Côte Basque > 81 NZ.

PERRIN, Paul Douglas　　　　　*Australia*
Qld.
b 26.3.40.
Lock, 1-0-0-1.
62 NZ−.
Fitter & turner. Son of Tom.

PERRIN, Thomas Drummond　　　*Australia*
NSW.
b 11; *d* 75.
Flanker/no 8, 2-1-0-1.
31 M+ NZ−.
Real estate. Father of Paul.

PERRINS, Victor Charles ('Vic')　　*Wales*
Welsh Youth, Newport.
b 44.
Hooker, 2-1-1-0.
70 SA= S+.
Steelworker/bricklayer. Wr > 69 NZ, A & Fj.

PERROTT, Edward Simcocks　　　*England*
Cheltenham Coll, O Cheltonians, Mdx.
b 16.9.1852; *d* 22.4.15.
Forward, 1-1-0-0.
1875 I+.
Bus in China; retired to Montgomeryshire.

PERRY, David Gordon　　　　　*England*
Clifton Coll, Cambridge Univ, Harlequins,
Bedford, Barbarians, London Cos, Surrey.
b 26.12.37.
No 8, 15-3-3-9 (6 − 2t).
63 F+ S+ NZ− NZ− A−; 64 NZ− W=(1t) I−;
65 W− I− F+ S=; 66 W−(1t) I= F−.
Packaging co dir. Blue 58. Oxford-Cambridge >
59 US. Nat Service with Parachute Rgt.

PERRY, Samuel Victor　　　　　*England*
King George V Sch Southport, Cambridge
Univ.
b 16.7.18.
Lock, 7-1-1-5.
47 W+ I−; 48 A− W= I− S− F−.
FRS. Prof of chemistry Birmingham Univ. Blue
46-7.

PERRY, William　　　　　　　*Wales*
Neath, Glam.
Lock, 1-1-0-0.
11 E+.
Police.

PESTEIL, Jean-Pierre　　　　　*France*
Béziers.
b 12.11.54 Vendres.
FH, 3-1-0-2 (9 − 3c 1p).

75 SA−(3c 1p); 76 A+ R−.
Municipal employee.

PETERKIN, W.A.　　　　　　　*Scotland*
Edinburgh Collegiate Sch, Edinburgh Univ.
Forward, 7-4-2-1 (2t).
1881 E=; 1883 I+; 1884 W+ I+(1t) E−; 1885
W= I+(1t).
Scottish 440y champ.

PETERS, James ('Darkie')　　　　*England*
Knowle Sch Bristol, Plymouth, Devon, Som.
b 1880 Salford; *d* − 3.54.
FH, 5-2-0-3 (6 − 2t).
06 S+ F+(1t); 07 I− S−(1t); 08 W−.
Dockyard worker Devonport. 1st coloured
player to app for E. Barrow RL 13.

PETIT, Charles　　　　　　　*France*
Le Lorrain.
b 5.1.04.
Lock, 1-0-0-1 (3 − 1t).
31 W−(1t).
Switched to RL.

PETRIE, Alexander Gordon　　　*Scotland*
Royal HS, Royal HSFP.
b 1852 Birkenhead; *d* 4.2.09 Edinburgh.
Forward, 11-4-4-3.
1873 E=; 1874 E−; 1875 E=; 1876 E−; 1877 I+
E+; 1878 E=; 1879 I+ E−; 1880 I+ E−.
Law. Ref S v I 1882. Pres SRU 1881-2.
Accomplished weightlifter, oarsman, hammer
thrower.

PEYRELADE, Henri　　　　　　*France*
Tarbes.
FH, 1-0-0-1.
40 BF−.

PEYROUTOU　　　　　　　　*France*
Périgueux.
SH, 2-1-0-1 (6 − 2t).
11 S+(2t) E−.

PFAFF, Brian Desmond　　　*South Africa*
Hilton Coll, Cape Town Univ, SA Univs, W
Prov.
b 2.3.30 Durban.
FH, 1-1-0-0.
56 A+.
Accountant. Capt SA Univs > 56-7 BI, F. Ckt
for W Prov 52-5.

PHELPS, Roderick　　　　　　*Australia*
N Sydney HS, NSW.
b 15.6.34.
Wing/FB, 23-5-1-17 (6 − 2t).
55 NZ− NZ+; 56 SA− SA−; 57 NZ− NZ−; 58
W− I−(1t) E− S− F− M+ NZ− NZ+ NZ−;

61 Fj+(1t) Fj+ Fj= SA− SA− F−; 62 NZ−
NZ−.
Dentist.

PHILLIPS, Alan John *Wales*
Kenfig Comp, Welsh Youth, Kenfig Hill,
Cardiff, Glam.
b 21.8.55 Kenfig Hill.
Hooker, 15-7-0-8.
79 E+; 80 F+ E− S+ I− NZ−; 81 E+ S− I+
F− A+; 82 I− F+ E− S−; BI > 80 SA.
Dir office cleaning business. Wales B v F 77, 78.
Cardiff v A 75, 84. 130t for Cardiff 72-85. Capt
Cardiff 85-6.

PHILLIPS, Bryn *Wales*
Aberavon.
b 4.10.1900 Merthyr.
Prop/lock, 5-1-1-3.
25 E− S− F+ I−; 26 E=.
Police. Huddersfield RL 26.

PHILLIPS, Charles *England*
Rugby Sch, Oxford Univ, Birkenhead Pk,
Cheshire.
b 14.8.1857; d 11.9.40.
Forward, 3-2-1-0.
1880 S+; 1881 I+ S=.
Solicitor/co dir. Blue 1876-9.

PHILLIPS, David Horace *Wales*
Dynevor GS, Trin Coll Carmarthen, Swansea.
b 24.8.28 Swansea.
Wing, 1-1-0-0.
52 F+.
HM.

PHILLIPS, Henry Percival *Wales*
('Sparrow') OBE
Clytha Sch, Newport.
b 1868 Machen; d 26.2.47 Newport.
Half-back, 6-4-0-2.
1892 E−; 1893 E+ S+ I+; 1894 E− S+.
Salesman/chipping agent.

PHILLIPS, Henry Thomas *Wales*
Newport.
b 22.6.03 Cross Keys; d 16.12.78.
Lock/prop, 9-2-0-7.
27 E− S− F+ I− NSW−; 28 E− S+ I− F−.
Miner/police.

PHILLIPS, Louis Augustus *Wales*
Monmouth Sch, Newport.
b 24.2.1878 Newport; kia 14.3.16 Cambrai.
Half-back, 4-3-0-1.
1900 E+ S+ I+; 01 S−.
Architect. Served WW1, Public Schools Battn,
refused commission; reached rank of Sgt, R
Welch Fusiliers. Amateur golf champ of W 07,
12; runner-up I champs 13.

PHILLIPS, Malcolm Stanley *England*
Arnold Sch Blackpool, Oxford Univ, Fylde,
Barbarians, Lancs.
b 3.3.36.
Centre/wing, 25-11-6-8 (15 − 5t).
58 A+(1t) I+ F+ S=; 59 W− I+ F= S=; 60
W+ I+ F= S+; 61 W−; 63 W+(1t) I= F+ S+
NZ− NZ−(1t) A−(1t); 64 NZ− W= I− F+(1t)
S−.
PA to man dir paint co. Blue 56-9. Once E rec
cap holder. Capt Lancs 62-5. Barbarians comm.

PHILLIPS, William David *Wales*
Cardiff.
b 16.8.1855 Cardiff; d 15.10.18 Cardiff.
Forward, 5-2-0-3.
1881 E−; 1882 I+; 1884 E− S− I+.
Rly official/accountant. Vice-capt Cardiff 1876-
7. Cardiff, WRU comm. IB rep 1887-07. Ref I v
S 89.

PHILLIPS, William John *New Zealand*
Te Mata Sch, Mako Mako, King Country,
Raglan, NZ Maoris, N Island.
b 30.1.14 Raglan; d 10.11.82 Raglan.
Wing, 3-2-0-1 (3 − 1t).
37 SA−; 38 A+ A+(1t).
Farmer. NZ Maoris > 35 A. NZ > 38 A.

PHILP, Andrew *Scotland*
Edinburgh Inst, Edinburgh Inst FP.
Centre, 1-1-0-0.
1882 E+.

PHILPONNEAU, Jean-François *France*
Montferrand.
b 23.11.50 Fort de l'Eau, Algeria; d 8.5.76.
Wing, 2-1-0-1 (4 − 1t).
73 W+ I−(1t).
Student. Killed by lightning.

PHIPPS, George C. *Ireland*
Rosslyn Pk, The Army.
Centre/wing, 5-1-0-4.
50 E− W−; 52 F+ W− E−.
The Army. Mjr in R Hants Rgt.

PHIPPS, James Alfred *Australia*
Barker Coll, Hawkesbury Coll, NSW.
b 31.12.31 Batavia, Java.
Centre, 11-3-0-8 (3 − 1t).
53 SA− SA+ SA− SA−; 54 Fj+(1t) Fj−; 55
NZ− NZ− NZ+; 56 SA− SA−.
Accountant. Took bro Peter's place 2nd Test v
NZ 55 when Peter inj before match. Peter never
played for A and is incorrectly credited by some
authorities as a capped player.

PIAZZA, André *France*
Montauban.
b 1.12.47 Moissac.

Wing, 2-0-0-2.
68 NZ− A−.
Office worker.

PICARD, T.   *France*
Montferrand.
Lock, 2-2-0-0.
85 Arg+ J+.
F > 85 Arg.

PICKARD, Jan Albertus Jacobus   *South Africa*
('Jan Bull')
Stellenbosch Univ, W Prov.
b 25.12.27 Paarl.
Flanker/no 8, 4-3-0-1.
53 A+ A+; 56 NZ+; 58 F−.
Wine taster/co dir. SA > 51-2 BI.

PICKERING, Arthur Stanley   *England*
Sedbergh Sch, Harrogate, O Dewsburians,
Headingley, Barbarians, Yorks.
b 24.3.1885 Dewsbury; d 17.2.69.
Centre, 1-0-0-1 (3 − 1p).
07 I−(1p).
Wool & waste merchant. Golf for Yorks.

PICKERING, David Francis ('Dai   *Wales*
Pick')
Cwrt Sart Comp, Neath VI Form Coll, Wales
SS, UWIST, Welsh Univs, Llanelli, W Wales.
b 16.12.60 Briton Ferry.
Flanker, 19-9-1-9 (12 − 3t).
83 E= S+ I+ F− R−; 84 S− I+ F− E+ A−; 85
S+(2t) I− F− E+ Fj+(1t); 86 E− S+ I+ F−.
Mgr/sports outfitter. Capt W v E,S,I,F 86.

PICKERING, Ernest Arthur Rex   *New Zealand*
Nelson Coll, Frankton, Waikato, N Island.
b 23.11.36 Te Kuiti.
Flanker, 3-2-0-1.
58 A+; 59 BI+ BI−.
Bank clerk/stock agent/finance co mgr. NZ > 57
A, 60 A & SA. Sec of Harlequins club. Bro John
rep Wellington 61-5.

PICKERING, Roger David Austin   *England*
Whitecliffe Mount Sch Cleckheaton, Hull Univ,
Bradford, Dax (F), Barbarians, Yorks.
b 15.6.43.
SH, 6-3-0-3.
67 I+ F− S+ W−; 68 F− S+.
Bus exec. Taught at Lycée de Garcons, Dax.

PICKLES, Reginald Clarence   *England*
Werrett MC
Bristol, Glos.
b 11.12.1895.
FB, 2-1-1-0.
22 I+ F=.
Served WW1, RE. MC 17.

PIENAAR, Zacharias Mattheus   *South Africa*
Johannes ('Gysie')
Dr Viljoen Sch Bloemfontein, UOFS, Jnr
Springboks, SA Forces, Barbarians, Gazelles,
Oribi, OFS.
b 21.12.54 Bloemfontein.
FB, 13-10-0-3 (14 − 2t 2p).
80 SAm+r BI+ BI+(1t) BI+ BI−(2p) SAm+
SAm+ F+(1t); 81 I+ I+ NZ− NZ+ NZ−.
Univ employee/Sgt SA Armed Forces. SA > 81
US (18 pts v Midwest).

PIERCE, Murray James   *New Zealand*
Comb Servs, Wellington.
b 1.11.57 Timaru.
Lock, 4-4-0-0.
85 E+ E+ A+ Arg+.
NZ > 84 A, 85 Arg. World XV > 86 SA.

PIERCE, Richard   *England*
Charterhouse Sch, Liverpool, Barbarians,
Lancs.
b 30.5.1874.
Forward, 2-0-0-2.
1898 I−; 03 S−.
Timber merchant. Lancs 1893-9.

PIERROT, Gilbert   *France*
Pau.
b 1888 Toulouse; d −.3.79.
Centre, 3-0-0-3.
14 I− W− E−.

PIKE, Sir Theodore Ouseley   *Ireland*
('Ted') KCMG CMG
The Abbey Tipperary, Trin Coll Dublin, Oxford
Univ, Lansdowne.
b 2.8.04 Thurles.
Prop, 8-5-0-3 (3 − 1t).
27 E− S+(1t) W+ NSW−; 28 F+ E− S+ W+.
Colonial service. Bro of Victor. CMG 53.
KCMG 56.

PIKE, Victor Joseph CB CBE   *Ireland*
DD
Bishop Foy Sch Waterford, Trin Coll Dublin,
Lansdowne, Leinster, The Army, Barbarians.
b 1.7.07; d −.2.86.
Hooker, 13-5-0-8 (3 − 1t).
31 E+ S+(1t) W− SA−; 32 E− S+ W+; 33 E−
W+ S−; 34 E− S− W−.
Chaplain General to The Army. One of 11
children of Tipperary clergyman, of whom 5
played prov rugby for Leinster & 3 became
bishops. Bishop Suffragan of Sherborne 60-76.

PIKE, Sir William Watson   *Ireland*
KCMG DSO
Kingstown Coll, Kingstown.
b 10.3.1860; d 22.6.41.
FB, 5-1-1-3.

1879 E−; 1881 E− S+; 1882 E=; 1883 S−.
Medicine. Maj Gen RAMC. Inter-prov hockey rep.

PILECKI, Stanislaus Joseph *Australia*
Brisbane, Qld.
 b 4.2.47.
Prop, 18-9-0-9.
78 W+ W+ NZ− NZ−; 79 I− I− NZ+ Arg−
Arg+; 80 Fj+ NZ+ NZ−; 82 S− S+; 83 US+
Arg− Arg+ NZ−.
Co dir. Of Polish descent. Rec no of apps for
Qld since 70. A > 78 NZ; 79 Arg; 80 Fj; 81-2 &
84 BI; Ar > NZ 82.

PILKINGTON, William Norman *England*
DSO
Clifton Coll, Cambridge Univ, St Helens
Recreation, Blackheath, Barbarians, Lancs.
 b 26.7.1877; *d* 8.2.35.
Wing, 1-0-1-0.
1898 S=.
The Army/co dir glass manufacturers. Blue
1896-7. Public Schs hurdles champ 1896; ath
blue (100y) 1897-9. Served WW1, Maj in S
Lancs Rgt; mentioned in despatches 3 times.
DSO 16, Bar 19. Died a bachelor, leaving nearly
£400,000 in his will.

PILLMAN, Charles Henry *England*
('Cherry') MC
Tonbridge Sch, Blackheath, Barbarians, Kent.
 b −.1.1890 Sidcup; *d* 58.
Flanker, 18-14-1-3 (26 − 8t 1c).
10 W+ I= F+ S+; 11 W− F+(2t) I− S+; 12
W+ F+(1c); 13 SA− W+(1t) F+(2t) I+(1t)
S+; 14 W+(1t) I+(1t) S+; BI > 10 SA 2-1-0-1.
Flour importer/London Corn Exchange. Bro of
Robert. Top scorer with 65 pts BI > 10 SA;
played FH in 2nd Test. Broke leg v S 14, ended
int career. Served WW1, Lt Dragoon Guards.
In WW2 Area Flour Officer for SE Division.
Golf for S of England v N.

PILLMAN, Robert Lawrence *England*
Merton Court Sch Sidcup, Rugby Sch,
Blackheath, London Cos, Kent.
 b 9.2.1893 Sidcup; *d* 9.7.16 Armentières.
Flanker, 1-1-0-0.
14 F+.
Solicitor. Bro of Cherry. Only cap v F 14, in
match missed by his bro because of broken leg.
Scratch golfer. Served WW1, R West Kent Rgt;
died of wounds.

PILON, Jean *France*
Périgueux.
 b 14.10.25 Bayonne.
FH, 2-1-0-1 (3 − 1t).
49 E−; 50 E+(1t).

PINCH, John *England*
Lancaster.
 b 1871 Lancaster; *d* 46 Lancaster.
Forward, 3-2-0-1.
1896 W+ I−; 1897 S+.
Dept mgr carpet manufacturers.

PINCHING, William Wyatt *England*
KCS Wimbledon, Cheltenham Coll, Guy's
Hosp.
 b 24.3.1851 Gravesend; *d* 16.8.1878 at sea.
Forward, 1-1-0-0.
1872 S+.
Medicine. Surg on SS Eldorado; lost overboard
1 day out from Colombo.

PINION, Godfrey *Ireland*
Methodist Coll Belfast, Collegians.
 b 1883; *d* 7.12.56 Belfast.
SH, 4-1-0-3 (2 − 1c).
09 E−(1c) S− W− F+.
Insurance mgr.

PIPER, Brian James Charles *Australia*
NSW.
 b 16.9.26.
FB, 12-4-1-7 (18 − 9c).
46 NZ− M− NZ−(2c); 47 NZ−(1c) S+(2c) I+
W−; 48 E+ F−; 49 M− M=(1c) M+(3c).
Dentist/medicine.

PIPER, Oliver James S. *Ireland*
Cork Constitution.
 b 1886 Aberavon; *d* −.
Forward, 8-2-1-5.
09 E− S− W− F+; 10 E= S− W− F+; BI > 10
SA 1-0-0-1.
Circus bus.

PIQUÉ, Jean *France*
Pau.
 b 17.9.35 Artix, Basses-Pyrénées.
Centre/wing, 18-11-2-5 (6 − 2t).
61 NZ− NZ− A+(1t); 62 S+ It+; 64 NZ− E−
W= It+ I+ SA+ Fj+ R+; 65 S+(1t) I= E−
W+ It+.
Hotelier/pork butcher. Coach F > 77 Arg; 78 J
& Can; 79 Fj & NZ; 80 SA; 81 A.

PIQUEMAL, Maixent *France*
Tarbes.
 b 07 Tarbes.
FB, 9-4-0-5.
27 I− S−; 29 I− G+; 30 S+ I+ E− G+ W−.

PIQUIRAL, Etienne *France*
RCF, Lyon.
 b 04 Perpignan; *d* 44.
No 8/flanker, 19-4-0-15 (9 − 3t).
24 S+(1t) I− E− W− R+ US−; 25 E−; 26 S−
(1t) I− E− W− M−; 27 I− S−(1t) W− E+ G+

325

G−; 28 E−.
Died behind German lines.

PITEU, Roger *France*
Pau, TOEC.
b 14.5.1899 nr Pau; *d* −.
SH, 15-2-2-11 (6 − 2t).
21 S+ W− E− I+(2t); 22 S= E= W− I−; 23
E−; 24 E−; 25 I− NZ− W− E−; 26 E−.

PITMAN, Isaac James KBE MP *England*
Summer Fields Sch Oxford, Eton Coll, Oxford
Univ, Harlequins.
b 14.8.01 Kensington; *d* 1.9.85 Chelsea.
Wing, 1-1-0-0.
22 S+.
Co dir/MP. Public Schs middleweight boxing
champ 19. Blue 21. Blues for ath & skiing 22.
Chmn R Soc of Teachers; designed Initial
Teaching Alphabet. Served WW2, RAF. Dir
Bank of E 41-5; dir of Organisation & Method at
the Treasury 43-5. Tory MP for Bath 45-64.
KBE 61.

PITZER, Gysbertus *South Africa*
N Transvaal.
b 8.7.39 Louis Trichard.
Hooker, 12-9-2-1.
67 F+ F+ F− F=; 68 BI+ BI= BI+ BI+ F+
F+; 69 A+ A+.
Electrician. SA > 69-70 BI.

PLANTEFOL, Alain ('Le *France*
Chinois')
RCF.
b 26.12.42 Colombes, Paris.
Lock, 11-5-2-4 (3 − 1t).
67 SA− SA+ SA= NZ− R+; 68 E+ W+
Cz+(1t) NZ−; 69 E− W=.
Car salesman.

PLANTEY, Serge *France*
RCF.
b 14.2.40 Salles, Gironde.
Wing/FH, 2-2-0-0.
61 A+; 62 It+.

PLUMMER, Kenneth Clive *England*
Bristol.
b 17.1.47.
Wing, 4-0-0-4.
69 W−; 76 S− I− F−.
Motor mechanic. 7 yrs between caps.

PLUMMER, Reginald Clifford *Wales*
Stanley
Long Ashton Sch, Bristol, Newport,
Barbarians.
b 29.12.1888 Newport; *d* 18.6.53 Newport.
Wing, 5-2-0-3 (6 − 2t).

12 S+(1t) I− F+(1t) SA−; 13 E−; BIuncap >
10 SA.
Hotelier. Served WW1, RE.

POCOCK, E.I. *Scotland*
Clifton Coll, Edinburgh W.
Back, 2-2-0-0 (1t).
1877 I+(1t) E+.
Indian Army.

PODEVIN *France*
SF.
Lock, 2-0-0-2.
13 W− I−.

POIDEVIN, Simon Paul *Australia*
Australian Univs, Sydney, NSW.
b 31.10.58.
Flanker, 33-20-1-12 (12 − 3t).
80 Fj+ NZ+ NZ− NZ+; 81 F+(1t) F+ I+ W−
S−(1t); 82 E− NZ− NZ− NZ−; 83 US+ Arg−
Arg+ NZ− It+ F= F−; 84 Fj+ NZ+ NZ−
NZ− E+(1t) I+ W+ S+; 85 C+ C+ NZ− Fj+
Fj+.
Student. Of French descent. Played for NSW
before Sydney. A > 80 Fj; 81-2 & 84 BI; 82 NZ;
83 It & F; 84 Fj. Overseas XV v Five Nations,
Twickenham 86.

POIRIER, G. *France*
SCUF.
Forward, 1-0-0-1.
07 E−.

POKERE, Steven Tahurata *New Zealand*
Southland, NZ Jnrs, S Island, Sassenachs, NZ
Barbarians, Auckland, NZ Maoris.
b 11.8.58 Hawera.
2nd five-eighth/centre, 18-15-1-2 (8 − 2t).
81 SA+; 82 A+(1t) A− A+; 83 BI+ BI+ BI+
BI+ A+ S= E−; 84 F+ F+ A+(1t) A+; 85 E+
E+ A+.
NZ > 81 R & F, 83 & 84 A, 83 S & E, 85 Arg.
World XV > 86 SA.

POLDEN, Stanhope Ernest *Ireland*
Wesley Coll, Clontarf.
b 24.3.1885 Dublin; *d* 14.10.58.
SH, 4-2-0-2.
13 W− F+; 14 F+; 20 F−.
Dublin Port & Docks Bd official. Pres IRU 33-
4.

POLLOCK, Harold Raymond *New Zealand*
('Bunk')
Petone West Sch, Petone, Wellington, N Island.
b 7.9.09 Petone; *d* 10.1.84 Otaki.
2nd five-eighth/centre/FB, 5-4-0-1 (29 − 9c 2d
1p).
32 A−(2c 1d) A+(1c 1d) A+(1c) A+(1c); 36 A+(1c)

A+(4c 1p).
NZ > 32 & 36 A.

POLLOCK, James Alan　　　*Scotland*
Newcastle RGS, Carnegie Coll, English
Students, Gosforth.
b 16.11.58.
Wing, 8-5-1-2 (8 − 2t).
82 W+(1t); 83 E+ NZ=(1t); 84 E+r I+ F+
R−; 85 F−.
PE teacher. Reserve for E Under 23s. English
Schs high jump finalist.

POLSON, Adam Henry　　　*Scotland*
Gala Acad, Gala.
b 19.11.07 Gala.
Flanker, 1-0-1-0.
30 E=.
Millman.

POMATHIOS, Michel　　　*France*
Agen, Lyon U, Bourg.
b 18.3.24 Bourg-en-Bresse.
Wing, 24-12-1-11 (18 − 6t).
48 I− A+(1t) S− W+(1t) E+(1t); 49 S− I+ E−
W+ Arg+ Arg+(1t); 50 S− I= W−; 51 S+ I−
E+ W+; 52 W−(1t) E−(1t); 53 S+ I− W−; 54
S+.
Commercial agent.

PONS, Pierre ('La Jaconde')　　　*France*
Toulouse.
b −; *d* −.3.81.
Hooker, 6-1-1-4.
20 S− E− W−; 21 S+ W−; 22 S=.

POOK, Tom　　　*Wales*
Newport.
b −; *d* c46.
Forward, 1-0-0-1.
1895 S−.
Holbeck RL c1899.

POOLE, Francis Oswald　　　*England*
Cheltenham Coll, Oxford Univ, Gloucester,
Sunderland, Barbarians, Glos, Durham Co.
b 17.12.1870; *d* 22.5.49 Market Drayton.
Forward, 3-2-0-1.
1895 W+ I+ S−.
Church. Blue 1891-4. Water polo blue 1892-5.
Ordained 1895. Spent 54 yrs in various curacies.

POOLE, Robert Watkins　　　*England*
Hartlepool OB, Hartlepool R, Barbarians,
Durham Co.
b 4.11.1874 Hartlepool; *d* c30.
FB, 1-0-0-1.
1896 S−.
Boilermaker. Like R.F. Oakes, born in
Hartlepool Militia Barracks, son of a sgt.
Broughton Rgrs RL 03. 2 E RL caps.

POPE, Alex Murray　　　*Australia*
Qld.
b 44.
Centre, 1-0-0-1.
68 NZ−r.
Probation officer.

POPE, Christopher Francis　　　*South Africa*
Cape Town Univ, W Prov.
b 30.9.52 Stellenbosch.
Wing, 9-4-1-4 (4 − 1t).
74 BI− BI− BI− BI=; 75 F+(1t) F+; 76 NZ−
NZ+ NZ+.
Medicine. SA > 74 F.

POPE, Edward Brian　　　*England*
Uppingham Sch, Cambridge Univ, Blackheath,
Barbarians.
b 29.6.11.
SH, 3-0-1-2.
31 W= S− F−.
Underwriting co dir. Blue 32. Served WW2,
RAF.

POPHAM, Ivan　　　*Ireland*
Cork Constitution.
Lock/No 8, 4-1-0-3.
22 S− W− F+; 23 F−.
Farmer.

PORRA, M.　　　*France*
Lyon.
b 06.
Hooker, 1-1-0-0.
31 I+.
Woodworker. RL.

PORTER, Clifford Glen　　　*New Zealand*
S Wellington Sch, Wellington Coll, Wellington
Coll OB, Wellington, Athletic, Hui Mai,
Horowhenua, N Island.
b 5.5.1899 Edinburgh; *d* 12.11.76 Wellington.
Flanker, 7-4-0-3 (12 − 4t).
25 F+(1t); 29 A−(1t) A−; 30 BI− BI+ BI+
BI+(2t).
Ptn paper bag manufacturing co. NZ (capt) >
24-5 BI,F & C (inj restricted int apps); 26 (capt)
& 29 A. Capt v BI 30.

PORTHAULT, Alain ('La　　　*France*
Gazelle')
RCF.
b 15.7.29 Paris.
Wing, 7-5-0-2 (9 − 3t).
51 S+(1t) E+ W+; 52 I−; 53 S+ I− It+(2t).
Rep F in 52 Olympics; reached 100m s-final.

PORTUS, Garnet Vere　　　*England*
Maitland HS (A), Sydney Univ, Oxford Univ,
Blackheath, Barbarians.
b 7.6.1883 Morpeth, NSW; *d* −.6.54.

FH, 2-2-0-0 (3 − 1t).
08 F+(1t) I+.
Church/university prof. Rhodes Scholar.
Ordained 11. Returned to A. Author of many
books on politics & economics.

POTEL, Albert   *France*
Bègles.
Prop, 1-1-0-0.
32 G+.

POTGIETER, H.J.   *South Africa*
OFS.
b 03; d 11.11.57 Mbabane, Swaziland.
2-1-0-1.
28 NZ+ NZ−.
Swaziland Public Works.

POTGIETER, Hermanus   *South Africa*
Lambertus
Kirkwood Sch, UOFS, Stellenbosch Univ, OFS.
b 11.1.53 Kirkwood.
Wing, 1-1-0-0 (4 − 1t).
77 Wd+(1t).
Schoolmaster.

POTTER, Robert Thomas   *Australia*
Qld.
b 42.
Wing, 1-1-0-0.
61 Fj+.
Solicitor.

POTTERTON, H. Norman   *Ireland*
St Andrews Coll, Wanderers.
b 3.4.1897; d 78.
No 8, 1-0-0-1.
20 W−.
Cattle salesmaster.

POTTS, John Maxwell   *Australia*
NSW.
b 21.2.36.
Centre, 5-0-0-5.
57 NZ− NZ−; 58 W− I−; 59 BI−.
Law.

POULTON (later POULTON-   *England*
PALMER), Ronald William
Dragon Sch Oxford, Rugby Sch, Oxford Univ,
Harlequins, Liverpool, E Midlands.
b 12.9.1889 Oxford; kia 5.5.15 Belgium.
Wing/centre, 17-14-0-3 (28 − 8t 1d).
09 F+ I+ S−; 10 W+; 11 S+; 12 W+ I+(1t)
S−; 13 SA−(1t) W+(1d) F+(1t) I+ S+; 14 W+
I+ S+(1t) F+(4t).
Bus. Blue 09-11. Hockey blue 09-11. 5t Oxford v
Cambridge 09 & 24 pts in 3 Univ Matches.
Served WW1, Lt R Berks Rgt; killed by sniper
Ploegsteert Wood. Implicit in his inheritance of
a fortune from the Rt Hon G.W. Palmer (d 13)

was a change of name, which he adopted after
his int career was over. See 'The Life of Ronald
Poulton', by E.B. Poulton, pub 19.

POWELL, Albert William   *South Africa*
('Bertie')
Kimberley, Griq W.
b 18.7.1873 Kimberley; d 11.9.48 Cape Town.
1-0-0-1.
1896 BT−.
Ckt for SA, 1 Test v E 1898. Played with bro
Jackie 3rd Test v BT, 1896.

POWELL, David Lewes ('Piggy')   *England*
Daventry GS, Long Buckby, Rugby,
Northampton, Barbarians, E Midlands.
b 17.5.42 Rugby.
Prop, 11-3-2-6.
66 W− I=; 69 I− F+ S+ W−; 71 W− I+ F=
S− S−; BI > 66 A, NZ.
Farmer.

POWELL, Graham   *Wales*
Ebbw Vale GS, Ebbw Vale.
b 17.11.32 Ebbw Vale.
Centre, 2-2-0-0.
57 I+ F+.
Schoolmaster/oil co rep. 1st Ebbw Vale player
capped.

POWELL, Jack   *Wales*
Cardiff, London Welsh.
b Merthyr.
Forward, 1-0-0-1.
06 I−.
Coal trimmer.

POWELL, Jack   *Wales*
Cardiff.
Wing, 1-0-0-1 (4 − 1d).
23 I−(1d).
Police/licensee. Bro of W.J.

POWELL, John Mercer ('Jackie')   *South Africa*
Kimberley, Griq W.
Half-back, 4-0-2-2.
1891 BT−; 1896 BT−; 03 BT= BT=.
Capt 2nd Test v BT 03. Longest int career (13
seasons) for SA, with B.H. Heatlie. Played with
bro Bertie 3rd Test v BT, 1896.

POWELL, Richard W.   *Wales*
Monmouth GS, Newport.
Forward, 2-1-0-1.
1888 S+ I−.

POWELL, Wickham C.   *Wales*
Christ's Coll Brecon, London Welsh,
Northampton, Welsh Guards, Wasps, The
Army, Barbarians.
b 05 Aberbeeg; d 73 SA.

Wing/SH, 27-14-2-11 (16 − 1t 2c 2d 1gm).
26 S− I+ F+; 27 E− F+ I−(1c); 28 S+ I− F−
(1t); 29 E− S+ F+ I=; 30 S− I+ F+(1d); 31
E=(1gm) S+ F+(1d) I+ SA−; 32 E+ S+ I−;
35 E− S− I+.
The Army/architect.

POWELL, Wickham James   *Wales*
Cardiff.
b 13.9.1892; *d* 20.3.61 Cyncoed, Cardiff.
Wing, 4-3-0-1 (6 − 2t).
20 E+(1t) S− F+(1t) I+.
Licensee. Bro of Jack. Rochdale Hornets RL
20.

POYDEBASQUE, François   *France*
Bayonne.
b −; kia WW1.
Centre/SH, 2-0-0-2.
14 I− W−.

PRAT, Jean ('Monsieur Rugby')   *France*
Lourdes.
b 1.8.23 Lourdes.
Flanker, 51-29-1-21 (145 − 9t 26c 5d 17p).
45 BF+(2c) BF−(1p) W−; 46 BF+(1t) I+
NZS− W+(1c); 47 S+(1c) I+(1t) W− E−(1p);
48 I− A+ S−(1p) W+ E+(1t); 49 S− I+(2c 2p)
E− W+ Arg+(1c) Arg+(1t 1p); 50 S−(1c) I=
E+ W−; 51 S+(1c 2p) E−(1t 1c 1p) W+(1c); 52
S+(1t 2c 1p) I−(1t 1c 1p) SA− W−(1c) E−
It+(1c 2p); 53 S+(1p) I− E− W− It+(1d); 54
S+ I+(1c) NZ+(1t) W−(2c 1p) E+(1c 1d)
It+(6c 2p); 55 S+(1t) I+ E+(2d) W−(1d) It+.
Hotelier. Scored 100th pt for F when converting
bro Maurice's t v I 54. Asst mgr F > 64 SA.

PRAT, Maurice   *France*
Lourdes.
b 17.9.28 Lourdes.
Centre, 31-18-0-13 (21 − 6t 1d).
51 I−; 52 S+ I− SA− W− E−; 53 S+ I− E−;
54 I+(2t) NZ+ W− E+(1t) It+(1t); 55 S+ I+
E+ W− It+; 56 I+ W− It+ Cz+(1t); 57 S− I−
W−(1t) It+ R+; 58 A+(1d) W+ I+.
PE instructor/hotelier. Played with bro Jean in
18 ints.

PRATT, Robert Henry ('Robin')   *Ireland*
Portora RS, Trin Coll Dublin.
b 24.12.11 Enniskillen.
FB, 5-1-0-4.
33 E− W+ S−; 34 E− S−.
Medicine.

PRATTEN, William Edgar   *England*
Marlborough Coll, Blackheath, Sidcup,
Barbarians, Kent.
b 29.5.07.
Lock, 2-0-0-2.
27 S− F−.

Co dir. Nephew of R. d'A. Patterson. Served
WW2, Maj RA.

PREECE, Ivor JP   *England*
Coventry, Barbarians, Warwicks, Midland Cos.
b 15.12.20 Coventry.
FH, 12-3-0-9 (3 − 1d).
48 I− S− F−; 49 F+(1d) S+; 50 W− I+ F−
S−; 51 W− I− F−; BI > 50 A, NZ 1-0-0-1.
Father of Peter. JP 64.

PREECE, Peter Stuart   *England*
King Henry VIII Sch Coventry, Coventry,
Barbarians, Warwicks.
b 15.11.49 Coventry.
Centre/wing, 12-4-0-8.
72 SA+; 73 NZ− W− I− F+ S+ NZ+; 75 I−
F− W− A−; 76 W−r.
Building soc employee. Son of Ivor. With Alan
Morley, E's most t in any tour match (4 v NSW
75).

PREEDY, Malcolm   *England*
Gloucester.
Prop, 1-0-0-1.
84 SA−.

PRENTICE, Clarence Warwick   *Australia*
NSW.
b 1891; *d* 48.
Flanker, 1-0-0-1.
14 NZ−.
Cattle market supervisor. Bro of Ward. RL.

PRENTICE, Frank Douglas   *England*
Wyggeston Sch, Westleigh, Leicester,
Barbarians, Leics.
b 1897; *d* 3.10.62.
No 8, 3-3-0-0.
28 I+ F+ S+; BI > 30 NZ 1-0-0-1, A 1-0-0-1.
Sec RFU 47-62. Capt BI > 30 A, NZ. Mgr RFU
> 36 SAm. E sel 32-47. Served WW1, RA.
Served WW2, Lt Col RASC.

PRENTICE, Warden Selby   *Australia*
NSW.
b 1886; *d* 69.
Centre, 6-3-0-3 (3 − 1p).
08 W−; 09 E+; 10 NZ− NZ+ NZ−; 12
US+(1p).
Bro of Clarence.

PRENTIS, Richard Basil   *South Africa*
Bros of Charity Coll, Diggers, Witwatersrand
Univ, Quaggas, Transvaal.
b 27.2.47 Krugersdorp.
Prop/lock, 11-10-0-1.
80 SAm+ SAm+ BI+ BI+ BI+ BI− SAm+
SAm+ F+; 81 I+ I+.
Industrial chemist. Prov debut 74.

PRESCOTT, Robert Edward *England*
('Robin')
Wells House Prep Sch, Marlborough Coll,
Oxford Univ, Harlequins, The Army, Comb
Servs, Guildford, Barbarians, Mdx.
b 3.4.13; *d* 18.5.75 Dartmouth.
Prop, 6-5-0-1 (3 − 1t).
37 W+ I+; 38 I+(1t); 39 W+ I− S+; RFU > 36
SAm.
Solicitor/ Sec RFU. Son of Ernest Prescott
(RFU pres 20-2); nephew of Curly Hammond;
bro A.E.C. won blue 28. Blue 32. Rep Oxford
Univ on RFU 51-62. E sel 49-59. V-pres RFU
62-3, but resigned in order to take up pro
appointment of sec.

PRESTON, Nicholas John *England*
Lancaster RGS, Nottingham Univ, Richmond.
b 5.4.58 Prestwich, Lancs.
Centre, 3-2-0-1 (4 − 1t).
79 NZ−; 80 I+ F+(1t).
Sales exec.

PRETORIUS, Nicholas F. *South Africa*
Transvaal.
Flanker, 4-2-0-2.
28 NZ+ NZ− NZ+ NZ−.
Ref SA v BI 4th Test 38.

PRÉVOST, Alfred ('Le Marquis') *France*
Albi.
b 5.5.1894 St-Girons; *d* − .10.74 Carbonne.
Flanker, 4-0-0-4 (3 − 1t).
26 M−; 27 I− S− W−(1t).

PRICE, Alfred Henry *Ireland*
St Columba's Coll, Trin Coll Dublin.
Flanker, 2-0-0-2 (3 − 1t).
20 S− F−(1t).
Medicine.

PRICE, Brian *Wales*
Newport, Barbarians.
b 30.10.37 Deri, Bargoed.
Lock, 32-14-4-14.
61 I+ F−; 62 E= S−; 63 E− S+ F− NZ−; 64
E= S+ I+ F= SA−; 65 E+ S+ I+ F−; 66 E+
S+ I− F+ A−; 67 S− I− F− E+; 69 S+ I+ F=
NZ− NZ− A+; BI > 66 A 2-2-0-0, NZ 2-0-0-2.
Schoolmaster/BBC production. Wales XV v Fj
64.

PRICE, Graham *Wales*
W Mon GS, Welsh SS, Alsager Coll, UWIST,
Pontypool, Mon, Barbarians.
b 24.11.51 Moascar, Egypt.
Prop, 41-25-1-15 (8 − 2t).
75 F+(1t) E+ S− I+ A+; 76 E+ S+ I+ F+; 77
I+ F− E+ S+; 78 E+ S+ I+ F+ A− A− NZ−;
79 S+ I+ F− E+; 80 F+(1t) E− S+ I− NZ−;
81 E+ S− I+ F− A+; 82 I− F+ E− S−; 83 E=

I+ F−; BI > 77 NZ 4-1-0-3; 80 SA 4-1-0-3; 83
NZ 4-0-0-4.
Lab technician/business. World's most capped
prop (53 inc 12 BI). Wales B v F 73, 74. W > 75
Far East; 78 A. Wales XV v Arg 76, R 79,
Maoris 82. Played for Pontypool as schoolboy.
Jaw broken by punch v A, Sydney 17.6.78. Mem
of legendary Pontypool Front Row. Welsh
Schools & Gwent senior shot & discus champ.
Autobiography 'Price of Wales' pub 84.

PRICE, Herbert Leo MC *England*
Bishop's Stortford Coll, Oxford Univ, Leicester,
Harlequins, Barbarians, Surrey.
b 21.6.1899; *d* 18.7.43 Manchester.
Flanker, 4-4-0-0 (6 − 2t).
22 I+ S+; 23 W+(1t) I+(1t).
HM. Served WW1, Lt S Wales Borderers; MC.
Blue 20-1. Blues for hockey (21-2) & water polo
(19-22). Ckt for Oxford. 13 apps for E at
hockey. Sel for E v S at both rugby & hockey on
same day, 18.3.22; chose rugby. Sc t v W 23
directly from kick-off; no Welshman touched
the ball.

PRICE, John *England*
Coventry.
Lock, 1-0-0-1.
61 I−.
Research engr. Moved to A.

PRICE, Malcolm John *Wales*
Welsh Youth, Pontypool, RAF.
b 8.12.37 Pontypool.
Centre, 9-4-1-4 (6 − 2t).
59 E+ S−(1t) I+(1t) F−; 60 E− S+ I+ F−; 62
E=; BI > 59 A 2-2-0-0, NZ 3-0-0-3.
Oldham RL.

PRICE, P.L.A. *England*
RIE Coll.
Half-back, 3-1-1-1.
1877 I+ S−; 78 S=.

PRICE, Raymond Allen *Australia*
NSW.
b 4.3.53.
Flanker, 8-5-1-2 (16 − 4t).
74 NZ−(1t) NZ= NZ−; 75 E+ E+(1t) J+
J+(1t); 76 US+(1t).
Carpenter. RL 76.

PRICE, Ronald E. *Wales*
RAF, Weston-super-Mare.
b 16.9.15 Trealaw.
Lock, 2-2-0-0.
39 S+ I+.
Electrician.

PRICE, Terence Graham *Wales*
Llanelli GS, New Dock Stars, Hendy, Leicester

Univ, Llanelli, London Welsh.
b 45 Hendy.
FB, 8-4-0-4 (45 − 9c 1d 8p).
65 E+(1c) S+(1c 2p) I+(1c 1d 1p) F−(2c); 66
E+(1c 2p) A−(1c 1p); 67 S−(1c) F−(1c 2p);
BIr > 66 A, NZ.
Schoolmaster/engrg. Grandson of Dai
Hiddlestone. Wales XV v Fj 64. Bradford N RL
67.

PRICE, Thomas William   *England*
St Mark's Sch, Gloucester, Cheltenham,
Barbarians, Glos.
b 26.7.14.
Prop, 6-2-0-4.
48 S− F−; 49 W− I− F+ S+.
Laundry employee/aircraft factory employee.

PRIDAY, Alun James   *Wales*
Glan-y-nant Sch, Whitchurch Boys' Sch,
Whitchurch GS, Penarth, Aberavon, RAF St
Athan, RAF, Cardiff, Rhiwbina, Glam,
Barbarians.
b 23.1.33 Whitchurch, Cardiff.
FB, 2-2-0-0.
58 I+; 61 I+.
Local govt clerk/draughtsman/rep/co dir.
English parents. Invited to attend English,
Welsh Trials 56; chose Wales. Sec Cardiff 72-86.

PRIMMER, Conrad James   *Australia*
Qld.
b 24.3.24.
Flanker/lock, 2-0-0-2.
51 NZ− NZ−.
Medicine.

PRINCLARY, Jean ('Le Prince')   *France*
Cavaillon, Brive.
b 15.7.12 Marseilles.
Prop, 10-6-0-4 (3 − 1t).
45 BF+(1t) BF− W−; 46 BF+ I+ NZS− W+;
47 S+ I+ W−.

PRINGLE, John Conrad   *Ireland*
Campbell Coll Belfast, NIFC.
b 8.11.1881; *d* 8.5.52.
Forward, 2-1-0-1.
02 S+ W−.
The Army. Lt Col RE.

PRINSLOO, Jan   *South Africa*
Transvaal.
b 35; *d* 28.7.66.
2-0-1-1.
58 F= F−.
Police. St Helens (E) RL.

PRINSLOO, Joshua ('Poens')   *South Africa*
N Transvaal.
b 11.10.35.

No 8, 1-0-0-1.
63 A−.
Police.

PRINSLOO, J.P. ('Boet')   *South Africa*
Stellenbosch Univ, Transvaal.
Wing, 1-1-0-0.
28 NZ+.

PRITCHARD, Cecil   *Wales*
Cross Keys, Pontypool.
Hooker, 8-3-1-4.
28 E− S+ I− F−; 29 E− S+ F+ I=.
Miner.

PRITCHARD, Charles Meyrick   *Wales*
Newport Intermed Sch, Long Ashton, Bristol,
Newport.
b 30.12.1882 Newport; *d* 14.8.16 No.1 CCS
France.
Forward, 14-8-1-5 (3 − 1t).
04 I−; 05 E+ S+ NZ+; 06 E+(1t) S+ I− SA−;
07 E+ S− I+; 08 E=; 10 F+ E−.
Shopowner. Served WW1, Capt in S Wales
Borderers; mentioned in despatches. Died of
wounds.

PRITCHARD, Clifford Charles   *Wales*
('Cliff')
W Mon GS, Newport, Pontypool.
b 1.10.1881 Pontypool; *d* 14.12.54 Pontypool.
Centre/extra back, 5-4-0-1 (6 − 2t).
04 S+ I−(1t); 05 NZ+; 06 E+ S+(1t).
Undertaker.

PROCTOR, Albert Charles ('Joe')   *New Zealand*
King Edward Tech Coll, Zingari-Richmond,
Otago, S Island.
b 22.5.06 Dunedin.
Wing, 1-0-0-1.
32 A−.
Accountant/fruit merchants mgr. NZ > 32 A.
Coach N Otago.

PROCTOR, Ian J.   *Australia*
NSW.
b 47.
Wing, 1-0-0-1.
67 NZ−.
Schoolmaster.

PROSSER, David Rees   *Wales*
Neath.
b 13.10.12; *d* 6.5.73 York.
Prop, 2-2-0-0.
34 S+ I+.
Colliery blacksmith. Bro of Glyn. York RL 34.

PROSSER, Frederick John   *Wales*
('Jack')
Cardiff.

b 15.12.1892 Newport.
Prop, 1-1-0-0.
21 I+.
Police.

PROSSER, Glyn   *Wales*
Neath.
b –; *d* –.1.73.
Flanker, 4-3-0-1.
34 E– S+ I+; 35 NZ+.
Miner. Bro of D.R. Sunday School teacher.
Huddersfield RL 36.

PROSSER, Roydon Barnett   *Australia*
Newington Coll, NSW.
b 18.2.42 Sydney.
Prop, 25-4-1-20.
67 E+ I– I– NZ–; 68 NZ– NZ– F+ I– S–;
69 W– SA– SA– SA– SA–; 71 SA– SA–
SA– F+ F–; 72 F= F– NZ– NZ– NZ– Fj+.
Marketing.

PROSSER, Thomas Raymond   *Wales*
('Pross')
Pontypool, Barbarians.
b 2.3.30 Pontypool.
Prop, 22-12-1-9 (3 – 1t).
56 S+ F+; 57 E– S– I+ F+(1t); 58 A+ E= S+
I+ F–; 59 E+ S– I+ F–; 60 E– S+ I+ F–
SA–; 61 I+ F–; BI > 59 A, NZ 1-0-0-1.
Bulldozer driver. Coach of Pontypool 70-86.

PROTHERO, Gareth John   *Wales*
Welsh Youth, Cardiff, Bridgend.
b 7.12.41 Beddau.
Flanker, 11-8-1-2 (3 – 1t).
64 S+ I+ F=; 65 E+ S+ I+ F–; 66 E+ S+ I–
(1t) F+; BI > 66 A, NZ.
Concrete factory worker. W > 64 SA. Wales
XV v Fj 64.

PROUT, Derek Henry   *England*
Cornwall Tech Coll, Launceston, Redruth,
Loughborough Colls, UAU, Northampton,
Barbarians, SW Cos, Cornwall.
b 10.11.42.
Wing, 2-0-2-0.
68 W= I=.
PE lecturer. Cornish 100y & 220y sprint champ.
Volleyball Assoc coach.

PRYCE-JENKINS, Thomas John   *Wales*
Llandovery Coll, Cambridge Univ, Bart's Hosp,
London Welsh.
b 1.2.1864; *d* 6.8.22 London.
Back, 2-1-0-1 (1t).
1888 S+(1t) I–.
Medicine. Fdr of London Welsh.

PUECH, Louis   *France*
Toulouse.

b 4.12.1896 Gorces, Lot; *d* –.
Lock, 5-2-0-3.
20 S– E– I+; 21 E– I+.

PUGET, Marcel   *France*
Toulouse.
b 28.9.40 Limoux, Aude.
SH, 17-6-2-9 (3 – 1d).
61 It+; 66 S= I+ It+; 67 SA– SA+ SA= NZ–;
68 Cz+ NZ– NZ– SA– SA–(1d) R–; 69 E–
R+; 70 W–.
Town Hall clerk.

PUGH, Charles Henry   *Wales*
Maesteg.
b 7.3.1896; *d* 23.1.51 Gowerton.
Lock/no 8, 7-1-0-6 (3 – 1t).
24 E– S– I–(1t) F+ NZ–; 25 E– S–.
Police.

PUGH, George Harold   *Australia*
NSW.
b 1890; *d* –.
Forward, 1-1-0-0.
12 US+.

PUGSLEY, Joseph   *Wales*
Cardiff, London Welsh.
b 10.5.1885 Swansea; *d* 13.6.76 Cardiff.
Hooker/prop, 7-6-0-1 (6 – 2t).
10 E– S+(1t) I+; 11 E+(1t) S+ F+ I+.
Docker/boilermaker. Salford RL 11.

PUIG, Alphonse   *France*
Perpignan.
b 01 Thuir; *d* –.12.74 Thuir.
Prop, 2-0-0-2.
26 S– E–.

PUJOL, T.   *France*
SOE Toulouse.
Wing, 1-0-0-1 (2 – 1c).
06 NZ–(1c)
Sc F's 1st c, v NZ 06.

PULLIN, John Vivian   *England*
Thornbury GS, Cirencester Agric Coll, Bristol
Saracens, Bristol, Barbarians, Glos.
b 1.11.41 Australia.
Hooker, 42-13-4-25 (3 – 1t).
66 W–; 68 W= I= F– S+; 69 I– F+ S+ W–
SA+(1t); 70 I+ W– S– F–; 71 W– I+ F= S–
S– P–; 72 W– I– F– S– SA+; 73 NZ– W–
I– F+ S+ NZ+ A+; 74 S– I– F= W+; 75 I–
W–r S+ A– A–; 76 F–; BI > 68 SA 3-0-1-2;
71 A, NZ 4-2-1-1.
Farmer. With I's Ken Kennedy, world's most
capped hooker, 49 inc 7 BI. E > 67 Can.
Barbarians > 69 SA. Capt E 13 times.

PULLMAN, Joseph J. *Wales*
Neath.
Hooker, 1-1-0-0.
10 F+.
Police.

PURCELL, Michael Peter *Australia*
Nudgee Coll, Qld.
b 6.9.45.
Lock/flanker, 3-1-0-2.
66 W+ S−; 67 I−.
Law.

PURCELL, Noel Mary *Ireland*
Belvedere Coll, Clongowes Coll, Trin Coll
Dublin, Lansdowne, Barbarians.
b 14.12.1891; *d* 62.
No 8, 4-1-0-3.
21 E− S+ W− F−.
Solicitor. Ref S v E 27. GB & I water polo;
Olympic gold medal 20.

PURDIE, William *Scotland*
Jedburgh GS, Jedforest.
b 24.6.10 Jedburgh.
Prop, 3-0-0-3.
39 W− I− E−.
Slater.

PURDON, Frank J. *Wales*
Newport, Swansea.
Forward, 4-1-0-3.
1881 E−; 1882 I+ E−; 1883 S−.
Uncle of W.P. Geen. Some sources state
Purdon played with H.M. Jordan for I v W 1884;
others believe it was J. McDaniel (Newport) &
Jordan.

PURDON, Henry *Ireland*
RBAI, NIFC.
Forward, 5-1-0-4.
1879 S− E−; 1880 E−; 1881 E− S+.

PURDON, William Brooke *Ireland*
RBAI, Methodist Coll, Queen's Coll Belfast.
b 28.11.1881; *d* 1.12.50.
SH/FH, 3-2-0-1 (3 − 1t).
06 E+(1t) S− W+.
Medicine. Maj Gen RAMC.

PURDUE, Charles Alfred *New Zealand*
Britannia, Southland.
b 10.6.1874 Mataura; *d* 10.10.41 Invercargill.
Forward, 1-1-0-0.
05 A+.
Storeman. Played with bro 'Pat' v A 05. Son
Jack rep Southland & NZ trial 39. Uncle of
George.

PURDUE, Edward ('Pat') *New Zealand*
Britannia, Southland, Orepuki.

b 1878 Dipton; *d* 16.7.39 Invercargill.
Forward, 1-1-0-0.
05 A+.
Rly ganger. Played with bro Charles v A 05.
Father of George. Another son Syd rep
Southland.

PURDUE, George Bambery *New Zealand*
Makarewa Sch, Orepuki Sch, Star, NZ Maoris,
Southland, S Island.
b 4.5.09 Invercargill.
Lock, 4-3-0-1 (3 − 1t).
31 A+; 32 A−(1t) A+ A+.
Truck driver/dir transport co. NZ > 32 A.
Served WW2. Son of 'Pat' & nephew of Charles.

PURDY, Stanley John *England*
Lawrence Sheriff Sch Rugby, Nottingham Univ,
UAU, Rugby, The Army, Comb Servs, Fylde,
Barbarians, Warwicks.
b 6.2.36.
Flanker, 1-0-1-0.
62 S=.
Management consultant.

PURKIS, Edwin Maurice *Australia*
NSW.
b 27.7.34.
Flanker, 2-1-0-1.
58 S− M+.
Salesman. RL.

PURSER, Francis Carmichael *Ireland*
OBE
Galway GS, Trin Coll Dublin.
b 16.9.1876; *d* −.2.34.
Wing, 3-1-0-2.
1898 E+ S− W−.
Medicine. Pres IRU 10-11. Pres RCPI; King's
Prof of Medicine Trin Coll Dublin.

PURVES, Alexander Buckholm *Scotland*
Haliburton Laidlaw
Fettes Coll, London Scottish, The Army.
b −.8.1886; *d* 20.9.45 London.
Wing, 10-6-0-4 (22 − 6t 1d).
06 W− I+ E−(1t) SA+(1t); 07 W+(1t) I+(1t)
E+(1t); 08 W−(1t) I− E+(1d).
The Army. Bro of W.D.C.L. Sc t in 6 successive
ints.

PURVES, William Donald *Scotland*
Campbell Laidlaw
Fettes Coll, Cambridge Univ, London Scottish,
Barbarians.
b 4.7.1888 Wimbledon; *d* −.
Lock, 6-2-0-4 (3 − 1t).
12 F+ W− I− SA−; 13 I+(1t) E−.
Farmer. Blue 07-9. Bro of A.B.H.L.

PURVIS, Neil Alexander *New Zealand*
John McGlashan Coll, Masterton, NZ Colts,
NZ Jnrs, Wairarapa-Bush, Upper Clutha,
Otago, S Island.
b 31.1.53 Cromwell.
Wing, 1-1-0-0.
76 I+.
Farmer. 9t NZ > 76 SA. Ckt for Otago 73.

PUTTER, D.J. ('Dick') *South Africa*
Potchefstroom Univ, W Transvaal.
b 13.2.32.
Prop, 3-2-0-1.
63 A+ A− A+.

PYKE, James *England*
St Helens Recreation.
b 8.2.1866 St Helens; *d* 17.5.41 St Helens.
Forward, 1-1-0-0.
1892 W+.
Glassworks mgr.

PYM, John Alfred MC *England*
Cheltenham Coll, RMA Woolwich, The Army,
Blackheath, Barbarians, Kent.
b 25.3.1891; *d* 9.2.69 Auckland.
SH, 4-3-0-1 (3 − 1t).
12 W+(1t) I+ S− F+.
The Army/farmer. Served in India, then WW1,
Capt RA. Wounded; mentioned in despatches
twice. MC & bar. Emigrated to NZ to take up
farming.

Q

QUAGLIO, Aldo *France*
Mazamet.
b 17.2.32 Saverdun, Ariège.
Prop, 13-8-2-3 (3 − 1t).
57 R+; 58 S− E− A+(1t) W+ I+ SA= SA+;
59 S+ E= It+ W+ I−.
Wool shop foreman. Roanne RL.

QUAID, Charles Edward *New Zealand*
Marist Bros' Sch Christchurch, E Christchurch
Sch, Linwood, Canterbury, Poneke,
Wellington, Southern, Otago, S Island.
b 17.8.08 Christchurch; *d* 18.12.84 Wellington.
Hooker, 2-2-0-0.
38 A+ A+.
Clerk. NZ > 38 A.

QUILIS, André *France*
Narbonne.
b 28.10.41 Coursan, Aude.
Wing/flanker/no 8, 5-1-2-2.
67 SA− SA= NZ−; 70 R+; 71 I=.
PE teacher.

QUINLAN, Sean Vincent Joseph *Ireland*
PBC Cork, Blackrock Coll, Highfield.
b 13.10.34 Cork.
Wing, 4-1-0-3.
56 F− E− W+; 58 W−.
Stores control system/co dir. Oldham RL.

QUINN, Brendan Thomas *Ireland*
Belvedere Coll, O Belvedere.
b 1.8.19 Dublin.
Wing, 1-0-0-1.
47 F−.
Local govt. Played in 3 Victory ints.

QUINN, Francis Peter *Ireland*
Belvedere Coll, Trin Coll Dublin, O Belvedere.
b 5.9.54 Dublin.
Wing, 3-0-0-3.
81 F− W− E−.
Management consultant. Living in
Johannesburg.

QUINN, James Patrick *England*
Wade Deacon HS Widnes, Aldershot Servs,
The Army, New Brighton, Sheffield Tg Coll,
Carnegie Coll, Harrogate, Barbarians, Hants,
Lancs.
b 19.2.30 Widnes; *d* 18.1.86 Leics.
Centre, 5-3-0-2.
54 W+ NZ− I+ S+ F−; BI > 55 SA.
PE teacher/PA/journalist. At school with Reg
Higgins. Rep R Mil Police in Nat Modern
Pentathlon Champ 49. Leeds RL 56; Cup
winners' medal 56, capt 59. LTA coach; also
swimming coach. Rugby corr for 'Sunday
Express' & for Radio Merseyside. Killed in car
crash driving home from E v W 86.

QUINN, Joseph Patrick MC *Ireland*
Blackrock Coll, Trin Coll Dublin, Barbarians.
b 23.11.1888 Dublin; *d* −.6.55.
Wing, 15-8-1-6 (27 − 9t).
10 E= S−; 11 E+ S+(1t) W− F+(1t); 12 E−
S+ W+; 13 E− W−(1t) F+(3t); 14 F+(1t) E−
(1t) S+(1t).
Medicine. Served WW1.

QUINN, Kevin Joseph *Ireland*
Belvedere Coll, O Belvedere.
b 14.3.23 Gort, Co Galway.
Centre, 5-2-1-2 (3 − 1p).
47 F− A−(1p); 53 F+ E= S+.
Medicine. Played in 3 Victory ints. Ckt for I 57-
9.

QUINN, Michael Anthony Mary *Ireland*
Newbridge GS, Bolton St Coll of Tech,
Lansdowne.
b 31.5.52 Dublin.
FH, 10-3-2-5 (18 − 2d 4p).
73 F+; 74 F− W= E+(1d) S+ P= NZ−; 77 S−

(1d 1p) F−(1p); 81 SA−(2p).
Architect. Ir > 81 SA.

QUINNELL, Derek Leslie *Wales*
Coleshill Sch, Welsh Youth, Llanelli,
Barbarians.
 b 22.5.49 Llanelli.
No 8/flanker/lock, 23-15-1-7 (8 − 2t).
72 F+r NZ−; 73 E+ S− A+; 74 S+ F=; 75
E+r; 77 I+r F− E+ S+; 78 E+ S+(1t) I+ F+
A− NZ−; 79 S+(1t*) I+ F− E+; 80 NZ−; BI
> 71uncap A, NZ 1-0-0-1; 77 NZ 2-1-0-1; 80 SA
2-1-0-1.
Sales rep/co dir. Bro in law of Barry John.
Wales B v F 71. W > 75 Far East; 78 A. Wales
XV v J 73; Tonga 74; Arg 76; R 79. Welsh XV v
NZ 74. Barbarians v NZ 73. Played on 4 winning
sides v NZ (Llanelli, BI (2) & Barbarians).
WRU sel 85-6. *Officially awarded to Terry
Holmes.

QUIRKE, John Michael *Ireland*
Thornton
Blackrock Coll, UC Dublin.
 b 26.6.44 Dublin.
SH, 3-1-0-2.
62 E− S−; 68 S+.
Bus exec/barrister.

R

RAAFF, J.W.E. ('Klondyke') *South Africa*
Griq W.
 b 1879; d −.7.49.
Prop, 6-2-3-1 (3 − 1t).
03 BT= BT=; 06 S− W+(1t) E=; 10 BT+.
Licensee.

RADFORD, William J. *Wales*
Newport.
 b −.4.1889 Newport; d 1.1.24 Newport.
Flanker, 1-0-0-1.
23 I−.
Docker. Played in unbeaten Newport XV 22-3.
Accidentally drowned in Newport Docks.

RAFTER, Michael *England*
St Brendan's Coll Bristol, St Luke's Coll,
Bristol.
 b 31.3.52 Bristol.
Flanker, 17-6-2-9.
77 S+ F− W−; 78 F− W− S+ I+ NZ−; 79 S=
I− F+ W− NZ−; 80 W+r; 81 W− Arg=
Arg+.
Schoolmaster/radio corr.

RALPH, A. Raymond ('Dicky') *Wales*
Pontywaun GS, Newport.
 b 21.1.08 Abercarn.
FH, 6-4-0-2 (17 − 3t 2d).

31 F+(2t) I+(1d) SA−; 32 E+ S+ I−(1t 1d).
Schoolmaster/approved sch HM. Capt Newport
32-3. Leeds RL 33; W v A 33, Challenge Cup
final medal 36.

RALSTON, Christopher Wayne *England*
('Rawley')
King William's Coll IOM, Richmond, London
Cos, Mdx.
 b 25.5.44 Hendon.
Lock, 22-7-1-14 (4 − 1t).
71 S− P−; 72 W− I−(1t) F− S− SA+; 73 NZ−
W− I− F+ S+ NZ+ A+; 74 S− I− F= W+; 75
I− F− W− S+.
Advertising exec. Sc E's 1st 4-pt t, v I 72.

RAMALLI, Cecil *Australia*
NSW.
 b 19.
SH, 2-0-0-2.
38 NZ− NZ−.
PRO. WW2 POW Japan.

RAMBAUT, Daniel Frederick *Ireland*
RS Armagh, Trin Coll Dublin.
 b 1860; d −.12.32.
Centre, 4-2-0-2 (3c).
1887 E+(2c) S− W−; 1888 W+(1c).
Medicine. Irish 120y hurdles champ.

RAMIS, Roger ('Le Ninou') *France*
Perpignan.
 b 29.3.02 Perpignan.
Centre, 3-0-1-2.
22 E= I−; 23 W−.

RAMSAY, Keith McKenzie *Australia*
Tamworth HS, Hawkesbury Agric Coll, NSW.
 b 27.8.14 Paddington; kia WW2.
No 8/flanker/lock, 4-1-0-3 (6 − 2t).
36 M+(1t); 37 SA−; 38 NZ− NZ−(1t).
Butcher/clerk.

RAMSDEN, Harold E. *England*
Bingley.
Forward, 2-1-1-0.
1898 S= W+.
Woollen manufacturer.

RAMSEY, Samuel H. *Wales*
Treorchy.
 b 1874 Scotland.
Forward, 2-0-1-1.
1896 E−; 1904 E=.
Colliery official. 8 yr gap between caps.

RANCOULE, Henri *France*
Lourdes, Toulon, Tarbes.
 b 6.2.33 Bram, Aude.
Wing, 27-19-3-5 (21 − 7t).
55 E+ W− It+(2t); 58 A+(1t) W+ It+ I+

SA=; 59 S+ It+(1t) W+; 60 I+(1t) It+(1t) R−
Arg+ Arg+; 61 SA= E= W+ It+ NZ− NZ−;
62 S+(1t) E+ W− I+ It+.
Hotelier.

RANDELL, Robert   *Wales*
Aberavon.
Lock, 2-1-0-1.
24 I− F+.
Foreman annealer tinplate works.

RANGI, Ronald Edward   *New Zealand*
Ponsonby, Auckland, NZ Maoris, Comb Servs,
N Island.
b 4.2.41 Auckland.
Centre, 10-8-0-2 (9 − 3t).
64 A+(1t) A−; 65 SA+ SA+(1t) SA−(1t)
SA+; 66 BI+ BI+ BI+ BI+.
RNZAF/Auckland Harbour Bd employee.
Maori Player of Year 64-5.

RANKIN, John George   *New Zealand*
Christchurch Boys' HS, HSOB, Canterbury,
Hutt Army, Wellington, S Island.
b 14.2.14 Christchurch.
Flanker, 3-2-0-1 (6 − 2t).
36 A+ A+(2t); 37 SA−.
Traveller/export mgr. NZ > 36 A. Canterbury
selector & coach 48-54. Son Alistair rep Victoria
(A) v SA 71. Ckt for Canterbury.

RANKIN, Ronald DFC Croix de   *Australia*
Guerre
Hurlstone HS, Sydney Tech, NSW.
b 14.
FB, 7-1-0-6 (27 − 6c 5p).
36 NZ−(1p) NZ−(2c 1p) M+(3c 1p); 37 SA−
SA−(1c 2p); 38 NZ− NZ−.
Schoolmaster. Served WW2.

RANSON, John Matthew   *England*
Birmingham Univ, Durham City, Rosslyn Pk,
Headingley, Selby, Barbarians, Durham Co, N
Midlands, Mdx.
b 26.7.38.
Wing, 7-1-1-5 (6 − 2t).
63 NZ−(1t) NZ− A−; 64 W=(1t) I− F+ S−.
Schoolmaster/brewer. Took hat-trick for
Northwood v MCC 68. Taught at Durham Sch
& Birmingham Univ. Joined Arthur Guinness &
Son as under-brewer 58.

RAPHAEL, John Edward   *England*
Merchant Taylors' Sch, OMT, Oxford Univ,
Surrey.
b 30.4.1882 Brussels; *d* 11.6.17 Remy,
Belgium.
Wing, 9-4-0-5 (3 − 1t).
02 W− I+ S+; 05 W− S− NZ−; 06 W− S+(1t)
F+.
Barrister. Blue 01-4. Water polo blue (02-4) &

ckt blue 03 (sc 130 in 1st inns), 04-5 (99 in 1st
inns). Also pl for Surrey CCC 03-6. Capt RFU
> 10 Arg. Called to Bar 08. Contested Croydon
for Lib 09 by-election. Served WW1, Duke of
Wellington's Rgt; d of wounds received on
Messines Ridge 7.6.17.

RAPIN, Achille   *France*
SBUC.
Centre, 1-1-0-0.
38 R+.

RAS, Wouter Johannes De Wet   *South Africa*
Harrismith Sch, UOFS, Natal, Gazelles, Oribis,
OFS.
b 28.1.54 Harrismith.
Centre, 2-2-0-0.
76 NZ+r; 80 SAm+r.
Salesman. 159 pts OFS Currie Cup 81. SA rec
335 pts 78. Nearly 2000 pts in 1st class rugby. 48
pts OFS v E Free State 31.5.77 (most pts by any
player in 1st class rugby in SA). SA > 80 SAm
(35 pts v British Sch OB, Montevideo).

RATHIE, David Stewart   *Australia*
Qld.
b 29.5.52.
Centre, 2-0-1-1.
72 F= F−.
Solicitor. Qld cricketer.

RAVENSCOURT, John   *England*
Rugby Sch, Oxford Univ, Birkenhead Pk,
Cheshire.
b 11.6.1857; *d* 18.8.02 Buenos Aires.
Forward, 1-1-0-0.
1881 I+.
Law. Blue 1877-8.

RAWLINSON, William Cecil   *England*
Welsh
Clifton Coll, Blackheath, RMC Sandhurst.
b 17.12.1855; *d* 14.2.1898 Northampton.
Forward, 1-1-0-0.
1876 S+.
The Army. Maj in Lincs Rgt.

RAYBOULD, William Henry   *Wales*
Cathay's HS Cardiff, Cambridge Univ, London
Welsh, Newport, Barbarians.
b 6.5.44.
Centre, 11-3-1-7 (3 − 1d).
67 S− I− F− E+(1d) NZ−; 68 I− F−; 70 SA=
E+ I− F+r; BI > 68 SA.
Schoolmaster/schs inspector. Blue 66.

RAYMOND, François   *France*
Toulouse.
Wing, 3-0-0-3.
25 S−; 27 W−; 28 I−.

RAYNAL, François *France*
Perpignan.
Flanker, 5-5-0-0 (5 − 1t 1c).
35 G+; 36 G+(1c) G+; 37 G+(1t) It+.

RAYNAUD, Firmin *France*
Carcassonne.
Wing, 1-1-0-0 (6 − 2t).
33 G+(2t).

RAZAT, Jean-Pierre ('Goupil') *France*
Agen.
b 15.10.40 Fumel.
FB, 4-1-1-2.
62 R−; 63 S− I+ R=.
PE teacher.

REA, Christopher William *Scotland*
Wallace
Dundee HS, St Andrew's Univ, W of Scotland,
Headingley, Barbarians.
b 22.10.43 Dundee.
Centre, 13-5-0-8 (9 − 3t).
68 A+; 69 F+ W− I− SA+; 70 F− W− I− A−;
71 F− W−(1t) E+(1t) E+(1t); BI > 71 A, NZ.
BBC. Scottish XV v Arg 69.

REA, Harold Halliday *Ireland*
Belfast Acad, Edinburgh Univ.
b 46.
Centre, 2-2-0-0.
67 A+; 69 F+.
Medicine.

READ, Henry Marvelle *Ireland*
St Columba's Coll Rathfarnham, Trin Coll
Dublin.
b 8.11.1888 Dungar, Roscrea; d 6.12.72
Dalkey.
SH, 13-6-1-6.
10 E= S−; 11 E+ S+ W− F+; 12 F+ E− S+
W+ SA−; 13 E− S−.
Pres IRU 55-6. Ckt for I.

REARDEN, James V. *Ireland*
CBC Cork, Castleknock Coll, Cork
Constitution.
b −; d 13.7.79.
Centre, 2-0-0-2.
34 E− S−.

REBUJENT, Raymond *France*
RCF.
Hooker, 1-0-0-1.
63 E−.
Switched to RL.

REDFERN, Steve *England*
Leicester.
Prop, 1-1-0-0.
84 I+r.

REDMAN, Nigel Charles *England*
Priory Comp Sch Weston-super-Mare, S Bristol
Tech Coll, Bath.
b 16.8.64 Cardiff.
Lock, 2-0-0-2.
84 A−; 86 S−r.
R Bath team-mate John Hall v S 86. E Colts 83.

REDMOND, Gerald Francis *England*
Western Hornets, Cambridge Univ, Bedford, St
Luke's Coll, Weston-super-Mare, Bristol, E
Cos, Som.
b 23.3.43.
No 8, 1-0-0-1.
70 F−.
Blue 69-71.

REDWOOD, Brian William *England*
Bristol GS, Exeter Univ, Bristol, Glos.
b 6.2.39.
SH, 2-0-2-0 (3 − 1t).
68 W=(1t) I=.
Personnel officer with Rolls Royce/sales co-
ordinator Rothmans. Played with one eye. E
sel.

REDWOOD, Charles Edward *Australia*
St Patrick's Coll Wellington, Toowoomba, Qld.
b 19.5.1878 Nelson, NZ; d 16.2.54 London.
Wing/FB, 4-0-0-4.
03 NZ−; 04 BT− BT− BT−.
Maltster.

REEDY, William Joseph *New Zealand*
White Star, Petone, Wellington, Athletic, N
Island.
b 1.4.39 Porirua.
Hooker, 2-1-1-0.
08 AW= AW+.
Rly workshops blacksmith.

REES, Aaron *Wales*
Maesteg.
Flanker, 1-0-0-1
19 NZA−.
Miner.

REES, Alan *Wales*
Glanafan GS, Welsh SS, Aberavon, Maesteg,
Llanelli.
b 17.2.38 Port Talbot.
FH, 3-1-1-1 (3 − 1d).
62 E= S−(1d) F+.
Pro cricketer/sports officer Borough of Afan.
Leeds RL 62. 216 apps Glam CCC 55-68.

REES, Arthur Morgan OBE *Wales*
Llandovery Coll, Cambridge Univ, RAF, Met
Police, London Welsh, Surrey, Barbarians.
b 20.11.12.
Flanker, 13-5-2-6.

34 E−; 35 E= S+ I− NZ+; 36 E= S+ I+; 37
E− S− I−; 38 E+ S−.
Metropolitan Police/Chief Constable of Staffs.
Team-mate of Cliff Jones & Vivian Jenkins at
Llandovery. Blue 33-4. Dir Derby Co AFC.

REES, Brian I. *Wales*
Neath GS, Cambridge Univ, London Welsh.
b 42.
Hooker, 3-0-0-3.
67 S− I− F−.
Medicine. Blue 63-6. W > 68 Arg.

REES, Clive Frederick William *Wales*
('Whizzer')
Llanelli GS, Loughborough Coll, London
Welsh, Barbarians, Reading.
b 6.10.51 Singapore.
Wing, 13-5-2-6.
74 I=; 75 A+; 78 NZ−; 81 F− A+; 82 I− F+
E− S−; 83 E= S+ I+ F−; BI > 74 SA.
Schoolmaster. W > 75 Far East. Wales XV v
Maoris 82. Wales B > 83 Spain. Capt London
Welsh 85-6 Centenary season. Welsh Schs sprint
champ.

REES, Daniel *Wales*
Swansea.
b 1876.
Centre, 5-4-0-1.
1900 E+; 03 E+ S−; 05 E+ S+.
Hull KR RL 05.

REES, Douglas *Wales*
Penclawdd, Swansea.
b 44.
FB 3-1-0-2 (9 − 3p).
68 S+ I−(1p) F−(2p).
Process operator.

REES, Evan B. *Wales*
Swansea.
b Cwmavon.
Centre, 1-0-0-1.
19 NZA−.
Dewsbury RL 19.

REES, Gary William *England*
Trent Coll, Nottingham.
b 2.5.60 Long Eaton.
Flanker, 4-1-0-3.
84 SA−r A−; 86 I+ F−.
Banking. E Under 23s > 82 It, 83 R.

REES, Harold Elgan *Wales*
Cwmtawe Sch, Welsh SS, Borough Rd Coll,
Neath.
b 5.1.54.
Wing, 13-7-1-5 (24 − 6t).
79 S+(1t) I+ F− E+(1t); 80 F+(1t) E−(1t) S+
I− NZ−; 83 E= S+(1t) I+(1t) F−; BI > 77

NZuncap 1-0-0-1; 80r SA.
Wales B v F 74-8, v A 78. Wales XV v Maoris
82.

REES, Harry *Wales*
Cardiff.
b −; *d* 78.
Lock/prop, 5-2-0-3.
37 S− I−; 38 E+ S− I+.
Police.

REES, John Idwal *Wales*
Swansea HS, Cambridge Univ, Swansea,
Barbarians, London Welsh.
b 25.7.10 Swansea.
Centre/wing, 14-8-1-5 (3 − 1t).
34 E− S+(1t) I+; 35 S+ NZ+; 36 E= S+ I+;
37 E− S− I−; 38 E+(1t) S− I+.
HM. Blue 31-2. Cowbridge GS HM 38-71.

REES, Joseph *Wales*
Amman Utd, Swansea.
b 3.6.1893; *d* 12.4.50 Swansea.
FB, 12-6-0-6 (7 − 2c 1p).
20 E+ S− F+ I+; 21 E− S− I+; 22 E+(2c); 23
E− F+(1p) I−; 24 E−.
School attendance officer. Served WW1.

REES, Lewis Morgan *Wales*
Treorchy, Cardiff.
b 17.1.10 Treherbert; *d* 21.12.76 Manchester.
Flanker, 1-0-0-1.
33 I−.
Dyer/brewery draysman. Oldham RL.

REES, Peter *Wales*
Gwendraeth GS, Llanelli, Tumble, Penygroes.
b 8.2.25 Penygroes.
Wing, 2-2-0-0.
47 F+ I+.
Power station shift mgr. Chmn, pres Llanelli.

REES, Peter M. *Wales*
Sheffield Univ, Newport.
b 38.
Wing, 4-3-0-1.
61 E+ S− I+; 64 I+.
Civil engr. W > 64SA.

REES, Theophilus Aneurin *Wales*
Llandovery Coll, Sherborne Sch, Oxford Univ.
b c1858; *d* 11.9.32 Merthyr.
Forward, 1-0-0-1.
1881 E−.
Solicitor/town clerk. WRU selector 1882.
Cricket MCC, Gentlemen of W. Town Clerk,
Merthyr.

REES, Thomas Edgar *Wales*
('Guardsman')
London Welsh, Welsh Guards, The Army.

b 22.8.04 Pontyclun; *d* 10.11.68 Oldham.
FB, 4-2-0-2 (4 − 2c).
26 I+(1c) F+; 27 NSW−(1c); 28 E−.
Coalminer/Army/gas bd employee/sheet metal
worker. Welsh Guards. Oldham RL.

REES, Thomas James   *Wales*
Bargoed, Cross Keys, Mountain Ash, Newport.
b 8.5.13 Fleur de Lys.
Prop, 8-4-1-3.
35 S+ I− NZ+; 36 E= S+ I+; 37 E− S−.
Miner. At over 18st, believed to be heaviest
man to play for Wales.

REES-JONES, Geoffrey Rippon   *Wales*
Ipswich Sch, Oxford Univ, London Welsh, E
Cos.
b 8.7.14 Bridgend.
Wing, 5-2-1-2 (6 − 2t).
34 E− S+; 35 I− NZ+(2t); 36 E=.
HM. Blue 33-5. Served WW2, Bde Major
Commandos, mentioned in despatches. HM of
King William Sch IOM.

REEVE, James Stanley Roope   *England*
Rugby Sch, Cambridge Univ, Harlequins,
Barbarians.
b 12.9.08 Kensington; *d* 6.11.36.
Wing, 8-3-2-3 (15 − 5t).
29 F+; 30 W+(2t) I− F+(1t) S=; 31 W= I− S−
(2t); BI > 30 A 1-0-0-1, NZ 3-1-0-2.
Barrister. Son of Judge Roope Reeve. Sc t in 1st
Test BI win v NZ 30. Killed in road accident.

REEVES, Frederick   *Wales*
Cross Keys, Newbridge.
b −; *d* 76.
SH, 3-2-0-1.
20 F+ I+; 21 E−.
Miner.

REGAN, Martin   *England*
West Pk GS St Helens, St Helens, Liverpool,
Blackheath, Barbarians, Lancs.
b 24.9.29 St Helens.
FH, 12-8-1-3 (3 − 1t).
53 W+ I= F+ S+; 54 W+ NZ− I+(1t) S+ F−;
56 I+ S+ F−.
Schoolmaster. Warrington RL.

REID, Alan Robin ('Ponty')   *New Zealand*
New Plymouth Boys' HS, Raglan, Waikato,
Frankton, Kereone, N Island.
b 12.4.29 Te Kuiti.
SH, 5-4-0-1.
52 A−; 56 SA+ SA+; 57 A+ A+.
Schoolmaster/mercer. NZ > 51 & 57 A (capt).
Waikato selector 66-9.

REID, Allan   *South Africa*
Diocesan Coll Rondebosch, Stellenbosch Univ,
W Prov.
b 1.10.1877 Cape Town; *d* 31.10.48.
Forward, 1-1-0-0 (3 − 1t).
03 BT+(1t).
Ckt for W Prov. Bro of Bert SA 06 (no Tests).

REID, B.C. ('Bunny')   *South Africa*
Border.
FB, 1-1-0-0.
33 A+.
Oil co rep.

REID, Carl   *Ireland*
RBAI, NIFC.
Centre, 4-2-0-2 (3 − 1t).
1899 S+(1t) W+ 1900 E−; 03 W−.

REID, Charles   *Scotland*
Edinburgh Acad, Edinburgh Academicals.
b 14.1.1864; *d* 25.10.09 London.
Forward, 20-12-4-4 (4t).
1881 I− E=; 1882 I+ E+; 1883 W+ I+(1t) E−
(1t); 1884 W+ I+ E−; 1885 W= I+(1t); 1886
W+ I+ E=; 1887 I+ W+(1t) E=; 1888 W− I+.
Medicine. Bro of James. Capped from sch, aged
17yrs 36days (see N.J. Finlay). Once S's rec cap
holder.

REID, Hikatarewa Rockcliffe   *New Zealand*
Western Heights HS, Ngongotaha, NZ Colts,
Bay of Plenty, Wasps, N Island.
b 8.4.58 Rotorua.
Hooker, 7-3-2-2 (8 − 2t).
80 A− A+(1t) 80 W+(1t); 83 S= E−; 85 Arg+
Arg=.
Insurance inspector. NZ > 80 A & Fj (broke leg
v ACT), NAm & W, 81 R & F, 83 S & E, 84 A,
85 Arg. World XV > 86 SA. Maori Player of
Year 80. Grandfather J. Hikatarewa rep NZ
Maoris 13.

REID, James   *Scotland*
Ayr Acad, Edinburgh Univ, Edinburgh W.
b 24.2.1851; *d* 29.7.08.
Forward, 5-2-1-2 (1t).
1874 E−; 1875 E=; 1876 E−; 1877 I+(1t) E+.
Sheriff Substitute for Banffshire. Bro of
Charles. Ump S v E 1881.

REID, John Lewis   *Ireland*
Epsom Coll, Oxford Univ, Richmond.
b 16.4.09 Bandon.
FH, 2-0-0-2.
34 S− W−.
Medicine.

REID, John Murray   *Scotland*
Edinburgh Acad, Edinburgh Academicals.
b 25.7.1876; *d* 25.5.67.

FB, 3-1-1-1.
1898 I+ E=; 1899 I-.
Medicine.

REID, Keith Howard   *New Zealand*
Wairarapa.
b 25.5.04 Clareville; *d* 24.5.72 Masterton.
Hooker, 2-0-0-2.
29 A- A-.
Farmer. NZ > 29 A. Wairarapa selector 39-52;
pres 50-9.

REID, Marshall Frederick CIE   *Scotland*
Loretto Sch.
b 3.8.1864; *d* -.4.25.
Centre, 2-1-0-1.
1883 I+ E-.
Co dir. Capped from sch.

REID, Patrick Joseph   *Ireland*
CBC Limerick, Crescent Coll, Garryowen.
b 17.3.24 Limerick.
Centre, 4-3-0-1 (3 - 1t).
47 A-; 48 F+(1t) E+ W+.
Brewery rep. Played in 2 Victory ints. Hockey
for I. Huddersfield RL.

REID, Sana Torium   *New Zealand*
Tolaga Bay HS, Paikea, E Coast, Country,
Hauiti, Hawkes Bay, Whakaki, NZ Maoris, N
Island.
b 22.9.12 Tokomaru Bay.
Lock, 9-5-0-4 (6 - 2t).
35 S+ I+ W-; 36 E- A+ A+(2t); 37 SA+
SA- SA-.
Slaughterman/agric contractor. NZ > 35-6 BI &
C, 36 A. NZ Maoris > 49 A. NZ Maoris selector
52-4.

REID, Terrence William   *Australia*
NSW.
b 20.9.34.
Flanker, 5-2-1-2 (3 - 1t).
61 Fj+ Fj+(1t) Fj= SA-; 62 NZ-.
Health inspector.

REID, Thomas Eymard   *Ireland*
('Colonel')
CBC Limerick, Garryowen, Barbarians.
b 3.3.26 Limerick.
Lock, 13-3-2-8.
53 E= S+ W-; 54 NZ- F-; 55 E= S-; 56 F-
E-; 57 F+ E- S+ W-; BI > 55 SA 2-1-0-1.
Sales rep. Emigrated to Can.

REID-KERR, James   *Scotland*
Greenock Acad, Greenock W.
Prop, 1-1-0-0.
09 E+; BI > 10 SA.
Cricket for S.

REIDY, Charles J. OBE   *Ireland*
Stonyhurst Sch, Cambridge Univ, London Irish,
The Army.
b 8.7.12 London.
Prop, 1-1-0-0.
37 W+.
The Army/professor. Ath for I.

REIDY, Gerald F.   *Ireland*
CBC Cork, UC Cork, Dolphin, Lansdowne.
b 13.5.26 Cork.
Flanker, 5-1-0-4.
53 W-; 54 F- E- S+ W-.
Office supplies co area mgr. Bro in law of Tom
Kiernan. Pres IRU 83-4.

REILLY, Norman Peter   *Australia*
Qld.
b 10.11.47.
Lock, 10-1-0-9.
68 NZ- NZ- F+ I- S-; 69 W- SA- SA-
SA- SA-.
Rep. RL.

RELPH, William Keith Linford   *Scotland*
Stewart's Coll, Stewart's Coll FP.
b 21.11.28.
Hooker, 4-2-0-2.
55 F- W+ I+ E-.
Co dir.

RENDALL, Paul Anthony   *England*
George
St Joseph's Sch Slough, England SS, Slough,
Bucks, Wasps, Mdx, S Cos.
b 18.2.54 London.
Prop, 5-1-0-4.
84 W- SA- SA-; 86 W+ S-.
England B v F 81, I 82. E > 81 Arg; 82 US, Can;
84 SA. England XV v Can 83.

RENNIE-TAILYOUR, Henry   *Scotland*
Waugh
Cheltenham Coll, RMA Sandhurst, RE.
b 9.10.1849 Mussorrie, India; *d* -.8.1921.
Forward, 1-0-0-1.
1872 E-.
The Army/man dir Guinness Brewery. Col in
RE. Rep Scotland at rugby & football (1873).
Played in 1st FA Cup final 1874, for RE v
Wanderers; in RE side which beat O Etonians 2-
0 to win FA Cup 1875. Kent CCC.

RENS, Ignatius Johannes   *South Africa*
('Bokspeen')
Transvaal.
b 19.7.29.
FH, 2-2-0-0 (19 - 5c 1d 2p).
53 A+(3c) A+(2c 1d 2p).
Dairy farmer. His d won Currie Cup for
Transvaal v Boland 52.

RENWICK, James Menzies   *Scotland*
Hawick HS, Hawick, Barbarians.
b 12.2.52 Hawick.
Centre/wing, 52-18-2-32 (67 − 8t 4c 4d 5p).
72 F+(1t) W−(1p) E+ NZ−; 73 F−; 74 W−
E+ I− F+; 75 I+(1t) F− W+ E− NZ−
A+(1t); 76 F−(1p) W− E+r; 77 I+ F− W−; 78
I− F− W−(1t) E− NZ−; 79 W− E= I= F−
NZ−; 80 I− F+(1c) W−(1t) E−; 81 F−(1c)
W+(2c 1p) E− I+ NZ− NZ−r(1d) R+
A+(1t); 82 E+ I−(2p) F+(1d) W+(1t 1d); 83
I−(1d) F− W−(1t) E+; 84 R−; BI > 80 SA 1-0-
0-1.
Electrician. S's most capped player; world's
most capped centre. Scottish XV v Arg 73; Tg
74, 77; Fj 82. S > 81 NZ. Scottish Schs
swimming champ.

RENWICK, William Norman   *Scotland*
Loretto Sch, Oxford Univ, London Scottish,
Edinburgh W, The Army.
b 29.11.14; kia 15.6.44 Italy.
Wing, 2-1-0-1 (6 − 2t).
38 E+(2t); 39 W−.
The Army. Blue 36-7.

RESIDE, Walter Brown ('Wattie') *New Zealand*
Gladstone, Wairarapa, NZ Maoris.
b 6.10.05 Masterton.
Flanker, 1-0-0-1.
29 A.
Farmer. NZ > 29 A.

RETIEF, Daniel Francois ('Daan') *South Africa*
Pretoria Univ, N Transvaal.
b 28.6.25 Lichtenburg.
No 8, 9-5-0-4 (12 − 4t).
55 BI− BI+ BI+(1t); 56 A+(1t) A+(1t) NZ−
NZ+(1t) NZ− NZ−.
Potato Bd employee. Converted from wing to
no 8 for SA.

REVALLIER, Daniel ('Sam')   *France*
Gaillac, Graulhet.
b 20.8.48 Rabastens.
Lock, 14-7-0-7.
81 S+ I+ W+ E+ A− A− R+ NZ− NZ−; 82
W− S− I+ R− Arg+.

RÉVILLON, Jean   *France*
RCF, CASG.
Wing, 3-0-0-3.
26 I− E−; 27 S−.

REW, Henry   *England*
Exeter Sch, Exeter, Blackheath, The Army,
Barbarians, Devon.
b 11.11.06; *d* 11.12.40.
Lock/prop, 10-5-2-3.
29 S− F+; 30 F+ S=; 31 W= S− F−; 34 W+
I+ S+; BI > 30 A, NZ 4-1-0-3.

The Army. Served WW2 as Maj; died of
wounds.

REYNECKE, H.J.   *South Africa*
W Prov.
Forward, 1-1-0-0 (3 − 1t).
10 BI+(1t).

REYNOLDS, Frank Jeffrey   *England*
Cranleigh Sch, O Cranleighans, RMC
Sandhurst, The Army, Blackheath, Barbarians,
Kent.
b 2.1.16 Canton, China.
FH, 3-2-0-1 (7 − 1t 1d).
37 S+; 38 I+(1t) S−(1d); BI > 38 SA 2-1-0-1.
The Army/hotel mgr. Hockey & ckt (2nd XI)
for Kent. Served WW2 Duke of Wellington's
Rgt; mentioned in despatches twice. Emigrated
to SA.

REYNOLDS, Leopold J.   *Australia*
King's Sch Parramatta, Sydney Univ, NSW.
Forward, 2-1-0-1.
10 NZ+r NZ−.

REYNOLDS, Ross John   *Australia*
Manly, NSW Country, NSW.
b 28.9.58.
No 8, 4-2-0-2 (4 -1t).
84 Fj+ NZ+(1t) NZ− NZ−.
A > 82 NZ.

REYNOLDS, Shirley   *England*
Christ's Hosp, Richmond, Barbarians.
b 1874; *d* 9.1.46 Epsom.
Forward, 4-1-1-2.
1900 W− I+ S=; 01 I−.

RHAPPS, John James ('The   *Wales*
Salford Lion')**
Penygraig.
b −.7.1877 Aberaman, Aberdare; *d* 23.1.50
Salford.
Forward, 1 1 0 0.
1897 E+.
Collier/licensee. Salford RL 1897. RL Lancs,
W. 4 RL Cup Final sides 1900, 02, 03, 06.
Groundsman/trainer at Ardwick Ath ground,
Manchester, until closure 1920s.

RHIND, Patrick Keith   *New Zealand*
St Bede's Coll, Christchurch, Canterbury, NZ
Army, S Island.
b 20.6.15 Lyttelton.
Prop, 2-2-0-0.
46 A+ A+.
Army/transport co man dir. Served WW2; 22
apps Comb Servs.

RHODES, John   *England*
Castleford, Yorks.

Forward, 3-1-0-2.
1896 W+ I− S−.
Glassblower. Hull KR RL 1897.

RIBÈRE, Eugène *France*
Perpignan, Quillan.
b 14.6.02 Thuir.
No 8/flanker, 34-12-0-22 (27 − 9t).
24 I−; 25 I−(1t) NZ−(1t) S−; 26 S− I− W−
M−(1t); 27 I−(1t) S− W− E+ G+ G−(1t); 28
S− NSW− I−(1t) E− G+ W+; 29 I− E−(1t)
G+; 30 S+ I+ E− W−; 31 I+(1t) S− W− E+
G+(1t); 32 G+; 33 G+.

RICE-EVANS, Walter *Wales*
Cowbridge GS, Crawfurd Coll Maidenhead,
Oxford Univ, Swansea.
b 10.9.1865; *d* 9.6.09 Neath.
Forward, 3-0-0-3.
1890 S−; 1891 E− S−.
Landed proprietor. Blue 1890.

RICHARDS, Alfred Renfrew *South Africa*
W Prov.
b 1868 Grahamstown; *d* 9.1.04 Salisbury,
Rhodesia.
Half-back, 3-0-0-3.
1891 BT− BT− BT−.
Capt v BT 3rd Test 1891. Ref SA v BT 4th Test
1896 & accused of bias in allowing SA winning t,
scored by Alf Larard. Cricket for SA, 1 Test v E
1895; bro Dicky played for SA 1888.

RICHARDS, Clifford *Wales*
Pontypool.
b 01 Hafodyrynys.
Wing, 5-3-1-1 (6 − 2t).
22 E+(1t) S= I+ F+; 24 I−(1t).

RICHARDS, David Stuart *Wales*
Neath GS, Welsh SS, Cardiff Coll, Swansea,
Barbarians.
b 23.5.54 Cwmgwrach.
Centre/wing, 17-8-1-8 (16 − 4t).
79 F− E+(1t); 80 F+(1t) E− S+(1t) I− NZ−;
81 E+ S− I+ F−(1t); 82 I− F+; 83 E= S+ I+
R−r; BI > 80 SA 1-0-0-1.
Wales B v F 75-7. W > 78 A. Wales XV v R 79,
Maoris 82. Barbarians v BI 77.

RICHARDS, Dean *England*
John Cleveland Coll Hinckley, England SS,
Roanne (F), Leicester.
b 11.7.63 Nuneaton.
No 8, 2-1-0-1 (8 − 2t).
86 I+(2t) F−.
Police. 1st E forward to score 2t on debut since
H. Wilkinson v W 29.

RICHARDS, Edward William *Australia*
Qld.

b −; *d* 28.
Forward, 4-0-0-4.
04 BT− BT−; 05 NZ−; 07 NZ−r.
Gold miner/Army. Bro of Tom.

RICHARDS, Ernest Edward *England*
Penryn, Plymouth A, Devon.
b 11.3.05 Plymouth.
SH, 2-1-0-1.
29 S− F+.
RN/bricklayer. London Highfield RL.

RICHARDS, Ernest Gwyn *Wales*
Bryncethin, Bridgend, Cardiff, Torquay Ath,
Devon.
b 22.12.05 Bryncethin; *d* 17.12.85 Bridgend.
FH, 1-0-0-1.
27 S−.
Miner. Uncle of K.H.L. Huddersfield RL 31.

RICHARDS, E.S. *Wales*
Swansea.
Forward, 2-0-0-2.
1885 E−; 1887 S−.

RICHARDS, Geoff *Australia*
Wasps (E), NSW.
FB, 3-2-0-1 (3 − 1p).
78 NZ−r NZ+; 81 F+(1p).
Ar > NZ 78.

RICHARDS, Idris ('The Bank') *Wales*
Cardiff.
b −; *d* 62.
Lock/no 8, 3-1-0-2.
25 E− S− F+.
Bank official. Capt Cardiff 23-4. Chmn Merthyr
RFC.

RICHARDS, Joseph *England*
Bradford, Yorks.
Forward, 3-2-0-1.
1891 W+ I+ S−.

RICHARDS, Kenneth Henry
Llewellyn *Wales*
Bridgend GS, Welsh SS, Bridgend, Cardiff,
Glam.
b 29.1.34; *d* 8.1.72 Bridgend.
FH, 5-2-0-3 (9 − 1t 2p).
60 SA−; 61 E+ S− I+(1t 2p) F−.
Schoolmaster. Nephew of Ernest Gwyn. Salford
RL 61. Killed in car accident.

RICHARDS, Maurice Charles
Rees *Wales*
Cardiff.
b 2.2.45 Ystrad.
Wing, 9-4-1-4 (21 − 7t)
68 I− F−; 69 S+(1t) I+ F=(1t) E+(4t) NZ−
NZ−(1t) A+; BI > 68 SA 3-1-1-1.

Scientific officer steel co/computer analyst. With W. Llewellyn & R.A. Gibbs most t (4) in int; with Gibbs most t (6) in Champ season. W's most t (3) in tour match, v Otago NZ 69. Wales XV v Fj 64. W > 69 NZ, A & Fj. Wales jnr long jump champ 63. Salford RL 69. 2 GB RL Tests. 2 Wales RL apps.

RICHARDS, Rees   *Wales*
Aberavon.
Forward, 3-3-0-0.
13 S+ F+ I+.
Miner. Wigan RL.

RICHARDS, Rex ('Tarzan')   *Wales*
Cross Keys, Newbridge.
b 4.2.34.
Prop, 1-1-0-0.
56 F+.
High diver. Lives in US.

RICHARDS, Stephen   *England*
Brookhouse
Clifton Coll, Oxford Univ, Richmond, Bristol, Sheffield, Mdx.
b 28.8.41 W Kirby.
Hooker, 9-3-1-5.
65 W− I− F+ S=; 67 A− I+ F− S+ W−.
Solicitor. Blue 62. Oxford-Cambridge > 63 E Africa, Rhodesia & SA. E > 67 Can.

RICHARDS, T. Bryan   *Wales*
Neath GS, Cambridge Univ, Swansea, London Welsh, Barbarians.
b 44.
FH, 1-0-0-1.
60 F−.
Schoolmaster. Blue 55.

RICHARDS, Thomas J. MC   *Australia*
Transvaal, Bristol, Glos, Qld, Biarritz (F).
b 1887 Vegetable Creek (now Emmaville), NSW; *d* −.9.35.
Prop, 3-2-0-1 (3 − 1t).
08 W−(1t); 09 E+; 12 US+.
Mining official/journalist. Bro of E.W. Olympic rugby gold medal 08. BIr > SA 10; pl in 3 Tests. WW1 gassed badly.

RICHARDS, T.L.   *Wales*
Maesteg.
No 8, 1-0-0-1.
23 I−.
Miner.

RICHARDS, Victor ('Shirts')   *Australia*
Randwick HS, NSW.
b 3.9.11; *d* 83.
Five-eighth/centre, 5-1-0-4.
36 NZ− NZ−r M+; 37 SA−; 38 NZ−.
Retailer.

RICHARDSON, Geoffrey Colin   *Australia*
NSW.
b 17.4.49 Taree, NSW.
Five-eighth, 9-2-0-7 (10 − 1t 1d 1p).
71 SA− SA− SA−; 72 NZ−(1d) NZ− Fj+; 73 Tg+(1t 1p) Tg− W−.
The Army/PE teacher. RL.

RICHARDSON, James Vere   *England*
Uppingham Sch, Oxford Univ, Birkenhead Pk, Richmond, Barbarians, Cheshire, Mdx.
b 16.12.03.
Centre, 5-5-0-0 (23 − 1t 8c 1d).
28 NSW+(3c) W+(2c) I+(1t 1d) F+(3c) S+.
Stockbroker/man dir. Blue 25. Hockey blue 25; played for Essex 24-6. Served WW2, Maj RA.

RICHARDSON, Johnstone   *New Zealand*
('Jock')
Normal Sch Dunedin, Alhambra, Otago, Waikiwi, Southland, Pirates, S Island.
b 2.4.1899 Dunedin.
Lock/flanker, 7-5-1-1 (3 − 1t).
21 SA+ SA− SA=; 24 I+ W+; 25 E+ F+(1t).
Clerk. NZ > 22 A, 24-5 BI (capt v I,W & E). Accountant-sec Southland. Otago shot putt champ 21-2. Moved to A to work in Public Works Dept.

RICHARDSON, Stanley John   *Wales*
Treherbert SMS, Aberavon.
b 1.4.49 Blaen-y-Cwm.
Prop, 2-1-0-1.
78 A−r; 79 E+.
Wales B v F 77. W > 78 A.

RICHARDSON, William Ryder   *England*
Manchester GS, Oxford Univ, Manchester, Lancs.
b −.9.1861; *d* 30.7.20.
Half-back, 1-1-0-0.
1881 I+
Blue 1881. 1st E player to be capped from sch. Sec R St George's GC, Sandwich; sec to Amateur Golf Champ comm. Served WW1, Lt in W Yorks Rgt.

RICHEY, H.A.   *Ireland*
Finchley GS, Trin Coll Dublin.
Forward, 2-1-0-1.
1889 W+; 1890 S−.

RICKARDS, Arnold Robert   *Wales*
Cardiff.
b 17.8.01 Thornbury.
Lock, 1-1-0-0 (3 − 1t).
24 F+(1t).
Police.

RICKARDS, Cyril Henry *England*
Rugby Sch, Cheltenham Coll, RMA Woolwich,
Gipsies.
b 11.1.1854; *d* 25.2.20.
Forward, 1-0-1-0.
1873 S=.
The Army.

RICKIT, Haydn *New Zealand*
Auckland, Waikato, NZ Maoris.
b 19.2.51 Taupo.
Lock, 2-2-0-0.
81 S+ S+.

RIDGEWAY, Ernest Charles *Ireland*
Dublin HS, Kilkenny Coll, Wanderers.
b 16.9.11 Dublin.
FB/centre, 5-4-0-1 (3 − 1t).
32 S+ W+; 35 E− S+(1t) W+.
Bus exec.

RIDLAND, Alexander James *New Zealand*
Star, Southland, S Island.
b 3.3.1882 Invercargill; *d* 5.11.18 France.
Hooker, 3-2-0-1.
10 A+ A− A+.
Blacksmith. NZ > 10 A. Served WW1, NZ
Rifle Bde; died of wounds during last week of
War.

RIKA, Wiremu See Heke, W.R.

RILEY, Norman M. *South Africa*
E Transvaal.
b 25.2.39.
FH, 1-0-0-1.
63 A−.
Cricket for NE Transvaal, OFS.

RILEY, Sidney Austin *Australia*
Ponsonby Sch, Bayfield Sch, Ponsonby,
Newtown, NSW.
b 18.4.1878 Auckland; *d* 31.3.64 Auckland.
1-0-0-1.
03 NZ−.
Industrialist. Auckland RL 12. Served with NZ
Army WW1. Nephew Brian played RL for NZ.

RIMMER, Gordon *England*
King George V Sch Southport, Wigan OB,
Waterloo, Lancs.
b 28.2.25 Southport.
SH, 12-3-0-9.
49 W− I−; 50 W−; 51 W− I− F−; 52 SA−
W−; 54 W+ NZ− I+ S+; BI > 50 SA 1-0-0-1.
Brewing/manufacturer's agent. Golf for Lancs.
Served WW2 Fleet Air Arm.

RIMMER, Laurance Ivor *England*
Birkenhead Sch, Oxford Univ, O Birkonians,
Bath, Cheshire, Dorset & Wilts.

b 31.5.35.
Flanker, 5-1-1-3.
61 SA− W− I− F= S+.
Schoolmaster. Blue 58. Oxford-Cambridge > 59
Far East. Ckt for Authentics & Free Foresters.
Coached rugby at RGS Lancaster & Dauntsey's
Sch.

RING, H. John *Wales*
Aberavon.
b 13.11.1900 Port Talbot; *d* 10.11.84 Wigan.
Wing, 1-0-0-1 (3 − 1t).
21 E−(1t).
Groundsman/Leyland Motors employee/pro
masseur. 76t Aberavon 20-1. Wigan RL 22,
Rochdale Hornets 32. Leading RL t scorer 4
consec yrs. RL for E, W & GB.

RING, Mark Gerarde ('Ringo') *Wales*
Lady Mary HS Cardiff, Cardiff Youth, Welsh
Youth, Cardiff.
b 15.10.62 Cardiff.
Centre, 5-1-1-3.
83 E=; 84 A−; 85 S+ I− F−.
Civil Service. Wales B > 83 Spain. W Player of
Year 85. Out of game for year after leg inj April
85. W baseball cap.

RINGER, Paul *Wales*
Cardigan GS, Madeley Coll, Poly of Wales,
Cardigan, Leicester, Ebbw Vale, Vichy,
Llanelli.
b 28.1.51 Aberporth.
Flanker, 8-4-0-4 (8 − 2t).
78 NZ−; 79 S+ I+(1t) F− E+(1t); 80 F+ E−
NZ−.
Property agent. Wales B v Arg 78. Wales XV v
R 79. Sent off E v W 80. Cardiff RL 81. 2 Wales
RL.

RINGLAND, Trevor Maxwell *Ireland*
Larne GS, Queen's Univ Belfast, Ballymena.
b 13.11.59 Belfast.
Wing, 21-8-1-12 (28 − 7t).
81 A−; 82 W+(1t) E+ F−; 83 S+ F+ W− E+;
84 F− W− E− S− A−; 85 S+(2t) F= W+(1t)
E+; 86 F− W−(1t) E−(1t) S−(1t); BI > 83 NZ
1-0-0-1.
Solicitor. Five Nations v Overseas XV,
Twickenham 86. 3t I v J 85.

RIORDAN, C.E. *South Africa*
Transvaal.
2-1-0-1.
10 BI+ BI−.

RIORDAN, William F. *Ireland*
CBC Cork, Cork Constitution.
b 30.8.1883; *d* 11.7.39.
Forward, 1-0-1-0.
10 E=.

RIPLEY, Andrew George   *England*
Greenway Comp Sch Bristol, Univ of E Anglia, Rosslyn Pk, Mdx.
b 1.12.47.
No 8, 24-8-1-15 (8 − 2t).
72 W− I− F− S− SA+, 73 NZ− W− I− F+ S+ NZ+ A+(1t); 74 S− I− F= W+(1t); 75 I− F− S+ A− A−; 76 A+ W− S−; BI > 74 SA.
Chartered accountant/banking. AAA 400m hurdles semi-finalist 78. Noted basketball player. Author of book 'Rugby Rubbish' pub 85.

RISMAN, Augustus Beverley   *England*
Walter
Cockermouth GS, Loughborough Coll, Manchester Univ, UAU, Cumberland, Lancs.
b 23.11.37 Salford.
FH/centre, 8-1-3-4 (8 − 1c 2p).
59 W− I+(1p) F= S=(1p); 61 SA− W− I−(1c) F=; BI > 59 A 2-2-0-0, NZ 2-1-0-1.
Schoolmaster. Sc t in BI 4th Test win v NZ 59. Lawn tennis for UAU & Cumberland. Leigh RL 61-6; Leeds 66. Son of Gus Risman, GB RL capt.

RITCHIE, George   *Scotland*
Edinburgh Acad, Merchiston Castle Sch, Merchistonians.
b 16.4.1848; *d* 31.1.1896.
Forward, 1-1-0-0.
1871 E+.
Brewer. Played in 1st int, S v E 1871.

RITCHIE, George F.   *Scotland*
Dundee HS, Dundee HSFP.
No 8, 1-0-0-1.
32 E−.
Wholesale grocer.

RITCHIE, James McPhail   *Scotland*
George Watson's Coll, Watsonians.
b 10.7.07; *d* 6.7.42 Rawalpindi.
Prop, 6-4-0-2 (3 − 1p).
33 W+ E+ I+; 34 W−(1p) I+ E−.
Insurance. Water polo international. Served WW2; died of enteric fever.

RITCHIE, James S.   *Ireland*
Methodist Coll Belfast, London Irish, Barbarians, Mdx.
b 11.12.26 Belfast.
Flanker, 2-0-0-2.
56 F− E−.
Mechanical engr. Son in law of W. E. Crawford. Capt I on 1st app.

RITCHIE, William Traill   *Scotland*
Wanganui Collegiate Sch NZ, Cambridge Univ, Barbarians.
b 11.3.1882 Dunedin; *d* 22.5.40 Timaru.
Wing, 2-1-0-1.
05 I− E+.
Farmer/chmn Timaru Harbour Board. Blue 03-4. Served WW1, NZ Field Artillery. At school excelled at ath, cricket & rowing.

RITSON, John Anthony Sydney   *England*
DSO OBE MC TD
Uppingham Sch, Durham Univ, Edinburgh Univ, Northern, Barbarians, Northumb.
b 18.8.1887 Pelton, Co Durham; *d* 16.10.57 Guildford.
Forward, 8-7-0-1 (6 − 2t).
10 F+ S+(1t); 12 F+; 13 SA− W+ F+ I+(1t) S+; BT(uncap) > 08 NZ.
The Army/mines inspector. Served WW1, Maj Durham LI. Mentioned in despatches twice; MC 17. DSO 18. HM Inspector for Mines in S & W. OBE 35.

RITTSON-THOMAS, George   *England*
Christopher
Dragon Prep Sch Oxford, Sherborne Sch, Oxford Univ.
b 18.12.26.
Flanker, 3-0-0-3 (3 − 1t).
51 W−(1t) I− F−.
Lloyd's. Blue 49-50. Swimming blue 49; Olympic trialist.

RIVES, Jean-Pierre   *France*
French Schs, French Univs, Toulouse, Barbarians (E), French Barbarians.
b 31.12.52 Toulouse.
Flanker, 60-39-3-18 (20 − 5t).
75 E+ S+ I− Arg+(1t) Arg+ R+; 76 S+ I+(1t) W− E+ US+ A+(1t) A+ R−; 77 W+ E+ S+ I+ Arg+ Arg= R+; 78 E+ S+ I+ W− R+; 79 I= W+ E− S+ NZ− NZ+ R+; 80 W− E−(1t) S− I+ SA−; 81 S+ I+ W+ E+ A− A−; 82 W− E− S−(1t) I+ R−; 83 E+ S+ I− W+ A= A+ R+; 84 I+ W+ E+ S−.
Court official/PR exec. F's most capped flanker. Capt F 34 times, most by any player. F > 80 SA (capt). Autobiography 'Jean-Pierre Rives − A Modern Corinthian' pub 86.

ROBB, Campbell Glynn   *Ireland*
Campbell Coll Belfast, Queen's Coll Belfast.
b 25.2.1882; *d* −.
Wing, 5-1-0-4 (3 − 1t).
04 E− S− W+; 05 NZ−; 06 S−(1t).
Medicine. Served in RAMC.

ROBB, G.H.   *Scotland*
Uppingham Sch, Glasgow Univ.
b −.9.1858; *d* −.
Forward, 2-0-1-1.
1881 I−; 1885 W=.

ROBBIE, John Cameron   *Ireland*
Dublin HS, Trin Coll Dublin, Greystones,
Cambridge Univ, Pontypool, Transvaal.
b 17.11.55 Dublin.
SH, 9-0-0-9 (9 − 3p).
76 A−(2p) F−(1p) NZ−; 77 S− F−; 81 F− W−
E− S−; BI > 80 SA 1-1-0-0.
Brewery exec. Capt I v W Schs ckt. Blue 77-8.
Emigrated to SA. Reserve SA v E 84.

ROBBINS, Graham Leslie   *England*
Fairfax HS, England Colts, Coventry,
Midlands.
b 24.9.56 Sutton Coldfield.
No 8, 2-1-0-1.
86 W+ S−.
Out of rugby for yr because of two operations
for cartilage inj. England B v I 85.

ROBBINS, Peter George Derek   *England*
Bishop Vesey GS Sutton Coldfield, Oxford
Univ, Moseley, Coventry, Barbarians,
Warwicks.
b 21.9.33.
Flanker, 19-11-4-4.
56 W− I+ S+ F−; 57 W+ I+ F+ S+; 58 W=
A+ I+ S=; 60 W+ I+ F= S+; 61 SA− W−; 62
S=.
Schoolmaster/exec/journalist. Blue 54-7.
Oxford-Cambridge > 55 US, Can, 56 Arg, 57 E
Africa & Rhodesia, 63 E Africa & SA (player-
mgr). Rugby corr 'Financial Times' & 'The
Observer'.

ROBERTS, Alan Dixon MC   *England*
Durham Sch, Cambridge Univ, Northern,
Barbarians, Northumb.
b 1887; *d* 1.9.40.
Wing, 8-5-0-3 (15 − 5t).
11 W−(1t) F+ I− S+; 12 I+(2t) S− F+(1t); 14
I+(1t).
Solicitor. Served WW1, Pte in R Fusiliers &
Capt in Welch Rgt; wounded.

ROBERTS, Barry Thomas   *Australia*
St Joseph's Coll, NSW.
b 3.10.33.
Wing, 1-0-0-1.
56 SA−.
Insurance.

ROBERTS, Cyril   *Wales*
Bryncoch, Neath.
b 19.12.30 Briton Ferry.
Wing, 2-1-0-1 (3 − 1t).
58 I+(1t) F−.
Metal Box.

ROBERTS, David Edward Arfon   *Wales*
Llandovery Coll, Welsh SS, Oxford Univ,
London Welsh, Langholm, Waterloo, Llanelli.

b 23.1.09.
SH, 1-0-0-1.
30 E−.
Schoolmaster/schools inspector. Served WW2,
Capt in RA.

ROBERTS, Edward James   *New Zealand*
Brooklyn Sch, St James, Wellington, Athletic,
N Island.
b 10.5.1891 Wellington; *d* 27.2.72 Wellington.
SH, 5-3-1-1 (4 − 2c).
14 A+ A+(1c) A+(1c); 21 SA− SA=.
Commercial traveller. NZ > 13 NAm, 14 A
(played in all 11 matches); 20 A. Father Harry
rep NZ 1884. Bros Harry & Len rep Wellington.
Rep Wellington at ckt.

ROBERTS, Edward John ('Ned')   *Wales*
Morfa Rgrs, Llanelli.
b 1868 New Dock Llanelli; *d* 40 Llanelli.
FB, 3-1-0-2.
1888 S+ I−; 1889 I−.
Tinplate millman. Played part of match Llanelli
v Gloucester 1888 at FB wearing overcoat
because of snowstorm.

ROBERTS, Ernest William OBE   *England*
Framlingham Sch, Merchant Taylors' Sch
Crosby, RNEC Keyham, RNC Dartmouth, RN,
Barbarians, Devon.
b 14.11.1878 Lowestoft; *d* 19.11.33
Manchester.
Forward, 6-0-0-6.
01 W− I−; 05 NZ−; 06 W− I−; 07 S−.
RN. Reached rank of Rear Adm. 1st Servs
player to capt int team, E v S 07. Served WW1,
Grand Fleet destroyers. RFU comm & sel.

ROBERTS, Evan   *Wales*
Llanelli.
b 1861 Llanelli; *d* 16.10.27 Llanelli.
Forward, 2-1-0-1.
1886 E−; 1887 I+.
Tinplater.

ROBERTS, Frederick   *New Zealand*
Thorndon Sch, Oriental, Wellington, N Island.
b 7.4.1881 Wellington; *d* 21.7.56 Wellington.
SH, 12-9-1-2 (11 − 2t 1c 1p).
05 S+ I+ E+ W−; 07 A+ A+ A=; 08 AW+(2t
1c 1p) AW+; 10 A+ A− A+.
Clerk. NZ > 05 A, 05-6 BI,F & NAm (30 apps),
07 & 10 A.

ROBERTS, Gareth John   *Wales*
Gowerton Comp, Welsh SS, UWIST, UAU,
Pontarddulais, Swansea, Cardiff.
b 15.1.59 Pontlliw.
Flanker, 2-1-0-1 (4 − 1t).
85 F−r E+(1t).
Pharmacist. Rec 21 apps for Welsh Schs. 12

times r for Wales. Wales B v F 78, 83-5. Wales B
> 83 Spain. Wales XV v Maoris 82. Team-mate
of E ints Tony Swift, Huw Davies in UWIST 9-0
v Exeter Univ UAU final 80.

ROBERTS, Geoffrey Dorling *England*
('Khaki') OBE QC
Rugby Sch, Oxford Univ, Harlequins, Exeter,
Barbarians, Devon.
b 27.8.1886; *d* 7.3.67.
Forward, 3-1-0-2 (6 − 3c).
07 S−; 08 F+(2c) W−(1c).
Law. Blue 07-8. Tennis blue. Called to Bar 12.
Served WW1, Maj Devonshire Rgt; 5 times
mentioned in despatches. Recorder of Exeter
32-46 & Bristol 46-60. Prosecutor at Nuremburg
War Trials.

ROBERTS, George *Scotland*
George Watson's Coll, Watsonians, Barbarians.
b 13.2.14 Edinburgh; *d* −.6.43 Japan.
FB, 5-3-0-2.
38 W+ I+ E+; 39 W− E−.
Outstanding golfer. Served WW2; died as
POW.

ROBERTS, Henry Flaxmore *Australia*
Qld.
b 39.
Five-eighth/centre, 4-1-1-2.
61 Fj+ Fj= SA− F−.

ROBERTS, H. Meirion *Wales*
Cardiff HS, Cardiff, Barbarians.
b 34 Aber, Bangor.
Centre, 8-3-0-5.
60 SA−; 61 E+ S− I+ F−; 62 S− F+; 63 I−.
Sales rep. Barbarians v SA 61.

ROBERTS, James *England*
Mill Hill Sch, Cambridge Univ, O Millhillians,
Sale, Barbarians, Mdx.
b 25.6.32.
Wing, 18-8-5-5 (18 − 6t).
60 W+(2t) I+ F= S+(1t); 61 SA− W− I−(1t)
F= S+(1t); 62 W= I+(1t) F− S=; 63 W+ I=
F+ S+; 64 NZ−.
Man dir. Blue 52-4.

ROBERTS, John *Wales*
Cardiff HS, Welsh SS, Cambridge Univ,
Cardiff, Barbarians.
b 08; *d* 68.
Centre/wing, 13-4-1-8 (15 − 5t).
27 E− S− F+(2t) I− NSW−; 28 E− S+(1t) I−
F−; 29 E− S+(2t) F+ I=.
Missionary/minister. Blue 27-8. Bro of Bill,
played against him, Cambridge v Oxford 28.
Missionary to Amoy, China 31. Took up
pastorate in Otterburn, Northumb 37. Same yr

played for Cardiff Ath, one match v Chepstow
in stockinged feet.

ROBERTS, Michael Gordon *Wales*
Colwyn Bay CS, Ruthin Sch, Liverpool, Colwyn
Bay, Trin Coll Dublin, Birkenhead Pk, Irish
Wolfhounds, Oxford Univ, Beacon Hill Boston
(US), London Welsh, Surrey, Barbarians,
London Cos.
b 20.2.46 St Asaph, N Wales.
Lock, 8-6-0-2 (4 − 1t).
71 E+ S+ I+ F+; 73 I+ F−; 75 S−; 79 E+(1t);
BI > 71 A, NZ.
Accountant/lecturer/sports marketing & travel
consultant. Blue 68. Wales B v F 70. W > 73
Canada. Wales XV v Tonga 74. One of 7 L
Welsh players on BI > A, NZ 71. Tournament
dir WRU Pro-Am Golf. Bro Dafydd double
bass player in Welsh National Youth Orchestra.

ROBERTS, Reginald Sidney *England*
Coventry, Warwicks.
b 11 Coventry.
Hooker, 1-1-0-0.
32 I+.
Huddersfield RL 32.

ROBERTS, Richard William *New Zealand*
Kaponga, Taranaki, Okaiawa, Hawera, N
Island, Comb Servs.
b 23.1.1889 Manaia; *d* 8.3.73 Okaiawa.
Centre, 5-5-0-0 (29 − 7t 4c)
13 A+(1t 3c) US+(3t); 14 A+ A+(1t) A+(2t
1c).
Farmer. NZ > 13 NAm, 14 A (capt). Served
WW1, NZ Rifle Bde; played for Comb Servs in
King's Cup & > SA 19. Leading NZ racehorse
owner.

ROBERTS, Sam *England*
Swinton.
FB, 2-1-0-1.
1887 W+ I−.

ROBERTS, Tom *Wales*
Risca, Newport.
b 1897.
Prop/lock, 9-5-1-3.
21 S− F+ I+; 22 E+ S= I+ F+; 23 E− S−.
Collier/police.

ROBERTS, Victor George *England*
Falmouth GS, Penryn, Swansea, Harlequins,
Barbarians, Cornwall.
b 6.8.24 Penryn.
Flanker, 16-7-0-9 (6 − 2t).
47 F+(1t); 49 W− I− F+ S+; 50 I+(1t) F− S−;
51 W− I− F− S+; 56 W− I+ S+ F−; BI > 50
A, NZ.
Customs & Excise official. Served WW2, Lt
RNVR. Capt E twice. Barbarians comm.

ROBERTS, William *Wales*
Cardiff HS, Welsh SS, Oxford Univ, Univ of
Rome, Cardiff.
b 20.2.09.
FH, 1-0-0-1.
29 E−.
Journalist/pig breeder. Blue 28-30. Bro of John.
Doctorate of Political Science in Rome. Served
WW2, Welsh Guards.

ROBERTSHAW, Albert Rawson *England*
Bradford, Barbarians, Yorks.
b 1861 Bradford; *d* 17.11.20.
Back/centre, 5-4-1-0.
1886 W+ I+ S=; 1887 W+ S+.
Bro of Percy. Introduced centre threequarter
theory to E 1886. His club, Bradford, helped
form NU 1895.

ROBERTSHAW, Percy *England*
Bradford.
Back, 0-0-0-0.
Bro of Rawson. With Harry Eagles awarded E
cap in the 1888 side that never played, because
of dispute over setting up IB. Neither player
made an int app.

ROBERTSON, Alexander *Scotland*
Hamilton
Ayr Acad, King William's Sch IOM, W of
Scotland.
Forward, 1-1-0-0.
1871 E+.
Played in 1st int, S v E 1871.

ROBERTSON (later *Scotland*
ROBERTSON-DURHAM), Alexander Weir
Edinburgh Acad, Edinburgh Academicals.
b 11.12.1877; *d* 28.10.41 Gullane.
Wing, 1-0-0-1.
1897 E−.
Chartered accountant.

ROBERTSON, Bruce John *New Zealand*
Hastings Boys' HS, Ardmore Coll, Counties,
Ardmore, N Island.
b 9.4.52 Hastings.
Centre, 34-23-2-9 (22 − 4t 2d).
72 A+ A+ S+; 73 E+ I= F−; 74 A+ A= A+;
74 I+; 76 I+(1t) SA− SA+ SA−(1t) SA−; 77
BI+ BI+(1d) BI+; 77 F−(1d) F+; 78 A+ A+
A− W+ E+ S+(1t); 79 F+ F− A−; 80 A+ A−
W+; 81 S+ S+(1t).
Schoolmaster/wine & spirits merchants sales
rep. NZ's most capped centre. NZ > 72-3 BI,F
& NAm, 74 A & Fj & I,W & E, 76 SA, 77 F, 78
BI, 79 A, 80r A & Fj; NAm & W. Bro Bill rep
Counties 80.

ROBERTSON, David Donaldson *Scotland*
Glasgow Acad, Cambridge Univ.

Wing, 1-0-0-1.
1893 W−.
Blue 1892.

ROBERTSON, Duncan *Scotland*
Edinburgh Acad, Edinburgh Academicals.
b 30.6.1851; *d* 29.9.07.
Forward, 1-0-1-0.
1875 E=.
Sheriff Substitute for Aberdeenshire.

ROBERTSON, Duncan John *New Zealand*
King Edward Tech Coll, Zingari-Richmond,
Otago, S Island.
b 6.2.47 Dunedin.
1st five-eighth/FB, 10-6-1-3 (4 − 1t).
74 A+(1t) A= A+

ROBERTSON, Ian *Scotland*
George Watson's Coll, Aberdeen Univ,
Cambridge Univ, London Scottish, Watsonians,
Barbarians.
b 17.1.45 London.
FH, 8-2-0-6 (9 − 1t 2d).
68 E−; 69 E− SA+; 70 F− W−(1t 1d) I−(1d)
E+ A−.
BBC. Blue 67. Scottish XV v Arg (2) 69.
Coached various sides, inc Cambridge Univ.
Racehorse owner.

ROBERTSON, Ian Jeffrey *Australia*
NSW.
b 51.
Wing, 2-2-0-0 (8 − 2t).
75 J+(2t) J+.

ROBERTSON, Ian Peter *Scotland*
Macintosh
George Watson's Coll, Watsonians.
b 1887; *d* 9.5.49.
Wing, 1-1-0-0 (6 − 2t).
10 F+(2t).
Chartered accountant.

ROBERTSON, Ian William *South Africa*
Rhodesia.
b 28.4.50 Salisbury, Rhodesia.
Centre/FB, 5-4-0-1 (3 − 1d).
74 F+ F+; 76 NZ+(1d) NZ− NZ+.
Commercial rep. Selected at centre v NZ, 1st
Test 76, played FB.

ROBERTSON, J. *Scotland*
Glenalmond Acad, Clydesdale.
b 5.5.1883; *d* −.
FH, 1-1-0-0.
08 E+.

ROBERTSON, Keith William *Scotland*
Melrose GS, Kelso HS, Melrose.
b 5.12.54 Hawick.

Wing/centre, 33-12-2-19 (30 − 6t 2d).
78 NZ−; 79 W− E= I=(1t) F−(1t) NZ−; 80
W− E−; 81 F− W+ E− I+ R+ A+; 82 E+ I−
F+ A+(1t) A−; 83 I− F−(1t) W− E+; 84 E+
I+(1t) F+ R−(1d) A−; 85 I−(1d) F− W− E−
(1t); 86 I+.
Dir motor sales co/financial consultant. Scottish
XV v J 76, Fj 82.

ROBERTSON, Lewis   *Scotland*
Cargilfield Sch, Fettes Coll, RMA Sandhurst,
London Scottish, US Portsmouth, The Army.
b 4.8.1883 Hawthornden; *d* 3.11.14 Ypres.
Forward, 9-3-0-6.
08 E+; 11 W−; 12 W− I− E+ SA−; 13 W− I+
E−.
The Army. Capt, Queen's Own Cameron
Highlanders; died of wounds.

ROBERTSON, Michael Alexander   *Scotland*
Stewart's Coll, Gala.
b 29.
Flanker, 1-1-0-0.
58 F+.
Cattle foods co sales dir.

ROBERTSON, Robert Dalrymple   *Scotland*
Highgate Sch, London Scottish, The Army.
Forward, 1-1-0-0.
12 F+.
The Army. One of few rugby ints to emerge
from football only school.

ROBILLIARD, Alan Charles   *New Zealand*
Compton
Ashburton HS, Christchurch, Canterbury, S
Island.
b 20.12.03 Ashburton.
Wing, 4-2-0-2.
28 SA− SA+ SA− SA+.
Jeweller. NZ > 24-5 BI,F & C, 26 A, 28 SA.
Father Fred, bros Noel, Guy & Jack played rep
rugby.

ROBINS, John Denning   *Wales*
Birkenhead Pk, Bradford, Yorks, RN,
Coventry, Barbarians.
b 17.5.26 Cardiff.
Prop, 11-7-1-3.
50 E+ S+ I+ F+; 51 E+ S− I= F−; 53 E− I+
F+; BI > 50 NZ 3-0-1-2, A 2-2-0-0.
Schoolmaster. Played for E in Servs int 44-5.
Coach at Loughborough Colls, Sheff Univ. 1st
BI coach, 66 > A, NZ.

ROBINS, Russell John   *Wales*
Pontypridd GS, Welsh SS, Pontypridd, The
Army, Yorks.
b 32 Pontypridd.
No 8/lock/flanker, 13-10-0-3 (3 − 1t).
53 S+; 54 F+ S+; 55 E+ S− I+ F+; 56 E+(1t)

F+; 57 E− S− I+ F+; BI > 55 SA 4-2-0-2.
NCB/Army teacher. Leeds RL 59.

ROBINSON, Arthur   *England*
Cheltenham Coll, Cambridge Univ, Hartlepool
R, Blackheath, Mdx.
b 8.11.1865 Darlington; *d* 9.4.48.
Forward, 4-3-0-1.
1889 NZN+; 1890 W− S+ I+.
Barrister. Blue 1886-7. Capped in 1888 E side
that did not play. Called to Bar 1890. Ckt for
Durham.

ROBINSON, Charles Edward   *New Zealand*
Bluff, Southland, S Island.
b 5.4.27 Bluff; *d* 4.3.83 Bluff.
Flanker, 5-4-0-1 (3 − 1t).
51 A+ A+ A+; 52 A− A+(1t).
Co supervisor. NZ > 51 A. 1t v A 52 after
switching to wing during match. Rep Southland
at rowing 45-8. Coach & comm Southland.

ROBINSON, Ernest T.   *England*
Coventry.
b 17.1.29.
Hooker, 4-2-1-1.
54 S+; 61 I− F= S+.
Engr. 7 yrs between caps.

ROBINSON, George Carmichael   *England*
('Tot') JP
Dame Allan's Sch Newcastle, Gosforth, Percy
Pk, Northumb, Blackheath, Barbarians.
b 1876; *d* 29.5.40.
Wing, 8-2-1-5 (24 − 8t).
1897 I−(1t) S+(1t); 1898 I−(1t); 1899 W−(1t);
1900 I+(2t) S=; 01 I−(1t) S−(1t).
Coal exporter. Sc t on all but 1 app for E. Rep
Northumb on RFU 23-40. E sel 21-9; pres RFU
39-40. JP 32-40. Scratch golfer.

ROBINSON, Ian R.   *Wales*
Cardiff, Barbarians.
b 21.2.46.
Lock, 2-0-1-1.
74 F= E−.
Transport mgr. Wales B v F 72. Wales XV r v J
73.

ROBINSON, John James   *England*
Appleby GS, Cambridge Univ, Headingley,
Burton, Barbarians, Midlands, Yorks.
b 28.6.1872 Burton; *d* 3.1.59 Leeds.
Forward, 4-2-0-2 (3 − 1t).
1893 S−; 02 W−(1t) I+ S+.
Solicitor. Blue 1892. Ckt blue 1894. Capped 10
yrs after 1st app, longest gap in int rugby.

ROBINSON, Thomas Trevor   *Ireland*
Hull DSO
Wesley Coll, Trin Coll Dublin, Wanderers.

349

b 17.11.1880; d 62.
FH, 10-3-0-7 (3 − 1t).
04 E− S−; 05 E+ S+ W−(1t) NZ−; 06 SA−;
07 E+ S− W−.
Medicine. Served WW1, Lt Col in RAMC.

ROBSON, Adam   *Scotland*
Hawick HS, Hawick, Edinburgh Coll of Art,
Edinburgh Univ, Barbarians.
b 16.8.28 Hawick.
Flanker, 22-7-2-13.
54 F−; 55 F− W+ I+ E−; 56 F+ W− I− E−;
57 F+ W+ I− E−; 58 W− A+ I− E=; 59 F−
W+ I− E=; 60 F−.
Schoolmaster. Barbarians > 57 Can. Pres SRU
84-5.

ROBSON, Alan   *England*
Northern, Northumb.
Hooker, 5-4-1-0.
24 W+ I+ F+ S+; 26 W=.
Bro in law of Herbert Whitley.

ROBSON, Matthew   *England*
George Heriot's Sch, Heriot's FP, Oxford Univ,
Blackheath, Barbarians, Northumb.
b 16.12.08; d 30.11.83 Edinburgh.
Centre, 4-2-1-1 (3 − 1t).
30 W+ I− F+(1t) S=.
Univ administrator/Colonial Service. Blue 29.
Served WW2, R W African Frontier Force.

ROCHE, Christopher   *Australia*
Brisbane State HS, Australian Schs, Qld Univ,
Brisbane, Qld.
b 9.9.58.
Flanker, 17-8-1-8 (12 − 3t).
82 S− S+ NZ− NZ+ NZ−; 83 US+(1t) Arg−
Arg+(1t) NZ− It+ F=(1t) F−; 84 Fj+ NZ+
NZ− NZ− I+.
Articled clerk. A > 81-2 BI (played as hooker v
Oxford Univ); 82 NZ; 83 It & F; 84 Fj; 84 BI.
Australian Player of Year 82. RL 85.

ROCHE, J.   *Ireland*
Wanderers.
Forward, 7-1-1-5 (2c).
1890 S− W=(1c) E−; 1891 E− S− W−; 1892
W+(1c).

ROCHE, Richard Edwin   *Ireland*
Garbally Pk Coll Ballinasloe, UC Galway,
Galwegians.
b 22.2.30 Woodford, Co Galway.
Wing, 4-1-1-2.
55 E= S−; 57 S+ W−.
Civil engr. 5ft 5in.

ROCHE, William Joseph   *Ireland*
Mungret Coll, UC Cork, Cardiff, Newport,
Barbarians.

b −; d 26.6.83 Bandon.
No 8/flanker, 3-0-0-3.
20 E− S− F−; BI > 24 SA.
Medicine. Played for Newport before & after
WW1. Entered for Welsh ABA middlweight
boxing champs, but did not box because there
were no other challengers. Kt of Malta.

ROCHON, Aimée   *France*
Montferrand.
Hooker, 1-1-0-0.
36 G+.

ROCYN-JONES, David Nathan   *Wales*
MD FRCS JP
The Leys Sch, Cambridge Univ, St Mary's
Hosp, Cardiff.
b 17.7.02 Abertillery; d 26.1.84.
FB, 1-0-0-1.
25 I−
Medicine. Son of Sir David, WRU pres 47-53.
Blue 23. WRU pres 64-5; chief medical officer.

RODD, John Adrian Tremayne   *Scotland*
Downside Sch, RNC Dartmouth, US
Portsmouth, RN, Comb Servs, Hants, London
Scottish, Barbarians.
b 35.
SH, 14-3-2-9.
58 F+ W− A+ I− E=; 60 F− W−; 62 F−; 64
F+ NZ= W−; 65 F− W− I−.
RN/merchant banker/dir sports trophies co.
Comb Servs v A 57; SA 61. Became Lord
Rennell. Related to Brian Boobbyer.

RODDY, Patrick Joseph   *Ireland*
St Mary's Coll, RCSI, Bective Rgrs.
b −; d 19.3.67.
Centre, 2-0-0-2.
20 S− F−.
Medicine.

RODERICK, William Buckley JP   *Wales*
Sidney Coll, Llanelli.
b 17.1.1862 Llanelli; d 1.2.08 Llanelli.
Forward, 1-1-0-0.
1884 I+.
Solicitor. Welsh cycling champ.

RODRIGO, Marius   *France*
Bordelais, Mauléon.
Lock/prop, 2-1-0-1.
31 I+ W−

RODRIGUEZ, Enrique Engardo   *Australia*
Cordoba, Arg, Warringah, NSW.
b 20.6.52 Arg.
Prop, 12-9-0-3.
84 Fj+ NZ+ NZ− NZ− E+ I+ W+ S+; 85 C+
C+ NZ− Fj+.
Played 15 times for Arg. Arg > E; F; NZ & SA

77-82; Arg > A 83, played in both Tests. Returned to settle in Sydney 84; qualified for A under local residential rule. Overseas XV v Five Nations, Twickenham 86.

RODRIGUEZ, Laurent *France*
Lannemazan, Mont-de-Marsan.
b 28.6.60 Poitiers.
Flanker/no 8/lock, 22-10-2-10 (8 − 2t).
81 A− A− R+ NZ− NZ−; 82 W− E− S− I+ R−; 83 E+ S+; 84 I+ NZ− NZ− R+; 85 E= S+ I= W+ J+(1t) J+(1t).
F > 81 A; 85 Arg. Five Nations v Overseas XV, Twickenham 86.

ROE, Robin MC *Ireland*
King's Hosp Sch, Trin Coll Dublin, Lansdowne, Barbarians.
b 11.11.28 Skierke, Ballybrophy, Co Leix.
Hooker, 21-7-2-12.
52 E−; 53 F+ E= S+ W−; 54 F− E− S+ W−; 55 F− E= S− W−; 56 F− E− S+ W+; 57 F+ E− S+ W−; BI > 55 SA.
Minister/Army chaplain. MC Aden 67.

ROGE, Lucien *France*
Béziers.
b 18.10.32 Cassenou, Herault.
Wing/centre, 15-10-1-4 (12 − 4t).
52 It+(1t); 53 E− W− It+; 54 S+ Arg+ Arg+(1t); 55 S+ I+; 56 W− It+(2t) E+; 57 S−; 60 S+ E=.
Dentist.

ROGERS, Chris D. *South Africa*
Milton HS Bulawayo, Wanderers, Zimbabwe, Gazelles, Transvaal, Barbarians.
b 10.10.56 Bulawayo, Rhodesia.
Hooker, 4-4-0-0.
84 E+ E+ SAm+ SAm+.
Motor mechanic.

ROGERS, Derek Prior ('Budge') *England*
OBE
Bedford Sch, City Univ, Bedford, Barbarians, E Midlands.
b 20.6.35.
Flanker, 34-10-6-18 (9 − 3t).
61 I−(1t) F= S+; 62 W= I+ F−; 63 W+ I= F+ S+ NZ− NZ− A−; 64 NZ− W= I−(1t) F+ S− (1t); 65 W− I− F+ S=; 66 W− I= F− S−; 67 A− S+ W− NZ−; 69 I− F+ S+ W−; BI > 62 SA 2-0-1-1.
Management consultant. Once E's rec cap holder. Capt E 7 times. E sel. OBE for servs to rugby.

ROGERS, John Henry *England*
Bromsgrove Sch, Moseley Woodstock, Moseley, Barbarians, Midland Cos.
b −; *d* −.3.22.

Forward, 4-2-0-2 (1t).
1890 W− S+ I+(1t); 1891 S−.
1st Moseley player to app for E. In Moseley XV that beat Cardiff 1886, their only defeat of season.

ROGERS, Walter Lacey Yea DSO *England*
Rugby Sch, Oxford Univ, The Army, Blackheath, Barbarians, Kent.
b 20.9.1878; *d* 10.2.48.
2-0-0-2.
05 W− I−.
The Army. Blue 1898-1900. Served WW1, RFA & RHA, Maj. Mentioned in despatches 3 times; DSO 18. Reached rank of Lt Col.

ROGERSON, John *Scotland*
Kelvinside Acad, Kelvinside Academicals.
FB, 1-0-0-1.
1894 W−.
Medicine.

ROLAND, Ernest T. *Scotland*
Merchiston Castle Sch, Edinburgh Academicals.
b −; *d* 1897.
Back, 2-1-0-1.
1884 I+ E−.

ROLLERSON, Douglas Leslie *New Zealand*
Wesley Coll, Massey Univ, Manawatu, NZ Jnrs, NZ Univs, London NZ (E), Mdx.
b 14.5.53 Papakura.
FB/1st five-eighth, 8-7-0-1 (24 − 1t 4c 2d 2p).
80 W+(2c 1p); 81 S+ SA+(1t 1c) SA− SA+(1c 1d 1p) R+(1d) F+r F+.
NZ > 76 Arg & Uruguay, 80 NAm & W, 81 R & F. Played in UK 79-80.

ROLLET, Jacques ('La Hire') *France*
Bayonne.
b 18.8.34 Bayonne.
Hooker, 5-4-0-1.
60 Arg+; 61 NZ− A+; 62 It+; 63 I+.
Electrician.

ROLLITT, David Malcolm *England*
Barnsley GS, Bristol Univ, Loughborough Colls, UAU, Bristol, Wakefield, Richmond, W Cos, S Cos, Glos.
b 24.3.43 Wombwell.
Flanker/no 8, 11-5-0-6 (3 − 1t).
67 I+ F− S+ W−; 69 I− F+(1t) S+ W−; 75 S+ A− A−.
Schoolmaster. Various teaching posts, inc Colston's, Bristol.

ROLLO, David Miller Durie *Scotland*
Bell Baxter Sch, Howe of Fife, Barbarians.
b 7.7.34.
Prop, 40-15-5-20.

59 E=; 60 F− W− I+ E− SA−; 61 F− SA−
W+ I+ E−; 62 F− W+ E=; 63 F+ W− I+ E−;
64 F+ NZ= W− I+ E+; 65 F− W− I− E=
SA+; 66 F= W− I+ E+ A+; 67 F+ W+ E−
NZ−; 68 F− W− I−; BI > 62 SA.
Farmer.

ROMÉRO, Henri   *France*
Montauban.
 b 11.7.36 Sigean, Aude.
No 8/flanker, 7-4-0-3.
62 S+ E+ W− I+ It+ R−; 63 E−.
Credit Agricole office worker.

ROMEU, Jean-Pierre   *France*
Montferrand.
 b 15.4.48 Tyrosse, Landes.
FH/FB, 34-21-3-10 (262 − 4t 27c 9d 55p).
72 R+(1c 3p); 73 S+(1d 3p) NZ+(1c 1p) E−
(1c) W+(1d 3p) I− R+(1d); 74 W=(1d 3p)
E=(1t 1c 1d 1p) S−(1d 1p) Arg+(1c 2p)
Arg+(3c 3p) R−(2p) SA− SA−r; 75 W− SA−
(1c 1d 3p) Arg+(1c 1p) Arg+(1t 2c 4p) R+(3c
1p); 76 S+(3p) I+(1c) W−(1c 1p) E+(1t 3c)
US+(1t 3c 5p); 77 W+(1c 2p) E+ S+(2c 1p)
I+(1p) Arg+(1d 4p) Arg= NZ+(1c 1d 3p)
NZ−(1p) R+(3p).
PE teacher. F's rec pts scorer. French rec 71 pts
(7 apps) F > SA 75, inc 14 pts 2nd Test.

RONCORONI, Anthony Dominic   *England*
Sebastian MC
Rossall Sch, W Herts, Richmond, E Midlands,
Midland Cos, Surrey.
 b 16.3.08; *d* 20.7.53.
Lock, 3-1-0-2.
33 W− I+ S−.
Snr exec 'Financial Times' advertising dept.
Served WW2 W Desert. POW; escaped through
It. Wounded in D-Day landings 44.

ROOKE, Charles Vaughan   *Ireland*
Trin Coll Dublin.
 b 1874; *d* 6.1.46 Wellington, NZ.
Forward, 19-7-2-10.
1891 E− W−; 1892 E− S− W+; 1893 E− S=
W−; 1894 E+ S+ W+; 1895 E− S− W−; 1896
E+ S= W+; 1897 E+ S−.
Minister. Sec Leinster RU.

ROOS, Gideon D.   *South Africa*
Stellenbosch Univ, W Prov.
2-1-0-1 (3 − 1t).
10 BI− BI+(1t).
Bro of Paul.

ROOS, Paul Johannes ('Polla')   *South Africa*
Stellenbosch Univ, W Prov.
 b 1880; *d* 22.9.48.
Flanker, 4-3-1-0.
03 BT+; 06 I+ W+ E=.

Schoolmaster/school inspector/politician. Bro of
Gideon. SA's 1st Tour capt > 06-7 BI, F;
described his players as 'De Springbokken' to
Press in UK. Mgr 1st Jnr Springboks > 32 Arg.
Strongly religious; once refused to play for W
Prov because it meant travelling on Sabbath.
When teaching in Pietersburg he cycled 70 miles
every Saturday to play in Pretoria & then cycled
back the same day to avoid travelling on
Sunday. Served as backbencher in SA
Parliament. Within hours of his final speech in
Parliament he died, one of the most revered
figures in SA rugby.

ROPER, Roy Alfred   *New Zealand*
New Plymouth Boys' HS, HSOB, Tukapa,
Taranaki, Comb Servs, N Island.
 b 11.8.23 Owhango.
Wing/centre, 5-3-1-1 (9 − 3t).
49 A−(1t); 50 BI=(1t) BI+(1t) BI+ BI+.
Chartered accountant. Treasurer Taranaki 52-
71. Rep W Coast in NZ ath champs. Son rep
Manawatu.

ROQUES, Alfred ('The Rock')   *France*
Cahors.
 b 17.2.25 Cozes-Moudenard, Tarn.
Prop, 30-22-5-3.
58 A+ W+ It+ I+ SA= SA+; 59 S+ E= W+
I−; 60 S+ E= W+ I+ It+ Arg+ Arg+ Arg+;
61 S+ SA= E= W+ It+ I+; 62 S+ E+ W− I+
It+; 63 S−.
Groundsman. Also known as 'Le Pepe
Duquercy'.

ROQUES, Jean-Claude   *France*
Brive.
 b 19.3.43 Brive.
FH, 4-3-1-0.
66 S= I+ It+ R+.
Accountant.

ROSE, David M.   *Scotland*
Jedforest.
 b 20.2.31 Jedburgh.
Wing, 7-1-0-6 (9 − 3t).
51 F−(2t) W+ I− E− SA−; 53 F−(1t) W−.
Mill employee/concrete co rep. Nephew of C.
McDonald. Huddersfield RL.

ROSE, Hugh Alexander   *Australia*
King's Sch Sydney, NSW.
 b 15.11.46.
Flanker/no 8, 13-2-0-11.
67 I− NZ−; 68 NZ− NZ− F+ I− S−; 69 W−
SA− SA− SA− SA−; 70 S+.
Schoolmaster.

ROSE, W. Marcus H.   *England*
Cambridge Univ, Coventry.
FB, 5-2-1-2 (41 − 1t 2c 11p).

81 I+(1t 1c) F−(4p); 82 A+(3p) S=(1p) I−(1c 3p).
Blue 79-81.

ROSENBERG, Wilfred *South Africa*
Sydney GS (A), Grey Coll, Witwatersrand Univ, Transvaal.
b 18.6.34 Sea Point, Cape Town.
Centre, 5-2-1-2 (6 − 2t).
55 BI+(1t) BI− BI+; 56 NZ−(1t); 58 F=.
Dentist/PR exec. Spent much of early life in A.
Leeds (E) RL.

ROSENBLUM, Rupert George *Australia*
The Scots Coll, NSW.
b 1.1.42.
Five-eighth, 3-1-0-2 (11 − 1t 1c 2p).
69 SA−(1c 2p) SA−; 70 S+(1t).
Solicitor.

ROSEWELL, John S.H. *Australia*
NSW.
b 1882; *d* −.
Forward, 2-0-1-1.
07 NZ− NZ=.
Labourer. RL 07.

ROSS, Alexander William *Australia*
Sydney GS, NSW.
b 24.11.05; *d* −.
FB, 9-5-1-3 (26 − 7c 4p).
29 NZ+; 30 BI+; 31 M+(1c 1p) NZ−(2c); 32 NZ− NZ−(1c); 33 SA+(1c); 34 NZ+(2c 3p) NZ=.
Medicine. NSW > 27 BI, F. Capt A 1st major tour > 33 SA; missed most of tour because of appendicectomy at start of tour.

ROSS, Andrew *Scotland*
Kilmarnock.
b 8.11.04.
Hooker, 2-1-0-1.
24 F− W+; BI > 24 SA.

ROSS, Andrew *Scotland*
Royal HS, Royal HSFP.
b 1879 Edinburgh; kia 6.4.16.
Forward, 5-2-0-3.
05 W− I− E+; 09 W− I+.
Marine engr. Sgt, 29th Canadians. In Arctic when war declared.

ROSS, Andrew Russell *Scotland*
George Watson's Coll, Loretto Sch, Edinburgh Univ, RMA Sandhurst, Barbarians.
b 13.1.1892 Juniper Green, Edinburgh; *d* 80.
Lock/flanker, 4-0-0-4.
11 W−; 14 W− I− E−.
Medicine.

ROSS, Daniel Joseph *Ireland*
Clongowes Coll, Belfast Acad, Belfast A.
b 1865; *d* 8.11.51.
Wing/centre, 4-0-0-4.
1884 E−; 1885 S−; 1886 E− S−.

ROSS, Edward Johnson *Scotland*
Fettes Coll, London Scottish.
Forward, 1-0-0-1.
04 W−.
Bro of James. Served in Indian Army.

ROSS, George Robert Porter *Ireland*
Portadown Coll, CIYMS.
b 1.11.25 Portadown.
No 8, 1-0-0-1.
55 W−.
HM.

ROSS, Graham Tullis *Scotland*
George Watson's Coll,, Watsonians.
b 5.7.28.
FH, 4-0-0-4.
54 NZ− I− E− W−.
Catering co dir.

ROSS, Iain A. *Scotland*
Hillhead HS, Hillhead HSFP.
b 15.12.28.
SH, 4-1-0-3.
51 F− W+ I− E−.

ROSS, James ('Jummy') *Scotland*
Cargilfield Sch, Fettes Coll, London Scottish, Barbarians.
b 15.2.1880 Rutherford, Roxburgh; kia 31.10.14 Messines.
Forward, 5-4-0-1.
01 W+ I− E+; 02 W−; 03 E+.
Stock Exchange. Bro of Edward. Pte, London Scottish Rgt.

ROSS, J.F. *Ireland*
NIFC.
Half-back, 1-0-0-1.
1886 S−.

ROSS, J.P. *Ireland*
Lansdowne.
Wing/centre, 4-0-0-4.
1885 E− S−; 1886 E− S−.

ROSS, Kenneth Innes *Scotland*
Boroughmuir Sch, Boroughmuir FP.
b 15.3.37.
Flanker, 11-5-1-5 (6 − 2t).
61 SA− W+ I+(2t) E−; 62 F− W+ I+ E=; 63 F+ W− E−.
Whisky sales rep. Glasgow-Edinburgh v A 57; SA 61. 1st Boroughmuir FP player to be capped by S.

ROSS, Norman G. *Ireland*
Foyle Coll, Malone.
No 8, 2-1-0-1.
27 F+ E−.
Sheep farmer. Born in A.

ROSS, William Alexander *Scotland*
Hillhead HS, Hillhead HSFP.
b 15.11.13; kia 28.9.42.
FH, 2-1-0-1.
37 W+ E−.
Chartered accountant/RAF.

ROSS, William McC. *Ireland*
RBAI, Queen's Univ Belfast, Barbarians.
b −; *d* 7.1.69.
Flanker, 9-3-0-6 (6 − 2t).
32 E− S+ W+(2t); 33 E− W+ S−; 34 E− S−;
35 NZ−.
Medicine. Ulster v NZ 35.

ROSS, William Scott *Australia*
Brisbane GS, Qld.
b 56.
Hooker, 13-7-0-6 (4 − 1t).
79 I− I− Arg+; 80 Fj+ NZ+ NZ− NZ+; 82
S− S+; 83 US+(1t) Arg− Arg+ NZ−.

ROSSBOROUGH, Peter Alec *England*
King Henry VIII Sch Coventry, O Coventrians,
Durham Univ, UAU, Brit Univs, Coventry,
Durham Co, Warwicks.
b 30.6.48 Coventry.
FB, 7-2-0-5 (34 − 1t 3c 1d 7p).
71 W−(1p); 73 NZ+(2c) A+(1c 2p); 74 S−(1d)
I−; 75 I− F−(1t 4p).
Schoolmaster. E Under 25s v Fj 70.

ROSSER, David William Albert *England*
Rochdale GS, O Rochdalians, Cambridge Univ,
Manchester, The Army, Wasps, London Welsh,
Barbarians, Hants.
b 27.3.40 Portsmouth.
Centre, 5-1-1-3.
65 W− I− F+ S=; 66 W−.
Schoolmaster. Blue 62-4. Oxford-Cambridge >
63 Africa, 65 Arg. Taught English at Dulwich
Coll 65-9 & Sherborne.

ROSSER, Melville A. *Wales*
Penarth.
b 18.4.01 Machen.
Centre/FB, 2-1-0-1.
24 S− F+.
Police/licensee. Selected as wing, switched to
FB v F 24 when B.O. Male suspended. Leeds
RL 24.

ROSSIGNOL, Jean-Claude *France*
('L'Oiseau')
Brive.

b 10.8.45 Grignols.
Prop, 1-1-0-0.
72 A+.
Municipal employee.

ROSSOUW, D.H. ('Daantjie') *South Africa*
Stellenbosch Univ, SA Univs, W Prov.
b 5.9.30.
Centre, 2-2-0-0 (3 − 1t).
53 A+(1t) A+.

ROTHERHAM, Alan *England*
Uppingham Sch, Oxford Univ, Coventry,
Richmond, Mdx.
b 31.7.1862; *d* 30.8.1898.
Half-back, 12-9-2-1 (2t).
1882 W+; 1883 S+(1t); 1884 W+(1t) S+; 1885
W+ I+; 1886 W+ I+ S=; 1887 W+ I− S=.
Barrister. Cousin of Arthur. Blue 1882-4. Called
to Bar 1888.

ROTHERHAM, Arthur *England*
Uppingham Sch, Cambridge Univ, St Thomas's
Hosp, Mdx W, Richmond, Coventry,
Barbarians, Surrey, Midland Cos.
b 27.5.1869; *d* 3.3.46.
SH, 5-1-1-3.
1898 S= W+; 1899 W− I− S−; BTuncap >
1891 SA.
Medicine. Cousin of Alan. Blue 1890-1. Asst
MO London Co Asylums; Visitor in Lunacy 31-
44.

ROTHWELL, Peter Ratcliffe *Australia*
N Sydney Tech HS, NSW.
FB, 4-1-0-3 (8 − 1c 2p).
51 NZ− NZ−(1c 1p) NZ−(1p); 52 Fj+.
Woolclasser.

ROTTENBURG, Harry *Scotland*
Kelvinside Academy, Loretto Coll, Cambridge
Univ, London Scottish, Barbarians.
b 6.10.1875 Glasgow; *d* 25.3.55.
FB, 5-2-2-1.
1899 W+ E+; 1900 W− I= E=.
Electrical engr. Blue 1898.

ROUAN, Jean *France*
Narbonne.
FB, 2-1-0-1.
53 S+ I−.

ROUCARIÈS, Gérard *France*
Perpignan.
b 13.8.32 Rivesaltes.
Lock, 1-0-0-1.
56 S−.
Wine grower.

ROUFFIA, Lucien *France*
Narbonne, Romans.

FB, 4-1-0-3.
45 BF− W−; 46 W+; 48 I−.

ROUGERIE, Jacques *France*
Montferrand.
Prop, 1-1-0-0.
73 J+.

ROUGHEAD, William Nicol *Scotland*
Rugby Sch, Edinburgh Academicals, Oxford
Univ, London Scottish, Barbarians.
b 19.9.05; d 22.4.75.
Hooker, 12-4-1-7.
27 NSW+; 28 F+ W− I− E−; 30 I− E=; 31 F+
W− I− E+; 32 W−.
Literary agent. Blue 24-6.

ROUGHLEY, David F.K. *England*
Beaumont Sch Warrington, Liverpool.
b 10.12.47 Warrington.
Centre, 3-1-0-2.
73 A+; 74 S− I−.

ROUJAS, R. *France*
Tarbes.
SH, 1-0-0-1.
10 I−.

ROUSSEAU, Willie P. *South Africa*
Diocesan Coll Rondebosch, Stellenbosch Univ,
Oxford Univ, W Prov.
b 11.8.06.
Centre, 2-1-0-1.
28 NZ+ NZ−.
Lawyer. Blue 29.

ROUSSET, Gérard *France*
Béziers.
b 21.1.53 Bour-les-Valence.
No 8, 2-1-0-1 (4 − 1t).
75 SA−; 76 US+(1t).
Municipal employee.

ROUSSIÉ, Max ('Mayou') *France*
Villeneuve.
b 15.7.12 Marmande; d 2.6.59 St Justin-des-
Landes.
SH, 4-3-0-1 (9 − 2t 1p).
31 S− G+(2t); 32 G+(1p); 33 G+.
PE teacher. Switched to RL. Died in motor
accident.

ROUX, Francois du Toit *South Africa*
('Mannetjies')
Stellenbosch Univ, W Prov, N Transvaal.
b 12.4.39.
Wing/centre, 27-18-2-7 (18 − 6t).
60 W+; 61 A+ A+(1t); 62 BI= BI+ BI+
BI+(2t); 63 A−; 65 A− A− NZ− NZ− NZ+
NZ−; 68 BI+ BI+(1t) F+ F+; 69 A+(1t) A+
A+ A+(1t); 70 I= NZ+ NZ− NZ+ NZ+.

Farmer/SAAF pilot. SA > 60-1 BI, F; r > 69-70
BI.

ROUX, Ockert Antonie *South Africa*
N Transvaal.
b 22.2.47 Pretoria.
Centre/FB, 7-0-3-4.
69 S− E−; 70 I= W=; 72 E−; 74 BI− BI=.
Quantity surveyor. SA > 68 F; 69-70 BI, F; 71
A.

ROW, Frank Leonard *Australia*
NSW.
b 28.1.1877; d 28.1.50.
Centre, 3-1-0-2.
1899 BT+ BT− BT−.
Banking. A's 1st capt. Bro of Norman.

ROW, Norman Edward *Australia*
NSW.
b 23.3.1883; d 28.10.68.
Prop, 6-2-1-3 (15 − 2t 3c 1p).
07 NZ− NZ=; 09 E+(1t); 10 NZ− NZ+(1c)
NZ−(1t 2c 1p).
Engr/tramways workshop mgr. Bro of Frank.

ROWAN, Norman Arthur *Scotland*
('Norrie')
Forrester HS, Boroughmuir.
b 17.9.51 Edinburgh.
Prop, 8-2-0-6.
80 W± E−; 81 F− W+ E− I+; 84 R−; 85 I−.
Building contractor. Scotland B.

ROWAND, Robert *Scotland*
Glasgow HS, Glasgow HSFP, Barbarians.
No 8/prop, 7-4-0-3.
30 F− W+; 32 E−; 33 W+ E+ I+; 34 W−.

ROWELL, Robert Errington *England*
Wymondham Coll, Loughborough Coll,
Leicester, Fylde, Waterloo, Leics, Lancs,
Midland Cos.
b 29.8.39.
Lock, 2-0-1-1.
64 W=; 65 W−.
Schoolmaster/tech rep.

ROWLAND, Ernest Melville *Wales*
Chardstock Coll, St David's Coll Lampeter,
London Welsh.
b 21.9.1864 Whitland, Pembs; d −.
Forward, 1-0-0-1.
1885 E−.
Son of a vicar. Sent down for term for violating
Coll discipline at St David's, Lent 1886. Name
taken from the books for gross violation of Coll
rules and discipline June 1886. Not ordained.

ROWLANDS, Charles Foster *Wales*
Aberavon.

355

b 1900 Blaengwynfi; *d* 10.11.58 Morriston.
Wing, 1-1-0-0.
26 I+.
Civil engr.

ROWLANDS, Daniel Clive　　　　*Wales*
Thomas ('Top Cat')
Ystradgynlais GS, Welsh SS, Abercarn,
Cwmllynfell Youth, Pontypool, Swansea.
b 14.5.38 Upper Cwmtwrch.
SH, 14-6-2-6 (3 − 1d).
63 E= S+(1d) I− F− NZ−; 64 E= S+ I+ F=
SA−; 65 E+ S+ I+ F−.
Schoolmaster/rep. Capt W on all 14 apps. WRU
coach 68-74. Selector 74-79, 82-85 (retired, then
returned because of ill-health of John Bevan).
Mgr W > 78 A & BI v Rest of World 86.

ROWLANDS, Gwyn　　　　*Wales*
RAF, Cardiff.
b 19.12.28 Berkhamsted.
Wing, 4-3-0-1 (13 − 1t 2c 2p).
53 NZ+(2c 1p); 54 E−(1t 1p) F+; 56 F+.
Medicine.

ROWLANDS, Keith A.　　　　*Wales*
Aberdare GS, Cardiff, Barbarians.
b 7.2.36 Brithdir.
Lock, 5-2-1-2.
62 F+ I=; 63 I−; 65 I+ F−; BI > 62 SA 3-0-1-2.
Business exec. WRU selector. IB rep 83−.

ROWLES, George R.　　　　*Wales*
Penarth.
Half-back, 1-0-0-1.
1892 E−.
Carpenter.

ROWLES, Peter G.　　　　*Australia*
NSW.
b 18.11.52.
Centre/Five-eighth, 2-1-0-1.
72 Fj+; 73 E−.
Schoolmaster. Manly RL.

ROWLEY, Alfred J.　　　　*England*
Coventry.
b 08 Coventry.
No 8, 1-0-0-1.
32 SA−.
Quality engr.

ROWLEY, Harrison Cotton　　　*New Zealand*
Banks
Southland Boys' HS, Mangatainoka, Bush,
Hunterville, Wanganui, Netherton, Thames
Valley, Kaitaia Pirates, N Auckland, N Island.
b 15.6.24 Cromwell; *d* 16.12.56 Waimate.
No 8, 1-0-0-1.
49 A−.

Stock agent. Died when car struck by train on
level crossing.

ROWLEY, Hugh Campbell　　　　*England*
Manchester GS, Bowdon & Lymm,
Manchester, Cheshire, Lancs.
b −.3.1854; *d* −.
Forward, 9-5-3-1 (3t).
1879 S= I+(1t); 1880 I+ S+; 1881 I+ W+(1t)
S=(1t); 1882 I= S−.
The Army. Served largely in India. His family
fdrs of Lancs CCC & Old Trafford.

ROY, Allan　　　　*Scotland*
Fettes Coll, Waterloo, Barbarians.
b −.5.11.
Lock, 6-3-0-3.
38 W+ I+ E+; 39 W− I− E−.
Jute merchant. Served WW2, Cameron
Highlanders.

ROYDS, Sir Percy Molyneux　　　　*England*
Rawson CMG CB MP
Eastmans Naval Sch Southsea, RNC
Greenwich, US Portsmouth, RN, Blackheath,
Barbarians, Kent.
b 1874; *d* 25.3.55.
Back, 3-1-1-1 (3 − 1t).
1898 S=(1t) W+; 1899 W−.
RN. Rear Adm. Ref W v F 21; F v I 23. Rep RN
on RFU 20-28. IB mem 27-49. E sel 28-31. RFU
Trustee 29-55; pres 27-8. Author of 1st
authoritative book on laws of game, 'The
History of the Laws of Rugby Football', pub 49.
Medal for rescuing diplomats at Peking 1900.
Served WW1, commanded HMS Canterbury at
Zeebrugge & Jutland; mentioned in despatches,
Legion d'Honneur, CMG 17. CB (mil) 24. Tory
MP for Kingston-on-Thames 37-45.

ROYLE, A.V. ('Artie')　　　　*England*
Broughton Rgrs.
FB, 1-1-0-0.
1889 NZN+.

ROXBURGH, James Russell　　　　*Australia*
King's Sch Sydney, NSW, Harlequins (E).
b 28.10.46.
Prop, 9-2-0-7.
68 NZ− NZ− F+; 69 W− SA− SA− SA−
SA−; 70 S+.
Schoolmaster. Played for Harlequins 71-2.

RUDD, Edward Lawrence　　　　*England*
St Edward's Coll Liverpool, Oxford Univ,
Liverpool, Barbarians, Lancs.
b 28.9.44 Liverpool.
Wing, 6-0-2-4.
65 W− I− S=; 66 W− I= S−.
Banking. Blue 63-4. In SAm for most of 65-6.

RUEBNER, George   *Australia*
Randwick HS, NSW.
b 30.8.42.
Wing, 2-0-0-2 (3 − 1t).
66 BI−(1t) BI−.
Sales mgr. RL.

RUIZ, André   *France*
Tarbes.
b 30.3.37 Semeac.
Centre, 2-0-0-2.
68 SA− R−.
Hairdresser. RL.

RUPERT, Jean-Joseph   *France*
Tyrosse.
b 7.3.38 St Jean-de-Marsacq, Landes.
Flanker, 14-9-2-3 (12 − 4t).
63 R=; 64 S− Fj+(1t); 65 E− W+ It+(1t); 66
S= I+ E+ W−(1t) It+; 67 It+(1t) R+; 68 S+.
Estate agent.

RUSSELL, Charles Joseph   *Australia*
('Boxer')
NSW.
b 1884; *d* −.5.57.
Wing, 5-1-1-3 (9 − 3t).
07 NZ− NZ− NZ=; 08 W−(1t); 09 E+(2t).
Warehouseman. Rec 23t A > BI 08-9. Olympic
rugby gold medal 08. RL.

RUSSELL, John ('Jack')   *Ireland*
St Colman's Coll Cork, UC Cork, Barbarians.
b 30.6.09 Cobh; *d* 13.5.77 Blarney.
Lock/flanker, 19-8-0-11 (6 − 2t).
31 F− E+ S+ W− SA−; 33 E− W+ S−; 34 E−
S−(2t) W−; 35 E− S+ W+; 36 E+ S+ W−; 37
E− S+.
Medicine.

RUSSELL, Richard Forbes   *England*
St Peter's Sch York, Cambridge Univ,
Leicester, Castleford, Cork, Yorks, Midlands.
b 5.4.1879 Bingham, Notts; *d* 30.5.60, Lezayre,
IOM.
Forward, 1-0-0-1.
05 NZ−.
Schoolmaster. Nephew of Sir Timothy Carew
O'Brien, Mdx & E Test ckter. Served WW1,
special constable IOM Police at Ramsey.
Taught at Fermoy, Co Cork.

RUSSELL, William L.   *Scotland*
Glasgow Academy, Glasgow Academicals,
Glasgow Univ.
Flanker, 4-1-0-3.
05 NZ−; 06 W− I+ E−.

RUTHERFORD, Donald   *England*
Tynemouth HS, Percy Pk, Preston
Grasshoppers, St Luke's Coll, Wasps,
Gloucester, Barbarians, Glos, Northumb.
b 22.9.37.
FB, 14-4-3-7 (36 − 6c 8p).
60 W+(1c 2p) I+(1c) F= S+(3c 1p); 61 SA−;
65 W−(1p) I− F+(2p) S=; 66 W−(1p) I=(1p)
F− S−; 67 NZ−(1c).
Schoolmaster/tech administrator RFU 69.

RUTHERFORD, John Young   *Scotland*
Selkirk HS, Scottish Schs, Jordanhill Coll of PE,
S of Scotland, Selkirk.
b 4.10.55 Selkirk.
FH, 37-16-4-17 (55 − 7t 9d).
79 W− E=(1t) I= F− NZ−; 80 I− F+(1t) E−
(1t); 81 F−(1t) W+ E− I+(1d) NZ− NZ−
A+(1d); 82 E=(1d) I−(1t) F+(1t) W+(1d)
A+(1d) A−; 83 E+ NZ=(2d); 84 W+ E+ I+
F+ R−; 85 I− F− W−(2d) E−; 86 F+ W−
E+(1t) I+ R+; BI > 83 NZ 1-0-0-1.
Schoolmaster/building soc mgr, insurance
consultant. S's most capped FH. Scotland B v I,
F. S > 77 Far East. Scottish XV v Fj 82. Sc t BI v
NZ 3rd Test 83. World rec half-back partnership
with Roy Laidlaw (30 apps to R 86).

RUTHERFORD, W.G.   *Ireland*
Tipperary.
Forward, 5-1-0-4.
1884 E− S−; 1885 E−; 1886 E−; 1888 W+.

RUTLEDGE, Leicester Malcolm   *New Zealand*
Riccarton HS, Wrights Bush, NZ Colts,
Southland, S Island.
b 12.4.52 Christchurch.
Flanker, 13-8-0-5.
78 A+ A+ A− I+ W+ E+ S+; 79 F+ F− A−;
80 A− A+ A−.
Stock agent. NZ > 78 BI, 79 A, 80 A & Fj.
Played RL as youth.

RYALLS, Henry John   *England*
Birkenhead Sch, New Brighton, Cheshire.
b 12.12.1858; *d* 17.10.49.
Forward, 2-2-0-0 (1t)
1885 W+(1t) I+.
Man dir music bus. E cap at New Brighton RFC.
Served WW1 on Disablement Comm. Pres
Music Industry Assoc of GB 17.

RYAN, Edmund G. ('Ted')   *Ireland*
Dolphin.
Prop, 3-1-0-2.
37 W+; 38 E− S−.
Bank mgr.

RYAN, James   *New Zealand*
Feilding Tech Coll OB, Petone, Wellington,
Manawatu, N Island, Comb Servs.
b 8.2.1887 Masterton; *d* 17.7.57 Feilding.
FB/2nd five-eighth, 4-3-0-1.
10 A−; 14 A+ A+ A+.

Army. RSM at end of WW1, reached rank of
Capt. NZ > 10 & 14 A. Capt Comb Servs 19.
One of 7 bros to rep Petone, 5 of whom rep
Wellington.

RYAN, James Gerard　　　　　*Ireland*
Castleknock Coll, UC Dublin.
b 1.4.17 Dublin; *d* −.7.78 Zambia.
Prop, 3-2-0-1.
39 E+ S+ W−.
Judge. Killed in motor accident.

RYAN, John　　　　　　　　*Ireland*
Rockwell Coll.
b −; *d* −.10.37.
Forward, 14-6-1-7 (3 − 1t).
1897 E+; 1898 E+ S− W−; 1899 E+ S+ W+;
1900 S= W−; 01 E+ S− W−(1t); 02 E−;
04 E−.
Farmer. Bro of Michael.

RYAN, John Robert　　　　*Australia*
NSW.
b 20.12.49; *d* 2.5.82 Sydney.
Wing, 6-6-0-0 (36 − 9t).
75 J+(3t); 76 I+(1t) US+(1t) Fj+(1t) Fj+(2t)
Fj+(1t).
Taxi driver. Penrith RL 77.

RYAN, Kevin James　　　　*Australia*
Qld.
b 26.8.34.
No 8, 5-2-0-3.
58 E− M+ NZ− NZ+ NZ−.
Insurance/barrister. Labor MP. RL 60.

RYAN, Michael　　　　　　*Ireland*
Rockwell Coll.
b 1871; *d* 19.8.47.
Forward, 17-7-1-9 (3 − 1t).
1897 E+ S−; 1898 E+ S− W−; 1899 E+ S+
W+; 1900 E− S= W−; 01 E+ S− W−; 03
E+(1t); 04 E− S−.
Farmer. Bro of John.

RYAN, Peter Francis　　　*Australia*
St Joseph's Coll, NSW.
b 2.4.40 Queanbeyan.
FB, 4-1-0-3 (6 − 3c).
63 E+(3c) SA−; 66 BI− BI−.
Laundry business. RL.

RYAN, Peter Henry　　　　*England*
Harrow Sch, Cambridge Univ, Richmond,
Barbarians, London Cos, Mdx.
b 1.10.30.
Flanker, 2-0-1-1.
55 W− I=.
Man dir. Ckt, Harrow v Eton 49. Blue 52-3. Sec
Rugby Ints Golfing Soc.

S

SADLER, Bernard Sydney　　*New Zealand*
('Joey')
Wellington Coll, Wellington Coll OB,
Wellington.
b 28.7.14 Wellington.
SH, 5-4-0-1.
35 S+ I+ W−; 36 A+ A+.
Co rep. NZ > 35-6 BI & C, 36 A. Knee inj in
club match 37 ended career. Coached various
sides.

SADLER, Edward H.　　　　*England*
R Signals, The Army.
b 12.
Flanker, 2-1-0-1 (3 − 1t).
33 I+(1t) S−.
Oldham RL.

SAGAR, John Warburton　　*England*
Durham Sch, Cambridge Univ, Castleford,
Barbarians, Yorks, Durham Co.
b 6.12.1878; *d* 10.1.41 Bournemouth.
FB, 2-0-0-2.
01 W− I−.
Schoolmaster/Sudan Civil Service. Blue 1899-
1900. Taught at Loretto Sch 02-3. Governor
Kardofan 17-22; of Wadi Halfa 22-4. Order of
the Nile 3rd class 22; 2nd class 24.

SAGOT, R.　　　　　　　　*France*
SF.
Centre, 3-0-0-3 (5 − 1t 1c).
06 NZ−; 08 E−; 09 W−(1t 1c).

SAHUC, André　　　　　　*France*
Métro.
No 8, 2-1-0-1 (3 − 1t).
45 BF+(1t) BF−.

SAHUC, Franz　　　　　　*France*
Toulouse.
FB, 1-1-0-0.
36 G+.

SAISSET, Olivier　　　　　*France*
Béziers.
b 7.6.49 Poujol-sur-Oub, Herault.
Flanker/no 8, 17-9-1-7 (8 − 2t).
71 R+; 72 S− I− A=(1t) A+; 73 S+ NZ+ E−
W+ I− J+(1t) R+; 74 I+ Arg+ SA− SA−; 75
W−.
Schoolmaster.

SALAS, Patrick　　　　　　*France*
Narbonne.
b 3.3.54 Narbonne.
Lock/prop, 7-3-0-4.

79 NZ− NZ+ R+; 80 W− E−; 81 A−; 82 Arg+.
Municipal employee.

SALINIÈ, René   *France*
Perpignan.
Centre, 1-0-0-1.
23 E−.

SALLEFRANQUE, Marc   *France*
Dax.
b 6.4.60 Dax.
FH/FB, 4-0-0-4 (19 − 2c 1d 4p).
81 A−(1d); 82 W−(1c 1p) E−(1c 2p) S−(1p).
France B v S 81.

SALMON, James   *New Zealand/England*
Lionel Broome
Wellington Coll, Kent Colts, Blackheath, NZ Colts, Athletic, Wellington (NZ), Harlequins.
b 16.10.59 Hong Kong.
New Zealand
Centre, 3-3-0-0 (4 − 1t).
81 R+(1t) F+ F+r.
England
Centre, 4-1-0-3.
85 NZ− NZ−; 86 W+ S−.
Schoolmaster at Wellington Coll/insurance broker. Went to NZ 79. NZ v Fj 80. NZ > R, F 81. Returned to UK. Enabled to play for E when IB altered qualification rules. E > 85 NZ.

SALUT, Jean ('Monsieur Jean')   *France*
TOEC.
b 14.4.43 Beaumont-de-Lomagne, Tarn et Garonne.
Flanker, 7-4-0-3 (3 − 1t).
66 R+(1t); 67 S−; 68 I+ E+ Cz+ NZ−; 69 I−.
Works mgr.

SAMATAN, Robert   *France*
Agen.
b 16.4.07 Toulouse.
Wing, 10-6-0-4 (9 − 3t).
30 S+ I+(1t) E− G+(1t) W−; 31 I+ S− W− E+ G+(1t).
Switched to RL.

SAMPLE, Charles Herbert OBE   *England*
Edinburgh Acad, Cambridge Univ, Durham Co, Northumb.
b 22.11.1862; *d* 2.6.38 Corbridge.
FB, 3-2-1-0 (1c).
1884 I+(1c); 1885 I+; 1886 S=.
Land agent. Blue 1882-4. Ckt for Northumb. Served WW1, Dist Commissioner for N Cos for Bd of Agric & Fisheries. OBE 18.

SAMPSON, J.H.   *Australia*
NSW.

Forward, 1-0-0-1.
1899 BT−.
Licensee.

SAMPSON, Ralph W.F. DSO   *Scotland*
DFC
London Scottish, Barbarians.
b S America.
Hooker, 2-0-0-2.
39 W−; 47 W−.
Played either side WW2. Served in War.

SAMUEL, D.   *Wales*
Swansea.
Forward, 2-2-0-0 (1 − 1t).
1891 I+(1t); 1893 I+.
Played with bro J., W v I 1891.

SAMUEL, Frederick   *Wales*
Mountain Ash.
b Llanelli.
FB, 3-2-1-0 (4 − 2c).
22 S=(1c) I+(1c) F+.
Colliery pipe fitter. Replaced unfit Joe Rees W v I 22 instead of nominated reserve, Daly James (Treorchy). Hull RL 22. RL Cup Final, Belle Vue, v Leeds 23.

SAMUEL, J.   *Wales*
Swansea.
Forward, 1-1-0-0.
1891 I+.
Played with bro D., W v I 1891.

SAMUELS, Theo A.   *South Africa*
Diocesan Coll Rondebosch, Kimberley, Griq W.
Wing/FB, 3-1-0-2 (6 − 2t).
1896 BT−(2t) BT− BT+.
Mining. Late r for inj F. Maxwell (Transvaal), scored SA 1st t, 2nd Test v BT 1896.

SANAC, André   *France*
Perpignan.
b 4.8.29 Trouillas.
Prop/lock, 10-5-0-5 (3 − 1t).
52 It+; 53 S+ I−; 54 E+; 56 Cz+; 57 S− I− E− W−(1t) It+.
Wine grower.

SANDERS, Donald Louis   *England*
('Sandy')
Ipswich YMCA, Harlequins, Barbarians, London Cos, E Cos.
b 6.9.24 Fulham.
Prop, 9-5-0-4.
54 W+ NZ− I+ S+ F−; 56 W− I+ S+ F−.
Sales mgr. Chmn RFU selectors 71; Central Dist CB rep. Served WW2 RNVR. Sec of E Rugby Ints Club.

SANDERS, Frank Warren *England*
Plymouth A, Devon.
b 24.1.1893; *d* 22.6.53.
Hooker, 3-3-0-0.
23 I+ S+ F+.
Chargeman HM Dockyard. Pres Devon Refs
Soc. Fdr, sec Plymouth Rowing Club. Sec Civil
Service Bowls Club, Plymouth.

SANDERSON, George Alfred *Scotland*
Royal HSFP.
b 9.8.1881 Edinburgh; *d* 23.11.57.
Forward, 4-2-0-2 (3 − 1t).
07 W+ I+(1t) E; 08 I−.
Wine merchant.

SANDERSON, James Lyon *Scotland*
Playfair
Edinburgh Academy, Edinburgh Academicals.
b 1852; *d* −.
FB, 1-0-1-0.
1873 E=.
Tea merchant.

SANDFORD, Joseph Ruscombe *England*
Poole
Allhallows Sch, Marlborough Coll, Oxford
Univ, Marlborough Nomads, Devon.
b 5.3.1881; *d* 19.7.16 Khartoum.
Centre, 1-0-0-1.
06 I−.
Sudan Civil Service. Blue 02-3. Hockey blue 03.
Acting Governor Omdurman 16.

SANGALI, François *France*
Narbonne.
b 8.9.52 Canet d'Aude.
Centre, 15-9-1-5 (4 − 1t).
75 I− SA− SA−; 76 S+ A+ A+ R−; 77 W+
E+(1t) S+ I+ Arg+ Arg= NZ+ NZ−.
Banking.

SANGWIN, Roger Dennis *England*
Sedbergh Sch, Hull & ER, Barbarians, Yorks.
b 2.12.37.
Centre, 2-0-1-1.
64 NZ− W=.
Architect.

SAPPA, Michel *France*
Nice.
Lock, 3-3-0-0.
73 J+ R+; 77 R+.

SARGENT, G.A.F. *England*
Gloucester.
Prop, 1-1-0-0.
81 I+r.
R Gloucester team-mate Phil Blakeway v I 81.

SARRADE, Robert *France*
Pau.
FH, 1-0-0-1.
29 I−.

SAUERMANN, Johannes *South Africa*
Theodorus ('Sakkie')
Transvaal.
b 16.11.44 Alberton.
Prop, 5-2-1-2.
71 F+ F= A+; 72 E−; 74 BI−.
Mining.

SAUX, Jean-Pierre *France*
Pau.
b 13.11.28 Paris.
Lock/prop, 22-14-2-6 (6 − 2t).
60 W+ It+ Arg+ Arg+; 61 SA= E= W+(1t)
It+ I+ NZ− NZ− NZ− A+; 62 S+ E+ W− I+
It+(1t); 63 S− I+ E− It+.
Insurance agent.

SAVAGE, Keith Frederick *England*
Leamington Coll for Boys, Leamington,
Loughborough Colls, Northampton,
Harlequins, E Midlands.
b 24.8.40.
Wing, 13-3-2-8 (3 − 1t).
66 W− I= F− S−; 67 A− I+ F− S+ W−(1t)
NZ−; 68 W= F− S+; BI > 66 A, NZ; 68 SA 4-
0-1-3.
Schoolmaster/bus exec. E > 67 Can.

SAVAGE, Laurence Theodore *New Zealand*
Nelson Coll, Univ, Canterbury, Wellington,
Bush, Mangainoka, S Island, NZ Univs.
b 17.2.28 Nelson.
SH, 3-0-0-3.
49 SA− SA− SA−.
Civil engr. NZ > 49 SA. NZ Univs selector 65-
77.

SAVITSKY, Michel *France*
La Voulte.
Lock, 1-1-0-0.
69 R+.

SAVY, Maurice *France*
Montferrand.
b 22.9.06 Clermont Ferrand.
FB, 5-3-0-2.
31 I+ S− W− E+; 36 G+.
FFR treasurer.

SAWYER, C.M. *England*
Broughton Wasps, Broughton, Lancs.
b 1856 Manchester; *d* 30.3.21.
Back, 2-2-0-0 (1t).
1880 S+; 1881 I+(1t).
Lancs CCC.

SAXBY, Leslie Eric *England*
Reading Sch, Gloucester.
b 19.5.1900 Bradfield.
Flanker, 2-0-0-2.
32 SA− W−.

SAXTON, Charles Kesteven *New Zealand*
Otago Boys' HS, Pirates, Otago, Timaru
HSOB, S Canterbury, Pirates, Southland,
Army, Canterbury, S Island.
b 23.5.13 Kurow.
SH, 3-3-0-0 (9 − 3t).
38 A+(2t) A+ A+(1t).
Traveller. NZ > 38 A. Mgr NZ > 67 BI,F & C.
Served WW2, Maj 19th Armoured Rgt. Capt
2nd NZEF > BI & Europe 44-5. NZRFU
council 56-71, pres 74, life mem 76. Author of
'The ABC of Rugby' pub 60.

SAYERS, Herbert James Michael *Ireland*
Stonyhurst Coll, RMA Sandhurst, Lansdowne,
The Army, Richmond, Barbarians, Surrey.
b 1.5.11; *d* −.12.43.
Flanker, 10-6-0-4 (3 − 1gm).
35 E− S+ W+; 36 E+ S+ W−; 38 W−; 39 E+
S+(1gm) W−.
The Army. 2t Brit Army v French Army 40.
Served WW2, Maj in RA; killed in air crash.

SAYLE, Jeffrey Leonard *Australia*
NSW.
b 25.8.42.
Flanker, 1-0-0-1.
67 NZ−.
Storeman/club mgr.

SAYROU, Joseph *France*
Perpignan.
Prop, 9-3-0-6.
26 W− M−; 28 E− G+ W+; 29 S− W− E−
G+.

SCHLEBUSCH, Jan Johannes *South Africa*
Jacobus
OFS.
b 5.5.49 Kroonstad.
Centre, 3-1-1-1.
74 BI− BI=; 75 F+.

SCHMIDT, Louis U. *South Africa*
N Transvaal.
b 6.2.36.
Flanker, 2-1-0-1.
58 F−; 62 BI+.
Mycologist.

SCHOEMAN, Johannes ('Haas') *South Africa*
Paarl Boys HS, Stellenbosch Univ, W Prov.
b 15.3.40 Prince Albert.
Flanker, 7-1-0-6.

63 A− A+; 65 I− S− A− NZ− NZ−.
Legal adviser.

SCHOFIELD, John Wood *England*
Uppingham Sch, Manchester Rgrs, Lancs.
b −.3.1858; *d* 3.5.31.
Forward, 1-1-0-0.
1880 I+.
Stockbroker.

SCHOLFIELD, John Arthur *England*
Sedbergh Sch, Cambridge Univ, Manchester,
Preston Grasshoppers, Harlequins, Barbarians,
Lancs.
b 6.4.1888; *d* 14.9.67.
Centre, 1-0-0-1 (3 − 1t).
11 W−(1t).
Insurance broker. Blue 09-10. Lancs CCC 2nd
X1 08. Capt R Birkdale GC. Served WW1, Capt
& Adjutant Manchester Rgt; wounded & POW.

SCHOLTZ, H.H. *South Africa*
W Prov.
2-1-0-1.
21 NZ− NZ+.
Wine farmer.

SCHULTE, Bernard G. *Australia*
Brisbane State HS, Qld.
b 18; *d* 54.
SH, 2-0-0-2.
46 NZ− M−.
The Army.

SCHULZE (later MILLER), *Scotland*
Douglas Gordon
Fettes Coll, Oxford Univ, London Scottish,
Surrey, Barbarians.
b 15.3.1881 Glasgow; *d* 17.5.56.
FB, 13-7-0-6 (4 − 1d).
05 E+; 07 I+ E+; 08 W− I− E+(1d); 09 W−
I+ E+; 10 W− I+ E−; 11 W−.
Schoolmaster. Taught at Christ's Coll Brecon.
Surrey v NZ 05.

SCHUTE, Frederick *Ireland*
Bradford, Wanderers, Yorks.
Forward, 2-0-0-2.
1878 E−; 1879 E−.
Father of Geoffrey.

SCHUTE, F. Geoffrey *Ireland*
Strangeways Coll, Trin Coll Dublin, Barbarians.
b −; *d* −.3.70.
Forward, 3-0-0-3 (3 − 1t).
12 SA−; 13 E− S−(1t).
Son of Frederick.

SCHWARZ, Reginald Oscar MC *England*
St Paul's Sch, Cambridge Univ, Richmond,
Barbarians, Mdx.

b 4.5.1875 Lee, Kent; *d* 18.11.18 France.
FH, 3-0-0-3.
1899 S−; 01 W− I−.
Stockbroker. Blue 1893. Ckt for Oxon 1899-1900, Mdx 01-5, SA (5 Tests v E 04, 07; 4 Tests A 10-11). MCC > 07 US. Served WW1, KRRC. Wounded, mentioned in despatches, MC. Died of influenza a week after Armistice.

SCOBIE, Sir Robert Mackenzie   *Scotland*
KBE CB MC
Wellington Coll, Cheltenham Coll, RMC Sandhurst, RE, The Army.
b 8.6.1893; *d* 23.2.69.
Centre, 3-0-0-3.
14 W− I− E−.
The Army.

SCOHY, Robert   *France*
BEC.
b 28.4.09 Tunis.
Hooker, 4-2-0-2 (3 − 1t).
31 S− W− E+ G+(1t).

SCORFIELD, Edward Scafe   *England*
RGS Newcastle, Percy Pk, Northumb.
b 21.4.1882 North Shields; *d* 66.
Lock, 1-1-0-0.
10 F+.
Engrg draughtsman/cartoonist. Tyneside Rowing Club 06-25. Cartoonist with 'Newcastle Chronicle' & 'Sydney Bulletin' in A.

SCOTLAND, Kenneth James   *Scotland*
Forbes
Heriot's, Heriot's FP, Cambridge Univ, R Corps of Signals, The Army, Leicester, Ballymena, Aberdeenshire, Barbarians.
b 29.8.36 Edinburgh.
FB/FH, 27-10-3-14 (71 − 7c 4d 15p).
57 F+(1d 1p) W+(1p) I−(1p) E−(1p); 58 E=; 59 F− W+(1p) I−(1p) E=(1p); 60 F− W− I+(1d) E−(3p); 61 F− SA−(1c) W+ I+(2c 1p) E−; 62 F− W+(1c) I+(1c 2p) E=(1p); 63 F+(1c 1d 1p) W− I+ E−(1d); 65 F−(1c); BI > 59 A 2-2-0-0, NZ 3-1-0-2.
Blue 58-60. Played in centre BI v NZ 4th Test 59. Ckt for S.

SCOTT, Charles Tillard   *England*
Tonbridge Sch, Cheltenham Coll, Cambridge Univ, The London Hosp, Blackheath, Barbarians, Kent.
b 26.8.1877; *d* 6.11.65.
Forward, 4-1-0-3.
1900 W− I+; 01 W− I−.
Medicine. Blue 1899. Cambs CCC. Served WW2 Maj LDV & Home Guard. R Humane Soc medal for saving life.

SCOTT, Dennis   *Ireland*
RS Dungannon, Stranmillis Teachers Coll, Malone.
b 19.11.33 Belfast.
No 8/flanker, 3-0-0-3.
61 F− SA−; 62 S−.
Schoolmaster. Emigrated to SA.

SCOTT, Donald Macdonald   *Scotland*
Dumfries Acad, Langholm Acad, Jordanhill, Langholm, Watsonians, The Army, Barbarians.
b 15.4.28 Langholm.
Wing/centre, 10-2-0-8.
50 I− E+; 51 W+ I− E− SA−; 52 F− W− I−; 53 F−.
Schoolmaster. Served in King's R Rifle Corps.

SCOTT, Edward Keith   *England*
Clifton Coll, Oxford Univ, St Mary's Hosp, Redruth, Harlequins, Barbarians, London Cos, Cornwall.
b 14.6.18 Truro.
Centre, 5-1-1-3.
47 W+; 48 A− W= I− S−.
Medicine. Son of Frank. Capt E 3 times. Ckt for OUCC (5 apps 38); Glos CCC (2 apps 37); Minor Cos (1 app 49). MCC > 51 Can.

SCOTT, Frank Sholl   *England*
Epsom Coll, Bristol, Glos, Devon.
b 9.1.1886 W Aus; *d* 4.2.52.
Wing, 1-0-0-1.
07 W−.
Medicine. Father of Edward Keith. Served WW1 RAMC. GP in A, then Cornwall 18-52.

SCOTT, Harry   *England*
Eccles, US Portsmouth, US Chatham, Manchester, Lancs.
b 7.11.26 Batley.
FB, 1-0-0-1.
55 F−.
Jnr draughtsman/forge & machine shop mgr. Manchester 50-63, capt 59-60. Lancs 51-61, capt 60-1.

SCOTT, James William   *Scotland*
Stewart's Coll, Stewart's Coll FP.
b 24.9.03; *d* 24.8.49.
Flanker/no 8/lock, 18-13-0-5 (6 − 2t).
25 F+ W+ I+ E+; 26 F+ W+ I− E+; 27 F+ W+ I− E+(1t) NSW+; 28 F+(1t) W− E−; 29 E+; 30 F−.

SCOTT, John Menzies Baillie   *Scotland*
OBE TD
Edinburgh Acad, Sedbergh Sch, Edinburgh Academicals, Barbarians.
b 6.10.1887; *d* 14.1.67.
Flanker, 21-8-0-13 (3 − 1t).
07 E+; 08 W− I− E+; 09 W− I+ E+; 10 F+

W− I+ E−; 11 F− W−(1t) I−; 12 W− I− E+
SA−; 13 W− I+ E−.
Writer to the Signet. Ref E v W 23.

SCOTT, John Phillip   *England*
Hele's GS, St Luke's Coll Exeter, Exeter,
Devon, Rosslyn Pk, Cardiff.
b 28.9.54 Exeter.
No 8/lock, 34-14-3-17 (4 − 1t).
78 F− W− S+ I+ NZ−; 79 S=r I− F+ W−
NZ−; 80 I+(1t) F+ W+ S+; 81 W− S+ I+ F−
Arg= Arg+; 82 I− F+ W+; 83 F− W= S− I−
NZ+; 84 S− I+ F− W− SA− SA−.
Schoolmaster/savings bank. E's most capped no
8. At 17 youngest ever forward to play in
England trial. E Under 23s v It 75; > 77 Can
(capt). E > 79 Far East, 81 Arg, 84 SA (capt).
Only man to capt Cardiff 4 consec seasons, 80-4.

SCOTT, John Stanley Marshall   *England*
Leas Sch Hoylake, Radley Coll, Birkenhead Pk,
Oxford Univ, Harlequins, London Cos,
Cheshire.
b 23.1.35.
FB 1-1-0-0.
58 F+.
Solicitor. Blue 57-8. Ckt for Authentics 58.
Crew mem America's Cup yachting challenger
'Sovereign' 64. Served in Malaya emergency,
Gurkha Rifles. Played for Negri Sembilan,
Malaya, 56.

SCOTT, J.S.   *Scotland*
St Andrew's Univ.
Flanker, 1-1-0-0.
50 E+.

SCOTT, Mason Thompson   *England*
Craigmount Sch, Cambridge Univ, Northern,
Blackheath, Barbarians, Northumb.
b 20.12.1865; *d* 1.6.16.
Half-back, 3-2-0-1.
1887 I−; 1890 S+ I+.
Co dir. Blue 1885-7. Bro of W.M.

SCOTT, P.   *South Africa*
Stellenbosch Univ, Transvaal.
4-1-0-3.
1896 BT− BT− BT− BT+.
Mining.

SCOTT, Peter Robert Ian   *Australia*
Telopea Pk HS, NSW.
b 1.1.40.
Centre, 2-0-0-2 (8 − 1c 2p).
62 NZ−(2p) NZ−(1c).
Civil service.

SCOTT, Robert   *Scotland*
Hawick.

Forward, 3-1-2-0.
1898 I+; 1900 I= E=.

SCOTT, Robert Desmond   *Ireland*
RS Dungannon, Queen's Univ Belfast.
b 2.10.41 Belfast.
Wing, 5-1-1-3.
67 E− F−; 68 F− E= S+.
Dental surgeon.

SCOTT, Robert William Henry   *New Zealand*
Ponsonby Sch, Ponsonby, Auckland, Comb
Servs, N Island.
b 6.2.21 Wellington.
FB, 17-10-1-6 (74 − 16c 2d 12p).
46 A+(5c) A+(1c 3p); 47 A+(2c) A+(3c 3p);
49 SA−(1c 1p) SA−(1p) SA− SA−(1c); 50
BI=(1p) BI+ BI+(1p) BI+(1c 1d); 53 W−; 54
I+(1c 1d 1p) E+(1c) S+(1p) F−.
Warehouseman/painter & decorator/men's
outfitter. RL for Ponsonby 39; served WW2 &
pl 19 times 2nd NZEF. Top scorer 72 pts NZ >
47 A; top scorer 60 pts (17 apps) NZ > 49 SA; >
53-4 BI,F & NAm. Often practised kicking in
bare feet. Overcame polio as a child. Co-author
with Terry McLean 'The Bob Scott Story' pub
56.

SCOTT, Thomas M.   *Scotland*
Highfield Acad, Gala Acad, Hawick.
Forward, 12-7-2-3 (9 − 3c 1p).
1893 E+; 1895 W+ I+ E+; 1896 W− E+(1c);
1897 I+(1c 1p) E−; 1898 I+(1c) E=; 1900 W−
I=.
Baker.

SCOTT, Tom   *Scotland*
Craigmount Sch, Langholm, Hawick.
b 8.3.1875; *d* 16.4.47.
Wing, 11-4-3-4 (6 − 2t).
1896 W−; 1897 I+ E−; 1898 I+(2t) E=; 1899
I− W+ E+; 1900 W− I= E=.
Tweed merchant. Pres SRU 18-20.

SCOTT, William Martin   *England*
Craigmount Sch, Cambridge Univ, Blackheath,
Northern, Barbarians, Northumb.
b 27.3.1870; *d* 26.2.44.
Half-back, 1-1-0-0.
1889 NZN+.
Blue 1888. Bro of M.T. Served WW1, Maj RE.
Known to have been one of 1st players to
employ dummy pass. Ckt for CUCC.

SCOTT, William Patrick   *Scotland*
Fettes Coll, W of Scotland, Barbarians.
b −.3.1880 Wishaw; *d* 1.6.48.
Forward, 21-11-2-8 (2 − 1c).
1900 I= E=; 02 I− E−; 03 W+ I+ E+; 04 W−

I+ E+; 05 W− I− E+(1c) NZ−; 06 W− I+ E−
SA+; 07 W+ I+ E+; BT > 03 SA.
Distiller. Pres SRU 35-6.

SCOULAR, John Gladstone   *Scotland*
St Bees Sch, Cambridge Univ, Barbarians.
 b 17.9.1885; *d* 7.9.53.
FB, 5-2-0-3.
05 NZ−; W− I+ E− SA+.
Mining engr. Blue 05-6.

SCOURFIELD, Thomas E.   *Wales*
Torquay Ath, London Welsh.
 b 09; *d* −.2.76 Can.
FB, 1-1-0-0.
30 F+.
Builder's labourer/groundsman. Huddersfield
RL 32. RL Cup Final 33.

SCOVELL, Rowland Hill   *Ireland*
Kingstown.
 b c1866; *d* −.2.39.
Wing, 2-0-0-2.
1883 E−; 1884 E−.

SCOWN, Alastair Ian   *New Zealand*
Patea Dist HS, Patea, NZ Jnrs, Taranaki, N
Island.
 b 21.10.48 Patea.
Flanker, 5-5-0-0 (4 − 1t).
72 A+ A+ A+(1t) W+r S+.
Farmer/racehorse stud breeder. NZ > 72-3 BI,F
& NAm. Patea comm.

SCRIMSHAW, George   *New Zealand*
Waitaki Boys' HS, Christchurch, Cust,
Canterbury, S Island.
 b 1.12.02 Islington; *d* 13.7.71 Christchurch.
Flanker, 1-0-0-1.
28 SA−.
Traveller. NZ > 28 SA.

SCRINE, George Frederick   *Wales*
Swansea.
 b 25.3.1882.
Forward, 3-2-0-1.
1899 E+ S−; 01 I+.
Plasterer/licensee. Scored t Swansea v NZ 05.
Led 'players' revolt' at Swansea RFC 06.

SCRIVEN, George JP FRGS   *Ireland*
Repton Sch, Trin Coll Dublin, Wanderers,
Blackheath.
 b 9.11.1856; *d* c33.
Forward, 8-0-0-8.
1879 S− E−; 1880 E− S−; 1881 E−; 1882 S−;
1883 E− S−.
Medicine. Ref E v S 1884; controversial match
in which E's winning t disputed & led to
cancellation of 1885 fixture & ultimately
formation of IB. Pres IRU 1882-3 & 1885-6.

SEALY, James W. KC   *Ireland*
Dublin HS, Trin Coll Dublin, Barbarians.
 b 19.3.1876; *d* 4.2.49.
Forward, 9-5-2-2 (6 − 2t).
1896 E+(1t) S= W+; 1897 S−; 1899 E+ S+(1t)
W+; 1900 E− S=; BT > 1896 SA.
High Court Judge. Pres IRU 27-8.

SEBÉDIO, Jean ('Le Sultan')   *France*
Tarbes, Carcassonne.
 b 6.12.1890 St Jean-de-Luz; *d* 12.6.51
Carcassonne.
Flanker/no 8, 9-2-2-5 (3 − 1t).
13 S−(1t) E−; 14 I−; 20 S− I+ US+; 22 S=
E=; 23 S−.
Business.

SEDDON, Robert L.   *England*
Broughton Rgrs, Lancs.
 b c1860; *d* 15.8.1888 W Maitland, NSW.
Forward, 3-1-1-1.
1887 W+ I− S=; BT > 1888 A, NZ.
Capt 1st BT tour > 1888. Died on tour,
drowned while sculling on River Maitland.

SEEAR, Gary Alan   *New Zealand*
Bayfield HS, Southern, NZ Colts, NZ Jnrs,
Otago, S Island, Fracasso San Dona (It).
 b 19.2.52 Dunedin.
No 8, 12-8-0-4 (11 − 2t 1p).
77 F− F+(1p); 78 A+ A+(1t) A− I+ W+ E+
S+(1t); 79 F+ F− A−.
Draughtsman. NZ > 76 SA, 77 F, 78 BI, 79 A.
Pl in It 79.

SEELING, Charles Edward   *New Zealand*
('Bronco')
Wanganui Dist HS, Pirates, Wanganui, City,
Auckland, N Island.
 b 14.5.1883 Wanganui; *d* 29.5.56 Stalybridge,
E.
No 8/flanker, 11-9-1-1 (6 − 2t).
04 BT+; 05 S+ I+ E+ W−; 06 F+; 07 A+(1t)
A+(1t); 08 AW+ AW= AW+.
Licensee. NZ > 05 A, 05-6 BI,F & NAm, 07 A.
Wigan RL (E) 10, playing his last RL match at
age 39. Killed in motor accident shortly before
planned return to NZ.

SÉGUIER, René   *France*
Béziers.
Wing, 2-2-0-0.
73 J+ R+.

SELBY, John Alexander   *Scotland*
Robertson
George Watson's Coll, Watsonians.
 b 28.7.1900 Port William; *d* 15.2.51.
SH, 2-2-0-0.
20 W+ I+.
Medicine.

SELLA, Phillippe   *France*
French Schs, France Jnrs, French Univs, Agen,
Barbarians (UK), French Barbarians.
b 14.2.62 Clairac.
Centre/wing, 28-18-3-7 (40 − 10t).
82 R− Arg+(2t) Arg+; 83 E+(1t) S+ I− W+
A= A+ R+; 84 I+(1t) W+(1t) E+(1t) S−
NZ− NZ− R+; 85 E= S+ I= W+ Arg− Arg+
J+; 86 S−(1t) I+(1t) W+(1t) E+(1t).
PE teacher. France B v W 81. F > 85 Arg.
Scored t in each of 4 Champ matches 86, feat
achieved only by P. Esteve, H.C. Catcheside &
A.C. Wallace. Five Nations v Overseas XV,
Twickenham 86.

SELLAR, Kenneth Anderson   *England*
('Monkey') DSO DSC
RNC Dartmouth, US Portsmouth, RNC
Greenwich, RN, Comb Servs, Blackheath,
Barbarians, London Cos, Hants.
b 11.8.06.
FB, 7-6-0-1.
27 W+ I+ S−; 28 NSW+ W+ I+ F+.
RN/stockbroker. Ckt for RN, Sussex & MCC.
Naval mem of R Yacht Squadron. Served WW2.
Many actions, inc leading landing craft on Sword
Beach during D-Day landings in Normandy.
DSC 44. DSO after leading assault on
Walcheren Island 44.

SELLARS, George Maurice   *New Zealand*
Victor
Napier St Sch Auckland, Ponsonby, NZ Maoris,
Auckland, N Island.
b 16.4.1886 Auckland; kia 7.6.17 Messines,
Belgium.
Hooker, 2-2-0-0.
13 A+ US+.
Shipwright. NZ > 13 NAm. Auckland Infantry
Rgt; killed carrying wounded comrade.

SEMMARTIN, Jean   *France*
SCUF.
FB, 2-0-0-2.
13 W− I−.
Commercial traveller.

SENAL, Georges   *France*
Béziers.
b 21.4.47 Poussan.
Lock, 6-2-0-4.
74 Arg+ Arg+ R− SA− SA−; 75 W−.
Municipal employee.

SENDIN, William D.   *South Africa*
Stockdale St Sch Kimberley, Griq W.
b − ; *d* 77 Kimberley.
Centre, 1-1-0-0 (3 − 1t).
21 NZ+(1t).
SA's lightest player (9st 6lb).

SENTILLES, Jean   *France*
Tarbes.
Centre, 4-0-0-4.
12 W− E−; 13 S− SA−.
Professor.

SERFONTEIN, David Jacobus   *South Africa*
('Divan')
Vanderbijlpark Sch, Stellenbosch Univ,
Defence (Cape Town), Gazelles, Barbarians,
Oribis, W Prov.
b 3.8.54 Krugersdorp.
SH, 19-15-0-4 (12 − 3t).
80 BI+ BI+ BI+ BI+ SAm+ SAm+
F+(1t); 81 I+ I+ NZ− NZ+ NZ− US+; 82
SAm+ SAm−; 84 E+ E+ SAm+(1t) SAm+.
Medicine. Capt SA v SAm 2 Tests 84. Prov
debut 76.

SERIN, Lucien   *France*
Béziers.
b 8.11.02 Antignac, Herault.
SH, 12-6-0-6 (3 − 1t).
28 E−; 29 W− E− G+; 30 S+ I+ E−(1t) G+
W−; 31 I+ W− E+.

SERRE, Paul ('L'Assassingue')   *France*
Perpignan.
Wing, 2-0-0-2.
20 S− E−.

SERVOLE, Leopold   *France*
Toulon.
FH, 7-5-0-2 (4 − 1d).
31 I+ S−(1d) W− E+ G+; 34 G+; 35 G+.
Co dir.

SEVER, Hal S.   *England*
Shrewsbury Sch, Sale, Barbarians, Cheshire.
b 3.3.10.
Wing, 10-6-1-3 (19 − 5t 1d).
36 NZ+(1t) W= I−(1t) S+; 37 W+(1d) I+(1t)
S+(1t); 38 W−(1t) I+ S−.
Actuary.

SEXTON, W.J.   *Ireland*
Garryowen.
Flanker, 1-0-0-1.
84 A−.

SHACKLETON, Ian Roger   *England*
Bradford GS, Cambridge Univ, Harrogate,
Bradford, Richmond, Yorks.
b 17.6.48 Shipley.
FH, 4-2-0-2 (3 − 1t).
69 SA+; 70 I+(1t) W− S−.
Schoolmaster/sponsorship consultant. Blue 68-
70.

SHACKLETON, James Alexander   *Scotland*
Pirie

Fettes Coll, London Scottish, Barbarians.
Centre, 7-2-2-3 (3 − 1t).
59 E=; 63 F+ W−; 64 NZ= W−; 65 I−
SA+(1t).
Insurance.

SHAMBROOK, Gregory George　　　*Australia*
Qld.
b 53.
Centre, 2-2-0-0.
76 Fj+ Fj+.
Marketing.

SHANAHAN, T.　　　*Ireland*
Lansdowne.
Forward, 5-1-0-4 (1t).
1885 E− S−; 1886 E−; 1888 W+(1t) S−.

SHAND, R.A.　　　*South Africa*
Griq W.
2-0-0-2.
1891 BT− BT−.

SHANKLIN, James Llewellyn　　　*Wales*
Greenhill GS Tenby, Welsh SS, Tenby, London
Welsh, Mdx, E Wales, London Cos.
b 11.12.48 E Williamston, Tenby.
Wing/centre, 4-2-0-2 (4 − 1t).
70 F+; 72 NZ−; 73 I+(1t) F−.
Brewery management trainee/wine, spirits
rep/sports goods shop proprietor. Played 13
seasons with London Welsh 68-80.

SHARP, Gregor　　　*Scotland*
Stewart's Coll, Stewart's FP, The Army.
b 20.4.34.
FH, 4-1-1-2.
60 F−; 64 F+ NZ= W−.
The Army. Served in R Corps of Signals.

SHARP, Richard Adrian William　　　*England*
OBE
Montpelier Sch, Blundell's Sch, Oxford Univ,
Redruth, RN, R Marines, Wasps, Bristol,
Barbarians, Cornwall.
b 9.9.38 Mysore, India.
FH, 14-7-4-3 (26 − 2t 4c 3d 1p).
60 W+ I+(1d) F= S+(1d); 61 I− F=; 62 W=
I+(1t 2c 1p) F−; 63 W+(2c 1d) I= F+ S+(1t);
67 A−; BI > 62 SA 2-0-0-2.
Schoolmaster/china clay co exec/journalist.
Came to UK 46. Blue 59-61. Capt E 5 times.
Asst master Sherborne 63-8. Rugby corr
'Sunday Telegraph'. OBE 86.

SHAW, Anthony Alexander　　　*Australia*
Qld.
b 20.3.53.
Flanker/lock, 36-20-0-16 (4 − 1t).
73 W− E−; 75 E+ E+ J+(1t) S− W−; 76 E−
I+ US+ Fj+ Fj+ Fj+ F− F−; 78 W+ W+

NZ− NZ− NZ+; 79 I− I− NZ+ Arg− Arg+;
80 Fj+ NZ+ NZ− NZ+; 81 F+ F+ I+ W− S−;
82 S− S+.
Insurance broker. Australian Player of Year 81.
A > 75-6 BI; 78 NZ; 79 Arg; capt A > 78 NZ;
80 Fj; 81-2 BI.

SHAW, Cecil Hamilton　　　*England*
Sedbergh Sch, Moseley, Midland Cos.
b 1.8.1879 Wolverhampton; *d* 13.11.64.
Forward, 6-2-1-3.
06 S+ SA=; 07 F+ W− I− S−.
Merchant. Served WW1, Capt RE.

SHAW, Frederick　　　*England*
Cleckheaton.
Forward, 1-0-0-1.
1898 I−.
Stonemason.

SHAW, Geoffrey Arnold　　　*Australia*
NSW.
b 27.12.48.
Centre, 27-12-1-14 (8 − 2t).
69 W− SA−r; 70 S+; 71 SA− SA− SA− F+
F−; 73 W− E−; 74 NZ− NZ= NZ−; 75 E+
E+ J+ J+(1t) W−; 76 E− I+(1t) US+ Fj+
Fj+ Fj+ F− F−; 79 NZ+.
Electrical engr. Capt A > 76 F, I.

SHAW, George Duncan　　　*Scotland*
Oundle Sch, Sale, Gala, Barbarians.
b 29.5.15 Galashiels.
Flanker, 6-1-0-5 (7 − 2c 1p).
35 NZ−; 36 W−; 37 W+(2c) I− E−(1p); 39 I−.
Textiles manufacturer. 1t 1c S of Scotland v NZ
35. Played in 6 Servs ints.

SHAW, Glyndwr　　　*Wales*
Cwmdulais SS, Welsh Youth, Neath.
b 11.4.51 Rhigos.
Prop, 12-5-2-5.
72 NZ−; 73 E+ S− I+ F− A+; 74 S+ I= F=
E−; 77 I+ F−.
NCB salvager. Wales XV v J 73. Widnes RL 77,
Wigan 81 £30,000 fee. 1 GB RL Test.

SHAW, G.M.　　　*Ireland*
Windsor.
b −; *d* -1.2.22.
FB, 1-0-0-1.
1877 S−.

SHAW, Ian　　　*Scotland*
Glasgow HS, Glasgow HSFP.
b 4.8.11.
Centre, 1-0-0-1 (4 − 1d).
37 I−(1d).
Played with bro Wilson v I 37.

SHAW, James Fraser *England*
King William's Sch IOM, RNEC Keyham,
Barbarians, Devon.
b 2.1.1878; *d* 23.7.41.
Forward, 2-1-1-0.
1898 S= W+.
RN. Served WW1 asst engr; later Engr Capt
HMS Invincible, Suffolk, Cordelia. Present at
Battles of Heligoland & Falklands Islands.
Mentioned in despatches 14. Father of actor
Robert Shaw.

SHAW, James Norrie MC *Scotland*
Edinburgh Acad, Stewart's Coll, Edinburgh
Academicals.
b 13.9.1896.
No 8, 2-1-0-1.
21 W+ I−.
Served WW1. Pres SRU 49-50.

SHAW, Mark William *New Zealand*
Kapiti Coll, Paraparaumu, Horowhenua, NZ
Colts, NZ Jnrs, Kia Toa, Manawatu, N Island.
b 23.5.56 Palmerston N.
Flanker/no 8, 29-21-2-6 (24 − 6t).
80 A− A+ A−r W+; 81 S+ S+ SA+(1t) SA−
R+ F+ F+(1t); 82 A+ A−(1t) A+(1t); 83
BI+(1t) BI+ BI+ BI+ A+ S= E−; 84 F+ F+
A−; 85 E+ E+(1t) A+ Arg+ Arg=.
Freezing worker. NZ > 80 A & Fj; NAm & W,
81 R & F, 83 & 84 A, 83 S & E, 85 Arg. Played
for Rest of World v BI, Cardiff 86 & Overseas
XV v Five Nations, Twickenham 86. Record
includes penalty t v F 81.

SHAW, Robert Wilson CBE *Scotland*
Glasgow HS, Glasgow HSFP, Barbarians.
b 11.4.13; *d* 23.7.79 Glasgow.
Wing/FH, 19-7-0-12 (28 − 8t 2c).
34 W− I+(2c) E−(1t); 35 W−(1t) I−(1t) E+
NZ−; 36 W− I− E−(1t); 37 W+(1t) I+ E−; 38
W+ I+ E+(2t); 39 W− I− E−(1t).
Played with bro Ian v I 37. Capt S 9 times. Pres
SRU 70-1.

SHAW, Terence W. *Wales*
Welsh Youth, Newbridge, Cardiff.
Lock, 1-0-0-1.
83 R−.
Wales XV v J 83.

SHEA, Jeremiah *Wales*
Newport.
b −.8.1892 Newport; *d* − .
Centre, 4-1-0-3 (19 − 1t 1c 2d 2p).
19 NZA−(1p); 20 E+(1t 1c 2d 1p) S−; 21 E−.
Docker/pro boxer. Wigan RL 21. Fought world
welterwt champ Ted Kid Lewis, non-title bout,
Mountain Ash 28.2.20. Also lost to Johnny
Basham in Welsh title bout.

SHEDDEN, David *Scotland*
Spiers Sch, W of Scotland, Barbarians.
b 24.5.44 Kilwinning.
Wing, 15-5-0-10 (8 − 2t).
72 NZ−; 73 F− W+ I+ E− P+(1t); 76 W− E−
I+; 77 I+ F− W−; 78 I− F−(1t) W−.
Industrial banker. Barbarians > 76 Can.

SHEEHAN, Michael Danaher *Ireland*
London Irish.
b −; *d* 3.11.74.
SH, 1-0-0-1.
32 E−.
CIE Limerick.

SHEHADIE, Sir Nicholas Michael *Australia*
OBE
NSW, Barbarians (UK).
b 15.11.26 Coogee.
Lock/prop, 30-8-1-21 (9 − 3t).
47 NZ−; 48 E+ F−; 49 M− M= M+ NZ+
NZ+; 50 BI− BI−; 51 NZ− NZ−(1t) NZ−; 52
Fj+ Fj−(1t) NZ−; 53 SA− SA+ SA− SA−; 54
Fj+ Fj−(1t); 55 NZ− NZ− NZ+; 56 SA−
SA−; 57 NZ−; 58 W− I−.
Business exec. 1st overseas int to app for
Barbarians, v A 48. A > 47-8 & 57-8 BI. Mgr A
> 81-2 BI. Lord Mayor of Sydney. Pres ARU
80.

SHEIL, Ainslie Glenister Ross *Australia*
Oxford Univ, Qld.
b 4.11.33.
Five-eighth, 1-0-0-1.
56 SA−.
Surgeon. Blue 58.

SHELFORD, Frank Nuki Ken *New Zealand*
Bay of Plenty, NZ Maoris, Wasps.
b 16.5.55 Waioeka.
Flanker, 4-4-0-0.
81 SA+ R+; 84 A+ A+.
NZ > 81 R & F, 83 S & E, 84 A, 85 Arg. World
XV > 86 SA.

SHELL, Roger Clive *Wales*
Aberavon.
b 9.9.47.
SH, 1-1-0-0.
73 A+r.
Schoolmaster. Wales XV v J 73. Only cap 83rd
minute r for Gareth Edwards.

SHEPHERD, David John *Australia*
Blundell's Sch, Victoria.
b 36 Devon, E.
Flanker, 5-3-0-2.
64 NZ+; 65 SA+ SA+; 66 BI− BI−.
Sales rep.

SHEPPARD, Austin. *England*
Bristol.
Prop, 2-0-0-2.
81 W−r; 85 W−.
Undertaker.

SHERIFF, A. Roger *South Africa*
Durban Tech, Transvaal.
b 12; *d* 51.
3-2-0-1.
38 BI+ BI+ BI−.
Engr. SA > 37 A, NZ.

SHERRARD, Charles William *England*
Rugby Sch, Blackheath, RE, The Army.
b 25.12.1849 London; *d* 21.
Forward, 2-1-0-1.
1871 S−; 1872 S+.
The Army. Played in 1st int, S v E 1871. Served
SA War 1879, SA War medal with clasp.
Reached rank of Col.

SHERRIFF, George Albert *England*
Saracens, Barbarians, London Cos, Mdx.
b 29.5.37.
No 8, 3-0-0-3.
66 S−; 67 A− NZ−.
Man dir stevedoring co. 1st played rugby at 24,
capped at 28.

SHERRY, Brendan Francis *Ireland*
Terenure Coll.
b 7.6.43 Cork.
SH, 6-3-1-2.
67 A+ E− S+ A+; 68 F− E=.
Chartered accountant.

SHERRY, Michael James *Ireland*
Aloysius
Mount St Joseph Coll Roscrea, UC Dublin,
Lansdowne.
b 21.6.51 Foxford, Co Mayo.
Flanker, 2-1-0-1.
75 F+ W−.
Solicitor.

SHEWRING, Harry Edward *England*
Colston Sch, Bristol, Som.
b 26.4.1882 Keynsham; *d* 27.11.60.
Centre, 10-3-1-6 (3 − 1t).
05 I− NZ−; 06 W− S+ F+ SA=; 07 F+(1t)
W− I− S−.
Bristol Waterworks employee. 250 apps & 67t
Bristol (capt 07-8). 45 apps Som (capt 07-8).

SHILLINGLAW, Robert Brian *Scotland*
Gala, KOSB, The Army.
b 38.
SH, 5-1-0-4.
60 I+ E− SA−; 61 F− SA−.
Builder. Whitehaven RL.

SHOOTER, John Henry *England*
Morley.
b 25.3.1875 Nottingham; *d* 13.8.22 Leeds.
Forward, 4-1-1-2.
1899 I− S−; 1900 I+ S=.
Coalminer. Hunslet RL 1900.

SHUM, Ernest Hamilton *South Africa*
Stellenbosch Univ, Transvaal.
b 17.8.1886; *d* 52.
Flanker, 1-1-0-0.
13 E+.
SA > 12-13 BI, F.

SHUTTLEWORTH, Dennis *England*
William OBE
Roundhay Sch, O Roundhegians, Headingley,
Blackheath, RMA Sandhurst, Halifax, Duke of
Wellington's Rgt, The Army, Comb Servs,
Barbarians, Yorks.
b 22.7.28 Leeds.
SH, 2-2-0-0.
51 S+; 53 S+.
The Army. Served Korea 53. Reached rank of
Lt Col. Army CB rep; pres RFU 85-6.

SIBREE, Herbert John Hyde MC *England*
Eltham Coll, Harlequins, Barbarians, London
Cos, Mdx.
b 9.5.1885; *d* 20.8.62 Tilehurst, Sussex.
SH, 3-2-0-1.
08 F+; 09 I+ S−.
Ship broker. Served WW1, Capt R Norfolk Rgt,
Artists Rifles. MC 16. Retired 59 after 55 yrs
service on Baltic Exchange.

SICART, Noël *France*
Perpignan.
No 8, 1-0-0-1.
22 I−.

SIDDELLS, Stanley Keith *New Zealand*
Wanganui Collegiate Sch, Victoria Univ,
Wellington, Pahiatua, Bush, N Island, NZ
Univs.
b 16.7.1897 Wellington; *d* 3.3.79 Pahiatua.
Wing, 1-0-1-0.
21 SA=.
Law. Served WW1, NZ Rifle Bde. Mayor of
Pahiatua; Commandant of local internment
camp WW2.

SIGGINS, John Allen Edgar *Ireland*
Methodist Coll Belfast, Armagh RS, Collegians,
Barbarians.
b 28.6.09 Belfast.
No 8, 24-11-0-13 (12 − 1t 3p).
31 F− E+ S+ W−(1t) SA−; 32 E− S+ W+; 33
E− W+(1p) S−; 34 E− S− W−; 35 E− S+
W+(1p) NZ−(1p); 36 E+ S+ W−; 37 E− S+
W+.

Insurance mgr. Ulster v NZ 35. Mgr BI > 55 SA. Irish sel. IB rep. Pres IRU 62-3.

SILK, Nicholas *England*
Lewes CGS, Oxford Univ, Harlequins, St Thomas's Hosp, Brit Univs, Sussex.
b 26.5.41 Lewes.
Flanker, 4-1-1-2.
65 W− I− F+ S=.
Medicine. Blue 61-3 (Capt 63). Capt Sussex 64-6. Career ended by knee injury 66.

SILLIÈRES, Jean *France*
Tarbes.
b 15.11.46 Marciac, Gers.
Wing, 8-4-2-2 (10 − 3t).
68 R−; 70 S+ I+(1t); 71 S+(1t) I= E=; 72 E+(1t) W−.
PE teacher.

SIMAN, Maurice ('Matelot') *France*
Montferrand.
b 12.7.24 Clermont Ferrand.
Wing, 6-2-1-3.
48 E+; 49 S−; 50 S− I= E+ W−.

SIMMERS, Brian Maxwell *Scotland*
Glasgow Acad, Loretto Sch, Glasgow Academicals.
b 26.2.40 Glasgow.
FH/centre, 7-3-0-4 (9 − 3d).
65 F− W−(2d); 66 A+; 67 F+(1d) W+ I−; 71 F−r.
Chartered accountant. Son of William.

SIMMERS, William Maxwell *Scotland*
Glasgow Acad, Glasgow Academicals, Barbarians.
b 7.8.04 Glasgow; *d* 14.11.72 Helensburgh.
Wing, 28-13-1-14 (18 − 6t).
26 W+ I− E+; 27 F+ W+ I− E+ NSW+; 28 F+(1t) W− I− E−; 29 F+ W− I+(1t) E+; 30 F−(1t) W+(2t) I− E−; 31 F+ W− I− E+; 32 SA− W− I−(1t) E−.
Chartered accountant. Father of Brian. Pres SRU 56-7.

SIMMS, Kevin G. *England*
Cambridge Univ, Liverpool.
Centre, 7-3-1-3.
85 R+ F= S+ I− W−; 86 I+ F−.
Blue 83-5.

SIMON, Harold James *New Zealand*
Southern, Otago, S Island.
b 7.3.11 Kingston; *d* 1.10.79 Karitane.
SH, 3-1-0-2.
37 SA+ SA− SA−.
Sugar boiler.

SIMPSON, Colin Peter *England*
Ipswich Sch, Ipswich, RMA Sandhurst, The Army, Combined Servs, BAOR, Harlequins, Wolfhounds, Barbarians, Suffolk, E Cos.
b 21.9.42.
Wing, 1-0-0-1.
65 W−.
The Army. Adjutant Wellington Coll CCF 68. Suffolk CCC.

SIMPSON, H.J. *Wales*
Cardiff.
Forward, 3-1-0-2.
1884 E− S− I+.
Solicitor/auditor. Capt W v I 1884, when 2 Irish players did not travel and were replaced by H.M. Jordan and F. Purdon. The identity of the missing Irish players has never been established.

SIMPSON, John George *New Zealand*
Ponsonby, Auckland, N Island.
b 18.3.22 Rotorua.
Prop, 9-4-1-4.
47 A+ A+; 49 SA− SA− SA− SA−; 50 BI= BI+ BI+.
Licensee/salesman. NZ > 47 A, 49 SA. Pl RL as youth. Served WW2. Knee inj v BI 50 ended career. Coach Takapuna, asst coach Auckland 57-62. Bowls for Wellington.

SIMPSON, John William *Scotland*
Dollar Acad, Royal HS, Royal HSFP, Barbarians.
b 1872; *d* 11.1.21.
Half-back, 13-7-2-4.
1893 I= E+; 1894 W− I− E+; 1895 W+ I+ E+; 1896 W− I=; 1897 E−; 1899 W+ E+.
Medicine. Ref I v W 06. Pres SRU 04-5.

SIMPSON, Paul D. *England*
Newcastle Poly, Gosforth, Bath.
b 7.6.58 Leeds.
Flanker, 2-1-0-1.
83 NZ+; 84 S−.
Computer salesman. Played RL at sch.

SIMPSON, Richard John *Australia*
NSW.
FB, 1-0-0-1 (4 − 2c).
13 NZ−(2c).
Compositor.

SIMPSON, Robert S. *Scotland*
Loretto Sch, Glasgow Acad, Glasgow Acads.
Flanker, 1-1-0-0.
23 I+.

SIMPSON, Thomas *England*
Rockcliff, Northumb, Barbarians.
Wing, 11-4-1-6 (9 − 3t).
02 S+; 03 W− I− S−; 04 I+(1t) S−; 05 I− S−;

06 S+(1t) SA=; 09 F+(1t).
Accountant with NE Rly Cos. Sec Northumb 25-32.

SIMPSON, Victor Lenard James *New Zealand*
Lyttelton, Poverty Bay, Canterbury.
b 26.2.60 Gisborne.
2nd five-eighth/centre, 2-1-1-0.
85 Arg+ Arg=.
NZ > 85 Arg. World XV > 86 SA.

SIMS, Graham S. *New Zealand*
Wanganui Boys Coll, Univ, Otago, NZ Univs, Suburbs, Canterbury, NZ Univs, S Island.
b 25.6.51 Featherston.
Centre, 1-1-0-0.
72 A+.
PE teacher/insurance agent. 5t Otago v W Coast 72. Coach Suburbs 76. Bro Howard rep Wairarapa 68-9 & Manawatu 70-1. Bro-in-law Ross Murray (NZ amateur golf champ) rep Otago 53.

SIMSON, Ernest David *Scotland*
Merchiston Castle Sch, Edinburgh Univ, London Scottish, The Army.
b 13.3.1882 Edinburgh; *d* 22.7.10 India.
Half-back, 17-10-0-7 (16 − 4t 1d).
02 E−; 03 W+ I+ E+(1t); 04 W− I+(1t) E+; 05 W− I− E+(1t) NZ−(1d); 06 W− I+ E−; 07 W+ I+ E+(1t).
Medicine. Cousin of John. Indian Medical Servs; died of cholera, aged 28.

SIMSON, John Thomas *Scotland*
George Watson's Coll, Watsonians, The Army.
b 21.10.1884; *d* 30.3.76.
Wing, 7-3-0-4 (6 − 2t).
05 NZ−; 09 W− I+ E+(1t); 10 F+ W−; 11 I− (1t).
Army Medical Service. Cousin of Ernest. One of the longest lived int players.

SIMSON, Ronald Francis *Scotland*
Edinburgh Acad, RMA Sandhurst, London Scottish, RA, The Army.
b 6.9.1890 Edinburgh; kia 14.9.14 Aisne.
Centre, 1-0-0-1 (3 − 1t)
11 E−(1t).
The Army. Lt, R Horse & R Field Artillery; 1st rugby int to be killed.

SINCLAIR, Desmond John *South Africa*
Transvaal.
b 14.7.28.
Centre, 4-2-0-2.
55 BI− BI+ BI− BI+.
Chiropractor. SA > 51-2 BI.

SINCLAIR, James Hugh *South Africa*
Transvaal.

b 16.10.1876 Swellendam; *d* 23.2.13 Yeoville.
Forward, 1-0-1-0 (3 − 1t).
03 BT=(1t).
Bank clerk/bus. Ckt for SA, 1069 runs, 63 wkts in 25 Tests. 1st SA to score 100 v a touring side, v Lord Hawke's XI 1899. J. Henry according to *Wisden*.

SITJAR, Michel ('Cocoye') *France*
Agen.
b 14.9.42 Valence d'Agen.
Flanker, 13-10-1-2 (3 − 1t).
64 W= It+ I+ R+; 65 It+ R+; 67 A+ E+ It+(1t) W+ I+ SA− SA−.
Photographer. RL.

SKEEN, Jack Robert *New Zealand*
Vermont St Marist Bros' Sch, Sacred Heart Coll, Marist, Auckland.
b 23.12.28 Auckland.
Flanker, 1-1-0-0.
52 A+.
Transport supervisor. Coach Marist. Rep Auckland at ckt.

SKENE, Alan L. *South Africa*
W Prov.
b 2.10.32.
Wing, 1-0-0-1.
58 F−.
Clerk. Wakefield Trin (E) RL 58 .

SKINNER, Alan James *Australia*
Sydney HS, NSW.
b 16.8.42.
Flanker/lock, 3-1-0-2.
69 W− SA−; 70 S+.
Business exec.

SKINNER, Kevin Lawrence *New Zealand*
Christian Bros' Sch Dunedin, Otago, Waiuku, Counties, S Island.
b 24.11.27 Dunedin.
Prop, 20-12-1-7 (3 − 1t).
49 SA− SA− SA− SA−; 50 BI= BI+ BI+ BI+; 51 A+(1t) A+ A+; 52 A− A+; 53 W−; 54 I+ E+ S+ F−; 56 SA+ SA+.
Grocer/coffee bar proprietor. NZ > 49 SA, 51 A, 27 apps 53-4 BI,F & NAm. Capt v A 52. Otago heavywt boxing champ 46, NZ champ 47.

SKRÉLA, Jean-Claude *France*
Toulouse.
b 1.10.49 Colomiers.
Flanker, 46-27-5-14 (24 − 6t).
71 SA= A−(1t) A+; 72 I− E+ W− I− A=; 73 W+ J+(1t) R+; 74 W= E= S− Arg+ R−; 75 W−r E+ S+ I− SA− SA− Arg+(1t) Arg+(1t) R+; 76 S+ I+ W− E+ US+ A+ A+ R−; 77 W+(1t) E+ S+ I+ Arg+ Arg= NZ+ NZ−

R+; 78 E+ S+ I+ W−(1t).
PE teacher.

SKRIMSHIRE, Reginald Truscott　　*Wales*
Monmouth Sch, Newport, Blackheath.
b 30.1.1878 Crickhowell; *d* 20.9.63 Worthing.
Centre, 3-1-0-2.
1899 E+ S− I−; BT > 03 SA.
Civil engr. Only Welshman on BT > 03 SA; 4t
BI v Kingwilliamstown.

SKUDDER, George Rupuha　　*New Zealand*
Te Aute Coll, Univ, NZ Univs, NZ Maoris,
Waikato.
b 10.2.48 Te Puke.
Wing, 1-1-0-0 (3 − 1t).
69 W+(1t).
Schoolmaster. NZ > 72-3 BI,F & NAm.

SKYM, Archibald　　*Wales*
Drefach, Tumble, Llanelli, Cardiff.
b 12.7.06 Drefach; *d* 15.6.70 Cardiff.
Lock/prop/flanker, 20-9-2-9 (6 − 2t).
28 E− S+ I− F−; 30 E− S− I+(1t) F+(1t); 31
E= S+ F+ I+ SA−; 32 E+ S+ I−; 33 E+ S−
I−; 35 E=.
Miner/police.

SLACK, Andrew Gerard　　*Australia*
Brisbane, Comb Servs, Qld.
b 24.9.55.
Centre, 27-16-0-11 (16 − 4t).
78 W+ W+ NZ− NZ+; 79 NZ+ Arg− Arg+;
80 Fj+; 81 I+ W−(1t) S−(1t); 82 E− S− NZ−;
83 US+(2t) Arg− Arg+ NZ− It+; 84 Fj+
NZ+ NZ− NZ− E+ I+ W+ S+.
Schoolmaster. A > 78 NZ; 79 Arg; 80 Fj (capt);
81-2 & 84 (capt) BI.

SLADEN, Geoffrey Mainwaring　　*England*
DSO DSC
RNC Dartmouth, US Portsmouth, RN, Hants.
b 3.8.04.
Centre, 3-1-0-2.
29 W+ I− S−.
RN. Served WW2, submariner (with HMS
Trident in surface attack on German cruiser
Prinz Eugen). DSC 40. DSO 42; bar 42.
Promoted Capt 46. Rep RN, Dorset at hockey;
RN, R Marines at ath.

SLATER, Jack T.　　*South Africa*
Kingswood Coll Grahamstown, E Prov.
b 16.4.01.
Wing, 3-2-1-0 (6 − 2t).
24 BI= BI+(1t); 28 NZ+(1t).
HM. Staff of Kingswood Coll 55. Inj ruled him
out of 2nd Test v NZ 28; never again selected.

SLATER, Stephen Hazleton　　*Australia*
NSW.

Forward, 1-0-0-1.
10 NZ−.
Warehouseman.

SLATTERY, John Fergus　　*Ireland*
Blackrock Coll, UC Dublin, Barbarians.
b 12.2.49.
Flanker, 61-24-7-30 (12 − 3t).
70 SA= F− E− S+ W+; 71 F= E− S+ W−; 72
F+ E+ F+; 73 NZ= E+ S− W− F+; 74 F−
W= E+ S+ P=(1t) NZ−; 75 E+ S− F+ W−;
76 A−; 77 S− F−; 78 S+ F− W− E− NZ−; 79
F= W− E+ S= A+ A+; 80 E− S+ F− W+; 81
F− W−(1t) E− S− SA− SA− A−; 82 W+ E+
S+ F−; 83 S+ F+ W− E+(1t); 84 F−; BI > 71
A, NZ; 74 SA 4-3-1-0.
Auctioneer/estate agent. World's most capped
flanker, 65 (4 BI). Capt I > 81 SA.

SLEMEN, Michael Anthony　　*England*
Charles
St Edward's Coll Liverpool, St Luke's Coll,
Liverpool.
b 11.5.51 Liverpool.
Wing, 31-15-2-14 (32 − 8t).
76 I− F−; 77 S+(1t) I+ F− W−; 78 F− W− S+
I+(1t) NZ−; 79 S=(1t) I− F+ W− NZ−; 80
I+(1t) F+ W+ S+(1t); 81 W− S+(1t) I+ F−;
82 A+ S= I−(1t) F+ W+(1t); 83 NZ+; 84 S−;
BI > 80 SA 1-0-0-1.
Schoolmaster. E's most capped wing.

SLOAN, Allen Thomson DSO　　*Scotland*
Edinburgh Acad, Edinburgh Academicals,
Edinburgh Univ, Barbarians.
b 30.12.1892; *d* 2.10.52.
FH, 9-4-0-5 (9 − 3t).
14 W−; 20 F+ W+(1t) I+ E−; 21 F− W+(1t)
I−(1t) E−.
Medicine. Father of D.A.

SLOAN, D.A.　　*Scotland*
Edinburgh Acad, Edinburgh Academicals,
London Scottish, Barbarians.
b 11.5.26.
Centre, 7-3-0-4 (9 − 3t).
50 F+ W− E+(2t); 51 W+ I−(1t) E−; 53 F−.
Accountant. Son of A.T.

SLOAN, Sir Tennant KCIE CSI　　*Scotland*
Glasgow Acad, Glasgow Academicals, Glasgow
Univ, Oxford Univ, London Scottish.
b 9.11.1884; *d* 15.10.72 Edinburgh.
Wing/centre, 7-4-0-3.
05 NZ−; 06 W− SA+; 07 W+ E+; 08 W−; 09
I+.
Indian Civil Service. Blue 08.

SLOANE, Peter Henry　　*New Zealand*
Whangarei Boys' HS, Hikurangi, N Auckland,
N Island.

b 10.9.48 Whangarei.
Hooker, 1-1-0-0.
79 E+.
Builder. NZ > 76 Arg & Uruguay, 79 E,S & It.
NZ (2) v Arg 79.

SLOCOCK, Lancelot Andrew   *England*
Noel
Marlborough Coll, Liverpool, Lancs.
b 25.12.1886 Wootton Warren, Warwicks; kia
9.8.16 Guillemont.
Forward, 8-3-0-5 (9 − 3t).
07 F+(1t) W− I−(1t) S−; 08 F+ W− I+ S−
(1t).
Cotton industry employee. Sec Liverpool 07-8.
Served WW1 King's Liverpool Rgt, 2nd Lt. See
A. Alcock.

SLOW, Charles F.   *England*
Northampton, Leicester, E Midlands.
b 11 Northampton; d 15.4.39.
FH, 1-1-0-0.
34 S+.
Killed in motor accident while serving with
RAFVR.

SMALL, Harold Dudley   *England*
Dundee HS SA, Witwatersrand Univ, Oxford
Univ, Barbarians.
b 7.1.22.
Flanker, 4-1-0-3.
50 W− I+ F− S−.
Mining engr. Served WW2, engr Merchant
Navy 42-6. Rhodes Scholar. Blue 49-50.
Returned SA 51, became mining engr; Anglo-
American Corp 68.

SMALLWOOD, Alistair   *England*
McNaughton
RGS Newcastle, Cambridge Univ, Gosforth
Nomads, Northumb, Leicester, Leics.
b 18.11.1892 Alloa.
Wing, 14-12-1-1 (25 − 7t 1d).
20 F+ I+ ; 21 W+(2t) I+ S+ F+; 22 I+(1t) S+;
23 W+(1d) I+(1t) S+(1t) F+; 25 I=(2t) S−.
Schoolmaster. Served WW1, Lt 5th Northumb
Fusiliers. Blue 19. Asst master Uppingham Sch;
master i/c rugby 19-52. Bassoonist with
Stamford Orchestra. Noted amateur gardener.

SMART, Colin Edward   *England*
Skinners Sch Tunbridge Wells, Cardiff Coll,
Newport, Kent.
b 5.3.50 Highbury.
Prop, 17-7-3-7.
79 F+ W− NZ−; 81 S+ I+ F− Arg= Arg+; 82
A+ S= I− F+ W+; 83 F− W= S− I−.
Schoolmaster/building soc employee. Invited to
join Wales Squad 74. E > 79 Far East, 81 Arg.

SMART, Sidney E.J.   *England*
Deacon's Sch Gloucester, Gloucester, Glos.
b 1888.
No 8/flanker, 12-10-0-2.
13 SA− W+ F+ I+ S+; 14 W+ I+ S+ F+; 20
W− I+ S+.

SMARTT, Frank Nangle Bury   *Ireland*
Dublin HS, Trin Coll Dublin, Barbarians.
b 24.12.1885; d −.2.65.
SH, 3-1-0-2.
08 E− S+; 09 E−.
Medicine. Fiji Medical Service.

SMEATON, Patrick Walker   *Scotland*
Edinburgh Acad, Edinburgh Academicals,
Edinburgh Univ.
b 12.11.1857; d 11.8.28.
Half-back/centre, 3-1-0-2.
1881 I−; 1883 I+ E−.
Chartered accountant/stockbroker.

SMEDDLE, Robert William   *England*
Durham Sch, Cambridge Univ, Durham City,
Blackheath, Durham Co.
b 14.7.08.
Wing, 4-1-0-3 (6 − 2t).
29 W+ I−(1t) S−; 31 F−(1t).
Stockbroker/bus. Blue 28-31. Durham CCC.
Served WW2, Capt in the Army.

SMITH, Alan Edward   *New Zealand*
Stratford Tech HS, Stratford, NZ Colts,
Taranaki.
b 10.12.42 Stratford.
Lock, 3-2-0-1.
69 W+ W+; 70 SA−.
Farmer. NZ > 67 BI,F & C, 70 A & SA. Coach
Stratford 78-9. Father E.C. Smith rep Taranaki
36-9; uncle John Walter rep NZ 25. Ckt for
Taranaki.

SMITH, Allan Ramsay   *Scotland*
Loretto Sch, Oxford Univ, Barbarians.
b 10.1.1875; d 31.3.26.
FB/wing/centre, 11-5-4-2.
1895 W+ I+ E+; 1896 W− I=; 1897 I+ E−;
1898 I+ E=; 1900 I= E=.
HM. Blue 1894-7.

SMITH, Arthur Robert   *Scotland*
Kirkcudbright Sch, Glasgow Univ, Scottish
Univs, Cambridge Univ, Gosforth, Ebbw Vale,
Edinburgh W, Barbarians.
b 23.1.33 Castle Douglas; d 3.2.75 Edinburgh.
Wing, 33-13-2-18 (56 − 12t 1c 6p).
55 W+(1t) I+ E−; 56 F+(1p) W− I−(1t) E−
(1p); 57 F+ W+(1t) I− E−; 58 F+ W−(1p)
A+(2p) I−(1t); 59 F− W+ I− E=; 60 F−(2t)
W− I+ E−(1t) SA−(1t 1c); 61 F− SA−(1t)
W+(1t) I+ E−; 62 F−(1p) W+ I+(2t) E=; BI

> 55 SA, 62 SA 3-0-1-2.
Investment analyst/co dir. Blue 54-7. S's most capped wing. Capt S 15 times. 5t (3 apps) S > 60 SA. Capt BI > 62 SA. Barbarians > 58 SA. Scottish long jump champ 53.

SMITH, Bruce Warwick   *New Zealand*
Hamilton OB, Waikato, NZ Jnrs, N Island, NZ Barbarians.
b 4.1.59 Wairoa.
Wing, 3-2-0-1.
84 F+ F+ A−.
NZ > 83 S & E, 84 A.

SMITH, C.C. ('Whacker')   *England*
Gloucester.
Wing, 1-0-0-1.
01 W−.
Deal porter.

SMITH, Cornelius Michael   *South Africa*
('Nelie')
OFS.
b 8.5.34.
SH, 7-2-0-5 (12 − 1t 3p).
63 A−(3p) A+; 64 W+(1t) F−; 65 A− A− NZ−.
SARB nat dir of coaching. Capt SA v F 64; v-capt SA > 65 A, NZ. SA coach 80; OFS coach.

SMITH, C.W. ('Tooki')   *South Africa*
Griq W.
3-0-0-3.
1891 BT−; 1896 BT− BT−.
Sports shop owner/SARB employee.

SMITH, Daniel   *South Africa*
Griq W.
1-0-0-1.
1891 BT−.

SMITH, David J.   *South Africa*
Zimbabwe.
Centre, 4-3-0-1.
80 BI+ BI+ BI+ BI−.

SMITH, Douglas William   *Scotland*
Cumming
Aberdeen GS, Aberdeen Univ, London Scottish, RAMC, The Army, Barbarians.
b 27.10.24 Aberdeen.
Wing, 8-3-0-5 (3 − 1t).
49 F+ W+(1t) I− E−; 50 F+ W− I−; 53 I−; BI > 50 NZ & A 1-1-0-0.
Medicine. Mgr BI > 71 A, NZ. Pres SRU 86-7.

SMITH, Dyne Fenton   *England*
Sherborne Sch, Richmond, R Fusiliers, Barbarians, Surrey.
b 21.7.1890 Brighton; d 28.8.69.
Lock, 2-1-1-0.

10 W+ I=; BT > 1900 SA.
Stockbroker. Served WW1, Maj R Fusiliers.

SMITH, Errol Ross   *Scotland*
Edinburgh Acad, Edinburgh Academicals.
b 1860; d 23.3.02.
Forward, 1-1-0-0.
1879 I+.

SMITH, Frank Bede   *Australia*
King's Sch, NSW.
b 1886; d 54.
Centre, 4-0-1-3.
05 NZ−; 07 NZ− NZ− NZ=.
Grazier. Olympic gold rugby medal 08. A > 08-9 BI.

SMITH, George A.C.   *South Africa*
E Prov.
b −; d 78.
FB, 1-0-0-1.
38 BI−.

SMITH, George Kenneth   *Scotland*
George Watson's Coll, Kelso, Oklahoma Univ US, Barbarians.
b 2.6.31 Edinburgh.
No 8/flanker, 18-6-1-11.
57 I− E−; 58 F+ W− A+; 59 F− W+ I− E=; 60 F− W− I+ E−; 61 F− SA− W+ I+ E−; BI > 59 A 2-2-0-0, NZ 2-0-0-2.
Farmer.

SMITH, George William   *New Zealand*
Wellesley St Sch Auckland, City, Auckland, N Island.
b 20.9.1874 Auckland; d 7.12.54 Oldham, England.
Wing, 2-2-0-0 (6 − 2t).
05 S+(2t) I+.
Meat processors employee/textiles employee.
NZ > 05 A, 05-6 BI,F & NAm (19t − broke collar bone v Munster). Oldham RL (E) 08-16. One of NZ's outstanding athletes; held 12 national titles from 100y to 440y hurdles 1898-04. Won 2 Australasian titles & AAA 120y hurdles 02. Set unofficial world rec 58.5s over 440y hurdles. As a jockey won NZ Cup on Impulse 1894.

SMITH, Harry Oswald   *Scotland*
George Watson's Coll, Watsonians, Edinburgh Univ.
b 1873; d 31.7.57.
Forward, 11-5-3-3 (5 − 1t 1c).
1895 W+(1c); 1896 W− I= E+; 1898 I+ E=; 1899 I− W+(1t) E+; 1900 E=; 02 E−.
Medicine. Pres SRU 45-7.

SMITH, Ian Scott   *Scotland*
Cargilfield Sch, Winchester Coll, Oxford Univ,

Edinburgh Univ, Barbarians.
b 31.10.03 Melbourne, Aus; d 18.9.72
Edinburgh.
Wing, 32-20-0-12 (72 − 24t).
24 W+(3t) I+ E−; 25 F+(4t) W+(4t) I+ E+;
26 F+ W+ I− E+(2t); 27 F+(2t) I− E+(2t); 29
F+ W− I+(1t) E+(2t); 30 F− W+ I−; 31 F+
W− I− E+(2t); 32 SA− W− I− E−(1t); 33
W+(1t) E+ I+; BI > 24 SA 2-0-0-2.
Chartered accountant/solicitor. Blue 23.
World's leading int try scorer. S's most t (8) in
Champ season, 25. Twice scored 4t in an int, v F
& W 25.

SMITH, Ian Sidney Gibson   *Scotland*
Heriot's Coll, Edinburgh Univ, London
Scottish, RADC, The Army.
b 16.6.44 Dundee.
FB, 8-2-0-6 (14 − 2t 1c 2p).
69 SA+(1t 1p); 70 F−(1t) W− I−(1c) E+; 71
F−(1p) W− I−.
Dentist.

SMITH, Ian Stanley Talbot   *New Zealand*
('Spooky')
King's HS, Pirates, Otago, NZ Colts,
Gimmerburn, Oamaru OB, N Otago,
Wyndham, Southland, Woodlands, S Island.
b 20.8.41 Dunedin.
Wing, 9-8-0-1 (6 − 2t).
64 A+ A+ A−; 65 SA+ SA+ SA+(2t); 66 BI+
BI+ BI+.
Stock buyer/farmer. NZ > 63-4 BI,F & C.

SMITH, John Burns   *New Zealand*
Kaikohe Dist HS, Kaikohu, N Auckland, NZ
Maoris, N Island.
b 25.9.22 Kaikohe; d 3.12.74 Auckland.
Centre, 4-2-0-2 (6 − 1t 1d).
46 A+(1t); 47 A+; 49 A− A−(1d).
Baker. Served WW2; pl Comb Servs 44-5. NZ >
47 A. Capt v A 49. Father-in-law of Mike
Parkinson. Not considered for NZ > 49 SA
because of colour bar in SA. 1st recipient of
Tom French Cup for outstanding Maori Player
of Year, 49. N Auckland selector 56. Father Len
rep N Island Country 12; bro Peter NZ 47 (no
Tests).

SMITH, John Hartley   *Ireland*
Methodist Coll Belfast, Queen's Univ Belfast,
London Irish, Collegians, Barbarians.
b 27.7.26 Dungannon.
Prop, 12-5-1-6.
51 F+ E+ S+ W= SA−; 52 F+ S+ W− E−; 54
NZ− F− W−.
Medicine. Emigrated to Can.

SMITH, John Vincent JP   *England*
Marling Sch Stroud, Cambridge Univ, Stroud,
Rosslyn Pk, The Army, Barbarians, Glos.

Wing, 4-1-0-3 (12 − 4t).
50 W−(1t) I+ F−(1t) S−(2t).
Catering/dir corn, agric merchants. Blue 48-50.
Ath blue 49. Pres Hawks Club 50-1. Army 44-8.
Glos CB rep 61-71; pres RFU 82-3. Fdr mem,
pres Minchinhampton RFC. Lib candidate
Stroud Gen Election 66. Author 'Good Morning
President. Rugby from the top' pub 85.

SMITH, J. Sidney   *Wales*
Cardiff.
Forward, 3-1-0-2.
1884 E− I+; 1885 E−.
Articled to Cardiff Town Clerk.

SMITH, Keith   *England*
Cross Green Sch Leeds, Roundhay.
b 19.11.52 Leeds.
Centre, 4-2-1-1.
74 F= W+; 75 W− S+.
Rent collector. Wakefield Trin RL 77.

SMITH, Lancelot Machattie   *Australia*
King's Sch, NSW.
b 1885; d 56.
Centre, 1-0-0-1.
05 NZ−.
Grazier/horse racing official.

SMITH, Michael Adam   *Scotland*
Glasgow Acad, Fettes Coll, Cambridge Univ,
London Scottish, Barbarians.
b 23.11.45 Liverpool.
Wing, 4-1-0-3 (3 − 1t).
70 W− I−(1t) E+ A−.
Medicine. Blue 66-7. Scottish XV v Arg (2) 69.

SMITH, Michael John Knight   *England*
OBE
Stamford Sch, Oxford Univ, Hinckley,
Leicester, Leics, Barbarians.
b 30.6.33 Broughton Astley, Leics.
FH, 1-0-0-1.
56 W−.
Administrative staff/gen mgr grandstands co.
Blue 54-5. Ckt blue 54-6 (477 runs in 3 apps v
Cambridge) − 43 apps OUCC 54-6; 28 apps
Leics CCC 51-55; 430 apps Warwicks CCC 56-75
(capt 57-67, asst sec 56-7); 50 apps E 58-72 (capt
25 times). OBE for services to ckt. CY 60.

SMITH, Philip Vivers   *Australia*
Sydney Boys HS, NSW.
b 15.7.46.
Centre, 8-1-0-7 (6 − 2t).
67 NZ−; 68 NZ− NZ− F+(1t) I− S−; 69 W−
(1t) SA−.
Audit clerk. RL.

SMITH, Reginald Allan   *Australia*
NSW.

374

b 13.1.48.
Lock, 22-10-1-11 (4 − 1t).
71 SA− SA−; 72 F= F− NZ− NZ−r NZ−
Fj+; 75 E+ E+(1t) J+ J+ S− W−; 76 E− I+
US+ Fj+ Fj+ Fj+ F− F−.
Civil service/min of agric.

SMITH, R.E.   *Ireland*
Lansdowne.
Forward, 1-0-0-1.
1892 E−.

SMITH, Robert Tait   *Scotland*
Kelso HS, Kelso.
b 08; *d* 7.4.58 Hawick.
Prop, 7-4-0-3.
29 F+ W− I+ E+; 30 F− W+ I−.
Baker.

SMITH, Ross Mervyn   *New Zealand*
Timaru Boys' HS, Christchurch, Canterbury, S
Island.
b 21.4.29 Ashburton.
Wing, 1-1-0-0.
55 A+.
Co mgr. 1st NZ to score over 100t in 1st-class
rugby (152 apps). Selector for Hawkes Bay &
Nelson Bays. Nephew of Alan Robilliard.

SMITH, S.H.   *Scotland*
Glasgow Acad, Glasgow Academicals.
Forward, 2-1-1-0.
1877 I+; 1878 E=.

SMITH, Simon Timothy   *England*
King Edward VI Sch Lichfield, Staffs SS,
Lancaster Univ, E Students, Lichfield, Fylde,
Cambridge Univ, Wasps, Staffs, Lancs,
Barbarians.
b 29.4.60 Baldock.
Wing, 9-3-1-5 (12 − 3t).
85 R+(1t) F= S+(1t) I− W−(1t) NZ− NZ−;
86 W+ S−.
England SS > 79 A. Blue 82-3. Ath blue.
Cambridge Univ > R, J; E Students > Far East.
E Under 23s.

SMITH, Stephen James   *England*
King's Sch Macclesfield, Loughborough Coll,
Sale, Lancs.
b 22.7.51 Stockport.
SH, 28-13-4-11 (8 − 2t).
73 I− F+ S+ A+; 74 I− F=; 75 W−r; 76 F−;
77 F−r; 79 NZ−; 80 I+(1t) F+ W+ S+(1t); 81
W− S+ I+ F− Arg= Arg+; 82 A+ S= I− F+
W+; 83 F− W= S−; BIr > 80 SA, r > 83 NZ.
Schoolmaster. E's most capped SH. Rugby corr
'Today' newspaper.

SMITH, Stephen Rider   *England*
Eltham Coll, Cambridge Univ, Aldershot Servs,

Richmond, Barbarians, Hants.
b 21.10.34 India.
SH, 5-1-2-2.
59 W− F= S=; 64 F+ S−.
Schoolmaster/educational missionary. Blue 58-9
(capt). Capt Richmond & Hants. Asst master
Harrow Sch. Left to become educational
missionary in India. Played for India v Ceylon
68.

SMITH, Thomas J.   *Scotland*
Gala.
b 31.8.53 MacMerry, E Lothian.
Lock, 4-1-1-2 (4 − 1t).
83 E+(1t) NZ=; 85 I− F−.
S > 84 R.

SMITH, Trellevyn Harvey   *England*
('Trevor')
Northampton.
b 3.4.20 Bedford.
Hooker, 1-0-0-1.
51 W−.
Motor engrg co.

SMITH, Wayne Ross   *New Zealand*
Putaruru HS, Belfast, Canterbury.
b 19.4.57 Putaruru.
1st five-eighth, 17-11-2-4 (10 − 1t 2d).
80 A−; 82 A+ A− A+(1d); 83 BI+ BI+ S=
E−; 84 F+ F+(1t) A− A+ A+; 85 E+ E+(1d)
A+ Arg=.
Oil co rep. NZ > 80 A & Fj, 83 S & E, 84 A, 85
Arg. NZ's most capped 1st five-eighth. Pl for
Rest of World v BI, Cardiff 86.

SMITH, William Ernest   *New Zealand*
Nelson Coll, Nelson, S Island.
b 9.3.1881 Wellington; *d* 25.5.45 Wellington.
Five-eighth, 1-1-0-0.
05 A+.
Clerk.

SMITHWICK, Frederick Falkiner   *Ireland*
Standish
Corrig Coll Kingstown, Monkstown.
Centre, 2-0-0-2.
1898 S− W−.
Minister. Capped from school. Served in R
Army Chaplains Dept.

SMOLLAN, Frederick C.   *South Africa*
Transvaal.
b 20.8.08.
3-2-0-1.
33 A+ A+ A−.
Bus/metal industry.

SMYTH, John Trevor   *Ireland*
Campbell Coll Belfast, Queen's Univ Belfast.
b 27.1.1897 Holywood, Co Down.

Flanker, 1-0-0-1.
20 F−.
Medicine. Lt Col in RAMC.

SMYTH, Patrick James   *Ireland*
Methodist Coll Belfast, Collegians, Barbarians.
b Raswarkin, Ballymena; *d* 12.1.28 Sydney,
NSW.
Forward, 3-3-0-0.
11 E+ S+ F+.
Bus. Capped from sch. Bro of Thomas &
William.

SMYTH, Robertson Stewart   *Ireland*
RS Dungannon, Trin Coll Dublin, Wanderers,
Barbarians.
b 1880 Banbridge, Co Down; *d* 5.4.16 London.
Forward, 3-1-0-2.
03 E+ S−; 04 E−; BT > 03 SA.
Medicine. Served WW1, Maj in RAMC,
mentioned in despatches; died from effects of
active service.

SMYTH, Thomas   *Ireland*
Ballymena Acad, Malone, Newport,
Barbarians.
b −.12.1884 Co Antrim; *d* −.5.28 London.
Forward, 14-4-1-9 (3 − 1t).
08 E− S+ W−; 09 E− S− W−; 10 E= S− W−
F+; 11 E+(1t) S+ W−; 12 E−; BI > 10 SA 2-1-
0-1.
Medicine. Bro of Patrick & William. Capt BI >
10 SA. Employed at R Gwent Hosp, Newport.

SMYTH, William S.   *Ireland*
Methodist Coll Belfast, Collegians.
b Raswarkin, Ballymena; *d* −.1.37 Belfast.
Forward, 3-1-0-2 (3 − 1t).
10 W− F+(1t); 20 E−.
Flax spinners co dir. Bro of Patrick & Thomas.
10 yrs between caps.

SNEDDEN, Robert C.   *South Africa*
Griq W.
1-0-0-1.
1891 BT−.
Capt v BT 2nd Test 1891.

SNOW, Eric McDonald ('Fritz')   *New Zealand*
Nelson, S Island.
b 19.4.1898 Nelson; *d* 24.7.74 Nelson.
No 8/flanker, 3-0-0-3.
29 A− A− A−.
Storeman. NZ > 28 SA, 29 A. Nelson comm &
selector. Bros Herbert & W.V. also rep Nelson.

SNYMAN, David Stephanus   *South Africa*
Lubbe ('Dawie')
Stellenbosch Univ, W Prov.
b 5.7.49 Johannesburg.
FH/FB, 10-6-0-4 (24 − 1t 1c 2d 4p).

72 E−(3p); 74 BI−(1d) BI−r F+ F+; 75 F+
F+; 76 NZ− NZ+(1d); 77 Wd+.
PE teacher. Bro of Jackie. 54 pts SA > 71 A.

SNYMAN, Jacobus Cornelius   *South Africa*
Pauw ('Jackie')
OFS.
b 14.4.48 Johannesburg.
FH, 3-0-1-2 (18 − 6p).
74 BI− BI−(3p) BI=(3p).
Sports organiser. Bro of Dawie.

SOANE, Frank ('Buster')   *England*
Clifton House Eastbourne, Oldfield Pk, Bath,
Barbarians, Som.
b 12.9.1866 Bath; *d* 32.
Forward, 4-1-0-3.
1893 S−; 1894 W+ I− S−.
Owner family pianoforte, music bus. Capt Bath
1890-8; 45 apps Som (capt 1896-9, sec 1896-9,
pres 1900).

SOBEY, Wilfred Henry   *England*
Mill Hill Sch, Cambridge Univ, O Millhillians,
Barbarians, London Cos, Hants.
b 1.4.05.
SH, 5-2-1-2.
30 W+ F+ S=; 32 SA− W−; BI > 30 A, NZ.
HM. Blue 25-6. BT > 27 Arg. Master Belmont
Prep Sch; Head Kingsfield Prep Oxhey, Herts.

SOLE, David Michael Barclay   *Scotland*
Glenalmond Sch, Scottish Schs, Exeter Univ,
UAU, Bath, Devon, Somerset, Anglo-Scots,
Toronto Scottish (Can).
b 8.5.62 Aylesbury, Bucks.
Prop, 2-1-0-1.
86 F+ W−.
Schoolmaster. 5 apps Scotland B. Spent some
time teaching in Can.

SOLER   *France*
Quillan.
Wing, 1-1-0-0 (6 − 2t).
29 G+(2t).

SOLOMON, Bert ('Barney')   *England*
Treleigh Rgrs, Redruth, Cornwall.
b 8.3.1885; *d* 30.6.61.
Centre, 1-1-0-0 (3 − 1t).
10 W+(1t).
Butcher. Mem of Cornwall XV which won
Olympic silver medal for rugby, as GB v A 08.
Son Alfred rep Devon/Cornwall v A 47.

SOLOMON, Frank   *New Zealand*
Apia Sch W Samoa, Levuka Sch Fiji, Seddon
Memorial Tech Coll, N Shore, Ponsonby, NZ
Maoris, Auckland, N Island.
b 30.5.06 Pago Pago, US Samoa.
Flanker/no 8, 3-3-0-0 (3 − 1t).

31 A+; 32 A+ A+(1t).
Commercial traveller. NZ > 32 A. Poverty Bay
selector 46-9. Coach Gisborne & Ponsonby.
Rep Auckland at rowing. Bro David rep NZ 35-
6 (no Tests); another bro George rep Waikato
37-8.

SOLOMON, Herbert John   *Australia*
The Scots Coll, NSW.
b 15.10.29 Randwick.
Wing/centre, 14-5-0-9 (12 − 2t 1d 1p).
49 M+ NZ+(1t); 50 BI− BI−; 51 NZ− NZ−;
52 Fj+(1t) Fj−(1d) NZ+ NZ−; 53 SA− SA+
SA−(1p); 55 NZ−.
Medicine. Capt A > 52, 55 NZ; 53 SA.

SOLOMONS, Bethel Albert   *Ireland*
Herbert
St Andrews Coll, Trin Coll Dublin.
b 27.2.1885; *d* 11.9.65.
Forward, 10-2-1-7.
08 E− S+ W−; 09 E− S− W− F+; 10 E= S−
W−.
Medicine.

SOMERVILLE, D.   *Scotland*
Edinburgh Inst, Edinburgh Inst FP.
Forward, 6-5-0-1 (2t).
1879 I+(1t); 1882 I+; 1883 W+ I+(1t) E−;
1884 W+.
Ckt for S.

SONNEKUS, Gerhardus   *South Africa*
Hermanus Henricus
Welkom Gimnasium Sch, UOFS, Gazelles,
OFS.
b 1.2.53 Senekal.
SH/no 8, 3-2-0-1 (4 − 1t).
74 BI−; 84 E+ E+(1t).
Accountant. Selected to play SH v BI 74,
although a no 8. Reverted to no 8 when next
capped 10 yrs later, v E 84.

SONNTAG, William Theodore   *New Zealand*
Charles
Kaikorai Sch, King Edward Tech Coll,
Kaikorai, Otago, S Island.
b 3.6.1894 Dunedin.
No 8, 3-0-0-3.
29 A− A− A−.
Electrical co proprietor. Selected NZ > 29 A on
35th birthday. Uncle rep Otago 1888-9.

SORO, Robert   *France*
Lourdes, Romans.
b 28.11.22 Odos.
Lock, 21-12-0-9 (6 − 2t).
45 BF+ BF− W−; 46 BF+ I+ NZS−; 47 S+ I+
W− E−(1t); 48 I−(1t) A+ S− W+ E+; 49 S−
I+ E− W+ Arg+ Arg+.

SORRONDO, Michel   *France*
Montauban.
b 16.7.19 Hendaye; *d* 24.7.76.
Centre, 6-2-0-4 (3 − 1t).
\ 46 NZS−; 47 S+ I+(1t) W− E−; 48 I−.
. Montauban RL.

SOULIÉ, Eugène   *France*
CASG.
Prop/no 8, 9-4-1-4.
20 E− I+ US+; 21 S+ E− I+; 22 E= W− I−.

SOURGENS, Joseph   *France*
Bègles.
b 3.9.03 Vehoux, Landes.
FH, 1-0-0-1.
26 M−.

SPAIN, Alexander William   *Ireland*
Blackrock Coll, UC Dublin.
b 22.9.1897 Cashel; *d* 24.2.83 Dublin.
1-0-0-1.
24 NZ−.
Medicine.

SPANGHÉRO, Claude   *France*
Narbonne.
b 5.6.48 Parra-sur-l'Hers, Aude.
Lock/no 8, 22-7-5-10 (8 − 2t).
71 E= W− SA− SA= A− A+(1t) R+; 72 S−
E+ W− I− A= A+; 74 I+ W= E= S− R−
SA−; 75 E+(1t) S+ I−.
Cattle dealer. Played with bro Walter in 7 ints.

SPANGHÉRO, Walter   *France*
Narbonne.
b 21.12.43 Parra-sur-l'Hers, Aude.
Lock/flanker/no 8, 51-25-6-20 (10 − 3t).
64 SA+ Fj+ R+; 65 S+ I= E− W+ It+ R+; 66
S= I+ E+ W− It+ R+; 67 S− A+ E+ SA−
SA− SA+ SA=(1t) NZ−; 68 S+ I+ E+ W+
NZ− NZ− NZ− A−(1t) SA− SA− R−; 69 S−
I− W=; 70 R+; 71 E= W− SA−; 72 E+(1t) I−
A= A+ R+; 73 S+ NZ+ E− W+ I−
Co proprietor. Played with bro Claude in 7 ints.
Capt F > 72 A.

SPARKS, Brian Anthonie   *Wales*
Cowbridge GS, St Luke's Coll Exter, Neath.
b 23.6.31 Llanhavan.
Flanker, 7-5-0-2.
54 I+; 55 E+ F+; 56 E+ S+ I−; 57 S−.
Police/schoolmaster. Halifax RL 57.

SPARKS; Robert Henry Ware   *England*
Plymouth A, Civil Service, Devon.
b 19.2.1899.
Prop/lock, 9-4-0-5.
28 I+ F+ S+; 29 W+ I− S−; 31 I− S− F−.
Chargehand HM Dockyard. Fell off motorcycle
on eve of W v E 30; place taken by Sam Tucker

377

who was flown to Cardiff on morning of match. Capt Plymouth A 34, Devon 34.

SPARROW, Willis   *Ireland*
Foyle Coll, Trin Coll Dublin.
FB, 2-1-0-1.
1893 W−; 1894 E+.

SPEED, Harry   *England*
Castleford.
b 19.8.1871 Castleford; d 3.7.37 Castleford.
Forward, 4-1-0-3.
1894 W+ I− S−; 1896 S−.
Collier/licensee. Castleford RL. E cap at Castleford RFC.

SPEIRS, Louis Moritz MM   *Scotland*
George Watson's Coll, Watsonians.
b 23.10.1885 Edinburgh; d −.4.49 Mexico.
Forward, 10-6-0-4.
06 SA+; 07 W+ I+ E+; 08 W− I− E+; 10 F+ W− E−; BI > 10 SA.

SPENCE, Frederick William   *England*
Fettes Coll, Birkenhead Pk.
b −.5.1867; d −.
Half-back, 1-1-0-0.
1890 I+.
Civil service. Emigrated A, JP for W Aus. R Humane Soc medal for saving person from drowning in Sydney Harbour.

SPENCE, Kenneth Magnus   *Scotland*
Loretto Sch, Oxford Univ, London Scottish, Barbarians.
b 21.11.29.
SH, 1-0-0-1.
53 I−.
Exec servs co dir. Blue 51-2.

SPENCER, E.   *Scotland*
Glasgow HS, Craigmount Inst, Clydesdale.
Centre, 1-1-0-0.
1898 I+.

SPENCER, Jeremy   *England*
Harlequins, St Jean-de-Luz (F).
b 27.6.39.
SH, 1-0-0-1.
66 W−.
Painter/weaver of tweeds. Held exhibition of his work with Spanish painter Juan Benito.

SPENCER, John Clarence   *New Zealand*
Mt Cook Sch, Melrose, Wellington, N Island.
b 27.11.1880 Wellington; d 21.5.36 Wellington.
Flanker, 2-2-0-0.
05 A+; 07 A+r.
Plumber. NZ > 03, 07 A. 1st NZ player to play as r, v A 07. RL 08, rep NZ 09. Three bros rep

Wellington; George accompanying J.C. on > 07 A.

SPENCER, John Sothern   *England*
Cressbrook Sch Kirby Lonsdale, Sedbergh Sch, Cambridge Univ, Headingley, Wharfedale, Barbarians.
b 10.8.47.
Centre, 14-5-0-9 (6 − 2t).
69 I− F+ S+ W− SA+; 70 I+ W− S−(1t) F− (1t); 71 W− I+ S− S− P−; BI > 71 A, NZ.
Solicitor. Son of Yorks solicitor. Blue 67-9 (capt 69). Capt E Under 25 v Fj 70.

SPIERS, John Edmunde   *New Zealand*
Onewhero HS, Pukekohe, Counties.
b 4.8.47 Otahuhu.
Prop, 5-5-0-0.
79 S+ E+; 81 R+ F+ F+.
Wool buyer. NZ > 76 Arg & Uruguay, 79 E,S & It, 80 A & Fj; NAm & W, 81 R & F.

SPIES, Johannes Jacobus   *South Africa*
N Transvaal.
b 8.5.45 Harrismith.
4-3-0-1.
70 NZ+ NZ− NZ+ NZ+.
Accountant/farmer. SA > 71 A.

SPILLANE, Augustine Patrick   *New Zealand*
Temuka Ath, S Canterbury, Temuka.
b 10.5.1888 Geraldine; d 16.9.74 Timaru.
2nd five-eighth, 2-1-0-1.
13 A+ A−.
Farmer. Bros Charles, William & Jack rep S Canterbury.

SPILLANE, Brian Jeremiah   *Ireland*
CBC Limerick, UC Cork, Irish Univs, Bohemians, Munster.
b 26.1.60 Cork.
No 8, 7-3-1-3
85 S+ F= W+ E+; 86 F− W− E−.
Medicine. 6ft 5in.

SPILLER, William John   *Wales*
Cardiff.
b 8.7.1886 St Fagan's; d 9.6.70 Cardiff.
Centre, 10-7-0-3 (16 − 4t 1d).
10 S+(1t) I+; 11 E+(1t) S+(2t 1d) F+ I+; 12 E− F+ SA−; 13 E−.
Police. Nominated 'best centre in Wales' 12. Scored 1st century in 1st class ckt for Glam CCC. Bowled for Glam.

SPONG, Roger Spencer   *England*
Mill Hill Sch, O Millhillians, E Midland W, Barbarians, Mdx.
b 23.10.06; d 27.3.80.
FH, 8-3-1-4.
29 F+; 30 W+ I− F+ S=; 31 F−; 32 SA− W−;

378

BI > 30 A 1-0-0-1, NZ 4-1-0-3.
Co dir family hardware bus/aircraft engrs. Capt
O Millhillians 30-1, chmn 67-71.

SPOONER, Reginald Herbert   *England*
Marlborough Coll, Marlborough Nomads,
Liverpool, Lancs.
b 21.10.1880 Litherland; d 2.10.61 Woodhall
Spa.
Centre, 1-0-0-1.
03 W−.
Land agent for Earl of Londesborough. Served
Boer War 1900, Manchester Rgt; WW1 Lincs
Rgt (Mons Star); made Capt 15. Ckt −
Marlborough Nomads, Lancs CCC, E (10 Tests,
v A 02, 12; v SA 12). CY 05.

SPRAGG, Alonzo Stephen   *Australia*
('Lonnie')
NSW.
b 2.10.1879; d 12.2.04 Brisbane.
Wing, 4-1-0-3 (17 − 3t 4c).
1899 BT+(1t 2c) BT− BT−(2t 2c) BT−.
Savings bank.

SPRING, Donal Eugene   *Ireland*
Mount St Joseph Coll Roscrea, Trin Coll
Dublin.
b 23.8.56 Tralee.
Lock, 7-3-1-3.
78 S+ NZ−; 79 S=; 80 S+ F− W+; 81 W−.
Law.

SPRING, Richard Martin   *Ireland*
Roscrea Coll, Trin Coll Dublin, Lansdowne.
b 29.8.50 Tralee.
FB, 3-1-1-1.
79 F= W− E+.
Barrister/MP. I's deputy PM.

SPRINGMAN (originally   *England*
SPRINGMANN), Herman Henry
Craigmount Sch Edinburgh, Liverpool, Lancs.
b 1859 Liverpool; d 17.10.36.
Forward, 2-0-2-0.
1879 S=; 1887 S=.
Cotton broker. Emigrated US after being
capped 1879; returned 7 yrs later to be capped
again, 1887. Bro of P. Springmann, Oxford blue
1877-8.

SPUNNER, H.F.   *Ireland*
Wanderers.
Half-back, 3-1-0-2.
1881 E− S+; 1884 W−.

SPURLING, Aubrey   *England*
Blackheath Proprietary Sch, Blackheath, Kent.
b 19.7.1856; d 26.3.45.
Forward, 1-0-1-0.
1882 I=.

Treas of Blackheath; Club's 1st historian. Bro of
Norman.

SPURLING, Norman   *England*
Blackheath Proprietary Sch, Blackheath, Kent.
b 15.2−.1864; d 20.7.19.
Forward, 3-1-2-0.
1886 I+ S=; 1887 W=.
Bro of Aubrey. Capped in 1888 E side that did
not play.

SQUIRE, Jeffrey   *Wales*
Newbridge GS, St Luke's Coll, Newport,
Pontypool, Barbarians.
b 23.9.51 Newport.
No 8/flanker, 29-16-1-12 (8 − 2t).
77 I+ F−; 78 E+ S+ I+ F+ A− NZ−; 79 S+
I+ F− E+; 80 F+ E− S+ I− NZ−; 81 E+ S−
I+ F− A+; 82 I− F+ E−; 83 E=(1t) S+ I+ F−
(1t); BIr > 77 NZ 1-0-0-1; 80 SA 4-1-0-3; 83 NZ
1-0-0-1.
Schoolmaster/dir sportswear co. Wales B v F 76.
W > 78 A. Wales XV v Arg 76r, R 79, Maoris
82. Replaced inj Roger Uttley BI > 77 NZ.

SQUIRES, Peter John   *England*
Ripon GS, St John's Coll York, Harrogate,
Yorks.
b 4.8.51 Ripon.
Wing, 29-12-2-15 (24 − 6t).
73 F+ S+(1t) NZ+(1t) A+; 74 S− I−(1t) F=
W+; 75 I− F− W− S+ A−(1t) A−(1t); 76 A+
W−; 77 S+ I+ F− W−; 78 F− W− S+(1t) I+
NZ−; 79 S= I− F+ W−; BI > 77 NZ 1-0-0-1.
Schoolmaster/rep. 49 apps Yorks CCC 72-6.

STACK, C.R.R.   *Ireland*
Armagh RS, Trin Coll Dublin.
Forward, 1-0-0-1.
1889 S−.

STACK, George Hall   *Ireland*
Raphoe Coll, UC Dublin.
b −; d −.11.1876.
Forward, 1-0-0-1.
1875 E−.
I's 1st capt, v E 1875.

STADDEN, William James Wood   *Wales*
('Buller')
Cardiff, Dewsbury.
b 1860; d 30.12.06 Dewsbury.
Half-back, 8-5-0-3 (1t 1d).
1884 I+(1d); 1886 E− S−; 1887 I+; 1888 S+
NZN+; 1890 S− E+(1t).
Butcher/licensee. 1st d for W, v I 1884.
Dewsbury RL c1894, 1st Welsh int to join RL.
Took own life.

STAFFORD, Richard Calvert   *England*
Bedford Mod Sch, Bedford.

b 23.7.1893 Bedford; *d* 1.12.12 Bedford.
Prop, 4-3-0-1.
12 W+ I+ S− F+.
Died of spinal cancer at 19, youngest age at
which an E player died.

STAFFORD, William Francis   *England*
Howard CB
Wellington Coll, RMA Sandhurst, RE, The
Army.
b 19.12.1854; *d* 8.8.42.
Forward, 1-1-0-0.
1874 S+.
The Army. Son of Maj-Gen W.J.F. Stafford.
Served Afghan War 1878-80; mentioned in
despatches. Served SA War 1899-02 (Queen's &
King's Medals). Retired as Brig Gen 11, but
returned to serve WW1, aged 60; mentioned in
despatches.

STAGG, Peter Kidner   *Scotland*
St Paul's Sch, O Paulines, Oxford Univ, Surrey,
Sale, Barbarians, Cheshire.
b 22.11.41 Twickenham.
Lock, 28-10-2-16.
65 F− W− E= SA+; 66 F= W− I+ E+ A+; 67
F+ W+ I− E− NZ−; 68 F− W− I− E− A+;
69 F+ W− I−r SA+; 70 F− W− I− E+ A−;
BI > 68 SA 3-0-1-2.
ICI technical rep. Blue 61-2. 6ft 10in, tallest
ever int player. Scottish XV v Arg (2) 69.

STANBURY, Edward   *England*
Plymouth A, Devon, Barbarians.
b 1897 Plympton; *d* 1.5.68 Plympton.
Flanker, 16-9-1-6 (13 − 5c 1p).
26 W= I− S−; 27 W+(1c 1p) I+(1c) S−(1c)
F−; 28 NSW+ W+ I+ F+ S+; 29 W+ I− S−
F+(2c).
Rating officer. Rep Devon on RFU 63-8.

STANDER, Jacobus Casparus   *South Africa*
Johannes ('Rampie')
OFS.
b 25.12.45 Cape Town; *d* −.8.80
Bloemfontein.
Prop, 5-3-1-1.
74 BI=r; 76 NZ+ NZ− NZ+ NZ+.
Lawyer. SA > 74 F.

STANDING, G.   *England*
Blackheath.
Forward, 2-2-0-0.
1882 W+; 1883 I+.
81 apps Blackheath 1881-5.

STANGER-LEATHES,   *England*
Christopher Francis
Sherborne Sch, Northern, Northumb.
b 9.5.1881; *d* 27.2.65.
FB, 1-0-0-1.

05 I−; BT(uncap) > 04 A, NZ.
Marine engr/ventilating engr. Capt co at ckt &
golf.

STAPELBERG, Willem P.   *South Africa*
N Transvaal.
b 29.1.47.
Wing, 2-2-0-0 (8 − 2t).
74 F+(1t) F+(1t).
Police.

STAPLETON, Edgar Thomas   *Australia*
NSW.
b 21.11.30 Sutherland.
Wing, 16-5-0-11 (22 − 5t 2c 1p).
51 NZ− NZ− NZ−; 52 Fj+(1t) Fj−(1t) NZ+
NZ−; 53 SA− SA+(1t 1c) SA− SA−(1t); 54
Fj+; 55 NZ−(1p) NZ− NZ+(1t 1c); 58 NZ−.
Electrician/licensee. Cousin of Bill Cerutti. 47
pts (12t) A > 55 NZ.

STARK, Kendrick James   *England*
Dulwich Coll, O Alleynians, HAC, TA, London
Cos, Surrey.
b 18.8.04.
Prop, 9-7-0-2 (5 − 1c 1p).
27 W+ I+ S−(1c 1p) F−; 28 NSW+ W+ I+ F+
S+.
Insurance. Served WW2, Capt RASC.
Mentioned in despatches.

STARKE, James J.   *South Africa*
Stellenbosch Univ, W Prov.
b 16.5.31.
Flanker, 1-0-0-1.
56 NZ−.
SAr > 56 A, NZ

STARKE, Kenneth T.   *South Africa*
Stellenbosch Univ, W Prov.
b − ; *d* 81.
Wing, 4-3-1-0 (13 − 3t 1d).
24 BI+ BI+(1t) BI= BI+(2t 1d).
Farmer.

STARKS, Anthony   *England*
Castleford.
b 11.8.1873 Castleford; *d* −.1.52 Hull.
Forward, 2-1-0-1.
1896 W+ I−.
Licensee. Hull KR RL 1897.

STARMER-SMITH, Nigel   *England*
Christopher
Magdalen Coll Sch Oxford, Oxford Univ,
Harlequins, Barbarians, Oxon, Surrey.
b 25.12.44 Cheltenham.
SH, 7-2-0-5.
69 SA+; 70 I+ W− S− F−; 71 S− P−.
Schoolmaster/TV commentator. Blue 65-6.
Master at Epsom Coll. Hockey for Oxon; ckt for

TA. Author of 'The Barbarians', official history, pub 77.

START, Sydney Philip *England*
Manchester GS, RNEC Keyham, US Portsmouth, RN, Devon, Surrey.
b 17.5.1879 Broughton, Manchester; *d* 14.12.69 Harrietsham, Kent.
SH, 1-0-0-1.
07 S−.
RN. Rear Adm. Joined RN 1894. Served WW1. ADC to King George V 31. Cambs CCC.

STEAD, John William *New Zealand*
Southland Boys' HS, Star, Southland, NZ Maoris, S Island.
b 18.9.1877 Invercargill; *d* 21.7.58 Bluff.
2nd/1st five-eighth, 7-7-0-0.
04 BT+; 05 S+ I+ E+; 06 F+; 08 AW+ AW+.
Bootmaker. 1st NZ capt in home Test, v BT 04. NZ > 03 A; v-capt 05-6 BI,F & NAm. In 42 NZ apps, never on losing side. NZ Maoris > 10 A. Mgr/coach NZ v SA 21. Bro Norman rep Southland & NZ Maoris. Co-author with Dave Gallaher 'The Complete Rugby Footballer' pub 06. Columnist for 'NZ Truth'.

STEEDS, John Harold *England*
St Edward's Sch Oxford, Cambridge Univ, Mdx Hosp, Saracens, Barbarians, Mdx.
b 27.9.16.
Hooker, 5-3-0-2.
49 F+ S+; 50 I+ F− S−.
Medicine. Blue 38. Served WW2, Surg Lt RNVR. Registrar Mdx Hosp 46-50, then GP.

STEEL, Anthony Gordon *New Zealand*
Christchurch Boys' HS, HSOB, Canterbury, Southland.
b 31.7.41 Greymouth.
Wing, 9-9-0-0 (21 − 7t).
66 BI+ BI+(1t) BI+(1t) BI+(1t); 67 A+(2t); 67 F+(1t) S+; 68 A+(1t) A+.
HM at Hamilton Boys' HS. NZ > 67 BI,F & C, 68 A & Fj. Coached clubs in A; Qld sel 74. NZ sprint champ 65-6; 9.6s best 100y time.

STEEL, John *New Zealand*
Greymouth Star, West Coast, Albion, Canterbury, S Island.
b 10.11.1898 Dillmanstown; *d* 4.8.41 S Beach.
Wing, 6-4-1-1 (9 − 3t).
21 SA+(1t) SA− SA=; 24 W+; 25 E+(1t) F+(1t).
Rly employee/licensee. Pro sprinter. NZ > 20 & 22 A, 24-5 BI,F & C (21t). Killed in motor accident.

STEELE, Harold William *Ireland*
Rainey Endowed Sch, Queen's Univ Belfast, Comb Univs, Ballymena, Ulster.
b 4.9.48 Cookstown.
No 8/lock, 10-4-1-5.
76 E+; 77 F−; 78 F− W− E−; 79 F= W− E+ A+ A+.
Agric adviser. Ireland B.

STEELE, Leo Brian *New Zealand*
Wellington Tech Coll, Onslow, Athletic, Wellington, Horowhenua, Shannon.
b 19.1.29 Wellington.
SH, 3-3-0-0.
51 A+ A+ A+.
Carpenter. NZ > 51 A. Jnr team coach at Athletic.

STEELE, William Charles *Scotland* **Common**
Langholm Acad, Langholm, Bedford, RAF, London Scottish, Barbarians.
b 18.4.47 Langholm.
Wing, 23-10-0-13 (22 − 6t).
69 E−; 71 F−(1t) W− I− E+ E+(1t); 72 F+ W− E+ NZ−; 73 F− W+(1t) I+ E−(2t); 75 I+(1t) F− W+ E− NZ−r; 76 W− E+ I+; 77 E−; BI > 74 SA 2-2-0-0.
PE instructor/RAF. Scottish XV v Arg 69, 73; Tg 74.

STEELE-BODGER, Michael Roland *England*
Rugby Sch, Cambridge Univ, Edinburgh Univ, Harlequins, Moseley, Co-optimists, Barbarians.
b 4.9.25.
Flanker 9-3-1-5.
47 W+ I− S+ F+; 48 A− W= I− S− F−.
Vet. Blue 45-6. E sel 53-68. Trustee RFU; pres 73-4. IB chmn & rep.

STEENEKAMP, J.G.A. *South Africa*
Potchefstroom Univ, Transvaal.
b 2.9.35.
1-0-1-0.
58 F=.

STEERE, Edward Richard George *New Zealand*
Napier Boys' HS, Napier HSOB, Hawkes Bay, N Island.
b 10.7.08 Raethi; *d* 1.6.67 Lower Hutt.
No 8/lock, 6-4-0-2.
30 BI− BI+ BI+ BI+; 31 A+; 32 A−.
Savings bank mgr. NZ > 29 & 32 A. Pres Wellington 60. Rep Hawkes Bay at shot putt & sprints, finishing 2nd in NZ sprint champ 34.

STEGGALL, John Cecil *Australia*
Toowoomba GS. Qld.
b 16.9.09 Geraldtown, WA.
Five-eighth/centre, 10-4-0-6 (9 − 3t).
31 M+(1t) NZ−; 32 NZ+ NZ−(1t) NZ−; 33

381

SA– SA+ SA– SA– ŞA+(1t).
Solicitor.

STEGMAN, Trevor Robert   *Australia*
NSW.
b 46.
Centre, 2-1-0-1.
73 Tg+ Tg–.

STEGMANN, Anton C.   *South Africa*
W Prov.
b 1884; *d* –.
Wing, 2-1-0-1 (3 – 1t).
06 S– I+(1t).
Minister. Bro of Jan. 16t in 18 apps SA > 06-7
BI, F.

STEGMANN, Johannes Augustus   *South Africa*
('Jan')
Stellenbosch Univ, W Prov, Diggers, Edinburgh
Univ, Transvaal.
b 21.6.1887 Bedford, Cape Prov.
Wing, 5-5-0-0 (15 – 5t).
12 S+(2t) I+(3t) W+; 13 E+ F+.
Dental surgeon. 9th child of family of 13. Bro of
Anton. SA > 12-13 BI, F. Retired from rugby to
study dentistry at Edinburgh Univ 18. Rep
Scotland as hurdler.

STEINTHAL (later PIETRIE),   *England*
Francis Eric
Bradford GS, Oxford Univ, Ilkley, Yorks.
b 21.11.1886 Bradford.
Centre, 2-2-0-0.
13 W+ F+.
Interior decorator/schoolmaster/professor. Blue
06. Served WW1, Capt R Fusiliers. Wounded
18. Emigrated to US 47. Asst professor of
German & French at Univ of California 56-61.

STEPHEN, A.E.   *Scotland*
W of Scotland.
Centre/wing, 2-1-1-0.
1885 W=; 1886 I+.

STEPHENS, Glyn   *Wales*
Neath.
b 29.11.1891 Neath; *d* 22.4.65 Neath.
Prop/lock, 10-5-0-5.
12 E– S+ I– F+ SA–; 13 E– S+ F+ I+; 19
NZA–.
Mining engr. Father of J.R.G. IB rep 54-5.
WRU pres 56-7.

STEPHENS, Ian ('Ikey')   *Wales*
Whitchurch Comp, Taffs Well, Bridgend.
b 22.5.52 Tongwynlais.
Prop, 13-6-0-7.
81 E+ S– I+ F– A+; 82 I– F+ E– S–; 84 I+
F– E+ A–; BIr > 80 SA 80; 83 NZ 1-0-0-1.
Casemaker. Wales B v F 79, 81. Wales B > 80

US, Canada. Wales XV v Maoris 82. Bridgend v
NZ 78. Called up to join BI > 80 SA as r while
touring with Wales B in NAm.

STEPHENS, John Griffiths   *Wales*
Aberystwyth CS, St David's Coll Sch, St David's
Coll Lampeter, Llanelli, RAF.
b 30.10.1893 Llanbadarn Fawr; *d* 14.5.56
Barton le Willows, Yorks.
Flanker, 4-3-1-0.
22 E+ S= I+ F+.
Minister. Entered St David's Coll 13.10.11,
same day as fellow future int I.T. Davies.
Served WW1 RFC. Ordained deacon 19, priest
20. Curate at Llanelli 19-22. RAF chaplain 22-8.

STEPHENS, John Rees Glyn   *Wales*
Llandovery Coll, Neath, Barbarians.
b 16.4.22 Neath.
No 8/lock, 32-19-0-13 (8 – 2t 1c).
47 E–(1t) S+ F+ I+; 48 I–; 49 S– I– F–; 51
F– SA–; 52 E+ S+ I+(1t) F+; 53 E– S+ I+
F+ NZ+; 54 E– I+; 55 E+ S–(1c) I+ F+; 56
S+ I– F+; 57 E– S– I+ F+; BI > 50 NZ, A 2-
2-0-0.
Farmer/cafe proprietor. Son of Glyn. Played in
4 Victory ints. Barbarians v SA 52, v NZ 54.

STEPHENS, Owen   *New Zealand/Australia*
George
Tauranga Boys' Coll, Tauranga Cadets, NZ
Jnrs, Bay of Plenty, Athletic, Wellington, N
Island, Sydney, NSW.
b 9.1.47 Paeroa, NZ.
New Zealand
Wing, 1-1-0-0.
68 F+.
Australia
Wing, 5-1-1-3 (8 – 2t).
73 Tg+(2t) Tg– W–; 74 NZ= NZ–.
Insurance rep. Moved to A 70, playing RL.
Reinstated 72. A > 73 E & W. Switched back to
RL 74 with Parramatta, later Wakefield Trin
(E). Father Mortimer rep Auckland RL 34 & E
clubs St Helen's & Rochdale Hornets. Bro rep
Waikato RU 70-6 & NZ Univs 73-7.

STEPHENSON, George Vaughan   *Ireland*
RBAI, Haileybury & ISC, Queen's Univ
Belfast, The London Hosp, Barbarians.
b 22.12.01; *d* 6.8.70.
Centre, 42-20-2-20 (94 – 15t 14c 7p).
20 F–; 21 E– S+(1t) W– F–; 22 E– S– W–
F+(1t); 23 E– S– W+ F–; 24 F+(1t) E– S–
(2t 1c) W+(1t) NZ–; 25 F+(1t) E= S– W+(1t
2c 1p); 26 F+(2t 1p) E+(1t 2c 1p) S+ W–(1c
1p); 27 F+(1c 1p) E–(1p) S+ W+(2t 2c 1p)
NSW–; 28 F+ E– S+(1t 2c) W+(2c); 29
F+(1t) E+ W=(1c); 30 F– E+ S+ W–.
Medicine. Bro of H.W.V. I's leading t scorer.

STEPHENSON, Henry William *Ireland*
Vaughan
Clanrye Sch Belfast, RNC Osborne, RNC
Dartmouth, US Portsmouth, RN.
 b 28.11.1900 Dromore, Co Down; *d* 58.
Wing, 14-5-1-8 (9 − 3t).
22 S− W− F+; 24 F+ E− S− W+ NZ−; 25 F+
E=(1t) S−(1t) W+(1t); 27 NSW−; 28 E−.
RN. Bro of George.

STENER, Guy *France*
PUC.
 b 11.2.31 Vichy; *d* −.12.67 Vichy.
Centre/wing, 5-3-1-1.
56 S− I+ E+; 58 SA= SA+.
Medical masseur.

STEVEN, P.D. *Scotland*
Heriot's Coll, Heriot's FP.
Wing, 4-0-0-4.
84 A−; 85 F− W− E−.
S > 84 R.

STEVEN, Robert *Scotland*
Edinburgh W, Barbarians.
Prop, 1-1-0-0.
62 I+.

STEVENS, Claude Brian ('Stack') *England*
Leedstown HS, Cornwall Tech Coll, Penzance-
Newlyn, Harlequins, Barbarians, Cornwall.
 b 2.6.41 Godolphin, Cornwall.
Prop, 25-10-1-14 (8 − 2t).
69 SA+; 70 I+ W− S−; 71 P−; 72 W− I− F−
S− SA+; 73 NZ+(1t) W− I− F+ S+ NZ+
A+; 74 S− I− F= W+; 75 I−(1t) F− W− S+;
BI > 71 A, NZ.
Farmer.

STEVENS, Ian Neal *New Zealand*
Palmerston N Boys' HS, Petone, NZ Jnrs,
Wellington, N Island, Diggers (SA).
 b 13.1.48 Waipawa.
1st five-eighth/SH, 3-3-0-0 (4 − 1t).
72 S+; 73 E+; 74 A+(1t).
Clerk. NZ > 72-3 BI,F & NAm, 74 A & Fj &
I,W & E, 76 Arg & Uruguay. Moved to SA late
70s.

STEVENSON, A.K. *Scotland*
Glasgow Acad, Glasgow Academicals,
Barbarians.
Prop, 4-2-1-1.
22 F=; 23 F+ W+ E−.

STEVENSON, A.M. *Scotland*
Glasgow Univ.
Forward, 1-0-0-1.
11 F−.

STEVENSON, George *Scotland*
Drummond
Hawick HS, Hawick, Barbarians.
 b 30.5.33 Hawick.
Centre/wing, 24-10-2-12.
56 E−; 57 F+; 58 F+ W− A+ I− E=; 59 W+
I− E=; 60 W− I+ E− SA−; 61 F− SA− W+
I+ E−; 63 F+ W− I+; 64 E+; 65 F−.
Whisky rep/engr.

STEVENSON, Henry James *Scotland*
Edinburgh Acad, Edinburgh Academicals,
Edinburgh Univ.
 b 12.7.1867; *d* 8.8.45.
Centre/FB, 15-11-1-3 (2d).
1888 W− I+; 1889 W+ I+(1d); 1890 W+ I+
E−; 1891 W+(1d) I+ E+; 1892 W+ I+ E−;
1893 I= E+.
Writer to the Signet. Ckt for S.

STEVENSON, James *Ireland*
RS Dungannon, Dungannon.
Half-back, 2-0-0-2.
1888 NZN−; 1889 S−.
Linen manufacturer. Bro of Robert.

STEVENSON, James Burton *Ireland*
RBAI, Queen's Univ Belfast, Instonians.
 b 28.8.29 Belfast.
Lock, 5-2-0-3.
58 A+ E− S+ W− F−.
Schoolmaster.

STEVENSON, Louis Edgar *Scotland*
St Peter's Sch York, Edinburgh Univ,
Cambridge Univ.
Forward, 1-0-0-1.
1888 W−.
Medicine. Blue 1884-5.

STEVENSON, Robert ('The *Ireland*
Major')
RS Dungannon, Dungannon, Lisburn.
 b 27.3.1866; *d* 60.
Forward, 14-2-3-9.
1887 E= S− W−; 1888 NZN−; 1889 S− W+;
1890 S− W= E−; 1891 W−; 1892 W+; 1893 E−
S= W−.
Linen manufacturer. Bro of James. One of I's
longest lived players. Pres IRU 12-13. Served
WW1.

STEVENSON, R.C. *Scotland*
Kirkcaldy HS, St Andrew's Univ, Barbarians.
Forward, 6-2-0-4.
10 F+ I+ E−; 11 F− W− I−; BI > 10 SA 3-1-0-
2.
Medicine.

STEVENSON, Ronald Cochran *Scotland*
Sedbergh Sch, London Scottish.

383

b 25.7.1873; *d* 12.2.34.
Forward, 6-3-1-2.
1897 I+ E−; 1898 E=; 1899 I− W+ E+.
Civil engr.

STEVENSON, T.H.   *Ireland*
Belfast Acad, Belfast A, Edinburgh Univ.
Centre, 7-3-1-3 (3 − 1t).
1895 E− W−; 1896 E+(1t) S= W+; 1897 E+
S−.
Medicine. Served with Army Medical Staff.

STEVENSON, W.H.   *Scotland*
Glasgow Acad, Glasgow Academicals, The
Army.
b −; *d* 72.
Prop, 1-1-0-0.
25 F+.
Indian Army.

STEWART, Albert Lewis   *Ireland*
RBAI, NIFC, Ulster.
b 19.2.1889 Belfast; kia 4.10.17 Ypres.
Centre, 3-2-0-1 (3 − 1t).
13 W−(1t) F+; 14 F+.
Chartered accountant. Ulster v SA 12. Served
WW1, Maj R Irish Rifles; mentioned in
despatches.

STEWART, Alexander Kenneth   *Scotland*
Haileybury & ISC, Edinburgh Univ.
b 30.8.1852; *d* 13.2.45.
Half-back, 2-0-0-2.
1874 E−; 1876 E−.
Medicine. Army Medical Staff.

STEWART, Allan James   *New Zealand*
Timaru Tech Coll, Timaru HSOB, S
Canterbury, Univ, NZ Univs, Canterbury, S
Island.
b 11.10.40 Temuka.
Lock, 8-6-1-1.
63 E+ E+; 63 I+ W+; 64 E+ S= F+; 64 A−.
Schoolmaster/oil co exec. NZ > 63-4 BI,F & C.
Father J. Stewart rep S Canterbury 36-7.

STEWART, Andrew Alec   *Australia*
NSW.
b 52.
Flanker/lock, 3-2-0-1.
79 NZ+ Arg− Arg+.

STEWART, Archibald Mathison   *Scotland*
Edinburgh Acad, Edinburgh Academicals,
Edinburgh Univ.
b 27.9.1890; *d* 18.9.74.
Forward, 1-0-0-1.
14 W−.
Medicine.

STEWART, Charles Alexander   *Scotland*
Reid
Merchiston Castle Sch, W of Scotland.
b 1858; *d* 26.2.1890.
Forward, 2-1-0-1.
1880 I+ E−.
Farmer.

STEWART, Charles Edward Bell   *Scotland*
George Watson's Coll, Kelso HS, Kelso.
b 23.12.36 Selkirk.
Flanker/no 8, 2-0-0-2.
60 W−; 61 F−.
Farmer.

STEWART, David Alfred   *South Africa*
Wynberg Boys HS, Villagers, W Prov.
b 14.7.35.
FH/centre, 11-7-1-3 (9 − 1t 2p).
60 S+; 61 E+ S+ F= I+; 63 A+ A− A+; 64
W+ F−(1t 1p); 65 I−(1p).
Draughtsman. SA > 60-1 BI, F.

STEWART, J.   *Scotland*
Glasgow HS, Glasgow HSFP.
Lock, 1-0-0-1.
30 F−.

STEWART, James Douglas   *New Zealand*
City, Auckland, N Island.
b 3.10.1890 Kaiapoi; *d* 5.5.73 Whangarei.
Wing, 2-1-0-1.
13 A+ A−.
4t Auckland v Southland 14.

STEWART, J.L.   *Scotland*
Edinburgh Acad, Edinburgh Academicals.
b 6.5.1894; *d* 6.8.71.
Flanker, 1-0-0-1.
21 I−.
Dir veterinary services, Gold Coast.

STEWART, Joseph William   *Ireland*
Coleraine AI, Queen's Univ Belfast, NIFC,
Preston Grasshoppers.
b 24.9.1900; *d* 58.
FB, 10-6-1-3.
22 F+; 24 S−; 28 F+ E− S+ W+; 29 F+ E+
S− W=.
Medicine. Served in Indian Medical Services.

STEWART, Kenneth William   *New Zealand*
Otago Boys' HS, Balfour, NZ Jnrs, Southland,
S Island.
b 3.1.53 Gore.
Flanker, 13-8-1-4.
73 E−; 74 A+ A= A+; 74 I+; 75 S+; 76 I+
SA− SA−; 79 S+ E+; 81 SA+ SA−.
Farmer. NZ > 72-3 BI,F & NAm, 74 A & Fj &
I,W & E, 76 SA, 79 E,S & It. NZ (2) v Arg 79.

384

STEWART, Mark S. *Scotland*
Stewart's Coll, Stewart's Coll FP.
Lock, 9-4-0-5.
32 SA− W− I−; 33 W+ E+ I+; 34 W− I+ E−.
Pres SRU 66-7.

STEWART, Ronald Terowie *New Zealand*
Timaru Boys' HS, HSOB, S Canterbury,
Christchurch, Canterbury, S Island.
b 12.1.04 Waikaia.
No 8/flanker, 5-3-0-2 (3 − 1t).
28 SA− SA+ SA−(1t) SA+; 30 BI+.
Stock & station employee. NZ > 24-5 BI,F & C,
26 A, 28 SA (19 apps). Southland comm.

STEWART, William Allan *Scotland*
The London Hosp.
b 23.10.1889 Launceston; *d* −.
Wing, 4-2-0-2 (24 − 8t).
13 F+(3t) W− I+(4t); 14 W−(1t).
Medicine.

STEYN, Stephen Sebastian *Scotland*
Lombard ('Beak')
Diocesan Coll Rondebosch SA, Oxford Univ,
Guy's Hosp, Barbarians.
b 10.11.1889 SA; kia 8.12.17 Palestine.
Wing, 2-0-0-2.
11 E−; 12 I−.
Medicine. Rhodes Scholar. Blue 11-12 (see
W.M. Dickson). Lt, RFA.

STILL, Ernest Robert *England*
Rugby Sch, Oxford Univ, Ravenscourt Pk.
b 14.7.1852; *d* 30.11.31.
Forward, 1-0-1-0.
1873 S=.
Solicitor/co dir. Blue 1871-3.

STIRLING, Robert Victor *England*
RAF, Comb Servs, Aylestone St James,
Leicester, Wasps, Barbarians, Kent, NLD.
b 4.9.19 Lichfield.
Prop, 18-10-1-7 (3 − 1t).
51 W− I− F− S+; 52 SA− W− S+ I+ F+; 53
W+ I= F+ S+(1t); 54 W+ NZ− I+ S+ F−.
RAF. Capt E 5 times. Rep RAF as heavywt
boxer 48-50. Served WW2, promoted from Ft
Sgt to Wg Cdr.

STOCK, Albert R. *Wales*
Newport.
b 18.4.1898.
Centre, 4-1-1-2.
24 F+ NZ−; 26 E= S−.
Butcher.

STODDART, Andrew Ernest *England*
Rev G.W. Oliver's St John's Wood Sch,
Harlequins, Blackheath, Barbarians, Mdx.
b 11.3.1863 S Shields; *d* 3.4.15 London.
Back, 10-6-1-3 (2t 1c 1gm).
1885 W+ I+; 1886 W+(1gm) I+ S=; 1889
NZN+(1t); 1890 W− I+(1t); 1893 W−(1c) S−;
BT > 1888 A, NZ.
Stockbroker/club sec. Only player to capt E &
BT at rugby & E at ckt. 1st player to kick gm in
int rugby. Capt E 4 times. Mdx CCC, E (16
Tests)) − capt E v A 1893-5. Stayed in A after
W.W. Read's 1887-8 ckt tour to await arrival of
1888 BT, which he capt when R.L. Seddon was
drowned during tour. CY 1893. Sec of Queen's
Club, venue of Univ Match. Took own life.

STODDART, Wilfred Bowring JP *England*
R Liverpool Inst, Liverpool, Barbarians, Lancs.
b 27.4.1871; *d* 8.1.35.
Forward, 3-1-0-2.
1897 W− I− S+.
Family bus. Ckt for Lancs CCC (capt), MCC;
Gentlemen v Players. Capt R Liverpool GC 10;
pres English Golf Union 26. Liverpool alderman
29. Cousin of G. Leather.

STOFBERG, Martinus Theunis *South Africa*
Steyn ('Theuns')
Grey Coll Bloemfontein, UOFS, OFS,
Gazelles, Oribis, Barbarians, SA Forces,
Defence (Pretoria), N Transvaal, W Prov.
b 6.6.55 Villiers.
Lock/flanker, 21-17-0-4 (24 − 6t).
76 NZ− NZ+; 77 Wd+; 80 SAm+ SAm+ BI+
BI+(1t) BI+ BI− SAm+(1t) SAm+ F+(1t); 81
I+ I+ NZ− NZ+ US+; 82 SAm+ SAm−; 84
E+ E+(1t).
Physiotherapist. Capt SA v SAm 1st Test 80,
NZ 1st Test 81, E 2 Tests 84. Oribis > 75 SAm.

STOHR, Leonard ('Jack') *New Zealand*
New Plymouth Boys' HS, Tukapa, Taranaki,
Comb Servs, N Island.
b 13.11.1889 New Plymouth; *d* 25.7.73
Johannesburg.
Wing, 3-2-0-1 (6 − 2t).
10 A I A A I (2t).
Chemist. NZ > 10 A. 1st player to kick 3p in
1st-class match, Taranaki v Wanganui 09.
Served WW1; rep Comb Servs in King's Cup &
> SA 19. Settled in SA 20.

STOKER, Ernest Wilson *Ireland*
RCSI, Wanderers.
Forward, 2-1-0-1.
1888 W+ S−.
Medicine. Played with bro Frank v W 1888.

STOKER, Frank Owen *Ireland*
Wanderers, Barbarians.
b 1866; *d* −.1.39.
Forward, 5-1-0-4.
1886 S−; 1888 W+ NZN−; 1889 S−; 1891 W−.

Medicine. Played with bro Ernest v W 1888. Wimbledon lawn tennis doubles champ 1890/3.

STOKES, Frederick   *England*
Rugby Sch, Blackheath, Kent.
b 12.7.1851 Blackheath; d 7.1.28 Basingstoke.
Forward, 3-1-1-1.
1871 S–; 1872 S+; 1873 S=.
Solicitor. Bro of Lennard. Bro in law of J.F. Green. E's 1st capt, v S 1871. Aged 24 when elected pres RFU 1874-5. One of 6 bros who played for Blackheath. Ckt for Kent CCC, Gentlemen v Players. Outstanding golfer. One of his sons served with HMS Powerful's Naval Bde in the relief of Ladysmith, SA. The other served as gunnery officer on HMS Temeraire WW1.

STOKES, Lennard   *England*
Sidney Coll Bath, Blackheath, Kent.
b 12.2.1856; d 3.5.33.
Back/FB, 12-8-3-1 (17c 2d).
1875 I+; 1876 S+(1c); 1877 I+(2c) S–; 1878 S=; 1879 S=(1c) I+(2c 1d); 1880 I+(1c) S+(2c); 1881 I+(2c) W+(6c) S=(1d). Medicine. Bro of Fred. Bro in law of J.F. Green. Capt Blackheath 1876-81. E's 1st capt v W, 1881. Capt 5 times in 12 apps. 80y d v S 1881. Rec 17c for E still stands. Pres RFU 1886-8; elected to RFU comm 1876, served for over 50 yrs. RFU Trustee 26-9. Ckt for Kent CCC. Utd Hosps sprint champ.

STOKES, Oliver S.   *Ireland*
Cork Bankers.
Forward, 2-0-1-1 (1t).
1882 E=(1t); 1884 E–.

STOKES, Patrick   *Ireland*
Blackrock Coll, UC Dublin, Garryowen.
b 3.4.1890; d 29.10.70.
No 8/flanker, 12-3-0-9 (12 – 4t).
13 E– S–(1t); 14 F+; 20 E– S– W– F–; 21 E– S+ F–(2t); 22 W–(1t) F+.
Medicine.

STOKES, Robert Day MBE   *Ireland*
Queen's Coll Cork.
Forward, 2-0-0-2.
1891 S– W–.
Medicine.

STONE, Albert Hodsdon   *Australia*
Sydney GS, NSW.
b 13; d 68.
Hooker, 3-0-0-3.
37 SA–; 38 NZ– NZ–.
Laboratory chemist.

STONE, Arthur Massey   *New Zealand*
Waikato, NZ Colts, Northern Maoris.

b 19.12.60 Auckland.
2nd/1st five-eighth, 4-4-0-0 (4 – 1t).
81 F+ F+; 83 BI+r; 84 A+(1t).
NZ > 81 R & F, 84 A.

STONE, Charles Gordon   *Australia*
Sydney GS, NSW.
SH, 1-0-0-1.
38 NZ–.
Radiologist.

STONE, Francis le Strange MC   *England*
Harrow Sch, Blackheath, Barbarians, London Co.
b 1886; d 7.10.38.
No 8, 1-1-0-0.
14 F+.
Solicitor. Capt Blackheath 10-11. Noted golfer. Served WW1, King's Own Hussars.

STONE, James Michael   *Australia*
NSW.
b 21.
Wing, 2-0-0-2.
46 M– NZ–.
Turf accountant.

STONE, Peter   *Wales*
Gowerton GS, UC Aberystwyth, Loughor, Llanelli, Swansea.
b 20.6.24 Loughor; d –.7.71 Bideford.
Flanker, 1-0-0-1.
49 F–.
Schoolmaster. Coach Barnstaple GS.

STOOP, Adrian Dura MC   *England*
Dover Coll, Rugby Sch, Oxford Univ, Harlequins, Surrey, Barbarians.
b 27.3.1883 London; d 27.11.57.
SH/FH, 15-8-2-5 (6 – 2t).
05 S–; 06 S+ F+(1t) SA=; 07 F+ W–; 10 W+ I= S+; 11 W– F+(1t) I– S+; 12 W+ S–.
Barrister. Bro of Fred. Served WW1, Capt in Queen's (R W Surrey) Rgt. Wounded Mesopotamia. MC 19. Blue 02-4. Sec, pres Harlequins; pres Surrey; RFU sel 27-31, pres 32-3; Central Dist rep 11-33. IB rep 23. Ref 1st Mobbs Memorial Match, E Midlands v Barbarians 21, mistakenly blowing no-side after 68 mins. After protests from spectators, players returned from changing–rooms to complete match.

STOOP, Frederick Macfarlane   *England*
Rugby Sch, RAC, Harlequins, Barbarians, Surrey.
b 17.9.1888 London; d 24.11.72.
Centre, 4-2-0-2.
10 S+; 11 F+ I–; 13 SA–.
Stockbroker. Played with bro Adrian 3 times for E. Served WW1, E Kent Rgt; Machine Gun

386

Corps (Armoured Cars) in Mesopotamia. Wounded; mentioned in despatches.

STOREY, Geoffrey Parnell   *Australia*
NSW.
b 04; *d* 75.
Lock, 2-2-0-0.
29 NZ+r; 30 BI+.
Solicitor. Bro of Keith. NSW > BI 27.

STOREY, Keith Parnell   *Australia*
NSW.
b 12.
FB, 1-0-0-1.
36 NZ−.
Accountant. Bro of Geoffrey.

STOREY, Norman John David   *Australia*
The Scots Coll, NSW.
b 5.10.36.
Five-eighth, 1-0-0-1.
62 NZ−.
Commercial pilot.

STOREY, Percival Wright   *New Zealand*
Waimate Sch, Zingari, S Canterbury, Comb Servs, S Island.
b 11.2.1897 Temuka; *d* 4.10.75 Timaru.
Wing, 2-1-0-1 (3 − 1t).
21 SA+(1t) SA−.
Traveller. Served WW1, Otago Infantry Battn; wounded at Passchendaele. Rep Comb Servs & > 19 SA. Played in all 10 matches & top scorer 47 pts NZ > 20 A. NZRFU sel 44.

STOUT, Frank Moxham MC   *England*
Gloucester, Richmond, Glos, Barbarians.
b 21.2.1877 Liverpool; *d* 30.5.26 Abbey Storrington, Sussex.
Forward, 14-2-2-10 (5 − 1t 1c).
1897 W− I−; 1898 I− S= W+(1t); 1899 I− S−; 03 S−; 04 W=(1c) I+ S−; 05 W− I− S−; BT > 1899 A, NZ; 03 SA.
Son of William Stout who won Diamond Sculls at Henley. Played with bro Percy 4 times for E. Only player to tour A, NZ 1899 & SA 03. 44 apps for Glos. Capt Richmond 03-5. Footballer (with Glos) before taking up rugby. Served WW1, Lt 20 Hussars; mentioned in despatches 16, 19.

STOUT, Percy Wyfold DSO OBE   *England*
Crypt GS, Gloucester, Richmond, Bristol, Barbarians, Glos.
b 20.11.1875; *d* 9.10.37.
Wing, 5-1-1-3 (3 − 1t).
1898 S= W+(1t); 1899 W− I− S−.
Co dir. Son of William Stout who won Diamond Sculls at Henley. Played with bro Frank 4 times for E. Football for Corinthian Casuals & Glos. Served WW1, Acting Capt Machine Gun Corps,

Egypt; DSO 17. Mentioned in despatches 5 times, Order of Nile (4th class), OBE (mil) 19.

STRACHAN, Donald John   *Australia*
NSW.
b 18.2.29 Orange, NSW.
Prop, 2-1-0-1.
55 NZ− NZ+.
Grazier.

STRACHAN, Gordon Matthew   *Scotland*
Ayr Acad, Glasgow Univ, Jordanhill Coll.
b 16.11.47 Littlemill, Ayrshire.
Lock/no 8/flanker, 5-4-0-1.
71 E+r; 73 W+ I+ E− P+.
PE teacher. Scottish XV v Arg 73.

STRACHAN, Louis Cornelius   *South Africa*
('Lucas')
Parys Sch, Transvaal.
b 12.9.07.
Flanker, 10-8-0-2.
32 E+ S+; 37 A+ A+ NZ− NZ+ NZ+; 38 BI+ BI+ BI−.
Police detective. SA > 31-2 BI.

STRAHAN, Samuel Cunningham   *New Zealand*
Wanganui Collegiate Sch, Oroua, NZ Jnrs, Manawatu, N Island.
b 25.12.44 Palmerston N.
Lock, 17-14-0-3.
67 A+; 67 E+ W+ F+ S+; 68 A+ A+ F+ F+ F+; 70 SA− SA+ SA−; 72 A+ A+ A+; 73 E−.
Farmer. NZ > 67 BI,F & C, 68 A & Fj, 70 A & SA.

STRANG, William Archibald   *New Zealand*
Southland Boys' HS, Timaru HSOB, S Canterbury, Temuka, S Island.
b 18.10.06 Invercargill.
2nd/1st five-eighth, 5-4-0-1 (13 − 1t 3c 1d).
28 SA− SA+(1d); 30 BI+(1c) BI+(1t 2c); 31 A+.
Farmer/stock buyer. NZ > 28 SA. Coach Timaru HSOB & army XVs during WW2. Bro Jim rep S Canterbury.

STRATHDEE, Ernest   *Ireland*
Belfast HS, Queen's Univ Belfast, Barbarians.
b −; *d* 17.7.71 Belfast.
SH, 9-7-0-2.
47 E+ S+ W− A−; 48 F+ W+; 49 E+ S+ W+.
Presbyterian minister/tv sports journalist. Played in 2 Victory ints. Died in hotel fire.

STRAUSS, J.A.   *South Africa*
W Prov.
Prop, 2-2-0-0.
84 SAm+ SAm+.

STRAUSS, Johan Hendrik　　　*South Africa*
Potgieter ('Pottie')
A. Bekker Sch, Diggers, Jnr Springboks,
Gazelles, Quaggas, Barbarians, Transvaal.
b 27.9.51 Alberton.
Prop, 3-3-0-0.
76 NZ+ NZ+; 80 SAm+.
Carpenter/building contractor. Gazelles > 72
Arg.

STRAUSS, S.S.F.　　　*South Africa*
Griq W.
1-0-1-0.
21 NZ=.
Business.

STREET, Norman Ogilvie　　　*Australia*
NSW.
b 1876; *d* 63.
Forward, 1-0-0-1.
1899 BT−.
Miner. Worked for a time in Lucknow, India.

STREETER, Stephen Frederick　　　*Australia*
NSW.
b 55.
Wing, 1-0-0-1.
78 NZ−.
Bulldozer driver.

STRINGER, Nicholas C.　　　*England*
Wasps.
b 4.10.60 Stanmore.
FB, 5-3-0-2.
82 A+r; 83 NZ+r; 84 SA−r A−; 85 R+.
Insurance salesman. E Under 23s v Netherlands
(10 out of 10 successful place-kicks), v English
Students 80; > 83 R. England B v F 81.
Formerly on ground staff at Lord's.

STRINGFELLOW, John Clinton　　*New Zealand*
Timaru Boys' HS, Greytown, Wairarapa,
Mangatainoka, Bush, Comb Servs, N Island.
b 26.2.05 Chertsey; *d* 3.1.59 Mauriceville.
FB/centre, 2-0-0-2 (3 − 1t).
29 A−r A−(1t).
Farmer. NZ > 29 A. Served WW2; Comb Servs
in BI 44-5.

STRONACH, R.S. CBE　　　*Scotland*
Glasgow Acad, Glasgow Academicals.
Forward, 5-3-0-2 (3 − 1t).
01 W+ E+; 05 W− I− E+(1t).
CBE 19.

STRONG, Edmund Linwood　　　*England*
Edinburgh Acad, Oxford Univ, Bath, Somerset.
b −.12.1862; *d* 20.3.45 Calcutta.
Forward, 3-3-0-0.
1884 W+ S+ I+.
Church. Blue 81-3. Ckt for S v G.F. Grace's XI.

Ordained 1887; curate St John the Divine
Kennington; served with Oxford Univ Mission,
Calcutta 1894-1900. Remained there until he d.

STRUXIANO, Philippe ('Struc')　　　*France*
Toulouse, Tarbes.
b 11.3.1891 Toulouse; *d* 56 Toulouse.
FH, 7-2-0-5 (6 − 3c).
13 W−(1c) I−; 20 S− E− W−(1c) I+ US+(1c).
Agricultural chemical producer.

STRYDOM, Coenraad Frederick　　*South Africa*
('Popeye')
Grey Coll Bloemfontein, OFS.
b 20.1.32 Kareedouw, Humansdorp.
SH, 6-2-1-3.
55 BI−; 56 A+ A+ NZ− NZ−; 58 F=.
Clerk.

STRYDOM, Louis J.　　　*South Africa*
N Transvaal.
b 27.10.21.
2-2-0-0.
49 NZ+ NZ+.
Prison officer.

STUART, Charles Douglas　　　*Scotland*
Pollokshields HS, W of Scotland.
b 18.5.1887 Glasgow; *d* 15.1.82 Glasgow.
Forward, 7-3-0-4 (3 − 1t).
09 I+; 10 F+ W− I+(1t) E−; 11 I− E−.
Engr/journalist. Bro of Ludovic. One of int
rugby's longest lived players.

STUART, Charles Parnell　　　*Ireland*
Clontarf.
b 2.4.1886; *d* 21.11.58.
1-0-0-1.
12 SA−.
Rly official.

STUART, Ian Malcolm Bowen　　　*Ireland*
Malvern Coll, Trin Coll Dublin, London Irish,
Barbarians, Surrey.
b 18.9.02 Dublin; *d* 3.8.69 US.
Lock/flanker, 2-0-0-2.
24 E− S−.
HM/PR. Designer of Barbarian FC badge &
crest.

STUART, Kevin Charles　　　*New Zealand*
St Bede's Coll, Marist, Canterbury, S Island.
b 19.9.28 Dunedin.
FB, 1-1-0-0.
55 A+.
Export marketing exec with stock agent. Ckt for
Canterbury 45-6. Bro of R.C.; another bro John
rep Canterbury 57. Cousin of J.C. Kearney.

STUART, Ludovic Mair *Scotland*
Glasgow HS, Glasgow HSFP, Bellahouston
Acad.
b 22.10.02; *d* 3.3.57.
Lock, 8-3-1-4 (3 − 1t).
23 F+ W+(1t) I+ E−; 24 F−; 28 E−; 30 I−
E=.
Solicitor. Bro of Charles.

STUART, Robert *Australia*
NSW.
b 13.6.1887; *d* 59.
Flanker, 2-1-0-1.
10 NZ+ NZ−.
Cooper. RL.

STUART, Robert Charles *New Zealand*
St Kevin's Coll, St Patrick's OB, Manawatu,
Univ, NZ Univs, Canterbury, Comb Servs, S
Island.
b 28.10.20 Dunedin.
No 8/flanker, 7−3-0-4 (3 − 1t).
49 A− A−; 53 W−; 54 I+(1t) E+ S+ F−.
Agric economist/dir Vocational Training
Council. Capt NZ > 53-4 BI,F & NAm. Served
WW2, Fleet Air Arm. NZRFU exec 74-80; NZ
rep on IB from 78. Bro of K.C.

STUART, Robert Locksdale *New Zealand*
Napier Boys' HS, Napier Tech Coll OB,
Hawkes Bay, Waipukurau HSOB, N Island.
b 9.1.48 Napier.
Prop, 1-0-0-1.
77 F−r.
Stock buyer. NZ > 77 F.

STUMBLES, Barry Donald *Australia*
Canberra HS, NSW.
b 27.9.48.
Lock, 4-1-0-3 (4 − 1t).
72 NZ−r NZ− NZ− Fj+(1t).
Schoolmaster. RL.

STURTRIDGE, Gordon Short *Australia*
Brisbane Boys' Coll, Melbourne Univ, Victoria.
b 07; *d* 16.9.63.
Centre, 9-4-0-5 (3 − 1t).
29 NZ+; 32 NZ+ NZ− NZ−; 33 SA− SA+(1t)
SA− SA− SA+.
Medicine. Pres Northampton (E) 50-63. 1st
Victorian to be capped.

SUDDON, Norman *Scotland*
Denholm Sch, Hawick, Barbarians.
b 28.6.43 Cavers, Roxburghshire.
Prop, 13-5-1-7.
65 W− I− E= SA+; 66 A+; 68 E− A+; 69 F+
W− I−; 70 I− E+ A−.
Hosiery. Barbarians > 69 SA.

SUGARS, Harold Sanderson *Ireland*
DSO MC
RS Dungannon, Trin Coll Dublin, Lansdowne,
Barbarians.
Forward, 3-0-0-3 (6 − 2t).
O5 NZ−; 06 SA−(2t); 07 S−.
Medicine. Served WW1.

SUGDEN, Mark OBE *Ireland*
Earlsfort House Dublin, Denstone Coll, Trin
Coll Dublin, Wanderers, Barbarians, Leinster.
b 11.2.02 Leek, Staffs.
SH, 28-16-2-10 (12 − 4t).
25 F+(1t) E= S− W+; 26 F+ E+ S+ W−; 27
E− S+ W+ NSW−; 28 F+ E−(1t) S+ W+; 29
F+ E+(1t) S− W=; 30 F− E+ S+ W−; 31 F−
E+ S+(1t) W−.
Schoolmaster. I's most capped SH. Ckt for I.
Distantly related to Danie Craven.

SULLIVAN, Donal Bartholomew *Ireland*
Clongowes Coll, UC Dublin.
b 28.8.1898 Mallow, Co Cork; *d* 26.4.74.
Centre/wing, 4-1-0-3.
22 E− S− W− F+.
Medicine.

SULLIVAN, John Lorraine OBE *New Zealand*
Tangarakau Sch, Tukapa, Taranaki, N Island.
b 30.3.15 Tahora.
Centre/wing/2nd five-eighth, 6-4-0-2 (9 − 3t).
37 SA+ SA−(2t) SA−; 38 A+(1t) A+ A+.
Carpenter/man dir oil co. NZ > 36 & 38 A.
Served WW2; leg inj while played for ME Army
42 ended playing career. NZRFU sel 54-60. Asst
mgr NZ > 60 A & SA. Bros Colin & George rep
Taranaki.

SULLIVAN, Peter David *Australia*
NSW.
b 19.3.48.
Flanker, 13-3-1-9 (4 − 1t).
71 SA− SA− SA− F+ F−; 72 F= F− NZ−
NZ− Fj+(1t); 73 Ig+ Ig− W−.
PE teacher. Capt A > W & E 73. RL.

SUMMERS, Richard Henry *Wales*
Bowlas JP
Cowbridge GS, Cheltenham Coll,
Haverfordwest.
b 30.7.1860 Haverfordwest; *d* 22.12.41
Haverfordwest.
Back, 1-0-0-1.
1881 E−.
The Army/police. Lived in India from 1882.

SUMMERSCALES, George *England*
Edward
Durham City, Durham Co.
b 1879; *d* 31.12.36 Durham.

Forward, 1-0-0-1.
05 NZ−.
Served WW1. 48 apps for Durham Co 1900-09,
& one in 20 when as a 41-yr-old sel he played v
Northumb when a player failed to arrive.

SUMMONS, Arthur James   *Australia*
Homebush GS, Teachers Coll Sydney, NSW.
b 13.12.35 Paddington.
Five-eighth, 10-1-1-8 (3 − 1t).
58 W− I−(1t) E− S− M= NZ− NZ+ NZ−; 59
BI− BI−.
Schoolmaster/sales exec/club mgr. RL.

SUTCLIFFE, John William   *England*
Bradford St Thomas Sch, Bradford,
Heckmondwike, Yorks.
b 14.4.1869 Shibden, Yorks; *d* 7.7.47
Bradford.
Wing, 1-1-0-0 (1t 1c).
1889 NZN+ (1t 1c).
Football for E: capped from Bolton W, kept
goal 5 times (v S 1895, 01; v W 1893, 03; v I
1895).

SUTER, Melvyn R. ('Snowy')   *South Africa*
Natal.
b 14.12.39.
2-0-0-2.
65 I− S−.
Electrician.

SUTHERLAND, Alan Richard   *New Zealand*
Marlborough Coll, Awatere, NZ Jnrs,
Marlborough, Opawa, S Island, Rhodesia.
b 4.1.44 Blenheim.
Lock/no 8/flanker, 10-6-1-3 (12 − 3t).
70 SA+ SA−; 71 BI−; 72 A+(1t) A+(1t)
A+(1t) W+; 73 E+ I= F−.
Farmer/sales rep/shearer. Did not play rugby at
sch. NZ > 68 A & Fj, 70 A & SA, 72-3 BI,F &
NAm, 76 SA. Took up coaching position in
Rhodesia 77; moved to SA to coach
Witwatersrand Univ. Bro Ray rep Marlborough
58-74.

SUTHERLAND, Walter Riddell   *Scotland*
Teviot Grove Sch Hawick, Hawick.
b 19.11.1890 Hawick; kia 4.10.18 Hulluch.
Wing/FB, 13-4-0-9 (12 − 4t).
10 W− E−; 11 F− E−(1t); 12 F+(2t) W−
E+(1t) SA−; 13 F+ W− I+ E−; 14 W−.
Sanitary inspector. Scottish Borders sprint
champ 11-14; rep S v I 11-13. 2nd Lt, Seaforth
Highlanders.

SUTRA, Gérard ('Sucette')   *France*
Narbonne.
b 22.3.46 Narbonne.
SH, 4-2-1-1.

67 SA−; 69 W=; 70 S+ I+.
Municipal employee.

SUTTON, Stephen   *Wales*
Nantyglo GS, Pontypool, S Wales Police.
b 17.2.58 Abertillery.
Lock, 2-1-0-1.
82 F+ E−.
Car components co/police.

SUTTOR, Dudley Colin   *Australia*
NSW.
b 10.4.1892 Cowra, NSW; *d* 62.
Wing, 3-1-0-2 (9 − 3t).
13 NZ− NZ−(1t) NZ+(2t).
Orchardist.

SVENSON, Kenneth Sydney   *New Zealand*
('Snowy')
Wanganui OB, Wanganui, White Star, Buller,
Athletic, Wellington, Moutere, Marlborough, S
& N Islands.
b 6.12.1898 Toowoomba, A; *d* 7.12.55 Raglan.
Wing, 4-4-0-0 (12 − 4t).
24 I+(1t) W+(1t); 25 E+(1t) F+(1t).
Licensee/farmer. NZ > 22 A, 24-5 BI,F & C
(23t), 26 A.

SWAIN, John Patterson ('Tuna')   *New Zealand*
Napier Tech Coll, Pirates, Hawkes Bay,
Athletic, Wellington, N Island.
b 02 Sydney, Aus; *d* 29.8.60 Eskdale.
Hooker, 4-2-0-2 (3 − 1t).
28 SA− SA+ SA− SA+(1t).
Mercer/farmer. NZ > 28 SA. Rep Wellington at
water polo.

SWAN, John Spence   *Scotland*
Madras Coll, St Andrew's Univ, REME, The
Army, London Scottish, Leicester.
b 14.7.30 St Andrews.
Wing, 17-6-0-11 (3 − 1t).
53 E−; 54 F− NZ− I− E− W−; 55 F− W+
I+(1t) E−; 56 F+ W− I− E−; 57 F+ W+; 58
F+.
The Army.

SWAN, Malcolm William   *Scotland*
Fettes Coll, Oxford Univ, London Scottish,
Barbarians.
b 4.12.34 Buenos Aires.
Lock, 8-3-1-4.
58 F+ W− A+ I− E=; 59 F− W+ I−.
Rep. Blue 57.

SWANNELL, Blair Inskip   *Australia*
Northampton, NSW.
b 20.8.1875 Olney, Bucks; kia 25.4.15
Gallipoli.
Forward, 1-0-0-1.
05 NZ−.

Of independent means. BT > A 1899, A & NZ 04. Served WW1, Major AIF.

SWARBRICK, David William   *England*
Kingswood Sch, Oxford Univ, Blackheath, Barbarians, Midland Cos, Mdx.
b 17.1.27.
Wing, 6-2-1-3.
47 W+ I− F+; 48 A− W=; 49 I−.
ICI. Blue 46-8. Oxford-Cambridge > 48 Arg. Capt Blackheath 50-2. Career cut short by head inj.

SWART, Josias Johannes   *South Africa*
Nicolaas ('Sias')
SW Africa.
b 29.7.34.
Wing, 1-0-0-1 (3 − 1t).
55 BI−(1t).
Welder/technical schoolteacher. 1st SA cap from SW Africa.

SWAYNE, Denys Harald   *England*
Bromsgrove Sch, Oxford Univ, St George's Hosp, Harlequins, London Cos, Herefordshire & Worcs, N Midlands, Glos, Mdx.
b 23.11.09.
Flanker, 1-0-1-0.
31 W=.
Medicine. Bro of J.W.R.. Blue 30-1. Ckt for Utd Hosps. Served WW2, RAMC; wounded in Normandy landings. GP at Stevenage.

SWAYNE, John Walter Rocke   *England*
MC TD
Bromsgrove Sch, Bridgwater & A, TA, Harlequins, Som.
b 27.5.06.
No 8, 1-1-0-0.
29 W+.
Solicitor. Bro of Denys. Capt Bromsgrove Sch, Bridgwater & Som. Served WW2, N Som Yeomanry. Squash & golf for Som; pres SW Golf Union 69.

SWEENEY, James Austin   *Ireland*
Blackrock Coll, Trin Coll Dublin.
b 29.5.1884 Dunloe, Co Donegal; *d* 6.9.44.
Forward, 3-1-0-2.
07 E+ S− W−.
Barrister/Indian Civil Service. 1st int from Blackrock Coll.

SWEENEY, Thomas Leo   *Australia*
St Joseph's Coll, Qld.
b 29.
FB, 1-0-0-1 (3 − 1p).
53 SA−(1p).
Hydro-electric engr.

SWEET, John Brunton   *Scotland*
Glasgow HS, Glasgow HSFP.
b 26.3.1892; *d* −.
Wing, 2-0-0-2.
13 E−; 14 I−.
Dentist.

SWEET-ESCOTT, Ralph Bond   *Wales*
King Henry VII Sch Coventry, Peterhouse Coll, Cambridge Univ, Blackheath, Cardiff, Penarth, Barbarians.
b 11.1.1869 Taunton; *d* 10.11.07 Johannesburg.
Half-back, 3-1-0-2.
1891 S−; 1894 I−; 1895 I+.
Architect/gold mines official. Son of Rector of Penarth. Glam CCC.

SWIERCZYNSKI, Christian   *France*
('Tarzan')
Bègles.
b 28.7.47 St-Magne.
Hooker, 2-0-1-1.
69 E−; 77 Arg=.
Police. 8 yrs between caps.

SWIFT, Anthony Hugh   *England*
Hutton GS, England SS, Swansea, UWIST, Bath.
b 24.5.59 Preston.
Wing, 7-1-2-4.
81 Arg= Arg+; 83 F− W= S−; 84 SA− SA−.
Accountant. England B v F 79, v I 80. Teammate with Huw Davies & Welsh int Gareth Roberts for UWIST v Exeter, UAU Cup final 80. E > 81 Arg, 82 US, Can. E Under 23s.

SYDDALL, James Paul   *England*
de la Salle Coll Salford, England SS, English Students, Portsmouth Poly, Waterloo, Lancs.
b 7.3.56 Swinton.
Lock, 2-0-0-2.
82 I−; 84 A−.
Quantity surveyor. Son of RL player. E > 82 US, Can. E Under 23s, England B.

SYKES, A.R.V.   *England*
Birkenhead Sch, Liverpool Univ, Blackheath, Barbarians.
Hooker, 1-1-0-0.
14 F+.

SYKES, Frank Douglas   *England*
St Paul's Coll Cheltenham, Huddersfield, Northampton, Boston (US), Barbarians, Yorks.
b 9.12.27 Batley.
Wing, 4-1-0-3 (3 − 1t).
55 F− S+(1t); 63 NZ− A−.
PE teacher. 8 yrs between caps. Capt Yorks 57-8. Served Sgt RAEC Singapore 47-9. Head of PE Northampton GS 54-66, in charge of rugby

from 60. Emigrated US, as promoter of rugby in Massachusetts.

SYKES, Patrick William　　　　　*England*
St John's Sch Leatherhead, Cambridge Univ,
Wasps, RAF, Comb Servs, London Cos,
Barbarians, E Cos, Mdx.
b 3.3.25 Vancouver.
SH, 7-5-1-1.
48 F−; 52 S+ I+ F+; 53 W+ I= F+.
RAF/artificial flower co employee/branch mgr
Burroughs Machines. War-time Servs int v
Kiwis 44. Capt Wasps. 16 apps E Cos. Chmn
Mdx sel.

SYMES, G.R.　　　　　*Ireland*
Monkstown.
FB, 1-0-0-1.
1895 E−.

SYMINGTON, Archibald William　　*Scotland*
Fettes Coll, Cambridge Univ, RAF.
b −.3.1892; *d* 8.5.41.
Lock, 2-0-0-2.
14 W− E−.
RAF. Blue 11-13.

SYNGE, John Samuel　　　　　*Ireland*
St Columba's Coll Dublin, Cambridge Univ,
Lansdowne.
b 12.7.06 Dublin; *d* 26.8.82.
Flanker, 1-0-0-1.
29 S−.
Nigerian Administrative Service. Blue 27.

SYRETT, Ronald Edward　　　　*England*
RGS High Wycombe, Wasps, RAF, London
Cos, Barbarians, Mdx.
b 5.1.31 Beaconsfield.
Flanker, 11-7-3-1 (3 − 1t).
58 W= A+ I+ F+; 60 W+ I+ F= S+(1t); 62
W= I+ F−.
Butcher/co dir sports outfitters. Bro in law of
J.E. Woodward. Pres Bucks Refs Soc.

T

TAAFE, Bruce Stanton　　　　*Australia*
Knox GS, NSW.
b 13.8.44.
Hooker, 3-0-1-2 (4 − 1t).
69 SA−; 72 F=(1t) F−.
Computer analyst.

TABERER, W.S.　　　　*South Africa*
Griq W.
1-0-0-1.
1896 BT−.

TAFFARY, Michel　　　　*France*
RCF.
b 25.5.50 Peyrehorade, Landes.
FB, 4-2-0-2 (6 − 2p).
75 W−(2p) E+ S+ I−.
Electricity co.

TAGGART, Thomas　　　　*Ireland*
Derry AI, Trin Coll Dublin.
b 1866; *d* −.2.45.
Forward, 1-0-0-1.
1887 W−.
Solicitor.

TAILLANTOU, Jean　　　　*France*
Pau.
Wing, 3-2-0-1 (9 − 3t).
30 I+ G+(3t) W−.

TAIT, John Guthrie　　　　*Scotland*
Edinburgh Acad, Edinburgh Academicals,
Edinburgh Univ, Cambridge Univ.
b 24.8.1861 Edinburgh; *d* 4.10.45.
Forward, 2-2-0-0.
1880 I+; 1885 I+.
Barrister/college principal. Blue 1880-2. Bro in
law of C.W. Cathcart.

TAIT, Peter Webster　　　　*Scotland*
Royal HS, Royal HSFP, Edinburgh Univ.
b 19.10.06; *d* 22.4.80 Edinburgh.
Hooker, 1-1-0-0.
35 E+.
Medicine.

TALLENT, John Arthur CBE　　　*England*
TD
Sherborne Sch, Cambridge Univ, Blackheath,
Barbarians, Kent, E Midlands.
b 8.3.11 Chislehurst.
Centre FH, 5-1-0-4 (9 − 3t).
31 S−(2t) F−(1t); 32 SA− W−; 35 I+. Asst
Schoolmaster/stockbroker. Blue 29-31. Asst
master Stowe Sch 32-6. Stock Exchange 36-9,
46-77. Served WW2, HAC; commanded 118
Rgt, Lt Col. OBE (mil) 46. Governor
Sherborne Sch 66. CBE for 'services to Rugby
football' 60. Central Dist CB rep 47. Pres RFU
59-60. Only player to have played centre & FH
for both Cambridge & England.

TAMPLIN, William Ewart　　　*Wales*
Cardiff, Barbarians.
Lock, 7-5-1-1 (24 − 3c 6p).
47 S+(2c 1p) F+(1p) I+(1p) A+(2p); 48 E=
S+(1c 1p) F−.
Police. Played in 5 Servs ints, 1 Victory int.

TANNER, Christopher Champain　　*England*
AM
Cheltenham Coll, Cambridge Univ, Richmond,

Barbarians, Gloucester, Glos.
b 24.6.08; kia 22.5.41 off Crete.
Wing, 5-2-1-2 (3 − 1t).
30 S=; 32 SA− W− I+ S+(1t).
Church. Blue 30. Ordained 35; curate Farnham
R 35-7; St Mary de Lode, Gloucester 37-9;
rector of Haslemere 39. Served WW2, RNVR
chaplain. Killed in action with HMS Fiji off
Crete 41. Albert Medal posthumously 42 for
saving wounded men after Fiji had been sunk.
He died within minutes of dragging one aboard
rescue ship. One survivor of Fiji's sinking was
fellow int, Vice Adm Sir Peveril William-
Powlett. Another rugby int, C.F.G.T. Hallaran,
also won rarely awarded AM (since replaced by
the George Cross).

TANNER, Haydn   *Wales*
Gowerton GS, Swansea, Cardiff, Penclawdd,
Barbarians.
b 9.1.17 Swansea.
SH, 25-12-2-11.
35 NZ+; 36 E= S+ I+; 37 E− S− I−; 38 E+
S− I+; 39 E− S+ I+; 47 E− S+ F+ I+; 48 E=
S+ F− I−; 49 E+ S− I− F−; BI > 38 SA 1-0-0-
1.
College master/industrial chemist/journalist.
Played either side of WW2. W's longest int
career (15 seasons). Played in 8 Servs ints, 4
Victory ints. Capt 1st Barbarians XV to play
overseas side, A 48. Barbarians comm.

TANNER, John Maurice   *New Zealand*
Auckland GS, Univ, Otago, Auckland, NZ
Univs, S & N Islands.
b 11.1.27 Auckland.
2nd five-eighth/centre, 5-4-0-1 (3 − 1t).
50 BI+; 51 A+ A+ A+(1t); 53 W−.
Dentist. NZ > 51 A, 53-4 BI,F & NAm. Bro
Murray rep Auckland 48-50.

TANNER, Kerry John   *New Zealand*
Takapuna GS, New Brighton, NZ Jnrs,
Canterbury, S Island.
b 25.4.45 Hamilton.
Prop, 7-5-1-1.
74 A+ A= A+; 74 I+; 75 S+; 76 I+ SA−.
Schoolmaster/licensee. NZ > 74 A & Fj & I,W
& E, 76 SA.

TANNER, William Henry   *Australia*
Qld.
b 27.12.1871; *d* −.
Forward, 2-1-0-1.
1899 BT+ BT−.
Labourer.

TARR, Donald James   *Wales*
Ammanford CS, Swansea, RN, US Portsmouth,
Hants, Barbarians.
b 11.3.10 Llandilofawr; *d* 4.6.80 Fareham.

Hooker, 1-1-0-0.
35 NZ+.
RN/schoolmaster. Broke neck W v NZ 35,
never played again.

TARR, Francis Nathaniel   *England*
Stoneygate Sch Leicester, Uppingham Sch,
Oxford Univ, Leicester, Headingley,
Richmond, Midland Cos.
b 14.8.1887 Derbyshire; kia 18.7.15 Ypres.
Centre, 4-2-0-2 (6 − 2t).
09 A− W− F+(2t); 13 S+.
Solicitor. Blue 07-9. Joined up on 1st day of
WW1.

TARRICQ, Pierre   *France*
Lourdes.
b 18.5.29 Labouheyre.
Wing, 4-4-0-0 (3 − 1t).
58 A+ W+(1t) It+ I+.
Office worker.

TASKER, William George   *Australia*
Newington Coll, NSW.
b 1892; kia 18.
Five-eighth, 6-1-0-5.
13 NZ− NZ− NZ+; 14 NZ− NZ− NZ−.
Served WW1.

TATE, Murray J.   *Australia*
NSW.
b 28.
Five-eighth, 8-3-0-5 (3 − 1t).
51 NZ−; 52 Fj+ Fj− NZ+ NZ−; 53 SA−; 54
Fj+(1t) Fj−.
Draughtsman.

TATHAM, William Meaburn   *England*
Marlborough Coll, Marlborough Nomads,
Oxford Univ.
b 30.7.1862; *d* 18.10.38.
Forward, 7-6-0-1 (1t).
1882 S− W+; 1883 I+(1t) S+; 1884 W+ I+ S+.
Church. Blue 1881-3 (capt). Ordained 1885;
curate of St Saviour's Folkestone 1885-90; St
Agnes Kennington 1890-2; vicar of Cantley, nr
Doncaster 1892-38. Acting chaplain to Forces in
SA War, 02.

TAVERNIER, Clovis   *France*
Toulouse.
Flanker, 1-0-0-1.
13 I−.

TAYLOR, Albert Russell   *Wales*
Cross Keys Mon, Barbarians.
b 15 Risca; *d* 9.10.65 Abergavenny.
Flanker, 3-1-0-2 (3 − 1t).
37 I−; 38 I+(1t); 39 E−; BI > 38 SA 2-1-0-1.
Police.

TAYLOR, Alfred Squire   *Ireland*
Campbell Coll Belfast, Belfast Univ, Edinburgh
Univ, Ulster.
b 6.7.1889; kia 31.7.17 Ypres.
Centre, 4-1-1-2 (5 − 1t 1c).
10 E= S− W−; 12 F+(1t 1c).
Medicine. Capt in RAMC attached to Highland
LI.

TAYLOR, Arthur Sneyd   *England*
Merchant Taylors' Sch, Cambridge Univ, Guy's
Hosp, Blackheath, Kent.
b 7.12.1859; *d* 31.7.17.
FB, 4-4-0-0.
1882 W+; 1883 I+; 1886 W+ I+.
Medicine. Blue 1879-81. Bro of Henry.
Contemporary of R.T. Finch at Pembroke Coll.
One of 3 bros who played for Blackheath. GP at
Surbiton.

TAYLOR, Charles Gerald   *Wales*
RNEC Keyham, RNC Greenwich, RN,
Ruabon, Blackheath.
b 1865 Ruabon; kia 24.1.15 Dogger Bank.
Back, 9-1-2-6 (1c).
1884 E− S− I+; 1885 E− S=; 1886 E−(1c) S−;
1887 E= I−.
RN. Served WW1, Engr Capt RN; died aboard
HMS Tiger. Ex-football player, noted athlete.
Pole vault champ of W.

TAYLOR, David Aubrey   *Australia*
Brisbane CEGS, Brisbane Univ, Qld.
b 11.11.44.
Flanker, 5-1-0-4.
68 NZ− NZ− F+ I− S−.
Geologist.

TAYLOR, David Robertson   *Ireland*
Queen's Coll Belfast, Edinburgh Univ.
b 26.10.1880; *d* −.11.41.
Centre, 1-1-0-0.
03 E+.
Medicine.

TAYLOR, Edward Graham   *Scotland*
Loretto Sch, Oxford Univ, Barbarians.
b 3.7.07; *d* 13.9.59.
Wing, 2-2-0-0.
27 W+ NSW+.
Chartered accountant. Blue 26-8.

TAYLOR, Ernest William ('Little   *England*
Billy')
Rockcliff, Barbarians, Northumb.
b 20.2.1869 Newcastle upon Tyne; *d* −.
Half-back, 14-7-0-7 (16 − 2t 3c 1gm).
1892 I+; 1893 I+(1t); 1894 W+(1t 1c 1gm) I−
(1c) S−; 1895 W+ I+ S−; 1896 W+(1c) I−;
1897 W− I− S+; 1899 I−.
Footwear retailer/cashier. Described as the

'prince of half-backs'. Ckt for Northumb. Capt
Whitley Bay GC; later a golf pro.

TAYLOR, Frank ('Sos')   *England*
Medway Street Sch Leicester, Medway OB,
Medway Ath, Leicester, Midland Cos, Leics.
b 4.5.1890; *d* −.10.56.
Prop, 2-2-0-0.
20 F+ I+.
Bro of Tim. Played for Leicester 11-24. Served
WW1, Leics Rgt.

TAYLOR, Frederick Mark ('Tim')   *England*
Medway St Sch Leicester, Medway OB,
Medway Ath, Leicester, Midland Cos, Leics.
b 18.3.1888; *d* 64.
FH, 1-1-0-0.
14 W+.
Bro of Frank. Played for Leicester 09-23.

TAYLOR, Henry Herbert   *England*
Merchant Taylors' Sch, St George's Hosp,
Blackheath, Kent.
b 1.9.1858; *d* 25.5.42.
Half-back, 5-3-1-1 (6t).
1879 S=; 1880 S+(2t); 1881 I+(3t) W+(1t);
1882 S−.
Medicine. Bro of Arthur. 1st E player to score
3t, v I 1881. Missed train to Edinburgh for S
match 1881; place taken by Frank Wright. Surg
R Alexandra Hosp for Children & Sussex Eye
Hosp.

TAYLOR, Henry Morgan   *New Zealand*
Christchurch Boys' HS, HSOB, Canterbury, S
Island.
b 5.2.1889 Christchurch; *d* 20.6.55
Christchurch.
SH/wing, 5-5-0-0 (12 − 4t).
13 A+r US+; 14 A+ A+(3t) A+(1t).
Man dir plumber's merchants. NZ > 13 NAm,
14 A (played in all 11 matches). Served WW1;
rep Trentham Military Forces. Rep Canterbury
at ckt 12-21.

TAYLOR, James D.   *Ireland*
Collegians.
Forward, 3-1-0-2.
14 E− S+ W−.
HM Customs & Excise.

TAYLOR, John ('Bas')   *Wales*
Watford GS, O Fullerians, Loughborough
Colls, London Welsh, Surrey.
b 21.7.45 Watford.
Flanker, 26-15-1-10 (25 − 4t 3c 2p).
67 S− I− F− E+ NZ−; 68 I− F−; 69 S+ I+(1t)
F= E+ NZ− A+(1t); 70 F+; 71 E+(2c) S+(1t
1c) I+ F+; 72 E+ S+(1t) F+ NZ−; 73 E+(1p)
S−(1p) I+ F−; BI > 68 SA; 71 A, NZ 4-2-1-1.
Schoolmaster/sponsorship consultant/journalist.

Wales XV (capt) v J 73. Rugby corr 'Mail on Sunday'.

TAYLOR, John Inglis *Australia*
NSW.
b 21.5.49.
Wing, 4-1-1-2 (4 − 1t).
71 SA−; 72 F=(1t) F− Fj+.
Veterinary science.

TAYLOR, John McLeod *New Zealand*
Menzies Ferry Sch, Wyndham Dist HS, Pirates, Otago, Wellington, NZ Army, S Island.
b 12.1.13 Mataura; *d* 5.5.79 Wellington.
FB, 6-4-0-2 (24 − 6c 4p).
37 SA+ SA− SA−; 38 A+(3c 2p) A+(2c) A+(1c 2p).
Public servant. Top scorer 45 pts NZ > 38 A. Served WW2. Coach, selector Wellington 54-62; chmn 69-73.

TAYLOR, John T. ('Long John') *England*
Castleford, W Hartlepool, Durham Co, Yorks.
b 26.5.1876; *d* 8.9.51 Ashington.
Centre/FB, 11-3-0-8 (5 − 1t 1c).
1897 I−; 1899 I−; 1900 I+; 01 W− I−; 02 W− I+ S+(1t); 03 W−(1c) I−; 05 S−.
Licensee. Renowned as drop kicker in club, co rugby. Capt his clubs & cos but not E.

TAYLOR, John Wilgar *Ireland*
RBAI, Queen's Univ Belfast, NIFC.
b 30.6.1859; *d* 16.12.24 Belfast.
Forward, 8-1-1-6.
1879 S−; 1880 E− S−; 1881 S+; 1882 E= S−; 1883 E− S−.
Medicine. Ump of abandoned match, I v S 1885.

TAYLOR, Murray Barton *New Zealand*
Matamata Intermed Sch, Matamata Coll, NZ Jnrs, NZ Colts, Waikato, N Island.
b 25.8.56 Hamilton.
1st/2nd five-eighth, 7-4-0-3 (3 − 1d).
79 F+ F− A−(1d); 79 S+ E+; 80 A− A+
Plumber. NZ > 76 Arg & Uruguay, 79 A, 79 E,S & It, 80 A & Fj; NAm & W.

TAYLOR, Norman Mark *New Zealand*
Dargaville HS, Reporoa, Bay of Plenty, Ngongotaha, Hawkes Bay, N Island, Wasps (E), Mdx (E).
b 11.1.51 Auckland.
Wing/2nd five-eighth, 9-5-0-4 (4 − 1t).
77 BI− BI+r; 77 F− F+; 78 A+ A+(1t) A−; 78 I+; 82 A−.
Insurance salesman/cleaning co mgr. NZ > 76 Arg & Uruguay, 77 F, 78 BI. Remained in UK after 78 tour to work in London.

TAYLOR, Ormonde B. *South Africa*
Natal.

b 5.6.37.
Wing, 1-0-1-0.
62 BI=.
Post Office.

TAYLOR, Philip Joseph *England*
('Noddy')
Wakefield, Duke of Wellington's Rgt, The Army, Blackheath, Loughborough Coll, Northampton, Barbarians, Yorks, Herts.
b 6.6.31 Wakefield.
No 8, 6-1-3-2.
55 W− I=; 62 W= I+ F− S=.
Schoolmaster/mgr timber importers/sales rep/PRO George Wimpey. 7 yrs between caps. Capt Northampton 61-3. Taught at Northampton GS.

TAYLOR, Reginald *New Zealand*
Inglewood Sch, Waimate, Taranaki, Clifton, N Island.
b 23.3.1889 Hillsborough, Taranaki; kia 20.6.17 Messines, Belgium.
Flanker, 2-1-0-1 (3 − 1t)
12 A+(1t) A−.
Served WW1, 6th Reinforcements.

TAYLOR, Robert Bainbridge *England*
Northampton GS, King Alfred's Coll Winchester, Barbarians, Hants, Northampton, E Midlands.
b 39.4.42 Northampton.
Flanker, 16-6-0-10 (6 − 2t).
66 W−; 67 I+ F− S+(1t) W− NZ−; 69 F+ S+ W− SA+; 70 I+ W− S− F−(1t); 71 S− S−; BI > 68 SA 4-0-1-3.
Schoolmaster. Capt E-W v S-I RFU Centenary Match 70. Basketball for Northants. Taught at Wellingborough GS from 65.

TAYLOR, Robert Capel *Scotland*
Glenalmond Acad, Glasgow Univ, Kelvinside-West, Kelvinside Academicals, Barbarians.
b 31.8.24.
Flanker, 4-1-0-3.
51 W+ I− E− SA−.
Medicine.

TAYLOR, Warwick Thomas *New Zealand*
Otago, Canterbury, NZ Colts, S Island Univs, NZ Univs.
b 11.3.60 Hamilton.
Centre/2nd five-eighth, 15-12-2-1 (12 − 3t).
83 BI+ BI+ BI+ BI+ A+(1t) S=; 84 F+(1t) F+(1t) A− A+; 85 E+ E+ A+ Arg+ Arg=.
NZ > 83 & 84 A; 83 S & E, 85 Arg. Inj v S 83. Played for Overseas XV v Five Nations, Twickenham 86.

**TAYLOR, William John. See
Kirwan-Taylor, W.J.**

TEAGUE, Michael C. *England*
Gloucester, Cardiff.
No 8, 3-0-0-3 (4 – 1t).
85 F–r NZ–(1t) NZ–.

TECTOR, William Richard *Ireland*
Kilkenny Coll, Mountjoy Sch, Trin Coll Dublin,
Wanderers.
b 16.4.29 Clonroche, Co Wexford.
FB, 3-0-1-2.
55 F– E= S–.
Schoolmaster.

TEDEN, Derek Edmund *England*
Taunton Sch, Richmond, Barbarians.
b 19.7.16; kia 15.10.40 Friesian Islands.
Prop, 3-2-0-1 (3 – 1t).
39 W+(1t) I– S+.
RAF. Served WW2, Pt Off.

TEDFORD, Alfred *Ireland*
Methodist Coll Belfast, Malone.
b 7.1.1877 Belfast; *d* 6.1.42.
Forward, 23-9-0-14 (18 – 6t).
02 E– S+ W–; 03 E+ S– W–; 04 E– S–
W+(2t); 05 E+ S+(1t) W– NZ–; 06 E+(2t)
S– W+ SA–; 07 E+(1t) S– W–; 08 E– S+
W–; BT > 03 SA.
Linen merchant. Pres IRU 19-20.

TEEHAN, Charles *Ireland*
PBC Cork, UC Cork.
b 6.5.19 Buttevant, Co Cork.
Prop, 3-2-0-1.
39 E+ S+ W–.
Dental surgeon.

TEGGIN, Alfred *England*
Broughton Rgrs, Lancs.
b 1860 Manchester.
Forward, 6-3-2-1 (1t).
1884 I+; 1885 W+(1t); 1886 I+ S=; 1887 I–
S=.
His club, Broughton Rgrs, helped form NU
1895.

TEITZEL, Ross Gordon *Australia*
Brisbane CEGS, Brisbane Univ, Qld.
b 20.3.46.
Flanker, 7-2-0-5.
66 W+ S–; 67 E+ I– F– I– NZ–.
Veterinarian.

TELFER, Colin McLeod *Scotland*
Royal HS, Hawick, Edinburgh Univ,
Barbarians.
b 26.2.47 Hawick.
FH, 17-9-0-8 (18 – 3t 2d).
68 A+; 69 F+ W– I– E–; 72 F+(1t 1d) W–
E+(1d); 73 W+(1t) I+ E– P+(1t); 74 W– E+
I–; 75 A+; 76 F–.

Investment analyst. Nephew of Hugh McLeod.
Scottish XV v Arg 73, Tg 74. Barbarians > 69
SA. SRU coach 84-5.

TELFER, James William *Scotland*
('Creamy') MBE
Gala Acad, Heriot-Watt Univ, Melrose,
Barbarians.
b 17.3.40 Pathhead, Midlothian.
No 8/flanker, 25-9-2-14 (9 – 3t).
64 F+ NZ= W– I+ E+(1t); 65 F– W– I–; 66
F= W– I+ E+; 67 W+(1t) I– E–; 68 E– A+;
69 F+(1t) W– I– E– SA+; 70 F– W– I–; BI
> 66 A 2-2-0-0, NZ 3-0-0-3; 68 SA 3-0-1-2.
Schoolmaster. Scottish XV v Arg (2) 69. S's
most capped no 8 (22 apps). Capt S 12 times.
Scotland B coach 74-81. Coach BI > 83 NZ.
SRU coach 80-4. Rector Hawick HS.

TENNENT, James MacWilliam *Scotland*
Merchiston Castle Sch, W of Scotland.
b 7.9.1888 Glasgow; *d* 19.3.55 London.
Half-back, 6-3-0-3 (12 – 4t).
09 W– I+ E+(2t); 10 F+(2t) W– E–.
Ref 7 ints 20-3. Ckt for S.

TERREAU, Maurice *France*
Bourg.
b 30.1.23 Bourg-en-Bresse.
FH/centre, 17-11-0-6 (15 – 5t).
45 W–; 46 BF+ I+ NZS–(1t) W+(2t); 47
S+(1t) I+ W– E–; 48 I– A+ W+(1t) E+; 49
S– Arg+ Arg+; 51 S+.

TETLEY, Thomas Spence *England*
Bradford, Yorks.
b 1856; *d* 15.8.24.
Back, 1-1-0-0.
1876 S+.
Worsted spinner. Acclaimed 100y sprinter.

TETZLAFF, Percy Laurence *New Zealand*
Huntly Dist HS, Hamilton Tech OB, Waikato,
Ponsonby, Auckland, N Island.
b 14.7.20 Taupiri.
SH, 2-2-0-0.
47 A+ A+.
Fitter & turner/engrg co mgr. NZ > 47 A.
Coach, comm & pres Ponsonby.

THEUNISSEN, Daniel Johannes *South Africa*
Stellenbosch Univ, Griq W.
b 1869; *d* 64.
1-0-0-1.
1896 BT–.

THEURIET, André *France*
SCUF.
b 30.3.1887 Paris; *d* –.
SH, 5-0-0-5.
09 E– W–; 10 S–; 11 W–; 13 E–.

Head of printing & publicity co. Rep France in 1500m in 08 Olympics.

THEVENOT, G. *France*
SCUF.
Forward, 3-0-0-3.
10 W− E− I−.

THIERRY, Robert *France*
RCF.
b 23.6.1893 Brienon-sur-Armançon;
d 23.10.73.
Flanker, 4-1-0-3.
20 S− E− W− US+.
Played with only one eye.

THIERS, Pierre *France*
Montferrand.
SH/flanker, 9-6-0-3 (17 − 7c 1p).
36 G+(1c) G+; 37 G+(3c) It+(3c); 38 G− G+;
40 BF−(1p); 45 BF+ BF−.

THIL, Paul *France*
Nantes.
b −; *d* 35 Nantes.
Flanker, 6-0-0-6.
12 W− E−; 13 S− SA− E− W−.
Rly official.

THIMBLEBY, Neil William *New Zealand*
Marton Dist HS, Taupo, Hawkes Bay, Hastings HSOB, Marist, Celtic.
b 19.6.39 Lower Hutt.
Prop, 1-0-0-1.
70 SA−.
Watersider. NZ > 70 A & SA. Hawkes Bay selector & coach 79-80.

THOM, David Alexander *Scotland*
Hawick HS, London Scottish, Barbarians.
b 16.2.10 Hawick; *d* 82.
Flanker, 5 1 0 4 (3 1t).
34 W−; 35 W−(1t) I− E+ NZ−.
Printing trade. Pres SRU 65-6.

THOM, George *Scotland*
Kirkcaldy HS, Kirkcaldy.
b −; *d* −.8.27 Brit Columbia.
Flanker/no 8, 4-3-0-1.
20 F+ W+ I+ E−.
Uncle of J.R.

THOM, James Robert *Scotland*
George Watson's Coll, Watsonians.
b 22.11.10 Kirkcaldy.
Prop/hooker, 3-3-0-0.
33 W+ E+ I+.
Forestry consultant UNO. Nephew of George.

THOMAS, Alan *Wales*
Newport, Barbarians, Cross Keys.
b 40.
Flanker, 2-0-1-1.
63 NZ−; 64 E=.
Engr.

THOMAS, Alun Gruffydd *Wales*
Port Talbot Co. Sch, Swansea, Cardiff, Llanelli, Barbarians.
b 26 Cwmavon.
Centre/wing/FH, 13-11-0-2 (6 − 1t 1d).
52 E+ S+ I+ F+(1d); 53 S+ I+ F+; 54 E− I+ F+; 55 S− I+ F+(1t); BI > 55 SA.
Sales mgr/oil co rep. WRU selector 63-8, pres 85-6. Asst mgr W > 64 SA. Mgr BI > 74 SA.

THOMAS, Barry Trevor *New Zealand*
Otahuhu Coll, Manukau, Auckland, Oriental, Wellington, N Island.
b 21.7.37 Auckland.
Prop, 4-3-0-1.
62 A+; 64 A+ A+ A−.
Plumber/sec & mgr Manukau RFC. Coach & comm Manukau. Father-in-law Sam Cameron rep Taranaki 10-25, Wanganui 24.

THOMAS, Beriah Melbourne Gwynne *Wales*
Ogmore Vale, St Bartholomew's Hosp, London Univ, Bridgend, Barbarians.
b 11.6.1896 Bridgend; *d* 23.3.66 Pontypridd.
Wing, 6-3-0-3 (6 − 2t).
19 NZA−; 21 S− F+ I+(1t); 23 F+(1t); 24 E−.
Medicine.

THOMAS, Brian Edwin *Wales*
Neath GS, Cambridge Univ, Neath.
b 18.5.40.
Lock/prop, 21-9-3-9 (3 − 1t).
63 E− S+ I− F− NZ−; 64 E= S+(1t) I+ F= SA−; 65 E+; 66 E+ S+ I−; 67 NZ−; 69 S+ I+ F= E+ NZ− NZ−,
Metallurgist. Blue 60-2. W > 64 SA; 69 NZ, A & Fj. Team mgr Neath RFC 83-6.

THOMAS, Charles *England*
Barnstaple Oaks, Barnstaple, Devon.
b 1875; *d* c35.
Forward, 4-2-0-2 (3 − 1t).
1895 W+ I+(1t) S−; 1899 I−.
One of the lightest forwards to be capped, 11st 3lb v W 1895.

THOMAS, Charles J. *Wales*
Newport, Barbarians.
Half-back/wing/centre, 9-3-1-5 (1 − 1t).
1888 I− NZN+; 1889 S− I−; 1890 S− E+ I=(1t); 1891 E− I+.
Farmer.

397

THOMAS, Cyril Rhys *Wales*
Glam Police, Bridgend, Blaengarw, Kenfig Hill,
Maesteg, Brit Police, Glam.
b 27.3.02 Bridgend; *d* 75.
Wing, 2-0-0-2 (3 − 1t).
25 E−(1t) S−.
Police. 58t for Bridgend 24-5 season.

THOMAS, David *Wales*
Aberavon.
b 39.
Centre, 1-1-0-0.
61 I+.
Civil engr. Wales XV v Fj 64.

THOMAS, David J. *Wales*
Swansea.
b 1880; *d* 19.10.25 Dunvant.
Forward, 10-7-1-2.
04 E=; 08 A+; 10 E− S+ I+; 11 E+ S+ F+ I+;
12 E−.
Collier.

THOMAS, David John *Wales*
Swansea.
b 30.3.09 Swansea.
Lock, 11-5-2-4.
30 S+ I=; 32 E+ S+ I−; 33 E+ S−; 34 E−; 35
E= S+ I−.
Police.

THOMAS, David Leyshon *Wales*
Briton Ferry, Bridgend, Neath.
b −.3.09 Neath; *d* 28.9.52 Neath.
Lock, 1-0-0-1.
37 E−.
Oil co employee. Bro of H.W.

THOMAS, Edward John Richard *Wales*
Ferndale Bd Sch, Ferndale, Penygraig,
Mountain Ash, Brigdend, Glam Police, Glam.
b 1881; kia 7.7.16 Mametz Wood.
Forward, 4-3-0-1.
06 SA−; 08 F+ I+; 09 S+.
Police. Served WW1, Sgt-maj in Welch Rgt,
Cardiff City Battn.

THOMAS, Edwin ('Beddoe') *Wales*
Newport.
b 1878; *d* −.11.61.
Forward, 6-5-0-1.
04 S+ I−; 09 S+ F+ I+; 10 F+.
Labourer/licensee.

THOMAS, George *Wales*
Newport.
Back, 3-1-1-1 (1t).
1888 NZN+(1t); 1890 I=; 1891 S−.
Pro sprinter.

THOMAS, Harold *Wales*
Swansea, Morriston, Llanelli, The Army.
FB, 1-1-0-0 (2 − 1c).
12 F+(1c).
The Army. Played in 2 Servs ints.

THOMAS, Harold Watkin *Wales*
Neath, Briton Ferry, Cimla.
b 19.2.14 Neath.
Lock, 6-2-1-3.
36 E= S+ I+; 37 E− S− I−.
Metal worker. Bro of D.L. Salford RL 37.
Served WW2, RSM in Maritime RA.
Mentioned in despatches.

THOMAS, Horace Wyndham *Wales*
Bridgend CS, Monmouth Sch, Cambridge Univ,
Swansea, Barbarians.
b 1891; kia 3.9.16 The Somme.
FH, 2-0-0-2.
12 SA−; 13 E−.
Business in India. Blue 12. Served WW1, 2nd Lt
in Rifle Bde.

THOMAS, Ivor *Wales*
Bryncethin, Torquay Ath, Devon.
b 30.4.1900.
Hooker, 1-0-0-1.
24 E−.
Miner/builder's labourer.

THOMAS, James Denzil ('Denzil *Wales*
Drop')
Llandeilo GS, Ystalyfera GS, Bangor Normal
Coll, Cardiff Coll, Cwmgors, Brynamman,
Bath, Neath, Llanelli.
b 29 Llandyfriog.
Centre, 1-1-0-0 (3 − 1d).
54 I+(1d).
Schoolmaster.

THOMAS, L.C. *Wales*
Cardiff.
Forward, 2-0-1-1.
1885 E− S=.

THOMAS, Malcolm Campbell *Wales*
Bassaleg GS, Welsh SS, Newport, Devonport
Servs, Barbarians.
b 25.4.29 Machen.
Centre/wing/FH, 27-15-2-10 (22 − 4t 2c 2p).
49 F−; 50 E+ S+(1t) I+(1t) F+; 51 E+(2t) S−
I= F− SA−; 52 E+(1c) S+(1c 2p) I+ F+; 53
E−; 56 E+ S+ I− F+; 57 E− S−; 58 E= S+ I+
F−; 59 I+ F−; BI > 50 NZ 2-0-0-2, A 1-1-0-0;
59 A, NZ 1-0-0-1.
RN/business exec. Barbarians > 58 SA.

THOMAS, Rees *Wales*
Pontypool.
b 1882 Caldicot; *d* 15.6.26.

Forward, 8-5-0-3 (3 − 1t).
09 F+ I+; 11 S+(1t) F+; 12 E− S+ SA−; 13
E−.
Miner. Warrington RL 13.

THOMAS, Richard Clement   *Wales*
Charles
Blundell's Sch, Welsh SS, Cambridge Univ,
Brynamman, Swansea, Harlequins, Barbarians.
b 28.1.29 Cardiff.
Flanker, 26-17-1-8 (3 − 1t).
49 F−; 52 I+(1t) F+; 53 S+ I+ F+ NZ+; 54
E− I+ F+ S+; 55 S− I+; 56 E+ S+ I−; 57 E−;
58 A+ E= S+ I+ F−; 59 E+ S− I+ F−; BI >
55 SA 2-1-0-1.
Wholesale butcher/auctioneer/journalist/wine
bar owner. Blue 49. Barbarians v NZ 54.
Author (with Geoffrey Nicholson) 'Welsh
Rugby' pub 80. Rugby corr 'The Observer'. Son
Mark played for Cambridge Univ, Swansea,
London Welsh.

THOMAS, Robert   *Wales*
Swansea.
b 1871; *d* −.2.10 Swansea.
Forward, 4-4-0-0.
1900 E+ S+ I+; 01 E+.

THOMAS, Rowland Lewis   *Wales*
Llandovery Coll, Univ Coll Hosp, London
Welsh, Llanelli.
b 1863 Whitland; *d* 21.1.49 Whitland.
Forward, 7-1-1-5.
1889 S− I−; 1890 I=; 1891 E− S− I+; 1892
E−.
Medicine. Fdr mem, 1st sec London Welsh
1885. Served WW1, medical officer in Welsh
Horse. Pres Whitland RFC. Ref. GP at St
Clears, Pembs 40 yrs.

THOMAS, Samuel Gethin   *Wales*
Llanelli.
b 1898 Llwynhendy; *d* 1.2.39 Llwynhendy.
Lock, 4-1-0-3.
23 E− S− F+ I−.
Grocer/sub-postmaster. Served WW1.

THOMAS, Stephen   *Wales*
Llanelli.
b 1865 Kidwelly; *d* −.10.37 Gowerton.
Forward, 3-2-0-1.
1890 S− E+; 1891 I+.
Tinplater. Replaced Jim Hannan v I 1891.

THOMAS, Watcyn Gwyn   *Wales*
Llanelli CS, Welsh SS, UC Swansea, Llanelli,
Swansea, Waterloo, Lancashire, Barbarians.
b 16.1.06 Llanelli; *d* 10.8.77 Birmingham.
No 8, 14-5-1-8 (6 − 2t).
27 E− S− F+(1t) I−; 29 E−; 31 E= S+(1t)
SA−; 32 E+ S+ I−; 33 E+ S− I−.

Schoolmaster. Capt 1st Welsh SS XV 24. Capt
Lancs, Co Champ winners 35. Coached England
Schs 19 Group. Autobiography 'Rugby-Playing
Man' pub 77. Merited mention in Oxford
Companion to the Literature of Wales, 86.

THOMAS, William Delme   *Wales*
Welsh Youth, St Clares, Llanelli, Barbarians.
b 12.9.42 Bancyfelin.
Lock, 25-15-1-9.
66 A−; 68 S+ I− F−; 69 E+ NZ− A+; 70 SA=
S+ E+ I− F+; 71 E+ S+ I+ F+; 72 E+ S+ F+
NZ−; 73 E+ S− I+ F−; 74 E−; BI > 66uncap
A, NZ 2-0-0-2; 68 SA 2(1r)-0-0-2; 71 A, NZ 2-1-
0-1.
Electricity linesman. 44 apps for BI, rec for
Welshman.

THOMAS, William Henry   *Wales*
Llandovery Coll, Welsh SS, Cambridge Univ,
Haverfordwest, London Welsh, Weston-super-
Mare, Llanelli.
b 22.3.1866 Fishguard; *d* −.10.21 Beccles.
Forward, 11-3-3-5.
1885 S=; 1886 E− S−; 1887 E= S−; 1888 S+
I−; 1890 E+ I=; 1891 S− I+; BT > 1888 A,
NZ.
Schoolmaster. Blue 1886-7.

THOMAS, William J.   *Wales*
Welsh Youth, Cardiff, Barbarians.
b 1.9.33 Bargoed.
Hooker, 2-0-0-2.
61 F−; 63 F−.
Engr's toolmaker.

THOMAS, William Llewellyn   *Wales*
Christ's Coll Brecon, Oxford Univ, Newport,
Barbarians.
b 6.5.1872; *d* 19.1.43.
Wing, 3-2-0-1.
1894 S+; 1895 E− I+.
Minister. Blue 1893-4.

THOMAS, W. Trevor ('Hocker')   *Wales*
Abertillery.
b 1909 Merthyr; *d* −.
Flanker, 1-0-0-1.
30 E−.
Miner. Oldham RL.

THOMPSON, Charles   *Ireland*
Methodist Coll Belfast, RS Dungannon,
Collegians.
Wing, 13-4-1-8 (9 − 3t).
07 E+ S−; 08 E− S+(1t) W−; 09 E− S− W−
(1t) F+; 10 E= S− W− F+(1t).
Timber trade.

THOMPSON, Edward George   *Australia*
Toowoomba GS, Qld.
b 06.
Prop/lock, 4-4-0-0.
29 NZ+ NZ+ NZ+; 30 BI+.
Bank mgr.

THOMPSON, Frederick   *Australia*
NSW.
b 1890; kia 18.
Hooker, 5-1-0-4 (3 − 1t).
13 NZ− NZ− NZ+(1t); 14 NZ− NZ−.
Bank mgr.

THOMPSON, Gerald W.   *South Africa*
('Tommy')
Rondebosch HS, W Prov.
b 4.10.1886 Carnarvon, Cape Prov; kia 30.6.16
Kangata, E Africa.
Hooker/prop, 3-3-0-0.
12 S+ I+ W+.
SA > 12-13 BI, F. Served WW1, Pte SA
Infantry.

THOMPSON, J.A.   *Ireland*
Queen's Coll Belfast.
Forward, 1-0-0-1.
1885 S−.

THOMPSON, John   *Australia*
Qld.
b −.7.1886 Warwick, Qld; *d* 78.
Flanker, 2-0-0-2.
14 NZ− NZ−.
Farmer. One of A's longest lived players.

THOMPSON, John Knox   *Ireland*
Stafford
RS Dungannon, Trin Coll Dublin.
b −; *d* c50.
Flanker/No 8, 8-2-0-6.
21 W−; 22 E− S− F+; 23 E− S− W+ F−.
Medicine.

THOMPSON, Joseph Francis   *Wales*
Abercarn, Cross Keys.
b 22.12.02 Hambrook, Glos; *d* 13.10.83 Leeds.
No 8, 1-0-0-1.
23 E−.
Miner/tram driver. Leeds RL 23 £300 fee.
Within 3 months of signing, 28.4.23, won Cup
Winners medal v Hull, Belle Vue. 390 apps for
Leeds (53t, 862 goals, 1883 pts). 12 GB RL, 8
Wales RL. 3 GB RL tours Australasia.
Received WRU cap Sept 75.

THOMPSON, Peter Donald   *Australia*
Qld.
Wing, 1-0-0-1.
50 BI−.
Hardware exec.

THOMPSON, Peter Humphrey   *England*
Leeds GS, Headingley, Waterloo, Barbarians,
Yorks.
b 18.1.29 Scarborough.
Wing, 17-10-4-3 (15 − 5t).
56 W− I+ S+ F−(1t); 57 W+ I+ F+ S+(1t); 58
W=(1t) A+ I+ F+(2t) S=; 59 W− I+ F= S=.
Sales mgr. Capt Headingley 56-7.

THOMPSON, Robert George   *Ireland*
Queen's Coll Cork, Lansdowne.
Forward, 1-0-0-1.
1882 W−.
Medicine. Army Medical Staff.

THOMPSON, Robert John   *Australia*
Rotorua BHS, Bay of Plenty, Maoris, W
Suburbs, WA.
b 8.3.47 Rotorua, NZ.
Hooker, 3-1-0-2 (6 − 1t 1c).
71 SA− F−r; 72 Fj+(1t 1c).
Springs manufacturer. A > 72 NZ. WA's 1st
cap; rec 18 pts WA v SA 71.

THOMPSON, Robin Henderson   *Ireland*
RBAI, Queen's Univ Belfast, Instonians,
Barbarians.
b 5.5.31 Belfast.
Lock/no 8, 11-3-0-8.
51 SA−; 52 F+; 54 NZ− F− E− S+ W−; 55
F− S− W−; 56 W+; BI > 55 SA 3-1-0-2.
Industrial chemist/journalist/tv reporter. Capt
BI > 55 SA. Warrington RL.

THOMSON, A.E.   *Scotland*
US Portsmouth.
Centre, 3-1-0-2.
21 F− W+ E−.

THOMSON, A.M.   *Scotland*
St Andrew's Univ.
Lock, 1-0-0-1.
49 I−.

THOMSON, Bruce Ewan   *Scotland*
Aberdeen GS, Oxford Univ.
b 19.11.30.
Prop, 3-0-0-3.
53 F− W− I−.
Schoolmaster/sales mgr/medicine. Blue 51-2.

THOMSON, George Thomas   *England*
Heath Sch Halifax, Halifax, Yorks.
b c1857; *d* 31.10.1889 Sydney, NSW.
Forward, 9-6-2-1 (1t).
1878 S=; 1882 I= S− W+(1t); 1883 I+ S+;
1884 I+ S+; 1885 I+.
Stuff merchant/manufacturer of sheeting. His
club, Halifax, helped form NU 1895. Capt
Yorks 1880-4. V-pres RFU 1884-7 whilst still
playing for E.

THOMSON, Hector Douglas　　*New Zealand*
('Mona')
Christchurch Boys' HS, Wellington Coll,
Oriental, Grafton, Auckland, Wanganui,
Wellington, S & N Islands.
b 20.2.1881 Napier; *d* 9.8.39 Wellington.
Wing, 1-1-0-0 (3 – 1t).
08 A W+(1t).
Civil servant. NZ > 05 A, 05-6 BI,F & NAm.
Arm inj 08 forced retirement. Bro Andrew rep
Wellington 06. Under-sec in NZ Immigration
Dept.

THOMSON, Ian Hosie Munro　　*Scotland*
Heriot's Coll, Heriot's FP, Edinburgh Univ,
The Army.
b 13.4.30.
FB, 7-1-0-6 (27 – 6c 5p).
51 W+(1c 1p) I–(1c); 52 F–(1c 2p) W– I–(1c
1p); 53 I–(1c 1p) E–(1c).
Served in R Corps of Signals.

THOMSON, J.S.　　*Scotland*
Glasgow Acad, Glasgow Academicals.
Forward, 1-1-0-0.
1871 E+.
Played in 1st int, S v E 1871.

THOMSON, Ronald Hew　　*Scotland*
Cambridge Univ, London Scottish, Barbarians.
b Finchley.
Wing, 15-6-1-8 (9 – 3t).
60 I+(1t) E– SA–; 61 F– SA– W+ I+ E–; 63
F+(1t) W– I+ E–; 64 F+(1t) NZ= W–.
Chartered accountant.

THOMSON, W.B.　　*England*
Bedford Modern Sch, Lewisham Pk,
Blackheath, W of Scotland.
b 1871 Matabeleland; *d* –.
FB/wing, 4-3-0-1 (3 – 1t).
1892 W+; 1895 W+(1t) I+ S–.

TIIOMSON, W.II.M.　　*Scotland*
W of Scotland.
Forward, 1-1-0-0.
06 SA+.

THOMSON, William John　　*Scotland*
Loretto Sch, Oxford Univ, W of Scotland.
b 18.4.1876; *d* 10.11.39.
Forward, 3-2-0-1 (6 – 1c 1gm).
1899 W+(1gm) E+(1c); 1900 W–.
Co dir. Blue 1895-6. Ckt for S.

THORBURN, Paul Huw　　*Wales*
Hereford Cathedr Sch, Herefordshire Schs,
Swansea Univ, S Gower, Welsh Univs, UAU,
Ebbw Vale, Neath.
b 24.11.62 Rheindalen, W Germany.
FB, 7-4-0-3 (80 – 7c 22p)

85 F–(1p) E+(2c 3p) Fj+(3c 2p); 86 E–(1c 3p)
S+(5p) I+(1c 3p) F–(5p).
Student. Wales B v F 1984. Neath rec 438 pts 84-
5. Longest p in int rugby v S 86, measured at
70yd 8 1/2in. Welsh rec 64 pts for season, 85-6.

THORNE, Graham Stuart　　*New Zealand*
Auckland GS, Univ, NZ Univs, Auckland, N
Transvaal.
b 25.2.46 Auckland.
Wing/centre, 10-7-0-3 (3 – 1t).
68 A+ A+(1t) F+ F+ F+; 69 W+; 70 SA–
SA+ SA– SA–.
Law student/bottle store owner/insurance
salesman/tv sports commentator. NZ > 67 BI,F
& C, 68 A & Fj (12t). 17t (inc 4t v NE Cape) NZ
> SA 70, most t for NZ in SA (total 19t from 20
apps inc A part of tour). Moved to SA 70; rep N
Transvaal & played in 2 SA trials before
returning to NZ.

THORNE, John David　　*England*
Bristol, Glos.
b 1.1.34.
Hooker, 3-2-1-0.
63 W+ I= F+.
Production controller shoe co.

THORNETT, John Edward MBE　　*Australia*
Sydney BHS, Sydney Univ, NSW.
b 30.3.35.
Flanker, 37-9-3-25 (3 – 1t).
55 NZ– NZ– NZ+; 56 SA– SA–; 58 W– I–
S–(1t) F– M= M– NZ+ NZ–; 59 BI– BI–;
61 Fj+ Fj= SA– SA– F–; 62 NZ– NZ= NZ–
NZ–; 63 E+ SA– SA+ SA+ SA–; 64 NZ–
NZ– NZ+; 65 SA+ SA+; 66 BI– BI–; 67 F–.
Engr. Bro of Dick. Capt A > 62, 64 NZ; 63 SA;
66-7 BI, F & Can.

THORNETT, Richard Norman　　*Australia*
NSW.
b 23.9.40.
Flanker/lock, 11-2-2-7 (6 – 2t).
61 Fj+(1t) Fj+ Fj= SA– SA– F–; 62 NZ–
NZ–(1t) NZ= NZ– NZ–.
Police/licensee/hotelier. Bro of John. Rep A
water polo Rome Olympics 60. 10 A RL Tests.

THORNHILL, Thomas　　*Ireland*
Wanderers.
b –; *d* 39.
Half-back, 4-1-0-3.
1892 E– S– W+; 1893 E–.
Barrister. Pres IRU 01-2.

THORNTON, Neville Henry　　*New Zealand*
Otahuhu Coll, Univ, Grammar, Auckland,
Otorohanga, King Country.
b 12.12.18 Otahuhu.
No 8, 3-2-0-1 (3 – 1p).

47 A+ A+(1p); 49 SA−.
Papakura HS principal. NZ > 47 A, 49 SA.
Served WW2; played for Comb Servs 44-5.
Coached Grammar club 53-4.

THORPE, Alan C. *Australia*
NSW.
Centre, 1-1-0-0.
29 NZ+r.
Clerk.

THRIFT, Harry *Ireland*
Dublin HS, Trin Coll Dublin.
b 24.12.1882; *d* 2.2.58.
Wing, 18-8-0-10 (15 − 5t).
04 W+(1t); 05 E+ S+ W− NZ−; 06 E+
W+(1t) SA−; 07 E+(1t) S− W−; 08 E−
S+(2t) W−; 09 E− S− W− F+.
Prof at Trin Coll Dublin. Pres IRU 23-4.

TIERNEY, Dennis ('Donough') *Ireland*
UC Cork, Barbarians.
b 15; *d* −.7.70.
Lock/prop, 3-1-0-2.
38 S− W−; 39 E+.
Medicine. Emigrated to Can.

TIGNOL, Paul *France*
Toulouse.
b 3.3.33 Toulouse.
Lock/no 8, 2-1-0-1.
53 S+ I−.

TILLIE, C.R. *Ireland*
Derry AI, Trin Coll Dublin.
Wing, 4-2-0-2 (1t).
1887 E+(1t) S−; 1888 W+ S−.

TILYARD, James Thomas *New Zealand*
Poneke, Wellington, Wanganui, N Island.
b 27.8.1889 Waratah, A; *d* 1.11.66
Dannevirke.
1st five-eighth, 1-0-0-1.
13 A−.
Labourer. Capt NZ > 20 A. Arrived in NZ at
early age. Rep Wellington at ckt 07-8. Bro Fred
rep NZ 23 (no Tests) & another bro Charlie rep
Wellington 19-20.

TIMBURY, Fredrick Richard *Australia*
Vaughan
Qld.
b 1885; *d* −.4.45 Sydney.
Forward, 2-1-0-1.
10 NZ− NZ+.
Solicitor.

TIMMS, Alec Boswell *Scotland*
Melbourne Univ, Edinburgh Univ, Edinburgh
W.
b Melbourne; *d* 5.5.22 Redhill, Surrey.

Centre, 14-8-1-5 (16 − 3t 1d 1p).
1896 W−; 1900 W− I=; 01 W+ I+ E+(1t); 02
W− E−; 03 W+(1p) E+(1d); 04 I+(1t) E+; 05
I−(1t) E+; BT > 1899 A.
Medicine. In practice for a time in Cardiff.

TINDALL, Eric Norman *Australia*
NSW.
b 45.
SH, 1-0-0-1 (4 − 1t).
73 Tg−(1t).

TINDALL, John C. ('Jackie') *South Africa*
Rondebosch HS, W Prov.
b 01; *d* 3.5.46.
FB, 5-3-0-2.
24 BI+; 28 NZ+ NZ− NZ+ NZ−.
Clerk. SA > 31-2 BI; seriously inj v London
Cos. Life saved by emergency operation.
Officials planned to cancel remainder of tour if
he died.

TINDALL, Victor Ronald *England*
Wallasey GS, Richmond, Liverpool Univ, RAF,
Comb Servs, Barbarians, Cheshire.
b 1.8.28.
Wing, 4-1-0-3.
51 W− I− F− S+.
Medicine. Cheshire Refs Soc 58-64. Ath for N
Cos AA. Served RAF 52-4. Consultant in
obstetrics & gynaecology Utd Cardiff Hosps; snr
lecturer Welsh Nat Sch of Medicine.

TINDILL, Eric William Thomas *New Zealand*
('Snowy')
Motueka Dist HS, Wellington Tech Coll,
Athletic, Wellington, N Island.
b 18.12.10 Nelson.
1st five-eighth, 1-0-0-1.
36 E−.
Accountant. NZ > 35-6 BI & C, 38 A. Served
WW2; capt 2nd NZEF in SA & UK 44-5. Ref
NZ v BI (2) 50 & NZ v A 55. Outstanding ckter,
rep Wellington & NZ 38-47 (in 29 apps for NZ
562 runs, 35 catches, 18 stumpings). NZ ckt
selector 55-6 & umpire NZ v E 59. Sons Peter &
Dennis rep Wellington at rugby. Co-author 'The
Tour of the Third All Blacks' pub 36.

TITLEY, Mark Howard *Wales*
Ysgol Gyfun Rhydfelen, Mid Glam Schs, E
Wales Schs, NE Surrey Coll of Tech, London
Welsh, Surrey, Bridgend, Swansea.
b 3.5.59 Swansea.
Wing, 10-4-0-6, (8 − 2t).
83 R−; 84 S−(1t) I+ F− E+ A−; 85 S+ I−
Fj+(1t); 86 F−.
Building site mgr. Wales B v F 82. Wales XV v J
83. Wales Player of Year 84.

TOBIAS, Errol George   *South Africa*
Swartberg HS Caledon, Villagers, SA Country
Dist, SARF, Boland, Proteas, Barbarians,
Barbarians (E).
b 18.4.50 Caledon.
Centre/FH 6-6-0-0 (22 − 1t 3c 4p).
81 I+ I+; 84 E+ E+(1t 1c) SAm+(2c 2p)
SAm+(2p).
SA > 80 SAm; 81 NZ, US.
Bricklayer/plasterer. 1st coloured Springbok.
Proteas > 71 BI; Barbarians > 79 BI.

TOBIN, Frank   *England*
Rugby Sch, Cambridge Univ, Liverpool, Lancs.
b 23.9.1849 Liverpool; *d* 6.2.27 Liverpool.
Half-back, 1-0-0-1.
1871 S−.
Merchant. Played in 1st int, S v E 1871. Capt
Liverpool 1870-2, pres 12-14, 19-20. Ckt blue
1870-2. Shooting expert. In bus in SAm. Knight
of Grace of the Order of St John of Jerusalem
16.

TOD, H. Borth   *Scotland*
Gala.
b −; *d* 31.12.62.
FB, 1-0-0-1.
11 F−.
Master baker.

TOD, J.K.   *Scotland*
Glasgow Acad, Glasgow Academicals.
Forward, 2-0-1-1.
1874 E−; 1875 E=.

TOD, John   *Scotland*
George Watson's Coll, Watsonians.
b 1862; *d* 9.9.35.
Forward, 8-5-2-1 (2t).
1884 W+ I+(1t) E−; 1885 W= I+; 1886
W+(1t) I+ E=.
Medicine.

TOD, N.S. ('Jacko')   *South Africa*
Natal.
Wing, 1-0-0-1.
28 NZ−.
Badly inj 2nd Test v NZ 28, never played for SA
again.

TODD, Alexander Findlater   *England*
Mill Hill Sch, Cambridge Univ, Blackheath,
Barbarians, Kent.
b 20.9.1873 Forest Hill, London; *d* 20.4.15
Ypres.
Forward, 2-1-1-0.
1900 I+ S=; BT > 1896 SA.
Blue 1893-5. Capt Kent. Berks CCC 1900, 10-
11. Served SA War, wounded at Diamonds Hill.
Served WW1, 3rd Battn Norfolk Rgt.
Mentioned in despatches. Died of wounds.

TODD, Andrew W.P. MC   *Ireland*
Shrewsbury Sch, St Andrews Coll, Trin Coll
Dublin.
b 6.7.1892; *d* −.3.42.
FB, 3-2-0-1.
13 W− F+; 14 F+.
Medicine. Served WW1, Maj RAMC.

TODD, R.   *England*
Allesley Coll Manchester, Manchester, Lancs.
b −.4.1847; *d* −.2.27.
Forward, 1-0-0-1.
1877 S−.

TOFT, Henry Bert   *England*
Manchester GS, Manchester Univ, RAF, Comb
Servs, Barbarians, Lancs.
b 2.10.09.
Hooker, 10-7-0-3.
36 S+; 37 W+ I+ S+; 38 W− I+ S−; 39 W+ I−
S+.
Schoolmaster/journalist. Capt every maj side for
whom he played. 64 apps Lancs. Appointed
RFU sel 39, took up duties after WW2, 45-52.
Taught at Manchester GS; Head R Latin Sch
Buckingham 39-48. Served WW2, signals
specialist RAF. Principal Bath Tech Coll 48-54;
SE Berks Coll of Ed 62. Rugby corr 'The
Observer' 52-66.

TOLHURST, Harold Ambrose   *Australia*
NSW.
b 4.7.09.
Wing, 2-1-0-1.
31 M+ NZ−.
Co dir. Ref A v NZ (2) 51.

TOLMIE, James Munro   *Scotland*
Glasgow HS, Glasgow HSFP.
b 20.11.1895; *d* 9.3.55.
Wing, 1-0-0-1.
22 E−.
Co dir.

TOMES, Alan James ('Toomba')   *Scotland*
Hawick HS, Heathfield GS Gateshead, Hawick,
Barbarians.
b 6.11.51 Hawick.
Lock, 41-15-2-24 (12 − 3t).
76 E+ I+; 77 E−; 78 I− F− W−(1t) E− NZ−;
79 W− E= I= F− NZ−; 80 F+ W− E−(1t); 81
F− W+(1t) E− I+ NZ− NZ− R+ A+; 82 E+
I− F+ W+ A+ A−; 83 I− F− W−; 84 W+ E+
I+ F+ R− A−; 85 W− E−; BI > 80 SA.
Bank official/Gas Board exec. Barbarians > 76
Can. Scottish XV v J 76, 77; Fj 82.

TONKIN, Arthur Edward Joseph   *Australia*
NSW.
b 19.10.22 Wagga, NSW.
Wing, 6-3-0-3 (14 − 2t 1c 2p).

47 S+(1t) I+(1t) W−; 48 E+(1c) F−(2p); 50 BI−.
PE teacher.

TOOTH, Richard Murray　　　*Australia*
Newcastle Tech, Sydney Univ, NSW.
 b 21.9.29.
Five-eighth/FB, 10-2-0-8 (22 − 2t 2c 4p).
51 NZ− NZ−(1t) NZ−; 54 Fj+(1c) Fj−; 55 NZ−(1t) NZ− NZ+; 57 NZ−(1c 2p) NZ−(2p).
Medicine.

TOOTHILL, John Thomas　　　*England*
Manningham, Bradford, Yorks.
 b 1866 Thornton, Bradford; d 29.6.47 Bradford.
Forward, 12-9-0-3 (1 − 1t).
1890 S+ I+; 1891 W+ I+(1t); 1892 W+ I+ S+; 1893 W− I+ S−; 1894 W+ I−.
Licensee. 50 apps Yorks 1892-5. Turned RL when his club, Bradford, helped form NU 1895.

TORREILLES, Serge　　　*France*
Perpignan.
 b 31.12.31 Baixas.
Wing, 1-0-0-1.
56 S−.

TORRENS, J.Desmond　　　*Ireland*
Portora RS, Bohemians, Barbarians.
 b 10.3.15; d 8.7.81 Biggleswade.
Centre, 4-2-0-2 (3 − 1t).
38 W−; 39 E+ S+(1t) W−.
Merchant draper/greyhound trainer.

TORRIE, Thomas Jameson　　　*Scotland*
Edinburgh Acad, Fettes Coll, Edinburgh Academicals.
 b 13.4.1857; d 18.6.13 St Andrews.
Forward, 1-1-0-0.
1877 E+.
Tea planter.

TOSSWILL, Leonard Robert　　　*England*
OBE
Marlborough Coll, Marlborough Nomads, Bart's Hosp, Exeter, Barbarians, Devon.
 b 12.1.1880; d 3.10.32 London.
Forward, 3-2-0-1.
02 W− I+ S+.
Medicine. After qualifying at Bart's (FRCS 03) continued studies in Vienna. Served WW1, Maj RAMC; twice mentioned in despatches. OBE 19. One of early BBC broadcasters on rugby.

TOURTE, Robert　　　*France*
St Girons.
Wing, 1-0-0-1.
40 BF−.

TOUZEL, Charles John Cliff　　　*England*
Wellington Coll, Cambridge Univ, Blackheath, Liverpool, Lancs.
 b 1855 Wirral, Cheshire; d 23.8.1899 Stroud.
Forward, 2-1-0-1.
1877 I+ S−.
The Army. Blue 1874-6. Capt 3rd Battn R Welch Fusiliers.

TOWELL, Alan C.　　　*England*
Leicester, Bedford.
Centre, 2-1-0-1.
48 F−; 51 S+.
Schoolmaster. Capt Bedford.

TOWERS, Cyril Henry Thomas　　　*Australia*
Randwick HS, NSW.
 b 30.7.06; d 8.6.85.
Centre, 9-5-1-3 (18 − 3t 3c 1p).
29 NZ+ NZ+(1p); 30 BI+; 31 M+ NZ−(2c); 34 NZ+(2t) NZ=; 37 SA−(1t 1c) SA−.
Bank official. NSW > 27 BI. Capt A v SA 37.

TOWERS, W.H.　　　*Wales*
Swansea, Hartlepool R, Durham Co.
Forward, 2-2-0-0 (1t).
1887 I+; 1888 NZN+(1t).

TOWNSEND, Lindsay James　　　*New Zealand*
Marist Bros' Sch Invercargill, Univ, Otago, Southern, Kamo, N Auckland, S Island.
 b 3.3.34 Mataura.
SH, 2-1-0-1.
55 A+ A−.
Insurance co mgr. Father L.G. rep Otago & Southland, as did uncle Frank.

TOWNSEND, W.H.　　　*South Africa*
Natal.
1-0-0-1.
21 NZ−.
Diamond digger. SA sel.

TRAVERS, Basil Holmes ('Jaika')　　　*England*
OBE
Sydney C of E GS NSW, Sydney Univ, Oxford Univ, Harlequins, Barbarians, N Suburbs (A), NSW.
 b 7.7.19 Sydney, NSW.
Flanker, 6-3-1-2 (4 − 2c).
47 W+ I−; 48 A− W=; 49 F+ S+(2c).
HM. Rhodes Scholar. Blue 46-7 (capt). Capt NSW v BI 50. NSW coach; A sel. Ckt blue − 23 apps OUCC 46-8. Ath blue (shot) 47. Swimming blue. Served WW2, Maj Australian Infantry. OBE (mil) 43; mentioned in despatches. Asst master Wellington Coll 48-9; Cranbrook Sch Sydney 50-2. Author of 'Let's Talk Rugger' pub 49 & 'The Captain General' pub 52.

TRAVERS, George ('Twyber')　　　*Wales*
Trin Church Sch Newport, Pill Harriers, Newport.
b 9.6.1877 Newport; *d* 26.12.45.
Forward, 25-21-0-4 (3 − 1t).
03 E+ S− I+; 05 E+ S+ I+ NZ+; 06 E+ S+ I− SA−; 07 E+ S− I+; 08 E+ S+ F+ I+ A+(1t); 09 E+ S+ I+; 11 S+ F+ I+.
Docker. Father of W.H. Played in 12 consec victories 07-11.

TRAVERS, William Henry　　　*Wales*
('Bunner')
Newport, Barbarians.
b 2.12.13 Newport.
Hooker, 12-5-0-7 (3 − 1t).
37 S− I−; 38 E+ S− I+; 39 E− S+(1t) I+; 49 E+ S− I− F−; BI > 38 SA 2-0-0-2.
Coal trimmer/licensee. Son of George. Played either side of WW2. 10 yrs between caps 8 & 9. Served WW2, 1st Mon Rgt. Played in 4 Servs, 1 Victory int.

TREADWELL, William Thomas　　　*England*
St Benedict's Sch Ealing, Guy's Hosp, Wasps, Barbarians, London Cos, Surrey.
b 13.3.39.
Hooker, 3-0-1-2
66 I= F− S−.
Dental surg. Private practice at Twyford, Berks.

TREHARNE, E. JP　　　*Wales*
Cowbridge GS, Pontypridd, Cardiff.
Forward, 2-0-0-2.
1881 E−; 1882 E−.
Medicine. Capped from sch.

TREMAIN, Kelvin Robin　　　*New Zealand*
('Bunny')
Auckland GS, Riversdale, Southland, Univ, NZ Univs, Manawatu, Lincoln Coll, Canterbury, Grammar, Hawkes Bay, Napier HSOB, S & N Islands.
b 21.2.38 Auckland.
Flanker/no 8, 38-30-3-5 (27 − 9t).
59 BI+ BI+ BI−; 60 SA− SA+ SA= SA−; 61 F+(1t) F+(1t); 62 A+(1t) A+ A=; 63 E+ E+; 63 I+(1t) W+; 64 E+ S= F+ A+ A+ A−; 65 SA+(1t) SA+(1t) SA−(1t) SA+; 66 BI+ BI+(1t) BI+ BI+; 67 A+(1t) E+ W+ S+; 68 A+ F+ F+ F+.
Farm appraiser/stock agent/travel agent. NZ's most capped flanker (36 apps, eq with Ian Kirkpatrick). NZ > 60 A & SA, 62 A, 63-4 & 67 BI,F & C, 68 A & Fj (1 app at prop).

TRENERY, W.　　　*South Africa*
Griq W.
1-0-0-1.
1891 BT−.
Mining.

TREVATHAN, David　　　*New Zealand*
Caversham Sch, Macandrew Rd Sch, Southern, Otago, Army, S Island.
b 6.5.12 Mosgiel Junction; *d* 11.4.86 Dunedin.
1st five-eighth, 3-1-0-2 (16 − 1d 4p).
37 SA+(1d 2p) SA− SA−(2p).
Milk factory employee. Coach Union & Alahambra clubs. Bro Tommy rep N Otago.

TREW, William John　　　*Wales*
Swansea.
b 1878 Swansea; *d* 20.8.26 Swansea.
Wing/FH/centre, 29-25-0-4 (39 − 11t 1c 1d).
1900 E+(1t) S+ I+; 01 E+ S−; 03 S−; 05 S+; 06 S+; 07 E+ S−; 08 E+(1t) S+(1t) F+(2t) I+ A+, 09 E+ S+(1t) F+(3t 1c) I+(1t); 10 F+(1t) E− S+; 11 E+ S+ F+ I+; 12 S+(1d); 13 S+ F+.
Boilermaker/licensee. Father in law of T.B. Day. Capt Wales 14 times. WRU comm 13. Merited mention in Oxford Companion to the Literature of Wales, 86.

TRICK, David Mark　　　*England*
Bryanston Sch, Plymouth A, England SS, England Colts, Tavistock, Bath, Som.
b 26.10.60 Dartford.
Wing, 2-0-0-2.
83 I−; 84 SA−.
Stockbroker. Ran 100m in 10.4s. E > 81 Arg, 84 SA. 3t England XV v Fj 82. England B v Ireland 82.

TRILLO, Jean　　　*France*
Bègles.
b 27.10.44 Condom, Gers.
Centre, 28-13-4-11 (19 − 6t).
67 SA+(1t) SA= NZ− R+; 68 S+ I+ NZ− NZ− NZ−(1t) A−; 69 I−(1t) E− W= R+; 70 E+(1t) R+; 71 S+ I+ SA−(1t) SA= A− A+; 72 S− A= A+ R+(1t); 73 S+ E−.
PE teacher.

TRISTRAM, Henry Barrington　　　*England*
Winchester Coll, Loretto Sch, Oxford Univ, Durham City, Fettesian-Lorettonians, Newton Abbot, Durham Univ, Devon.
b 5.9.1861 Hartlepool; *d* 1.10.46 Jersey.
FB, 5-4-1-0.
1883 S+; 1884 W+ S+; 1885 W+; 1887 S=.
HM. Blue 1882-4. Ckt for OUCC & Durham CCC. Described by Billy Bancroft as 'best-ever' FB. Author 'The History of Loretto School'.

TRIVETT, Richard Murray　　　*Australia*
Brisbane CEGS, Qld Univ, Qld.
b 42.
Centre, 2-0-0-2.
66 BI− BI−.
Veterinary surgeon.

TRIVIAUX, R. *France*
Cognac.
Flanker, 2-2-0-0.
31 E+ G+.

TROOP, Carlton Lang CBE *England*
St Peter's Sch York, RMC Sandhurst,
Harrogate OB, Devonport Servs, Richmond,
Aldershot Servs, The Army, Barbarians, Hants.
b 10.6.10 Malton.
No 8, 2-1-0-1.
33 I+ S−.
The Army. Served WW2, BEF. Various
postings after war, inc USAF Air Univ,
Washington & Air Attaché, Brit Embassy,
Stockholm. CBE (mil) 60. Emigrated to SA 67.

TROTT, R. Frank *Wales*
Cardiff, Barbarians.
FB, 8-2-1-5 (2 − 1c).
48 E= S+ F− I−; 49 E+ S−(1c) I− F−.
Electricity bd administrator. Sec Cardiff Ath
Club.

TRUMAN, Harry *Wales*
London Welsh, Llanelli.
b 11.12.09 Porth; *d* 26.7.84 Tenby.
Prop/lock, 2-0-1-1.
34 E−; 35 E=.
Carpenter/builder.

TRUMP, Leonard Charles *Wales*
Newport.
b 23.4.1887; *d* 9.6.48.
Prop/lock, 4-2-0-2.
12 E− S+ I− F+.
Labourer/potato merchant. Hull KR RL 12.

TRUTER, D.R. ('Pally') *South Africa*
Stellenbosch Univ, W Prov.
SH, 2-2-0-0.
24 BI+ BI+.

TRUTER, Jacobus Tredoux *South Africa*
('Trix')
Natal.
b 5.6.39.
Wing, 3-1-0-2 (3 − 1t).
63 A+; 64 F−; 65 A−(1t).
Electrician.

TUCK, Jack Manson *New Zealand*
Hamilton HS, HSOB, Waikato, Wellington.
b 13.5.07 Tikokino; *d* 23.3.67 at sea off
Whangaroa.
SH/FB, 3-0-0-3.
29 A− A− A−.
Timber mills co dir. NZ > 29 A. Inj forced
retirement 31. Died on board launch off
Whangaroa.

TUCKER, Colm Christopher *Ireland*
St Munchins Coll, Shannon.
b 22.9.52 Limerick.
Flanker, 3-0-1-2.
79 F= W−; 80 F−r; BI > 80 SA 2-1-0-1.
Brewery rep. Cousin of Tony Galvin,
Tottenham Hotspur & Republic of I footballer.

TUCKER, John Samuel *England*
St Nicholas & St Leonard Church Sch, Bristol,
The Army, Barbarians, Glos.
b 1.6.1895; *d* 4.1.73.
Hooker, 27-14-4-9 (6 − 2t).
22 W−; 25 NZ− W+ I= S− F+; 26 W= I− F+
S−(1t); 27 W+ I+ S− F−; 28 NSW+(1t) W+
I+ F+ S+; 29 W+ I− F+; 30 W+ I− F+ S=;
31 W=.
Solicitor's clerk/stevedore. Served WW1 RE;
wounded Battle of Somme. Not selected v W 30,
but was flown from Bristol to Cardiff to arrive
shortly before kick-off. See R.H.W. Sparks.

TUCKER, William Eldon *England*
Trin Coll Port Hope Can, Cambridge Univ, St
George's Hosp, Blackheath, Barbarians, Kent.
b 17.8.1872 Bermuda; *d* 18.10.53.
Forward, 5-3-0-2.
1894 W+ I−; 1895 W+ I+ S−.
Medicine. Father of W.E. Blue 1892-4. Half-
blue for billiards.

TUCKER, William Eldon CVO *England*
MBE TD
Sherborne Sch, Cambridge Univ, St George's
Hosp, Blackheath, TA, Barbarians, Mdx.
b 6.8.03 Bermuda.
No 8/flanker, 3-1-0-2.
26 I−; 30 W+ I−.
Medicine. Son of other W.E. Blue 22-5 (capt).
Served WW2; POW 40-3. Author of many
medical books. Hunterian lecturer R Coll Surg
58. CVO 54. MBE 44. TD 52.

TUCOO-CHALAT, Marcel *France*
PUC.
Lock, 1-0-0-1.
40 BF−.

TUKALO, Iwan *Scotland*
Royal HS, Scottish Schools, Edinburgh, Selkirk,
S of Scotland.
b 61.
Wing, 1-0-0-1.
85 I−.
Ukrainian father, Italian mother. Scottish clubs
joint top try scorer (24) 84/5. S > 85 US, Can; 84
R. Scotland B & Under 21s.

TUKE, Benjamin Burland *Ireland*
Athfurlong Coll Warwick, Bective Rgrs.
b 1870; *d* −.5.36.

Half-back, 9-3-0-6.
1890 E−; 1891 E− S−; 1892 E−; 1894 E+ S+
W+; 1895 E− S−.
Business.

TURK, Arthur Steven   *Scotland*
Langholm Acad, Langholm.
b 9.1.48 Cresswell.
Centre, 1-1-0-0.
71 E+r.
The Army/textile employee.

TURLEY, Patrick Noel   *Ireland*
Blackrock Coll, UC Dublin.
b 13.12.36 Co Laois.
Flanker, 1-0-0-1.
62 E−.
Schoolmaster. Gaelic football for Laois.

TURNBULL, Adrian Robert   *Australia*
Todd
Victoria.
b 36 UK.
Wing, 1-0-1-0.
61 Fj=.
Electronics co mgr.

TURNBULL, Bernard R. ('Lou')   *Wales*
Downside Sch, Cambridge Univ, Cardiff.
Centre, 6-0-0-6 (3 − 1t).
25 I−(1t); 27 E− S−; 28 E− F−; 30 S−.
Stockbroker. Bro of M.J. Blue 24-5. Capt
Cardiff 27-8, one of 6 bros who played for club.

TURNBULL, Frank Oliver   *Scotland*
Kelso HS, Kelso, Barbarians.
b 3.6.19.
Centre, 2-0-0-2.
51 F− SA−.
Forestry/farming. 31yrs 7mths when 1st capped.

TURNBULL, George Oliver   *Scotland*
Merchiston Castle Sch, RMA Sandhurst, W of
Scotland.
b 21.7.1877; *d* 14.1.70 Brighton.
Forward, 5-2-1-2 (3 − 1t).
1896 I= E+; 1897 I+(1t) E−; 04 W−.
Served in Indian Army.

TURNBULL, Maurice Joseph   *Wales*
Lawson
Downside Sch, Cambridge Univ, Cardiff.
b 16.3.06 Cardiff; kia 5.8.44 Normandy.
SH, 2-1-0-1.
33 E+ I−.
The Army. Served WW2, Capt S Wales
Borderers, Maj in Welsh Guards. Bro of B.R.
Hockey, ckt blue. Wales Hockey XI. Glam
CCC, England ckter. Wisden Ckter of Yr 31.

TURNBULL, Phipps   *Scotland*
Edinburgh Acad, Edinburgh Academicals.
b 3.4.1878; *d* 24.8.07 Newtonmore.
Centre, 6-3-0-3 (3 − 1t).
01 W+(1t) I+ E+; 02 W− I− E−.
Half-bro of Bruce Crole.

TURNBULL, Ross Vincent   *Australia*
NSW.
b 13.11.41.
Prop, 1-0-0-1.
68 I−.
Solicitor. Mgr A > 75-6 BI, US.

TURNER, Dawson Palgrave   *England*
Rugby Sch, Richmond.
b 15.12.1846; *d* −.2.09 Tunbridge Wells.
Forward, 6-3-2-1.
1871 S−; 1872 S+; 1873 S=; 1874 S+; 1875 I+
S=.
The Army. Played in 1st int, S v E 1871.

TURNER, Edward Beadon BEM   *England*
Uppingham Sch, O Uppinghamians, St
George's Hosp, Mdx.
b −.9.1854; *d* 30.6.31.
Forward, 3-3-0-0 (1t).
1875 I+; 1877 I+; 1878 I+(1t).
Medicine. Bro of Sir George. RFU comm 1878-
9. Held tricycle world recs from 2 to 25 miles,
beating all bicycle times.

TURNER, Frederic Harding   *Scotland*
Greenbank Sch, Sedbergh Sch, Oxford Univ,
Liverpool.
b 29.5.1888 Liverpool; kia 10.1.15 nr Kemmel.
Flanker, 15-4-0-11 (37 − 3t 14c).
11 F−(1c) W−(1t) I− E−; 12 F+(1t 5c) W− I−
(1t) E+ SA−; 13 F+(3c) W− I+(4c) E−; 14 I−
E−(1c).
Business. Blue 08-10. 5c v F 12, most by S player
(shared with J.W. Allan). Ckt for Oxford Univ
& Lancs CCC II. Lt, Liverpool Scottish Rgt.

TURNER, Frederick G.   *South Africa*
Greys HS Port Elizabeth, E Prov.
b 18.3.14.
Wing/centre/FB, 11-8-0-3 (32 − 5t 4c 3p).
33 A+ A− A+(1t); 37 A+ A+(1t) NZ−
NZ+(1t) NZ+(1t); 38 BI+ BI+(2c 2p) BI−(1t
2c 1p).
Clerk. 131 career pts for SA. Flown from Port
Elizabeth to Johannesburg to r Leon Barnard
1st Test v A 33, making him one of youngest
players (19yr 3mths) to appear for SA in a Test.
Barnard, ruled out by boil on an arm, was never
selected for SA. Coached Okey Geffin in place
kicking at Johannesburg Pirates.

TURNER, Sir George Robertson   *England*
KBE CB

407

Uppingham Sch, St George's Hosp, Mdx.
b 22.10.1855; *d* 7.4.41.
Forward, 1-1-0-0.
1876 S+.
Medicine/The Army/RN. Served WW1, Maj
Gen. CB 17. KBE (mil) 19.

TURNER, H.J.C.　　　　　　　　　*England*
Manchester, Lancs.
Forward, 1-0-0-1.
1871 S−.
Cotton trade. Played in 1st int, S v E 1871.

TURNER, John William Cleet　　　*Scotland*
Gala Acad, Kelso HS, Gala, Barbarians.
b 28.9.43 Hawick.
Centre, 20-8-0-12 (6 − 2t).
66 W− A+; 67 F+ W+ I− E−(1t) NZ−; 68 F−
W− I− E− A+; 69 F+; 70 E+(1t) A−; 71 F−
W− I− E+ E+; BI > 68 SA 4-0-1-3.
Insurance inspector.

TURNER, Martin Frederick　　　　*England*
Whitgift Sch, O Whitgiftians, Cambridge Univ,
Blackheath, Barbarians, London Cos, Surrey.
b 1.8.21.
Wing, 2-0-0-2.
48 S− F−.
Co dir. Blue 46. Co panel ref. Surrey CB rep;
RFU sel. Served WW2, Fleet Air Arm.

TURQUAND-YOUNG, David　　　　*England*
('Turkey')
Richmond, The Army, Barbarians.
Lock/no 8, 5-3-0-2.
28 NSW+ W+; 29 I− S− F+.
The Army. Rep the Army in modern
pentathlon. Lived in SA.

TURTILL, Hubert Sydney ('Jum') *New Zealand*
Christchurch, Canterbury, S Island.
b 1.2.1880 London; kia 9.4.18 France.
FB, 1-1-0-0.
05 A+.
Hardware merchants employee/licensee. Went
to NZ with parents 1884. Turned RL; NZ > 07
E. With St Helens 09-14. Served WW1, W
Lancs Rgt.

TUYNMAN, Steven Norman　　　*Australia*
Eastwood, NSW.
b 30.5.63.
No 8, 11-8-1-2 (4 − 1t).
83 F= F−; 84 E+ I+ W+(1t) S+; 85 C+ C+
NZ− Fj+ Fj+.
Trainee mgr. A Schs 80-2; capt > BI. Capt A
Under 21s > 83 NZ. Still at school when
selected for A > 82 NZ. A > 83 It & F. Credited
with t v W 84 at a push-over. Overseas XV v
Five Nations, Twickenham 86.

TWEEDALE, Eric　　　　　　　*Australia*
NSW.
b 22.
Prop, 10-4-1-5.
46 NZ− NZ−; 47 NZ− S+ I+; 48 E+ F−; 49
M− M= M+.
Co dir.

TWIGDEN, Timothy Moore　　*New Zealand*
Auckland GS, Grammar, Auckland, N Island.
b 14.5.52 Taumarunui.
Wing, 2-1-0-1.
80 A+ A−.
Savings bank officer. NZ > 79 E,S & It, 80 A &
Fj (concussed in final Test v A; did not go to Fj).
Won beach sprints in NZ surf life saving champs
73-4.

TWIGGE, Robert John　　　　*South Africa*
N Transvaal.
b 24.7.36.
1-1-0-0.
60 S+.

TWYNAM, Henry Thomas　　　　*England*
Sherborne Sch, Richmond.
b 1852; *d* 19.5.1899 Kensington.
Half-back, 8-7-1-0 (4t).
1879 I+(1t); 1880 I+; 1881 W+(1t); 1882 I=;
1883 I+(1t); 1884 W+(1t) I+ S+.
Solicitor.

TYDINGS, John Joseph ('Jim')　　*Ireland*
CBS Hassets Cross Limerick, Limerick Tech
Inst, Young Munster.
b 26.6.45 Limerick.
Wing, 1-1-0-0.
68 A+.
Clothing presser/textile machinist.

TYLER, George Alfred ('Bubs')　*New Zealand*
City, Auckland, N Island.
b 10.2.1879 Auckland; *d* 15.4.42 Auckland.
Hooker, 7-6-0-1 (5 − 1t 1c).
03 A+(1t); 04 BT+; 05 S+ I+ E+ W−; 06
F+(1c).
Boatbuilder/dockmaster Auckland Harbour Bd.
NZ > 05 A, 05-6 BI,F & NAm. Auckland
swimming champ pre-1900.

TYRRELL, Sir William KBE　　　*Ireland*
DSO
RBAI, Queen's Univ Belfast.
b 20.11.1885; *d* 29.4.68.
Forward, 9-4-0-5 (6 − 2t).
10 F+; 13 E− S− W− F+(2t); 14 F+ E− S+
W−; BI > 10 SA.
Medicine. Served WW1; DSO & Bar & Croix
de Guerre (Belgium) 18. KStJ 47. KBE 44. Pres
IRU 50-1. Air Vice Marshal RAF.

U

UDY, Daniel Knight *New Zealand*
Utd Greytown, Wairarapa, Greytown, N
Island.
b 21.5.1874 Greytown; *d* 29.7.35 Waikanae.
Hooker, 1-1-0-0.
03 A+.
Farmer. Cousin Hart Udy NZ > 1884 A.

UGARTEMENDIA, Jean-Louis *France*
St Jean-de-Luz.
b 10.7.43 Bayonne.
Hooker, 2-1-0-1.
75 S+ I−.
Naval mechanic.

ULYATE, Clive Anthony *South Africa*
St John's Coll Johannesburg, Hilton Coll,
Witwatersrand Univ, Transvaal.
b 11.12.33 Johannesburg.
FH, 7-3-0-4 (6 − 1t 1d).
55 BI− BI+ BI− BI+(1t 1d); 56 NZ− NZ+
NZ−.
Mining engr. Ckt for Transvaal.

UNDERWOOD, Adrian Martin *England*
King Charles I GS Kidderminster, St Luke's
Coll, Northampton, Exeter, E Midlands,
Devon.
b 19.7.40.
Wing/centre, 5-3-1-1.
62 W+ I= F+ S+; 64 I−.
Snr PE lecturer. Mem RFU coaching advisory
panel. Taught at Northampton GS & snr
lecturer at St Luke's Coll.

UNDERWOOD, Rory *England*
Barnard Castle Sch, E Colts, Middlesbrough,
Leicester, RAF.
b 19.6.63 Middlesbrough.
Wing, 12 5 1 6 (8 2t).
84 I+ F−(1t) W− A−; 85 R+ F= S+ I−(1t)
W−; 86 W+ I+ F−.
RAF pilot. Malaysian mother. E Under 23s v
English Students 82; > 82 It. England B v I 82.
Unable to tour E > 84 NZ, 85 SA because of
RAF duties. Five Nations v Overseas XV,
Twickenham 86.

UNWIN, Ernest James *England*
Haileybury & ISC, RMC Sandhurst, Rosslyn
Pk, The Army, Barbarians, E Cos.
b 18.9.12 Birdbrook.
Wing, 4-2-0-2 (9 − 3t).
37 S+(1t); 38 W− I+(1t) S−(1t); BI > 38 SA 2-
0-0-2.
The Army/corn merchant. Ckt for Suffolk CCC,
Essex CCC. Served WW2, Lt Col Mdx Rgt.

UNWIN, Geoffrey Thomas *England*
Marlborough Coll, Oxford Univ, Moseley,
Blackheath, Cheltenham, Derby, Barbarians,
Midlands.
b 1.6.1874; *d* 12.2.48.
FH, 1-0-1-0.
1898 S=.
Civil engr. Blue 1894-6.

UPRICHARD, Richard J.H. *Ireland*
('Hex')
Portadown Coll, Harlequins, RAF.
Centre, 2-1-0-1.
50 S+ W−.
RAF.

URBAHN, Roger James ('Spider') *New Zealand*
Plymouth Boys' HS, Stratford Tech HS,
Ardmore Tg Coll, Eltham, Taranaki, Okato,
New Plymouth HSOB.
b 31.7.34 Opunake; *d* 27.11.84 New Plymouth.
SH, 3-2-0-1 (3 − 1t).
59 BI+ BI+(1t) BI−.
Schoolmaster/journalist. NZ > 60 A & SA. Rep
Taranaki at ckt. Co-author with Don Clarke
'The Fourth Springbok Tour of NZ' pub 65.
Employed on 'Taranaki Daily News'.

UREN, Richard *England*
Waterloo, Barbarians, Cheshire.
b 26.2.26.
FB, 4-1-0-3 (7 − 2c 1p).
48 I−(2c) S−(1p) F−; 50 I+.
Rep Cheshire at golf. Took part in int &
Olympic yachting trials.

URLICH, Ronald Anthony *New Zealand*
Mt Albert GS, Otahuhu, Auckland, N Island.
b 8.2.44 Auckland.
Hooker, 2-0-0-2.
70 SA− SA−.
Draughtsman/tomato grower/salesman. NZ >
70 A & SA, 72-3 BI,F & NAm. Coach Otahuhu
78 80.

USHER, Charles Milne DSO OBE *Scotland*
Merchiston Castle Sch, RMA Sandhurst, US
Portsmouth, The Army, London Scottish,
Edinburgh W, Barbarians.
b 26.9.1891 Wimbledon; *d* 21.1.81
Haddington.
Flanker/no 8, 16-8-2-6 (6 − 2t).
12 E+(1t); 13 F+ W− I+(1t) E−; 14 E−; 20
F+ W+ I+ E−; 21 W+ E−; 22 F= W= I+ E−.
The Army. Capt S 7 times. Int career spanned
13 years. Served WW1, Gordon Highlanders;
POW. Played v F 20 in Paris during his
honeymoon.

UTTLEY, Ian Neill *New Zealand*
Wellington Coll, Univ, Wellington, NZ Univs,

Auckland, Mt Maunganui, Bay of Plenty.
b 3.12.41 Christchurch.
Centre, 2-2-0-0.
63 E+ E+.
Oil co exec. Various coaching & administrative
posts. Grandfather George rep Otago & N
Otago. Father Kenneth rep Otago 32-4.

UTTLEY, Roger Miles　　　　　*England*
Gosforth, Wasps.
b 11.9.49 Blackpool.
Flanker/lock/no 8, 23-12-2-9 (8 − 2t).
73 I− F+ S+ NZ+ A+; 74 I− F= W+; 75 F−
W− S+ A− A−(1t); 77 S+(1t) I+ F− W−; 78
NZ−; 79 S=; 80 I+ F+ W+ S+; BI > 74 SA 4-
3-1-0.
Schoolmaster.

UYS, Pieter de Waal　　　　　*South Africa*
Maitland HS Cape Town, N Transvaal.
b 10.12.37.
SH, 12-10-1-1.
60 W+; 61 E+ S+ I+ A+ A+; 62 BI= BI+; 63
A+ A−; 69 A+r A+.
Police. SA > 60-1 BI, F; 68 F.

UZZELL, Henry ('Harry')　　　　　*Wales*
Newport, London Welsh..
b 6.1.1883 Barton Regis, Glos; *d* 20.12.60
Bassaleg.
Hooker/prop, 15-11-0-4 (6 − 2t).
12 E− S+ I− F+; 13 S+ F+ I+; 14 E− S+
F+(2t) I+; 20 E+ S− F+ I+.
Innkeeper. Played either side of WW1. Mem of
'Terrible Eight'.

UZZELL, John Richard　　　　　*Wales*
Bargoed GS, Newport.
b 42.
Centre, 5-3-0-2.
63 NZ−; 65 E+ S+ I+ F−.
Schoolmaster.

V

VAILLS, Georges　　　　　*France*
Perpignan.
Hooker, 2-1-0-1.
28 NSW−; 29 G+.

VALENTINE, Alec R.　　　　　*Scotland*
RNAS, Anthorn.
b 23.2.28 Hawick.
Flanker, 3-0-0-3.
53 F− W− I−.
Bro of David.

VALENTINE, David Donald　　　　　*Scotland*
Hawick, KOSB, The Army, Barbarians.
, *b* 12.9.26 Hawick; *d* 14.8.76 Leeds.

Flanker, 2-0-0-2.
47 I− E−.
Licensee/cement co sales rep. Bro of Alec.
Huddersfield RL 47.

VALENTINE, James　　　　　*England*
Brindley Heath, Swinton, Lancs.
b 29.7.1866 Pendlebury; *d* 25.7.04 Barmouth.
Back, 4-1-0-3 (2 − 1c).
1890 W−; 1896 W+(1c) I− S−.
Licensee. 61t in 1889-90 season. Recalled to E
duty after 6 yrs, was barred when Swinton
joined NU 1896. Capped in 1888 E side that did
not play. Killed by lightning.

VALLOT, E.　　　　　*France*
SCUF.
Lock, 1-0-0-1.
12 S−.

VAN ASWEGEN, Henning　　　　　*South Africa*
Jonathan
Windhoek HS, UOFS, Stellenbosch Club, Jnr
Springboks, Gazelles, OFS, W Prov.
b 11.2.55 Okahandja.
Prop, 1-0-0-1.
81 NZ−.
Business. SA > 81 US.

VAN BROEKHUIZEN, Herman　　　　　*South Africa*
Dirk
W Prov.
b 17.6.1872 Netherlands; *d* 4.8.53.
1-1-0-0.
1896 BT+.
Ambassador to The Netherlands; chaplain to
President Kruger.

VAN BUUREN, Maurice　　　　　*South Africa*
Christiaan
Transvaal.
b 12.8.1865; *d* 51.
1-0-0-1.
1891 BT−.

VAN DEN BERG, Derek Sean　　　　　*South Africa*
Natal.
b 2.1.46 Cape Town.
4-3-0-1.
75 F+ F+; 76 NZ+ NZ−.
Medicine. Son of Mauritz. SA > 74 F.

VAN DEN BERG, Mauritz A.　　　　　*South Africa*
Durban Tech, W Prov.
b 10 Pretoria.
Flanker, 4-3-0-1.
37 A+ NZ− NZ+ NZ+.
Ice cream manufacturer. Father of Derek.

VAN DER MERWE, Albertus　　　　　*South Africa*
Johannes ('Bertus')

Worcester HS, Stellenbosch Univ, Boland.
b 14.7.29 Rawsonville, Cape Prov; *d* 74.
Hooker, 12-6-1-5.
55 BI+ BI− BI+; 56 A+ A+ NZ− NZ+ NZ−
NZ−; 58 F=; 60 S+ NZ−.
Wine farmer. Nephew of Alfred.

VAN DER MERWE, Alfred V.   *South Africa*
W Prov.
b 14.9.08.
Lock, 1-1-0-0.
31 W+.
Farmer. Uncle of Albertus. SA > 31-2 BI.

VAN DER MERWE, B.S. ('Fiks')   *South Africa*
N Transvaal.
1-1-0-0.
49 NZ+.
Police.

VAN DER MERWE, Hendrik   *South Africa*
Stefanus ('Stompie')
Hendrik Verwoed HS Pretoria, N Transvaal.
b 24.8.36.
Lock, 5-2-0-3.
60 NZ+; 63 A− A− A+; 64 F−.
Building inspector. SA > 60-1 BI.

VAN DER MERWE, Johannes   *South Africa*
Philmar
W Prov.
b 7.12.47 Uitenhage.
Centre, 1-0-1-0.
70 W=.
Schoolmaster. SA > 69-70 BI.

VAN DER MERWE, Philip   *South Africa*
Rudolph ('Flippie')
Diamantveld Sch Kimberley, Stellenbosch
Univ, W Prov, SA Country Dist, Gazelles, SW
Dist.
b 8.7.57 Dibeng.
Prop, 3-2-0-1.
81 NZ+ NZ− US+.
Military trainee. SA's heaviest player (20st 12lb
SA > 81 NZ). Overseas XV v Five Nations,
Twickenham 86.

VANDERPLANK, B.E.   *South Africa*
Natal.
b 29.4.1894.
2-1-1-0.
24 BI= BI+.
Farmer.

VAN DER SCHYFF, Jack Henry   *South Africa*
W Transvaal, Griq W.
b 11.6.28.
FB, 5-4-0-1 (10 − 2c 2p).
49 NZ+ NZ+ NZ+ NZ+; 55 BI−(2c 2p).
PT instructor/crocodile hunter/mining. 6 yrs

between caps. Dropped after missing c which
would have won 1st Test v BI 55.

VANDERSPAR, Charles Henry   *England*
Richard
Wellington Coll, Richmond.
b 1852; *d* 9.4.1877 Colombo, Ceylon.
Back, 1-0-1-0.
1873 S=.
Merchant. Bus in Ceylon, Singapore & A.

VAN DER WATT, Andrew   *South Africa*
Edward
Stellenbosch Univ, W Prov.
b 10.10.46 Krugersdorp.
Wing, 3-0-1-2.
69 S−r E−; 70 I=.
Schoolmaster. SA > 69-70 BI; 71 A. Noted
sprinter.

VAN DER WESTHUIZEN, J.C.   *South Africa*
Stellenbosch Univ, W Prov.
b 22.11.05.
Centre, 4-2-0-2 (3 − 1t).
28 NZ− NZ+ NZ−(1t); 31 I+.
Professor. Vice-capt SA > 31-2 BI, F; played
with bro 'Ponie' v I.

VAN DER WESTHUIZEN, J.H.   *South Africa*
('Ponie')
Stellenbosch Univ, W Prov.
b 4.11.09.
Wing, 3-3-0-0.
31 I+; 32 E+ S+.
Mining/insurance. SA > 31-2 BI, F; played with
bro JC v I.

VAN DE VYVER, Daniel   *South Africa*
Ferdinand ('Dirk')
St Andrew's Coll Grahamstown, W Prov.
b 10.
FH, 1-1-0-0.
37 A+.
Bank clerk.

VAN DRUTEN, Nicholas J.V.   *South Africa*
Stellenbosch Univ, Transvaal.
b 12.6.1898.
8-5-1-2 (6 − 2t).
24 BI+ BI+(1t) BI=(1t) BI+; 28 NZ+ NZ−
NZ+ NZ−.
Medicine.

VAN HEERDEN, Adrian Jacobus   *South Africa*
('Attie')
Stellenbosch Univ, Dublin Univ, Transvaal.
b 10.3.1898.
Wing, 2-0-1-1 (3 − 1t).
21 NZ−(1t) NZ=.
One of 2 sons of Dutch Reformed Church
minister, all 3 of whom played for Stellenbosch

Univ. Scored SA's 1st try v NZ. 5t v NSW (SA
> 21 A, NZ). Wigan (E) RL 23. Rep SA in
Olympics, 20 & 24.

VAN HEERDEN, Johannes   *South Africa*
Lodewikus ('Moaner')
Langenhoven Sch Pretoria, Jnr Springboks,
Transvaal, Pretoria, N Transvaal.
b 18.7.51 Pretoria.
Lock, 17-13-1-3 (4 − 1t).
74 BI− BI= F+ F+; 75 F+ F+; 76 NZ+ NZ−
NZ+ NZ+; 77 Wd+; 80 BI+(1t) BI+ BI−
SAm+ SAm+ F+.
Prison Dept/sports dealer/contractor.

VAN JAARSVELD, Christoffel   *South Africa*
Jacobus ('Hoppie')
Transvaal.
b 21.2.18.
1-1-0-0.
49 NZ+.

VAN JAARSVELDT, Desmond   *South Africa*
Charles
Plumtree Sch, Rhodesia.
b 31.3.29.
Flanker, 1-1-0-0 (3 − 1t).
60 S+(1t).
1st Rhodesian to capt SA, v S 60.

VAN NIEKERK, J.A. ('Jock')   *South Africa*
Wynberg HS, Rondebosch HS, W Prov.
b 1.6.07.
Wing, 1-0-0-1.
28 NZ−.
Mgr wine & fruit farm. Inj knee trying to
prevent practice ball going overboard on
steamship 'Windsor Castle' en route SA > 31-2
BI; inj worsened in 1st tour match v Midland
Cos. Never played again.

VANNIER, Michel ('Brin d'Osier')   *France*
RCF, Chalon.
b 21.7.31 Etain, Meuse.
FB, 43-28-3-12 (175 − 1t 44c 8d 20p).
53 W−; 54 S+ I+ Arg+(2c 2p) Arg+(3c 2d 1p);
55 S+(1p) I+(1c) E+(2c) W−(1c 1p) It+(3c
2p); 56 S− I+(1c 1d) W− It+(2c 1p) E+; 57 S−
I−(2p) E−(1c) W− It+(2c) R+(1d 4p) R+(1t
6c 1p); 58 S−(2p) E− A+ W+(2d) It+(1c 1p)
I+(1d); 60 S+(2c) E=(1p) W+(1c) I+ It+(4c)
R−(1c) Arg+(5c) Arg+(4c 1d); 61 SA=
E=(1c) W+(1c) It+ I+(1p) NZ− A+.
Engrg draughtsman. F's most capped FB. Inj F
> 58 SA, missed Tests.

VAN REENEN, George L.   *South Africa*
Stellenbosch HS, Stellenbosch Univ, W Prov.
b 14; *d* 12.11.68.
2-1-0-1 (6 − 2t).

37 A+(2t) NZ−.
Farmer/clerk.

VAN RENEN, Charles Gerhard   *South Africa*
W Prov.
b 23.8.1868; *d* 42.
3-1-0-2.
1891 BT−; 1896 BT− BT+.
Bro of William.

VAN RENEN, William A.   *South Africa*
W Prov.
b 1872; *d* 41.
2-1-1-0.
03 BT= BT+.
Bro of Charles.

VAN ROOYEN, George W.   *South Africa*
('Tank')
Transvaal.
b 1892; *d* 42 Runcorn, England.
Forward, 2-1-1-0.
21 NZ+ NZ=.
Driver. RL in E, Hull KR 23, Wigan 24, Widnes
30 .

VAN RYNEVELD, Clive Berrange   *England*
Diocesan Coll Cape Town, Cape Town Univ,
Oxford Univ, Barbarians.
b 19.3.28 Cape Town.
Centre, 4-2-0-2 (9 − 3t).
49 W− I−(1t) F+ S+(2t).
Advocate/politician. Son of R.C.B. Van
Ryneveld. Blue 47-9. Ckt blue − 28 apps OUCC
48-50 (capt 50); W Prov 46-7, 62-3 (capt 52-3,
57-8); 19 apps SA 51-8, inc tour of BI (capt v E
56-7, v A 57-8). Former SA MP (E London for
Progressive Party). Nephew of J.M.
Blankenburg, SA ckter.

VAN RYNEVELD, R. Clive B.   *South Africa*
Stellenbsoch Univ, W Prov.
Half-back, 2-1-0-1.
10 BI− BI+.
Father of C.B.

VAN SCHOOR, Ryk A.M.   *South Africa*
Rhodesia.
b 3.12.21 Philadelphia, Cape Prov.
Centre, 12-11-0-1 (6 − 2t).
49 NZ+ NZ+ NZ+; 51 S+(1t) I+(1t) W+; 52
E+ F+; 53 A+ A− A+ A+.
Tobacco farmer. SA > 51-2, carried off
unconscious v I. Defied medical advice,
returned to field & scored t.

VAN VOLLENHOVEN, Karel   *South Africa*
Thomas
N Transvaal.
b 29.4.35 Bethlehem, OFS.
Centre/wing, 7-4-0-3 (15 − 4t 1d).

55 BI− BI+(3t) BI− BI+(1t); 56 A+ A+(1d)
NZ−.
Pretoria Police/glassware co employee. 1st
player to score 3t in Test in SA, v BI 2nd Test
55. St Helens (E) RL.

VAN VUUREN, T.F.   *South Africa*
E Prov.
b 1889; *d* −.7.42.
Prop, 5-5-0-0.
12 S+ I+ W+; 13 E+ F+.
SA > 12-13 BI, F.

VAN WYK, Christiaan Johannes   *South Africa*
(**'Basie'**)
Vryburg Sch Potchefstroom, Transvaal.
b 5.11.23 Vryburg.
Flanker/hooker, 10-8-0-2 (18 − 6t).
51 S+(1t) I+(2t) W+; 52 E+ F+(1t); 53 A+
A−(1t) A+(1t) A+; 55 BI−.
Schoolmaster. SA > 51-2 BI, F; 56 A, NZ;
broke leg before 1st match in A. Inj ended
career.

VAN WYK, Jacobus Frederick   *South Africa*
Beatrix ('Piston')
N Transvaal.
b 21.12.43 Vereeniging.
Hooker, 15-9-2-4.
70 NZ+ NZ− NZ+ NZ+; 71 F+ F= A+ A+
A+; 72 E−; 74 BI− BI− BI=; 76 NZ+ NZ+.

VAN WYK, S.P.   *South Africa*
W Prov.
2-1-0-1.
28 NZ+ NZ−.
Medicine.

VAN ZYL, Ben-Piet   *South Africa*
W Prov.
1-1-0-0 (6 − 2t).
61 I+(2t).
Minister. SAr > 60-1 BI, F.

VAN ZYL, Christoffel Gert   *South Africa*
Petrus ('Sakkie')
OFS.
b 1.6.32.
4-1-0-3.
65 NZ− NZ− NZ+ NZ−.
OFS coach.

VAN ZYL, Gideon Hugo   *South Africa*
Paarl Gimnasium Sch, W Prov.
b 20.8.32.
Flanker, 17-12-4-1 (12 − 4t).
58 F=; 60 S+(2t) NZ+ NZ− NZ= NZ+ W+
I+(1t); 61 E+ S+ F= I+ A+ A+; 62 BI= BI+
BI+(1t).
Sports outfitter/business. BI > 60-1 BI, F.

VAN ZYL, Hendrik Jacobus   *South Africa*
(**'Hennie'**)
Ventersdorp HS Transvaal, Transvaal.
b 31.1.36.
Wing, 10-8-1-1 (18 − 6t).
60 NZ+(2t) NZ− NZ= NZ+ I+; 61 E+ S+ I+
A+(3t) A+(1t).
Co sec. 2t on Test debut. SA > 60-1 BI, F.

VAN ZYL, Pieter Johannes   *South Africa*
Poverville HS Cape Town, Stellenbosch Univ,
Boland.
b 23.7.33.
Wing, 1-1-0-0.
61 I+.
Motor business. SA > 60-1 BI.

VAQUER, Fernand ('Le   *France*
Maréchal')
Perpignan.
b 22.6.1889 La Tourbas-Elne; *d* 17.9.69.
Flanker/no 8, 3-1-0-2.
21 S+ W−; 22 W−.

VAQUERIN, Armand   *France*
Béziers.
b 21.2.51 Severac-le-Château, Aveyron.
Prop/lock, 26-11-4-11.
71 R+; 72 S− I− A=; 73 S+; 74 W= E= S−
Arg+ Arg+ R− SA− SA−; 75 W− E+ S+ I−;
76 US+ A+r A+ R−; 77 Arg=; 79 W+ E−; 80
S− I+.
Café proprietor.

VAREILLES, Charles   *France*
SF.
b −; *d* 30 Indo China.
Wing, 5-0-0-5 (4 − 1d).
07 E−; 08 E− W−(1d); 10 S− E−.
Planter.

VARENNE, François ('Popoff')   *France*
RCF.
b 26.7.26 Junay, Yonne.
Lock, 1-1-0-0.
52 S+.

VARLEY, Harry   *England*
Liversedge, Yorks, Lancs.
b 25.11.1868 Cleckheaton; *d* 21.11.15 Oldham.
SH, 1-1-0-0.
1892 S+.
Collier/licensee. Turned RL when his club,
Liversedge, helped form NU 1895. Capt
Oldham RL.

VARVIER, Theodore   *France*
RCF.
b −; kia WW1.
FH, 6-0-0-6.
06 E−; 09 E− W−; 11 E− W−; 12 I−.

VASSAL, Guy   *France*
Carcassonne.
SH, 2-2-0-0.
38 R+ G+.

VASSALL, Henry   *England*
Marlborough Coll, Oxford Univ, Marlborough
Nomads, Blackheath, Som.
b 22.10.1860; *d* 5.1.26 Repton.
Forward, 5-2-2-1 (3t).
1881 W+(3t) S=; 1882 I= S− W+.
HM. Uncle of Jumbo Vassall. Blue 1879-82;
capt 1881-2. 3t on int debut. Capt E twice.
Described as originator of tactical teamwork.
Treas RFU 1884-94. Author of 'Rugby
Football'.

VASSALL, Henry Holland   *England*
('Jumbo')
Bedford GS, Oxford Univ, Blackheath,
Barbarians, E Midlands.
b 23.3.1887 Wear, Devon; *d* 8.10.49.
Centre, 1-1-0-0.
08 I+; BT > 08 A, NZ.
Colonial service. Nephew of Henry. Blue 06-8.

VAUGHAN, David   *Australia*
NSW.
SH, 5-2-1-2.
83 US+ Arg− It+ F= F−.

VAUGHAN, Douglas Brian   *England*
Luton Sch, Cambridge Univ, RN, Headingley,
Harlequins, Devonport Servs, US Portsmouth,
Barbarians, Yorks, Hants, Devon.
b 15.7.25 Wrexham; *d* 19.4.77 Peel, IOM.
No 8/flanker, 8-2-1-5.
48 A− W= I− S−; 49 I− F+ S+; 50 W−.
RN/co dir. E sel 59-62 & 65-6. Ckt for RN &
Devon. Actively concerned in RN's 1st nuclear
submarines. Invalided from RN 64.

VAUGHAN, Geoffrey Norman   *Australia*
Homebush HS, Melbourne Univ, Victoria.
b 9.4.1933.
Prop, 6-1-1-4.
58 E− S− F− M+ M= M−.
Philosophy lecturer.

VAUGHAN-JONES, Arthur   *England*
US Portsmouth, RA, The Army.
b 25.9.09 Pontardulais, Glam.
Flanker, 3-2-0-1.
32 I+ S+; 33 W−.
The Army.

VAYSSE, Jean   *France*
Albi.
b 28.4.1900 Carmaux; *d* −.10.74 Albi.
Centre, 2-0-0-2.
24 US−; 26 M−.

VEITCH, James Pringle   *Scotland*
Royal HS, Royal HSFP.
b 1862 Penicuik; *d* 22.1.17.
FB, 7-5-1-1 (1c).
1882 E+; 1883 I+; 1884 W+ I+ E−; 1885
I+(1c); 1886 E=.

VELDSMAN, Pieter Eeden   *South Africa*
W Prov.
b 11.3.52 George.
1-1-0-0.
77 Wd+.

VELLAT, Edmond   *France*
Grenoble.
b 14.2.1897 Chambery; *d* −.
Wing, 5-2-0-3 (15 − 5t).
27 I− E+(1t) G+(2t) G−(2t); 28 NSW−.
Noted athlete.

VENTER, F.D. ('Floors')   *South Africa*
Heidelburg HS, Transvaal.
b 13.4.09.
Wing, 3-3-0-0.
31 W+; 32 S+; 33 A+.
Civil Service. Broke nose 1st match SA > 31-2
BI, F.

VERELST, Courtenay Lee   *England*
Charterhouse Sch, Liverpool, Lancs.
b 16.11.1855; *d* 9.1.1890 Ceylon.
Forward, 2-2-0-0.
1875 I+; 1878 I+.
Coffee planter.

VERGE, Cuthbert Arthur ('Jack')   *Australia*
NSW, Blackheath (E).
b 1882; kia 15 Egypt.
FB, 2-0-0-2.
04 BT− BT−.
Medicine. Played for Blackheath 07-8. Served
WW1, RAMC.

VERGER, André   *France*
SF.
b 28.5.06 Limoges; *d* −.4.78.
FH, 7-4-0-3 (8 − 2c 1d).
27 W−(1d) E+ G+; 28 I− E−(1c) G+(1c)
W+.

VERGES, André   *France*
SF.
Forward, 3-0-0-3.
06 NZ− E−; 07 E−.

VERNON, George Frederic   *England*
Rugby Sch, Blackheath, Mdx.
b 20.6.1856 London; *d* 10.8.02 Elmina, Gold
Coast.
Forward, 5-4-1-0.
1878 S= I+; 1880 I+ S+; 1881 I+.

Barrister. Called to Bar 1880. One of 1st line-out experts. Ckt for Mdx 1878-97; 1 app E v A in A, 1882.

VERSFELD, Charles ('Hasie')   *South Africa*
Hamiltons, W Prov.
Centre, 1-0-0-1.
1891 BT−.
Scored only t v 1891 BT, for Cape Town Clubs in 1st match. Played with bro Marthinus 3rd Test v BT, 1891. 2 other bros played v tourists in other matches. One of them, Loftus, became leading administrator in N Transvaal & Loftus Versfeld Stadium named after him .

VERSFELD, Marthinus   *South Africa*
Stellenbosch Univ, W Prov.
b 1868; *d* 41.
3-0-0-3.
1891 BT− BT− BT−.
Played with bro Charles 3rd Test v BT, 1891.

VIARD, Gérard   *France*
Narbonne.
b 19.5.45 St Jean-de-Luz.
No 8/flanker, 5-3-2-0.
69 W=; 70 S+ R+; 71 S+ I=.
Municipal employee.

VICKERY, George   *England*
Aberavon, Bath.
b 29.5.1879 Chard; *d* −.7.70.
Forward, 1-0-0-1.
05 I−.
Police. Father of Walter.

VICKERY, Walter   *Wales*
Aberavon.
b 25.10.09 Port Talbot.
No 8, 4-2-0-2.
38 E+ S− I+; 39 E−.
Docker. Son of George.

VIGERIE, Max   *France*
Agen.
b 28.11.06 Villereal.
Centre, 1-0-0-1.
31 W−.

VIGIER, Robert ('Popeye')   *France*
Montferrand.
b 15.12.26 Lanobie, Cantal.
Hooker, 24-14-2-8 (3 − 1t).
56 S− W− It+ E+ Cz+; 57 S− E− W− It+
R+ R+(1t); 58 S− E− A+ W+ It+ I+ SA=
SA+; 59 S+ E= It+ W+ I−.
Test motor driver.

VIGNE, J.T. ('Chubb')   *South Africa*
Transvaal.
Forward, 3-0-0-3.

1891 BT− BT− BT−.
Ckt for Griq W.

VIGNEAU, Armand   *France*
Bayonne.
Wing, 1-1-0-0 (3 − 1t).
35 G+(1t).

VIGNES, Christian   *France*
RCF.
b 5.6.34 Biarritz.
Centre/FH, 4-2-0-2 (3 − 1t).
57 R+(1t) R+; 58 S− E−.
Croupier/accountant.

VILE, Thomas Henry JP   *Wales*
Newport Intermed Sch, Pill Harriers, Newport,
Barbarians.
b 1.9.1883 Newport; *d* 30.10.58 Newport.
SH, 8-4-0-4.
08 E+ S+; 10 I+; 12 I− F+ SA−; 13 E−;
21 S−; BT > 04uncap A, NZ.
Soft drinks manufacturer. Played either side of WW1. Ref 13 ints 23-31. IB rep 46-53. WRU pres 55-6. High Sheriff of Mon.

VILJOEN, Joachim Frederik   *South Africa*
('Joggie')
Griq W.
b 14.5.45 Cape Town.
SH, 6-4-1-1 (6 − 2t).
71 F+(1t) F= A+(1t) A+ A+; 72 E−.

VILJOEN, Johannes Theodorus   *South Africa*
Natal.
b 21.4.43 Elliott.
Wing, 3-3-0-0 (6 − 2t).
71 A+(1t) A+(1t) A+.
16t (inc 5 v W Australia) in 10 apps SA > 71 A.

VILLA, Ernest   *France*
Tarbes.
Wing, 1-0-0-1.
26 M .

VILLAGRA, Jean   *France*
Vienne.
Hooker, 1-0-0-1.
45 BF−.

VILLAR, C.   *Scotland*
Edinburgh W.
Forward, 3-2-0-1.
1876 E−; 1877 I+ E+.

VILLEPREUX, Pierre   *France*
Lycée de Brive, Toulouse Univ, Toulouse.
b 5.7.43 Pompadour.
FB, 34-14-4-16 (163 − 2t 29c 1d 32p).
67 It+ I+ SA−(1p) NZ−(3p); 68 I+(2c 1p)
Cz+(1t 2c) NZ−(2p) NZ−(1p) NZ− A−(1c);

415

69 S−(1p) I−(2p) E− W=(1c 1p) R+; 70 S+ I+ W− E+(4c 1d 1p) R+(1c 3p); 71 S+(1t 2c 1p) I=(2p) E=(1c 1p) W−(1c) A−(1p) A+(1c 4p) R+(3c 3p); 72 S−(1c 1p) I−(1c 1p) E+(5c) W− (2p) I−(1c) A=(1c) A+(1c).
Professor of PE. 5c v E 72, most by Frenchman v IB opposition.

VILLET, John Villiers *South Africa*
Bellville Coll, Germiston Tech, W Prov.
b 3.11.54 Ceres.
Centre, 2-2-0-0.
84 E+ E+.
Draughtsman.

VINCENT, Sir Hugh Corbet *Wales*
Sherborne Sch, Christ's Coll Brecon, Trin Coll Dublin.
b 27.4.1862 Caernarvon; *d* 22.2.31 Treborth, Bangor.
Forward, 1-1-0-0.
1882 I+.
Solicitor. Played football for Carnarvon (sic) in FA Cup tie. Capped whilst student in Dublin. Stood as Tory candidate for Carnarfon Boro against David Lloyd-George in General Election 10. Mayor of Bangor 3 times. Kt 24.

VINCENT, Patrick Bernard *New Zealand*
Christchurch Boys' HS, Canterbury, Canterbury Tg Coll, Christchurch HSOB, S Island, Cantabrians.
b 6.1.26 Wataroa; *d* 10.4.83 Pittsburgh, US.
SH, 2-1-0-1.
56 SA+ SA−.
Schoolmaster/real estate/college administrator. 1st player to appear in 100 matches for Canterbury. Selector-coach for Canterbury 59-62. Moved to US 67. Coach various US sides & mgr US > 72 NZ. Pres N California RU 73-6; governor USARU 75-7. Died following an attack of asthma. Bros Bill & Bob rep W Coast.

VISAGIE, Petrus Jacobus ('Piet') *South Africa*
Griq W.
b 16.4.43 Kimberley.
FH, 25-18-3-4 (130 − 6t 20c 5d 19p).
67 F+ F+ F−(1c) F=(1d) 68 BI+(2c 2p) BI=(1p) BI+(1c 1p) BI+(2c) F+ F+; 69 A+(3c 3p) A+(1t 1c 2p) A+(1t 1c 1p) A+(2c 2p) S− (1p) E−(1c 1p); 70 NZ+(1d) NZ− NZ+ NZ+(1t); 71 F+(1d) F=(1d) A+(1d) A+(2t) A+(1t 3c 1p).
Statistician/mine paymaster. SA's most capped FH. 17 half-back apps with D.J. De Villiers. Most pts for SA in ints v IB countries (see H.E. Botha). 240 career pts for SA. Most pts (43, 4 apps) for SA in int series, v A 69. Most pts (25 v S Australia, 71) by SA player in match in A (tour total 55). Most pts (20 v Auvergne-Limousin, 68) by SA player in F. Bro Gawie

(Natal back) toured with SA to NZ, US (no Tests).

VISAGIE, Rudolf Gerhardus *South Africa*
('Vleis')
Rob Ferreira Sch Witrivier, Schoeman Pk, Gazelles, OFS.
b 27.6.59 Nelspruit.
Lock, 4-4-0-0.
84 E+ E+ SAm+ SAm+.
Clerk.

VISSER, Johann De Villiers *South Africa*
Voortrekker Sch, SA Schs, SA Under 19s, Defence (Cape Town), Barbarians, W Prov.
b 26.11.58 Cape Town.
Lock, 2-2-0-0.
81 NZ+ US+.
Flight mechanic SAAF. SA > 80 SAm. Barbarians > 79 BI.

VISSER, P.J. *South Africa*
Transvaal.
b − ; *d* 69.
1-0-0-1.
33 A−.
Gold mine official.

VIVIER, Stefanus Sebastian *South Africa*
('Basie')
OFS.
b 1.3.27 Pietersburg.
FB, 5-3-0-2 (11 − 4c 1p).
56 A+(1p) A+ NZ+(1c) NZ−(2c) NZ−(1c).
Police/mining. SA > 51-2 BI. Tour capt SA > 56 A, NZ. 165 career pts for SA. 16pts OFS v A 53. Surname sometimes spelled as Viviers.

VIVIÈS, Bernard *France*
Agen.
b 3.9.55 Rieumes..
FH, 9-4-1-4 (20 − 1c 2d 4p).
78 E+ S+ I+ W−(1d); 80 SA−(1c 3p) R−; 81 S+(1p) A−(1d); 83 A=r.
Restaurateur. Top scorer with 25 pts F > 80 SA. Replaced Lafond v A 83, but also inj & r by Pardo.

VIVYAN, Elliott John *England*
Stoke Sch Devonport, Devonport A, Devon.
b 6.1.1879 Devonport; *d* 3.12.35.
Wing, 4-1-1-2 (13 − 3t 2c).
01 W−; 04 W= I+(2t 2c) S−(1t).
Dockyard draughtsman. 1st player to score 10 pts in match for E, v I 01. Ldg ref.

VODANOVICH, Ivan Matthew *New Zealand*
Henry
Taumarunui, King Country, Marist, Wellington, N Island.
b 8.4.30 Wanganui.

Prop, 3-2-0-1 (3 − 1t).
55 A+(1t) A+ A−.
Menswear store ptn. NZRFU selector 67-72.
Asst mgr NZ > 70 A & SA. In business with
fellow All Black Tom Morrison.

VOGEL, Martin Leon *South Africa*
OFS.
b 22.10.49 Aliwal North.
Centre, 1-0-0-1.
74 BI−r.
Mining.

VOLOT, Marcel *France*
SF.
Hooker, 5-3-0-2.
45 W−; 46 BF+ I+ NZS− W+.

VOYCE, Anthony Thomas OBE *England*
Gloucester, Cheltenham, Richmond,
Blackheath, The Army, Barbarians, Glos.
b 18.5.1897; *d* 22.1.80 Gloucester.
Flanker, 27-19-3-5 (15 − 5t).
20 I+ S+; 21 W+ I+ S+ F+; 22 W− I+ F=(1t)
S+; 23 W+ I+(1t) S+(1t) F+; 24 W+ I+ F+
S+; 25 NZ− W+(1t) I= S− F+; 26 W= I− F+
S−(1t); BI > 24 SA 2-0-0-2.
Insurance broker. Played flanker, wing & FB on
BI > 24 SA because of spate of inj. Rep Glos on
RFU from 31-70. Pres RFU 60-1. OBE 62.
Served WW1, Glos Rgt; wounded in one eye.
Served WW2, Maj RASC.

W

WACKETT, John Arthur Sibley *England*
Welwyn, Rosslyn Pk, Herts.
b 27.9.30 Welwyn, Herts.
Hooker, 2-1-0-1.
59 W− I+.
Radio production mgr/hire mgr. Won 1st cap in
front row with Larry Webb, with whom he went
into bus 60.

WADDELL, Gordon Herbert *Scotland*
Fettes Coll, Scottish Schs, Cambridge Univ,
Stanford Univ US, London Scottish, Devonport
Servs, RN, Barbarians.
b 12.4.37 Glasgow.
FH, 18-6-3-9.
57 E−; 58 F+ W− A+ I− E=; 59 F− W+ I−
E=; 60 I+ E− SA−; 61 F−; 62 F− W+ I+ E=;
BI > 59 A, NZ; 62 SA 2-0-1-1.
Business exec. Blue 58-61. Son of Herbert.
Barbarians > 58 SA. Emigrated to SA; MP in
SA Parliament.

WADDELL, Herbert *Scotland*
('Napoleon') CBE

Glasgow Acad, Fettes Coll, Glasgow
Academicals, Barbarians.
b 19.9.02.
FH, 15-11-0-4 (45 − 7t 2c 5d).
24 F−(1d) W+(1t) I+(2t) E−; 25 I+(1d)
E+(1d); 26 F+ W+(1t 2c) I− E+(1t); 27
F+(2t) W+ I− E+(1d); 30 W+(1d); BI > 24
SA 3-0-1-2.
Stockbroker. Father of Gordon. At sch in F for
a time. Asst mgr Barbarians > 58 SA; mgr > 76
Can. IB mem 52-63. Pres SRU 63-4 &
Barbarians 74-86. Hon vice-pres SARB. Served
WW2, Col 1st Highland Light Infantry, The
Buffs; mentioned in despatches.

WADE, Albert Luvian *Scotland*
Dulwich Coll, London Scottish, Barbarians.
b 20.9.1884 Glasgow; kia 28.4.17 Oppy Wood,
Arras.
SH, 1-1-0-0.
08 E+.
Lt, Mdx Rgt (attached to Trench Mortar
Battery).

WADE, Charles Gregory KC *England*
KCMG
All Saints' Coll Bathurst NSW, King's Sch
Parramatta, Oxford Univ, Richmond, Mdx,
NSW.
b 26.1.1863 Singleton, NSW; *d* 26.9.23 Sydney.
Back, 8-8-0-0 (7t).
1882 W+(3t); 1883 I+(1t) S+; 1884 W+(1t)
S+; 1885 W+(1t); 1886 W+(1t) I+.
Barrister/politician. Blue 1882-4 (3t 1883). 1st
overseas player to app for E. Scored t on each of
4 apps v W. In 15 maj matches 1882-6 (for
Oxford, S of E & E) was on winning side every
time. Called to Bar 1886. QC 1891. Returned to
A, played for NSW v Qld, v BT 1888. Attorney-
Gen, Minister of Justice 04; NSW premier 07.
Agent-Gen for NSW in London 17-20. Justice of
NSW Supreme Court 20. KCMG 20.

WADE, Michael Richard *England*
Wyggeston Sch, Cambridge Univ, RAF,
Leicester, Barbarians.
b 38.
Centre, 3-1-1-1 (3 − 1t).
62 W= I+(1t) F−.
RAF/waiter. Blue 58-61.

WAGENAAR, Christo *South Africa*
Monument Sch Krugersdorp, Pretoria Univ, SA
Forces, N Transvaal.
b 11.3.52 Krugersdorp.
1-1-0-0.
77 Wd+.
Medicine.

WAHL, Johannes Joubert *South Africa*
('Ballie')

417

Stellenbosch Univ, W Prov.
1-1-0-0.
49 NZ+.

WAIDE, Shaun Lockhart   *Ireland*
Sedbergh Sch, Oxford Univ, NIFC.
b 8.8.12; d 84.
Wing, 5-3-0-2 (9 − 3t).
32 E−(1t) S+(1t) W+(1t); 33 E− W+.
Chmn, man dir chemical co. Blue 32.

WAITES, J.   *Ireland*
Bective Rgrs.
Forward, 7-1-1-5.
1886 S−; 1888 NZN−; 1889 W+; 1890 S− W=
E−; 1891 E−.

WAKEFIELD, Lord William   *England*
Wavell ('Wakers')
Craig Prep Sch, Sedbergh Sch, Cambridge Univ,
RAF, Leicester, Harlequins, Mdx..
b 10.3.1898 Beckenham; d 12.8.83 Kendal.
Flanker/lock/no 8, 31-20-3-8 (18 − 6t).
20 W− F+ I+(1t) S+; 21 W+ I+ S+ F+; 22
W− I+ F= S+; 23 W+ I+ S+ F+(1t); 24 W+
I+ F+ S+(1t); 25 NZ− W+ I= S−(1t) F+(1t);
26 W=(1t) I− F+ S−; 27 S− F−.
RAF/politician/co dir. Blue 21-2. Distinguished
in many sports inc ath (RAF 440y champ 20),
ckt (MCC) & skiing. Chmn Brit Ski Racing
Comm. Pres Brit Water Ski Fed. Pres Brit Sub
Aqua Club. Served WW1, RN Air Service,
transferred to RFC. Tory candidate for Swindon
34; elected MP 35. Served WW2, RAF pilot.
Tory MP for Marylebone 45-63. Played in
Centenary Match Rugby Sch 23. Capt E 13
times. 29 consec ints 20-26, E rec until beaten by
J.V. Pullin. Rep RAF on RFU 22-4. IB mem
54-61. Pres RFU 50-1. 1st Baron Wakefield of
Kendal 63.

WALDEN, Ronald John   *Australia*
NSW.
b 27.8.07.
Lock, 4-1-1-2.
34 NZ=; 36 NZ− NZ− M+.
Police. Mgr A > 49 NZ. Infection endangered
life 83; both legs amputated to save him.

WALDRON, Oliver Cornelius   *Ireland*
St Nessan's Coll Cork, UC Cork, Oxford Univ,
London Irish.
b 11.7.43 Cork.
Prop, 3-2-0-1.
66 S− W+; 68 A+.
Nuclear physicist. Blue 65-7.

WALDRON, Ronald   *Wales*
Neath.
b 34.
Prop, 4-3-0-1.

65 E+ S+ I+ F−.
Steelworker. Coach Resolven RFC, 76-8.

WALKER, Alan Keith   *Australia*
NSW.
b 4.10.25.
Centre, 5-1-0-4 (3 − 1t).
47 NZ−; 48 E+(1t) F−; 50 BI− BI−.
Clerk. Australian (not Tests) & Notts CCC
ckter. RL.

WALKER, Alfred P.   *South Africa*
Natal.
6-3-2-1.
21 NZ− NZ=; 24 BI+ BI+ BI= BI+.
Bro of Henry, father of Harry; 1st father & son
to become Springboks.

WALKER, Archibald   *Scotland*
Loretto Sch, Oxford Univ, W of Scotland.
b 29.6.1858; d 10.6.45.
Forward, 5-3-0-2.
1881 I−; 1882 E+; 1883 W+ I+ E−.
Distiller/merchant banker. Blue 1880. Played
with bro J.G. v E 1882, W 1883.

WALKER, Arthur Stanley   *Australia*
Billingsgate
NSW.
b 1893; d 58.
Five-eighth, 1-1-0-0.
12 US+.

WALKER, A.W.   *Scotland*
Cambridge Univ, Birkenhead Pk, Barbarians.
No 8/lock/flanker, 5-2-0-3.
31 F+ W− I− E+; 32 I−.
Leather co dir. Blue 29-30.

WALKER, Sir George Augustus   *England*
GCB CBE DSO DFC AFC
St Bees Sch, RAF, Blackheath, Cambridge
Univ, Barbarians, E Cos, Yorks.
b 24.8.12 Garforth.
FH, 2-1-0-1.
39 W+ I−.
RAF. Air Chief Marshal, highest ranked E
player. Ldg ref. Rep RAF on RFU 46-8 & 50-
65. Pres RFU 65-6. Entered RAF 34. Served
WW2, commanding bomber squadrons &
stations. DFC & DSO 41. CBE 45; lost an arm
in bomb explosion. AFC 56. CB 59. KCB 62.
Various high offices, inc Inspector Gen RAF 64-
7 & Deputy C in C Allied Forces, Central
Europe 67-70. GCB 69.

WALKER, Harry Newton   *South Africa*
Kearsney Coll Natal, OFS.
Prop, 4-2-0-2.
53 A+; 56 A+ NZ− NZ−.
Accountant. Son of Alfred.

WALKER, Harry W. *England*
Coventry, Barbarians, Warwicks.
b 11.2.15.
Prop, 9-3-1-5.
47 W+ I− S+ F+; 48 A− W= I− S− F−.
Machine tool fitter/licensee. Served WW2, the Army.

WALKER, Henry W. *South Africa*
Transvaal.
3-2-0-1.
10 BI+ BI− BI+.
Bro of Alfred.

WALKER, James George *Scotland*
Loretto Sch, Oxford Univ, W of Scotland.
b 9.10.1859 Glasgow; *d* 24.3.23 Ayr.
Forward, 2-2-0-0.
1882 E+; 1883 W+.
Barrister. Blue 1879-81. Pl with bro A. v E 1882, W 1883. Ckt blue 1882-3; also Mdx CCC & S.

WALKER, Lance Robert *Australia*
Cumberland HS Sydney, NSW Inst of Tech, Parramatta, Sydney, NSW.
b 26.10.55 Sydney.
Hooker, 2-1-0-1.
82 NZ+ NZ−.
Engr. Ar > 81-2 BI for Bruce Malouf.

WALKER, Michael *Scotland*
Bryanston Coll, Oxford Univ.
b 11.3.30 London.
Lock, 1-0-0-1.
52 F−.
Chief personnel officer. Blue 50-1.

WALKER, Roger *England*
Manchester, Berks W, Lancs.
b 18.9.1846; *d* 11.11.19 Reading.
Forward, 5-4-1-0.
1874 S+; 1875 I+; 1876 S+; 1879 S=; 1880 S+.
Touch-jdge S v E 1896. IB mem 1895-9. Pres RFU 1894-6. Mgr BT > 1896 SA.

WALKER, Samuel *Ireland*
RBAI, Instonians, Barbarians.
b 21.4.12 Belfast; *d* 27.1.72.
Hooker/prop, 15-6-0-9 (7 − 1t 2c).
34 E− S−; 35 E− S+ W+ NZ−; 36 E+ S+(1t) W−; 37 E− S+ W+(1c); 38 E− S−(1c) W−; BI > 38 SA 3-1-0-2.
Bank official/BBC commentator. Brit Army v French Army 40. Served WW2; mentioned in despatches 44-5. Capt BI > 38 SA, when team described as 'Lions' for 1st time.

WALKINGTON, Dolway B. *Ireland*
Trin Coll Dublin, NIFC.
FB, 8-1-2-5 (3 − 1d).
1887 E= W−; 1888 W+; 1890 W= E−; 1891

E− S− W−(1d).
Bro of R.B. Often wore monocle while playing. Scored I's 1st d.

WALKINGTON, R.B. *Ireland*
RBAI, NIFC.
FB, 10-0-1-9.
1875 E− E−; 1877 E− S−; 1878 E−; 1879 S−; 1880 E− S−; 1882 E= S−.
Bro of D.B. Pres IRU 1881-2.

WALL, Henry *Ireland*
Castleknock Coll, UC Dublin, Dolphin.
b 1.12.35 Cork.
No 8, 2-1-0-1.
65 S+ W−.
Veterinary surgeon.

WALLACE, Arthur Cooper *Scotland*
('Johnny')
Sydney GS, Sydney Univ, Glebe-Balmain, NSW, Oxford Univ, Blackheath, Barbarians.
b 5.10.1900 Sydney; *d* 3.11.75 Sydney.
Wing, 9-7-0-2 (33 − 11t).
23 F+; 24 F−(1t) W+(1t) E−; 25 F+(2t) W+(2t) I+(1t) E+(1t); 26 F+(3t).
Barrister/grazier. Rhodes Scholar. Blue 22-5. NSW > 21 NZ. Capt NSW > 27-8 GB & F. Scored t in each Champ match 25 (see H.C. Catcheside). Coach NSW & A v SA 37. Life mem & pres NSWRU.

WALLACE, James *Ireland*
Trin Coll Dublin, Wanderers.
b 30.10.1876; *d* 60.
Forward, 2-0-0-2.
04 E− S−; BT > 03 SA.
Played with bro Joseph v E & S 04.

WALLACE, Joseph *Ireland*
Trin Coll Dublin, Wanderers, Barbarians.
b 3.8.1878; *d* 29.1.67.
Forward, 10-4-0-6 (12 − 4t).
03 S W , 04 E− S− W+(1t), 05 E+(1t) S+(1t) W− NZ−; 06 W+(1t); BT > 03 SA.
Medicine. Played with bro James v E & S 04. Pres IRU 34-5.

WALLACE, Thomas *Ireland*
Coleraine AI, Queen's Univ Belfast, R Irish Fusiliers, RAMC, Cardiff, Newport, Barbarians.
b 25.4.1892 Ballymayo; *d* 9.9.54.
Centre, 3-0-0-3.
20 E− S− W−.
Medicine. Served WW1, then GP in Cardiff. 155 apps for Cardiff 19-25, capt 22-3. Capt W v E Civil Service int Cardiff 23.

WALLACE, William Joseph *New Zealand*
('Carbine')

419

Mt Cook Sch, Poneke, Wellington, Alhambra, Otago, N Island.
 b 2.8.1878 Wellington; *d* 2.3.72 Wellington.
FB/wing, 11-8-2-1 (50 − 4t 12c 2gm 2p).
03 A+(1c 2gm 1p); 04 BT+(1p); 05 S+ I+(3c) E+ W−; 06 F+(3t 2c); 07 A+(4c) A+(1t 1c) A=(1c); 08 AW=.
Iron foundry master. Pl in all 11 matches, NZ > 03 A; top scorer with 87 pts. NZ > 05 A, 05-6 BI,F & NAm (top scorer with 246 pts from 26 matches), 07 A. Career total 379 pts for NZ, rec for 50 yrs until bettered by Don Clarke. Mgr NZ > 32 A; co-mgr NZ Maoris > 35 A. NZRFU comm & exec 31-38. Reported to have scored t v Cornwall 05 wearing a sun hat.

WALLACE, William Middleton   *Scotland*
Edinburgh Acad, Cambridge Univ, Barbarians.
 b 23.9.1892 Edinburgh; kia 22.8.15 Sainghin, nr Lille.
FB, 4-0-0-4.
13 E−; 14 W− I− E−.
RFC. Blue 12-13.

WALLACH, Clarence ('Boss')   *Australia*
MC
Sydney GS, NSW.
 b −.11.1890 Sydney; kia 22.4.15 France.
Lock, 5-1-0-4.
13 NZ− NZ+; 14 NZ− NZ− NZ−.

WALLENS, J.N.S.   *England*
Waterloo.
FB, 1-0-0-1.
27 F−.

WALLER, Phillip Dudley   *Wales*
Newport, Som.
 b 28.1.1889 Bath; kia 14.12.17 Arras.
Forward, 6-6-0-0.
08 A+; 09 E+ S+ F+ I+; 10 F+; BT > 10 SA 3-1-0-2.
Engr. Worked with Tom Pearson. Stayed in SA after BT tour. Served WW1, 2nd Lt in SA Heavy Artillery.

WALLIS, Arthur Knight   *Ireland*
Wanderers.
 b −; *d* 05.
Forward, 5-1-0-4.
1892 E− S− W+; 1893 E− W−.
Bro of W.A., uncle of T.G. & Clive.

WALLIS, Clive O'Neill MC JP   *Ireland*
Cranleigh Sch, O Cranleighans, The Army, Wanderers.
 b 16.10.13 Dublin; *d* 26.10.81.
1-0-0-1.
35 NZ−.
The Army. Lt Col E Surrey Rgt. Nephew of Arthur & W.A.

WALLIS, Thomas Gill   *Ireland*
Wellington Coll, Wanderers, Barbarians.
 b 2.10.1892.
Centre/wing, 5-1-0-4 (14 − 1t 4c 1p).
21 F−(2c); 22 E−(1t) S− W−(1c) F+(1c 1p).
Co dir. Nephew of Arthur & W.A.

WALLIS, William Armstrong   *Ireland*
Wanderers.
 b −; *d* 25.
Forward, 5-1-0-4.
1880 S−; 1881 E− S+; 1882 W−; 1883 S−.
Bro of Arthur, uncle of T.G. & Clive.

WALLS, William Alexander   *Scotland*
Merchiston Castle Sch, Glasgow Acad, Glasgow Academicals.
 b 29.12.1859; *d* 19.2.36.
Forward, 10-7-1-2.
1882 E+; 1883 W+ I+ E−; 1884 W+ I+ E−; 1886 W+ I+ E=.
Merchant. Still active int player when ump S v I 1885. Pres SRU 11-12.

WALMSLEY, George   *Ireland*
Bective Rgrs.
 b 1869; *d* −.8.42.
Forward, 1-1-0-0.
1894 E+.

WALPOLE, A.   *Ireland*
Wesley Coll, Trin Coll Dublin, Barbarians.
 b 26.10.1865; *d* 24.6.10.
Centre, 2-0-0-2.
1888 S− NZN−.
The Army: Maj in RE.

WALSH, Edward J.   *Ireland*
Blackrock Coll, Lansdowne.
 b 1868; *d* 25.3.39.
Forward, 7-1-1-5 (4 − 2t).
1887 E= S− W−; 1892 E− S− W+(2t); 1893 E−.
Accountant gen Supreme Court of I. 120y hurdles champ of I.

WALSH, H.D.   *Ireland*
Portora RS, Trin Coll Dublin.
Forward, 2-0-0-2.
1875 E− E−.
Civil engr.

WALSH, James Austin   *Australia*
Homebush HS, NSW.
 b 26.
Hooker, 4-1-0-3.
53 SA− SA+ SA− SA−.
Real estate/building contractor.

WALSH, Jeremiah Charles   *Ireland*
PBC Cork, UC Cork, Sunday's Well, Barbarians.
b 3.11.38.
Centre, 26-8-2-16 (3 − 1t).
60 S− SA−; 61 E+ S− F− SA−; 63 E= S−
W+ NZ−; 64 E+ S− W− F−; 65 F= S+ W−
SA−; 66 F− S− W+; 67 E− S+ W+ F−
A+(1t); BI > 66 A, NZ.
Medicine.

WALSH, Patrick Bernard   *Australia*
NSW.
b − NZ; *d* −.
Forward, 3-0-0-3.
04 BT− BT− BT−.
The Army/rly porter. RL − later Huddersfield (E) RL.

WALSH, Patrick Timothy   *New Zealand*
Sacred Heart Coll Auckland, Ardmore, Auckland, Otahuhu, S Auckland, Papakura, Counties, Waiuka, Manurewa, NZ Maoris, N Island.
b 6.5.36 Kaitaia.
2nd five-eighth/FB/centre/wing, 13-10-0-3 (12 − 4t).
55 A+ A+ A−; 56 SA+ SA− SA+; 57 A+(1t)
A+; 58 A+(2t) A− A+; 59 BI+; 63 E+(1t).
Schoolmaster/insurance salesman/travel agent.
NZ > 57 A, 63-4 BI,F & C. NZRFU coach 69-71.

WALSHAM, Keith Percival   *Australia*
Wellington HS NSW, Newcastle Univ, NSW.
b 41.
Wing, 2-1-1-0 (3 − 1t).
62 NZ=; 63 E+(1t).

WALTER, Maurice Winn   *Scotland*
Merchiston Castle Sch, London Scottish, Hong Kong & Shanghai Bk.
b 4.1.1888 Yokohama; *d* 2.9.10 Worplesdon.
Centre, 0-5-0-3 (6 − 2t).
06 I+ E− SA+; 07 W+ I+; 08 W− I−; 10 I+(2t).
Banking. Selected E v I 06, chose S instead.
Died aged 22 of meningitis after playing ckt for his Bank side.

WALTERS, Nathaniel ('Danny')   *Wales*
Llanelli.
b 23.5.1875 Llanelli; *d* 22.2.56 Llanelli.
Forward, 1-1-0-0.
02 E+.
Licensee.

WALTON, Donald Cameron   *South Africa*
Natal.
b 5.4.39 Durban.
Hooker, 8-3-0-5.

64 F−; 65 I− S− NZ+ NZ−; 69 A+ A+ E−.
Rep. SA > 68 F; 69-70 BI.

WALTON, Ernest John ('Katie')   *England*
St Peter's Sch York, O Dewsburians, Oxford Univ, Castleford, Barbarians, Yorks.
b −.11.1879; *d* 8.4.47.
SH, 4-2-0-2.
01 W− I−; 02 I+ S+.
Bombay-Burmah Trading Corp in Bangkok.
Blue 1900-1.

WALTON, William   *England*
Castleford.
b 23.9.1874; *d* 1.6.40.
Forward, 1-0-0-1.
1894 S−.
Miner/licensee. Wakefield Trin RL 1895.

WANBON, Robert   *Wales*
Aberavon.
b 1944 Aberavon.
No 8, 1-0-1-0 (3 − 1t).
68 E=(1t).
Building labourer/licensee. St Helens RL 68.

WARD, Anthony Joseph Patrick   *Ireland*
St Mary's Coll, NCPE, Garryowen, Greystones.
b 8.10.54 Dublin.
FH, 17-3-2-12 (98 − 4c 3d 27p).
78 S+(1c 2p) F−(3p) W−(1d 3p) E−(1d 2p)
NZ−(2p); 79 F=(3p) W−(2c 3p) E+(1c 1d 1p)
S=(1p); 81 W− E− S− A−(4p); 83 E+r; 84 E−
(3p) S−; 86 S−; BIr > 80 SA 1-0-0-1.
Co dir. Champ rec 38 pts 78. BI most pts in int, 18 v SA 1st Test 80; also most pts sc v SA in Tests. 19 pts v ACT 79, most by I player (with Ollie Campbell) on tour. Football for Limerick Town AFC.

WARD, George   *England*
Belgrave, Leicester, Midland Cos, Leics.
b 19.3.1885; *d* 63.
Lock/no 8, 6-6-0-0.
13 W+ F+ S+; 14 W+ I+ S+.
Played for Leics 20-26.

WARD, Herbert   *England*
Bradford, Yorks.
b 1873 Bradford; *d* 18.2.55 Baildon.
FB, 1-1-0-0.
1895 W+.
Maintenance mechanic. Bradford RL 1899.

WARD, James Ibbotson   *England*
Tonbridge Sch, Gipsies, Richmond, Mdx.
b 24.4.1858; *d* 28.9.24 London.
Forward, 2-1-1-0.
1881 I+; 1882 I=.
Stock Exchange. Rowed for London RC at Henley 1879-81. HM Lt for City of London.

WARD, John Willie *England*
Castleford, Yorks.
b 29.1.1873 Castleford; *d* 30.4.39 Hemsworth.
Forward, 3-1-0-2.
1896 W+ I− S−.
Glassblower/hotel mgr. Castleford RL.

WARD, Peter ('Ginger') *Australia*
Southland, Marrickville, NSW, Auckland,
Hawke's Bay, Taranaki, Wanganui,
Queenstown (SA).
b 5.11.1876 Invercargill, NZ; *d* −.
Wing/Five-eighth, 4-1-0-3.
1899 BT+ BT− BT− BT−.

WARD, Ronald Henry *New Zealand*
Winton Dist HS, Gore Pioneer, Southland,
Pirates, Riverton, Hastings, Hawkes Bay,
Army, Canterbury, S Island.
b 1.12.15 Riverton.
Flanker, 3-2-0-1.
36 A+; 37 SA+ SA−.
Farmer. NZ > 36 A. Southland sel 57-61. Bro
J.C. rep Otago 42.

WARD, Thomas *Australia*
Qld.
b 1874; *d* 42.
Wing, 1-0-0-1.
1899 BT−.

WARD, William *Wales*
Risca, Cross Keys.
Lock, 2-2-0-0.
34 S+ I+.
Steelworker/tinplater.

WARDLOW, Christopher Story *England*
Creighton Sch Carlisle, Carlisle, Northampton,
Barbarians, NW Cos, Cumberland &
Westmorland.
b 12.7.42 Carlisle.
FB/centre, 6-2-1-3.
69 SA+r; 71 W− I+ F= S− S−.
Salesman/transport mgr. Played for Carlisle at
16.

WARFIELD, Peter John *England*
Durham Univ, Rosslyn Pk, Cambridge Univ.
Centre, 6-1-0-5.
73 NZ− W− I−; 75 I− F− S+.
Blue 74.

WARING, Frank W. *South Africa*
Cape Town Univ, W Prov.
b 7.11.08.
Centre, 7-5-0-2 (6 − 2t).
31 I+(1t); 32 E+; 33 A+ A−(1t) A+ A+ A−.
Grain broker/Cabinet minister. SA > 31-2 BI.

WARLOW, Douglas John *Wales*
Stebonheath Sch, Welsh Youth, Felinfoel,
Llanelli, Welch Rgt.
b 13.2.39 Dafen, Llanelli.
Prop, 1-0-1-0.
62 I=.
Steelworker/club steward. St Helens RL 63.

WARR, Antony Lawley ('Tim') *England*
Bromsgrove Sch, Oxford Univ, Weston-super-
Mare, Moseley, Harlequins, Wakefield,
Gloucester, Richmond, Barbarians, Mdx.
b 15.5.13 Selly Oak, Birmingham.
Wing, 2-2-0-0 (3 − 1t).
34 W+(1t) I+.
Schoolmaster. Blue 33-4. 4 apps OUCC 33-4.
Served WW2, R Glos Hussars. Various teaching
posts inc Harrow Sch from 46.

WARREN, J.P. *Ireland*
Kingstown.
Half-back, 1-0-0-1.
1883 E−.

WARREN, J.R. *Scotland*
Glasgow Acad, Glasgow Academicals.
Centre, 1-0-0-1.
14 I−.

WARREN, Robert Gibson *Ireland*
Rathmines Coll, Lansdowne.
b 1866; *d* 19.11.40.
Half-back, 15-2-2-11 (1t).
1884 W−; 1885 E− S−; 1886 E−; 1887 E= S−
W−; 1888 W+(1t) S− NZN−; 1889 S− W+;
1890 S− W= E−.
Pres IRU 1895-6. Ref S v E 1889, touch-judge I
v S 1896. IB rep 1887-1938; sec 1897.

WARREN, Ronald C. *Scotland*
Glasgow Acad, Glasgow Academicals.
Centre/FB, 5-2-2-1.
22 W= I+; 30 W+ I− E=.
8 yrs between caps.

WATERMAN, Alfred Clarence *New Zealand*
Auckland GS, Ihaewau, Kaeo, Kaitaia,
Whangarei City, N Auckland.
b 31.12.03 Auckland.
Wing, 2-0-0-2.
29 A− A−.
Post Office technician. NZ > 29 A.

WATERS, David Ralph *Wales*
Caerleon Comp, Magor, Newport, Barbarians.
b 4.6.55 Newport.
Lock, 4-2-0-2.
86 E− S+ I+ F−.
Ship's chandler/lorry driver. 6ft 6in son of
farmer. Wales B v F 83, 85. Chosen to r inj
Robert Norster v F, E 85, but missed caps

because matches postponed, and Norster hd regained fitness by time they were played. Ultimately r Norster who was banned from int rugby after being sent off Cardiff v S Wales Police Nov 85. Over 350 apps for Newport 76-86.

WATERS, Frank Henry   *Scotland*
Loretto Sch, Cambridge Univ, London Scottish.
b 2.12.08; *d* 18.10.54.
Lock, 7-1-1-5 (7 − 1t 2c).
30 F− W+(1c) I−(1t 1c) E=; 32 SA− W− I−.
Newspaper business mgr. Blue 27-9. Son of J.B. Banned by SRU for writing on the game; request for reinstatement not granted.

WATERS, John Alexander   *Scotland*
Selkirk HS, Selkirk, Barbarians.
b 11.11.08 Musselburgh.
Prop/no 8, 16-6-0-10.
33 W+ E+ I+; 34 W− I+ E−; 35 W− I− E+ NZ−; 36 W− I− E−; 37 W+ I− E−; BI > 38 SA 1-0-0-1.
Master butcher. Played in 3 Servs ints.

WATERS, Joseph Bow   *Scotland*
Loretto Sch, Cambridge Univ, Barbarians.
b 29.4.1882; *d* 30.6.54.
Forward, 2-2-0-0.
04 I+ E+.
Stockbroker. Blue 02-4. Father of F.H. Served WW1, Capt KOSB; Maj Special List.

WATHERSTON, J.G.   *Scotland*
Sedbergh Sch, Edinburgh W.
b 24.8.09.
Flanker, 2-1-0-1.
34 I+ E−.
Farmer. Uncle of W.R.A.

WATHERSTON, William Rory Andrews   *Scotland*
Sherborne Sch, London Scottish.
b 5.3.33.
Flanker, 3-2-0-1.
63 F+ W− I+.
Lloyds. Nephew of J.G.

WATKINS, David ('Dai') MBE   *Wales*
Welsh Youth, Newport, Barbarians.
b 5.3.42 Cwmcelyn, Blaina.
FH, 21-10-2-9 (15 − 2t 3d).
63 E− S+ I−(1d) F− NZ−; 64 E= S+ I+(1t) F= SA−; 65 E+(1d) S+ I+(1t) F−; 66 E+ S+ I− F+; 67 I− F−(1d) E+; BI > 66 A 2-2-0-0, NZ 4-0-0-4.
Tyre co rep/man dir Cardiff RL/finance co exec. Wales XV v Fj 64. W > 64 SA. Barbarians v A 67. Salford RL 67 for rec £16,000, Swinton 77. RL Cup final v Castleford 69. 6 GB RL, 16 Wales RL. 3 times RL leading goal kicker, 4

times leading pts scorer. World rec 221 pts 72-3, incl 13 goals v Keighley to equ Salford rec. Only RL player to have scored on every app for club over 2 seasons. Coach GB RL 77 World Cup. Man dir newly formed Cardiff RL 81, later coach in succession to John Mantle. MBE 86.

WATKINS, Edward   *Wales*
Neath.
b 27.9.1899 Neath; *d* 12.9.83 Neath.
SH, 4-1-0-3 (3 − 1d).
24 E− S− I−(1d) F+.
Council worker. Served WW1, RA. Halifax RL 24.

WATKINS, Edward   *Wales*
Caerphilly Sec Sch, Cardiff, RAF.
b 2.3.16 Caerphilly.
Lock/no 8, 8-4-0-4.
35 NZ+; 37 S− I−; 38 E+ S− I+; 39 E− S+.
Police/schoolmaster. Served WW2, RAF Special Investigations Branch. Played in 2 Servs ints. Wigan RL 39. Taught at Surbiton GS.

WATKINS, Emlyn   *Wales*
Blaina.
b 21.9.04 Blaina; *d* 15.5.78.
Flanker/no 8, 3-2-0-1 (3 − 1t).
26 S− I+ F+(1t).
Miner/office worker Oldham Municipal Waterworks. Leeds RL 26.

WATKINS, Eric Leslie   *New Zealand*
Wellington Coll, Wellington Coll OB, Wellington, Raetihi, Wanganui, N Island.
b 18.3.1880 Akaroa; *d* 14.8.49 Lower Hutt.
Forward, 1-1-0-0.
05 A+.
Contractor/labourer. Turned RL; NZ > 07 E.

WATKINS, Henry Vaughan ('Harry')   *Wales*
Llandovery, Llanelli.
b 1871 Trecastle; *d* 16.5.45 Llandovery.
Forward, 6-5-0-1 (3 − 1t).
04 S+ I−; 05 E+(1t) S+ I+; 06 E+.
Business/licensee. Chief Llandovery Fire Brigade. Chmn Carm Co Council. Emigrated Can, prominent in early Brit Columbia rugby. Capt Victoria v NZ 19.11.13.

WATKINS, John Arthur   *England*
Linden SMS, Gloucester, Glos.
b 28.11.47.
Flanker, 7-3-0-4.
72 SA+; 73 NZ− W− NZ+ A+; 75 F− W−.
Toolroom engr.

WATKINS, John Kingdon CBE   *England*
Epsom Coll, Devonport Servs, US Portsmouth, RN, Comb Servs, Barbarians, Som.

b 24.2.13; *d* 13.5.70.
3-2-0-1.
39 W+ I− S+.
RN/co dir. Rear Adm. Served WW2, OBE (mil)
45. CBE (mil) 67.

WATKINS, Leonard   *Wales*
Sherborne Sch, Oxford Univ, Llandaff.
b 7.12.1859; *d* 7.2.01 Entre Rios, Arg.
Half-back, 1-0-0-1.
1881 E−.
Moved to Arg 1882.

WATKINS, Michael John   *Wales*
Cwmcarn Sch, Gwent Sch, S Mon Youth,
Cwmcarn, Crumlin, Cardiff, Newport,
Barbarians.
b 9.1.52 Abercarn.
Hooker, 4-2-0-2.
84 I+ F− E+ A−.
Road haulage/engrg. Capt Wales on all 4 apps.
W > 78 A. Wales B v F 76, 79, 83. Wales XV v J
83.

WATKINS, Stuart John   *Wales*
Caerleon Coll, Newport, Barbarians.
b 5.6.41.
Wing, 26-14-3-9 (27 − 9t).
64 S+ I+(1t) F=(1t); 65 E+(2t) S+(1t) I+ F−
(1t); 66 E+ S+ I− F+(1t) A−; 67 S−(1t) I−
F− E+ NZ−; 68 E= S+; 69 S+ I+(1t) F= E+
NZ−; 70 E+ I−; BI > 66 A 2-2-0-0, NZ 1-0-0-1.
Sales rep. W > 64 SA; 69 NZ, A & Fj.
Barbarians v NZ 64, A 67.

WATKINS, William R.   *Wales*
Newport, St Luke's Coll, Barbarians.
b Treowen.
SH, 1-0-0-1.
59 F−.
Schoolmaster. Barbarians v SA 61.

WATSON, D.H.   *Scotland*
Glasgow Acad, Glasgow Academicals.
Forward, 3-2-0-1.
1876 E−; 1877 I+ E+.
Ref S v E 1881. Pres SRU 1880-1.

WATSON, Fischer Burges CBE   *England*
DSO
Ashdown House Forest Row, HMS Britannia,
US Portsmouth, RN, Barbarians, Surrey.
b −.9.1884; *d* 14.8.60.
Forward, 2-0-0-2 (3 − 1t).
08 S−; 09 S−(1t).
RN. Son of Rear Adm Burges Watson. Served
WW1, DSO 17. Served WW2, convoy service.
Twice mentioned in despatches. CBE 43 & bar
to DSO at 60 yrs old. Rear Adm.

WATSON, George W.   *Australia*
Qld.
b 6.1.1885; *d* −.
Wing, 1-0-0-1.
07 NZ−.
Clerk to chief sec's dept. RL; helped form Qld
RL.

WATSON, James Henry Digby   *England*
('Bungy')
King's Sch Canterbury, Edinburgh Acad,
Edinburgh Univ, Blackheath, The London
Hosp, Barbarians.
b 31.8.1890 Southsea; kia 15.10.14 at sea.
Centre, 3-3-0-0 (3 − 1t).
1914 W+ S+ F+(1t).
Medicine/RN. Son of James Donald Watson,
NZ non-test player. Reserve for S 12-13. Rep S
long jump 12. Edinburgh Univ middleweight
boxing champ. Served WW1, RN surg aboard
HMS Hawke; drowned when she was sunk by
German submarine.

WATSON, Richard ('Snipe')   *Ireland*
Wanderers.
b −; *d* 60.
1-0-0-1.
12 SA−.
Minister.

WATSON, William Sinclair   *Scotland*
Boroughmuir Acad, Boroughmuir, Barbarians.
b 7.1.49 Edinburgh.
No 8/flanker, 10-3-1-6.
74 W− E+ I− F+; 75 NZ−; 77 I+ F− W−; 79
I= F−.
Chartered accountant. Scottish XV v Arg 73, Tg
74, J 76.

WATSON, William Thornton   *Australia*
DSM MC
Newtown, NSW, Glebe-Balmain.
b 10.11.1887 Nelson, NZ; *d* 9.9.61 New York.
Flanker, 5-2-0-3.
12 US+; 13 NZ− NZ− NZ+; 14 NZ−.
Plantation mgr. Lived in Sydney from 11. Capt
AIF > 19 BI. Served WW1 & WW2. Vice-
Consul in New York.

WATT, Alexander Gordon   *Scotland*
Mitchell
Edinburgh Acad, Edinburgh Academicals,
RAMC, The Army.
Prop/no 8, 6-1-0-5.
47 F− W− I− A−; 48 F+ W−.
Medicine.

WATT, Bruce Alexander   *New Zealand*
Wanganui Tech Coll, Hunterville, NZ Jnrs,
Wanganui, Christchurch, Canterbury, S Island.
b 12.3.39 Marton.

1st five-eighth, 8-7-1-0 (9 − 2t 1d).
62 A+(2t) A+; 63 E+ E+; 63 W+(1d); 64 E+
S=; 64 A+.
Bank accountant. NZ > 62 A, 63-4 BI,F & C
(20 apps). Marlborough sel 76.

WATT, David Edward James   *England*
Bristol, Barbarians, Glos.
b 5.7.38.
Lock, 4-2-0-2.
67 I+ F− S+ W−.
Sales promotion exec.

WATT, James Michael   *New Zealand*
Wellington Coll, Univ, Otago, Wellington, NZ
Univs.
b 5.7.14 Dunedin.
Wing, 2-2-0-0 (6 − 2t).
36 A+(1t) A+(1t).
Prof of paediatrics. NZ > 36 A. NZ Univs 440y
titleholder 34-7; runner-up in NZ champs 37.
Father M.H. & bro M. rep NZ Univs.

WATT, William James   *Wales*
Llanelli CS, Carmarthen Tg Coll, Llanelli,
Leicester, Birkenhead Pk.
b 16.5.1890; d 16.9.50 Roehampton.
Centre, 1-0-0-1 (3 − 1t).
14 E−(1t).
Chartered accountant. Served WW1, wounded.
Pres London Welsh.

WATTS, David   *Wales*
Maesteg.
b 14.3.1886; kia WW1.
Lock, 4-3-0-1.
14 E− S+ F+ I+.
Miner. Mem of 'Terrible Eight'.

WATTS, James   *Wales*
Llanelli.
b 1878 Llanelli; d −.2.33.
Forward, 11-10-0-1 (6 − 2t).
07 E I S I I , 08 E I S+ F+ I+ A+, 09 S+
F+(1t) I+(1t).
Steelworker.

WATT, James Russell   *New Zealand*
Otago Boys' HS, Kaikorai, Otago, Gore
Pioneer, Southland, Athletic, Wellington, N
Island.
b 29.12.35 Dunedin.
Wing, 9-5-1-3(3 − 1t).
58 A−; 60 SA− SA+ SA= SA−; 61 F+ F+; 62
A+ A+(1t).
Bank official. 18t NZ > 57 A; 8t > 60 A & SA;
2t > 62 A.

WATTS, Murray Gordon   *New Zealand*
Stratford HS, Teachers Coll, NZ Jnrs,
Manawatu, New Plymouth HSOB, Taranaki.

b 31.3.55 Patea.
Wing, 5-2-0-3 (4 − 1t).
79 F+(1t) F−; 80 A− A+ A−r.
Schoolmaster. NZ > 79 A, 80 A & Fj. Bro
Allan rep Comb Servs 75.

WATTS, Wallace Howard   *Wales*
Newport, London Welsh..
b 25.3.1870 Chipping Norton; d 29.4.50
Richmond.
Forward, 12-5-0-7.
1892 E− S− I−; 1893 E+ S+ I+; 1894 E− S+
I−; 1895 E− I+; 1896 E−.
Business. Played final game for London Welsh,
11.

WEATHERSTONE, Laurence   *Australia*
John ('Spoon')
St Patrick's Coll, Bathurst, NSW Country,
NSW, ACT.
b 13.3.50.
Centre, 7-5-0-2 (8 − 2t).
75 E+ E+(1t) J+ J+ Sr−; 76 E− I+(1t).
Civil Service.

WEATHERSTONE, Thomas   *Scotland*
Grant
Stewart's Coll, Stewart's Coll FP, Edinburgh
Univ, Barbarians.
b 31.
Wing, 16-2-2-12 (9 − 3t).
52 E−; 53 I− E−(1t); 54 F− NZ− I− E− W−;
55 F−; 58 W− A+(1t) I−(1t) E=; 59 W+ I−
E=.

WEAVER, David   *Wales*
Swansea.
Wing, 1-0-1-0.
64 E=.
Metallurgist. Wales XV v Fj 64.

WEBB, Charles Samuel Henry   *England*
Devonport Servs, RN, Devon, Auckland.
Lock, 12-5-1-6.
32 SA− W− I+ S+; 33 W− I+ S−; 35 S−; 36
NZ+ W= I− S+.
R Marines. Emigrated NZ; played for Auckland
38.

WEBB, Desmond Stanley   *New Zealand*
Gisborne Boys' HS, Univ, Auckland, NZ
Univs, Whangarei HSOB, N Auckland.
b 10.9.34 Kawakawa.
Hooker, 1-1-0-0.
59 BI+.
Solicitor. Capt N Auckland 62-5.

WEBB, James   *Wales*
Abertillery.
b 1883 Coleford; d 4.2.55 Upper Soudley,
Glos.

Prop/lock, 20-18-0-2 (6 − 2t).
07 S−; 08 E+ S+ F+ I+ A+; 09 E+ S+ F+ I+;
10 F+ E+(1t*) S+ I+; 11 E+ S+ F+ I+(1t); 12
E− S+; BI > 10 SA 3-1-0-2.
Miner. St Helens RL 12. Played in 17 consec
victories 08-11. *Some sources credit this try to
T.H. Evans.

WEBB, James E.   *Wales*
Newport.
 b 1862; d 8.3.13 Newport.
FB/back, 2-1-0-1 (2 − 1c).
1888 NZN+(1c); 1889 S−.
Painter.

WEBB, J.W.G.   *England*
Northampton.
No 8, 3-1-0-2 (3 − 1t).
26 F+ S−(1t); 29 S−.
Bootmaker.

WEBB, Rodney Edward   *England*
Newbold Grange Sch, Coventry, Barbarians,
Midlands, Warwicks.
 b 18.8.43 Newbold-on-Avon.
Wing, 12-4-1-7 (6 − 2t).
67 S+(1t) W− NZ−; 68 I= F− S+; 69 I−
F+(1t) S+ W−; 72 I− F−.
Engr/sports goods shop owner. Warwicks
javelin champ. E > 67 Can. Bro Richard toured
BI, F with A 66-7.

WEBB, St Lawrence Hugh   *England*
(**'Larry'**)
St George's Sch Harpenden, Willesden Tech
Coll, Bedford, Aldershot Servs, Blackheath,
RE, Barbarians, Herts.
 b 7.3.31 Melbourne, A; d 30.5.78 at sea.
Prop, 4-1-2-1.
59 W− I+ F= S=.
Man dir plant hire co. Always held Australian
passport. E front row debut with John Wackett
who joined him in bus 60. Missing in private
aeroplane over English Channel.

WEBB, William   *Australia*
Wallaroos, NSW.
 b −; d 30.
Forward, 2-0-0-2.
1899 BT− BT−.

WEBSTER, Jan Godfrey   *England*
'Queen Mary's GS Walsall, Walsall, Moseley,
Staffs.
 b 24.8.46 Southport.
SH, 11-3-0-8.
72 W− I− SA+; 73 NZ− W− NZ+; 74 S−
W+; 75 I− F− W−.
Sports outfitter.

WEDGE, Thomas George   *England*
St Ives, Cornwall.
SH, 2-1-0-1.
07 F+; 09 W−.
Fisherman. Olympic silver medal for rugby, GB
(Cornwall) v A 08.

WEIGHILL, Robert Harold   *England*
George DFC
Wirral GS, Birkenhead Pk, Waterloo, RAF,
Harlequins, Leicester, Barbarians, Cheshire,
NLD.
 b 9.9.20.
No 8, 4-2-0-2.
47 S+ F+; 48 S− F−.
RAF/Sec RFU. Free-style swimming champ of
Cheshire 35-6. RAF rep on RFU 59-70. E sel 59-
64. Sec RFU 71-86. Sec to IB in succession to
John Hart 86. Served WW2, RAF Fighter
Command. DFC 44. ADC to HM The Queen
68.

WELLS, Bruce G.   *Australia*
NSW.
 b 37.
FH, 1-1-0-0.
58 M+.

WELLS, Cyril Mowbray   *England*
Dulwich Coll, Cambridge Univ, Harlequins,
Barbarians, Surrey.
 b 21.3.1871 London; d 22.8.63 St John's Wood.
Half-back, 6-2-0-4.
1893 S−; 1894 W+ S−; 1896 S−; 1897 W− S+.
Schoolmaster. Blue 1891-2. Ckt: blue 1891-3;
Surrey 1890-3; Mdx 1895-09 (inc co rec score 244
v Notts 1899); 4 times Gentlemen v Players; E v
S 1893. Taught at Eton Coll 1893-26.

WELLS, Gordon T.   *Wales*
Porth CS, St Luke's Coll, Cardiff, Barbarians.
Centre/wing, 7-5-1-1 (3 − 1t).
55 E+ S−; 57 I+ F+; 58 A+ E= S+(1t).
Schoolmaster.

WELLS, H.G.   *Ireland*
Bective Rgrs.
Wing, 4-2-0-2 (3 − 1t).
1891 S− W−; 1894 E+ S+(1t).
Dunlop, Coventry.

WELLS, John   *New Zealand*
Dargaville HS, Dargaville, N Auckland,
Athletic, NZ UNivs, Wellington, N Island.
 b 4.1.11 Dargaville.
Flanker, 2-2-0-0.
36 A+ A+.
Bank of NZ official. NZ > 36 A. Served WW2;
rep 2nd NZEF. Pres Athletic club 59-61 &
Wellington RU 69.

WELSH, Robert Brown   *Scotland*
Hawick HS, Hawick.
b 2.2.43 Hawick.
Centre, 2-0-0-2.
67 I− E−.
Joiner.

WELSH, Robin   *Scotland*
George Watson's Coll, Watsonians.
b 20.10.1869 Edinburgh; *d* 21.10.34.
Wing, 4-3-0-1(3 − 1t).
1895 W+ I+(1t) E+; 1896 W−.
Farmer. Cousin of W.H. Ref E v I 02 & 05; W v
E 03. Pres SRU 24-5. Rep GB at curling in
Olympics 24.

WELSH, William B.   *Scotland*
Hawick HS, Hawick.
b 11.2.07 Hawick.
No 8/flanker, 21-10-1-10 (3 − 1t).
27 NSW+(1t); 28 F+ W− I−; 29 I+ E+; 30 F−
W+ I− E=; 31 F+ W− I− E+; 32 SA− W−
I− E−; 33 W+ E+ I+; BI > 30 A, NZ 1-0-0-1.
London Highfield RL 33.

WELSH, William Halliday   *Scotland*
Merchiston Castle Sch, Edinburgh Univ.
b 4.9.1879; *d* 30.6.72.
Wing, 8-5-0-3 (12 − 4t).
1900 I+(2t) E+(1t); 01 W+ I+ E+; 02 W−(1t)
I− E−.
Medicine. Cousin of Robin. Pres SRU 38-9.

WEMYSS, Andrew ('Jock')   *Scotland*
Gala, Edinburgh W, Leicester, Barbarians.
b 22.5.1893 Galashiels; *d* 21.1.74 Edinburgh.
Flanker/prop, 7-2-2-3.
14 W− I−; 20 F+ E−; 22 F= W= I+.
Banking/journalist. Resumed int career despite
losing an eye WW2. Reprimanded by SRU for
writing about game when still playing.
Barbarians comm & records keeper.

WESSELS, J.J.   *South Africa*
Stellenbosch Univ, W Prov.
3-0-0-3.
1896 BI− BI− BI−.

WEST, Alfred Hubert   *New Zealand*
Matapu Sch, Hawera, Taranaki, N Island.
b 6.5.1893 Inglewood; *d* 7.1.34 Hawera.
No 8, 2-0-1-1.
21 SA− SA=.
Fencing contractor. NZ > 20 A, 24-5 BI,F & C.
Served WW1, gunner NZ Field Artillery.
Gassed, but recovered to rep Comb Servs in
King's Cup & > 19 SA. Hawera comm 22-6,
capt 27-9.

WEST, Bryan Ronald   *England*
Northampton GS, Loughborough Colls,

Northampton, Barbarians, E Midlands.
b 7.6.48.
Flanker, 8-3-2-3.
68 W= I= F− S+; 69 SA+; 70 I+ W− S−; BI
> 68 SA.
PE teacher. Wakefield Trin RL.

WEST, Leonard   *Scotland*
Fettes Coll, Edinburgh Univ, W Hartlepool,
Barbarians.
b −.5.1879; *d* 26.1.45 Hoddesdon.
Forward, 9-5-0-4.
03 W+ I+ E+; 05 I− E+ NZ−; 06 W− I+ E−.
Medicine. Took Hugh Monteith's place S v NZ
05.

WESTACOTT, David   *Wales*
Grange National Sch, Cardiff.
b 1882; kia 28.8.17 France.
Forward, 1-0-0-1.
06 I−.
Served WW1, Pte in Gloucester Rgt.

WESTBY, A.J.   *Ireland*
Monaghan Coll, Trin Coll Dublin.
Forward, 1-0-0-1.
1875 E−.

WESTFIELD, Robert E.   *Australia*
St Patrick's Coll Wellington, Sydney Univ,
Australian Univs, Randwick, E Suburbs, NSW,
Victoria.
b 25.5.07 Hunterville, NZ.
FB, 2-2-0-0.
29 NZ+ NZ+.
Advertising exec. NSW > 28 NZ. Capt A Univs
> 34 J.

WESTON, Henry Thomas   *England*
Franklin
Northampton, E Midlands.
b 9.7.1869 Yardley Gobion; *d* 5.4.55 Yardley
Gobion.
Forward, 1-0-0-1.
01 S−.
Farmer. Father of William Henry.

WESTON, Lionel Edward   *England*
Bedford Mod Sch, Loughborough Colls, W of
Scotland, Rosslyn Pk.
b 22.2.47 Much Wenlock.
SH, 2-0-0-2.
72 F− S−.
Schoolmaster.

WESTON, Michael Philip   *England*
Durham Sch, Richmond, Durham City,
Barbarians, Durham Co.
b 21.8.38 Durham.
Centre/FH, 29-11-6-12 (6 − 1t 1d).
60 W+ I+ F=(1t) S+; 61 SA− W− I− F= S+;

62 W= I+ F−; 63 W+ I= F+ S+ NZ− NZ−
A−; 64 NZ− W= I− F+ S−; 65 F+ S=; 66 S−;
68 F−(1d) S+; BI > 62 SA 4-0-1-3; 66 A 2-2-0-
0, NZ.
Auctioneer & estate agent. Once E's most
capped threequarter. Chmn E sels 85-6.
Durham CCC.

WESTON, V.G. *Scotland*
Kelvinside Acad, Kelvinside Academicals.
Flanker, 2-0-0-2.
36 I− E−.

WESTON, William Henry *England*
Oakham Sch, Northampton, Barbarians, E
Midlands.
b 21.12.05 Yardley Gobion.
Flanker, 16-10-2-4.
33 I+ S−; 34 I+ S+; 35 W= I+ S−; 36 NZ+
W= S+; 37 W+ I+ S+; 38 W− I+ S−; BT > 37
Arg.
Farmer. Son of H.T.F. Mem of E
Midlands/Leics XV v SA 31, the only team to
beat tourists.

WETTER, John James ('Jack') *Wales*
DCM
Newport.
b 29.12.1889 Newport; *d* 29.7.67 Newport.
Centre/SH/FH, 10-6-0-4 (14 − 4t 1c).
14 S+(1t) F+(2t) I+(1t); 20 E+ S− F+ I+(1c);
21 E−; 24 I− NZ−.
Docks crane driver/GWR employee. Bro of
Harry. Served WW1, S Wales Borderers.
Played either side of WW1. Baseball for W.

WETTER, William Henry *Wales*
('Harry')
Newport.
b 1880; *d* −.12.33 Newport.
Prop/lock, 2-0-0-2.
12 SA−; 13 E−.
Bro of Jack.

WHEATLEY, Arthur A. *England*
South St Sch Hillfields, Coventry, Warwicks,
Midland Cos.
b 9.12.08.
Lock, 5-4-0-1.
37 W+ I+ S+; 38 W− S+.
Haulier. Played with bro Harold 3 times for E.
Served WW2, Home Guard.

WHEATLEY, Harold F. *England*
Coventry, Warwicks.
b 25.12.12 Coventry.
Prop, 7-3-0-4.
36 I−; 37 S+; 38 W− S−; 39 W+ I− S+.
Haulier. Played with bro Arthur 3 times for E.

WHEEL, Geoffrey Arthur Derek *Wales*
Mumbles, Swansea, Barbarians.
b 30.6.51.
Lock, 32-22-1-9.
74 I= E−r; 75 F+ E+ I+ A+; 76 E+ S+ I+
F+; 77 I+ E+ S+; 78 E+ S+ I+ F+ A− A−
NZ−; 79 S+ I+; 80 F+ E− S+ I−; 81 E+ S−
I+ F− A+; 82 I−.
Toolmaker/brewery rep. Wales B v F 73. W >
75 Far East; 78 A. Welsh XV v NZ 74. Wales
XV v Arg 76. Barbarians > 76 Can. Capt
Swansea v NZ 80. Partnered Allan Martin 28
times. Played in 15 consec victories 75-78.
Football for Swansea City reserves before switch
to rugby 72. Select for BI > 77 NZ, failed
medical clearance and Moss Keane took place.
Sent off with Willie Duggan W v I 15.1.77, 1st
players dismissed in int in Cardiff.

WHEELER, George Herbert *Ireland*
Methodist Coll Belfast, Queen's Coll Belfast.
b 9.12.1864 Belfast; *d* 16.1.55 Belfast.
Centre, 2-0-0-2.
1884 S−; 1885 E−.
Solicitor/lecturer in law Queen's Univ.

WHEELER, James Reid *Ireland*
Methodist Coll Belfast, Queen's Univ Belfast,
Collegians, Barbarians.
b 1898 Belfast; *d* 23.3.73 Belfast.
FH, 5-1-0-4.
22 E− S− W− F+; 24 E−.
Medicine. Ref E v S 29,31,32; S v W 30, E v W
31. Pres IRU 59-60.

WHEELER, Paul J. *Wales*
Duffryn CS, Aberavon.
b 47.
FB, 2-0-1-1.
67 NZ−; 68 E=.

WHEELER, Peter John ('Brace') *England*
Brockley CS, O Brockleians, Leicester.
b 26.11.48 London.
Hooker, 41-17-2-22.
75 F− W−; 76 A+ W− S− I−; 77 S+ I+ F−
W−; 78 F− W− S+ I+ NZ−; 79 S= I− F+
W− NZ−; 80 I+ F+ W+ S+; 81 W− S+ I+
F−; 82 A+ S= I− F+ W+; 83 F− S− I− NZ+;
84 S− I+ F− W−; BI > 77 NZ 3-1-0-2; 80 SA 4-
1-0-3.
Insurance broker. E > 71 & 79 Far East, 81 US,
Can. Capt Leicester in 3 John Player Cup final
victories, 79-81.

WHELAN, Patrick Charles ('Pa') *Ireland*
Crescent Coll, Dublin Coll of Technology,
Garryowen.
b 2.5.50 Limerick.
Hooker, 19-3-2-14.
75 E+ S−; 76 NZ−; 77 W− E− S− F−; 78 S+

428

F− W− E− NZ−; 79 F= W− E+ S=; 81 F−
W− E−.
Quantity surveyor. Son in law of P.J. Reid.

WHETTON, Alan James   *New Zealand*
Auckland, NZ Colts, NZ Jnrs, N Island, NZ
Barbarians.
b 15.12.59 Auckland.
Flanker, 3-2-0-1.
84 A−r A+r; 85 A+r.
Bro of Gary. NZ > 84 A, 85 Arg.

WHETTON, Gary William   *New Zealand*
Auckland, NZ Colts, NZ Barbarians.
b 15.12.59 Auckland.
Lock, 19-17-1-1.
81 SA+ R+ F+ F+; 82 A+; 83 BI+ BI+ BI+
BI+; 84 F+ F+ A− A+ A+; 85 E+ E+ A+
Arg+ Arg=1.
Bro of Alan. NZ > 81 R & F, 84 A, 85 Arg. Inj
in W Prov Centenary match SA 83; missed tours
to A & S & E. World XV > 86 SA.

WHINERAY, Wilson James OBE *New Zealand*
Auckland GS, Martinborough, Waikaia,
Wairarapa, Rakaia, Mid-Canterbury, Univ,
Manawatu, NZ Colts, Lincoln Coll, Canterbury,
City, Waikato, Grammar, Auckland, S & N
Islands, NZ Univs.
b 10.7.35 Auckland.
Prop, 32-24-3-5 (6 − 2t).
57 A+ A+; 58 A+(2t) A− A+; 59 BI+ BI+
BI+ BI−; 60 SA− SA+ SA= SA−; 61 F+ F+
F+; 62 A+ A+ A= A+ A+; 63 E+ E+; 63 I+
W+; 64 E+ S= F+; 65 SA+ SA+ SA− SA+.
Business exec. NZ's most apps as capt (30, 58-
65). NZ > 57 & 62 A, 60 A & SA (made 3 out of
19 apps at no 8), 63-4 BI,F & C (1 app at no 8).
Studied business mangagement at Harvard
Business Coll, US. Coach various sides 70-4. NZ
'Sportsman of Year' 65. Mem Eden Pk Bd of
Control 80. NZ Univs heavywt boxing champ
56. NZ Wool Marketing Corp man dir 73 4.
OBE 61.

WHIPP, Peter John Milton   *South Africa*
Diocesan Coll Cape Town, Cape Town Univ,
Villagers, Jnr Springboks, Barbarians, W Prov.
b 22.9.50 East London.
Centre, 8-6-0-2 (4 − 1t).
74 BI− BI−; 75 F+; 76 NZ+ NZ+ NZ+; 80
SAm+ SAm+.
Clerk. SA > 74 F. Bro in law of N. V. H.
Mallett.

WHITE, Andrew ('Son')   *New Zealand*
Southland Boys' HS, Waikiwi, Southland,
Christchurch, Canterbury, S Island.
b 21.3.1894 Invercargill; *d* 3.8.68 Christchurch.
Lock/flanker, 4-4-0-0 (3 − 1t).

21 SA+; 24 I+; 25 E+ F+(1t).
Stock agent. NZ > 22 A, 24-5 BI.

WHITE, Charles J.B.   *Australia*
NSW.
b 1874; *d* −.10.41 Maitland.
Forward, 3-1-0-2.
1899 BT+; 03 NZ−; 04 BT−.
Carrier.

WHITE, Colin   *England*
Gosforth, NE Cos, North.
31.3.48 Newcastle-upon-Tyne.
Prop, 4-2-0-2.
83 NZ+; 84 S− I+ F−.
PE teacher/forestry worker. Lost 3 fingers in
forestry accident 78. England Squad 72.
England B v R 78. Won 1st cap at 34.

WHITE, David Mathew   *Scotland*
Kelvinside Acad, Glenalmond Acad, Kelvinside
Academicals, Oxford Univ, Barbarians.
b 21.11.43.
Centre, 4-2-0-2.
63 F+ W− I+ E−.
Grain merchant.

WHITE, Derek Bolton   *Scotland*
Dunbar GS, Gala.
b 30.1.58 Dunbar.
Flanker, 4-3-0-1 (4 − 1t).
82 F+ W+(1t) A+ A−.
Medical technician. Scottish XV v Fj 82.

WHITE, Donald Frederick   *England*
Wellingborough GS, Wellingborough O
Grammarians, Northampton, The Army, Comb
Servs, Barbarians, E Midlands, Midland Cos.
b 16.1.26 Earls Barton, Northants.
Flanker, 14-8-1-5 (6 − 2t).
47 W+(1t) I− S+; 48 I− F−; 51 S+(1t); 52
SA− W− S+ I+ F+; 53 W+ I= S+.
Co dir family shoe manufacturing bus
Northampton 44-61, 7 seasons as capt. E sel &
coach 69-71.

WHITE, Hallard Leo   *New Zealand*
Kawakawa Dist HS, Northcote, Auckland, N
Island.
b 27.3.29 Kawakawa.
Prop, 4-2-0-2.
54 I+ E+ F−; 55 A−.
Painter & paper hanger. NZ > 53-4 BI,F &
NAm. Coach & comm Auckland since 65.

WHITE, James   *South Africa*
Queen's Coll Queenstown, Border.
b 12 Queenstown, Cape Prov.
Centre/wing, 10-7-0-3 (10 − 2t 1d).
31 W+; 33 A+ A− A+ A+(1t) A−; 37 A+ A+
NZ−(1d) NZ+.

Clerk. Prov rugby at centre, FB, FH. SA > 31-2 BI.

WHITE, James Matthew *Australia*
St Stanislaus Coll Bathurst, NSW.
b 1893; *d* 35.
Forward, 1-0-0-1.
04 BT−.

WHITE, Jonathan Parker Laidley *Australia*
King's Sch Sydney, NSW.
b 27.2.35.
Lock/prop, 24-9-2-13.
58 NZ− NZ+ NZ−; 61 Fj+ Fj+ Fj= SA−
SA− F−; 62 NZ− NZ− NZ= NZ− NZ−; 63
E+ SA− SA+ SA+ SA−; 64 NZ− NZ− NZ+;
65 SA+ SA+.
Farmer.

WHITE, Maxwell Clarke *Australia*
St Joseph's Coll, Qld.
b 07; *d* 5.9.79.
Lock, 9-4-0-5.
31 M+ NZ−; 32 NZ+ NZ−; 33 SA− SA+
SA− SA− SA+.
Real estate. Bro of Bimbo. Bro in law of Walter Gordon Bennett.

WHITE, Michael MC *Ireland*
CBC Cork, Queen's Coll Cork.
b 2.2.1882; *d* 26.9.56.
Forward, 6-3-0-3.
06 E+ S− W+ SA−; 07 E+ W−.
Medicine. Served WW1, Lt Col in RAMC.

WHITE, Richard Alexander *New Zealand*
('Tiny')
Gisborne Dist HS, Feilding Agric Coll,
Gisborne HSOB, Poverty Bay, N Island.
b 11.6.25 Gisborne.
Lock, 23-15-1-7 (9 − 3t).
49 A− A−; 50 BI= BI+ BI+ BI+; 51 A+ A+
A+; 52 A−(1t) A+; 53 W−; 54 I+ E+ S+ F−;
55 A+ A+ A−; 56 SA+(1t) SA− SA+(1t)
SA+.
Sheep farmer/insurance underwriter. NZ > 51
A, 53-4 BI,F & NAm (pl in 30 out of 36
matches, rec for NZ player). Pl in 23 consec
Tests. Served WW2, J Force in Japan. Pres
Gisborne HSOB. Mayor of Gisborne 77. Son
David rep Canterbury 79-80. Farmed until inj in
tractor accident.

WHITE, Roy Maxwell *New Zealand*
Hastings Boys' HS, Petone, Wellington,
Trentham Army, Comb Servs, N Island.
b 18.10.17 Dannevirke; *d* 19.1.80 Wellington.
Flanker, 4-4-0-0 (3 − 1t).
46 A+(1t) A+; 47 A+ A+.
Engr. NZ > 47 A. Petone comm & Wellington
sel. NZ R Class yachting champ.

WHITE, Saxon William *Australia*
Sydney HS, NSW.
b 9.3.34.
Centre, 7-0-1-6.
56 SA− SA−; 58 I− E− S− M= M−.
Medicine/professor.

WHITE, Thomas Brown *Scotland*
Edinburgh Acad, Edinburgh Academicals,
Edinburgh Univ.
b 1.3.1866 Cumnock; *d* 6.7.39 Moffat.
Forward, 3-2-0-1.
1888 W− I+; 1889 W+.
Medicine.

WHITE, William George Searle *Australia*
('Bimbo') DFC
St Joseph's Coll, Sydney Univ, Qld.
b 13.
Lock, 10-4-1-5.
33 SA− SA+ SA− SA− SA+; 34 NZ+ NZ=;
36 NZ− NZ− M+.
Newsagent/sports goods salesman. Bro of Max.

WHITE, William James *Australia*
NSW.
b 08; *d* 77.
Wing, 1-1-0-0.
32 NZ+.
Fireman.

WHITEFOOT, Jeffrey *Wales*
('Hotfoot')
Bedwas Comp, S Mon Youth, Bedwas, Cardiff.
b 18.4.56 Bedwas.
Prop, 10-5-0-5.
84 A−r; 85 S+ I− F− E+ Fj+; 86 E− S+ I+
F−.
Mining electrician. Wales B v F 82, 83, 84.
Wales XV v J 83. Five Nations v Overseas XV,
Twickenham 86.

WHITELEY, Eric Cyprian Perry *England*
TD
Dulwich Coll, O Alleynians, HAC, Barbarians,
Surrey.
b 18.7.04.
FB, 2-0-0-2.
31 S− F−.
Chartered surveyor/produce merchant &
importer. Served WW2, Maj.

WHITELEY, W. *England*
Bramley, Yorks.
b c1871; *d* −.
Forward, 1-1-0-0.
1896 W+.
Leeds City Police.

WHITESTONE, Augustus *Ireland*
Mayberry

Armagh RS, Trin Coll Dublin.
Half-back, 5-0-0-5.
1877 E−; 1879 S− E−; 1880 E−; 1883 S−.
Medicine.

WHITFIELD, Jack *Wales*
Pill Harriers, Newport.
b 23.3.1893 Newport; *d* 26.12.27 Newport.
Lock, 12-6-1-5 (15 − 5t).
19 NZA−; 20 E+ S− F+ I+(1t); 21 E−; 22
E+(1t) S= I+(2t) F+(1t); 24 S− I−.
Foreman fitter/licensee.

WHITING, Graham John *New Zealand*
Taumarunui HS, Taumarunui, King Country,
NZ Jnrs, Athletic, N Island.
b 4.6.46 Wanganui.
Prop, 6-4-1-1.
72 A+ A+ S+; 73 E+ I= F−.
Mechanic/insurance agent. NZ > 72-3 BI,F &
NAm. Maritime RL 75.

WHITING, Peter John ('Pole') *New Zealand*
Auckland GS, Ponsonby, NZ Jnrs, Auckland, N
Island.
b 6.8.46 Auckland.
Lock, 20-12-3-5 (12 − 3t).
71 BI− BI+ BI=; 72 A+(1t) A+(1t) A+(1t)
W+ S+; 73 E+ I= F−; 74 A+ A= A+; 74 I+;
76 I+ SA− SA+ SA− SA−.
Schoolmaster/precious stones businessman. 6ft
6in, 17st 4lb. NZ > 72-3 BI,F & NAm, 74 A &
Fj & I,W & E, 76 SA.

WHITLEY, Herbert *England*
Durham Sch, Northern, Northumb.
b 26.8.03; *d* 75.
SH, 1-1-0-0.
29 W+; BI(uncap) > 24 SA 3-0-1-2.
Bank official. Bro in law of Alan Robson.
Served WW2, R Marines.

WHITSON, Geoffrey Keith *Wales*
Newport St Julian's HS, Newport.
b 4.12.30 Newport; *d* 18.5.84 Cwmbran.
Flanker, 3-3-0-0.
56 F+; 60 S+ I+.
Schoolmaster/sports centre mgr.

WHITTINGTON, Thomas Price *Scotland*
Merchiston Castle Sch, Merchistonians,
Edinburgh Univ.
b 12.8.1849; *d* 7.10.19 Neath.
Forward, 1-0-1-0.
1873 E=.
Medicine. Fdr mem Neath, W's oldest club.

WHITWORTH, R.J.E. *Scotland*
Bedford Sch, London Scottish.
Wing, 1-0-0-1.
36 I−.

WHYTE, David James *Scotland*
Bell Baxter Sch, Edinburgh W, St Andrew's
Univ, Scottish Univs, Oxford Univ, N Midlands,
Barbarians.
b 21.2.40.
Wing, 13-6-2-5 (6 − 2t).
65 W− I− E= SA+; 66 F=(1t) W− I+ E+(1t)
A+; 67 F+ W+ I− E−.
Schoolmaster. Blue 63. AAA long jump champ
59.

WICKHAM, Stanley *Australia*
Montgomery
Marist Sch Parramatta, W Suburbs, NSW.
b 1.1.1876 Parramatta; *d* −.3.60.
Centre, 5-0-0-5 (3 − 1p).
03 NZ−(1p); 04 BT− BT− BT−; 05 NZ−.
Clerk/business. Capt A v NZ 03, 1st int between
countries. Mgr A > 05 NZ. Asst mgr A > 08 BI.

WIGGLESWORTH, Henry John *England*
Thornes, Yorks.
b 1861; *d* 3.3.25 Leeds.
Back, 1-1-0-0.
1884 I+.
Warehouseman.

WIGHTMAN, Brian John ('Yeti') *England*
King Edward's Sch Birmingham, O Edwardians,
Loughborough Colls, UAU, Moseley,
Coventry, Rosslyn Pk, N Midlands.
b 23.9.36 Birmingham.
No 8, 5-1-1-3.
59 W−; 63 W+ I= NZ− A−.
Schoolmaster. E > 63 A, NZ. Emigrated to Can
64; played for Brit Columbia v NZ 67.

WILKINS, Dennis Thomas *England*
('Squire')
US Portsmouth, RN, Comb Servs, Roundhay,
Barbarians, Yorks.
b 26.12.24 Leeds.
Lock, 13-7-1-5.
51 W− I− F− S+; 52 SA− W− S+ I+ F+; 53
W+ I= F+ S+.
RN/marketing dir. Served WW2, Fleet Air Arm
pilot.

WILKINSON, Edgar *England*
Bradford, Yorks.
b 1863 Bradford; *d* 27.8.1896 Bradford.
Forward, 5-2-3-0 (2t).
1886 W+(1t) I+(1t) S=; 1887 W= S=.
His club, Bradford, helped form NU 1895.

WILKINSON, Harry ('Wilkie') *England*
Fettenhall Coll, Halifax, Yorks.
b 22.3.03.
Flanker, 4-2-0-2 (6 − 2t).
29 W+(2t) I− S−; 30 F+.
Co dir. Son of H.J.

WILKINSON, Harry James   *England*
Halifax, Yorks.
b 1864 Halifax; *d* 7.6.42 Halifax.
Forward, 1-1-0-0.
1889 NZN+.
Licensee/pattern dyer. Father of H. His club,
Halifax, helped form NU 1895.

WILKINSON, P.   *England*
Law Club.
Half-back, 1-1-0-0.
1872 S+.

WILKINSON, Richard W.   *Ireland*
Aravan Coll Bray, St Columba's Coll,
Wanderers.
b 24.3.15 Dublin.
Lock, 1-0-0-1.
47 A−.
Farmer.

WILKINSON, Robert Michael   *England*
St Albans Sch, Cambridge Univ, Bedford,
Barbarians.
b 25.7.51 Luton.
Lock, 6-1-0-5.
75 A−; 76 A+ W− S− I− F−.
Blue 71-3.

WILL, John George   *Scotland*
Merchant Taylors' Sch, OMT, Cambridge Univ.
b 2.9.1892; kia 25.3.17 Arras.
Wing, 7-2-0-5 (15 − 5t).
12 F+(1t) W−(1t) I−(1t) E+; 14 W− I− E−
(2t).
Blue 11-13. Lt, Leinster Rgt attached to RFC;
killed in air combat.

WILLCOCKS, T.J.   *England*
Buckfastleigh, Plymouth A, Devon.
Forward, 1-0-0-1.
02 W−.

WILLCOX, John Graham   *England*
Ratcliffe Coll, RMA Sandhurst, Fylde, The
Army, Oxford Univ, Harlequins, PUC,
Headingley, Malton, Lancs.
FB, 16-6-5-5 (17 − 4c 3p).
61 I− F=(1c) S+; 62 W= I+ F− S=(1p); 63
W+ I= F+(2p) S+(2c); 64 NZ− W= I−(1c)
F+ S−; BI > 62 SA 3-0-1-2.
Schoolmaster. Blue 59-62. Blue for boxing
(heavyweight) 60. Served in the Army 55-9.
Taught at Ampleforth Coll from 63. Sister
Sheila won European Horse Trials, Turin 57.

WILLIAM-POWLETT, Peveril   *England*
Barton Reibey Wallop KCB KCMG CBE DSO
Cordwalles Sch, RNC Osborne, RNC
Dartmouth, US Portsmouth, Blackheath, US
Devonport, Wanderers, RN, Hants.

b 5.3.1898 Abergavenny.
Prop, 1-1-0-0.
22 S+.
RN/colonial service. Joined RN at 17; reached
rank of Vice Adm. Polo for RN. Football for
RN Colls. Served WW1, Dardanelles & Battle
of Jutland. Served WW2; see C.C. Tanner.
Held many snr RN posts, in C in C S Atlantic 52-
4. KCB 53. Governor of S Rhodesia 54-9.
KCMG 59.

WILLIAMS, A.E.   *South Africa*
Griq W.
1-1-0-0.
10 BI+.

WILLIAMS, A.P.   *South Africa*
W Prov.
Wing, 2-2-0-0.
84 E+ E+.

WILLIAMS, Bleddyn Llewellyn   *Wales*
Rydal Sch, Cardiff, RAF, Barbarians.
b 22.2.23 Taff's Well.
FH/centre, 22-13-2-7 (21 − 7t).
47 E− S+(1t) F+ I+ A+; 48 E= S+(1t) F− I−
(1t); 49 E+ S−(1t) I−; 51 I= SA−(1t); 52 S+;
53 E− S+(2t) I+ F+ NZ+; 54 S+; 55 E+; BI >
50 NZ 3-0-1-2, A 2-2-0-0.
Co dir/steelworks official. Bro of Lloyd, one of 8
bros to play for Cardiff. Son Ashley also played
for Cardiff. Played in 3 Servs, 7 Victory ints.
Barbarians v A 48, v SA 52. Rec 185t for Cardiff
45-55, inc season rec 41 (48). Rugby corr
'Sunday People'.

WILLIAMS, Brinley   *Wales*
Bryncaerau, Llanelli.
b 3.4.1895 Llanelli.
Wing, 3-2-0-1 (12 − 4t).
20 S− F+(1t) I+(3t).
Steelworker. W's oldest surviving int. Batley RL
20, Leeds RL.

WILLIAMS, Bryan George   *New Zealand*
Mt Albert GS, Ponsonby, Auckland, N Island.
b 3.10.50 Auckland.
Wing/centre, 38-23-3-12 (71 − 10t 2c 1d 9p).
70 SA−(1t) SA+ SA−(1p) SA−(1t); 71 BI−
BI+(*1t) BI=; 72 A+(1t) A+(1t) A+(1t) W+
S+; 73 E+(1d) I= F− E−; 74 A+ A= A+; 74
I+; 75 S+(2t); 76 I+ SA−(1p) SA+ SA−(2p)
SA−(1p); 77 BI+(2c) BI−(3p) BI+ BI+ F−(1t
1p); 78 A+(1t) A+ A−; 78 I+r W+ E+ S+.
Barrister/solicitor. NZ's most capped wing (36
apps). 113 apps (rec 66t) for NZ. 14t NZ > 70 A
& SA. NZ > 72-3 BI,F & NAm, 74 A & Fj &
I,W & E, 76 SA (9t), 77 F (3 apps at FB), 78 BI.
Named 'Rugby Player of Decade' 80. Player-
coach Ponsonby. Bro Ken rep Auckland 68-9 &
NZ trial 68.* Record inc penalty t v BI 71.

WILLIAMS, Charles Derek *Wales*
Canton HS, Oxford Univ, Cardiff, Neath,
Barbarians.
b 28.11.24 Cardiff.
Flanker, 2-2-0-0 (3 − 1t).
55 F+; 56 F+(1t).
Co dir/licensee. Blue 45. Boxing blue. Chmn sel
Cardiff.

WILLIAMS, Christopher G. *England*
Gloucester, RAF.
FH, 1-0-0-1.
76 F−.
RAF.

WILLIAMS, Clifford *Wales*
Llangennech, RN, Llanelli, Cardiff, Bargoed.
b 20.4.1898 Llangennech; *d* 28.5.30 Cardiff.
Hooker, 2-0-0-2.
24 NZ−; 25 E−.
Miner/police. Served WW1, RN.

WILLIAMS, Clive *Wales*
Porthcawl Comp, Porthcawl, Aberavon,
Swansea.
b 2.11.48 Porthcawl.
Prop, 8-4-1-3.
77 E+ S+; 80 F+ E− S+ I− NZ−; 83 E=; BI
> 77 NZ; 80 SA 4-1-0-3.
Wales B v F 75, 76. Wales B > 83 Spain.

WILLIAMS, Cyril Stoate *England*
Truro Coll, Mill Hill Sch, Manchester Univ,
Manchester, Lancs.
b 17.11.1887 Stroud.
FB, 1-1-0-0.
10 F+.
Schoolmaster. Ldg ref & ckt umpire.

WILLIAMS, David Brynmor *Wales*
Cardigan GS, Cardiff Coll, Cardiff, Swansea,
Barbarians.
b 29.10.51 Cardigan.
SH, 3-1-0-2 (4 − 1t).
78 A−(1t); 81 E+ S−; BI > 77uncap NZ 3-1-0-
2.
Build soc branch mgr. Wales XV v Tonga 74. W
> 78 A. Wales B v F 76, 77. Wales B > 80 US,
Can. Barbarians > 76 Can. Welsh Schs high
jump champ. Runner-up in sprints, high jump
British Youth, British Schs champs. Bro
Gwynfor played for Cardiff, Cross Keys. Cardiff
RL 82 £15,000 fee. 1 Wales RL.

WILLIAMS, David M. *Australia*
Qld.
Flanker/no 8, 4-1-0-3.
13 NZ+; 14 NZ− NZ− NZ−.

WILLIAMS, David Owen *South Africa*
Diocesan Coll Rondebosch, W Prov.

b 16.6.13 Mowbray; *d* −.1.76.
Wing/FB, 8-6-0-2 (15 − 5t).
37 A+ A+(1t) NZ−(1t) NZ+ NZ+(1t); 38
BI+(2t) BI+ BI−.
Clerk. Of Welsh stock. SA's youngest tourist
(18yr 4mths when SAr > 31-2 BI).

WILLIAMS, Denzil *Wales*
Welsh Youth, Ebbw Vale, Vichy, Barbarians.
b 17.10.39 Trefil.
Prop, 36-19-5-12 (3 − 1t).
63 E− S+ I− F−; 64 E= S+ I+ F= SA−; 65
E+ S+ I+ F−; 66 E+ S+ I− A−; 67 F− E+
NZ−; 68 E=; 69 S+ I+(1t) F= E+ NZ− NZ−
A+; 70 SA= S+ E+ I−; 71 E+ S+ I+ F+; BI
> 66 A 2-2-0-0, NZ 3-0-0-3.
Steelworker. Wales XV v Fj 64. W > 64 SA; 69
NZ, A & Fj. Son Ian played for Tredegar,
Cardiff. Coach Rhymney RFC.

WILLIAMS, Edwin *Wales*
Neath.
b 14.10.1898 Cwmllynfell; *d* 31.1.83 Swansea.
SH/FH, 2-1-0-1.
24 NZ−; 25 F+.
Colliery fitter. Huddersfield RL 25.

WILLIAMS, Evan *Wales*
Eastern Sch Port Talbot, Aberavon.
b 18.6.06 Port Talbot; *d* 18.11.76 Leeds.
Centre, 2-0-0-2.
25 E− S−.
Blacksmith's striker/Civil Service. Leeds RL 25.
RL Cup Winners medals 32, 36. Served WW2,
RA. Awarded Imperial Services Medal.

WILLIAMS, Frank Llewellyn *Wales*
Cardiff HS, Brecon Coll, Cardiff, Wakefield,
Headingley, Yorks, Barbarians.
FH/centre, 14-8-1-5 (6 − 2t).
29 S+ F+ I=(1t); 30 E− S− I+ F+; 31 F+(1t)
I+ SA−; 32 E+ S+ I−; 33 I−.
Schoolmaster. Barbarians comm.

WILLIAMS, Gareth Powell *Wales*
('Sam')
Bridgend GS, Welsh SS, Cardiff Coll, Bridgend.
b 6.11.54 Merthyr Tydfil.
No 8/flanker, 5-2-0-3.
80 NZ−; 81 E+ S− A+; 82 I−; BIr/uncap > 80
SA.
Wales B v Arg 78, v F 78, 79, 81. Wales B > 80
US, Can. Uncapped when called up for BI > 80
SA while touring with Wales in NAm.

WILLIAMS, Gerald *Wales*
Heol Gam SMS, Welsh Youth, Bridgend,
Newport, Pontypridd, Glam Wdrs.
b 21.10.54 Swansea.
SH, 4-1-0-3.

81 I+ F−; 82 E−r S−.
Wales B v F 78, 81. Wales B > 80 US, Can.

WILLIAMS, Gerwyn *Wales*
Port Talbot SS, Devonport Servs, RN,
Loughborough Coll, London Welsh, Llanelli,
Barbarians.
 b 22.4.24 Glyncorrwg.
FB, 13-8-1-4.
50 I+ F+; 51 E+ S− I= F− SA−; 52 E+ S+ I+
F+; 53 NZ+; 54 E−.
PE dir. Barbarians v SA 52. Wales Schs ckt.
Coach Whitgift Sch, Croydon. Wrote 'Modern
Rugby', pub 64.

WILLIAMS, Graham Charles *New Zealand*
Rongotai Coll, NZ Jnrs, Wellington, N Island.
 b 26.1.45 Wellington.
Flanker, 5-5-0-0.
67 E+ W+ F+ S+; 68 A+.
Mechanic. NZ > 67 BI,F & C, 68 A & Fj (10t).
Rec 174 apps for Wellington 64-72.

WILLIAMS, Griff *Wales*
Aberavon Harlequins, Aberavon.
 b 30.6.07 Pontypridd.
Lock, 3-2-1-0.
36 E= S+ I+.
Building labourer/dry docker/steelworker.

WILLIAMS, Henry Raymond *Wales*
Llanelli GS, S Wales Borderers, St Luke's Coll,
Cardiff Coll, Felinfoel, Llanelli.
 b 13.11.27 Felinfoel.
Wing, 3-3-0-0 (3 − 1t).
54 S+(1t); 57 F+; 58 A+.
Schoolmaster. Coach Gwendraeth GS.

WILLIAMS, Johannes Gerhardus *South Africa*
N Transvaal.
 b 29.10.46 Johannesburg.
Lock, 13-7-2-4.
71 F+ F= A+ A+ A+; 72 E−; 74 BI− BI−
BI= F+ F+; 76 NZ+ NZ−.
Professor. On staff of Pretoria Univ..

WILLIAMS, John ('Jack') *Wales*
Blaina.
 b 1891 Blaina; d 6.12.65.
Prop, 7-5-0-2 (3 − 1t).
20 E+ S− F+ I+; 21 S− F+(1t) I+.
Colliery fireman. Full nickname Jack Williams
Punch.

WILLIAMS, John Edward *England*
Mill Hill Sch, The Army, Headingley, O
Millhillians, Harlequins, Sale, Barbarians,
London Cos, Mdx, Cheshire.
 b 31.1.32 Leeds.
SH, 9-3-1-5 (3 − 1t).
54 F−; 55 W− I= F− S+; 56 I+ S+(1t) F−; 65

W−; BI > 55 SA.
Bus agent. 9 yr gap between last 2 apps.

WILLIAMS, John Frederick *Wales*
Christ's Coll Brecon, Richmond, London
Welsh, Glam, Mdx, Barbarians.
 b 18.11.1882 Scathrog; d 28.8.11 Nigeria.
Forward, 4-3-0-1.
05 I+ NZ+; 06 S+ SA−; BT > 08 A, NZ.
Civil Service. Asst Resident Colonial Service
Nigeria where he died after contracting
blackwater fever.

WILLIAMS, John James *Wales*
Maesteg GS, Cardiff Coll, Bridgend, Llanelli,
Barbarians.
 b 1.4.48 Nantyffyllon.
Wing, 30-20-2-8 (48 − 12t).
73 F−r A+; 74 S+ I=(1t) F=(1t) E−; 75 F+
E+(1t) S− I+(1t) A+(3t); 76 E+ S+(1t) I+
F+(1t); 77 I+ F− E+ S+(1t); 78 E+ S+ I+(1t)
F+ A− A− NZ−; 79 S+ I+ F− E+(1t); BI >
74 SA 4-3-1-0; 77 NZ 3-1-0-2.
Schoolmaster/co dir. Wales B v Can 71, v F 72
(2). W > 73 Can; 75 Far East; 78 A. Wales XV v
J 73; Arg 76. Welsh XV v NZ 74. Rec 4t in series
BI v SA 74; also 6t BI v SW Dist 74, rec for BI in
SA. Barbarians v A 76. Barbarians > 76 Can.

WILLIAMS, John Lewis *Wales*
Cowbridge GS, Cardiff, Whitchurch, London
Welsh.
 b 3.1.1882 Whitchurch; kia 12.7.16 Mametz
Wood.
Wing, 17-15-0-2 (51 − 17t).
06 SA−; 07 E+(2t) S− I+(3t); 08 E+ S+(1t)
I+(2t) A+; 09 E+(1t) S+ F+(2t) I+; 10 I+(3t);
11 E+ S+(2t) F+(1t) I+; BT > 08 A, NZ.
Clerk Cardiff Coal Exchange. Served WW1,
Capt in Welch Rgt. Capt v F 11 because he
spoke French. Played in 14 consec victories 07-
11. 150t for Cardiff 03-14.

WILLIAMS, John Lewis *Australia*
Newington Coll, NSW.
 b 28.5.40.
Wing, 3-1-0-2 (3 − 1t).
63 SA− SA+(1t) SA−.
Clerk/commercial artist.

WILLIAMS, John Michael *England*
Rugby Sch, Cambridge Univ, Penzance-
Newlyn, Richmond, Barbarians, Cornwall.
 b 24.8.27.
Centre, 2-1-0-1.
51 I− S+.
Solicitor. Blue 49. Cornwall CCC.

WILLIAMS, John Peter Rhys *Wales*
Bridgend CS, Welsh SS, Millfield, St Mary's
Hosp, London Welsh, Bridgend, Barbarians.

b 2.3.49 Cardiff.
FB/flanker, 55-38-4-13 (36 − 6t 2c 3p)
69 S+ I+ F= E+ NZ− NZ− A+; 70 SA= S+
E+(1t 1c) I− F+(1c 2p); 71 E+(1p) S+ I+ F+;
72 E+(1t) S+ F+ NZ−; 73 E+ S− I+ F− A+;
74 S+ I= F=; 75 F+ E+ S− I+ A+; 76 E+(2t)
S+ I+ F+; 77 I+(1t) F+ E+(1t) S+; 78 E+ S+
I+ F+ A− A− NZ−; 79 S+ I+ F− E+; 80
NZ−; 81 E+ S−; BI > 71 A, NZ 4-2-1-1; 74 SA
4-3-1-0.
Orthopaedic surgeon. World's most capped FB
(62 inc 8 BI). W > 68 Arg; 69 NZ, A & Fj; 73
Can; 75 Far East; 78 A. Wales XV v J 73; Arg
76. Welsh XV v NZ 74. Barbarians v SA 70, NZ
73. Jnr Wimbledon champ 66, beating future
Davis Cup player David Lloyd.

WILLIAMS, Lloyd H.   *Wales*
Welsh Youth, Cardiff.
b 32 Taff's Well.
SH, 13-6-2-5.
57 S− I+ F+; 58 E= S+ I+ F−; 59 E+ S− I+;
61 F−; 62 E= S−.
Business rep. Bro of Bleddyn.

WILLIAMS, Mapson   *Wales*
Newport.
b 1895 Mackay, Queensland.
No 8, 1-1-0-0.
23 F+.

WILLIAMS, Oswald ('Ossie')   *Wales*
Coleshill Sch, Furnace, Welsh Guards, Llanelli,
Pontyberem, Felinfoel.
b 12.4.21 Llanelli.
Flanker, 7-3-1-3 (3 − 1p).
47 E− S+ A+; 48 E= S+ F−(1p) I−.
Steelworker. Cousin of Stanley.

WILLIAMS, Peter   *New Zealand*
Alhambra, Otago, S Island.
b 22.4.1884 Dunedin; *d* 30.8.76 Mosgiel.
Hooker, 1-1-0-0.
13 A+.
Farmer. NZ > 13 NAm. Selected > 14 A,
unable to travel.

WILLIAMS, Rhys Haydn   *Wales*
Ystalyfera GS, UC Cardiff, Llanelli, RAF,
Barbarians.
b 14.7.30 Cwmllynfell.
Lock, 23-14-2-7 (3 − 1t)
54 I+ F+ S+(1t); 55 S− I+ F+; 56 E+ S+ I−;
57 E= S− I+ F+; 58 A+ E= S+ I+ F−; 59 E+
S− I+ F−; 60 E−; BI > 55 SA 4-2-0-2; 59 A 2-
2-0-0, NZ 4-1-0-3.
Dir of Education. Barbarians > 57 Can 57; 58
SA. Mgr Wales B > 83 Spain. Barbarians
comm. Chmn WRU sel 85-6.

WILLIAMS, Richard Davies   *Wales*
Garnons
Magdalen Coll Sch, Cambridge Univ, RMC
Sandhurst, Brecon, Newport.
b 15.6.1856 Llowes, Radnorshire; kia 27.9.15
Loos.
Forward, 1-0-0-1.
1881 E−.
The Army. Served WW1, Lt Col in R Fusiliers.
Football for W.

WILLIAMS, Robert F.   *Wales*
Cardiff.
FB, 4-2-0-2.
12 SA−; 13 E− S+; 14 I+.
Clerk Cardiff Docks. Played minus three fingers
on one hand and partly paralysed ones on the
other.

WILLIAMS, S.G.   *England*
Devonport A, Devon.
Forward, 7-2-0-5 (6 − 2t).
02 W− I+(1t) S+(1t); 03 I− S−; 07 I− S−.
House decorator.

WILLIAMS, Stanley   *Wales*
Felinfoel, Llanelli.
b 1914 Llanelli; *d* 21.11.67 Llanelli.
Lock, 6-4-0-2.
47 E− S+ F+ I+; 48 S+ F−.
Steelworker/council worker. Cousin of Oswald.

WILLIAMS, Stanley Horatio   *England*
DSO
Newport Intermed Sch, Newport, Monmouth.
b 2.11.1886 Rogerstone, Gwent; *d* 30.4.36 at
sea.
FB, 4-2-0-2.
11 W− F+ I− S+; BTuncap > 10 SA 3-1-0-2.
Mines mgr. Reserve for W 10-11. Inj 3rd Test BI
v SA, carried off. Served WW1, Capt RFA.
Twice mentioned in despatches & DSO 17. Mgr
Ebbw Vale Iron Ore Mines Co. Lost overboard
when returning by sea from SAm 36.

WILLIAMS, Stephen Andrew   *Australia*
St Joseph's Coll, Australian Schs, Manly,
Sydney, NSW.
b 29.7.58.
Lock, 28-17-1-10 (4 − 1t).
80 Fj+ NZ+ NZ−; 81 F+ F+; 82 E− NZ−
NZ+ NZ−; 83 US+ Arg−r Arg+ NZ− It+(1t)
F= F−; 84 NZ+ NZ− NZ− E+ I+ W+ S+; 85
C+ C+ NZ− Fj+ Fj+.
Club administrator/stock market broker. 6ft 6in,
16st 12lb. A > 80 Fj; 81-2 & 84 BI; 82 NZ; 83 It
& F.

WILLIAMS, Sydney Arthur   *Wales*
Aberavon, The Army..
b 17.4.18 Aberavon; *d* 28.8.76.

Wing, 3-2-0-1.
39 E− S+ I+.
Cafe proprietor. Played in 7 Servs ints. Salford
RL 39.

WILLIAMS, Thomas   *Wales*
Pontypridd, Cardiff, Llwynypia.
b 1860 Llwynypia; d 4.2.13 Llwynypia.
Forward, 1-1-0-0.
1882 I+.
Solicitor. IB rep 01-8. Ref E v I 04. WRU vice-
pres, sel. Uncle of Willie Llewellyn.

WILLIAMS, T.   *Wales*
Swansea.
Forward, 2-1-0-1.
1888 S+ I−.

WILLIAMS, Tom   *Wales*
Swansea.
b 1887 Dunvant; d 9.9.27 Swansea.
Flanker, 6-4-0-2 (3 − 1t).
12 I−; 13 F+(1t); 14 E− S+ F+ I+.
Licensee. Mem of 'Terrible Eight'. Broke arm
W v I 12, stayed on. Served WW1, Capt in RE.
Elected to Gower RDC 25.

WILLIAMS, Trevor ('Tabor')   *Wales*
Cross Keys.
Lock/prop, 8-4-1-3.
35 S+ I− NZ+; 36 E= S+ I+; 37 S− I−.

WILLIAMS, Tudor   *Wales*
Swansea.
b c1892; d 24 Merthyr.
SH, 1-1-0-0.
21 F+.

WILLIAMS, Walter P.J.   *Wales*
Neath.
b 14.11.43; d −.3.85 Neath.
Prop, 2-0-2-0.
74 I= F=.
Stockbreeder/farmer. Took own life.

WILLIAMS, William A.   *Wales*
Garndiffaith, Newport.
SH, 3-2-0-1.
52 I+ F+; 53 E−.

WILLIAMS, William Arthur   *Wales*
Crumlin, Cross Keys.
b 29.12.05 Crumlin; d 4.11.73 Manchester.
Flanker, 4-1-0-3.
27 E− S− F+ I−.
Miner/licensee. Salford RL 27. 2 GB RL.

WILLIAMS, William Edward   *Wales*
Osborne
St John's Sch Leatherhead, Cardiff, London
Welsh.

b 15.12.1866; d 22.6.45 Chepstow.
Forward, 5-2-0-3.
1887 S− I+; 1889 S−; 1890 S− E+.
Inj in club match ended career 1890.

WILLIAMS, William Henry   *Wales*
('Buller')
Pontymister R, London Welsh.
b 1873 Pontlottyn; d 9.1.36 Barry Dock.
Forward, 4-4-0-0 (6 − 2t).
1900 E+ S+(1t) I+; 01 E+(1t).
Monumental mason & sculptor. Ckt for Glam
CCC.

WILLIAMS, William Leslie   *Wales*
Thomas
Devonport Servs, RN, Cardiff Tg Coll, Llanelli,
Cardiff.
b 21 Mynyddygarreg.
Wing/centre, 7-5-0-2 (9 − 3t).
47 E− S+(1t) F+ I+ A+; 48 I−; 49 E+(2t).
PE teacher. Hunslet RL 49.

WILLIAMS, William Owen   *Wales*
Gooding ('Stoker')
Swansea, Devonport Servs, RN Barbarians.
b −.11.29 Gower.
Prop, 22-16-0-6 (3 − 1t).
51 F− SA−; 52 E+ S+ I+ F+; 53 E− S+ I+
F+ NZ+; 54 E− I+ F+(1t) S+; 55 E+ S− I+
F+; 56 E+ S+ I−; BI > 55 SA 4-2-0-2.
Steelworker.

WILLIAMSON, Frederick   *Ireland*
William
Mountjoy Coll Dublin, Dolphin.
b 25.7.05 Wexford.
FB, 3-2-0-1.
30 E+ S+ W−.
Bank employee/holiday camp mgr.

WILLIAMSON, Rupert Henry   *England*
St Andrew's Coll Grahamstown SA, Oxford
Univ, Blackheath, Barbarians.
b 22.11.1886; d 16.3.46.
SH, 5-2-0-3 (6 − 2t).
08 W−(1t) I+(1t) S−; 09 A− F+.
Mining mgr in Transvaal 10-46. Rhodes
Scholar. Blue 06-8. Served WW1 in Africa.

WILLIMENT, Michael   *New Zealand*
Rongotai Coll, Univ, Wellington, NZ Univs, N
Island.
b 25.2.40 Wellington.
FB, 9-8-0-1 (70 − 1t 17c 11p).
64 A+(1c 2p); 65 SA+ SA+(2c) SA−(2c 1p);
66 BI+(1t 1c 2p) BI+(2c 1p) BI+(2c 2p)
BI+(3c 1p); 67 A+(4c 2p).
Schoolmaster/dir travel agency. 37 pts (4 apps) v
BI 66. Brabin Cup ckter.

WILLIS, William Rex　　　　　　　*Wales*
Cardiff, Barbarians.
b 25.10.24 Ystrad.
SH, 21-15-1-5.
50 E+ S+ I+ F+; 51 E+ S− I= F− SA−; 52
E+ S+; 53 S+ NZ+; 54 E− I+ F+ S+; 55 E+
S− I+ F+; BI > 50 NZ 1-0-0-1, A 2-2-0-0.
Cinema proprietor/business. Barbarians comm.

WILLIS, W.J.　　　　　　　　　*Ireland*
Lansdowne.
Back, 1-0-0-1.
1879 E−.

WILLOCKS, Charles　　　　*New Zealand*
S Otago HS, Clutha, Otago, S Island.
b 28.6.19 Balclutha.
Lock, 5-2-0-3.
46 A+ A+; 49 SA− SA− SA−.
Farmer. NZ > 47 A, 49 SA.

WILSON, Alfred William　　　　*Scotland*
Dollar Acad, Dunfermline.
Centre/FB, 3-2-0-1.
31 F+ I− E+.
Quarry master. Pres SRU 72-3.

WILSON, Arthur James　　　　　*England*
Glenalmond Sch, Northern, Camborne,
Camborne Sch of Mines, Camborne Students,
Cornwall.
b 29.12.1886; kia 1.7.17 Flanders.
Forward, 1-1-0-0.
09 I+.
Mines mgr/coffee planter. Olympic silver medal
for rugby, GB (Cornwall) v A 08. Mining in W
Africa; coffee planter in India. Pte in R Fusiliers
when kia.

WILSON, Bevan John　　　　　*Australia*
NSW.
b 20.9.27.
Prop, 2-2-0-0
49 NZ+ NZ+.
Schoolmaster. RL.

WILSON, Bevan William　　　*New Zealand*
Dunstan HS, Matakanui, NZ Jnrs, Otago, S
Island.
b 22.3.56 Dunstan.
FB, 8-5-0-3 (55 − 5c 15p).
77 BI+(1c 2p) BI+(2p); 78 A+(3p) A+(2c 1p)
A−; 79 F+(1c 3p) F−(1c 3p) A−(1p).
Farmer. NZ > 77 F, 79 A. Father Bill rep Otago
51-7.

WILSON, Charles Edward　　　　*England*
Dover Coll, Blackheath, The Army, Surrey.
b 2.6.1871 Fermoy, Co Cork; kia 17.9.14 River
Aisne, F.

Forward, 1-0-0-1.
1898 I−
The Army. Served in Boer War, Queen's R W
Surrey Rgt; mentioned in despatches. Fought at
relief of Ladysmith. Served in India. Capt when
kia. Légion d'Honneur.

WILSON, Charles Plumpton　　　*England*
Uppingham Sch, Marlborough Coll, Cambridge
Univ, Marlborough Nomads.
b 12.5.1859 Roydon, Norfolk; *d* 9.3.38.
Forward, 1-1-0-0.
1881 W+.
HM. Blue 1877-80. Ckt blue 1880-1. Cycling
blue 1879. Football for E (1883); Corinthian
Casuals; Hendon AFC.

WILSON, Charles Roy ('Chilla')　　*Australia*
Brisbane GS, Qld Univ, Qld, London Scottish
(E), Blackheath (E).
b 4.5.31.
Flanker/no 8, 4-1-0-3.
57 NZ−; 58 NZ− NZ+ NZ−.
Gynaecologist. Capt A > 58 NZ. Mgr A > 82
NZ; 83 It & F; 84 BI.

WILSON, Douglas Dawson　　　*New Zealand*
Christchurch Boys' HS, HSOB, Canterbury,
Oriental, Wellington, S Island.
b 30.1.31 Wanganui.
2nd five-eighth, 2-2-0-0.
54 E+ S+.
Insurance clerk/menswear retailer. NZ > 53-4
BI,F & NAm. Ckt for Canterbury.

WILSON, Dyson Stayt ('Tug')　　　*England*
Rydal Sch, King Edward VII GS Stafford, Met
Police, Harlequins, London Cos, Mdx.
b 7.10.26 Wilderness, SA.
Flanker, 8-5-0-3 (12 − 4t).
53 F+; 54 W+ NZ− I+(1t) S+(2t) F−(1t); 55
F− S+.
Police. To UK when 8. Returned to SA after int
career finished.

WILSON, Francis　　　　　　　*Ireland*
Boys Model Sch Belfast, St Luke's Coll Exeter,
CIYMS.
b 1.9.52 Belfast.
FB, 3-0-0-3.
77 W− E− S−.
Schoolmaster.

WILSON, George R.　　　　　　*Scotland*
Royal HS, Royal HSFP.
b 1868; *d* 08.
Centre/wing, 5-3-1-1.
1886 E=; 1890 W+ I+ E−; 1891 I+.

WILSON, Graham Alexander *Scotland*
Oundle Sch, Oxford Univ, Barbarians.
b 23.11.22.
Lock, 3-2-0-1 (3 − 1p).
49 F+ W+ E−(1p).
Blue 46-8.

WILSON, Guy Summerfield *England*
Tyldesley, Manchester, Birkenhead Pk,
Barbarians, Lancs.
b 30.8.07; *d* 8.7.79.
Wing, 2-1-0-1 (4 − 2c).
29 W+(1c) I−(1c); BT > 27 Arg.
Insurance broker.

WILSON, Hector William *New Zealand*
Ida Valley, Otago, S Island.
b 27.1.24 Beaumont.
Prop, 5-4-0-1 (3 − 1t).
49 A−; 50 BI+(1t); 51 A+ A+ A+.
Public Works employee. NZ > 51 A.

WILSON, Hugh Gilmer *Ireland*
Coleraine AI, RBAI, Dollar Acad, Glasgow
Univ, Malone.
b 11.4.1879; *d* 13.1.41.
Forward, 18-6-0-12.
05 E+ S+ W− NZ−; 06 E+ S− W+ SA−; 07
E+ S− W−; 08 E− S+ W−; 09 E− S− W−; 10
W−.
Medicine. Served WW1, RAMC.

WILSON, John Howard *Scotland*
George Watson's Coll, Watsonians.
b 3.3.30 Edinburgh.
Prop, 1-0-0-1.
53 I−.
Co dir.

WILSON, John Skinner *Scotland*
HMS Britannia, US Portsmouth, RN, London
Scottish.
b 10.3.1884 Trinidad; kia 31.5.16 Jutland.
Forward, 2-0-0-2.
08 I−; 09 W−.
RN. Lt Cdr on HMS 'Indefatigable' when sunk
off Jutland.

WILSON, J.S. CBE *Scotland*
Dundee HS, St Andrew's Univ, Barbarians.
Flanker/no 8, 5-2-0-3.
31 F+ W− I− E+; 32 E−.
Medicine.

WILSON, Kenneth James ('Tug') *England*
KGS Grantham, Kesteven, Cheltenham,
Gloucester, RAF, Comb Servs, Glos.
b 25.11.38 Newark.
Prop, 1-1-0-0.
63 F+.

RAF PT instructor/bus controller. RAF
heavywt boxing champ. Oldham RL, later capt.

WILSON, Lionel Geoffrey *South Africa*
('Speedy')
Wynberg Boys HS, False Bay, Hamiltons,
Villagers, W Prov.
b 25.5.33 Cape Town.
FB, 27-14-3-10 (6 − 1d 1p).
60 NZ= NZ+; 60-1 W+ I+ E+ F=; 61 I+ A+
A+(1p); 62 BI= BI+ BI+ BI+; 63 A+ A− A−
A+; 64 W+(1d) F−; 65 I− S− A− A− NZ−
NZ− NZ+ NZ−.
Assurance co mgr/insurance consultant. SA's
most capped FB. SA > 60-1 BI, F. 60 apps W
Prov. 17 yrs in snr rugby 50-66. Chmn Villagers.
W Prov Under 20s coach & W Prov comm.
SARB coaching panel. Lived 7 yrs NZ 80-6;
actively involved in coaching with Manawatu &
NZRU. Radio, newspaper rugby commentator.

WILSON, Nathaniel Arthur *New Zealand*
('Ranji')
Athletic, Wellington, Comb Servs, N Island.
b 18.5.1886 Christchurch; *d* 11.8.53 Lower
Hutt.
Lock/flanker, 10-7-1-2 (6 − 2t).
08 AW+ AW=; 10 A+(1t) A− A+; 13 A+(1t)
A−; 14 A+ A+ A+.
NZ > 10 & 14 A. Served WW1; rep Comb Servs
in King's Cup. Barred from > 19 SA because he
was classed as 'coloured' with English/West
Indian parentage. Selector for Wellington 22-6
& NZ 24-5. Pres Athletic 45-6. Bros William &
Sim rep Wellington.

WILSON, Norman Leslie *New Zealand*
Wairarapa Coll, Zingari-Richmond, Otago, S
Island.
b 13.12.23 Masterton.
Hooker, 3-3-0-0 (3 − 1t).
51 A+ A+(1t) A+.
Schoolmaster/oil co mgr. NZ > 49 SA, 51 A (pl
in 12 out of 13 matches). Coached various clubs.
TV commentaries since 72.

WILSON, Richard George *New Zealand*
Cathedral GS, St Andrew's Coll, Christchurch,
NZ Colts, NZ Jnrs, Canterbury, S Island.
b 19.5.53 Leeston.
FB, 2-1-0-0 (10 − 2c 2p).
79 S+(2c) E+(2p).
Sports store mgr. 272 pts (25 apps) for NZ. NZ
> 76 Arg & Uruguay (80 pts), 78r BI, 79 S,E &
It, 80 A & Fj. NZ (2) v Arg 79. Father George
rep Canterbury 49.

WILSON, Robert Little *Scotland*
Gala Acad, Gala, Barbarians.
b 1.7.26.
Prop, 8-1-0-7.

51 F− W+ I− E− SA−; 53 F− W− E−.
Motor engr.

WILSON, Roger Parker CIE   *England*
Liverpool Coll, Liverpool OB, Liverpool Univ,
Bart's Hosp, Lancs.
b 13.5.1870; *d* 12.12.43.
Forward, 3-2-0-1 (2 − 2t).
1891 W+ I+(2t) S−.
Medicine/Indian Army/prof of surgery.
Superintendent Dist & Central Jails in India 03-13.

WILSON, Ronald   *Scotland*
Fettes Coll, Brunel Univ, London Scottish.
b 1.7.54 Teddington, Mdx.
FH, 9-4-0-5 (3 − 1d).
76 E+ I+(1d); 77 E− I+ F−; 78 I− F−; 81 R+;
83 I−.
Building industry. Scottish XV v J 76, 77.

WILSON, R.W.   *Scotland*
Clifton Coll, W of Scotland.
b 4.2.1854; *d* 6.7.11.
Forward, 2-0-1-1.
1873 E=; 1874 E−.
Farmer. Moved to Brisbane.

WILSON, Stewart   *Scotland*
Pinner CGS, Oxford Univ, London Scottish,
Barbarians.
b 22.10.42.
FB, 22-8-3-11 (68 − 10c 16p).
64 F+(2c) NZ= W− I+(2p) E+(3c); 65 W−
(2p) I−(1p) E= SA+(1c); 66 F= W−(1p)
I+(1c) A+(1c 1p); 67 F+(2p) W+(1c) I−(1p)
E−(1c 2p) NZ−; 68 F−(1p) W− I−(2p) E−
(1p); BI > 66 A 1-1-0-0 & NZ 4-0-0-4.
ICI. Blue 63-4. Most c for BI in an int, 5 v A 66.

WILSON, Stuart Sinclair   *New Zealand*
Wairarapa Coll, Wellington Coll OB, NZ Colts,
Wellington, N Island.
b 22.7.53 Gore.
Wing/centre, 34-25-1-8 (76 − 19t).
77 F− F+(1t); 78 A+ A+(1t) A−(1t) I+
W+(1t) E+ S+; 79 F+(1t) F−(1t) A− S+(1t)
E+; 80 A− W+; 81 S+(1t) S+(3t) SA+(1t)
SA− SA+(1t) R+ F+(1t) F+(1t); 82 A+ A−
A+; 83 BI+ BI+ BI+(1t) BI+(3t) A+ S= E−.
Freezing co marketing rep. NZ's most t (19) in
Tests. NZ > 76 Arg & Uruguay, 77 F, 78 BI, 79
A, 79 E,S & It, 80 A & Fj; NAm & W, 81 R &
F, 83 A; S & E (capt; pl in all 8 matches). Wrote
(with Bernie Fraser) 'Ebony & Ivory. The Stu
Wilson, Bernie Fraser Story' pub 84.

WILSON, Vayro William DSC   *Australia*
Gympic GS, Brisbane Univ, Qld.
b 12; *d* 62.
Lock/prop, 5-0-0-5.

37 SA− SA−; 38 NZ− NZ− NZ−.
Schoolmaster. Capt A > 39 BI − tour
abandoned because of outbreak WW2.

WILSON, Walter Carandini CBE   *England*
DSO MC
Tonbridge Sch, US Portsmouth, The Army,
Richmond, Barbarians.
b 22.6.1885; *d* 12.4.68.
Wing, 2-0-0-2.
07 I− S−.
The Army/RAF. Served WW1, Leics Rgt. MC
14; wounded; mentioned in despatches 3 times;
DSO 15. Retired 32. Joined RAF 39; retired as
Group Capt 44. BOAC 44-5. Administrative dir
Greyhound Racing Assoc.

WILSON, W.H.   *Ireland*
Cheltenham Coll, Trin Coll Dublin, Bray.
b 25.11.1852; *d* 10.2.31 London.
Forward, 2-0-0-2.
1877 E− S−.
Stockbroker.

WILTSHIRE, Maxwell L.   *Wales*
Aberavon.
b 39 Sydney, A.
Lock, 4-1-1-2.
67 NZ−; 68 E= S+ F−.
Oil process worker.

WINDON, Colin James   *Australia*
Sydney GS, Brothers, NSW.
b 8.11.21.
Flanker/lock/no 8, 20-8-1-11 (33 − 11t).
46 NZ− NZ−; 47 NZ− S+ I+(1t) W−; 48
E+(2t) F−; 49 M−(1t) M=(1t) M+(1t)
NZ+(1t) NZ+(1t); 51 NZ− NZ− NZ−; 52 Fj+
Fj−(1t) NZ+(1t) NZ−(1t).
Traveller. Bro of Keith.

WINDON, Keith Stanley   *Australia*
NSW.
b 2.10.17.
Prop, 3-0-0-3.
37 SA− SA−; 46 M−.
Co dir. Bro of Colin. Pl either side WW2 − 9 yrs
between 2nd & 3rd cap.

WINDSOR, Robert William ('The   *Wales*
Duke')
Brynglas SMS, Cross Keys, Cardiff, Pontypool,
Mon, Barbarians.
b 31.1.48 Newport.
Hooker, 28-19-2-7 (3 − 1t).
73 A+(1t); 74 S+ I= F= E−; 75 F+ E+ S− I+
A+; 76 E+ S+ I+ F+; 77 I+ F− E+ S+; 78
E+ S+ I+ F+ A− A− NZ−; 79 S+ I+ F−; BI
> 74 SA 4-3-1-0; 77 NZ 1-0-0-1.
Steelworker. Wales B v F 72, 73. W > 73 Can;
75 Far East; 78 A. Wales XV v J 73; Arg 76; R

79. Welsh XV v NZ 74. Barbarians v NZ 74. Member of legendary Pontypool Front Row. 1st class career ended by slipped disc.

WINDSOR, John Clement　　　*Australia*
St Joseph's Coll, Brisbane Univ, Qld.
b 2.2.23.
FB, 1-0-0-1.
47 NZ−.
Medicine.

WINDSOR-LEWIS, Geoffrey　　　*Wales*
The Leys Sch, Cambridge Univ, Richmond, Barbarians.
b 7.4.36 Cambridge.
Centre, 2-1-0-1.
60 E− S+.
Estate agent. Blue 56-8. Son of Windsor Hopkin Lewis. Sec Barbarians. Asst mgr Barbarians > 69 SA, 76 Can.

WINFIELD, Herbert Benjamin　　　*Wales*
Cardiff, London Welsh.
b 1879 Nottingham; *d* 21.9.19 Porthcawl.
FB, 15-11-1-3 (50 − 14c 6p 1gm).
03 I+; 04 E=(2c 1gm) S+(3c 1p) I−; 05 NZ+; 06 E+(2c) S+ I−; 07 S−(1p) I+(2c 1p); 08 E+(2c 1p) S+ F+(2c 1p) I+(1c) A+(1p).
Laundry owner. Served WW1, Cardiff City Batn. Business partner with bro in law, E. Gwyn Nicholls. Killed falling off motorcycle.

WINMILL, Stanley ('Docker')　　　*Wales*
Cross Keys, Mon.
b 1889 Bedwellty; *d* −.40 Caerleon.
Prop, 4-2-0-2.
21 E− S− F+ I+.
Miner. Killed in accident at Nine Point Colliery. Mem of stay-down strike at Nine Point Colliery, 35.

WINN, Christopher Elliott　　　*England*
KCS Wimbledon, Oxford Univ, Rosslyn Pk, Barbarians, London Cos, Surrey, Sussex.
b 13.11.26 Beckenham.
Wing, 8-5-0-3 (9 − 3t).
52 SA−(1t) W− S+(1t) I+ F+; 54 W+(1t) S+ F−.
Sales mgr. Blue 50. Ckt blue − 38 apps OUCC 48-51; 15 apps Sussex CCC 48-52; 2 apps MCC 59-61. Married 55, Valerie Ball, Olympic athlete, ex-world rec holder for 880y & daughter of Sir Nigel Ball.

WINNING, Keith Charles ('Arch')　　　*Australia*
Brisbane GS, Qld.
b 2.2.28 Maleny, Qld.
No 8, 1-0-0-1.
51 NZ−.
Man dir chemical co. Capt A on only app.

WINTERBOTTOM, Peter James　　　*England*
Rossall Sch, E Colts, Seale Hayne Agric Coll, Exeter, Headingley.
b 31.5.60 Leeds.
Flanker, 19-6-2-11.
82 A+ S= I− F+ W+; 83 F− W= S− I− NZ+; 84 S− F− W− SA− SA−; 86 W+ S− I+ F−;
BI > 83 NZ 4-0-0-4.
Farmer. England B v F 81. E > 82 US, Can. England XV v Can 83. Played prov rugby in NZ; bro Michael played for Poverty Bay (NZ) v E 85.

WINTLE, Trevor Clifford　　　*England*
Lydney GS, Cambridge Univ, Rosslyn Pk, St Mary's Hosp, Northampton, Barbarians, Glos, Mdx, E Midlands.
b 10.1.40.
SH, 5-2-0-3.
66 S−; 69 I− F+ S+ W−.
Medicine. Blue 60-1.

WITHERS, Henry Hastings　　　*Ireland*
Cavendish ('Hal') DSO
Cheltenham Coll, RMA Sandhurst, The Army, Blackheath.
b 11.10.04; *d* 6.9.48.
No 8, 5-2-0-3.
31 F− E+ S+ W− SA−.
The Army. Served WW2, Lt Col RE.

WODEHOUSE, Norman　　　*England*
Atherton CB
HMS Britannia, US Portsmouth, RN, Barbarians, Hants.
b 18.5.1887 Notts; kia c4.9.41 at sea.
Forward, 14-10-0-4 (6 − 2t).
10 F+; 11 W− F+(1t) I− S+(1t); 12 W+ I+ S− F+; 13 SA− W+ F+ I+ S+.
RN. Served WW1, Lt. R Humane Soc silver medal for saving life 15. CB 39. ADC to HM King George VI. Served WW2; missing presumed drowned when in command of an Atlantic convoy having been recalled from retired list.

WOGAN, Lawrence William　　　*Australia*
Glebe, Glebe-Balmain, E Suburbs, NSW.
b 18.9.1890 Hokitika, NZ; *d* −.8.79 Sydney.
Centre, 6-1-0-5 (3 − 1t).
13 NZ− NZ− NZ+; 14 NZ− NZ− NZ−(1t).
A > 12 US.

WOLFE, E.J.　　　*Ireland*
Armagh.
b −; *d* −.2.33.
Centre, 1-0-1-0.
1882 E=.
Vicar of St John's Guernsey.

440

WOLFE, Thomas Neil   *New Zealand*
New Plymouth Boys' HS, NZ Colts, Univ, NZ
Univs, Wellington, Star, Taranaki, N Island.
b 20.10.41 New Plymouth.
1st/2nd five-eighth, 6-5-1-0.
61 F+ F+ F+; 62 A+ A=; 63 E+.
Soft drink co man dir. NZ > 62 A, 68 A & Fj.

WOLFF, Jean-Paul   *France*
Béziers.
b 61.
Lock/prop, 4-1-0-3.
80 SA− R−; 81 A−; 82 E+.
F > 80 SA.

WOLMARANS, Barend Johannes   *South Africa*
Oudtshoorn Sch, Teachers' Coll Wellington,
Boland, Jnr Springboks, SA Univs, SA Colls,
Gazelles, UOFS, OFS.
b 22.3.53 Oudtshoorn.
SH, 1-1-0-0 (4 − 1t).
77 Wd+(1t).
Schoolmaster. SA > 81 NZ, US. Teaches at
Grey Coll..

WOOD, Albert   *England*
Halifax.
Forward, 1-1-0-0.
1884 I+.
Emigrated A 1884.

WOOD, Alfred Ernest   *England*
Gloucester, Cheltenham.
b c1882 Bristol; *d* 15.2.63 Oldham.
FB, 3-2-0-1 (8 − 4c).
08 F+ W−(2c) I+(2c).
Engr's fitter. Oldham RL. Gave E cap to
employers, AV Roe (Aircraft) Ltd on
retirement. NB: the histories of OURFC &
RFU wrongly identified him with Alan Eustace
Wood, a blue 04 and a non-int.

WOOD, Alexander Thomson   *Scotland*
Royal HS, Royal HSFP.
b 30.4.1848 Fetteresso, Kincardine; *d* 26.10.05
Stonehaven.
Forward, 3-0-2-1.
1873 E=; 1874 E−; 1875 E=.

WOOD, Benjamin Gordon   *Ireland*
Malison
Crescent Coll, Garryowen, Barbarians.
b 20.6.31 Limerick; *d* 18.5.82 Limerick.
Prop, 29-10-0-19 (3 − 1t).
54 E− S+; 56 F− E− S+ W+; 57 F+ E− S+
W−; 58 A+ E− S+ W− F−; 59 E− S+ W−
F+; 60 E− S−(1t) W− F− SA−; 61 E+ S−
W− F− SA−; BI > 59 A, NZ 2-0-0-2.
Insurance inspector/licensee.

WOOD, Frederick   *Australia*
NSW.
b 23.1.1884 Staffs, E; *d* −.7.23.
SH, 12-2-1-9 (3 − 1t).
07 NZ− NZ− NZ=(1t); 10 NZ− NZ+ NZ−;
13 NZ− NZ− NZ+; 14 NZ− NZ− NZ−.
Clerk.

WOOD, George   *Scotland*
St Peter's Sch Gala, Gala.
b 19.4.05 Galashiels.
Wing, 5-0-0-5 (3 − 1t).
31 W− I−; 32 W− I−(1t) E−.

WOOD, George Harold   *Ireland*
Portora RS, Trin Coll Dublin.
b 6.9.1891; *d* −.2.80 Ipswich, Suffolk.
Wing/centre, 2-1-0-1 (3 − 1t).
13 W−; 14 F+(1t).
Medicine. Served WW1, RAMC.

WOOD, George William   *England*
('Pedlar')
Melbourne Rd Sch Leicester, Melbourne Rd
OB, Leicester, Nuneaton, Midland Cos, Leics.
b 5.2.1886; *d* 12.6.69 Leicester.
SH, 1-1-0-0.
14 W+.

WOOD, Maurice Edwin   *New Zealand*
Pashiatua, Bush, Woodville, Napier, Hawkes
Bay, Wellington, Christchurch, Canterbury,
Ponsonby, Auckland, S Island.
b 9.10.1876 Waipawa; *d* 9.8.56 Paraparaumu.
2nd five-eighth, 2-2-0-0.
03 A+; 04 BT+.
Loan co branch mgr. NZ long jump champ 04
(best 19ft 7 1/2in). Hawkes Bay ckt.

WOOD, Robert   *England*
Liversedge, Yorks.
b c1873; *d* −.
Half-back, 1-0-0-1.
1894 I−.
Licensee. Turned RL when his club,
Liversedge, helped form NU 1895.

WOOD, Robert Dudley   *England*
Liverpool OB, Barbarians, Lancs.
b 1873 Liverpool.
Forward, 3-0-0-3.
01 I−; 03 W− I−.

WOOD, Robert Norman   *Australia*
Qld.
b 48.
Lock, 1-1-0-0.
72 Fj+.
A > 69 SA; 72 NZ.

WOODBURN, J.C. *Scotland*
Kelvinside Acad, Kelvinside Academicals.
Wing, 1-1-0-0.
1892 I+.

WOODGATE, Edmund Elliot *England*
Dartmouth SMS, Kingswear, Paignton,
Barbarians, Devon.
b 21.1.22.
Prop, 1-0-0-1.
52 W−.
Mechanical foreman steelworks. Chepstow RFC
comm.

WOODHEAD, Ernest *England*
Huddersfield Coll, Edinburgh Univ, Dublin
Univ, Huddersfield.
b 2.2.1857 Huddersfield; *d* 10.6.44.
Forward, 1-1-0-0.
1880 I+.
Newspaper dir. Won Scottish Univs 440y title
for 3 yrs. Made only app for E as a late r v I
1880. A student in Dublin, he was called into
team because one of the E forwards was
suffering from sea sickness after ferry crossing.
Editor & chmn 'Huddersfield Examiner',
newspaper founded by his father.

WOODMAN, Frederick Akehurst *New Zealand*
Northland Coll, Ohaewai, NZ Jnrs, N
Auckland, NZ Maoris.
b 10.2.58 Kaikohe.
Wing, 3-2-0-1.
81 SA+ SA− F+.
Electrician. NZ v Fj 80. NZ > 80 NAm & W, 81
R & F. Bro T.B.K. pl for NZ Maoris & NZ > 84
A.

WOODROW, Alexander Norrie *Scotland*
Glasgow Acad, Merchiston Castle Sch, Glasgow
Academicals.
b 1867; *d* 26.2.16.
Wing, 3-2-1-0 (2c).
1887 I+ W+(2c) E=.

WOODRUFF, Charles Garfield *England*
('Peter')
Newport HS, London Civil Service, Civil
Service, Harlequins, Cheltenham, Barbarians,
London Cos, Kent, Glos.
b 30.10.20.
Wing, 4-1-0-3.
51 W− I− F− S+.
Air Ministry. Served WW2, navigator RAF.

WOODS, D.C. *Ireland*
Bessbrook.
Wing, 2-0-0-2.
1888 NZN−; 1889 S−.

WOODS, Samuel Moses James *England*
('Smudgy')
Sydney GS NSW, Brighton Coll, Cambridge
Univ, Wellington, Blackheath, Bridgwater,
Som, Barbarians.
b 14.4.1868 Ashfield, NSW; *d* 30.4.31.
Forward, 13-9-0-4 (5 − 1t 1c).
1890 W− S+ I+; 1891 W+ I+ S−; 1892 I+(1c)
S+; 1893 W− I+; 1895 W+(1t) I+ S−.
Blue 1888-90. Served WW1 Som LI, Devon
Rgt. One of 9 Blackheath players in E side v S
1895. Fdr mem Barbarians 1890. An established
ckter before Cambridge; 3 Tests A v E 1888.
When E rugby career finished, resumed int ckt
& played 3 Tests for E v SA 1895. Also played
for CUCC & Som CCC. CY 1889.
Autobiography 'My Reminiscences' pub 25.

WOODS, Thomas *England*
Bridgwater A, Som.
b 9.2.1883 Bridgwater; *d* 12.4.55 Rochdale.
Forward, 1-0-0-1.
08 S−.
Groundsman/licensee. Rochdale H RL 09.

WOODS, Tom *England*
Devonport Servs, US Portsmouth, RN,
Newbridge, Pontypool.
b ?Pontypool.
Lock, 5-5-0-0 (3 − 1t).
20 S+; 21 W+ I+ S+(1t) F+.
RN/colliery fitter. Wigan RL 21. Wales RL.

WOODWARD, Clive Ronald *England*
HMS Conway, E Colts, Loughborough Colls,
Harlequins, Leicester.
b 6.1.56 Ely.
Centre, 21-12-2-7 (16 − 4t).
80 I+r F+ W+ S+; 81 W− S+(1t) I+ F−
Arg=(2t) Arg+; 82 A+ S= I− F+(1t) W+; 83
I− NZ+; 84 S− I+ F− W−; BI > 80 SA 2-0-0-
2; 83 NZ.
Sales exec. Welsh SS final trialist, inj prevented
his played v A Schs. E Under 23s v It 76. 53 pts
BI > 80 SA (played 1 Test on wing). E > 82 US,
Can. Career hampered by inj; broke leg twice.
Wife Helen hockey int.

WOODWARD, John Edward *England*
RGS High Wycombe, O Wycombensians, RAF,
Wasps, Barbarians, Bucks, E Midlands, Mdx.
b 17.4.31 Wheeler End, Bucks.
Wing, 15-8-2-5 (21 − 6t 1p).
52 SA− W−(1t) S+(1t); 53 W+(1p) I= F+(1t)
S+(1t); 54 W+(2t) NZ− I+ S+ F−; 55 W− I=;
56 S+.
Butcher/sports goods retailer. Bro in law of Ron
Syrett. English Schs sprint champ.

WOOLDRIDGE, Charles *England*
Sylvester

442

Winchester Coll, Oxford Univ, Blackheath, Hants.
b 31.12.1858 Winchester; *d* 19.2.41.
Forward, 7-7-0-0.
1882 W+; 1883 I+ S+; 1884 W+ I+ S+; 1885 I+.
Solicitor. Product of football-playing sch. Blue 1882.

WOOLLER, Wilfred　　　　　　　　　*Wales*
Llandudno CS, Rydal Sch, Sale, Cambridge Univ, The Army, Cardiff, London Welsh, Barbarians.
b 20.11.12 Rhos on Sea.
Centre/wing, 18-8-2-8 (26 − 6t 1c 2p).
33 E+ S− I−; 35 E=(1t) S+(1t) I− NZ+; 36 E= S+(1t) I+; 37 E−(1t) S−(2t) I−; 38 S− I+(1p); 39 E− S+(1c 1p) I+.
Coal executive/insurance broker/pro ckter/journalist. Born of English parents. Blue 33-5. Ckt blue 35-6. 3t British Army v French Army, Stade Colombes, 40. Centre-forward Cardiff City 39. Served WW2, 77th Heavy AA Rgt, POW Java Feb 41 with Les Spence, Cardiff, WRU pres. Capt Glam CCC 47-60 (12078 runs, 892 wkts, 391 catches in 400 apps 38-62; 100 wkts & 1000 runs 54). Sec Glam CCC 46-78. E Test sel 52-8. Squash for W post-war. Corr for 'News Chronicle', 'Sunday Telegraph'.

WORDSWORTH, Alan John　　　　　*England*
Whitgift Sch, Cambridge Univ, Harlequins.
b 9.11.53 Thornton Heath.
FH, 1-0-0-1.
75 A−r.

WORTON, James Robert Bute　　　*England*
('John')
Haileybury & ISC, RMC Sandhurst, Harlequins, The Army, Comb Servs, Barbarians, Surrey.
b 31.3.01.
SH, 2-1-1-0.
26 W−; 27 W I.
The Army. Lt Col. Mem of Harlequin side which won 1st Mdx Sevens, 26. Served WW2, Mdx Rgt; retired with rank of Lt Col.

WOTHERSPOON, William　　　　　*Scotland*
Fettes Coll, Cambridge Univ, W of Scotland.
b 2.5.1868 Aberdour, Fife; *d* 19.8.42 Fleet, Hants.
Half-back, 7-4-0-3 (3t).
1891 I+(3t); 1892 I+; 1893 W− E+; 1894 W− I− E+; BT > 1891 SA.
Explosives co dir. Blue 1888-9.

WRENCH, David Frederick　　　　　*England*
Bryam
Sandbach Sch, Winnington Pk, Wilmslow, Leeds Univ, UAU, English Univs, Cambridge

Univ, Harlequins, Wolfhounds, Barbarians, Cheshire.
b 27.11.36.
Prop, 2-1-0-1.
64 F+ S−.
Schoolmaster. Blue 60. Ckt for Gentlemen of Herts. Taught at Haberdashers' Aske's. Led Brit Schs Exploring Soc's Expedition to Arctic Sweden 66.

WRIGHT, Cyril Carne Glenton　　　*England*
Tonbridge Sch, Cambridge Univ, Blackheath, Barbarians, Kent.
b 7.3.1887; *d* 15.9.60.
Centre, 2-1-0-1.
09 I+ S−.
Schoolmaster. Blue 07-8. Ckt blue 07-8. Taught at Dulwich Coll. Served WW1, Capt & Adjutant Durham LI.

WRIGHT, Francis Aitken MC　　　　*Scotland*
Edinburgh Acad, Edinburgh Academicals.
b 14.7.09; *d* 14.3.59.
Lock, 1-0-0-1.
32 E−.
Chartered accountant. Served WW2. Sec/treas SRU 51-4.

WRIGHT, Frank Thurlow　　　　　*England*
Edinburgh Acad, Edinburgh Academicals, Manchester, Lancs.
b 2.7.1862 Leigh; *d* 34 Marseilles.
Half-back, 1-0-1-0.
1881 S=.
Solicitor/resident mgr tea & rubber estates Ceylon. Won cap because H.H. Taylor missed train to Edinburgh.

WRIGHT, Hugh Brooks　　　　　　*Scotland*
George Watson's Coll, Watsonians.
b 1875 Inverary; *d* −.
Forward, 1-0-0-1.
1894 W−.
Engr.

WRIGHT, Ian Douglas　　　　　　*England*
Felixstowe GS, Worthing HS, St Luke's Coll, Rosslyn Pk, O Azurians, Northampton, London Cos, Sussex, Devon, Surrey.
b 24.12.45 Croydon.
FH, 4-1-1-2.
71 W− I+ F= S−r.
Schoolmaster. E Under 25s v Fj 70. Ckt for Sussex CCC. Taught at Bishop's Stortford Coll.

WRIGHT, James F.　　　　　　　　*England*
Bowling Old Lane Bradford, Idle, Bradford, Yorks.
b 1.4.1863 Bilborough, York; *d* 4.10.32.
Half-back, 1-0-0-1.
1890 W−.

Licensee/brewery rep. His club, Bradford, helped form NU 1895.

WRIGHT, John Cecil *England*
Sedbergh Sch, Crewe & Nantwich, Met Police, Brit Police, Newport, Mon, Mdx.
b 6.8.10.
Lock, 1-1-0-0.
34 W+.
Police/farmer. Met Police until served WW2 with 1st Battn King's Shropshire LI. E cap in Newport RFC. Farmed in Lincs & Dyfed.

WRIGHT, Kenneth James *Australia*
Marceilin Coll, NSW.
b 11.4.56.
Five-eighth, 9-5-0-4 (31 − 1t 3c 2d 5p).
75 E+(1d) E+(1c 1p) J+(1t); 76 US+ F− F−; 78 NZ−(1c 2p) NZ−(1d 1p) NZ+(1c 1p).
Accountant. 57 pts A > 78 NZ. E Suburbs RL 78.

WRIGHT, K.M. *Scotland*
Cheltenham Coll, RMA Sandhurst, London Scottish, RA, The Army.
b 6.9.04.
Flanker/no 8, 4-3-0-1.
29 F+ W− I+ E+.
The Army.

WRIGHT, Robert Aikin ('Robin') *Ireland*
Corrig Coll, RCSI, Monkstown.
b −; *d* 7.12.55.
FB, 1-1-0-0.
12 S+.
Medicine.

WRIGHT, Ronald W.J. *Scotland*
Edinburgh W.
Lock, 1-0-0-1.
73 F−.

WRIGHT, S.T.H. *Scotland*
Stewart's Coll, Stewart's Coll FP.
Prop, 1-0-0-1.
49 E−.

WRIGHT, Thomas *Scotland*
Trinity Sch Hawick, Hawick.
b 18.12.24 Hawick.
Centre, 1-0-0-1.
47 A−.
Monumental mason. Leeds RL 48.

WRIGHT, Thomas Peter *England*
Judd Sch Tonbridge, Tonbridge, Blackheath, Penarth, Cowbridge, Devizes, Barbarians, Kent.
b 28.2.31.
Prop, 13-5-4-4.
60 W+ I+ F= S+; 61 SA− W− I− F= S+; 62

W= I+ F− S=.
Agric contractor/brewery rep.

WRIGHT, William Henry George *England*
('Jock') ISM
Plymouth A, Devon.
b 6.6.1889; *d* −.
Prop, 2-1-0-1.
20 W− F+.
HM Dockyard Bermuda & Devonport. ISM 49.

WRIGLEY, Edgar *New Zealand*
Masterton, Wairarapa, Red Star, Wellington.
b 15.6.1886 Masterton; *d* 2.6.58 Huddersfield, England.
Five-eighth, 1-1-0-0 (3 − 1t).
05 A+(1t).
NZ's youngest int player, 19yrs 79days v A 05. Switched to RL; ;NZ > 07 E & signed for Huddersfield 08. Later Hunslet & Bradford N.

WYATT, Derek M. *England*
Colchester RGS, Oxford Univ, Bedford.
b 4.12.49 London.
Wing, 1-0-0-1.
76 S−r.
Publishing. Blue 81.

WYATT, Mark Anthony *Wales*
Brecon GS, Swansea Univ, British Univs, Swansea, Breconshire, Barbarians.
b 12.2.57 Crickhowell.
FB, 7-3-1-3 (53 − 1t 5c 13p).
83 E=(2p) S+(1c 3p) I+(1t 1c 3p) F−(1c); 84 A−(1c 1p); 85 S+(1c 4p) I−.
Research student. Wales B v A 81, F 82. Wales XV v Maoris 82, J 83.

WYLIE, Douglas S. *Scotland*
Stewart's-Melville FP.
Centre, 3-0-0-3.
84 A−; 85 W−r E−.
Normally plays FH for club.

WYLIE, James Thomas *New Zealand*
Univ, Auckland, N Island, NSW, Glebe.
b 26.10.1887 Galatea; *d* 19.12.56 Palo Alto, US.
Lock, 2-2-0-0 (3 − 1t).
13 A+ US+(1t).
Fruit shipper & wholesaler. Moved to A 10; A > 12 NAm. Returned NZ 13. NZ > 13 NAm. Remained in US to study at Stanford Univ where he coached rugby. Invited to kick-off California All Stars v NZ 53.

WYLLIE, Alexander John *New Zealand*
('Grizz')
St Andrew's Coll, Glenmark, Canterbury, S Island.
Flanker/no 8, 11-5-2-4 (8 − 2t).

70 SA+ SA−; 71 BI+ BI− BI=; 72 W+
S+(1t); 73 E+ I=(1t) F− E−.
Farmer. NZ > 70 A & SA, 72-3 BI,F & NAm.
210 apps for Canterbury 64-79, 100 as capt.

WYNESS, Melville R.K. ('Wang') *South Africa*
W Prov.
b 23.1.37.
Wing, 5-3-1-1 (3 − 1t).
62 BI= BI+ BI+ BI+(1t); 63 A−.

Y

YACHVILI, Michel *France*
Tulle, Brive.
b 25.9.46 Tulle, Corrèze.
Hooker/flanker, 15-5-2-8.
68 E+ W+ Cz+ NZ− A− R−; 69 S− I− R+;
71 E= SA− SA= A−; 72 R+; 75 SA−.
Municipal worker.

YANZ, Kenneth *Australia*
NSW.
b 18.5.24 Hornsby.
Lock, 1-0-0-1.
58 F−.
Motor mechanic.

YARRANTON, Peter George *England*
Willesden Tech Coll, Wasps, RAF, Comb
Servs, Barbarians, London Cos, Mdx.
b 30.9.24 Acton.
Lock, 5-3-0-2.
54 W+ NZ− I+; 55 F− S+.
RAF/operations officer Shell-BP. Rep RAF
swimming & water polo. Served WW2, with
over 3000 hours operational service mainly in
Burma & SE Asia as Ft Lt. Continued with
RAF until 58. Middx CB rep; pres Mdx 85-6.

YATES, Victor Moses *New Zealand*
Kaitaia Coll, Rarawa, N Auckland, NZ Maoris,
N Island.
b 15.6.39 Kaitaia.
No 8, 3-3-0-0 (3 − 1t).
61 F+ F+ F+(1t).
Farmer. NZ > 62 A. Outstanding Maori Player
of Year 61. RL 65. Father Moses & bro John rep
N Auckland; John NZ RL 54-7.

YEATES, R.A. *Ireland*
St Columba's Coll, Trin Coll Dublin.
Wing, 2-1-0-1.
1889 S− W+.

YIEND, William ('Pusher') *England*
Hartlepool R, Gloucester, Leicester, Keighley,
Peterborough, Barbarians, Durham Co.
b 1861 Winchcombe, Glos; *d* 22.1.39.
Forward, 6-5-0-1.

1889 NZN+; 1892 W+ I+ S+; 1893 I+ S−.
Rly traffic agent.

YOUNG, Sir Arthur Henderson *Scotland*
GCMG
Edinburgh Acad, Edinburgh Academicals,
Rugby Sch, RMA Sandhurst, Inniskilling
Fusiliers.
b 31.10.1854; *d* 20.10.38.
Forward, 1-0-0-1.
1874 E−.
The Army/colonial service. Governor of Straits
Settlements.

YOUNG, Arthur Tudor *England*
Tonbridge Sch, Cambridge Univ, Blackheath,
The Army, Kent.
b 14.10.01 India; *d* 22.6.33 Bareilly, India.
SH, 18-12-0-6 (6 − 2t).
24 W+ I+ F+(1t) S+; 25 NZ− F+; 26 I−(1t)
F+ S−; 27 I+ S− F−; 28 NSW+ W+ I+ F+
S+; 29 I−; BI > 24 SA 1-0-0-1.
The Army. 5ft 4 1/2in, 10st 7lb. Blue 22-4 (capt).
Died as ADC to Gen Sir Norman MacMullen,
GOC E Command, from pneumonia following
influenza.

YOUNG, Denis *New Zealand*
Christchurch Tech Coll, Coll OB, Canterbury,
Shirley, S Island.
b 1.4.30 Christchurch.
Hooker, 22-15-3-4.
56 SA−; 58 A+ A− A+; 60 SA− SA+ SA=
SA−; 61 F+ F+ F+; 62 A+ A+ A= A+; 63
E+ E+; 63 I+ W+; 64 E+ S= F+.
Cabinet maker/schoolmaster/travel agency dir.
NZ > 57 & 62 A, 60 A & SA, 63-4 BI,F & C.
139 apps for Canterbury 48-61. NZ jnr discus
champ.

YOUNG, Eric Templeton *Scotland*
Cargilfield Sch, Glasgow Acad, Glasgow
Academicals, Oxford Univ.
b −.5.1862; kia 28.6.15 Gallipoli.
Flanker, 1-0-0-1.
14 E−.
Served WW1, Capt, 8th Scottish Rifles.

YOUNG, George Avery *Wales*
Malvern Sch, Cardiff.
b 1863; *d* 23.1.1900 Penarth.
Forward, 2-0-0-2.
1886 E− S−.

YOUNG, Gordon *Ireland*
UC Cork.
FB, 1-0-0-1.
13 E−.
Medicine.

YOUNG, Jeffrey *Wales*
Garw GS, Blaengarw, Harrogate, RAF,
London Welsh, Bridgend, Yorks.
b 16.9.43.
Hooker, 23-15-1-7.
68 S+ I− F−; 69 S+ I+ F= E+ NZ−; 70 E+
I− F+; 71 E+ S+ I+ F+; 72 E+ S+ F+ NZ−;
73 E+ S− I+ F−; BI > 68 SA 1-0-0-1.
RAF. Jaw broken by Colin Meads NZ v W 69.

YOUNG, John Robert Chester *England*
Bishop's Vesey GS, O Veseyans, Oxford Univ,
Harlequins, Barbarians, London Cos,
Warwicks, Surrey.
b 6.9.37 Upton, Chester.
Wing, 9-4-2-3 (6 − 2t).
58 I+; 60 W+ I+ F= S+(1t); 61 SA− W−(1t)
I− F=; BI > 59 A, NZ 1-0-0-1.
Barrister. Blue 57-8. Ath blue 58-60. Oxford-
Cambridge > 57 E Africa. AAA 100y champ 56
(once ran 9.6s for 100y). Inj prevented his rep
GB in 56 Olympics & E in 58 Empire Games.
Called to Bar 61.

YOUNG, Malcolm *England*
QEGS Hexham, Cambridge Univ, Gosforth.
b 4.1.46 Mickley, Northumb.
SH, 10-4-1-5 (15 − 1t 4c 1p).
77 S+(1t) I+ F− W−; 78 F− W− S+(2c) I+(2c
1p) NZ−; 79 S=.
Section mgr.

YOUNG, Peter Dalton *England*
Clifton Coll, Cambridge Univ, Clifton, Rosslyn
Pk, Dublin W, Glos.
b 9.11.27.
Lock, 9-4-1-4 (3 − 1t).
54 W+ NZ− I+ S+(1t) F−; 55 W− I= F− S+.
RN/man dir tobacco co. Blue 49. Capt E v F & S
55 whilst played in Dublin.

YOUNG, Robert Graham *Scotland*
George Watson's Coll, Watsonians.
b 13.9.40 Edinburgh.
SH, 1-0-0-1.
70 W−.
Rep.

YOUNG, Roger Michael ('Koo- *Ireland*
Koo')
Methodist Coll Belfast, Queen's Univ Belfast,
Collegians, Barbarians.
b 29.6.43 Belfast.
SH, 26-12-4-10 (3 − 1t).
65 F= E+ S+(1t) W− SA−; 66 F− E= S−

W+; 67 W+ F−; 68 W+ A+; 69 F+ E+ S+
W−; 70 SA= F− E− S+ W+; 71 F= E− S+
W−; BI > 66 A 2-2-0-0, NZ 1-0-0-1; 68 SA 1-0-
0-1.
Dental surgeon. Emigrated to SA.

YOUNG, Thomas Eric Boswell *Scotland*
Loretto Sch, Durham Univ, Durham City.
b 1891; d 74.
Centre, 1-0-0-1.
11 F−.
Engr/Civil Service.

YOUNG, W.B. *Scotland*
City of London Sch, Cambridge Univ, King's
Coll Hosp, London Scottish, Barbarians.
Flanker, 10-5-0-5 (3 − 1t).
37 W+ I− E−; 38 W+ I+ E+; 39 W− I− E−;
48 E+(1t).
Medical missionary. Blue 35-7. 9 yrs between
caps.

YOUNGS, Nicholas Gerald *England*
Greshams Sch, England SS, Shuttleworth Agric
Coll, Bedford, Leicester.
b 15.12.59 W Runton, Norfolk.
SH, 6-2-0-4.
83 I− NZ+; 84 S− I+ F− W−.
Farm mgr/agric salesman. 9 schs caps. E Under
23 > 79 F, I; v Netherlands (capt) 80. England
B. England XV v Can 83.

Z

ZAGO, Fernand *France*
Montauban.
b 27.2.42.
Prop, 2-1-0-1.
63 I+ E−.
Butcher.

ZELLER, William C. *South Africa*
Umtate Boys HS, Natal.
Wing, 2-1-1-0.
21 NZ+ NZ=.
Lawyer. SA sel.

ZIMMERMAN, Maurice *South Africa*
('Zimmie')
Villiers Graaff HS, Cape Town Univ, W Prov.
b 8.6.11.
Wing, 4-4-0-0 (3 − 1t).
31 W+ I+(1t); 32 E+ S+.
SA > 31-2 BI; 4t SA v Midland Cos. SA sel.

446

BIBLIOGRAPHY

Most of the research for this book was conducted through correspondence with many of the listed players or their relatives. The other major sources of reference were books, newspapers, magazines and periodicals at the National Library of Wales at Aberystwyth, the British Library, the National Library at Dublin, and the National Newspaper Library at Colindale.

The chief newspapers referred to were: *The Times, The Guardian, The Observer, The Daily Telegraph, Western Mail, The Scotsman, Irish Times, Irish Independent, L'Equipe.*

Specialist rugby annuals: *Playfair Rugby Annual, Rothmans Rugby Yearbook, Rothmans Australian Rugby Yearbook, Rugby Almanack of New Zealand, Fédération Française de Rugby Annuaire Officiel, South African Rugby Annual.*

Specialist rugby histories:

History of Scottish Rugby (A. M. C. Thorburn, 1980)
History of Welsh International Rugby (J. D. Billot, 1970)
Men in Black (R. H. Chester & N. A. McMillan, 1978)
Encyclopedia of New Zealand Rugby (R. H. Chester & N. A. McMillan, 1981)
The Men in Green (Sean Diffley, 1973)
Springbok Saga (Chris Greyvenstein, 1978)
The Book of English International Rugby (John Griffiths, 1982)
Centenary History of the Rugby Football Union (U. A. Titley & Ross McWhirter, 1970)
The Barbarians (Nigel Starmer-Smith, 1977)
Fields of Praise (David Smith & Gareth Williams, 1980)
Rugby Football Internationals' Roll of Honour (E. H. D. Sewell, 1919)
History of Cardiff Rugby Club (D. E. Davies, 1975)
England Rugby (Barry Bowker, 1976)

Other reference books:

Dictionary of Welsh Biography, 1959
Oxford University Roll of Service (E. S. Craig, Ed, 1920)
War List of the University of Cambridge (G. V. Carey, 1921)
Alumni Cantabrigienses (J. & J. A. Venn, 1752-1900)
Alumni Oxonienses (J. Foster, 1715-1886, 1891-2)
Who's Who
Who Was Who
Dictionary of National Biography
(Schools) Calendars
The Times Obituaries
Crockford's Clerical Directory